DISCOVER AUSTRALIA
FISHING

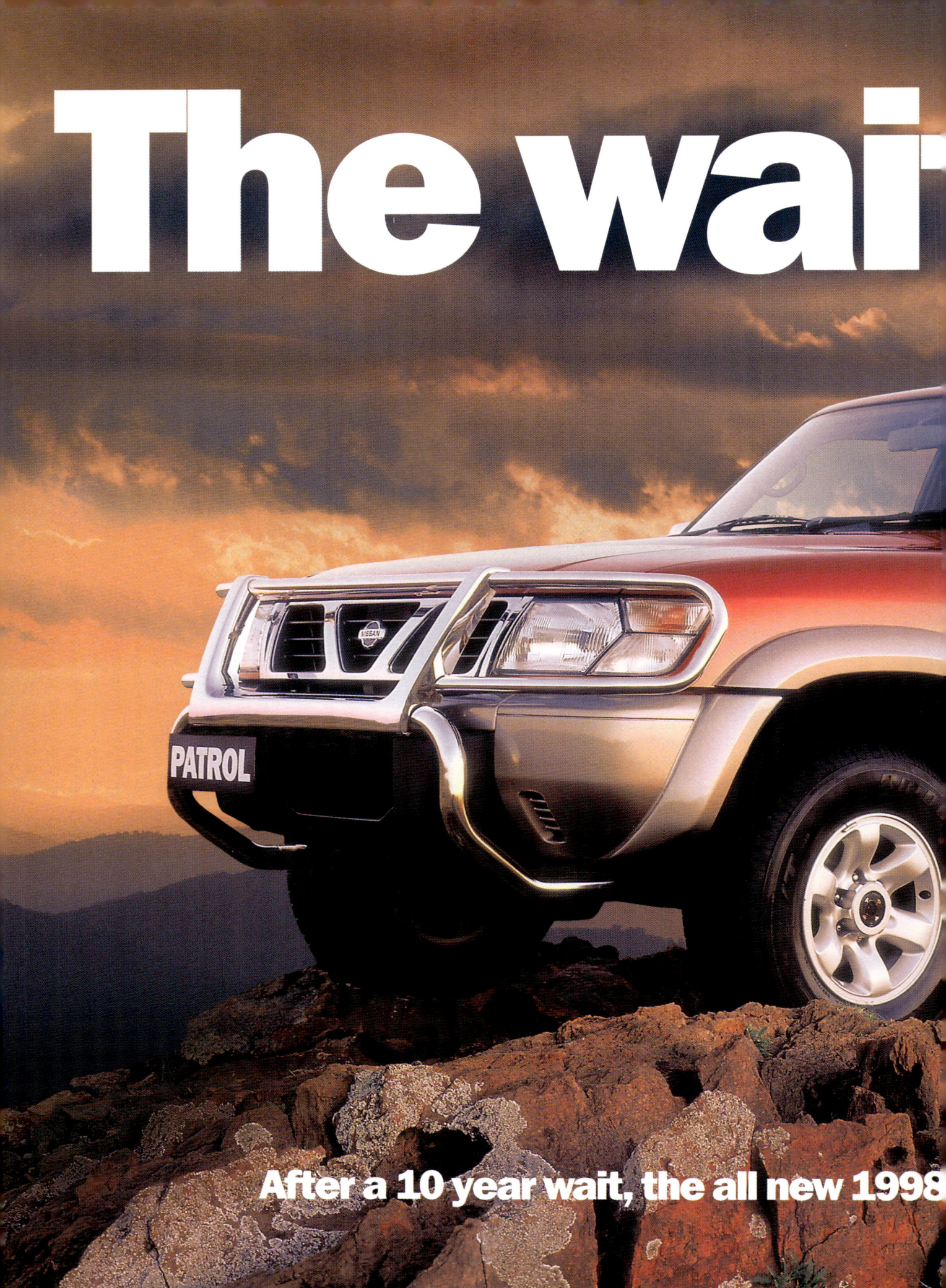

We'd like to introduce you to a *'reel'* smart card.

The Fishing Info Line Card is your membership to a club designed by anglers where you can take advantage of information, special offers and other opportunities to improve your fishing experience.

The Fishing Info Line Card is smart enough to hook you up with the latest in fishing information, from weather reports to marina locations and equipment hire. Smart enough to speak to local people who can update you on what's biting and what bait to use. Smart enough to negotiate some serious discounts on nearly everything related to fishing. Smart enough to know where you can go for the ultimate fishing adventure, what you'd need to take and where you can stay.

24 hours a day, all year long, Australia wide. It's no wonder then that successful anglers are turing to the Fishing Info Line Card and dialling in for the latest in fishing information. After all, it's the smart way to improve your catch and if your not hooked up, you won't reel in the big ones.

Where you can clean up with the Fishing Info-Line card:

YAMAHA 25% off lubricants in conjunction with an outboard service — **25% OFF**	**AVIS** 25% off standard rental rates, plus 5% off promotional rates. — **25% OFF**	**CLUB MARINE** 5% off all new Insurance policies — **5% OFF**
EAGLE 5% off all Eagle products — **5% OFF**	**SHIMANO** 5% off best price on selected lines. Selected lines will be changed regularly. — **5% OFF**	**TOYOTA** Toyota accessories when purchased from a Toyota dealer AND free roadside assistance to any card holder who purchases a new Toyota — **10% OFF**
LOWRANCE 5% off all Lowrance products — **5% OFF**	**ANSETT** 4% off air travel tickets when booked with Fishing Info-Line Travel — **4% OFF**	

Here's a net you *should* get tangled in.

Hooking into the world wide web, the Fishing Info Line web site (www.fishinfo.com.au), is the most comprehensive fishing site on the net.

By getting onto our new web site, you can access up to the minute info on just about anything related to fishing from what's biting to shopping from home. You can also access national weather reports updated every 1/2 hour, on line chat rooms, enter competitions for great prizes and even construct your own fishing web site.

With services like that, it's easy to see why people are rushing to get tangled up in this net!

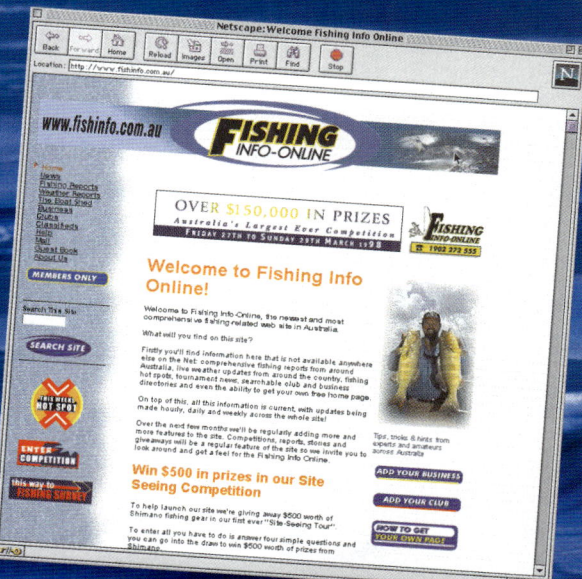

You bring the gear, we'll supply the adventure...

If you can conjure up the perfect fishing adventure, we can make it a reality. Whether it's somewhere in Australia or anywhere in the world, the Fishing Info Line Travel Service can get you there with no fuss and at a competitive rate.

Just name the adventure and we'll do the rest. After all, when you're travelling to fish, the only arrangements you want to make are what to pack and what to catch.

Making it easy... just pick up to hook up.
For information on how to hook into your Fishing Info Line Card call in at participating tackle shops, visit our web site or phone toll free on 1800 627 527.

DISCOVER AUSTRALIA
FISHING

Edited by Steve Starling

Publisher	Gordon Cheers	Map coordinator	Valerie Marlborough	Distribution maps	Deborah Clarke
Editorial consultants	Philippa Sandall, Steve Starling	Map editors	Jane Cozens, Denise Imwold, Jenny Lake, Heather Martin, Marlene Meynert, Janet Parker, Joan Sutter	Fish illustrations	Bernard Yau
Designer and managing editor	Siobhan O'Connor			Cover design	Bob Mitchell
				Photo research	Marie-Louise Taylor
Cartographer	John Frith			Publishing manager	Linda Watchorn
Cartography consultant	Bruce Whitehouse	Location maps	Robert Taylor, Warren Penney, Mike Gorman	Production coordinator	Sarah Sherlock

Published in Australia by
Random House Australia Pty Ltd
20 Alfred Street, Milsons Point, NSW 2061
Telephone 61 2 9954 9966
Fax 61 2 9954 9008
http://www.randomhouse.com.au

ISBN 0 09 183619 0

Sydney   New York   Toronto   London   Auckland   Johannesburg
and agencies throughout the world

First published in 1998

This publication and this arrangement is copyright
© Random House Australia Pty Ltd 1998
All maps © Random House Australia Pty Ltd 1998
Text © Random House Australia Pty Ltd 1998
Illustrations and photographs © Random House Australia Pty Ltd 1998
from the Random House Photo Library

Random House Australia Pty Ltd is the owner of the copyright subsisting in the original maps in this publication. Other than as permitted by the Copyright Act, no part of the maps can be reproduced, copied or transmitted in any form or by any means (electronic, mechanical, microcopying, recording, storage in a retrieval system or otherwise), without the prior written permission of Random House Australia Pty Ltd.

Random House Australia Pty Ltd will vigorously pursue any breach of their copyright. No part of this book may be reproduced without the prior written permission of Random House Australia Pty Ltd.

Random House Australia has made every effort to include the latest changes to all roads and highways at the time this publication went to press.

Use of maps: Should you be interested in using any of the maps or other material in this publication, please contact Sarah Sherlock. Telephone 61 2 9954 9966. Fax 61 2 9954 9008.

Cartographic coordinator: Gordon Cheers

The Publisher would be pleased to receive additional or updated material, or suggestions for future editions. Please address these to Gordon Cheers, Random House Australia Pty Ltd, 20 Alfred Street, Milsons Point NSW 2061, Australia. Telephone 61 2 9954 9966. Fax 61 2 9954 9008.

National Library of Australia
Cataloguing-in-Publication Data

Discover Australia: fishing
  Includes index
  ISBN 0 09 183619 0.

  1. Fishing – Australia – Guidebooks. 2. Australia – Guidebooks. I. Starling, Stephen.

799.10994

Printed by Dah Hua, Hong Kong
Film separation by Pica Colour Separation, Singapore

For information about purchasing books for use in mail order catalogues, as corporate gifts or as premiums, please contact Sarah Sherlock, Random House Australia. Telephone 61 2 9954 9966. Fax 61 2 9954 9008.

Photographs

Page 1: Fly casting in the Blue Mountains west of Sydney
Pages 6–7: Lord Howe Island—a dream trip come true

KEY TO ROAD MAPS

Legend for road maps

- Freeway with national route number
- Highway with State route numbers
- Major sealed road with Metroad number
- Minor sealed road
- Major unsealed road
- Minor unsealed road or track
- Total and intermediate road distances (km)
- Railway with station
- Railway (underground)
- Ferry route
- Walking track
- Major linear feature (as noted) — Dog Fence
- International airport
- Built-up area
- State or Territory capital
- Major regional centre
- Other towns
- Homestead
- Ruin
- Mine
- Landmark or tourist feature
- Bridge
- Gate
- Grid
- Bore, well or waterhole
- Tank
- Major river
- Watercourse
- Mountain peak
- Perennial lake
- Dry or intermittent lake
- Dry or intermittent lake in national park or reserve
- Prohibited Area boundary
- State or Territory border
- Marine park or reserve boundary
- Aboriginal land
- National or conservation park or reserve
- Coral reef

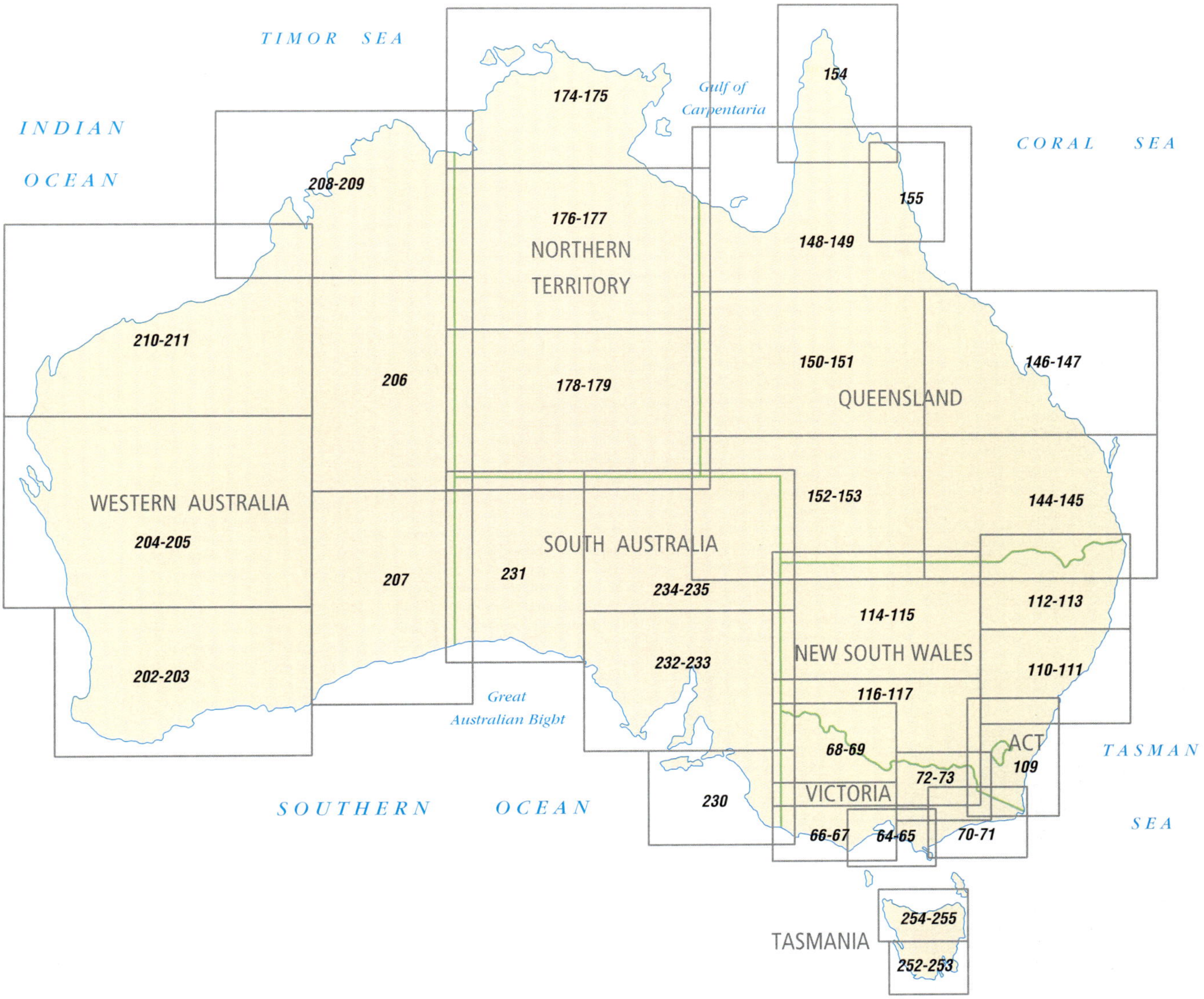

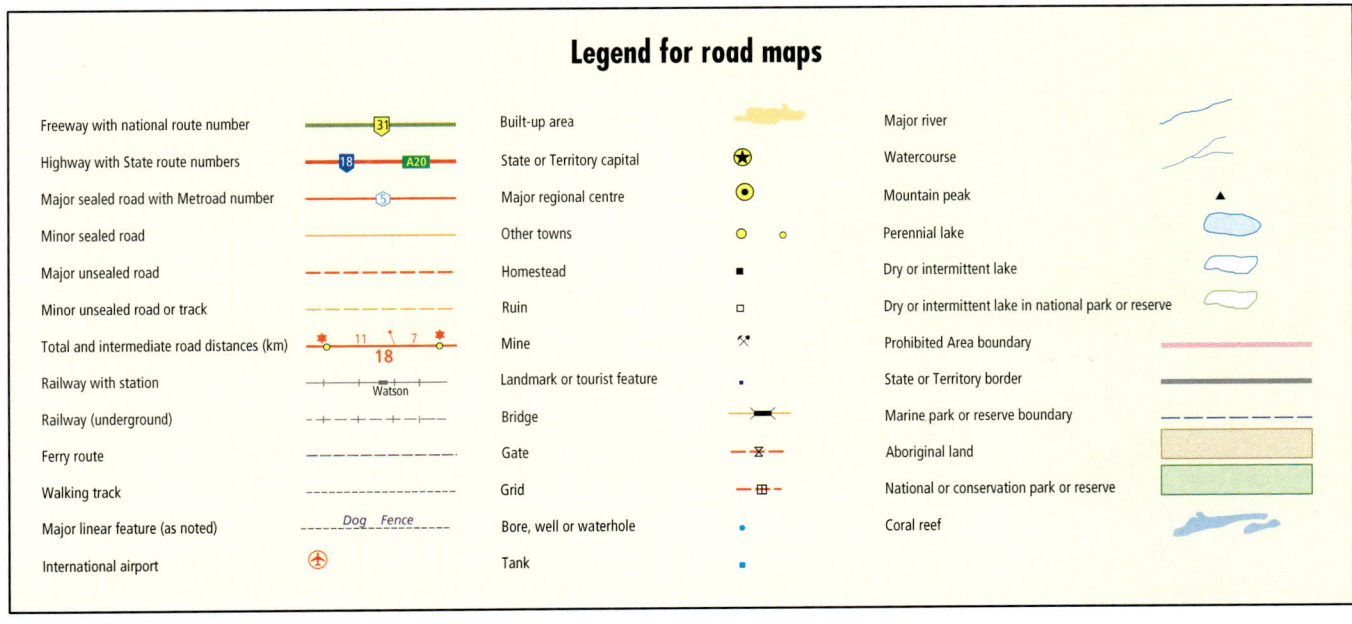

FOREWORD 11

Fishing is Australia's most popular pastime. It is also a unique activity that is enjoyed by people ranging in age from the very young to the very old.

I have known Steve Starling for more than 20 years. I first became aware of him when he was an enthusiastic young writer who had a vision... to make fishing his life. Well, he has certainly done that. He now enjoys a very high international profile. He is also, I might add, highly respected within all areas of angling in this country.

Steve works with me on my television program 'Rex Hunt Fishing Adventures'. While he is certainly a very accomplished presenter, he also excels in the technical side of fishing tackle and especially fish species. His knowledge of fish and their habits is amazing.

I am a very keen reader of all material on fishing and Australia has some of the best names in fishing in the print media. Steve Starling is certainly right up there with the very best of them.

He has that special talent that allows him to pass on his amazing ability as an angler through print and electronic media.

Technically, he is without peer. Steve also has the knack of writing so that beginners to the game can follow what he has to say.

Discover Australia: Fishing is a must for anyone who wants up-to-date, accurate information about our marvellous country and its fishing. The bonus is that Steve Starling has fished most of these places himself.

I present this publication to you. The publishers could not have asked a more qualified writer than Steve to put this material together. I am delighted they asked me to write the foreword. **Steve Starling is definitely the man to tell you about the fishing in our maaaaaagnificent country!**

Yibbida yibbida
Good fishing.

REX HUNT

CONTENTS

A fisherman cleans his catch

Key Map	9
Foreword	11
Introduction	14
About the Author	14
About the Contributors	15
How To Use This Book	16

PART 1: GEARING UP 17

Tackle Box	18
The Travelling Angler	26
Planning Your Trip	28
Safe Fishing	32
Catch of the Day	34

PART 2: GONE FISHING 36

VICTORIA 38
Port Phillip Bay 40 • Western Port 42 • Geelong and Corio Bay 44 • The Yarra River 46 • North-Eastern Estuaries 48 • Gippsland Lakes 50 • Lakes Entrance 52 • Wilsons Promontory and Corner Inlet 54 • Timber Lake 56 • Lake Eildon 58 • Dartmouth Reservoir and the Mitta Mitta River 60 • Trout Streams of South Gippsland 62 • Road Maps 64

NEW SOUTH WALES AND THE AUSTRALIAN CAPITAL TERRITORY 74
Sydney Harbour 76 • The Lower Hawkesbury and Broken Bay 78 • Hawkesbury–Nepean Bass Waters 80 • Botany Bay 82 • Georges River 84 • Gosford and Brisbane Water 86 • Port Stephens 88 • Lake Illawarra 90 • The South Coast 92 • Jervis Bay 94 • Batemans Bay and the Clyde River 96 • Lake Windamere 98 • Lake Glenbawn 100 • Lake Lyell 102 • The Capital's Lakes 104 • Trout Streams of the Australian Capital Territory 106 • Road Maps 109

QUEENSLAND 118
The Gold Coast 120 • Moreton Bay 122 • Moreton Island and North Stradbroke Island 124 • The Sunshine Coast 126 • Noosa to Tin Can Bay 128 • Fraser Island 130 • Fraser's Offshore Grounds 132 • Seventeen Seventy and Round Hill 134 • Hinze Dam 136 • Noosa River Bass 138 • Valley of Lakes 140 • The Golden West 142 • Road Maps 144

NORTHERN TERRITORY 156
Darwin Harbour 158 • Darwin Offshore 160 • Bynoe Harbour 162 • Shady Camp 164 • Dundee Beach 166 • The Daly River 168 • Kakadu and the South Alligator River 170 • East Alligator River 172 • Road Maps 174

WESTERN AUSTRALIA 180
Perth's Beaches 182 • The Lower Swan Estuary 184 • Cockburn Sound 186 • Hillarys Boat Harbour and Trigg Point 188 • Swan River Bream 190 • Rottnest Island 192 • Bunbury to Busselton 194 • South-West Corner 196 • Dongara and Geraldton 198 • South-West Trout Waters 200 • Road Maps 202

SOUTH AUSTRALIA 212
Adelaide's Jetties 214 • Adelaide Offshore 216 • The Port River and Outer Harbor 218 • The Fleurieu Peninsula 220 • The Coorong 222 • Murray Mouth Mulloway 224 •

Trout fishing in the New England region of northern New South Wales

South Australian Trout Waters 226 • Weekend on the Murray 228 • Road Maps 230

TASMANIA 236
The Derwent Estuary 238 • The Tasman Peninsula 240 • Bicheno and the Freycinet Peninsula 242 • St Helens 244 • Trout Streams around Launceston 246 • Arthurs Lake 248 • Lake Burbury 250 • Road Maps 252

DREAM TRIPS 256
Mallacoota 258 • East Gippsland Bream Rivers 260 • Shark Fishing off Phillip Island 262 • The Mighty Murray 264 • Big River Country 266 • Coffs Harbour 268 • Lord Howe Island 270 • The New South Wales Far South Coast 272 • The Snowy Mountains 276 • Cape York 278 • Mornington Island 282 • The Gulf of Carpentaria 284 • Exploring the Reef 286 • Cairns to Cape Tribulation 290 • Jessie River, Melville Island 292 • Cape Don and the Cobourg Peninsula 294 • Barra Base 296 • The Victoria River 298 • Vanderlin Island 300 • The Kimberley 302 • Broome and the Pearl Coast 306 • The Pilbara Coast 308 • The Mackerel Islands 310 • Dirk Hartog Island and Shark Bay 312 • Kalbarri and the Murchison 314 • Great Australian Bight 316 • Steel City Snapper 318 • Kangaroo Island 320 • Aboard the *Falie* 322 • Flinders Island 324 • Strahan and the Wild West Coast 326 • Tasmania's Central Highlands 328 • London Lakes 330

PART 3: WHAT FISH IS THAT? 332

Anatomy of a Fish 334 • Fish Distribution 335 • A to Z of Fish 336

PART 4: FISHING RULES & REGULATIONS 378

Victoria 381 • New South Wales 383 • Queensland 385 • Northern Territory 387 • Western Australia 388 • South Australia 389 • Tasmania 390

Index of Fish Species   391

Index of Place Names   392

Top right: A handsome mangrove jack
Centre right: Looking out over Gantheaume Point towards Cable Beach, near Broome in Western Australia — a dream destination
Bottom right: Boat anglers cleaning their catch after a day's successful fishing

INTRODUCTION

Welcome to *Discover Australia: Fishing*. This book is the latest in an ongoing series of Discover Australia titles from Random House Australia, each designed to help travellers and holidaymakers in their journeys around our magnificent island nation.

For a variety of reasons, today's recreational anglers are travelling further afield and more frequently in pursuit of their sport than at any time in the past. The aim of this publication is to provide a valuable source of reference and information for those travelling anglers, helping them to tap quickly and easily into the single most important ingredient in consistent fishing success: local knowledge.

To that end, *Discover Australia: Fishing* is a collaborative effort between more than half a dozen of this country's finest regional fishing writers and photographers — a hand-picked team who, between them, have more than 150 years worth of practical experience in all styles of fishing!

The combined result of such a wealth of expertise and know-how is a book that represents the most up-to-date and comprehensive source of information on locations, techniques, tackle, target species, rules and regulations ever offered to Australian anglers and those visiting our shores in pursuit of piscatorial pleasure. This publication literally does have *all* the answers to the many questions travelling anglers most commonly ask!

I am very proud to have been involved with the production of *Discover Australia: Fishing*, and I trust that you will enjoy owning and using it as you plan your next fishing getaway.

Cheers and tight lines,

STEVE STARLING

ABOUT THE EDITOR

Steve Starling, editor of *Discover Australia: Fishing* and the New South Wales' contributor, is a co-presenter of the weekly 'Rex Hunt Angling Adventures' program on Channel Seven and one of Australia's best known and most prolific fishing writers. He has written more than 15 books plus thousands of magazine articles, Australia's first fishing-related CD-ROM and various instructional videos. Steve is a regular columnist for *Modern Fishing*, *Rex Hunt's Fishing Australia* and *Canadian Sportfishing*, and his work has been translated into seven languages. He has cast a line in every state and territory of Australia, as well more than a dozen other countries, including Papua New Guinea, New Zealand, Fiji, Vanuatu, the Solomon Islands, Thailand, Finland, Norway, Russia, Canada, Britain, the United States and Japan.

ABOUT THE CONTRIBUTORS

Paul Worsteling

Patrick Brennan

Warren Steptoe

Alex Julius

Phil Stanley

Shane Mensforth

Mike Stevens

Paul Worsteling, Victorian contributor for *Discover Australia: Fishing*, writes regularly for several national titles and for the Victorian-based *South East Fishing* magazine. He owns and manages the same successful fishing tackle shop in Cranbourne where he has worked since the age of 15, and his life revolves almost completely around fishing!

Australian Capital Territory contributor **Patrick Brennan** is as happy casting a dry fly to a stream trout as he is trolling a skip bait for a marlin. He has fished in every Australian state and territory, as well as in Canada and Fiji. Patrick has six Master Angler awards from the Australian National Sportfishing Association (ANSA) and holds an Australian Fly Fishing Record for albacore tuna. In 1995, he established a guiding operation called Expert Fishing Systems.

A regular columnist for *Fresh Water Fish 'n' Tackle*, he has also contributed to *Fishing World*, *Saltwater Fishing Australia* and *Freshwater Fishing Australia*. These days, he enjoys sharing his wealth of knowledge with others and helping them learn the finer points of angling.

Queensland contributor **Warren Steptoe** is one of Australia's few successful full-time freelance fishing journalists, with regular features in *Modern Fishing*, *Modern Boating*, *Club Marine* and *Queensland Fishing Monthly* magazines. His other publishing credits have included *Playboy*, *Geo*, *NAFA*, *Fly Life* and the *Shimano Australia Year Book*. He confesses to being totally addicted to fishing in the more remote regions of northern Australia, particularly on Cape York Peninsula, and is happiest with a light baitcaster or fly rod in his hand and a pair of stout hiking boots on his feet. Warren is keenly involved in several fish management and environmental programs, and recently retired as the longest serving member in the history of Queensland's Sunfish Central Executive.

Darwin-based **Alex Julius** contributed sections on fishing in the Northern Territory. After a lengthy career in the Northern Territory Public Service, including a stint as Manager of Recreational Fishing Development, he set up his own media business in 1991. His mammoth publication—*National Australian Fishing Annual* (*NAFA*)—is now in its fifth edition. He also writes for other magazines, including *Fishing World*, to which he has contributed for more than 26 years. He is Executive Producer and Presenter of 'Fishing North Australia' on Darwin's Channel Eight, and resident fishing reporter on Channel Nine's 'Wide World of Sport'. He has produced a series of informative and highly entertaining videos on fishing throughout tropical Australia and Papua New Guinea.

Western Australian contributor **Phil Stanley** has been fishing the Wild West coast of Australia—from Esperance to the Kimberley region—for more than 25 years. He is one of Western Australia's best known angling columnists. Despite the demands of running a busy and successful fishing tackle shop, he still finds time to pen regular features and columns for *Overlander*, *Modern Boating*, *Modern Fishing* and *Western Angler* magazines, as well as undertaking fishing trips, often with his family—all of whom are keen anglers.

South Australian contributor **Shane Mensforth** has been a regular writer for fishing and outdoor publications for more than 20 years and is co-editor of *South Australian Angler* magazine. He has written four books on fishing, and contributed to many other publications. Often seen in 'Rex Hunt's Fishing Adventures', Shane also presents fishing segments on Adelaide's Channel Seven. He has fished all over Australia, as well as in Europe and throughout the South Pacific. While he is comfortable with most angling styles, he particularly enjoys slugging it out with sharks, tuna and other heavyweight game fish on serious 'stand-up' tackle.

Mike Stevens was born and bred in Tasmania, and is the Apple Isle's contributor for *Discover Australia: Fishing*. After a successful career in advertising with the *Examiner*, Mike has gone on to publish his own bimonthly fishing magazine, *Tasmanian Fishing and Boating News*.

He is involved in promoting fishing for children, and has been instrumental in the running junior fishing clinics as well as ongoing education programs for younger anglers. As part of his abiding interest in the future of the sport, Mike is an active member of the Tasmanian Recreational Fishing Advisory Committee. His favourite form of angling is fly casting for trout, but he also enjoys saltwater fishing for everything from flathead to tuna.

Bernard Yau, our fish illustrator, is a pharmacist who enjoys the challenge of illustrating new fish and meeting impossible deadlines.

HOW TO USE THIS BOOK

At its most basic level, successful angling involves understanding the three essential elements or ingredients of the sport: the fish, the locations where they live and the techniques and tackle used to catch them. Each of these issues is addressed in Discover Australia: Fishing ... and a few more besides.

The book is divided into four parts. Part 1, 'Gearing up', deals with techniques and tackle, and preparing for a fishing trip — whether it be a day trip or a major angling holiday. Part 2, 'Going fishing', is all about where to fish. Part 3, 'What fish is that?', is an A to Z guide to more than 80 species of fish commonly caught by recreational anglers. Part 4 is a comprehensive guide to the fishing rules and regulations in each state.

Rock fishing at Roebuck Bay near Broome, Western Australia

1 Gearing up

This section deals with what anglers need to know before they go fishing. There is information on what anglers should have in their tackle box, plus the various options open to them. There is also a guide for travelling anglers outlining what you need to consider when going fishing and a checklist for travelling anglers. 'Gearing up' also offers useful information on safe fishing and planning your fishing trip, as well as how to care for and prepare your catch once it is in the bag,

2 Going Fishing

'Going fishing' provides information on more than 200 fishing hot spots around Australia. The areas covered range from those suitable for day trips right up to more ambitious dream holidays. Also included are hot spots ideal for the odd weekend of piscatorial pleasure.

Each area covered has information on how to get there, the best time to fish and the major angling species to be found in that particular region. Where applicable, there is also information on special restrictions, warnings about possible dangers that need to be taken into consideration, ideas on accommodation and contact details for charter boats and fishing guides.

Not all areas have accommodation information. Where a hot spot is a popular holiday destination or within striking distance of major centres, this information has often been left to the angler to investigate, using traditional references such as phone books and travel agencies. The establishments listed are often provided as a starting point for anglers intending to travel to these destinations. Details are also given for more remote areas to assist readers where accommodation options are more limited.

3 What Fish Is That?

This A to Z guide looks at 80 or so of Australia's favourite salt and fresh-water angling species. With each species entry, we include the common and colloquial names, scientific names, description, size, distribution, fishing techniques and eating qualities. There are also fish species distribution maps and illustrations of major entries.

Dusky flathead

4 Fishing Rules and Regulations

This section is a state-by-state summary of Australian fisheries rules and regulations. The rules summarised in this section are only a few of a large range in force nationwide and were up to date at the time of going to press. This summary is simply a guide — rules change, so always check on the latest state of play *before* you go fishing.

At the end of the section on each state or territory for recreational anglers, you will also find a list of useful contact numbers.

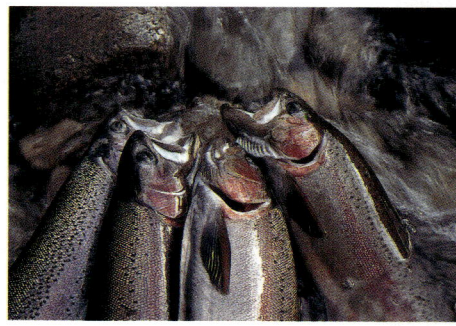
Above: Regulations apply in each state regarding the taking of certain species such as trout
Opposite: An angler cleaning his catch on the south coast of New South Wales

KEY TO LOCATION MAPS

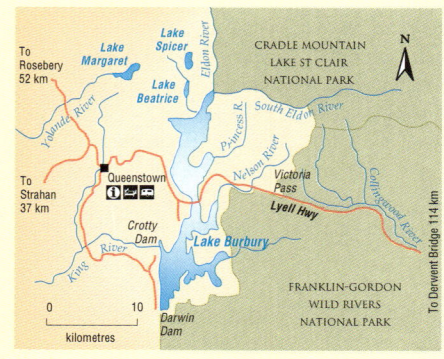

Each fishing destination has a 'mud map', provided as a guide to the area covered in the story and a basis from which anglers can gain their bearings. These maps are not intended for use as navigation aids, particularly in more remote areas or where more detailed information will be required for safe navigation through difficult or confusing waters.

Always carry detailed maps or charts of the area you wish to fish, especially if you are going out in a boat or fishing away from urban or regional centres.

LOCATION MAP LEGEND

Sealed/Unsealed Rd	Caravan Park
Four Wheel Drive	Camping Area
Walks	Accommodation
Rest Area (Picnic Area)	Information

Part 1

GEARING UP

TACKLE BOX

Since the middle of the 20th century, the fishing tackle industry has increasingly made use of modern materials such as nylon, high-impact plastics, fibreglass, polyethylene, titanium and various 'space-age' composites — particularly those based on carbon fibre or graphite. These strong, lightweight materials are now widely used in the manufacture of rods, reels, fishing lines and many other items of tackle.

Technological advances have made today's fishing tackle lighter, tougher and more efficient. In many cases, modern fishing gear is also less expensive, in real terms, than it has been at any time in the past.

Like practitioners of any sport, keen, consistently successful anglers need to stay abreast of the latest developments in tackle and techniques, and should be willing to try new ideas and equipment that have relevance to their favoured forms of fishing. On the other hand, it doesn't pay to become slavishly dependent on modern fashions. In the final analysis, there's no substitute for skill and know-how, and owning the best or most expensive gear on the market won't necessarily make you a great angler!

TERMINAL TACKLE

Fishing line and the various items attached to the end of that line are called terminal tackle or 'terminals'. This description includes line, leaders, traces, backing, hooks, sinkers, swivels, rings, floats, lures, flies and various other items.

Terminal tackle is available in a bewildering array of shapes, sizes and designs, with some hook makers, for example, listing tens of thousands of models in their catalogues. Most anglers, however, will never need to use more than a tiny percentage of the hooks, sinkers, lures, floats and swivels on the market. The secret lies in recognising which items are best suited to your specific fishing needs, and then making do with the simplest selection possible.

FISHING LINES

There are several types of fishing line available to the modern angler, and these may be roughly divided into two groups: multifilament lines and monofilament lines. As these names imply, multifilament lines are made from numerous fine strands of material which are woven, twisted or fused together, while monofilament lines consist of a single, extruded strand.

The most popular single-strand line is made from nylon and is called nylon monofilament or 'mono'. It is manufactured by melting chips or granules of nylon and then forcing or drawing the molten mixture through a nipple of a certain diameter and cooling the strand of line thus produced. This line is then wrapped onto spools of various sizes. Modern nylon monofilament is quite thin relative to its strength; it is also supple, resilient and available in a diverse range of colours, diameters and strengths (breaking strains). However, as good as modern nylon fishing line is, it is not indestructible. Exposure to abrasion and damaging forces such as ultraviolet radiation from the sun and various pollutants in the air and water will gradually weaken any nylon line.

Because of its susceptibility to adverse conditions, nylon fishing line has a limited life span. Nylon line may no longer be inexpensive, but it must still be regarded as an expendable item, and replaced regularly if unexpected breakages are to be avoided.

Experienced anglers refill or top-up ('top-shot') their reels with fresh line at least once a year.

The second type of fishing line on the market today has a multifilament construction. In the past, the most common multifilament lines were braided nylon, Dacron and Micron. Following the invention of nylon, the use of these lines was mostly restricted to some forms of big game fishing and as backing on fly reels. During the 1990s, however, this situation began to change with the arrival of a new breed of multifilament line called gel-spun polyethylene or GSP.

The advent of GSP 'super lines' has revived interest in multifilament lines. Today, GSP line is available in both a braided and a woven form, and as a heat-fused or 'fusion' style. Both forms offer very thin diameters for a given breaking strain, extremely low stretch rates and high levels of abrasion resistance.

Thanks to these advantages (and despite their relatively high prices), GSP lines are winning a small but growing share of the fishing line market, particularly amongst more experienced anglers fishing in very demanding situations.

FISH HOOKS

A fish hook is basically a curved or bent piece of wire with a point. Most hooks also have a barb of some sort, and the majority of modern hooks have eyes to which the line or leader may be tied.

The bigger hook makers offer catalogues listing thousands of hook patterns or styles, each offered in dozens of different sizes. However, the average angler will only need a handful of these.

All hook patterns catch fish, but different bends, shank lengths and wire gauges suit various types of bait and target species. Popular

A selection of the revolutionary new GSP 'super lines'

A lovely rainbow trout taken on fly fishing tackle

It is important to match hooks to baits

hook patterns include shapes known by traditional names such as O'Shaughnessy, Sneck, Carlisle, Viking and Limerick, as well as by descriptions such as long-shank and wide gap, or by various combinations of numeric and alphabetic codes.

Specialist hooks such as doubles, trebles, bait-holders and open-eyed models for ganging or linking are also available, as are an increasing variety of barbless patterns, intended to facilitate catch-and-release fishing.

Hooks are also offered in different metals, ranging from mild to high carbon steels and various grades of stainless steel. They may also be tempered or forged for increased strength and finished with bronze, cadmium, zinc, nickel, tin or even gold plating. Increasingly, manufacturers are also offering a choice of colours, usually in the form of an anodised coating in red, green, gold or black.

Many modern hooks are also acid etched to give them finer points. This process is popularly known as chemical sharpening.

More important than a hook's pattern is its size — particularly the width of its gape. More bites are missed and fish lost because a hook was the wrong size than because it was the wrong pattern.

Hook size is expressed via an unusual and confusing numbering system. Very small hooks carry the largest numbers — a No. 10 being a slightly bigger hook than a No. 12. The size of the hook continues to increase as the numeral decreases, up to a No. 1. At that point, the designation alters to an ascending number followed by a slash and a zero. Thus, the next size up from a No. 1 is a 1/0, followed by a 2/0, 3/0, 4/0 and so on.

The vast majority of fishing situations encountered by anglers in Australia are more than adequately covered by the 24 sizes between No. 12 and 12/0. Hooks smaller than No. 12 or No. 14 are mainly of interest to trout fly fishers or anglers targeting very small fish, while sizes larger than 12/0 are the sole province of heavy tackle game fishers pursuing sharks and marlin.

As the variation in size between each number hook is small, numbers can easily be skipped when putting together a collection of hooks. The following list of ten different sizes covers the vast majority of popular angling situations: Nos 12, 10, 8, 6, 4, 1, 2/0, 4/0, 8/0 and 10/0.

LEADERS AND TRACES

A leader or trace is a length of line at the working end of a rig constructed from material of a heavier or lighter gauge than the main line.

Some styles of fishing demand the use of a length of thicker, stronger nylon or even wire at the business end of the rig, in order to prevent hooked fish from biting through the line or abrading it with their teeth, gill covers or tails. This section of stronger line can also be a useful aid when landing fish.

In contrast, other forms of fishing call for a lighter, finer length of line ahead of the hook or fly, in order to reduce the chance of its detection by a timid fish.

Both types of leader or trace are available from tackle stores. The most common are 20 to 40 cm lengths of nylon-coated, multi-strand wire with a swivel at one end and a clip or snap at the other. These wire traces are useful when using light or medium tackle to catch fish with sharp teeth.

Commercially made tapered leaders for fly fishing are also popular, and are available from many specialist outlets.

Another product offered in some areas is the pre-snelled or snooded hook. This consists of a hook or hooks knotted to a length of nylon line with a loop or swivel at one end for attachment to the main line.

Bulk leader material of various types (mono or wire) is also available on spools or in hanks for those anglers who prefer to construct their own rigs.

SINKERS AND SHOT

Sinkers and shot are weights made from lead, lead alloy or other heavy substances which can be added to a fishing line or rig. They are intended to provide additional weight for casting, to take a line to the bottom, hold a bait at a desired level in the water, control the line in a strong current or balance a float so that it will register bites.

In nearly every case, the lightest sinker practicable under the prevailing conditions is the best one to use. Selecting the actual shape or design of the sinker is less important. Specialist

Ganged or linked hooks such as those used to catch this Japanese sea bream are especially useful for presenting larger baits

A tough leader or trace may help to prevent line breakages around structures such as Broome Jetty

TACKLE BOX

sinker shapes with useful applications are available, however, and these include bomb, snapper lead, star, helmet and spoon sinkers.

For most forms of fishing in Australia, ball, bean, bug and barrel sinkers are ideal. These all have a hole or channel through the centre so that they may be run freely on the main line or leader.

Split shot or shot are sinkers with a slice rather than a central line channel. They are held in place by being crimped or squeezed closed onto the line.

The sizing system for sinkers is less standardised than that used for hooks. Some makers number their sinkers beginning with the designation 00 for the smallest and moving up through 0 to 1, then 2, 3 and so on. However, it is also common practice to specify the weight in grams or ounces, especially for larger sinkers.

SWIVELS, CLIPS AND RINGS

The primary function of swivels is to prevent or reduce line twist, but they also make convenient sinker stoppers, spacers and rig connectors.

The commonest type of swivel is made from brass or steel, and is called a barrel swivel. Slightly stronger and more expensive is the box swivel. The torpedo swivel is stronger again, and best suited to very thick lines, while at the top of the range are various stainless steel ball-bearing swivels, which are particularly strong and effective.

Swivels are sized in a manner similar to that used for hooks: a No. 14 or the slightly larger No. 12 is the smallest swivel in most ranges. The size range No. 14 up to No. 4 covers most fishing situations. If larger swivels are needed, torpedo or ball-bearing models are best.

For optimum performance, always choose the smallest swivel suited to the line strength in use. In most cases, a swivel on which the wire of the eyelet is one-and-a-half to two times as thick as the main line is ideal.

Snaps, clips and snap swivels are safety-pin style devices made of brass or steel. They are commonly used to connect lures, leaders or even hooks to the line when frequent changes of terminal tackle are necessary.

Two types of rings are commonly used by anglers: split rings and solid brass rings. Split rings are similar to those found on a key ring and are made of brass or steel. They are mainly used for attaching hooks to lures. Solid brass rings make useful connectors, spacers and sinker stops when the twist-reducing properties of a swivel are not required.

FLOATS AND BOBBERS

Fishing floats are used to suspend a bait at a predetermined depth beneath the surface of the water, and also to give a visual indication of bites.

There are several styles of float. The most common is the stemmed float, which has a shaped

Above: *A collection of trolling lures*
Right: *Landing a large golden perch hooked on a lure at Lake Windamere in central western New South Wales*

body of foam, cork or wood, and a shaft of dowel, bamboo, plastic or metal. This shaft is fitted with either metal or plastic eyelets, or carries lengths of tightly fitting plastic tubing to hold the float to the line.

Floats without stems mainly take the form of bobby corks, 'bobbers' and bubble floats. Bobby corks are made of foam, cork, timber or hollow plastic. Most have a hole running through them to carry the line.

Floats of most types may be used either fixed on the line or allowed to run freely below a stopper of some sort. In general, fixed floats are best when fishing at relatively shallow depths, while running float rigs are preferred by anglers presenting a bait well beneath the surface.

LURES AND FLIES

A lure or fly is an artificial bait. Most are intended to represent a fish, prawn, crab, yabby or insect when pulled through the water or drifted along with the current. The major lure and fly types in use today include the following groupings.

METAL JIGS AND SLICES These are usually made of brass or cast metal and are chrome-plated or painted. They are cast and retrieved, jigged or trolled fairly rapidly to entice predatory species, mostly in salt water.

SPOONS Spoons look rather like the bowl of a tablespoon and are used in both fresh and salt

water. They may be cast and retrieved, jigged or trolled, usually at a slightly slower pace than jigs or slices.

SPINNERS Also called spinning blade lures or in-line spinners, spinners consist of a metal shaft or body and a rotating, spoon-like blade. They are most useful in fresh water, although they also appeal to smaller saltwater species. A variation is the spinnerbait, where the rotating blade is fixed to a coathanger-style arm extending above the lure's body.

SOFT PLASTICS These include rubber-tailed, lead-headed jigs, usually with just one hook instead of the trebles found on many other lures. They are best fished at slow to medium speeds with lots of stops and starts, and plenty of rod tip action.

TROLLING LURES While all lures may be trolled behind a moving boat, one large family of artificials is designed specifically for that purpose. Most have shredded, multi-strand plastic, vinyl or rubber skirts, and a rubber, resin or metal head. In most cases, the line is run through the middle of the lure and one or more hooks attached behind. They are used almost exclusively in salt water.

PLUGS AND MINNOWS These are fish- or insect-shaped lures constructed of timber or plastic. Most have a diving lip or bib which imparts a swimming action and causes the lure to dive beneath the surface. These lures are available in sinking and floating/diving models in a vast range of sizes and shapes.

POPPERS AND SURFACE LURES These are designed to remain on the surface, splashing, 'popping' or otherwise creating a fuss similar to that made by an injured bait fish or drowning insect. Most surface lures float at rest.

BAIT CATCHING RIGS These rigs consist of a string of two to seven small lures or flies rigged on short droppers. A sinker or metal lure is attached to the bottom end of the rig and a line tied to the opposite end. These rigs are extremely effective in the capture of bait species and also attract much larger predators at times.

FLIES Flies are a form of lure which is too light to be cast without the addition of extra weight to the line. They fall into two broad categories: 'dry' flies, which float on the surface of the water, and 'wet' flies, which sink or dive beneath the surface.

Traditionally, flies were made of natural fur and feathers, and used almost exclusively to catch trout and salmon. Nowadays, flies are made from all manner of natural and synthetic materials and are constructed in sizes and patterns that appeal to a broad range of fish in both fresh and salt water.

FISHING REELS

At its most basic, a fishing reel is a device for retrieving and storing line, although some models also play an important role in casting and when the angler is playing hooked fish. Many different styles, sizes and models of fishing reel are available, and each is suited to one or more specific types of fishing.

The simplest reel of all is a **handline** or **hand-caster**, which is typically used without a fishing rod. The most common hand-caster is a ring-shaped spool, often with a central crossbar. By holding this in one hand and swinging a weighted line in the other, it is possible to execute a reasonable cast with a handline, although handlining is really at its best in fishing situations that allow the line to be simply dropped into the water or lobbed a short distance.

Beyond the handline or hand-caster, there are six common styles or families of reel in widespread use throughout Australia today.

THREADLINE OR SPINNING REELS Spinning reels are also known as threadlines or fixed-spool reels, as well as by various colloquial names such as 'eggbeaters' and 'coffee grinders'.

Spinning reels are characterised by having spools that remain stationary when casting, with line spilling over the lip of the spool. To retrieve line, a metal or plastic bail arm is engaged. Driven by the reel's revolving rotor head, this bail arm wraps line around the stationary spool as the handle is cranked. The spool itself only rotates when line is pulled from the reel against the drag or slipping clutch, or via some form of preset 'bait-runner' line feeding device.

Spinning reels should always be located underneath the rod, although the distance from the butt to the reel depends on the weight of the tackle

A selection of lure fishing tackle used for trout fishing

and the individual preferences of the angler. They are made in both right- and left-hand retrieve versions, although most modern types are ambidextrous, with the handle able to be moved easily from the right to the left side.

These reels are much favoured by both lure and bait fishers in fresh and salt water. They are particularly well suited to casting light weights and fishing with lines up to 15-kg breaking strain.

Threadline (spinning) tackle may be used in a variety of angling environments

TACKLE BOX

Centrepin reels are most commonly used by luderick or blackfish specialists

A pair of trevally caught using a fly reel in salt water

CLOSED-FACE REELS Closed-face reels are also known as spincast reels or spin-casters. Most are small to medium reels best used in freshwater or estuarine environments, although the largest models have some limited applications in general saltwater angling.

These reels are characterised by a conical or semi-spherical metal or plastic nose-cone which covers the spool. A hole in the centre of this cover permits the passage of line, which is picked up and wrapped around the stationary spool by one or more spring-loaded pins mounted on the internal rotor head. As with spinning reels, the spool of a closed face reel only rotates when line is pulled from the reel against the preset tension of the drag.

Closed-face reels are used on top of the rod, and are often coupled with special baitcaster or plug rods featuring a trigger grip or pistol-style butt configuration. They are made in both right- and left-hand drive, although some types are ambidextrous.

To cast a closed-face reel, a thumb button or lever is depressed, retracting the pick-up pins and securing the line against the inside of the spool cover. Releasing the button or lever allows line to flow freely over the lip of the spool and out through the hole in the cover.

Closed-face reels are easy to use and accurate over short casting distances. Great care must be taken to prevent corrosion in these reels, however, especially when they are being used around salt or brackish water.

BAITCASTER REELS Baitcasters or baitcasting reels are also known as plug reels. They are small to medium overhead reels with a revolving spool, and most are fitted with a level-wind or line-laying device. Despite their name, these reels are used more often to cast lures than with natural baits.

The axle-mounted spool of a baitcaster turns to recover line as the handle is cranked, as well as to pay out line when a cast is made. The spool will also rotate to yield line against the tension of the drag when a fish is hooked.

Baitcasting reels are designed to be used on top of a rod, and are often coupled with specialist baitcaster or plug rods featuring a trigger or pistol-grip butt configuration. A button, lever or thumb-bar is used to disengage the gears prior to casting. With the reel in free-spool, the angler uses his or her thumb to restrain the line, lifting it when a cast is made and lightly 'feathering' or thumbing the spinning spool to prevent over-runs and backlashes.

Most baitcasters have the handle on the right-hand side and cannot be adapted for left-handed cranking. Some manufacturers, however, also offer left-hand models.

Because the spool spins when a cast is made, over-runs and tangles are always a possibility. These potential problems deter many newcomers from trying baitcasters. All quality baitcasters are fitted with anti-backlash devices of one type or another, however, and with a reasonable amount of practice, most users can soon achieve trouble-free casting.

While more expensive and slightly more difficult to master than spinning and closed-face reels, baitcasters offer superior drag performance, line capacity, casting accuracy and control over hooked fish. For this reason, they are greatly favoured by experienced anglers undertaking demanding styles of angling in fresh and salt water.

OVERHEAD REELS Overhead reels are also called multipliers or revolving drum reels. They are almost identical in design to baitcasting reels, but are generally larger and do not usually feature a level-wind line-laying device.

As their name implies, overhead reels sit on top of the rod. They vary in size from the dimensions of a large baitcaster right up to giant, lever drag game reels capable of holding a kilometre or more of 60-kg line! Some are intended for casting while others — especially the larger game and trolling reels — are not.

Over-runs and backlashes are potential problems when casting overhead reels, due to the revolving spool. Modern cast controls featuring mechanical, centrifugal or magnetic spool brakes remove some of the risks, but there is still no substitute for practice and an 'educated thumb'.

Once mastered, overheads offer superb performance and are much favoured by anglers who regularly need to throw their baits or lures long distances, or battle big, active fish.

SIDECAST REELS Although sidecast reels originated in Britain during the 19th century, they are rarely used outside Australia these days. In fact, the world's only major manufacturer of sidecast reels — the Alvey company — is located in the suburbs of Brisbane.

A sidecast is essentially a centrepin reel with a spool that can be twisted or rotated through 90° so that it may be cast in the manner of a fixed-spool reel, with the line flowing off over the lip of the spool.

To recover line once a cast is completed, the spool is twisted back until it is once more aligned with the rod. This simple but innovative feature

A tailor landed while using a sidecast reel

A baitcaster or plug reel, lure and silver perch

turns the sidecast into one of the most effective casting reels ever built, especially when combined with light and ultra-light baits and lures. In essence, sidecasts offer the powerful direct drive and sensitivity of a centrepin, combined with the easy casting capabilities of a spinning reel. They also require the minimum of care and maintenance. For these reasons, they have long been popular with Australian saltwater anglers, particularly those fishing from beaches, ocean rocks and jetties.

The main disadvantages of sidecast reels are the potential line twist generated by the rotation and re-alignment of the spool, their relatively slow retrieve speed and the need to use a longer than normal rod with large diameter runners.

CENTREPINS AND FLY REELS
Centrepins are amongst the most basic of all fishing reels. They consist of a line storage spool revolving on metal bushes or ball bearings attached to an axle, which is in turn mounted to a back plate. Most are direct drive, with no gears, although some have drag or clutch systems.

Centrepins are not widely used in Australia today, with the exception of blackfish reels and fly reels. The only significant group of Australian anglers who rely on free-running centrepin reels are the luderick or blackfish specialists of the Australian east coast, many of whom still find these simple but effective reels ideal when float fishing in moving water.

In contrast, fly reels are modified centrepins designed specifically for fly fishing. Although constructed in a very similar manner to other centrepins, fly reels do incorporate certain distinctive features.

Most fly reels are fitted with line guards, constantly engaged ratchets or clickers, and at least a rudimentary drag system. Most are also characterised by the holes drilled in their spools and back plates to reduce the weight of the reel and allow the fly line and backing to dry after use.

FISHING RODS
In its most basic form, a fishing rod is an extension of an angler's arm. It allows a baited line, fly or lure to be manipulated and presented in ways that would be almost impossible by hand. Mated to a reel designed for casting, a rod will also allow a sinker or lure to be cast a considerable distance. Just as importantly, a fishing rod allows large fish to be battled and tired out on relatively fine, light line, and greatly aids in the landing of these fish.

The second half of the 20th century has seen natural rod-building materials such as cane and timber almost totally replaced, first by solid fibreglass, then by hollow or tubular fibreglass, and later by various forms of graphite or carbon fibre composites. Thanks to these advances, today's top-quality fishing rods are lighter, stronger and more responsive than any which have come before them.

MULTI-PIECE AND TELESCOPIC POLES
Fishing poles are intended for use without a reel. They have reached a pinnacle of development in the hands of European coarse or match fishers, and Japanese specialists pursuing species such as *ayu* and *hera*.

While some poles may be as short as a metre or two in length, most are much longer, with some measuring between 10 and 12 m. Because of their length, these poles are usually constructed in multiple sections which either pull apart or telescope together for storage and transportation.

The angler's line is attached to the tip of the pole or fed down through the middle of the top section to an internal anchoring point. Rubberised shock absorbers or lengths of pole elastic are sometimes used to avoid line breakages when large fish are hooked.

SPINNING RODS
Spinning or threadline rods are intended for use with spinning reels. They range from ultra-light, single-handed 'flick sticks' of 1.5 m and less up to heavy duty, double-handed spinning rods measuring anywhere from 2 to 4 m in length.

Using a rock/surf rod with a large threadline reel

TACKLE BOX

A snapper taken on heavy baitcaster tackle

Today, these rods are made almost exclusively from hollow, high-modulus fibreglass, graphite, Kevlar, boron, or a combination of those substances. Their straight handles or grips may be constructed from rubberised materials such as Hypalon and Duralon, or from cork or even strong cord wrapped around the rod shaft or blank.

BAITCASTER OR PLUG RODS
Baitcaster or plug rods are designed to be used with baitcasting reels, smaller overheads and closed-face reels, all of which are intended to be used on top of the rod. Many of these rods feature a butt or handle with a moulded pistol-grip or trigger design, although there has been a more recent trend towards the use of straight butts, especially on heavier, double-handed plug rods.

Baitcaster or plug rods range from light and ultra-light single-handed models measuring anywhere from 1.5 to 2.2 m in length, up to double-handed versions typically measuring between 1.8 and 2.5 m.

Quality baitcaster rods are typically fitted with as many as eight or even nine line guides. Such a large number of runners is needed to keep the line clear of the blank under load, and to remove potential friction points. In contrast, small numbers of baitcaster rods (as well as spinning rods) are now available with no guides whatsoever—the line runs through the centre of the blank instead. These are called inter-line or inner-line rods.

SIDECAST RODS
Rods intended for use with sidecast reels, especially when fishing from beaches, ocean rocks, breakwalls or jetties, are usually quite long (3 to 4.5 m) and have their reel seats located no more than 10 to 20 cm from the butt end of the rod. These sidecast rods typically carry between four and six runners or line guides, with the guide nearest the reel (the 'stripper') having an inside diameter of at least 5 cm to facilitate easy line flow and long casts.

BOAT, SPORT AND GAME RODS
Boat rods and those designed specifically for offshore sport and game fishing cover a range of angling options. However, most are characterised by being relatively short (1.4 to 2.2 m) and are intended primarily for fighting fish and controlling lines rather than casting. Several types of reels may be used on these rods, including centrepins (snapper winches), sidecasts, medium to large threadlines and various overheads. Each of these reel styles calls for a slightly different type of rod.

The rod styles most specifically designed for offshore sport and game fishing are jig rods and game or trolling rods. These are primarily intended for use with overhead reels, and most are designed to be used with just one or two specific line test 'classes', as set down by the rules and regulations of various fishing organisations.

These rods usually carry between five and eight line guides or runners, and these may be either fixed guides or special roller runners. Many are also fitted with a slotted butt cap intended to fit into a gimbal belt worn by the angler.

ACCESSORIES AND PARAPHERNALIA
In addition to those items of tackle directly involved with the fishing process, anglers also require a range of other odds and ends. The number and complexity of these accessories varies with the type of fishing being undertaken, but generally there's a need for something in which to store and transport terminal tackle and other equipment, as well as a knife for cutting bait, trimming lines and cleaning the catch. In some cases, anglers will also need a landing net or a gaff, or both, in order to secure the catch, and some form of hook-removing device.

Once again, simplicity is the best policy. For many anglers, a simple plastic bucket and a cheap knife may be all the accessories needed at first. By starting in this way, with nothing more than the absolute basics, it's easy to add items as new needs become apparent.

TACKLE BOXES
Every angler needs to develop a workable system for tackle storage and transportation. For a boat fisher, this may consist of a chest-style tackle box, while for the more mobile rock or beach angler, a couple of small, snap-top containers in a haversack or shoulder bag may prove to be a better solution.

The separate, modular system involving small tackle boxes offers many advantages, including the ability to carry only that gear which is needed for a particular outing.

Most anglers also find it worthwhile to keep a reserve of terminal tackle at home and to carry just enough for immediate use in their working tackle box or boxes. A cupboard or chest of drawers of the kind designed to hold screws, nuts and bolts, sewing equipment and the like is ideal for home tackle storage.

HAVERSACKS AND CARRY BAGS
Rock, beach or shore-based river and lake anglers often need to carry their gear a considerable distance. Light haversacks, day packs or shoulder bags are ideal for this purpose. Simple shoulder bags with single straps are sufficient for lightweight saltwater work and most freshwater scenarios. An advantage is their ability to be easily swung off the shoulder and set aside on the bank while casting or playing a fish.

Canvas or nylon A-frame day packs are also well suited to many fishing needs, although the angler who carries lots of gear, or also needs space for camping equipment, extra clothing and

A small hand gaff has been used to land this mackerel tuna

food, should definitely consider purchasing a larger, H-frame hiking pack.

Some boat fishers and travelling anglers also find considerable merit in soft, circular, kit bag style luggage for transporting reels, small tackle boxes, lunch, a camera and dry clothing.

FISHING KNIVES Most anglers soon discover the need for at least two knives in their fishing kit: a rugged, general purpose blade and a more specialised filleter.

The general-purpose or bait knife should be relatively inexpensive and have a reasonably wide, stiff blade made of hard stainless steel. A scaler or rope cutting saw on the back of the blade can be useful, as is a built-in bottle opener. Some of the lighter skindivers' knives on the market are ideal for this application.

The second knife should be a more expensive, high-quality filleter with a long, narrow and slightly flexible blade. Ideally, this blade will be made of slightly softer stainless or high carbon steel than the general-purpose knife to facilitate fast, easy sharpening on a stone or steel.

Both knives should have handles that offer a good grip, even when wet, and they need to be stored in stiff, hard plastic pouches or sheaths.

GEAR FOR LANDING FISH Anglers who pursue larger, more active species, use light lines or fish from boats, piers, high rock ledges or steep banks may need to use a net or gaff to secure their catch safely.

A generous, sturdy landing net is usually best where the target species run from 500 g up to 7 or 8 kg in weight. Bigger fish generally demand the use of gaffs.

A gaff consists of a stout hook fixed securely to a pole made of aluminium, fibreglass, bamboo or wood. It is used to impale and lift a fish that has been fought to the bank, shore or boat.

A second style of gaff—called a flying gaff— is intended for really big, active fish and has a detachable head attached to a cable or rope. When a big fish is gaffed with such a device, the head detaches from the handle and the fish is secured by way of the rope, which is normally cleated off to a strong point in the boat.

Still another type of gaff can be clipped to a taut, nylon fishing line and allowed to slide down to the water on a length of cord. This is known as a cliff gaff, and is an invaluable tool when fishing from very high rock ledges, cliffs or tall piers and jetties.

HOOK REMOVERS, CLIPPERS AND OTHER TOOLS Hook removers, line cutters or trimmers and pliers or folding, multi-purpose tools containing pliers and screwdrivers are also very handy accessories for most kinds of fishing, as is a set of weighing scales or spring balances.

A pair of ordinary nail clippers or small scissors makes a useful line trimmer for cutting lighter nylon and gel-spun polyethylene lines. Always use side cutters or special heavy-duty wire cutters with hardened jaws when working with wire and very heavy nylon leader materials.

Hook removers include simple plastic disgorgers, long-nosed pliers, surgical artery forceps, button-hooks of strong wire attached to a sturdy handle and specialised 'hook-out' style pliers manufactured expressly for the task.

All these tools should be kept close at hand or stored in a belt sheath ready for immediate use.

BAIT GATHERING GEAR
Anglers who gather or collect their own bait supplies need a range of accessories and tools.

Bait pumps (also called yabby pumps, worm pumps or nipper guns) are used to gather squirt worms, sand worms, yabbies (pink nippers) and other productive baits from sand or mud flats exposed at low tide. If the flats are covered by water, it may be necessary to deposit the contents of the pump into a sieve or colander, which retains the baits and allows the sand and mud to fall through onto the ground or into the water.

A fine-mesh prawn scoop net can be used to gather prawns, shrimp and small fish for bait, but always check on the legality of these devices and any regulations concerning their size and shape that may apply in your area before using one.

Mullet and other small bait fish can also be caught in traps baited with bread, or with the aid of cast or drag nets, where these are legal. In addition, mullet, yellowtail, slimy mackerel and other small bait fish can be berleyed into an area then fished for using light lines and tiny hooks baited with fish flesh, prawn pieces, dough or mince meat. These small bait fish can be kept alive for a time in a bucket if the water is periodically changed. For longer term storage and transportation, it may be necessary to replenish the dissolved oxygen in the water via a battery-operated aerator or air pump, powered either by flashlight batteries or a 12-volt car or motorcycle battery.

TIDAL TABLES, MAPS AND CHARTS
Tide charts are an essential tool for all anglers fishing in salt or brackish water. Compiled by institutions such as the Flinders University of

Hooked up to a jumping Australian salmon at sunset

South Australia, these charts are reproduced throughout the country by a wide range of organisations and companies.

Tide charts usually indicate moon phases, and show approximate times and levels of high and low tide for a given location (such as Fort Denison in Sydney Harbour), as well as indications of local variations for locations where the tide occurs earlier or later than the mean times stated on the tables. Some also include the times of sunrise and sunset. This is all-important information when planning a fishing trip.

Much can also be done to improve the outcome of any fishing trip by studying maps or charts of the areas to be fished.

Offshore anglers can obtain Admiralty charts from good chandleries and speciality mapping outlets, while shore-based, estuary and inland fishers can also benefit greatly from the study of topographical maps. These are available from the Central Mapping Authority (CMA), AUSLIG, State Lands Departments and other organisations.

It is also possible for anglers to check on land ownership and rights of access to waterways through the Cadastral map register, Pastures Protection Board stock route maps and forestry department maps.

THE TRAVELLING ANGLER

Increasingly, it seems that successful fishing and travel go hand in hand. Each year, more and more Australian anglers are hitting the road in search of greener piscatorial pastures. There are many reasons for this trend: notably the combination of higher disposable incomes, better roads, improved standards of infrastructure in remote regions and a boom in the number of professional guides, fishing lodges and charter services now operating throughout the country.

Sadly, a deteriorating general standard of fishing, especially in waters close to our larger cities and towns, is another motivating factor driving many anglers to look further afield in the pursuit of their sport.

The truth is, more anglers with better equipment, greater skills and higher levels of expectation are chasing fewer and fewer fish on most of our southern and urban waterways. As fish numbers in these areas decline, angling attention naturally shifts elsewhere. Over the past decade or two, the most clearly identifiable directions for this shift have been from the south of our nation towards the north, and from densely populated stretches of coast or river to more remote areas.

Careful selection and packing of gear is essential, especially when travelling to isolated locations

CHANGING PATTERNS

Of course, there's nothing particularly new about this fascination with distant waters. Even back in the days when our parents and grandparents were making the shift from Rangoon cane poles to fibreglass rods, it was every suburban angler's dream to load up the family car with gear and head north to the sun-baked realm of barramundi and coral trout.

In those days, this was a serious adventure, complete with a long list of potential hazards. It was also relatively expensive and took more time than the average annual holidays allowed. For these reasons, few working families ever realised their dreams. Most members of those earlier generations had to wait until retirement to make their big trip.

The 1970s and early 1980s marked a golden era for the great road safari. At that time, the ranks of serious travellers were dominated by retired couples and small parties of young, single people — mostly men — seeking adventure before settling into full-time jobs or tertiary studies.

Times change, and while those two groups are still well represented along the Gibb River Road or on the Bruce Highway, several important new elements have now joined the ranks of piscatorial pilgrims. The first of these are family groups taking advantage of better roads, more flexible holiday schedules and comfortable, air-conditioned 4WD vehicles.

The second is a new generation of fishing traveller, those who choose to fly to their dream destination in a few short hours aboard a jet aircraft, then link up with a friend, fishing guide, tour operator, lodge or charter boat for a week or two of intensive fishing action.

BE PREPARED

Regardless of the mode of transportation or the final destination, a major fishing trip represents a significant investment of time, effort and money. It's not something to be embarked upon lightly. Those who enjoy their angling travel adventures most are generally the same people who put the greatest effort into planning and preparing for the event.

One of the most important keys to success lies in selecting the right tackle to take on any fishing trip. In this regard, it makes very good sense to base your choice of equipment around the types of gear with which you are most comfortable and familiar. If that means using tackle that's a little heavier or lighter than normally recommended for a particular task, or choosing a spinning (threadline) reel where some experts recommend a baitcaster, it doesn't really matter. Within certain boundaries, such variables come down to individual tastes and preferences.

Obviously, if your intended trip targets only one or two types of fish in a couple of specific locations, you can cut down dramatically on the amount of gear taken and be much more specialised in its selection. On the other hand, if you're likely to sample a broad range of fishing opportunities, you will need to be well enough prepared — within reason — to meet any likely eventuality.

THE ESSENTIAL TRIO

For most fishing safaris that take in a mix of freshwater and saltwater angling opportunities, you will require a bare minimum of three rod-and-reel outfits or 'combos'.

The first of these should be a light, single-handed spinning (threadline) outfit. This should consist of a 1.7- to 2.2-m rod capable of accurately and repetitively casting lures, baits or sinkers in the 5- to 20-g weight range. This would be mated to a small or medium spinning reel filled with 2- to 5-kg breaking strain line. Ideally, this reel will have a spare spool, allowing one spool to be filled with 2- or 3-kg line and the other with 4- or 5-kg line.

This outfit can be used to target bream, whiting, garfish, flathead, tommy rough, trout, perch and many other species in southern salt and fresh waters, as well as sooty grunter, jungle perch, tarpon (ox-eye herring), saratoga and smaller billabong barramundi in the north. It is also ideal for most bait-catching purposes.

The second essential travelling combo is the classic barra or snapper outfit. This may be based on either a spinning (threadline) or baitcaster reel loaded with 6- to 12-kg line. The rod, which may be a double- or single-handed model, should be between 1.8 and 2.2 m in length and capable of effectively and accurately casting lures, sinkers or baits weighing between 15 and 40 g. Ideally, this rod will have a butt configuration that fits easily into a rod holder when trolling from a boat.

The nature of the third outfit in this essential trio will be dictated by the areas to be visited and the likely breakdown between shore-based and boat fishing opportunities. For anglers intending to do a lot of land-based fishing, especially in the southern half of the continent, a surf or rock casting outfit built around a 3.2- to 4-m rod and medium to large spinning, overhead or sidecast reel filled with 8- to 12-kg line is likely to be the best choice.

For keen boat anglers, a combo intended for offshore trolling, jigging, live baiting, dead baiting and bottom fishing is highly desirable. This should be based on a quality star or lever drag overhead reel capable of holding at least 350 m of 12- to 20-kg line and mated to a suitable rod in the 1.6- to 2.2-m length range. This rod should have a slotted gimbal fitting at the butt, so that it will key into a rod holder or fighting belt if necessary.

Anglers intending to pursue a mix of saltwater boat and shore fishing should consider carrying both of these outfits, thereby turning the 'essential trio' into an 'essential quartet'.

Remember, however, that these three or four outfits represent the *minimum* tackle requirements needed to handle a reasonably wide range of Australian fishing requirements. Many keen anglers will opt to carry additional, specialised outfits to be used in specific locations and when targeting certain species, as well as one or more back-up combos and possibly also a few handlines.

PRE-TRIP MAINTENANCE

It's one thing to have the right gear for the job. It's quite another to have it in tip-top shape.

Well before your big trip, you should strip all your reels of line, service and lubricate them thoroughly and re-spool them with new line. If you don't feel qualified to service your own gear, have it done for you by a reputable tackle shop.

At the same time, go over your rods thoroughly from butt to tip. Check all the guide or runner inserts for cracks and the bindings for frays, and replace them where necessary.

Empty all your terminal tackle and lures out onto sheets of newspaper, clean your tackle boxes and check all the hooks, rings, swivels and so on for signs of rust or other damage. Once again, replace any suspect items before carefully re-stocking the tackle box.

Finally, when you're completely happy with everything, pack it carefully for the trip. Tackle boxes should be locked where possible and rods placed in soft cloth bags inside stout PVC rod tubes, with the screw caps taped firmly in place or locked to deter inquisitive fingers.

TRANSPORTING TACKLE

Clearly, you'll need something to pack all your fishing gear into, as well as to transport your clothing, toiletries, camera gear and so forth. If you're flying to your destination, try to limit yourself to just *three* items of baggage, consisting of a large duffel or kit bag, a tackle box or camera bag, and a rod tube (either a commercially made tube, or one constructed at home from tough PVC sewer pipe).

Hard tackle boxes are quite good for transporting quantities of lures, terminal items, spools of line and even reels, but the newer generation of soft-sided, modular tackle packs with a collection of smaller plastic boxes inside are even better, and add considerable flexibility to the task of packing for different fishing trips.

Whatever forms of luggage you choose, make sure that they can be securely locked, and that your name, address and telephone number are clearly displayed on the outside.

A CHECKLIST FOR TRAVELLING ANGLERS

The following list of 20 items or groups of items should be regarded as the bare essentials for any travelling angler embarking on an extended fishing trip into new or unknown territory.

- A minimum of three or four rod-and-reel combos intended to cover the broadest possible range of fishing opportunities
- Large tackle box or soft-sided tackle pack, well stocked with terminal tackle, lures, floats, etc.
- Basic tackle repair and maintenance kit and collection of spare parts
- At least one bulk spool of spare line for each reel
- Hook-out device or long-nosed pliers
- Lure de-snagging device and length of strong cord
- High-quality, multi-purpose folding belt tool
- File, hook hone and/or sharpening stone
- Large landing net and/or sturdy hand gaff
- Heavy-duty bait or general purpose knife in a stout sheath with belt loop
- Quality filleting knife
- Tape measure and/or hand-held weighing scales (spring balance)
- Fish-handling or tailing glove made from Kevlar or similar tough material
- Line trimmers and/or wire cutters
- Leader material, including single strand and multi-strand wire
- Insect repellent (including spray and lotion styles)
- Broad-brimmed hat (or peaked cap with neck flap)
- SPF 15+ sunscreens (including lotions and lip creams)
- Quality polarised sunglasses
- Camera with spare batteries and film

Gear should be well organised and packed when travelling to any fishing destination

PLANNING YOUR TRIP

The act of travelling to exciting new angling locations is not, in itself, a guarantee that you will automatically enjoy exceptional fishing! In fact, many footloose fishers come home from major expeditions rather disappointed with their results, and with a newfound respect for the calibre of angling available on their own doorstep.

Making use of professional fishing guides, charter boats or specialist angling lodges while on the road may well swing results in your favour. However, you still shouldn't expect immediate and spectacular results simply because you've travelled a relatively long distance to go fishing.

Chances of success are dramatically increased by careful planning and pre-trip research. Efforts in this area are usually repaid many times over, and can spell the difference between an extremely enjoyable and memorable expedition ... and one that burns brightly in your memory for all the wrong reasons.

DOING YOUR HOMEWORK

Closely examine all the books, magazine articles and other material you can find concerning the destinations you plan to visit on your trip, and carefully read any brochures or other literature supplied by tourism associations and commercial operations such as fishing guides, lodges and charter boats operating in those areas. Be alert for what's *not* said in this promotional literature, as much as for what is! If you do intend to use a guide, lodge or charter service, contact the operators of this business well in advance and ask for references, including the names of past clients whom you can call or write to for an honest assessment. If the operators are serious — and confident about their performance — they should have no hesitation in supplying such contacts.

CHOOSING WHEN TO GO

Deciding where to go on your big fishing trip and who to fish with is at least half the battle ... the rest lies in deciding *when* to go. Each region of Australia has its peak angling season and, unfortunately, these don't always coincide neatly with the best and most comfortable times to travel. Furthermore, no two seasons are exactly the same, and cyclic anomalies such as drought, flood, storms and the like can impact adversely upon the best-laid travel plans.

Many anglers plan their northern or tropical fishing safaris for the southern winter months of June, July, August and early September. This decision is typically based on a desire to escape the worst of the southern chill, and the knowledge that the weather will almost certainly be warm, stable and dry in the tropics at this time of year.

There's certainly no denying that travelling conditions can be extremely pleasant in the tropics during the dry season months. Cape York, the Gulf of Carpentaria, the Top End and the Kimberley are at their most 'user-friendly' during July and August, with nights cool enough for comfortable sleeping (you may even need a blanket!) and long days of dry heat under clear, blue skies. Sadly, the standard of fishing on offer doesn't always match the weather at these times.

The fishing 'up north' is often relatively slow during the months of July, August and early September, particularly in estuaries, rivers and billabongs. Water temperatures are at their lowest, and the activity levels of many fish (especially barramundi) tend to decline significantly as a result. In addition, prevailing south-east trade winds blow almost every day on the east coast of Queensland and in the Gulf of Carpentaria. These often reach 20 knots or more by mid-afternoon and seriously curtail most open-water activities.

Despite these negatives, there's still some great fishing to be had in the tropics during late winter, particularly for species such as billfish, mackerel and most reef-dwelling fish. In more remote regions, such as Kakadu, Arnhem Land or the Kimberley, visitors should also be able to find at least *some* barra, mangrove jacks, threadfin salmon, queenfish, trevally and various other estuarine and inshore species at this time.

At the opposite end of the spectrum, it's rather foolhardy to plan your big tropical trip for the middle of the wet season! Although it's widely promoted these days by tourism authorities as the 'green season', and some exceptional fishing is available from late December until the middle

El Questro Station in the Kimberley region of Western Australia is dramatically situated

Travelling to a fishing dream destination by light plane is often part of the adventure

ABORIGINAL COMMUNITIES AND LAND

Much of inland Australia and parts of the far north are Aboriginal land. These areas can be cattle stations that are now owned and run by Aboriginal communities, or vast areas of former reserve land that have been deeded to an Aboriginal community as freehold land or areas of Crown land that have been handed back to a particular group of Aboriginal people. In the Northern Territory, more than 50 per cent of the land is now owned by Aboriginal groups, while in other states this proportion is less.

Permits and Access

You need an access permit to enter or cross most Aboriginal land. While some are easy to obtain, such as the permits required to use the Gunbarrel Highway west of Uluru, other areas are almost impossible to enter.

For further information and requirements concerning access permits, you should write to or contact the relevant Aboriginal land authority. Remember to allow plenty of time before your planned trip, as it can take some time to get a reply.

Portaging a canoe through rapids on the Clarence River in northern New South Wales

Riding camels at sunset on Cable Beach in Broome, Western Australia — sometimes fishing is just one of the attractions on offer

PLANNING YOUR TRIP

Surf fishing on Flinders Island in the Bass Strait, an attractive southern destination

of April, travelling north during this period can be a chancy business. Cyclones, tropical depressions and fierce monsoonal downpours are par for the course. As a result, many northern roads — even major highways — can be closed to all traffic for days or weeks at a time.

Still, there are often lengthy spells of settled weather during the wet season (particularly on the east and west coasts). This is when southern visitors can expect to strike patches of better-than-average estuary and inshore action around the larger centres such as Townsville, Cairns and Broome. Just remember that travelling north at such times is a gamble, and it pays to build a considerable degree of flexibility into your schedule.

Between these two extremes lie the post-wet 'run-off' and the pre-wet 'build-up' periods. Generally speaking, these include the six or seven weeks from late April until early June and a somewhat longer period from the end of September until early or mid-December. Most experienced northern anglers would agree that these two 'shoulder' periods offer the finest fishing opportunities in Australia's tropical regions.

Only by thoroughly doing your homework before a trip will you uncover such information and be able to plan your itinerary accordingly.

PERSONAL PREPARATION

As well as planning your trip thoroughly and having your tackle and other gear in good order, it pays to be in reasonable physical shape yourself before departing on a major fishing trip. This doesn't necessarily mean working out at the gym every day for a month beforehand, but it does extend to getting several good night's sleep during the preceding week, doing a bit of walking to stretch those office-bound muscles and avoiding overindulgence in rich food or alcohol. This also applies during the plane trip or drive to your chosen destination.

Similarly, if you have a nagging cold, upset stomach, any major muscular aches and pains, or a problem with your teeth, it makes very good sense to see someone about it *before* you leave home. The last place you want to spend your valuable (and limited) holiday time is in a dentist's chair or a doctor's surgery.

Many keen anglers find that it's also a good idea to commence a course of vitamin supplements at least a week or two before departing on any major fishing expedition, and to keep this up for the duration of the trip. Vitamin C may help to ward off colds and sniffles — which are all too easy to pick up in planes or crowded, air-conditioned airport terminals — and a vitamin B complex is an excellent buffer against the bites and stings of sandflies and mosquitoes. These insects may still bite you after taking a course of vitamin B, but reactions to their bites are usually much less severe as a result of the vitamins.

Naturally, if you're headed overseas to places such as New Guinea, the Solomons or Vanuatu, it's important to see your family doctor well ahead of departure and obtain a prescription for anti-malarial tablets, as well as seeking advice regarding the necessity of having shots to ward off various other bugs. At the very least, take this opportunity to have a tetanus booster, which is something *all* anglers should do every six or seven years, and an inoculation against hepatitis A.

BE METHODICAL

Once you've done your homework and planning, picked when and where to go, prepared your gear and attended to your personal wellbeing, it's vitally important to be completely methodical in

BASIC 4WD EQUIPMENT, SPARES AND TOOLS

While some of the following may not be required for a day trip to Moreton Island or the like, carrying them does make sense for longer trips. If travelling for a more extended period, you could include a more comprehensive range of tools and spares.

BASIC EQUIPMENT ALWAYS TO BE CARRIED
Basic recovery equipment
Basic first aid kit
Fire extinguisher
CB radio
Tool kit and spare parts (see list)
10 litres of water (in semi-remote and remote desert country, you'll need much more)
Map of area and surrounds
Matches, compass, torch, knife
Space blanket

BASIC SPARES TO CARRY
Radiator hoses, heater hoses
Fan belts (an emergency Uni-Belt is handy and easier to fit)
Fuses, globes, electric wire
Spark plugs, plug leads, points
Coil, condenser
Tyre tube

BASIC TOOLS TO CARRY
Set of ring and open-end spanners (to suit your vehicle)
Adjustable spanner, plug spanner
Wheel brace, jack and jacking plate (30 cm x 30 cm x 2.5 cm board)
Screwdrivers/Phillips head screwdriver
Hammer, chisel
Hacksaw and spare blades
Files, including a points file
Pliers and wire cutters
Feeler gauges
Tyre levers
Pump and pressure gauge for tyres
Tube/tyre repair kit
Battery jumper leads
Repair manual
WD40 or similar aerosol lubricant

Heli fishing in the Kimberley region of Western Australia

your final packing and preparation. Make a comprehensive checklist and tick each item off as it goes into the rod tube, tackle box or bag. If tickets or other travel documentation are involved, triple check that you have them on you before leaving home, and give yourself plenty of time to reach the airport for checking-in and boarding.

The more methodical and conservative you are, the lower your stress levels will be and the more you'll enjoy the entire experience of travelling... After all, it's meant to be fun!

A MATTER OF ATTITUDE

Finally, a word about attitude and the travelling angler... If you set off on your big fishing adventure with extremely high expectations and a very specific set of fishing-related goals, there's a strong chance that you'll come home disappointed. If, on the other hand, you set out with a more flexible approach, a desire to learn and a willingness to be surprised and delighted by what you find along the way, you'll most likely have the time of your life.

Australia is still one of the luckiest countries on earth in terms of the recreational angling opportunities on offer. That doesn't necessarily mean, however, that the standard of fishing will always be either easy or outrageously good. What it does mean is that the experience of being there and actually doing it will be unforgettable — and after all, isn't that why we travel?

TEN COMMANDMENTS FOR TRAVELLING ANGLERS

Travelling to find fish can be great fun. In fact, going fishing in new locations and catching species you've never encountered before is one of the most exciting and rewarding aspects of the sport. However, angling travel is not without its potential pitfalls.

To help you avoid some of the most common mistakes, we've prepared the following 'Ten Commandments for Travelling Anglers'. Stick to these and you won't go too far wrong!

1. First, do your homework. Learn as much as you possibly can about your intended destination well before you leave home. Dig out old magazine articles, talk to friends who've been there and phone a reputable information provider such as the Fishing Info Line (1902 727 555) for an up-to-date report. (You can also check out their Internet site.)
2. Plan your trip in detail. Draw up an itinerary and make a thorough list of everything you need to take, then tick each item off as you pack. Double-check all the really important things, such as air tickets, passports, money, travellers cheques, credit cards, reels, lures and the like.
3. Make all your bookings and travel arrangements through a reputable operator — ideally, a travel company that specialises in fishing. (There are several of these in Australia, and most of them advertise in the monthly fishing magazines.)
4. Buy any new tackle needed for your trip from a reputable tackle shop. Not only will they be able to cater to your more specialist requirements, but also chances are that at least someone on the staff will have been where you are going, or know a bit about it — and that sort of first-hand knowledge is absolutely priceless.
5. If you're using a lodge, guide or charter boat service, make contact with the operator a week or two before the trip by phone or fax. In a short, courteous communication, establish that they are expecting you on the correct date and for the right period of time, and that they plan to undertake the types of fishing in which you're most interested. Also, if you intend to use any of their tackle, check that it's the right sort and in good repair.
6. Take out travel insurance to cover the loss of fares through forced cancellations and the loss or damage of any baggage or tackle, as well as personal injury. Travel insurance is money well spent!
7. Pack wisely. Large, soft-sided but extra tough duffel or kit-style bags are much better than hard suitcases. Pack all rods in extra-strong PVC tubes after first padding them with soft cloth bags or bubble wrap. Label every item of baggage with your name, address and telephone number.
8. Check carefully on any baggage weight or size restrictions before you leave home. Many smaller airlines, in particular, are very strict in this area, and some stipulate a limit of 12 or 15 kg per person.
9. Give yourself plenty of time to make any travel connections. Avoid becoming stressed. Be relaxed and positive... After all, this is your well-deserved holiday, and it is supposed to be fun! Consider the trip itself as part of the adventure, rather than as a chore that must be endured just to get where you're going.
10. Take a decent camera and plenty of film with you. Photographs (or videos) from a great trip will keep the memory alive for many, many years.

SAFE FISHING

Although recreational fishing is great fun and an extremely healthy outdoor activity, it can potentially be as dangerous as any other sport, particularly if certain common sense rules are ignored.

As fishing, by its very nature, takes place on and around water, there is always a risk of falling into that water. For this reason, all anglers should learn how to swim well, and should also master at least some basic lifesaving skills. If you can't swim 100 m and tread water for 5 to 10 minutes while fully clothed, you are taking a major risk each time you go fishing. Not only that, you are also placing others, who may need come to your aid in an emergency, at considerable risk.

MENTAL ATTITUDE

Perhaps the most important aspect in all water safety matters is mental attitude. Anglers should always be aware of the risk of falling, being knocked, tipping or washing into the water while fishing—either from the shore or from a boat.

If you think about this aspect of the sport every time you fish, and ask yourself the simple questions 'What would I do if I fell in?' and 'Where would I try to come ashore?', you will be much better prepared to handle such an emergency should it arise. Shock and panic are always your major enemies in such a crisis, and mental preparedness is the best way to avoid them.

BASIC FIRST AID

Besides water safety skills, all anglers should also have at least some knowledge of basic first aid.

Common injuries suffered by anglers include cuts and punctures from knives, hooks, fish teeth or spines and oysters or coral, as well as falls,

Using long-nosed pliers to remove the hooks from a dusky flathead landed with the aid of a net

sunburn, heat stroke and hypothermia or exposure. Anglers should possess the basic skills needed to treat such ailments, and have access at all times to an adequate first aid kit.

Undertaking a St John Ambulance or Red Cross course in first aid is also highly recommended. Barring this, all anglers should at least read a few textbooks on first aid and familiarise themselves with such basic lifesaving techniques as mouth-to-mouth (expired air) resuscitation and cardiac massage; know how to stop or reduce bleeding, treat burns and deal with other common injuries; and adequately be able to treat snake bites and venomous fish stings.

SUN SENSE

Awareness of the dangers of prolonged exposure to sunlight has increased greatly in recent years. Most anglers now understand that excessive amounts of ultraviolet radiation can potentially cause skin cancers, especially now that the earth's protective ozone layer appears to be breaking down, at least in the higher latitudes towards both poles.

When fishing or boating, get into the habit of wearing a broad-brimmed hat and quality sunglasses (ideally, polarised glasses). Do this every time you go outside, even in winter.

On particularly hot, bright days, cover up even more thoroughly with a lightweight, long-sleeved shirt or blouse, and long trousers. Apply a sunscreen to exposed areas of skin and make sure you choose a water resistant lotion with an SPF factor of 15+ or higher.

Excessive exertion in high temperatures can also cause sunstroke and dehydration. Keep your fluid intake up (not alcohol!) and avoid stressful activities during the hottest hours of the day.

DANGEROUS MARINE LIFE

Some fish are potentially dangerous to handle. Certain species—including Spanish mackerel, wahoo, barracuda, tailor and many species of shark—have very sharp teeth and powerful jaws.

Others—including stonefish, the various rock cods and scorpion fishes, fortescues, bullrouts, stingrays, catfish, gurnard and even flathead—carry spines or spikes that can inject venomous material into an unwary hand or foot. This threat

The dogtooth tuna has powerful jaws and sharp teeth that can cause serious injury to careless or unwary anglers

FIRST AID CHECKLIST

A basic first aid kit including a manual from the Australian Red Cross should always be carried, and restocked as items are used so that the kit is always complete. Anglers should carry as many of the following items as possible.

- Antiseptic fluid (Betadine, Dettol or similar)
- Antiseptic cream
- Eye bath and eyestream drops
- Assorted sticking plasters, strips and spots
- Steristrip wound closures
- Elastic and crepe bandages for sprains and snake bite
- Sterile gauze bandages (50 and 75 mm)
- Triangular bandages to support limbs and hold dressings in place
- Adhesive tape, cotton wool, tissues
- Scissors, safety pins
- Thermometer
- Calamine lotion, Stingose or similar for insect bites
- Fine-point tweezers

ranges from the mildly toxic, anticoagulant mucus of the flathead to the life-threatening venom of the stonefish.

Still other fish pose a threat because of their sheer bulk and power. Large cobia, kingfish and tuna are all capable of knocking anglers off their feet and even breaking bones with their thrashing tails. Then there are the fish with specific problem areas, such as the sharp, roughened bills or spears of sailfish and marlin; the stout, serrated dorsal spines of leatherjackets and boarfish; and the strong electric charge of the numbfish or torpedo ray.

In addition to fish, sharks and rays, many other aquatic creatures are potentially hazardous. These include the blue-ringed octopus, various stinging jelly fishes (particularly the sea wasp or box jelly), venomous cone shells, stinging corals, sea snakes and estuarine crocodiles, to name just a few of the more obvious threats.

Finally, there are those fish that are poisonous if eaten. These include the highly toxic toad fishes and puffers, and also certain tropical species known to carry the potentially life-threatening ciguatera toxin. (Common carriers of ciguatera include Chinaman fish, red bass, red paddletails, fusiliers, large coral trout and even Spanish mackerel. Anglers visiting tropical areas should always seek local advice on the likelihood of encountering this problem.)

The more you know about these potentially dangerous fish and other marine creatures and the threats they pose, the less likely you are to be injured while handling them.

As a rule, be especially careful when dealing with any new or unfamiliar species. If in doubt, use tough gloves, fish-handling tongs and grippers, or wrap the fish in a wet towel or hessian bag before removing the hook with a pair of long-nosed pliers or a special disgorger. Never eat unidentified or suspect seafood.

Learn as much as you can about the fish you catch and other potentially hazardous forms of marine life in order to avoid injury or illness.

CLEANING UP OUR ACT

Almost as important as our personal health and safety while fishing is the care and respect we show towards the angling environment and those with whom we share it.

Sadly, anglers appear to be amongst the worst litterers in the community, and the litter they commonly leave — especially discarded nylon fishing line, plastic bags, lure packaging and various tackle wrappers — is amongst the most dangerous and long-lasting.

There are no longer any excuses for this kind of behaviour. We know the damage caused by discarded plastics and other waste products, and we understand how simple it is to avoid this damage. So, take your rubbish home with you and dispose of it correctly. While you're at it, pick up a little of that left by others.

We can take this conservation role one step further by being eternally vigilant in defence of our fisheries and their habitats. There is no

ROCK FISHING SAFETY

Fishing from the ocean rocks around our coastline is a potentially dangerous pastime that continues to claim many lives and cause serious injuries every year, particularly in New South Wales and Western Australia, where this form of angling is most popular.

The majority of rock fishing fatalities occur when anglers are washed from ledges or platforms by heavy seas or large waves. However, falls from cliffs and steep slopes, or injuries resulting from landslides and rock falls, also contribute to the annual toll.

The application of a little common sense can greatly reduce the risks associated with rock fishing. Adhering to the following ten 'golden rules' of rock fishing safety should ensure that you enjoy a long and trouble-free lifetime of 'rock-hopping':

Ten Golden Rules of Rock Fishing Safety
1. Never fish from the ocean rocks alone.
2. Don't go rock fishing if you can't swim.
3. Always tell someone where you are going and when you will return.
4. Have an action plan in case of emergency.
5. Wear appropriate footwear and clothing.
6. Carry a throwable flotation device or wear a buoyancy vest.
7. Never climb on ropes or ladders of uncertain age and strength.
8. Avoid turning your back on the sea.
9. Observe your chosen fishing spot from a safe distance for at least 15 minutes before venturing out onto it.
10. Finally, remember that no fish or item of snagged tackle is worth risking your life!

shame in reporting the wrongdoings of others to the relevant authorities. Indeed, the shame today is in looking the other way and upholding the 'she'll be right' tradition to the detriment of our priceless and fragile environment.

Caring for the health of our angling environment is as important as caring for our own health

CATCH OF THE DAY

One of the prime motivations for going fishing is the promise of a delicious meal of fresh seafood. These days, we are constantly reminded of the importance of a healthy diet, and it has been clearly established that fish is one of the healthiest forms of protein available. At the same time, seafood prices have sky-rocketed, putting many species of fish and crustacea into the 'luxury' bracket. Catching your own represents a major saving, as well as a chance to enjoy seafood at its freshest and most nutritious.

If the fish you catch are to taste their best, they must be handled correctly between the water and the frying pan or grill. They must also be prepared in a way which brings out their flavour, without destroying the vitamins and minerals locked inside.

CARING FOR THE CATCH

The basis of any personal philosophy of angling ethics must be founded on a deep respect for the fish you catch. This begins with the simple acknowledgment that fish are living creatures, and that those intended for the table should be killed as quickly and humanely as possible.

Caring for your catch begins the very moment a fish is landed. Fish destined for the table may be kept alive for short periods in a keeper net or live bait tank after capture. Generally speaking, however, most fish should be killed promptly with a sharp blow to the head, then immediately 'bled'.

To kill and bleed most fish, simply sever one or more gill arches with a sharp knife after striking the fish on the head with a heavy, blunt instrument. Better still, cut right through the 'throat latch' area under the gills and bend the fish's head back sharply in order to sever the spinal column.

After killing and bleeding the fish, it should be laid flat in a shaded spot and covered with a wet sack or towel. Ideally, place it on ice in an insulated cooler or styrofoam box.

Bacteria of many sorts begin to grow and multiply in the stomach cavities and blood of all fish from the very moment of death, causing gradual deterioration of the flesh, loss of nutrients and, in the worst cases, a risk of serious food poisoning. The formation of these bacteria is greatly accelerated by heat, but will also occur in cool weather. Regardless of weather conditions, always aim to clean your catch within an hour or two of landing it, and try your best to get the fish onto ice or into a refrigerator within three or four hours of capture. This is especially critical on very hot days and in tropical areas.

CLEANING AND PREPARING THE CATCH

To clean or gut most fish, slice the fish open along the belly, from the vent to the gills. Be careful not to rupture the stomach and other organs with your knife point.

After opening the stomach cavity, lift out all the organs inside and cut them free. You should also remove the gills and as much of the kidney (which form a 'blood line' along the roof of the stomach cavity) as possible. A spoon, round-bladed knife, scrubbing brush or square of hessian or similar rough material can be very useful in removing this blood line.

After cleaning, wash the carcass thoroughly in the coolest water available. Wherever possible, saltwater fish should be washed in clean salt water, as fresh water can leach out the flavour. For the same reason, never leave gutted fish or fish fillets soaking in water for more than a few minutes at a time.

If you wish to remove the fish's scales, do so using the back of your knife or a specially designed fish scaler, working in short, sharp strokes from the tail towards the head.

Increasingly, however, many anglers are opting to leave the scales on their catch, filleting and skinning the fish just prior to cooking it. Certainly, leaving the scales on helps to retain moisture and prevent the catch from drying out and deteriorating.

Fish can be prepared in a number of ways: as fillets, steaks or cutlets, or the entire carcass may be left intact. Each method suits a different range of species and cooking techniques. You will find these various approaches detailed in better seafood cookbooks and in some of the pamphlets distributed by the fish marketing authorities and their equivalents in various states and territories.

Once thoroughly cleaned and chilled, fish may be stored in the refrigerator (below 5°C) for at least three or four days prior to consumption, or frozen for up to six months. Remember, however, that some deterioration and loss of flavour is inevitable if fish are kept in this way. Most species are best if eaten within 48 hours of their capture.

FREEZING FISH

To freeze fish, the fillets or whole carcasses should first be tightly wrapped in plastic film or aluminium foil, taking care to exclude as much air from the package as possible. They should

Good fish handling begins the moment the fish is landed and continues all the way to the table

A large catch of reef fish taken in tropical waters

then be brought down to a temperature well below 0°C (ideally about –15°C) as rapidly as possible and held there until needed.

One very successful way of freezing fillets, steaks and fish pieces is to place them in a container of very cold sea water or salted tap water. The entire container is then frozen, making sure none of the fish flesh protrudes above the surface of the ice. Although it means taking up rather a lot of space in the freezer, this method generally yields a superior product.

To thaw frozen fish, lift the packages out of the freezer and place them in the normal section of the refrigerator around 24 hours prior to cooking. In cool weather, the frozen fish may be covered with a cloth and left on a bench or some other shaded part of the kitchen. A microwave oven can also be used to thaw frozen fish. Thawing should not be accelerated by immersing the fish in hot water, however, or by leaving the package in direct sunlight. Both methods promote the rapid development of harmful bacteria.

Once thawed, fish flesh should be refrigerated, and then consumed within 24 hours. It should never be re-frozen.

COOKING FISH

To really enjoy the flavours of fresh seafood, stick to simple recipes. Avoid heavy sauces and complex cooking techniques. Try grilling small fish whole, or pan-frying fillets and cutlets in a little olive oil. Many fish are also delicious when barbecued, baked whole in the oven (conventional or microwave), or wrapped in aluminium foil and cooked in the coals of a campfire.

Regardless of the cooking method chosen, be careful not to overcook fish. Timing is critical in seafood cookery, and it pays to err slightly on the underdone side, rather than ruin the meal by cooking the flavourful juices out of that prize catch.

Unlike some red meats, there is little risk in eating underdone or even raw fish of most species (although there are exceptions). In fact, certain cultures—such as the Japanese—make great use of raw fish, and the end result is almost always a pleasant surprise to those doubtful consumers who eventually decide to 'give it a go'. Some even come to enjoy the experience on a regular basis!

RESPECTING YOUR CATCH

Remember, the underlying spirit of sport fishing is a contest between person and fish. This matching of wits between the hunter and prey is older than humankind itself, yet it still touches a basic chord within us, and satisfies a deep-seated urge to provide sustenance for ourselves and others. Few modern sports satisfy this need so completely as angling.

For fishing to be truly enjoyable and rewarding, regardless of the beauty and peace in our surroundings, there must always be the expectation of a catch. Fishing is nothing without the promise of fish. They, alone, are the magic ingredient which can transform a pleasant walk along the beach or a day on the water into a consuming passion that recognises no distinctions of age, sex, race or class. In an age of terrible pressures on our natural resources, it would serve us all well to remember the absolute importance of fish to our sport ... Without them, there is no magic.

LIMITING YOUR KILL

Today, many popular Australian recreational angling species are subject to bag and size limits, as well as various other controls (see 'Rules and regulations', pp. 378–90). For the most part, these restrictions are generous, and the majority of anglers would be delighted to fill a limit for any species. However, situations do occasionally arise when it is possible to catch large quantities of fish with relative ease. Whether the species in question is protected by legal limits or not, we owe it to ourselves and to future generations of Australians to practise restraint at these times.

Those happy occasions when fish are plentiful and willing provide the perfect opportunity to observe, experiment and learn. They allow anglers to try new techniques or test unused items of tackle that may later improve results during tougher times when fish are harder to catch. Always treat a 'hot bite' as a valuable learning experience, rather than as a chance to fill the freezer!

CATCH-AND-RELEASE

As an extension of the philosophy of limiting one's kill, an increasing number of modern anglers are choosing to release all or at least part of their catch, even when targeting species that are highly regarded as table fish. Such behaviour is most widespread amongst freshwater anglers pursuing bass, barramundi and trout, but is quickly gaining popularity elsewhere in the fishing world.

Catch-and-release angling emphasises the challenge and reward of finding a fish, inducing it to bite and playing it to the bank or boat. The entire process of the 'hunt' may be enjoyed without the need for a 'kill'. This allows fragile fish stocks to be preserved and means that a single fish may be enjoyed by several anglers, greatly enhancing its value as a recreational resource.

Although still in its relative infancy in Australia, catch-and-release fishing is clearly the way of the future, especially if we are to maintain healthy fisheries in hard-hit areas. Certainly, this has proven to be the case in many parts of North America and Europe. Those anglers who are yet to return a large, highly desirable fish to the water alive and watch it swim off are denying themselves a unique experience. If you haven't done so already, try it ... It feels good!

Rex Hunt and Rhonda Burchmore ham it up with a tiny snapper on Sydney Harbour ... the fish was carefully released, of course! Always observe size and bag limits in the areas where you fish

Part 2

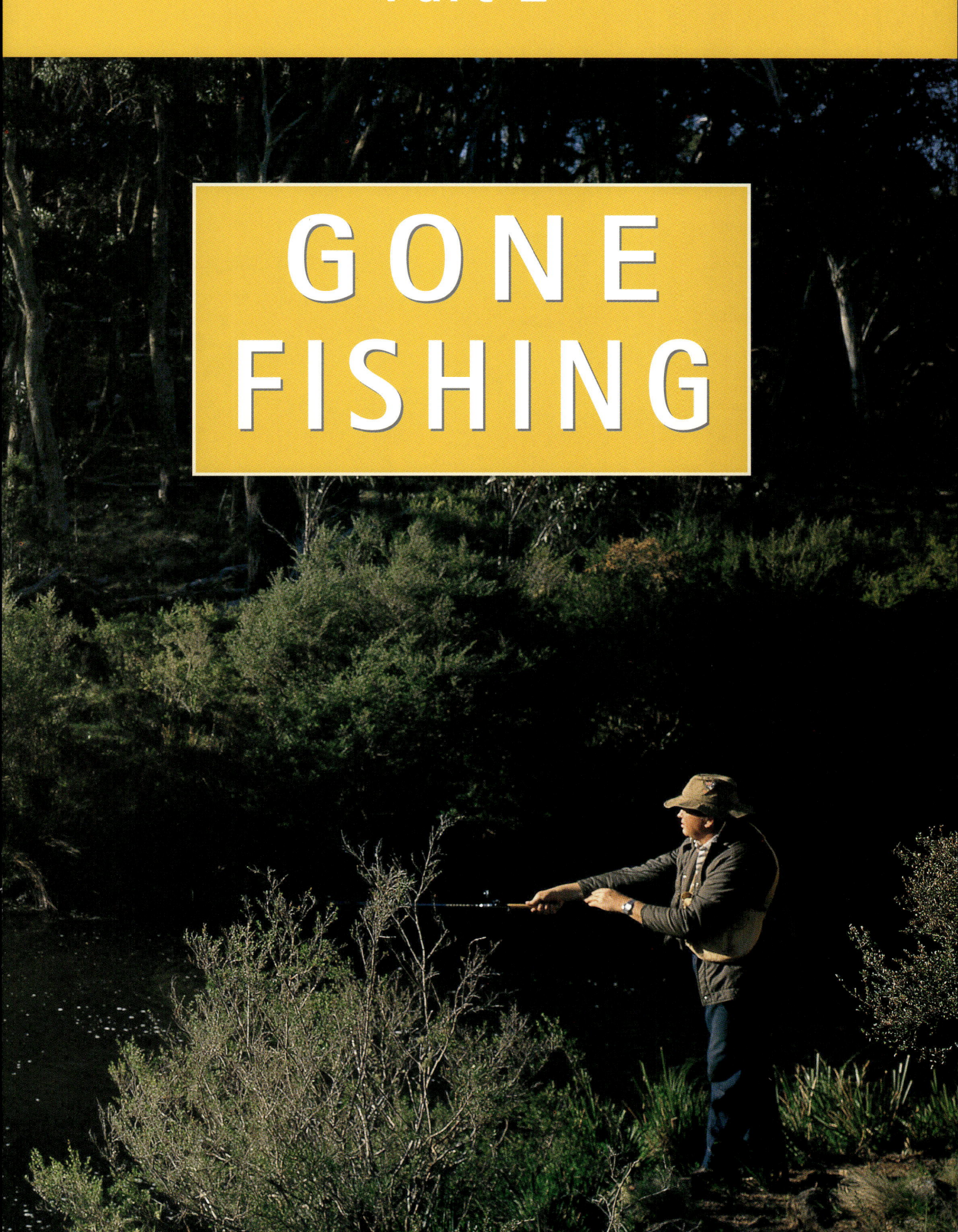

GONE FISHING

VICTORIA

FISHING HOT SPOTS

- Port Phillip Bay (pp. 40–1)
- Western Port (pp. 42–3)
- Geelong and Corio Bay (pp. 44–5)
- The Yarra River (pp. 46–7)
- North-Eastern Estuaries (pp. 48–9)
- Gippsland Lakes (pp. 50–1)
- Lakes Entrance (pp. 52–3)
- Wilsons Promontory and Corner Inlet (pp. 54–5)
- Timber Lake (pp. 56–7)
- Lake Eildon (pp. 58–9)
- Dartmouth Reservoir and the Mitta Mitta River (pp. 60–1)
- Trout Streams of South Gippsland (pp. 62–3)

Although it is Australia's second smallest state (after Tasmania), Victoria's land area of just less than 228 000 square kilometres actually means it is much larger than many European countries, including England, Austria and Hungary! Within its extensive borders, Victoria contains a very diverse range of land forms, from the arid semi-deserts of the north-west to the high alpine regions of the central north and the lush coastal plains of the east and south-east.

Its waterways are similarly varied and include cold mountain brooks, big meandering western rivers, natural and artificial lakes, long beaches, rocky promontories and the open seas of Bass Strait and the Southern Tasman.

Melbourne's skyline from the banks of the Yarra

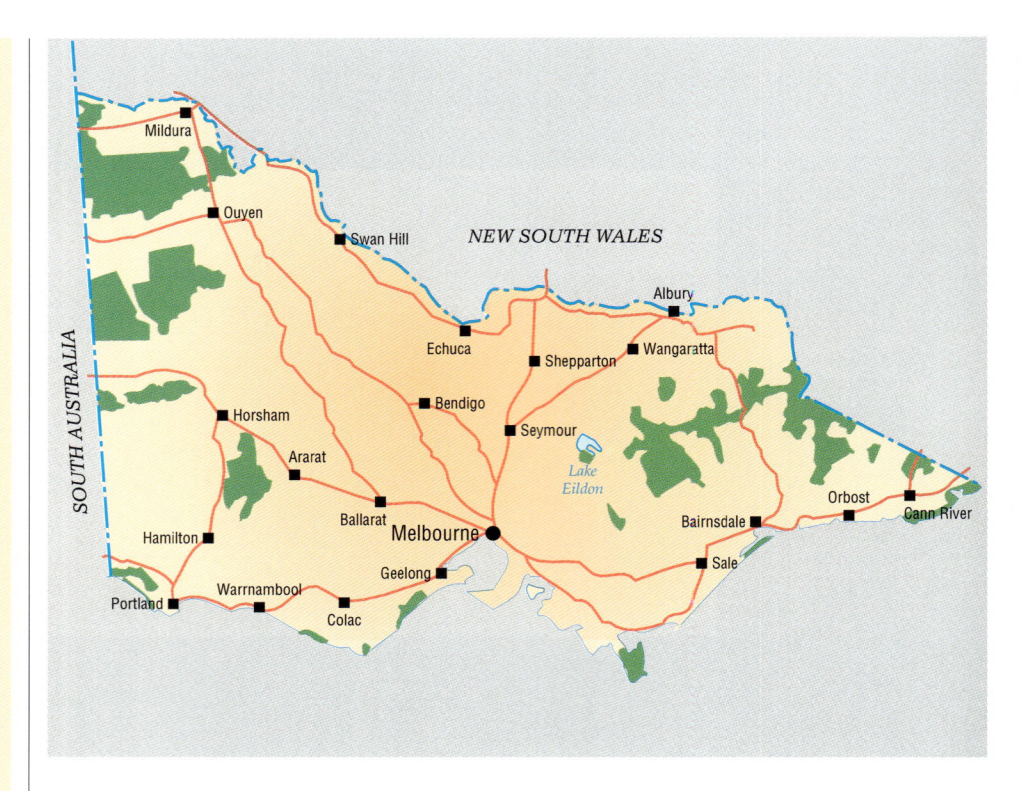

The four seasons are quite clearly defined in Victoria—more so than in most other parts of the mainland—and many first-time visitors have commented on the distinctly 'European' feel of the place, be it in the cosmopolitan surrounds of downtown Melbourne or the cultivated farmlands of the Goulburn Valley and Gippsland regions.

In many ways, this green and pleasant state has more limited recreational angling options than the other mainland states, mostly because of its climate, geography and population density, which is the highest of any region in Australia by a significant degree. Yet, despite this, Victorian anglers are amongst the most numerous, and certainly the keenest, in the land. Victoria offers some exciting fishing opportunities for local and visiting anglers alike. Indeed, there is some brilliant fishing to be had. However, it tends to occur in more isolated pockets than in most other states, and is often heavily dependent on weather, time of year and other prevailing conditions. As a rule, anglers work harder in Victoria than in any other Australian state to bring home a reasonable catch of fish.

In the relatively recent past, a big part of the problem with Victoria's fisheries stemmed from the management practices of government agencies such as the Fisheries Division of the Department of Conservation and Natural Resources (DCNR). This was perhaps best demonstrated by the tragic decline of snapper stocks in Port Phillip Bay from the 1960s onwards and what used to be an almost total lack of control over the state's once excellent trout fisheries.

Happily, there now seems to have been a general turnaround in this situation—largely driven by a powerful ground swell of public opinion. Sensible salmonid (trout and salmon) regulations have now been introduced, including closed seasons and bag limits. There may even be light at the end of the tunnel concerning depleted saltwater fisheries such as Port Phillip Bay's remnant snapper stocks, although it is a little early yet to break out the celebratory champagne!

Despite these recent significant improvements in the state of play, it is still true that Victorian anglers tend to travel further and more often in the pursuit of their sport than most other Australians. They are much more likely to cross state borders in the hope of finding better fishing.

It is also true that Victoria is not high on the list of preferred angling destinations amongst Australians living in other states and territories. Nonetheless, there are very nice surprises in store for those who give Victoria a chance, and who take the time to explore some of the less travelled corners of the Garden State thoroughly. Several of these fascinating backwaters and byways are examined in detail in this chapter, along with many of Victoria's larger and better known angling waters.

OPPOSITE PAGE:
Top left: *Tidal River on Wilsons Promontory*
Top right: *A small freshwater stream near Bright*
Bottom left: *View over the expanse of Port Phillip Bay from Mount Martha*
Bottom right: *Fishing on Ninety Mile Beach*

Contact Numbers

For the latest information on Victorian regulations call one of the numbers shown below:

FISHERIES INFORMATION LINE
(03) 9643 3533

**DEPARTMENT OF CONSERVATION AND
NATURAL RESOURCES OFFICES**

Alexandra	(03) 5772 0200	Horsham	(03) 5381 1255	Portland	(03) 5523 3232
Bairnsdale	(03) 5152 0400	Kerang	(03) 5452 1237	Sale	(03) 5144 3048
Ballarat	(03) 5337 0782	Lakes Entrance	(03) 5155 1539	Shepparton	(03) 5831 1777
Benalla	(03) 5761 1611	Mallacoota	(03) 5158 0219	Swan Hill	(03) 5033 1290
Bendigo	(03) 5444 6666	Melbourne	(03) 9651 3728	Traralgon	(03) 5172 2111
Box Hill	(03) 9296 4400	Mildura	(03) 5022 3000	Wangaratta	(03) 5721 5022
Colac	(03) 5233 5533	Mornington	(03) 5975 4779	Warrnambool	(03) 5561 9950
Cowes	(03) 5952 2509	Noojee	(03) 5628 9507	Wodonga	(03) 6055 6111
Geelong	(03) 5226 4667	Orbost	(03) 5161 1222	Yarram	(03) 5182 5155

PORT PHILLIP BAY

IN BRIEF

MAP REFERENCE: PAGE 64 E5
GETTING THERE Port Phillip Bay lies south of the city of Melbourne
BEST TIME TO FISH October to May
BEST TIME TO TRAVEL Year-round
MAJOR ANGLING SPECIES Snapper, whiting, flathead, barracouta and squid
WARNINGS The Rip, at the narrow entrance to Port Phillip Bay, is a particularly hazardous area subject to very strong tides and rough conditions. The whole of Port Phillip Bay can become extremely rough in strong winds. Great care should also be exercised when boating in and around the busy shipping channels

The vast expanse of water that forms Port Phillip Bay is Melbourne's favourite aquatic playground and attracts an immense amount of recreational fishing attention each year, particularly during late spring, summer and autumn. Considering its proximity to Australia's second largest city and the considerable pressures placed upon it over the past two centuries, the fishing in Victoria's largest body of semi-enclosed tidal water is still quite reasonable. Unfortunately, the legendary snapper runs of old are today only a pale shadow of their former glory, but some very good 'reds' are still taken each year, along with far larger numbers of flathead, King George whiting, garfish, barracouta, squid and other southern species.

Limited shore-based fishing opportunities do exist around Port Phillip Bay, particularly from the various jetties, wharves and other artificial structures. The best results, however, are achieved by boat anglers.

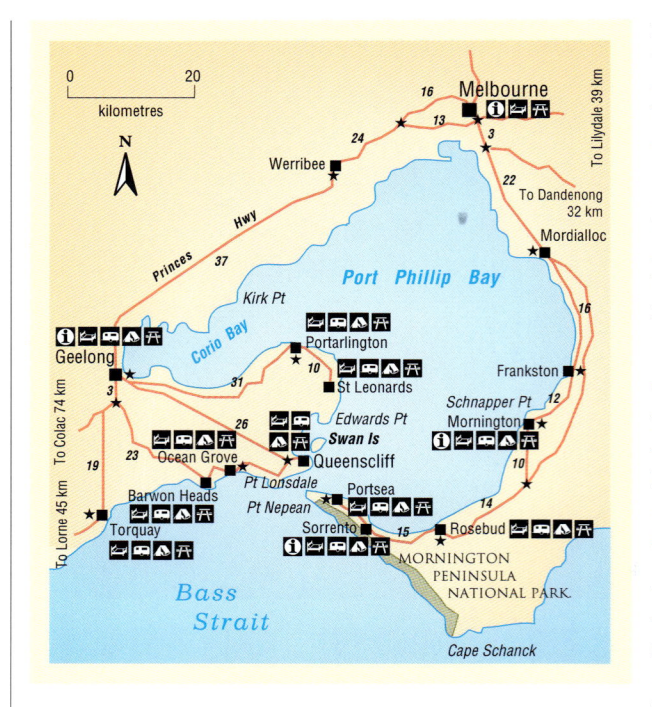

FLATHEAD BY THE THOUSAND

Flathead are by far the most common catch from the waters of Port Phillip Bay and during the summer months countless thousands of 'frogs' (as they're popularly known in Victoria) are taken by recreational anglers. While generally small (with many under or just on the minimum legal length of 25 cm), these little fish provide hours of entertainment and many welcome meals, especially for casual anglers.

Drifting in a boat is definitely the most productive method for catching flathead in Port Phillip Bay, with baits such as half pilchards, pilchard fillets, fish strips, whitebait and squid pieces attracting the best results. Casting from jetties and piers will also produce flathead, especially if the angler's bait is slowly retrieved across the sea bed.

Plenty of action is provided at times by huge schools of small barracouta. These fish will eagerly grab baits and lures all over the bay and sometimes become a nuisance for those pursuing more desirable target species.

THE MAIN PRIZE

The most attractive of all the target species available in Port Phillip Bay is the mighty snapper, and it is this fish that draws the greatest following amongst anglers.

Sadly, snapper numbers in the bay declined dramatically through the late 1980s and early 1990s, resulting in a series of very poor seasons. On the brighter side, recent efforts to reduce and ultimately phase out the impact of scallop dredging and certain other forms of destructive commercial fishing in Port Phillip Bay appear to be working. As a result, the standard of snapper fishing may gradually improve, although only time will tell.

From late September onwards (particularly after the AFL Grand Final has been played), thousands of boats of all sizes begin to gather over the bay's known snapper grounds and marks. Peak snapper action usually occurs in late October and November, tapering off through December and into January before hitting a second, less spectacular peak in February or March.

Snapper hot spots vary with the seasons, and can even change from day to day, but locations with a solid reputation for producing snapper include grounds off Point Cook, Kirk Point and Portarlington on the western side of Port Phillip Bay, as well as Sandringham, Black Rock, Beaumaris and the reefs off Mordialloc and Patterson River in the east.

PINKIES AND REDS

Many of the snapper caught in Port Phillip Bay these days, particularly during summer, are 'pinkies' from less than legal size up to 1 kg or so. A smattering of larger fish continues to be taken, however, especially by serious anglers who are willing to fish through the night. These include reasonable numbers of 'reds' in the 3- to 7-kg range, with the occasional monster of 9 kg or better still showing up every year.

A few snapper also continue to be caught during the winter by anglers hardy enough to brave the frigid conditions, but there are a lot of hours between bites.

A flathead moving along the bottom of the bay, near Rosebud on Port Phillip Bay's eastern shore

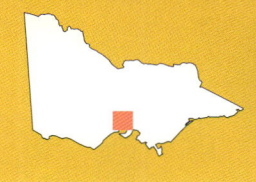

Popular snapper baits in Port Phillip Bay include pilchards, fish flesh strips or chunks (particularly strips of tuna or bonito), flathead and barracouta fillets, live or dead garfish, squid, octopus and cuttlefish. For the small fish or 'pinkies', half pilchards, pilchard fillets and cut fish flesh baits generally produce the most consistent results.

Snapper Tactics

Anglers fishing the upper portion of Port Phillip Bay tend to use 'floater' baits with little or no lead. A small sinker the size of a pea is usually more than enough weight. However, the stronger tidal run in the lower (southern) portion of the bay often necessitates the use of heavier sinkers in the 60-g range.

Berleying definitely improves snapper catches. While many anglers simply cut up a few pilchards and toss them out near their baits, a berley bag or dispenser located near the sea bed is a better option in any sort of current.

A view of Port Phillip Bay across Mornington Beach

Delicious Whiting and Other Catches

While snapper are regarded as Port Phillip Bay's most exciting inhabitants, many people prefer to fish for the delicious King George whiting. These fish are often abundant over broken rubble grounds, near weed beds and on sand patches close to shore.

King George whiting mostly run from 250 to 700 g, with the odd exceptional specimen weighing more than 800 g. They begin to show up in numbers during late November or early December, hitting their peak in mid-summer and slowly tapering off as autumn arrives.

The fondness of these tasty little fish for inshore gravel areas and sandy patches amongst relatively shallow weed beds means that they are easily accessible, even to smaller trailer boats. In addition, they often bite right through the day, although dawn, dusk and tide changes are usually the peak times.

The humble mussel, which grows on rocks, piers and jetties around the bay, is a choice whiting bait, although these shellfish are becoming increasingly difficult to find in any numbers. Luckily, Jap clams, pipis and tenderised squid and cuttlefish can usually be relied upon to produce a catch of these marvellous little fish if mussels can't be obtained.

Other fish found in good numbers in the same areas as whiting include garfish, leatherjackets and red mullet. The gars, in particular, are a firm favourite with many anglers, and these fish grow to impressive sizes in the waters of Port Phillip Bay.

Berley is essential when chasing garfish, and some of the best mixtures contain breadcrumbs, bran, pollard. One of the many commercially prepared mixes available can be used as well, and a dash of tuna oil also helps. Float-suspended baits of maggots (gentles), small worm or prawn pieces and little strips of fish flesh or squid are best for tempting garfish.

Both calamari and aero ('arrow') squid are sometimes caught throughout Port Phillip Bay, too. Most of these cephalopods fall to the charms of a slowly worked pawn-style squid jig or 'jag'.

Queenscliff and The Rip

The southern end of Port Phillip Bay — beyond a line drawn roughly from Indented Head on the Bellarine Peninsula to Rosebud or Rye on the Mornington Peninsula — takes on a more oceanic nature than the upper bay, thanks to the healthy flush of water pushing in and out through the notorious Rip with each change of tide.

Encounters with ocean-going species such as Australian salmon, silver trevally, yellowtail kingfish, sharks and even tuna are more likely in this area, and there are also reasonable numbers of whiting, snook, pike, learherjackets and the odd snapper to be had.

Big yellowtail kingfish (including the odd specimen in excess of 25 kg) feed right in The Rip at times, and there was a strong surge of interest in targeting these tackle busters through the 1980s. However, numbers appear to have declined, and catching yellowtail kingfish in The Rip today is a chancy affair at best, and one mostly pursued by experienced, dedicated crews who know exactly how to handle the potentially treacherous currents and standing waves of this turbulent area.

Southern bluefin tuna also make a very occasional showing in The Rip, but targeting these torpedoes is even more problematic than chasing the area's kingies. Most are hooked by accident and few are landed.

More consistent sport can be had by trolling or casting for Australian salmon, snook (short-finned sea pike) and barracouta, which often feed in the lower bay, their schools signposted by wheeling flocks of sea birds. Usually running between 1 and 3 kg, the salmon are best tackled by stopping the boat and casting metal lures at the schools, or by trolling around the fringes of the same schools with small chromed lures, minnows, Christmas tree–style skirted lures or even pieces of clear plastic tubing slipped over stainless steel hooks. Snook respond better to the combination of spoons or small minnow lures rigged behind a diving board, planer or paravane.

There are some very nice whiting to be had on the gravel and sand grounds inside the Kelp Patch, in Nepean Bay and off bayside ports such as Rosebud, Rye, Sorrento, Portsea and Queenscliff. The same areas also produce 'pinkies' and the odd larger snapper, as well as silver trevally and the occasional gummy or school shark.

Squid are also abundant at times in the lower bay, and may even be taken right in The Rip itself, especially on slack water at the change of tides.

WESTERN PORT

IN BRIEF

MAP REFERENCE: PAGE 65 H5

GETTING THERE Western Port lies about 60 km south-east of Melbourne along the South Gippsland Highway
BEST TIME TO FISH September to May
BEST TIME TO TRAVEL Year-round
MAJOR ANGLING SPECIES Snapper, gummy shark, elephant shark, King George whiting, flathead, leatherjackets, garfish, mullet and trevally
SPECIAL RESTRICTIONS Channel speed limits must be observed at all times
WARNINGS Western Port is a very intense tidal zone. Caution should be taken in all areas when boating
CHARTER BOATS AND FISHING GUIDES
Corporate Fishing Charters, telephone (03) 9654 2022; Rex Hunt's Shimano Explorer, telephone (03) 9589 4035; Katrina-Louise Charters, telephone (03) 9584 8301; information on the area is available from Paul Worsteling's Cranbourne Fishing Tackle, telephone (03) 5996 6500

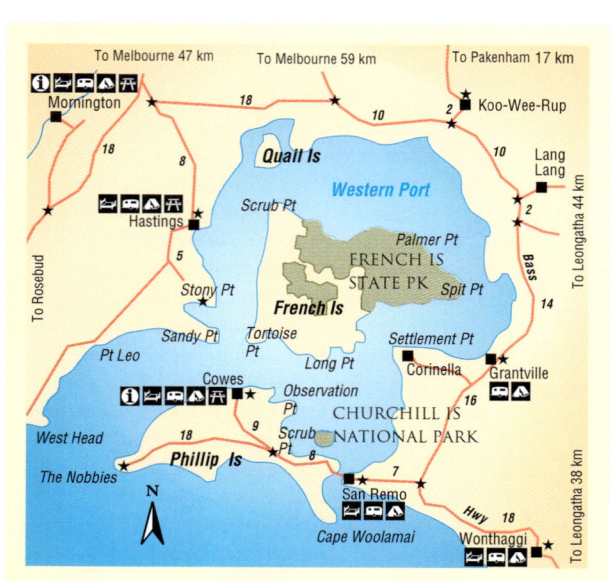

Corinella boat ramp of the eastern side of Western Port, near Settlement Point

Western Port is home to some big snapper, gummy sharks, King George whiting and an amazing marine creature known as the elephant shark. The waters of Western Port provide a unique fishing experience due to the large displacement of water caused by the size of its western entrance.

For Port Phillip Bay anglers, the tide change is nothing more than a fish-rich time when predators begin to move in search of food. For Western Port anglers, however, fishing success will come only when the angler has a thorough understanding of the tide and its movement patterns. As a result, Western Port anglers must consider the best time for fishing, where to target specific species in relation to the stage of the tide, the best rig to use, the correct bait and presentation, and which outfit will best suit their needs.

Best Times To Fish

As with most fishing scenarios, the best time to fish Western Port is about one hour either side of the change of tide. This is when the angler can fish relatively deep water with minimal weight.

As the tide turns, water speed will gradually increase until it is unfishable. There are also better times for fishing at different times of the week and month. The idea is to find a tide change with minimal difference between high and low (neap tide). A 'low' high tide fished through to a 'high' low tide will mean less water movement and, obviously, easier fishing conditions.

Another important point to remember when fishing the area is that big fish are not necessarily always found in the deepest water. In fact, most snapper catches take place in 15 m of water or less, with big gummy sharks preferring a depth of around 8 m.

The advantage in fishing shallower water is that only half the lead is required and it is possible to fishing well past the change of tide. Fishing early morning, late afternoon, overcast days or at night will also improve the angler's chances in the shallows and increase productive fishing time immensely.

Rigs, Techniques and Tackle

The best rig for targeting snapper, gummy sharks and elephant sharks in Western Port is a simple fast-water running-sinker rig. Utilising the correct ingredients is crucial to the rig's overall performance.

A bomb or teardrop sinker is allowed to run freely on the main line on a running-sinker clip. This is stopped by a ball bearing swivel with up to

The marina at Hastings on the bay's western side

2 m of 15-kg trace used. The trace length is vital to perfect bait presentation as its length allows the bait to waft slowly in the current.

An overhead reel capable of holding around 300 m of 10-kg line should be used in conjunction with a fast taper 2- to 2.2-m rod. The rod should have a light tip for bite detection and a strong butt section for lifting heavy fish in fast water.

Fishing Hot Spots

Western Port has something to offer every angler, from the holidaying school kids catching mullet off the Warneet Jetty to big game anglers targeting a large shark off The Nobbies. In fact, one of the bay's great attractions is the multitude of land-based options that it has to offer.

Inlets at the northern end of Western Port such as Sawtells and Rutherford consistently produce yellow-eye mullet, small Australian salmon, flathead, trevally and whiting in season. In these areas, pipis and pilchard fillets fish work well, particularly on a paternoster rig with No. 6 long-shank hooks.

When heading south towards Phillip Island, anglers can take a right-hand turn down Jetty Lane to find themselves at the Lang Lang Jetty. High tide is the only time to fish as it is a 200-m cast to the water on the low tide! This pier produces gummies weighing up to 8 kg, good mullet and an occasional snapper.

Stockyard Point offers land-based anglers the chance to hook a big shark — either a gummy or elephant. On low tide, it is possible to cast directly into the channel with a surf rod and this usually has good results.

Corinella, Newhaven and Cowes piers are also well worth a mention, with captures of big bronze whalers, thresher sharks and mulloway becoming more and more common. The many beaches and rock platforms on Phillip Island produce salmon weighing up to 4 kg, a healthy run of sweep and good bags of whiting in season.

A large elephant shark taken from the waters of Western Port

As with most locations, boat anglers are at a definite advantage in Western Port as they are able to move from one place to another through the maze of channels in search of good fishing.

Western Port begins firing around September, when the first run of decent snapper begin to make their way up the Long Reef with reds well over the old 20-lb (9-kg) mark always a possibility. This run of fish keeps anglers happy until Christmas, when the seasonal run of King George whiting makes its appearance along the middle spit at Hastings, filtering into the many smaller 'nursery' channels around the Tooradin area.

Elephant Shark Action

By early to mid-March, the elephant shark invasion begins in the lower reaches around the Corinella–Rhyll area. In more recent times, this has brought with it schools of tailor and salmon and mulloway weighing up to 30 kg.

When the elephants are on, anglers wait at the Corinella ramp for up to three hours just to get their boat in and out of the water. Believe it or not, it is worth the wait as the elephant is a hard-fighting, good-eating adversary. It is not unusual to land 50 elephant sharks in a session. When fished on 2- to 4-kg line, the fight is intense to say the least. Obviously, anglers must remain sensible and generally the vast majority of such a catch is released unharmed.

In a nutshell, Western Port has something to offer everyone and plenty of fish of varying species to go round. While anglers mustn't gain the impression that fishing this area will be easy, they should also realise that with a little hard work and smart thinking, the opportunities are endless. The key here is to work the tides carefully, thus increasing the angler's chances of success.

GEELONG AND CORIO BAY

IN BRIEF

MAP REFERENCE: PAGE 64 E5

GETTING THERE Geelong is 76 km south-west of Melbourne along the Princes Highway, on the shores of Port Phillip Bay
BEST TIME TO FISH October to May
BEST TIME TO TRAVEL Year-round
MAJOR ANGLING SPECIES Snapper, whiting, flathead, barracouta and squid
WARNINGS The Rip, at the narrow entrance of Port Phillip Bay, is a particularly hazardous area subject to very strong tides and rough conditions. The whole of Port Phillip Bay can become extremely rough in strong winds. Great care should also be exercised when boating in and around the busy shipping channels

Commercial fishers unloading a scallop catch at Geelong

Part of the much larger Port Phillip Bay system, the body of water known as Corio Bay is roughly bounded by Point Wilson to the north and the extensive Bellarine Peninsula to the south. The city of Geelong lies at Corio Bay's western end, on the shores of an area of partially enclosed water known as the Corio Bay Inner Harbour or simply Geelong Harbour.

Much the same general standard of fishing found elsewhere in Port Phillip Bay can also be enjoyed at times throughout Corio Bay and inside the Inner Harbour waters adjacent to Geelong. As a bonus, this area also offers slightly better protection from strong winds than the more open expanses of the main bay itself.

In addition to the usual Port Phillip Bay piscatorial targets of flathead, snapper, King George whiting, gummy sharks, garfish, mullet, leatherjackets and squid, various other fish including silver trevally, juvenile Australian salmon (so-called 'bay trout'), chopper tailor (sometimes called 'skippies' in Victoria) and even mulloway (jewfish) all turn up in the waters of Corio Bay from time to time, although their appearances here tend to be anything but consistent or predictable these days.

Corio Bay Hot Spots

Acknowledged hot spots within the Corio Bay region include Port Lillias and nearby Bird Rock. These areas are especially good for gummy sharks, flathead and the occasional snapper.

Rippleside Jetty, Cunningham Pier and Fishermans Jetty, as well as several other platforms in the region, are all favoured locations for land-based anglers pursuing flathead, King George whiting, leatherjackets, garfish and squid.

The deeper shipping channels running off Clifton Springs and Point Richard are frequented by boat anglers chasing snapper, particularly during the spring to autumn season. However, those fishing from boats should exercise considerable caution whenever anchoring in these areas, especially at night, and avoid the busier shipping lanes. It is also absolutely essential to display approved navigation and riding lights after dark.

Several other offshore grounds, low reefs and rubble patches lying adjacent to areas of coastline further south around the Bellarine Peninsula — such as Portarlington, Steeles Rocks, Grassy Point, Indented Head and St Leonards — also offer access to reasonably consistent flathead, whiting, snapper and squid fishing, with fair to good boat launching facilities available at most of the aforementioned bayside locations and suburbs.

A little further afield, although not strictly part of Corio Bay itself, the relatively shallow waters of Swan Bay, on the south-eastern side of the Bellarine Peninsula, can also produce the odd whiting and some fine catches of flathead, including the occasional larger-than-average specimen of 'frog' or 'yank', as they are locally known.

Big Winter Reds

Corio Bay is perhaps most famous in Victorian angling circles for the big, winter-time snapper still occasionally taken from its waters by both shore-based and boat anglers. This rather unique fishery gained a great deal of prominence during the late 1960s and the 1970s, thanks in no small part to the appearance of a series of magazine articles in the popular angling press detailing the capture of numerous big 'reds' from these seemingly unlikely waters. Sadly, however, the calibre of this winter snapper 'run' declined rather dramatically through the late 1980s, and has only recovered slightly in more recent times.

These days, the capture of a large winter 'red' from Corio Bay typically entails the investment of a considerable amount of time and effort. Nonetheless, such is the quality of these fish that many anglers regard such an investment as being entirely worthwhile.

Sunset over Corio Bay at Geelong — a prime time to start fishing

Proven hot spots for these 'out-of-season' winter or resident snapper include Limeburners Point and Bay, the Grammar School 'lagoon' and several stretches of nearby shoreline, and the Point Lillias–Bird Rock area described earlier.

RESIDENT FISH

It seems that a certain percentage of larger-than-average snapper do not leave the confines of Corio Bay at the end of April, preferring to over-winter in relatively shallow, protected areas such as those described. Here, they feed on the abundance of small crabs, shellfish, squid and octopus that also call these estuarine waters home.

Although these big winter 'reds' are certainly no longer a sure bet, specialist anglers who are willing to put in long, cold nights fishing around the Corio Bay foreshores—from both the bank and from small boats—still take a sprinkling of 6- to 10- or even 11-kg specimens every year between May and October. Not surprisingly, however, most of these anglers remain rather tight-lipped about their occasional successes!

The majority of these big winter snapper fall to lightly weighted baits of fish flesh, whole pilchards, squid, octopus or crab fished on the bottom, usually under cover of darkness. However, it is not entirely unknown for the odd snapper to be taken during daylight hours, especially in overcast or rainy weather, and in the days immediately following major storms and strong gales.

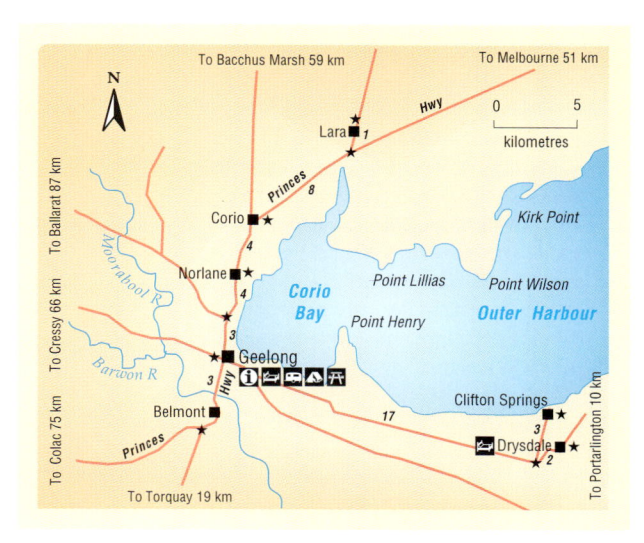

Fishing boats moored near Geelong. Commercial fishing pressure has no doubt played a part in the area's declining catches

THE YARRA RIVER

IN BRIEF

MAP REFERENCE: PAGE 64 G3

GETTING THERE The Yarra River runs through the heart of Melbourne
BEST TIME TO FISH November to June, in the evening and at dawn on the tide change
BEST TIME TO TRAVEL Year-round
MAJOR ANGLING SPECIES Bream, trevally, mullet, mulloway and garfish
SPECIAL RESTRICTIONS Not all sections of the river are accessible and an inland angling licence is required

The Yarra River flows through the heart of metropolitan Melbourne and for this reason it is often ignored by recreational anglers who struggle under the misapprehension that quality fishing and city living cannot coexist.

The Yarra certainly has its fair share of problems. The water always looks dirty, floating debris is a constant reminder of some people's lack of respect for the environment and it can be extremely hard to find parking when there are major events on at Flinders Park and the Melbourne Cricket Ground.

Despite all this, the Yarra River came alive in the late 1980s and has fished extremely well for a wide variety of species ever since. There are several reasons for the improved fishing. The main one is a reduction in pollutants emptied into the river, which in turn has seen a steady improvement in environmental factors that have led directly to better fishing.

Regeneration of the once muddy bottom has seen regrowth of weed beds, barnacles and other fish-attracting structures. As the habitat slowly returned to something approximating its former glory, so, too, did the fishing, with a first-class bream fishery now located on Melbourne's doorstep.

Another reason for an increase in fish captures from the Yarra River is the increasing sophistication of the angling methods now used. Relatively new fishing techniques such as coarse angling lend themselves to the species found in the river. Both bream and mullet respond extremely well to ground bait (berleying) techniques and, as a direct result of this, coarse angling has become very popular and highly successful in the Yarra.

The Yarra River and Melbourne city skyline make a stunning vista at night

Above: *A large mulloway taken from the Yarra River at night on a squid bait*
Left: *A catch of southern bream landed in early spring*

The Hotties

The mouth of the Yarra spills into Port Phillip Bay at Williamstown and, in doing so, passes one of its most popular fishing locations, 'The Warmies'. Also known as 'The Hotties', this area provides excellent fishing when the Newport Power Station warms the water in the area. Access is via Douglas Parade or North Road, Newport, and when the action is 'hot', it is definitely a case of standing room only.

Many species are targeted in this area, with bream, mullet and small tailor the main fare. A traditional running sinker rig will usually achieve the best results, with a No. 6 long-shank hook effective on both bream and mullet. These fish respond well to sand worms, bass yabbies, shrimps, raw chicken and peeled prawns soaked in tuna oil.

At different times of the year, large schools of salmon and garfish also make their way into the Hobsons Bay–Warmies area. These fish will respond best to a berley trail of breadcrumbs, pellets and tuna oil, with maggots (gents), small fish and pipis the most effective offerings. In this situation, the angler should use a pencil or quill float with a 1- to 1.5-m leader.

As seasonal species come and go from this area without much warning, visiting anglers should ensure that they have a range of tackle on hand to suit a variety of fishing applications, including coarse techniques and the use of telescopic poles.

Yarra River Bream

Bream are the main target of anglers fishing the river as they are available from the mouth at The Warmies right through to Abbotsford. The stretch of water that is most productive, however, is between The Warmies and where the Maribyrnong and Yarra rivers meet. June and July are the best months to fish this area as the bream enter the river from Port Phillip Bay in preparation for their spawning run.

Both sides of the river near the Westgate Freeway bridge are good areas for bream, with anglers casting towards the pylons. Bass yabbies tend to work well here and small crabs gathered from the rocks are also a top local bait.

The bream fishing may be best in the Yarra's lower reaches, but it is by no means confined to this area. On any given day, bream anglers can be found right along the Yarra as it slowly winds its way through the city towards Port Phillip Bay. In more recent times, the swinging bridge at South Bank has proved a popular haunt, with bream measuring up to 35 cm a regular catch.

Anglers fishing this area with live bait such as bass yabbies also put themselves in with a chance to catch small mulloway, or soapies as they are also known, weighing up to 1 kg or so. It is best to release these small mulloway as this not only helps to ensure a future population, but, as the name suggests, they also don't taste all that wonderful.

Snapper and Mulloway

A small band of anglers dedicate their fishing time on the river solely to snapper and mulloway. Several magnificent specimens are taken each year, with snapper weighing in excess of 6 kg and mulloway ranging from 1 to 30 kg and beyond.

Although some snapper and mulloway are taken almost accidentally by anglers targeting bream and the like, the serious fish are generally taken by serious anglers.

Fresh and live baits are crucial for mulloway, while snapper are a little less fussy. Squid, octopus, fish fillets or live mullet should be enough to temp a big mulloway, but the wait may be a long one. Anglers targeting these prize species should fish exclusively at night and may increase their chances of a strike by slowly retrieving the bait once it has made its way to the river bed.

With such a wide variety of fish on offer so close to the stress and pressure of city life, it is no wonder the Yarra has received so much fishing attention in recent years. With its proximity to the heart of Melbourne and a stunning city backdrop, this river makes the perfect day trip for locals and visiting anglers alike.

THE NORTH-EASTERN ESTUARIES

IN BRIEF

MAP REFERENCE: PAGE 71 K5

GETTING THERE Mallacoota is about 520 km east of Melbourne and 600 km south of Sydney — turn off the Princes Highway at Genoa
BEST TIME TO FISH August to May
BEST TIME TO TRAVEL Year-round
MAJOR ANGLING SPECIES Bream, flathead, luderick, whiting, mullet, tailor, mulloway and estuary perch
SPECIAL RESTRICTIONS Specific regional bag limits can sometimes apply to particular species in Mallacoota Inlet, especially when this system is closed to the sea. Check the current rules before fishing
WARNINGS Access to the sea across Mallacoota Bar (when open) is potentially hazardous and very difficult at low tide. Seek local advice first

The Bottom Lake at Mallacoota, in Victoria's north-east, is subject to considerable fishing pressure

Sometimes known — only partially in jest — as the 'Victorian Riviera', the far north-eastern portion of Victoria, between its border with New South Wales and the extensive Gippsland Lakes system, is an immensely popular area with tourists, many of whom come here specifically to fish.

One of this region's greatest charms is its surprisingly mild climate, which is generally more pleasant and predictable than the weather experienced closer to Melbourne, and may even be superior to that typically encountered on the far south coast of New South Wales.

Despite being a good five or six hours by road from Melbourne, the towns, caravan parks and camping grounds of the north-east fill up on most weekends between October and May, and are especially busy during the Christmas and Easter holiday breaks. Regardless of these crowds and the obvious pressures they place on the region's fish stocks, good catches are regularly made, and there are still numerous little pockets within the north-east corner of Victoria that remain lightly fished and provide excellent opportunities for the more adventurous angler.

MALLACOOTA INLET

The popular resort of Mallacoota is dealt with in greater detail on pp. 258–9, but is covered here as a major component of Victoria's north-eastern estuary region.

The Mallacoota Inlet or lake is an extensive, relatively shallow waterway lying just south of he border and surrounded by Croajingolong National Park. Fed by a dozen or more rivers and creeks, this estuary system is effectively divided into a Bottom Lake and Top Lake by a deep, constricted run aptly known as The Narrows.

When Mallacoota Inlet is open to the sea, the Bottom Lake receives a strong tidal flush each day and generally contains clean, saline water. However, tidal movement in the Top Lake is more restricted and less powerful, and this shallower, heavily weeded body of water becomes quite brackish in nature and may even have a layer of almost fresh water on top after periods of rain.

The fishing and abalone diving township of Mallacoota is situated on the western shore of the larger Bottom Lake, and it is hardly surprising that this area receives the greatest fishing pressure. Some fine catches of flathead and bream are taken in the Bottom Lake, particularly during summer and autumn. These fish may be caught by drifting, anchoring or even walking and wading the banks and shallows, or fishing from the various public jetties along the lake's western shorelines.

Best baits for bream include live bass yabbies (nippers), sand worms, small crabs and prawns. While flathead will also take these same baits, better results are usually achieved by using small, live mullet ('poddies'), whole whitebait and bluebait, or artificial lures such as soft plastic-tailed jigs, metal spoons and diving minnows.

Hot spots in the Bottom Lake include the Allen Head area, John Bull Light and Goodwin Sands, but any stretches of broken weed bed and sand flat are well worth a try, especially for flathead and sand whiting. Bream and luderick tend to be more prolific around deeper points and isolated rocks, such as those near Goat and Horse islands and off Captains Point.

Upstream, the deeper waters of The Narrows are the acknowledged hot spot in this system for mulloway or jewfish. Specimens weighing up to 30 kg have been taken here, although fish a third to half that size are more likely. Most of these fall to live baits, usually fished at night.

A flathead taken in one of the lakes

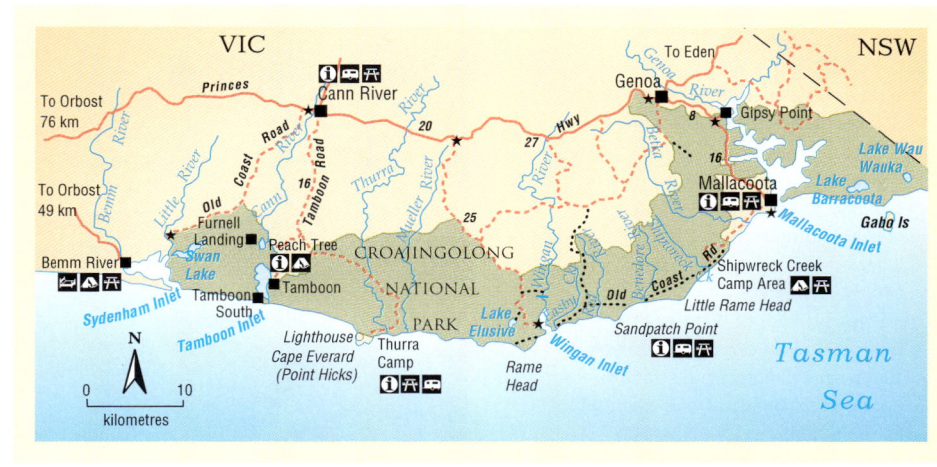

The Top Lake receives less fishing pressure than the lower end of the system, and looks somewhat less productive at first glance. However, its shallow, weedy waters do contain some excellent fish, including a scattering of surprisingly large dusky flathead.

The delightful little village of Gipsy Point and its waterside pub make a great stepping-off point for anglers working the Top Lake and its various feeder streams, including the productive Wallagaraugh and Genoa rivers. There is an excellent run of southern bream in these rivers during late winter and spring each year, and the famous Bull Ring hole on the Wallagaraugh, not far above Johnsons Bridge, has produced some amazing catches over the years. Sadly, however, both the number and size of fish taken here seems to have declined a little in recent times.

There are also some good bass and estuary perch to be had higher up in these rivers. Summer and autumn are the best time to target these fish on either natural baits or lures.

WINGAN AND TAMBOON INLETS

These two modest estuary systems lie south and west of Mallacoota, and are often overlooked by anglers on their way to better known locations. Both, however, offer some fine fishing at times.

Access to Wingan Inlet is via the West Wingan Road, off the Princes Highway north of Cann River. It is a small, attractive estuary with a good population of flathead, bream, mullet and the odd bass or estuary perch. A boat is useful, but not essential, as reasonable action can be had while wading the flats at the inlet's lower end.

Further west, on the Melbourne side of Point Hicks (the first part of the Australian mainland sighted by the crew of the *Endeavour* in 1770) is the somewhat larger estuary system known as Tamboon Inlet. This delightful tidal lake and river is reached by turning off the highway at Cann River and proceeding some 20 km to Furnell Landing, where boats can be launched.

When the mouth of Tamboon Inlet is closed and its water level high, navigation is reasonably easy. However, when it's open, things can be rather tricky, especially at low tide.

Tamboon holds the same mix of estuarine species as Mallacoota and Wingan inlets, including some thumping big bream, good flathead and a few bass and estuary perch. Top spots include Pelican Point and the flats around the small island where the Cann River enters the main lake, below Furnell Landing.

BEMM RIVER AND SYDENHAM INLET

Bemm River is without doubt one of the best known and most productive estuaries in all of Victoria, with a well-earned reputation for producing great catches of southern bream, luderick and estuary perch. Although results have declined a little in recent years, the Bemm River and Sydenham Inlet are still well worth fishing.

Bream, which are the system's major target species, can be caught all year round, but are definitely at their best and most predictable in late winter and spring. Top bream spots include the Mahoganys area, Bobs Bay, Pelican Point and the location known as Siberia.

One of the more interesting aspects of bream fishing in the Bemm River system is the fact that most experienced anglers prefer not to anchor in the soft mud and weed, but instead use long, wooden poles which they push into the bottom and to which they tie off. A pole at each end of the boat is best, and provides a solid mooring.

Sand worms are the number one bait for bream in this system, followed by live bass yabbies, fresh or frozen prawns and spider crabs. Limited but productive bait pumping grounds lie around the mouth of the Bemm River, where it enters Sydenham Inlet, but sand worms can also be purchased from several shops in the area.

In addition to bream, the Bemm is renowned for its large luderick or blackfish, which also fancy a live sand worm. There are also some sand whiting, mullet, flathead, tailor and estuary perch to round out anglers' catches in the Bemm River and Sydenham Inlet.

The inlet at Thurra River in Croajingolong National Park

GIPPSLAND LAKES

IN BRIEF

MAP REFERENCE: PAGE 70 E6

GETTING THERE Bairnsdale is approximately 280 km east of Melbourne along the Princes Highway
BEST TIME TO FISH July to May
BEST TIME TO TRAVEL Year-round
MAJOR ANGLING SPECIES Bream, flathead, luderick, whiting, mullet, tailor, mulloway and estuary perch
WARNINGS The open waters of the Gippsland Lakes can become extremely choppy and dangerous in strong winds. Boat owners should always exercise extreme caution
CHARTER BOATS AND FISHING GUIDES Fishing charter boat the *Mulloway*, telephone (03) 5155 3304; Port Side Boat Hire, telephone (03) 5155 3832

Estuarine species such as mullet are found in the Gippsland Lakes system

The vast network of interconnected tidal waterways collectively known as the Gippsland Lakes forms one of south-eastern Australia's largest estuary systems. This system has close to 400 square km of open lake, in addition to the more sheltered and enclosed waters of at least five or six significant tributary rivers and various smaller creeks, backwaters and swamps. The Lakes National Park and Gippsland Lakes Coastal Park cover for much of the area between the lakes and Bass Strait.

The main lakes in the Gippsland system are King, Victoria, Reeve and Wellington, while the six major rivers are the Tambo, Nicholson, Mitchell, Avon, Thompson and La Trobe. In addition, there is an extensive area of tidal waterway around the township of Lakes Entrance itself, including the system's mouth or entrance, and the North Arm. Some of the more significant parts of this enormous system—notably Lakes Entrance itself and the area's three most famous bream rivers (the Tambo, Nicholson and Mitchell)—are dealt with in greater detail on pp. 52–3 and pp. 260–1.

This entire area of eastern Victoria is very popular with tourists and visiting anglers, and local businesses cater particularly well to their needs. Many visitors to the Gippsland Lakes stay in waterside resorts, units and caravan parks, while others choose to hire a houseboat, and this latter option is certainly a wonderful way to explore the diverse, interconnected waterways that comprise the magnificent Gippsland Lakes.

THE INFLUENCE OF TIDES

Interestingly, the Gippsland Lakes had no permanent entrance to the sea until one was created by human intervention in 1889. Before that date, the system only cut its way to the sea intermittently when inundated by flood waters, usually at a point around Ocean Grange. The creation of a permanent mouth at the pleasant seaside township of Lakes Entrance has turned this system into a tidal one, although the impact of these tides and the size of their daily fluctuations diminish markedly as one moves further west, up the chain of lakes.

The Gippsland Lakes' most westerly body of water—Lake Wellington—experiences very little tidal flush and is almost fresh in nature for much of the year. It is also shallow, weedy and not of great interest to anglers, although it does hold a few good bream, along with its more abundant eels and the introduced European carp.

The area between the artificial entrance to the lakes and the village of Metung experiences the greatest tidal influence. As a result, it produces more 'oceanic' fish species, such as tailor, Australian salmon, silver trevally and mulloway (jewfish), as well as common estuarine targets such as southern and eastern black bream, luderick (blackfish), flathead of several types, flounder, garfish and mullet.

Top fishing spots in this lower part of the Gippsland Lakes include North Arm, Bullock and Rigby islands, Reeves Channel and Bancroft Bay.

Lake King is also quite close to the entrance and experiences quite strong tidal influences. It is a reasonably large expanse of water averaging 4 to 6 m in depth, and acts as a major highway for fish moving in and out of the system, producing excellent angling results at times for flathead, bream, mullet, tailor and trevally, in particular.

Like every other open body of water in the Gippsland Lakes, Lake King can become extremely rough and dangerous in strong winds, particularly westerlies, and boat anglers should be especially careful.

FISHING IN LAKES KING AND VICTORIA

One of the best spots to fish in Lake King is the McMillan Strait area, between Paynesville and Raymond Island. Despite playing host to moderately heavy boat traffic, this stretch of water produces flathead, bream, whiting and flounder, especially in the change-of-light periods during the late afternoon or evening, and again in the early morning. Other worthwhile locations are the area around the beacon at the aptly named Bream Reef, and the wooden pilings which mark the entrance to the Tambo River mouth. For boat fishers, the entire lake is also well worth trolling for tailor and even the odd Australian salmon, especially during summer and autumn.

Lake Victoria is a long, relatively narrow body of water running south-west from Lake King. The popular holiday resorts of Loch Sport and Hollands Landing lie on its shores, and its waters have a good reputation for producing catches of bream, especially in any slightly deeper holes near the more prominent points.

One of the best areas for bream in this entire region is McLennans Strait—a long, narrow channel upstream of Hollands Landing that links Lake Victoria to Lake Wellington. In many ways, this strait has much more in common with a river than a lake, and should be fished accordingly, whether from a boat or off the shore.

Lake Reeve is a long, narrow arm of water running off Lake King and down along the back of Ninety Mile Beach, past Loch Sport. Although not fished all that heavily, Lake Reeve can also produce some good bream, flathead and mullet.

Cleaning the day's catch

Boat owners may also cross the lake and walk out onto the beach itself, where excellent surf casting opportunities exist for those targeting salmon, mullet, gummy and school sharks, and even the very occasional mulloway or jewfish.

An aerial view of the Lakes National Park looking towards the ocean across a portion of the Gippsland Lakes

LAKES ENTRANCE

IN BRIEF

MAP REFERENCE: PAGE 70 E6

GETTING THERE Lakes Entrance is about 390 km east of Melbourne along the Princes Highway
BEST TIME TO FISH Year-round depending on target species
BEST TIME TO TRAVEL Year-round
MAJOR ANGLING SPECIES Bream, flathead, mullet, salmon, garfish, perch, tailor, carp, and mulloway
WARNINGS Caution should be taken when crossing the ocean bar because of the strong tides and shifting sands
ACCOMMODATION Hibiscus Lodge, telephone (03) 5155 1768; Road Nite Caravan Park, telephone (03) 5155 2750; Lakes Central Hotel, telephone (03) 5155 1977; Eastern Beach Van Park, telephone (03) 5155 1581
CHARTER BOATS AND FISHING GUIDES The *Mulloway* (fishing charter boat), telephone (03) 5155 3304; Port Side Boat Hire, telephone (03) 5155 3832

Aerial view of Ninety Mile Beach and Lakes Entrance

Lakes Entrance is best known to many as a popular summer tourist destination on Victoria's East Gippsland coast, but it is also a haven for anglers, being one of the rare locations where all the popular styles of fishing (beach, offshore, estuary and river) can be experienced all year round.

Lakes Entrance is also special in that it offers access to land-based locations where the once-a-year or occasional angler, families or non-boat owners can enjoy the pleasures of wetting a line.

The township of Lakes Entrance is built on the narrow peninsula between North and Cunninghame arms at the far eastern end of the Gippsland Lakes. It is only a short walk across the Cunninghame Arm footbridge to the famous Ninety Mile Beach. Various points along this beach provide excellent surf fishing, with the main target species being Australian salmon and gummy sharks, although mullet, tailor and flathead are not uncommon catches. Big mulloway and various shark species apart from the gummy are also taken from time to time.

The best locations in the area to target both salmon and gummy sharks are at Eastern, Lake Tyers and Pettman beaches, all of which are east of the township of Lakes Entrance. Eastern Beach is a two-minute drive from the town centre, Lake Tyers is a ten-minute drive and Pettmans only half an hour by car. The latter is a renowned gummy beach and for some reason accounts for more of these sharks than any other beach in the region. Paternoster rigs seem to work best and preferred baits are pilchard, squid and eel. The latter two baits, which are much tougher, are the answer if crabs become a problem. Australian salmon are abundant throughout the year, although winter is the best time. The warmer months are prime gummy shark time.

OFFSHORE ACCESS

Access to the waters offshore from Lakes Entrance is via the artificial entrance, which in the wrong conditions can be treacherous. This should not act as a complete deterrent to the offshore angler, but simply as a warning to check bar conditions before heading out.

A variety of species await the angler in the waters of Bass Strait and none is more keenly sought than the big snapper that call this area home from November to April each year. Snapper weighing almost 15 kg have been taken in recent years and the many reefs, which are easily detected by sounders, are obviously the best place to fish. The snapper are available all year round, but the winter run only sees fish in the 3- to 4-kg range, with efforts to tackle them often limited by poor weather. Summer provides much better conditions and bigger snapper.

The best places to target snapper are the Four Mile Reef and Six Mile Reef, which are directly off Lakes Entrance and, as their names suggest, are 4 miles (6.5 km) and 6 miles (9.5 km) offshore.

Gummy sharks are also a common catch and several other species are available, too. These include flathead (both sand and tiger), trevally, barracouta, salmon, slimy mackerel, King George whiting, sand whiting and many reef species including Sergeant Baker and gurnard.

Those wanting to tangle with a bigger catch can target the many species of larger sharks, including whalers, threshers, makos, hammerheads and seven-gills. The February to March period is a good time to fish as there are usually plenty of skipjack or striped tuna around, which adds to the shark activity in the area. Yellowfin have also been sighted here at this time and it is not uncommon to see marlin free-jumping in the waters off Lakes Entrance. While both are rare catches, it should be remembered that few anglers actually target these species.

Estuary Angling

As mentioned, Lakes Entrance is situated on a small peninsula and its closeness to the entrance to the Gippsland Lakes contributes to the excellent angling for a variety of estuary species. Many areas around the township have gained a reputation as 'hot spots' for certain varieties of fish, and they always seem to produce the goods.

Bream are the most sought-after estuarine fish in this region and one of the best places to tackle these fine eating fish is also one of the most accessible. The post office jetty in Cunninghame Arm is an excellent place to start any bream fishing expedition and, although this particular jetty has gained a solid reputation for bream catches, most of the jetties along Cunninghame Arm are suitable. The best bream bait is definitely sand worms, but fresh prawns, shrimps and pipis will also work.

Other catches off these jetties include King George whiting, trevally and spotty salmon (juvenile Australian salmon). Salmon become more prevalent on the run-in tide and at this time are often taken off Bullock Island, which is right near the entrance to the lake system and can be easily reached by car.

The rock walls around Kalimna are another popular land-based location and they attract literally thousands of luderick (blackfish) anglers annually. Green lettuce weed presented under a float is a popular offering with these anglers. A long, 3- to 4-m rod is handy in this situation to reach over the rock walls, but it is not a necessity.

The many channels and weed beds around Lakes Entrance are also home to good numbers of King George whiting, which are caught all year round. Three of the better locations are on

Fishing boats safely at anchor in Lakes Entrance as a storm front approaches from the south

Ninety Mile Beach offers excellent surf fishing for Australian salmon

the southern shore of Cumminghame Arm, Hopetoun Channel and in the stretch of water between Kalimna Jetty and Rigby Island. Sand worms or pipis will do the trick, and it pays to keep baits moving ever so slowly as this seems to entice the whiting to bite.

Exploring the Lakes

There are certainly plenty of land-based locations to be found in and around Lakes Entrance, but hiring one of the large range of craft available in the North Arm provides the opportunity to get out on the water and visit the many creeks and inlets in the area.

Further down the lake system, the area towards Metung also provides excellent fishing for whiting, but large dusky flathead enter the equation in this region, too, with live mullet the premier temptation.

The region's three big bream rivers—the Tambo, Nicholson and Mitchell—are all within half an hour's travelling distance by car of Lakes Entrance. The Tambo River is undoubtedly the best of the three, and is also the closest to Lakes Entrance. The bream are usually biting somewhere in the Tambo and it is normally simply a case of finding out where. Some of the better performing places are the cliffs in the upper reaches, Bennetts Brook (on the Metung Road), Rough Road and the mouth.

Fresh local glassies or 'smig' usually produce the best-quality fish, but are only available at certain times of the year. If they are unavailable, it pays to try sand worms, shrimps and prawns.

Each of the three rivers also holds good numbers of yellow-eye mullet, with estuary perch not uncommon in the Tambo and Mitchell. The perch will be best tempted by live unweighted baits and small minnow or yabby lures. For those more adventurous anglers, a Crazy Charlie fly fished on a seven-weight fly rod will sometimes work wonders, too.

WILSONS PROMONTORY AND CORNER INLET

IN BRIEF

MAP REFERENCE: PAGE 65 N7

GETTING THERE Welshpool is about 200 km south-east of Melbourne along the South Gippsland Highway

BEST TIME TO FISH September to May

BEST TIME TO TRAVEL Year-round

MAJOR ANGLING SPECIES Bream, flathead, luderick, whiting, mullet, snapper and estuary perch

SPECIAL RESTRICTIONS Permits are required for overnight excursions outside of designated camping areas in Wilsons Promontory National Park. Ballots are sometimes necessary in order to allocate limited camping spaces during peak periods. Contact the ranger for details, telephone (03) 5680 9555

WARNINGS Both the enclosed waters of Corner Inlet and the open waters of Bass Strait can become extremely dangerous in strong winds. Boat owners should exercise caution at all times

ACCOMMODATION Camping is allowed within Wilsons Promontory National Park in several areas, telephone (03) 5680 9555; camping and caravan sites, flats and lodges are also available within the park at Tidal River, telephone (03) 5680 9500 for details of flat and lodge accommodation

Whisky Bay in Wilsons Promontory National Park

A huge, granite headland that thrusts deep into the waters of Bass Strait, Wilsons Promontory forms the southernmost point of the Australian mainland. To its north, the shallower and more protected waters of Corner Inlet are a boating and fishing paradise with a wide range of angling options. The entire area has a fascinating human history that extends from earliest Aboriginal times to the whaling and sealing days of the 19th century and beyond. Today, it is one of Victoria's most popular holiday destinations.

Wilsons Promontory—better known simply as The Prom—and its scrub lands, forests, headlands and pristine beaches are now largely protected from undesirable development by the existence of the 49 000-hectare Wilsons Promontory National Park. This important park contains more than 700 species of native plants, as well as abundant bird and animal life. Various walks, ranging from 10-minute strolls to rugged overnight excursions (for which permits are required), are available throughout the park, and some of these offer access to excellent fishing locations.

FISHING ON THE PROM

Fishing on and around Wilsons Promontory itself is best accessed via the settlement of Tidal River, with its often busy camping and caravan sites, flats and lodges. These typically become packed with visitors at holiday time, particularly during the warmer months. Making bookings and reservations in advance is essential.

Where permitted and accessible, beach and rock fishing around the shoreline of Wilsons Promontory both produce decent catches of King George whiting, flathead, mullet, Australian salmon, gummy sharks, sweep, parrot fish and the like. The Darby and Tidal rivers both contain limited numbers of bream, estuary perch, mullet and luderick (blackfish), although it should be noted that fishing on Tidal River is not permitted upstream of the Tidal River Road.

In fact, the overall status of recreational fishing in many of Victoria's national parks — including Wilsons Promontory — was under review at the time of publication, and intending visitors should check the current state of play before planning a fishing trip to this region.

Port Albert and Corner Inlet

Corner Inlet or Corner Basin is a vast, shallow, expanse of estuarine water located on the eastern side of Wilsons Promontory and connected to the open ocean via a deeper, often fast-flowing passage called the Singapore Channel. Inside the estuary, this passage divides into four smaller channels.

The fishing grounds of Corner Inlet are some of the best and most productive in Victoria. The basin itself features vast areas of shallow banks where worms, yabbies, shrimps, crabs and other invertebrate food sources thrive. This forage base supports a healthy fish population consisting primarily of flathead, whiting, mullet, trevally, garfish and flounder.

In the deeper channels and adjacent ocean waters, these estuarine species are joined by snapper, salmon, gummy sharks, school sharks, pike, snook and barracouta. In particular, the area has a reputation for producing some enormous snapper, including the odd monster in the 12- to 16-kg range, particularly during spring and early summer. Catches of these very large fish declined somewhat during the 1980s and early 1990s, but appear to have improved slightly in more recent times.

Port Albert, Port Welshpool, Barrys Beach and Port Franklin all offer access to the waters of Corner Inlet, as well as providing different levels of accommodation and some limited services for visiting anglers. There is an excellent concrete launching ramp at Port Welshpool that will handle trailer boats of all sizes. There are also two long piers that provide reasonable shore-based angling at times, particularly for silver trevally when these popular fish are on the bite.

Port Welshpool itself lies some two-and-a-half hours drive east of Melbourne, along the South Gippsland Highway. There are only a handful of shops and a caravan park in the village, but bait and other facilities are available at the slightly larger township of Welshpool, five minutes inland.

Corner Inlet can become very choppy in anything stronger than a moderate wind because it is so broad, shallow and exposed. Boat fishers should exercise extreme care at all times while navigating its waters. The same is even more true of the open ocean waters beyond, which are often particularly rough.

Further offshore, outside Corner Inlet, boat anglers enjoy more great snapper fishing, as well as abundant snook, pike, trevally, flathead, gummy sharks, yellowtail kingfish and various other species, when the weather permits. Further out again, there are large sharks, tuna of several species and even marlin to be had in the deeper waters adjacent to the Bass Strait oil rigs in summer and autumn. However, this is a very long run through open, rough water, and should only be undertaken by experienced crews in large, seaworthy vessels.

One of the many beaches within Wilsons Promontory National Park

Dusky flathead such as this specimen are often taken by rock and beach anglers

TIMBER LAKE

IN BRIEF

MAP REFERENCE: PAGE 64 A6

GETTING THERE Colac is 150 km south-west of Melbourne along the Princes Highway
BEST TIME TO FISH October to May
BEST TIME TO TRAVEL Year-round
MAJOR ANGLING SPECIES Murray cod, golden perch, brown trout and rainbow trout
SPECIAL RESTRICTIONS Timber Lake is a privately owned lake situated on private property. Access is only available through Clearwater Fishing Tours, telephone (03) 5282 1466. Fishing is strictly on a catch-and-release basis

Preparing to release a pretty cod taken on a deep-diving plug

Privately owned and operated 'pay-to-fish' angling destinations are a relatively new phenomenon on the Australian freshwater fishing scene, but one that appears set to flourish over the next few years. There are several reasons for this trend, not the least of which is the growing number of keen freshwater anglers now competing for fishing opportunities on this dry continent's limited public rivers, lakes and dams.

Pay-to-fish businesses offer a viable alternative for many freshwater anglers, especially those who are becoming increasingly disillusioned with the growing crowds and falling catch rates now evident on so many public waters, particularly in the more populous southern states.

Intelligently set up and well-run private fisheries are capable of reducing pressure on those public waters. They also offer a unique set of angling opportunities to keen anglers who don't mind paying a reasonable fee for the luxury of fishing in uncrowded locations with healthy fish populations. Certainly, such businesses are now thriving in many other countries, including Britain and the United States. There is no reason to believe that they won't enjoy a similar boom here in Australia.

One such successful operation is based at Timber Lake, not far outside the major rural centre of Colac, in the delightful Otway region of Victoria. Timber Lake is some two hours drive south-west of Melbourne and about an hour's drive from Geelong via the Princes Highway.

MEADE'S CLEARWATER TOURS

Timber Lake is a delightful, 16-ha, privately owned artificial dam set in rolling hill country some 10 or 15 km east south-east of Colac.

The brains and sweat behind Timber Lake is Rob Meade, who runs a one-man guided angling business called Clearwater Fishing Tours out of his rural home at Lara, near Geelong.

As well as taking his paying clients fishing on various public streams and lakes in south-western Victoria, Rob has established exclusive access to a string of private lakes and dams that contain everything from silver perch and golden perch (yellowbelly) to 5-kg tiger trout (hybrid brown trout–brook trout crosses). The jewel in the crown of this operation, however, is definitely Timber Lake.

This attractive impoundment is 1.5 km long, some 400 m wide, and looks for all the world like a small-scale model of the famous Lake Mulwala, on the Murray River near Yarrawonga.

The lake is almost evenly divided between a heavily timbered southern section, with lots of closely set trees that were left standing in place when the dam filled, and a much more open and broad main basin. The distinction between these two sections is so clearly defined that the impoundment can almost be treated as two distinct lakes rolled into one.

Quite reasonable numbers of brown and rainbow trout averaging 700 g to 1 kg in weight and sometimes topping 3 kg swim in the open end of the big dam, making occasional forays into the timbered section. These fish often provide excellent sport, especially during major insect hatches in spring and early summer when feeding trout can be readily targeted on fly gear. It is the much larger native fish species lurking in and around the lake's stands of drowned timber, however, that are of greatest interest to most anglers.

A typical Timber Lake cod of about 4 kg

Murray Cod and Golden Perch

Timber Lake contains a fighting fit population of darkly hued Murray cod up to at least 10 or 12 kg in weight, plus a scattering of very respectable golden perch or yellowbelly, including the occasional specimen in the 6-kg plus class. There are also plans to stock the hard-fighting native freshwater species Australian bass into Timber Lake in the near future.

Strictly Catch-and-Release

Timber Lake is run on a strictly catch-and-release basis. In a typical day, anglers target cod, golden perch or trout, depending on the season and weather conditions. Lures with barbless hooks are most commonly used, and many anglers opt to target Murray cod and golden perch on fly fishing tackle with barbless hooks.

To date, fishing results have generally been outstanding, especially in the peak autumn months from late February until April, when everything in the lake seems to be 'on the chew'. It is extremely rare to experience a fishless day at this time of year. Boat and tackle are provided for visiting anglers as part of the overall service.

The Timber Lake operation provides anglers with a unique opportunity to target big freshwater fish on lures and flies. It is one of the new breed of personalised, environmentally friendly, services now available to discerning sport fishers who want not only to catch fish, but also to learn something about those fish and the various techniques used to target them.

Rob Meade works the trees at Timber Lake, where he operates an excellent guiding service

LAKE EILDON

IN BRIEF

MAP REFERENCE: PAGE 72 D7

GETTING THERE The township of Eildon lies about 160 km north-east of Melbourne along the Maroondah and Goulburn Valley highways

BEST TIME TO FISH October to May

BEST TIME TO TRAVEL Year-round

MAJOR ANGLING SPECIES Brown trout, rainbow trout, Murray cod, redfin, European carp and roach

SPECIAL RESTRICTIONS Adults require an inland angling licence to fish these waters. New freshwater fishing regulations now apply to all Victorian waters; these should be carefully checked. Boating is prohibited on Eildon Pondage

WARNINGS The open waters of Lake Eildon can become very rough in strong winds. Eildon Pondage is fast flowing and cold during major releases of water from the dam. Great care should be exercised around its shores, especially if wading

ACCOMMODATION Camping facilities are available in Eildon State Park, telephone (03) 5775 2788 or (03) 5772 0200, and Fraser National Park, telephone (03) 5772 1293 or (03) 5773 2208

Lake Eildon, in central Victoria, is a vast body of fresh water created by the construction of Eildon Dam during the 1950s. This major structure greatly increased the holding capacity of the existing Sugarloaf Dam, which was first built across the Goulburn River in the early 1920s to provide water for irrigation.

With a surface area of 13 830 ha when full, a maximum depth of nearly 80 m in places and some 500 km of shoreline featuring several major arms, a multitude of small bays and many tributary creeks and rivers, Lake Eildon offers a broad range of fishing opportunities for both shore-based and boat anglers.

This area has long been a favourite with Victorian holiday makers and travelling anglers, many of whom visit on a regular basis to stay in weekenders, camping and caravan parks or other forms of accommodation around the lake's extensive shores. Houseboating on the lake is also immensely popular, with many privately owned and rental houseboats plying Eildon's waters each weekend and holiday period.

FISHING IN LAKE EILDON

Most anglers visit Lake Eildon to pursue its populations of naturally spawned and stocked brown and rainbow trout, although many also keenly target the more abundant (but usually quite small) redfin or English perch. An increasing number of anglers are also coming here specifically to fish for European carp and roach, which also abound in the lake's waters.

Brown trout are generally more abundant in these waters than rainbows, although the latter are usually easier to catch. While most of the trout encountered will weigh 1 kg or less, the odd brown to 3 kg is still likely to turn up occasionally.

The biggest, most consistent catches of trout at Lake Eildon are taken by trolling with spoons, minnows, Tasmanian-style lures or combinations of natural baits such as dragonfly larvae (mudeyes) or worms and Cowbell or Ford Fender flasher rigs.

Reasonable catches of trout may also be made at times by spinning (lure casting), bait fishing or fly fishing from the lake's shores or from a drifting, anchored or moored boat. Carp, roach and small redfin can, however, be a nuisance at times when fishing with natural baits.

SEASONAL TRICKS

Generally speaking, the best trout fishing in Lake Eildon's main basin and the area downstream towards the dam wall occurs in late spring, summer and early autumn. During the heat of midsummer, it may be necessary to employ downriggers, paravanes, lead-core line or similar devices in order to reach trout holding deeper in the water column—near the thermocline, or layer of sudden temperature change. In late autumn, winter and early spring, better trout fishing—especially for the lake's larger browns—is typically experienced in the upper arms of Eildon, near the inflows of major feeder streams such as the Goulburn, Jamieson, Howqua and Delatite rivers.

Redfin are best targeted during the warmer months of the year, especially in the shallower, northern half of Lake Eildon. Good catches of redfin are often taken here by boat anglers 'bobbing' or jigging with baits and lures near submerged timber. While most of these 'reddies' are small, the occasional 1-kg plus specimen is always on the cards.

BOOMING COD FISHERY

Although primarily thought of as a trout and redfin fishery, Lake Eildon has gained increasing prominence in recent years as a result of the standard of fishing now offered by the Murray cod that have been stocked into its waters since the late 1980s and early 1990s.

Most of these cod—including the occasional specimen in excess of 18 or 20 kg—are taken by anglers slow trolling reasonably large, deep-diving lures or plugs along steep, rocky shorelines and near sunken timber in the Delatite Arm of

Carp are abundant in Lake Eildon

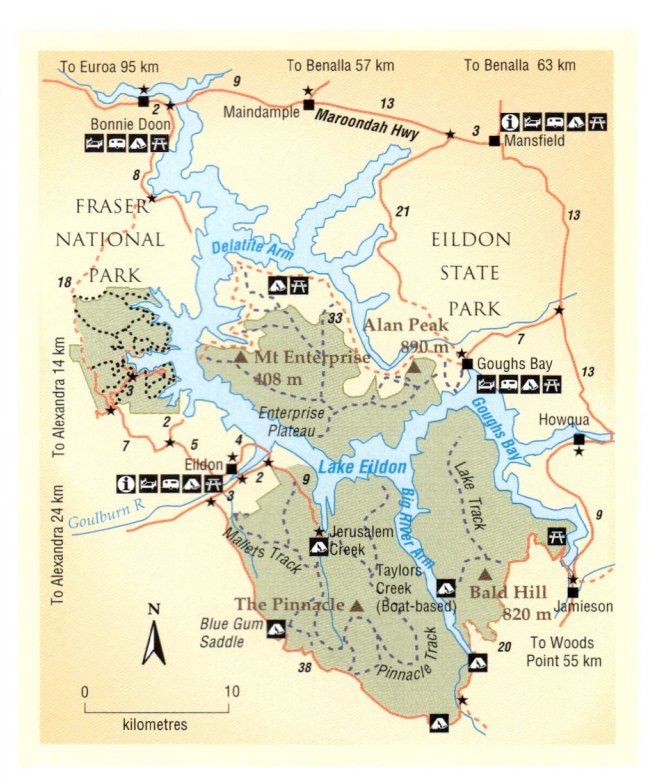

Lake Eildon at dawn — the best fishing results are often experienced early and late in the day

the lake during summer. Encounters with Murray cod are slowly spreading to other areas, however, including the Big River and Goulburn arms.

OTHER INHABITANTS

Native Macquarie perch were abundant in the lake until the 1960s, but have gradually disappeared, perhaps as a result of direct competition with carp and other introduced species, as well as as a consequence of the effects of a deadly virus (EHNV), thought to be transmitted by infected redfin. Attempts by Victorian Fisheries to reintroduce Macquarie perch by stocking adult fish taken from Dartmouth Reservoir have so far met with only limited success.

The population of exotic cyprinids — including European carp, goldfish, roach and, to a much lesser extent, tench — continues to increase in this impoundment, no doubt to the detriment of more desirable species. It remains to be seen if continued liberations of native predators such as Murray cod will have any appreciable impact on these noxious exotics. The release of golden perch (yellowbelly) and possibly even chinook ('quinnat') salmon is also mooted for Lake Eildon, and will certainly add to the diversity of species on offer.

On the negative side of the ledger, mercury levels in many fish sampled from Lake Eildon (particularly larger redfin) are disturbingly high. The regular consumption of large meals of these fish is not recommended.

THE PONDAGE

Eildon Pondage is a relatively shallow, 150-hectare regulating dam situated directly downstream of the main wall at Lake Eildon. It is stocked regularly (at least once each year) with surplus brood stock trout from Snobs Creek Hatchery, and regularly produces big browns and rainbows in the 1- to 4-kg size range. These trout are taken on baits, lures and flies cast from the shore, as boating is not permitted on the Pondage.

Eildon Pondage is an interesting put-and-take fishery, especially for those keen to catch a very big trout. Its banks can become rather crowded at times, however, especially when word gets out that some big fish have recently been liberated and are coming on the bite.

Brown trout are more prolific than rainbow trout in Lake Eildon

DARTMOUTH RESERVOIR AND THE MITTA MITTA RIVER

IN BRIEF

MAP REFERENCE: PAGE 73 K5

GETTING THERE The village of Mitta Mitta is about 100 km south-east of Albury–Wodonga along the Kiewa Valley, Murray Valley and Omeo highways
BEST TIME TO FISH October to May
BEST TIME TO TRAVEL October to May
MAJOR ANGLING SPECIES Rainbow trout, brown trout, Macquarie perch and redfin
SPECIAL RESTRICTIONS In addition to regular Victorian freshwater fishing regulations, there are specific closed seasons and bag limits on the taking of Macquarie perch from Dartmouth Reservoir and its feeders. Anglers should check on the current status of these rules before fishing
WARNINGS Dartmouth Reservoir's open waters can become rough in strong winds. Extreme weather conditions are possible at any time of the year in high alpine regions. Check road conditions before travelling and always carry suitable clothing
ACCOMMODATION Dartmouth Lodge, telephone (02) 6072 5511
CHARTER BOATS AND FISHING GUIDES
Angling Expeditions Victoria, telephone (03) 5754 1466

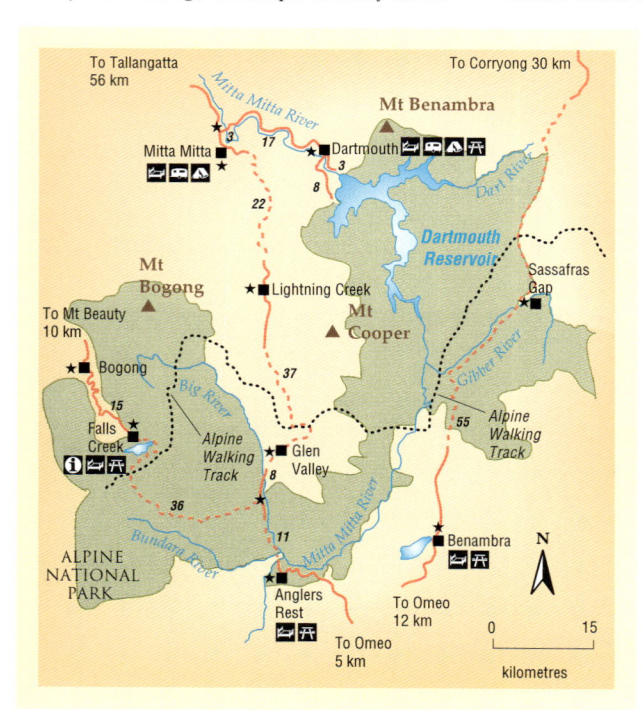

Light, single-handed spinning tackle is ideal for catching trout such as this rainbow

Dartmouth Reservoir and the small township of Mitta Mitta lie high on the north-western slopes of the Victorian Alps, 100 km or so south-east of the twin Murray River border cities of Albury and Wodonga. This is particularly scenic and impressive country, consisting of steep, heavily forested mountains, deep valleys and twisting rivers fed directly from the nearby winter snowfields of Mount Buffalo, Mount Beauty and the ruggedly beautiful Bogong High Plains.

The best access to Dartmouth Reservoir, especially for those people with vehicles towing caravans or boats, is via Albury–Wodonga along a well-signposted and sealed road. This route follows the picturesque Mitta Mitta River past the rural settlements of Eskdale and Mitta Mitta before climbing up to the village of Dartmouth itself. Further on still lies the dam wall viewing area and the popular Six Mile Creek boat ramp on Dartmouth Reservoir's shores.

An alternative route from Bairnsdale, in Gippsland, via Omeo, Anglers Rest, Glen Valley and Sunnyside, offers some stunning alpine vistas. This road is generally slower and more demanding, however, with many twisting turns and sections of unsealed gravel road that make it unsuitable for towing boats or caravans.

While the lake itself does not seem to fish quite as well these days as it did during the 1980s, the region around Dartmouth Reservoir still offers an interesting range of freshwater fishing opportunities and attracts reasonable numbers of visiting anglers from all over Victoria and southern New South Wales. Nonetheless, it is nearly always possible to find a secluded stretch of river or a quiet bay, even during peak holiday time.

FISHING IN DARTMOUTH RESERVOIR

The construction of Dartmouth Reservoir was a joint venture between Victoria, New South Wales and South Australia. As well as producing hydroelectricity for the Victorian grid, the lake is intended to provide back-up water for Lake Hume during drought periods.

The dam itself is situated in a spectacular V-shaped gorge on the Mitta Mitta River. The highest of its kind in the southern hemisphere, Dartmouth's dam wall consists of a massive earth- and rock-fill embankment towering some 180 m from base to crest. The vast lake held back behind this wall has a storage capacity of 4 million megalitres and its backed-up waters stretch more than 40 km up the Mitta Mitta River.

Dartmouth Reservoir has a mostly forested shoreline of more than 150 km in length, including many secluded inlets and steep, timbered hillsides. These natural features make it an interesting and pleasant place to visit. The lake is primarily fed by the Mitta Mitta River, which also receives the waters of the Big River, falling from the slopes of Mount Bogong, Victoria's highest peak. Other feeders flowing into Dartmouth include the Gibbo and Dart rivers, as well as numerous smaller creeks that tumble from the surrounding high country.

Recreational angling species available in the lake include brown trout, rainbow trout and native Macquarie perch, as well as a few Murray cod and possibly the occasional trout cod.

Although opportunities for shore-based fishing around the lake are somewhat limited

A stunning view across nearby Mt Feathertop at last light

by a shortage of access tracks and the ruggedness of the terrain, good sport can be had from the relatively clear stretches of bank adjacent to the boat launching area. This is especially so for those fishing fresh, natural baits such as scrub worms and mudeyes (dragonfly larvae) at dawn, dusk and through the night.

Dartmouth Reservoir, however, is mainly a boat angler's waterway. The best fishing is available to those operating craft with motors of sufficient horsepower to allow easy exploration of this very extensive lake system.

AFLOAT ON DARTMOUTH

Boat anglers on Dartmouth Reservoir may choose from several effective techniques, including trolling, drifting and casting, or tying up to the abundant drowned trees in order to soak a bait.

Throughout much of the year, trolling is the most productive method, especially for those seeking trout. Popular trolling lures include all the famous impoundment trout-takers such as spoons, minnows and Tasmanian-style lures.

As effective and enjoyable as lure trolling can be, there is no doubt that one of the most efficient techniques on this lake is the dead slow trolling of mudeye or scrub worm baits in conjunction with Cowbell or Ford Fender flasher rigs. As in most freshwater trolling, the best results are achieved by staying close to drowned treelines, steep shorelines and rocky bluffs. Late in the evening, however, many good trout are taken in the more open, seemingly featureless waters of the main basin, near the launching area.

The occasional Macquarie perch will be picked up while trolling, but those specifically seeking this species should try casting natural baits in amongst the sunken timber, especially near river or creek inflows in the narrower arms of the reservoir. Although several changes of location may be required until a patch of Macquaries or 'Maccas' is encountered, because of their schooling nature, once one is hooked, reasonable action usually follows.

All adult anglers must possess a current Victorian Inland Angling Licence to fish Dartmouth Reservoir and any freshwater streams surrounding it, and a closed season applies to the taking of Macquarie perch. In addition, bag limits are imposed on both trout and perch. As these seasons and limits change from time to time, it is advisable to check first with the local fisheries inspector. Current fishing regulations are also clearly signposted around the lake.

ALONG THE MITTA MITTA

The Mitta Mitta River below the dam wall and all the way downstream to the village Eskdale and beyond is another favourite destination with freshwater anglers.

As long as the discharge of water from the dam is not too great, this delightful river offers very good to excellent fly fishing, spinning and bait fishing for healthy stocks of brown and rainbow trout, redfin and the very occasional trout cod. (Trout cod are an endangered species and should be returned to the water alive if accidentally hooked.)

Most of the trout encountered in the Mitta Mitta River are smallish fish in the 200- to 800-g range, although larger specimens are always on the cards, particularly closer to the dam wall itself and in the partially backed-up waters above the small regulating weir below the main wall.

Similarly, the redfin of the Mitta Mitta are mostly small fish, although an odd plate-sized example will occasionally be taken further downstream, particularly on minnow-style lures and small diving plugs or crayfish imitations.

Introduced European carp are also present in the Mitta Mitta River in increasing numbers. These noxious pests are not much sought-after by anglers, however, apart from those who enjoy coarse fishing with light tackle for these hard-fighting, but otherwise rather disagreeable fish.

Trout fishing on the Mitta Mitta River below Dartmouth's dam wall

TROUT STREAMS OF SOUTH GIPPSLAND

IN BRIEF

MAP REFERENCE: PAGE 65 K4

GETTING THERE Tarago Reservoir is about 125 km east of Melbourne and this area is an easy day trip from that city
BEST TIME TO FISH Different streams produce better at different times, but winter is the best period
BEST TIME TO TRAVEL April to October
MAJOR ANGLING SPECIES Brown trout, rainbow trout, blackfish, eels and redfin
SPECIAL RESTRICTIONS See freshwater regulations on pp. 381–2
ACCOMMODATION Accommodation ranging from caravan parks to hotels and motels can be found in the nearby major towns

Any close examination of a detailed map of South Gippsland will reveal many thin, blue lines, which create a complex and tangled web. These thin, blue lines are the creeks, streams and rivers that weave their way through the many valleys of the South Gippsland region.

As small as many of these watercourses appear, their potential to hold trout should not be underestimated. It is hard to imagine why or how trout would find their way into some of these areas. The fact is, however, that they do, and these fish are there for the taking by anglers in possession of a little stream craft.

One such waterway is the Tarago River, a classic South Gippsland trout stream flowing through forested country to which access is difficult above the Tarago Reservoir. This small river flows into the Tarago Reservoir at Neerim South and is worth a special mention as it is one of South Gippsland's premier trout streams, holding good numbers of extremely large trout. The reservoir itself is a 200-hectare domestic water storage which was closed to fishing in 1977 to minimise the risk of contamination of the domestic water supply. It still holds trout of well in excess of 4 kg.

From late June through to November, huge brown trout and rainbow trout move up out of the Tarago Reservoir and into the river to spawn on the many gravel beds. Until the recent introduction of a closed season for trout in Victorian waters, these fish were readily taken on large trout pattern minnow lures and on glo bug-style flies. Many of these fish remain in the river above the reservoir well into November, however, and therefore still offer a great target for both lure and fly anglers alike.

Below the reservoir, the river is a much better prospect for fishing with a fly rod or lure casting, as it flows through open, hilly country until meeting up with the Bunyip River at Longwarry. From here it becomes the Main Drain and makes its way into the upper reaches of Western Port.

Sea-run brown trout are occasionally taken by anglers fishing the Main Drain at Koo-Wee-Rup, just a couple of hundred metres from its entrance into Western Port. Anglers fishing here mainly target Australian salmon and mullet, and so the trout are usually taken on pipis, whitebait and bluebait. These sea-run fish are not particularly common, but they usually hit the scales at around 3 or 4 kg when caught.

SUCCESSFUL LURE FISHING

As with the many other small streams in the South Gippsland area, the most effective method for catching trout in the Tarago River is with small, floating/diving minnow lures. For most situations, 2-kg line on a small long-cast reel will be more than adequate. The rod should be no

A handsome South Gippsland brown trout from a tiny stream

Some South Gippsland streams are well suited to fly fishing

longer than 1.6 m, and preferably shorter to help combat the obstacles provided by the profusion of overgrown timber and shrubs.

The reason that lure casting is so successful throughout these areas is because it enables the angler to fish every square centimetre of the river with relative ease and deadly effectiveness. It is not unreasonable to fish a 5-km stretch of river in a single session of lure casting.

Bait fishing, on the other hand, is a waiting game that may tie the angler to one pool for lengthy periods. A good compromise is to drift unweighted baits down runs and into the strike zones. A simple bunch of wriggling garden worms fished on a running sinker rig will account for a fair catch of fish, even in the smallest of streams. Freshwater blackfish or 'slipperies' weighing up to 1 kg and eels are also on the cards for the bait angler when fishing this region.

Hundreds of Rivers

The beauty of the area surrounding the Tarago Reservoir is that there are so many rivers, creeks and tributary streams to investigate. There is nothing like the excitement of casting your bait, lure or fly into a new pool or run for the first time, filled with the anticipation of what the next corner may hold.

You can also fish the La Trobe River, which eventually empties into Lake Wellington at Gippsland Lakes, as well the Toorongo River, the Loch River, Icy Creek and the Tanjil River as it flows into Blue Rock Lake, all of which are very close to the Tarago. The Bunyip and Lang Lang rivers, too, are well catered for in terms of trout stocks.

Apart from these more popular waters, there are many other streams in South Gippsland that could best be described as trickles. However, even streams that, in places, narrow to less than 30 cm in width should never be underestimated when it comes to taking trout! The size of the trout in these tiny streams tends to be on the smaller side, with most fish averaging 500 g or less. At first, this may sound a little disappointing, but even a small fish taken out of a tiny stream can provide a huge buzz for anglers. To add to the excitement, the odd monster to 3 or 4 kg is always a possibility.

In short, if you can't step over it, don't drive past it. This simple rule of thumb should keep you heading in the right direction as you investigate new locations and pursue varied techniques in the many 'thin, blue lines' that flow throughout South Gippsland.

While often small and overgrown with timber and shrubs, Gippsland rivers and streams such as this offer fine fishing

67

A
B
C
D
E
F
G
1
2
3
4
5
6
7
8
9
10
Waterloo
Glenbrae
Waubra
Mount Beckworth
Smeaton
Daylesford
Coomoora
Little Hampton
Tylden
Woodend North
Rochford
Woodend
Hesket
Romsey
Mt Misery
Addington
Coghills Creek
Allendale
Kingston
Creswick North
Blampied
Eganstown
Musk
Lyonville
Trentham
Fern Hill
Darraweit Guim
Lake Learmonth
Learmonth
Creswick
Mount Prospect
Bullarto
Trentham East
Mount Macedon
New Gisborne
Monegeetta
Trawalla
Bald Hills
Newlyn
Leonards Hill
Newbury
Macedon
Bolinda
Nerring
Burrumbeet
Windermere
Miners Rest
Dean
Spargo Creek
Barrys Reef
Blackwood
Riddells Creek
Brewster
Cardigan Village
Mollongghip
Bullengarook
Gisborne
Clarkefield
Mena Park
Lake Burrumbeet
Wendouree
Clarkes Hill
Blakeville
Lerderderg Gorge Forest Pk
Pootilla
Springbank
Couangalt
Kalkallo
Leigh Creek
Wallace
Greendale
Mickleham
Carngham
Ballarat
Bungaree
Gordon
Korobeit
Sunbury
Yuroke
Mount Emu
Haddon
WESTERN
Sebastopol
Mt Clear
Dunnstown
Millbrook
Ballan
Myrniong
Coimadai
Oaklands Junction
Ross Creek
Toolern Vale
Mortchup
Snake Valley
Mt Helen
Yendon
Mt Egerton
Werribee Gorge SP
FWY
Diggers Rest
Bulla
Greenvale
Buninyong
Smythesdale
Pittong
Scarsdale
Scotsburn
Lal Lal
Lal Lal Res
Fiskville
Bacchus Marsh
Melton
Sydenham
Tullamarine
Napoleons
Newtown
Linton
Clarendon
Bungal
Melton Sth
Sydenham West
Italian Gully
Mt Doran
Mount Wallace
Parwan
Rockbank
Keilor
Enfield
Rowsley
Melton Res
Exford
Coburg
Brunswick
Mannibadar
Deer Park
MIDLAND
Brisbane Ranges NP
Cape Clear
Grenville
Sunshine
Footscray
Elaine
Beremboke
Balliang East
Chartwell
Truganina
Willowvale
Pitfield
Illabarook
Dereel
Mount Mercer
Durdidwarrah
Balliang
One Tree Hill
Laverton
Rokewood Junction
Meredith
Hoppers Crossing
Woodbourne
Steiglitz
Altona
Wallinduc
Corindhap
Werribee
Mount Bute
Rokewood
Quiney Hill
Sheoaks
You Yangs Forest Park
Altona Bay
Bamganie
Anakie
Warrambine
Point Cook
Little River
Werneth
Maude
Lethbridge
Campbells Cove
Berrybank
Rothwell
Werribee South
Shelford
Gow Hill
Lara
PRINCES
Port
Cressy
Teesdale
Avalon Airport
Mt Rebecca
Bannockburn
Lovely Banks
Kirk Point
Phillip
Foxhow
Corio
Avalon
Point Wilson
Point Richards
HAMILTON
Inverleigh
Murgheboluc
Jetty
Lake Corangamite
Wingeel
Batesford
Norlane
Portarlington
Lake Martin
Barpinba
HWY
Fyansford
Corio Bay
Lake Murdeduke
Stonehaven
Geelong
Clifton Springs
Point George
Bellarine
Indented Head
Pelican Point
Mt Pollock
Gnarwarre
Highton
Eurack
Belmont
Drysdale
St Leonards
Dreeite
Mount Moriac
Ceres
Leopold
Lake Beeac
Beeac
The Cap
Grovedale
Wallington
Mannerim
Edwards Point
Wool Wool
Alvie
Warrion
Salt Lake
Mt Gellibrand
Winchelsea
Marshall
Waurn Ponds
Swan Bay
Lake Modewarre
Moriac
Lake Connewarre
Swan Island
Coragulac
Connewarre
Queenscliff
Freshwater Creek
Wurdiboluc Res
Cororooke
Irrewarra
Ingleby
Barwon Heads
Ocean Grove
Point Lonsdale
The Rip
Lake Colac
Breamlea
Nalangil
Angahook-Lorne State Park
Portsea
Warncoort
Birregurra
Bellbrae
Sorrento
Pirron Yallock
Larpent
Colac
Torquay
Blairgowrie
Elliminyt
Jan Juc
Bambra
Rye
Tulloh
Bells Beach
Point Addis
Mornington Peninsula Nat Park
The Cups
Yeodene
Deans Marsh
Anglesea
Barongarook
Rd
Lookout Hill
St Andrews Beach
Eastern View
Kawarren
Aireys Inlet
Murroon
Cape Schanck
Barwon Downs
Benwerrin
Fairhaven
Big Hill
Gellibrand
Forrest
Lorne Forest Park
Paterson Bay
Carlisle State Pk
Lorne
Point Grey
Charleys Creek
Barramunga
Artillery Rocks
RANGE
Beech Forest
Separation Creek
Ferguson
Ocean
Wye River
Weeaproinah
Haines Junction
Wyelangta
Kennett River
Cape Patton
OTWAY
Wongarra
Skenes Creek
Apollo Bay
Paradise
Great
Glenaire
Otway Nat Park
Marengo
Blanket Bay
Point Lewis
Cape Otway
Point Franklin
144°
38°
39°
N

0 10 20 30 40 50
kilometres

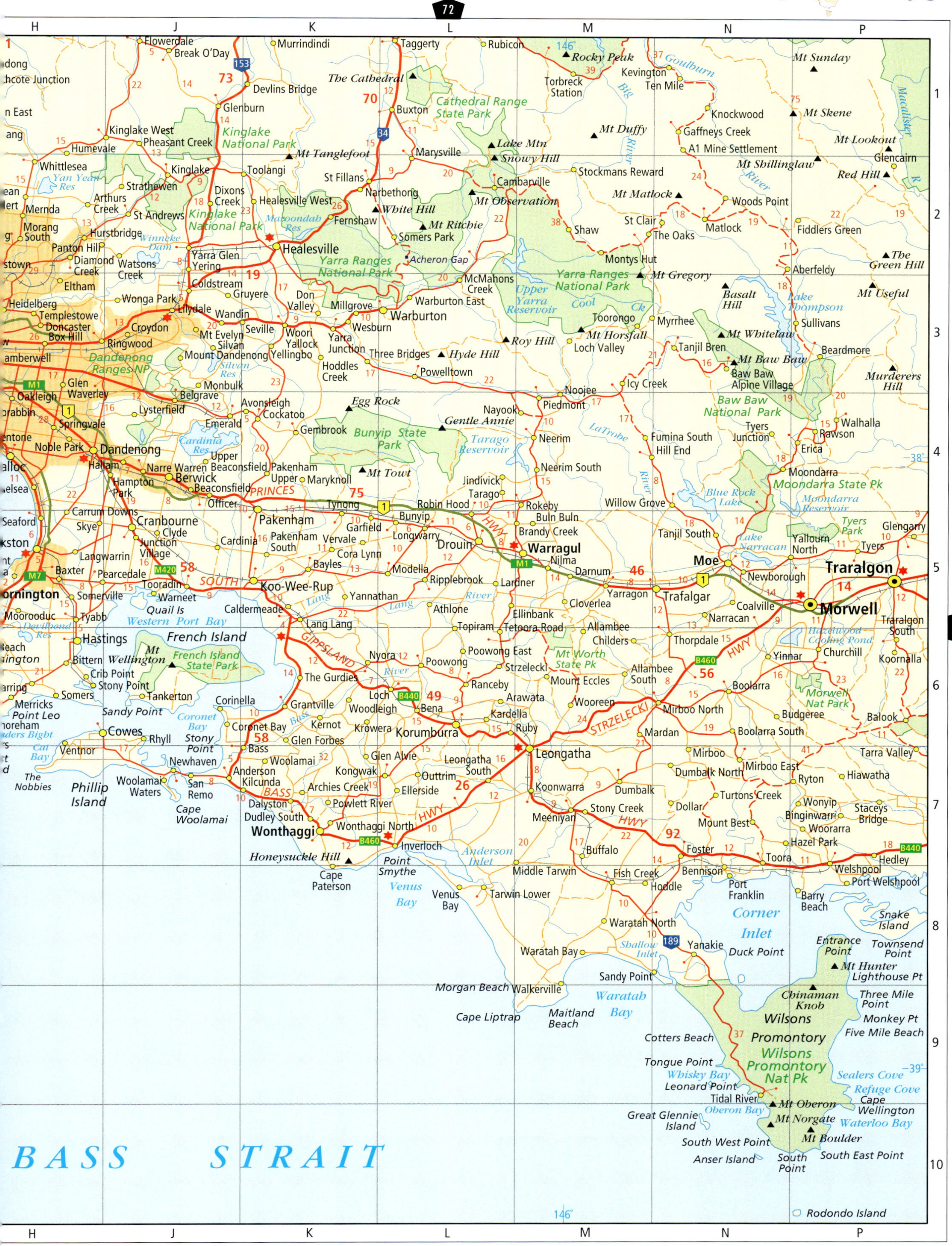

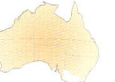

66 South-West Victoria

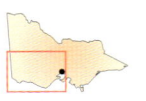

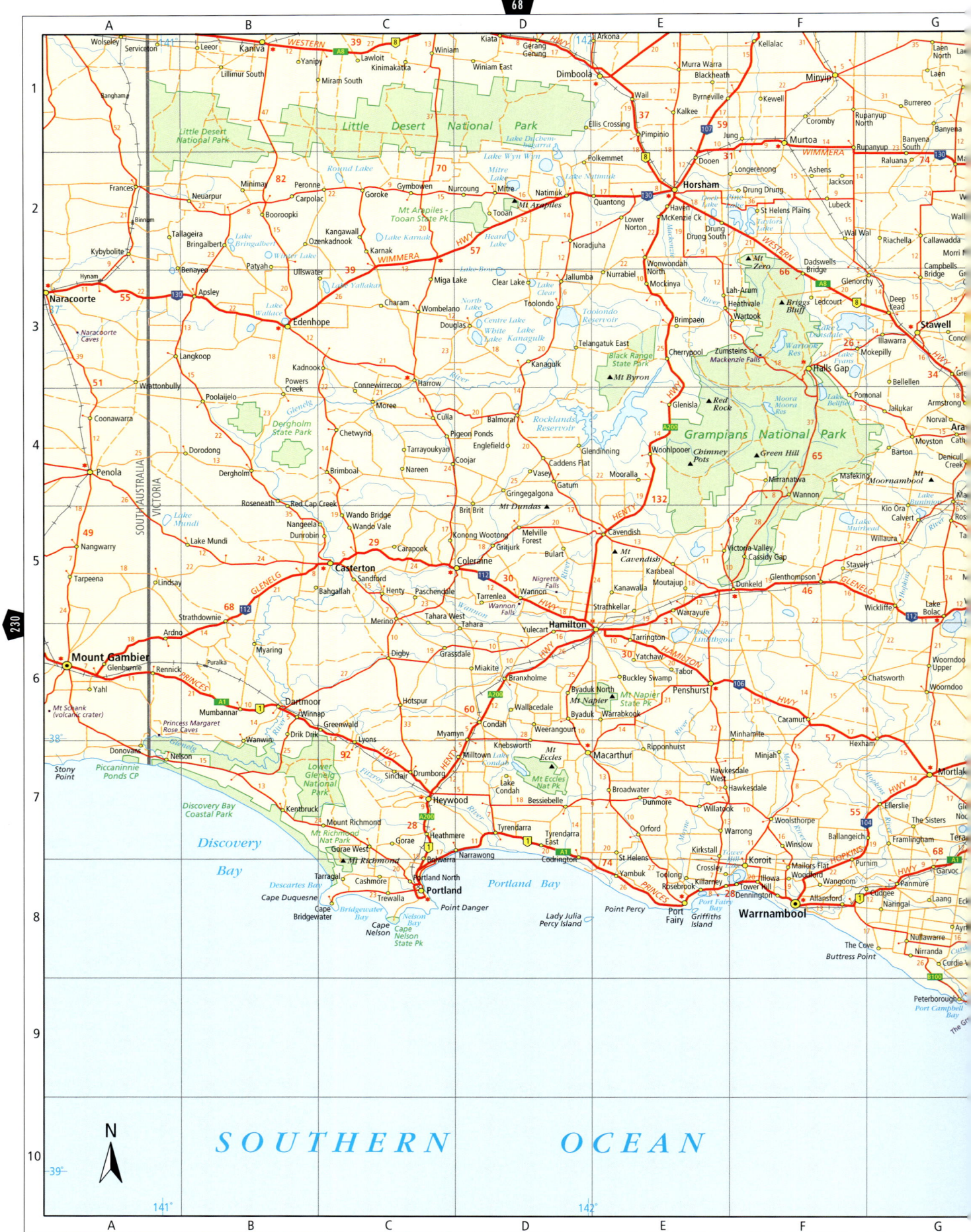

0 10 20 30 40 50
kilometres

69

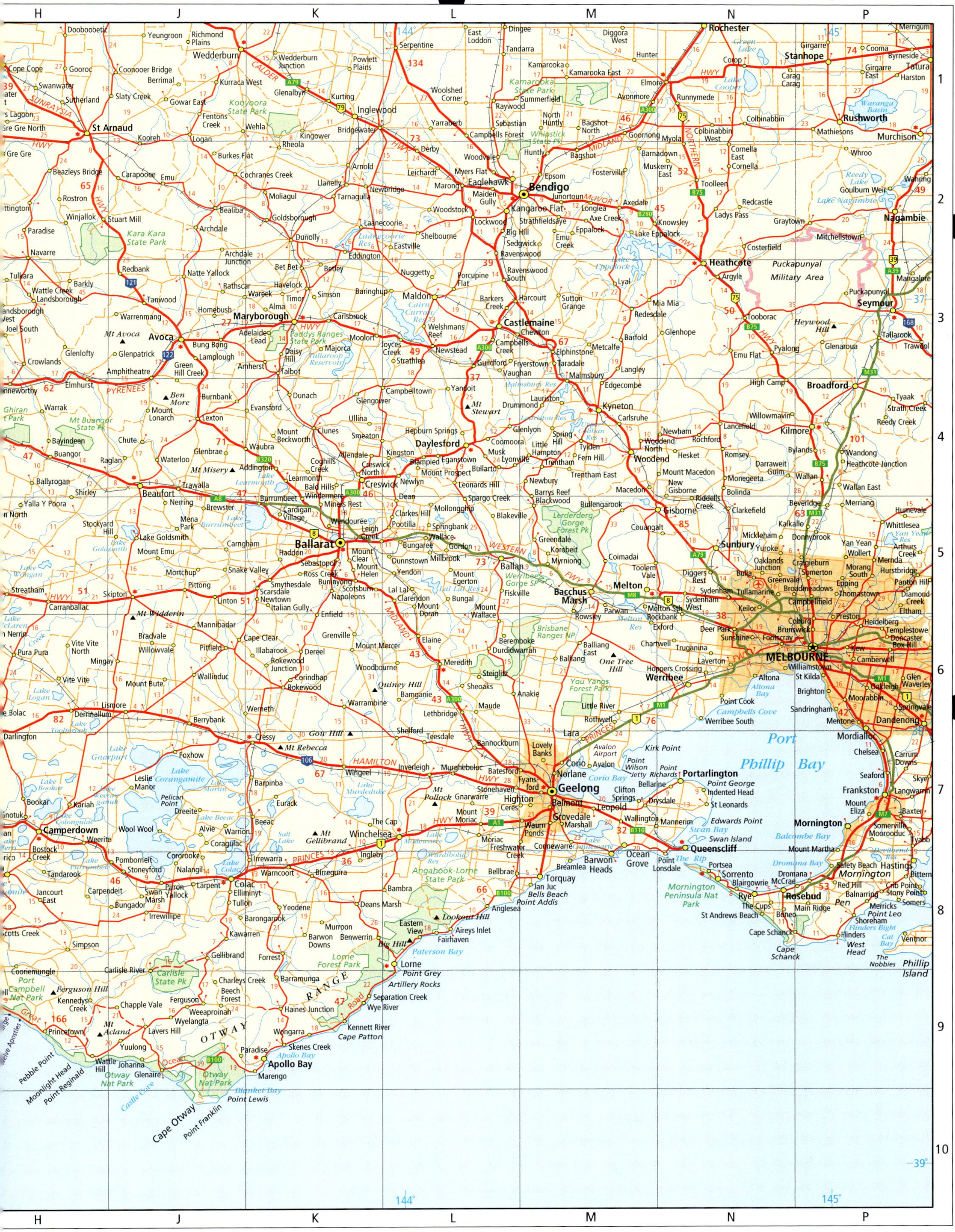

72

65

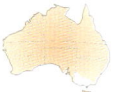

68 NORTH-WEST VICTORIA

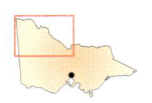

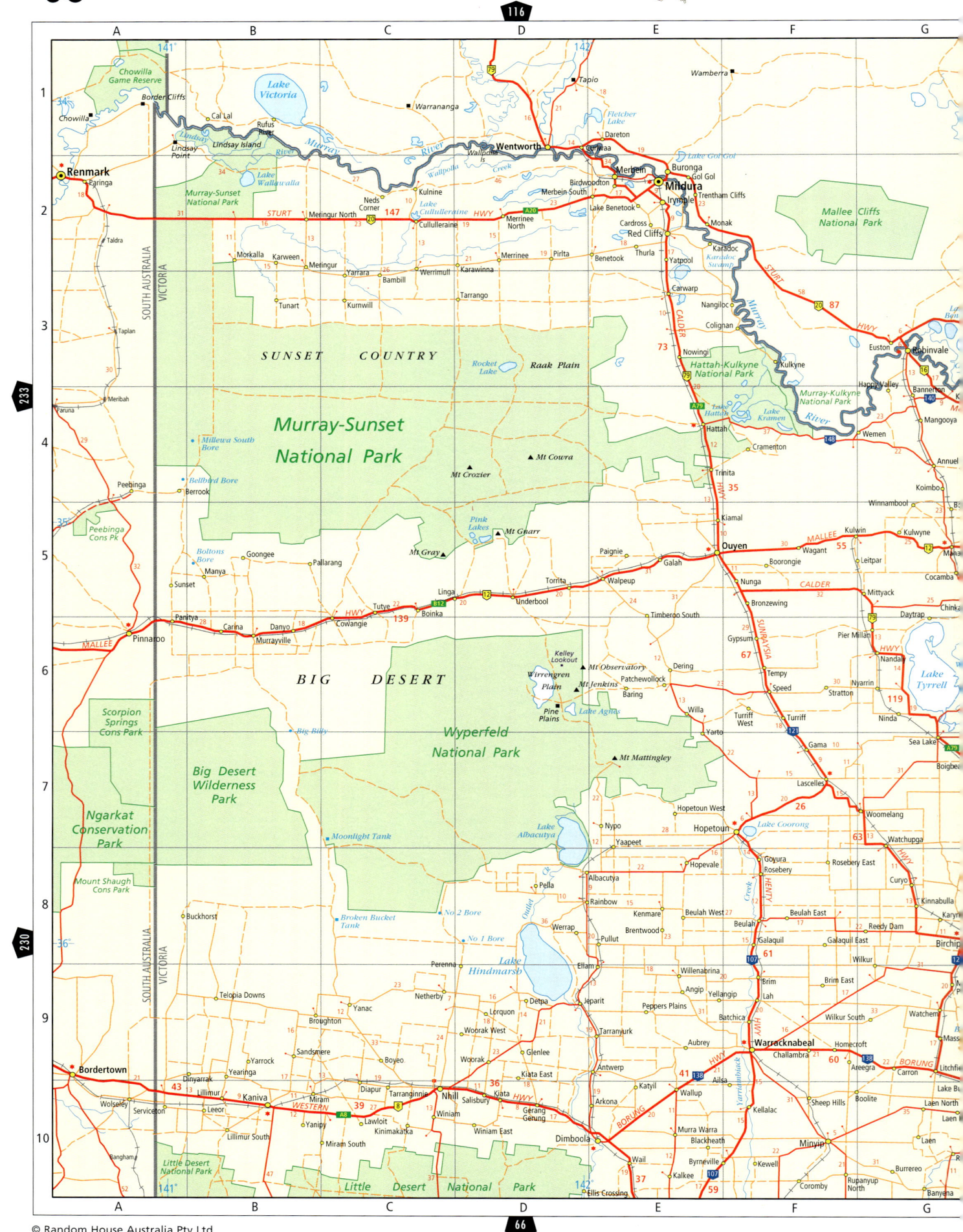

0 10 20 30 40 50
kilometres

116

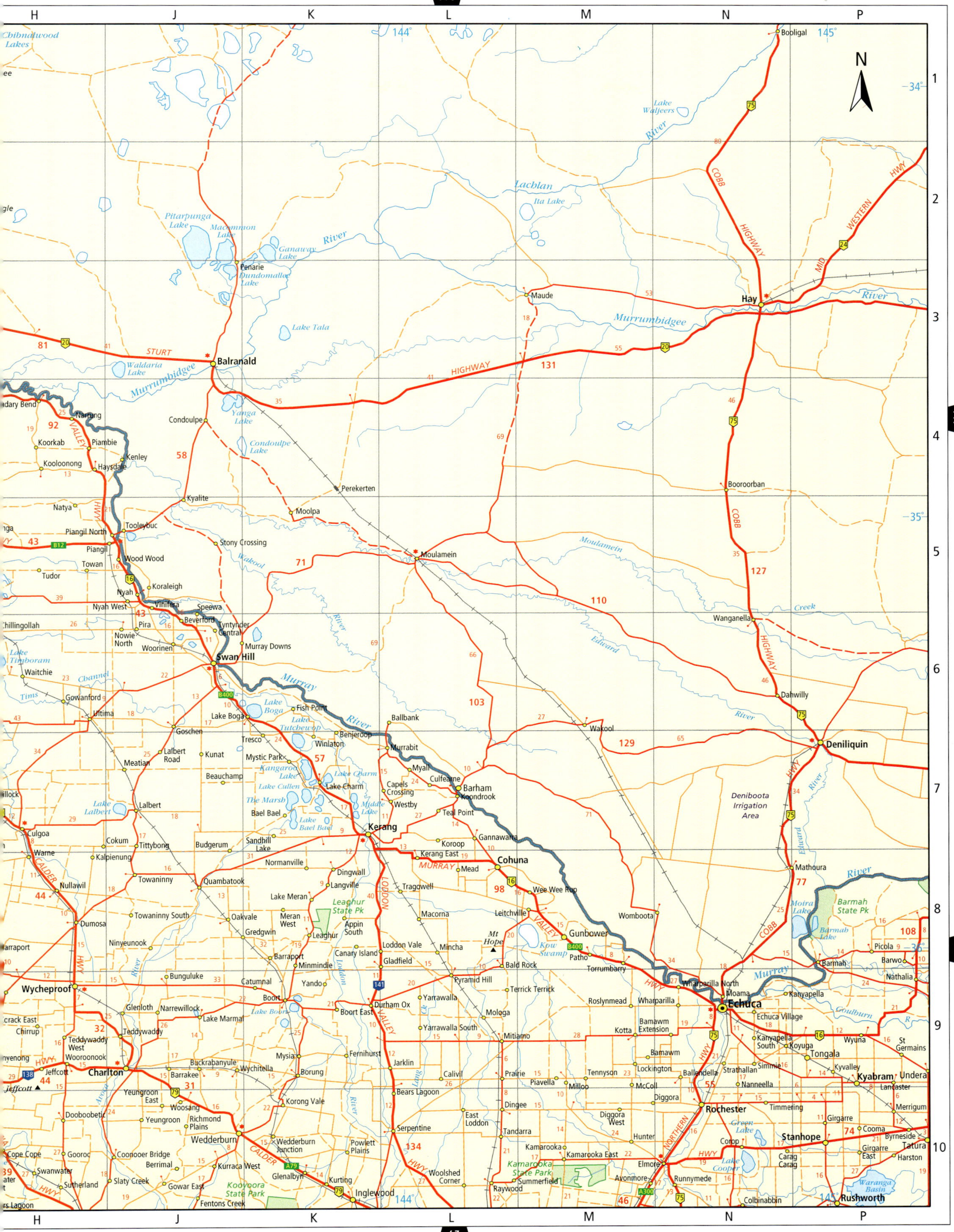

117
72
67

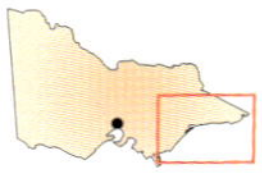

73
72
65
A B C D E F G
1 2 3 4 5 6 7 8 9 10
147°
148°
Edi
Carboor Upper
Buffalo River
Eurobin
Mt Emu
Lightning Creek
Toke Gibbo
King Valley
Whitfield
Cheshunt
Dandongadale
Anderson Peak
Mt Buffalo National Park
Lake Buffalo
Mount Buffalo Chalet
The Hump
The Horn
White Hill
Porepunkah
Bright
Germantown
Freeburgh
Tawonga
Mount Beauty
Bull Hill
Mt Bogong
Mt Cooper
Alpine National Park
Mt Murphy
Johnnies Top
Clover Power Station
Bogong
Alpine National Park
Christmas Creek
Mt Misery
Forest Hill
Buckland
Wandiligong
Typo
Mt Warrick
Abbeyard
Mt Mary
Harrietville
Mt Feathertop
Falls Creek
Rocky Valley Reservoir
Glen Wills
Glen Valley
Mt Fraser
Uplands
Mt Pendergast
Moscow Peak
Mt Cobberas
Lake William Hovell
Mt Typo
Mt Angus
Twin Knobs
Bogong High Plains
RANGE
Lake Omeo
The Brothers
The Brothers
Mt Wombargo
Alpine National Park
Mt McIver
Mt Sugarloaf
Mt Loch
Hotham Heights
Mt Hotham
Anglers Rest
Benambra
Hinnomunjie
Bingo Munjie North
Brumby Hill
Forlorn Hope
Mt Selwyn
Mt Murray
Dargo High Plains
Dinner Plain
Cobungra
Road
Mt Battery
Round Hill
Mt Shanahan
Mt Nunniong
Wulgulmerang
The Pinnacle
Mirimbah
The Viking
Mt Stirling
Mt Blue Rag
Cobungra
Omeo
Bindi
Mt Seldom Seen
Mt Buller
Mount Buller Alpine Village
The Pimple
Mt Howitt
Wonnangatta
Basalt Knob
DIVIDING
Treasures
Mt Livingstone
OMEO
Mt Bindi
Mt Statham
The Bluff
Mt Darling
The Governor
Mt Darling
Mt Phipps
Dogs Grave
Cassilis
Tongio
Tongio West
Swifts Creek
Mt Nugong
Alpine
Crooked River
Treasure
Mt Birregun
Doctors Flat
Green Hills
Mt Sunday
GREAT
National Park
Mt McAdam
Mt Cynthia
Mt Ewen
Mt Delusion
Brookville
Ensay North
Timbarra
Gillingall
Mt Reynard
Howittville
Wongungarra
Ensay
Seldom Seen
Dawson City
Pretty Boy Saddle
Mt Arbuckle
Mt Dawson
Mt Steve
Nicholson
Dogtown
Stirling
Holstons
Dingo Knob
Crooked River
Mt Victoria
Macalister
East Pinnacle
Dargo
Mt Lookout
Glencairn
Castle Hill
Waterford
Morris Peak
Forktown
Tambo Crossing
Buchan Caves
Red Hill
Bruni Knob
Lamb Hill
Freestone
Mt Sugarloaf
Echo Point
Tabberabbera
Mt Hoad
Buchan South
Castleburn
Deptford
Pheasant Hill
Double Bridges
Spanker Knob
Fiddlers Green
Mt Ronald
Mt Hump
Mt Blomford
Cobbannah
Licola
Avon Wilderness Park
Bullumwaal
Mitchell River Nat Park
Mt Little Dick
The Green Hill
Davey Knob
Clifton Creek
Wiseleigh
Bruthen
Mt Useful
Big Hill
Mt Angus
Wright Hill
Mt Ray
Mount Taylor
Nowa Nowa
Morgan
Iguana Creek
Mossiface
Lake Tyers State Park
Sullivans
Rocky Knob
Avon
Glenaladale
Woodglen
Lindenow
Wy Yung
Sarsfield
Tambo Upper
Culloden
The Fingerboards
Walpa
Lucknow
Nicholson
Swan Reach
Colquhoun Hill
Lake Tyers
Beardmore
Mt Margaret
Valencia Creek
Stockdale
Lindenow South
Bairnsdale
Johnsonville
Kalimna West
Murderers Hill
Glenmaggie Reservoir
Maffra West Upper
Briagolong
Fernbank
Lake King
Kalimna
Lakes Entrance
Lake Tyers
Glenmaggie
Coongulla
Boisdale
Bushy Park
Eagle Point
Paynesville
Metung
Walhalla
Thomson
Seaton
Newry
Munro
PRINCES
Delvine
Forge Creek
Raymond Is
Rawson
Erica
Heyfield
Maffra
Tinamba
Stratford
Bengworden
Goon Nure
Pt Best
Point Wilson
Cowwarr Weir
Cowwarr
Riverslea
Meerlieu
The Lakes NP
Mt Lookout
Denison
Airly
Perry Bridge
Pelican Point
Toongabbie
Winnindoo
Bundalaguah
Nambrok
Clydebank
Lake Victoria
Moondarra Reservoir
Nambrok West
Myrtlebank
Cobains
Lake Wellington
Holland Landing
Loch Sport
Tyers Park
Kilmany
Fulham
RAAF Base East Sale
Seacombe
Beach
Tyers
Glengarry
LaTrobe
Sale
Wurruk
The Heart
Gippsland Lakes Coastal Park
Kilmany South
Longford
Lake Coleman
Traralgon
Flynn
Rosedale
Dutson
Morwell
HYLAND
Flynns Creek
Holey Plains State Park
Deadman Hill
Paradise Beach
Golden Beach
Hazelwood Cooling Pond
Merriman
Willung
Delray Beach
Churchill
Traralgon South
Hiamdale
Gormandale
Stradbroke West
Stradbroke
Flamingo Beach
Glomar Beach
Koornalla
Willung South
Mile
Carrajung
Toms
Cap
Creek
Carrajung South
Giffard West
The Honeysuckles
Morwell Nat Park
Blackwarry
Seaspray
Balook
Tarra-Bulga Nat Park
GIPPSLAND
Giffard
Macks Creek
Wonwron
Darriman
Jack Smith Lake
Tarra Valley
Hiawatha
Devon
Ninety
Greenmount
SOUTH
Woodside
Woodside Beach
Wonyip
Staceys Bridge
Alberton West
Yarram
Hunterson
SOUTHERN
Binginwarri
Alberton
McLoughlins Beach
Woorarra
Tarraville
St. Margaret Island
Manns Beach
Welshpool
Hedley
Port Albert
Port Welshpool
Shallow Inlet
Sunday Island
Kate Kearney Entrance
Barry Beach
Clonmel Island
Snake Island
Port Albert Entrance
Entrance Point
Townsend Point
Mt Hunter
Lighthouse Point
Chinaman Knob
Three Mile Point
A1
B500
B440
188
1
HWY
TAMBO

0 10 20 30 40 50
kilometres

109

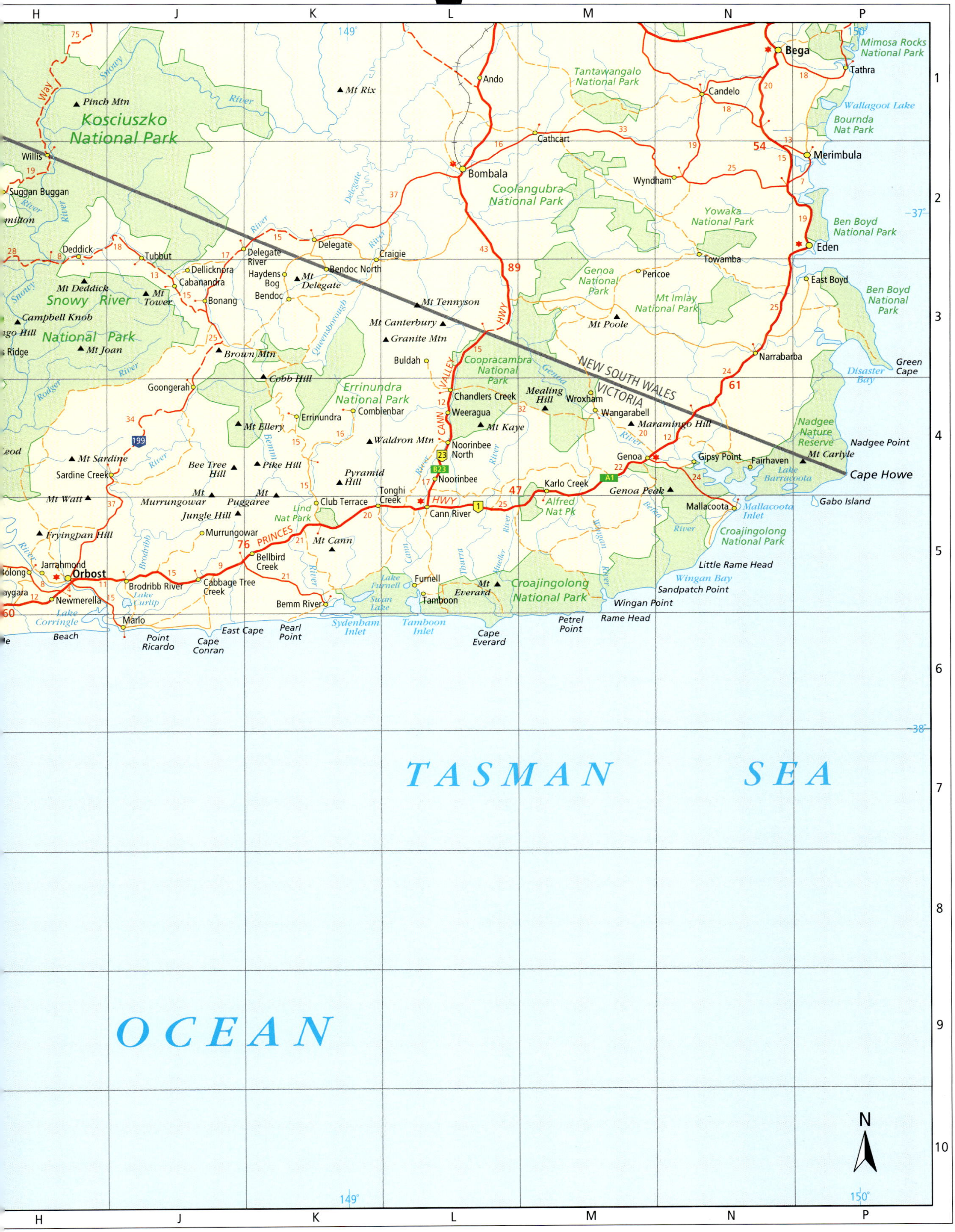

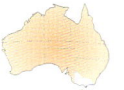

72 North-East Victoria

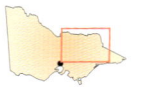

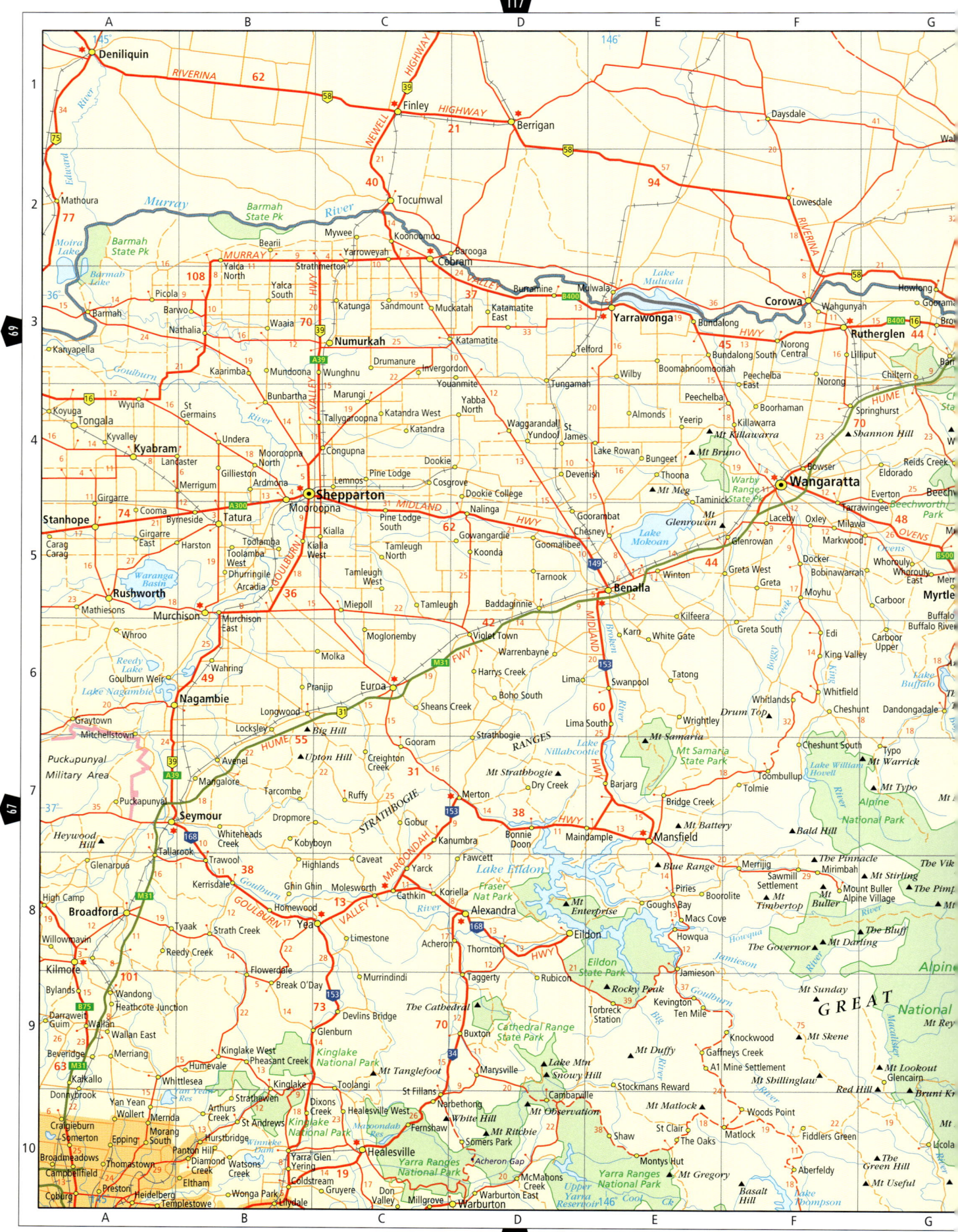

117
109
109
71
70

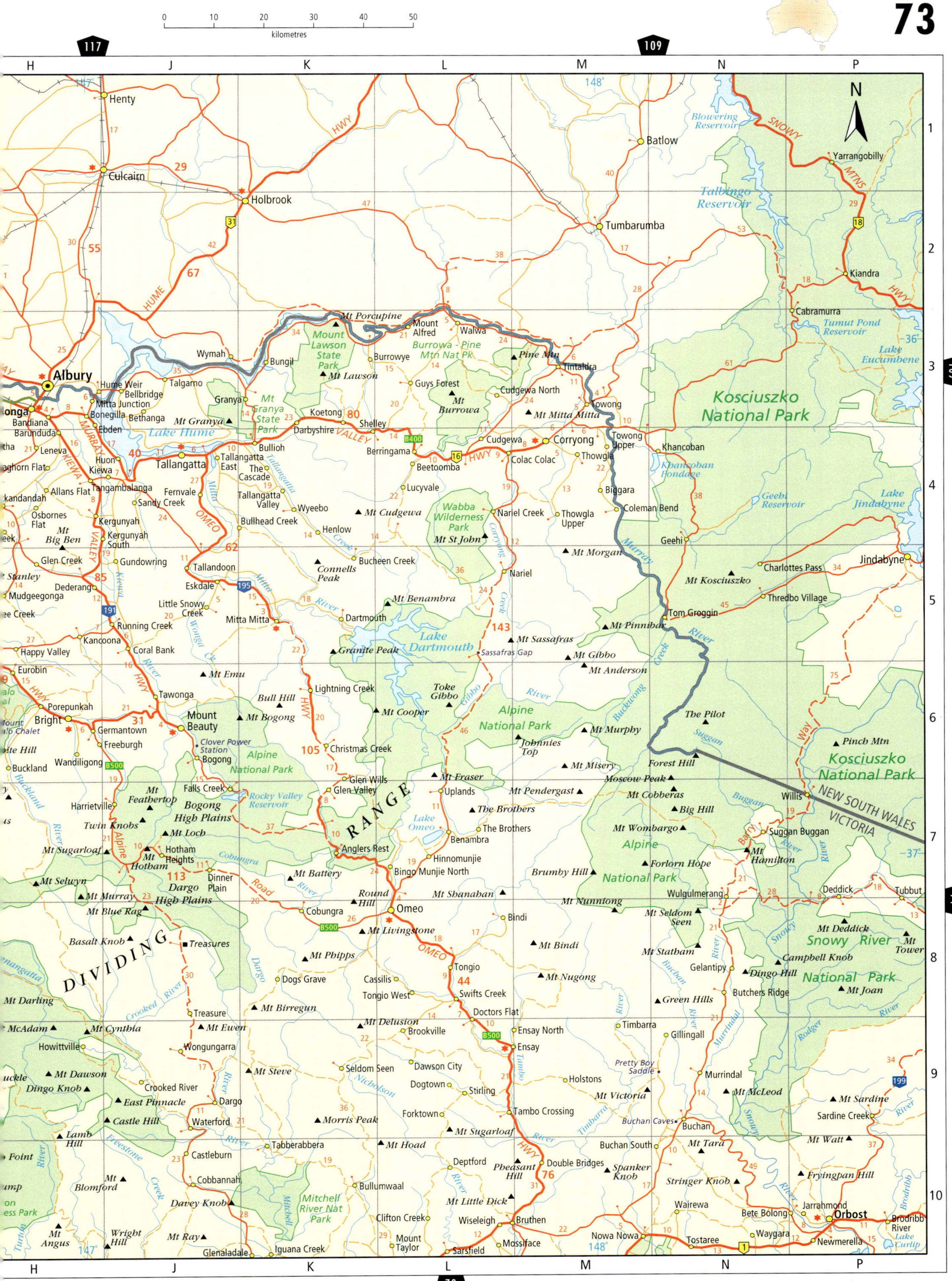

NEW SOUTH WALES AND THE AUSTRALIAN CAPITAL TERRITORY

FISHING HOT SPOTS

- Sydney Harbour (pp. 76–7)
- The Lower Hawkesbury and Broken Bay (pp. 78–9)
- Hawkesbury–Nepean Bass Waters (pp. 80–1)
- Botany Bay (pp. 82–3)
- Georges River (pp. 84–5)
- Gosford and Brisbane Water (pp. 86–7)
- Port Stephens (pp. 88–9)
- Lake Illawarra (pp. 90–1)
- The South Coast (pp. 92–3)
- Jervis Bay (pp. 94–5)
- Batemans Bay and the Clyde River (pp. 96–7)
- Lake Windamere (pp. 98–9)
- Lake Glenbawn (pp. 100–1)
- Lake Lyell (pp. 102–3)
- The Capital's Lakes (pp. 104–5)
- Trout Streams of the Australian Capital Territory (pp. 106–8)

Despite being the most populous state in Australia, and home to its largest city, New South Wales still offers an excellent range of angling opportunities to its residents, as well as to the many travellers from interstate and overseas who visit each year.

With a coastline that stretches all the way from the subtropical waters of the north to the cool, temperate seas of the south, the state has a particularly diverse selection of saltwater species on offer. These include such tropical visitors as Spanish mackerel, cobia, mangrove jacks, giant trevally and emperor in the north to cold-water types such as barracouta, snook, southern bream, King George whiting and warehou or 'snotty' trevalla in the far south. In between, temperate species such as eastern black bream, luderick, tailor, Australian salmon, drummer, groper, silver trevally, snapper, morwong, flathead, leatherjackets, kingfish, sand whiting, garfish, mullet and mulloway tend to dominate inshore and estuarine catches.

New South Wales has a relatively narrow continental shelf (particularly off the South West Rocks area in the north and Narooma–Bermagui to the south) and warm currents that wash its coast each summer and autumn. As a result, it boasts excellent offshore sport and game fishing action, particularly for tuna, marlin and sharks.

The most famous big game ports in this state include Bermagui and Port Stephens, but excellent bluewater fishing is available off most parts of the coast, and Sydney itself is home to a large and active offshore fleet. Between December and May each year, large numbers of sizeable marlin, tuna and sharks are hooked directly off the city, many of them within sight of the high-rise buildings and towers of the CBD.

New South Wales and Australian Capital Territory anglers are also particularly well catered for on the freshwater front. The Snowy Mountains and Monaro high country of the south offer the best and most extensive trout fishing on the mainland, and pockets of fair to good trout water also exist in the Southern Highlands, Blue Mountains, Central Western Slopes, Barrington Tops and New England districts.

Like most mainland trout waters, all these areas are highly susceptible to the severe droughts that regularly grip the state. During favourable periods, however, they offer world-class trout fishing—a fact clearly recognised by the staging of the World Fly Fishing Championships here in late 1999.

Sunrise over Swansea on the New South Wales Central Coast

Eastern-flowing rivers on the coastal plains of New South Wales—especially those unaffected by major dam construction—also offer freshwater anglers reasonable to excellent sport with Australian bass, as well as smaller numbers of other species such as estuary perch, mullet, herring, eels and the protected eastern cod of the Clarence River system.

Inland, numerous western-flowing streams and rivers pour from the Great Dividing Range, meander across the flat plains of the west and eventually feed into the mighty Murray–Darling system on its way to the Southern Ocean in South Australia. Sadly, these western rivers have been seriously degraded by dam and weir construction, water abstraction, pollution and salination, not to mention the spread of the introduced and noxious European carp. As a result, native fish numbers have dramatically declined in many areas. Nonetheless, Murray cod, golden and silver perch and eel-tailed catfish are still targeted—with mixed success—by many keen inland anglers.

Ironically, the brightest spots here are the numerous dams or impoundments constructed throughout the 20th century to meet the growing demands of country towns, irrigators and power generators. Despite the damage wrought to our western rivers by these dams, their backed-up waters now provide a valuable freshwater fishing resource for anglers. Regular stocking by government agencies, clubs, associations and individuals has assured excellent fishing in these impounded waters for many years to come.

New South Wales remains a lucky state in fishing terms—in spite of the ravages of development and the considerable pressures imposed by its large (and growing) population. It has much to offer the avid angler.

Below: *A view from Sydney Harbour looking towards the city centre*
Right: *Fishing from a canoe at Clarrie Hall Dam*
Bottom: *Looking south over Gerringong and Werri Beach towards Seven Mile Beach*

Contact Numbers

Information on fisheries rules and regulations in New South Wales or the Australian Capital Territory can be obtained by telephoning one of the numbers shown below. Numbers for New South Wales regional offices are given on p. 384.

FISHERIES INFORMATION SERVICE — NSW
(02) 9566 7802

FISHERMAN'S WATCH — NSW (24 hours)
1800 043 536

ENVIRONMENT ACT
(02) 6207 2117
(02) 6207 2120

SYDNEY HARBOUR

IN BRIEF

MAP REFERENCE: PAGE 111 H9

GETTING THERE Sydney Harbour runs through the very heart of the city of Sydney and is accessible from many points

BEST TIME TO FISH September to June

BEST TIME TO TRAVEL Year-round

MAJOR ANGLING SPECIES Bream, flathead, whiting, tailor, luderick (blackfish), trevally and leatherjackets

SPECIAL RESTRICTIONS Shore access to most islands in Sydney Harbour is strictly controlled. Some may be visited with a permit, others are off-limits. The same is true of certain mainland locations, including the old Quarantine Station at North Head. It should also be noted that fishing is not allowed in parts of Homebush Bay, and that fish from the more polluted areas of the Parramatta River should not be eaten. Beyond the Ryde Bridge, heavy metal and organochlorine deposits in the sediment have led to total bans on the consumption of fish caught in these waters. Check current notifications of restrictions

WARNINGS Boat traffic is extremely heavy at most times on Sydney Harbour. Be especially vigilant in main shipping channels or when drifting and anchoring, particularly at night

CHARTER BOATS AND FISHING GUIDES Craig McGill's Fish-About Tours, telephone (02) 9498 7340

Sydney Harbour is one of the best known urban waterways in the world, and an icon of Australian life. It also provides some surprisingly good fishing opportunities for a body of water surrounded by more than 4 million people!

Over the centuries since European settlement, Sydney Harbour and its fish populations have taken a severe beating from pollution, foreshore development, overharvesting and intense boating traffic. Fishing in the Harbour certainly ain't what it used to be, and the big snapper that were still being pulled from its waters on a reasonably regular basis as recently as 20 or 30 years ago are now largely a thing of the past.

On the positive side, Sydney Harbour water quality has improved somewhat in recent times, thanks to the advent of deep-water sewage outfalls and a gradual improvement in the control of storm water run-off and industrial pollution. Dolphins are once again being seen as far upstream as the Harbour Bridge, and good catches of kingfish and other pelagic species are once again being taken each summer in the lower reaches. Sharks have also returned to the Harbour in reasonable numbers. Compared with harbours in some other major cities around the world, Sydney's jewel is still in relatively good shape, and well worth casting a line into!

PORT JACKSON AND MIDDLE HARBOUR

The Lower Harbour—known officially as Port Jackson—is bounded at its seaward extremity by an imaginary line between the North and South heads, with Sydney Harbour Bridge generally being regarded as its upper limit. On the northern side of the Lower Harbour, Middle Head and Grotto Point mark the entrance to Middle Harbour, and a line between Dobroyd Head and Inner North Head effectively separates the North Harbour, or Manly Cove as it is more commonly known, from the main harbour.

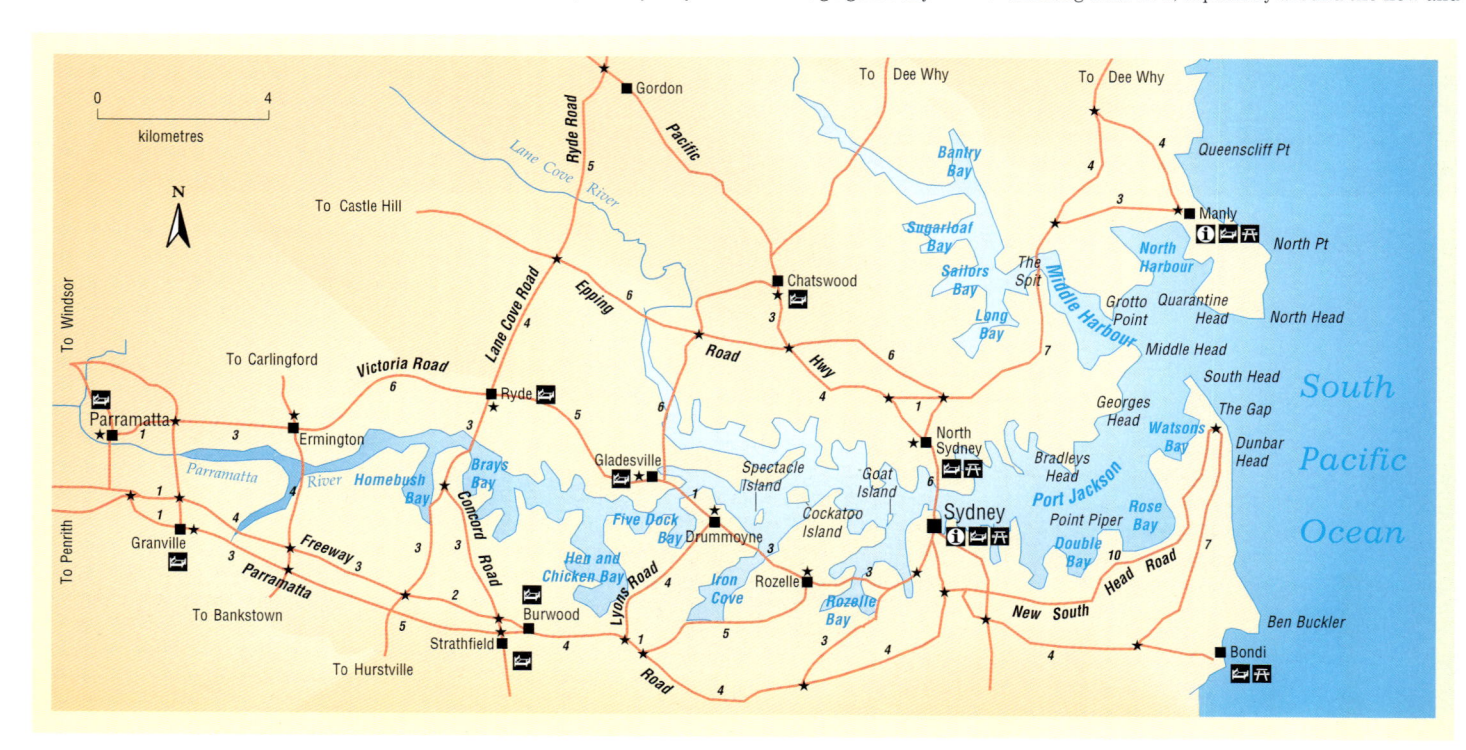

The Lower Harbour is flushed twice a day by a strong tidal flow, especially around the new and

full moon periods, and as a result it has relatively clean water and an interesting mixed population of oceanic and estuarine fish species.

Around North Head and Inner North Head, Dobroyd Head, Grotto Point, Middle Head, Georges Head and Inner South Head, it is possible to catch black and silver drummer, blue groper, large, sea-going luderick, trevally, bream, pike, leatherjackets and various other reef and estuary fish, as well as passing pelagics such as tailor, Australian salmon, bonito, 'rat' kingfish, frigate mackerel and the odd mackerel tuna.

Further into Sydney Harbour, bream, whiting, flathead, luderick, flounder and leatherjackets take over as the most consistent targets, with schools of hard-feeding tailor often evident on the surface, especially in autumn and early winter. The odd school mulloway is also encountered, mostly at night.

Some surprisingly large yellowtail kingfish are to be found under the various navigation markers and buoys in the Lower Harbour, particularly from November until March, when they will sometimes respond to live fish baits, whole fresh squid or even lures and flies. Early morning is the best time to target these hard-fighting hoodlums.

Anglers targeting mixed bags of bream, flathead, whiting and trevally would do best to anchor near submerged features out of the main shipping channels, berley heavily and fish with lightly weighted baits of fresh harbour prawns, yabbies, fish flesh strips, small live fish and, of course, blood worms. Good spots for such activities include Sow and Pigs, Bottle and Glass, the reefy patches around Shark Island, off Chowder Head, Clifton Gardens and Point Piper, to name just a few. These are also good areas for tailor.

As well as being one of the most famous and beautiful harbours in the world, Sydney Harbour offers some excellent fishing opportunities

Many of the Harbour's better bream spots can be fished from the shoreline, too, especially in Middle Harbour. Here, the Spit Bridge, Willoughby Bay, Long Folly Point, Fig Tree Point, Sailors Bay, Sugarloaf Point and the area under the Roseville Bridge are all proven bream producers, particularly on a rising tide at dusk, dawn or through the night.

In fact, the best times to fish anywhere in the Harbour are generally from very early morning—well before dawn—until about an hour or two after sunrise, and again late in the afternoon and into the night. However, if you are boating at such times, be extra careful of ferries, pleasure boats and large ships! Make sure your vessel is fitted with all the necessary navigation lights and stay out of the busy shipping channels.

Further up the Harbour, towards the Harbour Bridge, good luderick are taken on green weed baits around many of the points, rock retaining walls and boat moorings, with bream, silver trevally or barely legal snapper always a chance on a blood worm, prawn or fish fillet bait cast a little further out. Unusual baits such as cooked chicken, raw skirt steak and even tripe also take their share of fish here, especially big bream.

Another fish worth watching for anywhere in the Harbour, particularly during the cooler months, is the delicious and unusual John dory. These are best targeted with small live baits, and usually hang around wharves, pontoons, moorings, swimming baths and similar structures.

THE UPPER HARBOUR AND PARRAMATTA RIVER

Upstream from the Harbour Bridge, Sydney Harbour becomes much more estuary-like. It is also somewhat more polluted and degraded, with less daily tidal flush and more run-off from upriver. Nonetheless, the Upper Harbour still offers some surprisingly good fishing, especially for bream. Some of the best spots are around the rock walls, piers, docks and wharf pilings of Walsh Bay, Pyrmont, the Sydney Fish Markets at Blackwattle Bay, Drummoyne and Balmain.

In addition to bream, these locations offer luderick, leatherjackets, silver trevally, flathead and the odd legal snapper or school mulloway. Yellowtail and slimy mackerel are also thick at times, and schools of chopper tailor show up regularly in autumn and early winter.

Further upstream, beyond the Gladesville Bridge and on towards the Ryde Bridge at Meadowbank, water quality becomes a serious consideration. Although there are still many fish to be caught, it's probably unwise to eat your catch. This is particularly true of Homebush Bay, beyond the Ryde Bridge, where heavy metal and organochlorine deposits in the sediment have led to total bans on the consumption of fish caught from these waters. It's important to keep up to date with notifications of restrictions.

Much to the surprise of some anglers, there is often exceptional bream fishing available — especially on lures — in the Parramatta River between Hen and Chicken Bay and the Silverwater Bridge or beyond. This fishing should, however, be regarded as purely for sport. All fish should be returned to the water because of their likely contamination with heavy metals, pesticides and so on.

Shore-based anglers fishing in Sydney Harbour with Glebe Point Bridge in the background

THE LOWER HAWKESBURY AND BROKEN BAY

IN BRIEF

MAP REFERENCE: PAGE 111 H7

GETTING THERE Broken Bay and the Lower Hawkesbury River define the northern boundary of the city of Sydney and are less than an hour's drive from the CBD
BEST TIME TO FISH Year-round
BEST TIME TO TRAVEL Year-round
MAJOR ANGLING SPECIES Bream, flathead, whiting, tailor, luderick (blackfish), mulloway (jewfish), hairtail, bass and estuary perch
WARNINGS Tidal flows in Broken Bay and the Lower Hawkesbury can be very strong at times. Care should be exercised, particularly when anchoring
ACCOMMODATION Lakeside Caravan Park, North Narrabeen, telephone (02) 9913 7845; Hawkesbury River Tourist Accommodation Centre, telephone (02) 9985 7090
CHARTER BOATS AND FISHING GUIDES MV *Careel* Fishing Charters, telephone (02) 9973 2797

Despite two centuries of urban development, significant pollution from the nearby metropolis and years of overharvesting of its fish and invertebrate populations by commercial netters, the lower Hawkesbury River system and its associated estuarine arms to the north and south continue to produce surprisingly good fishing for a broad range of species. As a result, the Lower Hawkesbury remains one of the most popular estuary fishing locations in New South Wales and attracts a significant amount of recreational angling pressure throughout the year — especially at holiday time.

The Hawkesbury River's resilience in the face of so much attention and mistreatment is mute testimony to its strength and recuperative powers, although it's doubtful if it can survive another century of abuse without suffering dramatic collapses of its natural ecosystems and ecology.

BROKEN BAY AND PITTWATER

Broken Bay is a broad, deep, natural harbour at the mouth of the Hawkesbury River system. It was formed millions of years ago when sea levels rose to inundate an old river valley. The entrance to Broken Bay is marked on the northern side by Box Head and to the south by Barrenjoey Head and its prominent lighthouse. Westward from an imaginary line between these two points, the bay may be classified as an estuary, although it remains rather oceanic in nature, at least as far upstream as Lion Island and Middle Head.

Pittwater is an extensive bay system running south behind Barrenjoey Headland. Although shallower in many areas than Broken Bay itself, Pittwater is also more oceanic than estuarine in character, and is regularly flushed by tides from the open sea beyond the heads.

Not surprisingly, an interesting mix of sea-going and estuarine fish are taken in Broken Bay and, to a lesser extent, Pittwater. These include species such as snapper, tailor, salmon, trevally, pike, drummer and groper, as well as more typical estuary targets such as bream, flathead, whiting, blackfish, mulloway (jewfish), leatherjackets, garfish, mullet and flounder. Bait fish including yellowtail and slimy mackerel are also seasonally abundant, as are prawns and squid.

Schools of true pelagic species such as skipjack (striped tuna), bonito, frigate mackerel and even mackerel tuna will also enter the lower bay at times and travel upstream at least as far as Lion Island. Tailor and salmon schools are also commonly seen feeding on the surface in these waters at certain times of the year (most notably during spring and, to a lesser extent, autumn).

MIXED BAGS

Drifting with natural baits for mixed bags of flathead, whiting, flounder and other species is an especially popular angling technique during the warmer months, particularly near the entrance to Pittwater and north of Lion Island near the entrance to Paddys Channel and Brisbane Water.

Anchoring in these same areas and berleying can also produce similar mixed catches, as well as bream and snapper, although the latter species often tend to be undersized these days, as a result of decades of dramatic overharvesting by nets, traps and lines.

A little further upstream, the Flint and Steel area has a very good reputation for producing big bream and mulloway, while opposite it, on the estuary's northern shore, Patonga is a great place to chase bream and good-sized dusky flathead with either baits or lures.

SURFACE ACTION

Pursuing surface fish such as tailor and salmon can also be an exciting option on the more open waters of Broken Bay. These fast-moving pelagic fish are best caught by motoring quickly within range of a feeding school, cutting the engine and casting a small metal lure or jig ahead of the travelling fish before retrieving it rapidly back to the drifting boat. Trolling is generally much less effective than casting, but may work at times.

Surface fish are somewhat less common inside Pittwater itself, although smaller 'chopper' tailor certainly do visit these waters, particularly off Mackerel Beach and Soldiers Point. Better bets are the flathead, whiting, bream, blackfish and flounder that feed on the shallow sand flats and around various boat moorings, jetties, pontoons, reefs and points throughout Pittwater. These are best targeted with fine lines and fresh or live natural baits. Early morning and late evening tend to be the best periods for fishing here, as boat traffic is generally much lighter at these times than during the middle of the day.

Prawning and crabbing (for blue swimmers and the occasional mud crab) are also very

Looking out across Pittwater to Barrenjoey Headland and the mouth of Broken Bay

productive at times in Pittwater, as well as in some of the more sheltered arms and coves of Broken Bay itself.

THE LOWER HAWKESBURY

The Hawkesbury River can be roughly divided into two distinct sections. The first of these is the Lower Hawkesbury, which runs from a line between Juno Point and Challenger Head upstream to about Spencer. The second section is the Upper Hawkesbury, from Spencer upstream to at least Windsor or Yarramundi and the junction of the Grose River. (This is dealt with separately in Hawkesbury–Nepean Bass Waters on pp. 80–1.)

The Lower Hawkesbury is an extensive and heavily fished area that includes such major tributaries and arms as Cowan, Mooney Mooney, Mangrove and Berowra creeks, as well as Dangar, Spectacle, Long, Milson and Bar islands. It is also crossed by several major highway and railway bridges. Fishing in the Lower Hawkesbury is dominated by popular estuary species, notably bream, blackfish (luderick), flathead, mulloway (jewfish), whiting, mullet and garfish. Top spots for these fish include the various feeder creeks (especially Cowan) and the areas around the bridges, points and islands between Dangar Island and Berowra Point.

Waters immediately adjacent to oyster leases, prominent points and other significant structures (both natural and artificial) often tend to produce the most consistent angling results, especially for bream, which are typically at their best and biggest in late summer, autumn and early winter.

Excellent angling results are often achieved by selecting a likely spot, mooring a boat fore and aft across the tide close to shore and berleying with soaked bread, chicken pellets, boiled wheat and the like while fishing lightly weighted natural baits such as live yabbies (nippers), fresh or live prawns, blood worms and small estuary crabs. These baits should be presented on relatively light tackle and cast parallel to the shore, into the current-borne berley stream or trail. This technique typically produces good bags of bream, the odd flathead and an occasional school mulloway.

Luderick or blackfish specialists will usually adopt a similar approach, but will berley instead with a chopped green weed and sand mixture before presenting green weed baits under a float on small hooks and light tackle.

For big mulloway or jewfish, try the deeper points, holes and areas around bridge pylons at night using live yellowtail and mullet, whole or cut squid, whole small octopus, pilchards or fresh fillets of tailor, mullet and blackfish.

THE ENIGMATIC HAIRTAIL

A particularly interesting fishery in this area involves the pursuit of the enigmatic hairtail, especially during the cooler months of the year. These long, silvery fish with their fearsome fangs first enter Broken Bay from the open ocean in late April or May, and are often encountered in good numbers at deep-water spots such as Portuguese Bay, lower down in the Hawkesbury River system.

Later, in June and July, the hairtail will move upriver, particularly into the Cowan Creek system, and often take up residence around Akuna Bay, in deeper parts of Coal and Candle Creek and in Jerusalem Bay. Most years, they disappear rather abruptly some time during late August or, at the latest, in early September.

Hairtail are best targeted at night using whole pilchards on very sharp ganged (linked) hooks. Fresh fish fillets or small live yellowtail will also tempt these fish. Once located, large catches are sometimes possible. It should be noted, however, that a bag limit is now in force for this species, so be sure to check the current regulations before going fishing.

Near Spencer, the mighty Hawkesbury narrows somewhat and becomes much more riverine in nature, although it is still strongly tidal, at least as far upstream as its junction with the Colo River, opposite Lower Portland, and usually well beyond, to the Windsor–Richmond area. Here, bass, estuary perch, mullet, eels and carp become the dominant species. Reasonable catches of bream and blackfish and even the occasional mulloway may still be encountered, particularly during dry years, when brackish water extends well upstream on a making (rising) tide.

HAWKESBURY–NEPEAN BASS WATERS

IN BRIEF

MAP REFERENCE: PAGES 110 G8 AND 111 H7

GETTING THERE Wisemans Ferry is about 70 km north-west of Sydney
BEST TIME TO FISH Year-round
BEST TIME TO TRAVEL Year-round
MAJOR ANGLING SPECIES Bass, estuary perch, eels, mullet and carp
SPECIAL RESTRICTIONS Fishing is prohibited immediately below the wall of Warragamba Dam and for 1 km downstream
ACCOMMODATION Houseboats can be hired from Wisemans Ferry, and further down the Hawkesbury at Akuna Bay and Brooklyn; Del Rio Riverside Resort, Webbs Creek via Wisemans Ferry, telephone (02) 4566 4330; accomodation is also available at Wisemans Ferry and at the historic Settlers Arms Inn in St Albans
CHARTER BOATS AND FISHING GUIDES Hawkesbury River Bass Fishing Tours, telephone (02) 4576 3318 or 014 047 813

View of the Hawkesbury River as it winds past Leets Vale south of Wisemans Ferry

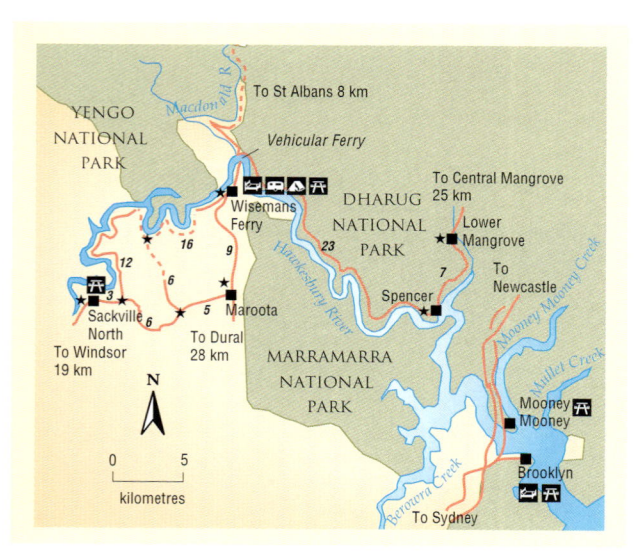

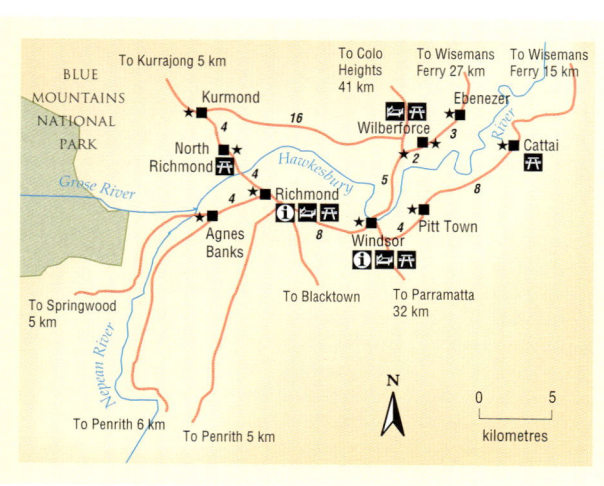

The Hawkesbury River system is one of the largest and most important coastal catchments on the entire eastern seaboard of Australia. It has played a vital role in the history of this region, particularly in the development of the city of Sydney since European settlement at the end of the 18th century.

The Hawkesbury system's numerous and extensive tributaries drain a significant portion of coastal New South Wales. Some rise high in the Blue Mountains, far to the west of Sydney. Others flow down from the Wollemi Valley and Wollemi Plateau to the north, and still more from the Southern Tablelands and Wollondilly Valley, to the south-west.

One arm of the main southern artery of this river system is held back by Warragamba Dam, near Wallacia, to form Lake Burragorang, which provides much of Sydney's water needs. From here, the Nepean River runs generally north, effectively defining the western limits of Sydney as it flows past Penrith, before becoming the Hawkesbury River proper and swinging east around Richmond and Windsor towards the distant sea.

The Hawkesbury River can be divided into two distinct sections. The first of these is the Lower Hawkesbury, from a line between Juno Point and Challenger Head in Broken Bay, upstream to about Spencer. The second section is the Upper Hawkesbury, from Spencer upstream to at least Windsor or Yarramundi and the junction of the Grose River. Above this, the river is more correctly referred to as the Nepean.

Fishing in the Lower Hawkesbury is dominated by popular estuary species such as bream, flathead and mulloway, while fresh and brackish water species tend to take over further upstream, especially above Wisemans Ferry.

TIDAL INFLUENCES

Below Richmond and Windsor, the Hawkesbury is subject to significant tidal influences. By the time it picks up the Colo and Macdonald rivers and reaches Wisemans Ferry, it is a true estuary, ultimately going on past Spencer and joining with Berowra and Cowan creeks to form the vast, natural harbour known as Broken Bay.

Between Spencer and Wisemans Ferry to the west, estuarine species such as bream, luderick (blackfish), flathead and mulloway (jewfish) continue to dominate most angler's catches, although the occasional estuary perch and bass also begin to appear in some bags, particularly in winter and spring.

Above Wisemans Ferry, bream and the odd mulloway are still encountered, but bass and estuary perch become the dominant angling species. Here, a tidal rise and fall is still evident, but it lags many hours behind the tidal cycle experienced at the mouth of Broken Bay.

The tidal influence finally begins to wane beyond Windsor until it disappears completely above Richmond.

Winter Bass

The very best bass fishing in the tidal stretch of river from a little below Wisemans Ferry upstream to the Colo River junction tends to occur along deep, rocky shorelines in autumn, winter and spring. This fishery is related to the downstream movement of mature bass into these tidal waters in preparation for spawning, and for this reason, most modern anglers tend to release all or most of the bass that they catch at such times.

Quite large numbers of generally small 'resident' bass continue to be taken here right through the summer. Incredibly heavy ski boat traffic can become a real nuisance for anglers at this time of year, however, especially during holiday periods or on warm, sunny weekends.

A boat of some sort is needed to get amongst the best of this Hawkesbury River bass action, and the top technique is to drift or use an electric motor to stay within casting range of the shore while peppering likely spots with lures such as deep-diving plugs and spinnerbaits. Surface lures can also be effective in the late afternoon or early morning, especially during spring and summer.

Trolling with medium to deep-diving plugs and minnows can also be highly effective at times. This is best done in 3 to 7 m of water close to the edge along broken, rocky shorelines. As well as providing good catches of bass, trolling tends to turn up the occasional estuary perch, including some prime specimens in the 1- to 2.5-kg range.

Once a concentration of bass or perch has been found by trolling, many anglers prefer to anchor or drift and cast lures or flies into the school.

Further Upstream

Further upstream, near Windsor and Richmond, bass fishing action is often more consistent through spring, summer and early autumn. The majority of fish taken here tend to be of a modest size, although specimens of more than 40 cm in length and 1 kg in weight are always on the cards.

Heavy aquatic weed growth in this stretch of river — especially during prolonged dry spells — tends to preclude the use of deep-diving lures and dramatically limits the effectiveness of trolling. Much better results are usually achieved by using shallow-running plugs or minnows and spinnerbaits. Some excellent morning and evening action is also available for those casting surface lures, poppers and topwater flies into the pockets and gaps between weed beds or under the trailing fronds of bankside willow trees.

Bait fishers in this stretch usually target the noxious, introduced European carp, but may also encounter large eels, mullet, catfish, Nepean herring and even the occasional bream. Whaler sharks — including the odd specimen of genuine man-eating proportions — were once reasonably common this far upstream, but are more rarely encountered these days.

The Nepean River

Further upstream again, the Nepean River proper continues to hold fair to good populations of Australian bass, at least as far upriver as Camden and Douglas Park, although the movement of fish into and out of this stretch of water is severely curtailed by as many as a dozen weirs along the river's length.

Other species present in the Nepean above and below Penrith include long- and short-finned eels, European carp, 'wild' goldfish, mullet, eel-tailed catfish, herring and the occasional trout. All of these fish become slightly more abundant downstream of the Nepean's junction with the Warragamba River, near Wallacia, and even the odd Murray cod has been reported here, although it's uncertain where these fish originated.

The endangered and protected Macquarie perch also occurs sporadically in the Nepean, but these fish are a rare catch these days and should always be returned carefully and quickly to the water if inadvertently hooked.

A Shadow of Its Past

Around Penrith and beyond, the Nepean still produces quite reasonable bass fishing action at times, especially in summer, although most of the fish encountered here are on the small side, with the vast majority measuring between 20 and 30 cm.

European carp and large, feral goldfish are also abundant in this stretch, as are some big eels and hefty mullet, particularly below the various weirs. Both brown and rainbow trout turn up from time to time, too, especially after heavy rains in the cooler months. Most of these trout are washed over the spillway of Warragamba Dam during flooding, and it is something of a miracle that they can survive such a long drop!

Sadly, the Nepean River today is only a shadow of its former self and both its water quality and aquatic biodiversity are in serious decline. These days, those anglers who fish the Upper Nepean regularly do so mostly because this river is handy to their place of abode, rather than out of choice — this is certainly not a waterway to which one would travel any great distance specifically to fish!

An Australian bass taken from the Hawkesbury

The vehicular ferry at Wisemans Ferry, one of several found along the Upper Hawkesbury

BOTANY BAY

IN BRIEF

MAP REFERENCE: PAGE 111 H9

GETTING THERE Botany Bay lies in the south-eastern suburbs of Sydney
BEST TIME TO FISH Year-round, but generally best from September to June
BEST TIME TO TRAVEL Year-round
MAJOR ANGLING SPECIES Bream, flathead, whiting, tailor, luderick (blackfish), leatherjackets and silver trevally
SPECIAL RESTRICTIONS There is a strict exclusion zone permanently in force around the oil loading jetty at Kurnell
WARNINGS Boat traffic is heavy at times on Botany Bay and in the lower Georges River. Be especially careful in main shipping channels or when drifting and anchoring, particularly at night
ACCOMMODATION There are caravan parks, hotel and motels close to or on Botany Bay, particularly around Brighton and on the Sutherland peninsula to the south
CHARTER BOATS AND FISHING GUIDES Ross Hunter's Game Fishing Charters, telephone (02) 9534 2378; Brighton Bait and Tackle, telephone (02) 9567 1226

Situated in the south-eastern suburbs of Australia's largest city, Botany Bay is a rather heavily degraded, modified and overfished urban waterway. Yet it continues to produce fair to reasonable recreational angling results — very much in spite of the efforts of humans rather than because of them!

As well as having an important place in the European history of Australia, Botany Bay was also once an extremely valuable fish nursery and feeding ground, with extensive shoreline mangrove forests and adjacent tidal swamps and wetlands that acted as giant water filters, as well as valuable bird rookeries and wildlife habitats. Most of these areas disappeared long ago under concrete, asphalt and brick, although pockets of vital sea grass beds and mangrove estuary still remain, particularly on the more isolated and less developed southern shores and in Woolooware Bay, and Botany Bay is also home to an important nesting site for little terns.

Botany Bay's major feeder stream, the Georges River, has suffered a similar environmental fate to the bay itself and that of so many other urban waterways. In fact, parts of this estuary system were recently found to be so heavily polluted with heavy metals, organochlorines and other hazardous wastes that the eating of fish from specified locations has now been totally banned on public health grounds.

Having said all that, a surprising number of people still continue to enjoy fair to very good

Returning to the lower Georges River after catching a silver trevally in Botany Bay

recreational angling on and around these waters, and reasonable catches are still made here with amazing regularity.

THE VANISHING BAY

Looking at a series of revised maps spanning several recent decades, one could be forgiven for concluding that Botany Bay is actually shrinking! The construction of airport runway extensions far out into the bay and the so-called 'reclamation' of land for the Port Botany container and shipping terminals have certainly taken their toll on this much abused waterway. Despite this continuing encroachment, however, there is still plenty of aquatic territory left within Botany Bay for fish, and also for the many anglers who chase them. The most reliable stand-by species in Botany Bay are bream, flathead, silver trevally and tailor.

Leatherjackets, luderick (blackfish), sand whiting, yellowtail (also called 'yakkas' or 'bung') and snapper (usually undersized) round out the bulk of most angler's catches from this body of water, although occasional surprises turn up in the form of yellowtail kingfish (especially near the heads), the odd hairtail and a very occasional mulloway, particularly in and around the mouth of the Georges River.

Blue swimmer crabs are also present in catchable numbers from time to time, mostly during the warmer summer months.

RELIABLE HOT SPOTS

Watts Reef, which lies to the east of the oil refinery wharf at Kurnell, is probably the best known fishing spot in the entire bay, with a reputation for producing good to excellent catches of bream at times, especially during the night in late summer, autumn and early winter.

A hot-water outlet just to west of this same wharf at Kurnell is another very good fishing location for boat owners, but anglers should not try to move in too close to the long jetty itself, as a strict exclusion zone is enforced around it for safety reasons. Massive quantities of flammable petroleum products are unloaded here almost every day, and a stray spark or naked flame could easily result in major catastrophe. For this reason, security guards strictly enforce a no-go area of several hundred metres around the facility, and will not hesitate to chase away boats that stray too close. Repeat offenders may well find themselves liable to prosecution.

The Kurnell Groynes—a series of short, artificial rock walls or breakwaters extending out from the southern shore—can provide reasonable land-based fishing, especially for luderick (blackfish) and bream, as do the structures enclosing the swimming baths and the various jetties at Dolls Point, Ramsgate and Brighton le-Sands on the western shoreline, as well as the rock walls either side of the entrance to the Cooks River at Kyeemagh.

Many shore-based anglers also fish from the banks of the Cooks River a little further upstream. The most commonly encountered species here are bream, mullet and luderick. While this waterway was extremely polluted and almost devoid of aquatic life as recently as the 1980s, it has been cleaned up somewhat in more recent times and is undergoing a partial revival as an ecosystem. Nonetheless, it is probably still not advisable to eat too many meals of fish from the Cooks River on a regular basis.

ON THE DRIFT

Back out on Botany Bay itself, the areas adjacent to the airport runway extensions and container port facilities occasionally turn on good action for bream and silver trevally, while surface-feeding tailor schools are likely to pop up almost anywhere in the bay, especially around Christmas time (when they're mostly small) and again in autumn (when they're likely to be a bit larger).

Tailor can be taken on lures or baits such as pilchards and whitebait. They are best targeted by motoring within casting range, cutting the motor and drifting while casting. Silver trevally and flathead, along with the odd bream, often hang under these feeding tailor schools.

Similarly, a quiet drift across any sand, mud or weed patches in the bay will often produce catches of flathead (mostly duskies, with the odd sand and spiky flathead thrown in for variety), although many of these fish will be slightly smaller than the 33-cm minimum legal length, and must therefore be returned to the water alive.

The lower Georges River, beyond the Captain Cook Bridge and on past the Tom Uglys Bridge, also fishes reasonably well at times for bream, luderick, flathead, whiting, tailor and even the odd mulloway, especially under the bridges themselves at night. This area is dealt with separately, along with the rest of the Georges River as far upstream as Liverpool, on pp. 84–5.

Flathead are a popular target species in Botany Bay

GEORGES RIVER

IN BRIEF

MAP REFERENCE: PAGE 111 H9

GETTING THERE The Georges River runs through Sydney's southern suburbs, from south of Liverpool to Sans Souci and Taren Point in the east, and into Botany Bay

BEST TIME TO FISH Year-round, but generally best from September to June

BEST TIME TO TRAVEL Year-round

MAJOR ANGLING SPECIES Bream, flathead, whiting, luderick (blackfish) and mulloway (jewfish)

SPECIAL RESTRICTIONS Fishing is restricted in parts of the upper Georges River, and fish from more polluted stretches should not be eaten. Check current notifications of these restrictions

WARNINGS Boat traffic is heavy at times in the lower Georges River. Be especially careful in main shipping channels or when drifting and anchoring, particularly at night

Native birds such as kookaburras are common in the bushland found along the Georges River

The Georges River is fed by several smaller tributaries, which flow mostly north out of the high escarpment country and heathlands behind Wollongong and the southern suburbs of Sydney. The Georges River itself continues north past Campbelltown, Minto, Ingleburn, Macquarie Fields and Casula before swinging to the east just beyond Liverpool and twisting around Chipping Norton past Milperra and Panania to East Hills and Picnic Point.

Below its confluence with Salt Pan Creek, which joins the river on its northern side near Lugarno, the lower Georges River becomes much broader and more obviously tidal in nature. There are numerous bays and rocky inlets, many of which support oyster farming operations.

The Georges is joined here on its southern side by the Woronora River and flows under the main railway bridge of the Illawarra line, then on past the aptly named Oyster Bay to Tom Uglys Bridge on the Princes Highway and the newer Captain Cook Bridge that runs in a high arc from Taren Point, on the south side, to Sans Souci, in the north.

Beyond the Captain Cook Bridge, the river joins with the open waters of busy Botany Bay. This structure can therefore effectively be considered as the river's downstream boundary.

GOOD AND BAD NEWS

While it must once have been a healthy and vibrant waterway teeming with aquatic life, the Georges River has suffered serious degradation and decline since the early days of European settlement on this continent. Running, as it does, through the fast-growing southern and south-western suburbs of Sydney, the river has been heavily polluted for many years by urban and industrial run-off. It has also been overfished, especially by commercial netters.

Recently, parts of this river's estuary system were discovered to be so heavily polluted with long-lasting heavy metals, organochlorines and other potentially hazardous wastes that the catching and eating of fish or any other seafood from specified locations is now totally banned on public health grounds. (Anglers should carefully check the current boundaries of these closures before going fishing and observe any warning signs or notices on the shoreline or at boat launching ramps.)

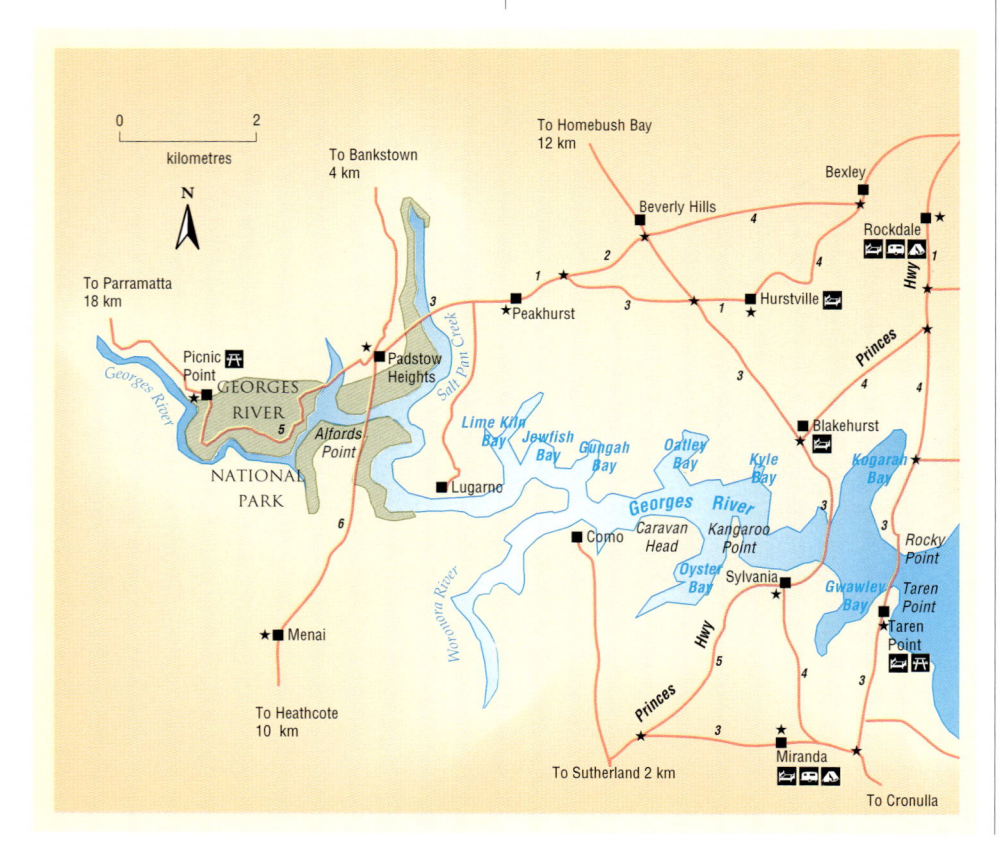

This pollution problem also casts a dark cloud over the long-term viability of the river's oyster growing operations. Oyster farmers are already forced to utilise expensive cleaning and flushing processes to ensure the safety of their produce.

Nonetheless, some positive trends in the control and reduction of polluted run-off in recent decades has led to at least a partial recovery of natural ecosystems in many stretches of the Georges River. It is to be hoped that, over time, this important estuary system can be further restored. Meanwhile, many recreational anglers continue to enjoy fair to good sport while casting a line into its less-than-pristine waters.

Fishing the Georges River

The lower Georges River, between the Captain Cook Bridge at its confluence with Botany Bay and the railway bridge at Como, attracts the greatest amount of attention from both shore-based and boat anglers.

This lower stretch of river fishes reasonably well at times, especially for bream, luderick (blackfish), dusky flathead, sand whiting, small tailor and even the odd mulloway or jewfish, especially under and adjacent to the bridges themselves at first or last light and through the night. Most of these jewies are taken by keen, specialist anglers using live baits or large dead baits, although a few are also hooked each year by unsuspecting bream fishers.

Further upstream, beyond Oyster Bay and Salt Pan Creek, water quality and the possible contamination of resident fish with heavy metals and other toxins increasingly becomes an issue of serious concern, although some very fine bream certainly hang around the various oyster leases and other significant structural elements—both natural and artificial.

Dusky flathead can also be caught on baits or lures over the sand and mud flats in this stretch. The most reliable 'lizard' action occurs during the warmer months of the year, from October to May. Casting and retrieving lures such as diving minnows, plugs, spoons or jigs around sandy flats in bays and inlets at such times can be an especially pleasant way to spend a few hours, especially during the last half of the run-out (ebb) tide.

The Upper Georges River

Much higher upstream—towards Liverpool and even beyond—the Georges River still contains a few hardy bass and estuary perch, as well as numerous introduced European carp, goldfish, eels and some gigantic mullet. Fshing in this area could not truly be described as pleasant, however, and only a foolhardy angler would consider eating fish taken from these heavily polluted waters on anything like a regular basis!

Many of the fish found in this upper stretch of the Georges River tend to congregate in the areas immediately below various weirs and barrages, and provide reasonable sport for anglers at such times. The frequent presence of sores and other abnormalities on these fish, however, is a good indicator of persistent water quality problems in this system.

The upper, freshwater reaches of the river and its tributaries once held excellent bass populations and even scattered stocks of the now endangered Macquarie perch. While bass have hung on in many pockets, Macquarie perch are virtually unknown from these waters today.

Above left: *The Georges River National Park runs along part of the southern and northern banks of the Georges River*
Above right: *Eastern black or yellowfin bream are a prime target amongst Georges River anglers*

GOSFORD AND BRISBANE WATER

IN BRIEF

MAP REFERENCE: PAGE 111 H7

GETTING THERE Gosford is about 80 km north of Sydney along the Pacific Highway
BEST TIME TO FISH Year-round, but September to June is generally best
BEST TIME TO TRAVEL Year-round
MAJOR ANGLING SPECIES Bream, flathead, whiting and luderick (blackfish)
SPECIAL RESTRICTIONS Angling is prohibited within the Bouddi Marine Sanctuary near Gosford. Check the status of all marine sanctuary boundaries and other area restrictions before going fishing. Crab and other traps are prohibited in Brisbane Water
WARNINGS Numerous shallow areas present hazards to navigation, especially at low tide
ACCOMMODATION The Central Coast has numerous types of accommodation available, from caravan parks and holiday units to hotels and resorts

The New South Wales Central Coast region is normally regarded as that stretch of the coast lying between the northern headland of Broken Bay and the current-scoured Swansea Channel, at the mouth of Lake Macquarie. Most of this region is populous, built-up and rather heavily developed, but it retains many of its natural attractions and still offers a fine standard of recreational fishing for visitors and locals alike.

The main urban focal point at the southern end of the Central Coast is the large town of Gosford, which extends along the shores of Brisbane Water and has a permanent population in excess of 45 000 people. To the west of Gosford lies Brisbane Water National Park, which is renowned for its displays of wildflowers in the spring and for the many Aboriginal rock carvings and art sites to be found within its borders.

Nearby Beaches

One of Gosford's greatest attractions — and a major reason for its ongoing popularity as a holiday and retirement destination, as well as a commuter base for Sydney workers — is the number and standard of nearby beaches. Not surprisingly, these beaches are also popular with surf casting anglers.

Top ocean beaches in the area include Killcare, MacMasters, Copacabana, Avoca, Terrigal, Wamberal and Forresters. All produce fair to very good catches of whiting (mostly in summer), as well as bream, tailor, flathead, Australian salmon and other common surf-casting targets. The odd mulloway or jewfish is also taken from these beaches, although serious jewie specialists normally head north to The Entrance beach (especially North Entrance) when chasing these highly prized predators.

Forresters Beach, in particular, once had a reputation for also producing the occasional big snapper after a prolonged period of heavy seas, although such catches are rather rare today.

On the Rocks

The Gosford region is also well catered for in terms of rock fishing spots, with famous ledges such as The Skillion at Terrigal producing great mixed catches of bread and butter fish such as

There are many excellent rock fishing locations on the Central Coast

bream, drummer and luderick (blackfish), as well as seasonal lure or bait spinning action on tailor, bonito, salmon and small to medium yellowtail kingfish. Frigate mackerel and mackerel tuna or kawa kawa also turn up in numbers here at times.

Other rock spots worthy of attention include Crackneck (north of Forresters), Spoon Bay, Grannys, Cod Hole, Flat Rock, High Rock or Splashy and the northern end of Avoca. All of these locations offer mixed bags, with surface fish within casting range on occasion, particularly from the more exposed headlands.

Rock fishers in this region should carefully note and observe the boundaries of the Bouddi Marine Reserve. This reserve is part of the Bouddi National Park and extends over Maitland Bay, between MacMasters Beach and Killcare. Marine life is totally protected in this area and fishing of all types was prohibited along this stretch of coast at the time of writing.

BOUNTIFUL BRISBANE WATER

Brisbane Water is a broad, shallow and almost completely enclosed northern arm of Broken Bay, connected to that much larger body of water via the relatively narrow Paddys Channel at Woy Woy and The Rip, near Booker Bay.

Despite its shallow average depth, Brisbane Water can be particularly productive for bream and sand whiting, as well as for dusky flathead, blue swimmer crabs and the odd big mud crab. (Anglers should carefully note that nets or traps cannot legally be used here, and therefore crabs must be caught on a baited line.)

The areas around Brisbane Water's many oyster leases, oyster racks and similar structures are best for those anglers chasing bream, particularly at first and last light or through the night. A sparse berley trail of cut tuna, bonito or mullet pieces and a fresh slab or cube of the same fish flesh on a No. 1 to 2/0 hook attached to a lightly weighted line will often produce the goods here, although more conventional offerings such as prawns, yabbies and crabs also work well.

Paddys Channel is justifiably renowned for producing some very big sand whiting, bream and dusky flathead. This is one area where oversized whiting weighing up to 750 g and even more can be taken right through the winter months, usually by fishing at night with blood worms, live prawns or small soldier crabs.

The pick of the bream spots to be found in Paddys Channel are the oyster leases upstream of Pelican Island, and these tend to fish best in autumn or early winter.

Good luderick or blackfish are also available throughout this entire estuary system. These fish mostly fall to specialist anglers who berley with a mixture of chopped green weed and sand, then fish suspended green weed baits under a fine float rigged on traditional blackfish tackle.

Waratahs are a common sight in Brisbane Water National Park during the spring wildflower season

PORT STEPHENS

IN BRIEF

MAP REFERENCE: PAGE 111 K5

GETTING THERE Nelson Bay is about 210 km north-east of Sydney on the southern side of Port Stephens
BEST TIME TO FISH Year-round, but generally best from September to June
BEST TIME TO TRAVEL Year-round
MAJOR ANGLING SPECIES Bream, flathead, whiting, tailor, luderick (blackfish), mulloway (jewfish), snapper, offshore reef fish and game species
SPECIAL RESTRICTIONS Check the status of all marine sanctuary boundaries, military reserves and other area restrictions before fishing
WARNINGS The waters of Port Stephens, particularly near its broad entrance to the sea, can become extremely choppy when tide and wind direction are opposed. Caution should be exercised at such times
CHARTER BOATS AND FISHING GUIDES Nelson Bay Tackle, telephone (02) 4984 1415; Albatross Offshore Fishing Charters and Expeditions, telephone Freecall 1800 805 543

A young angler poses briefly with a striped marlin before returning it to the water off Port Stephens

The blue waters and coastal foreshores of the vast estuary or harbour system called Port Stephens, north-east of Newcastle, provide a particularly popular holiday destination, especially amongst people travelling from Sydney, Newcastle and the inland centres of central northern New South Wales. Many of these holiday makers and their families have been coming to this particular area on the central north coast of New South Wales for decades, and some ultimately aspire to retire here.

For these regulars, as well as for growing numbers of newer visitors, recreational fishing is one of the region's major attractions. Anglers are well catered for around Port Stephens, especially in terms of bait and tackle outlets, hire boat operations, houseboats, camping grounds, affordable holiday accommodation, launching ramps and marinas.

Jetty at Tea Gardens on the northern shore of Port Stephens

GAME FISHING MECCA

The vast natural harbour known as Port Stephens is amongst New South Wales' best known game and sport fishing ports. At the end of summer each year, it is the venue for the Port Stephens Inter-Club Tournament, the largest regular game fishing event of its kind staged anywhere in the southern hemisphere.

The wide continental shelf and offshore reefs immediately adjacent to Port Stephens provide prime feeding grounds for striped and black marlin, tuna of several types, yellowtail kingfish and various sharks, especially during the period from December until June each year. More exotic northern wanderers such as Spanish mackerel, cobia and even sailfish also turn up in smaller numbers at times, but it is probably the abundant marlin that attract most serious offshore angling visitors to Port Stephens.

In particular, the inshore grounds between the heads and Broughton Island, and further offshore out to the 50 or 60 fathom (100 m) line, play host to incredible quantities of juvenile black marlin and mid-range striped marlin during some seasons. Even in a 'quiet' year, the game and sport fishing here is better than that experienced off many other east coast harbours. When the Port Stephens grounds 'fire', however, this location is truly world class, especially for marlin in the 40- to 100-kg range.

Further offshore, these sought-after fish are joined by larger representatives of the same species, as well as big blue marlin, large tuna, wahoo, dolphin fish (mahi mahi) and half a dozen species of sharks, including some giant tigers and whites weighing as much as 500 kg apiece or more!

Bread and Butter Fishing

For those with less ambitious goals, the reefs, coastal washes and islands closer to Port Stephens also produce excellent snapper, bream, morwong, teraglin, jewfish, trevally, kingfish and various other species, while the extensive drifting grounds regularly turn up good catches of flathead and silver trevally, plus the odd snapper and morwong.

Hot spots for bottom, reef and sport fishing action include V-Reef, Gunsight Reef, Cabbage Tree, Little and Shark islands. Further offshore and northwards, Broughton Island has an especially good reputation amongst dedicated snapper and mulloway (jewfish) specialists.

Squid are also abundant at times around Broughton Island, while the shallower waters close to this island's shores hold excellent populations of blue groper, black drummer (rock blackfish), luderick (blackfish), bream and leatherjackets.

Fishing in a runabout at Mungo Beach in Myall Lakes National Park just to the north of Port Stephens

Land-based Hot Spots

For land-based anglers, the steeply sloping, rocky headland at Tomaree, on the southern side of Port Stephens, is an absolute Mecca for those pursuing longtail (northern bluefin) tuna, mackerel tuna, bonito, kingfish, cobia and sharks from the ocean rocks. The occasional Spanish mackerel is also hooked here.

While some of these fish (especially mackerel tuna and bonito) can be caught in almost any month of the year, peak activity for bigger fish — especially longtails — usually occurs between September and May.

Live baits including yellowtail, mullet, slimy mackerel and garfish may be caught inside the bay and carried out to the rocks in buckets or, on occasion, taken from the front of the fishing ledge itself. Slimy mackerel, in particular, form thick schools here on occasion and may be taken on small lures, multi-hook jig rigs (sabikis) or even a white-painted barrel sinker running freely above a hook. Yellowtail, garfish and even mullet may also be berleyed up at times and captured for bait. As is so often the case, however, days which see plenty of big fish activity are often the toughest on which to catch a live bait!

Estuary Action

Inside Port Stephens itself, the opportunities for estuary fishing are varied and abundant. There are excellent runs of bream, especially in autumn and early winter, while dusky flathead become a prime target from mid-September until May, with the largest specimens often landed during October.

Sand whiting, blackfish (luderick), tailor, jewfish (mulloway), garfish and flounder are also taken at hot spots such as Salamander Bay, Lemon Tree Passage, Corrie Island and up into the Karuah River and the Myall River, near the popular holiday destination of Tea Gardens.

Big schools of mackerel tuna or kawa kawa, along with the occasional heavyweight longtail tuna and smaller patches of skipjack or striped tuna, once made regular forays into the port itself during spring, travelling at least as far upstream as Salamander Point, although this occurrence is no longer as commonplace as it was in the 1970s and early 1980s. It's still worth watching carefully for the flocks of sea birds and frothing patches of water that mark the progress of these pelagics into the harbour, however, especially from late August until November each year.

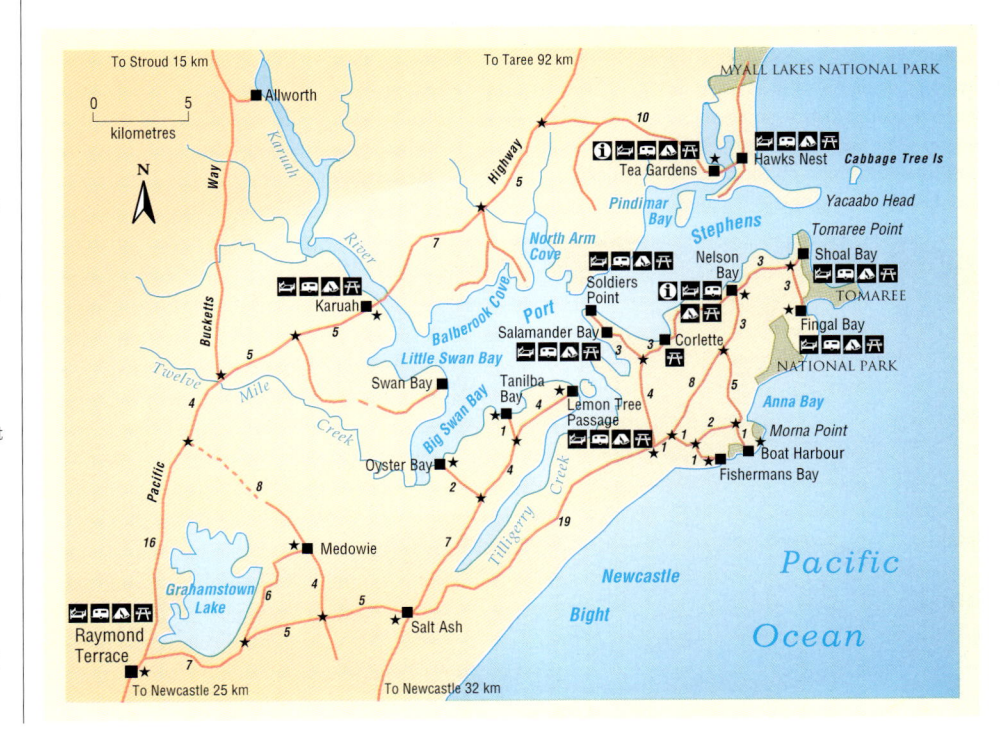

LAKE ILLAWARRA

IN BRIEF

MAP REFERENCE: PAGE 109 G3

GETTING THERE Wollongong is 80 km south of Sydney along the Princes Highway; scenic coastal route via Royal National Park and Lawrence Hargrave Drive
BEST TIME TO FISH October to June
BEST TIME TO TRAVEL Year-round
MAJOR ANGLING SPECIES Bream, flathead, whiting, luderick (blackfish) and prawns
SPECIAL RESTRICTIONS A well-signposted area of the warm water outlet at Tallawarra Power Station is closed to all angling
WARNINGS Many shallow areas pose a hazard to navigation and the lake can become very choppy in strong winds
ACCOMMODATION Lake Illawarra Village Caravan Park, telephone (02) 4295 1773
CHARTER BOATS AND FISHING GUIDES Wollongong Boat Charter, telephone (02) 4234 1340

Lake Illawarra, situated in Wollongong's southern suburbs, is a large, relatively shallow tidal lake some 95 km in circumference. Despite obvious environmental degradation from pollution, urban run-off, siltation, overharvesting by commercial fishers and constant attention from the recreational sector, this extensive body of water still produces some surprisingly good catches of both fish and prawns for local and visiting anglers.

The shallow, weedy waters of Lake Illawarra are actually highly fertile and are frequented by large numbers of bream, luderick (blackfish), flathead, whiting, mullet, leatherjackets and garfish. While the vast majority of these fish are juveniles using the lake as a nursery area in which to feed and grow, reasonable numbers of larger, adult fish are also present. When any of these species are 'on the bite', word quickly spreads and local anglers flock to the lake.

Lake Illawarra is also an immensely popular destination with those pursuing school and king prawns with legal scoop or drag nets, especially during the warmer months of the year. Successful recreational prawners tend to concentrate their efforts on the so-called 'dark' periods or phases of the moon, from four or five nights after the full moon until the onset of the new moon, some ten days later. Prawning is typically most productive on any 'dark' phase that occurs between late November and March.

SOME HOT SPOTS

While the lake's main entrance channel, at Windang, is regarded by many hopefuls as the best spot for both angling and prawning, there's also some very good fishing to be had along the lake's inner foreshores at times. This is particularly so on the eastern and northern sides of Lake Illawarra, between the entrance and the mouth of Mullet Creek.

Here, small to middling dusky flathead, bream and whiting can often be found close to shore along the edges of the abundant ribbon weed

A catch of sand whiting taken from Lake Illawarra

beds and around various jetties, boat moorings and rock retaining walls. These may be targeted with fresh, natural baits such as prawns, yabbies (nippers) and marine worms or, especially in the case of the flathead, with various lures and flies.

Luderick or blackfish are also abundant at times in this area of the lake. Although many of these fish are small, some good specimens are available for those berleying with a mixture of chopped green weed and sand while presenting local green weed baits on small hooks and specialist blackfishing float tackle.

Hot spots for all of these species on the lake's northern side include the deeper areas around Bevans or Inspectors Island, The Humps, the Mud Hole, Primbee Point, the back of the Illawarra Yacht Club, Kelly Reef, Stoney Point and the Berkeley foreshore.

On the southern side of the lake, Native Dog Reef (which is clearly marked) is well worth a try, as are The Oaks, the mouth of Macquarie Rivulet, the entrance to Wollingurry Creek and the warm-water outlet at Tallawarra Power Station, although it should be noted that an area here is closed to angling and well signposted.

Railway Point, to the north of the power station outlet, is also worth a try at times for luderick, while an unmarked reef called Robinsons, situated in the bay to the north of Railway Point, produces some good bream for those able to locate it using a depth finder or sounder.

THE LAKE'S TRIBUTARIES

Mullet Creek and Macquarie Rivulet, two small streams flowing into the lake's western side, also provide some of the best bream fishing in the area. The latter, in particular, still has some reasonable bass in its upper tidal and freshwater reaches.

Both of these creeks are crossed by highway bridges that offer reasonable access to stretches of bank for land-based anglers. The number of cars parked beside these bridges and in nearby public reserves is a good indication of the quality of fishing available at any time. Word soon spreads among anglers of a decent 'run' of bream or luderick (blackfish).

Large mullet are also abundant in these creeks during the warmer months. These fish can sometimes be attracted and excited with a berley trail of floating bread pieces, then targeted with bread and dough baits or small bread-imitating flies.

Further upstream, the odd bream persists, along with some very large eels and a few bass and estuary perch.

Prawning is popular in Lake Illawarra

Lake Illawarra with Tallawarra Power Station in the background

THE SOUTH COAST

IN BRIEF

MAP REFERENCE: PAGE 109 G3

GETTING THERE Kiama is about 120 km south of Sydney along the Princes Highway
BEST TIME TO FISH October to June
BEST TIME TO TRAVEL Year-round
MAJOR ANGLING SPECIES Bream, flathead, whiting, drummer, salmon, tailor, luderick, snapper, game fish and reef species
SPECIAL RESTRICTIONS Some rock fishing spots may only be reached across private property. Seek permission first
WARNINGS Heavy seas make many of the exposed rock fishing locations in this area dangerous
ACCOMMODATION Easts Van Park, Kiama, telephone (02) 4232 2124; Seven Mile Beach Holiday Park, Gerroa, telephone (02) 4234 1340
CHARTER BOATS AND FISHING GUIDES Kiama Charter Services, telephone (02) 4237 8496; Guided Fishing and Canoeing, Nowra, telephone (02) 4443 7597

Fishing at sunrise on Seven Mile Beach south of Gerroa

Lying within easy daytripping distance of Sydney, the New South Wales south coast region—bounded by Wollongong in the north, Nowra to the south and the Illawarra escarpment to the west—has witnessed significant growth and development since the 1970s. The population has increased markedly in that time, with a resultant inevitable decline in the health and abundance of many fish stocks. Nonetheless, some very good catches are still made here.

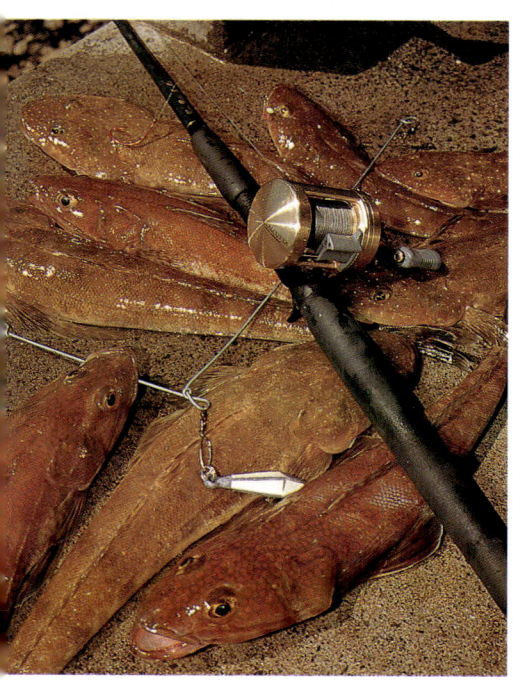

A catch of flathead taken while drifting offshore

KIAMA, GERRINGONG AND GERROA

The strikingly attractive stretch of coastline running from Bombo Beach, just north of Kiama, to Black Head and Seven Mile Beach at Gerroa is an area that remains immensely popular with tourists and visiting anglers alike.

Rock fishing is particularly popular here, with Kiama's Blowhole Point, Kendalls, Bubbly, Marsdens, the Little Blowhole and Easts High all being famous locations that once produced some great land-based snapper action. Nowadays, however, they do so only under exceptional circumstances—usually following prolonged periods of heavy storm surge in spring or summer.

These rock ledges and a string more like them running further south all the way to Black Head at Gerroa still offer good luderick (blackfish), drummer (rock blackfish), groper and the odd bream and trevally, as well as playing host to seasonal influxes of tailor, salmon, frigate mackerel, bonito and 'rat' (school-sized) yellowtail kingfish. The occasional heavyweight king and passing tuna are also hooked from the Blowhole Point at Kiama, or Campbells and Finneys rocks, just north of Gerringong, as well as from Black Head in Gerroa. All of these rock platforms are susceptible to large swells and heavy seas, and many lives have been lost here over the years, so extreme caution should always be exercised by rock fishers.

BEACH FISHING PROSPECTS

While the surf just north of the mouth of the Minnamurra River has a reputation for turning on some big whiting and bream at times, Bombo Beach north of Kiama and Werri and Walkers beaches, near Gerringong, are all surprisingly poor producers of fish, save for the infrequent appearance of a school of salmon or the odd flathead, bream and whiting, especially in summer and autumn. Good catches of mullet are taken from the ends of these beaches in summer.

Further south, Seven Mile Beach, which stretches in a long sweep from Gerroa past Shoalhaven Heads and on to Comerong Island, is generally a much better surf fishing prospect for all of the species mentioned, and also produces a handful of big mulloway or jewfish each year, mostly near Shoalhaven Heads.

SOUTH COAST ESTUARIES

Excluding Lake Illawarra (which is dealt with on pp. 90–91), the major estuary in the northern part of this region is the Minnamurra River. This waterway is something of a disappointment from an angling perspective. Best prospects here are flathead, bream, whiting and luderick (blackfish), particularly from the areas above, below and between the highway and railway bridges. There is also an occasional small to middling bass to be found higher up in the system.

The biggest and most important estuary on the south coast is the Shoalhaven River, and it offers a wider and generally more positive range of prospects. The Shoalhaven estuary still manages to produce quite satisfactory fishing at times. The best of it occurs between the golf course, just upstream of the twin Nowra bridges, and the artificial canal that links this system to the somewhat healthier Crookhaven River between Shoalhaven Heads and Greenwell Point.

Drifting or lure casting for flathead in summer, fishing fresh local baits around rocky reefs in autumn for bream, and casting squirt worms or green weed for luderick (blackfish) in spring are the pick of the seasonal options along the lower Shoalhaven.

A few decent mulloway or jewfish are still taken here, too, particularly near the ends of the Canal, at the mouth of Broughton Creek and in deeper stretches just downstream of Nowra itself. There is rather a lot of water between these fish, however, and it is usually only the very patient angler who is rewarded with a big jewie.

BASS FISHING OPPORTUNITIES

Further upstream, the Shoalhaven remains a reasonable bass river with large numbers of generally small fish on tap from Longreach and Burrier through Gradys to Coolendel and beyond, especially in the summer months.

Sadly, the construction of Tallowa Dam at the Shoalhaven's junction with the Kangaroo River during the mid-1970s effectively tore the heart out of what was once a vast and magnificent freshwater fishing system, and arguably one of the finest bass waters to be found south of Sydney.

This dam denies migrating bass access to at least 70 per cent of their former home range and dramatically degrades both the quantity and quality of water available to these fish in the Shoalhaven River's lower reaches.

On a brighter note, stocking of hatchery-bred bass in the impounded waters above Tallowa has generated an exciting new put-and-take bass fishery in Lake Yarrunga and the upper Shoalhaven and Kangaroo rivers, although these wonderful fish now share their new home with increasing numbers of noxious and unwanted European carp.

THE OFFSHORE SCENE

There are good boat launching facilities at Kiama, Shoalhaven Heads and Greenwell Point, the last two having all-weather ramps that offer access to the open ocean through the entrance of the Crookhaven River, where the bar is reasonably well behaved in most fishable seas.

An ocean ramp in Boat Harbour, at Gerringong, is suitable for boats up to about 6 m in length, but should be avoided on the dead low tide or when heavy swells from the east and north-east create a dangerous surge.

The most famous offshore fishing grounds on the south coast of New South Wales are The Banks, south east of Greenwell Point and north east of Currarong, along with the various deep water canyons beyond them, and those wide of Jervis Bay. These areas produce excellent sport and game fishing at times for tuna, yellowtail kingfish, marlin and sharks.

The area between Kiama and Crookhaven Heads also has its share of deep-water features, most notably the Kiama Canyons. These well-known commercial drop-lining grounds are regularly visited by tuna, billfish, sharks and other bluewater species, particularly when the warm currents are running hard in the period from January until June.

A series of reefs and rubble patches in 50 to 70 fathoms (90 to 140 m) of water offshore from the coast between Kiama and Greenwell Point attracts plenty of attention from deep-water bottom fishers and charter boat crews, who mostly drift for rubberlip (silver) and jackass morwong, nannygai, sand and tiger flathead, sweep and the occasional snapper.

The same area also sees lots of commercial trapping activity for both fish and crays (lobsters), and the ropes and floats on these traps attract quantities of dolphin fish in summer and autumn. Most of these are juveniles in the 1- to 2-kg range, but a small, live bait fished alongside the buoys will sometimes turn up a 5- to 15-kg specimen.

Closer to shore, various reefs, rubble patches, gravel beds and sandy areas are fished at anchor or on the drift for morwong, snapper, flathead, leatherjackets, sweep, pig fish, groper, trevally, teraglin and the like.

Drifting in the sandy bays not far off Werri Beach and Seven Mile Beach can be especially productive for sand flathead at times, although these fish should be measured carefully, as at least one in three will usually be under the 33-cm minimum legal length. Some boat anglers prefer to anchor on relatively shallow marks such as the Big Bombie and the Corrugations, south of Gerroa, or around Rangoon Island, at the entrance of the Minnamurra River. Here they berley and fish lightly weighted floater baits of pilchards, fish flesh strips and prawns.

These locations once produced outstanding catches of snapper. Most of these fish were in the 500-g to 2.5-kg range, but a good sprinkling of larger 'reds' also turned up from time to time.

For whatever reason, the inshore snapper fishery in this region crashed disastrously during the early 1990s and legal-length reds became an unusual catch. Interestingly, reasonable quantities of small snapper have reappeared over recent seasons, and anglers are quietly hopeful that their numbers may continue to increase slowly.

Other species taken on these shallow marks include silver trevally, bream, tailor, bonito, salmon, 'rat' kings, leatherjackets and the occasional teraglin, as well as numerous less desirable types such as Sergeant Baker, red rock cod, Maoris, sweep and pike. Large schools of bait fish, including slimy mackerel and yellowtail, are often present inshore, as well, and proven bait grounds exist just outside Kiama Harbour and in the so-called 'Hole', 400 m or so south south-west of Chips, at Gerroa.

The Hole was once a famous (and rather secret!) mark for big jewfish (mulloway) in the 10- to 30-kg range, as well as being known for its phenomenal run of 6- to 20 kg kingfish in late summer and autumn. The big kings have simply failed to show since the early 1990s, however, and only those dedicated anglers who invest a phenomenal amount of effort and persistence are still rewarded with good jewfish at this spot today.

JERVIS BAY

IN BRIEF

MAP REFERENCE: PAGE 109 G4

GETTING THERE Jervis Bay is about 34 km south-east of Nowra and 195 km south of Sydney by road
BEST TIME TO FISH October to June
BEST TIME TO TRAVEL Year-round
MAJOR ANGLING SPECIES Bream, flathead, salmon, tailor, luderick (blackfish), snapper and various game and reef species
SPECIAL RESTRICTIONS Much of Beecroft Peninsula is still used by the Defence Department as a live firing range. Periodic closures apply. Check local newspapers. A fee is payable for entrance into the Jervis Bay National Park. Specified areas around and within Jervis Bay are declared marine reserves or sanctuaries. Check current regulations with national parks rangers or fisheries officers before fishing
WARNINGS Heavy seas make many of the exposed rock fishing locations in this area dangerous. It is extremely inadvisable to leave the main tracks within the Beecroft Peninsula firing range, or to touch any items of military ordnance found there
CHARTER BOATS AND FISHING GUIDES Simo's Afloat Chartered Tours, telephone (02) 4441 5889

The Drum and Drumsticks fishing ledge is famed for its deep-water access

An angler fishing from the rocks on the southern side of Jervis Bay

One of the largest and most spectacular natural harbours on the New South Wales coast, Jervis Bay continues to play an important role in Australia's defence preparedness as a naval port and military target range. The entire area is also recognised today as a uniquely valuable site in terms of its ecological, environmental and cultural significance. This has been acknowledged through the creation and expansion of the Jervis Bay National Park and the establishment of a number of marine preservation zones, both within and adjacent to the bay.

Today, Jervis Bay attracts increasing numbers of tourists, as well as a growing local population. The big challenge next century will lie in balancing the often conflicting demands of tourism, development and the military with the priceless natural resources of this region.

BEECROFT PENINSULA

Two long headlands partially enclose the massive body of water known as Jervis Bay, and both peninsulas provide a number of very good rock and beach fishing locations. The best known and most heavily fished of these promontories is the northern headland, known as Beecroft Peninsula.

Beecroft Peninsula is the site of some of the most famous fishing ledges in Australia. These deep-water locations—with a proven reputation for producing everything from luderick and drummer to tuna and marlin—include Little and Big Beecroft, Old Mans Hat, Eves Ravine, The Drum and Drumsticks, Crocodile Head, Neverfail, Devils Gorge, the Three Graves and, moving inside the bay itself, the Outer Tubes, Plank, Docks and Inner Tubes.

As well as being a prime area for shore-based fishing, however, Beecroft Peninsula is also a military target range, and is therefore subject to defence department controls and periodic closure to all public access. Boom gates, check points and both road and helicopter patrols are used to enforce such closures, and their timing is well publicised in local papers and on bulletin boards displayed in nearby Currarong and at the entrances to the target zone.

Some fish are available from the locations mentioned during every month of the year, but the big, fast-swimming sport and game species that attract so much attention are more prolific from January until May, when crowds can be a real problem, particularly on weekends.

It should also be noted that many of these spots—particularly those on the exposed ocean side of the headland—are very dangerous in heavy seas and can only be reached by walking (and sometimes climbing) through the rough coastal terrain along overgrown bush tracks and down steep, cliff-edged paths. Obviously, extreme care should be exercised in this area at all times!

JERVIS BAY

Inside Jervis Bay itself is a vast, partially sheltered harbour-like environment that offers a broad range of fishing habitats and styles, with target species that include both estuarine and open ocean types. It must always be remembered, however, that these waters can become extremely rough in a strong blow, and that sudden southerly and westerly storm fronts commonly strike this stretch of coast.

A boat fishing mark worthy of particular attention is the Middle Ground, lying between the heads. This area frequently produces snapper, yellowtail kingfish and even the odd mulloway or jewfish, as well as a host of other reef and pelagic species.

Further back in Jervis Bay, bomboras or 'bombies' off Long Nose Point and several other headlands fish well for snapper, bream, tailor and salmon. This is especially the case in a moderate sea or following a prolonged period of heavy storm surge. Target Beach and its adjacent headlands also offer top-class shore fishing on occasions for salmon, tailor, drummer, bream and groper.

Along the western side of the bay, reef and gravel patches off Huskisson and Vincentia continue to produce reasonable snapper on occasion, as well as bream, drummer, groper and the like, while the dazzlingly white beaches between Callala Bay and Murrays Beach see runs of whiting, bream and small to middling flathead.

Various creeks flowing into Jervis Bay (notably Currambene Creek, at Huskisson) also hold good estuary fish, although several zones of marine reserve have recently been declared in these and other areas on and around Jervis Bay, and anglers should check carefully on the status of these reserves before they go fishing.

On the southern side of the bay, beyond the sanctuary of Bowen Island, some excellent general rock-hopping and beach fishing is to be had between Murrays and Steamers beaches. Hot spots here include Green Rock, Devils Elbow, The Pimple, The Old Light, Stoney Creek, Salt Rock, Brookes Rock, and Corangemite or St Georges Head. Most of these can produce excellent luderick, drummer, groper, bream, sweep, salmon, tailor, bonito, mackerel tuna and the odd big kingfish and snapper. These areas are all very dangerous in heavy seas.

Much of the coastline around Jervis Bay is stunningly beautiful

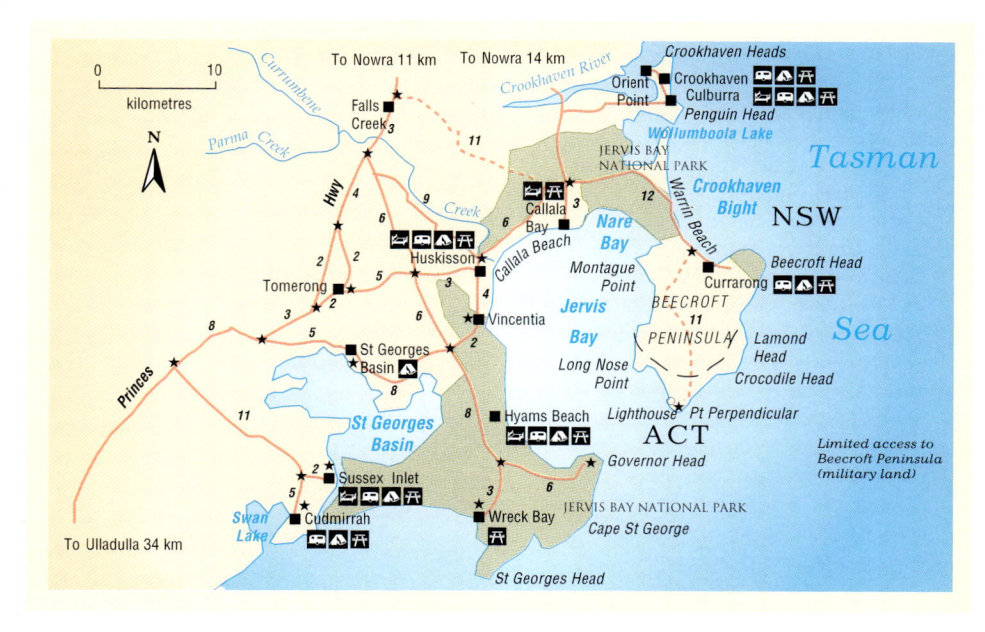

BATEMANS BAY AND THE CLYDE RIVER

IN BRIEF

MAP REFERENCE: PAGE 109 E6

GETTING THERE Batemans Bay, at the foot of Clyde Mountain, is about 280 km south of Sydney along the Princes Highway and 150 km from Canberra
BEST TIME TO FISH October to June
BEST TIME TO TRAVEL Year-round
MAJOR ANGLING SPECIES Bream, flathead, whiting, salmon, tailor, luderick (blackfish), mulloway (jewfish), snapper, bass and various game and reef species
SPECIAL RESTRICTIONS A permit from the National Parks and Wildlife Service is required to land on the Tollgate Islands
WARNINGS Heavy seas make many of the exposed rock fishing locations in this area dangerous. Conflicting tide and wind directions can also create hazardous conditions for small craft on the Clyde River estuary
CHARTER BOATS AND FISHING GUIDES OB 1 Charters, telephone Freecall 1800 641 065; Baitrunner Charters, telephone (02) 4472 6646;

Above: Bass fishing above Shallow Crossing on the Clyde River
Below: Rugged coastline in Murramarang National Park

Just a two-hour drive from Canberra, Batemans Bay—or 'The Bay' as it's better known—is a favourite holiday spot for people living in the national capital. As a result, it experiences significant influxes of visitors on almost every weekend, and is particularly busy during public and school holiday periods.

Lying on the southern shores of the broad Clyde estuary, Batemans Bay is a modern and fast-growing community that offers a full range of services to locals and visitors. It is an especially popular fishing destination, and boasts several good boat ramps, tackle stores, charter services and hire boat outlets.

BATEMANS BAY AND THE CLYDE RIVER

The Clyde is one of the last major untamed rivers of southern New South Wales and it offers a fine standard of fishing for many species, especially during the warmer months from November until June.

Upstream, particularly in the area between Shallow Crossing and Yadboro, the Clyde is a famous bass water, producing reasonable numbers of mostly small fish. Clyde River bass are dark, handsome and rather secretive fish that do not appear to grow quite as quickly, nor as large, as some other bass populations. Any Clyde bass of more than 800 g is a very good fish, although truly exceptional specimens of up to 2 kg are still encountered from time to time, particularly in the higher reaches.

Best bass action occurs from late November until April, and most fish succumb to lures or flies fished on or near the surface during spells of warm weather. These bass are particularly fond of feeding on terrestrial insects, and pre-stormfront termite hatches in November and early December can produce spectacular action.

Access to most freshwater stretches of the Clyde is through private property, and many land owners in this region are rather unsympathetic to intending anglers.

Below Shallow Crossing, bream, flathead, mullet and the odd estuary perch become the dominant species, with increasing numbers of whiting, luderick, leatherjackets and garfish lower down the river. Around Batemans Bay itself, more oceanic species such as yellowtail, trevally, pike, slimy mackerel, juvenile snapper and small groper also penetrate well into the estuary, particularly during dry spells.

The Clyde also has a well-deserved reputation for producing big mulloway or jewfish, including the odd specimen weighing more than 20 kg. As with most south coast mulloway fisheries, however, considerable time and effort are usually required to produce a result.

The Tollgate Islands group and its associated reef system, lying in the broad mouth of the Clyde estuary, provides some excellent boat fishing at times for bream, snapper, salmon, tailor, kingfish and smaller fare such as garfish, sweep and pike.

Further offshore, the relatively wide continental shelf adjacent to Batemans Bay sees seasonal influxes of yellowfin tuna, skipjack, sharks and marlin, with some of the best action often occurring in the 40 to 70 fathom (80 to 140 m) depth zone north-east of the bay, where rows of fishtrap buoys are often clearly evident. Further out, the deeper waters of the continental drop-off and canyons boast abundant albacore, tuna and most other game fish during the first six months of the year.

Fine rock and beach fishing opportunities also exist around Batemans Bay, with the rugged stretch of coastline in the Murramarang National Park, to the north, being particularly interesting and challenging for the keen rock-hopper. In fact, Snapper Point, at the northern edge of this park, is a famous destination for dedicated land-based game fishers, lure casters and snapper specialists.

Estuary fishing on the Clyde River

LAKE WINDAMERE

IN BRIEF

MAP REFERENCE: PAGE 110 D5

GETTING THERE Mudgee is about 270 km north-west of Sydney by road
BEST TIME TO FISH September to May
BEST TIME TO TRAVEL Year-round
MAJOR ANGLING SPECIES Golden perch, silver perch and Murray cod
SPECIAL RESTRICTIONS The Cudgegong River below Lake Windamere is now a gazetted trout stream and normal seasonal closures apply here
WARNINGS This lake can become choppy in strong winds. Boating near the dam wall and fishing from the wall are prohibited. Low water levels expose numerous submerged trees and shallow areas, posing a hazard to navigation
ACCOMMODATION Cudgegong Waters Park, telephone (02) 6358 8462

This moderately large (353 000 megalitres) artificial lake or impoundment lies in the central western district of New South Wales, close to the picturesque wine-growing centre of Mudgee. It is representative of the many impoundments now producing fine freshwater angling throughout New South Wales and south-eastern Queensland, largely as a result of dramatic increases in hatchery-bred fish liberations or stockings during the late 1980s and 1990s. Other popular dams of this type in New South Wales include Chaffey, Split Rock, Glenbawn, Wyangala and Burrinjuck.

Lake Windamere offers fair to excellent fishing for several native freshwater species — primarily golden perch or yellowbelly and silver perch, with smaller numbers of Murray cod and a sprinkling of eel-tailed catfish also taken from time to time.

At the time of writing, Lake Windamere was blessedly free from the scourge of both European carp and English perch or redfin. Common 'feral' goldfish (including some specimens weighing up to 2 kg and more) are reasonably common in Windamere's waters, however, and are often mistaken by visitors for the more damaging and virulent common carp.

PICTURESQUE AND PRODUCTIVE

The construction of Windamere Dam across the Cudgegong River during the early 1980s created Lake Windamere, a picturesque and productive freshwater fishery that now offers some of the finest angling opportunities for large golden perch or yellowbelly in all of New South Wales. These native freshwater fish typically run between 1 and 5 kg in this lake, although exceptional specimens weighing up to 8 kg and slightly more are certainly not unheard of at Windamere.

In addition to golden perch, Lake Windamere also contains reasonable numbers of Murray cod, including a scattering of fish of more than 8 or 9 kg, as well as abundant silver perch, the occasional eel-tailed catfish and introduced 'wild' goldfish (not to be confused with the closely related European carp).

The very best fishing at Lake Windamere typically occurs along the banks and weed bed edges in spring, early summer and autumn, with successful anglers using small to medium deep-diving lures or natural baits such as worms, shrimps and yabbies. Trolling with larger deep-diving lures can also be effective at times, especially when targeting Murray cod in the late summer or autumn months.

Above: Golden and silver perch are more likely to be found among structures such as drowned trees
Left: A golden perch or yellowbelly

Hot spots for both golden perch and Murray cod include most of the steeper, rocky shorelines and promontories, as well as areas of sunken or submerged timber. As a rule of thumb, the cod prefer slightly deeper water than yellowbelly.

Silver perch and small numbers of catfish are mostly taken on natural baits in shallower bays or amongst the many stands of drowned trees in the lake itself and further upstream in the flooded Cudgegong River. The majority of silver perch caught in this manner weigh less than 1 kg, although some monsters up to 4 kg have been taken in the past, especially by lure anglers chasing yellowbelly and cod.

Catfish all but disappeared from the lake within a few years of it first filling, but have staged a very modest comeback following restocking efforts by local clubs. Their numbers are generally still far too low, however, to make them anything other than an incidental catch.

Proven Locations

Well-known and proven fishing locations around Lake Windamere include the aptly named Cod Run, Shitty Corner, the rock wall at Limestone Creek, Deception Bay, Mystery Bay, The Eagles Nest, various causeways and stone retaining walls and those limited areas of the dam wall itself and its immediate surrounds where angling is permitted (check the signs).

Naturally, different locations produce varying results as the lake's water level fluctuates. As a general guide, look for points or steep banks with adjacent weed beds and pockets of structure such as drowned trees and rock piles. Closely examining the shoreline topography while Windamere's level is low can provide valuable clues for finding fish when the water eventually rises, as can talking to anglers who fish this area regularly.

Boat or Bank?

Lake Windamere may be fished effectively from boats or from the shore. The best results are often experienced within a narrow, 5-m band of the bank. This is especially the case in spring and early summer when the resident golden perch are at their most active and aggressive. While trolling parallel with the bank or around submerged weed beds and islands is highly effective at times, many boat anglers prefer to pull their vessels ashore and cast baits or lures from the bank itself, especially if a concentration of fish is encountered.

The only limiting factor for shore-bound hopefuls is the lack of access opportunities across private property and Department of Water Resources or Soil Conservation land. For this reason, boat owners typically enjoy better results, thanks to their ability to range further afield and seek out more remote locations.

Cabins, on-site caravans, caravan sites, tent site and boat launching facilities are all available at Cudgegong Waters Park, which is on the Mudgee–Rylestone road running on the southern side of Lake Windamere. A small shop at the

Boat-based anglers are able to explore the more remote reaches of Lake Windamere

park's kiosk also sells basic groceries, ice and a few simple fishing supplies. There is a small charge for entering the boom gates into the park.

At the time of writing, the closest fuel supply was located in the village of Ilford, some 19 km away from Lake Windamere towards Lithgow, and this was only open during normal business hours. More services and longer fuel retailing hours are available in Mudgee itself, some 25 or 30 km in the opposite direction.

LAKE GLENBAWN

IN BRIEF

MAP REFERENCE: PAGE 110 G3

GETTING THERE Scone is about 310 km north-west of Sydney along the New England Highway via Muswellbrook. Lake Glenbawn lies 15 km south-east of Scone
BEST TIME TO FISH September to May
BEST TIME TO TRAVEL Year-round
MAJOR ANGLING SPECIES Australian bass, golden perch, silver perch, eel-tailed catfish and Murray cod
SPECIAL RESTRICTIONS Boating near the dam wall is prohibited
WARNINGS This lake can become choppy in strong winds. Low water levels expose numerous submerged trees and shallow areas, posing a hazard to navigation. Avoid swimming or drinking lake water during blue-green algae blooms
ACCOMMODATION Lake Glenbawn is in the Hunter Valley region, where a multitude of accommodation is available ranging from self-contained cabins and caravan parks to resorts and boutique hotels

Golden perch are abundant in Lake Glenbawn, although big bass are the major drawcard

Lake Glenbawn is an artificial impoundment on the upper Hunter River, situated south-east of Scone and north-east of Muswellbrook. This famous wine-growing region is about four hours drive from the northern and north-western suburbs of Sydney, and is therefore a feasible weekend and long weekend destination for freshwater anglers living in Australia's largest city.

The earth- and rock-fill dam wall across the Hunter at Glenbawn is controlled by the New South Wales Department of Water Resources. It was first constructed in 1958, but was significantly enlarged during 1986 to reach its present height, which is well in excess of 75 m.

Lake Glenbawn holds up to 750 000 megalitres of water when full. Nonetheless, it is a reasonably modest-sized water storage compared to many others in the state, and can be thoroughly explored in a day or two from a small vessel propelled by an outboard motor of 15- to 40-horsepower.

Stocked Fish

Quite large quantities of brown and rainbow trout fingerlings have been stocked into the backed-up waters of Lake Glenbawn over the years. While small numbers of these introduced fish are still occasionally encountered in the Hunter River immediately downstream of the dam, trout fishing in the lake itself has never been a viable pursuit.

Clearly, like many lower altitude impoundments in the northern half of New South Wales, Lake Glenbawn is simply too warm to support a healthy trout fishery, and all efforts expended to establish one here represent a waste of money and resources that could better have been directed elsewhere. Thankfully, the same certainly cannot be said of Australian native fish, several species of which now thrive in Lake Glenbawn.

The star performers amongst the species introduced into this lake over the past decade or so have been Australian bass (which were native to the Hunter River system prior to the construction of dams such as Glenbawn) and golden perch or yellowbelly, which have been translocated from western-flowing watersheds and now thrive in their new home. (Interestingly, Lake Glenbawn is the only eastern watershed impoundment in New South Wales that receives regular liberations of both golden and silver perch fry with the support and backing of New South Wales Fisheries—an organisation normally opposed to translocation of western species.)

Famous for Big Bass

Nowadays, Lake Glenbawn is without doubt one of the most famous big bass waters in New South Wales, with stocked fish of this species occasionally obtaining massive sizes here, as well as in nearby Lake St Clair or Glennies Creek Dam.

Bass well in excess of 3 kg have been officially recorded from both of these Hunter Valley lakes, although frequent reports and rumours of fish in the 4- to 5-kg plus class almost always turn out to be flights of fancy.

While there is a great deal of talk about 'monster' bass in Glenbawn (and Lake St Clair), as with most impounded bass fisheries, smaller fish in the two- to four-year-old age group dominate anglers' catches. These bass typically measure between 25 and 40 cm and weigh up to 1.2 kg. Fish weighing more than 1.5 kg remain the exception rather than the rule.

Heavyweight Goldens

The real heavyweights in Lake Glenbawn are its golden perch or yellowbelly. The largest of these officially recorded at the time of writing weighed a staggering 15 kg. Specimens of more than 7 kg are far from uncommon, and goldens in the 2- to 6-kg range are regarded as 'average' for this fertile body of water.

Silver perch appear to have fared less spectacularly in Lake Glenbawn and are only occasionally taken by anglers, while eel-tailed catfish provide good sport for bait fishers, especially those confined to the shores of the impoundment.

Over the years, there have also been several unauthorised and technically illegal liberations of Murray cod into the waters of Lake Glenbawn, and isolated specimens of this highly prized species—including the odd fish of more 10 kg in weight—are still encountered from time to time by anglers targeting bass and golden perch.

Proven Techniques

Popular and productive angling techniques at Lake Glenbawn include trolling from boats, casting and retrieving lures from the shore or boats and bait fishing.

Over the long run, trolling with small to medium deep-diving plugs tends to produce more bass and golden perch than any other technique, especially in the main basin of the lake and towards the dam wall itself. However, casting and retrieving is becoming more popular each year, and this technique certainly has its place at Lake Glenbawn.

As with most impoundments that contain good stocks of golden perch, excellent result are sometimes obtained on this species during spring and early summer by casting and retrieving deep-diving lures in the 10-m wide band of water immediately adjacent to steeper shorelines and rocky points. This may be done from a boat or off the bank itself.

Finding Fish

One of the greatest keys to success at Lake Glenbawn lies in locating actively feeding fish. The bass here often form moderately large mid-water schools over and around submerged structures such as drowned river beds and hilltops, although some of these fish also maintain their river-dwelling habits and spend a great deal of time lurking amongst tangles of submerged timber and fallen trees. Hooking a 2-kg bass close to such cover is certainly an adrenalin-charged experience, as these fish are amongst the hardest fighting freshwater adversaries available to Australian anglers.

Golden perch are generally a little easier to find, especially in spring and early summer, when they relate closely to weed bed edges, steep banks, points and drop-offs.

A shore-based angler at Lake Glenbawn

Silver perch are particularly fond of standing timber in the backs of inlets, while catfish prefer soft bottom strata, gently sloping shorelines and large, shallow bays. Murray cod are not really plentiful enough in Lake Glenbawn to be specifically pursued and targeted.

Troublesome Algal Blooms

Traditionally, one of the greatest problems associated with fishing at Lake Glenbawn has been the propensity for the impoundment to experience massive 'blooms' of potentially toxic blue-green algae during the warmer months of the year—particularly from mid-November until March or early April.

These blooms are aggravated by the run-off of nutrient-rich water from surrounding agricultural land and the very high surface temperatures sometimes experienced in backwaters of the lake. Such phenomena can adversely affect angling results by reducing visibility and making fish—especially bass and perch—rather lethargic and difficult to catch.

Because of the frequency with which these blooms have tended to occur over recent years, many keen Glenbawn regulars prefer to concentrate their angling efforts in the lake on the period from mid- or early September until early November, not visiting again until late March or April. The annual occurrence of these algal blooms is by no means a certainty, however, nor do they always affect the entire lake. It is therefore still possible to enjoy some excellent sport right through the summer period, even in mid-December and January.

A handsome bass taken on a spinnerbait

LAKE LYELL

IN BRIEF

MAP REFERENCE: PAGE 110 E8

GETTING THERE Lithgow is about 140 km west of Sydney on the Great Western Highway. The turn-off to Lake Lyell is opposite the Donnybrook Hotel at Hartley, 10 km east of Lithgow. From the turn-off, it is less than 10 km to the dam wall and recreational reserve
BEST TIME TO FISH Year-round, but best from March to November
BEST TIME TO TRAVEL Year-round
MAJOR ANGLING SPECIES Brown trout, rainbow trout, yabbies and Australian bass
SPECIAL RESTRICTIONS Boating is prohibited close to the dam wall, the 'bubbler' and the spillway. The 'no-go' area is marked by buoys. Fishing immediately downstream of the dam is also prohibited
WARNINGS Sudden storms and very cool weather are always possible at Lake Lyell, especially in winter or early spring

The artificial impoundment known as Lake Lyell (also known in some literature as Lilyvale) is one of a string of dams just west of the Blue Mountains that have been built in the Lithgow–Wallerawang region. Their primary purpose is to supply water to local coal-burning power plants used to generate electricity for the New South Wales grid.

Construction of the original 47-m high rock-fill embankment of Lyell Dam across the upper Coxs River was completed in 1983, and stocking of trout began almost as soon as the lake filled.

During the mid-1990s, the spillway of this dam was raised by some 3 m to increase the lake's storage capacity. This extra capacity was needed to supply additional cooling water to the large, relatively new power plant at Mount Piper, northwest of Lithgow.

FLUCTUATING FORTUNES

Over the years since the construction of the dam, Lake Lyell has produced varying standards of angling. After an initial flurry of very good trout fishing in the mid- to late 1980s, trout catches tapered off somewhat. Increased stocking rates and the raising of the dam spillway to enlarge the impoundment's capacity appear, however, to have provided a much-needed shot in the arm for this fishery. Catch rates picked up again in the mid- to late 1990s, only to decline once more as a result of severe drought and falling water levels.

Such fluctuating piscatorial fortunes are not at all uncommon in artificial impoundments, especially those whose primary function is to supply water for irrigation, power generation or industry. Yet, despite its ups and downs (literally), Lake Lyell is today regarded as a reasonably reliable producer of both brown and rainbow trout, particularly during the cooler months of the year. With only limited natural spawning and recruitment of 'wild' trout from the upper Coxs River and other feeders, however, continued stocking will be needed to maintain this as a viable trout fishery into the 21st century.

BASS AND YABBIES

Interestingly, 10 000 hatchery-bred Australian bass fry were also stocked into Lake Lyell on a trial basis during 1995 by New South Wales Fisheries. At the time of writing, reports on the success or failure of this worthwhile experiment were still rather sketchy, although there's no reason to believe that this impoundment couldn't be turned into a reasonable mixed fishery over time, with trout and bass in the same water.

It's also worth noting that Lake Lyell contains excellent stocks of large, healthy yabbies, which appear to be the western strain *Cherax destructor* species or an allied variety. Whatever the case, many switched-on anglers supplement their catches from the lake—particularly in summer—with a few dozen of these tasty crustaceans.

FISHING IN LAKE LYELL

Lake Lyell can be fished both from the bank and out of boats (internal combustion engines of all sizes are allowed here, although there are speed restrictions in some areas). There are several functional boat launching sites, the best and most convenient being the concrete ramp located in the picnic reserve, near the dam wall.

Lake Lyell's trout are taken by all popular methods, including bait fishing, trolling, lure casting and fly fishing. Deep trolling (anywhere between 5 and 15 m or even more beneath the surface of the water) with the aid of a downrigger

Yabbies taken from the stomach of a large brown trout from Lake Lyell

Despite its fluctuating water levels, Lake Lyell can still provide some good trout fishing within a couple of hours of travel from Sydney

typically produces the best and most spectacular catches, however, including the occasional brown trout weighing 4.5 kg or better, especially in winter and spring.

There can be some excellent sight fishing for trout around the banks at times, particularly in late spring or early summer. Various fly patterns or small lures will catch these fish if carefully presented. Many fly fishers favour beetle or nymph patterns in this situation, but long leaders, careful casts and drab or camouflaged clothing are essential for success.

Fly fishing from the banks at night with large wet flies such as Craig's Nighttimes, Woolly Buggers and Taihape Ticklers can also be quite productive, especially during the warmer months or when the lake is rising over areas that have been dry for some time. A few very large trout (usually browns) are taken this way each year, as well as plenty of average fish in the 500-g to 1.5-kg range (both browns and the lake's more prolific rainbows). Flats and bays along the eastern shoreline of Lake Lyell's main basin tend to be best for this style of fishing.

In summer, when water skiers are often out on the lake in numbers, fishing is generally best very early in the morning, and again late in the evening or through the night. In winter and spring, trout may be caught all day, especially if the weather is overcast and drizzly (as it often is).

THE BUBBLER

Lake Lyell is equipped with a large aerator pump situated not far from the dam wall. This device, commonly known amongst anglers as the 'bubbler', is activated from time to time during summer to promote water circulation, prevent stratification or layering, and maintain water quality.

When the bubbler is switched on, it becomes a real fishing hot spot. This mechanism increases oxygen content in the water, creates a strong current and drives many small forage fish and other food items to the surface. Here, packs of opportunistic trout often hunt them in a spectacular manner, slashing the water like feeding tailor or tuna at times!

Unfortunately, the bubbler is located within a strictly enforced no-go zone near the dam wall. This area is clearly marked by a string of buoys and boating is not permitted here for safety reasons. Anglers are therefore forced to cast lures and flies towards the bubbler from a steep section of rocky bank adjacent to it, or to position their boats right up hard against the line of marker buoys and cast from there. Both approaches can produce good catches.

NOT TO BE UNDERESTIMATED

While there are definitely better and more consistent trout fisheries in Australia, and even within New South Wales, few lie within two hours drive of western Sydney. This certainly helps to explain Lake Lyell's increasing popularity as a freshwater angling venue.

Nonetheless, this rather pretty little body of water should never be underestimated, as it continues to produce more than its share of exceptionally big trout for those willing to invest the necessary time and effort — as well as fair catches of average-sized fish in between the 'lunkers' and 'wall hangers' that all anglers dream of catching.

THE CAPITAL'S LAKES

IN BRIEF

MAP REFERENCE: PAGE 109 C5

GETTING THERE Lakes Burley Griffin, Ginninderra and Tuggeranong all lie within the Canberra metropolitan area
BEST TIME TO FISH September to May
BEST TIME TO TRAVEL Year-round
MAJOR ANGLING SPECIES Golden perch, Murray cod, carp, redfin and trout
SPECIAL RESTRICTIONS Several lakes in the Canberra region are closed to fishing and internal combustion engines may not be used on Lake Burley Griffin, Lake Ginninderra and Lake Tuggeranong
WARNINGS These lakes can become very choppy in high winds
ACCOMMODATION Various levels of accommodation are available throughout Canberra
CHARTER BOATS AND FISHING GUIDES Expert Fishing Systems, telephone (02) 6247 9707

Sunset over Lake Burley Griffin, a productive time of day for fishing

Canberra is not often considered as an angling destination other than by its residents, yet within the borders of the Australian Capital Territory lie six major lakes. They include Lake Burley Griffin, which is in the city centre; Lake Ginninderra, which is in the northern suburban centre of Belconnen; and Lake Tuggeranong, which is in the southern suburban centre of Tuggeranong.

The remaining three lakes are Cotter, Bendora and Corin dams. These last three are closed to fishing of any kind, as they form part of the capital's water supply.

Over the years, the three main fishing lakes have developed a sound reputation as productive fisheries for both native and introduced species.

An excellent aspect of Canberra's design means that the three main lakes are right in the middle of built-up areas so it is only a short walk, bike ride or drive for any resident to cast a line. Before- and after-work 'stealth missions' are commonly practised in the Canberra region.

Lake Burley Griffin, Lake Ginninderra and Lake Tuggeranong all have boating restrictions which prevent the use of petrol-powered vessels but do allow the use of canoes or electrically powered craft. Almost inevitably, there is some degree of bureaucracy involved in getting to use your electrically powered boat on any of the lakes. This involves obtaining a permit from the relevant authorities. Further information regarding this can be obtained from any of the local tackle stores.

LAKE BURLEY GRIFFIN

Lake Burley Griffin was filled in 1964 as a result of the damming of the Molonglo River. It is the largest and oldest of the Canberra lakes and, as with all of them, the shoreline is generally well manicured. This makes for a very aesthetically pleasing environment, as well as relatively easy access to potential fishing spots.

Between 1981 and 1995, the lake was stocked with a variety of species including more 100 000 Murray cod and 150 000 golden perch. There have also been stockings in past years of brown and rainbow trout, and silver perch.

The trout were originally very successful and the lake provided very good fishing for them. For a variety of reasons, however, their success has waned. From time to time, trout do make a reappearance and offer some pretty good fishing, but the lake could not be considered a consistent trout fishery. Luckily, the native freshwater fish began to establish themselves as the trout stocks declined, and these are now the most sought-after of the angling species.

Lake Burley Griffin also has a substantial population of carp and redfin. While generally not highly prized by anglers, these offer a sporting introduction to fishing. Experienced anglers looking for a quick and easy 'fishing fix' will also target them on fly or coarse fishing tackle. In fact, Lake Burley Griffin has recently hosted several national coarse fishing events.

One problem Lake Burley Griffin has had in the past is poor water clarity. This was usually the case after heavy rainfall. The lake often stayed dirty for several weeks, making many types of fishing, especially lure fishing, very difficult. At one stage, it was said that the Water Police used Lake Burley Griffin as their training area for zero visibility dives. This situation seems to be improving. It now takes a substantial period of heavy rain to dirty the water and only a few days for it to clear—at least by local standards, where visibility that exceeds 40 to 50 cm is enough to cause considerable excitement!

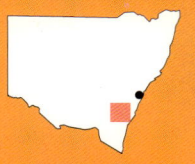

The mainstay of the Burley Griffin native fishery are its golden perch or yellowbelly. The lake now has a well-established population of these fish, which provide very consistent fishing. An average size would be between 1.5 and 2.5 kg, with fish in excess of 4 kg being caught regularly. When conditions are suited to lure fishing, medium to large deep-diving lures in sharply contrasting colours are proven producers.

As one might expect, the more productive lure fishing areas for golden perch are the deeper sections of the lake which follow the old river course. These areas include sections of the Molonglo River Arm, Blue Gum Point, Black Mountain Peninsula, Yarramundi Reach and the basin at Scrivener Dam.

For the bait fisher, there are several other spots which can be productive, including the northern end of Kings Avenue Bridge and Acton Peninsula. The most productive baits include live yabbies, wood grubs, bardi grubs and witchetty grubs.

BIG MURRAY COD

Probably the greatest surprise to anglers not familiar with the Australian Capital Territory is the potential of Lake Burley Griffin to produce big Murray cod. Every summer regular reports of cod in the 10- to 25-kg range buzz through local tackle shops and fishing clubs, and appear in local newspaper fishing columns. Targeting these big cod, however, requires careful planning, preparation and perseverance.

There is an abundance of food for these fish in the form of carp, redfin and golden perch, so they can be hard to tempt. Any deep-diving, strongly swimming lure or plug will do the job, but those wanting to get serious should think big. Larger lures will be more likely to tempt a big cod. Anglers who do manage to entice a cod need to be prepared for fish that have been conservatively estimated to grow in excess of 50 kg. As with all big fish, it may be necessary to put in plenty of hours to target these large cod successfully, but this time will be pleasantly interrupted by respectable golden perch or redfin.

LAKE GINNINDERRA

Lake Ginninderra was first filled in 1976 by the damming of Ginninderra Creek, and it is now well populated with both native and introduced species. Between 1981 and 1995, Ginninderra was stocked with nearly 60 000 Murray cod and 150 000 golden perch. Other species such as trout and silver perch have not proven to be successful stocking species here and have been virtually discontinued save a few incidental stockings.

Ginninderra, like Burley Griffin, is no sparkling, crystal clear spring, although it is not quite as bad as Canberra's most famous waterway. It also has a large carp and redfin population which provides plenty of entertainment for budding or bored anglers.

Golden perch or yellowbelly are the most abundant of the more desirable species and can be caught using either baits or lures. Some of the best locations include the rock wall at the dam, the deeper section of the spillway basin, the Water Police wharf and the adjacent rock wall, as well as some deeper rocky points. Golden perch between 800 g and 2 kg are most common, with the odd fish of more than 3 kg being taken from time to time. Deep-diving lures in small to medium sizes are best and, as with Burley Griffin, sharply contrasting colours work well. Best natural baits include scrub worms, grubs and yabbies.

Murray cod seem to be caught more frequently in Ginninderra than Burley Griffin. There are very respectable specimens available here, ranging from 6 to 15 kg. The locations mentioned for golden perch are also the more productive spots for cod.

Many of the big cod caught in Lake Ginninderra are taken on baits, ranging from the simple garden worm to large wood or bardi grubs. For the angler with an electrically powered boat, trolling lures along the edge of the weed beds, as well as any of the other locations mentioned, is a good technique for targeting both golden perch and Murray cod.

LAKE TUGGERANONG

This is the most recently constructed of all the Australian Capital Territory lakes. The lake had a rather disappointing start, with very little return from stocking programs, and the construction of a large shopping mall on the lake's shores was

A golden perch taken while lure casting into the rock walls

blamed for its pollution problems. In recent times, however, the lake has started to produce some respectable, albeit limited, catches of both golden perch and Murray cod. Lake Tuggeranong also hosts a large carp and redfin population.

The artificial rock walls are the best locations for targeting perch and cod, using either lures or baits. The same lures and baits described for the other two lakes are suitable for Lake Tuggeranong. This lake promises some good fishing potential, provided it is given due stocking attention and suitable environmental management.

Preparing to release a Murray cod hooked in Lake Ginninderra

TROUT STREAMS OF THE AUSTRALIAN CAPITAL TERRITORY

IN BRIEF

MAP REFERENCE: PAGE 109 C5

GETTING THERE The streams discussed here all lie within an hour's drive of Canberra
BEST TIME TO FISH October to May
BEST TIME TO TRAVEL Year-round
MAJOR ANGLING SPECIES Brown trout, rainbow trout and redfin
SPECIAL RESTRICTIONS Normal New South Wales and Australian Capital Territory trout fishing regulations apply
WARNINGS Extreme weather conditions are possible at any time of year, especially at higher altitudes. A good-quality topographic map is essential for gaining access to many fishing spots on the Cotter and Queanbeyan rivers
ACCOMMODATION Various levels of accommodation are available throughout the Canberra region
CHARTER BOATS AND FISHING GUIDES Expert Fishing Systems, telephone (02) 6247 9707

It may come as a surprise to some people, but within the borders of the Australian Capital Territory, or just beyond, there are many streams that hold good populations of brown and rainbow trout. Some of the main rivers of interest to trout anglers in this region include the Gudgenby, Goodradigbee, Cotter and Queanbeyan rivers. The waters of all these streams eventually flow into the Murrumbidgee River.

Sadly, this once mighty river has suffered serious environmental degradation and carp infestation in the Canberra region over the past 20 years, which has affected the quality of fishing for both natives and trout. Its various tributaries, however, have fared much better, and all have populations of trout which are worthy of pursuit.

THE GUDGENBY RIVER

The Gudgenby River is situated in the south of the Australian Capital Territory in spectacular surrounds. The higher sections of the river are quite rugged, with the terrain being steep and access often difficult. The river flows quite rapidly through these sections and is formed mainly of rapids and plunge pools.

There are good populations of rainbow trout in these higher areas. These little battlers are in excellent condition and respond well to thoughtfully placed lures or flies.

Lower down, the river transforms into a more tranquil, slow-flowing river lined with willow trees. The river is quite small and narrow by any standard, with the occasional larger pool downstream. Here, the weed beds and undercut banks hold some respectable brown trout. One thing to remember about the Gudgenby is that you should always be prepared to come across a reasonable trout in just about any section of the river.

THE GOODRADIGBEE RIVER

The Goodradigbee River actually flows just to the west of the Australian Capital Territory. Its source is in the high country near Tantangara Reservoir, and it eventually flows into Burrinjuck Dam. The Goodradigbee is also the main trout spawning tributary for Burrinjuck.

This river offers some superb trout fishing for both browns and rainbows. The higher section to

A beautifully coloured rainbow trout taken with a minnow lure from the Goodradigbee River

The Cotter River, below Bendora Dam, offers some spectacular scenery and fine trout fishing

south-west of the Australian Capital Territory is, however, in rugged and difficult terrain. Some areas will require a 4WD vehicle and land owner's permission to gain access to the river, but the fishing can be well worth the extra effort! Other sections are far more accessible, but, as would be expected, are heavily fished.

The Goodradigbee River is a recognised trout river and is governed by seasonal closures during spawning season. Caring anglers enjoy good fishing for quality brown trout before the close of season and rainbows at the opening, making sure they release the bulk of their catch.

Bait, lure and fly fishing are all productive techniques in the right sections of the river. Lure and fly fishers, in particular, will enjoy fishing the Goodradigbee immensely. Of all the rivers in the region, this one offers the most consistent fishing for quality trout.

THE COTTER RIVER

Not all sections of the Cotter River are open to fishing and it should also be noted that all three dams on the Cotter River (Cotter, Bendora and Corin) are totally closed to fishing. Be sure to make yourself aware of the fishable sections of this river before you begin to enjoy it.

The Cotter River flows through subalpine terrain in the higher country and pine plantations in the lower sections. The entire river is virtually free of development and is very picturesque. The shortish section of the river from immediately below Cotter Dam through to where it joins the Murrumbidgee River is easily accessible and dotted with public camp sites and picnic grounds.

Until recent times, it still produced some very good trout fishing. Unfortunately, carp have now infested this section of the river and although a few trout are still caught, not many serious anglers make the effort. After heavy rains, however, trout often come over the dam wall at Cotter and provide some pretty good, albeit short-lived, fishing in this stretch, especially in the large pool immediately beneath the dam wall.

Upstream of Cotter Dam, from the confluence of Pierces Creek, there is more than 20 km of river where fishing is permitted, to a point just below Bendora Dam. This section is also governed by seasonal closures. The water hosts some fun fishing for small- to medium-sized rainbow trout. The early season (October) can produce some very respectable rainbows which have not yet returned downstream to the Cotter Dam.

The easiest spot at which to gain access to this stretch by conventional vehicle is Vanitys Crossing. Here, you can fish either upstream or downstream. There is minimal opportunity to walk along the banks in this area and most anglers prefer to wade in the river. Much of the river is shallow enough to allow this.

Other areas are accessible with the aid of 4WD vehicles or some strenuous hiking. If considering either of these options, a good-quality 1:25 000 topographic map is essential. This area is a maze of forestry and fire trails which can keep you driving round in circles for days if you don't prepare yourself.

Those keen to add a bit of hiking to their adventure should be warned that the terrain is quite steep and this is definitely not a 'stroll in the park'. The vegetation is also dense, which makes for demanding hiking. The rewards, however, are some very spectacular scenery more reminiscent of North America than Australia, and some lightly fished waters.

The quality of fishing in this part of the Cotter River is largely determined by the amount of flow, which is regulated at Bendora Dam. High or rising levels definitely offer the best fishing.

Sight casting is possible in the clear waters of the Queanbeyan River

TROUT STREAMS OF THE AUSTRALIAN CAPITAL TERRITORY

Bearing in mind that the river is relatively shallow, it takes some anglers a couple of trips of spooking fish to work out just how little cover some trout need. Fly and lure casters fish their way up looking for the slightest hint of cover and fishing it thoroughly.

Lure casters should stick with small, shallow- to medium-depth lures or the ever popular bladed spinners. Fly fishers can enjoy some dry fly fishing in this river using basic patterns such as Royal Wulff or Red Tag. Nymphing is also productive. The best way of covering your options is to use a larger Wulff pattern with a small nymph under a 20-cm dropper.

In this part of the Cotter River, there are also small populations of Macquarie perch, river blackfish and trout cod. All are totally protected and must be released unharmed back into the river. Basically, if you catch something that is not a trout, let it go with minimal handling and fuss.

The Queanbeyan River

The Queanbeyan River runs through the New South Wales town of Queanbeyan, which is right on the border of the Australian Capital Territory. It joins the Molonglo River, which then flows into Canberra's main lake, Lake Burley Griffin. Upstream of the town of Queanbeyan, the river is dammed at Googong Reservoir.

The stretch of river between the Molonglo junction and the boundary fence of Googong Reserve below Googong Dam has the potential to produce some quality trout fishing. This, however, is dependent upon a couple of factors.

When trout populations in Lake Burley Griffin are good, they will often run upstream into the Queanbeyan River. Also, when Googong Dam is overflowing, trout often go over the wall. Those that survive are usually decent-sized fish and provide anglers with good sport. There are also resident fish to keep anglers amused between these events.

The Queanbeyan River, upstream of Googong Dam, provides some excellent trout fishing for those prepared to make the effort to get there. Googong Dam is quickly developing a reputation as a genuine big trout fishery and fish of this calibre also inhabit the upstream sections of the Queanbeyan River. Much of the land is privately owned and permission is required to gain access. There are some sections which are accessible after a reasonable walk. Like all proposed trips to new grounds, get a good-quality map and study it thoroughly. Seasonal closures also apply to this part of the river.

Small Streams

Some other spots worth checking out include Paddys River, Orroral River and Condor Creek. All three hold trout in good numbers, although not at any great size.

A mountain stream near Canberra — although small, such waters can provide good sport

AUSTRALIAN CAPITAL TERRITORY FISHING RULES AND REGULATIONS

Recreational fishing in Canberra and the Australian Capital Territory is administered by Environment ACT. At the time of writing, fisheries rules and regulations for waters within the Australian Capital Territory were being overhauled to bring them more closely into line with those in New South Wales.

When we went to press, no angling licence was required, but this and a number of other regulations look likely to change during 1998. So, it is absolutely essential to check the current state of play before fishing in Australian Capital Territory waters.

Bag, Size and Other Regulations
What was the story when we went to press?

- There was a blanket bag limit of 10 fish per person per day (any species or combination of species) for all Territory waters and a minimum legal lenght of 25 cm for all trout species.

- The use of fish roe (eggs) as bait was completely prohibited, and it was illegal to stock or translocate fish in Territory waters without a permit.

- Regulations governing the number of rods, reels and hooks per angler and various closures — seasonal and permanent — applied to certain waters,

- Although there were no specific rules regarding carp or redfin, Environment ACT advise that it is not illegal to return these fish to the water, but that if you kill them, please do so humanely.

Check First!
Before fishing in any waters in the Australian Capital Territoy, or those nearby waters partially or completely under its control, call Environment ACT for the most up-to-date information on rules and regulations.

ENVIRONMENT ACT
(02) 6207 2117
(02) 6207 2120

South-East New South Wales

109

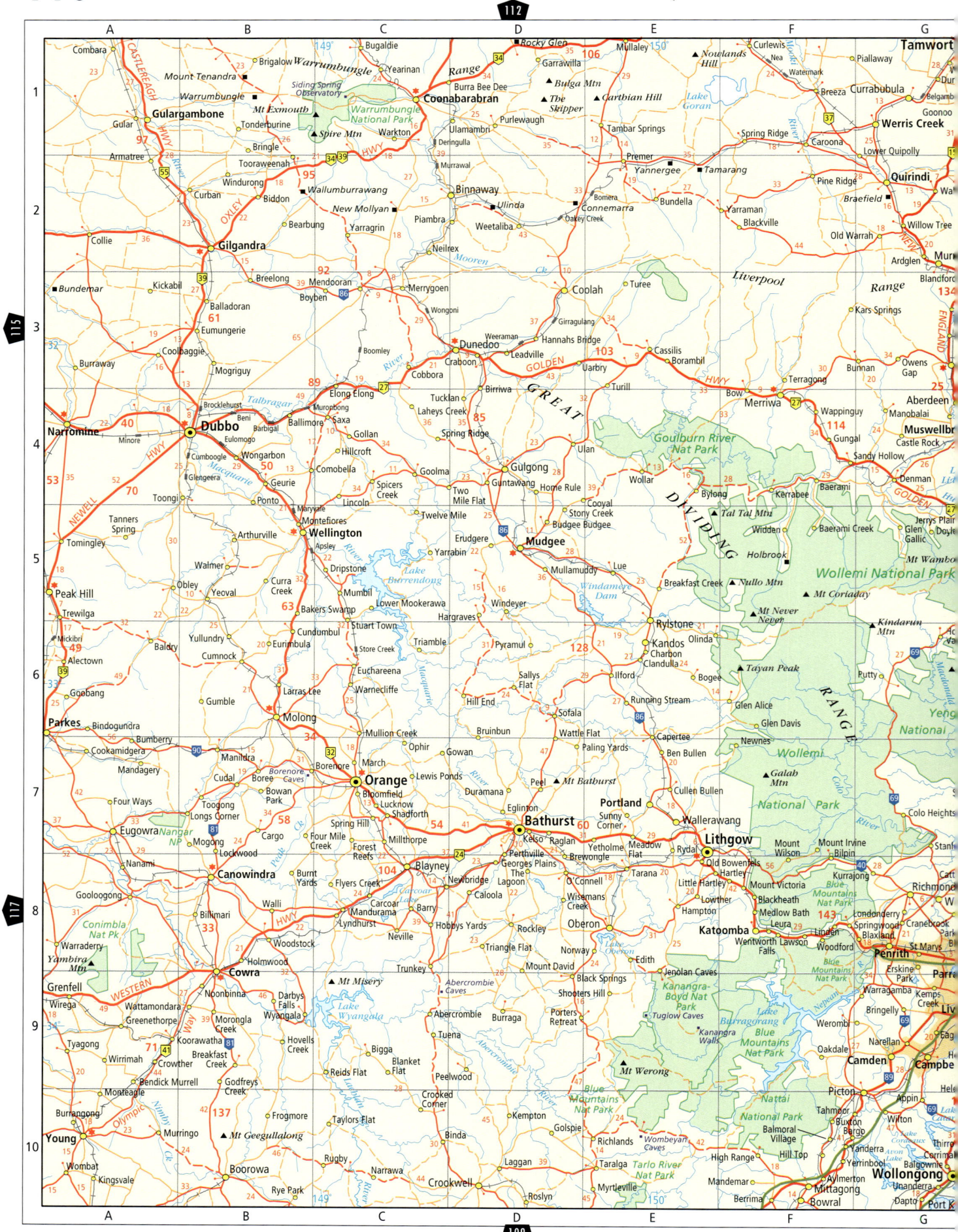

110 CENTRAL-EAST NEW SOUTH WALES

0 10 20 30 40 50
kilometres
113
H J K L M N P
1 2 3 4 5 6 7 8 9 10
N
Aberbaldie
Glen Morrison
Dungowan
Weabonga
Woolomin
Chaffey Res
Bowling Alley Point
Ogunbil
Niangala
Mt Sugarloaf
Brackendale
Riamukka
Nowendoc
Nundle
Hanging Rock
Vombramurra
Barry
DIVIDING
RANGE
Bralga Tops
Barnard River
Thunderbolts
Nowendoc River
Woko Nat Pk
Timor
Ellerston
Barrington Tops National Park
Moonan Flat
Upper Bowman
Woolooma
Belltrees
Mt Barrington
Rawdon Vale
Copeland
Maudville
Gloucester Tops
Faulkland
Davis Creek
Mt Royal
Gap
Barrington Tops National Park
Salisbury
Chichester
Chichester Dam
Underbank
Bowmans Creek
Halton
Munni
Bendolba
Bandon Grove
Main Creek
Fosterton
Lake St Clair
St Clair
Allynbrook
Gresford
Dungog
Tyraman
Camberwell
Glendon Brook
Wallarobba
Brookfield
Clarence Town
Martins Creek
Vacy
Paterson
Redbournberry
Singleton
Branxton
Greta
Belford
Woodville
Rothbury
Rutherford
Maitland
Broke
Abermain
Metford
Yellow Rock
Cessnock
Kurri Kurri
Bellbird
Pelaw Main
Paxton
Kearsley
Kitchener
Ellalong
Wollombi
Brunkerville
Laguna
Cooranbong
Bucketty
Cedar Brush Creek
Morisset
Dora Creek
Kulnura
Yarramalong
Jilliby
Dooralong
Wyee
Central Mangrove
Peats Ridge
Calga
Wyong
Tuggerah
Ourimbah
Gosford
Kariong
Terrigal
Woy Woy
Brisbane Water NP
Bouddi NP
Killcare
Umina
Brooklyn
Broken Bay
Palm Beach
Ku-ring-gai Chase NP
Mona Vale
Terrey Hills
Narrabeen
Long Reef Point
Manly
North Sydney
Port Jackson
SYDNEY
Bondi Junction
Hurstville
Botany
Caringbah
Botany Bay
Cronulla
Port Hacking
Bundeena
Royal National Park
Kemps Pinnacle
Kangaroo Flat
Mt Banda Banda
Mt Werrikimbe
Werrikimbe National Park
Upper Rollands Plains
Yarrowitch
Mt Seaview
Myrtle Scrub
Mount Seaview
Forbes River
Kindee
Yarras
Bellangry
Pappinbarra
Pembrooke
OXLEY
HWY
Raffles Peak
Ellenborough
Bagnoo
Beechwood
Wauchope
Port Macquarie
Tacking Point
Byabarra
Herons Creek
Kendall
Bulga
Elands
Comboyne
Mooral Creek
Bobin
Number One
Central Lansdowne
Lansdowne
Apple Tree Flat
Cedar Party
Coopernook
Bretti
Manning River
Tibbuc
Mount George
Rookhurst
Wingham
Taree
Killawarra
Tinonee
Bohnock
Kimbriki
Barrington
Burrell Creek
Gloucester
Forbesdale
Rainbow Flat
Krambach
Nabiac
Dyers Crossing
Stratford
Craven
Bunyah
Bucketts Way
Wards River
Coolongolook
Wootton
Markwell
Stroud Road
Stroud
Pacific Palms
Boolambayte
Bulahdelah
Bungwahl
Booral
Girvan
Nerong
Allworth
Bombah Point
The Broadwater
Mungo Brush
Limeburners Creek
Karuah
Seaham
Wallalong
Swan Bay
Port Stephens
Tea Gardens
Hawks Nest
Soldiers Point
Shoal Bay
Nelson Bay
Raymond Terrace
Medowie
Anna Bay
Boat Harbour
Williamtown
Beresfield
Sandgate
Fern Bay
Wallsend
Stockton
Port Hunter
Newcastle Bight
Newcastle
Broadmeadow
Boolaroo
Warners Bay
Charlestown
Toronto
Redhead
Belmont
Lake Macquarie
Swansea
Gwandalan
Catherine Hill Bay
Lake Munmorah
Doyalson
Budgewoi
Noraville
Norah Head
Tuggerah Lake
The Entrance
South Kempsey
Hat Head NP
Kundabung
Crescent Head
Rollands Plains
Limeburners Creek NR
Point Plomer
Saltwater Lake
Telegraph Point
Blackmans Point
Lake Innes
Lake Innes Nature Res
Lake Cathie
Bonny Hills
Queens Lake
Kew
North Haven
Laurieton
Watson Taylor Lake
Johns River
Coralville
Crowdy Bay National Park
Moorland
Crowdy Head
Harrington
Manning Point
Farquhar Inlet
Old Bar
Wallabi Point
Diamond Beach
Hallidays Point
Failford
Tuncurry
Forster
Forster Keys
Wallis Lake
Coomba
Elizabeth Bay
Elizabeth Beach
Blueys Beach
Smiths Lake
Sugarloaf Bay
Myall Lake
Seal Rocks
Boolambayte Lake
Myall Lakes National Park
Broughton Island
PACIFIC HWY
SOUTH PACIFIC OCEAN
TASMAN SEA
152°
153°
-32°
-33°
-34°

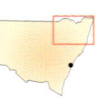

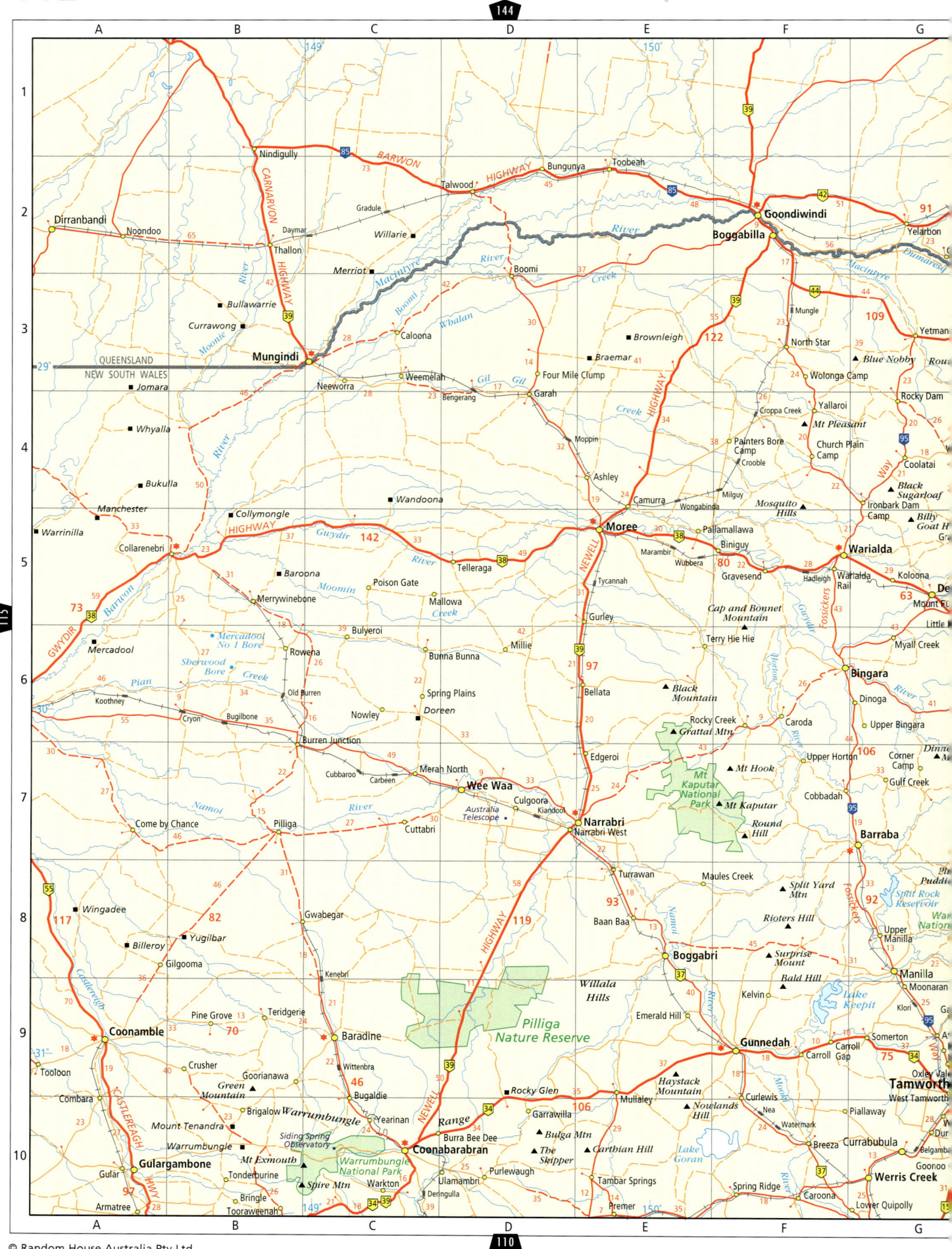

112 North-East New South Wales

0 10 20 30 40 50
kilometres
145
111
H J K L M N P
1 2 3 4 5 6 7 8 9 10
Warwick
Karara
Lake Leslie
Main Range National Park
Rockbrae
Emu Vale
Lake Moogerah
Killarney
Legume
Old Koreelah
Urbenville
Dalveen
Wylie Creek
Rivertree Peak
Tooloom
The Summit
Liston
Stanthorpe
Amosfield
Pikedale
Browns Mtn
Limevale
Sundown National Park
Glen Aplin
Ballandean
Girraween Nat Pk
Bald Rock National Park
Boonoo Boonoo Nat Park
Boonoo Boonoo
Texas
Mt Gunyan
Glenlyon
Silver Spur
Lake Glenlyon
Wallangarra
Sunnyside
Tarban
Mingoola
Mole River
Riverton
Bonshaw
Mt Bowman
Maidenhead
Round Hill
Kathida
Tenterfield
Bryans Gap
Leechs Gully
Sandy Hill
Drake
Black Mtn
Surface Hill
Billyrimba
Bluff Rock
Sandy Flat
Bolivia
Torrington
Stannum
Tent Hill
Emmaville
Strathbogie
Deepwater
Ashford
Pindari Dam
Bukkula
Tree Hill
Kings Plains Nat Park
Kings Plains
Dundee Rail
Dundee
Wellingrove
Nullamanna
Sapphire
Inverell
Elsmore
Swan Vale
Matheson
Glen Innes
Stonehenge
Red Range
Yarrowford
Bald Nob
Glen Elgin
Black Mtn
Gilgai
Stannifer
Carters Mtn
Stanborough
Tingha
Kangaroo Camp
Maybole
Glencoe
Pinkett
Mount Mitchell
Ben Lomond
Wandsworth
Llangothlin Lake
Backwater
Tenterden
Llangothlin
Wards Mistake
Bundarra
Georges Mtn
Guyra
Baldersleigh
Abington
Pine Mtn
Black Mountain
Joeys Knob
Mt Davidson
Aberfoyle
Torryburn
Kingstown
Yarrowyck
Mitchells Flat
Armidale
Waterfall
Hillgrove
Wollomombi
Jeogla
Round Mtn
Rocky River
Uralla
Castle Doyle
Gostwyck
Enmore
Oxley Wild Rivers National Park
Longford
Kentucky
Borah Mtn
Wollun
Baynes Mtn
Moona Plains
Walcha
Walcha Road
Woolbrook
Moonbi
Limbri
Aberbaldie
Glen Morrison
Weabonga
Dungowan
Brackendale
Mt Sugarloaf
Niangala
Woolomin
Chaffey Res
Bowling Alley Point
Ogunbil
Riamukka
Yarrowitch
Myrtle Scrub
Mount Seaview
Mt Seaview
Kangaroo Flat
Mt Werrikimbe
Werrikimbe National Park
Mt Banda Banda
Kemps Pinnacle
Upper Rollands Plains
Forbes River
Kindee
Yarras
Ellenborough
Beechwood
Pappinbarra
Pembrooke
Bellangry
Rollands Plains
Telegraph Point
Blackmans Point
Port Macquarie
Kundabung
Crescent Head
Limeburners Creek NR
Point Plomer
Saltwater Lake
Kempsey
South Kempsey
Hat Head NP
Korogoro Point
Hat Head
Sherwood
Frederickton
Turners Flat
Gladstone
Smithtown
Kinchela
Jerseyville
Smoky Cape
Arakoon
South West Rocks
Trial Bay
Clybucca
Willawarrin
Toorooka
Kookaburra
Daisy Plains
Oven Mtn
Bellbrook
Comara
Georges Creek
Five Day Creek
Burrapine
Talarm
Bulingary
Eungai
Warrell Creek
Macksville
Scotts Head
Grassy Head
Stuarts Point
Nambucca Heads
Bowraville
Missabotti
Valla Beach
Urunga
Killiekrankie Mtn
New England National Park
Point Lookout
Majors Point
Ebor
Darkwood
Bellingen
Brierfield
Thora
Raleigh
Repton
Mylestom
Sawtell
Boambee
Coffs Harbour
Valery
Bonville
Dorrigo
Dorrigo NP
Brooklana
Megan
Cascade
Bostobrick
North Dorrigo
Fernbrook
Hernani
Wongwibinda
Cathedral Rock NP
Monkey Point
Tyringham
Dundurrabin
Paddys Plain
Billys Creek
Marengo Plain
Mt Hyland Nat Res
Chaelundi Mtn
Clouds Creek
Guy Fawkes River National Park
Red Herring Hill
Nymboida
Glenreagh
Towallum
Lowanna
Ulong
Nana Glen
Coramba
Korora
Moonee Beach
Emerald Beach
Sandy Beach
Woolgoolga
Arrawarra
Corindi Beach
Red Rock
Kungala
Halfway Creek
Yuraygir National Park
Wooli
Bare Point
Minnie Water
Pillar Valley
Braunstone
Coutts Crossing
OBX Creek
Buccarumbi
Dalmorton
Louis Point
Newton Boyd
Mann River Nature Res
Nymboida National Park
Grafton
South Grafton
Tucabia
Ulmarra
Koolkhan
Copmanhurst
Jackadgery
Cangai
Gibraltar Range NP
Gibraltar Range
Washpool National Park
Timbarra
Gordon Brook
Coaldale
Barretts Creek
Woodford Dale
Lawrence
Tyndale
Brooms Head
Sandon
Sandon Bluffs
Yuraygir National Park
The Bald Knob
Angourie
Wooloweyah Estuary
Yamba
Iluka
Maclean
Harwood
Chatsworth
Mororo
Mulloway Point
Bundjalung National Park
Tabbimoble
Whiporie
Camira Creek
Baryulgil
Wyan
Rappville
Coombell
Busbys Flat
Alice
Ellangowan
Woodburn
Evans Head
Snapper Point
Broadwater
Broadwater NP
Dungarubba
Wardell
Coraki
Tatham
Yorklea
Greenridge
Tuckurimba
Empire Vale
Ballina
Wollongbar
Alstonville
Lismore
Lennox Head
Bexhill
Goolmangar
Bentley
Casino
Woodview
Fairy Hill
Mallanganee
Tabulam
Mummulgum
Theresa Creek
Doubtful Creek
Dyraaba Central
Ettrick
Bonalbo
Old Bonalbo
Paddys Flat
Cedar Point
Kyogle
Rock Valley
The Channon
Dunoon
Modanville
Rosebank
Nashua
Bangalow
Suffolk Park
Byron Bay
Goonengerry
Mullumbimby
Brunswick Heads
Ocean Shores
Wooyung
Burringbar
Pottsville Beach
Uki
Kunghur
Nightcap Nat Pk
Mt Matheson
Nimbin
Cawongla
Blue Knob
Horseshoe Creek
Eden Creek
Wiangaree
Roseberry
Grevillia
Old Grevillia
Mount Lion
Lindesay View
Cougal
Woodenbong
Dalman
Mt Barney
Mt Barney Nat Park
Rathdowney
Tamrookum
Laravale
Numinbah Valley
Lamington Nat Park
Springbrook Nat Park
Bald Mtn
Border Ranges NP
Tyalgum
Chillingham
Numinbah
Murwillumbah
Bogangar
Condong
Tumbulgum
Kingscliff
Chinderah
Bilambil
Banora Point
Fingal Head
Tweed Heads
Coolangatta
Burleigh Heads
Mudgeeraba
Lake Coolmunda
Tank Mtn
GREAT DIVIDING RANGE
MT LINDESAY HWY
BRUXNER HWY
GWYDIR HWY
NEW ENGLAND HWY
OXLEY HWY
PACIFIC HWY
Summerland Way
Richmond Range
Coast Range
SOUTH PACIFIC OCEAN
TASMAN SEA
N
29°
30°
31°
152
153

114 North-West New South Wales

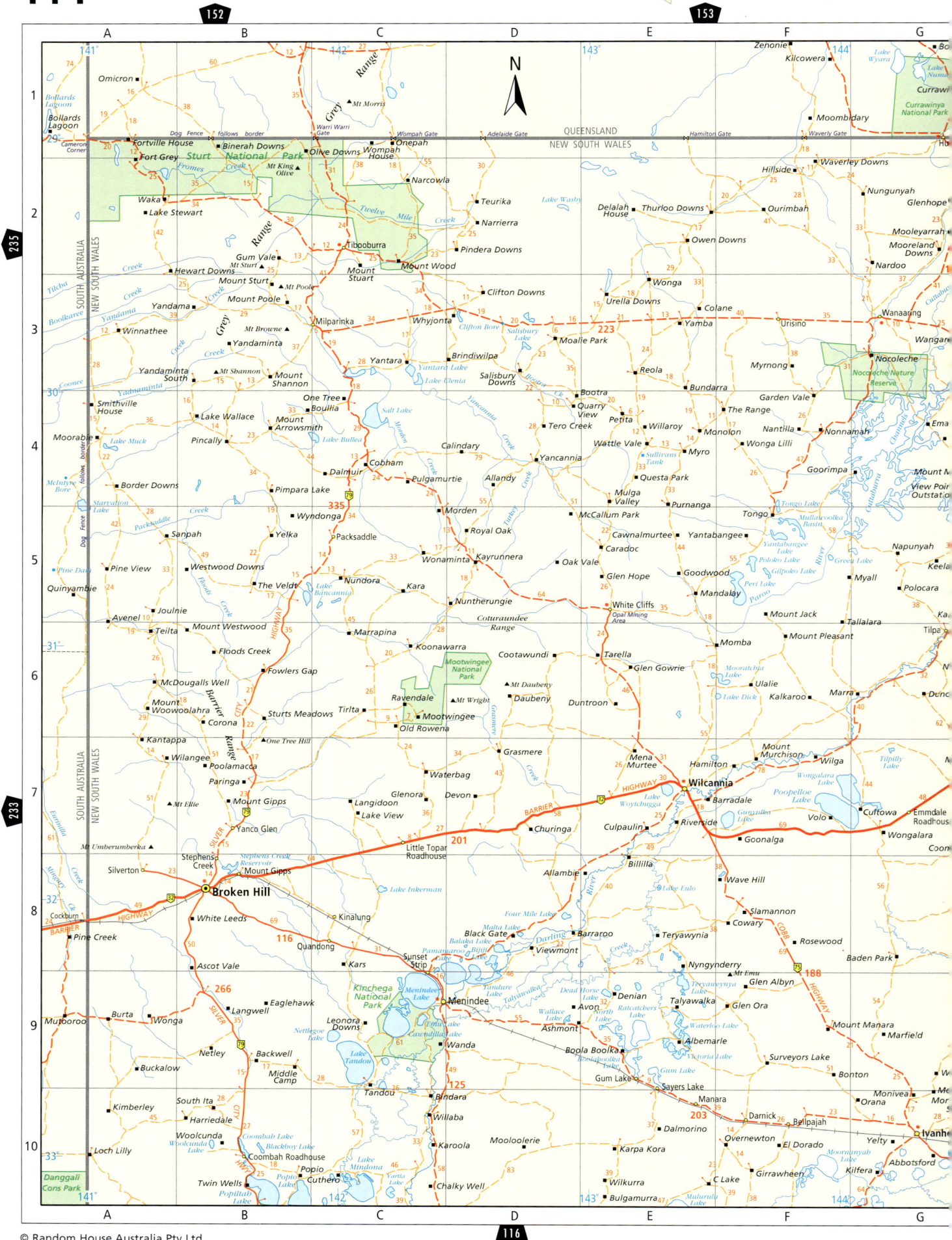

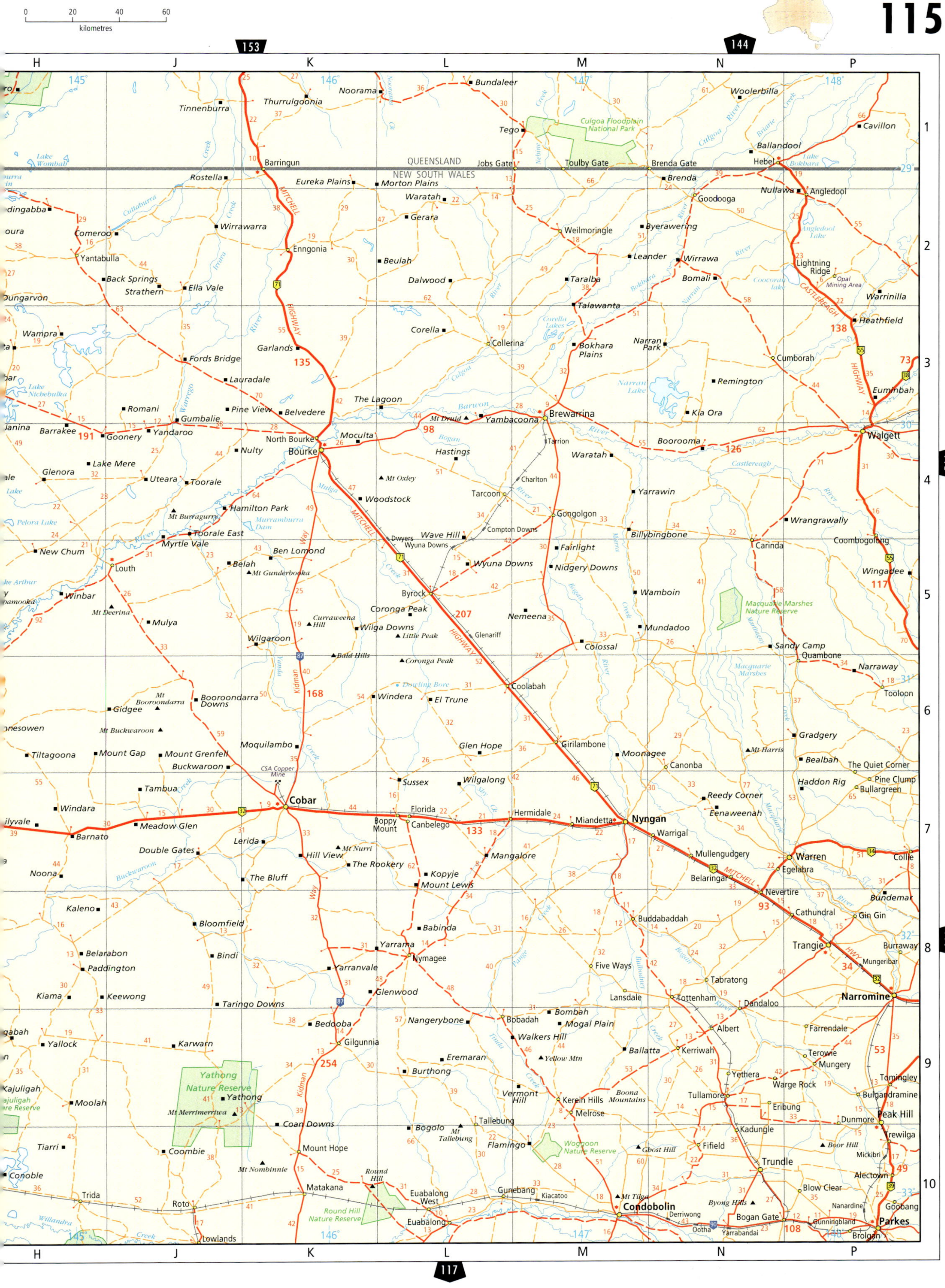

0 20 40 60
kilometres
153
144
112
110
117
H J K L M N P
1 2 3 4 5 6 7 8 9 10
145°
146°
147°
148°
29°
30°
31°
32°
33°
QUEENSLAND
NEW SOUTH WALES
Tinnenbura
Thurrulgoonia
Noorama
Bundaleer
Tego
Culgoa Floodplain National Park
Woolerbilla
Cavillon
Ballandool
Hebel
Lake Bokhara
Lake Wombah
Barringun
Jobs Gate
Toulby Gate
Brenda Gate
Rostella
Eureka Plains
Morton Plains
Brenda
Goodooga
Nullawa
Angledool
Waratah
Gerara
Weilmoringle
Byerawering
Angledool Lake
dingabba
Comeroo
Wirrawarra
Enngonia
Beulah
Leander
Wirrawa
Lightning Ridge
Opal Mining Area
Yantabulla
Back Springs
Strathern
Ella Vale
Dalwood
Taralba
Bomali
Coocoran Lake
Warrinilla
Dungarvon
Talawanta
Heathfield
Wampra
Corella
Collerina
Corella Lakes
Bokhara Plains
Narran Park
Cumborah
Garlands
Fords Bridge
Lauradale
Remington
Eumimbah
Lake Nichebulka
Narran Lake
The Lagoon
Romani
Pine View
Belvedere
Gumbalie
Barwon
Mt Druid
Yambacoona
Brewarrina
Kia Ora
Janina
Barrakee
Goonery
Yandaroo
North Bourke
Moculta
Tarrion
Boorooma
Walgett
Bourke
Nulty
Hastings
Waratah
Castlereagh
Lake Mere
Glenora
Uteara
Toorale
Mt Oxley
Charlton
Tarcoon
Yarrawin
Woodstock
Hamilton Park
Mt Burragurry
Murramburra Dam
Pelora Lake
Gongolgon
Wrangrawally
Compton Downs
Toorale East
Myrtle Vale
Dwyers
Wave Hill
Wyuna Downs
Billybingbone
Carinda
Coombogolong
New Chum
Ben Lomond
Fairlight
Louth
Belah
Mt Gunderbooka
Wyuna Downs
Nidgery Downs
Wingadee
Lake Arthur
Winbar
Byrock
Wamboin
Mt Deerina
Corongo Peak
Currawenna Hill
Nemeena
Macquarie Marshes Nature Reserve
Mulya
Wilga Downs
Little Peak
Glenariff
Mundadoo
Wilgaroon
Colossal
Sandy Camp
Quambone
Bald Hills
Coronga Peak
Macquarie Marshes
Narraway
Dowling Bore
Coolabah
Tooloon
Mt Booroondarra
Booroondarra Downs
Windera
El Trune
Gidgee
onesowen
Mt Buckwaroon
Gradgery
Moquilambo
Glen Hope
Girilambone
Mt Harris
Tiltagoona
Mount Gap
Mount Grenfell
Moonagee
Bealbah
Buckwaroon
Canonba
The Quiet Corner
CSA Copper Mine
Sussex
Wilgalong
Haddon Rig
Pine Clump
Bullargreen
Tambua
Reedy Corner
Windara
Cobar
Florida
Hermidale
Eenaweenah
ilyvale
Meadow Glen
Boppy Mount
Canbelego
Miandetta
Nyngan
Barnato
Warrigal
Double Gates
Lerida
Mt Nurri
Mullengudgery
Warren
Collie
Hill View
Mangalore
Noona
The Rookery
Kopyje
Egelabra
The Bluff
Mount Lewis
Belaringar
Nevertire
Bundemar
Buckwaroon
Kaleno
Cathundral
Gin Gin
Buddabaddah
Bloomfield
Babinda
Belarabon
Yarrama
Trangie
Burraway
Bindi
Nymagee
Mungeribar
Paddington
Five Ways
Yarravale
Tabratong
Kiama
Keewong
Glenwood
Lansdale
Tottenham
Narromine
Taringo Downs
Dandaloo
Bedooba
Nangerybone
Bobadah
Bombah
Mogal Plain
Farrendale
gabah
Albert
Yallock
Karwarn
Gilgunnia
Walkers Hill
Ballatta
Kerriwah
Terowie
Eremaran
Yellow Mtn
Mungery
Yathong Nature Reserve
Burthong
Yethera
Tomingley
Warge Rock
Kajuligah
Yathong
Vermont Hill
Kerein Hills
Boona Mountains
Tullamore
Bulgandramine
Moolah
Mt Merrimerriwa
Melrose
Eribung
Peak Hill
Coan Downs
Tallebung
Dunmore
Tiarri
Bogolo
Mt Tallebung
Kadungle
Trewilga
Coombie
Mount Hope
Flamingo
Woggoon Nature Reserve
Ghost Hill
Fifield
Boor Hill
Mt Nombinnie
Trundle
Mickibri
Conoble
Round Hill
Alectown
Trida
Matakana
Eubalong West
Gunebang
Kiacatoo
Mt Tilga
Byong Hills
Blow Clear
Roto
Condobolin
Derriwong
Narardine
Goobang
Round Hill Nature Reserve
Euabalong
Bogan Gate
Gunningbland
Parkes
Willandra
Lowlands
Ootha
Yarrabandai
Bogan
MITCHELL
HIGHWAY
Kidman Way
CASTLEREAGH HIGHWAY
MITCHELL HWY
Culgoa River
Narran River
Bokhara River
Barwon River
Bogan River
Darling River
Warrego River
Paroo River
Cuttaburra
Mulga Creek
Irrara Creek
Yanda Creek
Marra Creek
Macquarie River
Duck Creek
Crooked Creek
Gunningbar Creek
Lachlan River
191
135
98
126
207
168
133
93
34
254
53
49
108
138
73
117
71
55
38
32
87
90
39

116 South-West New South Wales

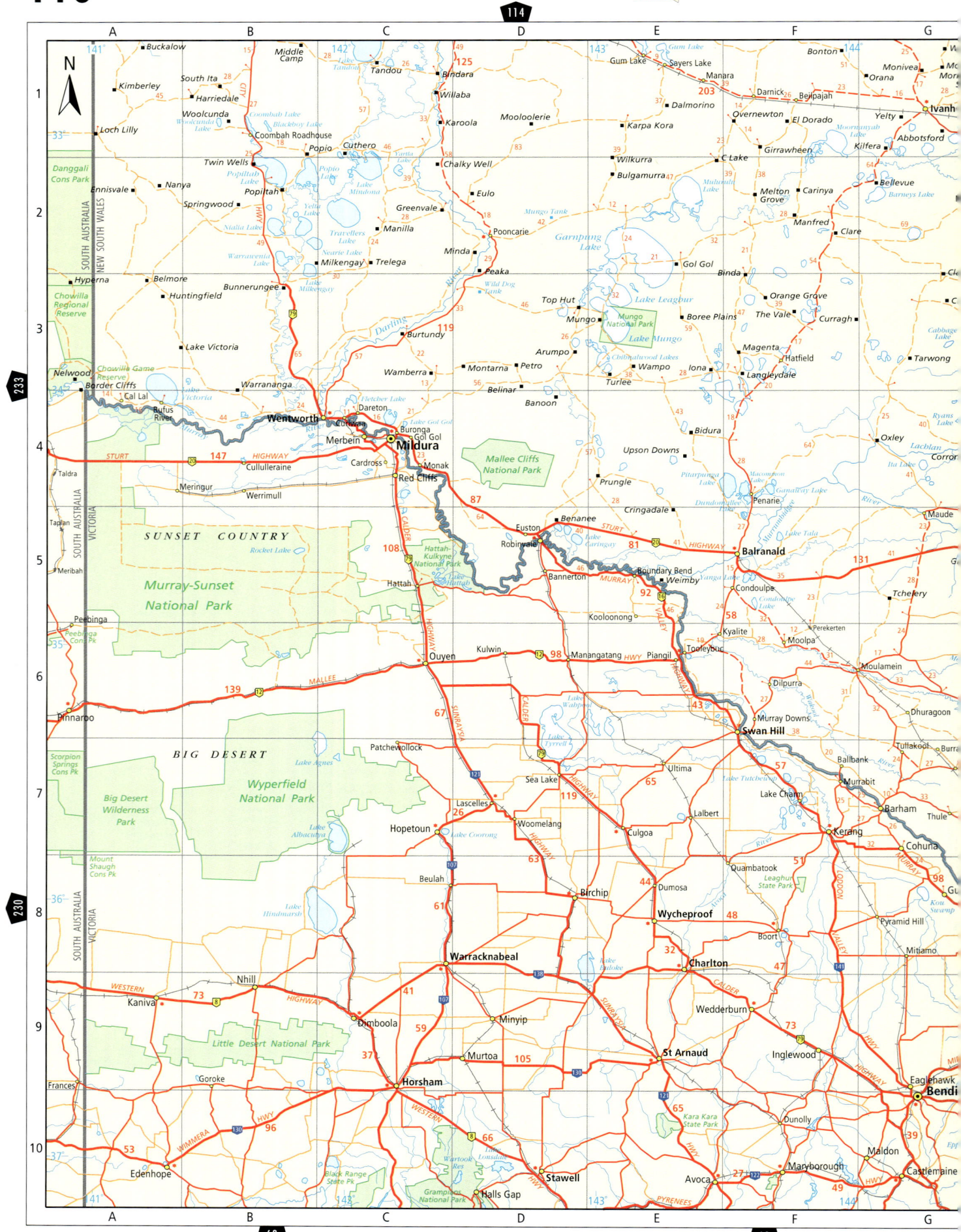

0 20 40 60
kilometres

115

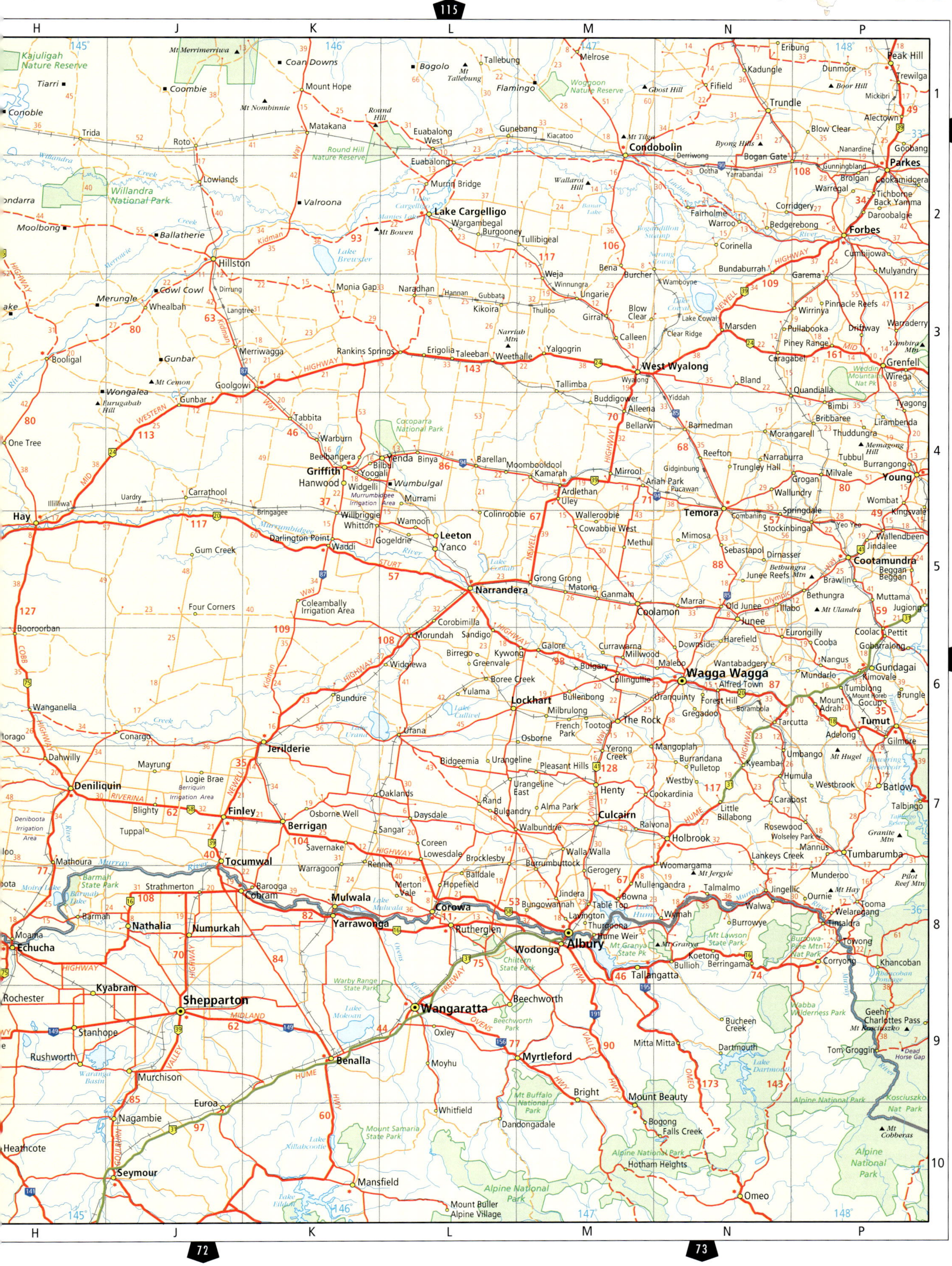

110

109

72

73

QUEENSLAND

FISHING HOT SPOTS

- The Gold Coast (pp. 120–1)
- Moreton Bay (pp. 122–3)
- Moreton Island and North Stradbroke Island (pp. 124–5)
- The Sunshine Coast (pp. 126–7)
- Noosa to Tin Can Bay (pp. 128–9)
- Fraser Island (pp. 130–1)
- Fraser's Offshore Grounds (pp. 132–3)
- Seventeen Seventy and Round Hill (pp. 134–5)
- Hinze Dam (pp. 136–7)
- Noosa River Bass (pp. 138–9)
- Valley of Lakes (pp. 140–1)
- The Golden West (pp. 142–3)

The aptly named Sunshine State is a Mecca for visitors of all persuasions, but especially for keen recreational anglers. Few other Australian states, with the possible exception of Western Australia, offer such a diverse range of opportunities and so many wonderful places to cast a line, and *none* has a more extensive list of desirable fish species for the angler to pursue.

From the hot, dry Channel Country of the southern and central interior, through the rugged ranges and deep chasms of the Great Divide, to the sun-drenched coast and Great Barrier Reef of the tropical north, Queensland is a piscatorial paradise that could well have been designed by a celestial committee of avid anglers! In all too many instances, however, Queensland's fishing history since European settlement has been one of paradise lost.

By the early 1980s, many important fish stocks in Queensland were in a parlous state. Some were teetering on the brink of oblivion as a result of rampant overharvesting and environmental degradation, and much of blame for this situation was directly attributable to the march of so-called 'progress', as reflected in the state's rapid population growth and economic development over preceding decades.

After many years of what is widely regarded as having been a mixture of mismanagement and undermanagement through the 1960s, 1970s and 1980s, however, the powers-that-be in Queensland (both bureaucratic and political) finally appear to have recognised the true value of this state's considerable fresh and saltwater fisheries. These resources are now being husbanded in a more sustainable manner for the maximum benefit of all Australians.

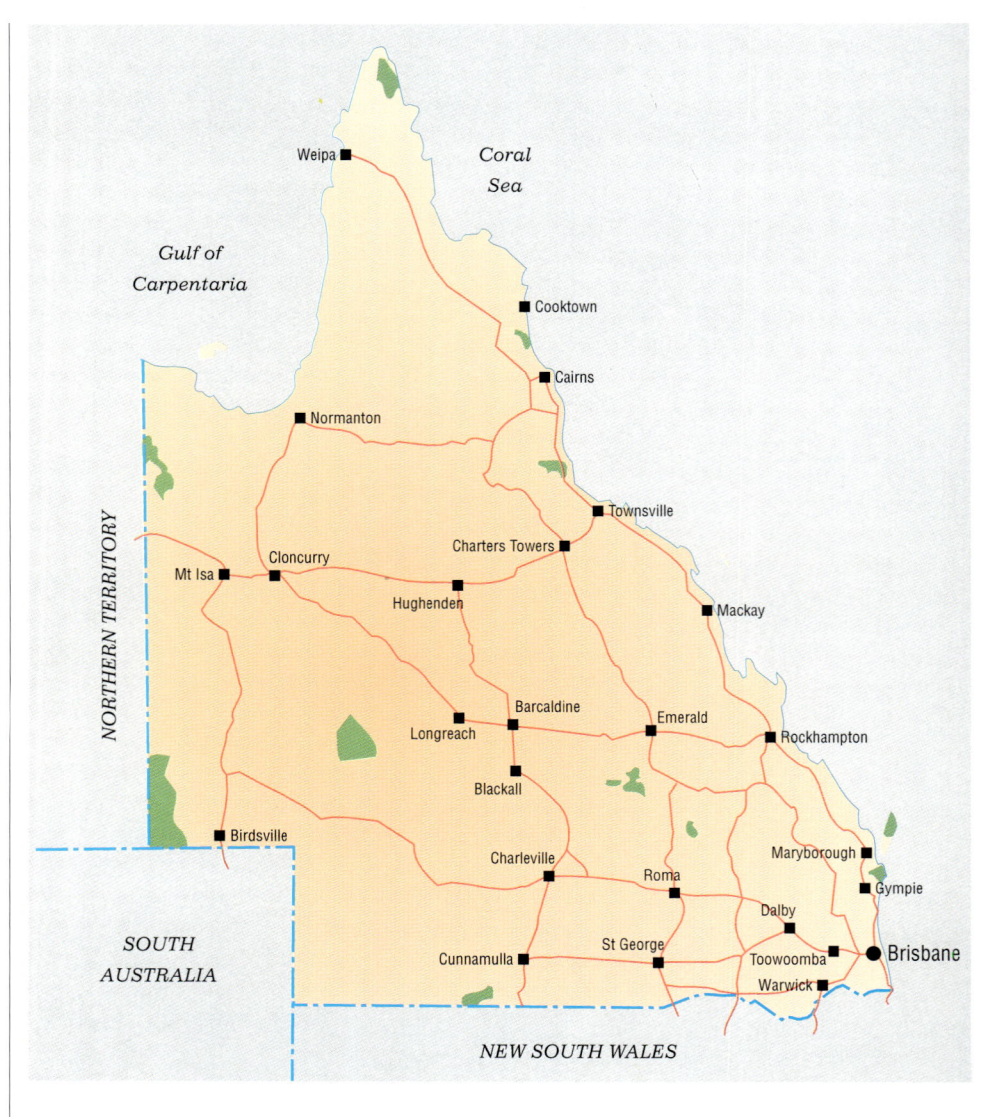

Much of the credit for this newfound attitude must go to motivated and dedicated recreational anglers who — acting both alone and in concert with others of a similar bent — have coerced, cajoled and convinced the elected and non-elected keepers of the public purse to take better care of Queensland's diminishing fisheries resources.

Today, there is reason for guarded optimism. Despite recent netting bans in specific locations, barramundi remain a relatively rare catch in popular spots such as the Hinchinbrook Channel or Cairns Inlet, where they were once plentiful, and the unique Mary River cod has recently been classified as an endangered species. In many areas, however, clear progress is being made.

One shining example is the opening of large water supply reservoirs and impoundments in the south-east of the state to carefully managed recreational angling, and the successful stocking of these waterways with Australian bass, golden perch, Murray and Mary River cod, saratoga and other sport fish species. Parallel development is evident further north, where giant dams such as Tinaroo, on the tablelands above Cairns, are being transformed into significant angling assets, thanks to intelligent, large-scale stocking programs.

Also heartening is the advent and general acceptance of stricter size, bag and gear limits throughout the recreational sector, along with closed seasons, fish tagging, improved research and education programs. At the same time, commercial fishing operations are coming under increasing public scrutiny, and their less desirable and less sustainable practices are being openly questioned, as are the activities of land developers, local councils and others who would destroy mangrove forests, de-snag rivers or pump untreated effluent and other pollutants into waterways in the quest for a quick buck.

This important change in attitude is evident even at the grass roots level of the Queensland fishing fraternity. Today, concepts such as sport fishing, catch-and-release and environmental sustainability are gaining increasing acceptance, heralding a more enlightened era in the history of this state's fisheries.

Right now, Queensland is a wonderful place for a fishing holiday... and there's every reason to believe that it will only get *better* in coming years!

Contact Numbers

Information on fisheries rules and regulations in Queensland can be obtained by telephoning one of the numbers listed on this page.

QUEENSLAND FISHERIES MANAGEMENT AUTHORITY

Bowen	(07) 4786 3444	Mackay	(07) 4951 8724
Brisbane	(07) 3860 3506	Maryborough	(07) 4123 7722
Bundaberg	(07) 4153 7800	Mooloolooba	(07) 5444 4599
Cairns	(07) 4052 7404	Noosa	(07) 5449 7555
Gladstone	(07) 4976 0729	Port Douglas	(07) 4099 5160
Gold Coast	(07) 5583 5500	Rockhampton	(07) 4936 0218
Hervey Bay	(07) 4125 3989	Roma	(07) 4622 9999
Ingham	(07) 4776 1611	Thursday Island	(07) 4069 1772
Karumba	(07) 4745 9142	Townsville	(07) 4772 7311

FISHERIES ENFORCEMENT HOT LINE
(24 Hours)
1800 017 116

Top left and right: Moreton Island is right on Brisbane's doorstep and offers some excellent beach, rock, reef and offshore fishing opportunities
Above: Lake Wivenhoe in Queensland's Valley of Lakes west of Brisbane
Right: An aerial view of Indian Head in Fraser Island's Great Sandy National Park

THE GOLD COAST

IN BRIEF

MAP REFERENCE: PAGE 145 N8

GETTING THERE Southport and Surfers Paradise lie 70 km south of Brisbane along the Pacific Highway
BEST TIME TO FISH Year-round
BEST TIME TO TRAVEL Year-round
MAJOR ANGLING SPECIES Bream, flathead, whiting, tailor, trevally, snapper, mulloway, mackerel and various reef species
SPECIAL RESTRICTIONS Internal combustion engines are not permitted on Hinze Dam
WARNINGS The Seaway and The Broadwater can become very rough in strong winds. All tidal areas are subject to powerful currents and there are potentially dangerous bars at the ocean entrances
CHARTER BOATS AND FISHING GUIDES Gold Coast Offshore Fishing Co., telephone 0412 147 170; Game Striker Charters, telephone 018 761 293; Age of Reason Charters, telephone 018 760 259

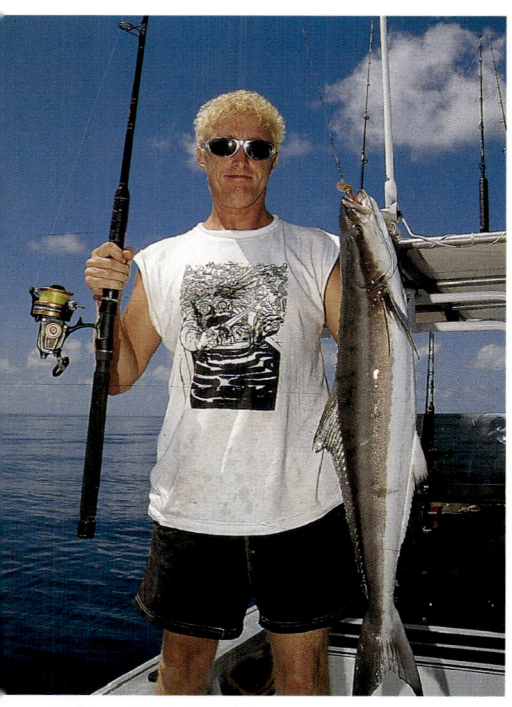

Cobia or black kingfish are a highly prized catch from ocean waters off the Gold Coast

Better known to many visitors from around Australia and overseas for its glitzy strip of beach-front, high-rise apartments, night spots, shops, restaurants, surfing beaches and other tourists attractions, the heavily developed and densely populated Gold Coast region of south-eastern Queensland also remains a prime recreational fishing destination. Despite significant — and sometimes detrimental — alterations to the natural environment, the Gold Coast's extensive estuarine waterways and offshore fishing grounds continue to produce a comparatively high standard of angling.

Many of the holiday makers who come here with other activities in mind would be amazed to see some of the catches regularly made by successful anglers working these waters.

SOUTHPORT AND THE BROADWATER

The extensive area of semi-enclosed estuarine water stretching south and west from Jumpinpin, at the top of South Stradbroke Island, to the Southport Bar, and including Coombabah Lake and the Coomera and lower Nerang rivers, has been greatly modified by human activities over the past century. Many areas of this waterway have changed dramatically in appearance and topography, particularly since the early 1970s.

The most significant modifications have been those involved with the construction of the new Seaway and the Wave Break Island, situated behind the bar at the entrance of the Seaway off Southport, towards the southern end of the expanse of water known as The Broadwater.

These changes have certainly altered the standard of fishing and the mix of species on offer in these waters, and many anglers would argue that at least some of these changes have been for the better. Certainly, offshore and deep-water species such as trevally, tailor, yellowtail kingfish and mulloway (jewfish) have become more common inside the lower estuary reaches since the construction of the new Seaway, as have seasonal tropical visitors such as tarpon (ox-eye herring), queenfish and mangrove jacks.

Estuarine species including bream, whiting, flathead and luderick are nowadays more likely to be encountered in good numbers further inside the system, especially northward towards Jumpinpin and in the various rivers and tidal lakes feeding this vast system. However, excellent bream and luderick fishing is also available around the various retaining walls and wave breaks of the new artificial structures.

SPECIES AND TECHNIQUES

For bluewater anglers, the modified entrance to the Seaway provides safer and more consistent access to adjacent offshore fishing grounds that continue to produce excellent catches of snapper and other reef species, as well as spotted and Spanish mackerel, various tuna, cobia, marlin and sailfish at certain times of year.

Inside The Broadwater, one the most popular and abundant species remains the sand or summer whiting. These delicious little fish are caught in good numbers and sizes, mostly between September and May each year. However, a few whiting can also be taken right through the mild winter months at certain proven locations.

Many of the best whiting catches are taken at night or in the early hours of the morning, around first light, before the level of boat traffic increases. The pick of the baits for targeting these fish is the blood worm, with local Cribb Island worms offering a very good substitute.

As the whiting action begins to taper off in April or May, the emphasis shifts to bream, which are traditionally present in huge numbers, especially up around Jumpinpin. It's not uncommon to find bream schooled up in any one of the deeper gutters off the edges of the many sand banks in this area, while oyster leases and other structures also attract these popular fish in large numbers.

Most recognised bream baits — especially yabbies (pink nippers) and prawns — work well, but mullet gut is also a prime fish taker, especially during and after a big 'fresh', when the water is discoloured by significant amounts of run-off.

Dusky flathead are the other mainstay species for estuary anglers throughout The Broadwater and its many tributaries. While some flatties — especially smaller specimens — can be caught year-round, the bigger 'lizards', as they're popularly known, become much more active during September. This big fish activity peaks in October or early November, and then tapers off a little through the summer.

Today, many of these fish are taken by slowly trolling deep diving minnow-style lures along gutters, channels and weed bed edges in 2 to 5 m of water, particularly while travelling with the current on a the run-out (ebb) tide. Other flathead fall to cast and retrieved lures or more traditional natural baits such as pilchards, sardines, whitebait, fish strips, small live or dead mullet, prawns and yabbies fished around drop-offs, creek mouths and gutter junctions.

These days an average Broadwater 'lizard' will weigh anywhere from 400 g to 2.5 kg, although monsters in the 3- to 9-kg range are still taken on a reasonably regular basis. Many anglers choose to release these larger female fish and keep just a few smaller flathead for a meal.

THE NERANG RIVER

The Nerang River enters The Broadwater at its southern end, after passing behind the hotels and high-rise apartments of downtown Surfers Paradise. Although lined for much of its lower length with houses, shops and apartments, and playing host to myriad fast-moving water craft, the Nerang estuary still produces good to excellent catches of whiting, bream and dusky flathead, particularly at night and in the early hours of the morning, just before and after first light.

There are also some hefty mangrove jacks living in this stretch of water. Most of these fish take up residence on deeper rock bars or other oyster-encrusted outcrops, while some also hang around pylons, moorings, embankments and various structures. These mangrove jacks are not easy to catch, preferring to feed in 3 to 5 m of water when the tidal run or current is running at its hardest. For those anglers willing to invest the necessary effort trolling deep-diving lures or drifting live baits, however, some stunning fish in the 2- to 4-kg plus class are available.

Higher up the Nerang lies Hinze Dam, which holds back a body of fresh water officially known as Advancetown Lake. This pretty stretch of water has been well stocked with Australian bass, and provides superb fishing, especially on a warm spring or early summer evening. Fishing in Hinze Dam and the upper Nerang River below the dam wall is dealt with in more detail on pp. 136–7.

The Broadwater runs behind the hotel and high-rise apartment strip of Surfers Paradise

A 'squire'-sized snapper from offshore waters

MORETON BAY

IN BRIEF

MAP REFERENCE: PAGE 145 N6

GETTING THERE Moreton Bay is on the south-east coast of Queensland — Brisbane lies on the shores of Moreton Bay and the Gold Coast is adjacent

BEST TIME TO FISH Year-round

BEST TIME TO TRAVEL Year-round

MAJOR ANGLING SPECIES Bream, whiting, flathead, longtail tuna, mackerel tuna, spotted mackerel and cobia

SPECIAL RESTRICTIONS Areas closed to fishing near Redcliffe, Jumpinpin and the Gold Coast

WARNINGS Extreme caution should be taken around bar entrances at Caloundra, South Passage, Jumpinpin and the Southport Seaway. Small boats fishing in their vicinity must take care during periods of strong tidal flow. Open water sections of Moreton Bay become uncomfortable when wind speeds reach 15 knots and progressively more dangerous if they strengthen

CHARTER BOATS AND FISHING GUIDES Check Yellow Pages for details or ask advice at local tackle stores; Alibi Charters Offshore Reef Fishing, telephone 0412 235 460

Moreton Bay is formed behind a series of sand barrier islands: Moreton Island, North Stradbroke Island and South Stradbroke Island. (Fishing on Moreton and North Stradbroke islands is covered in greater detail on pp. 124–5.) Even residents of Brisbane who have never fished there before are often surprised to learn that access to the better fishing spots in Moreton Bay requires either a 4WD vehicle or a boat.

For those who do not own or have access to a 4WD, the best fishing in Moreton Bay is from Bribie Island at the northern end of the bay. Pumicestone Passage, which separates Bribie from the mainland, was recently closed to commercial netting. This will inevitably focus more attention on this area from recreational anglers, who should find better and better fishing as Pumicestone recovers.

Pumicestone Passage can be treated as a large estuary system which is, almost entirely, only fishable from a boat. Bribie Island, however, unlike all the other islands in Moreton Bay, is at least connected to the mainland by a bridge. People wishing to sample some of the rather good calm-water beach fishing around the southern part of the island can get there in the family car.

Bribie Island's southern beaches at Skirmish Point and in the suburbs of Woorim and Bongaree are within easy walking distance of various roads. The several waterside parks and reserves make them eminently suited to family fishing outings. The main catch is the everpresent summer or sand whiting. Live worms available from local bait shops are the best bait. Yabbies pumped fresh from any sand flat in Pumicestone Passage or beach worms caught from Bribie Island's eastern beach are both worthwhile substitutes. Skirmish Point also regularly produces tailor.

With the aid of a boat, the entire length of Pumicestone Passage is fishable from ramps in the vicinity of the bridge, in the Caloundra area (at the northern entrance to Pumicestone Passage) or at Toorbul or Donnybrook.

There is some bankside fishing available in Brisbane's bayside suburbs (the Redcliffe Peninsula in the north and the Wynnum to Redland Bay area to the south), and also around the port at the mouth of the Brisbane River. Generally speaking, however, the fishing here is not as productive as in other parts of Moreton Bay.

Apart from Pumicestone Passage, Moreton Bay can be divided into two distinct areas: the northern open-water section from Caloundra down the eastern side of Bribie Island to where Peel Island in the south marks a change to the more sheltered waters extending south all the way to the Southport Seaway, where the Gold Coast begins.

SOUTHERN MORETON BAY

The southern section of Moreton Bay shelters behind North and South Stradbroke islands. A gap between the two is a typical southern Queensland bar entrance. The area immediately west of it is called Jumpinpin. 'The Pin', as locals know it, is an expansive mangrove wetland in an almost pristine state. The Gold Coast has encroached somewhat with canal estates creeping towards Jumpinpin from the south. Largely, however, the southern end of Moreton Bay remains a fantastic area of fish habitat and most of it has been protected from development

The very southern part of Moreton Bay is known as the Southport Broadwater. Some shore-based fishing—without the need for a 4WD vehicle—is available from the Seaway entrance's southern breakwall. Here, a tailor-style surf rod casting a Western Australian pilchard is the preferred rig amongst regulars. Tailor, trevally and an odd mulloway will usually comprise most of the catch.

Both the Broadwater and Jumpinpin areas are justifiably famous for bream 'runs', consistent catches of quality whiting and their flathead fishing. The Broadwater and Jumpinpin are best accessed by boat—indeed, the latter is only accessible by boat.

During winter, bream spawn near the Southport and Jumpinpin bars. Peaks of activity occur during the full-moon periods in July and August. The classic southern Queensland 'Sloppy Joe' rod mounted with a sidecast reel accounts for most bream.

Flathead fishing is best in spring as both smaller male and the larger female flathead congregate near the bar opening to spawn in September and October. Lure fishing for flathead has gained an enormous following in southern Queensland in recent years, and flathead may be caught on lures at Jumpinpin and in The Broadwater all year round.

Sand whiting are available the entire year in southern Moreton Bay, although their popular name of summer whiting correctly indicates that the best fishing for this species is during the warmer months. Specialist whiting anglers tend to use an extra-soft version of the traditional 'Sloppy Joe', fine line and very light sinker weights to target big whiting. Various local worms, such as the Cribb Island variety, dug fresh and fished live are the best baits.

The Southport Broadwater area is easily accessible from several ramps; a good street directory will soon locate these. The Broadwater is several kilometres by water from ramps at Jacobs Well and Cabbage Tree Point to reach Jumpinpin. There are also private ramps and a marina nearby. These charge for launching, but have secure storage for cars and trailers if anglers are out fishing overnight.

At anchor in the shallows of eastern Moreton Bay

NORTHERN MORETON BAY

North of Peel Island, Moreton Bay opens out into a body of water expansive enough to require boats suited to offshore use. Northern Moreton Bay is big, wide, open and shallow, and deserves the utmost respect.

While a 12-foot (3.7-m) tinny may catch a lot of fish from southern Moreton Bay, it has no place in the north. Popular ramp access points include the boat harbour complexes at Manly, south of the Brisbane River mouth, and at Scarborough on the Redcliffe Peninsula. Some prefer to launch their boats in the Brisbane River itself. Smaller ramp facilities at Wellington Point and Cabbage Tree Creek at Shorncliffe are also popular. The ramps in Pumicestone Passage near the bridge to Bribie Island are often used to fish the very northern part of Moreton Bay.

Fishing in northern Moreton Bay has four aspects: sand crabbing, fishing for whiting, reef fishing and fishing for open-water pelagic species such as mackerel and tuna.

Using what is locally known as a 'dilly' (witch's hat has long proven to be the most effective way of catching sand crabs in the bay. Sand crabs are found anywhere in the shallower waters of Moreton Bay's many sand bank systems, particularly in the southern area of Moreton Bay around Wynnum–Manly (Green, St Helena and Mud islands) and near the banks guarding the western edge of the South Passage bar between Moreton and North Stradbroke islands.

These areas are equally good places to fish for the small yet tasty winter (diver) whiting in the cooler months. Summertime brings the larger summer whiting.

Coral reefs near Mud, Green, St Helena and Peel islands and artificial reefs placed west of the Rous Channel (the Harry Atkinson Reef) and near Cowan Cowan (Curtin Artificial Reef) are the focus for reef fishing. Mostly the catch comprises small snapper (squire), sweetlip and parrot fish. The more southerly reefs hold big bream, too. The artificial reef near Cowan Cowan produces better quality snapper, particularly if fished at night, as it is situated in more open water. In addition, monster cobia take up residence here in spring.

Spinning the open waters of northern Moreton Bay by following flocks of working sea birds and casting baitfish-profiled metal lures at lurking mackerel and tuna has been developed into an art form by Brisbane sport fishers. Longtail and mackerel tuna are the main tuna species. Spotted mackerel were once the most popular target species, but unfortunately their numbers have been depleted considerably over the past decade by commercial ring netting.

The high-speed retrieve threadline reels and powerful two-handed spin rods they're matched to have become known nationwide as 'Moreton Bay spin sticks' as a result of their popularity on northern Moreton Bay.

Longtail or northern bluefin tuna frequently visit Moreton Bay

MORETON ISLAND AND NORTH STRADBROKE ISLAND

IN BRIEF

MAP REFERENCE: PAGE 145 N6

GETTING THERE Moreton Island and North Stradbroke Island lie off the coast of Brisbane
Moreton Island — barge to Kooringal and The Wrecks departs Lytton (near the mouth of the Brisbane River), telephone (07) 3895 1000; barge to Bulwer departs Scarborough Boat Harbour, telephone (07) 3203 6399
North Stradbroke Island — barge to Dunwich departs Toondah Habour, Cleveland, telephone (07) 3286 6666
BEST TIME TO FISH January and February for marlin; April for sailfish; summer to autumn for other pelagic species; winter for reef fish; year-round for bream, whiting, dart and flathead; late winter for tailor
BEST TIME TO TRAVEL Year-round
MAJOR ANGLING SPECIES Black marlin, sailfish, Spanish mackerel, cobia, wahoo, snapper, sweetlip, pearl perch, bream, whiting, dart, flathead and tailor
SPECIAL RESTRICTIONS Camping permits required for Moreton Island, telephone (07) 3408 2710
WARNINGS Extreme caution should be taken around South Passage Bar
CHARTER BOATS AND FISHING GUIDES Many available – check Yellow Pages for details

---

Brisbane and the worries of an urban existence are a world away from Moreton and North Stradbroke islands, despite their proximity to Queensland's capital. Although officially a suburb of Brisbane, Moreton Island is true wilderness only accessible from the mainland by boat.

There are no sealed roads on Moreton Island and as for 'townships'... there is Kooringal at the southern end of the island; Cowan Cowan on the central western coast, near Tangalooma Resort; and Bulwer, near the northern tip of the island's west coast. These townships or villages mostly consist of weekender-style cottages, and while Bulwer and Kooringal do have a shop and service station each, the 'streets' are sand and 4WD only.

North Stradbroke is somewhat more 'civilised', with bitumen roads, at least on the northern part of the island. The three settlements—Amity Point, Point Lookout and Dunwich—are connected by sealed road. The entire southern section is 4WD territory, however, the eastern beach being the only way to drive from Point Lookout in the north to the southern end of the island. There is a road across the centre of North Stradbroke Island past the Blue Lake National Park. This does reach the eastern beach, but once there, to travel north or south means either walking or using a 4WD.

Point Lookout is the main holiday area on North Stradbroke. It has a famous pub, used as the base for the 'Straddie Classic' fishing competition, and a variety of accommodation from up-market units to rental cottages. There are also several camping and caravan areas near Point Lookout and at adjacent Adder Rock.

Point Lookout is a large, rocky headland with many rock fishing spots accessible from graded walking tracks. These are well signposted.

As always, caution and local advice as to which places are safe to fish in varying sea conditions are essential before fishing from the rocks in the Point Lookout area. Fish species available from this headland include good bream, tailor and even the mighty Spanish mackerel.

Point Lookout, Amity and Dunwich each possess all the facilities of any coastal village. The vehicular ferry and water taxi services to North Stradbroke Island depart from Toondah Harbour in the Brisbane suburb of Cleveland.

Beach fishing with the aid of a 4WD vehicle for getting around is similar on both Moreton and North Stradbroke. The only exception is that the western beach on 'Straddie' (as locals know it) is mangrove habitat and not accessible, whereas almost the full perimeter of Moreton Island is.

Cape Moreton and the nearby North Point are the only rock outcrops on Moreton Island. These have great rock fishing, although anglers of course need to observe all the necessary safety precautions when fishing from the rocks.

SURF FISHING

The triangular-shaped Moreton Island has a 'surf' beach down its eastern coastline and 'calm' beaches along its northern and western shores.

The eastern beach is one of the best tailor fishing spots in Queensland, being surpassed only by Fraser Island. Late winter brings the tailor run along Moreton Island's eastern beach., although astute reading of formations along the beach will locate a few tailor at any time of the year. Good gutters along the eastern beach also produce bream, dart and whiting all year round.

Moreton's northern beach is the best part of the island for quality whiting, particularly in the area near Yellow Patch (a coloured sand cliff marked on maps) and Comboyuro Point, the island's north-west extremity. The western beach, being calmer, doesn't have the same well-defined formations and is more popular as a camping area. Good catches of flathead are made from the western beach in spring.

The Tangalooma wrecks are a popular fishing spot on Moreton Island's western side

Passage Bar. Typically these are known by their water depth (the Twenty Nines, Thirty Five Fathom Reef, etc.) and all have enough boats on them on any weekend with good weather to make locating productive bottom-fishing grounds relatively easy.

OFFSHORE HOT SPOTS

There is a proliferation of shallow reefs off Moreton Island's eastern beach, many of which are only 300 to 500 m offshore. These fish well for smaller snapper and sweetlip, especially at night.

Deep Tempest (rising from around 90 m of water) and Shallow Tempest (rising from around 30 or 40 m of water) are the two well-known reefs south-east of Moreton Island's Cape Moreton. There is also a collection of rock areas rising from the bottom around the Cape Moreton area. Flinders Reef is the only one which actually protrudes from the water. It is situated approximately due north of Cape Moreton. Flinders is an extensive area of dry rock useful as a mark to locate nearby Smith Rock and the huge Hutchison Shoal. Brennan Shoal and Roberts Shoal are both to the east of Cape Moreton. Hendersons Rock is several kilometres south, east of Moreton's largest sand hill, Mount Tempest. All of these are notable hot spots for reef and pelagic sport fish.

Locating Cape Moreton's billfish may be a somewhat less precise science, but it is often easier. Small black marlin and sailfish are to be found in the proximity of the 40-m depth line near Cape Moreton, where large baitfish shoals congregate. The favoured technique locally is to troll either rigged baits or skirted lures until a concentration of bait fish is located, then switch to deep-drifted live baits.

Moreton Island is a national park, so camping is regulated and requires a permit. In some areas, camping is restricted to designated camping sites. Cottages are available for rent at Bulwer and Kooringal, but these are rarely advertised and are usually rented through word of mouth. There's also the resort at Tangalooma.

BOAT FISHING

Visiting Moreton and North Stradbroke islands by boat requires a long haul across Moreton Bay. Offshore from both islands, reef fishing for snapper and other favourites such as sweetlip and pearl perch is both popular and productive. Sport fishing is also available here for a mix of tropical and subtropical speedsters, with some of the best small black marlin and sailfish grounds in the world. Other pelagics cruising the waters off the islands are Spanish mackerel, wahoo, cobia, yellowtail kingfish and several tuna species.

The launching site used to reach the offshore grounds depends upon which area one intends to fish. To fish the northern Moreton Island area near Cape Moreton, the best launch site is from either the Bribie Island ramps or Scarborough Boat Harbour on the Redcliffe Peninsula.

Between Moreton and North Stradbroke islands lies the South Passage Bar. Huge volumes of water move in and out between the two islands, making South Passage particularly dangerous. Local knowledge of this bar is absolutely essential. Due to the bar's massive size, even locals who cross it regularly mark the channel on their GPS as they exit. Later in the afternoon, when the sun sinks, it is difficult to locate a clear passage through the breakers.

Days Gutter, a sheltered anchorage near Moreton Island's Kooringal township, is often used as an overnight anchorage by boats fishing offshore from Moreton and North Stradbroke islands.

Flat Rock, Boat Rock and Shag Rock are three protruding rocks or bomboras in the vicinity of Point Lookout. Flat Rock, being in deeper water, is perhaps the most attractive to pelagic fish. Big Spanish mackerel and cobia often frequent this area.

Brisbane's reef fishers have a number of favourite reefs reached by crossing the South

Trolling off Flat Rock, Point Lookout

THE SUNSHINE COAST

IN BRIEF

MAP REFERENCE: PAGE 145 N4

GETTING THERE Noosa Heads lies about 150 km north of Brisbane just off the Bruce Highway
BEST TIME TO FISH Year-round
BEST TIME TO TRAVEL Year-round
MAJOR ANGLING SPECIES Bream, flathead, whiting, tailor, trevally, snapper, mulloway, mackerel and various reef species
SPECIAL RESTRICTIONS Vehicles are not permitted within the Noosa National Park. Sections of the Noosa River may also be closed to angling or boating. Check current regulations before fishing
WARNINGS The bars at the mouths of some rivers along this coast are shallow and may be treacherous in rough seas. Be especially careful when onshore winds oppose run-out tides
CHARTER BOATS AND FISHING GUIDES Noosa Blue Water Charters, telephone (07) 5449 9355; Mooloolaba Reef and Game Charters, (07) 5444 3735

The Sunshine Coast, which begins about 100 km north of Brisbane, runs from about Caloundra or Maroochydore in the south to Rainbow Beach, Tin Can Bay and the southern end of Fraser Island in the north. It is centred on the attractive coastal resort town of Noosa Heads, which serves as the Sunshine Coast's unofficial 'capital'.

An immensely popular holiday destination, the Sunshine Coast has fortunately escaped the worst excesses of commercialism and the all-pervading 'develop or perish' mentality that appears to have gripped the Gold Coast throughout the 1960s, 1970s and 1980s. As a result, although settled by a large influx of new residents during that same period, the Sunshine Coast and its mountainous, ruggedly beautiful hinterland areas have retained a fair slice of their original charm and natural attractions. Today, residents of this region are keen to see this trend maintained, and there are strict controls over the direction and scope of any future developments.

Life here is generally rather laid back and unhurried, especially in comparison with the hustle and bustle of the Gold Coast, and the entire area exudes a year-round holiday atmosphere—a feeling greatly enhanced by the mild to hot weather that normally prevails, even during the winter months.

Excellent fishing opportunities exist right along this stretch of coast—from freshwater bass rivers to coastal estuaries, beaches, rocky headlands and offshore reefs.

MOOLOOLABA — PLACE OF SNAPPER

The Aboriginal word 'mooloolaba' is said to mean 'place of the snapper', and good numbers of these very popular marine fish are still caught on the many reefs and gravel patches beyond the mouth of this safe harbour at the southern edge of the city of Maroochydore.

There is also some reasonable to good estuary fishing to be had upstream in the Mooloolah River itself, despite extensive canal developments and the removal of many mangrove stands and other natural features.

A little further to the north, the Maroochy River is another highly productive waterway, particularly for bream, whiting, flathead, tailor and the occasional mulloway or jewfish, as well as smatterings of mangrove jacks and estuary cod. Top spots within this popular estuary include Goat Island, Channel Island, Chambers Island, the Motorway Bridge, the Cod Hole, Eudlo Creek, Petrie Creek and the Bli Bli Bridge area.

Fishing off Teewah Beach often produces good catches

The Maroochy River at sunset

ON THE BEACH

Moving north again from Maroochydore, there are some excellent surf fishing beaches running between the Maroochy River mouth and Noosa Heads. These include Mudjimba, Marcoola, Yaroomba, Coolum, Peregian, Marcus and Sunshine beaches.

All of these surf beaches produce fair to excellent tailor catches, especially in mid-winter and early spring, as well as some very good sand whiting, bream, flathead, swallowtail dart and the occasional mulloway or jewfish.

Visiting anglers are advised to look for well-formed holes, gutters and sandbank edges and use fresh, natural baits when prospecting these beaches. It also pays to watch the locals and ask their advice concerning locations, rigs and baits. As in all surf fishing, any gathering of anglers at a particular section of a beach is well worth investigating!

North of Noosa, Teewah and Cooloola beaches produce similar results, and once again a peppering of surf casters along these stretches is a sign the fishing is good. The wreck of the *Cherry Venture* on the beach south of Double Island Point is a very popular spot, especially after rough seas. This northern portion of the Sunshine Coast is dealt with in greater detail on pp. 128–9.

Rock Fishing Ledges

Most of the rock ledges and headlands along this stretch of coast are also highly productive fishing spots at times. Some visitors might be taken aback by the relatively shallow water and sandy sea beds around many of these rocky outcrops, but make no mistake about it, they still attract some great fish.

The thing to remember is that many of these fish will be temporary visitors on their way north or south along the coast, and that these ledges generally have smaller numbers of 'resident' fish than the deeper rock fishing locations more familiar to southern anglers. This can tend to result in 'boom or bust' fishing—anglers either do very well indeed or miss out completely.

The relatively small Noosa National Park is considered by many anglers to contain some of the finest rock fishing spots in Queensland, with a great variety of fish on offer. Again, this area is dealt with more thoroughly elsewhere, under the regional heading of Noosa to Tin Can Bay.

The Sunshine Offshore Scene

There's also some great fishing to be had offshore along this beautiful stretch of coast. North Reef, to the north-west of Noosa Heads, is particularly productive in summer, especially after rough weather. It fishes best around dusk on the making or building (waxing) moon, most notably for snapper and various other reef species.

Moving back down the coast, the Sunshine Reefs, off Sunshine Beach to the south of Noosa Heads, fish well all year round, providing catches of snapper and mixed reef fish, as well as mackerel (Spanish, school and spotted), yellowtail kingfish and the odd cobia or black kingfish.

Mudjimba Island, offshore just north of the Maroochy River, and Chardons Reefs, wide of Sunshine Beach, both tend to fish at their best in late winter, spring and early summer. The action at both these spots can often be a little hit-and-miss in nature, however, as with so much of the angling along this stretch of coast.

The Pinnacles, at the northern end of the extensive Barwon Banks off Maroochydore, and the Barwon Banks themselves, fish well all year round. The best results are usually obtained in mid- to late autumn, winter and spring because of the strong currents that so often run during summer and early autumn.

The very best general bait on all the reefs off Noosa and the southern portion of the Sunshine Coast is definitely the Western Australian blue pilchard. Pilchards may be either fished in pieces, cubes or fillets on single hooks, or presented whole on flights of three to five ganged (linked) hooks, usually in the 3/0 to 6/0 size range.

Other viable alternatives when it comes to choosing offshore baits include squid, mullet, prawns, and cuttlefish. Small live yellowtail can also be big fish takers at times, as can lures such as minnows, jigs and poppers.

Finally, boat fishers headed offshore along this popular stretch of coast should note that the bar at the mouth of the Noosa River is shallow and sometimes dangerous. Local knowledge should always be sought before attempting a crossing in anything other than dead calm conditions.

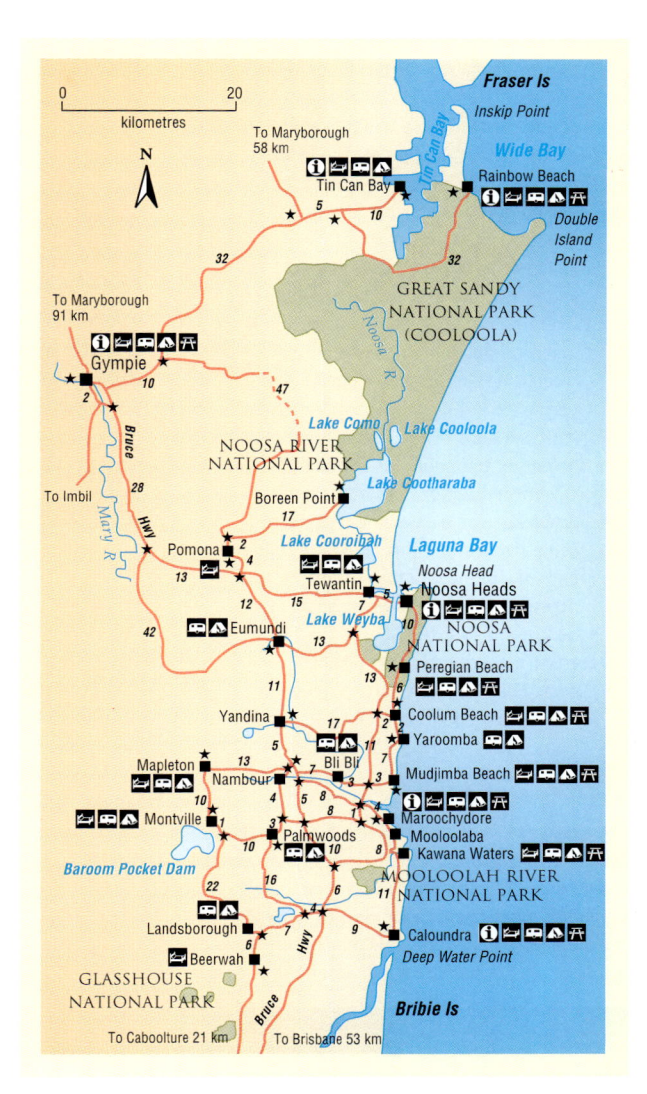

Western Australian pilchards are the best bait for offshore fishing

NOOSA TO TIN CAN BAY

IN BRIEF

MAP REFERENCE: PAGE 145 N4

GETTING THERE Noosa Heads is about 150 km north of Brisbane just off the Bruce Highway, Tin Can Bay is another 115 km north via the main road, through Gympie
BEST TIME TO FISH Year-round
BEST TIME TO TRAVEL Year-round
MAJOR ANGLING SPECIES Bream, flathead, whiting, tailor, trevally, snapper, mulloway, mackerel and various reef species
SPECIAL RESTRICTIONS Vehicles are not permitted within the Noosa National Park. Sections of the Noosa River may also be closed to angling or boating. Check current regulations before fishing
WARNINGS The bars at the mouths of some rivers along this coast are shallow and may be treacherous in rough seas. Be especially careful when onshore winds oppose run-out tides
CHARTER BOATS AND FISHING GUIDES Noosa Blue Water Charters, telephone (07) 5449 9355; Mooloolaba Reef and Game Charters, telephone (07) 5444 3735

The sheltered waters of Noosa Sound

The extensive Sunshine Coast region, north of Brisbane, is centred on the extremely attractive and pleasant coastal resort of Noosa Heads, which has a permanent population somewhere in excess of 6000 people. This modest number of inhabitants is swollen for much of the year by large influxes of tourists, who flock to this sun-drenched part of south-eastern Queensland to enjoy its wonderful surfing beaches and other natural attractions, as well as the unhurried pace, colourful cultural features, shops and great restaurants that now typify the Noosa lifestyle.

Most visitors to the Sunshine Coast spend the bulk of their holidays in and around Noosa itself, or at one of the other resort towns such as Nambour, Maroochydore, Buderim or Caloundra that are dotted throughout the southern section of this region. Yet it should be remembered that the Sunshine Coast actually extends well north beyond Noosa Heads, and runs all the way north to Double Island Point, Tin Can Bay and the narrow stretch of water separating the southern end of Fraser Island from the mainland. This extensive northern half of the Sunshine Coast is much less densely settled than the southern portion and dominated by long beaches, striking headlands and the vast coastal wilderness and wetlands of the Cooloola National Park.

Not surprisingly, some excellent fishing opportunities are available right along this less peopled stretch of coast—from the freshwater bass waters of the upper Noosa River to the extensive ocean beaches, rocky ledges and numerous offshore reefs, as well as the estuarine waters of Tin Can Bay itself.

ROCK FISHING HOT SPOTS

The relatively small Noosa National Park is considered by many anglers to contain some of the finest rock fishing locations available in all of Queensland, with a great variety of fish species on offer at various times of the year.

Access to rock ledges within the park is via various well-established walking trails, although good catches of fish can often be taken within 100 m of the main car park at Laguna Bay, which turns on some excellent fishing at times for big 'blue nose' bream and many other species.

Some lovely tailor can be taken here early in the morning, especially in winter, and large mulloway or jewfish are often available at dawn, dusk and through the night at almost any time of the year. Competition for space with surfboard riders, however, can be something of a problem during daylight hours, especially when a decent swell is running and some good breaks are available for the surfers.

For those seeking a little more solitude and willing to walk a few extra kilometres, locations such as Dolphin Point, the Fairy Pools, Hells Gate, Oyster Rock, Lion Rock and Paradise Cave are well worth the additional effort, with the last three being best reached by walking north from the end of Sunshine Beach.

OFFSHORE FROM NOOSA

Offshore, there's also some terrific fishing to be enjoyed along this beautiful stretch of coast. In particular, North Reef, situated to the north-west of Noosa Heads, is a productive mark in summer and autumn, especially during the period following a spell of rough weather. This location often produces its best results on the making or building (waxing) moon for snapper and other species, including tropical mackerel. Action is often best from first light until an hour or so after sunrise.

Numerous other reefs and pinnacles lie off the coast between Noosa Heads and Double Island Point, although access and launching facilities for trailer boats are rather limited. Nonetheless, on the right day, excellent sport is available for seaworthy craft ranging north from Noosa or south from Tin Can Bay.

Offshore fishing along the Sunshine Coast is dealt with in more detail on pp. 126–7.

THE NOOSA RIVER

The tannin-stained waters of the Noosa River and its associated lake systems—lakes Weyba, Doonella, Cooroibah, Cootharba and Cooloola—represent a magnificent wetland that offers all of the usual estuary action in its tidal stretches (especially around Tewantin), as well as some excellent bass fishing in its dark, tea-coloured freshwater reaches.

For better or worse, access to some of the upper parts of the Noosa River system is now rather problematic. This entire situation was once again under review at the time of writing, and should be carefully checked before making a

Noosa is a great spot for beach fishing

Dolphin Point overlooking Laguna Bay in Noosa National Park

visit. (Bass fishing on the Noosa River is dealt with in greater detail on pp. 138–9, and that section is accompanied by a more thorough examination of the access question.)

Surf Fishing Action

Not surprisingly, surf or beach fishing is immensely popular along the entire Sunshine Coast, and some of the better beaches in the southern half of this region—locations such as Mudjimba, Marcoola, Yaroomba, Coolum, Peregian, Marcus and Sunshine beaches—are household names amongst keen, east coast surf casters.

North of Noosa, Teewah and Cooloola beaches, in particular, produce similar results to the southern beaches already mentioned (described in more detail on pp. 126–7, while the wreck of the *Cherry Venture*, on the beach south of Double Island Point, is a very popular surf angling spot, especially after a period of rough seas.

Major surf fishing targets along this stretch of coast include sand whiting, bream, swallowtail dart, tailor, flathead and mulloway (jewfish), although surprises often turn up in the form of golden trevally, snub-nosed dart (permit) and even an occasional bonefish! Pelagic species such as spotty mackerel, mackerel tuna (kawa kawa) and Watson's leaping bonito also venture inshore close enough at times to be reached by a long cast with a lure from these clean, golden beaches, adding an interesting dimension to the overall surf fishing picture.

Rainbow Beach and Tin Can Bay

At the northern end of the strip popularly known as the Sunshine Coast lies Inskip Point and the towns of Rainbow Beach and Tin Can Bay, both of which look out across a relatively narrow, current-scoured channel to the southern end of Fraser Island. This is a popular stepping-off point for visitors to the big, sandy island, who use the vehicular ferries operating here to transport their 4WDs across the narrow strip of water.

Tin Can Bay and the inlet of the same name offer excellent estuary fishing opportunities for all of the usual species, especially during the summer months. The area has a delightfully quiet, country-style atmosphere, in contrast to the more modern amenities and slightly faster pace of nearby Rainbow Beach.

There are boat ramps at Tin Can Bay, Carlo Point and Bullock Point, allowing access to the partially enclosed waters of the inlet. It should be noted, however, that the main channel between Inskip Point and Fraser Island can become extremely rough, particularly when a run-out tide opposes an onshore wind from the east or south-east. For this reason, boat anglers should exercise extreme caution at all times when operating in this area.

Also, many of the smaller creeks in Tin Can Bay—most of which produce good fishing and crabbing—drain almost entirely on a very low tide, and unwary boaters can easily become stranded or trapped for hours at a time.

Double Island Point, to the east, offers some very challenging rock fishing opportunities. It is also a popular venue for small boat anglers chasing bottom fish. Sport and game species such as big 'green-back' tailor, schools of tuna, mackerel, yellowtail kingfish and cobia may be targeted as well, with live or dead baits. For a real thrill, they can be hooked on skipping poppers or minnow-style lures cast from a drifting boat back into the foamy, aerated wash zones around the headlands and adjacent rocks or bomboras.

FRASER ISLAND

IN BRIEF

MAP REFERENCE: PAGE 145 N2

GETTING THERE It is about 240 km by road from Brisbane to Rainbow Beach and the vehicular ferry (no bookings necessary) that crosses to the southern end of Fraser Island. Hervey Bay and the port of River Heads are another 60 km further north

BEST TIME TO FISH Year-round

BEST TIME TO TRAVEL April to October

MAJOR ANGLING SPECIES Tailor, bream, flathead, whiting, dart, tarwhine, trevally, snapper, mulloway, mackerel and various reef species

SPECIAL RESTRICTIONS You require a vehicle access permit to drive on Fraser Island and this must be fixed to your windscreen. If you intend to camp anywhere other than the commercial camping areas at Dili and Cathedral beaches, you need a camping permit, telephone Brisbane (07) 3327 8185, Gympie (07 5482 4189) or Rainbow Beach (07) 5486 3160. Normal highway road rules apply when driving (4WD) on the eastern beaches of Fraser Island. Extreme caution should be exercised near pedestrians and other beach users

WARNINGS Take care at all creek crossings and in soft sand. Always check tides and partially deflate tyres before travelling on beaches. Dingoes are prolific on Fraser Island and have been known to cause problems, especially with children. Under no circumstances should dingoes be fed

CHARTER BOATS AND FISHING GUIDES Time-n-Tide Charters has a live-aboard charter vessel offering excellent reef and sport fishing, telephone (07) 4125 5444; Sid Boshammer, professional sport fishing guide, telephone (07) 4125 1755

Dingoes are commonly seen on Fraser Island

Fraser Island, the world's largest sand island, has golden beaches, coloured sands, beautiful, crystal clear freshwater lakes, rainforest and abundant wildlife, including dingoes. To add to the spectacle, whales migrate through these waters from August until October each year.

On top of being a terrific holiday destination, Fraser is famous for the calibre of fishing on offer from its extensive beaches and in the surrounding warm waters. Here, hot currents from the tropical north mix with cooler, southern waters, providing a fascinating mix of fish species and some exceptional sport at times.

To the west and north of the island lies the vast expanse of Hervey Bay, bounded to the north-west by Bundaberg and Burnett Heads, and to the south by the Mary River estuary. Between these two points are Elliot Heads, Woodgate, Burrum Heads, Hervey Bay, River Heads, Pialba and Urangan. A little further inland is the provincial city of Maryborough, with a population of close to 30 000 people. This entire region draws tourists and travelling anglers from all over Queensland and much further afield. It is also an essential stop-over for round-Australia adventurers, foot-loose retirees and other sunseekers escaping the chill of a southern winter.

Much More than Tailor

Fraser Island is best known in angling circles for the calibre of beach fishing available in the surf along its extensive eastern shoreline. In particular, the annual Fraser Island tailor run—which begins in late autumn or winter and builds to a crescendo by spring—is legendary. This phenomenon still attracts large crowds of anglers, despite dramatically declining catches in more recent times and the imposition of a closed season in September to protect breeding populations of these popular but hard-hit fish.

While the tailor run remains a major drawcard, especially with diehard Fraser Island surf fans, there is much more to the beach fishing on this unique island than simply standing shoulder-to-shoulder with hordes of fellow anglers and flinging gang-hooked pilchards in the pursuit of a bag of choppers.

Fraser Island's gutters, holes and banks offer superb surf fishing opportunities for sand whiting, bream, tarwhine, golden trevally, mulloway or jewfish, sharks, flathead and—most abundant of all—the ubiquitous swallowtail dart. And while the tailor action is almost always best from June until October, many of these other species are far more abundant in the summer and autumn months.

Whiting, trevally and dart, in particular, are at their most willing from November until May, while the bream fishing in April, May and June can be outstanding. Mulloway can turn up at any time, but are most prolific when baitfish schools are plentiful, and often hunt the smaller, earlier run of tailor in autumn and winter.

Finding Fish in the Surf

Finding fish on Fraser Island's beaches requires much the same skills as reading beaches anywhere else, except that there is a lot more likely terrain to choose from on this giant sand island than on most stretches of mainland coast.

Holes and gutters show up as darker areas with unbroken swells, while shallow banks and flats are signalled by pale green or aquamarine water overlaid with plenty of foam and surf break. Both areas produce fish, with the holes and gutters being a better bet for bream, mulloway and tailor, while the shallower banks are prime feeding grounds for whiting, dart and flathead.

Perhaps the best fish indicator of all on Fraser Island's beaches, however, is the presence of a collection of parked vehicles and a cluster of expectant anglers. If one or more of these hopefuls is leaning back against a bending rod, so much the better!

ROCKY HEADLANDS

Separating the major surf beaches on Fraser Island are a number of weathered rocky headlands. The most famous of these are Indian Head and Waddy Point in the north.

At times, all of these headlands offer excellent fishing opportunities. Most are anything other than user-friendly, however, especially when compared with the flat sandstone ledges so prevalent in many other parts of the country.

Extreme caution should always be exercised on Fraser's rocks, as they are steep, slippery and prone to inundation by larger-than-average waves. However, for the prudent rock-hopper, they offer valuable vantage points for pursuing all of the species commonly encountered in the surf, as well as larger pelagic fishes such as school and Spanish mackerel, cobia, bonito, longtail tuna, mackerel tuna and large sharks.

THE WESTERN SIDE

The western side of Fraser Island is very different from the surf-pounded eastern shore. It consists primarily of mangrove forests, tidal flats, protected beaches, low headlands and myriad small estuaries. These winding estuaries are home to prolific numbers of bream, whiting, flathead, mullet ... and sandflies! There are also smaller populations of highly prized tropical sport fish, including mangrove jack, estuary cod, queenfish, trevally, threadfin salmon and even the occasional barramundi.

All of these estuaries and flats are best fished from a boat, but great care must be exercised, as many of them drain almost completely on a low tide or become land-locked thanks to the shallow bars and banks at their mouths. Spending six hours marooned in a sandfly-infested creek on a hot summer's day is bad enough, but being forced to overnight in the same location can be quite harrowing for both those involved and their loved ones left behind ... so, watch the tides!

In recent years, the extensive sand and mud flats along the south-western shore of Fraser Island have gained great prominence in sport fishing circles, most notably because of the big schools of hard-pulling golden trevally that swim here from late October until May. These goldens, which frequently run from 6 to 9 kg in weight, are increasingly being pursued (usually on a catch-and-release basis) by lure and fly casting specialists who enjoy the thrill of sight casting to such a worthy adversary in shallow water. This is not easy fishing, especially by late summer or autumn when the tailing trevally become rather 'gun shy'. However, tangling with even one of these skinny water speedsters on light line can make a trip to the island worthwhile!

Other visitors to the flats include big flathead, queenfish and threadfin salmon, as well as small numbers of 'his highness and shyness', the bonefish. Stingrays and sharks are also plentiful, so take care when wading.

THE OFFSHORE SCENE

If the shore, flats and estuary fishing on Fraser Island is good, then the offshore reef fishing and trolling (which is dealt with in greater detail on pp. 132–3) can only be classed as exceptional. This is especially so off the north and north-eastern corners, which receive very little commercial or recreational boat fishing pressure.

The biggest problem here is access. Boats must make the very long and exposed run across the bay from mainland ports such as Hervey Bay, negotiate the sometimes treacherous bar at the southern end of the island or be launched directly into the surf at places such as Waddy Point.

Once at sea, the potential is almost unlimited. Commonly encountered offshore species include several types of wrasse (usually called 'parrots' in this region), sweetlip, big red emperor, snapper, pearl perch, cod, cobia, trevally, yellowtail kingfish, amberjack, school and Spanish mackerel, wahoo, tuna of various types, dolphin fish, sailfish, marlin and sharks. More than enough, in fact, to keep any adventurous boat fisher happy!

Above: Surf fishing for tailor, dart and bream on Fraser Island
Right: A big red emperor from a Fraser Island reef

Activity at Orchid Beach during a big fishing competition held each year in autumn

FRASER'S OFFSHORE GROUNDS

IN BRIEF

MAP REFERENCE: PAGE 145 N1

GETTING THERE It is about 240 km by road from Brisbane to Rainbow Beach and Inskip Point, where the vehicular ferry crosses to the southern end of Fraser Island (no need to make a booking). Once on Fraser, the eastern beach is the easiest route to travel when towing a boat

BEST TIME TO FISH December to May for coral trout, wahoo and Spanish mackerel; winter for snapper; December and January for spotted mackerel; December for billfish in Hervey Bay; and December to May offshore

BEST TIME TO TRAVEL Year-round

MAJOR ANGLING SPECIES Spanish and spotted mackerel, longtail and mackerel tuna, wahoo, black marlin, red emperor, coral trout, sweetlip, parrot fish, trevally and snapper

SPECIAL RESTRICTIONS A permit is required to travel on Fraser Island. Camping permits are required at Wathumba and Waddy Point, telephone (07) 3227 8185

WARNINGS Beware of eating large specimens of any coral reef related species taken from Platypus Bay due to a high occurrence of ciguatera poisoning in fish from the area

ACCOMMODATION Camping and resorts on Fraser Island and in Hervey Bay

CHARTER BOATS AND FISHING GUIDES Time-n-Tide Charters, telephone (07) 4125 5444; Sid Boshammer, telephone (07) 4125 1755

Fabulous Fraser Island

For generations people who fish have flocked to Fraser Island. It has only been since the advent of the big fishing competition based at Orchid Beach, however, that much attention has been focused on offshore fishing from this massive sand island.

Boats mounted on fat-tyred trailers aren't a rare sight any more on Fraser. The fantastic reef fishing on the Gardner Banks east of Waddy Point and Indian Head makes the camping area at Waddy a crowded place at times. Yet what is coming to light now is the sport and game fishing potential in the waters off Fraser Island.

There has been some attention given to sport fishing on the Hervey Bay side of the island, where lure casting for spotted mackerel and longtail and mackerel tuna has been practised for many years. Also, the somewat erratic run of baby (15 to 25 kg) black marlin in Hervey Bay has been the subject of articles in fishing magazines for a decade.

Now, however, a couple of properly equipped boats have come to Hervey Bay and 'wider' grounds off Breaksea Spit (the huge sand spit projecting more than 30 km north from Fraser) are proving to be a hot spot the likes of which hasn't come to light in a very long time.

The reason this has taken so long is the difficulty involved in reaching Fraser's offshore grounds. Any one of them is a long way from anywhere. This is something that has to be considered before anglers venture offshore from Fraser Island as it means that help is also a long way away. Those fishing offshore from Fraser must be prepared to be entirely reliant on their own resources in the event of an emergency.

Technology helps. EPIRBs and modern radio communications are a must. When all is said and done, however, there is still much to recommend the simple, old-fashioned 'buddy' system. Always travel in the company of another boat.

Island Logistics

If fishing the Hervey Bay (western) side of the island, it is 16 km across the island from Orchid Beach to the only secure anchorage north of the boat harbour at Urangan. This anchorage is in Wathumba (pronounced 'watoomba') Creek.

It is 50 km by water from Urangan Boat Harbour to Wathumba Creek. The only difficulty faced here is that, even for outboard-powered boats that are able to tilt their drive units up to negotiate shallow sand bars at the mouth, entry to Wathumba can really only be relied upon at the top half of the tide.

Once inside the creek, though, there is always a deep hole where even large inboard boats may

Beach launching at Waddy Point, Fraser Island

Fighting a fish on a calm day in the waters of Hervey Bay off Fraser Island

anchor and stay afloat at low tide. At high tide, there is normally at least a couple of metres of water over the sand at the entrance.

An obvious and seemingly simple method of avoiding a 50-km over-water journey to Wathumba would be to cross the island towing a boat on a trailer, then simply launch the boat off the beach. The problem here is that the sands on Fraser Island's western beach are not hard like those of the eastern beach. Soft spots have trapped so many vehicles on the western beach that it is generally considered untrafficable.

Trailering a boat up the eastern beach is not difficult provided the trailer and towing vehicle are set up for soft surfaces and beach launching. This option is cramped, however, by the narrow, winding nature of the track from Orchid Beach to Wathumba Creek.

REALISTIC OPTIONS

The most realistic options to fishing the Hervey Bay side of Fraser Island are based on travelling over water from the launch ramp at Urangan Boat Harbour. As the island is orientated in such a way that it provides protection from prevailing south-east winds, the journey from Urangan is relatively comfortable provided the winds stay from the south-east. Winds from the north with any westerly aspect, however, are decidedly unfriendly on Hervey Bay.

Getting fuel to Wathumba means either carrying it aboard or having a 4WD travel up separately to act as a fuel truck. While both options are somewhat limiting, there's simply no other choice.

If anglers are not living aboard their boat, there's a national park camping ground on the southern bank of Wathumba Creek. This is not popular with boating visitors, however, as the channel normally runs along the other side of the creek several hundred metres away.

There are no facilities in place on the northern bank of Wathumba Creek, although it is rated by most people as a better camp site.

A MULTITUDE OF PELAGICS

Lure casting to the multitudinous schools of pelagic species working under massive flocks of feeding sea birds is the most readily available fishing on the Hervey Bay side of Fraser Island. There's great reef fishing along the inside of the island, too, but the bottom here tends to be what locals call 'coffee rock reef', which is fairly flat and difficult to read.

Off Rooneys Point, extensive areas of more prominent reef where pinnacles and drop-offs can be found are much easier to identify. Significantly, Hervey Bay charter boats fish the Rooneys Point area, passing by reefs further south on their way to get there.

Conventional trolling techniques off the west coast connect with a variety of pelagic species, including good numbers of Spanish mackerel. However, ciguatera poisoning has been a problem in Hervey Bay in the past, the culprit being Spanish mackerel often enough for the taking of the species to be banned from this part of Hervey Bay (known as Platypus Bay).

GAME FISHING OPTIONS

Small black marlin frequent Hervey Bay at times, although predicting those times has proven difficult so far. Now that large, fast offshore boats working from the Hervey Bay side can reach the Light Ship marking the northern extremity of Breaksea Spit, or the Sandy Cape Shoal and Spit Bommie to the east of the shallows, sport and game fishing off Fraser has opened up somewhat.

The bomboras add phenomenal numbers of small trevally and reef species to the list of possibilities to be taken offshore from Fraser.

The Light Ship is one of those dream hot spots where sport and game fishing has been explored only enough to tantalise. Larger billfish and the full gamut of pelagic species call the Light Ship area home and much more will be heard of this hot spot now that there is infrastructure in place to reach it.

Boats on trailers custom built for beach travelling and surf launching are becoming an increasingly common sight on Fraser Island. The advent of Great Sandy National Park has brought with it a much improved bypass track climbing above Middle Rocks between Indian Head and Waddy Point. This improved access makes it possible for larger boats to be towed on the island.

Waddy Point shelters a national park camping area sited under the frontal dune. Here the beach faces north, making it ideal for launching a boat. Obviously, a heavy swell precludes beach launching. In reasonable conditions, however, Waddy Point is as good as surf beach launches get.

Off Waddy Point lie the Gardner Banks or, more specifically, North Gardner Bank, South Gardner Bank, the Gravel Patch and North Reef. Big red emperor, coral trout and snapper are the attraction here. Equally impressive, if not as often keenly pursued, are monster Spanish mackerel and wahoo. The potential of the billfishing on the Gardner Banks remains another tantaliser. If reports from people fishing the Gardners are anything to go by, there's a hot spot here just waiting to be explored.

Wahoo are one of the many species available

SEVENTEEN SEVENTY AND ROUND HILL

IN BRIEF

MAP REFERENCE: PAGE 147 L9

GETTING THERE Miriam Vale is about 480 km north of Brisbane along the Bruce Highway. Seventeen Seventy is 55 km east by road from Miriam Vale

BEST TIME TO FISH Year-round

BEST TIME TO TRAVEL Year-round, but avoid periods of heavy rain

MAJOR ANGLING SPECIES Spanish and spotted mackerel, cobia, giant trevally, queenfish, flathead, whiting, grunter and mud crabs

SPECIAL RESTRICTIONS Camping permits are required in Eurimbula National Park, telephone (07) 4972 1993

WARNINGS Sections of the road from Miriam Vale to Seventeen Seventy are unsealed and can be rough

ACCOMMODATION Camping at Eurimbula Creek, Seventeen Seventy and Agnes Waters; cottages available at Seventeen Seventy, Agnes Waters and Turkey Beach

The creeks in this area hold plenty of mud crabs

The first question that everyone asks is 'Why is it called Seventeen Seventy?' The answer is that Lieutenant James Cook first set foot in Round Hill Creek in the year 1770. Thus, the small coastal village now tucked away in the lee of Round Hill Head, along the southern bank of Round Hill Creek, was named Seventeen Seventy.

As a fishing spot, the Round Hill area has a lot to offer. For starters, there's Round Hill Creek itself, a productive little estuary which has been closed to commercial netting for many years. Heading north, there's Eurimbula Creek, which is also closed to commercial netting and is within Eurimbula National Park, then Middle Creek.

Middle Creek is the southern entrance to an extensive mangrove wetland stretching north some 15 km to Bustard Head. Bustard Head is, in fact, an island separated from the mainland by mangroves. Behind Bustard Head is the northern entrance of the wetland system. Effectively an estuary, it is called Pancake Creek.

All the mangroves, Bustard Head and the associated rocky reefs offshore from the head account for much of the interest in Seventeen Seventy. That's not all, however.

The road to Seventeen Seventy is not the only access route to launching a boat bound for Bustard Head. To the north-west of Bustard Head lies Rodds Peninsula. In its turn, the peninsula guards Rodds Bay, another expansive area of mangrove wetlands, access to which can be gained via another of the region's small coastal settlements known as Turkey Beach. Many regular visitors to the area actually prefer Turkey Beach as a jumping-off point for Bustard Head. This is all to do with how the coastline faces relative to the strong south-east trade winds often experienced here.

A glance at a map shows why. It's a down-sea run back to Turkey Beach, while Seventeen Seventy lies directly upwind—an uncomfortable direction of travel in all excepting the best boats.

REACHING SEVENTEEN SEVENTY

There are two ways to reach the Round Hill area: by turning off the Bruce Highway towards Lowmead, or by heading for Seventeen Seventy further north at Miriam Vale. Either way, there's a certain amount of unsealed road to travel before reaching Seventeen Seventy. The road to Seventeen Seventy has a reputation for being rough and demands caution, especially if your vehicle is towing a boat or trailer.

The road to Seventeen Seventy first touches the coast 6 km away from the settlement at Agnes Water. Agnes Water is perhaps the faster growing community of the two because of the space constraints at Seventeen Seventy.

Both Agnes Water and Seventeen Seventy have camping areas. Rental accommodation is available in both places, too. The boat ramp at Seventeen Seventy is also quite a good one.

On the Seventeen Seventy road, there's a signpost marked Eurimbula National Park. This marks the access track to a national park camping area at Eurimbula Creek and to Middle Creek further north. There is a rough ramp at Middle Creek, but be warned that this road is definitely recommended for 4WDs only.

FISH AND CRABS

Round Hill Creek at Seventeen Seventy does not have a bar on its entrance as such. However, entry at low tide in big swell conditions can certainly be hazardous. High tide is much safer.

At high tide, the mouth of Eurimbula Creek is only a few kilometres away. It's impossible to enter Eurimbula at low water.

Up the creek amongst the mangroves is the place to look for mangrove jacks. These lure destroyers are prolific in all mangrove creeks along this part of the coast, including those in Rodds Bay.

Middle Creek, too, has an entrance which is shallow and hazardous at low water. As it is not closed to commercial netting, it generally doesn't fish as well as Round Hill and Eurimbula creeks.

Mud crabs are a major item of interest throughout this entire area—not surprisingly perhaps given the extent of the mangrove systems. Despite heavy commercial crabbing, it's still well worth running a few pots.

If a boat large enough to be slept aboard is being used, Pancake Creek is sufficiently sheltered and has deep enough water to be a popular anchorage for passing yachts. The upper reaches of the estuary here fish well, but are a little hard to gain access to in larger boats. In a smaller boat, it's possible to enter the upper end of the Pancake Creek estuary by travelling at high tide through mangrove channels from Middle Creek. A good sense of direction is essential to find a way through this maze.

Offshore Opportunities

Off Bustard Head lie three rock bomboras named Inner, Outer and Middle rocks. These are a natural focus point for pelagic species travelling down the Queensland coast and, although not widely known, are an acknowledged hot spot for big Spanish mackerel and cobia. At the end of summer, huge giant trevally also frequent these rocks, as well as Bustard Head itself.

Back towards Round Hill from Bustard Head, Bustard Bay sees a run of the smaller spotted mackerel pass through in early summer.

Mackerel tuna and a few longtail tuna are to be found in Bustard Bay off and on throughout the year. In autumn and sometimes into early winter, large queenfish can be found working under feeding birds anywhere between Rodds Peninsula and Round Hill. Queenfish up to 8 kg and better come close inshore and can be taken off the rocks, particularly off the front of Round Hill Head. Great rock fishing at Round Hill and Bustard Head is too often overlooked.

A smaller boat launched at Turkey Beach will be kept busy fishing the myriad mangrove channels in Rodds Bay. To venture to Bustard Head from either Turkey Beach or Seventeen Seventy requires a capable offshore boat.

Unfortunately, there is nowhere to camp at Turkey Beach. However, some of the cottages there are available for rental through real estate agents in Miriam Vale.

The road to Turkey Beach is sealed and it is only 24 km from the Bruce Highway to Turkey Beach, another reason why some boat-based anglers prefer this location as a launch site to Bustard Head.

Spanish mackerel are a prime angling target in the waters around Seventeen Seventy and Round Hill

Seventeen Seventy and Round Hill offer some excellent rock fishing for a mix of northern and southern species

HINZE DAM

IN BRIEF

MAP REFERENCE: PAGE 145 N8

GETTING THERE Southport and Surfers Paradise lie 70 km south of Brisbane along the Pacific Highway; Advancetown is 25 km south-west of Southport

BEST TIME TO FISH Year-round, but best from September to May

BEST TIME TO TRAVEL Year-round

MAJOR ANGLING SPECIES Australian bass, golden perch, silver perch, spangled perch and Mary River cod

SPECIAL RESTRICTIONS Internal combustion engines are not permitted on Hinze Dam, and a permit must be obtained before fishing and boating here. Special conditions apply to the catching and keeping of endangered Mary River cod — check the current status of these restrictions before fishing

WARNINGS Sudden storms are possible on Hinze Dam, especially in summer. These may greatly hinder the return of non-powered craft to the launching area. Buoyancy vests should be worn at all times in small craft

Looking out towards Surfers Paradise across Hinze Dam in the Gold Coast hinterland

Not far from the bright lights and noisy night spots of heavily urbanised south-eastern Queensland lies a delightful freshwater fishing venue that offers both visiting and local anglers a peaceful escape from the glamour and glitz of the nearby Gold Coast. It also provides anglers with a wonderful opportunity to lock horns with some hard-fighting Australian native fish in truly delightful surroundings.

The lower Nerang River is well known to most Gold Coast visitors. Its tidal estuary joins the busy Broadwater at Narrow Neck, near Southport, after passing between the luxury houses and high-rise apartments of downtown Surfers Paradise. This stretch of the Nerang is a well-known hot spot for whiting, bream and flathead, and can produce some hefty mangrove jacks and the odd estuary cod, too.

Further upstream, however, the Nerang River is a freshwater stream, and home to reasonable populations of native Australian bass, mullet and eels. Higher up again, its headwaters actually lie within the mountainous border country of the Lamington National Park, not far from the 1120-m peak of Mount Hobwee.

ADVANCETOWN LAKE

In its middle reaches, south-west of the township of Nerang and just a few kilometres from the villages of Advancetown and Gilston, the Nerang River is held back by the 44-m high wall of Hinze Dam. This dam impounds a moderately large volume of fresh water with a surface area of 970 hectares when full. Officially known as Advancetown Lake, it is almost always referred to by locals and visitors alike simply as Hinze Dam.

Primarily intended as a water supply reservoir for the fast-growing Gold Coast region, this relatively new lake has also proven to be a very useful and popular recreational resource. It now offers an interesting, alternative sport fishery for those anglers seeking a change from the primarily saltwater diet of the region.

SUCCESSFULLY STOCKED

Since 1991, this pretty stretch of impounded water has been well stocked with hatchery-bred Australian bass, silver perch, golden perch (yellowbelly) and smaller numbers of the endangered Mary River cod. All of these fish have thrived in their new home and grown quite rapidly. The lake is also home to large numbers of mostly small spangled perch, which can be something of a nuisance at times, especially for bait fishers.

While catches of silver and golden perch have increased in recent years, and the odd Mary River cod is now also turning up, Australian bass remain the prime target for most sport fishers visiting Hinze Dam. These handsome, hard-fighting fish often provide superb action, particularly on a warm spring or early summer evening.

Most of the bass encountered in Hinze Dam these days will measure between 30 and 40 cm in length and range in weight from 500 g to 1 kg or slightly more. Smaller fish from recent liberations are often encountered and the occasional larger specimen from earlier stockings is also on the cards. These older specimens could include exceptional fish up to 50 cm in length and 2.5 kg or more in weight, although such trophy bass are extremely rare anywhere, and Hinze Dam is certainly no exception to that rule.

FISHING STRATEGIES

Fishing at Hinze Dam — with baits, lures or flies — may be done from the lake's bank or from canoes, kayaks, punts and other small craft. Internal combustion engines are strictly prohibited on this water supply reservoir. Electric thrusters, on the other hand, are permitted. Canoes are also available for hire at the dam, and there is nothing to stop visitors from fitting their own electric motors to these craft.

Trolling compact, deep-diving minnows and plugs parallel to the lake's shoreline in 3 to 8 m of water is a particularly effective strategy for catching bass and other species in Hinze Dam, especially during the day.

Productive areas include the deep bays and points on the lake's western shore and the eastern bank of the Pine Creek arm which, as well as bass, also produces good numbers of golden perch or yellowbelly. Plenty of mostly small bass are taken along the shoreline directly opposite the launching ramp at the recreation area as well, while a submerged hilltop to the west of this cove known as Brett's Bump produces some good golden perch and the odd bass. A small electronic fish finder or depth sounder proves invaluable for finding such underwater features.

Casting and retrieving really comes into its own early and late in the day, and some excellent fly fishing opportunities occur on warm, summer evenings when small to middling bass are often seen 'rising' prolifically in the waters immediately adjacent to the recreation area and boat ramps. At such times, a deer hair bug or small fly rod popper cast near any obvious surface disturbances and worked slowly across the water like a drowning insect will often elicit a spectacular strike.

Downstream of the Dam

Bass were native to the upper tidal and middle freshwater stretches of the Nerang River prior to the construction of Hinze Dam, and small numbers of these fish continue to live and reproduce naturally in the river downstream of the wall. This population has been significantly increased by 'escapee' bass and other fish washed over the spillway during floods.

It is a fact of life that many adult bass approaching spawning condition will sieze any opportunity offered to migrate downstream, especially during the winter (pre-spawn) period. No doubt thousands of mature bass have travelled over the wall of Hinze Dam during high-flow periods driven by exactly such urges. While the fall of 44 m probably kills or injures some of these fish, many others survive unscathed and take up residence in the river below.

The calibre of bass fishing available downstream from Hinze Dam has increased as a result of this 'recruitment' of new stock from the lake, and the odd silver and golden perch may also be encountered here nowadays, as well as a very occasional Mary River cod. This area is best fished from the bank by casting floating/diving plugs and various surface lures.

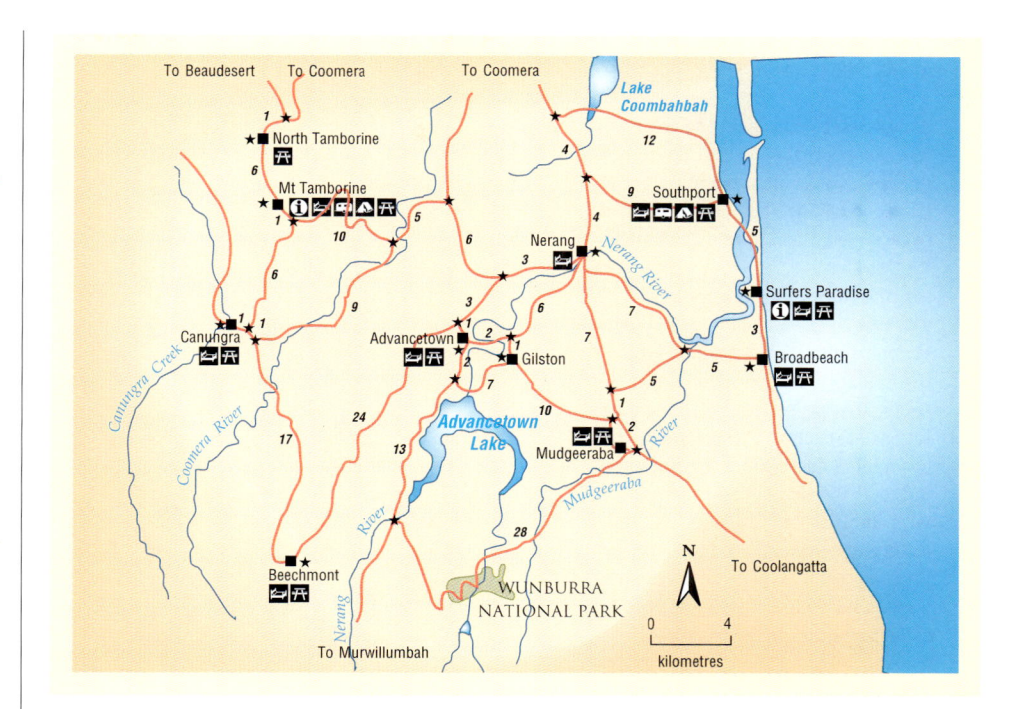

Above: *A fine Australian bass taken from the waters of Hinze Dam on a diving lure*
Below: *Carefully releasing a bass back into the water*

NOOSA RIVER BASS

IN BRIEF

MAP REFERENCE: PAGE 145 M4

GETTING THERE Seek local advice on how to reach Harry Springs Hut. There is a boat ramp in Lake Cootharaba at Boreen Point, and canoe launching only at Elanda Point. Access is via Cooroy from the Bruce Highway
BEST TIME TO FISH September to May
BEST TIME TO TRAVEL Year-round, but avoid periods of heavy rain and just after as roads become inaccessible
MAJOR ANGLING SPECIES Australian bass
SPECIAL RESTRICTIONS New regulations concerning bass fishing were being introduced at the time of publication. Check with Queensland Fisheries Management Authority, telephone (07) 3225 1848. Camping permits required for Harry Springs Hut. Power boat restriction on some part of upper Noosa — telephone as per camping permit. The entire upper Noosa has a 4-knot speed limit
WARNINGS Lake Cootharaba can be hazardous for canoes in strong winds
ACCOMMODATION National park camping area at Harry Springs Hut, telephone (07) 5449 7364 or (07) 5485 3245; private camping ground at Elanda Point, telephone (07) 5485 3165
CHARTER BOATS AND FISHING GUIDES Contact via Davo's Bait and Tackle at Noosaville, telephone (07) 5449 8099. Canoes available for hire from camping ground at Elanda Point, telephone (07) 5485 3165

In southern Queensland, only the Noosa River's catchment still flows undisturbed through the coastal heathlands. The river's entire catchment is contained within Great Sandy National Park and the upper Noosa remains one of the prettiest and most pristine waterways in Australia.

For the Noosa bass fishery, this has two effects: one good and the other not so good, at least as far as bass anglers are concerned.

Bass anglers in southern Queensland have long treasured the Noosa bass fishery. Even before the introduction of the current two-fish bag limit, the vast majority of people fishing the Noosa treated it as purely a catch-and-release fishery — a practice that continues today. As a result, the fishing in this area remains excellent and has, in fact, improved since 1985 when those same bass anglers were successful in lobbying for a halt to commercial netting of bass migrating downstream to spawn during winter.

The 'not so good' aspect of bass angling on the upper Noosa is that, being in a national park, much of the river has been closed to power boats.

Anglers wishing to fish above a certain point on the upper Noosa must either paddle or row to do so. Electric motors are permitted upstream as far as the Noosa River–Teewah Creek junction. As this is more than 10 km upstream of the closure point for power boats, however, covering such distances under electric power is often impractical.

At present, exactly where the closure begins is under review. There is a signpost on the river bank marking the power boat closure so anglers need not worry about inadvertently doing the wrong thing. A phone call to the regional national parks office will help when planning a trip.

Notwithstanding the power boat closure, a boat or canoe is essential to fish the upper Noosa River effectively. There is limited bank access near the Harry Springs Hut camping area and from some designated national park walking tracks along the river. However, the sedge-lined nature of the Noosa's banks makes fishing from them quite difficult.

Harrys Hut

Harry Springs Hut camping area is perhaps the best way to gain access to the upper Noosa's bass fishery. Harrys Hut, as locals call it, is reached via a series of forestry roads and finally a vehicular track through the Great Sandy National Park after turning off the Bruce Highway at the Cooroy exit then travelling via the small historic township of Kin Kin. It is quite easy to become lost amongst the secondary roads here, so advice from someone who has been to Harrys Hut before is essential. All the forestry roads and the track through the national park are unsurfaced and can become impassable after heavy rain. When dry, the unsealed sections are rough, but trafficable in a sensibly driven conventional vehicle.

Camping permits are required to camp at Harrys Hut, or any of the other designated campsites upriver from there. These are available from the national parks office at Elanda Point; the Sir Thomas Hitley Information Centre at Kinaba (if entering Great Sandy National Park from Lake Cootharaba); the Gympie office of the Department of Environment or from a self-registration box beside the information board at Harrys Hut. Please note that camping other than at designated sites is not allowed in this section of Great Sandy National Park.

Downstream of Harrys Hut, the river (which is more than 100 m wide in front of the hut) threads its way through a snaggy section appropriately known as The Narrows. All of the river above the Sir Thomas Hitley Information Centre is subject to a 4-knot speed limit. In some parts of The Narrows, even this is too fast. Contact with submerged timber is the norm—but it's a great place to look for bass. Above Harrys Hut, the river remains wide for the entire 16 km to the junction of Noosa River and Teewah Creek. Neither of these waterways is then navigable, although adventurous folk in canoes might make their way a little further upstream.

Data collected from a tagging program conducted by the Queensland branch of the Australian National Sportfishing Association and the Fisheries Division of the Queensland Department of Primary Industries indicates that the best bass fishing is found between The Narrows (near the entrance to Lake Como) and upstream to the designated national park camp site No. 5. This is the area, it is hoped, that will remain open to power boats.

FISHING THE NOOSA SYSTEM

A small dinghy powered by an outboard motor (possibly with an electric motor to use while lure casting) is the best way to fish for bass on the upper Noosa. If launching from Harrys Hut, there is no ramp so boat, motor and all gear must be carried to the water's edge.

Harrys Hut is also a favoured launching site for bass anglers using canoes. They can be launched from Elanda Point, too, and canoes are available for hire here as well. However, it is some distance to paddle across the lake past the information centre, then through a series of shallow lakes, before entering the river proper again at the entrance to The Narrows.

Lake Cootharaba can become rough and hazardous for canoes in strong winds, making it advisable not to attempt crossing the lake between Elanda Point and the information centre at such times. It is also advisable to obtain a map of this section of the lakes and the river entrance at the information centre to avoid any confusion.

The area between Kinaba and Harrys Hut is called the 'Everglades'. It, and indeed the whole Noosa River, is an exceptionally scenic and truly beautiful place. The Noosa's water is stained dark red—it appears almost black in places—by the tannins from plants in the catchment's surrounding heath (this country is called 'wallum' locally). When there is no wind, reflections in his dark water are so mirror-like that it can be difficult to aim a lure properly—a fine excuse for sending one into the clutches of a shrub!

Whether fishing from a dinghy or a canoe, there is one piece of advice valuable to all first-time Noosa bass anglers: use small lures. Being at almost the northern extreme of their range, the bass in the Noosa River have a smaller average size than that of those in the Queensland–New South Wales border region.

Dedicated bass anglers prefer to cast lures around bankside structures. However, in the Noosa, there are so many of these that slow trolling along the sedge banks and snag piles can be more effective. As with bass fishing anywhere, the summer months provide the best fishing—although, as this area is so far north, fine fishing is available all year round if you fish above Harrys Hut to avoid fish engaged in the spawning run.

The upper Noosa River provides a tranquil setting for bass angling

VALLEY OF LAKES

IN BRIEF

MAP REFERENCE: PAGE 145 M5

GETTING THERE Esk is approximately 100 km north-west of Brisbane
BEST TIME TO FISH September to May
BEST TIME TO TRAVEL Year-round
MAJOR ANGLING SPECIES Bass, golden perch, silver perch, spangled perch, catfish, garfish, saratoga, Mary River cod and Murray cod
SPECIAL RESTRICTIONS Permits are required for boating on most of these lakes and several have strict bans on the use of internal combustion engines. Access and camping may also be limited at some locations. It should also be noted that there is a zero bag limit for the endangered Mary River cod in the entire Mary River basin
WARNINGS Larger lakes such as Wivenhoe can become very choppy in strong winds. Violent storms are reasonably common, especially in summer
ACCOMMODATION Excellent camping facilities exist at Somerset Park, Kirkleigh, Logans Inlet and Cressbrook Dam
CHARTER BOATS AND FISHING GUIDES Ranger Big Bass Fishing Safaris, Ravensbourne, telephone (07) 4697 8237 or 015 039 629; Beach and Bush Fishing Adventures, telephone (07) 5444 6280

The area known as the Valley of Lakes lies to the west and north-west of Brisbane and consists of a string of artificial dams or impoundments on the upper Brisbane River and its tributaries, as well as several adjacent watersheds.

Since the 1980s, this region has become one of the best known and most popular destinations for inland angling in all of Australia. Thanks to significant fish stocking by government agencies and private self-help groups, the lakes in this region are now well populated with a range of native fish species and consistently produce outstanding angling action.

As a result of its many attractions, the Valley of Lakes area now receives considerable fishing pressure, and an active, ongoing re-stocking scheme will be essential in order to sustain viable fishing results well into the future. Ultimately, this may necessitate some form of 'user-pays' contribution from visiting and local anglers alike.

LAKE SOMERSET

One of the oldest stocked impoundments or artificial lakes in Australia, Lake Somerset is located on the Stanley River, a tributary of the Brisbane River, and lies between the townships of Esk and Kilcoy, about 120 km north-west of Brisbane.

Construction of this dam commenced in 1933, but was interrupted by World War II, and it was not completed until 1959. In addition to the flooded area, which covers 4212 ha when the dam is at full capacity, anglers can also enjoy access to many kilometres of the Upper Stanley River, almost upstream to the town of Kilcoy.

The dam has been sporadically stocked with fish for more than 25 years, although serious stocking did not begin until the mid- to late 1980s. Today, a large population of Australian bass provides excellent sport in all but the coldest of the mid-winter months. Some of the largest Australian bass ever recorded have come from these waters, including exceptional specimens of 4 kg and more. These fish can be found in all of their familiar haunts. Somerset bass also have a

A typical golden perch taken from Lake Somerset

tendency to school in mid-water over relatively featureless areas of lake bed, especially in summer. When this occurs, a depth sounder is invaluable for locating the schools, and excellent catches can be made by trolling, casting or jigging.

Golden perch or yellowbelly thrive in Lake Somerset, and specimens weighing 10 kg and even more have been caught here. Golden perch are best targeted during the early spring months in relatively shallow waters near the lake's edge. Later, in summer, they tend to move into deeper water adjacent to steeper banks and cliffs.

Somerset also holds spangled and silver perch—particularly in the sunken timber at the lake's northern end, while eel-tailed catfish are spread throughout the lake. A few saratoga are present, but are not often caught. There are also some very large snub-nosed garfish to be had by those fishing baits on small hooks and float tackle.

The dam has been stocked with small numbers of hatchery-bred fry of the endangered Mary River cod, and occasional catches of this species are now being reported, with the odd fish up to 10 kg or more turning up each year.

Excellent camping facilities exist at Somerset Park, below the dam wall, and at Kirkleigh, some 10 km north along the lake's western shore.

Boat launching ramps are found at Kirkleigh and The Spit. A boating permit is required, but there are no engine restrictions. The lake is used for water skiing and, occasionally, for ski racing, and these activities may adversely affect the fishing on the main basin in summer. At such times, it is best to head for the more sheltered arms or heavily treed areas of the lake.

LAKE WIVENHOE

The Queensland government started building Wivenhoe Dam in 1971, primarily as a water supply and flood mitigation storage for the city

Ranger Big Bass Fishing Safaris operate several of these US-built boats on the lakes

of Brisbane. It is 150 km upstream from the mouth of the Brisbane River, and lies some 80 km by road to the north-west of Brisbane.

When full, Lake Wivenhoe has a capacity of more than 1 million megalitres, a surface area of at least 10 000 ha and a shoreline in excess of 400 km, making it the second largest impoundment in Queensland today. In fact, the backed-up waters of this vast lake extend more than 50 km upstream, all the way to Lake Somerset.

This large lake is well stocked with Australian bass, and has produced some exceptionally big specimens to lengths of 60 cm and more, and weights in excess of 4 kg.

Wivenhoe is rather unique in that it fishes well for these very large bass during mid-winter, with fish weighing more than 2.5 kg regularly being caught between May and September, both on lures and natural baits such as live shrimps.

Golden perch, eel-tailed and fork-tailed catfish, saratoga, silver perch, banded grunter and large garfish are also present. Unfortunately, the noxious and exotic tilapia has also been caught here, as well as in Lake Somerset. It is an offence to return this species to the water, either dead or alive, and any catches of tilapia should be reported to authorities and their carcasses retained for scientific examination.

The large catfish population in Wivenhoe can make summertime fishing for golden perch or bass a rather difficult proposition, as the fork-tailed catties, in particular, will attack anything in the water, including most lures and flies. In summer, bass are best targeted on surface flies and poppers, and these top-water artificials also produce an occasional big saratoga.

Camping facilities exist only at Logans Inlet, with limited day access to the public boat ramps and picnic grounds. Despite the enormous size of this lake, boat operators are limited to using electric motors, oars, paddles or sail.

Boating access elsewhere on Wivenhoe is also very limited, although small punts and canoes can be launched at the northern end of the lake, and there are three boat ramps at the southern, more exposed end. A boating permit is required, and this may be obtained from the administration office near the dam wall, or from one of the rangers operating throughout the area.

With its vast expanse of water, limited access and regular re-stocking, Lake Wivenhoe will clearly, in time, become one of Australia's principal and premier freshwater fisheries.

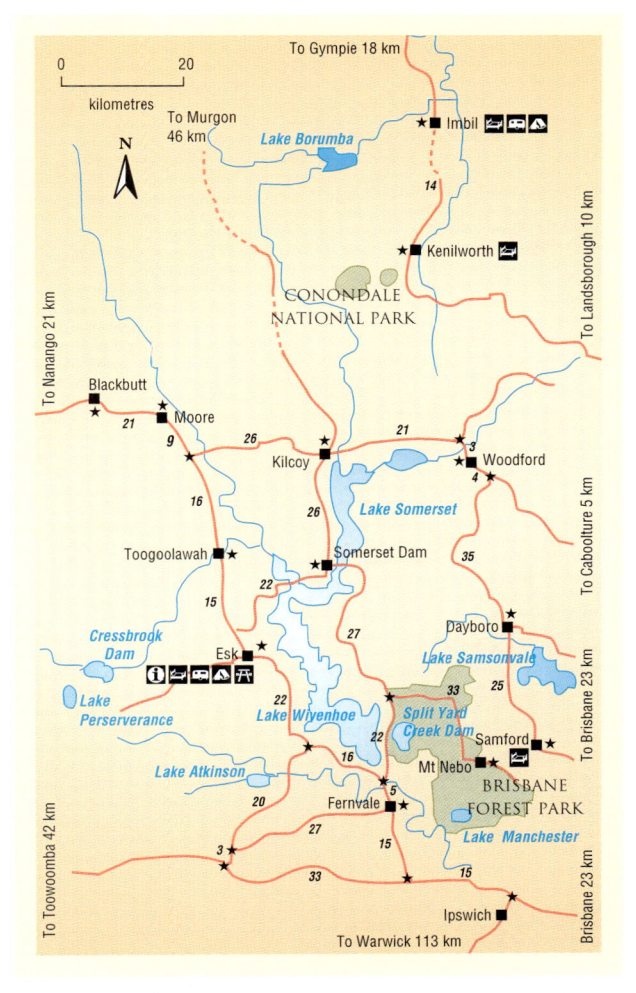

CRESSBROOK AND COOBY DAMS

Lying between Crows Nest and Ravensbourne, some 40 km west of the town of Esk, Cressbrook Dam is a favoured haunt for many keen anglers from the large inland city of Toowoomba, about 50 km to the dam's south-west.

The relatively small Cressbrook Dam (it covers 517 ha) is a picturesque lake with excellent launching and picnic facilities, and a relatively new camping ground.

Cooby Dam is located between Cressbrook and Toowoomba, near Meringandan. A much smaller lake than Cressbrook, it has a surface area of just 301 ha when at full capacity.

Cressbrook Dam first opened to fishing in 1993, although it has been regularly stocked with native species since 1988. Cooby opened in mid-1991, and has also been stocked since 1988. Permits are required to boat and fish on both lakes, and these may be obtained from rangers and local shops. Cressbrook has a blanket 8-knot speed limit for all craft, but outboard engines are permitted. Boating at Cooby, on the other hand, is limited strictly to vessels powered by electric motors, oars, paddles or sail.

An active local fish stocking association has ensured the future viability of both of these fisheries, with huge numbers of fish having been stocked since 1988. More than half a million golden perch (yellowbelly) fingerlings have now been released, along with around a quarter of a million silver perch. Some 150 000 Australian bass had been liberated into Cressbrook by the beginning of 1998, but no bass have been stocked into the waters of nearby Cooby Dam.

Cressbrook has also been stocked with garfish, which continue to breed there, as well as a small number of saratoga. Both lakes have eel-tailed catfish and Cressbrook boasts plenty of small spangled perch. Both impoundments, however, will no doubt ultimately become best known for their large stocks of cod. Some 15 000 Mary River cod have been released in Cressbrook, while 12 000 western Murray cod have been released at Cooby.

Fish in both of these small lakes respond well to lures trolled around weedbed edges and drop-offs, with deep-diving plugs being the best option. The spring and summer months tend to produce the most consistent fishing, although reasonable catches can also be made during winter by using live, natural baits. Cressbrook also offers some very good summertime surface activity on flies and top-water lures, particularly around dusk in the waters near the picnic area, where bass often rise to the top, leaving clearly visible swirls.

A pair of 1-kg bass taken from Lake Somerset

THE GOLDEN WEST

IN BRIEF

MAP REFERENCE: PAGE 144 E8

GETTING THERE Toowoomba is 128 km west of Brisbane along the Gore Highway; St George is a further 275 km west
BEST TIME TO FISH September to May
BEST TIME TO TRAVEL March to September
MAJOR ANGLING SPECIES Golden perch, Murray cod, eel-tailed catfish and silver perch
ACCOMMODATION A range of accommodation is available in the larger regional towns
CHARTER BOATS AND FISHING GUIDES Information about fishing in this region is available from Mullet Gut Marine, Ruthven St, Toowoomba, telephone (07) 4632 9770

There's something of a puzzle in the way that Brisbane's keen freshwater anglers have traditionally travelled north to the Noosa River, or south into northern New South Wales, to pursue their sport. The boom in freshwater fishing generated by Queensland's dams and impoundments coming on line only serves to deepen this mystery, because nearly all of the new sweetwater enthusiasts attracted by these fisheries have completely overlooked some fine freshwater fishing a similar travelling time away in a different direction—to the west.

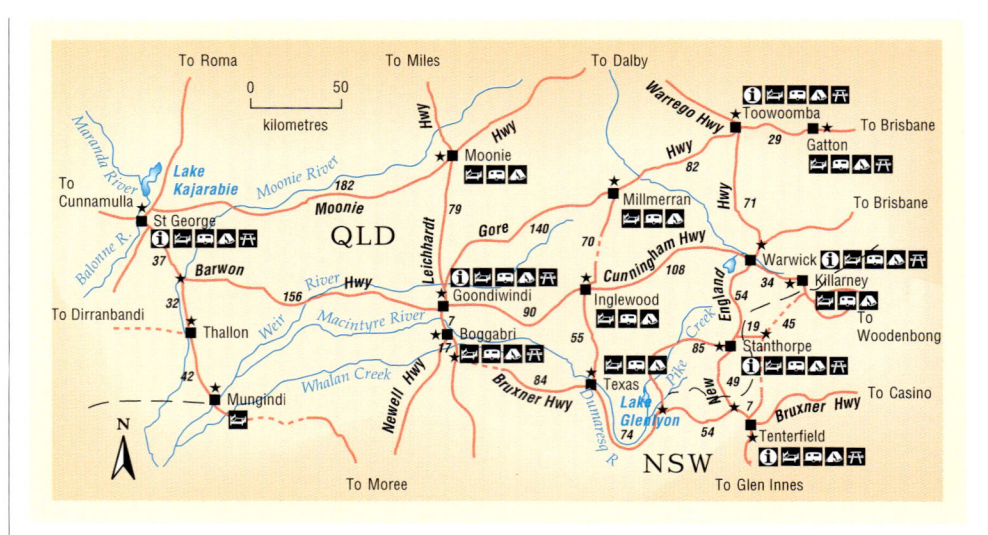

This perplexing situation remains, despite the best efforts of the people at the Toowoomba and Golden West Regional Tourist Association, who have even gone to the trouble of producing a brochure and map detailing some 51 fishing spots in the region west of Toowoomba, past Roma and St George, south into New South Wales (past Goondiwindi and Mungindi), and north to Taroom and Injune.

Setting a travel limit of four hours or so by road from Brisbane may not get you to Roma and Goondiwindi, but it certainly will get you to a string of publicly accessible fishing spots along the Condamine River from Pittsworth and Milmerran out to the Dalby–Chinchilla area.

Also within that theoretical four-hour travel radius are areas around the New South Wales border in the Stanthorpe and Tenterfield regions.

Only slightly further afield, within a five-hour radius, are dams such as Glenlyon and Boondooma, the latter being one of Queensland's finest stocked impoundments. Leslie Dam, near Warwick, is yet another well-stocked impoundment, and it is within two to three hours drive of most parts of Brisbane. Still another dam coming on line is Lake Barambah, near Murgon. This body of water is perhaps better known as Bjelke-Petersen Dam.

All in all, there is enough freshwater fishing within weekend tripping distance of Brisbane to keep the keenest freshwater angler happily exploring for years!

TARGET SPECIES AND TURBID WATERS

The basic target fish in these waters are golden perch, silver perch, Murray cod and freshwater eel-tailed catfish (commonly called 'jewies' by local anglers). There are also bass in Lake Barambah and Boondooma Dam, and ample numbers of the eager, if small, spangled perch, which are especially good fun for kids of any age.

Water levels are a critical factor throughout much of Australia and certainly present difficulties in this area. This is as applicable to the gorges of the upper slopes of the Great Divide as it is to the flatland flood plains further west. To the uninitiated, the often turbid appearance of the water adds another negative element. It's worth remembering, however, that western watershed species such as golden perch call turbid waters home for most of their lives.

Fishing on a rocky outcrop in Lake Leslie near Warwick, three hours drive from Brisbane

Lure fishing has become extremely popular in southern Queensland since the impoundment fishing boom began and perhaps the unsuitability of very turbid water for serious lure fishing helps to explain why some of the best freshwater fishing in the country has thus far been overlooked. Nonetheless, for those prepared to fish with bait when necessary, saving their lure fishing for suitable water conditions, great fishing is certainly here for the taking.

Access and Information

For anglers keen to visit the Golden West region, the best place to start is by obtaining one of the Regional Tourist Association brochures. These are distributed through tourist information facilities in the region and can also be obtained from the association's head office in Toowoomba. They are also available from Mullet Gut Marine tackle store in Toowoomba.

Fishing spots in the Golden West region are largely based on access points where roads cross or pass close by rivers. Many of these locations have informal camping areas where overnight camping is not only permitted under local by-laws, but is also encouraged. However, most of these have no facilities. Wheel tracks heading into the scrub often lead to better camp sites.

A small boat or canoe is almost always the key to the best fishing in western rivers. There are usually some spots to fish off the bank, but a boat greatly expands one's horizons. It's worth remembering, however, that launching ramps are virtually non-existent and getting a boat into and out of the water may require some physical effort.

Even given reasonable rains and an end to the prolonged droughts experienced in the late 1980s and mid-1990s, rivers such as the Condamine typically consist of a chain of waterholes, connected by a largely dry, sand river bed. The holes are sometimes several kilometres in length and only accessible at one point, which is why a small boat or canoe is practically a necessity.

Baits and Rigs

There's little argument that the best natural bait to use throughout the Golden West region is live shrimps. Often, these can be caught in situ in a trap baited with chicken, meat or fish scraps. Night time is always better for shrimp trapping.

Crayfish (yabbies) will also be caught in baited traps, and these make good baits, too. Earthworms are a convenient bait to carry, just in case the shrimp traps don't produce results. Worms are a reasonable bait rather than the best, and tend to produce more catfish than golden perch, silver perch or cod.

A standard running sinker rig is the most popular option locally. Use of a leader is generally preferred, although the number of snag-ups encountered may eventually dictate the choice of a rig where the sinker is allowed to run freely right down onto the eye of the hook.

A live shrimp fished 1 or 2 m under a running float and presented in the vicinity of snag piles and fallen timber is often preferred by more dedicated and successful local anglers.

When water conditions are suitable, standard lure fishing techniques involving either casting or trolling do not differ significantly from those employed successfully on a bass stream or, for that matter, along northern barramundi rivers.

One area where lure fishing can be practised on a regular basis is in the headwaters and border river country around Stanthorpe and Tenterfield. The biggest problem visiting anglers face here is access. Almost all of the Severn River, the Mole, Tenterfield Creek and, further downstream, the Macintyre and Dumaresq (pronounced 'dew-merrick') rivers flow through private property. Astute reading of detailed local maps, however, and the use of canoes will allow access to some exciting water, especially when there has been enough rain for the rivers to flow well without actually flooding.

Stout Boots and Strong Legs

Stout boots and equally stout legs are necessary to reach many areas of the gorge country when permission for access can be obtained. Sadly, however, land holders in this region are generally reluctant to grant access, even if anglers can overcome the difficulty of finding out how to contact them in the first place.

On a brighter note, the slump in Australia's rural economy has encouraged some land owners in the border rivers and Great Divide region to supplement their income with low-key tourism ventures. Some operators boost their fisheries by stocking, and the result is excellent fishing, kept healthy through strict catch-and-release policies. The best way to locate these operations is through tourist information facilities in regional centres.

As for the dams and impoundments in the Golden West, fishing all of them generally requires a boat. Impoundment fishing has become an angling style with its own unique ways. These vary little from Somerset to Glenlyon or Boondooma. The most important thing to remember is not to overlook the wide range of freshwater fishing available within a weekend's drive of Brisbane!

A rugged walking track beside the Severn River near Lake Glenlyon

A nicely coloured golden perch from the headwaters of the Great Divide

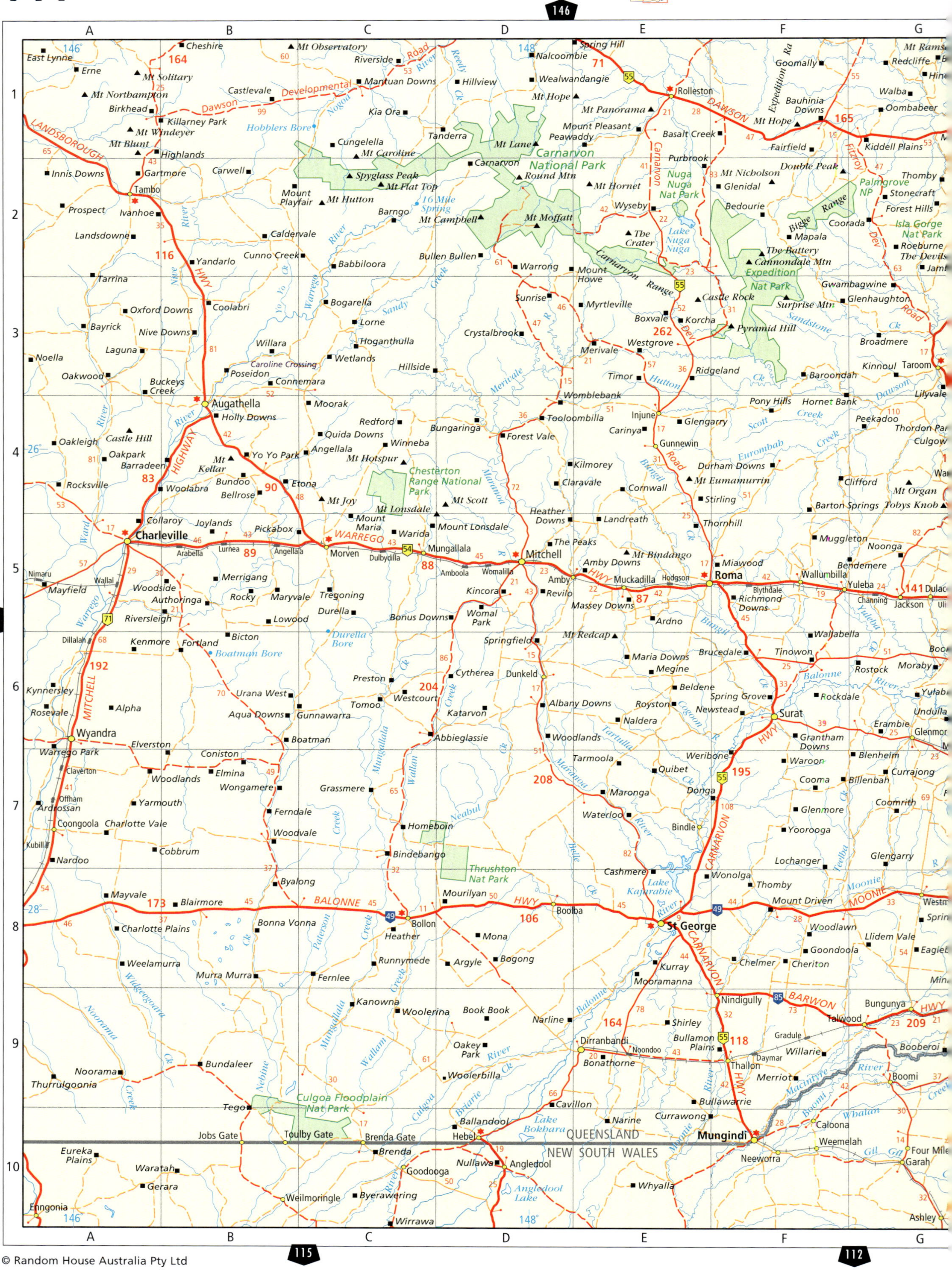
146
153
115
112
A
B
C
D
E
F
G
1
2
3
4
5
6
7
8
9
10
East Lynne
Cheshire
Erne
Mt Solitary
Mt Northampton
Birkhead
Killarney Park
Mt Windeyer
Mt Blunt
Highlands
Innis Downs
Gartmore
Tambo
Prospect
Ivanhoe
Landsdowne
Yandarlo
Tarrina
Oxford Downs
Coolabri
Bayrick
Nive Downs
Laguna
Noella
Oakwood
Buckeys Creek
Augathella
Holly Downs
Oakleigh
Castle Hill
Oakpark
Barradeen
Mt Kellar
Rocksville
Woolabra
Bundoo
Bellrose
Collaroy
Joylands
Charleville
Arabella
Lurnea
Pickabox
Angellala
Nimaru
Mayfield
Wallal
Woodside
Authoringa
Riversleigh
Dillalah
Kenmore
Fortland
Bicton
Boatman Bore
Kynnersley
Alpha
Rosevale
Wyandra
Warrego Park
Claverton
Elverston
Coniston
Woodlands
Elmina
Offham
Ardrossan
Yarmouth
Wongamere
Coongoola
Charlotte Vale
Kubill
Nardoo
Cobbrum
Mayvale
Blairmore
Charlotte Plains
Weelamurra
Murra Murra
Noorama
Thurrulgoonia
Bundaleer
Tego
Jobs Gate
Toulby Gate
Culgoa Floodplain Nat Park
Eureka Plains
Waratah
Gerara
Enngonia
Mt Observatory
Riverside
Mantuan Downs
Castlevale
Hobblers Bore
Kia Ora
Cungelella
Mt Caroline
Spyglass Peak
Mt Flat Top
Mount Playfair
Mt Hutton
Barngo
Caldervale
Cunno Creek
Babbiloora
Bogarella
Lorne
Hoganthulla
Willara
Wetlands
Caroline Crossing
Poseidon
Connemara
Moorak
Redford
Quida Downs
Angellala
Winneba
Yo Yo Park
Mt Hotspur
Etona
Mt Joy
Mount Maria
Chesterton Range National Park
Warida
Morven
Dulbydilla
Merrigang
Rocky
Maryvale
Tregoning
Lowood
Durella
Durella Bore
Urana West
Aqua Downs
Gunnawarra
Boatman
Tomoo
Preston
Westcourt
Grassmere
Ferndale
Woodvale
Byalong
Bonna Vonna
Fernlee
Kanowna
Woolerina
Brenda Gate
Brenda
Goodooga
Weilmoringle
Byerawering
Wirrawa
Hillview
Tanderra
Carnarvon
16 Mile Spring
Mt Campbell
Bullen Bullen
Hillside
Bungaringa
Mt Scott
Mt Lonsdale
Mount Lonsdale
Mungallala
Amboola
Bonus Downs
Cytherea
Katarvon
Abbieglassie
Homeboin
Bindebango
Thrushton Nat Park
Mourilyan
Bollon
Heather
Runnymede
Argyle
Mona
Bogong
Book Book
Oakey Park
Woolerbilla
Ballandool
Hebel
Nullawa
Angledool
Angledool Lake
Spring Hill
Nalcoombie
Wealwandangie
Mt Hope
Mt Panorama
Mount Pleasant
Peawaddy
Mt Lane
Carnarvon National Park
Round Mtn
Mt Hornet
Mt Moffatt
Warrong
Mount Howe
Carnarvon Range
Sunrise
Myrtleville
Crystalbrook
Merivale
Womblebank
Tooloombilla
Forest Vale
Kilmorey
Claravale
Heather Downs
Landreath
The Peaks
Mt Bindango
Mitchell
Womalilla
Amby Downs
Amby
Muckadilla
Hodgson
Kincora
Revilo
Massey Downs
Womal Park
Springfield
Mt Redcap
Maria Downs
Dunkeld
Megine
Albany Downs
Woodlands
Tarmoola
Maronga
Waterloo
Cashmere
Boolba
St George
Kurray
Mooramanna
Narline
Dirranbandi
Noondoo
Bonathorne
Cavillon
Narine
Lake Bokhara
Whyalla
QUEENSLAND
NEW SOUTH WALES
Rolleston
Basalt Creek
Purbrook
Nuga Nuga Nat Park
Wyseby
The Crater
Lake Nuga Nuga
Boxvale
Korcha
Westgrove
Timor
Injune
Carinya
Gunnewin
Cornwall
Ardno
Beldene
Royston
Naldera
Quibet
Donga
Bindle
Lake Kajarabie
Shirley
Bullamon Plains
Thallon
Bullawarrie
Currawong
Mungindi
Neeworra
Goomally
Expedition Ra
Bauhinia Downs
Mt Hope
Fairfield
Mt Nicholson
Double Peak
Glenidal
Bedourie
Bigge Range
Mapala
Coorada
The Battery
Cannondale Mtn
Expedition Nat Park
Castle Rock
Surprise Mtn
Pyramid Hill
Ridgeland
Glengarry
Pony Hills
Durham Downs
Mt Eumamurrin
Stirling
Thornhill
Miawood
Roma
Blythdale
Richmond Downs
Wallumbilla
Muggleton
Bendemere
Yuleba
Channing
Jackson
Brucedale
Tinowon
Spring Grove
Newstead
Surat
Rockdale
Grantham Downs
Weribone
Warroon
Cooma
Glenmore
Yoorooga
Lochanger
Wonolga
Thomby
Mount Driven
Woodlawn
Goondoola
Chelmer
Cheriton
Nindigully
Talwood
Gradule
Willarie
Daymar
Merriot
Caloona
Weemelah
Redcliffe
Walba
Oombabeer
Kiddell Plains
Thomby
Palmgrove NP
Stonecraft
Forest Hills
Isla Gorge Nat Park
Roeburne
The Devils
Gwambagwine
Glenhaughton
Broadmere
Kinnoul
Taroom
Baroondah
Lilyvale
Horse Bank
Peekadoo
Thordon Park
Clifford
Mt Organ
Barton Springs
Tobys Knob
Noonga
Bendemere
Rostock
Moraby
Erambie
Glenmorgan
Blenheim
Billenbah
Currajong
Coomrith
Glengarry
Lliden Vale
Bungunya
Booberoi
Boomi
Four Mile
Garah
Ashley
LANDSBOROUGH
MITCHELL
WARREGO
BALONNE
CARNARVON
DAWSON
MOONIE
BARWON
HWY
Developmental Road

0 20 40 60 80 100
kilometres

147

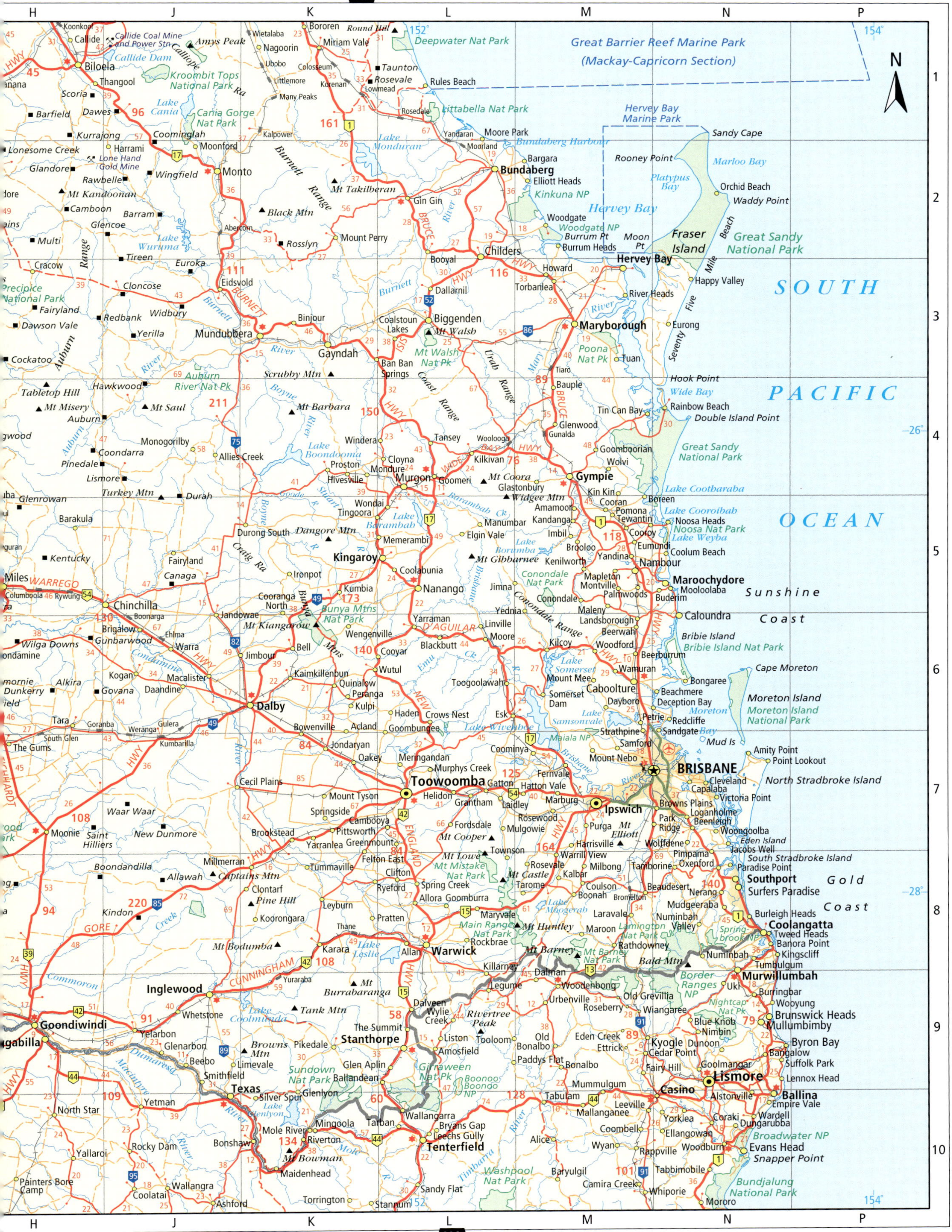

113

149

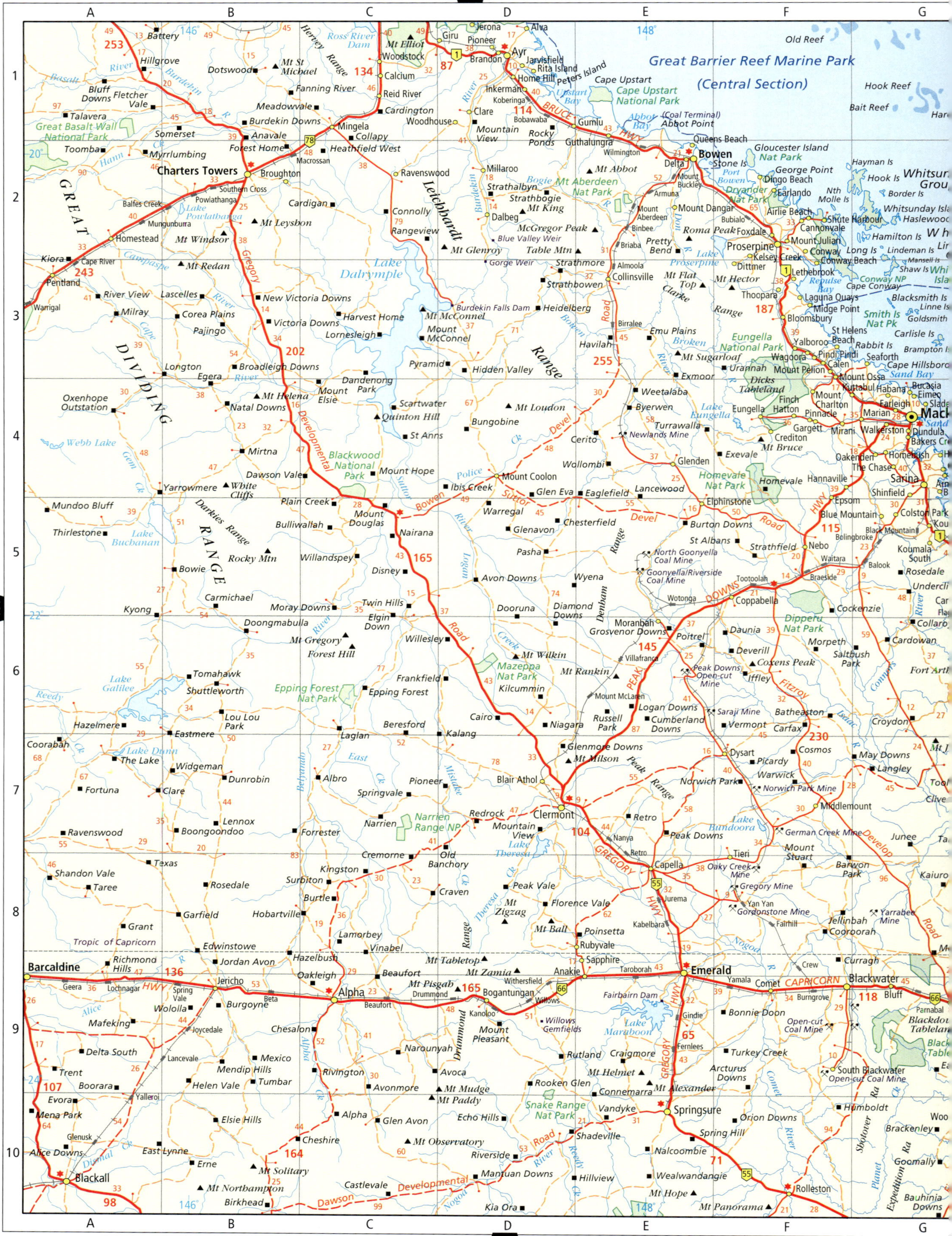

A
B
C
D
E
F
G
1
2
3
4
5
6
7
8
9
10
Great Barrier Reef Marine Park
(Central Section)
Old Reef
Hook Reef
Bait Reef
Hayman Is
Hook Is
Whitsunday Group
Border Is
Whitsunday Island
Haslewood
Lindeman Is
Shaw Is
Whitsunday Islands
Conway NP
Cape Conway
Blacksmith Is
Linne Is
Goldsmith
Smith Is Nat Pk
Carlisle Is
Brampton Is
Cape Hillsborough
Sand Bay
Battery
Hillgrove
Dotswood
Mt St Michael
Hervey Range
Ross River Dam
Mt Elliot
Woodstock
Calcium
Reid River
Giru
Jerona
Alva
Pioneer
Brandon
Ayr
Jarvisfield
Rita Island
Home Hill
Peters Island
Cape Upstart
Cape Upstart National Park
Upstart Bay
Inkerman
Kokeringa
Clare
Bobawaba
Gumlu
Mountain View
Rocky Ponds
Guthalungra
Abbot Bay
(Coal Terminal)
Abbot Point
Queens Beach
Wilmington
Bowen
Gloucester Island Nat Park
Stone Is
Port Bowen
George Point
Dingo Beach
Dryander Nat Park
Earlando
Nth Molle Is
Airlie Beach
Shute Harbour
Cannonvale
Mount Julian
Proserpine
Kelsey Creek
Conway
Conway Beach
Lethebrook
Repulse Bay
Laguna Quays
Midge Point
Bloomsbury
St Helens Beach
Yalboroo
Rabbit Is
Seaforth
Pindi Pindi
Calen
Wagoora
Mount Pelion
Mount Ossa
Kuttabul
Habana
Bucasia
Eimeo
Slade Point
Mount Charlton
Farleigh
Finch Hatton
Pinnacle
Marian
Mackay
Gargett
Mirani
Walkerston
Dundula
Bakers Creek
Homebush
Oakenden
The Chase
Sarina
Hannaville
Shinfield
Epsom
Colston Park
Blue Mountain
Black Mountain
Belingbroke
Nebo
Koumala South
Waitara
Balook
Rosedale
Braeside
Undercliffe
Cockenzie
Carmila
Collaroy
Cardowan
Saltbush Park
Fort Arthur
Croydon
May Downs
Langley
Clive
Middlemount
Junee
Burdekin
Bluff Downs
Fletcher Vale
Talavera
Great Basalt Wall National Park
Somerset
Toomba
Myrrlumbing
Charters Towers
Burdekin Downs
Anavale
Forest Home
Broughton
Mingela
Collapy
Heathfield West
Macrossan
Cardington
Woodhouse
Ravenswood
Millaroo
Strathalbyn
Bogie
Mt Aberdeen Nat Park
Strathbogie
Mt King
Dalbeg
McGregor Peak
Blue Valley Weir
Table Mtn
Mt Abbot
Delta
Mount Buckley
Armuna
Mount Aberdeen
Mount Dangar
Bubialo
Binbee
Roma Peak
Foxdale
Briaba
Pretty Bend
Almoola
Collinsville
Mt Flat Top
Mt Hector
Dittmer
Thoopara
Clarke Range
Strathmore
Strathbowen
Gorge Weir
Mt Glenroy
Leichhardt
Southern Cross
Powlathanga
Balfes Creek
Lake Powlathanga
Mungunburra
Homestead
Cardigan
Mt Leyshon
Connolly
Rangeview
Mt Windsor
Kiora
Cape River
Pentland
Mt Redan
Lake Dalrymple
Warrigal
River View
Lascelles
Milray
Corea Plains
Pajingo
New Victoria Downs
Victoria Downs
Harvest Home
Lornesleigh
Burdekin Falls Dam
Mt McConnel
Mount McConnel
Heidelberg
Birralee
Emu Plains
Broken River
Havilah
Eungella National Park
Mt Sugarloaf
Urannah
Exmoor
Dicks Tableland
Eungella
Lake Eungella
Great Dividing Range
Longton
Egera
Broadleigh Downs
Dandenong Park
Pyramid
Hidden Valley
Oxenhope Outstation
Mt Helena
Mount Elsie
Natal Downs
Scartwater
Quinton Hill
St Anns
Mt Loudon
Bungobine
Weetalaba
Byerwen
Turrawalla
Newlands Mine
Cerito
Glenden
Exevale
Wollombi
Webb Lake
Mirtna
Blackwood National Park
Mount Hope
Dawson Vale
Mount Coolon
Ibis Creek
Glen Eva
Eaglefield
Lancewood
Homevale Nat Park
Homevale
Elphinstone
Yarrowmere
White Cliffs
Mundoo Bluff
Plain Creek
Mount Douglas
Warregal
Glenavon
Chesterfield
Burton Downs
St Albans
Strathfield
Thirlestone
Lake Buchanan
Darkies Range
Bulliwallah
Nairana
Pasha
North Goonyella Coal Mine
Goonyella/Riverside Coal Mine
Rocky Mtn
Willandspey
Disney
Avon Downs
Wyena
Tootoolah
Coppabella
Wotonga
Bowie
Carmichael
Kyong
Moray Downs
Twin Hills
Elgin Down
Dooruna
Diamond Downs
Denham Range
Moranbah
Grosvenor Downs
Dipperu Nat Park
Doongmabulla
Mt Gregory
Forest Hill
Willesley
Poitrel
Daunia
Morpeth
Deverill
Coxens Peak
Villafranca
Peak Downs
Open-cut Mine
Iffley
Mt Wilkin
Mazeppa Nat Park
Mt Rankin
Kilcummin
Tomahawk
Shuttleworth
Lake Galilee
Epping Forest Nat Park
Epping Forest
Frankfield
Mount McLaren
Logan Downs
Saraji Mine
Batheaston
Cumberland Downs
Vermont
Carfax
Russell Park
Hazelmere
Lou Lou Park
Eastmere
Laglan
Beresford
Kalang
Cairo
Niagara
Glenmore Downs
Mt Wilson
Dysart
Cosmos
Picardy
Warwick
Norwich Park
Norwich Park Mine
Coorabah
Lake Dunn
The Lake
Widgeman
Dunrobin
Albro
Springvale
Pioneer
Blair Athol
Fortuna
Clare
Narrien
Narrien Range NP
Redrock
Clermont
Mountain View
Retro
Lake Bundoora
German Creek Mine
Ravenswood
Lennox
Boongoondoo
Forrester
Old Banchory
Lake Theresa
Nanya
Peak Downs
Mount Stuart
Texas
Cremorne
Tieri
Capella
Oaky Creek Mine
Barwon Park
Shandon Vale
Taree
Rosedale
Kingston
Surbiton
Craven
Peak Vale
Gregory Mine
Yan Yan
Gordonstone Mine
Yarrabee Mine
Burtle
Mt Zigzag
Florence Vale
Jurema
Jellinbah
Coorooran
Grant
Garfield
Hobartville
Lamorbey
Mt Ball
Poinsetta
Kabelbara
Fairhill
Tropic of Capricorn
Edwinstowe
Vinabel
Rubyvale
Sapphire
Crew
Curragh
Barcaldine
Richmond Hills
Jordan Avon
Hazelbush
Oakleigh
Mt Tabletop
Mt Zamia
Anakie
Taroborah
Emerald
Yamala
Comet
Blackwater
Bluff
Geera
Lochnagar
Spring Vale
Jericho
Beta
Alpha
Beaufort
Mt Pisgah
Drummond
Withersfield
Bogantungan
Willows
Fairbairn Dam
Burngrove
Parnabal
Blackdown Tableland
Wololla
Burgoyne
Mafeking
Joycedale
Chesalon
Kanoloo
Mount Pleasant
Willows Gemfields
Lake Maraboon
Gindie
Bonnie Doon
Open-cut Coal Mine
Delta South
Mexico
Lancevale
Narounyah
Rutland
Craigmore
Fernlees
Turkey Creek
Trent
Mendip Hills
Rivington
Avoca
Mt Helmet
Arcturus Downs
South Blackwater Open-cut Coal Mine
Boorara
Helen Vale
Tumbar
Avonmore
Mt Mudge
Mt Paddy
Rooken Glen
Connemarra
Mt Alexander
Evora
Yalleroi
Mena Park
Elsie Hills
Alpha
Glen Avon
Echo Hills
Snake Range Nat Park
Vandyke
Springsure
Humboldt
Orion Downs
Glenusk
Cheshire
Mt Observatory
Shadeville
Spring Hill
Brackenley
Alice Downs
East Lynne
Riverside
Nalcoombie
Gomally
Erne
Mt Solitary
Mantuan Downs
Hillview
Wealwandangie
Blackall
Mt Northampton
Castlevale
Dawson Developmental Road
Mt Hope
Rolleston
Birkhead
Kia Ora
Mt Panorama
Bauhinia Downs
Expedition Ra
Planet
Shotover
Gregory Developmental Road
Peak Downs Hwy
Capricorn Hwy
Bruce Hwy
Gregory Hwy
Bowen Developmental Road
Suttor Developmental Road
Dawson Developmental Road
146°
148°
20°
22°
24°

151

144

0 20 40 60 80 100
kilometres

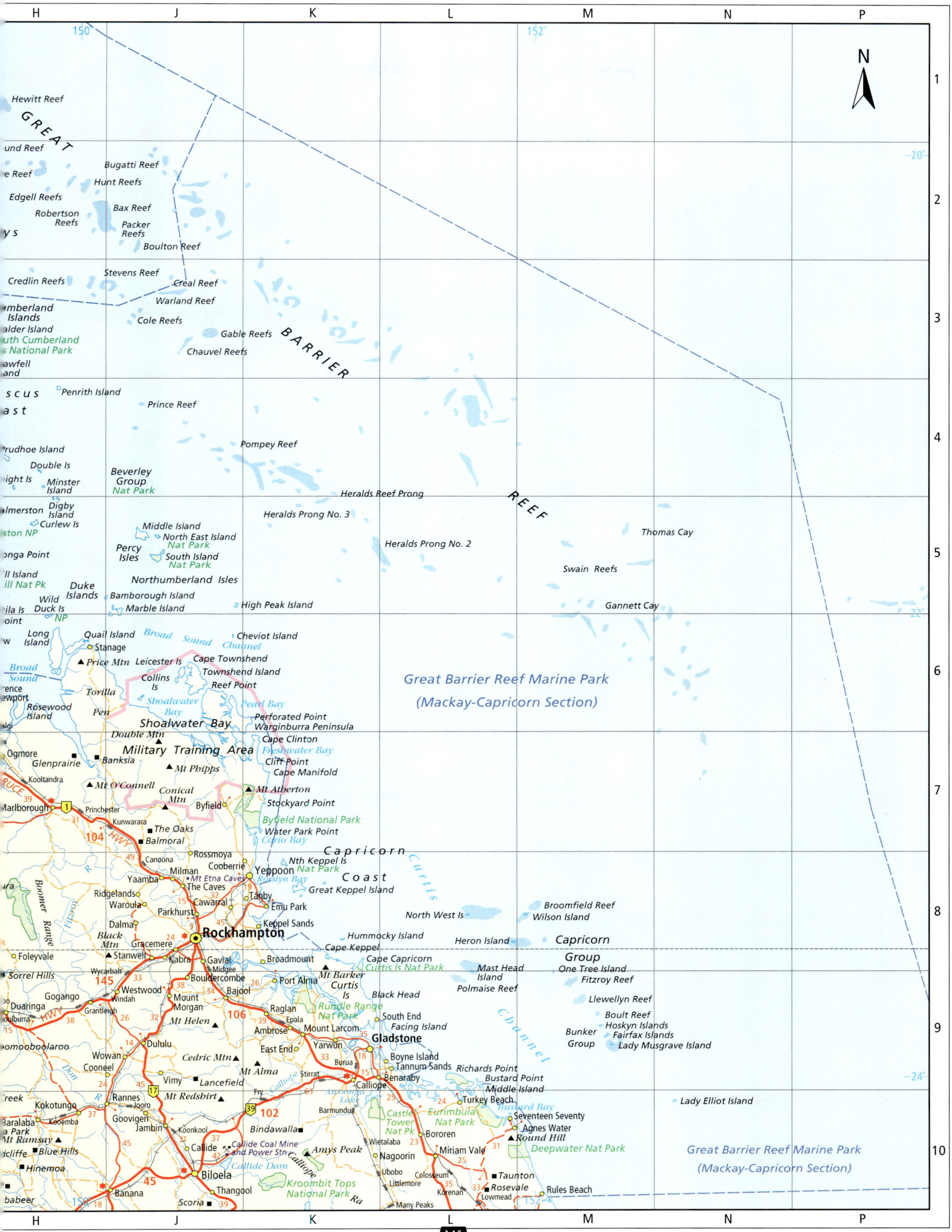

145

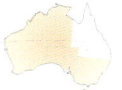

148 North Queensland

54

0 20 40 60 80 100
kilometres
H J K L M N P
1 2 3 4 5 6 7 8 9 10
CORAL SEA
SOUTH PACIFIC OCEAN
GREAT BARRIER REEF
Great Barrier Reef Marine Park (Cairns Section)
Great Barrier Reef Marine Park (Central Section)
GREAT DIVIDING RANGE
Great Dividing Range
Coen
Silver Plains
Hedge Reef
Corbett Reef
Claremont Point
Davie Reef
Tydeman Reef
Waterwitch Passage
Old Silver Plains
Eden Reef
Stewart
Foxs Lookout
Flinders Group Nat Park
Stanley Is
Flinders Is
Bathurst Bay
Cape Melville
Twin Peaks
Bathurst Head
South Warden Reef
Yarraden
Princess Charlotte Bay
Beabey Hill
Ninian Bay
Barrow Pt
Mid Reef
Crescent Reef
Annie
Lily Vale
Wakooka Outstation
Cape Bowen
Howick Is
Howick Group NP
Hicks Reef
Red Point
Day Reef
Cooks Passage
Marina Plains
Murdoch Point
Yonge Reef
New Bamboo
Cape Melville National Park
Brown Peak
Lizard Island Nat Park
Cormorant Passage
Flat Top Hill
Saddle Hill
Eagle Is
Musgrave
Breeza Plains Outstation
Black Hill
Martin Reef
Ribbon Reef
Glen Garland
Lakefield National Park
Kalpowar
Jack Lakes
Lookout Point
Rocky Islets Nat Park
Munburra
Lakefield
Mt Norkwa
Starcke Nat Park
Cape Flattery
Dixie Outstation
Starcke
New Dixie
Glenrock
Elderslie
Hann River Roadhouse
Mt Jack
Kalinga
Koolburra Mtn
Lakefield National Park
Battle Camp
Cape Bedford
Louisiana
Koolburra Outstation
Old Laura
Hope Vale Aboriginal Community
Nob Point
Hazelmere
Endeavour
Endeavour River NP
Fairview
Marton
Cooktown
Killarney
Olive Vale
Mt Cook NP
Walker Bay
Osterland Reef
Laura
Black Mtn Nat Park
Archer Point
Kimba
Forsberg Pt
Gill Patches
Pinnacles
Crocodile
Helenvale
Rossville
Cairns Reef
Cruiser Pass
Fairlight
Springvale
Cedar Bay Nat Park
Cedar Bay
Rattlesnake Point
Lakeland
Ayton
Strathleven
King Junction
Mt Lukin
Wujal Wujal
Weary Bay
Mt Emma
Mt Hann
Degarra
Agincourt Reefs
Mt Daintree
Palmerville
Maytown (ruins)
Mt McDowall
Cape Tribulation Nat Park
Mackay Reef
Palmer River Roadhouse
Cape Tribulation
Maiden Peak
Thornton Beach
St Crispin Reef
Alexandra Bay
Rudder Reef
Mt Mulgrave
Mt Hurford
Woods Peak
Maitland Downs
Daintree National Park
Daintree
Twyford
Cape Kimberley
Snapper Is
Opal Reef
Tongue Reef
Mount Mulgrave
Wonga
Dayman Point
Norman Reef
Groganville
Mt Spurgeon
Miallo
Newell
Batt Reef
Holmes Reef
Mt Elephant
Mossman
Mossman Gorge
Cooya Beach
Port Douglas
Trinity Opening
Hastings Reef
Burke
Gamboola
Bellevue
Hurricane
Mount Carbine
Maryfarms
Craiglie
Pebbly Beach
Michaelmas Reef
Wrotham Park
Rumula
Julatten
Trinity Bay
Oyster Reef
Arlington Reef
Mount Molloy
Ellis Beach
Clifton Beach
Trinity Beach
Flora Reef
Hann Tableland National Park
Kuranda
Yorkeys Knob
Machans Beach
Green Is Nat Park
Nychum
Koah
Stratford
Yarrabah
Moore Reef
Bulimba
Mount Mulligan
Kingsborough
Biboohra
Cairns
Fitzroy Island Nat Park
Elford Reef
Kays Mtn
Mareeba
White Rock
Thornborough
Edmonton
Sudbury Reef
Blackdown
Rookwood
Grey Peaks NP
Mungana
Chillagoe
Wolfram
Mutchilba
Walkamin
Dimbulah
Tinaroo Falls
Gordonvale
Chillagoe-Mungana Caves Nat Park
Calcifer
Fluorspar
Tolga
Lake Tinaroo
Deeral
Bellenden Ker
Jubilee Mtn
Verdure
Atherton
Yungaburra
Gibson Reef
Torwood
Almaden
Petford
Herberton
Babinda
Bramston Beach
Bolwarra
Irvinebank
Malanda
Butchers Ck
Howie Reef
Tate Tin Mines
Ootann
Koorboora
Tarzali
Bartle Frere
Miriwinni
Fischerton
Millaa Millaa
Daradgee
Flying Fish Point
Hall-Thompson Reef
Mt May
Gilmore Mine
Kaban
Goondi
Innisfail
Etty Bay
Bulleringa Nat Park
Ravenshoe
South Johnstone
Mourilyan Harbour
Adelaide Reef
Abingdon Downs
Bullock Creek
Mount Garnet
Innot Hot Springs
Mourilyan
Cowley
Potter Reef
Mt Emu
Gingerella
Cowley Beach
Taylor Reef
Burlington
Barwidgi
Morecambe
Cardstone
Japoon
Kurrimine Beach
Lyndbrook
Sundown
Koombooloomba
Tully Falls
Silkwood
El Arish
Bingil Bay
Eden Vale
Van Lee
Barney Knob
Mission Beach
Campbell Mtn
Dagworth
O'Briens Creek
Gemfields
Gunnawarra
Lake Koombooloomba
Tully
Dunk Island
Mt Departure
Silky Oak Creek
South Mission Beach
Cabana
Springfield
Euramo
Hull Heads
Tully Heads
Ironhurst
Brooklands
Fewhurst
Mt Poole
Forty Mile Scrub National Park
Tiger Hill
Otter Reef
Hot Springs
Talaroo
Mount Surprise
Kirrama
Edmund Kennedy NP
Rockingham Bay
Goold Island Nat Park
Minnamoolka
Glen Ruth
Cape Richards
Cape Sandwich
Durham
Eveleigh
Yaramulla
Blencoe Falls
Kennedy
Britomart Reef
Hinchinbrook Island
Georgetown
Glen Harding
Herbert River Falls
Meadowbank
Mt Thorn
Cardwell
Riverview
Undara Volcanic National Park
Lumholtz Nat Park
Trunk Reef
Mt Bowen
Hinchinbrook Island National Park
Donnyville
Mt Webster
Mt Tabletop
Kens Bluff
Wairuna
Rib Reef
Lornvale
Rosella Plains
Abergowrie
George Point
Hopkinson Reef
Bowl Reef
Einasleigh
Mt Misery
Bowman Hill
Long Pocket
Lucinda
Forsayth
Wirra Wirra
Narrawa
Lake Lucy
Macknade
Halifax
Pelorus Is
Orpheus Island Nat Park
John Brewer Reef
Trebonne
Ingham
Spring Creek
Valley of Lagoons
Carpentaria Downs
Conjuboy
Upper Stone
Forrest Beach
Curacoa Is
Great Palm Island
Mt Bentley
North Head
Mt Helpman
Robinhood
Wyandotte
Mt Lee
Toobanna
The Oaks
Mywyn
Kidston
The Lynd Junction
Camel Creek
Mt Fox
Bambaroo
Halifax Bay
Havannah Island
Davis Reef
Cobbold Gorge
Oasis Roadhouse
South Head
The Lynd
Greenvale Nickel Mine
Greenvale
Kangaroo Hills
Hidden Valley
Moongobulla
Acheron Island
Broadhurst Reef
Mt Lyall
Blue Range
Paluma
Paluma Range Nat Park
Rollingstone
Herald Island
Bairds Table Mtn
Christmas Creek
Mt Halifax
Magnetic Island
Ewan
Taravale
Toolakea
Saunders Beach
Nat Park
Picnic Bay
Mt Lookout
Blue Range
Yabulu
Pallarenda
Cape Cleveland
Fog Creek
North Knob
Lyndhurst
Clarke River
New Moon
Bluewater
Townsville
Bowling Green Bay Nat Park
Hanns Table Hill
Oak Park
Teddy Mtn
Pandanus Creek
Blue Water Springs Roadhouse
Tabletop
Thuringowa
Garbutt
Stuart
Alligator Creek
Cape Bowling Green
Bellfield
Werrington
Mt Mackay
Laroona
Star
Nome
Bowling Green Bay
Niall
Antill Plains
Jerona
Montgomery Range
Big Ben
Battery
Hervey Range
Ross River Dam
Mt Elliot
Giru
Alva
Blackbraes
Oak Valley
Maryvale
Pioneer
Woodstock
Brandon
Ayr
Strathpark
Hillgrove
Dotswood
Mt St Michael
Calcium
Jarvisfield
Rita Island
Peters Island
Castle Hill
Mt Louisa
Home Hill
Cape Upstart
Chudleigh Park
Clarke Hills
Bluff Downs
Fletcher Vale
Fanning River
Reid River
Inkerman
Middle Park
Nulla Nulla
Meadowvale
Cardington
Upstart Bay
Cape Upstart National Park
Kings Knob
Talavera
Clare
Maiden Springs
Burdekin Downs
Woodhouse
Mingela
Mount Norman
Great Basalt Wall National Park
Collapy
Mountain View
Rocky Ponds
Bobawaba
Gumlu
Abbot Bay
Cuba Plains
Somerset
Anavale
Heathfield West
Guthalungra
Reedy Springs
Toomba
Forest Home
Cargoon
Myrrlumbing
Macrossan
Wilmington
Pretty Plains
Mt Courtney
Charters Towers
Broughton
Ravenswood
Millaroo
Mt Abbot
Mount Sturgeon
Mount Emu Plains
Lake Cargoon
Killarney
Southern Cross
Bogie
Peninsula Developmental Rd
Kennedy Hwy
Gregory Developmental Rd
Bruce Hwy
Cook Hwy
Flinders Hwy
144°
146°
148°
14°
16°
18°
20°

151

146

150 Outback Queensland

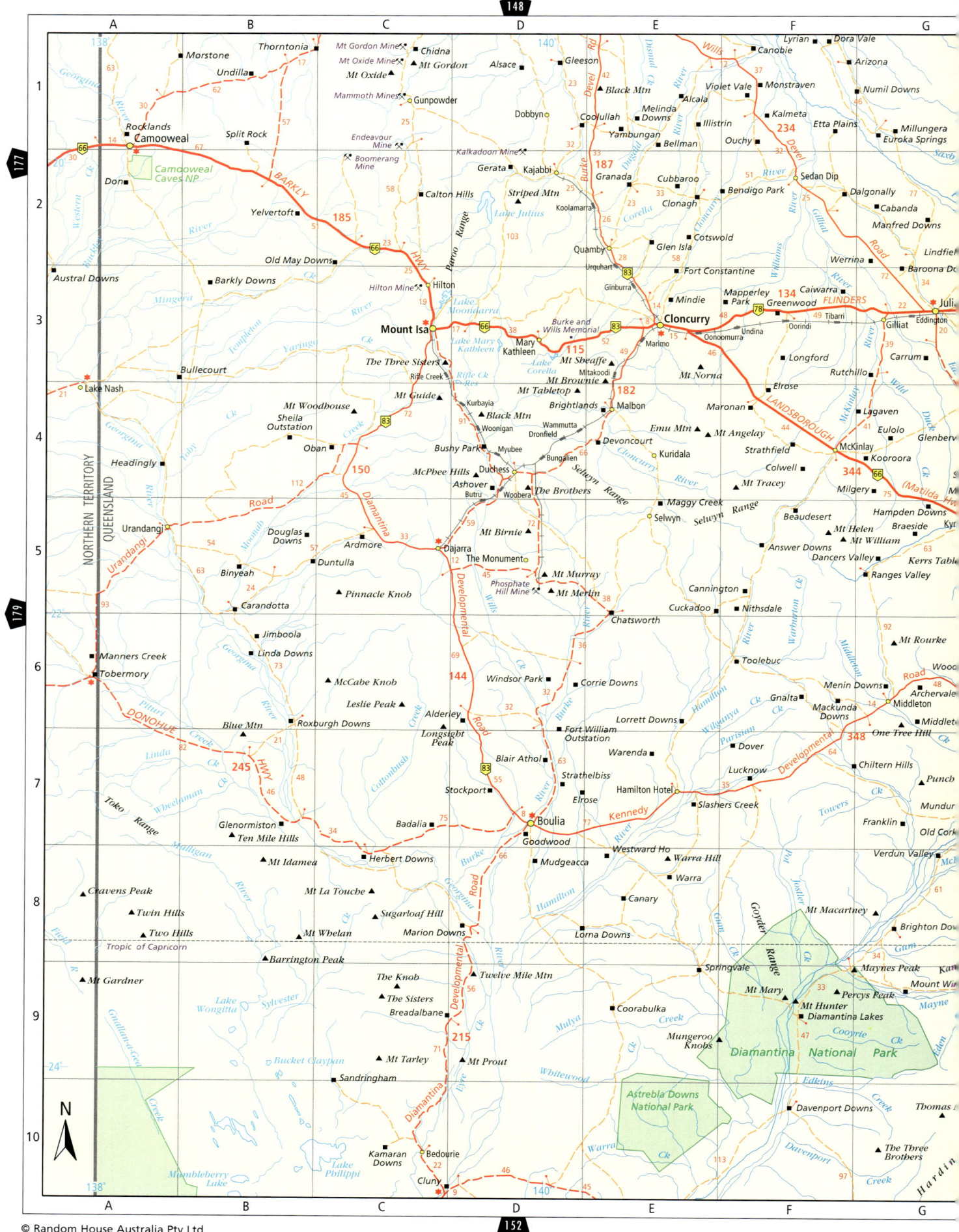

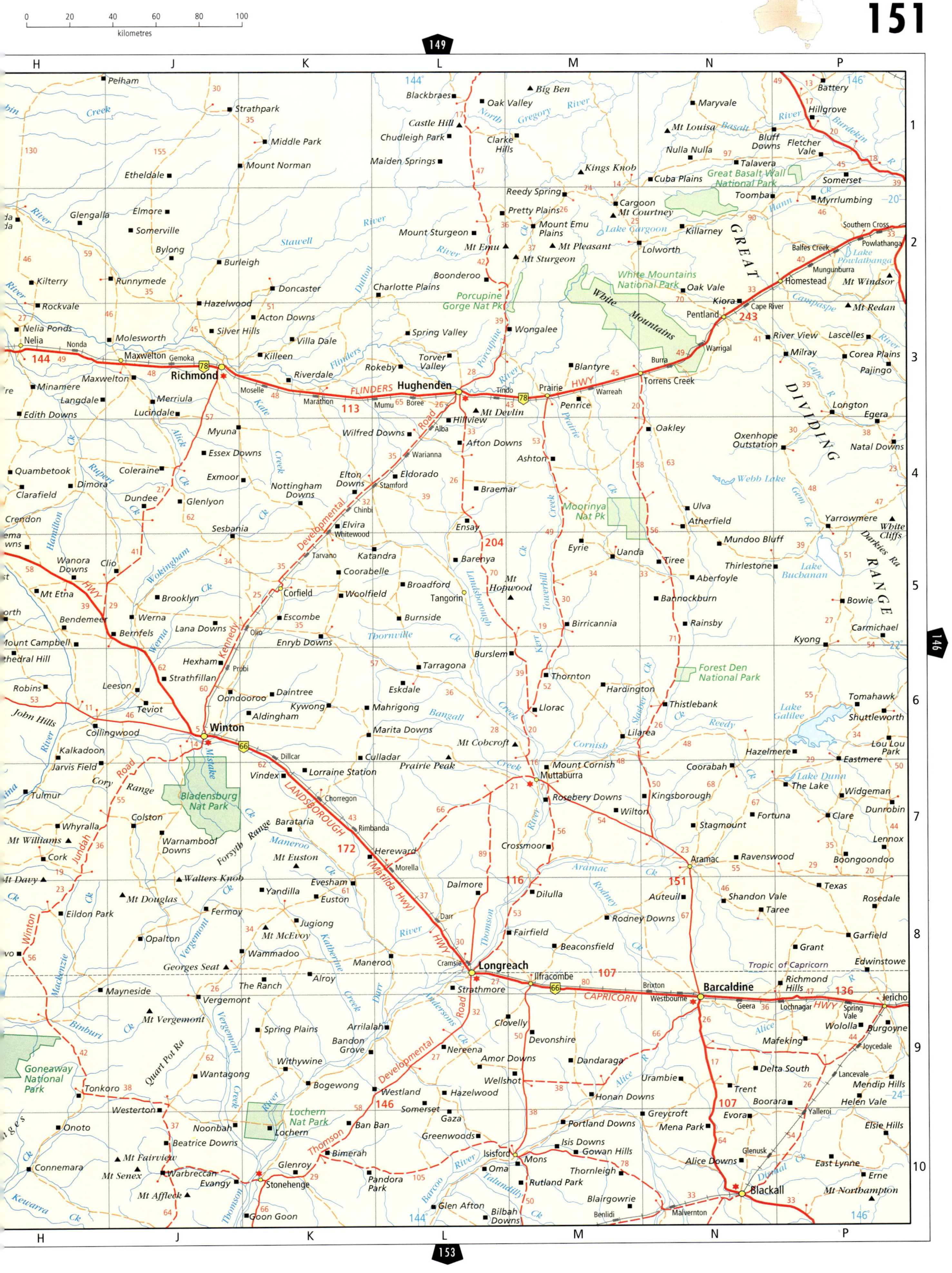
0 20 40 60 80 100
kilometres
149
153
146
H J K L M N P
1 2 3 4 5 6 7 8 9 10
Pelham
Strathpark
Middle Park
Mount Norman
Etheldale
Elmore
Glengalla
Somerville
Bylong
Burleigh
Kilterry
Runnymede
Rockvale
Hazelwood
Doncaster
Acton Downs
Silver Hills
Villa Dale
Nelia Ponds
Nelia
Nonda
Molesworth
Maxwelton
Gemoka
Richmond
Killeen
Riverdale
Minamere
Maxwelton
Langdale
Merriula
Lucindale
Edith Downs
Myuna
Essex Downs
Quambetook
Coleraine
Dimora
Exmoor
Clarafield
Dundee
Glenlyon
Crendon
Sesbania
Wanora Downs
Clio
Mt Etna
Brooklyn
Bendemeer
Werna
Bernfels
Lana Downs
Mount Campbell
Hexham
Strathfillan
Robins
Leeson
Teviot
John Hills
Collingwood
Winton
Kalkadoon
Jarvis Field
Cory
Range
Tulmur
Bladensburg Nat Park
Colston
Whyralla
Mt Williams
Cork
Mt Davy
Warnambool Downs
Walters Knob
Mt Douglas
Eildon Park
Fermoy
Opalton
Georges Seat
Mayneside
Vergemont
Mt Vergemont
Binburi
Goneaway National Park
Tonkoro
Westerton
Onoto
Connemara
Mt Senex
Mt Fairview
Warbreccan
Evangy
Mt Affleck
Kewarra
Noonbah
Beatrice Downs
Wantagong
Quart Pot Ra
Blackbraes
Oak Valley
Big Ben
Castle Hill
Chudleigh Park
Clarke Hills
Maiden Springs
Mount Sturgeon
Mt Emu
Mt Sturgeon
Boonderoo
Charlotte Plains
Porcupine Gorge Nat Pk
Spring Valley
Wongalee
Torver Valley
Rokeby
Hughenden
FLINDERS HWY
Moselle
Marathon
Mumu
Boree
Tindo
Prairie
Warreah
Mt Devlin
Hillview
Alba
Wilfred Downs
Afton Downs
Warianna
Ashton
Elton Downs
Eldorado
Stamford
Nottingham Downs
Chinbi
Braemar
Elvira
Whitewood
Ensay
Tarvano
Katandra
Coorabelle
Barenya
Broadford
Tangorin
Mt Hopwood
Corfield
Woolfield
Burnside
Escombe
Ojio
Enryb Downs
Thornville
Burslem
Tarragona
Probi
Oondooroo
Daintree
Eskdale
Aldingham
Kywong
Mahrigong
Marita Downs
Dillcar
Culladar
Mt Cobcroft
Prairie Peak
Lorraine Station
Vindex
Chorregon
Rimbanda
Barataria
Maneroo
Mt Euston
Hereward
Morella
Evesham
Yandilla
Euston
Jugiong
Mt McEvoy
Wammadoo
Maneroo
Alroy
The Ranch
Spring Plains
Arrilalah
Bandon Grove
Withywine
Bogewong
Westland
Lochern Nat Park
Lochern
Ban Ban
Bimerah
Glenroy
Stonehenge
Pandora Park
Goon Goon
Darr
Dalmore
Cramsie
Longreach
Strathmore
Ilfracombe
Clovelly
Devonshire
Nereena
Amor Downs
Wellshot
Hazelwood
Somerset
Gaza
Greenwoods
Isisford
Mons
Oma
Rutland Park
Glen Afton
Bilbah Downs
Maryvale
Mt Louisa
Bluff Downs
Fletcher Vale
Battery
Hillgrove
Nulla Nulla
Talavera
Kings Knob
Cuba Plains
Great Basalt Wall National Park
Somerset
Reedy Spring
Cargoon
Mt Courtney
Toomba
Myrrlumbing
Pretty Plains
Mount Emu Plains
Lake Cargoon
Killarney
Southern Cross
Mt Pleasant
Lolworth
Balfes Creek
Powlathanga
Lake Powlathanga
Mungunburra
White Mountains National Park
Oak Vale
Homestead
Mt Windsor
Kiora
Cape River
Mt Redan
Pentland
River View
Lascelles
Warrigal
Milray
Corea Plains
Blantyre
Burra
Torrens Creek
Pajingo
Penrice
Longton
Egera
Oakley
Oxenhope Outstation
Natal Downs
Webb Lake
Moorinya Nat Pk
Ulva
Atherfield
Yarrowmere
White Cliffs
Mundoo Bluff
Eyrie
Uanda
Tiree
Thirlestone
Lake Buchanan
Aberfoyle
Bannockburn
Bowie
Birricannia
Rainsby
Carmichael
Kyong
Forest Den National Park
Thornton
Hardington
Tomahawk
Llorac
Thistlebank
Lake Galilee
Shuttleworth
Lilarea
Lou Lou Park
Hazelmere
Eastmere
Mount Cornish
Muttaburra
Coorabah
Lake Dunn
The Lake
Widgeman
Rosebery Downs
Kingsborough
Wilton
Fortuna
Dunrobin
Clare
Stagmount
Lennox
Crossmoor
Aramac
Ravenswood
Boongoondoo
Dilulla
Auteuil
Shandon Vale
Taree
Texas
Rosedale
Rodney Downs
Fairfield
Beaconsfield
Garfield
Grant
Edwinstowe
Tropic of Capricorn
Barcaldine
Richmond Hills
Brixton
Westbourne
Geera
Lochnagar
Jericho
Spring Vale
CAPRICORN HWY
Wololla
Burgoyne
Mafeking
Joycedale
Dandaraga
Urambie
Delta South
Lancevale
Mendip Hills
Trent
Honan Downs
Booroa
Helen Vale
Portland Downs
Greycroft
Mena Park
Evora
Yalleroi
Elsie Hills
Isis Downs
Gowan Hills
Glenusk
Thornleigh
Alice Downs
East Lynne
Erne
Blackall
Mt Northampton
Blairgowrie
Benlidi
Malvernton
GREAT DIVIDING RANGE
Darkies Ra
White Mountains
LANDSBOROUGH (Matilda Hwy)
Developmental Road
Kennedy
Thomson
Barcoo
Alice
Landsborough
Towerbill
Cornish
Aramac
Rodney
Flinders
Porcupine
Dutton
Stawell
Gregory
North
Burdekin
Campaspe
Cape
Tabletop
Kate
Alick
Rupert
Hamilton
Wokingham
Mistake
Forsyth Range
Katherine
Maneroo
Anderson
Talundilly
Jundah
Mackenzie
Winton
Vergemont
Thomson
Dismal
144
113
172
204
116
151
107
136
146
243
78
66

152 SOUTH-WEST QUEENSLAND

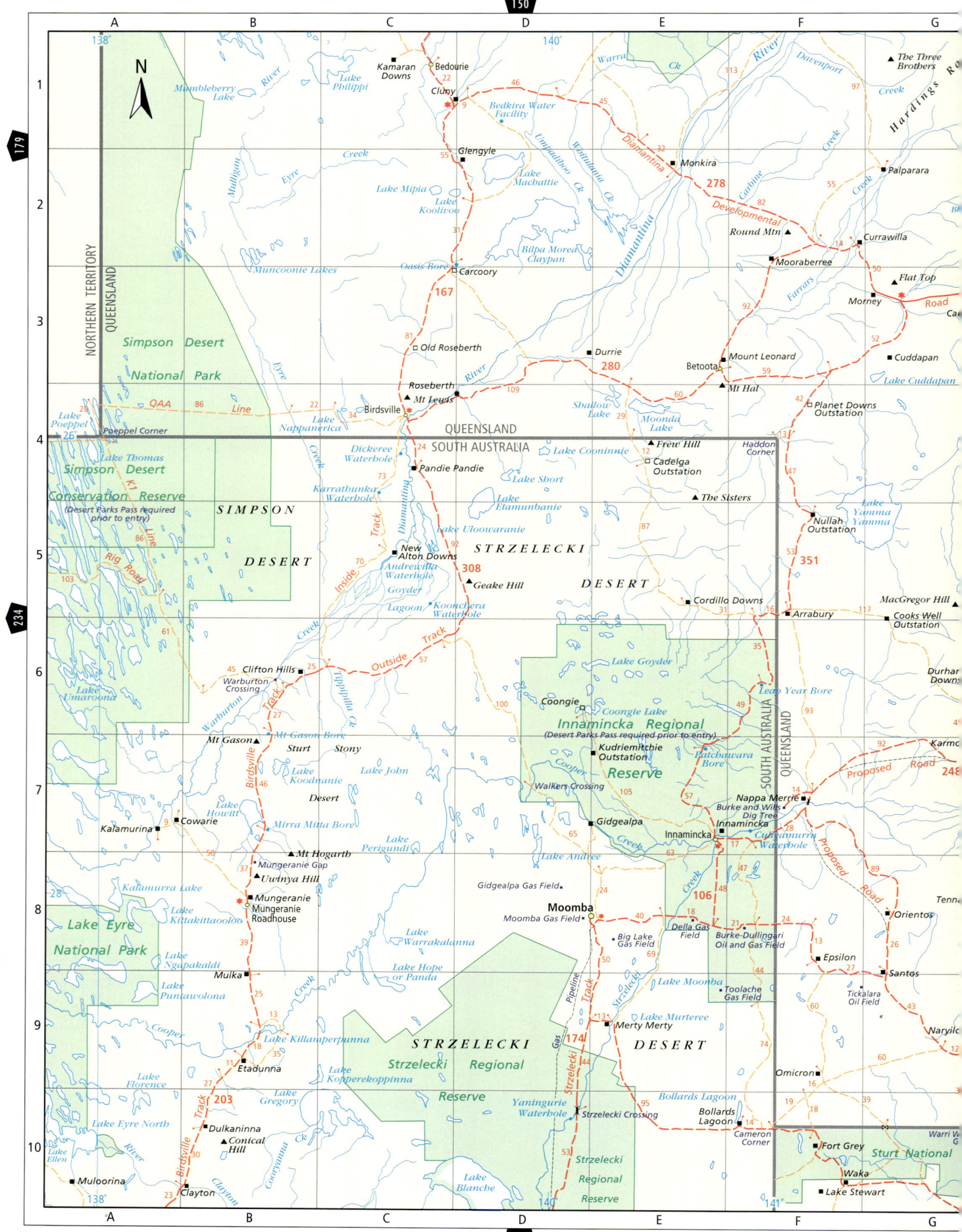

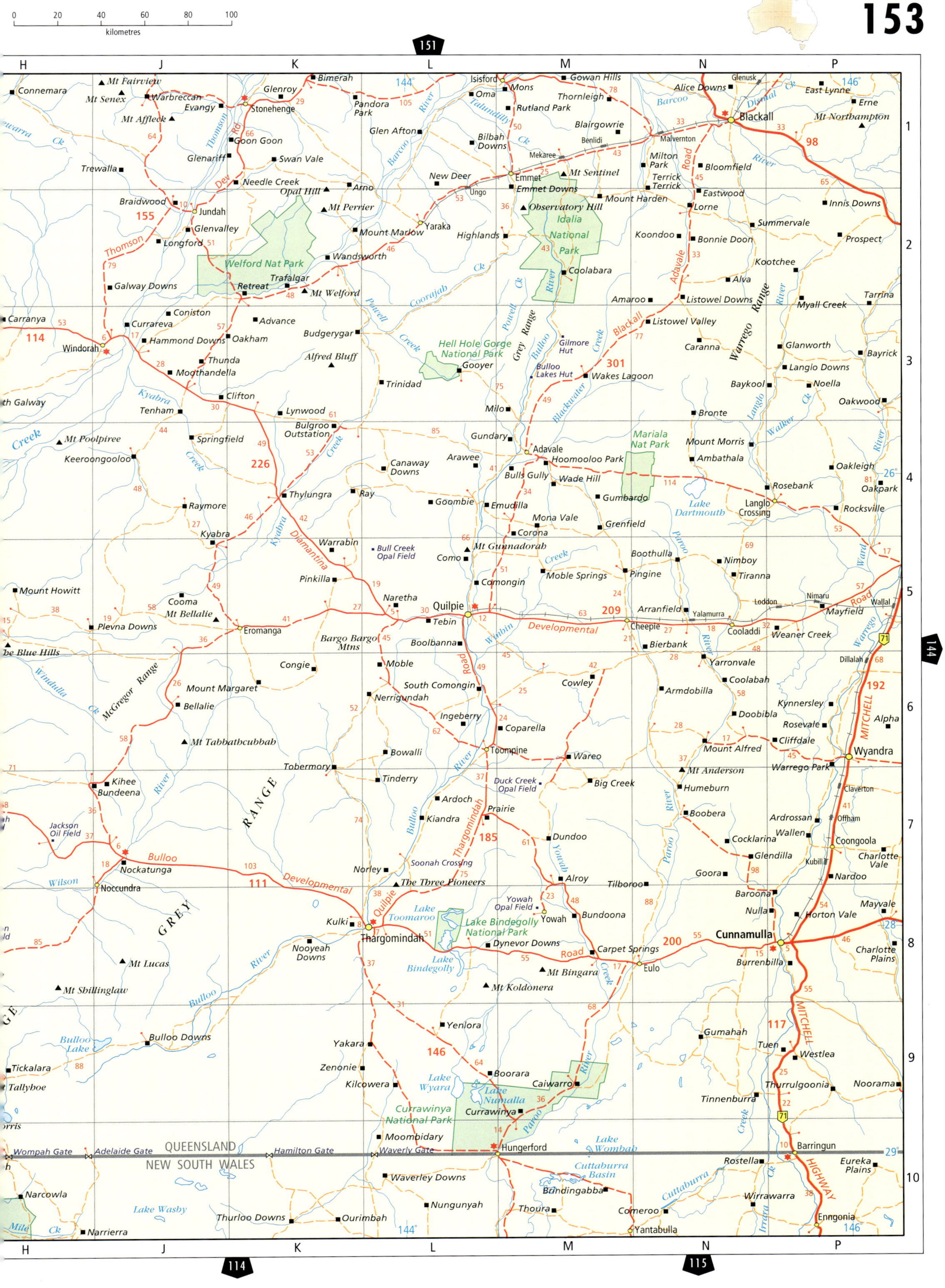
0
20
40
60
80
100
kilometres
151
114
115
144
H
J
K
L
M
N
P
1
2
3
4
5
6
7
8
9
10
Connemara
Mt Fairview
Mt Senex
Warbreccan
Evangy
Stonehenge
Glenroy
Bimerah
Pandora Park
Isisford
Oma
Mons
Gowan Hills
Thornleigh
Rutland Park
Blairgowrie
Benlidi
Alice Downs
Glenusk
East Lynne
Erne
Blackall
Mt Northampton
Mt Affleck
Goon Goon
Glenariff
Swan Vale
Glen Afton
Bilbah Downs
Mekaree
Malvernton
Milton Park
Bloomfield
Trewalla
Needle Creek
Opal Hill
Arno
New Deer
Ungo
Emmet
Emmet Downs
Mt Sentinel
Terrick Terrick
Eastwood
Innis Downs
Braidwood
Jundah
Mt Perrier
Yaraka
Observatory Hill
Mount Harden
Lorne
Summervale
Glenvalley
Longford
Mount Marlow
Highlands
Idalia National Park
Koondoo
Bonnie Doon
Prospect
Thomson
Welford Nat Park
Wandsworth
Coolabara
Kootchee
Galway Downs
Retreat
Trafalgar
Mt Welford
Alva
Amaroo
Listowel Downs
Tarrina
Myall Creek
Carranya
Coniston
Currareva
Advance
Hammond Downs
Oakham
Budgerygar
Windorah
Hell Hole Gorge National Park
Gilmore Hut
Listowel Valley
Caranna
Glanworth
Bayrick
Thunda
Moothandella
Alfred Bluff
Gooyer
Bulloo Lakes Hut
Wakes Lagoon
Langlo Downs
Trinidad
Baykool
Noella
Clifton
Tenham
Lynwood
Milo
Bronte
Oakwood
Bulgroo Outstation
Gundary
Mariala Nat Park
Mount Morris
Mt Poolpiree
Springfield
Adavale
Ambathala
Keeroongooloo
Canaway Downs
Arawee
Hoomooloo Park
Oakleigh
Bulls Gully
Wade Hill
Rosebank
Oakpark
Thylungra
Ray
Goombie
Emudilla
Gumbardo
Lake Dartmouth
Langlo Crossing
Rocksville
Raymore
Mona Vale
Grenfield
Kyabra
Corona
Warrabin
Bull Creek Opal Field
Mt Gunnadorah
Como
Boothulla
Nimboy
Tiranna
Pinkilla
Comongin
Moble Springs
Pingine
Mount Howitt
Cooma
Naretha
Quilpie
Arranfield
Loddon
Nimaru
Wallal
Mayfield
Mt Bellalie
Tebin
Developmental
Cheepie
Yalamurra
Cooladdi
Weaner Creek
Plevna Downs
Eromanga
Bargo Bargo Mtns
Boolbanna
Bierbank
Dillalah
The Blue Hills
Congie
Moble
Yarronvale
Cowley
Coolabah
McGregor Range
Mount Margaret
South Comongin
Armdobilla
Nerrigundah
Kynnersley
Alpha
Bellalie
Ingeberry
Doobibla
Rosevale
Coparella
Mt Tabbatbcubbah
Toompine
Mount Alfred
Cliffdale
Wyandra
Tobermory
Bowalli
Wareo
Warrego Park
Mt Anderson
Kihee
Bundeena
Tinderry
Duck Creek Opal Field
Big Creek
Humeburn
Claverton
Ardoch
Prairie
Boobera
Ardrossan
Offham
Jackson Oil Field
Kiandra
RANGE
Dundoo
Cocklarina
Wallen
Coongoola
Bulloo
Nockatunga
Soonah Crossing
Glendilla
Kubill
Charlotte Vale
Norley
Alroy
Tilboroo
Goora
Nardoo
Wilson
Noccundra
The Three Pioneers
Baroona
Yowah Opal Field
Yowah
Bundoona
Nulla
Mayvale
Horton Vale
Kulki
Lake Toomaroo
Lake Bindegolly National Park
Thargomindah
Dynevor Downs
Carpet Springs
Cunnamulla
Charlotte Plains
GREY
Nooyeah Downs
Lake Bindegolly
Road
Eulo
Burrenbilla
Mt Lucas
Mt Bingara
Mt Koldonera
Mt Shillinglaw
Yenlora
Gumahah
MITCHELL
Tuen
Bulloo Lake
Bulloo Downs
Yakara
Westlea
Tickalara
Zenonie
Boorara
Lake Wyara
Kilcowera
Caiwarro
Thurrulgoonia
Noorama
Tallyboe
Lake Numalla
Tinnenburra
Currawinya National Park
Currawinya
Moombidary
Wompah Gate
Adelaide Gate
QUEENSLAND
Hamilton Gate
Waverly Gate
Hungerford
Lake Wombah
Barringun
NEW SOUTH WALES
Cuttaburra Basin
Rostella
Eureka Plains
Waverley Downs
HIGHWAY
Narcowla
Bindingabba
Cuttaburra
Wirrawarra
Lake Wasby
Nungunyah
Thoura
Comeroo
Engonia
Thurloo Downs
Ourimbah
Narrierra
Yantabulla
Diamantina
Grey Range
Warrego
Paroo
Barcoo
Blackwater

154 Cape York

CAIRNS AND SURROUNDING AREAS

155

NORTHERN TERRITORY

FISHING HOT SPOTS

- Darwin Harbour (pp. 158–9)
- Darwin Offshore (pp. 160–1)
- Bynoe Harbour (pp. 162–3)
- Shady Camp (pp. 164–5)
- Dundee Beach (pp. 166–7)
- The Daly River (pp. 168–9)
- Kakadu and the South Alligator River (pp. 170–1)
- East Alligator River (pp. 172–3)

With a land area of just less than 1.4 million square kilometres, the Northern Territory is almost twice as large as New South Wales, and six times bigger than Victoria. However, the Northern Territory's very modest population of around 150 000 — around half of whom live in Darwin and its surrounding communities — ensures that this remains one of the most sparsely peopled and relatively unspoiled parts of Australia.

The northern half of this largely untamed tropical region — an area popularly known as the Top End — represents one of the world's last great recreational fishing frontiers, and is attracting an increasing amount of attention amongst travelling anglers from Australia and the rest of the world.

Recognising the immense importance of recreational angling to their fast-growing economy, successive Territory governments have worked diligently since the early 1980s both to protect and enhance fish populations and the environmental resources upon which this lucrative sport fishery is based, and also to develop the infrastructure to cope with a steadily growing number of anglers.

Throughout this same period, commercial exploitation of fish stocks has been strictly controlled and recreational activities carefully regulated to ensure a sustainable future for fishing, especially for more important target species such as the mighty barramundi — the universally acknowledged icon of Northern Territory sport fishing.

Today, the Territory is reaping the benefits of these far-sighted policies as it attracts an increasingly large slice of the sizeable annual expenditure on recreational angling generated by Australian and overseas anglers.

Not surprisingly, it now also leads the rest of Australia in terms of the number, variety and integrity of its professional fishing guides, charter services, lodges and safari camps. These pay-to-fish operations are becoming increasingly relevant and necessary in order to cater to the needs of so many visiting anglers in a remote region that remains potentially harsh, unforgiving and even dangerous for the inadequately prepared traveller.

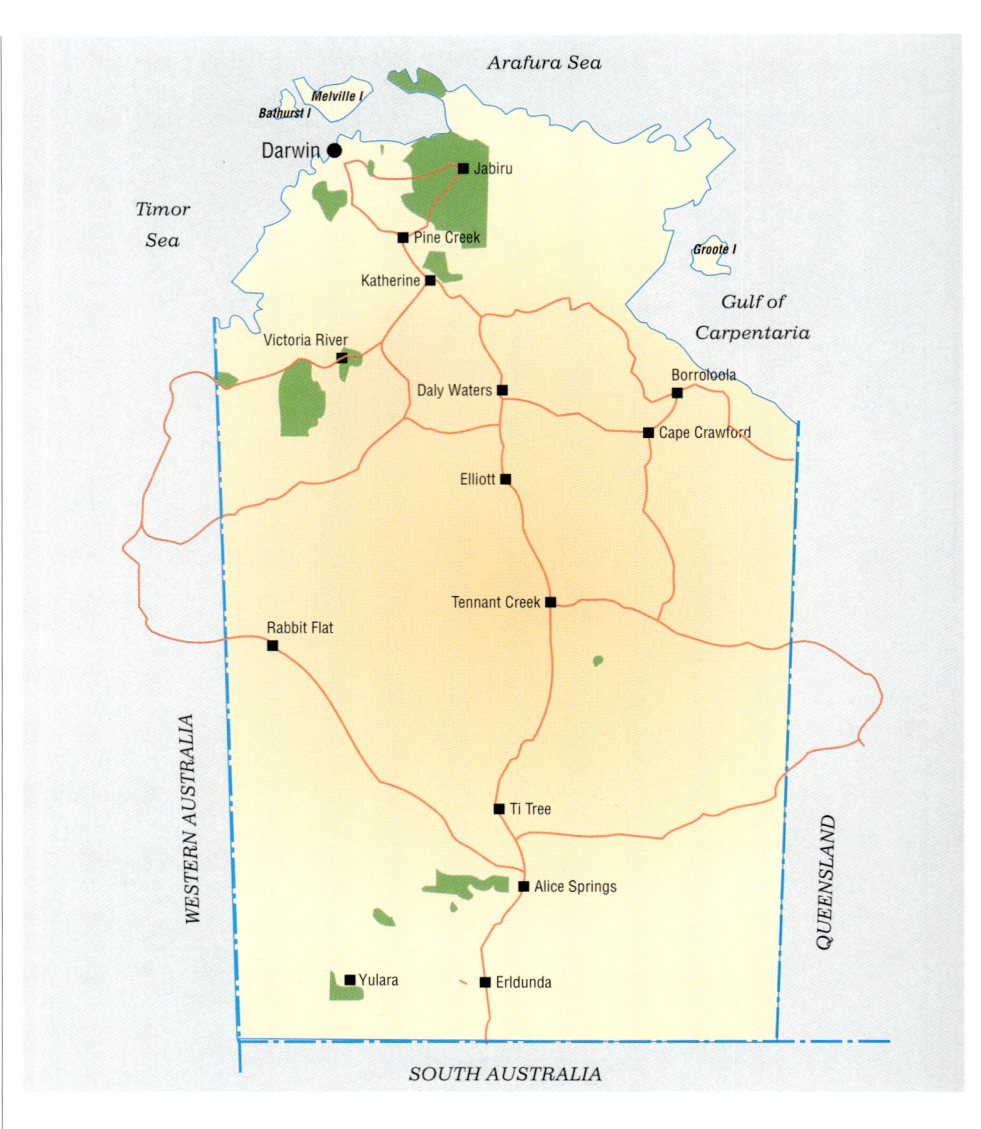

The remaining issue to be resolved for recreational angling in the Northern Territory is the vexing question of public access to Aboriginal lands and waters, World Heritage areas and national parks. Increasingly, recreational anglers and tourists find that entry to these extensive tracts of land is being cut off or restricted. This trend intensifies the pressures on the remaining portions of the Top End, as well as denying anglers a chance to sample some of the most exciting and potentially valuable fishing hot spots on earth. Those concerned need to hammer out an agreement that establishes a workable balance between the preservation of native title rights, natural heritage values, pastoral leaseholds, mining operations and public use for recreation.

Even taking into consideration any difficulties presented by the dynamic and occasionally confusing land and water access issue, however, the Territory remains — at least in recreational angling terms — one of the luckiest parts of the luckiest country on earth. It is truly a fishing paradise, and one of the sport's last great frontiers.

CONTACT NUMBERS

Anyone wishing to purchase maps or the video 'Sportfishing Australia's Northern Territory', or to obtain information on rules and regulations from the Fisheries Division of the Northern Territory, Department of Primary Industry and Fisheries should contact the Fisheries Division Licensing Office, GPO Box 990, Darwin NT 0801.

RECREATIONAL FISHING OFFICE
(08) 8999 4395

Reports of illegal fishing activity should be directed immediately to:
POLICE FISHERIES ENFORCEMENT HOTLINE
1800 89 1136

HOW TO BE CROCODILE WISE

In areas where estuarine crocodiles may be present you should follow this code:

- Be aware of crocodiles — keep your eyes open
- Do not feed or otherwise interfere with crocodiles
- Avoid areas where large crocodiles or their nests have been seen
- Camp at least 50 m from the water's edge
- Stand at least a few metres back from the water's edge when fishing and don't stand on logs overhanging deep pools
- If you're going for a swim, pick a shallow spot, e.g. over a rapid; don't swim in deep, dark waters; always swim in a group rather than alone
- Dispose of fish offal and any other animal refuse well away from camp sites; the carcasses of dead animals attract crocodiles
- Don't set a regular routine in these areas, such as cleaning fish on the side of a river at the same spot each day. Saltwater crocodiles are cunning hunters and have been known to observe such behaviour and wait for an opportune moment to attack
- Always take note of any warning signs — they are there for a reason

Saltwater crocodiles occur in all Top End rivers

The Dripstone Cliffs in Casuarina Coastal Reserve on the northern outskirts of Darwin

Aerial view of a meandering river in the Northern Territory

DARWIN HARBOUR

IN BRIEF

MAP REFERENCE: PAGE 174 D4

GETTING THERE Darwin Harbour is on the foreshores of the city itself, with boat ramp access at several locations
BEST TIME TO FISH April to December
BEST TIME TO TRAVEL May to November
MAJOR ANGLING SPECIES Barramundi, golden snapper (fingermark), black jewfish, pikey bream, threadfin salmon, blue salmon and queenfish
SPECIAL RESTRICTIONS Fishing is not permitted in Doctors Gully Fish Reserve
WARNINGS Various rock reefs become exposed at different tide levels in the harbour arms. These present potential hazards to navigation
ACCOMMODATION Accommodation of all levels is available in Darwin
CHARTER BOATS AND FISHING GUIDES HotSpot Fishing Tours can arrange fishing trips with accredited charter boat operators and fishing guides, telephone Freecall 1800 809 035

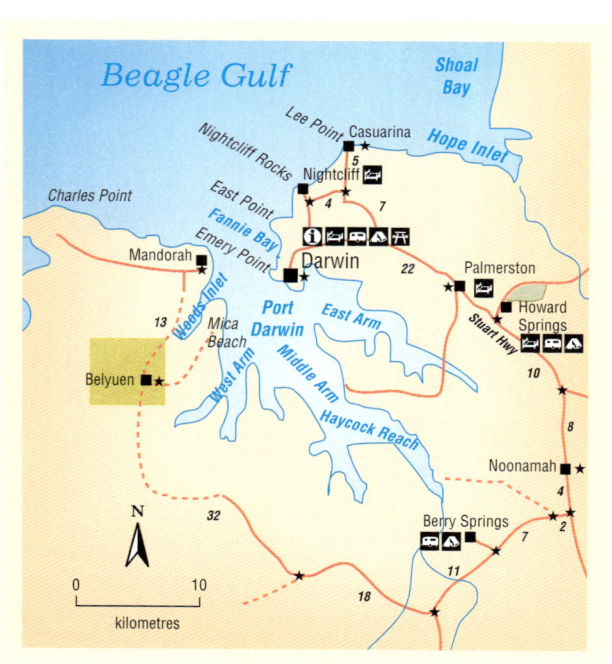

Sunrise over Darwin Harbour

Although Darwin is a capital city in every sense of the word, its immense, beautiful harbour offers a quality of fishing normally only encountered in far more remote parts of northern Australia. There are several reasons for this.

First, Darwin has a population of only 75 000 people and its nearby waters are subjected to relatively little fishing pressure compared with other capital city harbours. Secondly, Darwin Harbour is huge—many times the size of Sydney Harbour—and includes several adjoining estuaries, referred to locally as harbour arms, which in turn boast hundreds of creeks and rivulets. Thirdly, practically the entire foreshore of Darwin Harbour and its arms are lined with mangroves, a primary habitat and food source at the bottom of the food chain. Finally, this imposing body of water is flushed regularly by tidal movement of up to 7 m. Each sweep of the tide brings with it rich sources of food for angling target species, which either sit and wait in ambush for the tucker to arrive, or hitch a ride on the strong tidal currents.

Visitors to the Top End will generally be surprised at the easy access to different areas. There are formed concrete boat ramps at many locations and Darwin Harbour contains a lion's share. Using a 3.6-m to 4.6-m aluminium boat with adequate horsepower is standard practice in the harbour. A boat of this size is suitable for fishing the deep-water harbour itself during favourable sea conditions and ideal for venturing right up the harbour arms at any time.

SEASONAL OPTIONS

Of course, where to fish and at what time of day are dependent on several factors, not least of which is the Top End's dynamic seasonal calendar. The two main seasons are the 'Dry' and the 'Wet'. The dry season is usually from May until September inclusive. It is a beautiful time of year—warm with clear, blue skies by day and star-filled skies at night. South-east winds of varying intensity predominate during the dry season, and anglers intent on fishing the exposed main harbour in small boats need to work around the south-easterlies.

The Top End wet season gets under way in about December, often ending quite abruptly around mid-March. Fishing Darwin Harbour during this period is governed entirely by wet season activity. During a bout of monsoonal rain is not the time to be out fishing, and wet season storms can be fierce. However, breaks in the Wet can be productive—the two- to three-month period before the Wet (known as the 'build-up') is an excellent time to fish Darwin Harbour for most species and the weather is usually quite favourable at this time of year.

Most anglers visiting the Territory rate barramundi a priority, and there's great barra fishing to be had in Darwin Harbour's arms. There are four arms: East Arm, Middle Arm, West Arm and Woods Inlet. The build-up period leading to the wet season is prime barra time in the arms. The best fishing is during the spring tide phases when there is considerable tidal movement. Typically, a good day's fishing can be expected when the low tide is between 0.5 and 1.5 m.

WORKING THE TIDES

Lure casting is the most popular fishing style in the harbour's arms, and a very successful style it is at that. Most barramundi are caught on the bottom half of the tide by anglers casting lures at tidal gutters where dirty water is flowing off the mud banks into clear water. It helps if you can see bait fish working in the murky water as it increases the chance of a barra or two being there. These gutters are easily found along the foreshore of any of the harbour arms, but anglers can often do better poking up some of the larger creeks, particularly in the bigger East and Middle arms.

For some reason, harbour arm barramundi tend to stop biting during the quiet hour or two right at the bottom of the tide when there is no tidal run. Once the tide starts to push in again, however, the alert angler can find excellent fishing, especially if they once again target the muddy gutters. The tactic is to look for bait fish congregating in the gutters and moving up towards the mangroves with the rising tide. Mullet and other bait fish know they are safe once the tide rises into the tangled mangrove roots, but it's a deadly waiting game when a barramundi, salmon or other large predatory fish moves into the gutter beforehand.

There are many exposed rock bars in Darwin Harbour that regularly produce quality barramundi. Again, casting lures around the rocks is the preferred technique.

Tactics and Techniques

Small-to-medium swimming minnow lures work best in Darwin Harbour when fishing for barramundi. Shallow-to-medium divers are the norm, but lead-head soft plastics bounced across the mud and over submerged rocks sometimes work when all else fails. When all lures are unsuccessful, a lightly weighted live mullet will usually make the difference between a feed of fresh barra and nothing to show but the bodily wear and tear from a steamy day amongst the mangroves and mud.

There are many opportunities for bait fishing with handlines in Darwin Harbour. The bombing of Darwin during World War II, Cyclone Tracy and the ongoing program to create artificial reefs have resulted in many harbour wrecks which are home to various tropical reef species, including the highly regarded black jewfish. Generally encountered in small schools of 8- to 15-kg fish, the black jewfish is best fished for on the change of the tide using a heavy handline, weighted to the bottom, with a strong 9/0 to 12/0 hook baited with whole squid or fish bait. Black jewfish bite all year round in Darwin Harbour.

Bread and Butter Fishing

Southern anglers may be surprised to learn of the annual bream run in Darwin Harbour. The run occurs for a couple of months in the middle of the dry season when the weather is at its coolest. The best fishing is from sunset into the night, and most anglers concentrate their efforts on boat fishing along the eastern shore of Darwin Harbour. The target species here is pikey bream, which has dark blue lips, but is otherwise very similar in appearance to the southern silver bream.

The golden snapper (fingermark bream) is also a popular reef fish with Darwin anglers, and tasty plate-size specimens can be caught readily in the harbour arms when there is plenty of tidal movement. The top half of the tide is usually the best, fishing with squid bait at creek junctions, over rocky or shaly bottom or adjacent to rock bars.

For land-based anglers, the Stokes Hill Wharf below the city is a prime location. During the dry season, on neap tides (those with minimal tidal movement), floating pilchard baits catch a variety of pelagic species, including Spanish mackerel and queenfish. Even better jetty fishing can be experienced off the Mandorah Jetty on the opposite side of the harbour to the city.

A lovely catch of black jewfish from Darwin Harbour

Jetty fishing in Darwin Harbour, a popular pursuit among local anglers

DARWIN OFFSHORE

IN BRIEF

MAP REFERENCE: PAGE 174 D4

GETTING THERE Depart from Darwin city — road access to Darwin via Stuart and Arnhem Highways

BEST TIME TO FISH April to December

BEST TIME TO TRAVEL May to October

MAJOR ANGLING SPECIES Golden snapper, red-throat emperor, black jewfish, Spanish mackerel, longtail tuna, giant trevally, queenfish, sailfish and marlin

WARNINGS Wet season storms can be both sudden and fierce

ACCOMMODATION Accommodation of all levels is available in Darwin

CHARTER BOATS AND FISHING GUIDES HotSpot Fishing Tours can arrange day and extended fishing trips with accredited charter boat operators, telephone Freecall 1800 809 035

A combination of current-verging rock peninsulas, inshore and offshore shallow reefs, tropical islands, healthy reef and pelagic stocks, and abundant bait fish congregations provides Darwin bluewater anglers with myriad options for great fishing.

Perhaps the most famous location — and also the closest to Darwin — is Lee Point at the northern end of suburban Casuarina Beach. Lee Point pokes out like an extended finger for nearly a kilometre, its seaward end exposed only on the lowest of tides. The point marks the southern entrance to the nutrient-rich Shoal Bay system, with its mangrove-lined saltwater creeks and the small but imposing Howard River itself. This area is popular with the dinghy brigade as much as it is with larger boat owners. The closest boat access to Lee Point is from either Nightcliff ramp or Buffalo Creek ramp, although launching from the latter is only possible on the top half of the tide. Throughout the dry season, the main target species is the Spanish mackerel, and some world-class fish are caught off Lee Point. In fact, on a weekend morning or afternoon, it is not unusual to find dozens of boats anchored off the point, berley slicks evident and ganged pilchard or garfish baits streaming in the current. To add to this activity, other boats can usually be seen trolling big minnows around the point and out to nearby Angler's Reef.

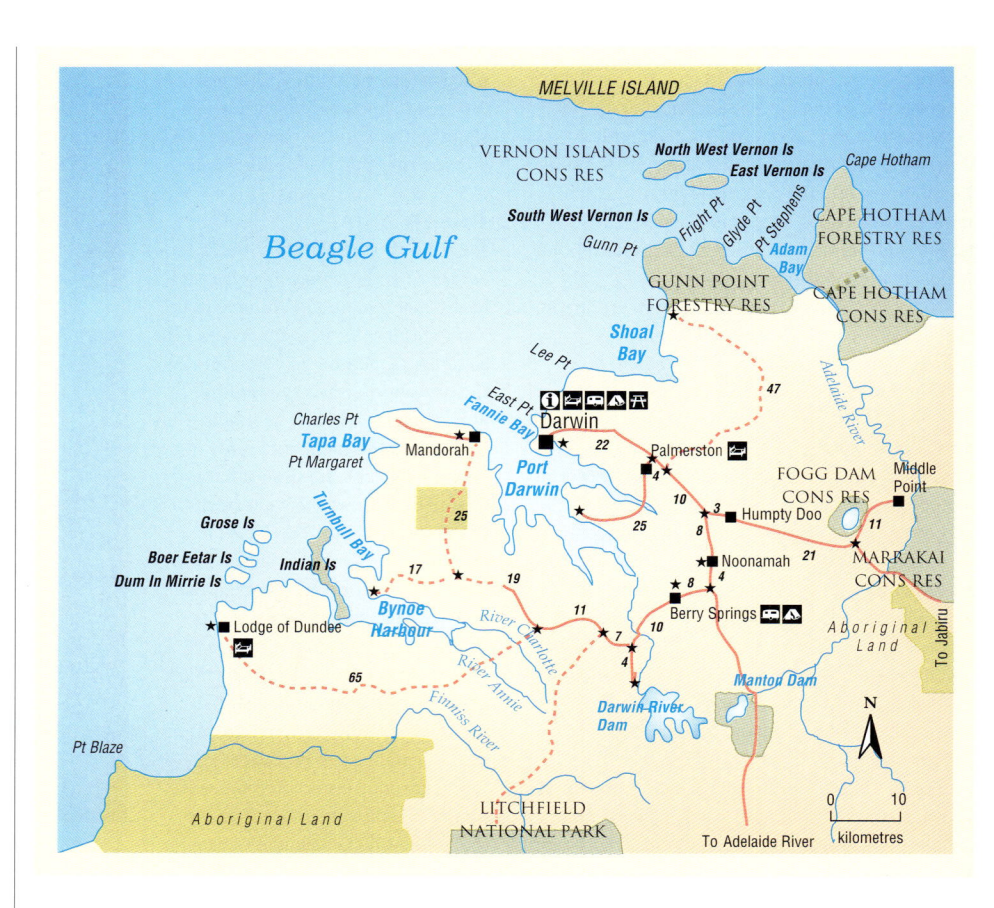

Bottom bouncers *can* catch a feed of fish at Angler's Reef, but the best catches come from the nearby Bottlewasher artificial reef.

Releasing a sailfish near the Fenton Patches

THE VERNON ISLANDS

The Vernon Islands to the north of Darwin are accessible from Darwin boat ramps or from the Leaders Creek ramp on the Gunn Point peninsula. Strong tidal currents wind through the islands and their many shallow reefs, making the area ideal habitat for the hard-fighting giant trevally. These fish are best caught by trolling pencil poppers or deep-diving minnows, but can often be difficult to land amongst the sharp coral and shallow rocky reefs. Two consistent trevally spots are Henry Ellis Reef off South West Vernon Island and Smith Reef off North West Vernon Island.

The best reef fishing is in the deeper holes or channels between the islands, particularly if you focus your efforts on the changes of tide when currents are not a problem. A popular channel is between South West Vernon Island and Gunn Point. Using heavy handlines or robust rod-and-reel outfits, anglers can often make good catches of black jewfish and golden snapper (fingermark).

At the tip of Gunn Point itself are the famous Blue Holes. Rather like lakes in the reef, they are only accessible near the top of the tide. Small reef fish, queenfish and trevally are the dominant catch.

FENTON PATCHES

About 30 km to the north-west of Darwin, on an area known as the Fenton Patches, a large complex of artificial reefs has become established as one of Darwin's best offshore fishing spots. It is also a popular attraction for scuba divers. Comprising various derelict hulks and heavy construction material, the artificial reef has been built in a hexagonal pattern, with the wreck of the *Marchart 3* forming the middle reef. Six other reefs are positioned a nautical mile apart and in a six-sided pattern around this central wreck.

Several of the reefs are buoyed 50 m to the north of their exact position. They are home to most Darwin reef species, including black jewfish, and are also patrolled regularly by vast schools of gold-spot and giant trevally. The Fenton Patches artificial reef complex can be fished right through neap tidal phases, but on spring tides strong currents restrict fishing to the turn of the tide.

In recent years, the areas immediately west of Fenton Patches and for several kilometres to the north have been proven as sailfish and marlin grounds. These billfish species are not prolific, but experienced anglers will generally bag or tag one every two or three trips.

Charles Point Patches

Charles Point Patches, about 20 km west of Darwin, is a renowned golden snapper and black jewfish spot. The patches are slightly offshore from the tip of the peninsula, which is marked by a lighthouse, and are best fished on a rising neap tide during the first few hours after first light in the morning. Good reef fishing is also available just inside the point itself, where a series of dropping ledges provides the ideal habitat for various species.

Around Charles Point and heading roughly south-west are a series of tidally exposed reefs leading on to the Grose Islands. It is quite feasible to fish parts of this large area in a day trip from Darwin. Anglers heading around Charles Point will first encounter Kellaway Reef, Fish Reef and Middle Reef. Drop-offs around these reefs provide the best reef fishing, particularly when a voracious school of golden snapper moves under the boat. Fish Reef is also frequented by schools of queenfish, which provide great light-tackle sport on trolled poppers and minnows.

Quail Island and Bass Reef

Quail Island is at the top of the Grose Islands chain. Its shallow waters are not usually productive for reef fish, but trolling around Quail Island and nearby Bare Sand Island will sometimes yield large queenfish or trevally.

For anglers desperate to catch a Spanish mackerel, there is no better ground within a day's reach of Darwin than Bass Reef, just 7 km west of Quail Island. On a rising neap tide during the dry season, a steady trail of crushed pilchards will soon attract hordes of mackerel in the 10- to 15-kg range. During hot sessions, double and even triple hook-ups on floating pilchard baits are the norm.

A very large Spanish mackerel from the Lee Point grounds off Darwin

Lorna Shoal, to the west of Bass Reef, marks the extremity of a comfortable day-fishing trip for a typical trailer boat departing from Darwin. There is wonderful reef fishing to be experienced at Lorna Shoal—not only for golden snapper and the occasional black jewfish, but also for tasty red-throat emperor (sweetlip) which often queue up to take the baits.

Wide of Darwin are two areas known as South Gutter and North Gutter. These extensive grounds offer exciting reef fishing, but are best fished on the drift due to their expanse and often prevailing strong currents. North Gutter is the most consistent, and is recognised as the home of some of the biggest golden snapper in Top End waters. It is also at the northern extremity of the billfish grounds.

Less ambitious pelagic fishermen troll the fringes of the gutter for giant trevally and Spanish mackerel, or chase longtail and mackerel tuna schools, casting small metal lures when a feeding pack comes within range.

BYNOE HARBOUR

IN BRIEF

MAP REFERENCE: PAGE 174 C4

GETTING THERE Bynoe Harbour is about 120 km south-west of Darwin by road, on the southern side of the Cox Peninsula
BEST TIME TO FISH March to January
BEST TIME TO TRAVEL April to December
MAJOR ANGLING SPECIES Barramundi, mangrove jack, threadfin salmon, blue salmon, estuary rock-cod, golden snapper, black jewfish, queenfish, giant trevally and Spanish mackerel
WARNINGS Rock bars in some creeks require careful navigation; extensive pearling leases in the harbour also require careful navigation
ACCOMMODATION There is bungalow-style accommodation at Crab Claw Island Fishermen's Village, telephone (08) 8978 2313
CHARTER BOATS AND FISHING GUIDES HotSpot Fishing Tours can arrange day fishing trips and extended fishing safaris with accredited operators, telephone Freecall 1800 809 035

Bynoe Harbour is less than two hours drive from Darwin heading south-west, which makes it a quite feasible destination for day fishing trips from that city. There are also plenty of sandy camping spots with no facilities on the harbour's eastern shore, although access is by 4WD only. Accommodation and facilities are available at Crab Claw Island Fishermen's Village on the western side of the harbour.

Longtail tuna are prolific during the dry seaason

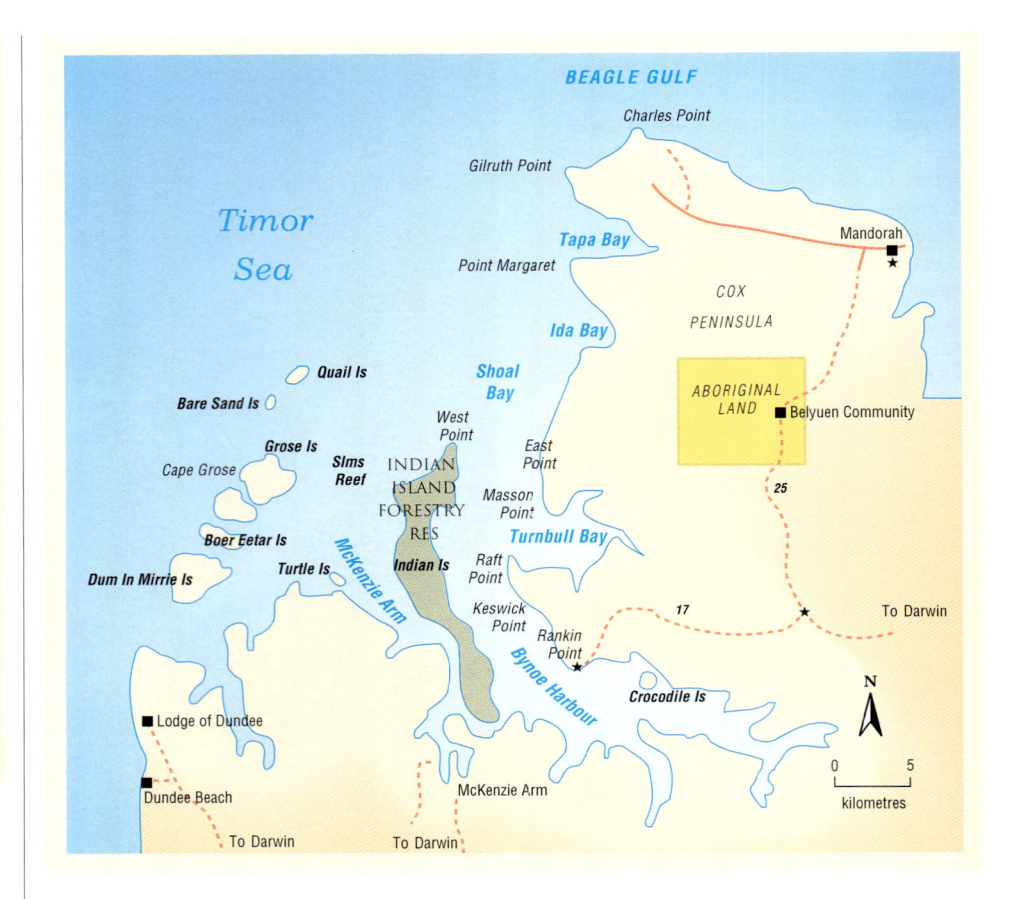

If you are camping or daytripping, you can launch your boat relatively easily (except at low tide) from the boat landing at Keswick Point on the eastern side of Bynoe Harbour. At high tide, small trailer boats can also be launched from the beach at scenic Raft Point. Anglers with large trailer boats usually head for Bynoe by sea all the way from Darwin. In good weather, the voyage typically takes an hour and a half.

There are dozens of significant creeks and hundreds of smaller creeks flowing into Bynoe Harbour. The estuary and its creeks are littered with rock bars and tidal gutters, all of which are capable of producing exciting lure and bait fishing action. Barramundi, threadfin salmon, blue salmon, mangrove jack, estuary cod and small golden snapper are all caught along the creeks, particularly when there is plenty of tidal movement. A couple of hours either side of a 1- to 1.5-m low tide is prime fishing time. Anglers can begin fishing an hour after high tide, however, casting lures around those rock bars which be totally exposed near the bottom of the tide.

The vast majority of creeks in Bynoe Harbour are on the western shore and anyone crossing the harbour must negotiate extensive pearl leases to get to the other side. Many of the rock bars are up the creeks and some are not evident until the bottom half of the tide. Caution should therefore always be exercised when exploring the creeks. Anglers should also take care not to become stranded above a rock bar on the falling tide.

OUTSTANDING JEWFISH

Although you can catch most tropical reef-dwelling species in and around Bynoe Harbour, this area is best known for the and size and numbers of black jewfish that are caught. The vast bottom terrain of Bynoe is honeycombed with deep holes, ledges and drop-offs, and black jewfish abound.

Spots to try for this species include just out in front of Raft Point, where the sea bed deepens dramatically; on and below the ledge which runs for some distance about a kilometre out on the southern side of Indian Island; and adjacent to Sims Reef, where there is a very deep hole. Night-time fishing seems to be the best for jewfish in Bynoe Harbour — usually on neap tides when tidal movement is minimal, but in some spots on spring tides, right on the turn.

Other Species

Golden snapper (fingermark bream) are prevalent throughout Bynoe Harbour. Normally caught bottom-fishing with bait, in shallow- to medium-depth water, 'goldies' occasionally grab a lure or small trolled mullet bait. A golden snapper caught on a lure or trolled bait can be a good clue to the presence of other fish. Fishing the same spot with squid head baits will often yield many more snapper.

Golden snapper grow to more than 10 kg in the Top End, and some very large specimens are caught near and outside the entrance to Bynoe Harbour. One area which is renowned for producing whopper golden snapper at night is along the ledge between Bynoe Harbour and Tapa Bay. This ledge is well marked on the nautical chart for the area.

Bynoe Harbour is also well known for its queenfish population. Big queenfish tend to patrol rocky points and sand bars with deep channels running alongside. A queenfish patch is best located by trolling a skipping popper across the surface and a small diving minnow about 2 m below. A falling tide with plenty of movement is favoured. A good spot to try is the eastern tip of Indian Island.

Small- to medium-sized giant trevally sometimes accompany the queenfish schools, and bigger lone fish can turn up anywhere.

Bynoe Harbour is close to some of Darwin's hottest dry season Spanish mackerel grounds. Big mackerel sometimes find their way right into the harbour, but it is the offshore that excels. From Bynoe, it is only a short trip out to Bass Reef (see Darwin Offshore, pp. 160–1). On an incoming tide, the ledge between the harbour entrance and Tapa Bay is good Spanish mackerel country, and is best fished at anchor with floating baits in a pilchard berley trail.

If you do not have a global positioning system (GPS), a good trick on the offshore reefs is to troll the area and drop a marker buoy as soon as a mackerel strikes a lure or swimming bait. The fish will often congregate on a pinnacle and won't move far to take a lure. A buoy simplifies the task of pinpointing the strike zone so that trolling time can be put to the most effect.

During the early dry season months, schools of longtail tuna work the nutrient-rich waters in front of Bynoe Harbour. These aren't big fish by east coast standards, averaging 5 kg and rarely seen at more than 10 kg. However, they are fun to catch and make excellent sashimi.

Bynoe Harbour's offshore reef fishing scene is excellent. It is a shorter distance by sea to Lorna Shoal and Bass Reef from Bynoe than it is from Darwin Harbour. As a bonus, it is also close to the Roche Reefs, which are renowned for their red-throat emperor or sweetlip.

The beaches between the mangroves along the eastern shore can sometimes produce quality fish for land-based anglers. A day trip timed to coincide with the top half of a rising tide is the best strategy. Small mullet—which can be caught along the shore with a cast-net—make excellent live bait. It is not unusual for land-based anglers fishing with live mullet baits to catch black jewfish, queenfish, trevally and even barramundi off the beaches.

Bynoe Harbour may not be one the Northern Territory's most exotic locations, but it is handy to Darwin and fairly protected... and there is hardly a species caught in the Top End that is not available from Bynoe.

Fighting a big queenfish from the beach at Bynoe Harbour

SHADY CAMP

IN BRIEF

MAP REFERENCE: PAGE 174 E4

GETTING THERE Shady Camp is about 180 km east of Darwin on the Mary River—access via Stuart and Arnhem Highways, then unsealed road to Shady Camp

BEST TIME TO FISH March to May in the tidal section; September to December in the freshwater lagoon

BEST TIME TO TRAVEL Year-round depending on weather and unsealed road conditions

MAJOR ANGLING SPECIES Barramundi

SPECIAL RESTRICTIONS Access to Shady Camp is through Shady Camp Reserve; normal restrictions pertaining to Northern Territory parks apply

WARNINGS Large saltwater crocodiles inhabit these waters and anglers should stay out of the water and away from the water's edge

ACCOMMODATION Resort, budget and serviced camping accommodation is available at several locations close to Shady Camp; camping is permitted for a minimal fee at Shady Camp Reserve

CHARTER BOATS AND FISHING GUIDES HotSpot Fishing Tours can arrange day and extended accommodated fishing packages with accredited guides, telephone Freecall 1800 809 035; boat hire is available on site from Shady Camp Boat Hire, telephone Freecall 1800 242 177

Mention the words 'big barra' and it wouldn't be out of place to say 'Shady Camp' in the same breath. In recent years, this troubled, inappropriately named fishing spot has become a Mecca for anglers seeking that one barramundi of a lifetime.

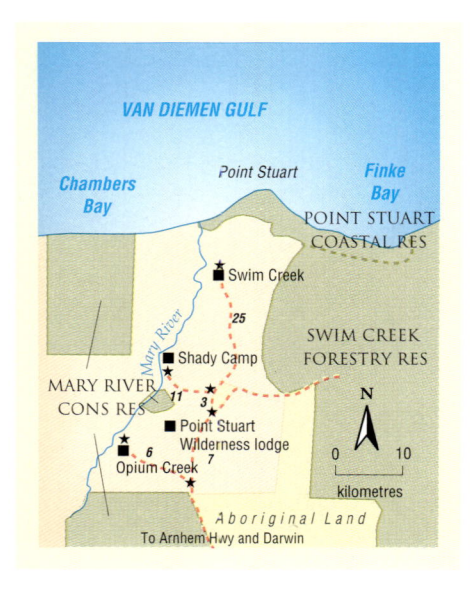

Situated at the bottom end of the Mary River, where the tidal salt water comes to an abrupt halt at an artificial rock barrage, this once lush wetland environment has given way to exotic mimosa infestation and ghostly forests of paperbarks which have been killed by relentless saltwater intrusion. It has become an engineering nightmare to stem the flow of salt water and one that comes at a huge cost—both in terms of dollars and in the negative effect on the aquatic environment—as a result of the construction of dozens of floodplain barrages in an effort to hold back the tide. Unfortunately, these barrages also restrict the flow of flood waters to the sea and through the once fast-flowing feeder creek mouths to the river. The result has been the loss of precious wetland habitat and remedies thus far have sacrificed far too many fish. Sadly, it is an environmental problem that only time and human ingenuity properly applied will fix.

And yet the big barra keep coming. At the end of the wet season, in late March and April, schools of great fish power their way up the Mary River to Shady Camp, where they are targeted by anxious anglers in boats sometimes parked anchor to stern along the banks of the hot spots. The most famous of these is the S-bend, about 10 km down the river from the Shady Camp barrage.

The best fishing takes place one to three hours after the turn of a big tide. It is these big tides that rise against the receding flow of flood, carrying schools of frantic sea mullet and the massive predatory fish that feed on them. When the big barramundi are running, it is nothing for a couple of dozen 15- to 25-kg specimens to be caught by the boats in an afternoon session. There are also often plenty of smaller fish to keep the interest up in between bites from the whoppers.

Big Barra Tactics

For many anglers, the presence of so many boats is off-putting, regardless of the booty on offer. For those willing to give it a go, however, the tactics are simple. Anchor with the fleet so as not to impede the casting of others, and toss big diving minnows into the flowing current and swirling eddies, retrieving them just fast enough to maintain lure action.

The period from March to May offers the best fishing at Shady Camp. Barramundi can be caught right along the tidal system by casting lures to any colour-change run-offs that are encountered or trolling lures wherever the water is deeper than 2 m and visibility is to a depth of more than 30 cm.

One of the best spots is the rock barrage right where boats are launched at Shady Camp. Some caution is required at the barrage because Shady Camp is home to a huge population of saltwater crocodiles. Regardless of this, there always seem to be plenty of keen anglers willing to take the risk. As the wet season flow diminishes, the bottom, tidal side of the barrage becomes too shallow for launching and negotiating by boat, let alone attempting to catch a barra. Around the top of the tide, however, casting lures from the barrage to the downstream salt water can be highly productive.

Casting lures from the barrage to the permanent freshwater lagoon on the top side of the Shady Camp barrage can also produce results, particularly at night, if you're game.

The Barrage and Lagoon

A few Darwin anglers specialise in fishing from the barrage, concentrating their efforts during the early morning, the late evening and at night. The area within 100 m either side of the barrage is restricted to fishing with an artificial lure or fly with one single-point hook only, and these specialist anglers have adapted conventional minnows and poppers accordingly. The trick is to replace all the standard trebles with one single-point 4/0 to 6/0 straight-shank hook fitted to the middle eyelet of the lure. Conventional single-hook soft plastic barramundi lures also work well off the barrage.

Boats can be launched into the Shady Camp freshwater lagoon immediately above the barrage at any time. The lagoon is about 4 km long and is typical of many lagoons across the Top End. Its

Shady Camp is home to an astonishing number of saltwater crocodiles

banks are lined with beds of lotus lilies, the edges of which can be trolled. Anglers also cast lures for barramundi to gaps in the lilies.

A large freshwater barramundi from Shady Camp lagoon

There are not many snags which can be easily fished in Shady Camp lagoon, but two submerged rock bars offer excellent fishing. The most productive barra fishing time in the lagoon is late in the dry season—from September until the wet season commences in December or January.

The first rock bar is located about two-thirds of the way up the lagoon. It stretches approximately halfway across from the right-hand side going up and is about 150 m long. The best way to find it is to troll along the right-hand bank with an eye on a reliable depth sounder. The second rock bar is only 500 m or so from the top of the lagoon, commencing on a slight S-bend before zig-zagging from side to side for a couple of hundred metres on the straight section leading to the lagoon's end. It is further easily located by the patch of sparse dead paperbarks that take up a large area to the right. These trees also form a small rookery for egrets, sea eagles and other wetland birds. Typically with the approaching wet season, anglers should see upwards of half a dozen occupied and vacant nests high in the trees.

Top Techniques

Trolling small to medium minnows that swim 2 to 2.5 m deep across the rock bars seems to produce the best results. Lures that occasionally bump across the rocky bottom are swimming at the right depth. Prime fishing time is from dawn until about 11 a.m., at which time the heat of the day late in the year puts the fish off the bite. The fishing picks up again late in the afternoon and excellent fishing can be had trolling right up until about 9 o'clock at night.

At the very top of the lagoon is a fork with a wide pool of water on the right and a narrow channel straight ahead, which during most dry seasons becomes unnavigable due to constricting water and lilies. However, around the fork junction and in the pool itself, barramundi, tarpon (ox-eye herring) and, in some years, saratoga can be caught by casting sinking soft plastic lures and rattling lures. It's something to try when all else fails.

Finally, it should be noted that the tidal section of Shady Camp is closed to fishing from 1 October to 31 January. Also, a special bag limit of two barramundi in possession with a minimum size of 55 cm applies. For 100 m either side of the barrage, only artificial lures and flies may be used, and they may only have one single-point hook attached.

DUNDEE BEACH

IN BRIEF

MAP REFERENCE: PAGE 174 C4

GETTING THERE Dundee Beach is on Fog Bay, about 160 km south-west of Darwin — access via Stuart Highway, and then sealed and unsealed road
BEST TIME TO FISH March to December
BEST TIME TO TRAVEL April to December
MAJOR ANGLING SPECIES Barramundi, blue salmon, golden snapper (fingermark), black jewfish, red-throat emperor (sweetlip), Spanish mackerel, longtail tuna, giant trevally, queenfish, sailfish and marlin
WARNINGS Wet season storms can be both sudden and fierce
ACCOMMODATION Lodge of Dundee provides cabin-style accommodation, powered sites for caravans and camping facilities, telephone (08) 8978 2557
CHARTER BOATS AND FISHING GUIDES HotSpot Fishing Tours can arrange day and extended charter fishing trips with on-board or lodge accommodation, telephone Freecall 1800 809 035. Hire boats are available from Dundee Beach Boat Hire, telephone (08) 8978 2688

Access to some of the best bluewater fishing available in the Top End is only two hours drive from Darwin, at Dundee Beach. Add to that the wonderful facilities on-site for angling parties, including families, and it's no wonder this destination is regularly used as a weekend retreat by Darwin residents.

The area known as Dundee Beach extends for several kilometres south from Native Point along the shores of Fog Bay, which is to the south-west of Darwin. Access to the bay and beyond is from the Lodge of Dundee, which is reached via bitumen and formed gravel road from Darwin.

At the lodge, there is camping and budget accommodation, full amenities and a concrete boat ramp. The area is suitable for both small and large fishing boats, with ample opportunities for land-based action, too.

Large trailer boats can be towed from Darwin or driven by sea to a waiting, mostly calm anchorage in front of the Lodge of Dundee. Only a short distance to the north, anglers will often find good pelagic fishing at the lower end of the extensive Roche Reefs.

Trolling minnows and skipping popper lures around the coral bombies and reef edges are likely to entice a strike from either a queenfish, giant trevally, barracuda, coral trout, longtail tuna or mackerel. Most tropical reef fish can also be caught in the area.

The most-recognised angling value of Dundee Beach is its access and proximity to the excellent fishing grounds off Point Blaze to the south-west and further down the coast to the fabulous Peron Islands. Close in to rocky Point Blaze and the adjoining Point Jenny, anglers can troll for queenfish, trevally and mackerel. Pelagic activity is often pinpointed by the presence of frenzied birds hovering and diving over the schools.

OFFSHORE FROM POINT BLAZE

Heading straight out from Point Blaze in a westerly direction (see map, p. 168), anglers will first encounter patches of rocky bottom, which can be fished for both golden snapper (fingermark bream) and black jewfish.

Schools of medium to large snapper patrol these patches — which are approximately 5 km offshore — and the fishing can be hectic at times. First-time golden snapper anglers are often surprised at how voracious a school of snapper can be, and then equally surprised at how quickly they can go off the bite when a hooked fish is lost. When that happens, experienced snapper fishermen pull the pick and go looking for a fresh, unsuspecting school.

The Lodge of Dundee at Dundee Beach

tides, particularly on the turn, anglers fishing the bottom can sometimes experience jewfish action at a frantic pace.

The Peron Islands run in a north-westerly direction with a shallow, rocky causeway between them. Access through the causeway is risky except at the top of a big tide.

There are not many tropical fish species that can't be caught at the Perons, but the best fishing is undoubtedly along the west coast of the islands. From the bottom of South Peron to the top of North Peron, rocky peninsulas and sand cays offer excellent sportfishing for queenfish, trevally and mackerel. Just offshore from the west side of North Peron, patches of reef can be drifted or anchored on and fished for good catches of red-throat emperor (sweetlip), golden snapper, coral trout and red emperor.

Approximately 10 km to the west of the Perons is a large complex of reefs known as Bateman Shoal. Sharp pinnacles rise to within 5 m of the surface at Bateman Shoal, and at times anglers encounter vast schools of Spanish mackerel and trevally species, with the occasional cobia or sailfish thrown in for interest. Understandably, reef fishing can also be exceptional on the shoal.

SMALL BOAT OPPORTUNITIES

Anglers with small trailer boats or even car-toppers have plenty of opportunities for quality fishing around Dundee Beach. Only 1 km straight out from the lodge is a small reef which produces good catches of black jewfish at night. Black jewfish are also caught around inshore rocky outcrops along the beach. These outcrops are exposed for all but the highest of tides.

There's good saltwater barra fishing to be had around Dundee, too. The exposed rocky outcrops can be trolled or cast to for barramundi. At the top of the tide and for a couple of hours afterwards, anglers can also target barramundi at rocky mainland points along the coast immediately south of the lodge. Even further south are the Finniss River and the Little Finniss. Barramundi are regularly caught in these systems, but are best fished for on neap tides with little movement when the water is clear enough to be productive.

The top of a big tide is by far the best time to fish from the shore at Dundee. Anglers can begin fishing right in front of the lodge where a half-pilchard bait hurled out and anchored to the bottom is a proven technique for catching blue salmon, golden snapper and even jewfish. Anglers can also walk from one rocky point to the next, casting lures for barramundi. In fact, the artificial rock groyne next to the boat ramp is as good a place as any to begin trying for barra.

The Lodge of Dundee is only a short drive from Six-Pack Creek, where a small boat ramp provides access to the southern end of Bynoe Harbour. The ramp is only useable during the top half of the tide, but the creek itself fishes well for barramundi, salmon and the occasional mangrove jack. It's also a good creek to drop a few pots for a feed of mud crabs.

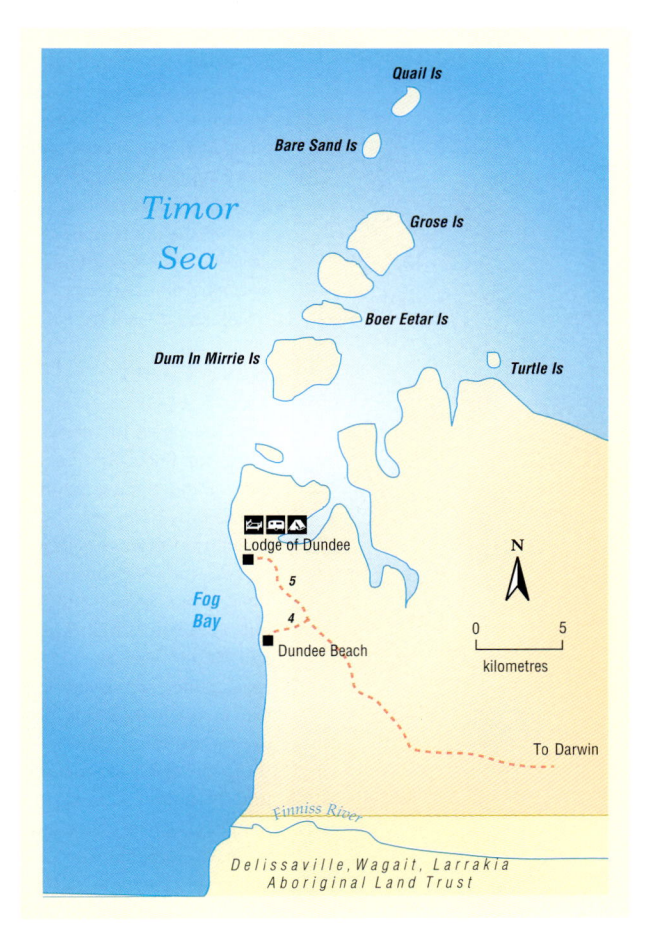

Out wider and slightly north is popular Bowra Shoal. This is excellent Spanish mackerel country during the Top End dry season. At times, it also attracts vast schools of both longtail and mackerel tuna, and is recognised as one of the Northern Territory's best billfish grounds. For reef fishermen, a feed for the table is rarely a problem, with the prospect of catching not only the more common golden snapper and red-throat emperor, but also the highly prized red emperor.

Although squid baits are favoured for reef fishing, a good tip for red emperor is to use shark-flesh baits. The incidental capture of small sharks while reef fishing will provide plenty of opportunities to obtain this preferred bait.

THE PERON ISLANDS

There are patches of reef along much of the coast and inshore areas from Point Blaze to the Peron Islands, a vast area which will usually keep reef anglers both occupied and happy. However, most angling parties go all the way to the Perons — and for good reason.

There are two islands: North Peron and South Peron (see map, p. 168). South Peron is within 2 km of the mainland, just off Channel Point. The channel itself is very deep with strong currents surging through it on big tides. However, on small

Massive golden snapper or fingermark bream can be caught offshore from Dundee Beach

THE DALY RIVER

IN BRIEF

MAP REFERENCE: PAGE 174 C5

GETTING THERE The Daly River settlement is 232 km south of Darwin along the Stuart Highway and then unsealed road
BEST TIME TO FISH April to July
BEST TIME TO TRAVEL May to September
MAJOR ANGLING SPECIES Barramundi
SPECIAL RESTRICTIONS Permits and special entry restrictions apply in all Aboriginal lands and some national parks, parts of which may be totally closed to entry. Specific fishing regulations and limits are also in force on certain waterways. Check the current status of all rules and regulations before going fishing
WARNINGS During spring tides, a significant tidal bore (wave) may be encountered on the Daly River and boat owners should be especially careful when mooring craft along the banks. Saltwater crocodiles inhabit all inshore areas, estuaries and river systems in the Top End, often extending well above the upper tidal limits into fresh water — observe all warning signs.
Many roads in the Top End are suitable for 4WD vehicles only, and may be totally impassable from late November until late May or early June
Cyclones and severe tropical storms can occur at any time from November to May
ACCOMMODATION Daly River Mango Farm, telephone (08) 8978 2464

Butterfly Gorge on the Daly River

The Daly River system, some 230 km south-west of Darwin, is one of the Top End's largest coastal river systems, draining a huge area of the Northern Territory including vast tracts of remote country around Katherine, far away to the south-east.

The lower section of the Daly, in particular, sees a great deal of fishing pressure from keen Territorians and interstate visitors alike, and this is understandable in light of the excellent catches of barramundi that this big river continues to produce year after year.

The Daly is also the usual venue for two of the nation's largest barra fishing tournaments or competitions: the Barra Nationals and the long-running Barra Classic. Both of these high-profile invitation events are staged between late April and early June each year, and attract hundreds of contestants from all over Australia and even further afield.

It's not surprising that the organisers of these major competitions have settled on the Daly as an ideal venue for their big events. As well as good numbers of average fish, this tidal river system regularly turns up some of the heaviest barramundi seen west of Darwin, with specimens of 10 kg, 15 kg, 20 kg and even occasionally 25 kg being taken, particularly by anglers trolling lures in the many snag-lined holes and stretches downstream of Browns Creek and the Mango Farm.

BEST EARLY AND LATE

As is the case with most of the Top End's big rivers, barramundi fishing results on the Daly River are typically at their very best early in the year, during the post-wet season run-off period in late March, April and May. However, reasonable catches can also be taken from this productive river right through the dry season and into the humid build-up to the next big wet, especially by smart, methodical anglers willing to work the deeper snag piles and rock bars carefully with diving minnow-style lures capable of running 3 to 5 m below the surface when trolled.

A quality depth sounder or fish finder and a good knowledge of the workings of this river's powerful and sometimes confusing tides are also important keys to consistent success on the Daly. It should also be noted that most of the legal barramundi caught on lures in this river system each year fall to trolled deep diving minnows, especially after about the middle of April. This is one area where casting and retrieving lures is significantly less effective for most of the year than trolling, and this is particularly so in the middle of the cooler dry season.

Exceptions to this rule of thumb occur in the brief run-off period immediately following the wet. The timing of this period varies somewhat from year to year, but those who strike it just right can anchor at the mouths of various feeder creeks and enjoy excellent results by casting and retrieving lures or bulky flies around the colour changes, eddies and current edges.

BAIT FISHING ALTERNATIVES

Later on, during the quieter times of the dry season, some very good catches are sometimes taken by bait anglers fishing with live cherabin or

CAMPING AND TOURING ETIQUETTE

One of the greatest disappointments of a trip to a pristine wilderness is to come across a delightful camping site marred — no, vandalised — by rubbish! For everybody's sake:

- Leave the camp site clean and take *all* your rubbish out with you. *Don't* bury it, as wild animals, other people and flooding rivers can uncover the junk and spread it over the countryside
- Use a shovel to dig a deep hole for your toilet requirements; keep the hole away from running water and other campers
- Set up camp well away from any stock or water point
- Don't use soap, shampoo or detergent in streams, waterholes, dams or water troughs. Use a bucket or a bush shower well away from the water to wash and rinse yourself. Also use a bucket to wash clothes and dishes, away from where animals and other humans may drink. Nobody likes to drink water tainted by soap!
- Take care with fire — clear an area around the fireplace before lighting it. Before you leave, make sure the fire is well and truly out
- Use old fireplaces — don't erect new ones. Observe all fire restrictions
- Observe all rules and regulations pertaining to the use of public land
- Keep to constructed vehicle tracks, never 'bush bash'
- Avoid areas which are easily damaged, such as swamps and vegetated sand dunes
- Respect wildlife
- Respect private land. Always ask permission before crossing pastoral land
- Leave gates as you find them
- Observe all park regulations; when in doubt, consult the ranger

macrobrachium (large freshwater prawns or shrimps) right in the middle of various submerged snag piles. A heavy handline is the favoured tool for this style of fishing. When a decent barramundi is hooked, it must be hauled out as quickly as possible to avoid having the line entangled or cut amongst any of the tangles of dense timber beneath the surface of the water.

It is also possible to cast live cherabin baits on lighter conventional gear around snags and creek mouths, although anglers pursuing this form of fishing must expect to lose a certain amount of fish and terminal tackle. An alternative approach is to jig in the same areas with rattling, sonic-style lures, soft plastics or artificial plastic and rubber prawns. Once again, however, the attrition rate to snags and fish can be rather high.

A large barramundi taken while trolling in the Daly River

KAKADU AND THE SOUTH ALLIGATOR RIVER

IN BRIEF

MAP REFERENCE: PAGE 174 F4

GETTING THERE Jabiru, on the eastern edge of Kakadu National Park, lies 254 km east of Darwin along the Stuart and Arnhem highways

BEST TIME TO FISH March to November

BEST TIME TO TRAVEL May to October

MAJOR ANGLING SPECIES Barramundi, saratoga and ox-eye herring (tarpon)

SPECIAL RESTRICTIONS Permits and special entry restrictions apply in all Aboriginal lands and some national parks, parts of which may be totally closed to entry. An entry fee is also charged for entry into Kakadu National Park. Specific fishing regulations and limits are in force on certain waterways; on the South Alligator River, fish may only be cleaned at the boat ramp cleaning table. Check the current status of all rules and regulations before going fishing

WARNINGS Saltwater crocodiles inhabit all inshore areas, estuaries and river systems in the Top End, often extending well above the upper tidal limits into fresh water — observe all warning signs
Many roads in the Top End are suitable for 4WD vehicles only, and may be totally impassable from late November until late May or early June
Cyclones and severe tropical storms can occur at any time from November to May

ACCOMMODATION Wildman River Wilderness Lodge, telephone (08) 8978 8912

Most tourists travelling to the Top End eventually get around to visiting Kakadu National Park, which is probably the Northern Territory's second most famous natural attraction after Uluru (Ayers Rock), in the arid Red Centre.

A greater egret in the wetlands of Kakadu National Park

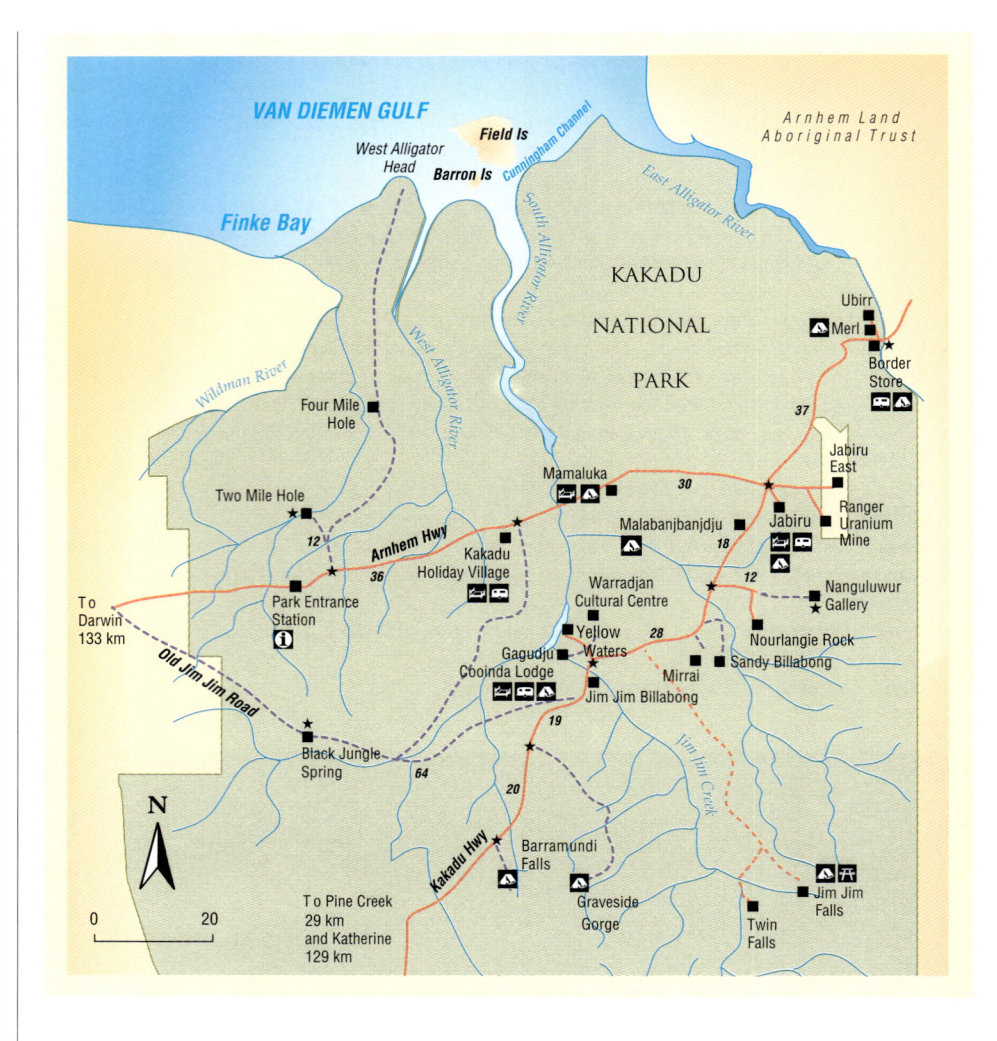

At approximately 20 000 square km, Kakadu is Australia's largest national park, and a listed World Heritage area of environmental, cultural and historical significance to all Australians.

There is some wonderful recreational angling available within the park, although access to the best of this is increasingly being restricted and even denied by Parks Australia, the federal bureaucracy which has replaced the former National Parks and Wildlife Service (NPWS).

While there are sound reasons for some of these restrictions, others do not appear to be valid conservation measures. Recreational angling lobby groups are constantly arguing the case for more, rather than less, access to the fresh and tidal waters within Kakadu.

At the time of writing, however, Kakadu National Park administration's unstated but implicit anti-angling regime was clearly in the ascendancy.

Yet there are many areas within Kakadu National Park and along its borders where recreational angling is not only possible, but also highly productive. The most famous of these is the South Alligator River itself.

THE SOUTH

'The South', as most Territorians call it, produces excellent barramundi fishing, particularly during the weeks immediately following the cessation of heavy rains at the end of the monsoonal wet season. The timing and intensity of this post-wet season barra bite varies from year to year, but usually occurs from late March or early April until late May or even into early June.

The most productive fishing styles vary, from casting shallow running lures at creek mouths and drains immediately after the wet to trolling deeper diving lures in the main channels and adjacent to various rock bars as soon as the main flush of receding flood waters slows down in mid- to late April.

Waterway near Jabiru in Kakadu National Park

There are many submerged rock bars in the South Alligator River, and anglers trolling these spots — as well as along the various snag-lined banks — catch some truly huge barramundi, especially in late April and May.

Reasonable to very good barramundi fishing is also available along the South Alligator River and in its floodplain billabongs throughout the rest of the year, including the middle of the dry season. Athough the action certainly does tend to taper off in the cooler months of July and August, it slowly improves again through the months of September and October, peaking once more in the build-up to the wet season, during November and even into early December.

THE BILLABONGS OF KAKADU

Places such as Yellow Waters and the various lagoons or waterholes along the extensive flood plain of the South Alligator River also offer some of the best-known and most accessible billabong and lagoon barramundi action in the Top End.

Sight fishing with lures or flies to individual cruising barramundi is often possible here, especially late in the dry season. However, standard casting and trolling methods also work well, regularly producing both freshwater

A barramundi taken from a freshwater waterhole in Kakadu

barramundi and saratoga. These smaller, isolated waters are particularly exciting to fish at night if noise-making surface lures such as poppers and fizzers or top-water flies are used. Great care should always be exercised on or around these waterways after dark, however, as this is when saltwater crocodiles are also at their most active and dangerous!

EAST ALLIGATOR RIVER

IN BRIEF

MAP REFERENCE: PAGE 174 F3

GETTING THERE The East Alligator River is on the eastern perimeter of Kakadu National Park and flows through Arnhem Land; Border Store is 279 km east of Darwin along the Stuart and Arnhem Highways, then sealed road to Border Store

BEST TIME TO FISH March to April downriver; March to December upriver

BEST TIME TO TRAVEL March/April to December depending on road access after the wet season

MAJOR ANGLING SPECIES Barramundi

SPECIAL RESTRICTIONS Visitors to Kakadu National Park must pay entry fees and obtain camping permits as required

WARNINGS Saltwater crocodiles inhabit these waters and anglers should stay out of the water and away from the water's edge; rock bars and mud banks pose navigational hazards at different stages of the tide

ACCOMMODATION Park camping ground near river, budget accommodation at Border Store, all levels of accommodation at Jabiru township

CHARTER BOATS AND FISHING GUIDES HotSpot Fishing Tours can arrange accommodated fishing safaris to the East Alligator River, telephone Freecall 1800 809 035

The East Alligator River is about 280 km east of Darwin and part of its length forms the border between Kakadu National Park and Arnhem Land. Kakadu is renowned for its natural beauty and wetlands, and the East Alligator is no exception.

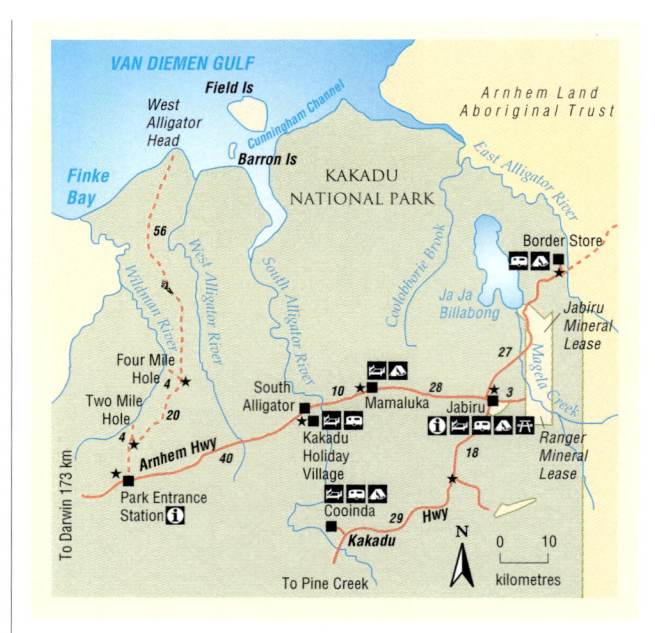

Bird watching, bushwalking and river cruises are popular with visitors to the area, and it is also possible to see some fine Aboriginal rock art while you are there.

Permits are required to enter Kakadu and anglers heading for the East Alligator can camp at designated grounds near the river, where there are toilet and shower amenities on site. Basic accommodation is available at Border Store, with all levels of accommodation on offer at the uranium township of Jabiru about 60 km from the river.

The best fishing at the East Alligator occurs as soon as the river becomes accessible after the wet season. Cahills Crossing, where the Oenpelli Road leaves Kakadu to enter Arnhem Land, is always worth a cast, particularly on the downstream side during a rising tide. Tides larger than 6 m rise right over the top of the crossing, but the best fishing is just before the water becomes level with the crossing. At this time, mullet are moving up with the tide and become stuck below the crossing, presenting an easy target for feeding barramundi.

The upriver side of Cahills Crossing also produces the occasional barramundi that has moved down to the crossing to engage mullet as they come over the top on the tide.

For mullet, a rising tide at Cahills Crossing is a nerve-racking experience; for anglers, it's a good opportunity for land-based barra fishing. Unfortunately, man is not the only large predator known to hunt at the crossing—the occasional saltwater crocodile will also move in and feed at the appropriate time, and caution should be exercised as there has been at least one fatal crocodile attack at this location in relatively recent times.

FISHING THE RUN-OFF

Serious Top End anglers with boats don't usually bother with the crossing at the East Alligator River. Straight after the wet season, they head downstream to fish the mouths of feeder creeks coming off the flood plains. Like most major tidal rivers in the Territory, at the end of the Wet the submerged flood plains drain excess water through these feeder creeks. The fishing is excellent, particularly when the draining water is dark and clear, forming a strong colour contrast to the main river flow. Small fish, crustaceans, tadpoles and frogs come out of these creeks and barramundi often lay in wait in ambush mode. Anglers need only anchor within casting range of the mouth and colour change, and work steadily through the tackle box until a lure of the right size, colour, depth and action is uncovered.

The feeder creeks start only about 5 km downstream, but around low tide anglers need to be careful getting over one particular rock bar, which extends practically the width of the river.

MAGELA CREEK

There are at least a dozen creeks that can fire after the Wet. The biggest, and without doubt the most popular, is Magela Creek. This long feeder creek begins right up near Jabiru and winds its way down through paperbark swamps until it empties in the main river more than 40 km downstream from the crossing. In the dry season, once the flood waters have dissipated, Magela

Many anglers prefer to use lures or flies when chasing barra, but live and dead baits can also be effective

The East Alligator River flows through some magnificent terrain

Creek is tidal only. Muddy and accessible only on the top of the tide, it's not worth being there. When it's flowing strongly, however, pumping tea-coloured water into the main river, Magela Creek offers barra fishing as good as one can expect anywhere.

There are several places to fish and a number of techniques to try in the Magela. The mouth of the creek is always worth a shot. Boats should be anchored just inside and lures should be cast around the colour change that invariably exists on the bottom (downstream) side of the mouth. Another technique is to motor quietly about 100 m into the creek and drift down to the mouth and around in the eddy which usually works when the creek is pumping strongly, casting to the edges on either side. The first of the incoming tide often provides the best barramundi fishing at the Magela Creek mouth.

Motoring up the creek, there is often good fishing at little drains flowing into the main stream. A typical drain is half a metre wide at its mouth and recessed into a small bay which provides shelter for barramundi out of the normally raging current. The technique is to anchor fairly close to the drain and cast to and about its mouth where one or, at the most, two fish will be holding up. When the creek is running strongly, there are many drains to fish, which is why it pays to grab a fish or two then move on to another drain rather than wait for more barra to arrive. With this approach, anglers can move up and down the Magela, returning to drains and catching barramundi regularly. The hitch is that the current is usually so strong that landing quality fish without pulling anchor and following them requires testing your tackle to the fullest.

Another good spot in Magela Creek is the fork near the top of the tidal influence. The left-hand arm (when travelling upstream) invariably flows much more strongly than the right-hand arm, and there is always a distinct colour variation between the two streams. When the fish are on, anglers can actually alight from their boat and fish off the bank right at the fork.

On a big rising tide, when the barramundi are not feeding at the fork, motoring up either stream right up onto the flood plain will yield barra at little creeks and eddies along the way. It's important for fishing success to proceed quietly and to stop the boat to cast ahead of it to a likely spot. This is because the water, especially up the left arm, is crystal clear and the channel is narrow, both of which mean that lurking barramundi can be easily spooked.

Above the Crossing

Upriver from Cahills Crossing, the East Alligator River never fishes to the potential of the downriver side immediately after the wet season. However, once the hot period is over, there is better boat fishing on the top side because the water remains clear. Right through the dry season, casting to snags or trolling regularly produces quality barramundi, and night fishing can be very good. Best of all, the East Alligator escarpment scenery on the top side is breathtaking.

Finally, note that a bag limit of two barramundi in possession with a minimum size of 55 cm is proposed in the forthcoming Kakadu Plan of Management. Check regulations before fishing.

174 The Top End, Northern Territory

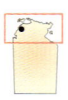

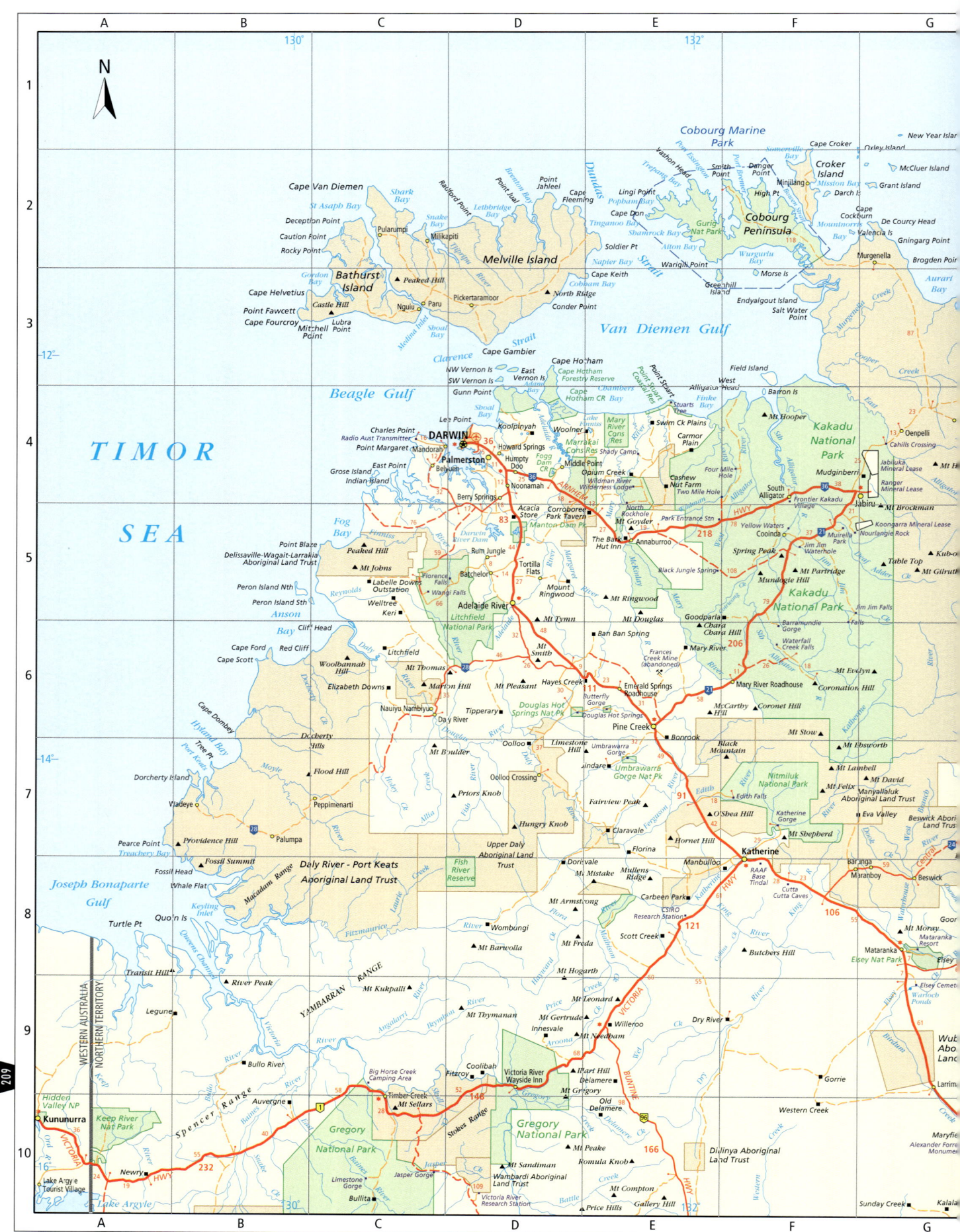

0 20 40 60 80 100
kilometres

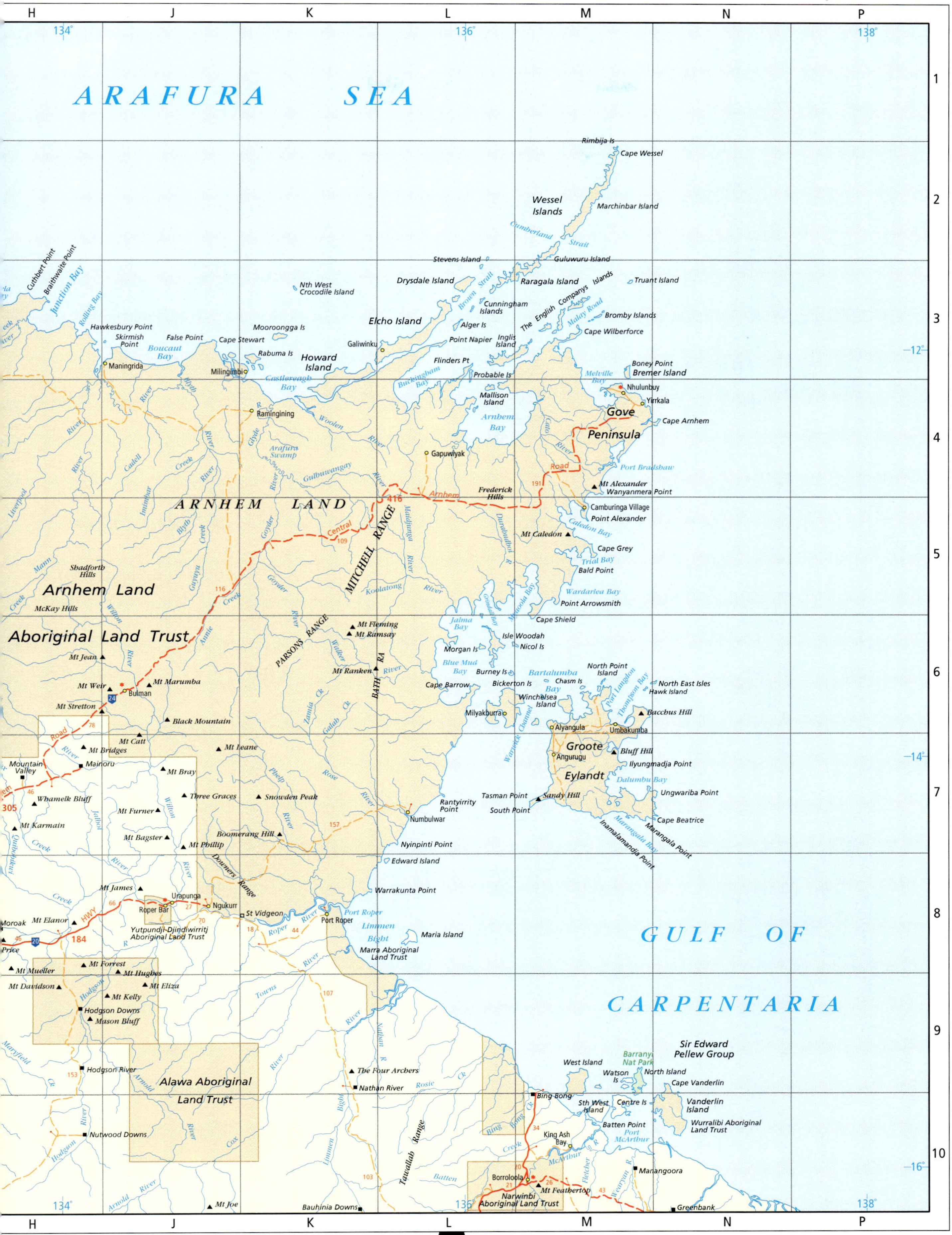

176 Central Northern Territory

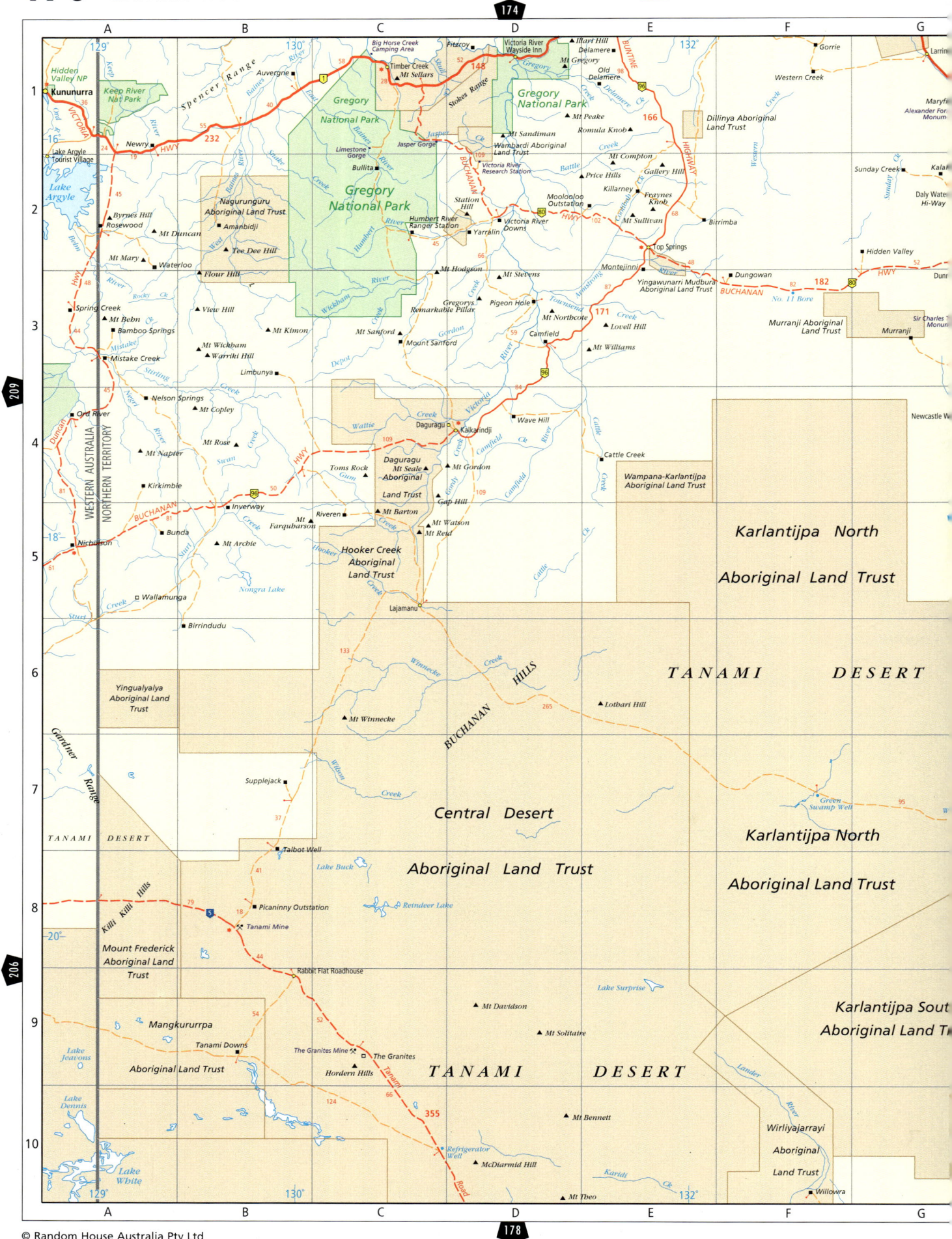

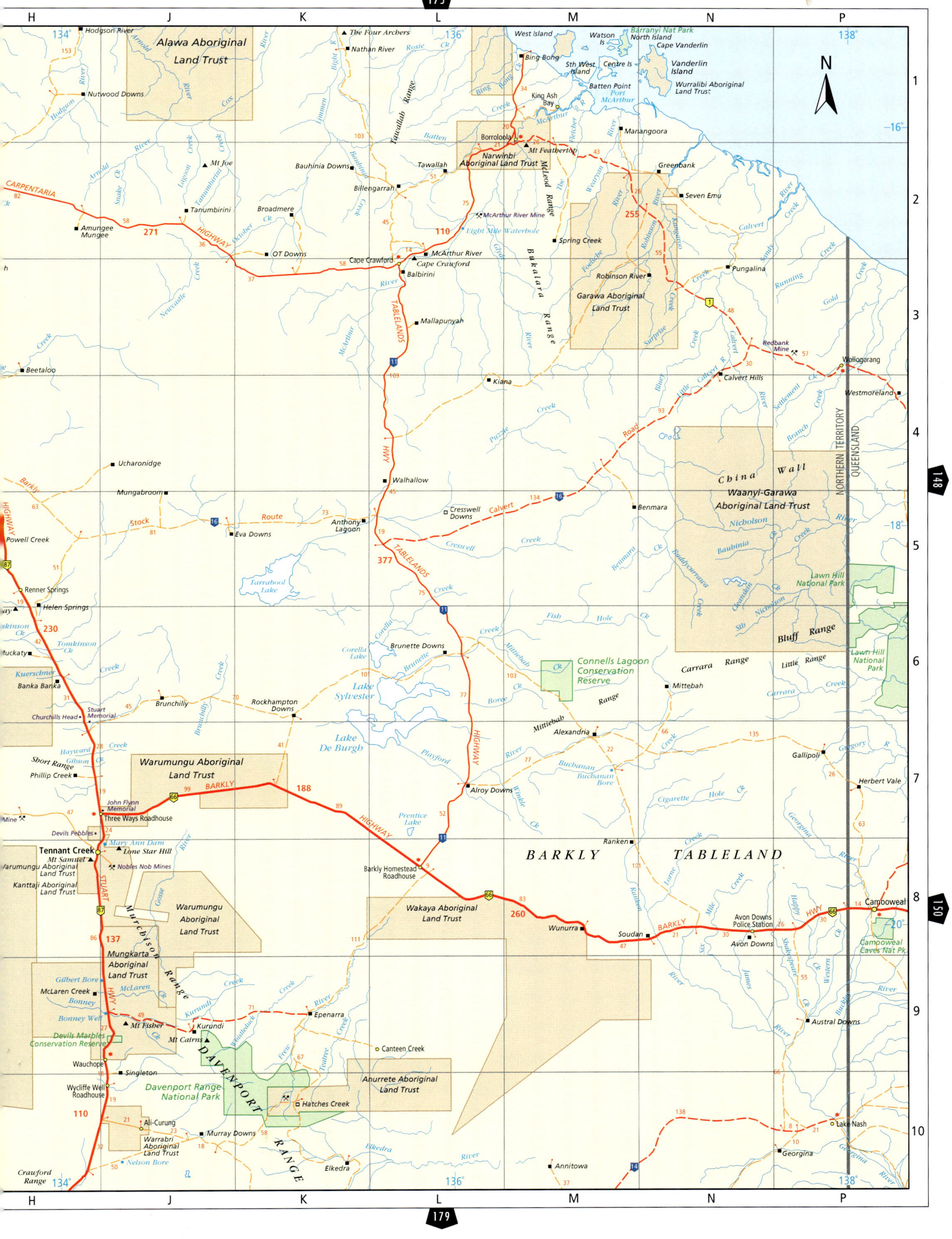

0 20 40 60 80 100
kilometres
175
179
148
150
H J K L M N P
1 2 3 4 5 6 7 8 9 10
134°
136°
138°
16°
18°
20°
N
Alawa Aboriginal Land Trust
Hodgson River
Nutwood Downs
Mt Joe
Tanumbirini
Amungee Mungee
CARPENTARIA HIGHWAY
271
Broadmere
OT Downs
The Four Archers
Nathan River
Tawallah Range
Bauhinia Downs
Tawallah
Billengarrah
Borroloola
Mt Featherton
Narwinbi Aboriginal Land Trust
McArthur River Mine
Eight Mile Waterhole
110
McArthur River
Cape Crawford
Balbirini
Mallapunyah
TABLELANDS
Bukalara Range
Spring Creek
West Island
Watson Is
Barranyi Nat Park
North Island
Cape Vanderlin
Vanderlin Island
Sth West Island
Centre Is
Batten Point
Port McArthur
King Ash Bay
Wurralibi Aboriginal Land Trust
Bing Bong
Manangoora
Greenbank
Seven Emu
255
Robinson River
Garawa Aboriginal Land Trust
Pungalina
Redbank Mine
Wollogorang
Calvert Hills
Westmoreland
NORTHERN TERRITORY
QUEENSLAND
China Wall
Waanyi-Garawa Aboriginal Land Trust
Lawn Hill National Park
Bluff Range
Beetaloo
Kiana
Ucharonidge
Walhallow
Mungabroom
Stock Route
Eva Downs
Anthony Lagoon
Cresswell Downs
Calvert Road
Benmara
Powell Creek
377
Tarrabool Lake
Renner Springs
Helen Springs
230
Muckaty
Banka Banka
Churchills Head
Stuart Memorial
Brunchilly
Rockhampton Downs
Brunette Downs
Corella Lake
Lake Sylvester
Lake De Burgh
Connells Lagoon Conservation Reserve
Carrara Range
Little Range
Mittebah
Alexandria
Buchanan Bore
Gallipoli
Herbert Vale
Warumungu Aboriginal Land Trust
Short Range
Phillip Creek
BARKLY HIGHWAY
188
John Flynn Memorial
Three Ways Roadhouse
Devils Pebbles
Tennant Creek
Mt Samuel
Lone Star Hill
Mary Ann Dam
Nobles Nob Mines
Warumungu Aboriginal Land Trust
Kanttaji Aboriginal Land Trust
Alroy Downs
Prentice Lake
Barkly Homestead Roadhouse
BARKLY TABLELAND
Ranken
Wakaya Aboriginal Land Trust
260
Wunurra
Soudan
Avon Downs Police Station
Avon Downs
Camooweal
Camooweal Caves Nat Pk
STUART HWY
137
Mungkarta Aboriginal Land Trust
Murchison Range
Gilbert Bore
McLaren Creek
Bonney Well
Devils Marbles Conservation Reserve
Mt Fisher
Kurundi
Mt Cairns
Epenarra
Canteen Creek
Wauchope
Singleton
Wycliffe Well Roadhouse
Davenport Range National Park
DAVENPORT RANGE
Hatches Creek
Anurrete Aboriginal Land Trust
Ali-Curung
Warrabri Aboriginal Land Trust
Murray Downs
Nelson Bore
Crawford Range
Elkedra
Annitowa
Austral Downs
Lake Nash
Georgina

178 Southern Northern Territory

0 20 40 60 80 100
kilometres

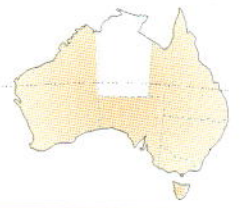

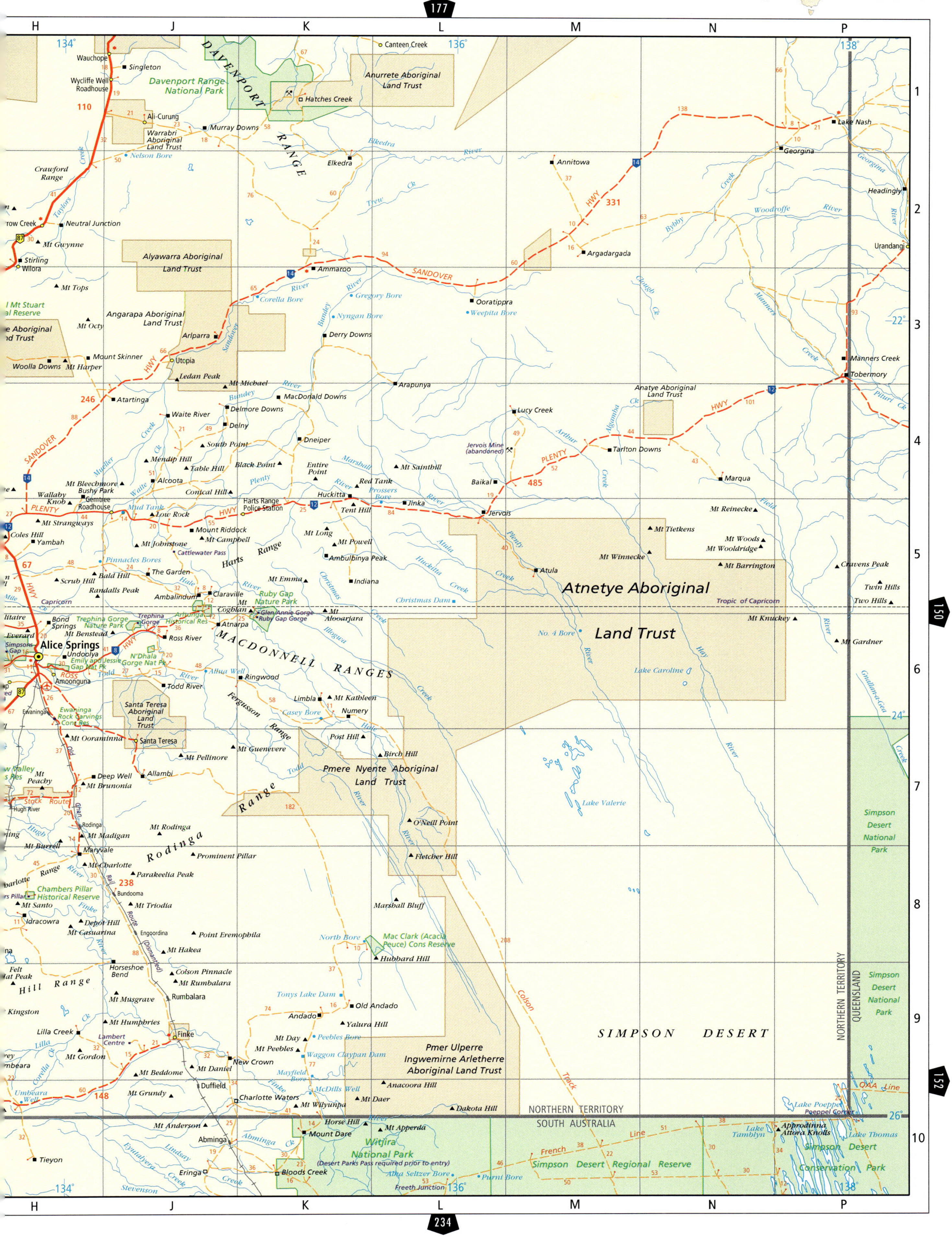

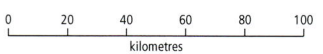

WESTERN AUSTRALIA

FISHING HOT SPOTS

- Perth's Beaches (pp. 182–3)
- The Lower Swan Estuary (pp. 184–5)
- Cockburn Sound (pp. 186–7)
- Hillarys Boat Harbour and Trigg Point (pp. 188–9)
- Swan River Bream (pp. 190–1)
- Rottnest Island (pp. 192–3)
- Bunbury to Busselton (pp. 194–5)
- South-West Corner (pp. 196–7)
- Dongara and Geraldton (pp. 198–9)
- South-West Trout Waters (pp. 200–1)

Western Australia is far and away our largest state, occupying fully one-third of the entire continent. Its coastline is also immense, running all the way from the wave-lashed desert cliffs of the Great Australian Bight to the shallow gulfs and muddy estuaries of the Northern Kimberley, with countless golden beaches, rugged headlands, estuaries, bays, flats, islands and reefs scattered in between. Not surprisingly, Western Australia also has the most diverse marine ecology and the widest array of saltwater fishing opportunities to be found anywhere in Australia — if not the world. These run the full gamut — from cool-water species such as King George whiting, Australian salmon, tommy rough and southern bluefin tuna in the far south to barramundi, sailfish, mangrove jacks and Spanish mackerel in the north, with a vast area of potential overlap between all of the various tropical, subtropical and temperate Indian Ocean species stretching right along the state's western seaboard.

Perhaps the only regard in which Western Australia can be said to have received less than its fair share of blessings is in terms of its freshwater fishing opportunities. Being a relatively dry state, there are few major river systems, especially south of the Tropic of Capricorn, and almost no permanent, natural lakes. Nonetheless, pockets of surprisingly good trout and redfin angling now exist in the south-west corner, while the north offers barramundi, grunter, chanda perch and some of the biggest and most prolific fork-tailed catfish to be found anywhere in the world.

As would be expected in a state of such size and diversity, preferred fishing techniques, favoured baits, proven rigs and even the most popular common names for many of Western Australia's fish species vary considerably from one stretch of coast to another.

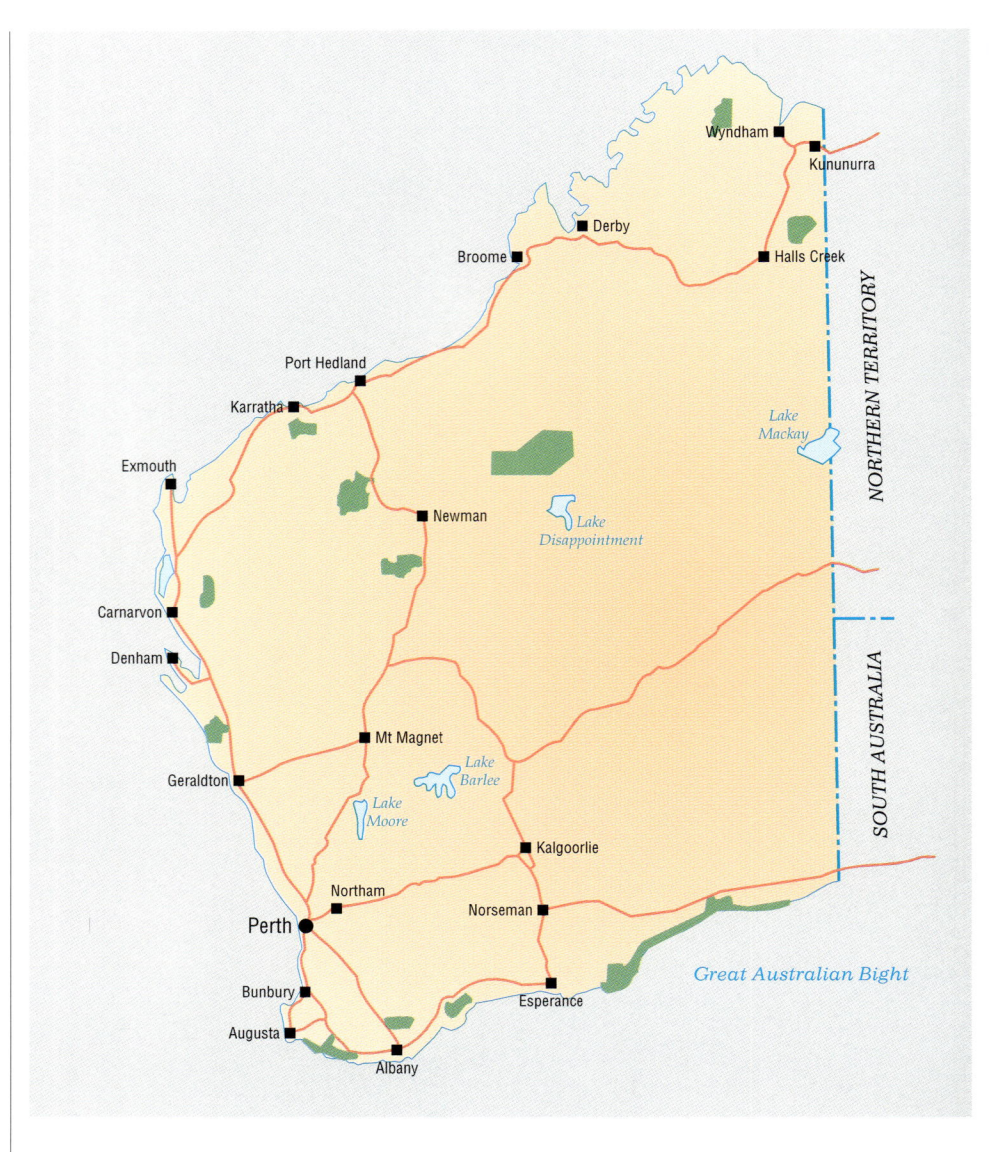

In addition, as well as the active pursuit of bony fish, sharks and rays for sport and for the table, West Australian anglers enjoy a long tradition of targeting invertebrate creatures such as marron (freshwater crayfish), rock lobsters, prawns, blue manna crabs, mud crabs, abalone, scallops and oysters. Fisheries management and enforcement agencies have had to take all of these factors into consideration when framing and constantly refining Western Australia's fishing rules and regulations. The result is a rather complex set of recreational angling laws, but one which appears to be working quite well.

The most significant challenges and limitations facing anglers are the sheer distances between many locations, the relative lack of infrastructure and services in more isolated areas and some access difficulties in Aboriginal reserves, pastoral holdings, mining leases and national parks. For the most part, however, the major dilemma lies in deciding which of the thousands of hot spots to visit first, and what species or group of species to target. It's a problem that many anglers from less fortunate regions would simply love to have!

CONTACT NUMBERS

Information on fishing rules and regulations in Western Australia can be obtained by telephoning the following Fisheries Department offices.

Perth	(08) 9482 7333
Bunbury	(08) 7212 598
Mandurah	(08) 9535 1240

FISHWATCH HOT LINE (24 hours)
1800 815 507

Top: *A view north across the Swan River estuary towards Perth's city centre*
Bottom left: *The chequerboard-patterned lighthouse at Bunbury on Western Australia's south-west coast*
Bottom right: *Serpentine Falls on the Serpentine River close to Perth, one of the state's lesser trout streams*

PERTH'S BEACHES

IN BRIEF

MAP REFERENCE: PAGE 202 B4

GETTING THERE Perth is the capital of Western Australia and is serviced regularly by air, rail and coach services
BEST TIME TO FISH September to May
BEST TIME TO TRAVEL Year-round
MAJOR ANGLING SPECIES Tailor, tommy rough (herring), Australian salmon and mulloway

Fishing at sunset on Mandurah Beach to the south of Fremantle

With its population of a little more than one million people and an extremely pleasant Mediterranean-style climate, Perth is often nominated as Australia's most attractive and 'livable' city. Certainly, its inhabitants are extremely proud of their home town, and regard themselves as fortunate indeed to live in such a delightfully cosmopolitan metropolis.

Dominated by the broad waters of the Swan River estuary, Perth is built for the most part on a relatively flat, sandy coastal plain, backed by the low foothills of the Darling Escarpment in the east and washed by the warm, blue waters of the Indian Ocean to the west.

Recreational angling is immensely popular amongst Perth and Fremantle residents, and there is also a strong tradition of seafood harvesting, tied closely to the seasons—from the cool to mild winter with its moderately heavy rainfall through to the long, hot and often very dry summer.

A String of Beautiful Beaches

The Perth region boasts a string of gorgeous ocean surf beaches, each washed by the blue waters of the Indian Ocean. These stretch all the way from Mandurah in the south to Lancelin in the north, although the true metropolitan

Cottesloe Beach is a popular angling venue, although it can become rather crowded on a hot day

beaches are usually regarded as being those which lie between Woodman Point, near Coogee, and Hillarys Boat Harbour, just north of Sorrento Beach (an area covered on pp. 188–9 in much greater detail).

Included in this long stretch of coast are Coogee Beach and Fremantle's South Beach, both on the southern side of the Swan River estuary mouth, as well as Port Beach, Cottesloe, North Cottesloe, Swanbourne, City Beach, Floreat, Scarborough, North Beach, Watermans and Sorrento, all of which lie to the north of the Swan.

These various sandy strands are separated from each other by low, rocky headlands and more extensive reefs such as the famous Trigg Point, as well as by various breakwaters, groynes and retaining walls, which are usually referred to as 'moles' in Western Australia.

Major Target Species

As well as being immensely popular with swimmers, surfers, sunbathers and beachcombers, the clean sands of Perth's wave-washed beaches also see a great deal of recreational angling pressure, especially when a strong run of tailor or Australian salmon move in close to the coast.

Sadly, Australian salmon appear to be much more uncommon in Perth's inshore metropolitan waters these days than they were three or four decades ago, no doubt as a result of commercial overharvesting and the depletion of pilchard (mulie) schools closer to shore. Nonetheless, good catches of salmon are still taken here from time to time, and there are even indicators of a gradual recovery in their numbers in more recent times, which bodes well for the future.

Mulloway (known in some eastern states as jewfish, but almost never referred to by that name in the West) are also found along these metropolitan ocean surf beaches, particularly when bait fish schools and tailor numbers are strong and good holes or gutters are evident close to shore, within casting range of anglers.

Mulloway on these city beaches run all the way from barely legal 'schoolies' to outstanding fish of 20 kg and more, but the majority of those encountered by surf anglers will typically weigh between 6 and 16 kg.

Most of these highly prized fish are taken by specialist anglers fishing at dawn, dusk or through the night with larger baits, although a surprising number of mulloway also succumb to a whole pilchard or mulie intended for tailor and salmon, even in mid-morning or afternoon.

In addition to tailor, Australian salmon and mulloway, Perth's metropolitan beaches and the rocky or reefy areas dividing them are home to large shoals of the ubiquitous and ever popular tommy rough or ruff — a small cousin of the Australian salmon known almost exclusively in Western Australia as herring or Australian herring.

The metropolitan surf also contains tasty yellowfin or sand whiting, mullet and tarwhine, plus the usual small sharks and rays, and even an occasional much larger shark. These species round out the range of fish commonly available to surf casting anglers close to the city, although surprises certainly do turn up from time to time.

Best Beach Fishing Spots

The best and most consistent beach fishing spots close to the city of Perth include the famous Swanbourne Drain, parts of City Beach, most of Floreat Beach and the Brighton Road area, although other areas also sometimes produce some very good catches. Local knowledge should always be sought concerning what's biting and where. Staff at local tackle stores — especially those situated close to the beaches themselves — are often excellent sources of valuable information.

Another tip is to watch closely the more successful local surf anglers. When they begin to gather close together at a particular location, chances are something worthwhile is biting, or is about to do so! Newcomers won't necessarily be welcome if they barge into such a gathering, but a cautious approach and friendly greeting will often secure a place amongst the action.

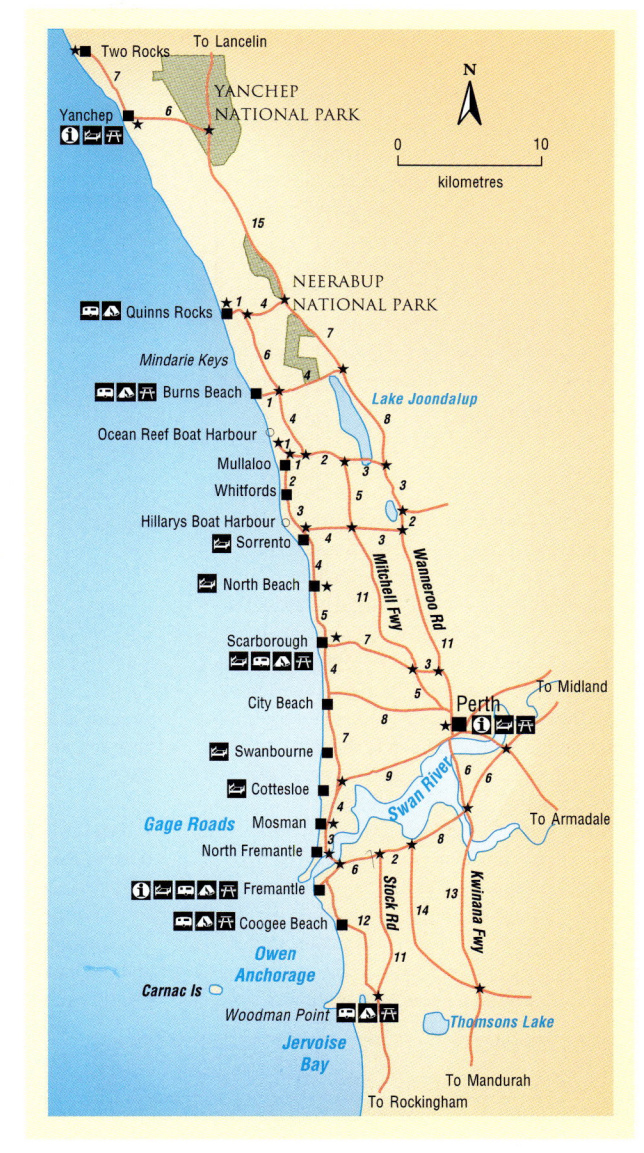

Tailor are very popular around Perth and are making a comeback under new fishing regulations

THE LOWER SWAN ESTUARY

IN BRIEF

MAP REFERENCE: PAGE 202 C4

GETTING THERE The Swan River winds its way through the suburbs of Perth before emptying into the Indian Ocean north of Fremantle. Perth is the capital of Western Australia and is serviced regularly by air, rail and coach services
BEST TIME TO FISH Year-round, but September to May is generally best
BEST TIME TO TRAVEL Year-round
MAJOR ANGLING SPECIES Tailor, flathead, flounder, bream, cobbler (catfish) and mulloway

---

Dominated by the broad waters of the Swan River estuary, which winds through many of Perth's leafy suburbs, this city is home to many keen anglers. In addition to pursuing various fish species, these anglers also regularly target the delicious prawns and blue manna crabs that are so abundant in the Swan estuary.

Nearby Fremantle—a wonderful seaside city with a busy port and a strong maritime tradition—stands on the southern head of the Swan River estuary mouth. 'Freo', as it is known locally, is a haven for both fish and fisherpeople.

Many anglers cast their lines from the various docks, wharves, groynes and moles around Fremantle in search of tommy rough (herring), trevally (skippy), small tailor, tarwhine, garfish and slimy or blue mackerel, as well as heftier targets such as bonito, larger tailor, Australian salmon and even the occasional mulloway. As popular as these coastal locations are, however, far more anglers choose to fish in the nearby Swan estuary.

PRODUCTIVE WATERS

Despite many years of reasonably heavy fishing pressure and at least some pollution from the surrounding city, the Swan's extensive waters remain highly productive for both the occasional and the more dedicated angler. This large estuary system can effectively be divided into two fairly distinct areas. From the busy harbour mouth at Fremantle and upstream as far as the aptly named Narrows Bridge, the lower Swan is a broad body of water that receives regular tidal flushing and hosts an interesting mix of both oceanic and estuarine species.

Above this bridge, and particularly beyond Heirisson Island and East Perth, the river narrows considerably and begins to twist and meander between its banks. Here, it is less marine in nature and often remains discoloured for prolonged periods following winter rains, with quite low salinity levels.

The productive lower Swan is home to a broad range of fish species, most notably flathead, flounder, tailor, cobbler (catfish) and mullet.

Being for the most part a sandy, relatively shallow waterway, the lower Swan estuary forms a natural haven for flathead and flounder in particular. These popular, bottom-dwelling flatfish are found here on a year-round basis, although in winter both flathead and flounder are mainly confined to the deeper, saltier holes, and are therefore a little more difficult to catch at this time than in the warmer months.

FLICKING LURES

Parts of the Swan lend themselves perfectly to lure fishing for flathead and even flounder, particularly in the area west from an imaginary line between Point Walter and Point Resolution, and taking in all of Freshwater Bay.

Keen anglers can spend many pleasant hours here in the warmer months, wading the shorelines and sand spits or drifting the shallows in a boat while casting and retrieving lures such as metal spoons, minnows, plugs and soft-plastic tailed jigs or bucktails.

While lure fishing for flathead (mostly of the bar-tailed variety), anglers will often spot a flounder following their lure. On such occasions, it is sometimes possible to change to a smaller lure or a natural bait quickly, lower this offering carefully ahead of the waiting flounder and jiggle it slightly to induce a strike.

Conventional bait fishing for these bottom-dwelling species with school prawns, whitebait and blue sardines is also highly successful at times. It can become rather frustrating, however, when large numbers of pesky blowfish or 'blowies' move in and ferociously attack these baits.

CHASING TAILOR

Tailor will also be encountered in the lower Swan by anglers using the techniques described for flathead and flounder. These voracious predatory fish are generally small, averaging 20 to 30 cm in

Flathead are readily taken on lures in the Swan River

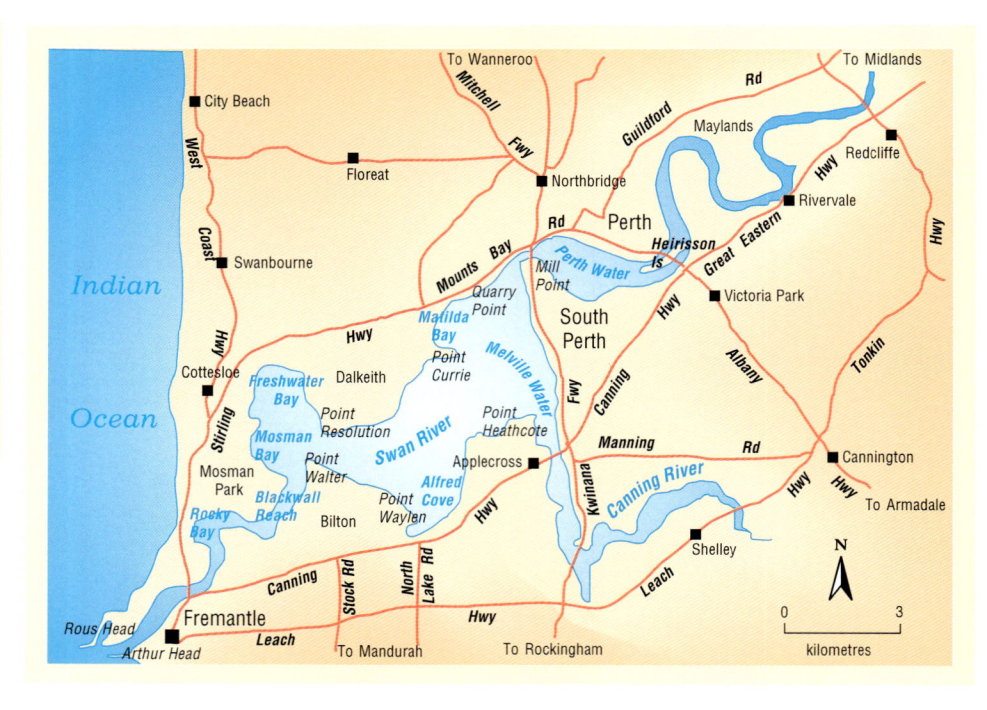

Perth's city skyline provides a picturesque backdrop for some excellent estuary fishing

length, but what they lack in size is more than made up for in ferocity and numbers.

For this reason, great care should be exercised not to breach current bag and size limits governing the capture of this popular species, which is staging a major comeback after serious declines during the 1980s.

Any hot summer's evening in Perth sees the jetties of the lower Swan crammed with anglers fishing for tailor, mostly using whitebait on small ganged hooks or various light, flashy lures.

THE SWAN'S BIGGEST PRIZE

Without doubt, the greatest prize on offer in the lower Swan estuary is the mulloway, sometimes known colloquially in these parts as 'river king' or 'silver king'. With the exception of the odd whaler shark, mulloway are the Swan's biggest predator, regularly attaining weights of 10 to 15 kg and very occasionally topping 25 kg.

During daylight hours, mulloway are normally found in the deeper holes around Swan Reach, Mosman Bay or Freshwater Bay, but they will sometimes move into slightly shallower water at night to feed, and it is at such times that the majority of these highly prized and sought-after fish are caught. Live baits are the most successful offering for mulloway, the best types being trumpeter, tailor, mullet and yellowtail, although the humble frozen mulie (Western Australian blue pilchard) also produces the odd fish, as do fillet baits, squid and octopus.

Boat fishing for mulloway is usually done in the deeper areas of the Swan, while the land-based angler can choose from any one of a number of piers, landings or yacht club jetties, where fishing from these structures is permitted. The foreshore adjacent to the old Swan Brewery site, below Kings Park, is another favourite mulloway spot with those fishing from land.

FURTHER UPSTREAM

Above The Narrows and Heirisson Island, southern black bream become the prime target species, although some of these fish are also taken further downstream, especially after heavy winter rains.

As a rule of thumb, Swan River bream favour the estuary's upper reaches, where the water is brackish and salinity levels lower. However, they do exhibit clear seasonal movements, mostly related to rainfall patterns.

Some of the best areas, especially in autumn, winter and spring, are beneath The Narrows and Canning bridges, while the fishing further upstream generally improves towards summer, with the bream favouring any snaggy areas. They are often found close to the pylons of jetties and bridges, and near old boat moorings, as well as around fallen trees and logs.

Bream are caught on a variety of baits. The most consistent of these are fresh or live river prawns and live blood worms, although other baits such as whitebait, mulie fillets, mussels and crabs can also work quite well. A running sinker rig is best, so that a biting bream feels as little resistance as possible when it picks up the bait and moves off with it.

Bream fishing in the Swan River is covered in greater detail on pp. 190–1.

COCKBURN SOUND

IN BRIEF

MAP REFERENCE: PAGE 202 B5

GETTING THERE Cockburn Sound lies about 30 km south of Fremantle. Launch at Fremantle, Jervoise Bay, Grain Terminal (moderate ramp only), Palm Beach or Cape Peron

BEST TIME TO FISH Year-round (mornings are generally calmest); September/October for the pink snapper run

BEST TIME TO TRAVEL February to April generally offer the best weather

MAJOR ANGLING SPECIES Herring (tommy rough), silver trevally, sand whiting, King George whiting, garfish, tailor and pink snapper

SPECIAL RESTRICTIONS Access to Garden Island limited to daylight hours on the northern end. Normal size and bag limits apply (visitors will need to obtain a readily available brochure for detailed information), except for pink snapper. For this species, a boat limit of 4 fish of more than 70 cm exists from 1 September to 31 December, with no more than 2 fish measuring more than 70 cm per angler

WARNINGS Cockburn Sound is navigable year-round, but be alert for winter storms and strong wind warnings

A large flathead by Western Australian standards

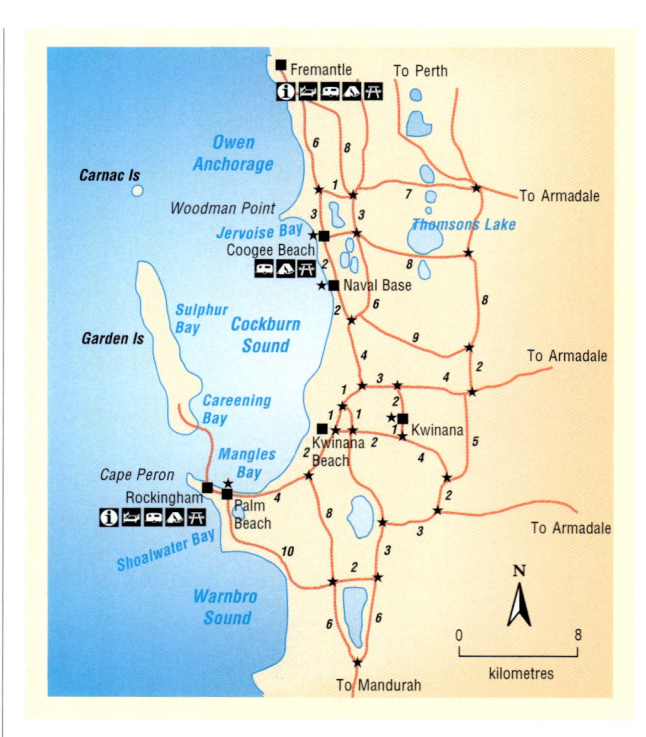

The lack of estuaries along Western Australia's coastline is partially offset by the fantastic scope of the ocean-washed Cockburn Sound, which stretches from Fremantle to Rockingham, and is sheltered for much of its length by Garden Island.

Heavy industry dominates the shoreline, but this shouldn't put boat anglers off as the water quality is excellent given the built-up nature of the area. These waters offer fine fishing, mostly for smaller species. They do yield some monsters at times, however, especially if there is a late spring snapper run, which often sees boats wall-to-wall around coral and gravel spots.

The snapper fishing is so productive in Cockburn Sound that special regulations exist to govern the number of fish per angler and per boat. Essentially, the run is a spawning one, meaning the fish are easy prey to both professional and amateur anglers. It is important to protect stocks and any measures taken to do so will be appreciated by anglers of the future. A bonus of the snapper angler's night vigil is an occasional very large mulloway. Many stingrays also inhabit Cockburn Sound, even in shallow waters, providing plenty of excitement and putting decent bends in rods.

The crown jewel of Cockburn Sound is the King George whiting, with some specimens tipping the scales at more than 1 kg, even heavier if taken outside the sound. At the back of Garden Island and near Rottnest, the odd King George will weigh nearer to 3 kg — and these are some fish on the right gear!

King George whiting are a year-round option. These fish school in December/January, when bag limits (20 fish per day) can easily be achieved. Most anglers are content with just a few of these outstanding specimens — they are fantastic to catch and one of Western Australia's finest table fish.

Sand whiting abound almost all year round and hordes of small ones and thick-as-your-wrist specimens are as likely as not to take a bait. Add herring (tommy rough), silver trevally, garfish, leatherjacket, snook, tailor, a few flathead (including the large blue spot species), flounder, trumpeter and tailor to this list and you have a vibrant fishery for the small boat angler. Rock areas at the top of Cockburn Sound, near Carnac Island and the Mewstone, hold schools of large tailor. Early risers cast pilchard baits and lures into the white water to good effect.

Generally better results for Cockburn hopefuls are obtained with the careful use of berley — a container set about 2 to 3 m below the water is a good option. Slow-release berley forms an important element, with the berley 'pot' including all manner of fish and crustacea scraps. If the bite slows, a quick jiggle results in the weight needed to sink the pot and move it up and down, releasing more berley.

Squid and blue swimmer crab numbers are huge in Cockburn Sound. The autumn and spring months are the best for squidding. Drifting is the best method of finding the squid, making sure plenty of action is imparted to the jig. Colour is a personal preference; the depth at which the lure works is a far bigger factor. It is important that the lure runs near to, but not along, the bottom. It makes sense to have a squid jig suspended from a float while you are fishing, the berley attracting attention from these creatures, too, and a freshly caught squid provides excellent bait.

Look for squid in water about 5 to 8 m deep, preferably over weeds. Closer to Garden Island, cuttlefish also attack squid jigs. These strange-looking cephalopods are certainly as tasty as squid, but with a greater capacity to blacken a boat or angler with their ink.

The summer months are best for crab hunting. Although drop nets are the preferred option, divers with wetsuits, snorkel, fins and heavy gloves dive for blue swimmer crabs near

Carnac Island, sitting at the top of Cockburn Sound, forms a sheltered boundary where large seals take advantage of the calm seas and sandy beaches

the Causeway at Rockingham. Very long ropes for drop nets are needed in Cockburn Sound near the Grain Terminal (about 20 to 25 m). If blues are found, however, they can sometimes be huge.

Finding Fish

Finding fish requires careful selection of a spot, then anchoring so that berley flows across a fish-holding area. Look for sand clearings near weed, so that the berley draws the fish towards you, away from the weed itself. Fishing on or too close to the weed results in hordes of unwanted fish such as butterfish, trumpeter or wrasse taking the baits. Fishing in about 6 to 8 m of water often works well. Anglers should choose deeper parts if drift fishing is a possibility. Drifting over a sandy patch or along an edge is dynamite for catching succulent sand whiting.

A surface rig with a small hook suits species such as garfish and herring. Add a small ball sinker about 30 to 40 cm above the hook and it becomes a universal rig, still picking up the occasional herring and garfish, but readily catching King George whiting, sand whiting or silver trevally. A No. 6 hook is suitable for this type of fishing—a chemically sharpened style is recommended. Use only as much weight as is necessary for the cast, or to find the bottom on a drifting session.

Neatly cut portions of river prawn make top bait, as they appeal to all the fish species. Make sure this bait is as fresh as possible. Squid is another good choice and sand worm is also favoured. At times, pieces of sardine or pilchard have been snaffled with relish by hungry King George whiting.

Light rods are the order of the day—a rod measuring around 2 m is fine—with small reels chosen to complement the rod. Lines of around 5 to 6 kg are adequate for the mostly small fish. The newer style braided and gel-spun lines, with their low-stretch characteristics, are finding favour, particularly for the quick-biting whiting. A landing net is essential in any boat, as the King George whiting, especially, readily flicks itself off a hook.

Shore fishing in Cockburn Sound is limited by access, sadly allowing nowhere near the scope for the land-based angler that the boat owner enjoys. Woodman Point Jetty is popular, yielding herring, garfish, sand whiting, tailor, yellow-eye mullet, squid, rays and silver trevally at times. The rock walls around the ship-building area offer good fishing where the angler is able to gain access. Woodman Point itself has a couple of small rock walls where herring and whiting are taken.

Lots of people fish from Palm Beach Jetty in Rockingham. It's an excellent platform from which anglers of all ages can try their luck.

Cockburn Sound is a welcome treasure for Perth's small boat anglers, in spite of the surrounding industry and constant threat of future development. It isn't the province of the huge boat either—only a small craft is needed to enjoy the wonderful marine life available right at Perth's front door.

HILLARYS BOAT HARBOUR AND TRIGG POINT

IN BRIEF

MAP REFERENCE: PAGE 202 B4

GETTING THERE Easy access along West Coast Drive — access from Perth CBD via Mitchell Freeway and Karrinyup Road, North Beach Road or Hepburn Avenue. There are excellent boat-launching facilities at Hillarys Boat Harbour

BEST TIME TO FISH Year-round. Sun-up and sundown for tailor, and into the night

BEST TIME TO TRAVEL Year-round except for storms; winter months the best from shore, apart from when targeting tailor

MAJOR ANGLING SPECIES Herring (tommy rough), tailor, garfish, silver trevally, mulloway, small sharks and whiting. Also, for boat anglers, pink snapper, West Australian jewfish, breaksea cod, baldchin groper, blue morwong, Samson fish and mackerel (summer)

WARNINGS Watch for waves, especially on reef areas; boat anglers must always consider weather and ocean conditions

ACCOMMODATION Numerous facilities ranging from caravan parks and chalets to five-star hotels

CHARTER BOATS & FISHING GUIDES Up-to-date information can be obtained from the tackle stores at Hillarys Boat Harbour; Mills Charters operate from Hillarys, telephone (08) 9246 5334; Sea Venture Boat Charters operate from Ocean Reef Boat Harbour, telephone (08) 9405 4248

Samson fish cause mayhem when hooked in near-reef areas, fully testing both angler and gear

Just a couple of kilometres offshore from Hillarys Boat Harbour, the occasional city skyscraper is visible to the east, indicating just how accessible the Hillarys, Sorrento and Trigg Island areas are to Perth's CBD. Add to this a fair expectation that anglers will actually catch fish and it is little wonder that fishing enjoys such huge popularity in the West Australian capital.

A summer's evening sees this stretch of coast dotted with hopeful anglers, all keen to take advantage of a tailor run. At these times, fish weighing up to 2 kg attack pilchard baits with the speed and tenacity characteristic of the species. Although found here year-round, tailor are more popular in the summer season, when techniques for successful tailor angling are within everyone's reach. Long rods are the order of the day — short sticks are better left for the rock walls of Hillarys Boat Harbour. There is generally plenty of swell around and longer rods allow for casting over the breakers, keeping the line above the water. Longer rods also give better clearance over reefs and rock edges.

Standard baits are pilchards, usually called 'mulies', and these are threaded on a gang of hooks — four 4/0 tarpon-style hooks are perfect for the task. This same set-up is suitable for other shore-hugging species such as mulloway and small sharks, and even for pink snapper on the odd occasion.

BEST BAITS AND RIGS

Some anglers prefer to fish the rock walls or beaches with whitebait or sardines. Again, a set of linked (ganged) hooks better suits these baits. A fair degree of force is necessary for a long cast in the Hillarys–Trigg Point area, and the linked hooks impaled in the bait helps to keep that bait on the line. Tailor are still captured with these smaller baits, as are herring (tommy rough), silver bream, silver trevally (which especially love sardines), flathead, flounder, sand whiting and sometimes King George whiting.

When fishing from the rock walls at Hillarys, anglers can attract small blue or slimy mackerel with berley. In fact, the careful use of berley increases one's chances dramatically for nearly all species. Yellowtail and garfish, too, are sometimes around in large numbers and small baits such as prawn pieces, squid, sand and blood worms and maggots are good for these, as well as for herring and whiting. A variety of cages and floats are used to dispense the berley, all with one thing in common: they 'personalise' the small area around a bait, attracting fish to that precise spot. Berley is generally inserted each cast for best results. The autumn and winter months yield better catches of herring and yellow-eye mullet. (The latter species is often called 'pilch' in Western Australia.)

In the Trigg Reef area, an unweighted mulie (pilchard), or one rigged with a small ball sinker above

The reef-dwelling harlequin fish, with its iridescent blue markings, adds spectacular colour to any catch

the hooks, is utilised for 'baitcasting'. This is a deadly technique for tailor especially, but suitable for a variety of applications along this section of coast. Trigg Blue Hole is a singularly famous spot, best fished in winter for tailor, salmon, mulloway and silver bream. A stand-out feature here is the use of tripods by local anglers. While it does offer good fishing, the Blue Hole is definitely for the experienced angler only.

Lures used along this coast are mostly selected for their long casting qualities and fast-action metal styles are best. There are a variety of heavy metals on tackle shop shelves — 30 to 60 g are good all-round weights. Poppers able to be cast a long distance are great for tailor around the reef spots at Trigg, with floating styles allowing the angler to explore water right over broken reefs, where tailor love to hang out.

A few anglers specialise in catching cobbler (estuary catfish) — mostly using worms or maggots — close to shore from the rock walls at Hillarys Boat Harbour.

Herring can be sought all year round, but a large run of these fish occurs in autumn. April, May and June see vast numbers of the mighty little fish hell-bent on taking baits. Maggots are the most often used baits, but prawns, squid and worms are also ideal options. Artificial maggots work well, especially in conjunction with one or two of the real thing on the hook. In late autumn, yellow-eye mullet (known locally as 'pilch') are present in numbers. The techniques for catching them are similar to those used for herring, and red meat baits such as ox heart are popular.

The highly prized West Australian jewfish is keenly pursued by anglers along this stretch of coast

THE GATEWAY TO ADVENTURE

Hillarys Boat Harbour is the gateway to adventure. On the right day, anglers in small boats have to travel out only a few kilometres in order to find plenty of small fish such as herring, (tommy rough), skippy (silver trevally) and garfish. These can be readily berleyed to the boat and caught using baits such as worms, prawns, maggots or squid. Hordes of sand whiting can also be found, usually by drifting over sandy areas, with some lucky anglers hooking into very large King George whiting. South of Hillarys, off the suburb of Scarborough, is another reliable spot for sand whiting.

The offshore reef near Trigg and Hillarys is a favoured hunting ground for large tailor. Anglers should cast their baits and lures right next to the reef for the best results, but care is needed to handle the boat in the usually swelly conditions. The Three Mile Reef, extending from Scarborough to Ocean Reef, attracts plenty of attention, and tailor fishing on exposed reef areas is a favourite pastime in this area. In the channels further out from Three Mile Reef, pink snapper are caught.

The famed West Australian jewfish is more often caught closer to shore in winter and spring along this stretch of coast than in many other areas. Baldchin groper and breaksea cod are both highly prized and not unusual in a good bag, and a harlequin fish adds spectacular colour to a catch.

Echo sounders are almost mandatory, except when fishing the exposed reef and island areas. The best technique is to search for a 'lump' (reef) or a significant drop-off, then drift over the area. Heavy weights are sometimes required for the baits to reach the bottom. 'Coral' areas hold fine fish and are worth drifting over or anchoring nearby in the hope of results.

Throughout the year, Samson fish may well attack baits, offering first-class action and demonstrating how well they deserve their name. From January to March, when the waters are warmer, mackerel species are often taken by trollers using large lures or garfish baits. It is not uncommon for deep sea anglers to hook an odd Spanish mackerel either, and there are always plenty of sharks.

Charter operations work daily from Hillarys Boat Harbour. Their experienced crews know special spots where clients will encounter some of the area's marine treasures. A word of caution if you are not a good sailor: the west coast is noted for its waves.

SWAN RIVER BREAM

IN BRIEF

MAP REFERENCE: PAGE 202 C4

GETTING THERE The Swan–Canning river system winds through Perth before emptying into the Indian Ocean just north of Fremantle. Access is available by foot from many car parks or by boat

BEST TIME TO FISH Early morning and late evening

BEST TIME TO TRAVEL Year-round

MAJOR ANGLING SPECIES Black bream, mulloway, flathead, flounder, grunter, giant herring

SPECIAL RESTRICTIONS Digging of worms allowed in specified areas only

CHARTER BOATS & FISHING GUIDES No specific guides or charters operate in the Swan–Canning system. Bluewater Tackle in Morley is in the heart of bream country, telephone (08) 9375 9800

Swan River black bream are an exciting and challenging target species. For starters, they are a handsome fish, the term 'black' belying the vibrant golden sheen of their scales as these powerful fish are first brought from the water. Add to this their strong runs and ability to find cover or a snag when hooked and black bream stand out as fascinating adversaries. They are never easy to catch, increasing the challenge for both the beginning angler and the dedicated bream specialist.

The gradual increase in the size and number of bream in the Swan–Canning estuary system is a success story in itself. After years of heavy netting of spawning stock in a confined area, this practice was banned, and the results of that move are now being seen. What was considered a trophy fish of 2 kg ten years ago is today being dwarfed by 3-kg monsters. Fish weighing 1 to 1.5 kg are now relatively commonplace.

As the the fishery has improved, so, too, have the tactics for catching black bream. In place of the common worm, a variety of baits are being employed, with lures and even saltwater fly becoming commonly used options.

Finding Black Bream

Bream are a year-round target, with schools heading well upriver as far as Caversham in the warm summer months and as near to the sea as Mosman Bay, only a few kilometres from Fremantle Harbour in winter. Most of the activity among anglers occurs from the Narrows Bridge to Guildford, and as far as the Rivervale Bridge over the Canning River.

Looking for bream involves two major techniques: fishing structures such as bridges, pylons, jetties, wrecks and fallen timber, or fishing the flats for foraging fish. Bream love to hang about a structure, where there's sure to be a ready food supply. Anglers would do well to follow the old fishing rule: 'Find the structure, find the fish.'

The boating clubs that exist along the Swan–Canning are prime black bream country, although for the land-based angler access to most of these is limited through 'Members Only' signs. Anglers owning or being able to use boats don't suffer the same restrictions, however, and drifting a bait past the many pylons or anchoring and casting a bait work well.

Baits must always be as fresh as possible. The southern black bream is a fussy fish, so the whole prawn must be in good condition, without any blackening of the head. Live baits and fresh bony herring are top of the list, with a fresh batch of king prawns also included in this list. Bait shop prawns are fine, but as with all baits of this type, they must be kept cool for best results. Blood

Boat moorings, jetties and other man-made structures all attract feeding bream

worms are another top bait—again, the fresher the better. There are designated areas in the river system for digging worms, but tackle shop worms will also do the job. Some of the biggest black bream caught in recent times have been taken with a fillet of bony herring, a co-inhabitant of the Swan–Canning estuary.

LURING BREAM

Lures cast near jetties and pylons or trolled immediately alongside make for exciting angling—a small bibbed minnow is likely to be whacked by the powerful fish. Turning the bream away from the pylon is the next challenge facing the angler as these muscular fish are particularly expert at tangling the line around any object in an effort to evade capture.

Using light line in the open water is fine, where the bream has fewer places to shelter, but the big fish will make short work of light line around pylons or tree stumps. A fair amount of drag needs to be employed for the same reason. It is better to catch the fish quickly regardless of whether keeping or releasing one's catch. A landing net is essential in this type of fishing.

The selected lure should be about 40 to 60 mm long, with medium-depth divers the best in most of Perth's water. Don't be afraid to use a slow retrieve—just enough to have the lure swimming enticingly past the bream's resting spot. Soft lures work well, but don't last long, as the pesky blowfish make short work of the important fine tails which make these lures so attractive. It is better to stick to hard plastic or wooden styles. These same lures will also catch flathead and flounder, sometimes in the same water.

Lures that are fish look-a-likes are the most favoured, although yabby styles are popular, too. There is enormous choice available, one common factor appearing to be a touch of fluorescent colouring somewhere on the lure.

OPEN-WATER BREAM

The second major area in which anglers can track down the black bream involves more speculative fishing—trying open water and flats with the same range of baits and lures. Instead of working for the fish around a pylon or tree, anglers should generally cast the bait and leave it, awaiting the arrival of feeding fish. Deep river holes are better fished this way. So, too, are flats near riverbanks where sea grasses hold shrimp schools and where hungry bream expect to find food with the rise and fall of the tide. However, deeper waters provide the better option for getting away from the blowfish.

Bony herring fillet is good for this style of fishing, as it is better able to withstand the 'pickers' and its strong smell attracts fish. It is also possible that one of the many mulloway in the area will take a liking to such a bait.

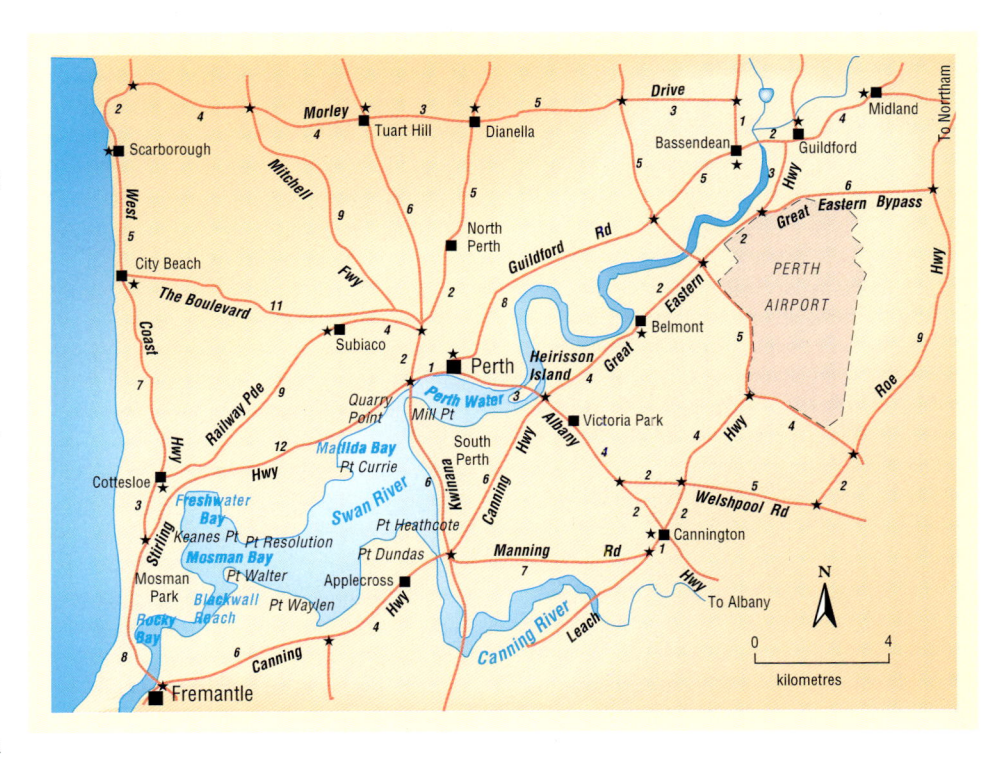

Using berley in the Swan–Canning estuary is not recommended. Although it can attract target fish, the perennial blowfish will also be tempted and snatch all the beautiful baits the angler has saved for those treasured black bream.

SEASONS AND TACKLE

Winter months are better for fishing structures; the summer is more suitable for angling in the deeper holes in the cool of day, speculating over flats at other times and at high tide. Summer is also best for trying around fallen trees and stumps.

Spots such as Maylands, Belmont and East Perth are top year-round propositions. One of the beauties of the Swan–Canning estuary is that shore fishing is as productive as that from a boat, bringing it into everyone's reach.

Tackle is simplicity itself. Line and hook are enough, but a medium-action rod of any length is better to cover more ground. Generally, brown-coloured lines are preferred, as are brown hooks. Rigs, too, are as basic as they come: a bait keeper-style hook with the slices in its shank and as small a sinker as possible, with none being the best option. A short monofilament trace line of about 8 to 10 kg is suitable, but never use a wire trace or clip on the single hook. Size 1/0 to No. 4 hooks are about right, with No. 1 or No. 2 being best for all-round use.

Bream bite throughout the day and night, generally with increased activity in the early morning and evening. As with all fishing, the middle of the day is the least likely time to catch a bream, yet a rod set in a holder, with the bait sitting quietly while your lunch is prepared, is a relaxing way to fish. The tap-tap on the line, or its sudden tightening, then a quivering rod and rattling drag, is sure to shatter the riverbank peace. If it is a large Swan River black bream buzzing sideways, with the line cutting the water as the fish tries to gain its freedom, then this is what bream angling is all about. Soon the gleaming golden-bronze flanked fish may be in the net, fins thrust out defiantly.

More and more anglers are starting to target bream on lures

ROTTNEST ISLAND

IN BRIEF

MAP REFERENCE: PAGE 202 B4

GETTING THERE Rottnest Island lies 21 km off the coast of Perth and is serviced regularly by ferries. It also has an airstrip for light planes

BEST TIME TO FISH Year-round, but September to May is generally best

BEST TIME TO TRAVEL Year-round

MAJOR ANGLING SPECIES Whiting, snapper, Australian salmon, tailor, garfish, tommy rough (herring), bream, trevally (skippy), Samson fish, West Australian jewfish, various other reef, sport and game species

SPECIAL RESTRICTIONS Accommodation and camping on Rottnest Island is controlled by the Rottnest Island Authority, telephone (09) 9372 9729. The number of visitors is capped during peak holiday seasons, so advance bookings are essential

WARNINGS Occasional 'king waves' are experienced along this stretch of coast, especially in winter — rock anglers should take particular care. Large great white sharks are also occasionally encountered around Rottnest and pose a potential threat to swimmers and divers, particularly during the warmer months

ACCOMMODATION Information about staying on Rottnest Island can be obtained from the Rottnest Island Authority, telephone (08) 9372 9729 or (08) 9372 9752 (visitors centre); Rottnest Hotel, telephone (08) 9292 5011; All Seasons holiday apartments, telephone (08) 9292 5161

Lying some 21 km north north-west off the coast of Fremantle is the ruggedly beautiful Rottnest Island, which owes its unusual name to the abundant, wallaby-like quokkas that still call it home. On seeing these creatures and their numerous nests during his brief visit to the island in 1696, Dutch explorer Willem de Vlamingh was reminded of giant rats. As a result, a corruption of the Dutch term for 'rats' nests' has survived to this day as a less than flattering name for a truly delightful location.

The island was eventually settled by small numbers of Europeans after 1831, and served as the site for a penal colony from the late 1830s until as recently as 1931, the open water between its shores and the mainland obviously deterring escape. Today, however, people are much keener to get to this island jewel than escape from it!

With its myriad sheltered bays, picture postcard coves, small beaches, rocky points and fish-rich reefs, Rottnest or 'Rotto' is truly Perth's favourite aquatic playground. It is the number one holiday destination for most Western Australians living between Bunbury and Lancelin, as well as for many other visitors from much further afield.

Rottnest is a low-lying, sandy island with stabilised, vegetated dunes rising to a height of about 20 m above sea level and numerous rocky outcrops thrusting into the sea. Its beaches are composed of clean, white sand which contrasts dramatically with the surrounding aquamarine waters, through which submerged reef and weed patches remain clearly visible for a surprising distance offshore, especially on sunny days.

Fishing is available all year round in the waters lapping Rottnest Island. While piscatorial activity tends to peak in the warmer half of the year, some keen anglers actually prefer the cooler winter months, when crowds on the island are much smaller and the pressure on fishing is dramatically reduced.

PROLIFIC HERRING

The most prolific fish species found at Rottnest Island would have to be the little tommy rough or ruff—better known to most Western Australians by the somewhat confusing title of herring or Australian herring.

These small, golden-speckled cousins of the Australian salmon regularly run from 200 to 400 g in weight and very occasionally approach twice that size. However, what they lack in bulk they more than make up for in sheer numbers and their willingness to bite!

Float tackle is ideal for targeting herring or tommy rough, and one of the favourite techniques employed in Western Australia involves the use of a large wooden float called a 'blob'. This float features holes or internal cavities that can be filled with berley to attract, excite and concentrate both tommy rough and garfish, which are also plentiful here at times. Productive berley mixtures include soaked stale bread, bran, pollard, fish pastes and pet food, although keen tommy rough anglers often have their own 'secret' recipes.

Several baits are usually rigged at varying distances below the blob float on small hooks. The

Boats at anchor in Thomson Bay, Rottnest Island

most productive offerings include maggots (also known as 'gentles'), pieces of prawn, sections of marine worm, small squid strips, dough, bread, cheese and the various commercial or packet long-life bait mixtures. However, tommy rough occasionally become so ravenous that they will bite quite freely at bare hooks! On occasions such as this, small lengths of coloured plastic tubing or sections of drinking straw placed on the hook will catch these little fish one after another.

OTHER TARGETS

Some very nice Australian salmon are sometimes taken around Rottnest Island, particularly near its more rugged and exposed western end. Big tailor, yellowtail kingfish and Samson fish are also a chance for the shore-based angler here, along with a very occasional mulloway.

Silver drummer or buffalo bream (commonly referred to in Western Australia as buff bream) are also abundant in shallow areas right around Rottnest Island. While not especially prized as table fish, they can provide excellent sport, as do the many small trevally (skippy) which are also encountered here in good numbers, especially during the spring and summer months.

Silver drummer are common around Rottnest Island

Sand or yellowfin whiting and even a few King George whiting are also taken by shore-based anglers casting from the island's beaches and rocky points.

To achieve the best results with King George whiting, however, a boat is needed to reach the sand and fine gravel patches scattered amongst the surrounding reefs where these highly sought-after table fish prefer to feed.

OFFSHORE FISHING

Further offshore from Rottnest Island and in deeper water, there is some superb reef fishing to be had for the revered West Australian jewfish (sometimes spelt 'dhufish'). Pink snapper, red snapper (a large member of the nannygai clan), Samson fish, blue morwong or queen snapper, and various other bottom and mid-water fish are available here, too.

The shipping channel between Rottnest Island and the port of Fremantle also yields some very big snapper at times, as do the waters around nearby Garden Island and inside Cockburn Sound. Carnac Island produces occasional good trevally catches, as well as a range of other species. (Fishing in Cockburn Sound—especially for pink snapper—is dealt with in much greater detail on pp. 186–7.)

Rottnest Island is also the hub of sport and game fishing in southern Western Australia. Spanish mackerel, shark mackerel, dolphin fish (mahi mahi), wahoo, tuna of several types, various sharks and some very big marlin (mostly Indo-Pacific blues) are on offer over the Rottnest Trench and along the edge of the continental shelf, as well as in waters much closer to the island itself, particularly during late summer and autumn each year.

All-in-all, Rottnest Island has something to offer every angler and holiday maker, and its continued prominence as Western Australia's favourite vacation destination is certainly easy enough to understand!

BUNBURY TO BUSSELTON

IN BRIEF

MAP REFERENCE: PAGE 202 B7

GETTING THERE Bunbury is about 190 km south of Perth — access via National Highway One; Busselton is a further 52 km south of Bunbury
BEST TIME TO FISH Year-round, although autumn weather is the calmest and coincides with the salmon run
BEST TIME TO TRAVEL Friendly climate in summer, but attractive all year
MAJOR ANGLING SPECIES Tailor, herring, sand whiting, King George whiting, squid, silver trevally, salmon, mulloway, garfish, bream in rivers; pink snapper, jewfish, sharks, tuna, bonito for boat anglers
WARNINGS Boating is fairly safe, but water and weather conditions need to be monitored carefully, especially once out of the shelter of Geographe Bay. Shore fishing from rocks on the ocean side of the region (south from Yallingup) can be dangerous
ACCOMMODATION Many units, chalets, hotels, motels and caravan parks
CHARTER BOATS AND FISHING GUIDES None available, seek local advice at tackle shops

Beach fishing is popular during the warmer months, especially when the tailor run is on

Just a couple of hours drive south of Perth, Bunbury sits at the top of the vast and beautiful Geographe Bay, with rugged Cape Naturaliste jutting westwards at the bay's southern end to form a fishing and water sports playground. This area, with Bunbury as its focal point, is a major centre for Western Australian tourism. There is beautiful forest and coastal scenery nearby, as well as golf courses and the wineries of the world-renowned Margaret River region to the south. Visitors can enjoy dining at fine restaurants, swimming, diving and snorkelling, sailing and water skiing Also, rather than simply serving as a launching point to Geographe Bay, Bunbury is the gateway to a diverse fishery — beach, rock, jetty, freshwater and river. For the keen angler, it is a difficult choice — what to fit into a weekend?

Small boat angling is foremost. The shape of Geographe Bay offers protection from the prevailing south-westers, the state's sea breeze. If Western Australia has nothing else, it has plenty of wind — more than its share, in fact — and this is a factor that fishing parties must take into account. Although Geographe Bay is mostly fishable all year round, north-westerlies need to be watched carefully. So, too, does venturing too far out beyond the bay's limits, where strong currents and the west coast's famous waves make conditions for the experienced only. At times, however, the bay is delightfully tranquil and these days are diamonds.

FISHING OPTIONS

Anglers using bigger craft enjoy catching large West Australian jewfish, which are as plentiful around the off-shore reefs here as anywhere. Pink snapper and Samson fish add to the larger species found in this region, and even sharks and tuna species are likely to be decked at times. Favoured baits are octopus and squid, while pilchards are best presented on a gang of hooks — four 4/0 tarpon-style are perfect for the 'mulie' (pilchard). The new line styles made from gel-spun polyethylene fibres, with their low-stretch characteristic, are ideal for this deeper water fishing. Berleying helps tremendously, especially if the berley is able to be released near the sea bed.

Mulloway are sought by both boat and shore anglers. The shipping channels off Bunbury are productive, as are smaller channels out from Busselton. Beach anglers often try for this species along the surf stretches both north and south of Bunbury, and at the 'Cut', built as an entrance to the Leschenault Estuary. The Collie River is another good hunting ground for mulloway. Excellent black bream and cobbler (catfish) fishing is available here, too. The large Leschenault Estuary is popular for crabbing, prawning and whiting fishing, and garfish are readily berleyed. Try a river prawn or worm bait for the Collie River's black bream. Small bibbed minnow lures are also able to entice strikes from this species.

BREAD AND BUTTER FISHING

Pursuing smaller species such as King George whiting, sand whiting, herring, skippy (silver trevally), garfish, leatherjackets and other estuary

Busselton Jetty, formerly used for shipping, is now a popular fishing platform for anglers of all ages

odds-'n-sods in Geographe Bay make for great fishing, despite the built-up nature of the region. Blue swimmer crabs are prevalent and squid, too, are present in large numbers. A drift over sandy areas just off the shoreline is likely to yield good catches of King George and sand whiting. Occasionally bigger fish such as snook will also take a swipe. Anchor near weed beds or adjacent to the few reefs in Geographe Bay and use a berley pot (preferably one that sinks 2 or 3 m) to bring up the fish.

An underwater mountain of old tyres has created an artificial reef about 6 km north of Dunsborough. This feature has quickly attracted a diverse range of fish and marine life. In late 1997, the decommissioned Australian naval ship the *Swan* was sent to the bottom about 4 km out from the shore near Busselton to create another artificial reef for anglers and divers.

Beach anglers need long casts for general surf fishing, and morning and evening tailor runs have beaches such as Wannerup, Peppermint Beach, Bunbury's Town Beach, Myalup and Binninngup dotted with hopefuls. Pilchard baits on a gang or flight of hooks work well for tailor (the summer months are best), and for salmon in autumn and early winter. Lures sometimes turn a trick — heavy metal spinners or slices are effective, as are popper styles. The white sand beaches immediately north of Busselton are busy on summer evenings, as families fish the nightly tailor raid. Recent seasons have seen an improvement in the number of tailor, after many years of poor catches. Beach and rock spots all the way to Cape Naturaliste itself are worth trying.

Smaller baits such as sardines and whitebait allow mixed bag catches. Tailor will still take these offerings and herring, snook, whiting, silver trevally, silver bream and flathead may also find themselves in the bag. A key element to shore fishing along the Bunbury–Busselton coast is the 'personalising' of berley. A berley float (for long casts), a wire or plastic cage, or a berley sinker will increase your chances. Berley should be added to these before each cast.

Mixed Bags

Busselton Jetty reflects the shallow nature of the water around the edges of Geographe Bay. This mile-long jetty is one of the lengthiest in the southern hemisphere. When the jetty was used for shipping, it needed this length to reach deeper water where larger boats could draw enough water. Nowadays, it forms an excellent fishing platform for young and old, and is fishable year-round in most weather conditions. There is always something to be caught: tommy rough (herring), silver trevally, prolific garfish, silver bream, squid, crabs, mulloway, pike, bonito in some years (especially from January to March) and small sharks all hit the deck at times.

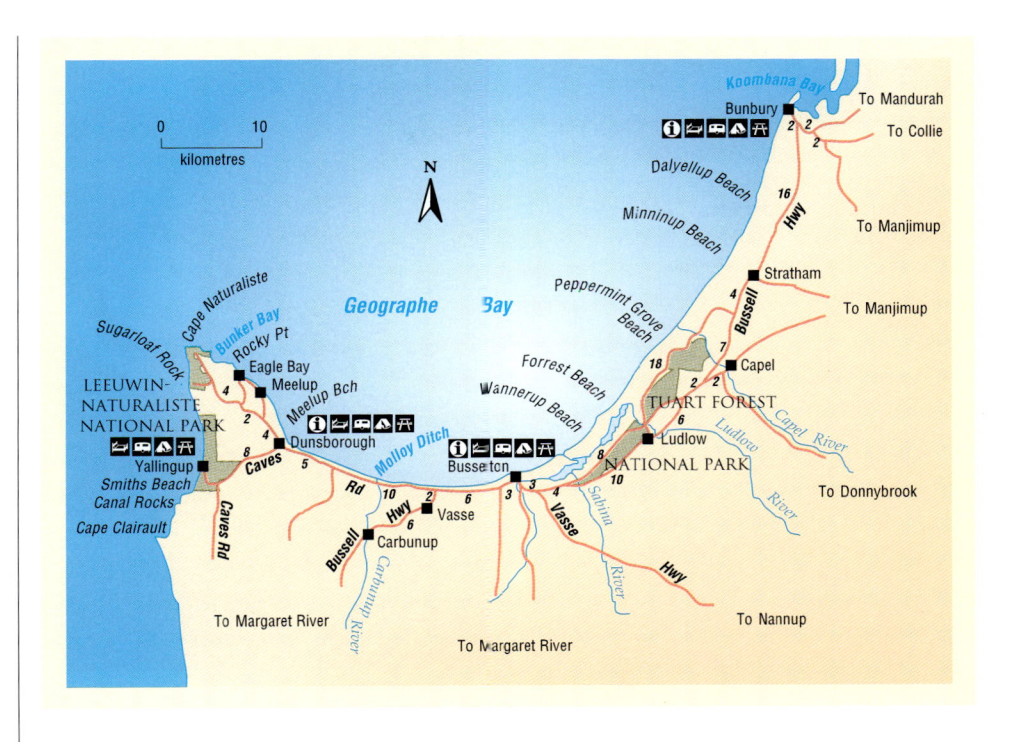

Long casts are not required and even handlines are effective. However, the use of berley substantially increases the chances of success. Lightweight berley cages are ideal for surface-feeding species such as garfish and herring. Also, no one should venture onto this treasured structure without a squid jig.

A small donation is requested from those visiting the jetty, as the Busselton townspeople funded the major renovations needed to save the outstanding platform. Ongoing maintenance is both necessary and expensive.

At Bunbury, the inner harbour rock walls allow for relaxed angling for tailor and mulloway, and drop-netters also try for blue swimmer crabs from boths the walls and boats.

Australian Salmon

Autumn is salmon time for the south-west corner of Western Australia. Large schools of these powerful fish come within casting distance of the shore in this region. Southern rock and reef spots near Dunsborough are favoured fishing spots, as are the surf beaches north of Bunbury. The use of pilchard baits is the way to go, with popper lures being the best artificial choice, especially near rocky areas.

Rock fishing is quite safe along this part of the coast, except on rare occasions. Around the corner to Yallingup and further south, however, it is a different story and great care must be taken.

The strong flavour of the Australian salmon is not for everyone. Many anglers prefer to catch and release this torpedo-like fish, which is better regarded as a sporting challenge than as a food fish. If salmon are to be kept, bleeding and icing them down makes for a better meal. The fillets make fine eating if barbecued soon after the salmon has been caught, and this oily fish also lends itself superbly to smoking. With saltwater fly fishing increasing in popularity, the Australian salmon has become a highly prized adversary for exponents of the fly. Largish Deceiver patterns are effective, with outfits from seven-weight upwards offering good sport.

A monster King George whiting from Geographe Bay

SOUTH-WEST CORNER

IN BRIEF

MAP REFERENCE: PAGE 202 A7

GETTING THERE Bunbury is about 190 km by road south from Perth, Busselton is 52 km south of Bunbury and Augusta is a further 145 km south from there

BEST TIME TO FISH September to May

BEST TIME TO TRAVEL Year-round

MAJOR ANGLING SPECIES Whiting, snapper, Australian salmon, garfish, tommy rough (herring), bream, trevally (skippy), West Australian jewfish, various other reef and sport species

SPECIAL RESTRICTIONS In some areas, regulations limit recreational boating activities that may interfere with the pursuit of salmon schools by commercial fishers during the designated netting season. Details are signposted at most launching ramps

WARNINGS Weather changes are possible at any time and so-called 'king waves' are also experienced along this stretch of coast, especially in winter — rock fishers should take particular care. Large great white sharks are reasonably abundant in coastal waters here and pose a potential threat to swimmers and divers, particularly during the warmer months

Falls on the Margaret River near the township of the same name

The south-west corner of Western Australia — an extensive region stretching from from Bunbury to Augusta — is an area that is attracting an increasing amount of interest from tourists and travellers these days, thanks in no small part to its famous wineries, great surfing beaches, pristine stretches of coast, majestic karri and jarrah forests, and excellent recreational fishing opportunities.

In many ways, the delightful township of Margaret River, lying in the middle of this region, has become its unofficial capital. Today, there is almost always some kind of festival, celebration, exhibition or organised event going on in this busy little settlement of 1500 souls. Even if there's not, visitors will still be able to find plenty to see or do.

From Margaret River, it is possible to strike southward towards rugged Cape Leeuwin, where the Indian and Southern oceans meet in a clash of often titanic forces, or head north to the more sheltered waters of Geographe Bay and Busselton.

Both directions offer myriad places to cast a line, and an appealing list of potential target species that includes Australian salmon, herring (tommy rough), bream, garfish, mullet, whiting, trevally, snapper, West Australian jewfish, Samson fish, mulloway, tuna and sharks — to name just a few of the more commonly encountered types.

GEOGRAPHE BAY TO MARGARET RIVER

Geographe Bay is a large body of relatively shallow ocean water stretching between Bunbury and Cape Naturaliste. The pleasant seaside resort of Busselton, with a population of around 6500 people, lies at the southern apex of this sweeping bay and is a very popular holiday destination with anglers from all over the lower half of Western Australia.

At Busselton, Geographe Bay enjoys some protection from southerly winds, but is largely open to breezes from all other points of the compass, at least until one moves west towards Dunsborough and Meelup, where the bulk of Cape Naturaliste itself provides a buffer of sorts against prevailing summertime afternoon sea breezes from the west and south-west.

By far the most popular angling species along this beautiful stretch of coast is the Australian herring or tommy rough (also spelt tommy ruff in some literature). While these oily, strong-flavoured little fish can be caught in good numbers throughout the year, their peak season usually occurs around April or early May. Yellow-eye mullet (known locally as 'pilch') and garfish are also taken in good numbers by light tackle bait anglers in the summer and autumn months, along with the tommy rough.

Australian salmon migrate through the waters of this area from February until late April or early May each year, and the many rocky headlands

View across to the lighthouse at Cape Leeuwin

along the coast between Dunsborough and Redgate, just south of the Margaret River, make ideal spots for those chasing these hard-fighting fish. However, great care should always be exercised, as many of these rock ledges can become extremely dangerous in a heavy swell.

Top rock fishing spots in this area for anglers wishing to target salmon include Rocky Point, Bunker Bay, Sugarloaf Rock, Smiths Beach, Canal Rocks, Wyadup, Little Injidup and Big Injidup.

Australian salmon are a common catch in this region

Silver trevally or 'skippies' are another very popular target species for both shore and boat anglers in this region. These fish are mostly taken on whole whitebait and blue sardines presented on ganged hooks, often fished in conjunction with a berley trail. An occasional yellowtail kingfish or big Samson fish is also hooked from the more exposed rocky headlands such as Sugarloaf, especially by those anglers using live herring (tommy rough) and other large baits on heavier tackle. The same areas also yield the odd West Australian jewfish, blue groper, mulloway or big shark, while surface-feeding schools of bonito and juvenile southern bluefin tuna may be encountered within casting distance of shore at times. A cliff gaff of some sort is essential for landing larger specimens of any of these fish at most of the spots mentioned.

Basic boat launching facilities are available at Dunsborough, Canal Rocks and Gracetown. Boat anglers fishing off this rugged stretch of coast regularly encounter West Australian jewfish, pink snapper, queen snapper, blue groper and silver trevally (skippy). There are also sharks, tuna and even the occasional marlin for those anglers with greater aspirations.

Boat fishing in the slightly more sheltered waters of Geographe Bay itself, especially offshore from Dunsborough and Busselton, produces good catches of silver trevally and whiting, while Samson fish, yellowtail kingfish, southern bluefin tuna and pink snapper may all be encountered at Naturaliste Reef when the weather conditions are favourable.

Geographe Bay is also one of the prime destinations in all of Western Australia for those targeting the sweet and delicious blue manna (blue swimmer) crabs that are so popular.

AUGUSTA AND FLINDERS BAY

Augusta, with a population of around 500 people, is one of the oldest towns in all of Western Australia and lies on the shores of Hardy Inlet, near the mouth of the pretty Blackwood River, some 30 km south of Margaret River.

There are some lovely southern black bream in the lower and middle reaches of both the the Blackwood and Margaret rivers, while trout may also be encountered further upstream, along with the big, black crayfish known as marron.

Inshore and estuary angling near Augusta and in Flinders Bay produces herring (tommy rough), garfish, mullet (pilch), King George whiting, sand whiting, flathead and juvenile Australian salmon. Further offshore, there is some excellent reef and bottom fishing for the highly prized West Australian jewfish, as well as big Samson fish, pink and red snapper, blue morwong (queen snapper), breaksea cod and various other species.

Signs at popular rock fishing spots in this area warn anglers of the danger of the so-called 'king waves' that regularly sweep in from the west and south, particularly in winter. However, when conditions are favourable, rock-hoppers take some fine catches of Australian salmon, pike, silver trevally, tommy rough, Samson fish, sweep and the occasional large tailor, while specialist anglers casting long distances into deeper water even pull out a few succulent West Australian jewfish — a much sought-after species normally thought of as the sole province of the offshore boat fisher.

Southern bluefin tuna migrate along this stretch of coast in numbers at certain times of year, and there are even some big marlin and broadbill swordfish swimming in the deep waters beyond the continental shelf. However, few serious efforts have yet been made by recreational anglers and specialist game or sport fishers to target these species.

DONGARA AND GERALDTON

IN BRIEF

MAP REFERENCE: PAGE 204 C8

GETTING THERE Geraldton is about 425 km from Perth along the Brand Highway — about 5 hours drive
BEST TIME TO FISH Essentially year-round, but the summer months are best for tailor
BEST TIME TO TRAVEL Spring and autumn
MAJOR ANGLING SPECIES Tailor, mulloway, West Australian jewfish, pink snapper, whiting, baldchin groper, sharks
SPECIAL RESTRICTIONS Only crayfishing professionals permitted on Houtman Abrolhos islands
WARNINGS The region is noted for its big seas — while reef fishing is fairly safe, small boat users must always exercise caution
ACCOMMODATION Numerous motels, units and caravan parks, especially in Geraldton and Dongara; S Bend Caravan Park at Greenough, telephone (08) 9926 1072; caravan parks and some units at Horrocks and Northampton
CHARTER BOATS AND FISHING GUIDES Regular charters available from Geraldton to Houtman Abrolhos waters. Check the local Yellow Pages or ask the local tackle shops for recommendations

---

Windsurfers simply love Geraldton, which says much about the nature of its weather! Couple this with the sight of Greenough's leaning trees, with their trunks running at seeming impossible angles almost horizontal to the ground, and one gets an idea of just how windy this portion of the coast is. The prevailing south-westerlies are very strong, causing the trees to grow with a bend to the north-east, often with their foliage actually touching the ground. However, the spring wildflower season just inland from this section of coast is superb.

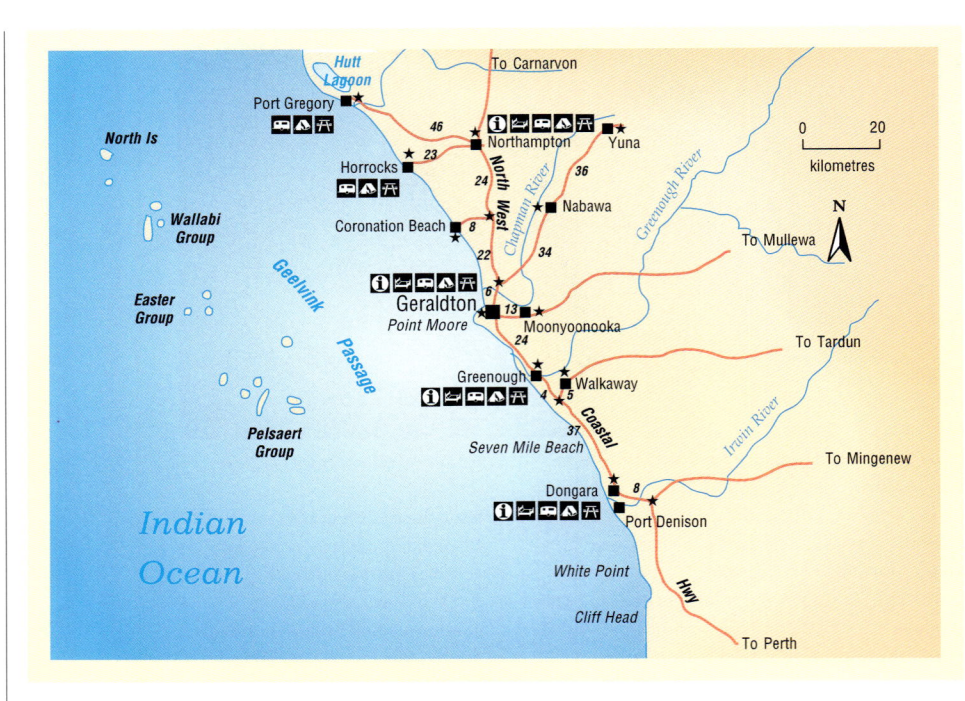

The fishing here is dictated by the wind and waves, yet it is very productive — the shore angling, in particular, is among the best on the Western Australian coast. Boat fishing is also outstanding. In fact, so highly regarded is the fishery that Geraldton has hosted the Australian Angling Championships, with spectacular success.

Surf beaches and low rock platforms allow anglers with the usual heavy surf outfits to catch tailor, mulloway, tommy rough (herring), whiting and silver trevally from the shore. Tailor are the outstanding feature of such places as Seven Mile, Nine Mile and Flatrocks.

It is better to use a 4WD to reach Duncans and Lucys, which are both behind the S Bend Caravan Park at Greenough.

The Greenough River mouth is another low rock platform offering excellent beach fishing, with tailor still the major target species.

Greenough is also one of only a few places in Western Australia where the famed West Australian jewfish is caught from the shore; the reefy, rocky nature of the water suits this highly prized fish. An occasional baldchin groper is caught, too, reflecting this coast's nearness to the prolific Houtman Abrolhos islands, famed as commercial crayfishing grounds.

Crayfish lovers even walk craypots to the edge of the reef here, plopping them over on the chance of collecting a few of these succulent creatures. Boat anglers from Geraldton have a much easier job, catching plentiful reef crayfish and western rock lobsters. An indication of the abundance of these crustaceans is the huge commercial cray fishery based in the town.

The Greenough River has supported some decent black bream in the past, but has suffered heavily from overfishing.

LIMITED ACCESS

Areas offshore from between Dongara and Geraldton experience little recreational fishing pressure because of the rugged nature of the coastline and the very limited access for small boats. For those able to launch boats at the towns themselves, offshore angling is sensational, with West Australian jewfish, pink snapper, baldchin groper, coral trout, Samson fish, mackerel, tailor,

There's plenty of great fishing country along this stretch of coast

sharks of several types and silver trevally all common catches.

Big boats often travel to the Houtman Abrolhos, but occupants have to stay on board as only professional crayfishers are allowed on the low islands making up the group. It is exciting news, then, that the state government is looking to open the islands to recreational fishing development.

Small craft are able to venture a few kilometres offshore, the shipping channels straight out from Geraldton's large harbour being a good place to start looking for fish. Beware, however, of fishing too close to the reef, where the constant surf and substantial swell can cause serious problems. This is a dangerous coast for the unwary or ill-prepared boat fisher.

NORTH MEETS SOUTH

Larger boats give access to fabulous fishing offshore. The deeper waters yield many jewfish, large schools of pink snapper, baldchin groper, Samson fish, Spanish mackerel, emperor and various cod species. The Houtman Abrolhos marks the boundary between north and south in west coast fishing, and tropical species mix with those from the temperate south. Heavy tackle is generally required, with 15- to 24-kg rod and reel combinations proving perfect.

Although the water is shallow around the islands in the Abrolhos, heavy weights are needed for most outside fishing. Thick handlines will do the job, too, with the most successful baits being octopus, squid and pilchards.

Fishing the beaches near Geraldton itself is productive. Again, tailor are the major adversary, and it's not impossible to take home the bag limit of eight fish on a reasonably regular basis.

Separation Point is known for its excellent reef fishing from either shore or boat. Silver trevally are often caught here, as well as herring, tailor and whiting. Boat anglers can add Samson fish, coral trout and mackerel to this list, especially around Point Moore, at the southern end of the town. From the northern side of Point Moore, garfish, tailor and herring are often captured. The rock wall sheltering the harbour has fine fishing for Samson fish, tailor, mulloway, sharks and whiting, while in the harbour itself, crabs are drop-netted and squid, herring, some tailor and mulloway are caught.

Early morning tailor fishing action at Greenough south of Geraldton

STANDARD TACKLE

The standard surf and rock tackle usual in most of Western Australia is best for the task. This is typically based on 3.5- to 4-m rods, with around 10-kg line on a spinning or sidecast reel.

Pilchard ('mulie') baits are the most likely selection, used almost always on a gang of hooks. Star sinkers are ideal for surf beaches, but spoon sinkers prove better around reef areas. Aside from the much-used mulie, heavy metal lures are also popular for tailor, as are popper styles, especially heavy ones able to be cast long distances.

North of Geraldton, Sunset Beach and Drummonds Cove are great morning and evening fishing spots, with snook, tailor, garfish, herring, whiting, sharks and mulloway among the possibilities. Access to the coastline is restricted by natural barriers further to the north of the region—river mouths being a good option and 4WD vehicles allowing easier access.

The Buller River mouth is best for tailor, whiting and dart, while at Coronation Bay some big mulloway are landed. At the Oakagee River mouth, pink snapper, mulloway, various sharks and tailor are regularly seen among catches.

A 4WD vehicle is needed to reach the Bowes River mouth, where exciting fishing is on tap for mulloway, tailor and heaps of sharks. If rock holes are worked well, the fabled West Australian jewfish, taken from the shore, makes for a truly memorable capture.

A QUIET BACKWATER

Horrocks Beach is a quiet yet beautiful backwater, a little bay offering shelter to a few crayfishing boats. It is possible to launch small craft from the beach, although ocean surge can be a problem at times. Once at sea, however, wonderful fishing is possible only a couple of kilometres from shore, over vast coral beds.

Horrocks is one of those overlooked locations which tourists and anglers often drive past on their way to better known places further north. If those same people only knew what they were missing, they would no doubt stop!

West Australian jewfish abound here, as do pink snapper, with Samson fish, baldchin groper, silver trevally and coral trout often boosting catches. Squidding is productive and, as is found all along this coast, crayfishing is a way of life for amateur and professional alike. Some of the finest mulloway fishing along the west coast is also available from beaches here and tailor are readily captured.

Certainly, Western Australia's mid-west coast is pure adventure. It represents an oustanding opportunity to fish some wild water for big fish, from both shore and boat.

SOUTH-WEST TROUT WATERS

IN BRIEF

MAP REFERENCE: PAGE 202 C5

GETTING THERE Access via South West Highway from Armadale to Waroona, Harvey and Collie to access dams, continuing to Bridgetown, Nannup, Manjimup, Pemberton and Walpole for river and private dam fishing. Bridgetown is about 280 km south of Perth

BEST TIME TO FISH Summer in rivers and spring for impoundments

BEST TIME TO TRAVEL Year-round, but can be very hot in summer

MAJOR ANGLING SPECIES Brown and rainbow trout, and redfin

SPECIAL RESTRICTIONS Closed season for trout in many south-west rivers from May to August. Marron season strictly limited to a few weeks in January

WARNINGS The bushfire danger is high in summer months and there are many snakes in south-west areas. Anglers should exercise care when walking through bush

CHARTER BOATS AND FISHING GUIDES Shan and Mary Low at Nannup, telephone (08) 9756 1207; Pat Stubberfield, Sports Locker, Manjimup, telephone (08) 9777 1881

The south-west corner of Western Australia provides a stark contrast to the mostly dry expanses of this huge state. Here, thick groves of large trees flank the roadways — tall, majestic tuarts, karri, jarrah and gum trees casting long shadows across the country. The south-west corner is the wettest part of Western Australia, and the trees reflect this. This is the home of the West's temperate freshwater fishery. It is small, but much loved, needing plenty of care to maintain at current levels. Very few trout hatch in the wild here and re-stocking is constantly necessary.

River fishing for trout is at its best in the upper Blackwood River, Donnelly River, Lefroy Brook and the Warren River near Manjimup, and the accessible parts of the Shannon and Gordon rivers.

Freshwater inhabitants of this region include redfin, rainbow trout and brown trout — all introduced species. Unlike trout, redfin perch have little trouble reproducing and breed prolifically. In fact, at times there are so many of these fish in dams and rivers that the population consists mostly of small, stunted redfin.

Trout are the 'holy grail' of the freshwater scene, and anglers go to great lengths to find 'wild' fish, often pushing through dense undergrowth to discover pools that may hold trout. The rewards are high, and rainbows or browns weighing up to 3 kg are not unknown. These are greatly treasured by their captors, especially if caught on fly gear.

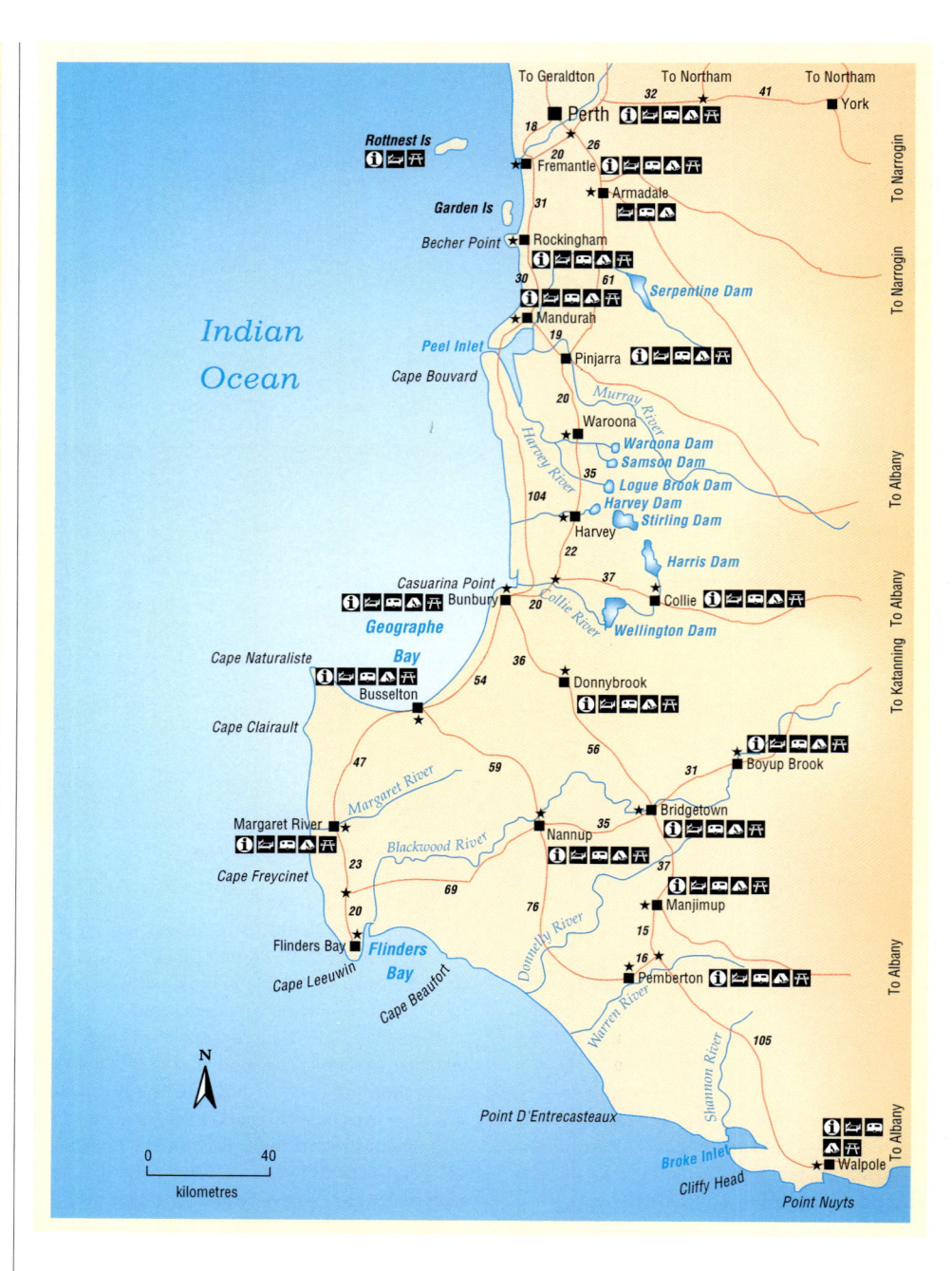

Areas around Pemberton, Nannup and Manjimup are the best for 'wild' river trout. Spinning or lure casting is an easier option than fly fishing in these places because of the often dense nature of the undergrowth. Most big rivers are difficult to wade, leaving bridges and a few well-trodden spots for the angler to try.

Winter rain causes heavy flows in Western Australia's south-west rivers. When the trout season opens on 1 September, the rivers usually still have substantial amounts of water flushing through their mostly narrow valleys. During the hot summer, rivers typically become a series of pools, often tranquil, with shadowed surfaces where the angler is able to spot the rise of a trout as it finds its evening meal.

SPRING TROUT FISHING

Spring fishing for trout in the south-west occurs mostly in impoundment areas, such as Waroona Dam, Harvey Weir or Logue Brook. Fly fishers utilise four-, five- or six-weight outfits, with dry flies often being the first tried, but nymphs and wet flies are also included in the tackle box and often take the bulk of fish caught.

Spinning is also popular. Little metal spinners with revolving blades are perfect for the task. The flashing blades of these can be turned at very slow speeds, imitating struggling fish or swimming insects. Bladed spinners are a versatile lure, and if the slow, twirling action isn't doing the trick, try an erratic retrieve, or even a dash of speed to excite the fish.

Lures for trout and redfin need to be small, making them by nature light, so that light threadline or spinning gear is essential for easy casting. Lines of 2- and 3-kg breaking strain are ideal, making it not only possible to cast the little weights, but increasing the fun, too.

WORKING STRUCTURE

The value of casting right next to a rock or fallen tree cannot be underestimated, except during the usual late afternoon rise, when trout will often cruise in open water. At other times, trout regularly hold behind a log, tuft of grass, rock or drop-off, either waiting for something to swim by or sheltering in the cool. This is an exciting way to fish—swimming a small minnow lure enticingly past a set of rocks in a pool, only to see a perch or trout charge out and seize it.

Small bibbed minnow style lures, either in a fish pattern or the popular yabby format, are easily fished and effective in lakes and streams. As with the spinners, work the lure right down to its slowest speeds, at times just enough to give it the seductive wobble so characteristic of this lure type. Lure selection is governed by the depth of water, so a range of minnow styles needs to be carried. Short, light spinning rods in the 1.6- to 1.8-m range are perfect for casting these little lures.

Not many Western Australian anglers use bait for trout. A few try worms dug from the river bank, maggots or meat baits such as cubes of liver. Live yabbies and small freshwater minnows are both natural baits. Note that it is illegal to use tiny marron. (Marron are Western Australia's large freshwater crayfish, and are keenly sought during their short open season. Heavy fines are stringently applied for taking undersize or out-of-season marron.)

Logue Brook Dam is one of Western Australia's finest impoundment fisheries

CLOSER TO PERTH

The Serpentine and Murray rivers, nearer Perth, both hold small populations of trout, along with a lot more redfin perch. Summer months are easier to fish here, and spots on the Murray near Dwellingup—in the hilly gorge country—are best. Sections immediately below the foothills in the Murray have, in recent years, also become one of the better 'wild water' trout spots around Perth.

Waroona Dam trout angling has been restricted somewhat by the numbers of redfin perch, which have become the predominant species. Despite this, some excellent trout are still captured in season, mostly with wet fly, although lures allow anglers to cover more ground. Canoes and small boats give anglers good coverage of fishable areas.

Drakesbrook Reservoir, immediately below Waroona Dam, holds many redfin and marron, while Logue Brook Dam is among the state's best impoundments and fishes best in autumn and spring. Samson Dam and Stirling Dam are similar in nature to Waroona, and all three support good marron populations and are dotted with hopefuls during the strictly limited marron season.

Harvey Dam is at its peak for trout in spring and early summer, but Harvey anglers fish with lures and baits for sizeable redfin perch all year round—in the little Harvey Weir below the main dam, as well as in the larger dam.

Wellington Dam near Collie is huge and fishes best for redfin, as well as receiving plenty of attention during the marron season.

PRIVATE WATERS

An exciting aspect for lovers of trout fishing is the increase in the number of private dams where both brown trout and rainbow trout are stocked. Here, entrepreneurs enhance their properties while also allowing keen anglers a chance to ply their skills with fly and lure on a pay-to-fish basis.

Bob McCarthy's dam at Williams, well inland and among fairly dry farming country, is a tribute to that farmer's tenacity in creating an artificial fishery against the odds.

Trout Association members also enjoy group access to some of these stocked dams in the south-west, and joining such an organisation makes great sense for those wishing to sample these excellent and little known fishing opportunities.

Beautiful trout water near Wellington Mills

202 South-West Western Australia

0 20 40 60 80 100
kilometres
205
207
H J K L M N P
1 2 3 4 5 6 7 8 9 10
120°
122°
30°
32°
34°
Pigeon Rocks
Mt Manning Range
Mt Manning Nature Reserve
Hunt Range
Davyhurst
Goongarrie
Menangina
Goongarrie Nat Park
Lake Goongarrie
Lake Owen
237
Ponton Creek
Lake Rebecca
Pinjin
Queen Victoria Spring Nature Reserve
Bungalbin Hill
Mount Vetters
Rowles Lagoon Nature Reserve
Mt Carnage
Ora Banda
Credo
Carbine
Broad Arrow
Kanowna
Yindi
Yangan Hill
Lake Penny
Jubilee Mine
Black Flag
White Flag Lake
Watt Hills
Lake Deborah East
Lake Roe
Cundeelee Aboriginal Land
Ponton
Cundeelee Community
Lake Yindana
Steeple Hill
Kalgoorlie
Boulder
West Kalgoorlie
Bonnie Vale
Mount Burges
Lake Yindarlgooda
Koolyanobbing
Timberfield
Hannan Lake
Stoneville
Curtin
Avoca Downs
Blamey
Karonie
Chifley
Coonana
Zanthus
Lake Seabrook
Coolgardie
HWY
Bullabulling
Mount Monger
Cowarna Downs
Woolibar
COOLGARDIE
Duladgin Rock
Yellowdine Nature Res
Boorabbin Nat Park
EASTERN
Woolgangie
Nepean Nickel Mine
Kambalda NR
Kambalda
Kambalda West
Southern Cross
GREAT
Karalee
Boorabbin
188
Victoria Rock
Victoria Rock Nature Res
Lake Lefroy
Harris Lake
Yellowdine
Strawberry Rocks
Marvel Loch
Burra Rock Nature Reserve
Widgiemooltha
Lefroy
Lake Robin
Cockatoo Tank
Toomey Hills
170
Binyarinyinna Rock
Cave Hill NR
Cave Hill
Cowan Hill
Higginsville
Lake Cowan
Dulcie Jean Tank
Jilbadji Nature Reserve
Barker Lake
Skeleton Rock
Hayes Hill
ESPERANCE
Sandalwood Rock
McDermid Rock
Killaloe Hill
EYRE
Fraser Range
Newman Rock
Mt Holland
Mt Day
Mt Thirsty
Norseman
HIGHWAY
Southern Hills
Lake Johnston
Mt Kirk
Lake Kirk
Woolyeenyer Hill
Noondoonia
Balladonia Hotel
Rocks
North Ironcap
Lake Cronin
Marble Rock
Lake Hope
Dundas Nature Reserve
Lake Hurlstone NR
Lake Hurlstone
Middle Ironcap
Bremer Range
Lake Dundas
Gilmore Rocks
Lake Gilmore
Holt Rock
Lake Varley
Digger Rocks
Mt Andrew
Varley
Frank Hann National Park
Kumari
Booanya Rock
Lake Fox
Lake Ace Nat Res
Lake Ace
Peak Charles
HWY
206
Mt Gibbs
Lake Tay
Lake Sharpe
Peak Charles Nat Pk
Salmon Gums
Nature Reserve
Coragina Rock
Rays Rock
Lake Camm
Circle Valley
Lake Mends
Lake King
Pyramid Lake
River
Red Lake
Lake Pallarup
Mt Ridley
Grass Patch
Lake Halbert
Mt Heywood
Pine Hill
Dunn Rock Nat Res
Mount Madden
Truslove
Griffiths Nat Res
Truslove Townsite Nature Reserve
Mt Burdett
Kau Rock Nat Res
Beaumont Nat Res
Cape Arid
Mt Dean
Mt Symmons
National Park
Lake Cobham
Mt Short
Young
Cascade
Scaddan
Lake Morris
Lake Magenta
Cheadanup Nat Res
Speddingup
Muntz Nat Res
Ravensthorpe
Jerdacuttup
Oldfield
COAST
Lort
Gibson
Burdett South NR
The Diamonds Hill
Boyatup Hill
SOUTH
Kundip Nat Res
Phillips
187
River
Munglinup
HWY
Dalyup
Condingup
Fitzgerald
Hamersley
Lake Shaster
Lake Gore
Pink Lake
Cape Le Grand National Park
Yungarup Hill
Esperance
Esperance Bay
Fitzgerald River National Park
Jerdacuttup Lakes
Stokes National Park
Duke of Orleans Bay
Yokinup Bay
Mt Arid
Sandy Bight
Mt Pasley
Cape Pasley
Hopetoun
Bat Cave Point
Culham Inlet
Twelve Mile Beach
Starvation Boat Harbour
Powell Point
Mason Bay
Lake Shaster NR
Shoal Cape
Stokes Inlet
Fanny Cove
Barker Inlet
Butty Head
11 Mile Beach
Mt Le Grand
Cape Le Grand
Dunn Rocks
Rossiter Bay
Lucky Bay
Hammer Head
Cape Arid
Twin Bays
Fitzgerald Inlet
Point Charles
Point Ann
Mt Bland
Trigelow Beach
Gordon Inlet
Recherche Archipelago Nature Reserve
Middle Island
Mondrain Island
Archipelago of the Recherche
Salisbury Island
Bremer Bay
Point Henry
Dillon Bay
Cape Knob
SOUTHERN OCEAN

204 CENTRAL-WEST WESTERN AUSTRALIA

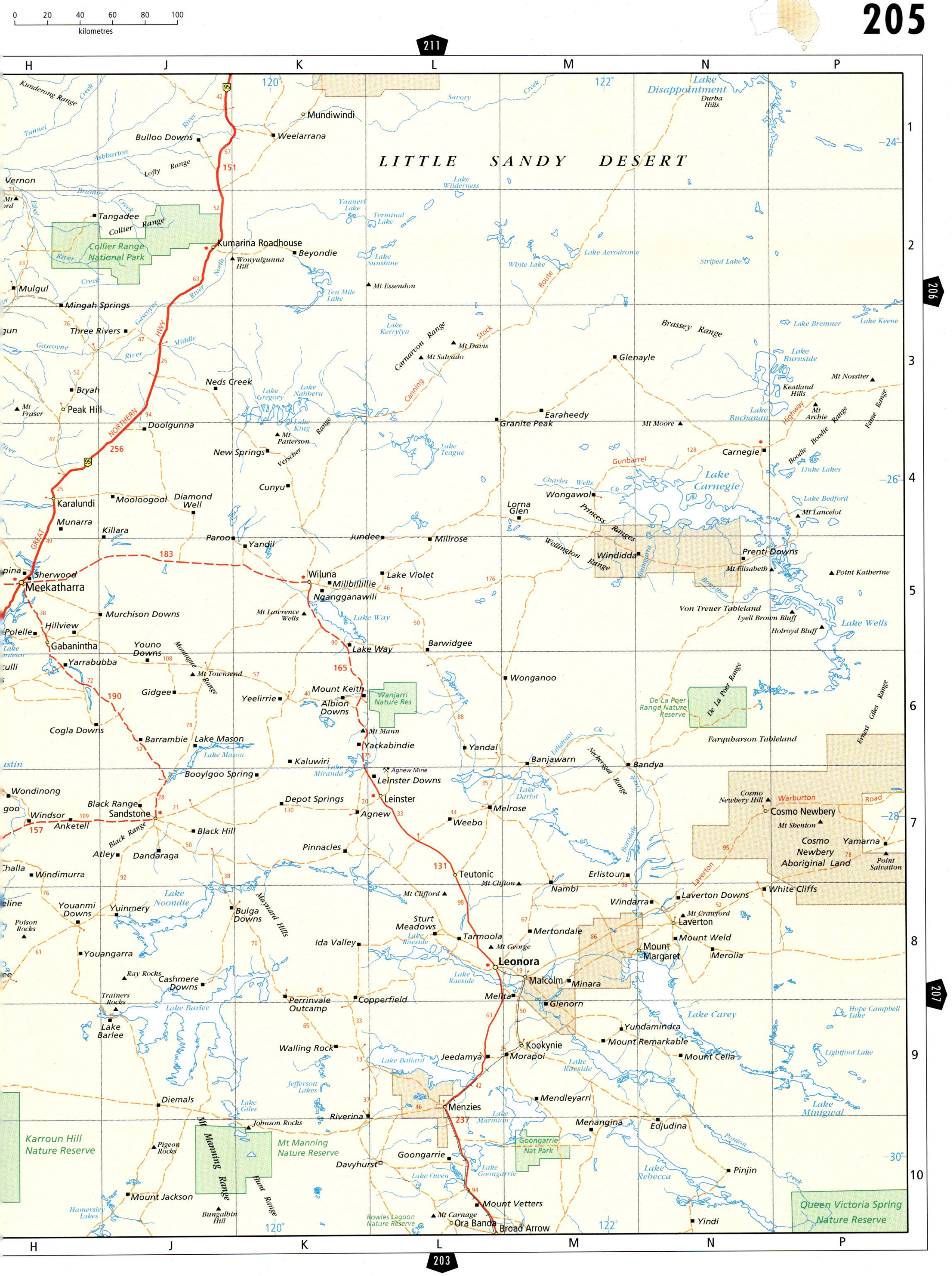

0 20 40 60 80 100
kilometres
211
203
206
207
H J K L M N P
1 2 3 4 5 6 7 8 9 10
120°
122°
24°
26°
28°
30°
LITTLE SANDY DESERT
Kunderong Range
Tunnel
Creek
Bulloo Downs
Weelarrana
Mundiwindi
Savory
Creek
Lake Disappointment
Durba Hills
Ashburton
River
Lofty Range
Vernon
Brumby
Creek
Lake Wilderness
Yanneri Lake
Terminal Lake
Tangadee
Collier Range
Collier Range National Park
River
Kumarina Roadhouse
Beyondie
Wonyulgunna Hill
North
River
Lake Sunshine
White Lake
Lake Aerodrome
Striped Lake
Route
Ten Mile Lake
Mt Essendon
Mulgul
Mingah Springs
Gascoyne
Three Rivers
Gascoyne
River
Middle
HWY
Lake Kerrylyn
Carnarvon Range
Mt Davis
Mt Salvado
Stock
Canning
Brassey Range
Lake Bremner
Lake Keene
Glenayle
Lake Burnside
Mt Nossiter
Keatland Hills
Mt Archie
Lake Buchanan
Highway
Range
Fame Range
Boodie Range
Boodie
Bryah
Peak Hill
Mt Fraser
NORTHERN
Doolgunna
Neds Creek
Lake Gregory
Lake Nabberu
Lake King
Mt Patterson
Range
Earaheedy
Granite Peak
Mt Moore
Lake Teague
New Springs
Verscher
Gunbarrel
Carnegie
Linke Lakes
Lake Carnegie
Charles Wells
Ck
Cunyu
Wongawol
Princess
Ranges
Lake Bedford
Mt Lancelot
Karalundi
Mooloogool
Diamond Well
Lorna Glen
Munarra
Killara
Paroo
Yandil
Jundee
Millrose
GREAT
Wellington Range
Windidda
Prenti Downs
Mt Elisabeth
Point Katherine
183
Sherwood
Meekatharra
Wiluna
Millbillillie
Ngangganawili
Lake Violet
Bonython
Creek
Von Treuer Tableland
Lyell Brown Bluff
Holroyd Bluff
Lake Wells
Murchison Downs
Mt Lawrence Wells
Lake Way
Hillview
Polelle
Gabanintha
Youno Downs
Montague Range
Lake Way
Barwidgee
Yarrabubba
Mt Townsend
Wonganoo
Gidgee
190
165
Yeelirrie
Mount Keith
Albion Downs
Wanjarri Nature Res
De La Poer Range Nature Reserve
De La Poer Range
Giles Range
Ernest
Cogla Downs
Mt Mann
Barrambie
Lake Mason
Lake Mason
Yackabindie
Yandal
Erlistoun
Ck
Farquharson Tableland
Kaluwiri
Lake Miranda
Agnew Mine
Leinster Downs
Banjawarn
Bandya
Booylgoo Spring
Neckersgat Range
Wondinong
Windsor
Anketell
157
Black Range
Sandstone
Black Range
Black Hill
Depot Springs
Leinster
Agnew
Lake Darlot
Melrose
Weebo
Cosmo Newbery Hill
Warburton
Road
Cosmo Newbery
Mt Shenton
Cosmo Newbery Aboriginal Land
Yamarna
Point Salvation
Atley
Dandaraga
Pinnacles
Teutonic
Mt Clifton
Erlistoun
Laverton
Nambi
White Cliffs
Windimurra
Lake Noondie
Maynard Hills
Mt Clifford
Windarra
Laverton Downs
Youanmi Downs
Yuinmery
Bulga Downs
Poison Rocks
Sturt Meadows
Lake Raeside
Tarmoola
Mertondale
Mt Crawford
Laverton
Mount Weld
Youangarra
Ida Valley
Mt George
Leonora
Mount Margaret
Merolia
Ray Rocks
Cashmere Downs
Lake Raeside
Malcolm
Minara
Trainers Rocks
Lake Barlee
Perrinvale Outcamp
Copperfield
Melita
Glenorn
Lake Carey
Hope Campbell Lake
Lake Barlee
Yundamindra
Mount Remarkable
Kookynie
Walling Rock
Lake Ballard
Jeedamya
Morapoi
Lake Raeside
Mount Cella
Lightfoot Lake
Jefferson Lakes
Mendleyarri
Diemals
Lake Giles
Menzies
Lake Minigwal
Riverina
Lake Marmion
Johnson Rocks
Menangina
Edjudina
Karroun Hill Nature Reserve
Mt Manning Range
Mt Manning Nature Reserve
Goongarrie Nat Park
Pigeon Rocks
Goongarrie
Ponton
Davyhurst
Lake Owen
Lake Goongarrie
Lake Rebecca
Pinjin
Creek
Hunt Range
Mount Jackson
Mount Vetters
Queen Victoria Spring Nature Reserve
Hamersley Lakes
Bungalbin Hill
Rowles Lagoon Nature Reserve
Mt Carnage
Ora Banda
Broad Arrow
Yindi

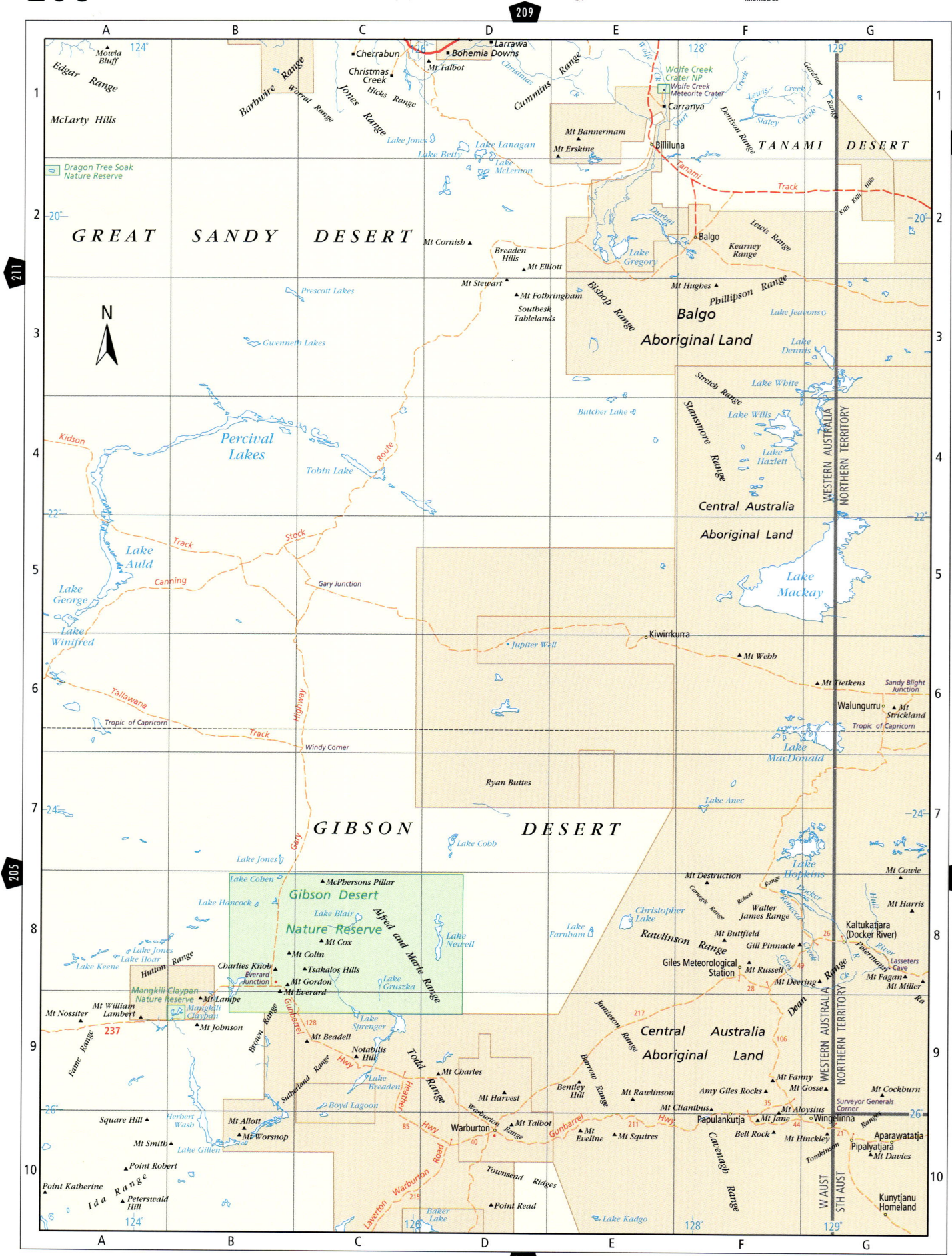

206 Central-East Western Australia

South-East Western Australia

207

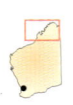

208 The Kimberley, Western Australia

0 20 40 60 80 100
kilometres

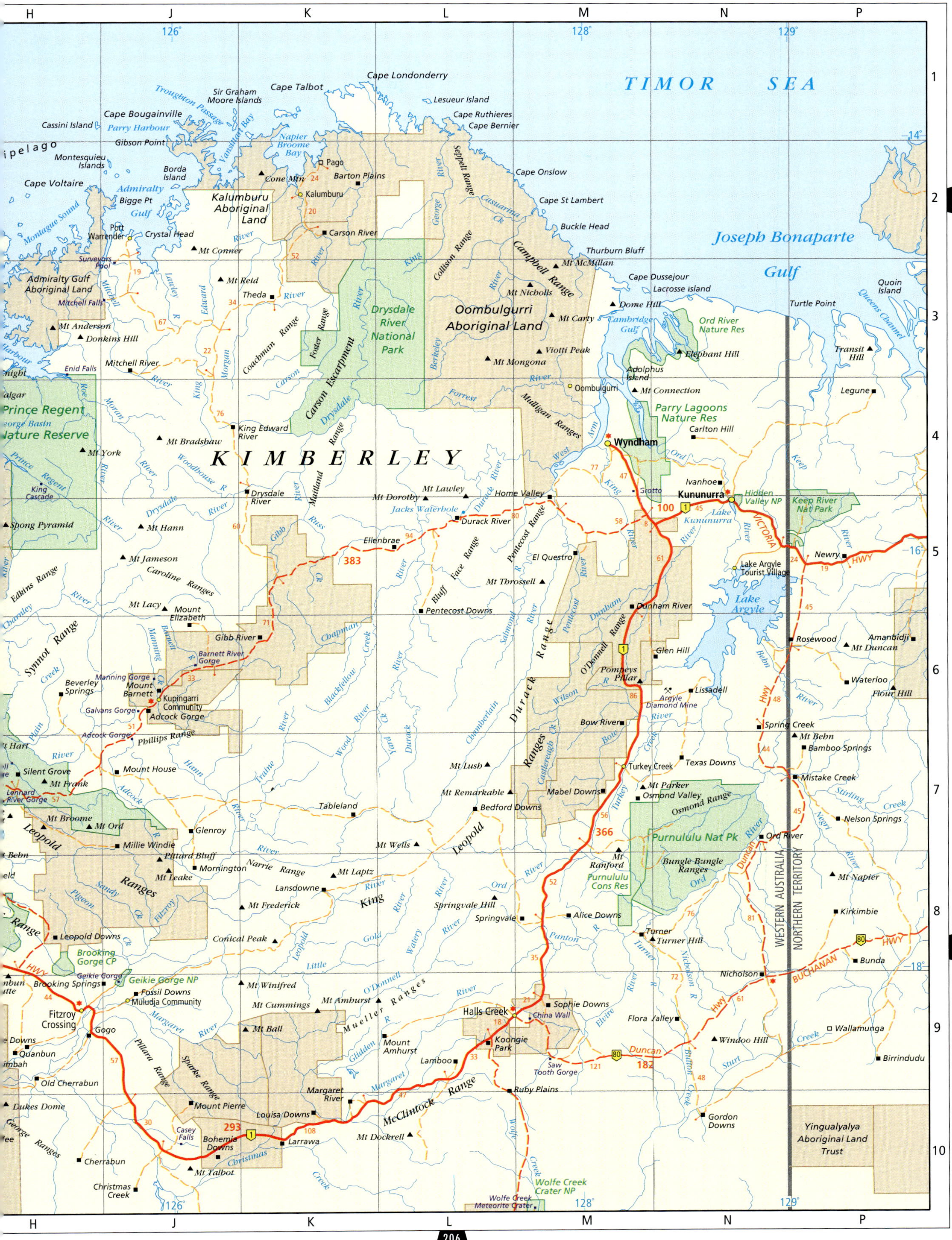

206

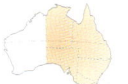

210 The Pilbara, Western Australia

0 20 40 60 80 100
kilometres

208

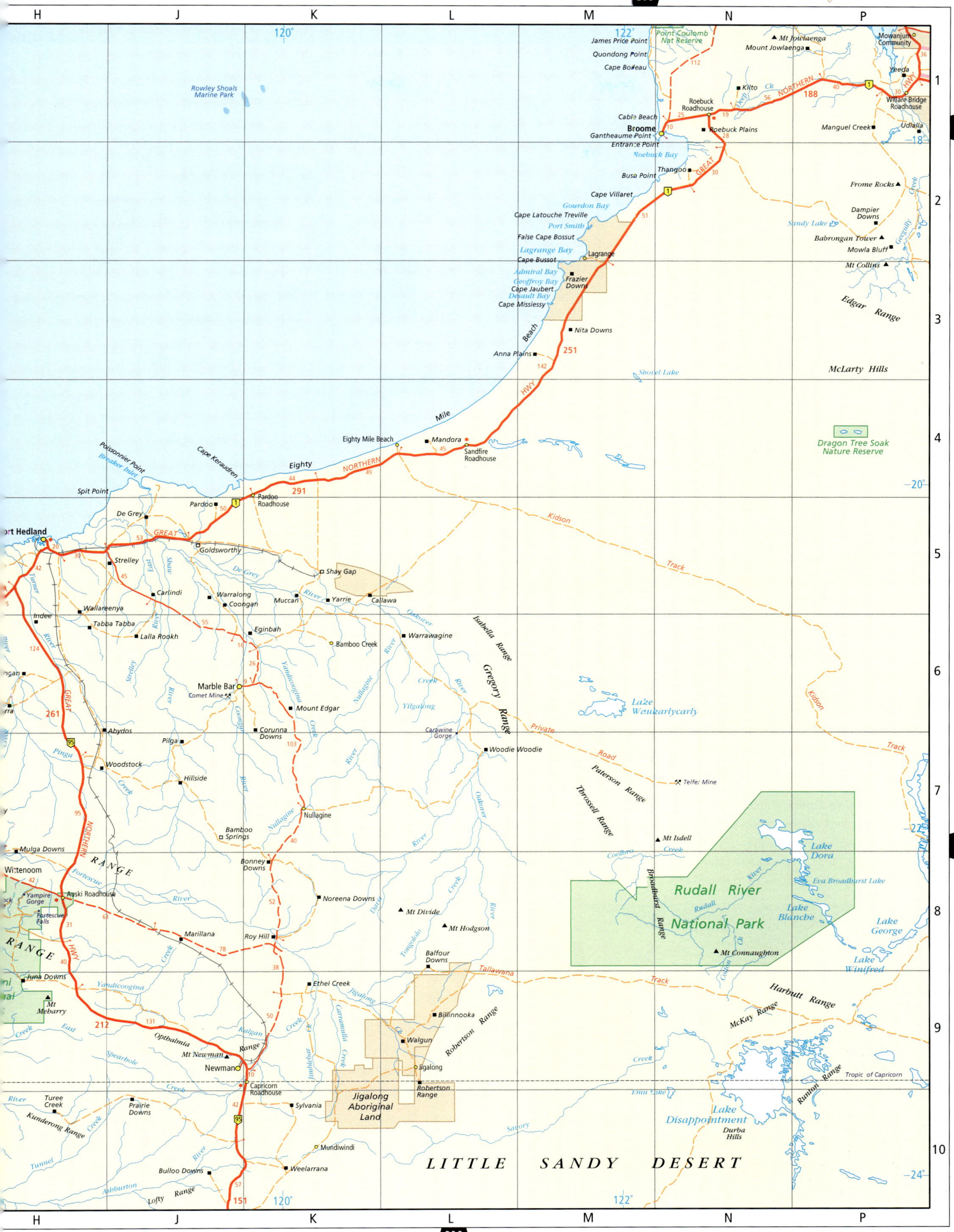

208
206
205

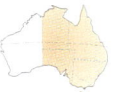

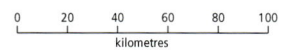

SOUTH AUSTRALIA

FISHING HOT SPOTS

- Adelaide's Jetties (pp. 214–15)
- Adelaide Offshore (pp. 216–17)
- The Port River and Outer Harbor (pp. 218–19)
- The Fleurieu Peninsula (pp. 220–1)
- The Coorong (pp. 222–3)
- Murray Mouth Mulloway (pp. 224–5)
- South Australian Trout Waters (pp. 226–7)
- Weekend on the Murray (pp. 228–9)

South Australia is the driest of all our states, with almost two-thirds of its interior classified as true desert. The population density in the arid inland region—mostly north of the 32 parallel of latitude—is extremely low, and comparable with remote areas in the Northern Territory and the Kimberley region in Western Australia.

The vast majority of South Australians live in the relatively fertile south-eastern corner, bounded by the Victorian border to the east, Port Augusta to the north and Ceduna to the west. In fact, more than one million South Australians live in the attractive capital city of Adelaide and its surrounding centres, situated along the western shores of Gulf St Vincent. This area enjoys a so-called 'Mediterranean' climate with cool, wet winters and hot, dry summers, which explains its appeal to residents and visitors alike, and its worldwide prominence as a wine-growing region.

Not surprisingly, most recreational fishing in South Australia is also concentrated in the state's more populated south-eastern corner. It is dominated by estuary, bay, coastal and inshore angling for bread-and-butter marine species such as tommy rough, whiting, mullet, southern bream, snapper, garfish, snook, sweep, mulloway and Australian salmon. Smaller numbers of keen anglers also head further offshore into the Southern Ocean in search of bluewater species including tuna, yellowtail kingfish, Samson fish, assorted deep-reef dwellers and various sharks.

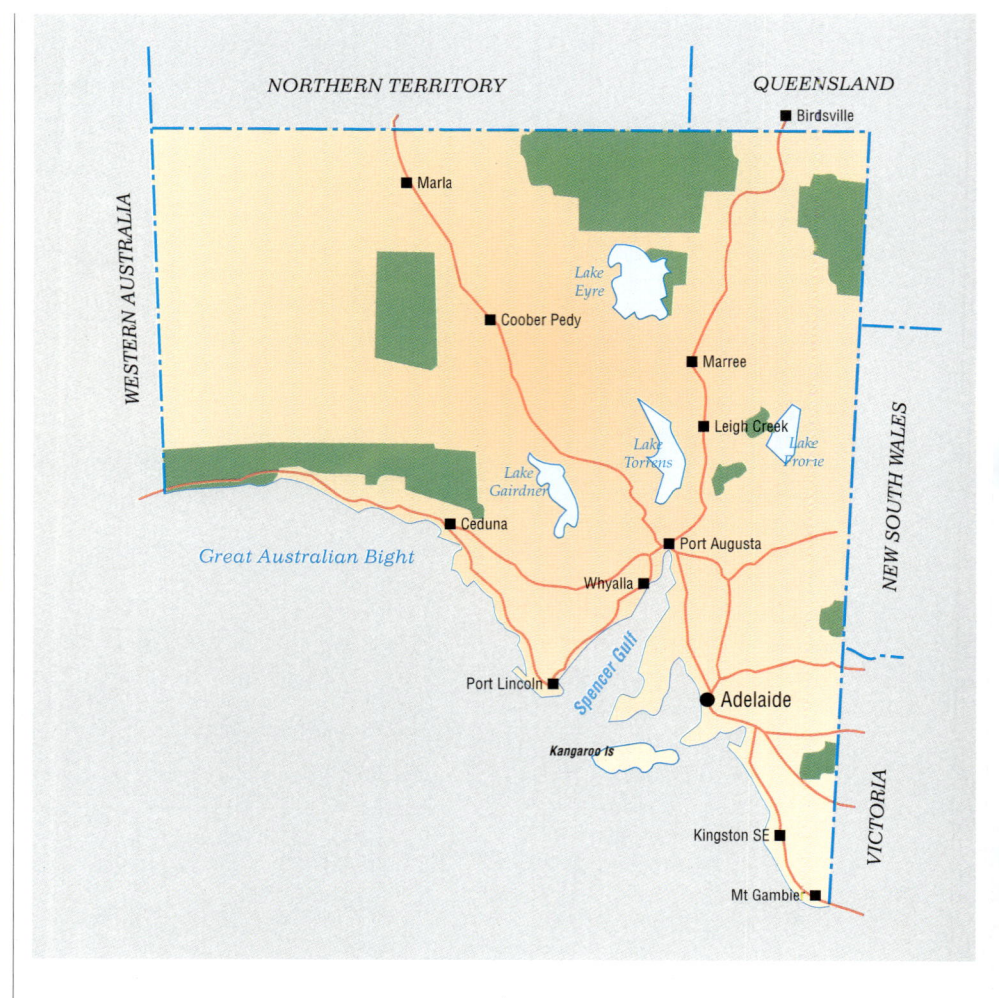

In contrast, freshwater fishing has a lower overall profile in South Australia than any other state, although reasonable numbers of anglers do fish for native and introduced species such as callop (golden perch), Murray cod and carp along the lower Murray River, and some also pursue trout and redfin in the small streams, lakes and farm dams of the south-eastern corner. South Australian freshwater fishing opportunities are generally limited, however, by low rainfall figures and a scarcity of permanent streams and lakes, as well as by the degraded water quality and heavily modified environments of the lower Murray River.

In some ways, the Festival State's recreational fishing opportunities could be classified as being rather limited in terms of the range of species and angling styles on offer—especially when compared with states such as Queensland, Western Australia and even New South Wales. However, what South Australian angling lacks in this regard is more than made up for by the dedication and commitment of its sizeable fishing fraternity.

Crow Eaters, as South Australians are sometimes fondly referred to by those from other states, are recognised as being amongst our keenest and best-informed anglers, and many of them are willing to travel vast distances and invest considerable amounts of time and effort in the pursuit of piscatorial pleasure.

The strength and importance of recreational fishing in South Australia is clearly reflected in the active, 'hands-on' management strategies of its fisheries administrators, not to mention the state's consistently high per capita boat

Fishing off a jetty near Second Valley on the Fleurieu Peninsula

ownership figures, the ongoing bait and tackle consumption of its inhabitants, and their hunger for books and periodicals dealing specifically with the subject of fishing in this region.

Recreational angling is clearly alive and well in South Australia, and appears to have a very bright future as we proceed into the next century.

CONTACT NUMBERS

Anyone wishing to obtain further information on fisheries rules and regulations in South Australia should telephone one of the Fisheries Division or other numbers listed below.

Adelaide	(08) 8226 2311
Kadina	(08) 8821 3242
Kingston	(08) 8767 2358
Mount Gambier	(08) 8724 2942
Port Adelaide	(08) 8449 1432
Port Lincoln	(08) 8688 3488
Streaky Bay	(08) 8626 1247
Whyalla	(08) 8648 8187

FISHWATCH HOT LINE (24 Hours)
1800 065 522

RECFISH AUSTRALIA
1800 686 818

Above: *The sweeping arc of the beach at Port Noarlunga, south of Adelaide*
Below: *Dramatic coastline near The Gap in Innes National Park on the Yorke Peninsula*

ADELAIDE'S JETTIES

IN BRIEF

MAP REFERENCE: PAGE 233 J10

GETTING THERE Adelaide is the capital of South Australia. It is serviced regularly by air, rail and coach services
BEST TIME TO FISH September to May
BEST TIME TO TRAVEL Year-round
MAJOR ANGLING SPECIES Tommy rough, garfish, whiting, squid, crabs, sharks and rays
SPECIAL RESTRICTIONS Some jetties and other structures may not be open to fishing or general public access; check with the Fisheries Division information service, telephone (08) 8226 2311

Variously known as the Festival City, City of Light and City of Churches, Adelaide is a pleasant, friendly metropolis with a population of more than one million people who are particularly well served in terms of public amenities, cultural and artistic events, sporting facilities, recreation areas and park lands. The region's climate is described as being 'Mediterranean', with hot, dry summers and cool, moderately wet winters.

All in all, South Australia's capital has a well-deserved reputation for being a fine place to live, work and raise a family. The members of its large fishing fraternity are also amongst the keenest to be found anywhere in the country.

The western seaside suburbs of Adelaide—from St Kilda in the north to Brighton in the south—lie along the shores of the relatively shallow Gulf St Vincent, which provides a range of both shore- and boat-based fishing opportunities for most southern saltwater species. The city is less well catered for in terms of estuary angling venues, these being limited to the enclosed waters of Port Adelaide's Outer Harbor, the Port River and West Lakes. Nonetheless, these waters also provide a reasonable standard of angling at times. When it comes to land-based fishing opportunities, however, many residents of Adelaide turn to the city's jetties.

Port Noarlunga jetty, south of Adelaide, is a popular location with local anglers

PRODUCTIVE JETTIES

Jetty or pier fishing is particularly popular with both Adelaide-based anglers and visitors to the city. The better jetties regularly produce fair to reasonable catches of tommy rough (ruff), garfish, mullet, yellowfin or sand whiting, and squid, as well as the odd snapper, mulloway, shark or large ray (particularly eagle rays) for the more adventurous angler.

Naturally enough, light tackle with small hooks and baits are best employed to target the tommy rough, garfish, mullet and small whiting that make up the lion's share of the catch taken from most of these jetties, especially during daylight hours. However, nocturnal hopefuls in search of a big ray or shark—and always mindful of the slim chance of encountering a big mulloway or snapper—tend to choose much sturdier gear and larger offerings.

It is also possible to catch sand and blue crabs from some of these jetties with witch's hat nets or similar legal devices, particularly during the summer and early autumn months, when the shallow gulf waters are at their warmest.

The jetty at Glenelg in Adelaide's southern suburbs

One of the most productive fishing jetties in and around Adelaide is the popular structure at Port Noarlunga, some 30 km south of the city. Other productives jetties can be found in the seaside suburbs of Brighton, Glenelg, Henley Beach, Grange, Semaphore and Largs Bay. The new purpose-built fishing jetty adjacent to the mangroves at Garden Island, inside the harbour, is also becoming increasingly popular amongst anglers chasing bream, garfish, juvenile salmon (so-called 'salmon trout') and mullet. There is even the outside chance of a school mulloway turning up here, especially at night.

A Valuable Resource

Once used for a variety of purposes, including the servicing of small ships and ferries, many of the major coastal jetties between Port Noarlunga and Port Adelaide are now maintained almost entirely for the benefit of recreational anglers. They represent a valuable resource for Adelaide's anglers, particularly those who don't own or have access to boats.

Sadly, the more exposed of these coastal jetties are at times prone to major damage from the severe winter storms that occasionally rip in across the Gulf St Vincent from the west and south-west. Unfortunately, funds are not always immediately available to repair those structures that are damaged in this way, or which simply deteriorate over time.

For this reason, some of the jetties or piers mentioned here may not be open to the public at certain times.. while others are occasionally undergoing repairs and upgrades that can severely limit their usefulness as fishing platforms. Still others have been significantly shortened over the years by repeated storm damage, and do not provide the same general standard of fishing today that they did in the 1950s and 1960s.

It pays to check on the current state of play in this regard by contacting the South Australian Department of Primary Industry's Fisheries Division information service in Adelaide, or by speaking to the staff in any of the city's major tackle stores.

A fine catch of garfish taken from one of Adelaide's jetties

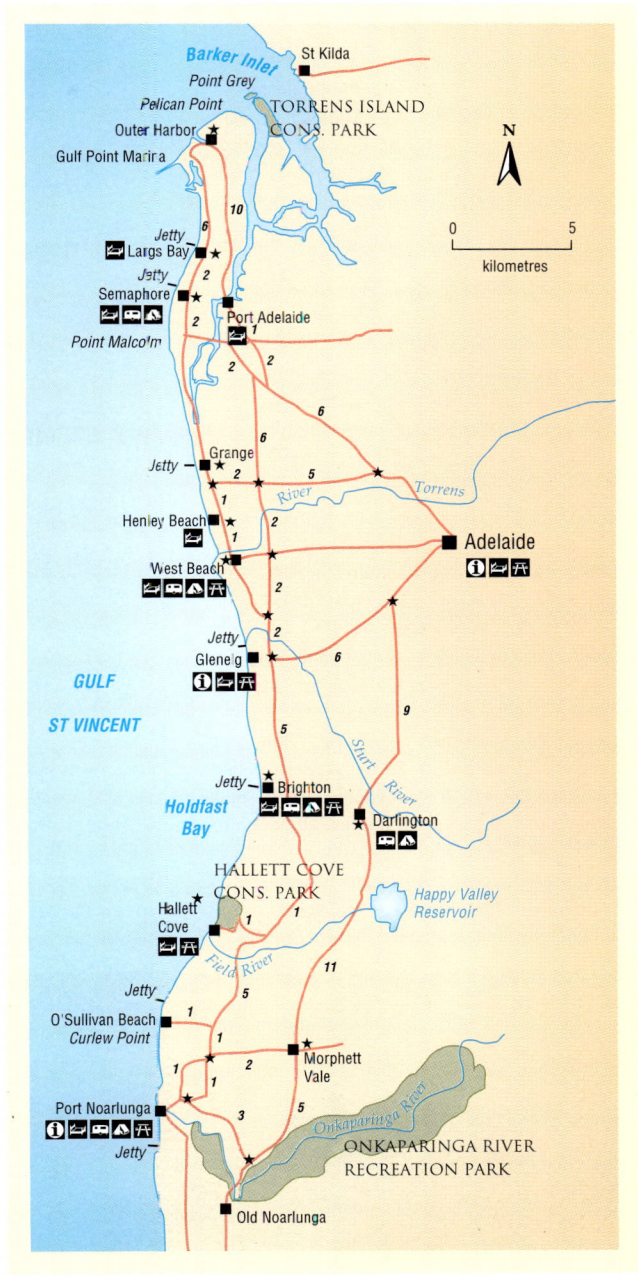

ADELAIDE OFFSHORE

IN BRIEF

MAP REFERENCE: PAGE 233 H8

GETTING THERE Boat launching ramps are available at North Haven Marina, Glenelg and O'Sullivan Beach Marina — access to Adelaide via National Highway One
BEST TIME TO FISH Year-round, although summer is the windiest season
BEST TIME TO TRAVEL Year-round
MAJOR ANGLING SPECIES Snapper, whiting, tommy rough, garfish, squid, small sharks
WARNINGS In summer, the afternoon sea breeze can be hazardous for small boats
CHARTER BOATS AND FISHING GUIDES North Haven Charter Services, telephone (08) 8449 1491; Kingfisher Charters, telephone (08) 8346 6756

Adelaide has an active, vibrant offshore boat fishing scene. Situated on the eastern shores of the Gulf St Vincent, the city's waters are largely immune from the effects of ocean swell and thus provide small boat anglers with plenty of opportunity to fish almost all year round.

As the gulf's waters are relatively shallow and not greatly influenced by ocean currents, pelagic fish are rarely seen off Adelaide. However, there are plenty of highly regarded alternatives such as King George whiting and big snapper to keep the throng of small boat enthusiasts well satisfied.

Adelaide's offshore waters are largely devoid of natural reef, but artificial fish-aggregating structures have been successfully deployed in several areas, solely for the use of recreational anglers. These include tyre reefs and disused sunken ships, most of which attract and hold popular school fish in good numbers according to season. All of these artificial reefs are prominently marked and well patronised, particularly by those anglers who target whiting and snapper.

BOATING FACILITIES

Adelaide's offshore anglers are well catered for in terms of boat ramps and marina facilities. The North Haven Marina complex, at the northern end of the metropolitan foreshore, boasts a six-lane launching ramp, bait and tackle store, excellent boat wash-down facilities and a Coast Guard base. There is also plenty of trailer parking space, which can be a problem at some other metropolitan boat ramps.

Adjacent to the public launching facility at North Haven lies the Cruising Yacht Club of South Australia, which accommodates the bulk of Adelaide's larger recreational and game fishing boats. It is here that a couple of charter fishing operators moor their craft.

The Glenelg boat launching complex has been at the centre of controversy for several years. Located at the mouth of the Patawalonga River, its entrance is often blocked by a menacing sand bar which restricts access on a falling tide. Car parking is also limited at Glenelg, but because of its convenient location near the middle of the metropolitan coast, this facility still attracts plenty of trailer boat anglers.

The O'Sullivan Beach Marina, situated in Adelaide's southern suburbs, caters for thousands of trailer boat anglers, the bulk of whom operate between Brighton and Port Noarlunga. Although this facility is smaller than North Haven, it has its own bait and tackle outlet, first class wash-down facilities, ample parking space and a double-lane ramp with boarding pontoons. O'Sullivan Beach makes a very convenient launching point for those with larger trailer boats wishing to travel across Gulf St Vincent. Noted snapper and whiting areas such as Tapley and Troubridge Shoals, off the bottom end of Yorke Peninsula, are well within reach of O'Sullivan Beach in favourable weather.

SEASONS AND WEATHER PATTERNS

As a result of its unique geography, Gulf St Vincent often seems to create distinctive weather and sea conditions that can differ markedly from those in other parts

Fishing offshore from Adelaide in the waters of Gulf St Vincent

Coastline near Troubridge Point on Gulf St Vincent

of the state. Adelaide is situated roughly two-thirds of the way up the gulf on its eastern side and is thus subject to a 'funnelling' effect when the prevailing winds blow onshore. Winds from the south and south-west often create a short, steep chop that makes offshore boating difficult and uncomfortable.

Summer is undoubtedly the windiest time of year in the Gulf St Vincent. Incessant overnight south-easterly winds swing to the south-west most afternoons between November and February, regularly topping 25 knots and building nasty seas. Only when the weather is really hot does Gulf St Vincent remain calm and fishable all day during the summer months.

Autumn and winter are by far the most stable seasons for offshore fishing. The months of March through to May see light winds and low seas in the gulf and, apart from the odd north-westerly buster, June, July and August also usually provide pleasant, calm conditions.

Springtime is often an unpredictable period that yields a mixture of weather extremes. Seas can be smooth for several consecutive days, then chop up for a week with the arrival of a strong cold front. Unfortunately, weather conditions such as these regularly coincide with some of Adelaide's best offshore fishing.

Fish Varieties and Where To Find Them

Adelaide is famous within national angling circles for two fish—the King George whiting and the magnificent snapper. Both are available in good numbers, but those anglers who specialise in one or both naturally achieve the best results. However, there is a lot more to Adelaide's offshore fishing scene than just these 'big two'.

Snapper are found right along the Adelaide coast, from Port Stanvac in the south up to Port Gawler, north-west of the city. They vary in size from just legal (38 cm) 'ruggers' to 16-kg giants, with bigger specimens probably more common than the little guys.

Of all the big snapper hotspots offshore from Adelaide, the Outer Harbor shipping channel is easily the most consistent. The reds average better than 10 kg apiece from the channel, but it isn't uncommon to catch them at 14 kg or even more. Berley and patience are the keys to success while fishing the edges of the Outer Harbor channel.

King George whiting are widespread throughout Gulf St Vincent and, despite considerable fishing pressure, they are still easy to locate and catch offshore from Adelaide. Most of the artificial reefs hold whiting in good numbers, especially the Grange tyre reef, which is easily accessible from both the North Haven and Glenelg boat ramps. Other very popular whiting locations include the Goannas (an area of sea grass and broken ground north of Adelaide), Semaphore Reef, the wrecks of the *Norma* and the *John Robb*, and the Glenelg tyre reef.

Garfish are extremely popular offshore targets during the warmer months and are regularly found in company with tommy rough and slimy mackerel. These surface feeders are easily located right along the metropolitan coast, but tend to congregate over the artificial reefs and larger seagrass beds.

Squid, or southern calamari, are keenly sought by Adelaide's offshore set and now rival some of the more traditional top table fish in popularity. They can be found without much trouble along the inshore weed beds and over low reefs. Marino, Hallett Cove and Port Noarlunga are among the better locations for catching squid.

Best Baits

The Goolwa cockle, which is readily available from Adelaide tackle outlets, is by far the most popular offshore bait. The cockle will catch King George whiting, tommy rough, garfish, mackerel and even small snapper.

Blowfly maggots (known in South Australia as 'gents') are also very popular, particularly with garfish and tommy rough specialists, and Western Australian pilchards are the number one choice with those who chase big snapper.

A 10.5-kg snapper taken in Adelaide's Outer Harbor shipping channel

THE PORT RIVER AND OUTER HARBOR

IN BRIEF

MAP REFERENCE: PAGE 233 J9
GETTING THERE Via Port Adelaide — access to Adelaide from National Highway One
BEST TIME TO FISH Year-round, depending on target species
BEST TIME TO TRAVEL Year-round
MAJOR ANGLING SPECIES Mulloway, bream, mullet and juvenile Australian salmon
SPECIAL RESTRICTIONS There is no access to Outer Harbor's northern breakwater and several clearly marked wharf areas. Speed restrictions apply to small boats in designated areas
WARNINGS The Port River is flanked by mud banks, which can be hazardous for the unwary boat operator at low tide

Adelaide's Port River isn't really a river in the strictest terms. Rather, it is a natural canal which flows between the artificial West Lakes system and Gulf St Vincent. It branches roughly halfway along its length, and the North Arm offshoot forms the eastern shores of Torrens and Garden islands. The river eventually empties into Gulf St Vincent through Outer Harbor, at the northern extremity of Adelaide's metropolitan foreshore.

As is the case with most waterways adjacent to a capital city, the Port River carries a large volume of commercial shipping. It also accommodates plenty of dockside industry, which means that its water quality isn't exactly pristine. Despite this, however, the river continues to yield quality fishing from both small boats and shore. It is also a favoured haunt for sailing and bird-watching, the latter particularly around the St Kilda mangroves.

The mighty mulloway is undoubtedly this area's number one angling drawcard, although as is the case with mulloway fishing anywhere in Australia, only those prepared to put in the hours and the effort catch big 'butterfish' (as they are known locally) with any regularity.

Sheltered as it is from strong winds, the Port River is enormously popular with Adelaide's 'tinny' brigade. Those with small aluminium dinghies can fish in complete safety, particularly in the river's higher reaches which pose little risk even when the exposed waters of Gulf St Vincent are totally out of the question. A 4-m aluminium boat with a small-capacity outboard is all that is needed to chase anything from mullet to mulloway.

SHORE-BASED FISHING OPTIONS

Although the recent closure and demolition of some wharves has seriously reduced the range of land-based alternatives around the Port River, resourceful anglers still manage to pull plenty of good fish. Bream are available right along the river's main thoroughfare, with Hindmarsh Reach (between the Jervois and Railway Bridges) and Snowdens Beach probably the pick of the bunch.

The North Arm, particularly between the Torrens Island Bridge and the wrecks, is also good for bream and yellow-eye mullet, as are the creeks on the eastern side of the St Kilda Channel. School mulloway can be taken from the shore in the North Arm at times, but are generally a better proposition from a boat.

Unfortunately, the long wharf at Outer Harbor is now closed to recreational fishing. Some mighty mulloway catches have been made there over the years, including many fish weighing more than 30 kg, but the wharf now seems lost forever. The adjacent Outer Harbor breakwater, however, may still be fished and, for those keen enough to traverse its rocky length, mulloway, snook, salmon and the occasional snapper are viable targets.

THE PORT RIVER BY BOAT

As mentioned, even small boats can be used to fish the Port River successfully. In fact, the manoeuvrability afforded by a car-topper sized dinghy is often an advantage when fishing around wharves, bridges and partly submerged wrecks.

There are several reasonable concrete launching ramps to choose from, including the dual-lane facility on Garden Island, one at Birkenhead, another near the sailing club and the old ramp at the northern end of Outer Harbor. All Port River ramps are best used when the tide is well up. Also, security for cars and trailers parked near the ramps after dark has traditionally been a problem.

Yellow-eye mullet are prolific throughout the entire system, but are most readily found along the mangrove fringes around Torrens and Garden

Port River's Tragedy Dock is very popular with land-based anglers

winter and early spring are probably the best periods for targeting these fish.

Practically every angler who regularly fishes the Port River would love to do battle with a 20-kg mulloway, but the truth is only a select few ever realise that ambition. Mulloway are present in various sizes thoughout the entire year, with the true giants usually at their peak between late April and July. Those who specialise in this species generally concentrate their efforts in a handful of locations, including the North Arm junction, the Quarantine Station and the edges of the shipping channel on the river's eastern side.

Serious mulloway fishing often means spending long, cold nights at anchor, regularly catching nothing except the proverbial cold. However, when that 20- or 30-kg fish snaffles a live bait and powers off into the darkness, all previously unsuccessful sorties suddenly seem irrelevant.

THE BEST BAITS

As with most estuary systems, live or locally procured baits stand alone when fishing the Port River. Several varieties of marine worm can be dug or pumped from the mud flats at low tide, all of which are dynamite on bream, mullet and school mulloway. Local rock crabs, easily gathered from beneath shoreline rocks or around mangrove roots, also work very well, particularly on larger bream.

islands. The most successful technique when targeting mullet is to anchor near the mangroves in just a metre of water on a rising tide, then berley heavily with stale bread and mincemeat. Catches of several dozen are common and most are of a good size.

Tying up alongside the old wharves in the Port River's upper reaches can produce plenty of big bream, particularly from dusk through until early evening. Bream bite all year round, but late

Fishing opposite the lighthouse at Port Adelaide on the Port River

Large bream such as this 1-kg specimen are available throughout the entire Port River system

Live bait accounts for at least 90 per cent of all mulloway caught in the Port River, with mullet, garfish, trumpeters and Australian salmon all effective in certain locations. Those who fish exclusively for the winter run of big mulloway or 'jewies' generally prefer large yellow-eye or 'jumper' mullet, but live squid are also extremely effective if they are available. Fortunately, those anglers who have neither the time nor the inclination to gather their own bait are well served by tackle stores in and around Port Adelaide. Top-quality frozen baits such as prawns, anchovies, pilchards, whitebait and craytail will all catch fish and these are available in convenient packaging and at reasonable prices. The fact that several stores are open until 9 or 10 o'clock at night adds to the appeal of using frozen baits.

TIMES AND TIDES

Dawn, dusk and the early hours of the evening seem to be the best times to fish the Port River and Outer Harbor. Bream and mulloway definitely prefer diminishing light to full darkness, while mullet and Australian salmon can be taken at practically any time.

Mulloway specialists generally prefer to fish the slower tides and tide changes, as live baits are definitely more effective away from strong currents. Ideal tidal conditions for mid-winter mulloway would be a high water peaking well after dark, followed by 1 m or less of run-out towards low water.

THE FLEURIEU PENINSULA

IN BRIEF

MAP REFERENCE: PAGE 230 A5

GETTING THERE The Fleurieu Peninsula lies south of Adelaide on the south-eastern side of Gulf St Vincent — access via Main South Road from Adelaide

BEST TIME TO FISH Year-round, but autumn provides most stable weather

BEST TIME TO TRAVEL Year-round

MAJOR ANGLING SPECIES Snapper, whiting, silver trevally, snook, squid, tommy rough, Australian salmon and garfish

WARNINGS Strong tidal rips occur in Backstairs Passage between the Fleurieu Peninsula and Kangaroo Island

ACCOMMODATION Abundant caravan parks, motels, resorts and units

CHARTER BOATS AND FISHING GUIDES Cape Jervis Charter, telephone (08) 8598 0222; Fleurieu Charters, telephone (08) 8598 0264; Victor Harbor Boat Charter, telephone (08) 8552 7475; Double Impact Charters, telephone (08) 8552 5943; Paradise Cove Boat Charters, telephone (08) 8322 7161

Essentially, the Fleurieu Peninsula marks the boundary between Gulf St Vincent and the Southern Ocean. Its southernmost tip is also the closest point between the mainland and Kangaroo Island, which is separated from the peninsula by a narrow corridor of water known as Backstairs Passage. European explorers Matthew Flinders and Nicolas Baudin charted the Fleurieu coast in 1802 and were taken by its exceptional beauty.

The relatively high annual rainfall in this region has meant that the Fleurieu Peninsula has long been a renowned dairy farming region. Today, however, it also accommodates thousands of permanent residents and almost as many weekend visitors. It is undoubtedly the most popular weekend getaway venue for Adelaide folk and attracts a huge number of recreational anglers during the warmer months.

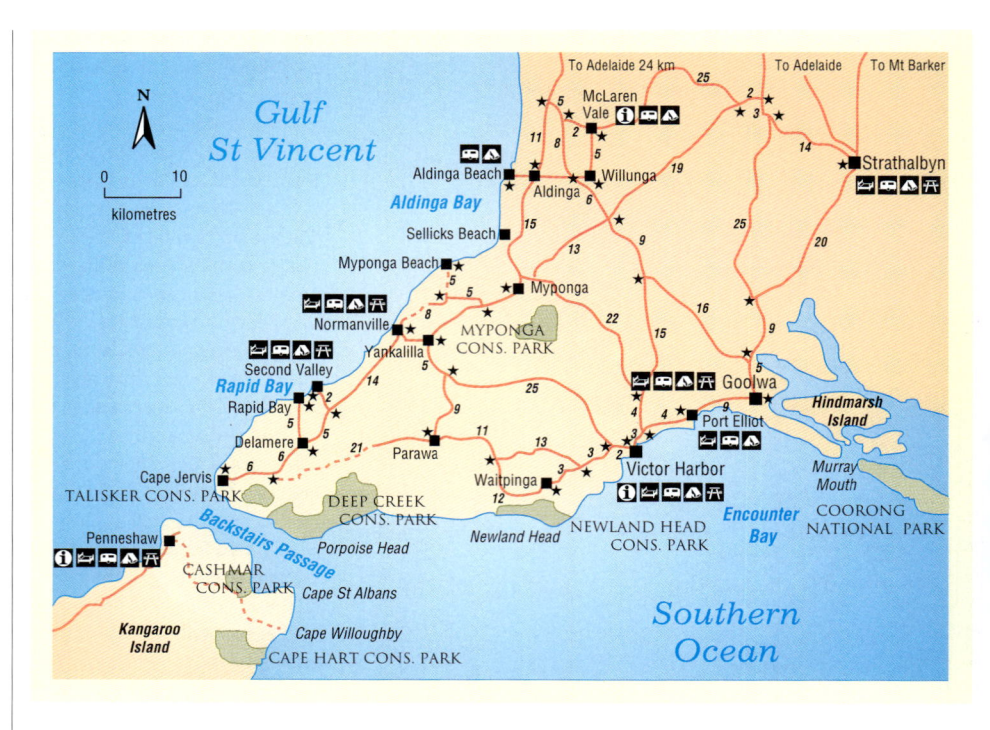

Victor Harbor is the Fleurieu Peninsula's principal settlement with a population of around 12 000 permanent residents. However, this number swells to more than 30 000 during the summer holiday season, pushing available accommodation to the limit. Cape Jervis, Rapid Bay, Second Valley and Normanville may all be small coastal hamlets with limited facilities, but they also have the drawcard of terrific fishing.

One of Fleurieu Peninsula's most appealing and convenient features is its relative proximity to Adelaide. Victor Harbor is only an hour's drive from the capital's southern suburbs and it's only half an hour further on from there to Cape Jervis. Fortunately, despite this accessibility, the fishing remains in good shape.

LAND-BASED FISHING OPPORTUNITIES

Rock, beach and jetty anglers have plenty to get excited about when they plan a weekend on the Fleurieu Peninsula. In fact, few other parts of South Australia can boast such a cross-section of land-based fishing possibilities in such a small area. There are half a dozen productive jetties, a couple of legendary surf beaches and enough low cliffs and headlands to keep the keenest rockhopper entertained.

Rapid Bay Jetty, roughly 80 km south of Adelaide, is undoubtedly the state's most popular angling pier outside of the Adelaide metropolitan area. It belongs to BHP and is open to anglers at all times except when a bulk carrier ship is tied up to load gypsum. It is a long jetty which is best known for big catches of squid, tommy rough, silver trevally and garfish. During the summer months, it also attracts huge yellowtail kingfish, but these are difficult to tempt with anything but live squid, and even harder to land once hooked!

Most of the other Fleurieu jetties are much shorter, but still excellent venues for catching tommy rough, garfish and squid. Screwpile Jetty, on Victor Harbor's Granite Island, turns up some real surprises from time to time, including big snapper, sharks and the occasional mulloway of up to 25 kg.

Waitpinga and Parsons beaches, situated just west of Victor Harbor, were once among South

This 16-kg yellowtail kingfish was taken on one of the Fleurieu's offshore reefs during the warmer months

Australia's premier salmon fishing locations, but local commercial netting has unfortunately taken a heavy toll. Australian salmon are still taken from these beaches, but no longer with such regularity nor at such a consistent size. Salmon of up to 1 kg are plentiful, as are big yellow-eye mullet. Some monster mulloway turn up occasionally for those prepared to fish into the night.

Inexplicably, Waitpinga is perhaps the only beach in South Australia to yield tailor. These fish are not caught regularly, but when they do grab a salmon lure or pilchard, they are almost always 5 kg or better. A couple of tailor pulled from the Waitpinga beach's western end back in the 1980s weighed a staggering 9 kg each!

Rock anglers can pull plenty of sweep from the waters between Cape Jervis and Victor Harbor, along with Australian salmon, leatherjackets and the odd big snapper. Be warned, however, this is a turbulent stretch of coastline which regularly claims the lives of those who are either unprepared or oblivious to the potential danger. Anglers must take extreme care at all times if they are fishing in this area.

OFFSHORE FROM THE FLEURIEU PENINSULA

Because of its location between gulf and ocean waters, the east and west coasts of Fleurieu Peninsula are radically different. From Rapid Head eastwards, the influence of the ocean swell is evident on all but the calmest days, while gulf weather and sea conditions dominate from Rapid Bay all the way up to Adelaide.

There are several launching facilities from which trailer boat anglers may choose, with Cape Jervis, Wirrina and Victor Harbor undoubtedly the best. The O'Sullivan Beach marina, in Adelaide's southern suburbs, also provides convenient access to the Fleurieu Peninsula's western shores in favourable weather.

Backstairs Passage, which fronts the Cape Jervis ramp and small boat basin, is a highly productive, but difficult piece of water to fish. Despite heavy commercial fishing pressure, this stretch of water still yields big snapper in the summer months, as well as trevally, snook, Australian salmon, squid and sharks. However, as Backstairs Passage is subject to enormous tidal influence, it is only possible to fish there for just a few hours each day and then only when weather conditions permit.

A view across to Granite Island from Victor Harbor, on the eastern side of the Fleurieu Peninsula

Victor Harbor's offshore reef systems, while similarly affected by fresh winds for at least half of the year, have become enormously popular with trailer boat anglers in recent times. There are two major reefs, known simply as the Inner and Outer grounds, which produce silver trevally to 5 kg, big snook, warehou (sea bream), snapper and slimy mackerel.

These reefs definitely fish best in the warmer months, but persistent south-easterly winds between December and March render them inaccessible to small boat operators on an annoyingly regular basis. Ocean swell often builds quite alarmingly after sustained periods of wind from this quarter, making outside conditions quite hazardous for the inexperienced.

The eastern end of Kangaroo Island is within easy reach of both Cape Jervis and Victor Harbor, as are the Pages Islands and Tunkalilla. Some huge King George whiting come from these areas, with fish measuring up to 55 cm in length quite common. Nannygai (red snapper), snook, salmon, kingfish and sweep are also regulars along the cliffs and over offshore reefs.

As the Fleurieu Peninsula is well endowed with offshore charter fishing services, it isn't mandatory actually to own a boat in order to sample the action. Most of the charter skippers operating out of Victor Harbor and Cape Jervis are former professional fishermen who know their home waters intimately and regularly put clients on to top-class fishing. These fellows are also adept at finding somewhere to fish with success and in comfort when weather conditions keep the trailer boat fleet at home.

The Normanville Jetty at sunset

THE COORONG

IN BRIEF

MAP REFERENCE: PAGE 230 A6

GETTING THERE Goolwa is 85 km south-east of Adelaide and 20 km east of Victor Harbor, at the north-western edge of the Coorong National Park
BEST TIME TO FISH September to May
BEST TIME TO TRAVEL Year-round
MAJOR ANGLING SPECIES Bream, mulloway, mullet and Australian salmon
SPECIAL RESTRICTIONS Camping permits are required within the Coorong National Park and strict rules apply to those operating 4WD vehicles in this area; contact the national parks office in Meningie on (08) 8575 1200 or the Salt Creek Visitor Centre on (08) 8575 7014 for details
WARNINGS Although narrow, the estuarine waters of the Coorong can become very choppy in strong winds. In addition, numerous shallow sand banks present navigation hazards
ACCOMMODATION Camping within the Coorong National Park; caravan parks and motels in the nearby townships of Meningie, Strathalbyn and Goolwa

Surprisingly, the south-eastern corner of the Festival State is a region often overlooked by Adelaide-based anglers, as well as many of those travelling from further afield seeking a new location to cast a line. However, this delightful area offers some excellent fishing opportunities, particularly during the late spring, summer and early autumn months. It also offers a range of striking, sometimes harsh scenery and many isolated stretches of coastline, several of which featured prominently in the popular Australian movie *Storm Boy*.

Important centres in the region include Victor Harbor, with a population in excess of 5500; Port Elliot, with slightly more than 1000 inhabitants; and Goolwa, opposite Hindmarsh Island, with some 2500 residents. This last town is the gateway to the Murray Mouth and Coorong regions, and a popular staging point for keen anglers.

The Murray Mouth

Just south-east of Goolwa is the spot where the mighty Murray–Darling River system finally joins the Southern Ocean, after first passing through the broad, shallow expanses of Lake Alexandrina and Lake Albert. This estuary has been greatly modified over the past century through the construction of long barrage walls and locks intended to prevent the intrusion of salt water into the lower Murray.

As a result of all these changes and the general degradation of the natural environment, the Coorong's lakes and lower river reaches are now mostly populated by the introduced and noxious European carp. However, the long estuarine arm known as the Coorong Lagoon—which runs south from Hindmarsh Island behind the Younghusband Peninsula, before ending in a series of salty waterholes beyond Chinamans Well—can still offer some very fine fishing, as do the region's long surf beaches and the Murray Mouth area itself (see pp. 224–5).

Beach fishing opportunities are particularly attractive to many visitors, with some great Australian salmon on tap at times, as well as gummy and school sharks, mullet, rays and the occasional big mulloway or large whaler shark. A 4WD vehicle, however, is essential to reach the best of these spots.

Exploring the Coorong

The Coorong's name is derived from the Aboriginal word 'kurangh', meaning a long, narrow body of water. The Coorong Lagoon is a fascinating and unique estuary system of sheltered, tidal water with an average depth of less than 3 m. It is separated from the open sea by a narrow finger of rolling sand hills known as the Younghusband Peninsula. The entire region teems with native birds and wildlife, and is a nature reserve of considerable significance. Summer sees an influx migratory birds and Cape Barren geese, swelling the already significant number of bird species here.

Camping permits are required by anyone wishing to stay overnight, and 4WD activities are strictly controlled because of the Coorong's importance and fragile ecosytem. Those intending to visit should contact any South Australian Tourism office, or call into the National Parks offices at Meningie or Salt Creek to obtain more details and apply for a camping permit.

A small boat launched at Goolwa or Hindmarsh Island allows access to most of the Coorong's fascinating and beautiful 130-km length, and freely enables anglers to pursue the abundant southern bream, mullet, juvenile Australian salmon (often called salmon trout in this part of the world) and prolific school mulloway that call this extensive system home.

Specific fishing restrictions and regulations on the taking of certain species—most notably mulloway—are in force throughout the Coorong. Anglers should thoroughly familiarise themselves with these special rules before fishing the area.

In the Surf

The Ninety Mile Beach, on the ocean side of the Younghusband Peninsula, is relatively remote

Looking out across the shallow waters of the Coorong Lagoon

A surf angler on the Younghusband Peninsula in Coorong National Park

and quite lightly fished. A reliable 4WD vehicle is necessary for access, and there are several crossing points towards the south-eastern end of the Coorong—between Salt Creek and the Twenty-Eight Mile Crossing.

Strict restrictions apply to the use of off-road vehicles in this area, and the route north along Ninety Mile Beach from Tea Tree Crossing is completely closed to traffic from late October until Christmas each year, in order to protect nesting hooded plovers.

Although often lacking in distinct features such as prominent holes and gutters, this long beach produces reasonable catches of Australian salmon, yellow-eye mullet, gummy sharks and rays, as well as the odd mulloway and even a very occasional tailor.

One of this region's main claims to fame is the abundance of Goolwa cockles (pipis). These are found mainly on Goolwa Beach, which lies to the west of the Murray Mouth. Goolwa cockles are one of South Australia's favourite baits, especially for whiting, and are so numerous on Goolwa Beach that they support a thriving local bait-gathering industry, as well as attracting keen anglers willing to collect their own bait supplies. Regulations exist to govern the harvesting of these bivalve molluscs, and these should be carefully checked before collecting any cockles or other invertebrates for bait or human consumption.

MURRAY MOUTH MULLOWAY

IN BRIEF

MAP REFERENCE: PAGE 230 B6

GETTING THERE From the township of Goolwa, travel to surf beach car park, then by 4WD vehicle to the river mouth
BEST TIME TO FISH October through May, depending on river conditions
BEST TIME TO TRAVEL Year-round
MAJOR ANGLING SPECIES Mulloway
SPECIAL RESTRICTIONS The beach 4WD speed limit is 40 kph
WARNINGS The Murray Mouth is subject to strong tidal rips which have claimed anglers' lives, so always take extreme care if wading
ACCOMMODATION Camping only

After meandering its way through three states, the mighty Murray River eventually ends its journey to the Southern Ocean just a few kilometres east of the small township of Goolwa. The exit is via Lake Alexandrina, which abuts the Coorong, one of Australia's largest estuary systems. The interchange of water in this region is quite complex, with a substantial barrage separating fresh from salt to the west of the Murray Mouth, and the tremendous tidal outflow from the Coorong to the east.

Both fish and bird life in the Coorong are diverse and a wonder for lovers of nature. The Coorong's expansive flats and profusion of channels provide fabulous small boat fishing, particularly for bream, flounder, Australian salmon, mullet and school mulloway. So prolific are the small mulloway at times that the region has its own bag and size limits for the species. Unlike other parts of South Australia, Coorong mulloway have a reduced minimum legal size of 46 cm and a daily bag limit of 10 fish per angler.

However, it is the big fish—the 20- to 30-kg giants—that grab the angling limelight in this area and these are caught right in the river mouth itself. Most of the fishing is done at night time with heavy lures and, although it is a great place to be when the big mulloway are on, it is quite dangerous for the inexperienced. One unfortunate angler lost his life late in 1997 after being washed out to sea and others have been close to a similar fate on several occasions.

PREPARING FOR A WEEKEND

Number one item on the prerequisites list for a trip to the mouth of the Murray River is a reliable 4WD vehicle. It is roughly 11 km from the Goolwa Beach car park to the river mouth and the sand is regularly soft and difficult to negotiate. Vehicles with inadequate ground clearance and thin tyres often get into trouble in the beach's particularly soft sections and getting bogged to the axles at night time can be a traumatic experience. The ideal vehicle for Murray Mouth access is a powerful 4WD with wide tyres and plenty of ground clearance. Reducing tyre pressure also helps traction in ultra-soft sand, so a portable compressor is handy to reinflate the tyres after leaving the beach on the way back out.

Other accessories include a lightweight shovel and stout tow rope, both of which can help save the day in the event of a serious sand bog.

Most anglers who spend a weekend at the Murray Mouth do so in small, easy-to-erect tents or camper trailers. These can be sited well back from the surf line near the base of the sand hills, where they are out of the way of passing vehicles.

THE MULLOWAY OF A LIFETIME

It is the natural berleying effect of the river outflow that attracts mulloway in large schools from outside ocean waters. When the Murray volume increases due to upstream activity (usually snow melt from the Victorian alpine regions), the outflow at the river mouth increases dramatically. At times, literally thousands of dead or dying carp and redfin come down with the flow, many of which find their way out through the mouth. This situation attracts all manner of predators and in

Monster mulloway are the reward for those who invest the necessary time and effort

particular some enormous mulloway. These fish wait just outside the surf line until the ebb tide gets underway, then move into the narrow channel, constantly on the look-out for an easy meal. This is where a specialised form of lure casting can really pay dividends.

The technique is to cast the lure as far as possible from the shoreline, let it sink, then retrieve it quite slowly. The run-out tide will bring the lure around in a gradual arc and, if it bumps its way past the nose of a marauding mulloway, a strike usually results. Sometimes it's a case of casting for hours on end before a hook-up is made, but when the big mulloway are there in numbers and really on the prowl, the action can be fast and furious. This is surf casting at its very best!

The majority of big mulloway hooked in the Murray Mouth run long and hard, straight out to sea because of the strong ebb tide. This is where large spool capacity is vital and well-constructed terminal tackle comes into its own.

Many an inexperienced surf caster at the Murray Mouth has hooked that elusive 25-kg fish, only to have it escape due to a poorly tied knot or inadequate leader material. Most Murray Mouth regulars tie a short double at the end of their main line (using a bimini twist), then attach a metre or so of heavy monofilament via an albright knot. A quality snap swivel is then used to facilitate lure changes. This system provides the ultimate in knot strength (the bimini is quoted as being a close to 100 per cent knot) and offers plenty of abrasion resistance against sharp gill rakers, fins and tails. Mastering both the bimini twist and the albright knot requires a little practice, but they are very handy in a wide range of fishing situations.

Likewise, the rod/reel combination used on big Murray Mouth mulloway needs to be top quality and well maintained. The reel spool should hold at least 400 m of line, which is usually of between 10- and 15-kg breaking strain, and the drag must be smooth and positive. These are heavy, powerful fish that will inevitably find flaws in shoddy equipment, so it pays to have the tackle side of things well sorted out before any Murray Mouth excursion.

It is also wise to carry a short-handled gaff for the moment that big, golden-flanked mulloway hits the shore break. Collapsible metal shank gaffs which can be easily carried on a belt are ideal, as long as they are strong enough for the job.

Top-quality surf casting tackle is mandatory for catching big mulloway at the river mouth

An aerial view of the mouth of the Murray River, with the Coorong estuary in the background

SOUTH AUSTRALIAN TROUT WATERS

IN BRIEF

MAP REFERENCE: PAGE 233 J9

GETTING THERE The major trout waters lie within the south-east corner of the state. Most are accessible from sealed roads
BEST TIME TO FISH March to November
BEST TIME TO TRAVEL Year-round
MAJOR ANGLING SPECIES Brown and rainbow trout, and redfin
SPECIAL RESTRICTIONS No closed season, but as most South Australian trout waters flow through private property, permission must be sought prior to fishing
FLY FISHING OPERATORS Rosebank Farm, telephone 019 697 657; South Australian Trout Tours, telephone (08) 8250 6020

South Australia is generally regarded as the driest state in one of the world's driest continents, so it is no surprise to learn that substantial inland waterways are few and far between. With the obvious exception of the Murray, South Australia has a mere handful of permanent rivers, none of which carry native fish of any significance.

The same applies to lakes and impoundments. Lake Alexandrina, at the bottom end of the Murray, is infested with carp. Although trout stocking has been attempted here on several occasions, it has been largely unsuccessful. Blue and Valley lakes, near Mount Gambier in the state's south-east, have also been stocked sporadically, but they, too, have failed to sustain viable trout populations.

However, while conditions for trout in South Australia may not be ideal, both brown trout and rainbow trout have been introduced and, in a few cases, have done reasonably well. Due to climatic and geographical conditions, there is little, if any natural spawning, so the wellbeing of the state's trout stocks rests solely with an artificial breeding program. The South Australian Fly Fishers Association operates its own hatchery and is responsible for most of the browns and rainbows available to anglers. These dedicated folks receive very little government assistance and rely heavily on private funding to carry on their work.

As the trout don't breed in the wild, there has never been a need for a closed season, so the only restriction facing anglers is a minimum legal length of 28 cm for both brown trout and rainbow trout.

Although the majority of South Australia's reservoirs are populated with redfin and a few trout, they are totally off-limits to fishing. This situation has been discussed at government level with a view towards possibly opening one or more impoundments to recreational anglers, but to date no action has been taken.

On the other hand, a high percentage of privately owned farm dams are liberally stocked with trout and perch, which appear to do quite well. Once again, the Fly Fishers Association seeds most dams and, in some cases, has exclusive fishing rights for these impoundments.

SOUTH AUSTRALIA'S BETTER TROUT WATERS

As much of the north of South Australia is hot and arid, most permanent rivers are found within a couple of hours' drive of Adelaide. Public access to the rivers is limited and those who fish them usually do so by seeking permission from land owners. The majority of farmers don't mind anglers crossing their property, as long as stock are not interfered with and gates are left as found — a cardinal rule when visiting rural properties.

The Onkaparinga River, just south of Adelaide, is undoubtedly South Australia's most famous trout water. Originating in the Mount Lofty Ranges, the Onk (as it is best known) meanders through the southern suburbs before eventually reaching Gulf St Vincent at Port Noarlunga. It is, in its lower sections at least, a deep, slow-flowing river flanked by rocky gorges and rolling hills.

The Onkaparinga is heavily fished because of its closeness to suburban Adelaide. However, consistent trout stockings ensure that the population remains in good shape and it regularly produces some lovely browns and rainbows. Pre-metrics double-figure trout are taken from the Onkaparinga occasionally, as are some big redfin. The Finniss River, a little further south, is a favourite fly fishing stream, although the recent appearance of carp has seen water quality diminish. Should the carp population become established, it's a safe bet the Finniss will no longer be stocked with trout.

Both the Hindmarsh and Inman rivers, which flow into the Southern Ocean near Victor Harbor, carry limited numbers of trout. These are not easy waters to fish, but brown trout and rainbow trout weighing up to 2 kg are there for those with the necessary patience and expertise.

The streams north of Adelaide, while subject to extreme heat during the summer months, are among the state's most reliable trout producers. The rivers Light, Wakefield and Broughton all receive consistent stockings of brown and

Lures such as this shallow-running minnow account for many of the trout taken in South Australia

rainbow fingerlings. Moreover, despite a less than favourable climate, the fish do well. As all three waterways carry plenty of yabbies, minnows and shrimp, growth rates are high and the trout's condition factor is exceptional.

The River Light flows through the delightful township of Kapunda, just a short drive from the renowned Barossa Valley. Both lures and flies work nicely on the Light, with large, flashy wet flies scoring consistently with the rainbow population. This river's brown trout are invariably more difficult to catch and usually fall to nymphs or to small dries when the conditions are right.

Both the Wakefield and Broughton rivers are deep, clear and slow flowing, which means that the trout they carry are rarely easy to catch. Lure tossers pull the occasional rainbow, but live baiters and experienced fly casters seem to do best. Although the purists may cringe at the thought, a small yabby fished beneath a light quill float is probably the most effective fishing system for either of these rivers.

The Broughton River flows quite close to the lovely Clare Valley, another of Australia's most famous wine-producing regions. It is quite convenient and certainly enjoyable to turn a day's trout fishing on the Broughton into a great weekend by staying overnight in the township of Clare and visiting the wineries as well.

Private Trout Waters — A Convenient Alternative

While South Australia has several 'pay-by-the-kilo' trout farms which attract plenty of young and novice anglers, it also has a couple of more serious small impoundment fisheries set up especially to cater for fly casters.

Rosebank Farm, south of Adelaide, is a beautiful property which offers top notch fishing for rainbow trout weighing up to 3 kg or more. So well run and organised is Rosebank that the State Fly Fishing Titles are regularly held here.

South Australian Trout Tours, based at Kalangadoo near Mount Gamber, also offers fly fishing in several large and picturesque lakes. Both brown trout and rainbow trout in excess of 3 kg have been taken on this property, with wet fly fishing the most productive method. Transport to and from Adelaide, as well as meals and farmhouse accommodation, are included in the South Australian Trout Tours package.

Both of these operations are catch-and-release only, but anglers are each given a couple of plate-sized rainbow trout to take home if so desired. Rates are quite reasonable and exclusive bookings are available for those who prefer to fish alone or with a small group.

Fly casting at dawn on the Onkaparinga River, South Australia's most popular trout water

WEEKEND ON THE MURRAY

IN BRIEF

MAP REFERENCE: PAGE 233 L8

GETTING THERE Murray Bridge is 80 km east of Adelaide along National Highway One; Mannum is 23 km north of Murray Bridge
BEST TIME TO FISH October to May
BEST TIME TO TRAVEL Year-round
MAJOR ANGLING SPECIES Golden perch (callop), redfin perch, Murray cod, carp and freshwater crayfish (yabbies)
SPECIAL RESTRICTIONS All carp captured should be killed humanely and disposed of away from the water
FLY FISHING OPERATORS Caravan parks, camping grounds and motels can be found at various places along the Murray River. Houseboats are also available for hire

The Murray River's red ochre cliffs catch the late afternoon sun

The River Murray may no longer flow clear and clean as it once did, but thousands of recreational anglers still flock to its banks each year. While European carp have long since taken over as the dominant fish species, the native varieties continue to battle on against all odds. The Murray cod, golden perch, silver perch and eel-tailed catfish not only have to contend with the carp menace, but also with varying water quality due to damming and upstream agricultural activity.

Doom and gloom aside, however, the Murray remains one of the most beautiful and serene locations in South Australia for a weekend fishing vacation. Its red ochre cliffs, gently swaying willows and profusion of birdlife make it especially appealing to those people who enjoy escaping the pace of modern life and winding down for a couple of days.

It is possible to camp alongside the river in any number of locations. There are designated camping grounds adjacent to most riverside towns and these are well patronised during the warmer months. Some folk prefer to pitch a tent well away from civilisation and do their own thing. Either way, the Murray is a charming place for a camping holiday.

Without doubt, the best way to spend a weekend on the river is to hire a houseboat. This provides very comfortable accommodation and the mobility to explore as much, or as little, water as desired. Houseboats are generally expensive, but as they can accommodate several couples or two or three families, the hire fee can often be divided equally to reduce the outlay.

Murray Fish Species

Both catfish and silver perch are now extremely uncommon in the South Australian section of the Murray. It would appear that these two native species have all but succumbed to the river's environmental problems and they are now totally protected. Golden perch or callop, on the other hand, appear much more hardy and remain a viable target species downstream from Mildura.

Murray cod are, as they always have been, the Murray's glamour fish, but they, too, are now few and far between. The Fisheries Division of the South Australian Department of Primary Industry imposed a temporary moratorium on their capture in the early 1990s, but this has since been lifted and they may again be taken legally.

The carp menace looks like being part of the Murray forever — unless scientists can come up with some miraculous biological control. However, rather than bemoaning something they cannot change, anglers should simply have to grin and bear the European import, fishing around it wherever possible for more desirable native species, or simply enjoying the sport of catching these noxious pests and doing their bit to help control carp numbers in the process.

A Murray Houseboat Weekend

A major prerequisite of any houseboat holiday is booking early. Most of the better houseboats are booked up to 12 months in advance during the popular summer and autumn seasons, so to avoid disappointment it's essential to select dates and pay a deposit to secure a weekend booking.

Most houseboats are pre-fuelled and completely ready to go when clients arrive after work on a Friday afternoon. If there is sufficient daylight, it's simply a matter of casting off and motoring to a likely-looking spot to spend the first night.

Apart from riverside reserves, there are few locations along the South Australian section of the Murray which are off-limits to houseboats, so all that's required are a tranquil setting and a couple of strong bankside trees as mooring points. Also, as the majority of houseboats have a

View across the Murray River near Mannum

rear swimdeck, it is a simple matter to set two or three fishing rods from the deck, then go about cooking dinner. Dusk can be a productive period, particularly for native species, and it isn't unusual to pull a golden perch or two between carp bites at this time of day.

Those anglers who are serious about catching native fish during their houseboat vacation usually set several shrimp traps overnight, and these should yield a good supply of live bait for the following morning. Shrimp traps are best baited with fish frames, meat or even a can of pet food with a couple of small punctures in the lid. The most likely spot to catch shrimp and small yabbies is in close to the bankside reeds.

Being up early next morning is the key to success in targeting golden perch. If there are any golden perch feeding in the general area, they will take live shrimps readily and definitely bite best for the first hour after sunrise. From that point onwards, carp will be the number one contenders, regardless of the bait used.

It is sensible to take advantage of the houseboat's mobility by moving along the river during the day and then settling on another likely fishing location by late afternoon. Some houseboat hire operators actually provide small dinghies for their clients, which open opportunities to fish a range of locations in the general area of mooring. If this is the case, anchoring the dinghy 20 m off the bank and casting back into the reeds or willow roots is often more productive than working the other way around, as native fish regularly feed right in close to the bank as daylight diminishes.

Some keen anglers actually fish from the houseboat through the night. Although the hours of darkness rarely yield consistent action, both Murray cod and golden perch occasionally turn up to provide a welcome bonus. Some big cod, in particular, have been taken at night on live yabbies.

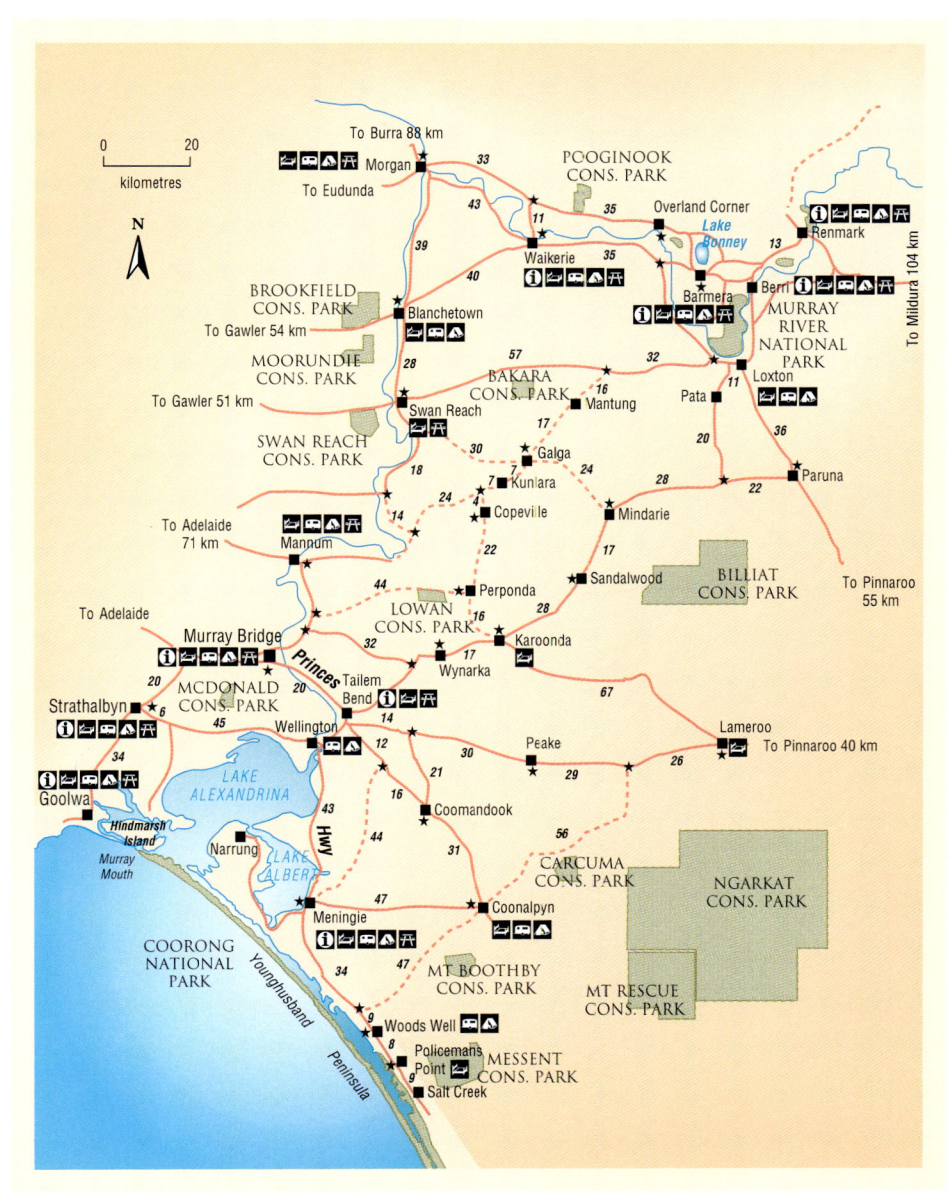

If the boat is due back by late Sunday afternoon, it is wise to begin the return trek by mid-morning. Stopping along the way, usually on the opposite bank to that followed on the way up, makes for a pleasant journey, especially if children are involved. Carp will be the daytime catch and, although they're not much good to eat, they are great fish for kids to practise on and big carp have the ability to fight hard if the tackle is light enough. Just remember, it is illegal to return captured carp to the water in South Australia, so all those caught must be killed humanely and disposed of properly. Fortunately, they make great yabby bait!

This young angler has landed a small carp on a shrimp bait and paternoster rig

0 20 40 60 80 100
kilometres

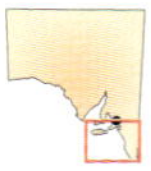

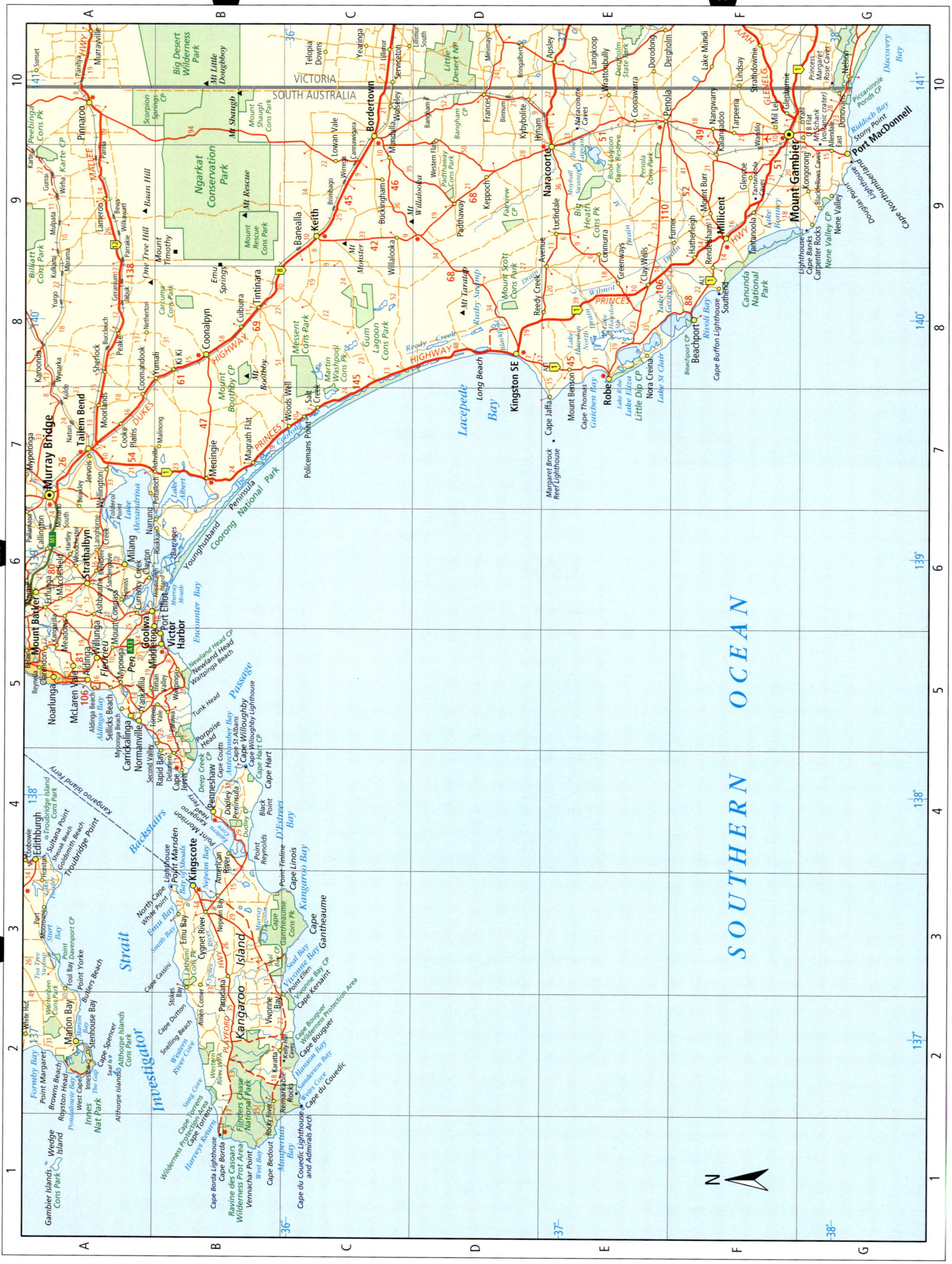

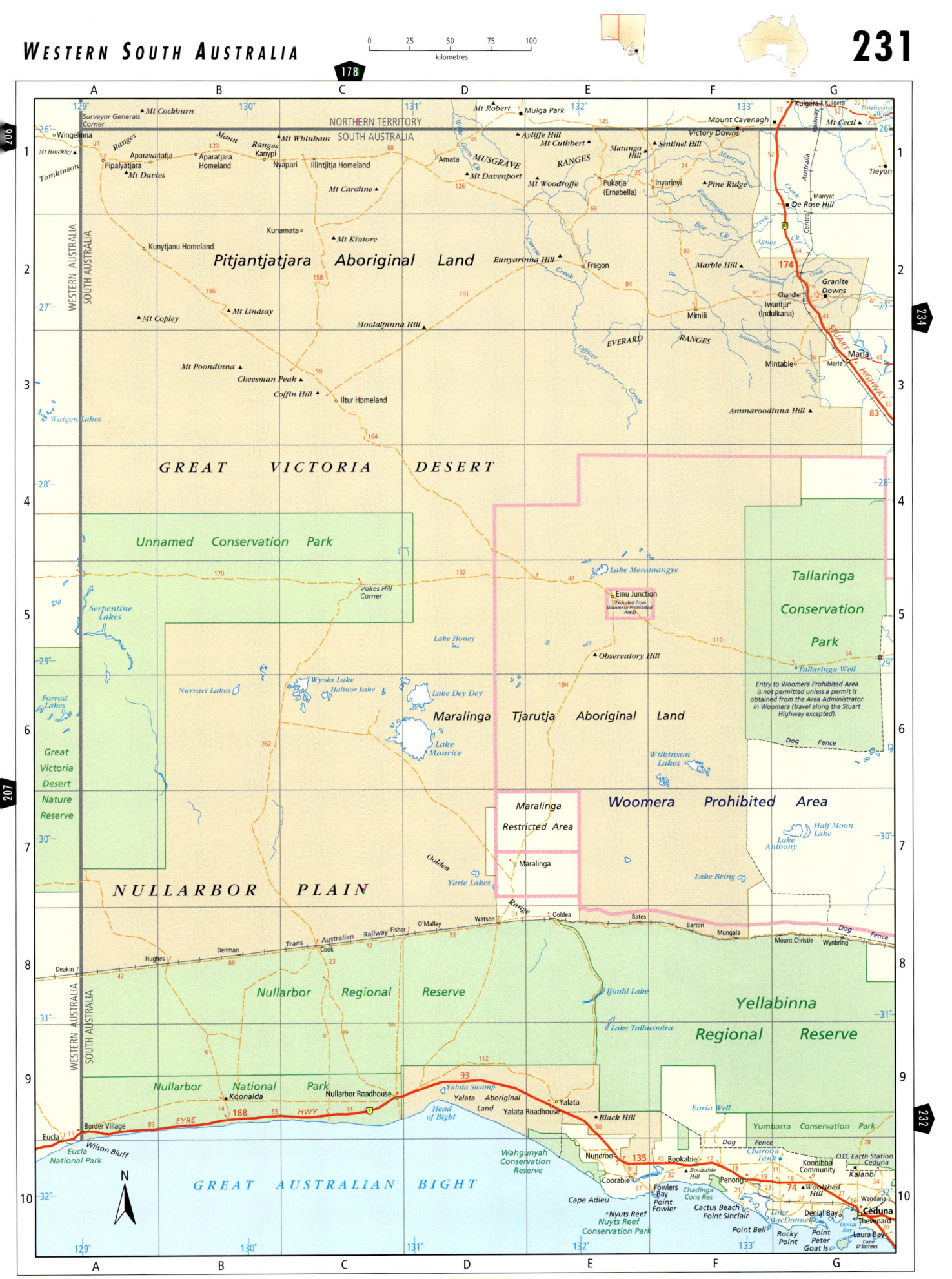

Western South Australia

231

232 CENTRAL-EAST SOUTH AUSTRALIA

0 20 40 60 80
kilometres

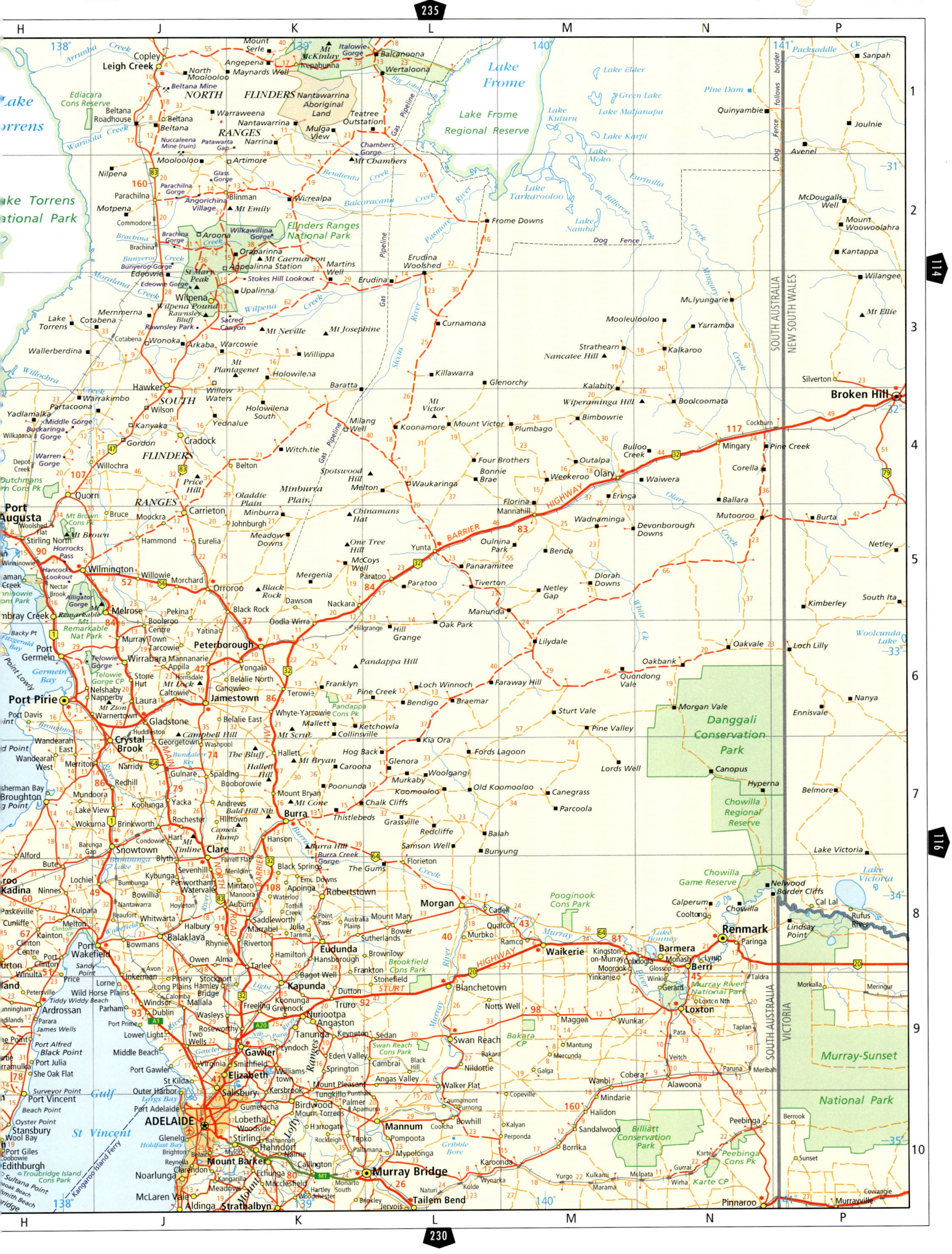

179

NORTHERN TERRITORY
SOUTH AUSTRALIA
Charlotte Waters
Mt Anderson
Abminga
Mount Dare
Horse Hill
Mt Apperda
Witjira National Park
(Desert Parks Pass required prior to entry)
Tieyon
Eringa
Bloods Creek
Dalhousie Springs
Dalhousie
Freeth Junction
Purni Bore
Alka Seltzer Bore
Macumba Well
SIMPSON DESERT
Mt Britton
Hamilton
Pedirka
Old Ghan Rail Route (Dismantled)
PEDIRKA DESERT
Lambina
Mount Sarah
Mt Sarah
Flood detour
Fogartys Claypan
Todmorden
Macumba River
Macumba
Marla
Welbourn Hill
STUART HIGHWAY
Oodnadatta
Allandale
Wintinna
Mt Willoughby
Mt Dutton
Mount Dutton
Algebuckina Bridge
Cadney Homestead (Roadhouse)
Cadney Park
Mt Arckaringa
Arckaringa
Mount Willoughby
Copper Hill
North Peake
Mt Kingston
Mt Denison
Warrina
England Hill
Evelyn Downs
Mount Barry
Peake
Edwards Creek
Mt Barry
Pootnoura
Nilpinna
Mt Margaret
Derangunabula Hill
Duff Creek
Tallaringa Conservation Park
Dog Fence
Mount Clarence
Box Creek
Oodnadatta Track
Mabel Creek
Manguri
Coober Pedy
Lake Cadibarrawirracanna
Anna Creek
William Creek
Irrapatana
Lake Eyre
Halligan Bay
Hambidge Point
Elliot Price Cons Park
Bonython Headland
Belt Bay
Lake Callara
Beresford
Kewson Hill
Coward Springs
Hamilton Hill
Curdimurka
Lake Eyre National Park
Woomera Prohibited Area
Lake Phillipson
Wirrida
Lake Wirrida
Ingomar
Central Australia Railway
McDouall Peak
Mirikata
Gina
Stuart Creek
Commonwealth Hill
Billa Kalina
The Twins
Millers Creek
Carne Outstation
Carne
Bulgunnia
Haggard Hill
Mount Eba
Mulgathing
Mt Sabine
Mattawearra Lagoon
Curdlawidny Lagoon
Partridge Lakes
Mentor Outstation
Bon Bon
Vivian Wells
Parakylia
Red Lake
Olympic Dam Mine
Andamooka
Lake Torrens National Park
Olympic Dam
Roxby Downs
Mount Vivian
Borefield Road

231

232

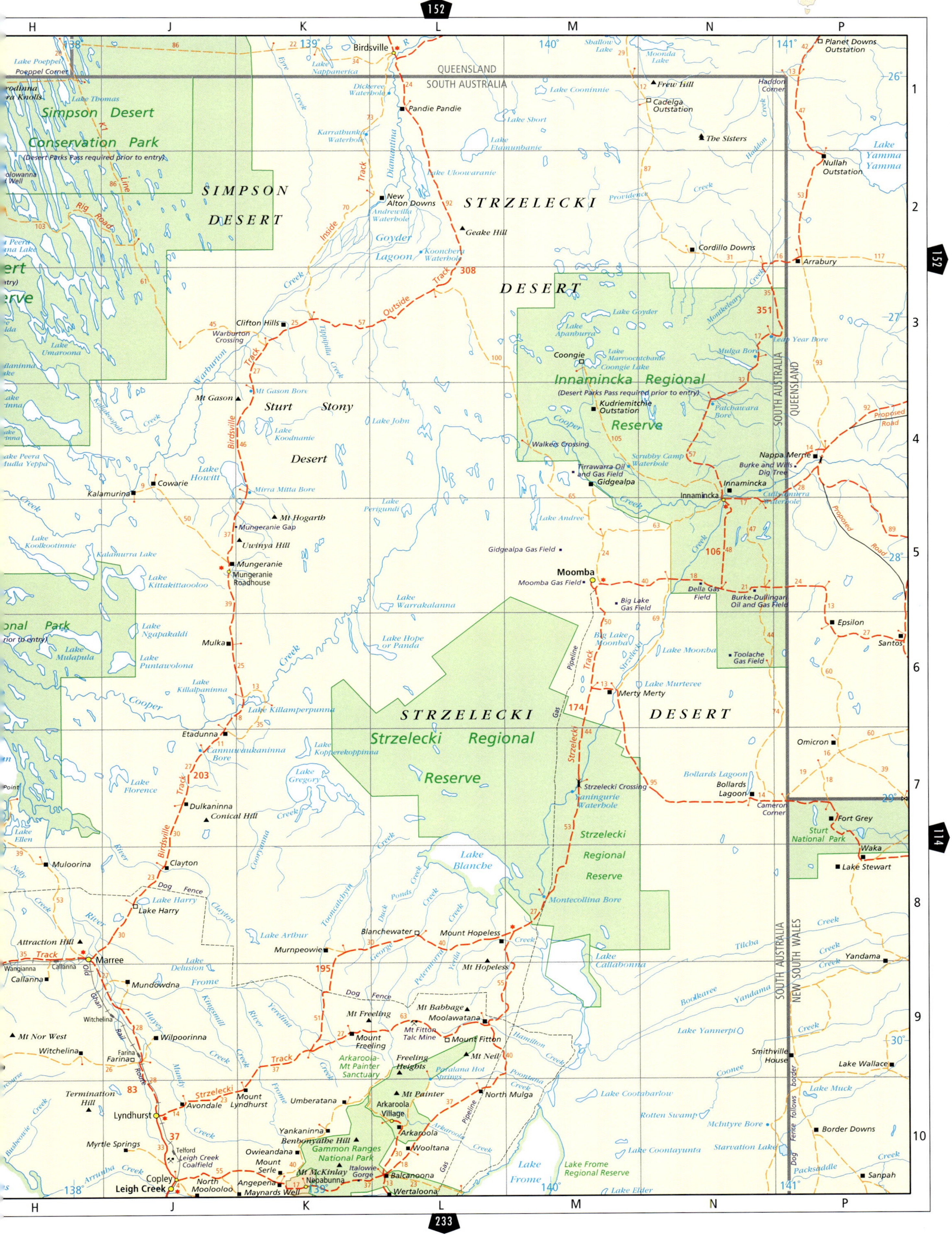
0 20 40 60 80
kilometres
152
233
114
H J K L M N P
1 2 3 4 5 6 7 8 9 10
QUEENSLAND
SOUTH AUSTRALIA
NEW SOUTH WALES
Birdsville
Lake Nappanerica
Poeppel Corner
Lake Poeppel
Lake Thomas
Simpson Desert
Conservation Park
(Desert Parks Pass required prior to entry)
K1 Line
Rig Road
SIMPSON
DESERT
Dickeree Waterhole
Pandie Pandie
Karrathunka Waterhole
Diamantina
Inside Track
New Alton Downs
Andrewilla Waterhole
Goyder Lagoon
Kooncheera Waterhole
Geake Hill
Outside Track
Lake Coorinnie
Lake Short
Lake Etamunbanie
Lake Ulooowaranie
Shallow Lake
Moonda Lake
Frew Hill
Cadelga Outstation
The Sisters
Haddon Corner
Haddon
Providence
Creek
Planet Downs Outstation
Nullah Outstation
Lake Yamma Yamma
Cordillo Downs
Arrabury
STRZELECKI
DESERT
Lake Goyder
Lake Apanburra
Coongie
Lake Marroocutchanie
Coongie Lake
Mulga Bore
Leap Year Bore
Montebeleary
Innamincka Regional Reserve
(Desert Parks Pass required prior to entry)
Kudriemitchie Outstation
Patchawarra Bore
Cooper
Walkers Crossing
Scrubby Camp Waterhole
Tirrawarra Oil and Gas Field
Gidgealpa
Innamincka
Nappa Merrie
Burke and Wills Dig Tree
Cullyamurra Waterhole
Proposed Road
Lake Andree
Gidgealpa Gas Field
Moomba
Moomba Gas Field
Della Gas Field
Burke-Dullingari Oil and Gas Field
Big Lake Gas Field
Epsilon
Santos
Big Lake Moonba
Lake Moonba
Toolache Gas Field
Lake Murteree
Merty Merty
DESERT
Clifton Hills
Warburton Crossing
Warburton
Lake Umaroona
Tippipilla Creek
Mt Gason Bore
Mt Gason
Sturt Stony Desert
Lake Koodnanie
Lake John
Kallakoopah
Lake Howitt
Cowarie
Kalamurina
Mirra Mitta Bore
Lake Perigundi
Mt Hogarth
Mungeranie Gap
Uwinya Hill
Mungeranie
Mungeranie Roadhouse
Birdsville Track
Lake Koolkootinnie
Kalamurra Lake
Lake Kittakittaooloo
Lake Warrakalanna
Lake Ngapakaldi
Lake Mulapula
Lake Puntawolona
Lake Hope or Panda
Mulka
Lake Killalpaninna
Lake Killamperpunna
Cooper
Etadunna
Cannuwaukaninna Bore
Lake Kopperekoppinna
Lake Gregory
Lake Florence
Dulkaninna
Conical Hill
Coongyanna
STRZELECKI
Strzelecki Regional Reserve
Gas Pipeline
Strzelecki Track
Strzelecki Crossing
Yaningurie Waterhole
Strzelecki Regional Reserve
Montecollina Bore
Bollards Lagoon
Cameron Corner
Omicron
Fort Grey
Sturt National Park
Lake Stewart
Waka
Lake Blanche
Muloorina
Clayton
Dog Fence
Lake Harry
Clayton
Toonatchynia
Duck Ponds Creek
Lake Arthur
Blanchewater
Mount Hopeless
Murnpeowie
Mt Hopeless
Lake Callabonna
Attraction Hill
Marree
Track
Wangianna
Callanna
Lake Eyre Delusion
Frome
Mundowdna
Kingsmill
Yerelina
Peternorrna
Dog Fence
Mt Babbage
Moolawatana
Mt Freeling
Mt Fitton Talc Mine
Mount Fitton
Mount Freeling
Hamilton Creek
Mt Neil
Arkaroola-Mt Painter Sanctuary
Freeling Heights
Paralana Hot Springs
Poontana Creek
Mt Nor West
Witchelina
Wilpoorinna
Farina
Hayes
Mundy
Termination Hill
Strzelecki Track
Mount Lyndhurst
Umberatana
Mt Painter
Arkaroola Village
North Mulga
Lyndhurst
Avondale
Yankaninna
Benbonyathe Hill
Gammon Ranges National Park
Arkaroola
Wooltana
Myrtle Springs
Telford
Leigh Creek Coalfield
Owieandana
Mount Serle
Mt McKinlay
Italowie Gorge
Nepabunna
Balcanoona
Copley
Leigh Creek
North Moolooloo
Angepena
Maynards Well
Wertaloona
Lake Frome
Lake Frome Regional Reserve
Lake Elder
Lake Cootabarlow
Rotten Swamp
Lake Coontayunta
Starvation Lake
McIntyre Bore
Lake Yannerpi
Coonee
Bookaree
Yandama
Tilcha
Smithville House
Lake Wallace
Lake Muck
Border Downs
Packsaddle
Sanpah
Fence follows border
Dog Fence
138°
139°
140°
141°
26°
27°
28°
29°
30°

TASMANIA

FISHING HOT SPOTS

- The Derwent Estuary (pp. 238–9)
- The Tasman Peninsula (pp. 240–1)
- Bicheno and the Freycinet Peninsula (pp. 242–3)
- St Helens (pp. 244–5)
- Trout Streams around Launceston (pp. 246–7)
- Arthurs Lake (pp. 248–9)
- Lake Burbury (pp. 250–1)

Tasmania is the smallest state of Australia, with a surface area of slightly more than 68 000 square km and a population of fewer than half a million people. It is also Australia's only island state, divided from the mainland by the often rough and cold waters of Bass Strait.

It has often been said that much of Tasmania has a very European look and feel, with its high, snow-clad mountains, vast forests, natural lakes, rolling green meadows and quaint, country villages. Certainly, parts of it remind one of Switzerland or Austria at first glance, while other areas are vaguely reminiscent of Scotland, or perhaps England's Lakes District. Yet it is also uniquely Antipodean with its unusual fauna and flora, ancient trees, crisp, clean air, striking landforms and very Australian population.

Nonetheless, it is perhaps fitting that this most 'European' part of modern Australia is also the most famous in international sport fishing circles not for the quality and abundance of its native fish species, but rather for the exceptional standard of trout angling which its cool inland rivers and lakes offer.

Brown trout from Europe were successfully introduced to Tasmanian waters after several earlier, failed attempts during the middle of the 19th century, and have thrived in their new home. Later, around the turn of the 20th century, these speckled aristocrats of the sweetwater were joined by their more colourful, rambunctious counterparts from North America—the hard-fighting, high-jumping rainbow trout.

Today, well-established and often self-supporting populations of both brown and rainbow trout—along with pockets of brook trout (brook char) and Atlantic salmon—dominate recreational angling in Tasmania.

The excellent standard of trout fishing on offer throughout Tasmania today attracts growing numbers of local anglers, visitors from the mainland and, increasingly, overseas tourists to the Apple Isle. They come to sample the breathtaking scenery, unpolluted waters, delicious foods and wines, and—most importantly—Tasmania's wild, cunning and extremely challenging trout.

In contrast, keen Tasmanian saltwater anglers remain relatively few in number, and many seem to prefer the use of nets (still legal for amateurs in this state at the time of writing) to rod and reel or line fishing. Similarly, the Apple Island's marine fisheries fail to attract much serious attention from tourists, despite the fact that its nutrient-rich seas actually abound with fish life and offer some very exciting angling opportunities.

There is considerable potential for marine angling around the island's picturesque coastline. A small but growing number of dedicated local anglers are beginning to explore these saltwater possibilities more fully, and they are increasingly being joined by a trickle of interested sea and estuary fishing pioneers from across Bass Strait.

All-in-all, the future for recreational angling in Tasmania appears bright. Not only is the ongoing maintenance of its world-class salmonid fisheries assured, but this is also accompanied by a growing awareness of the riches on offer in the seas surrounding this clean, green island state.

CONTACT NUMBERS

Anyone wishing to obtain information on fishing rules and regulations in Tasmania should contact one of the following organisations.

INLAND FISHERIES COMMISSION
(03) 6223 6622

PARKS AND WILDLIFE
(03) 6233 6556

MARINE RESOURCES (Recreational)
(03) 6233 6234

FISHERMAN'S WATCH
(24 Hours)
1800 005 555

FISHWATCH HOT LINE (24 hours)
1800 815 507

Top: *Looking out over Coles Bay towards The Hazards on the Freycinet Peninsula*
Left: *The Douglas River in Douglas-Apsley National Park near Bicheno on Tasmania's east coast*
Above: *Tasmania is renowned for its trout fishing*

THE DERWENT ESTUARY

IN BRIEF

MAP REFERENCE: PAGE 253 K4

GETTING THERE The Derwent estuary is right on Hobart's doorstep
BEST TIME TO FISH Year-round
BEST TIME TO TRAVEL Year-round
MAJOR ANGLING SPECIES Flathead, whiting, flounder, Australian salmon, barracouta, bream, silver trevally, bastard trumpeter, warehou, trout, garfish, leatherjackets, mullet and squid
SPECIAL RESTRICTIONS Strict rules and regulations apply to the taking of trout and salmon in all Tasmanian waters. Fishing off many city wharves is now also restricted, so check first

While Tasmania is best known for the exceptional standard of its freshwater trout fishing, the Apple Isle's estuaries and coastal waters can also offer excellent fishing opportunities, and this is even true of the relatively busy tidal waterways on Hobart's doorstep.

Hobart is a delightful maritime city with a strong sense of history, and much of it lies along the south-western shores of the River Derwent estuary—a broad, attractive stretch of tidal water with much to offer the angler. The river itself attracts its fair share of recreational anglers.

The Constitution Dock area and harbour foreshores represent a very popular venue for fisherfolk of all ages and levels of expertise—especially when there's a strong 'run' of schooling migratory fish such as silver trevally, warehou (snotty trevalla) or barracouta in attendance. At such times, it can be standing room only on the more productive piers and rocky points. However, for much of the year, the lower Derwent and Hobart foreshore region is delightfully devoid of crowds, and it's almost always possible to find a quiet cove or bay to cast a line.

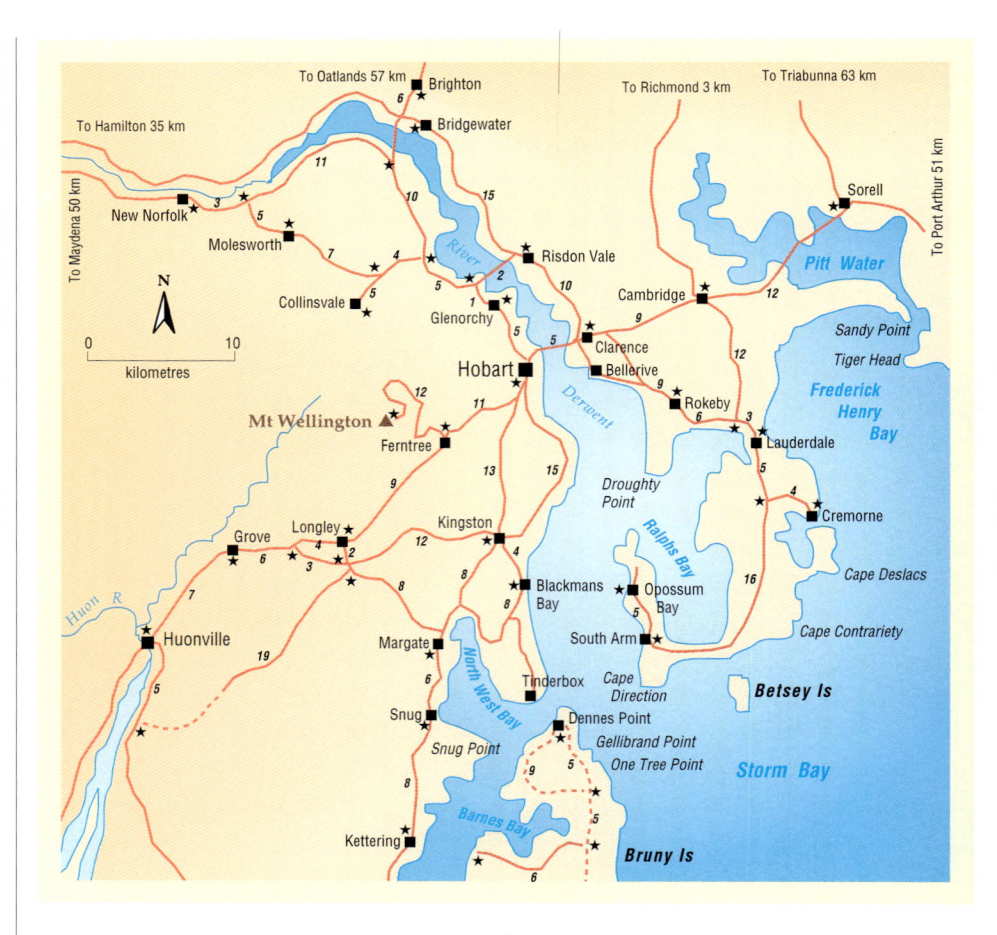

FISH OF THE DERWENT

Tasmania's Derwent estuary has a lot to offer both the local and visiting angler, from 200-g trout and 1-kg southern bream to 100-kg thresher sharks!

Along the lower Derwent, there are abundant bays and coves, all of which produce fish at different times of the year. Boat and shore-based anglers typically target the region's prolific flathead, sea perch, rock cod, barracouta, warehou (snotty trevally), school whiting, silver trevally, Australian salmon and squid, as well as sea-run trout (particularly in winter and spring) and 'escapee' Atlantic salmon from the various fish farms of southern Tasmania, when these are available.

There are two main types of flathead present in the River Derwent: the sand flathead and the king or tiger flathead. The sand flathead is the more common of the two. It is caught mostly from boats and jetties, and off various beaches along the lower reaches of the river. Tiger flathead are caught in the same general areas, but seem to prefer slightly deeper water and are mostly landed by boat anglers.

The best approach for both species is to drift (if fishing from a boat) or slowly retrieve line if shore casting. Top baits include fillets or strips of fish flesh, especially those taken from oily species such as barracouta or cowanyoung (known locally as horse mackerel).

Today, many sport fishers prefer to cast and retrieve or troll for flathead using lures, jigs or flies on relatively light tackle. These techniques also turn up other species, including barracouta, Australian salmon and the odd sea-run trout.

Barracouta are often encountered in the river in large numbers, and may turn up anywhere from the mouth of the estuary upstream to the Bowen Bridge. They are actively targeted by many locals, who enjoy their pink, slightly oily flesh either cooked or smoked.

The best methods for catching barracouta include bait fishing under floats, spinning and trolling, with a fine wire trace being essential to prevent repeated bite-offs, regardless of the technique employed.

Fishing boats at Constitution Dock on Hobart's River Derwent

Although welcomed by some anglers, barracouta will often take baits, lures and flies intended for other fish, and can sometimes make a nuisance of themselves.

Large silver trevally are other occasional visitors to the Derwent. With some of these hard-fighting fish running between 3 and 4 kg, it's not surprising that their appearance—even if it only lasts a week or two—attracts so much local attention. Although these fish will respond to a range of baits, many anglers prefer to target the bigger trevally with lures such as chrome spoons.

Each year, usually in late summer or autumn, schools of warehou, known locally as snotty trevalla, also enter the River Derwent. Once again, it doesn't take long for word of their arrival to sweep through the fishing grapevine, and hundreds of anglers soon line Macquarie Wharf and the surrounding areas of shoreline in pursuit of these very tasty table fish.

Bellerive Marina on the River Derwent, with Mount Wellington in the background

Good catches of warehou are regularly taken at such times, usually with the aid of a little berley. Floating or lightly weighted baits are most effective, although offerings fished on or near the sea bed can work well on occasion. Warehou also respond well to small lures and flies. With an average weight of 500 g to 1.5 kg, they provide good sport, as well as an excellent meal.

The warehou's eating qualities are good when fresh, whether fried, baked, grilled or smoked. However, warehou don't keep well and become rather soft after freezing, so it's best to take only enough fish for your immediate needs and resist the temptation to amass a 'cricket score' catch.

Southern bream are reasonably common in the Derwent estuary, too, most notably in the middle reaches between Bridgewater and the Bowen Bridge area. This stretch of river is particularly productive for bream in winter and spring. Later, around Christmas and New Year, good bream are often encountered further downstream, around the wharves and docks of Hobart itself—especially if there's been a reasonable amount of spring and summer rainfall.

Best bream baits include prawns, 'pretty fish', cut fish flesh, crabs, mussels and shrimps. These should be fished on fine, lightly weighted lines.

The vast majority of bream catches are made from shore-based locations such as boat docks, jetties and rocky points, and bream anglers often score a welcome bonus in the form of a silvery sea trout or two. Sea-run trout are a highly prized catch in the Derwent estuary, and are being targeted by a small but growing band of devotees.

These fish are mostly estuary-dwelling brown trout, or fish that descend briefly into brackish water from areas further upstream towards New Norfolk or Macquarie Plains. However, the occasional rainbow and Atlantic salmon escaped from nearby fish farms may also be encountered, adding considerable spice to proceedings.

Sea-trout fishing often peaks between September and Christmas, although a few of these attractive, hard-fighting and delicious fish are present in the lower Derwent all year round and will succumb to lures, flies and small dead baits such as whole 'pretty fish'.

Remember, however, that the taking of trout and salmon in Tasmanian waters is governed by a reasonably complex set of rules and regulations. You should carefully check the current status of these laws before targeting salmonids—in either fresh or salt water.

Derwent Hot Spots

Fishing hot spots within the Derwent estuary include the Piersons Point–Iron Pot area, which marks the effective downstream extremity of the estuary and offers access to the more open waters of Storm Bay, with its mix of inshore and offshore species. There is a good boat ramp at Tinderbox, but anglers fishing this stretch should note the existence of a marine reserve running between Tinderbox and Bruny Island.

Ralphs Bay is a large, reasonably enclosed area of water on the lower estuary's eastern side, noted for its big flathead, as well as mullet, Australian salmon and the odd escapee Atlantic salmon. Punchs Reef, just off Tranmere and not far from the Tasman Bridge, is a popular location for boat anglers seeking cod, morwong, trevally, garfish and Australian salmon. Trevally are also targeted from the shore here, especially around Bellerive and Howrah. Sandy Bay is readily fished from both shore and boat, and offers flathead, garfish, mullet, morwong and Australian salmon.

The stretch of river from the Tasman to Bowen bridges is not as highly rated as the lower Derwent estuary, but some good bream come from the Lindisfarne Bay area at times, and there are always a few sea trout (sea-run browns) to be had from August until October.

Otago Bay, upstream of Bowen Bridge on the eastern shore, produces some stud bream each year, including the odd one on lures and flies. Trout—both sea-run and resident—are also available here throughout much of the year.

Above Bridgewater and up towards New Norfolk, the major target species are bream and trout. Trout are at their best from September until Christmas, with the bream taking over in summer and early autumn. It should be noted, however, that fishing is only permitted here during the trout open season, and adults must hold a current inland angling licence when fishing in these waters.

THE TASMAN PENINSULA

IN BRIEF

MAP REFERENCE: PAGE 253 M6

GETTING THERE Eaglehawk Neck is 100 km south-east of Hobart along the Tasman and Arthur highways
BEST TIME TO FISH September to May
BEST TIME TO TRAVEL Year-round
MAJOR ANGLING SPECIES Flathead, trumpeter, barracouta, morwong, cod, Australian salmon, albacore, bluefin tuna, sharks and marlin
WARNINGS Violent weather changes are likely at any time on Tasmanian ocean waters and huge swells and high seas are always possible, especially further south. Care should also be exercised when crossing bars at harbour or river entrances

Best known as the site of Port Arthur—one of Australia's most infamous convict settlements—the Tasman Peninsula is a relatively large area of maritime land joined to the main body of south-eastern Tasmania by a very narrow neck or isthmus near Dunalley. This natural land bridge separates Blackman Bay to the north-east from Norfolk Bay in the south-west, and an artificial canal at this point offers small vessels a welcome shortcut on their way to and from Hobart.

Further south, the Tasman Peninsula is almost cut in two again at picturesque Eaglehawk Neck, where 100 m or less of rocky and sandy land divide the comparatively sheltered waters of Eaglehawk Bay from the often rough open ocean of the Tasman Sea itself. Strictly speaking, the area north of this isthmus is known as the Forestier Peninsula, although most people speak of the entire region simply as the Tasman Peninsula.

Major and minor settlements on the peninsula include Murdunna, Eaglehawk Neck, Penzance, Taranna, Port Arthur, Nubeena and Premaydena, although the permanent population of each of these centres is relatively small. However, visitors greatly swell the peninsula's resident population, especially in summer.

RICH SOUTHERN SEAS

The continental shelf off this awe-inspiring stretch of coast is narrow and full of dramatic physical features. Regular upwellings of cold water mixing with warmer currents from the north during the first six months of the year also ensure massive concentrations of bait species such as cowanyoung (horse mackerel) and squid, which in turn attract many larger predators.

Weather permitting, the offshore sea fishing can be exceptionally good here. Migratory pelagic species such as albacore, skipjack (striped) tuna and even the occasional yellowfin tuna begin to arrive off the Tasman Peninsula in late January or early February, and are soon joined by sharks of several species and reasonable numbers of large striped marlin.

Most of the albacore encountered off the Tasman Peninsula weigh between 2 and 8 kg, although some will run to 15 or even 20 kg, and possibly more. Most are taken on trolled lures, and they are found closer to the coast here than almost anywhere else in Australia.

A little further offshore, there are also known to be quantities of broadbill swordfish, although recreational anglers are yet to target this most highly prized of billfish seriously in these southern waters. Striped marlin can also be reasonably abundant here on occasion, and are being hooked in increasing numbers as angling pressure increases and becomes more sophisticated.

Barracouta are incredibly prolific at various times in these cool waters. This can be seen as either a boon or a bane, depending upon your attitude towards these long, skinny and tooth-some fish. At certain times, it can be almost impossible to target other species successfully with a bait or lure when a 'razor gang' of hungry barracouta is present.

THE BLUEFIN RUN

Towards the end of February or early March, the first waves of southern bluefin tuna arrive in the waters off the Tasman Peninsula in numbers. It is these handsome, hard-fighting pelagic fish that are most highly prized by south-east Tasmanian game and sport fishers.

These early arrivals are mainly 'schoolies'—bluefin from 10 to 20 kg—but there is also likely to be the occasional 'bottle fish' (a specimen weighing more than 45 kg) mixed in with them.

The chances of encountering a 'bottle' or 'two bottle' (90-kg plus) southern bluefin tuna increase as the season progresses through March and into April or early May. In fact, southern bluefin tuna of more than 150 kg have been taken off Eaglehawk Neck at this time of year.

In good seasons, big bluefin tuna may still be caught in late May, but by the end of that month or early June, it is generally too bitter, cold and rough for most amateur anglers to even think about venturing out to sea!

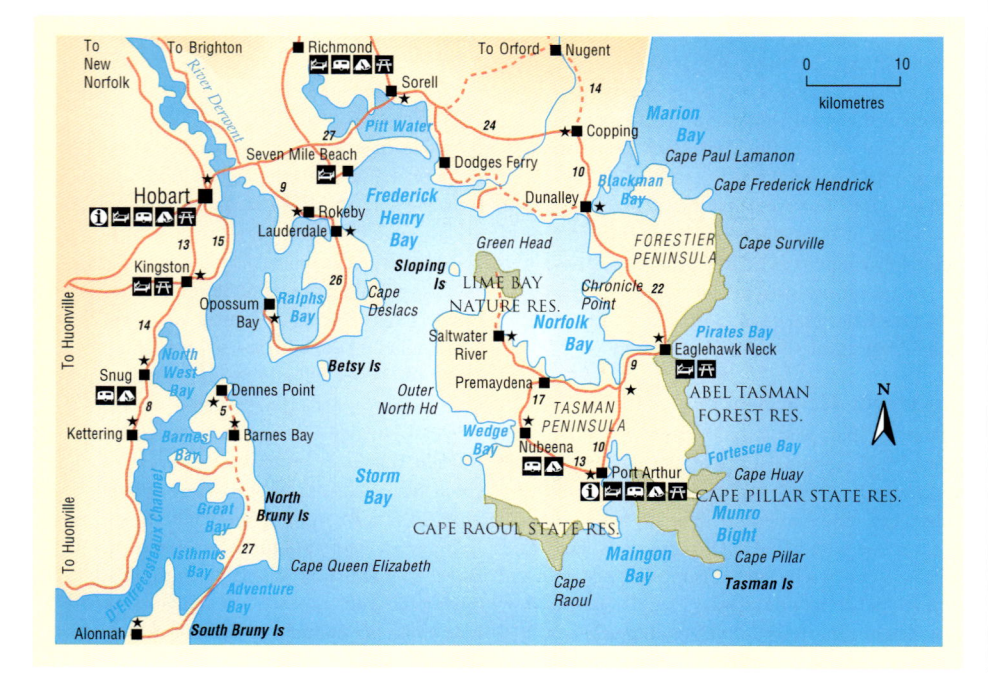

The Devils Kitchen near Eaglehawk Neck

Tasman Peninsula Hot Spots

Hot spots for most of the pelagic species include the reef-strewn waters around the Hippolyte Rocks, off Fortescue Bay, as well as the area off The Lanterns and the deeper waters east and south of Cape Pillar and Tasman Island, with its inspiring sea cliffs and remote lighthouse.

Bottom fishing in the same general areas produces flathead, cod, ling, Tasmanian or striped trumpeter, morwong, wrasse and several other species, with the big, delicious trumpeter— weighing up to 20 kg and even more at times— being amongst the most sought-after of all piscatorial targets in this region.

The shallower, more sheltered waters of Norfolk and Frederick Henry bays, on the Tasman Peninsula's western side, also hold prolific numbers of flathead, flounder and mullet. In fact, enclosed water fishing for flathead, small to medium Australian salmon, flounder, mullet and big southern bream is also good in the bays and estuaries along many other parts of this coast. Further upstream, most rivers in the south-east contain at least some wild, sea-going brown trout and small numbers of Atlantic salmon and rainbow trout that have escaped from the floating pens of nearby fish farms.

A good boat ramp is available at Pirates Ba. While another ramp at Fortescue Bay offers more immediate access to the best fishing grounds, it also lies at the end of an often rough gravel road. A third boat ramp at Garden Point, south of Port Arthur, is best suited to those wishing to confine their activities to the Tasman Island area.

A trailer boat trolling near The Lanterns on the Tasman Peninsula

A Weather Eye

Weather is a major factor when considering any sea fishing opportunities in the far south-east of Tasmania, and great care should always be exercised, especially by boat fishers. Antarctic gales from the south and south-west can strike without much warning, making these some of the roughest and most treacherous ocean waters in the world.

The most stable climatic period in the south-east tends to run from mid- or late February until the end of March. At this time, the sea may be relatively kind and the skies blue for days or even weeks at a time, although there is certainly no iron-clad guarantee of this!

Looking across to the lighthouse on Tasman Island near Cape Pillar on the Tasman Peninsula

BICHENO AND THE FREYCINET PENINSULA

IN BRIEF

MAP REFERENCE: PAGE 255 P9

GETTING THERE Bicheno is 180 km north-east of Hobart along the Tasman Highway. Freycinet National Park lies 39 km south of Bicheno — there is limited vehicular access within the park
BEST TIME TO FISH September to June
BEST TIME TO TRAVEL Year-round
MAJOR ANGLING SPECIES Flathead, Australian salmon, bream, morwong, trumpeter, albacore, tuna, sharks and rock lobsters
WARNINGS Violent weather changes are likely at any time on Tasmanian ocean waters and huge swells and high seas are always possible

View of Carp Bay from Cape Tourville, on the eastern side of the Freycinet Peninsula

While St Helens to the north and the Tasman Peninsula further south tend to be better known as top-class saltwater angling destinations — particularly when it comes to offshore sport and game fishing — Tasmania's mid-east coast, around Bicheno, Great Oyster Bay and the Freycinet Peninsula, also offers some tremendous fishing opportunities in very picturesque and sparsely populated surroundings.

With a permanent population of just 700 or so inhabitants, the seaside village of Bicheno itself is a busy fishing port with a fascinating maritime history. Once an important staging point for whalers and sealers from around the world, most of the commercial fishing effort off Bicheno these days is focused on the capture or harvest of southern rock lobsters, abalone and various finfish such as the highly prized orange roughy.

Recreational anglers working out of this harbour in tough, seaworthy boats chase seasonal pelagic fishes such as albacore and various tuna, as well as bread-and-butter species including flathead, cod, morwong, trevally, trumpeter, Australian salmon, wrasse (blue-throated parrot fish) and the ever-present barracouta.

Recreational snorkelling and scuba diving are also popular pursuits in the cool, clear waters off Bicheno, and several of the region's charter fishing vessels double as dive boats.

Rock lobsters or crayfish are a favourite target with many recreational fishers and divers, as well as the commercial sector, and are taken by hand as well as in pots or with rings. Abalone harvesting is also actively pursued by recreational anglers. However, strict regulations apply to the taking of these extremely valuable crustaceans and molluscs, and the current rules should be carefully checked before attempting to take either lobsters or abalone.

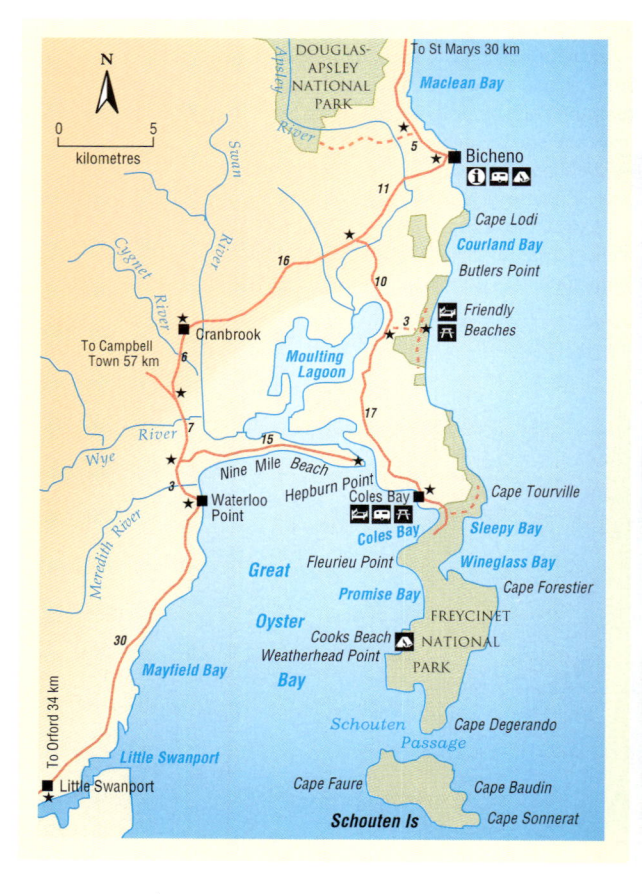

FREYCINET PENINSULA AND SCHOUTEN ISLAND

The scenic Freycinet Peninsula and Schouten Island lie south of Bicheno, forming the Freycinet National Park. Wineglass Bay, on the eastern side of the peninsula, is a particularly striking seaside location, and one that features regularly in tourist brochures, posters and advertisements for the state of Tasmania. To the west of the Freycinet Peninsula, Great Oyster Bay and the town of Swansea enjoy a reasonable amount of shelter from east and north-east winds, and are popular destinations with anglers seeking flathead, squid and other inshore species, including isolated pockets of whiting.

The main pier at Swansea and another at Coles Bay can both offer excellent catches of squid, as well as small Australian salmon, pike

A pair of sizeable Tasmanian trumpeter

and cowanyoung (horse mackerel). Mayfield Beach and Little Swanport are also worth a try for the same species.

The estuaries in this area—especially the Swan River—also contain some very good southern bream populations, as well as large garfish and tasty leatherjackets.

The Friendly Beaches, which lie between Bicheno and the Freycinet Peninsula, are well known for their surf fishing. Good catches of Australian salmon are sometimes taken here, as well as the odd gummy shark.

Schouten Passage, between Schouten Island and the peninsula, is often turbulent and difficult to fish, but produces big flathead, wrasse and the odd Tasmanian trumpeter.

Further south, the tip of Schouten Island is home to schools of ravenous barracouta, while further offshore, albacore, southern bluefin and yellowfin tuna and several species of shark are available seasonally.

SHORE-BASED FISHING VARIETY

As with most Tasmania's east coast, jetty and rock fishing are available throughout this region, with sweep, Australian salmon, ling, cod, flathead, blue-throated parrot fish (wrasse), barracouta, pike and snook on offer, along with seasonal runs of warehou or snotty trevalla, and silver trevally.

There are also some as yet almost untouched fisheries for luderick (blackfish) here at sizes that would be regarded as very impressive indeed on the Australian mainland!

Right: View from Coles Bay towards the Hazards on the Freycinet Peninsula
Below: Fishing boats at anchor in the harbour of the small settlement of Bicheno

ST HELENS

IN BRIEF

MAP REFERENCE: PAGE 255 P6

GETTING THERE St Helens is 260 km north north-east of Hobart along the Tasman Highway, and about 160 km east of Launceston
BEST TIME TO FISH September to June
BEST TIME TO TRAVEL Year-round
MAJOR ANGLING SPECIES Flathead, garfish, Australian salmon, morwong, albacore, tuna, sharks and marlin
WARNINGS Violent weather changes are likely at any time on Tasmanian ocean waters and huge swells and high seas are always possible. Care should be exercised when crossing bars at harbour or river entrances, such as the one near St Helens
ACCOMMODATION Facilities ranging from hotels and self-contained cabins to campsites can be found in and around St Helens

Nestled at the back of Georges Bay, on Tasmania's temperate north-east coast, is the town of St Helens. St Helens is regarded as the unofficial capital of what some people have described — only partly in jest — as the Apple Isle's 'Riviera'.

There is certainly no denying that the climate here is generally much more mild than anywhere else in this southern island state, and the region experiences longer summers and less severe winters than the rest of Tasmania.

The saltwater fishing around St Helens can be exceptionally good, too, and it is increasingly being seen — both at home and further afield — as the saltwater sport and game fishing epicentre of Tasmania, with a reputation for producing consistent catches of many species using a wide range of tackle and techniques.

PELAGIC NOMADS

As well as abundant resident reef and bottom fish, the St Helens area also experiences a regular influx of migratory species each season.

From about the end of January, relatively warm ocean currents from the north begin to lick the east coast of Tasmania, bringing with them pelagic fishes from the temperate and subtropical seas further north. These seasonal visitors include albacore, several types of tuna, sharks and even marlin. All of these predators are particularly abundant around some of the reef patches and banks east and south-east of the harbour entrance at St Helens, including famous grounds such as Merricks, as well as further offshore, towards the edge of the relatively narrow continental shelf.

When the warm ocean currents run hard here in February and March, vast schools of albacore, skipjack (striped) tuna and yellowfin tuna are often evident, along with mako and blue sharks and more than the odd striped marlin. Bluefin tuna also visit these waters in late summer and autumn, although they are not generally as large nor as numerous as the bluefin encountered further south.

Looking across Beerbarrel Beach near St Helens

A pair of yellowfin tuna taken while trolling off St Helens in north-eastern Tasmania

REEF AND BOTTOM FISHING

Reef and bottom fishing off St Helens is also extremely productive, and regularly produces good catches of flathead, cod, morwong, gurnard and barracouta, as well as the occasional large silver trevally, bastard and striped trumpeter and even small to mid-size yellowtail kingfish and decent gummy sharks on occasion.

Hot spots for both bottom and sport or game fishing include Merricks, Pulfers, Middle Ground and Eddystone reefs, all of which rise abruptly from moderately deep water and hold vast numbers of bait fish and squid, which in turn attract larger predators.

Further offshore, big striped trumpeter, blue-eye trevalla, hapuka and similar deep-water delicacies can be added to this list. Broadbill swordfish, thresher sharks and several other big game prizes are also known to lurk here.

Boat anglers fishing along this stretch of coast are well serviced, with five boat ramps currently available, including three in Georges Bay, one at Binalong Bay and one at Burns Bay. The last two ramps mentioned offer direct ocean access in suitable weather, eliminating the need to negotiate the sometimes treacherous St Helens bar.

ESTUARY AND BAY ACTION

Inshore, the Georges River, Georges Bay and, more notably, the Scamander River estuary a little further south, are renowned for their stocks of big southern bream, including more than a few fish well above the 1.5-kg mark.

Juvenile Australian salmon, massive garfish and even some of the less common Tasmanian species, such as luderick and small snapper, are also prolific in most north-eastern estuarine areas such as Georges Bay at times, and provide excellent sport and many delicious meals.

ROCK AND BEACH FISHING

Local beaches, headlands and rocky points, particularly those running north from St Helens for 15 km or so, are all capable of providing excellent angling. This is especially the case for good-sized Australian salmon to 3 kg and better, as well as mixed bags of mullet, flathead, skate and gummy sharks.

Shallow, reef-strewn areas along this lightly fished stretch of shoreline also produce good numbers of leatherjackets, wrasse (blue-throated parrot fish), pike and bastard trumpeter, to name just a few of the more common varieties regularly encountered here.

St Helens makes the perfect base for any saltwater fishing holiday, and has something to offer anglers of all persuasions and all levels of skill or commitment.

TROUT STREAMS AROUND LAUNCESTON

IN BRIEF

MAP REFERENCE: PAGE 255 K6

GETTING THERE All streams described here lie within 45 minutes drive of central Launceston
BEST TIME TO FISH Entire trout season (see p. 390)
BEST TIME TO TRAVEL Year-round
MAJOR ANGLING SPECIES Brown trout
SPECIAL RESTRICTIONS Seek permission before fishing on private property. Access from bridges does not necessarily give you the right to fish a property or river. If property owners are asked politely, permission to fish is rarely denied
ACCOMMODATION Accommodation of all levels is available, from camping to four-star hotels in Launceston; colonial cottage and riverside accommodation is also available in several locations

The Launceston area contains many of Tasmania's best trout fishing streams: from the Macquarie River—famous for its red spinner hatch—to the North Esk, South Esk, Meander and St Patricks rivers. All these streams and several others besides offer excellent sport.

Macquarie River

The Macquarie is arguably Tasmania's most famous trout stream. Starting at Tooms Lake, the Macquarie River is what David Scholes describes in *Fly Fisher in Tasmania* as a 'flat river'. Nowhere along its length is it bubbling and boisterous.

From the very beginning of the trout season in August, the Macquarie produces fish. When the winter and spring floods break the banks and water covers the adjacent flats, trout move out to feed. A virtual smorgasbord of grubs, beetles, worms and other food is suddenly available and the fish take full advantage of this.

A small brown trout taken on a minnow-style lure

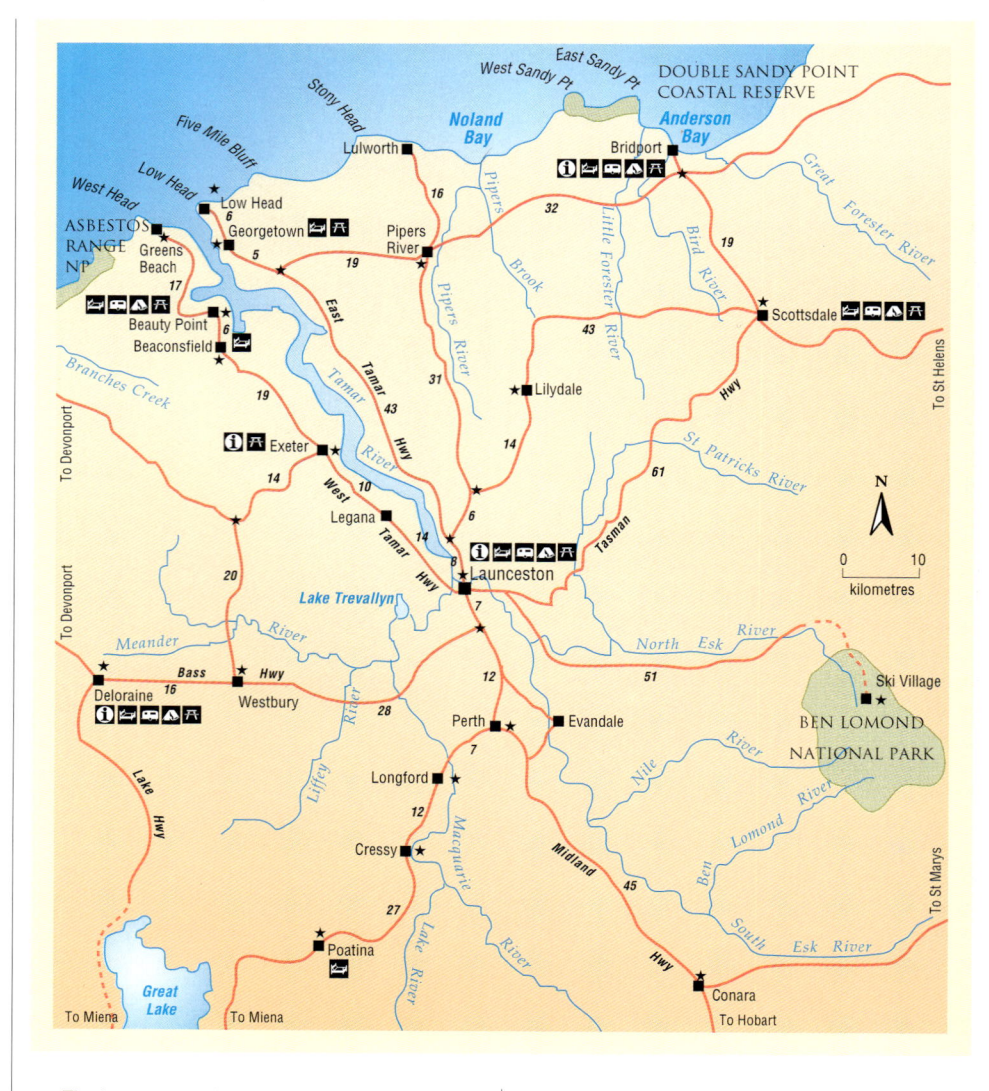

The best time to fish the floods is when the river is still rising and filling the depressions and backwaters. Look for areas without water flowing too strongly through them as they flood. Once the level starts to drop, the fish move quickly back to the main river channel. During flooding, a worm or wet fly such as a Woolly Worm or Wigram's Robin is usually all that is necessary to produce some good action.

The Macquarie River is at its best in October and November, and again in March and April, when the red spinner hatch brings out both the trout and ardent fly fishers. Due to the open nature of this river, calm weather is necessary, as a breeze can quickly ruin a fly fisher's day.

Above Cressy, the Macquarie often suffers from low flow levels during summer, while below this it is replenished with large volumes of water from the Poatina power station that flows through Brumbys Creek for most of the summer.

The Macquarie is most highly regarded as a fly fishing water, but there are no restrictions on methods and both lure and bait fishers also enjoy the fruits of their labours.

It should be noted that the bag limit is five fish per day on the Macquarie River.

Brumbys Creek

Despite the impression created by its name, Brumbys Creek is really three small impoundments held back by low weirs.

Brumbys' water level is quite variable, as it is supplied with water from Great Lake via Poatina power station. This can lead to levels that vary not only day to day, but also often by the hour.

Regardless of the water level, the fishing can be tremendous, with fish of 2 kg and better taken regularly and fish of up to 5 kg available below the bottom weir. The top weir is open to fishing with flies and artificial lures only. Access to all the weirs is excellent.

South Esk River

The South Esk is an excellent water that is largely underfished. From its headwaters at the back of Ben Lomond throughout its 200-km length to Lake Trevallyn, almost in the centre of Launceston, this river offers fine trout fishing.

Much of the South Esk is quite a distance from the road, but if property owners are politely asked, permission to fish is rarely denied. All accepted fishing methods are popular here, including bait, lure and fly fishing.

Although the fish in the upper reaches, above Mathinna, are small they can be quite challenging. Below Mathinna, fish of 2 kg are often caught in the many riffles, runs and pools. Pools and runs continue all the way downstream to below Perth. It is only in the last few kilometres that the river becomes wider, the pools much bigger and wading impossible. There is quite some pressure on the river by farmers for irrigation and, at the height of summer, flows can become rather low.

The best fishing is from Evandale to Mathinna. Black spinner hatches start in September, followed by red spinner hatches, beetle falls and grasshoppers. During autumn, ant falls are common.

For the fly fisher, this variety can bring both rewards and frustration when trying to fool a trout. However, black spinners (fly patterns) in several sizes will bring most fish undone.

By far the most popular lure is a small metal spinner, while a humble garden worm will usually reward the bait fisher. Summer is also the time for grasshoppers and it is then that both fly and bait fishers make the most of the presence of these insects.

Fighting a brown trout on the South Esk River

Meander River

The Meander River rises at the foot of the Western Tiers and flows into the South Esk River at Hadspen, west of Launceston.

The headwaters of this river are stony, broken riffles that can be fished with fly, bait or small spinning blade lures. These waters can be quite productive all the way down to Deloraine and, although the fish are small, large bags can be expected. Sizes vary, with fish up to 500 g being common.

From a few kilometres above Deloraine all the way to Hadspen, the Meander River flows through pastures with many long, deep pools and short riffles. Much of the river is difficult to access, although some of it is now being cleared of riverside willows.

Early mornings and evenings are the best time to fish. In the bigger pools, specimens of up to 1.5 kg are taken at these times of day. October and November produce the best fishing, and action is good again in autumn.

Like many of Tasmania's rivers, the Meander River suffers from low summer flows, while flood fishing at any time of the year is often exceptional. For those anglers catching the river as it floods, the banks can be very productive, with fish searching the many flats for food.

St Patricks River

St Patricks River is a delightful small stream that flows into the North Esk River at Watery Plains. Unlike many of the other rivers around Launceston, the St Pat's, as it is better known, fishes well during the height of summer. This is largely due to a canopy of trees that keep the water cool. It is not until summer that the water warms and the trout here become really active.

The most productive area of this river is in the Diddleum Plains region, where large bags can be caught on worms, small lures or any small fly. A modest, self-sustaining population of rainbows is also present in the upper reaches of the St Patricks River, alongside the resident browns.

North Esk River

Another delightful stream that deserves close attention is the North Esk. Curling around the back of Mount Barrow, this river, like the South

A brown trout taken on fly tackle

Esk, ends its journey in the city of Launceston. For most of its length, the North Esk is a series of pools, riffles and runs. Some areas are accessible to fly and lure, but many others are almost completely overgrown with willows.

The upper section—down to the Burns Creek bridge—has some excellent fishing. Fly, lure and bait anglers all do well at times and even in summer there is usually a reasonable flow.

Sight fishing to trout is the ultimate sport here, and during late summer grasshoppers bring the bigger fish out to feed. Look for pasture up to the edge of the river for the best grasshopper fishing.

Fly fishers should use a black beetle, black spinner, Royal Wulff or nymph for best results. In the mid- to lower section of the river, a few huge trout to 4.5 kg are taken each year on wattle grubs. These big fish usually only appear at night in the large, deep holes, when most anglers are off the river.

In the tidal reaches below St Leonards, large sea-run and estuary-dwelling trout are also caught during the August to October period, as they chase whitebait up the river. Baits or lures are generally the best way to fool these big fish.

ARTHURS LAKE

IN BRIEF

MAP REFERENCE: PAGE 255 J9

GETTING THERE Arthurs Lake lies south of Launceston in the Western Tiers region — it is 115 km from Launceston and about 130 km from Hobart
BEST TIME TO FISH Entire trout season (see p. 390)
BEST TIME TO TRAVEL September to May
MAJOR ANGLING SPECIES Brown trout
WARNINGS There are many submerged rocks and stumps in this lake, especially in the Cowpaddock area as the water drops below 2 m from full. Most are not marked. Proceed with caution when within 100 m of shore. All streams flowing into the lake are closed to fishing, as is the water for a 50-m radius around the mouth
ACCOMMODATION Great Lake Hotel is only 15 minutes drive away, telephone (03) 6259 8163; Compleat Angler Lodge, 15 minutes drive away, telephone (03) 6259 8179; camping grounds are located at Pump House Bay and Jonah Bay. The grounds at Pump House Bay have showers, water and toilets, while at Jonah Bay only toilets are provided. Informal camping occurs at many other places around the lake — this is not encouraged

Arthurs Lake is, without doubt, Tasmania's premier trout fishery. It produces magnificent fishing from the start of the trout season until the very end. Access is also very good and all legal methods are open to anglers, including bait fishing, lure casting, trolling and fly fishing. Arthurs Lake holds brown trout only and these fish are totally self-sustaining.

Covering an area of 6460 ha, Arthurs Lake is quite large, yet it is not an excessively deep lake, the maximum depth being around 8 m. Originally, the lake was made up of two separate bodies of water: Sand Lake and Blue Lake. A small dam was built across the Lake River outfall in 1922–23, but it was not until 1964 that a 15-m high dam was completed and, in 1965, the two lakes became one. Today the only water that flows down the original Lake River (via Woods Lake) is for riparian water rights, the bulk of the water being pumped uphill into Great Lake. The Hydro Electric Corporation then gains better use of the water from Great Lake through the Poatina power station.

During the trout fishing season of 1966, the average weight of fish from Arthurs climbed to about 2.7 kg — probably the highest ever for this region. More recently, during the season of 1996–97, the average was still excellent at something more than 1.5 kg, with 2-kg fish common and an occasional 3- to 4-kg trout being taken. This is very good for a water that receives some of the heaviest angling pressure in Tasmania.

PRODUCTIVE METHODS

Arthurs Lake can be fished using any legal method, from a boat or from the shore. Top techniques include 'polaroiding', spinning from the shore and drift spinning. In fact, there is fishing here for everyone. There are midge hatches, mayfly hatches and caddis hatches, and it doesn't matter how many boats are on the lake, there is always plenty of room.

December is probably the best month of all for Arthurs, as the fish can be found right in along the shore, while later they move away into deeper water. The mayfly hatches also really get under way early to mid-December.

To be successful, it is important for anglers to investigate all methods and options here. Too many people fish with little thought as to what the fish are doing. Lure anglers all too often stick with one lure or one type of lure when changing could make all the difference. If there is no action on a shallow swimming lure, try a deep diver instead. Move around, too. Try fishing the rough, windswept shores for a change, and remember that what works one day won't necessarily work the next. Experimentation is the key.

BAIT FISHING

Traditionally, bait fishing at Arthurs Lake was done with wattle grubs, and these are available at most tackle shops. Lately, though, mudeye (dragonfly larvae) fishing has taken on a higher

A brown trout taken from Arthurs Lake

profile. This has probably been due to increased availability of mudeyes through tackle stores. (Note that it is illegal to catch mudeyes and use them for bait except in the water you are fishing.)

Mudeyes are uncommon in Arthurs, therefore they must usually be bought from a tackle store. The favoured method is to use a greased line of 2 to 3 kg with the bait suspended under a bubble float. A size 10 to 12 hook is most common. Try any area around the many flooded trees. This method is probably the most productive and consistent of all in Arthurs Lake.

MIDGE HATCHES

One of the best times to fish Arthurs is when a midge hatch occurs. There are seldom many boats out at these times, and there is often lots of action. These hatches occur from early October onwards. First light is best and you need to be on the water before dawn.

All areas of Arthurs Lake have midge hatches and probably the best is the one known as The Morass. Fish can be difficult to catch, though. If they won't take a dry, try a small, black sinking nymph and move it slightly as the fish approaches. A small black beetle will also often work and much of the time it is possible to use a Red Tag. Presentation is more important than imitation, and the importance of this cannot be overemphasised.

The midge hatch is usually over by 9 a.m., but warm evenings can also be spectacular for midges. The shore in the lee of the land is best by far, especially after a day that is not too windy. Take the boat into the shore and then drift out. If there is no action, try the rough shore or cast a wet fly.

MAYFLY HATCHES

Mayfly hatches occur from early December until late February. This fishing commonly occurs during 'office hours' — from 10 a.m. until 4 p.m — although sometimes it can go through until 6 or 7 p.m. The mayfly dun hatch can be spectacular. Overcast conditions are best and rain or storms won't stop the hatch — in fact, they often make it better!

Drifting in a boat is the most popular method and, once again, the presentation is more important than the fly pattern selected. Probably the best fly to employ is a size 12 emerger pattern or a dun, clipped off underneath so that it floats low in the water. A floating nymph is also used by many anglers and is as good as any fly.

The best areas for fishing the mayfly hatch are Cowpaddock, The Opening, Jonah Bay, Seven Pound Bay, Duck Bay, Creely Bay, The Morass and Hydro Bay.

GUM BEETLES

Gum beetles can arrive on the water on any warm day, although some say that their appearance is most likely two days after a cold snap. This can happen from 11.30 a.m. and it is best when there are just a few on the water. The Morass area is best during a gum beetle fall and this is where the largest fish in the lake live.

If the beetle fall is too large it can be very short lived and can often ruin fishing for a couple of days. A Red Tag up to a size 10 is a great fly during a gum beetle fall.

LURE FISHING

When it comes to lure fishing, the rougher the weather, the better! Concentrate on water about 4 m deep and fish as close to shore as possible. A wind blowing along the shore is preferred and, if in a boat, drift down the shore with the wind. Green and gold devon style lures are best for drift spinning. For trolling, the Tasmanian or cobra style lures are excellent. A bibbed minnow for the deeper water is also very good. Always use an anti-kink keel with the spinners and a loop knot to tie on the lure. This gives the lure a better action.

Trolling is best around the old Sand Lake area (north-eastern end). Run lines and lures at varying lengths and depths. In bright, sunny conditions, the old lake bed area of the Blue Lake can sometimes save the day.

TROUT FOOD

Food for trout is abundant in Arthurs Lake, and crustaceans are the most plentiful group. It is these crustaceans that give the fish their superb pink flesh.

Common crustaceans found here include isopods, amphipods and decapods. Chironomids, or midges, are also in abundance as are caddis, aquatic worms, bivalves and, to a smaller, more localised extent, mayflies.

Two native galaxiids (small fish) are also common to the waters: the Arthur paragalaxias and *Galaxias tanycephus*. These live around the lake margins amongst rocks and scrub. Please note, however, that it is illegal to use galaxiids as bait, either live or dead.

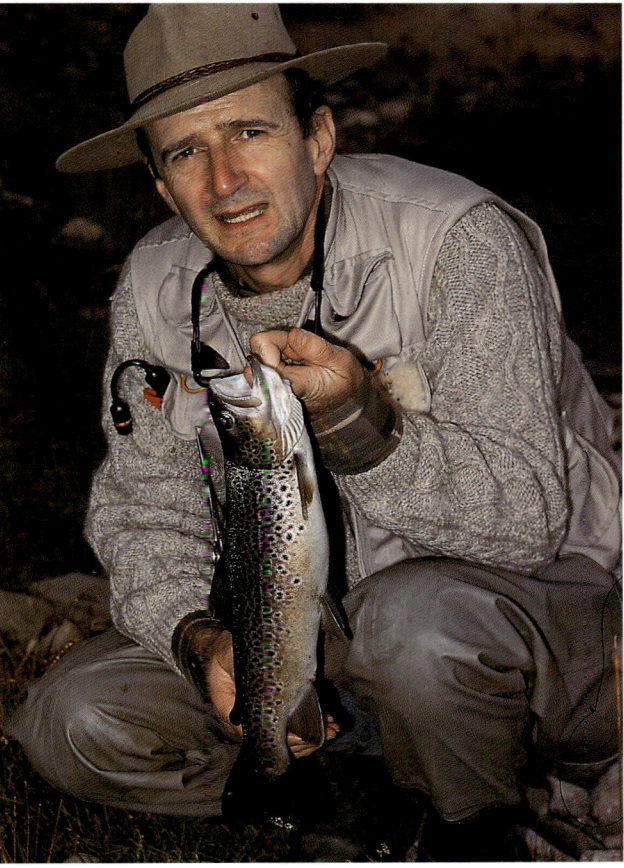

A nice brown trout taken on fly tackle

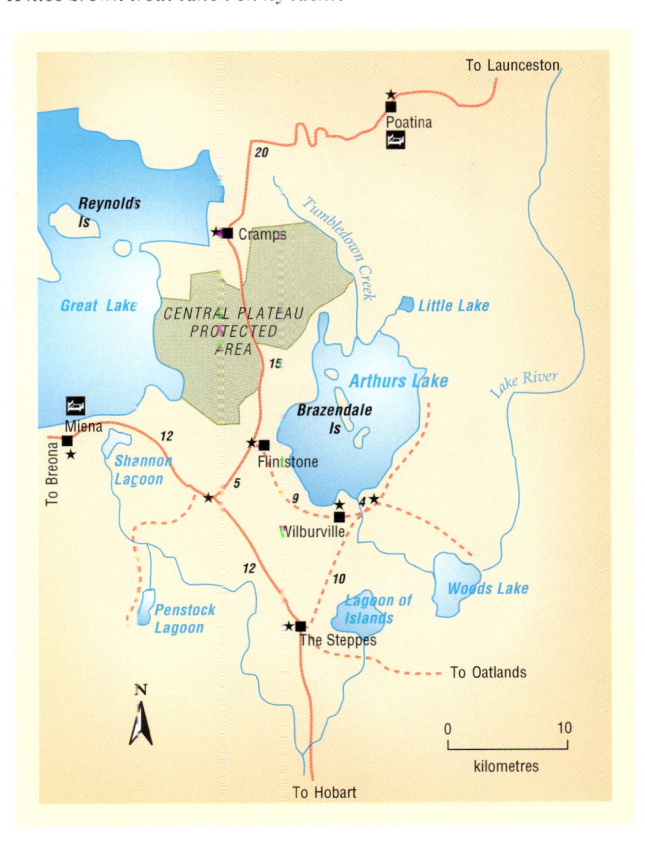

LAKE BURBURY

IN BRIEF

MAP REFERENCE: PAGE 254 D9

GETTING THERE Lake Burbury lies just east of Queenstown and about 260 km north-west of Hobart along the Lyell Highway. It is 3½ hours drive from Hobart and 4 hours drive from Launceston
BEST TIME TO FISH September to May
BEST TIME TO TRAVEL Year-round
MAJOR ANGLING SPECIES Brown and rainbow trout
ACCOMMODATION Casual camping around the shores or basic accommodation at Queenstown

Although only constructed in 1991, Lake Burbury has well and truly come of age as a trout fishery over the past couple of years. The flooding of large button grass plains by an 80-m high rock fill dam between Mount Huxley and Mount Jukes created a long expanse of water which is basically two lakes, with several large arms. It was predicted by some that it would become a water of giant trout, similar to Lake Pedder during the 1970s. However, this was not to be.

Far from being a big fish water, Lake Burbury has become a big numbers water, probably due to the many inflowing streams. Wind lane fishing by fly fishers is at its best here, with competent fly casters sometimes catching 30 fish or more in an early morning session. So often anglers speak of the 'good old days', but at Lake Burbury, the good old days are happening now!

At 235 m above sea level, Lake Burbury is much lower than the Central Highlands, most of which lies at around 1000 m. Thus, the weather at Burbury is often milder—although, as it located near Tasmania's west coast, wind and rain can be constant companions. The prevailing westerlies blow incessantly at times and snow often covers the surrounding peaks.

Shore anglers will find the going tough, apart from an area of the western shore for 3 to 4 km either side of Bradshaws Bridge. Another area that is open to shore-based anglers is part of the eastern shore where the Lyell Highway was drowned, although this side of the lake is very exposed to the prevailing westerlies. Some other areas offer reasonable shore fishing, but these are only accessible with a boat and in reality it is also better to fish these areas from a boat.

A brown trout taken on an ultra-light jig

BAIT FISHING

Mudeyes (dragonfly larvae) are by far the most successful bait at Lake Burbry and there is little reason to use any other. Natural baits cannot be brought in from other waters and it is a good idea to either collect mudeyes from the lake itself or to buy them from a local outlet. These are collected under licence and are readily available between October and March. Check any of the tackle and general stores in the area. Anglers should not introduce any bait from interstate, as this puts Tasmania's fishery at risk.

The best method with mudeyes is to use a size 12 or 14 hook with a live mudeye under a small bubble float. The line should be greased to float and should be free running through the float. A stopper should be attached about 30 cm above the hook. Cast out and let the mudeye pull line through the float. If there is no action after 20 minutes or so, retrieve and recast to another area. (Note that two rods can be used for bait fishing and trolling if a second rod fee is paid.)

LURE FISHING

Although much has been written about fly fishing at Lake Burbury, lure fishing is the most popular type of fishing practised here. Trolling is without doubt the most common method used, followed by drift spinning. Tradition dictates that Tasmanian Cobra-style lures are the most popular and these are used either flat-lining, in conjunction with lead lines, or occasionally on downriggers. Downriggers are probably underutilised in Tasmania, but old habits die hard. Minnow-style lures also work well, and may be flat-lined or fished deeper.

Lures are best trolled close to shore. Drifting amongst the trees and casting lures can also bring a lot of action. A floating bibbed lure cast amongst the trees can be a tremendous fish catcher, as it can be cranked down to the snags and then backed up by pausing, and cranked down again, enticing any trout in the area.

Fly Fishing

Fly fishing is another method that can be enormously effective on Lake Burbury at times. Some fly fishers, particularly during suitable weather, catch their bag limit several days in a row. Often this happens early in the morning, before the sun hits the water, especially along 'wind lanes'. (Wind lanes are slicks that concentrate available food into a smorgasbord that trout find irresistible.)

The early part of the day—from the first glow of dawn until the sun hits the water—can be the most exciting of all for fly fishers. If the weather is kind and wind lanes have formed paths across the lake, anglers will find lots of hungry fish. A boat is needed to get to these trout, and their numbers are often amazing.

Trout swim up and down these wind lanes gobbling everything in their path. Although they may appear easy to catch, fly casters need to be spot on with their presentation. Fast and accurate casts are the key and if anglers can manage a genuine 15-m cast, there are times when they can hook fish several casts in a row.

Once the sun hits the water, the action will usually slow or stop. Sometimes, however, even with a substantial ripple on the water, the wind lanes will remain obvious and fishing in this manner can continue for several hours.

Later in the day, fly fishing usually means going subsurface. Normally, a weighted wet fly is required, with a sinking mudeye pattern 'counted down' to the right depth proving a good bet.

Evening fishing with a floating mudeye pattern fly can bring fly fishers some of their most exciting action. Squinting to watch the fly against the barely lit sky and seeing a fish porpoise and slurp it off the surface can take your breath away!

Weather is really the key to fishing Lake Burbury and unfortunately good weather is not all that common on the west coast. Look for a big, lingering high-pressure system over Lake Burbury and then hurry! The fishing at such times can be the best Tasmania has to offer, but it may not last for long.

PREPARING FOR EXTREMES

Weather conditions can change very rapidly in Tasmania, especially in the far south, along the west coast or at higher altitudes. Even in midsummer, anglers should be prepared at any time to encounter extreme weather conditions, including strong winds, heavy rain, very low temperatures and even sleet or snow. December blizzards are certainly not unknown in the Central Highlands and Western Tiers!

- Always carry extra warm clothing and be prepared to dress in layers to avoid exposure and hypothermia. This could involve the use of full length thermal underwear, woollen or synthetic over-garments in various thicknesses and an exterior shell or jacket capable of repelling moisture and cutting wind without causing excessive condensation from sweating during periods of exertion.
- Remember also that a great deal of heat can be lost from the head during exposure to extreme weather, so always wear a hat and carry a beanie or balaclava for emergency use. In addition, pack extra energy-rich food such as chocolate or barley sugar and, if possible, take a vacuum flask of warm liquid such as soup, cocoa, coffee or tea.
- Be sure to tell someone exactly where you are going and when you expect to return, and discuss an action plan that they should put into motion if you are more than an hour or two overdue.
- Finally, it should be stressed that, as well as dealing with the possibility of exposure to extreme weather, you must also be wary of the high levels of ultraviolet radiation from the sun Tasmania receives during the long days of summer. Always wear a broad-brimmed hat and apply high-quality sunscreen lotion with an SPF factor of 15+ when spending time in the outdoors, particularly during the highest risk period between 11 a.m. and 3 p.m. on summer's days.

A brown trout taken while trolling a lake in typical Tasmanian weather

Lake Burbury's rainbow trout are dark and heavily speckled

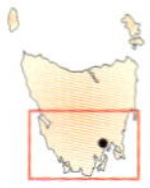

254
A
B
C
D
E
F
G
1
2
3
4
5
6
7
8
9
10
145°
145°30'
146°
146°30'
42°30'
43°
43°30'
Macquarie Heads
Ocean Beach
Strahan
Regatta Point
Swan Basin Picnic Ground
Cape Sorell
Lynchford
Crotty Dam
Darwin Dam
Teepookana Forest Res
Sophia Pt
Liberty Pt
Table Head
Sloop Point
Macquarie Harbour
Gorge Point
Gould Pt
Sarah Is
Rum Pt
Kelly Basin
Birthday Bay
Gulley Point
Varna Bay
Hibbs Bay
Point Hibbs
Spero Bay
Endeavour Bay
High Rocky Point
Low Rocky Point
Elliott Bay
Nye Bay
Elliot Point
Mulcaby Bay
Brier Holme Head
Svenor Point
Wreck Bay
James Kelly Basin
Davey Head
North Head
Point St Vincent
Port Davey
Hilliard Head
Stephens Bay
Mutton Bird Island
Window Pane Bay
Doorstop Bay
Mt Karamu
South West Cape
Telopea Point
Wilson Bight
New Harbour
Cox Bight
Cox Bluff
Red Point
Red Point Hills
Louisa Bay
Louisa Island
Havelock Bluff
Ile du Golfe
Point Cecil
Point Vivian
Prion Bay
Surprise Bay
Shoemaker Point
De Witt Island
Flat Witch Island
Walker Island
Maatsuyker Island
Maatsuyker Group
SOUTHERN
OCEAN
Victoria Pass
LYELL HWY
A10
B24
Raglan Ra
Lake Burbury
Mt Alma
Mt Rufus
Cheyne Ra
Derwent Bridge
Mt King William I
Mt King William II
Mt King William III
Mt Darwin
Mt Sorell
West Coast Ra
Frenchmans Cap
Franklin-Gordon Wild Rivers National Park
Lake Rufus
Lake Richmond
Engineer Range
Cracroft Hills
Mt McCall
Deception Range
Western Plains
Goodwins Peak
Norway Ra
Elliot Ra
Prince of Wales Range
Mt Humboldt
D'Aguilar Range
Mt Lee
Princess Range
Nicholls Ra
Denison Range
The Pleiades
Hamilton Range
Southwest Conservation Area
Moores Valley
Mt Lewis
Charles Range
Gordon Dam
Serpentine Dam
Strathgordon
Teds Beach
Mt Sprent
Lake Gordon
Clear Hill
Tiger Ra
Lake Curly
Wylds Craig
Starfish Hill
Mt Osmund
Lawson Range
Rookery Plain
Double Peak
Frankland Range
The Coronets
McPartian Pass
Lake Pedder
Mt Solitary
Scotts Peak
Scotts Peak Dam
Edgar Dam
Mt Giblin
Folded Range
White Monolith Range
Propsting Range
Piners Peak
De Witt Range
Mt Hean
Davey Gorge
Lost World Plateau
Settlement Point
Mt Hesperus
Arthur Range
Mt Orion
Lake Jupiter
West Portal
Southwest National Park
Mt Norold
Ripple Mtn
Rugby Ra
Mt Rugby
Erskine Ra
Rowitta Plains
Bathurst Harbour
Spiro Range
Mt Pollux
Federation Peak
Cracroft Gorge
Lake Geeves
South West Cape Range
Melaleuca Range
Mt Melaleuca
Ray Range
Mt Counsel
Mt Louisa
Ironbound Range
Mt Victoria Cross
Precipitous Bluff
New River Lagoon
Mt Bobs
Bobs Knobs
Sib Picton Range
Mt Picton
The Razorback
Bronte Park
London Lakes
Lake Big Jim
Laughing Jack Lagoon
Lake King William
Butlers Gorge Power Station
Bronte Lagoon
Bradys Lake
Lake Binney
Tarraleah
Tarraleah Power Station
Wayatinah
Wayatinah Lagoon
Wayatinah Power Station
Lake Catagunya
Catagunya Power Station
Lake Repulse
Repulse Power Station
Misery Plateau
Mount Field Nat Park
Mt Field West
Lake Belton
Skiing
Tim Shea
Mt Mueller
Tyenna
Ibsens Peak
Frodshams Pass
Creepy Crawly Walk
Mount Wedge Forest Res
Mt Bowes
Mt Eliza
Mt Anne
Lake Judd
Gallagher Plateau
Mt Weld
Snowy Range

0 10 20 30
kilometres

255

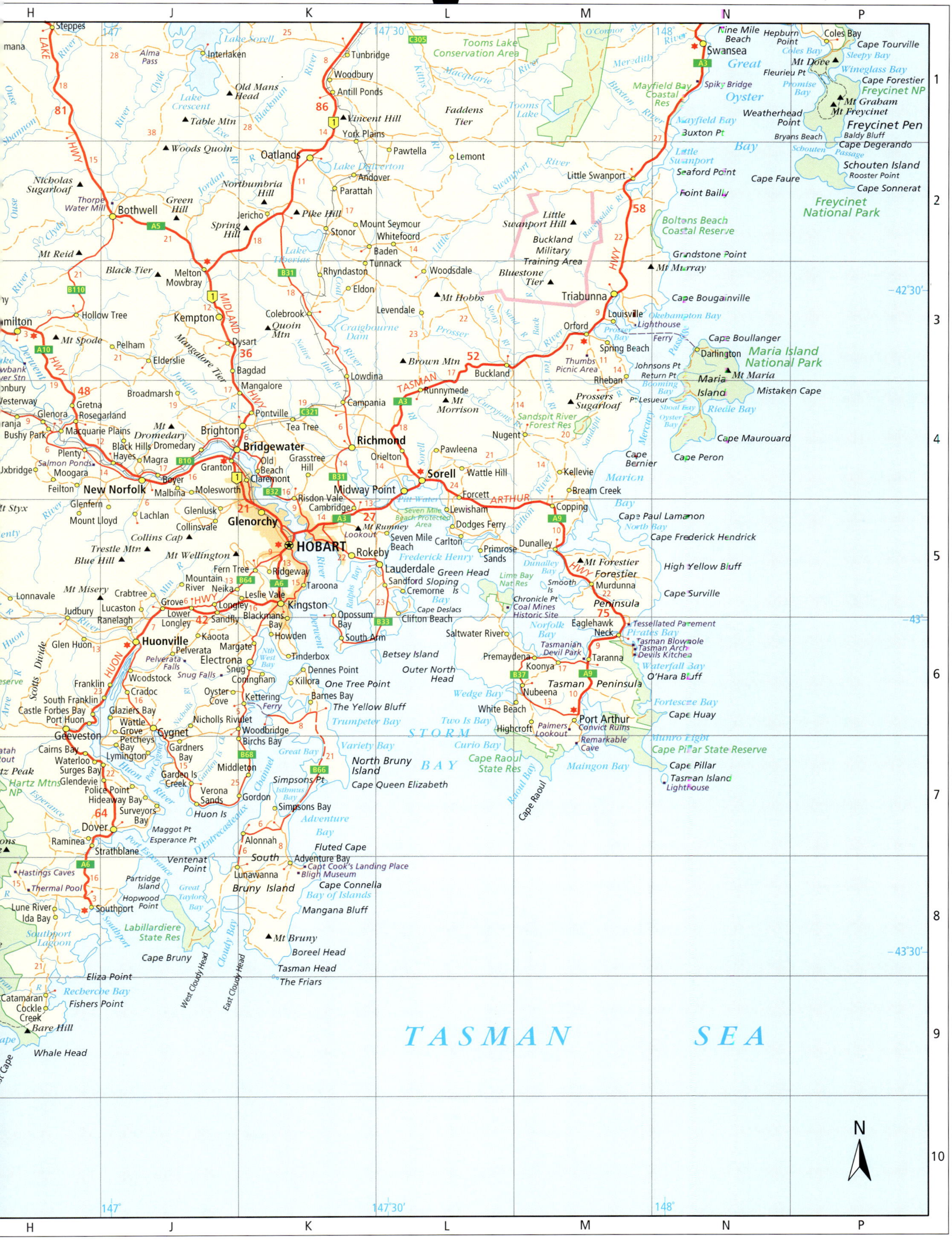

A
B
C
D
E
F
G
1
2
3
4
5
6
7
8
9
10
145°
145°30'
146°
40°30'
41°
41°30'
42°
N
Cape Keraudren
Coulomb Bay
Cape Rochon Lighthouse
Three Hummock Island
Cape Adamson
South Hummock
Hope Channel
Cuvier Bay Lighthouse
Hunter Island
Goodwill Point
Walker Channel
Walker Island
Hunter Passage
Trefoil Island
Woolnorth Point
Ransonnet Bay
Cape Grim
Valley Bay
Woolnorth
Kangaroo Island
Robbins Island
Guyton Point
Flat Topped Bluff
Bluff Point
Studland Bay
Cape Elie
Robbins Passage
Montagu Is
Stony Pt
Montagu
Perkins Island
Perkins Bay
Highfield Historic Site
North Point
Half Moon Bay
Lighthouse
The Nut Chairlift
Stanley
Circular Head
The Nut
Sawyer Bay
Duck Bay
Smithton
Mella
Wiltshire
Port Latta
Rocky Cape Lighthouse
Rocky Cape Nat Park
Mt Cameron West
Ann Bay
Welcome River
Montagu River
Christmas Hills
Smokers Bank
Forest
Crayfish Creek
Hellyer
Rocky Cape
Green Point
Marrawah
Redpa
Togari
Brittons Swamp
Irishtown
South Forest
Mengha
Sisters Beach
Boat Harbour Beach
West Pt
BASS HWY
Bond Tier
Alcomie
Lileah
Montumana
Sisters Creek
Boat Harbour
Lighthouse
Table Cape
Mawson Bay
Sherstons Hill
Edith Creek
Nabageena
Mawbanna
Flowerdale
Wynyard
Seabrook
Arthur Pieman Protected Area
Duck River
Roger River
Myalla
Moorleah
Lapoinya
Bluff Hill Point Lighthouse
Trowutta
Wedge Plains
Dip Falls
Milabena
Somerset
Arthur River
Gardiner Point
Dip Range
Lower Mount Hicks
Burnie
Calder
Oldina
Upper Mount Hicks
Heybridge
Howth
Sulphur Creek
Penguin
Milkshakes Hills Forest Reserve
Meunna
Preolenna
Elliott
Mooreville
Stowport
Kanunnah Bridge
Lake Chisholm Forest Reserve
Neasey Plains
Yolla
West Ridgley
Upper Stowport
Cuprona
Ulverstone
Turners Beach
Leith
Devonport
Nelson Bay
Julius River Forest Res
Campbell Range
Henrietta
Ridgley
West Pine
Forth
Don
Blue Peak
Takone
Natone
Camena
Mt Duncan
Gawler
Couta Rocks
Hellyer
Tewkesbury
Upper Natone
Riana
North Motton
Abbotsham
Spreyton
Eugenana
Temma
Richardson Point
Horton
Hampshire
Highclere
South Riana
Spalford
Kindred
Melrose
Paloona
Tarleton
Balfour
Hellyer Gorge State Res
Hazard Bay
Mt Balfour
Mt Frankland
Thornton R
Gunns Plains
Heka
Preston
Central Castra
Paloona Power Station
Lwr Barrington
Mt Bertha
Parawee
Warringa
Gunns Plains Cave
Lower Wilmot
Lake Paloona
Barrington
Mt Hazelton
Upper Castra
Nook
Devils Gate Power Station
St Valentines Peak
Nietta
Sheffield
Kenneth Bay
Leven Canyon
Wilmot
Sandy Cape Lighthouse
Guildford
Loongana
South Nietta
West Kentish
Mt Norfolk
Mt Bischoff
Erriba
Roland
Paradise
Waratah
Talbots Lagoon
Black Bluff
Staverton
Claude Road
Mt Cleveland
Winterbrook Falls
Mt Roland
Luina
MURCHISON HWY
Mt Pearce
Mt Cattley
Lake Gairdner
Moina
Gowrie Park
Mt Claude
Mersey
Savage River
Whyte
Lake Lea
King Solomon Cave
Arthur Pieman Protected Area
Lake Cethana
Lorinna
Liena
Mayberry
Mt Meredith
Middlesex Plains
Marakoopa Cave
Mole Creek
Blackguards Hill
Mt Ramsay
Hatfield
Dove
Emu Plains
Western Bluff
Mt Donaldson
Meredith Range
Mt Charter
Vale
Mt Remus
Pencil Pine Visitor Centre
Lemonthyme Power Station
Rupert Point
Corinna
Cradle Valley
Devils Gullet Lookout
Hardwicke Bay
Pieman River State Reserve
Mt Livingstone
Burns Peak
Dove Lake
Lake Parangana
Conical Rocks Point
Yarrana Hill
Mackintosh Dam
Mt Romulus
Cradle Mtn
Borradaile Plains
Fisher Bluff
Reece Dam
Lake Mackintosh
Lake Mackenzie
Rowallan Power Stn
Bastyan Dam
Tullah
Lake Will
Clumner Bluff
Rosebery
Mt Black
Granite Tor
February Plains
Duck Ck
Renison Bell
Murchison Dam
Victoria Peak
Overland Track
Granville Harbour
Williamsford
Mt Murchison
Lake Rowallan
Walls of Jerusalem
Lake Pieman
Chalmers
Montezuma Falls
Mt Read
Mt Pelion West
Mt Jerusalem
Mt Heemskirk
Cradle Mountain
Lake Adelaide
Mt Agnew
Zeehan
Lake Murchison
Mt Ossa
Lake Louisa
Walls of Jerusalem National Park
Lake Plimsoll
Wallace
Lake Myrtle
Lake Meston
Mt Zeehan
Trial Harbour
Mt Tyndall
Lake St Clair National Park
Lake Malbena
Little Henty R
Lake Margaret
Eldon Peak
Eldon Bluff
Lake Olive
Lake Norman
Henty Glacial Moraine
South Eldon River
Travellers Rest Lake
Lake Ina
Henty River
Mt Lyell
Lake Burbury
Pyramid Mtn
Mt Olympus
Lake St Clair
Henty Dunes
Tully
Queenstown
Gormanston
Mt Owen
Cheyne Ra
Mt Rufus
Lynchford
Victoria Pass
LYELL HWY
Derwent Bridge
Strahan
Macquarie Heads
Ocean Beach
Regatta Point
Crotty Dam
Mt Alma
Raglan Ra
Cape Sorell
Swan Basin Picnic Ground
King River
Teepookana Forest Res
Lake Burbury
Laughing Jack Lagoon
Franklin
Lake King William
Pine Cove
Darwin Dam
Loddon
Mt King William I
Sophia Pt
West Coast Range
Mt Darwin
Frenchmans Cap
Butlers Gorge Power Station
Mt Sorell
King Island
0
10
kilometres
Cape Wickham Lighthouse
Disappointment Bay
Cape Farewell
Phoques Bay
Egg Lagoon
Lake Martha Lavinia
Lavinia Point
New Year Island
Christmas Island
Whistler Point
Yambacoona
Lavinia Nature Reserve
Reekara
Counsel Hill
KING ISLAND
Cowper Point
Loorana
Sea Elephant Bay
Currie Harbour
Currie
Pegarah
Naracoopa
Fraser Bluff
Parenna
Yarrah Creek
Lymwood
Fitzmaurice Bay
Bold Head
Cataraqui Point
Grassy
Calcified Forest
Mt Stanley
Big Lake
Surprise Bay
Seal Bay
Stokes Point
144°
40°
Bass Strait Ferry

252

0 10 20 30
kilometres
H
J
K
L
M
N
P
1
2
3
4
5
6
7
8
9
10
Flinders Island
0 10 20
kilometres
N
148°
Outer Sister Island
Inner Sister Island
Lighthouse
Stanley Point
Blyth Point
Palana
FURNEAUX
Killiecrankie Bay
Mt Killiecrankie
Killiecrankie
Mt Tanner
B85
FLINDERS
Leeka
Roydon Is
Tanners Bay
ISLAND
Marshall Bay
C802
Babel Island
Lighthouse
Cat Island
Sellars Point
Sellars Lagoon
40°
Emita
Memana
Furneaux Lookout
The Patriarchs
Blue Rocks
Walkers Lookout
Arthur Bay
Mt Levenstborpe
Cameron Inlet
Chalky Island
Long Point
Parrys Bay
Whitemark
C803
GROUP
B85
Logan Lagoon
Big Green Island
East Kangaroo Island
Fotheringate Bay
Ranga
Strzelecki Peaks
Lady Barron
Pot Boil Point
Trousers Point
Strzelecki Nat Park
Little Green Is
Great Dog Island
Mt Chappell Island
Little Dog Is
Pigs Head Point
Vansittart Island
Goose Island
Franklin
Sound
Puncheon Point
147°30′
Mt Chappell Island
148°
Great Dog Island
Strzelecki NP
Little Dog Is
Vansittart Island
Goose Island
Lighthouse
Franklin
Pigs Head Point
Anderson Island
Sound
Puncheon Point
Tin Kettle Island
Deep Bay
Apple Orchard Point
Badger Island
Long Island
Cape
Mt Munro
Barren Island
Harleys Point
Cape Barren Island
Double Peak
Cape Sir John
Mt Kerford
Thunder and Lightning Bay
Preservation Island
Vansittart Island
Wombat Pt
Sloping Pt
Kent Bay
Cone Pt
40°30′
Armstrong Channel
Forsyth Island
Passage Island
Clarke Island
Black Point
Lookout Head
Moriarty Bay
Moriarty Point
BANKS STRAIT
Swan Island
Cape Portland
Ringarooma
Bay
Waterhouse Island
Boobyalla Beach
Waterhouse Point
Ringarooma Coastal Reserve
Great Musselroe Bay
Poole
Cape Naturaliste
Croppies Point
Sth Croppies Point
Tomahawk
Boobyalla
Stumpys Bay
Waterhouse Protected Area
Big Waterhouse Lake
Mt William
Cod Bay
West Sandy Point
St Albans Bay
East Sandy Point
Anderson Bay
Shortys Point
Granite Point Coastal Res
87
Purdon Bay
Gladstone
Eddystone Point
Lighthouse
Eddystone Point
Stony Head
Noland Bay
Double Sandy Pt Coastal Res
Bridport
B82
Mt Cameron
41°
Five Mile Bluff
Lulworth
Stony Head Military Area
Beechford
Weymouth
Bellingham
The Banca
South Mount Cameron
Ansons Bay
Low Head
Port Dalrymple
West Head
Low Head
58
B82
B84
Mt Horror
Sharon Point
dger Head
Greens Beach
Lefroy
Pipers Brook
19
Pioneer
Herrick
Bay of Fires Coastal Reserve
George Town
Pipers River
North Scottsdale
Winnaleah
Kelso
Clarence Point
Bell Bay
Tippogoree Hills
Warrentinna
Bay Of Fires
Bakers Beach
Beauty Point
Asbestos Range Nat Park
Retreat
Golconda
Jetsonville
Scottsdale
Derby
Sorell
Rowella
Blumont
Nabowla
Tonganah
Branxholm
Big Lagoon
The Gardens
Beaconsfield
Kayena
54
Tunnel
Wyena
Tulendeena
Weldborough
Sidmouth
Lebrina
West Scottsdale
43
Lower Turners Marsh
Springfield
Cuckoo
Sloop Lagoon
Deviot
Ledgerwood
Mt Paris Dam
Hillwood
Lisle
Cuckoo Hill
Ringarooma
Mt Pearson
Binalong Bay
Mount Direction
Karoola
66
A3
Goulds Country
Humbug Point State Rec Area
Sassafras
43
Paper Beach
Lilydale
South Springfield
Gravelly Beach
Lalla
Mt Arthur
55
George
St Helens Pt
Holwell
Exeter
Blackwall
Underwood
Myrtle Bank
Talawa
Pyengana
St Helens Point State Rec Area
Winkleigh
Lanena
Windermere
Turners Marsh
Hollybank Forest Reserve
TASMAN
Mt Victoria Forest Reserve
Mt Victoria
St Columba Falls State Reserve
St Helens
Stieglitz
West Frankford
B71
Dilston
Targa
Patricks
Parkside
Parnella
Frankford
Rosevears
Paterson
Tayene
Mt Young
St Helens Island
Glengarry
A8
Rocherlea
Mt Barrow
Mt Saddleback
Dianas Basin
Legana
A7
Nunamara
Loila Tier
Parkham
Bridgenorth
Ben Nevis
Evercreech Forest Res
Beaumaris
Birralee
Mowbray
Upper Scamander
Scamander Forest Res
B72
Rosevale
Launceston
Scamander
Reedy Marsh
Selbourne
Prospect
Norwood
Burns Creek
Weetah
Lake Trevallyn
Musselboro
Henderson Lagoon
Elizabeth Town
Westwood
Youngtown
North Esk
Upper Blessington
Mathinna
Falmouth
Meander
White Hills
C401
35
41°30′
BASS
HWY
Hadspen
Relbia
Ben Lomond Cons Area
Deloraine
Lemana
Westbury
Hagley
49
Carrick
Breadalbane
Blessington
Ski Village
Legges Tor
Mt Nicholas
Red Hills
Osmaston
Pateena
B41
Western Junction
A4
Four Mile Creek
B52
Perth
Evandale
Cornwall
Ironhouse Point
Montana
Glenore
Oaks
Ben Lomond National Park
St Marys
Quamby Brook
Cluan
Whitemore
Toiberry
Longford
Deddington
Mangana
Stacks Bluff
Quamby Bluff
Golden Valley
Bishopsbourne
35
Clarendon
Storys Creek
Elephant Pass
Meander
Bracknell
C416
Fingal
Chain of Lagoons
Liffey
Nile
Rossarden
Liffey Forest Res
Liffey Falls
Drys Bluff
Cressy
MIDLAND
Picaninny Point
65
Projection Bluff
Blackwood Creek
B53
C515
A3
Templestow Lagoon
Wild Dog Tier
Hummocky Hills
74
Douglas Apsley National Park
Seymour
Long Point
Epping Forest
B42
A4
Mt St John
Maclean Bay
Breona
Poatina
Mt Blackwood
24
Cleveland
Avoca
St Pauls Dome
Mother Lords Plains
26
ESK
C301
Birdlife and Animal Park
Central Plateau Protected Area
C522
C520
Conara
Royal George
Mt Henry
Bernacchi
Reynolds Is
Reynolds Neck
Cramps
Harding Falls Forest Res
Bicheno
Liawenee
TIERS
Great Lake
Little Lake
Millers Bluff
Snow Hill
95
B51
Elizabeth
Cape Lodi
A5
Campbell Town
Meetus Falls Forest Res
Courland Bay
Arthurs Lake
B34
TASMAN
Tods
Mt Augusta
Cygnet
C302
Moulting Lagoon
Miena
Flintstone
Lake Leake
42°
Barren Tier
Shannon Lagoon
Mt Penny West
Ross
Hobgoblin
334
Cranbrook
Friendly Beaches
Mt Peter
Wilburville
Mt Franklin
Mt Paul
A5
Penstock Lagoon
Woods Lake
Lake Sorell
86
Nine Mile Beach
Hepburn Point
Coles Bay
Lake Echo
Steppes
Lagoon of Islands
Tooms Lake Conservation Area
Swansea
Cape Tourville
Waddamana
Interlaken
Sleepy Bay
Alma Pass
Tunbridge
Meredith
Great
Mt Dove
Wineglass Bay
Lakes
Woodbury
Old Mans Head
Mayfield Bay Coastal Res
Spiky Bridge
Fleurieu Pt
Promise Bay
Cape Forestier
Freycinet NP
Oyster
Antill Ponds
Lake Crescent
Faddens Tier
Tooms Lake
Mt Graham
Mt Freycinet
Dee Lagoon
81
Vincent Hill
Mayfield Bay
Weatherhead Point
Freycinet Pen
Lake Echo Power Station
Table Mtn
York Plains
147°30′
Buxton Pt
Bay
Bryans Beach
Baldy Bluff
Cape Degerando
147°
148°

253

DREAM TRIPS

FISHING HOT SPOTS

- Mallacoota (pp. 258–9)
- East Gippsland Bream Rivers (pp. 260–1)
- Shark Fishing off Phillip Island (pp. 262–3)
- The Mighty Murray (pp. 264–5)
- Big River Country (pp. 266–7)
- Coffs Harbour (pp. 268–9)
- Lord Howe Island (pp. 270–1)
- The New South Wales Far South Coast (pp. 272–5)
- The Snowy Mountains (pp. 276–7)
- Cape York (pp. 278–81)
- Mornington Island (pp. 282–3)
- The Gulf of Carpentaria (pp. 284–5)
- Exploring the Reef (pp. 286–9)
- Cairns to Cape Tribulation (pp. 290–1)
- Jessie River, Melville Island (pp. 292–3)
- Cape Don and the Cobourg Peninsula (pp. 294–5)
- Barra Base (pp. 296–7)
- The Victoria River (pp. 298–9)
- Vanderlin Island (pp. 300–1)
- The Kimberley (pp. 302–5)
- Broome and the Pearl Coast (pp. 306–7)
- The Pilbara Coast (pp. 308–9)
- The Mackerel Islands (pp. 310–11)
- Dirk Hartog Island and Shark Bay (pp. 312–13)
- Kalbarri and the Murchison (pp. 314–15)
- Great Australian Bight (pp. 316–17)
- Steel City Snapper (pp. 318–19)
- Kangaroo Island (pp. 320–1)
- Aboard the *Falie* (pp. 322–3)
- Flinders Island (pp. 324–5)
- Strahan and the Wild West Coast (pp. 326–6)
- Tasmania's Central Highlands (pp. 328–9)
- London Lakes (pp. 330–1)

The hand-picked collection of very special destinations described in the next section of the book includes many of Australia's most desirable and highly regarded recreational fishing hot spots. A visit to any one of these fish-rich regions could aptly be described as a 'dream trip' for the vast majority of keen anglers.

A few of the locations described on the following pages are extremely remote and difficult to reach, while others represent private or limited-entry fisheries where visitors must book well in advance and pay for the privilege of casting a line. In contrast, however, the bulk of these dream destinations lie much closer to 'civilisation' and are relatively well serviced in terms of road, rail or air access, accommodation, professional guides, charter boats, tourist services and various other forms of infrastructure. In many instances, anyone with even a modest sense of adventure and a willingness to explore the wealth of angling opportunities available beyond their own backyard is free to visit these places and sample their delights, and tens of thousands of us choose to do exactly that every year.

The dream destinations dealt with here cover the full geographic, climatic and piscatorial spectrum— from alpine and subalpine trout waters in the far south of Australia to mangrove-lined estuaries and coral-fringed islands in our tropical north. What they all share, however, is a potential standard of recreational sport fishing that justifiably remains the envy of well-informed anglers, not only from right around Australia, but also from all over the globe. The fact is, each one of these destinations is capable of offering truly world-class fishing.

Having said that, it must be stressed that even the 'hottest' of angling locations will not necessarily produce outstanding fishing results all the time, nor for every hopeful visitor. Even dream destinations have their quiet periods and 'off' days or weeks. Experienced anglers accept this fact and plan their fishing expeditions accordingly. They choose optimum periods to visit a particular location, take the most suitable tackle and use the best techniques available for the task at hand. And still, on occasion, they will miss out, draw a blank or get 'skunked', to borrow the rather apt American parlance for a no-fish day.

It must always be remembered that recreational fishing is a game of both skill and chance. There are simply no iron-clad guarantees. If we all hooked fish every time we dropped a line into the water, our sport would be called 'catching' rather than 'fishing'—and it would instantly lose a great part of its inherent charm and appeal.

Even when visiting the very best of our angling hot spots—including the destinations described in these pages—it pays to remember that there is much more to fishing than simply catching fish. Travellers are well advised to slow down and absorb their surroundings. Take the time to smell the flowers and feel the crunch of clean sand beneath bare feet. Admire the views, listen to the locals and sample the delights of regional foods, wines or crafts. Above all, open your senses to the rich stimuli offered by any new location... then go fishing—and enjoy yourself!

The Great Barrier Reef, one of Australia's World Heritage areas

257

Top: *Gantheaume Point, near Broome, in the late afternoon*
Above left: *Beach fishing on Flinders Island*
Right: *Alpine pools in the Snowy Mountains, New South Wales*

MALLACOOTA

IN BRIEF

MAP REFERENCE: PAGE 71 N5

GETTING THERE Mallacoota is 542 km east of Melbourne along the Princes Highway

BEST TIME TO FISH Year-round, but winter mornings can be brisk when chasing bream and flathead

BEST TIME TO TRAVEL Year-round, although out-of-holiday periods may be better because of this region's popularity

MAJOR ANGLING SPECIES Flathead, bream, whiting, mulloway, gummy shark, trevally, garfish and tailor

SPECIAL RESTRICTIONS Specific regional bag limits can sometimes apply to particular species in Mallacoota Inlet, especially when this system is closed to the sea. Always check the current rules before fishing

WARNINGS Access to the sea across Mallacoota Bar (when open) is potentially hazardous and very difficult at low tide. Seek local advice first

ACCOMMODATION Bluewater Cabins, telephone (03) 5158 0261; Gipsy Point Lodge, telephone Freecall 1800 063 556; Foreshore Camp Park, telephone (03) 5158 0300

CHARTER BOATS AND FISHING GUIDES Ferry and Boat Hire Service, telephone (03) 5158 0555; Mallacoota Bait and Tackle, telephone (03) 5158 0050

In the far east of Victoria's Gippsland region lies the township of Mallacoota. Even though it is a five- to six-hour drive from Melbourne, this town sees its population swell enormously during holiday periods. Serious anglers and those who just come to enjoy the tranquillity are drawn back time after time. As well as boasting some of the best estuary fishing in the Victoria, Mallacoota also offers bushwalks in the Croajingolong National Park and walks and swimming along kilometres of unspoiled coastline.

This large waterway system that attracts so many visitors each year is comprised of two lakes, Top and Bottom, divided by a deep channel called The Narrows. Feeding these two lakes are the Wallagaraugh and Genoa rivers, plus many smaller tributaries. The town of Mallacoota itself is situated on the Bottom Lake near the entrance to the ocean, with good fishing only a stone's throw from the local tackle shop.

Major target species in Mallacoota Inlet include bream, estuary perch, mulloway, tailor, luderick, whiting and garfish.

The fish that Mallacoota is renowned for, however, is the dusky flathead. This extensive estuary system is the home of the giant flathead, with many anglers actually devoting a lifetime to catching these piscatorial bottom-dwellers.

TARGETING FLATHEAD

Over the past decade or so, lure fishing for flathead has come a long way, having seen the introduction of a much larger range of soft plastics and minnow type lures.

Anglers who prefer a more passive style of fishing can use a small plastic bait trap to collect live 'poddy' mullet for bait. When the trap is left in the shallows with a breadcrumb and tuna oil blend, it should not take long to collect a healthy handful of live baits.

For those anglers seriously targeting big flathead, the Goodwin Sands is a great place to start. These shallow waters allow lure anglers to pull their boats up on the sand and get out to wade the flats while casting lures to likely lies. Bait anglers can also use the sands to their advantage by nosing up onto the flats and casting live mullet out over the drop-offs. Allan Head and Swimming Point are both popular flathead destinations in the Bottom Lake.

The wharf in the town of Mallacoota itself also produces some huge flathead. Fish of up to 4 kg are regularly taken on baits ranging from frozen prawns to bluebait and whitebait.

In the Top Lake, the Palmer Bank and Smellys Inlet offer the best flathead potential, and the many sand banks in the Genoa River are particularly popular with locals.

BIG MULLOWAY HAUNTS

The mulloway is another prize species in this estuary system. Serious mulloway anglers use only the best live baits and tend to fish at night. Live salmon, mullet and tailor all work well.

The tranquillity of Mallacoota Inlet

Although there are mulloway throughout the system, most of the fishing effort is concentrated around The Narrows as these fish tend to congregate in the deeper holes, especially after rain. A deep hole at Cape Horn on the Genoa River also produces its fair share of fish.

One of the most frustrating things about mulloway is that they are normally hooked on light tackle while targeting much smaller species, such as bream. In this situation, the angler has little chance of success, as 2- or 3-kg line is no match for fish weighing up to 35 or 40 kg! With care, patience and skill on the part of the angler, however, some very large specimens can be landed on this light tackle on occasion.

Mallacoota Bream

The southern black bream is also abundant in this estuarine system. During autumn, the bream run in Mallacoota's Bottom Lake, with bass yabbies being the number one bait.

Several outlets in the town sell yabbies, but it is much more rewarding to take a bait pump and gather your own. The islands adjacent to the boat ramp, including Rabbit Island, are productive bait-gathering grounds, and it normally doesn't take long to collect more than enough baits for a bream-fishing session.

By mid-June, the majority of bream fishing is done in the Top Lake, as the bream congregate in preparation for their spawning run up the rivers. Bream spawn in the rivers between August and October, and this is an intense time for anglers targeting this species.

The best baits to use while the bream are spawning are sand worms, bass yabbies and peeled prawns. The Bull Ring, a deep hole found above Johnson Bridge on the Wallagaraugh River, consistently produces great catches of these fish during this period.

With lure casting becoming more and more popular among anglers, the catch rate of estuary perch in this region has also increased in recent years. The perch are nearly always found along the shoreline and never too far from cover. Electric motors or oars are used to navigate within casting distance of a good snag, where small minnow and yabby imitations are used to deceive the fish. This is an exciting new trend that is sure to grow in years to come.

Surf Fishing Opportunities

The many ocean surf beaches around Mallacoota also provide some hot fishing action with several species available. Australian salmon, mullet and yellowfin or eastern black bream are prime targets. Anglers who fish the full moon in conjunction with a rising tide, when the beaches are largely free of weed, put themselves in the running for gummy sharks weighing up to 20 kg and large seven-gill sharks.

Pelican on a private jetty on the Bottom Lake

Tip Beach and Secret Beach are the two prime locations for these night-time adventures. A large threadline, sidecast or overhead reel spooled with at least 300 m of 12- or 15-kg line should be fished on a medium to heavy 3.5- to 4-m rod. The best bait is octopus, and this can be collected around the Bottom Lake's many private jetties.

The Betka River system can be found approximately 3 km out of town along the aerodrome road and, although the fishing is patchy at times, the river mouth can produce some fine catches of land-based bream and flathead. The shallow waters also offer a great opportunity for bait collection, with poddy mullet and sand worms available.

Offshore from Mallacoota

The offshore waters beyond Mallacoota's often treacherous bar are also well worth a look if the entrance is open. Tallaberga Island produces consistent flathead captures of fish around the 1-kg mark and regular gummies while bottom bashing. This area also produces the occasional kingfish and some nice pinkie snapper.

Gabo Island is a fishing mecca for big flathead, gurnard, gummy sharks and snapper. Anglers who troll lures around the island's south-west corner put themselves in with a big chance to catch kingfish and large pike. Good calamari are also available along the islands western shoreline on imitation prawn jigs.

Further out to sea, Mallacoota also offers great game fishing potential with the possibility of yellowfin tuna, marlin and a wide variety of sharks. Offshore game fishing in this region has always been held back because of the poor access to the ocean waters. Hopefully, in years to come, Mallacoota will have serious ocean launching facilities and Victorian game fishing may be on the map in a big way.

A small black bream taken from Mallacoota's Top Lake

EAST GIPPSLAND BREAM RIVERS

IN BRIEF

MAP REFERENCE: PAGE 70 E6

GETTING THERE Bairnsdale is 280 km east of Melbourne, at the junction of the Princes and Omeo highways
BEST TIME TO FISH August to May
BEST TIME TO TRAVEL Year-round
MAJOR ANGLING SPECIES Southern black bream, mullet and estuary perch
SPECIAL RESTRICTIONS Adults require an inland angling licence to fish in some parts of these waters — always check first
WARNINGS The unprotected open waters of the Gippsland Lakes can become very rough in strong winds

Looking out across Lake King

Still known to many keen southern estuary anglers simply as the 'Big Three', the trio of major coastal rivers flowing into the Gippsland Lakes of eastern Victoria are the Tambo, the Nicholson and the Mitchell. All three names are synonymous with bream fishing, and have been since the earliest days of recreational angling in Victoria.

Unfortunately, the 'Big Three' don't fish quite as spectacularly nor as consistently today as they did back in those early days, nor even as well as they did in the 1960s and 1970s. Both the numbers and average sizes of fish caught in these rivers have declined — sometimes rather dramatically — over the intervening years, and it can only be hoped that the relatively recent imposition of stricter bag and size limits helps to preserve and even restore depleted southern bream stocks in this popular region.

Any restoration of the 'Big Three' to something approaching their former piscatorial glory seems unlikely, however, at least while commercial harvesting of fish continues in the area.

One of the direct results of the overall decline in the standard of bream fishing along East Gippsland's 'Big Three' rivers in recent years has been a distinct drop in tourist numbers visiting the area, especially in spring, when bream runs associated with the fish's upstream spawning cycle are traditionally at their very best. While this slump in angling-related tourism is obviously a disaster for local businesses — many of which are now struggling for survival or have folded — the downturn can actually be something of a bonus for those who still keenly fish these rivers.

Today, it is sometimes possible to have a productive stretch of water almost entirely to one's self in late winter or early spring, particularly during mid-week periods. Such a luxury was virtually unknown 10 or 15 years ago.

ALONG THE TAMBO

Despite declining bream catches, the Tambo River remains a very popular venue for both bank and boat anglers. It is probably the pick of the 'Big Three' these days, especially in terms of the number of fish likely to be encountered.

The Tambo's popularity with bank anglers is a direct result of the many roads and tracks running alongside or close to its lower and middle reaches. These thoroughfares allow access to both sides of the river along almost its entire fishable length.

Boat anglers favour the Tambo River, too, because it is well protected (at least in parts) from almost all weather and wind conditions, including the very strong westerlies and sou'westers that so commonly blow in spring.

Southern bream aggregate in the Tambo from late July or early August, when dense wattle blooms paint the banks in their rich, golden hue, until at least early or mid-October, although a few fish are available here right throughout the year. As well as bream, there are dusky flathead,

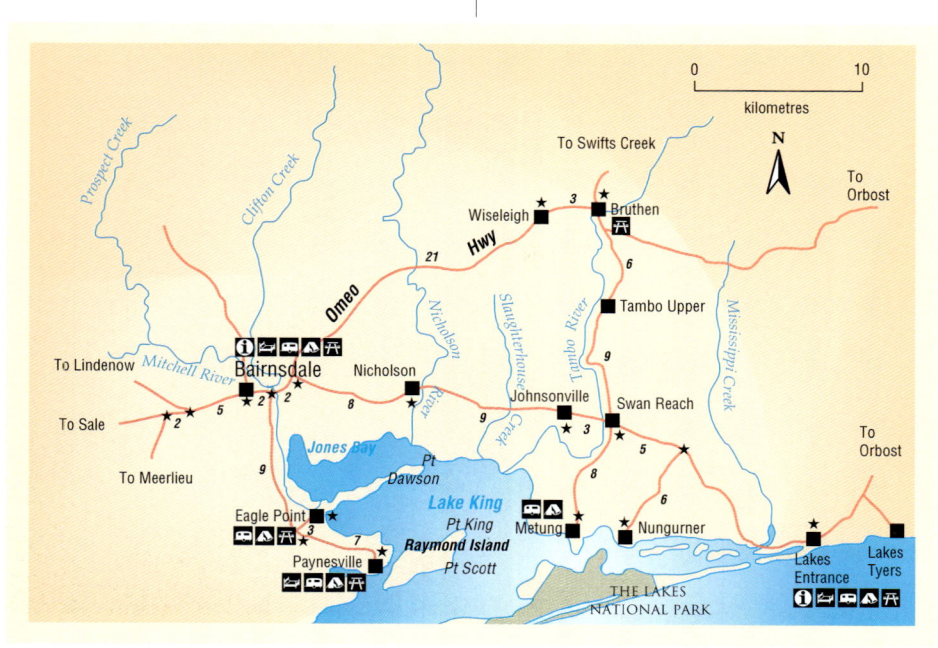

It is also a more difficult spot for shore-based anglers to work effectively. Bank fishing options are limited to the boat ramp and jetty area, just below the Princes Highway on the Melbourne side of the river, and a few other spots further upstream near the Omeo Highway.

As a result of these access difficulties, the Nicholson tends to remain more popular with boat anglers than those confined to the shore, although reasonable bank fishing bags are taken at times.

In addition to southern black bream, the Nicholson River also offers a few luderick or blackfish, good numbers of mullet (mostly yellow-eye mullet, which are often referred to locally as 'golden eyes') and the odd dusky flathead, as well as estuary perch, eels and the introduced European carp a little further upstream.

MITCHELL RIVER SURPRISES

The Mitchell River has its origins on the Dargo High Plains, where it is formed by the confluence of the Dargo and Wonnangatta rivers. Several other small streams also join it above the town of Bairnsdale, where it passes under a major road bridge on the Princes Highway. The Mitchell eventually enters Lake King via a channel between raised, parallel banks known as the Silt Jetties. These natural levees extend well out into and across Lake King, almost enclosing the area known as Jones Bay to the north. Shore-based fishing from these arms or levees can be quite good at times, particularly on their river sides.

Bream, estuary perch and mullet are the most abundant species in the Mitchell, although there are also a few luderick, tailor, garfish and the odd flathead in its lower reaches. All of these estuarine fish are found upstream only as far as the Water Works rock barrier, some 5 km above Bairnsdale. Beyond that point, there are eels, a few bass and even the odd trout.

Indeed, one of the little known aspects of all these Gippsland rivers—but most especially of the Mitchell—is the presence of small populations of trout in their upper and middle reaches, and the occasional appearance of estuarine dwelling or so-called 'sea-run' brown trout in the slightly brackish waters of their lower, tidal sections. Local anglers aware of this surprising phenomenon occasionally take some lovely trout here on baits, lures and even flies while casting in stretches of estuarine water most people would think of purely as bream and mullet country.

Finding and catching these elusive sea trout is rarely easy, but it is certainly well worth the effort involved, particularly when the fish in question tops the 2- or 3-kg mark, as they sometimes do.

All in all, while they 'ain't what they used to be' in angling terms, the East Gippsland's 'Big Three' rivers are still well worth a second look—and not only for their bream!

luderick (blackfish), mullet and small chopper tailor or 'skippy' present in the river's lower section, along with estuary perch and perhaps the odd bass in the upper reaches, particularly around Bruthen. Most of these fish are at their best in the warmer months, from late spring until the middle or end of autumn.

THE PRETTY NICHOLSON

The Nicholson is arguably the prettiest of the 'Big Three' Gippsland rivers, although it tends not to produce quite as many bream as the other two.

A pre-bag limit haul of southern bream from the Tambo River

Boating on the Tambo River in early spring, when the wattle is in bloom

SHARK FISHING OFF PHILLIP ISLAND

IN BRIEF

MAP REFERENCE: PAGE 65 H6

GETTING THERE Phillip Island is about 135 km south of Melbourne along the South Gippsland and Bass highways
BEST TIME TO FISH November to April — conditions are best in a northerly wind
BEST TIME TO TRAVEL Year-round
MAJOR ANGLING SPECIES Mako shark, thresher shark, blue shark, bronze whaler shark and seven-gill shark
SPECIAL RESTRICTIONS The taking of great white sharks was under review in Victoria at the time of publication and it is probable that this species will become protected
WARNINGS Bass Strait is a dangerous waterway and local knowledge is advised
ACCOMMODATION Killunda Caravan Park, telephone (03) 5678 7260; San Remo Caravan Park, telephone (03) 5678 5220; New Haven Caravan Park, telephone (03) 5956 7227; Coleshill Lodge (self-contained units), telephone (03) 5956 9304
CHARTER BOATS AND FISHING GUIDES Corporate Fishing Charters, telephone (03) 9654 2022; Rex Hunt's *Shimano Explorer*, telephone (03) 9589 4035; San Remo Fish and Dive, telephone (03) 5678 5426; *Sharon Lee II*, telephone (03) 5678 5346

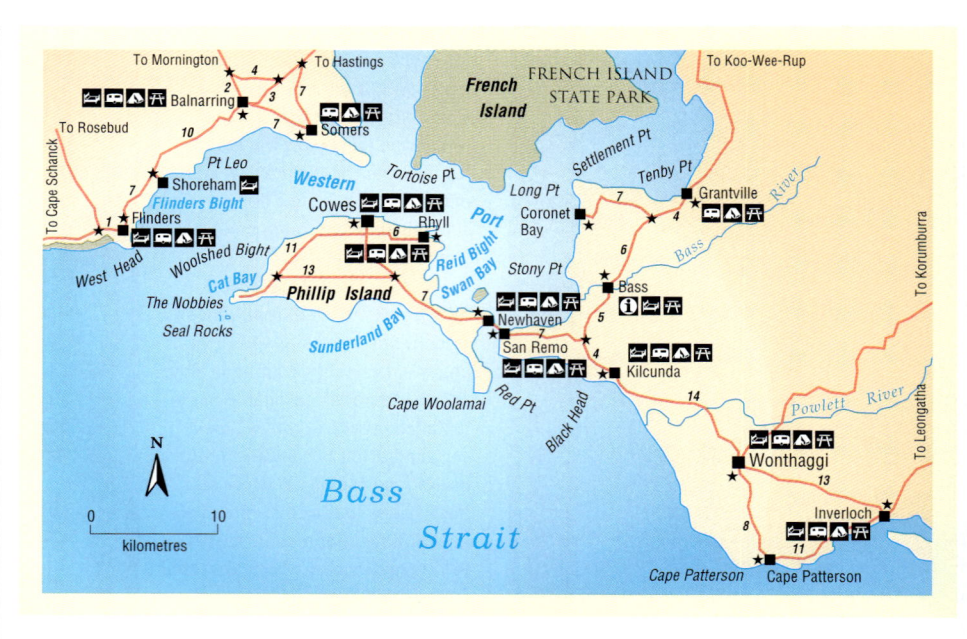

In recent years, a small band of anglers have discovered a new frontier of game fishing in Victorian waters. Laying berley trails in pursuit of a variety of species of sharks is nothing new, but it has never been done with such success as it has lately in the offshore waters of Phillip Island and the Bass Strait beaches. Threshers, makos, blues, hammerheads, bronze whalers and great whites are all a possibility in this world-class fishery only an hour's drive from metropolitan Melbourne. It should be noted, however, that great whites are now protected in most Australian waters.

Between the months of November and May, the stretch of water between Cape Schanck and Cape Paterson comes alive, with surface water temperatures reaching 21°C and higher. These warm waters bring with them many schools of bait fish, including barracouta, slimy mackerel, salmon and yakkas (yellowtail). As with many other forms of fishing, a natural progression occurs: the predators follow the prey and it isn't long until reports of shark activity begin to filter through.

Cape Schanck, at the southern tip of Mornington Peninsula west of Phillip Island

BEATING THE WEATHER

Unfortunately, Bass Strait is often not a good place to be in a boat. The relatively shallow waters, coupled with large southern swells, can make for an uncomfortable and at times dangerous outing. There is a way around this, however, and it has allowed even the smallest of trailer boats to head offshore in search of some serious sharking action.

During summer, which just happens to be the most productive time for sharks, Melbourne experiences many days of hot, northerly winds. These favour the shark angler immensely. Due to the position of Phillip Island and surrounding land formations, these hot northerlies blow directly offshore, flattening the swell and thus allowing anglers to fish on calm seas, even in gales.

Unlike many other game fishing hot spots, here the angler doesn't have to travel a long way offshore for action. In fact, more often than not, the best fish are taken within a kilometre of shore, and occasionally from land-based rock platforms such as Punchbowl and Black Head.

Even though The Nobbies, at the western entrance to Western Port, are renowned for shark captures, amateur anglers more often tend to frequent the eastern entrance waters these days.

PLANNING A TRIP

When planning an offshore trip anywhere in the vicinity of Phillip Island, one fact that must be considered is where anglers will launch their vessels. The Newhaven public ramp is closest to the action, but with rocks flanking both of its sides and a gradient that resembles the Nullarbor Plain, it is a waste of time at most stages of the tide, especially high water. The yacht club ramp which is situated only 10 m away is superb, but it is guarded by a heavy padlock and chain, and only on special occasions is permission given for launching by non-club members.

Anglers travelling from Melbourne and surrounding suburbs tend to use either the Stony Point or Corinella ramps, as both of these are safe and accessible at all stages of the tide. The only drawback is that the fishing grounds are about 30 km by boat from Stony Point and not a lot closer to Corinella.

A note of caution to anglers: take great care as you approach the last port channel marker in Cleeland Bight prior to entering Bass Strait. The tide rips through this area at a rate of knots and, when the wind is against the tide, glassy seas soon turn to extremely choppy waves.

Catching a Shark

Now that anglers are safely out on the water, the decision that they face is which species of shark to target and, more importantly, which area to fish in an effort to find them. This decision is normally made a little easier by the weather. If things are looking good, anglers normally head offshore in search of makos and blues. If the weather is unsettled, however, threshers start to look more and more promising. This is because these sharks can be caught within 100 m of the shoreline, making it easy to tuck the boat in under the cliffs around Punchbowl Rocks in an effort to get out of the wind. More importantly, boat fishers are able to get home quickly if necessary.

The 40- to 50-m depth line off Cape Woolamai is the place to find makos. One specimen of 275 kg was taken there in January 1994.

Although some very large makos are taken in this area, most specimens tend to fall between the 10- and 50-kg marks, which is perfect for anglers targeting their first shark or for those who are looking for big thrills on light line.

When targeting makos, a heavy berley trail should be employed, with pellets, bread, tuna oil and fish offal the key ingredients. As with all forms of berley, keeping the trail unbroken is the key. Then it becomes a waiting game.

The best baits for makos include barracouta, live fish such as salmon and slimy mackerel, skipjack or striped tuna fillets and squid. By far the best bait, however, is a single pilchard, especially when the shark presents itself at the boat's transom prior to being hooked.

The trace should be made of 100- to 200-kg nylon-coated wire and be at least 3 m in length with an 8/0 to 10/0 live bait hook most successful. The rod and reel will vary — anything from 6- to 24-kg stand-up tackle is appropriate, depending on the size of the shark.

Anglers who target makos should be prepared for anything, as it is while fishing for makos that great whites, whalers and blues often appear and sometimes cause havoc. Many an angler has been scared out of his or her wits by a 5-m great white having a curious nibble on the outboard when all that was expected was a 15-kg mako!

The closer offshore reefs, around the 15- to 25-m mark, are where the angler is most likely to encounter the thresher shark, which offers blistering runs and incredible acrobatics when hooked. The tactics for chasing these small-mouthed fish eaters are similar to those used when chasing makos. The major differences are the use of 80- to 100-kg nylon-coated wire, no larger than an 8/0 live bait hook and a trace that has a minimum length of 3 to 4 m to resist abrasion from the shark's unusually large tail.

The berley trail is also scaled down a little and fishing is done at anchor. Baits are set at varying depths and floated out under balloons. Once again, single pilchards are the best bait, but these can be hard to fish when the area's barracouta are ravenous.

The shallow waters in which these threshers are found off Phillip Island also make record captures on light line a real possibility. In December 1997, a pending world record thresher shark of 89.4 kg was taken on 6-kg line just off Punchbowl Rocks. Exactly one week later, the same angler battled a shark of around 60 kg on 4-kg line for more than three hours before the line gave way at the boat's side.

Quality table fish such as snapper, big flathead and whiting add to the excitement of fishing this area, often ensuring a good feed on even the slowest of days.

This shark fishing action is not only available to boat anglers. Several threshers and bronze whalers are taken from popular land-based locations each season. These hot spots include Pyramid Rock, Shelly Beach, Punchbowl Rocks, Black Head and Harmers Haven. It is not an easy task targeting a large shark off the rocks, but it is possible, and very rewarding when successful.

Top: Small mako sharks such as this one abound in the waters off Phillip Island
Above left: A 55-kg thresher shark taken off Phillip Island by game fishers targeting this species
Above right: A magnificent blue shark taken on fly tackle in Bass Strait, near Phillip Island

THE MIGHTY MURRAY

IN BRIEF

MAP REFERENCE: PAGE 69 L7

GETTING THERE The twin cities of Albury–Wodonga are 560 km south-west of Sydney and 309 km north of Melbourne along the Hume Highway

BEST TIME TO FISH Upper reaches, October to May; downstream, year-round

BEST TIME TO TRAVEL Year-round, but outback areas may be very hot from November to March

MAJOR ANGLING SPECIES Brown and rainbow trout (upper Murray), European carp, golden perch, Murray cod, trout cod and redfin

SPECIAL RESTRICTIONS It should be noted that the endangered trout cod is totally protected. A special trout cod protection zone exists between Yarrawonga Weir and Tocumwal road bridge — no fishing is permitted here during the normal Murray cod closed season (September to December)

WARNINGS The areas immediately downstream of major weirs or dams (especially Hume Weir) are subject to large releases of fast-flowing and very cold water at times. The Murray also contains a multitude of submerged snags which are capable of seriously damaging boats and motors. Great caution should be exercised when boating here

CHARTER BOATS AND FISHING GUIDES B & C Fishing Tours, Echuca, telephone (03) 5482 4618 or 018 576 526

Paddle boat and barge on the Murray River near Echuca

Sadly, big Murray cod such as this one are no longer common in the Murray River itself

The mighty Murray River, which forms the border between New South Wales and Victoria for much of its length, is Australia's largest and best known inland waterway. Despite serious degradation over the past century or so, it remains a vitally important icon amongst freshwater anglers in the southern half of this dry nation.

The Murray is normally regarded as beginning where the Indi and Swampy Plains rivers join, just upstream of the Bringenbrong Bridge, on the back road between Khancoban and Corryong. Some people still consider the Indi River — which rises high in the alpine border country between the Victorian and New South Wales' snowfields — to be part of the Murray itself. Technically, at least, this is not the case.

Beyond the confluence of these two alpine trout streams, the willow-lined upper Murray twists northward and then west through grazing country, picking up other feeders such as the Tooma River, Corryong Creek and Cudgewa Creek, all of which also contain good trout stocks, as does the Murray River itself at this point.

Around Thologolong, the upper Murray theoretically joins the backed-up waters of the vast artificial reservoir known as Lake Hume. When this impoundment is at anything less than full capacity (which is usually the case), backed-up waters may not be encountered until the river reaches an area between Bungil and Talgarno.

LAKE HUME

Lake Hume is also fed by waters flowing north out of alpine Victoria along the Mitta Mitta and Kiewa rivers, and provides a valuable angling resource, especially when filled to more than 50 per cent of its capacity. The lake has been well stocked over the years with trout and native species, and also contains large populations of noxious European carp and redfin or English perch. However, its greatest claim to fame is probably the size of its golden perch or yellowbelly, which very occasionally top the 10-kg mark.

Below the high, concrete wall of Hume Weir, the Murray is usually a classic tail race fishery, almost as far downstream as the twin cities of Albury and Wodonga. In other words, when water is being released from the dam, the flow rates here are very high and the water extremely cold.

Some of the largest trout on the Australian mainland are taken here at such times, including monster browns up to 8 kg in weight! These are normally targeted on heavy, sinking lures such as locally made lead fish with their bright feather tails.

When flow rates are more modest, good stocks of golden perch or yellowbelly also move upstream into this stretch of river. Carp, redfin and the occasional Murray cod or trout cod are also taken here at times, although it should be carefully noted that trout cod are completely protected and must be returned to the water alive.

ALBURY TO MULWALA

Downstream of Albury, the Murray River begins to slow and broaden into lazy meanders. The water here becomes much warmer and is often discoloured — thanks in no small part to the mud-sifting behaviour of the many European carp that now call it home. By the time the Murray reaches the backed-up reaches of Lake Mulwala, downstream of Corowa, trout are virtually unknown from its turbid waters. The dominant species are now the ever-present carp, along with golden perch, Murray cod and redfin.

Lake Mulwala itself — the water impounded by Yarrawonga Weir — is justifiably renowned as one of the better Murray cod fisheries left in Australia, and still produces thousands of these sought-after green fish for anglers every year, including a handful of monsters in the 20- to 40-kg range. Most of these are taken on big, slow-trolled, deep-diving lures or on natural baits such as bardi grubs, yabbies, shrimps and worms.

While the rarer big cod attract most media attention, smaller examples in the 40- to 60-cm range remain a far more common catch here, as they do elsewhere. Anglers should remember that strict size and bag limits are in force governing the taking of these wonderful fish, and that there's a closed season from 1 September until 30 November (inclusive) each year.

Yarrawonga to Swan Hill

The Murray River immediately downstream of Yarrawonga Weir and on to Cobram or Tocumwal offers some of the better angling opportunities still on offer in this heavily degraded waterway. While introduced carp continue to outnumber all other species, reasonable stocks of Murray cod and golden perch remain, along with the very occasional silver perch. This is also one of the last natural strongholds of the endangered and protected trout cod, and for that reason the river here is totally off-limits to all fishing during the Murray cod closed season from September to December. (Anglers should carefully check the downstream boundary of this closure, which was recently moved from Barooga to the road bridge at Tocumwal, thus extending the protection zone.)

Downstream from Yarrawonga Weir and all the way to Echuca and well beyond, the Murray has a special attraction for anglers and other holiday makers. Its tree-lined banks and lazily swirling waters typify the look and feel of the southern interior or 'outback', and provide a delightful setting for any camping or fishing trip, especially in spring or autumn.

In this lightly populated region, the Murray River meanders around countless bends, many fringed with clean, sandy beaches, and is bordered along almost its entire length by thick forests of red gum trees, which are home to a wide variety of wildlife.

Bush tracks provide good access to the river here for much of the year, although heavy rain can make them muddy, greasy and impassable to anything but a serious 4WD vehicle.

Boat launching is also rather restricted, with decent ramps only available at Cobram, Tocumwal and Echuca. Various rough earth ramps can be pushed into service, however, when water levels are suitable. Lighter boats, car toppers and canoes can simply be manhandled down the bank.

Fishing the Lower Murray

Beyond Swan Hill, the now muddy and carp-infested Murray River meanders north to Robinvale, thence on to Mildura and Wentworth, where it is joined by the Darling River. From here, it eventually flows west into South Australia and on towards its ultimate confluence with the Southern Ocean, at Murray Mouth.

Fishing and holi-daying (particularly houseboating) along this lower stretch of the Murray are dealt with in far greater detail on pp. 228–9.

Downstream of Yarrawonga Weir, the main drawcard for anglers remains the promise of mixing it with Australia's biggest and most sought-after native freshwater species, the Murray cod.

Sadly, while still present in this much maligned river (and occasionally encountered at weights in excess of 35 kg), the Murray cod has dramatically declined in numbers. Today, exotic European carp are definitely the dominant species in this river, far outnumbering natives such as cod, golden perch, silver perch and eel-tailed catfish.

That is certainly not to say that keen anglers cannot effectively target remnant populations of native fish with reasonable success. In fact, some surprisingly good catches of cod and yellowbelly, in particular, continue to be taken here. All the same, the mighty Murray is today only a pale shadow of its former self.

It stands as mute testimony to the abuse inflicted upon this fragile continent in less than two centuries of European habitation. Saving the ailing Murray–Darling system from complete and possibly irreversible environmental collapse will surely pose one of the greatest challenges facing all Australians during the first two decades of the 21st century.

Fishing in the Murray River near Echuca in New South Wales

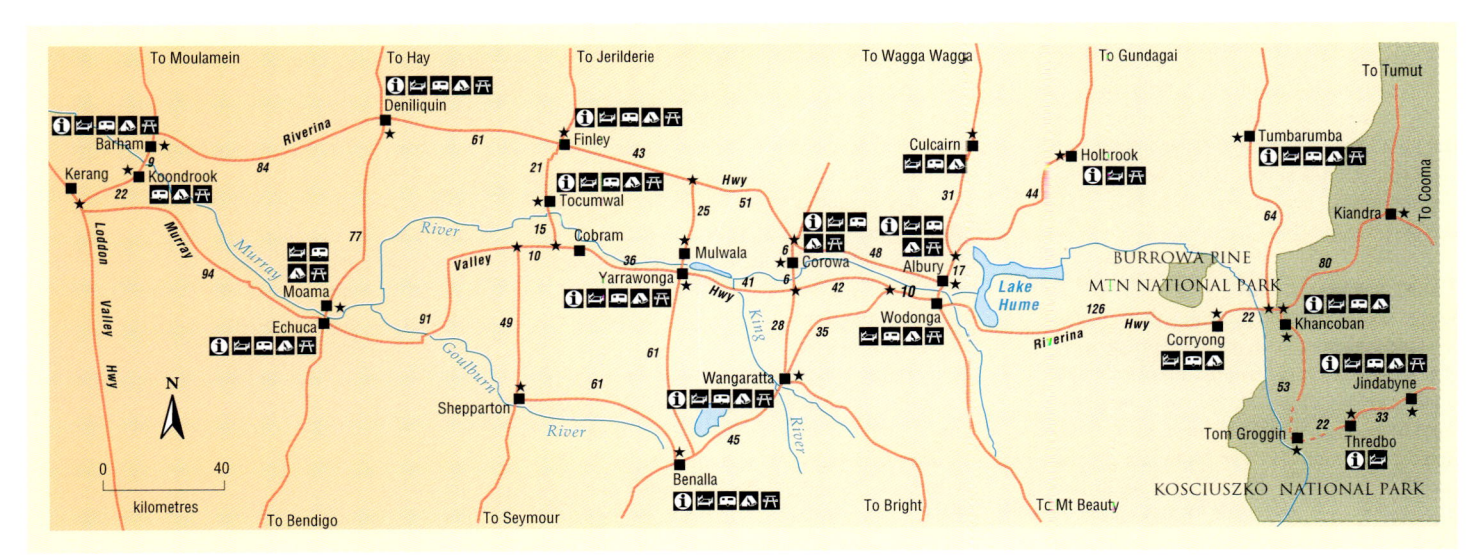

BIG RIVER COUNTRY

IN BRIEF

MAP REFERENCE: PAGE 113 N4

GETTING THERE Grafton is about 350 km south of Brisbane and 650 km north of Sydney along the Pacific Highway
BEST TIME TO FISH Year-round
BEST TIME TO TRAVEL Year-round
MAJOR ANGLING SPECIES Bream, flathead, whiting, tailor, luderick (blackfish), mulloway (jewfish) and bass
SPECIAL RESTRICTIONS The beaches south of Evans Head are part of an RAAF gunnery range and are subject to periodic closure. The east coast or Clarence River cod is totally protected, and any specimens accidentally hooked must be returned to the water immediately
WARNINGS The Clarence River and its tributaries are subject to periodic flooding. Sudden, dramatic rises in river height sometimes occur with very little warning
CHARTER BOATS AND FISHING GUIDES Rob Lockwood's Kingfisher Adventures, telephone (02) 6643 2866; Osprey II, telephone (02) 6646 3330

The large wedge of northern coastal New South Wales centred on Grafton and bounded by the Washpool National Park in the west, Bundjalung National Park to the north and Sandon River to the south is often known as Big River Country, in recognition of the mighty Clarence River system that serves as its main aquatic artery.

In many ways, the Clarence district and its massive river can be regarded as defining the southern boundary of the east coast's true subtropical zone. Sugar cane and bananas thrive here, and tropical fish such as fork-tailed catfish, tarpon (ox-eye herring) and mangrove jack are occasionally taken alongside more familiar species including Australian bass, bream, whiting and flathead.

This region is a justifiably famous recreational fishing destination. It attracts numerous tourists and holiday makers from Brisbane in the north and Sydney to the south, as well as regular visitors from all over regional New South Wales and Queensland.

YAMBA AND ILUKA

Yamba is a fishing and prawning town of about 3500 people situated on the southern shores of the Clarence River mouth. Iluka is a much smaller settlement—less than half the size of Yamba—located on the northern headland of the same river mouth. The two towns are connected via a ferry service, or by road over the bridge at Harwood, north of Maclean. This area is famous for its fishing opportunities, and despite years of

Aerial view of the Clarence River near Yamba

intensive commercial activity by trawlers, netters and trappers, it continues to produce good to excellent results for those willing to invest a little time and effort in the pursuit of their sport.

The Clarence River estuary, between Grafton and its mouth, is one of the most prolific fish producers in New South Wales, and may be fished either from the bank or a boat. Breakwalls at the river's entrance and in its lower reaches provide excellent land-based platforms for anglers targeting tailor, mulloway (jewfish), bream, blackfish, flathead and whiting, and Yamba's famous Middle Wall is one of the best known fishing hot spots in the entire region.

Where the North and South walls extend offshore from the river mouth, they also offer access to migratory pelagic species including tuna, mackerel, kingfish and cobia, as well as numerous sharks and mulloway, especially after floods.

Extensive sand flats within the vast estuary system and adjoining Lake Wooloweyah hold many whiting, bream and flathead, as well as crabs and prawns in season. Good catches of dusky flathead and other species are taken by drift fishing all the way up the river to well beyond Harwood, where the Pacific Highway crosses the Clarence, and at least as far as Maclean and Lawrence at times.

There are several boat ramps in Yamba. These offer anglers the choice of fishing within the Clarence estuary system or heading offshore to various reefs and gravel patches offering reliable action for snapper, teraglin, pearl perch, leatherjackets, flathead and numerous other bottom-dwelling species.

Woody Head, Iluka and the north bank of the Clarence estuary are reached from a well-signposted turn-off to Iluka, 65 km south of Woodburn. Iluka also has several boat ramps, and smaller boats may be launched near the hotel and upstream at an old ferry approach near the power lines.

ROCK AND BEACH LOCATIONS

This entire area also boasts many fine rock and beach fishing locations. These include Woody Head, Iluka Bluff, Little Bluff and Frasers Reef on the northern side of the river mouth. On the southern side, Yamba and nearby Angourie offer access to excellent rock fishing from Flat Rock, Green Point and Angourie Point, while further south lies Yuraygir National Park and a number of prime rock fishing platforms that receive a little less angling pressure by virtue of their isolation.

Tailor, bream, mulloway, drummer, groper and other rock species are abundant from all of these rocky headlands at times, as are big surface fish such as Spanish mackerel, longtail tuna, mackerel tuna, yellowtail kingfish and cobia. The beaches in between produce whiting, bream, tailor, flathead, dart and the occasional big mulloway or jewfish.

The front of Shelley Head, in the Yuraygir National Park, is a particularly good rock fishing spot that is accessible via 5- or 6-km walking trails from either Angourie Point or Red Cliff. The turn-off to Red Cliff is located at Maclean, on the

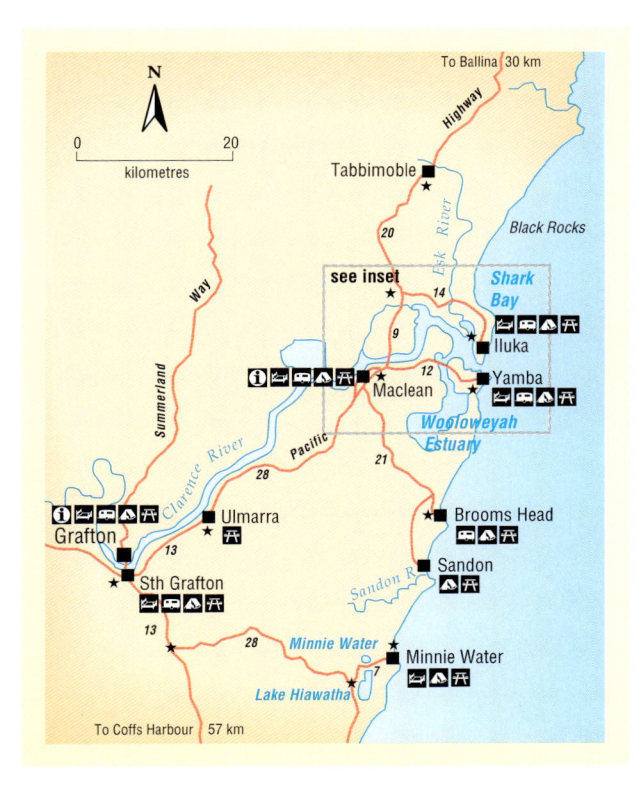

Pacific Highway. This same road leads to nearby Brooms Head and the beautiful Sandon River.

Brooms Head is a small village with a caravan park and store. It offers good beach and rock fishing, especially for tailor, and there is also reef fishing offshore. It is possible to beach launch a boat at Brooms Head, but extreme care should be exercised at all times.

The Sandon River lies south of Brooms Head and marks the end of this particular coastal road, with the Sandon's southern shores being reached via Minnie Waters to the south, along a 4WD track. The Sandon has a boat ramp that provides access to prolific reefs offshore and to the small estuary itself. Whiting, bream and flathead are the major targets in the estuary, along with the occasional mangrove jack taken around the rock bar further upstream.

THE CLARENCE RIVER

Rising high in the rugged mountain rainforests of the Great Dividing Range along the New South Wales–Queensland border, and fed by tributaries flowing in from as far afield as Glen Innes, Guyra and Ebor, the Clarence is a truly massive system. It remains one of the last great untamed and undammed rivers of Australia's south-east.

The highest feeders of the Clarence hold scattered, marginal populations of introduced trout, but as the branches of this mighty river tumble from the high escarpments and join together, unique native species become its dominant inhabitants.

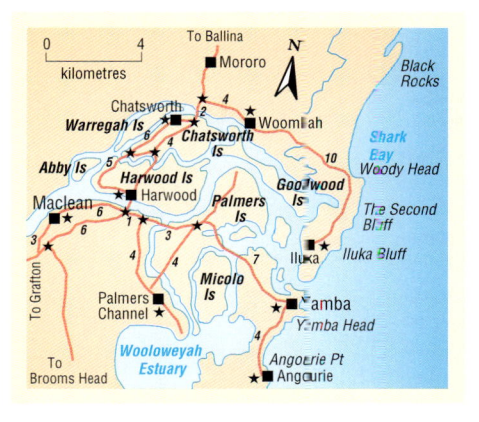

First and foremost amongst these—in terms of both size and importance—is the once threatened and still protected east coast or Clarence River cod. A kissing cousin of the western Murray cod—a species from which it developed in the relatively recent evoluionary past—the east coast cod is a strikingly attractive, highly territorial species possibly capable of reaching 30 or even 40 kg in exceptional cases, but more common in the 1- to 10-kg size range.

Sadly, east coast cod numbers declined dramatically through the 20th century, until rescued from the brink of extinction in the 1980s. Related fish in the Richmond and Brisbane rivers, further north, were not so lucky, and had disappeared completely by the 1960s, while only remnant populations of the Mary River cod survive in that south-eastern Queensland river.

Today, thanks to their protected status and careful restocking of depleted stretches of river, Clarence cod numbers are bouncing back. One day, limited sport fishing (probably on a purely catch-and-release basis) may even be reintroduced for this challenging, hard-fighting species. Meanwhile, any angler accidentally hooking one of these magnificent native fish while targeting eel-tailed catfish or bass should carefully unhook it without excessive handling and return it quickly to the water.

Other fish in the freshwater reaches of this river system include eel-tailed catfish, Australian bass, Nepean herring, eels and the very occasional golden perch or yellowbelly (possibly escapees from farm dams). Of these, it is the bass that attract greatest interest and attention from anglers.

CLARENCE BASS

The rugged Clarence Gorge, upstream from Copmanhurst, acts as an effective natural barrier to the free movement of bass for years at a time. Occasionally, however, it is inundated by massive flooding, allowing fish of all sizes to move in both directions and thereby maintain a healthy population of bass above the gorge in rivers like the Mann, Nymboida and the upper Clarence itself.

Because the Clarence River is bounded by private land along many stretches, access to these regions can be tricky. Adventurous anglers who launch canoes at Buccarumbi, Jackadgerry or Cangai, however, can occasionally enjoy exceptional sport.

More accessible and consistent bass fishing action is available downstream of the Gorge, near Fine Flower and Copmanhurst, as well as in lower Clarence tributaries such as the Orara, Coldstream and Esk rivers and Sportsmans Creek. Here, bass are often taken right alongside other brackish water species such as estuary perch, bream, flathead and the occasional ox-eye herring (tarpon) and mangrove jack.

There are some excellent rock fishing locations in northern New South Wales

COFFS HARBOUR

IN BRIEF

MAP REFERENCE: PAGE 113 N7

GETTING THERE Coffs Harbour is about 420 km south of Brisbane and 550 km north of Sydney along the Pacific Highway
BEST TIME TO FISH Year-round
BEST TIME TO TRAVEL Year-round
MAJOR ANGLING SPECIES Bream, flathead, whiting, tailor, luderick (blackfish), snapper, mulloway (jewfish), mackerel, tuna, bass and various other reef, sport and game species
SPECIAL RESTRICTIONS Areas around the Solitary Islands group off Coffs Harbour and Woolgoolga have been declared as marine reserves and certain activities are prohibited. Anglers should check on the current status of these reserves before fishing near these islands. The east coast or Clarence River cod is totally protected, and any specimens accidentally hooked must be returned to the water immediately unharmed

The lighthouse on South Solitary Island

Originally named Korffs Harbour after Captain John Korff, who sought shelter here in 1847, this well-known northern New South Wales port actually began life as two small towns situated some 3 km apart. Over time, these settlements grew together and their name was eventually 'Australianised' to become Coffs Harbour.

Today, Coffs Harbour is a thriving regional centre with a population in excess of 23 000 people and a well established fruit-growing industry celebrated by the Big Banana theme park and nearby World of Agriculture exhibit.

In addition to agriculture, Coffs Harbour is home to a range of light manufacturing industries and services. Tourism plays an increasingly important role in the city's survival and development, however, and it is particularly well placed to service the needs of holiday makers.

Situated almost midway between Sydney and Brisbane, Coffs Harbour forms the hub of a stretch of coastline that is justifiably renowned as a vacation or retirement destination. This region is blessed with some of the most pleasant weather to be found anywhere in Australia, and its golden beaches are lapped by warm, blue waters that rarely drop below 16°C, even in winter, and often top 25°C during the first six months of the year.

Recreational fishing is one of the area's greatest tourist drawcards, and there are plenty of opportunities for beach, rock, estuary and offshore anglers to pursue their sport.

AN ANGLER'S MECCA

Coffs Harbour is a real angler's mecca, with many fishing hot spots — especially for land-based fishers — situated very close to the city centre itself. Particularly good areas close to Coffs include Boambee Beach to the south, which is well known for its tailor, bream, whiting, dart and school mulloway (jewfish). The aptly named Bream Hole, just south of the harbour's eastern wall, is another popular and productive location, while the harbour rock walls themselves, its southern headland and Muttonbird Island, which is connected to the mainland by the north wall, are also prime land-based spots.

The seaward side of Muttonbird Island and the far end of the east harbour wall, in particular, are rock fishing locations right on the edge of town capable of producing everything from tailor, bream, drummer and mulloway to big Spanish mackerel, cobia and longtail tuna at times.

Park Beach, to the north of Coffs Creek mouth, is the town's main surfing beach and can become rather crowded during periods of hot weather. Good gutters here also produce bags of whiting, dart, bream, tailor and the occasional mulloway. Just like Boambee Beach to the south (and most other surf beaches in this area), there are also good populations of large beach worms to be had on Park Beach.

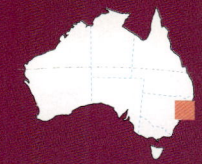

Macauleys Head, at the northern end of Park Beach, produces all of the usual rock-dwelling species. As with most of the headlands in this region, Macauleys can turn on some big mulloway at times, especially after a spell of rough weather. Interestingly, this is one region where keen anglers deliberately target big mulloway or jewfish on lures, even outside of flood times, and some monsters have been taken on large, strong-actioned minnows and plugs fished off heavy tackle, particularly at dawn and dusk.

Diggers Beach, between Macauleys and the Blue Gutter at Diggers Head, is another popular surfing beach that also produces reasonable fishing, while rock species and the odd decent snapper are taken from the headlands at both ends, particularly from ledges such as Jarrets Rock, the rather dangerous Sunday Seat and the Blue Gutter itself.

Local Estuaries

Coffs Creek is a relatively small estuary that produces quite reasonable catches of bream, flathead, whiting and blackfish (luderick) at times, as well as the very occasional mangrove jack. There are also a few bass to be had in this creek west of the Pacific Highway, and some big mud crabs in the upper tidal reaches.

Further inland, behind Coffs, the Orara River (a southern tributary of the Clarence River system) holds good bass, Nepean herring, catfish and a sprinkling of protected east coast cod, although any of the latter species accidentally hooked while targeting bass must be carefully unhooked and returned immediately to the water.

South of Coffs Harbour, Bonville Creek is recognised as one of the more southerly locations capable of producing reasonably reliable mangrove jack action for those who put in the effort with lures or live baits. Flathead, bream and whiting are usually better bets, however, especially for visiting anglers.

While these smaller creeks can be quite productive at times, most keen estuary anglers prefer to travel south to the Bellinger River near Urunga, the Nambucca River at Nambucca Heads or even the Macleay, at South West Rocks, in order to pursue their sport. Others go north to Wooli or the delightful little Sandon River.

Offshore from Coffs

Coffs Harbour is blessed with a big, safe harbour, extensive marina facilities and good boat launching ramps. This infrastructure, combined with the excellent standard of fishing available offshore, helps to explain why Coffs is such a popular boat fishing base.

Offshore action starts as close as the wash zones around Pig, Muttonbird and Little Muttonbird islands, where tailor, snapper, bream, trevally, drummer, groper, bonito and mackerel tuna (kawa kawa) may all be caught, along with the occasional larger target in the form of a mulloway, Spanish mackerel, cobia or tuna.

Further out, any decent reef patch, rubble ground, hole, peak or pinnacle revealed by the use of a depth sounder is likely to produce snapper, morwong, kingfish, Samson fish, pearl perch, pigfish, teraglin and other reef or bottom-fishing varieties. Sandy areas are well worth a drift for flathead. Live baits suspended near the surface while drifting will also catch mackerel on these grounds, especially in early autumn.

While many reef fishers also prefer to drift, better results are often obtained by carefully anchoring just upcurrent of a bottom feature and laying down a sparse berley trail of cut fish pieces and bait scraps before presenting lightly weighted offerings of whole or cut pilchards, tuna flesh, fresh squid, octopus or large prawns. Such tactics regularly produce some wonderful snapper, along with teraglin, jewfish, kings and Samson fish. Further out, in deeper water, the delicious pearl perch is likely to show up in catches, and mackerel often make a good showing around Easter.

Moving north, The Wash, wide of Woolgoolga, is a prominent bombora or reef over which the sea breaks in all but the calmest of conditions, creating a zone of aerated white water that attracts bait species and predators alike. The Wash is particularly renowned for producing big tailor, Spanish mackerel, cobia and yellowtail kingfish, although drummer, groper and big bream also call it home.

Further offshore from this same stretch of coast lie the Solitary Islands, and the reef-strewn waters surrounding these beautiful islands present plenty of excellent opportunities for boat anglers chasing snapper, pearl perch, mulloway, Spanish and spotted mackerel, tuna of several types, trevally, yellowtail kings and Samson fish, to name just a few of the more common and popular species likely to be encountered.

It should be carefully noted, however, that parts of the Solitary Islands' group are included in a marine reserve. Certain activities are restricted or even prohibited within areas of this reserve. It is important to check the current status of these restrictions and the boundaries of any special zones well before going fishing.

Fighting a large striped marlin offshore from Coffs Harbour

Year-round Game Fishing

These days, Coffs Harbour is rapidly developing a serious reputation as a year-round game and sport fishing port of considerable significance. As well as light and medium tackle targets including mackerel, kingfish, wahoo, dolphin fish and school tuna, the waters wide of Coffs also see regular influxes of larger predators including big tuna, marlin and some heavyweight sharks.

This is one of the few ports in New South Wales where marlin—including very large Indo-Pacific blues to 300 kg and more—can be hooked during every month of the year, even in the normally 'quiet' period from July to November.

This same time frame sees good quantities of yellowfin tuna in the 15- to 45-kg range travelling through the waters off Coffs, along with some solid striped marlin and hard fighting mako sharks. There is also an as yet largely untapped potential for catching broadbill swordfish and big-eye tuna on rod and reel in the deep waters beyond Coffs Harbour's narrow continental shelf.

Snapper are prolific on the reefs off Coffs Harbour

LORD HOWE ISLAND

IN BRIEF

GETTING THERE Lord Howe Island lies in the South Pacific Ocean 702 km north-east of Sydney and almost due east of Port Macquarie. It is serviced regularly by flights from Sydney, Port Macquarie and Brisbane
BEST TIME TO FISH Year-round
BEST TIME TO TRAVEL Year-round
MAJOR ANGLING SPECIES Yellowtail kingfish, wahoo, yellowfin tuna, dolphin fish (mahi mahi), marlin, whaler sharks, bluefish, double headers, Australian salmon and silver drummer
SPECIAL RESTRICTIONS The maximum number of visitors to Lord Howe island is capped. Advance bookings are essential
ACCOMMODATION There are numerous lodges and guest houses on the island
CHARTER BOATS AND FISHING GUIDES Several charter boats operate from the island. For specialist fishing trips, contact Gary Crombie of Oblivienne Charters, telephone (03) 6563 2155

Lord Howe Island's sheltered lagoon offers a range of angling opportunities

Lord Howe Island is a true jewel of the South Pacific. It is hardly surprising that almost everyone who visits this magnificent location eventually returns, nor that many go on to become 'regulars', spending at least one holiday on Lord Howe each year or two for the rest of their lives! There is just something very magical and incredibly special about this place that seems to call people back again and again.

Many first-time visitors to Lord Howe Island are amazed when they closely study a map and finally come to realise that this is not a 'tropical' island in the true sense of that word. It lies well south of the Tropic of Capricorn, and is not even off the Queensland coast, as so many people seem to expect. In fact, Lord Howe Island is actually on almost exactly the same latitude as Port Macquarie, in northern New South Wales—well south of mainland ports such as Coffs Harbour.

Yet the feeling on Lord Howe is undeniably that of a tropical paradise, and this is not dispelled in any way by the abundance of swaying palm trees or the aquamarine intensity of the lagoon shallows, where colourful schools of fish flash amongst bright coral outcrops. It should never be forgotten, however, that this is the southernmost hard coral island to be found anywhere in the world, nor that Lord Howe Island owes its balmy climate and lush vegetation more to the constantly warm ocean currents that bathe its shores than its geographic location.

A Plethora of Species

In addition to being a holiday getaway of almost unmatched appeal, Lord Howe is a true angler's paradise. Since being put firmly on the sport fishing map in the 1980s, it has joined a short list of the most desirable and talked about fishing destinations in all of Australia.

Marlin, tuna of several types, massive numbers of yellowtail kingfish, whaler sharks, wahoo, dolphin fish or mahi mahi, silver trevally of world record size, spangled emperor, delicious bluefish, thumping great silver drummer, Australian salmon and the unique double header wrasse are all amongst Lord Howe's regular piscatorial targets. There are many others on the inventory as well, including more than a few surprises. For example, some huge bonefish, schools of juvenile milkfish and secretive snub-nosed dart or permit have all been encountered here, and there are days when anglers literally cannot guess what will next grab their baits, lures or flies.

At the bread-and-butter end of the spectrum, Lord Howe's lagoon, surf beaches, rocky coves and sheltered bays are also endowed with more than enough big garfish, whiting, mullet, small trevally and other 'pan fish' species to keep the casual angler or family fisher happy.

Kingfish Heaven

Lord Howe Island is probably most famous in fishing circles for the abundance and size of its yellowtail kingfish. While they may have become slightly harder to catch in recent years (probably as a direct response to angling pressure), these pugnacious predators still swarm here in numbers long since forgotten on Australia' east coast.

Most Lord Howe kingfish run between 2 and 12 kg, although there are enough 'greenbacks'— a local term for fish in excess of 15 or 16 kg—to add spice to any offshore or rock fishing trip. These green and gold torpedoes can be found anywhere from the jetty right in front of the town to well beyond the continental shelf, but the reef-strewn waters surrounding that awesome rock spire known as Balls Pyramid— an hour's boat ride south of the island—is the best place of all to find these fish, especially in their larger sizes.

Once located, Lord Howe kingies respond to jigs, trolled minnows and other lures, poppers, dead baits and live baits, although live baits tend to produce the largest specimens these days.

A big kingfish taken in the shadow of Balls Pyramid

A Carpet of Grey

If yellowtail kingfish sometimes seem to exist in plague proportions at Lord Howe Island, then so, too, do sharks. Whalers predominate, although the odd hammerhead shows up offshore and some very big tigers can also be found hanging around the reef entrances at times.

The whalers are at their most prolific in mid- to late summer, often tearing hooked fish to pieces and generally making a nuisance of themselves. These predators hunt in packs, and usually appear just as a big kingfish or yellowfin tuna is pumped into view after a long, hard fight. Occasionally, there are so many sharks that the water seems to be turning grey, as if a new land mass is rising from the depths!

At such times, the best approach is to move and look for a new fishing area—usually in deeper water—and hope that the 'brat pack' can be left behind in the shallows.

Game and Sport Fishing

The deep, blue seas around Lord Howe Island play host to strong seasonal influxes of pelagic game fish. Black, blue and striped marlin, as well as some big sailfish, have all been taken from these waters, although blacks in the 60- to 200-kg range are the most common billfish, along with a smattering of Indo-Pacific blues.

Most Lord Howe marlin are taken on trolled skirted lures, which have the bonus of also being highly attractive to other game species common in these waters, notably yellowtail kingfish, wahoo and the odd dolphin fish or mahi mahi.

Yellowfin tuna are year-round visitors to Lord Howe, although the period from January through May offers the greatest numbers of these beautiful fish, while winter is the time to target bigger specimens over the 50-kg mark.

Wahoo are also thickest during the first six months of the year, but can turn up at any time when the warm currents are running. Deep-diving magnum minnows and bibless trolling lures are ideal for targeting these living lightning bolts of the sea, some of which top 30 kg.

Reef and Bottom Fishing

Bottom fishing at Lord Howe can turn up some real surprises. Aside from the expected hauls of kingfish, whaler sharks, big silver trevally and spangled emperor, species such as black cod (which are protected and must be released), the odd red emperor and even the occasional giant snapper topping 10 kg in weight are all likely to show up in the catch.

Sea Breezes

If Lord Howe Island has one downside (apart from the expense of getting there and the moderately high price of most island holiday packages), it is the fact that the wind blows quite briskly on at least two days out of every three and sometimes reaches gale force strength, especially in winter.

While this phenomenon can be very annoying for visitors, the island's sheer bulk and its two towering mountains (Gower and Lidgbird) ensure there's always a sheltered lee shore somewhere, so fishing is still possible, even in the strongest blow ... and after all, there's always tomorrow.

A double-header or hump-headed wrasse

THE NEW SOUTH WALES FAR SOUTH COAST

IN BRIEF

MAP REFERENCE: PAGE 109 E7

GETTING THERE Merimbula is approximately 470 km by road from Sydney, 580 km from Melbourne and 270 km from Canberra
BEST TIME TO FISH October to June
BEST TIME TO TRAVEL Year-round
MAJOR ANGLING SPECIES Bream, flathead, whiting, Australian salmon, tailor, luderick, snapper, game fish and southern reef species
SPECIAL RESTRICTIONS Landing on Montague Island is only allowed with a permit from National Parks. Some roads and access tracks into national parks (particularly south of Eden) have recently been closed and entry permits may be required, even for hikers
WARNINGS Heavy seas make many of the exposed rock fishing locations in this area extremely dangerous. Caution should always be exercised when rock fishing. Also, the Narooma and Merimbula bars (harbour entrances) are potentially hazardous to vessels in some sea conditions. Seek local knowledge first
CHARTER BOATS AND FISHING GUIDES Darryl's Discount Tackle and Dive, Narooma, telephone (02) 4476 2111; Bermagui Boat Charters, Bermagui, telephone 018 397 635; K9 Fishing Charters, Merimbula, telephone (02) 6495 1934; Freedom Charters, Eden, telephone (02) 6496 1209

Saltwater Bay in Ben Boyd National Park south of Eden

The region defined as the far south coast of New South Wales can best be said to begin beyond the Clyde River at Batemans Bay and extend all the way to the Victorian border—a distance of some 250 km. This is a truly delightful coastal area that has always been extremely popular with Victorian and Canberran visitors, but less so with those from further north in New South Wales, who have traditionally looked to that state's north coast and portions of south-eastern Queensland for their favoured holiday destinations.

If the far south coast of New South Wales has a significant drawback for the travelling angler, it is the region's less-than-perfect weather. Winters here are relatively long and significantly more severe than those experienced around Sydney, and the fishing action tends to be very slow during the coolest part of the year. Therefore, peak fishing on the far south coast—at least in terms of consistent results with popular species—is generally best confined to the warmer months of the year.

NAROOMA AND MONTAGUE ISLAND

The well-known tourist port of Narooma, overlooking the clean, aquamarine waters of Wagonga Inlet, is a major holiday destination for people from all over southern New South Wales, the Australian Capital Territory and Victoria. Narooma becomes a hive of bustling activity every Christmas and Easter holiday period, with its population swelling to many times the usual figure of around 3500 permanent residents.

Wagonga Inlet provides very good to excellent fishing for bream, dusky flathead (including some absolute monsters), luderick (blackfish), sand whiting, tailor, silver trevally, leatherjackets, garfish and the like, as well as the odd big mulloway or jewfish, particularly during the warmer months. Juvenile snapper (also known as 'cockney bream' or red bream) are also abundant inside the inlet at times. While many of these fish are under the legal minimum length, a few 'keepers' also turn up in some catches.

A black marlin taken in the waters off the New South Wales far south coast

Because it has no major freshwater feeders or tributaries, and is flushed twice daily by strong tides, Wagonga Inlet tends to stay stunningly clean and clear, even after heavy rain. Also, this inlet is not fished commercially by professional netters (at least, not legally!), so its aquatic flora and fauna remain in a far more natural and undisturbed state than is the case with many other south coast estuary systems, which are hammered hard by the commercial sector.

Rock, beach and breakwall fishing in the Narooma area is also extremely worthwhile, with the ledges below the famous and very picturesque golf course being justifiably renowned as top spots to lure or bait cast for Australian salmon, tailor and bonito, or search for resident drummer and groper.

It is as a stepping-off point for boat fishers, however, that Narooma is most famous. Thanks to its shallow and sometimes dangerous entrance bar, the term 'infamous' might actually be far more suitable!

Despite several well-publicised fatalities and many more close shaves, the Narooma Bar is actually quite tame on three days out of any four. The trick lies in knowing when to stay at home!

The offshore attractions between Narooma and Bermagui are many, but one stands out from the rest. Some 6 or 8 km east south-east of Narooma and 22 km north north-east of Bermagui, lies one of Australia's best-known and most legendary fishing spots, Montague Island.

Over the years, the area around this island has produced more big yellowfin tuna (including a score of specimens over the 100-kg mark) than any other location in the country. Sadly, however, catches have declined dramatically in number, if not in size, since the early 1990s.

Yellowfin tuna are not the only species present in these rich waters. Marlin, sharks, bonito and

THE NEW SOUTH WALES FAR SOUTH COAST

View across a rocky beach in Mimosa Rocks National Park, north of Tathra

Bermagui to Tathra

If Narooma is this region's tourism jewel, then Bermagui is certainly its fishing capital. A classic seafaring port whose entire existence is tied to the bounty of the ocean, Bermagui waxes and wanes between sleepy village and bustling resort with the passage of the seasons. It has been an icon of Australian game fishing since American novelist Zane Grey first visited the town in the 1930s.

Bermagui is justifiably renowned as a premier game and sport fishing port, with exceptional catches of tuna, sharks and marlin taken each year by its well-established charter fleet and flotilla of visiting and local trailer boats. With a much safer harbour entrance than Narooma and the presence of prolific grounds such as the Four, Six and Twelve Mile Reefs, its narrow continental shelf and reasonable proximity to Montague Island, 'Bermi' or 'Berma' is ideally placed to serve as a base for the dedicated offshore angler.

Shore and estuary fishing is also available here and, in particular, the string of small estuaries, coastal lagoons and tidal lakes along the picturesque coastline between Bermagui and Tathra offer excellent action at times for bream, flathead, whiting, luderick, mullet, garfish and other species.

The pick of these systems are Cuttagee, Murrah, Wapengo, Nelson lakes and lagoons, and the Bega River estuary (Mogareka Inlet). Most of these areas offer their best results from December until April. Further upstream, the Bega River still has some nice bass. Finding them in the silted, braided channels, however, is certainly not easy.

South of the Bega River mouth (which is often closed), a long surf beach sweeps around to the fast-growing village of Tathra, with its rocky headlands, bays and famous old steamer wharf.

Now renovated and repaired, this heritage-listed timber platform offers excellent fishing for everything from yellowtail, slimy mackerel, tailor and trevally to salmon, kingfish, the odd tuna and some very big sharks. It even has its own tackle shop, and a quaint little cafe that serves excellent cappuccinos!

Tathra also boasts one of the safest and best-serviced ocean boat ramps on the south coast. Nestled in sheltered Kianinny Bay, this ramp offers quick access to the sea in all but the heaviest of southerly swells. It also allows trailer boat fishers to reach some superb flathead, morwong and snapper grounds, as well as the seasonal sport and game fishing action of the narrow continental shelf and deeper canyons beyond.

Merimbula and Pambula

The Merimbula–Pambula area is one of Victoria's favourite holiday getaway destinations, and becomes an extremely busy tourist centre from early December until late April each year. Many of these visitors from south of the border come here specifically to fish, and most pursue bread-and-butter species such as bream, flathead and whiting in the two major lake systems, as well as several smaller coastal estuaries that intermittently run to the sea between Wallagoot Lake in the north and Twofold Bay in the south.

Merimbula Lake is the best known of these estuaries. Its Top Lake, in particular, produces reasonable catches of flathead, bream, luderick and chopper tailor throughout the warmer months, as well as the occasional mulloway or jewfish to 15 kg or better and, surprisingly, some very big whiting on cold winter's nights.

The entrance to Merimbula Lake, although shallow, is navigable on most tides even for reasonably large vessels, and gives access to some excellent offshore fishing. Its bar has a nasty and largely undeserved reputation for treachery, but is usually quite tame in all but the sort of seas that would confine sensible sailors to the shore. The low concrete road bridge downstream of the boat ramp is a far greater problem, effectively preventing the passage of larger trailer boats on some stages of the tide.

Nearby, the restored and rebuilt Merimbula Wharf is almost as popular a fishing platform as its sister structure in Tathra, although not quite as productive in terms of fish numbers these days.

Eden, Twofold Bay and Wonboyn

Once considered as a possible site for Australia's national capital because of its deep, natural harbour, Eden is today one of the busiest commercial fishing ports in New South Wales. This area also provides excellent fishing opportunities and services for recreational anglers.

Not generally recognised as a major tourist destination in the same league as Merimbula or Narooma, Eden remains less crowded in the peak holiday period than many other southern coastal centres. That fact, combined with its surprising variety of fishing options, makes the area something of a well-kept secret amongst keener anglers.

This region — particularly the long promontory of Green Cape, to the south — also represents a geographic boundary zone for many types of fish. Wandering southern species such as King George whiting and southern bream may be encountered around Eden at times, along with all the regular east coast targets.

Within the vast expanse of the aptly named Twofold Bay, both shore and boat anglers can usually find a sheltered location to fish, regardless of the wind and sea conditions.

schools of yellowtail kingfish regularly frequent the seas around Montague Island. At times, tropical speedsters such as wahoo and dolphin fish or mahi mahi also swim here in good numbers. For the bottom fisher, snapper, kingfish, trevally, morwong, leatherjackets, sweep and flathead round out the picture.

The best fishing around Montague Island usually occurs between November and July, with the big yellowfin tuna action (when it still happens) peaking from mid-April until late June.

Deep-sea anglers proudly displaying their catch, including morwong

Boat anglers drifting these waters take reasonable catches of flathead, as well as leatherjackets, whiting, sweep, silver trevally and the occasional snapper. Further offshore, outside the bay, seasonal reef, sport and game fishing action is similar to that experienced off the better known southern ports such as Narooma and Bermagui.

Shore-based anglers are also well catered for, with piers, beaches and various rock platforms, the most famous being those on Green Cape — one of the Meccas of land-based game fishing for kingfish, tuna and sharks.

South of Green Cape lies Disaster Bay. At the back of this bay, one of the most delightful little estuary systems in the entire region joins the sea. Wonboyn Lake and the river of the same name are famous for producing very good catches of bream, flathead, luderick, whiting, mullet and tailor. In the summer months, this system is also one of the best on the far south coast for mulloway or jewfish, with specimens up to 12 or 14 kg being taken quite regularly, especially by keen night-time anglers.

Further up the river, more bream, some very big flathead, the odd bass and isolated pockets of estuary perch also provide sporadic action, particularly in late summer, autumn and spring.

To the north and south of the Wonboyn Lake's often shallow entrance, rock platforms and surf beaches turn on good catches of tailor and salmon almost all year round for those casting lures, flies or whole pilchard baits, as well as a few hefty gummy sharks in the summer and autumn months.

Further offshore, Disaster Bay still boasts some of the finest flathead drifting on the far south coast, and is visited seasonally by schools of Australian salmon, yellowtail kingfish and tuna of several species. Although not as productive today as it was 20 or 30 years ago, Wonboyn is still a very worthwhile fishing destination, and a great place for a family holiday — as, indeed, is the entire far south coast of New South Wales.

A jackass morwong lying on top of a catch of gurnard perch with distended swim bladders

THE SNOWY MOUNTAINS

IN BRIEF

MAP REFERENCE: PAGE 109 A6

GETTING THERE Cooma is approximately 420 km by road from Sydney and 115 km from Canberra

BEST TIME TO FISH October to May, although good winter fishing also available

BEST TIME TO TRAVEL October to May; snow may close roads in mid-winter

MAJOR ANGLING SPECIES Brown, rainbow and brook trout and land-locked Atlantic salmon

SPECIAL RESTRICTIONS Closed seasons apply in all streams and rivers in this area. There are bag, size and tackle restrictions on the taking of trout and salmon. Some areas of the high country lie within Kosciuszko National Park and access is controlled, restricted or subject to entry fees

WARNINGS Extreme weather conditions are possible at any time of the year in high alpine regions. Check road conditions before travelling and always carry suitable clothing and emergency supplies

CHARTER BOATS AND FISHING GUIDES Steve Williamson, Trout Guide, Jindabyne, telephone (02) 6456 1342 or 018 024 436; Alpine Angler Tackle Store, Cooma West, telephone (02) 6452 5538

A brace of browns from the Eucumbene River

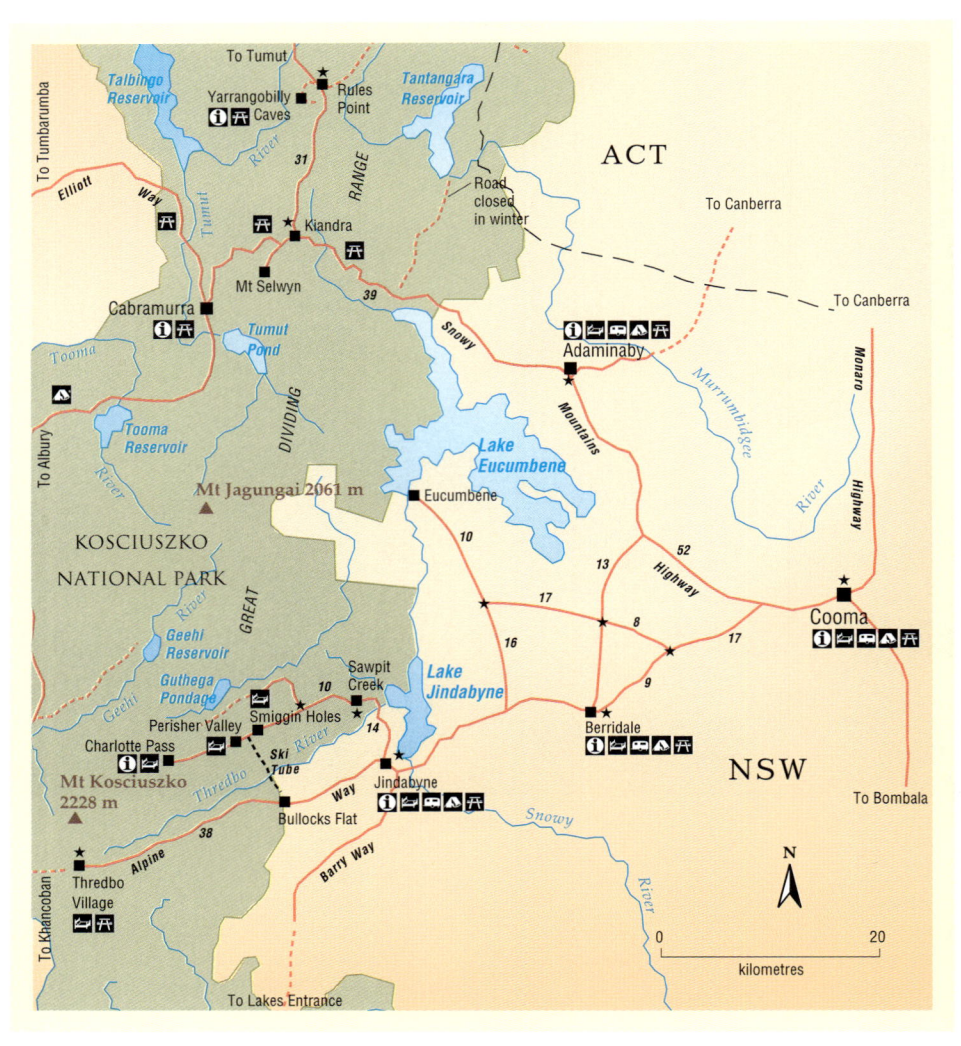

Created during the construction of the massive Snowy Mountains Scheme (SMS) during the 1950s and 1960s, Lakes Eucumbene and Jindabyne are today the two most striking jewels in the crown of mainland trout fishing, and represent extremely popular destinations for the country's growing freshwater angling fraternity.

Both lakes are massive bodies of water—particularly Eucumbene—and are well stocked with trout. These fish include 'wild' trout (especially browns) spawned in the various feeder streams of the two lakes, as well as hatchery bred fingerlings released in large numbers each year. In addition to abundant brown and rainbow trout, Lake Jindabyne also contains a reasonable population of land-locked Atlantic salmon, bred and stocked by the staff at nearby Gaden Hatchery, as well as a sprinkling of attractively marked brook trout (which are actually a char, rather than a true trout) from the same establishment.

In addition to the two big lakes described in detail here, there are various smaller impoundments and some excellent trout streams and rivers in the Snowy Mountains region. These streams are open to angling between October and June each year. Notable amongst them are the Eucumbene, Thredbo (Crackenback), Snowy, Gungarlin and upper Murrumbidgee rivers and their various tributaries.

LAKE EUCUMBENE

As mentioned, the two major lakes in the Snowy Mountains were formed by the damming of the Eucumbene and Snowy River systems during the late 1950s. Lake Eucumbene lies at a higher altitude than Lake Jindabyne and is therefore cooler for a greater part of the year. Its many shallow bays do warm quickly in late spring and early summer, however, kick-starting a food chain of aquatic life that sees prolific shallow-water feeding by the lake's generous trout population.

This factor, combined with the presence of excellent spawning beds in the upper Eucumbene River, conspire to provide ideal trout habitat and to ensure that fish densities and growth rates in Lake Eucumbene remain very high.

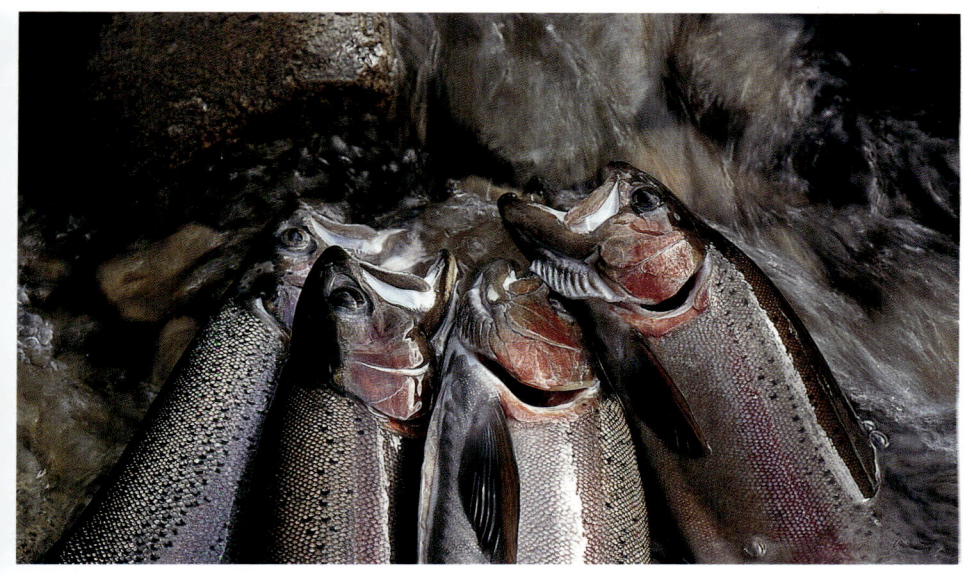

A fine catch of rainbow trout from alpine waters

While a few fish can be caught almost anywhere in Lake Eucumbene during every week of the year, there is a general movement of trout throughout this large lake with the passage of the seasons.

During the height of summer, concentrations of fish occur in deeper water towards the lower (downstream) end of the lake. These fish make regular nocturnal and early morning or late afternoon forays into the adjacent shallow bays to hunt yabbies, snails, small fish and insect nymphs such as dragonfly larvae or 'mudeyes'. Hot spots at this time of year include Middlingbank, Buckendera, Fryingpan Arm, Braemer Bay and Eucumbene Cove.

Later, in autumn, many fish—but especially the lake's abundant 'wild' brown trout—begin o move up the lake towards the Providence Arm in preparation for their spawning run into the Eucumbene River and its smaller tributary creeks. At this time, fishing action picks up around Seven Gates, Anglers Reach, Providence Arm and at Providence Portal itself, as well as in the mouth and lower reaches of the upper Eucumbene River.

In late autumn and early winter, the action is concentrated around Providence Portal, where a large tunnel discharges cold water from Tantangara Reservoir, and in the lower and middle stretches of the Eucumbene River itself, at least until the stream fishing season closes at the beginning of June.

In spring, hungry post-spawn fish spread back down through the main basin of the lake and into its many arms, and the entire cycle begins anew.

LAKE JINDABYNE

At first glance, Lake Jindabyne appears much less fertile and prolific than Eucumbene, but this smaller, lower lake with its rocky shores, sandy beaches and gravel banks also contains lush weed beds. These harbour a multitude of the tasty invertebrate life forms favoured by hungry trout. As a rule of thumb, Jindabyne's trout are slightly less numerous, but somewhat larger on average than their Eucumbene counterparts.

The presence of Atlantic salmon and brook trout (brook char) in Jindabyne also adds to this lake's appeal, with the promise of a Jindabyne 'grand slam' (catching a rainbow, brown, brookie and Atlantic salmon in a single day) bringing many keen anglers back again and again.

Similar fish movements to those already described for Eucumbene occur within Lake Jindabyne, with the major spawning river here being the Thredbo or Crackenback. Another very interesting phenomenon occurs in Lake Jindabyne, however, and one that is keenly anticipated by many anglers.

During late winter and early spring, this lake's water level begins to draw down dramatically due to hydroelectric generation and the trapping of potential run-off in the form of snow on nearby mountain peaks. Yabbies hibernating in their bankside burrows are forced to evacuate their homes en masse at such times and follow the receding waterline as it falls. Hungry trout—particularly post-spawn browns—actively target these crustaceans in the shallow lake margins.

As a result, superb shore fishing action is often experienced between late June or July and October, with the peak occurring in August and September; especially during spells of settled weather associated with slow-moving high-pressure systems. At such times, it is possible to walk the shores of the lake wearing polarised sunglasses and sight as many as 30 or 40 cruising trout in a single day!

These fish—which run anywhere from 600 g to 4 kg—are best targeted with wet flies or small lures that imitate the lethargic, cold-numbed crayfish shuffling through the shallows, although good catches are sometimes taken on baits such as lightly weighted scrub worms flicked out from the shore.

Like their Eucumbene counterparts, Jindabyne trout also respond well to trolled lures throughout much of the year. Deep fishing techniques utilising downriggers or lead-core line are generally more effective here, however, particularly in mid-summer and mid-winter. Prime trolling depths are usually around the 4- to 8-m mark, with 5 m being a particularly 'hot' zone.

Productive areas in Lake Jindabyne include Stinky Bay, the various islands, Hatchery, Hayshed and Rushes bays, the East Jindabyne shoreline and 'bubbler', the Kalkite Arm, Waste Point and the Thredbo and Snowy River arms.

The lakes and streams of this region are fed by alpine snowfields

CAPE YORK

IN BRIEF

MAP REFERENCE: PAGE 154

GETTING THERE The Jardine River is 2640 km north of Brisbane. From Cairns, it is 974 km by road to the tip of Cape York (4WD only). There are scheduled and charter flights from Cairns to Bamaga, Horn Island and Weipa

BEST TIME TO FISH April to December

BEST TIME TO TRAVEL May to October

MAJOR ANGLING SPECIES Barramundi, saratoga, mangrove jack, trevally, queenfish, mackerel and reef species

SPECIAL RESTRICTIONS Permits and special restrictions apply in some Aboriginal reserves and national parks. You need a ferry and access permit to enter all areas north of the Dulhunty River. This can be obtained from the Injinoo Community Council, telephone (07) 4069 3252, or at the ferry on the Jardine River. You need a permit from the DEH to camp in national parks. There is a closed season on the taking of barramundi in Queensland (usually November through February), as well as various other fishing restrictions. These may change from time to time. Check the current rules and regulations before fishing

WARNINGS Saltwater crocodiles inhabit all estuary and river systems on Cape York, often extending well above the upper tidal limits — observe all warning signs. Many roads are 4WD only, and may be totally impassable from late November until May. Don't take a caravan and only use good off-road trailers. Cyclones and severe tropical storms can occur at any time between November and May. Make sure you carry plenty of water and fuel for the long distances involved

ACCOMMODATION Contact the Far North Queensland Promotion Bureau, telephone (07) 4051 3588; Punsand Bay Safari and Fishing Lodge, telephone Freecall 1800 079 006; Pajinka Wilderness Lodge, telephone Freecall 1800 802 969; Seisia Village Campground, Bamaga, telephone (07) 4069 3285; Weipa Camping and Caravan Park, telephone (07) 4069 7871

CHARTER BOATS AND FISHING GUIDES Punsand Bay Safari and Fishing Lodge, telephone Freecall 1800 079 006; Hyperspace Sportfishing Tours, telephone (07) 4725 5258; Cape York Rod and Rifle Safaris, telephone (07) 4069 3243; Carpentaria Seafaris, telephone (07) 4096 5632; Dave Donald Sportfishing, telephone (07) 4039 1863

The tip of Cape York, the northernmost point of mainland Australia

Cape York Peninsula extends northwards from an imaginary line linking the cosmopolitan east coast city of Cairns with the Gulf of Carpentaria, in the west. North beyond Cooktown, this vast wilderness is sparsely populated and largely unspoiled, with few roads and only a scattering of small towns, Aboriginal settlements and pastoral holdings. The major centres are Laura, Musgrave, Coen, Weipa, Bamaga and Seisia, although several of these are little more than villages. Road access is generally via 4WD vehicles, and is usually limited to the dry season (May through October). For the rest of the year, most travel on Cape York is undertaken by air or sea.

Cape York is the northernmost point of Australia and an abundant range of animals and bird life, rainforests, crystal clear streams, tropical savanna, coral reefs and islands are found there. There are also several magnificent national parks, including Cape Melville National Park, Iron Range National Park, Jardine River National Park, Lizard Island National Park and Mungkan Kaanju National Park.

Cape York (along with Arnhem Land in the Northern Territory and the Kimberley region of Western Australia) represents the true frontier for modern sport fishers because of its immense size, tiny population and largely untamed nature. It is the last remnant of the exceptional standard of angling action that must once have been available right across the tropical north of this country.

This remote region attracts tens of thousands of visitors each year. Many make the long and sometimes challenging journey by 4WD vehicle to The Top during the dry season. Others fly in aboard scheduled or charter aircraft to airstrips at Weipa, Bamaga or Horn Island, in Torres Strait.

Many visitors are attracted to Cape York by the area's extensive fishing opportunities, and few are disappointed by what they find. Generally, the standard of estuary and inshore angling, in particular, improves noticeably as one travels north beyond Cape Melville and Princess Charlotte Bay, onto Cape York itself.

PRINCESS CHARLOTTE BAY

This vast expanse of relatively shallow, choppy and often discoloured water is fed by several major rivers, notably the Normanby, Kennedy,

Reef species such as the fingermark pictured here respond well to jigs

Hann and Morehead. These rivers and Princess Charlotte Bay itself offer fair to very good fishing for all of the usual tropical species, with results largely dictated by the weather, season and recent activity levels of commercial netters.

Princess Charlotte Bay provides many travelling anglers heading north along the east coast with their first really good chance to tangle with the legendary barramundi in reasonable numbers and sizes, although even here, the barramundi fishing can be rather disappointing at times. Best results are likely immediately after the wet season (April or early May) and again just prior to the onset of heavy rains (late October and November).

It should be noted, however, that a closed season currently applies to the taking of barramundi in Queensland waters, and this usually runs from 1 November to 1 February each year. During this period, all barramundi must be carefully returned to the water alive.

Best results on barramundi, mangrove jack, estuary cod, fingermark and the other popular tropical estuary species often occur close to oyster-encrusted rock bars adjacent to river mouths, as well as near snags, undercut banks and gutters or creek junctions within the river systems themselves. Many experts prefer to concentrate on the last half of the run-out tide, although some rock bars fish best around high water. These rivers and the shallower, mud-bottomed bays at their mouths can also produce excellent hauls of delicious mud crabs for those equipped to target them.

Further offshore, pelagic action for trevally, mackerel, barracuda, queenfish and tuna (mostly mackerel tuna and longtails) reaches a peak from June to October, although this period also coincides with the strongest and most consistent south-easterly trade winds. These winds can create conditions that are anywhere from uncomfortable to unbearable or even downright dangerous, and small boat fishers should be especially cautious when venturing offshore.

THE JACKY JACKY

A vast, tidal estuary system, the Jacky Jacky is one of the largest of such systems in the north. It has myriad bends and forks, and literally hundreds of kilometres of mangrove-lined banks to explore.

Despite the size and relatively pristine nature of the Jacky Jacky, fishing results may sometimes be disappointing, especially for the casual visitor. Regular success in this system demands an intimate knowledge of the area's fickle tides and a good understanding of the habits of its fish. For this reason, it is best attacked with the help of local knowledge or a professional guide.

Good results are sometimes obtained simply by launching a dinghy or punt into one of the twisting river arms near the Bamaga airstrip and travelling upstream or downstream, casting lures or baits around any of the creek junctions, snag piles and undercut banks encountered along the way. Barramundi, tarpon (ox-eye herring), javelin fish (grunter), cod, mangrove jack, fingermark and trevally are the most likely customers. Take care not to lose your way in the maze of channels, especially as evening approaches!

TORRES STRAIT ISLANDS

These numerous islands are scattered like stepping stones between the tip of Cape York Peninsula and the southern coast of Papua New Guinea. They offer visitors a chance to experience a little known slice of Australian indigenous culture in an exotic, tropical setting surrounded by warm, blue waters.

These same waters are also home to a veritable plethora of table and sport fish, especially mackerel of several species, tuna, trevally, queenfish, barracuda, coral trout, emperor and sweetlip, as well as less common contenders such as cobia, giant herring and even the occasional sailfish and marlin.

Thursday Island, the best-known destination in the chain, is relatively small and quite densely populated. For these reasons, it does not offer the same quality or diversity of angling as some of its neighbours such as Horn Island (where the airport is), Prince of Wales, Possession, Hammond, Moa and Badu islands.

Best results in the islands are often achieved by trolling deep-diving minnow lures or rigged garfish around reef edges and isolated rocks or bomboras. Anchoring or drifting and fishing the bottom with baits or jigs can also be highly effective at times. Be careful because the combination of very strong tidal currents and south-easterly trade winds can quickly turn Torres Strait into a dangerous stretch of water.

CAPE YORK

Seisia Jetty is a very popular land-based fishing spot

SEISIA JETTY

For visiting anglers without boats, the concrete shipping jetty or wharf at Seisia, on the coast not far from Bamaga, provides the best shore-based angling opportunities in the whole region. Some stunning captures have been made here, including giant trevally to 25 kg and more, big Spanish mackerel, cobia, queenfish, barracuda and even the odd barramundi.

The reason for the jetty's productivity as a fishing spot is quickly evident to any keen observer. Tens of thousands of silvery northern herring (known locally as sardines) call the area home, and dense schools can usually be found sheltering nervously under the wharf. These bait fish shoals are regularly decimated by predators, and the loud, watery detonations of their feeding activity provide a stark contrast to the peaceful gurgling of water around the pilings, or the cries of terns and other sea birds circling above.

The best fishing often occurs at dawn and dusk, although short, intense bursts of activity can occur at any time of the day or night, depending on the tidal flow and bait fish concentrations. Unweighted or lightly weighted live sardines are the favoured bait, although rapidly retrieved metal lures, minnows and bucktail jigs all take their share of fish.

A long-handled net or gaff is required to safely land large fish here, although those without access to such a device can sometimes improvise by walking their catch to the nearby beach and landing it there.

THE JARDINE RIVER

This famous northern river is one of the jewels of Cape York and a must-see destination for many visitors. Flowing strong and fresh for much of the year, it has a limited tidal area and is therefore better known for its two freshwater sport fish, the barramundi and the saratoga. In fact, this river gives its name to the scientific title of the unique northern saratoga (*Scleropages jardini*), whose range begins here, or slightly to the east, and extends westward to Darwin.

Many stories exist to explain the phenomenal freshwater discharge of this stream, which apparently exceeds the run-off attributable to Cape York's annual rainfall. The most popular theory is that the Jardine River is fed by subterranean aquifers, some of them flowing deep under Torres Strait, all the way from the mountainous highlands of Papua New Guinea. Whatever the reason, the river's output of fresh, tannin-stained water is prodigious. Besides the barramundi, saratoga and tarpon (ox-eye herring) common throughout its upper and middle reaches, the Jardine offers exceptional fishing around its mouth at times for large queenfish and big, bruising trevally. Nearby Muttee Head is also the regional hot spot for black jewfish or northern mulloway every April and early May, with a strong run of fish to 30 kg and better. Most of these are taken on squid or herring baits presented on heavy handlines.

McDONALD, DOUGHBOY, JACKSON AND SKARDON RIVERS

The rivers of north-western Cape York—from Vrilya Point south to Port Musgrave—offer some of the most exceptional angling opportunities in the entire country, with abundant small to medium barramundi, lots of mangrove jack, fingermark, javelin fish, cod, threadfin salmon, trevally, tarpon and, in their higher reaches, saratoga and sooty grunter. The Skardon, in particular, also boasts exceptional numbers of mud crabs.

Around the river mouths and a short distance offshore swim large schools of queenfish, trevally, school and Spanish mackerel, tuna of several types, giant herring, milkfish and cobia. The numerous small reef patches dotting these waters are home to emperor, coral trout, big cod, tropical nannygai (sea perch) and a dozen or more other species.

This area's remoteness is both the major reason for its piscatorial productivity and a

Low tide on a Cape York beach

The northern saratoga is a popular sport fishing target in the Jardine River

significant hurdle for visiting anglers. Fortunately, however, the stretch of coast from Seisia to Weipa is well serviced by a very professional charter operation called Carpentaria Seafaris, which operates a comfortable mother ship and a fleet of sport fishing dinghies.

This largely catch-and-release operation caters specifically for fly and lure anglers keen to taste the temptations of the pristine waters of north-western Cape York Peninsula. While not cheap, it represents one of the best value-for-money angling getaways in the tropics today.

WEIPA REGION

The bauxite mining centre of Weipa offers all the services and amenities one would expect from a town of some 2500 people, plus a few that might come as a surprise to the jaded traveller.

Weipa has comfortable camping and caravan parks, and motel accommodation of several standards, plus a full range of shops, businesses and services, from medical to mechanical.

The fishing is surprisingly good, even close to town, and simply gets better as one travels north and south from the port. Barramundi and a host of other sport and table fish are often encountered within sight of the town itself, while further offshore, big Spanish mackerel are one of the most popular targets of the area's keen army of resident anglers.

Several large rivers flow into Albatross Bay, on either side of Weipa, and these, along with the tributaries of Port Musgrave to the north, offer excellent estuary fishing opportunities for all the usual tropical targets, particularly barramundi, mangrove jack, fingermark, grunter, salmon and trevally.

Weipa makes the perfect base for an extended northern stay and serious assault on the abundant fishing prospects of western Cape York Peninsula.

A pair of delicious coral trout from a shallow reef

A large queenfish landed on fly gear on Cape York Peninsula

MORNINGTON ISLAND

IN BRIEF

MAP REFERENCE: PAGE 148 B5

GETTING THERE Mornington Island lies in the Gulf of Carpentaria just off the Queensland coast near Burketown. Commercial and charter flights operate to the island, and it is also accessible to those with their own private aircraft

BEST TIME TO FISH Early and late in the season

BEST TIME TO TRAVEL April to October (although the middle of this period is often cooler, it's also often more windy)

MAJOR ANGLING SPECIES Giant herring, queenfish, Spanish mackerel, giant and golden trevally, barracuda, longtail and mackerel tuna, sweetlip, red emperor and coral trout

SPECIAL RESTRICTIONS Mornington Island is an Aboriginal community. Access is only allowed through Birri Lodge fishing resort

ACCOMMODATION Birri Lodge, telephone (07) 4745 7277

CHARTER BOATS AND FISHING GUIDES Birri Lodge, telephone (07) 4745 7277

Tucked away in the Gulf of Carpentaria north of Mount Isa and west of Cairns, Mornington Island is an inconsequential-looking piece of topography with an awesome angling reputation. This low, barren island produces fishing of international standing for some of tropical Australia's most exciting game fish.

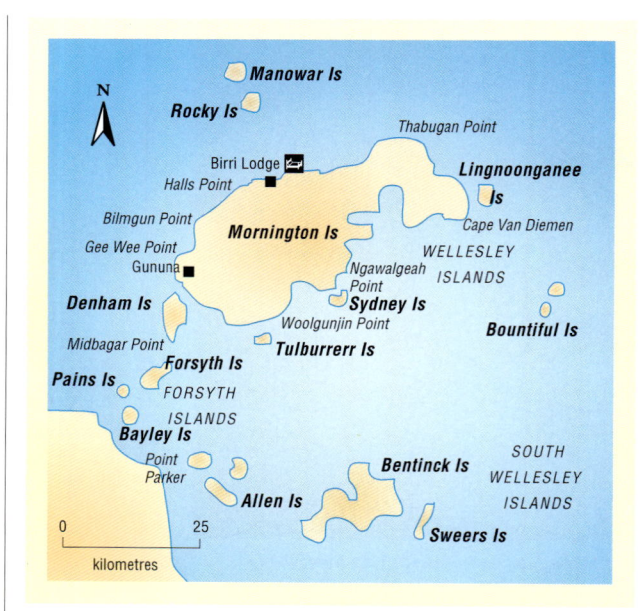

There is one fish in particular, however, that makes Mornington Island a stand-out destination for sport fishers—the giant herring. This species is actually quite widespread in Australia, yet while giant herring are sometimes encountered elsewhere, it is only at Mornington and a few other areas of the Gulf of Carpentaria that these fish can be regularly and successfully targeted.

So what's so special about giant herring? It all boils down to one word: speed!

Although not quite classic flats fish in the vein of the famous bonefish, the giant herring at Mornington Island are found feeding on schools of bait fish over flats across the northern shore. Here the water can be anything from 1.5 to 5 m deep. So, flats fishing as seen overseas with anglers wading or being 'poled' up to fish from specially built boats isn't the way it happens.

In most aspects, fishing for giant herring at Mornington Island is much the same as lure casting for mackerel or tuna, except that pound for pound, a giant herring would outdistance and outrun any mackerel or tuna ever seen. Spectacular jumps, often more than 2 m clear of the water, and absolutely scorching runs from a fish shaped like a jet fighter and powered by a deeply veed tail make for a fish to excite by any standards.

Silvered to a sheen that has been accurately described as 'chromed', the giant herring is a sport fish with few peers. And Mornington Island is one of the few places in the world where giant herring are present in numbers and eminently catchable. They alone would be enough to put Mornington Island on the proverbial map, but in fact they're only the start!

LIMITED ACCESS

Mornington Island is an Aboriginal community not freely open to outsiders except for people fishing out of Birri Lodge fishing resort. Situated on the northern side of the island, Birri nestles in behind the beach, beside its own airstrip.

Some clients fly to the island in their own planes (after checking with resort operators about the current state of the strip, of course. Most come to Mornington on commercial flights to Gununa, a township on the southern side of the island where the resort's operators pick them up and transport them to Birri to the north.

Birri is a low-key resort, and fishing is the accepted reason for its existence. Star ratings are irrelevant. In such remote locations, it's sufficient to say the accommodation is comfortable and the atmosphere always congenial. Fishing is from outboard-powered centre consoles, well suited to any fishing technique including lure casting and fly fishing. Many visitors to Mornington, however, are more intent on reef fishing.

REEF FISHING

Reef fishing at Mornington is always productive. The average catch doesn't match the size or variety of species found on the Great Barrier Reef, but there are ample stocks of red emperor, sweetlip and coral trout to be had. The resort operators limit the number of fish people may

A rocky shoreline on Mornington Island

take with them in a deliberate and successful attempt to ensure stocks remain sustainable. Nonetheless, fresh-caught reef fish is alway a feature of the cuisine at Birri Lodge.

Still, while most people go to Mornington simply to fish, it is definitely the sport fishing that gives the place its hotspot rating.

SPORT FISHING

In their turn, queenfish, giant and golden trevally, Spanish mackerel and giant herring all turn on the action at Mornington.

During the northern dry season (the southern winter), strong south-east trade winds blast the entire Gulf. This bring to light another good thing about Birri. As it is situated on the northern side of the island, the trade winds here are offshore winds. Even when these winds are at their worst, Mornington Island offers a degree of protection which allows the fishing to continue thanks to the sheltering lee. And the worst of the trade winds in July and August is when big Spanish mackerel prowl the waters off Mornington.

Mornington's other sport fish are more or less present all year round, although it's fair to say that they are often more reliable early and late in the season.

Birri resort closes in December and doesn't reopen until April when the rains (and cyclones) are finished. The period immediately after the resort reopens is usually the time giant herring are present and feeding most actively. While bursts of giant herring activity continue to occur throughout the dry season, this is the period when the herring are at their most predictable.

Similarly, queenfish frequent the waters near the resort all year round. When on the boil, queenfish action at Mornington can be incredible. There are few experiences in fishing to surpass a queenfish frenzy, and Mornington is one place where this happens with regularity.

Typically, a trolling pattern in maintained along the northern coast of the island until queenfish are found. At least one popper should be kept splashing along the surface at all times. When it is tackled by a horde of leaping, cartwheeling queenfish, it's a fair assumption that queenfish have been found!

Once the fish are located, casting poppers and lures keeps the action going until fish or fishers eventually tire. Fly fishers who become involved find their whole concept of fly fishing being rearranged by takes that can occur anytime from when a fly touches down to when it's lifted out for the next cast. Queenfish, like giant herring, are

a fly fishing target of international significance with potential long overdue to be realised.

Giant trevally and golden trevally are regularly found in company with queenfish aggregations. Barracuda are another addition to an already long and exciting list of Mornington offerings.

BUILD-UP ACTION

Perhaps the best time for queenfish and their hangers-on is the last month or so before the resort closes. This period is known in the north as the wet season 'build-up'. The weather can be torrid and the later in the year, the hotter and hotter it gets. But then, so does the fishing.

High-speed spinning tackle of the 'Moreton Bay spin stick' style, fishing line classes from 4 to 10 kg and a variety of metal spoons and baitfish profiles are essential gear for sports fishers at Mornington. A good stock of both skipping and 'blooper' poppers is an absolute must.

Fly fishers should take an 8, 9 or 10 weight outfit. The rod should be of the faster tapered style mounted with a reel loaded with several hundred metres of backing. A pair of weight-forward saltwater taper lines (a floating and a sinking) covers the options. An intermediate line could also be useful. Baitfish-style flies and 'popper' types in sizes from a No. 1 hook up to as big as you can handle in the often windy conditions are the basic patterns. Successful flies include Lefty's Deceiver, Clouser Deep Minnow, Dahlberg Diver, variants, Slider, Sillicone, Bob's Banger, Pink Thing, Surf Candy and Joe Brook's Blonde.

Top right: Coming ashore on a Mornington beach
Bottom left: The giant herring is one of Mornington's most highly prized species
Bottom right: Coral trout abound in the reef-strewn shallows around Mornington Island

THE GULF OF CARPENTARIA

IN BRIEF

MAP REFERENCE: PAGE 148

GETTING THERE Normanton is approximately 2150 km north north-west of Brisbane
BEST TIME TO FISH March to November
BEST TIME TO TRAVEL April to October
MAJOR ANGLING SPECIES Barramundi, mangrove jack, cod, javelin fish, threadfin salmon, trevally, queenfish, mackerel and various reef and game species
SPECIAL RESTRICTIONS There is a closed season on the taking of barramundi in Queensland (usually November through February), as well as various other fishing restrictions. These may change from time to time. Check the current rules and regulations before fishing
WARNINGS Saltwater crocodiles inhabit all estuaries and river systems around The Gulf, often extending well above the upper tidal limits — observe all warning signs. Many roads are 4WD only, and may be totally impassable from late November until May. Cyclones and severe tropical storms can occur at any time between November and May

Sunset over the Gulf of Carpentaria

The Gulf of Carpentaria is a vast, relatively shallow body of warm, often turbid tropical water separating Queensland's Cape York Peninsula from Arnhem Land in the Northern Territory.

Consisting in most parts of a mud, silt or sand bottom strata with just the odd outcrop of rock or coral, the Gulf, as it is popularly known, is nonetheless and extremely fertile body of water. This is due, in no small part, to the number of major rivers and estuary systems emptying into it, particularly from the east and south.

The Gulf of Carpentaria is especially famous for its abundant prawn stocks, and the commercial fishery for these succulent crustaceans attracts a large fleet of trawlers. These same prawns also attract vast numbers of fish into the area, and play a major role in the overall fertility of the Gulf region.

In some ways, the Gulf lacks the obvious aesthetic charms of the Coral Sea coast in north-eastern Queensland. Missing, for the most part, are the crystal clear, aquamarine waters, fringing reefs and white, sandy beaches of the Great Barrier Reef, replaced instead by mud flats, mangrove forests, salt pans and low, scrubby islands. Nonetheless, the Gulf of Carpentaria holds a special place in the hearts of all serious anglers, thanks to the incredibly high standard of recreational fishing still on offer in so many of its more remote waterways.

KARUMBA AND NORMANTON

Most of the prawn trawlers in the Gulf fleet call the small port of Karumba, at the mouth of the Norman River, home. Further upstream and some 70 km south-east of Karumba lies the larger town of Normanton, with a permanent population of around 1200 people. Normanton's population is constantly swelled by visitors throughout the dry season, however, many of whom use it as a stop-over and stepping-off point for exploring and fishing the extensive tracts of low, marshy land and winding waterways of the region.

Coastal rivers such as the Flinders, Norman, Saxby and Carron all offer fair to very good barramundi fishing in their lower and middle reaches, particularly from late March or April until June and again in October and November (check the current closed seasons before fishing). Further upstream in each of these long, winding and often muddy rivers, the area's barramundi are joined by sooty grunter (black bream), fork-tailed catfish and pockets of saratoga.

Trolling with minnow-style lures and bait fishing with live prawns, shrimps or small fish are popular ways of taking barramundi in this region. A boat of some sort is almost essential for good fishing, however, as is a sound knowledge and understanding of the area's large and often rather erratic tidal fluctuations.

HISTORIC BURKETOWN

Well to the west of Normanton lies the small village of Burketown, the Gulf's oldest European settlement. Named after the famous explorer Robert O'Hara Burke, who passed through in 1861, Burketown has had a rather chequered history, punctuated by epidemics of tropical disease in the early days and its near destruction by a major cyclone in 1976.

A commercial fishing boat on the Norman River near Normanton

Today, Burketown is another popular stop-over and staging point for adventurous travellers and keen anglers intent on sampling the delights of the lower Gulf region.

The Gregory, Nicholson and Alexandra River systems all run to the sea through a complex series of deltas near Burketown. Each of these is well known, particularly in their middle and lower stretches, for fine barramundi fishing.

Higher up these same rivers, especially in the upper Gregory and the O'Shannassey, whose headwaters rise very close to those of the southward-flowing Georgina system, sooty grunter, catfish, archer fish and freshwater long tom are also prolific. Some of these waters also hold pockets of northern saratoga.

Lower down, towards the tidal reaches, barramundi take over as the prime target species, while closer still to the sea, mangrove jacks, estuary cod, threadfin salmon and small queenfish are more abundant, along with the ever-present trevally species, fork-tailed catfish, sharks, rays and sawfish. Mud crabs are also prolific in this area, and make a popular target for locals and visitors alike.

As with most of the Top End and Gulf, access to and travel within this area is very difficult, uncomfortable and potentially hazardous during the wet season (which usually runs from late November through April or even into May), but becomes much easier and more pleasant from July until October. Unfortunately, the latter period is also the quietest for fishing—especially barra fishing—and those keen on sampling good sport should carefully time their visit for the periods immediately after or just before the 'big wet'.

ISLANDS OF THE GULF

An extensive archipelago known as the Wellesley, South Wellesley and Forsyth islands lies in the lower end of the Gulf of Carpentaria, offshore to the north-west of Burketown. This group includes Mornington Island (the largest of the Wellesleys), as well as Bentinck, Denham, Forsyth, Sydney, Bountiful and Sweers islands, plus many smaller outcrops. Excellent fishing exists around all of these areas, as well as in the relatively small estuaries on the larger islands, most notably the Sandlewood River on Mornington Island.

There is also a long-established fishing lodge on the Aboriginal-controlled Mornington Island, and from here anglers can fish for barramundi, cod of several species, mangrove jacks, barracuda, mackerel, queenfish, cobia, prolific numbers of trevally and a wide variety of reef species. This is also one of the most reliable and productive areas in Australia for catching (or at least hooking!) the spectacular and highly prized giant herring or 'ladyfish'. (Fishing at Mornington Island is dealt with in greater detail on pp. 282–3.)

South-east of Mornington, in the South Wellesley Islands, lies the much smaller Sweers Island, where another, more modest fishing lodge caters primarily for fly-in reef anglers and those keen to catch the big Spanish mackerel, tuna and queenfish that are prolific in these waters at times.

Both Mornington and Sweers are serviced by air charter services and are also accessible to anglers arriving in their own light aircraft.

Evening sun illuminates the cliffs of Sweers Island in the South Wellesley group

Queenfish are abundant in Gulf of Carpentaria waters

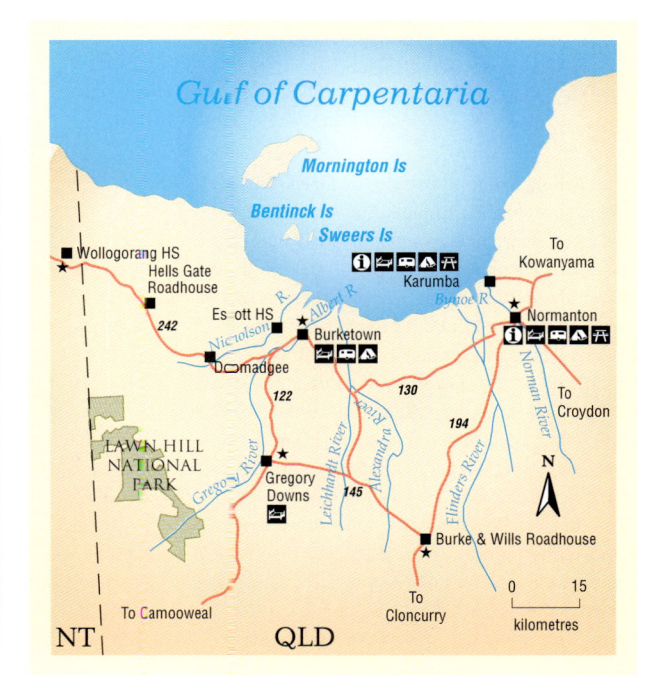

EXPLORING THE REEF

IN BRIEF

MAP REFERENCE: PAGES 146–9 AND 154–5

GETTING THERE The Great Barrier Reef stretches from about Gladstone in the south all the way to Cape York. Cooktown is about 330 km north of Cairns via Mossman and Lakeland

BEST TIME TO FISH Year-round

BEST TIME TO TRAVEL May to November

MAJOR ANGLING SPECIES Various reef and game fish species

SPECIAL RESTRICTIONS Remember that the entire Great Barrier Reef is a national park and there are a number of restrictions on anglers, divers and boat users in certain areas. The Great Barrier Reef Marine Park Authority controls the reef and the seas surrounding it. The authority administers zoning restrictions and regulations, some of which affect fishing. It is a good idea to have an up-to-date zoning map of the area in which you plan to fish. Zoning maps are available from local fishing tackle shops or newsagents. If in any doubt, check with the Great Barrier Reef Marine Park Authority (GBRMPA), telephone (07) 4750 0700. They have detailed zoning maps of the reef. Remember, some areas are completely closed to fishing, others may only be trolled over and in some, anchoring is prohibited. Ignorance of these restrictions is no excuse for breaking the law.

WARNINGS Trade winds prevail across the Great Barrier Reef for most of the year. Its remoteness makes careful planning, emergency reserves and appropriate experience a must for boat fishers

CHARTER BOATS AND FISHING GUIDES Check local Yellow Pages for details

---

Of all fishing dreams, visiting the Great Barrier Reef is close to the ultimate. Endless reef in myriad intricate patterns of gloriously hued coral, crystalline water, sand so white it hurts your eyes, gracefully arching palms ... and always-hungry fish in numbers so thick it's hard to keep them off your line! Like many other dreams, those things actually do exist. The reality of fishing the Great Barrier Reef, however, is inevitably different.

To begin with, there are the trade winds. Constant strong winds, 20 knots plus, are not part of any fishing dream. They're a fact of life on the Great Barrier Reef, however, for most of the year anyway. Then there are the distances involved. The reef is a long way off the coast. It comes closer to shore north from Cooktown, but that is a long way to tow a boat, and the road certainly isn't bitumen all the way!

All of which begs the question: is fishing the Reef just a dream, and an impossible one at that? The answer is a qualified no.

REALISTIC GOALS

All it takes to realise the dream of fishing the Great Barrier Reef from your own boat is to accept that, for the most part, the Reef itself is out of reach of most trailerable boats. If you lower your sights a fraction, though, a large number of inshore reefs, continental shelf islands and so on can be included in the picture because many of these are certainly accessible for those with trailerable boats. Most people, however, do include these areas in their mental picture of the Great Barrier Reef; therefore, the fact that they're not actually part of the Reef proper may go comfortably unnoticed.

Even so, visiting inshore reefs, continental shelf islands, coral cays and so on is not a thing to be undertaken lightly. Great amounts of logistical planning are required. These areas are remote from the comforts of home and the facilities of boating life that those operating close to populated centres take for granted.

Even visiting those areas that are not strictly part of the Great Barrier Reef proper generally involves using an offshore-capable boat. Basically, the bigger and more comfortable the boat, the better. Thanks to those incessant trade winds,

Above: *The transparent waters of the reef edge fire any angler's imagination*
Bottom right: *A beautiful hump-headed wrasse taken from reef waters*

the inshore waters along the entire Queensland coast can be expected to be rough for much of the year. Deeply veed hulls of 5.5 to 6 m and more are the most popular boat in north Queensland, and with good reason.

THE BIG WET

There's only one time of the year when the trade winds can be expected to ease and that is during the wet season. At this time, a strong air stream that comes predominantly from the south-east, due to high-pressure systems moving across the Great Australian Bight and out into the Tasman Sea, is stalled by the encroachment of monsoonal troughs moving south from the Equator. The heavy rains brought by the monsoons, however, preclude much small boat activity (and road travel in far north Queensland, often as not), so the wet season proper is as inadvisable for fishing the Reef as the trade wind season.

Luckily, each year during November and early December there occurs a period when the wet season is building up. The trade winds become stalled for days on end, while the monsoonal troughs have not yet made it far enough south to bring concentrated rain.

The build-up, as it's called in the north, is when lighter winds prevail, sometimes for day after day after day. Significantly, the build-up is the time of year when most north Queensland locals consider fishing the Great Barrier Reef.

WHERE TO GO

Having picked the right time, and with access to a big, comfortable boat which carries plenty of fuel and a trailer robust enough to travel to far north Queensland, visitors are faced with a choice of destinations. North Queensland is a big place, and thinking of trailer boats and the Reef means thinking of the coast between Cooktown and the Capricorn area, a distance of about 1500 km in all.

Cooktown these days still remains a quiet, little coastal town. It has a good ramp and, from Cooktown, a 25-km radius covers several reef complexes. In the build-up period, a boat capable of round trips of 150 to 200 km will even be able to reach the outer edges of the Great Barrier Reef proper. The main drawback these days to using Cooktown as a launching point is that fact that it is not yet accessible by an all-bitumen road. One of its main access routes, the coast road via the Daintree and Bloomfield, is 4WD only in parts. Nonetheless, the road to

EXPLORING THE REEF

THE CIGUATERA RISK

Ciguatera (pronounced sig-a-terra) is a toxin found in the flesh of certain fish in tropical waters in some areas. Thought to be caused by the ingestion of tiny organisms called dinoflagelates that live on dead and damaged areas of coral, ciguatera is a cumulative toxin that tends to be concentrated in the flesh of some higher order predators. These large fish consume smaller forage fish, and thereby accumulate significant quantities of the toxin over time.

Species known to be carriers in Australia's tropical and subtropical areas include red bass, Chinaman fish, red paddletails, fusiliers, coral trout and Spanish mackerel. Other possible carriers are barracuda, jobfish, dogtooth tuna, certain trevallies and the various emperors. Generally speaking, the risk of ciguatera poisoning increases with the size of the fish eaten, particularly in the case of Spanish mackerel and coral trout.

The problem appears to be area specific. Some regions of northern Australia are largely free of ciguatera; others fall into the medium- or high-risk categories. So, when fishing in tropical waters, always seek local advice on the ciguatera risk category of the area before eating your catch.

Symptoms of ciguatera poisoning include:

- dizziness
- nausea
- diarrhoea
- lethargy
- a tingling sensation in the fingers and toes
- temperature sense reversals (meaning hot water feels icy cold and vice versa)

In extreme cases, poisoning can lead to breathing difficulties, loss of consciousness and even death.

If you suspect that you may have suffered ciguatera poisoning, consult your doctor and avoid eating high-risk species from known ciguatera areas as the toxin is cumulative in humans as well, and repeated exposure even to relatively low doses may prove to be life threatening.

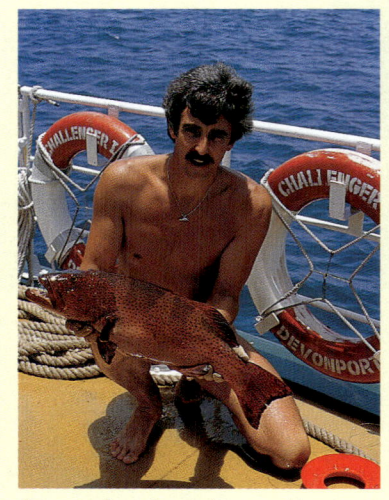

Some reef species such as coral trout are known carriers of the ciguatera toxin

Looking towards Purtaboi Island from Dunk Island

Cooktown via the Atherton Tableland is improving all the time and it's already a realistic proposition for stout trailers carrying well tied down boats.

Around Cairns, ramps in the Daintree River at Port Douglas, in Cairns itself and a little further south in the Russell Heads area provide some of the best jumping-off points for reaching the Reef along the entire Queensland coast. It's around 60 km in a straight line from any of these places to the outer reef. Travelling this distance, however, is hardly necessary when islands such as the Low Islets, Fitzroy Island and High Island lie within 20 km of a ramp. Accessible inshore reefs include Arlington, Michaelmas, Sudbury and Batt, all of which are around 40 km from a ramp.

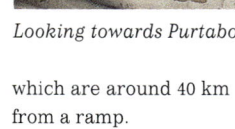

Moving south, the Dunk Island region is accessible from Hull Heads and Mission Beach. There are some problems with ramps at these places, especially at low tide. Given good weather and a high-tide launch, however, the Family Islands group (which includes Dunk) are well within daytrip reach. East of Dunk, the Beaver Cay area is a known marlin and sailfish hot spot. The national park camping ground on Dunk Island is an ideal base from which to explore and eliminates the problems of the tide.

Near Townsville, the Palm Island group, the Rattlesnake group and nearby Magnetic Island are all within reach of ramps at Forrest Beach, Balgal and Townsville, respectively.

At Bowen, the distances are stretched a little more. The Gloucester Island National Park camping area is nearly 60 km from the ramp in Bowen Harbour (Port Denison). Great fishing near Bowen, however, makes it all worthwhile.

The Whitsundays, part of the Cumberland and Northumberland Island groups, need no introduction. Again, distances stretch the limits of trailerable boats, although a Whitsunday assault launched using a bareboat charter yacht as a mobile base is very feasible, especially for groups. (See the fact box on p. 289 for more details.)

THE CAPRICORNIA COAST

This Capricornia Coast is so named because the Tropic of Capricorn (the beginning or the end of the tropics, depending on how you look at it) passes through the region. Capricornia, that is the Keppel Islands and their many associated islands, rocks and bomboras, is another fantastic area on the inner reef that is feasibly explorable from a larger trailerable boat.

At Rosslyn Bay Boat Harbour near Yeppoon, there's a ramp which can handle any trailer boat, with a security car park for tow vehicles and trailers. A national park camp site on North Keppel is one accommodation option out on the islands. Great Keppel has a resort, with nearby Wapparaburra Haven for stricter budgets. Several islets have cabins which may be rented by enquiring at real estate agents in Yeppoon.

The last option for exploring the Reef is the Capricorn–Bunker group, which is a long way offshore and out of reach of trailerable boats. However, Lady Musgrave, Tryon, North West and Masthead islands all have national park camping areas. As with all areas covered by the marine park, all regulations must be strictly observed and fishing is not allowed in certain zones.

These islands are serviced by barges working out of Gladstone. Reaching the Capricorn–Bunker group is a matter of organising a large enough group to make chartering a barge feasible, booking an island and then organising the formidable logistics of a week or more on a true tropical paradise. The barges are large enough to carry dinghies on their decks. These boats cannot be of the size necessary to reach other areas of the Reef as they must be manhandled from the barge to the water once the island is reached. 'Tinnies' of around 3.8 m in length are ideal and quite well suited to fishing and snorkelling around the sheltered side of the islands.

So there, in a nutshell, is a guide to fishing the Great Barrier Reef from a trailerable boat — a possible dream!

Red emperor are a highly-sought-after catch on the Great Barrier Reef

THE WHITSUNDAY ISLANDS

Mention the Whitsunday Islands and many Australians immediately conjure mental images of tourist resorts filled to overflowing with happy holiday makers. In reality, however, the Whitsundays Group covers a vast area, and the various popular tourist resorts represent only a tiny percentage of the region's total land area. In fact, it will surprise many first-time visitors to discover that vast tracts of the Whitsundays remain amongst the most natural and unspoiled locations on the east coast of Queensland! As well as a plethora of gorgeous islands, sheltered coves, beaches and coral reefs, the Whitsundays offer a multitude of fishing and cruising prospects for the boat-based angler, whether operating a trailer boat from the mainland or chartering one of the many available vessels.

All the usual tropical and subtropical inshore and offshore species mix together here in the many channels and reef complexes that surround the islands. There's also some fine sport and game fishing on offer in slightly deeper water to the east and north-east of the archipelago. Proserpine and the nearby coastal ports of Airlie Beach, Shute Harbour and Conway Beach all provide ideal stepping-off points for those wanting to fish the Whitsunday Islands, and each has a thriving 'bare-boat' charter fleet, offering fully equipped yachts, with or without experienced crews. There are well-known resorts on Lindeman, Hamilton, South Molle and Hayman, plus lesser known getaways on some of the other islands.

To be consistently successful when fishing in this area, it is often necessary to venture onto the more exposed eastern sides of the islands, and to troll a lure, drop a jig or soak a bait well away from the usual anchorages and cruising grounds.

On the bottom-fishing front, species such as the various emperors, cod, sweetlip, coral trout and the like are still available in reasonable numbers in and around the Whitsundays. Top spots include Langford Island and its associated reef system, Hook Passage, Mackerel Bay and the entire eastern side of Hook Island, as well as parts of the reef surrounding Deloraine Island and the area near Cid Island. The major pelagic species encountered in the Whitsundays are mackerel (school, spotted and Spanish), queenfish, trevally of several types, various small tunas and cobia or black kingfish. There are also reasonable numbers of small marlin and big sailfish to the north and east of the islands, particularly in late winter and spring.

The Spanish mackerel run along this stretch of coast traditionally hits its peak between July and October each year, although a few decent mackerel are available in almost any month. The same is true of queenfish, tuna and cobia. Productive areas for these surface fish include the exposed eastern sides of islands, especially around any prominent points and bomboras. The waters around Langford and Deloraine islands, Haslewood Island, Solway Pass and even those around South Molle Island are particularly good for trolling, lure-casting, jigging and 'floater' fishing with lightly weighted baits.

An aerial view of Whitsunday Island's Whitehaven Beach

CAIRNS TO CAPE TRIBULATION

IN BRIEF

MAP REFERENCE: PAGE 155 D5

GETTING THERE Cairns is about 1670 km north of Brisbane along the Bruce Highway, with the Great Barrier Reef to the east, Atherton Tableland to the west, and Daintree River and Cape Tribulation to the north
BEST TIME TO FISH March to November
BEST TIME TO TRAVEL April to October
MAJOR ANGLING SPECIES Barramundi, mangrove jack, estuary cod, javelin fish, salmon, trevally, queenfish and various reef and game species
SPECIAL RESTRICTIONS There is a closed season on the taking of barramundi in Queensland (usually November through February), as well as various other fishing restrictions. The rules change from time to time, so it is essential to check current regulations before fishing. The entire Great Barrier Reef is a national park and there are a number of restrictions on anglers, divers and boat users in certain areas. Zoning maps are available from local fishing tackle shops or newsagents, or from the Great Barrier Reef Marine Park Authority, telephone (07) 4750 0700
WARNINGS Saltwater crocodiles inhabit estuary and river systems in this region, sometimes ranging beyond the upper tidal limits — so observe all warning signs. Some roads may be cut by flood waters for short periods from late November until late May. Cyclones and severe tropical storms can occur at any time between November and May
CHARTER BOATS AND FISHING GUIDES Tanderra Charters and Fishing Exclusive — contact Marlin Marina Tours, telephone (07) 4052 1966; Restless Charters, Port Douglas, telephone 015 212 444; Peter Haynes Sportfishing Charters, telephone (07) 4033 2398

Boating on the Daintree River north of Cairns

Many visitors, from both within and outside Australia, rightly regard Cairns as a convenient gateway to the tropical north and to the natural wonders of the Great Barrier Reef. Despite the attractions of the region, however, the fishing, especially within daytripping distance of the city, has deteriorated dramatically in recent decades. Today, many visitors return home disappointed after a fishing trip to Cairns. The area still offers some great angling opportunities, however, it is just that these days you usually have to venture further afield to find consistent piscatorial action.

The extensive stretch of tropical coastline running north from Cairns past the Daintree River and on to Cape Tribulation offers a wide variety shore-based, estuarine and offshore fishing. Even here, visiting anglers shouldn't expect to find an untouched fishing paradise, especially for keenly sought-after species such as the mighty barramundi.

Barramundi fishing along the north-eastern seaboard deteriorated markedly in the three or four decades following World War II and is only slowly recovering today, thanks to improved management practices. The mangrove-lined estuaries on this coastline, however, offer the keen visiting angler at least the chance of a barramundi or two. Other inshore and estuarine species such as mangrove jack, estuary cod, pikey bream, bar-tail flathead, fingermark, javelin fish, trevally and barracuda all remain reasonably abundant, as do many offshore and reef species.

CAIRNS TO DAINTREE

Cairns is a big, cosmopolitan city and deserves its place as the unofficial capital of the far north in every way. As may be expected of an area as heavily settled and hard fished as Cairns, the local angling is not quite up to past standards. Trinity Inlet, however, still produces its share of fish, including some good fingermark bream, mangrove jacks, javelin fish and barramundi. Most of these are taken by a dedicated band of local bait fishers using live prawns, yabbies or herring fished around the snags.

Making use of local knowledge is the key to successful fishing. Visiting casual anglers who lack local connections or decide not to use of one of the area's excellent professional guiding services more often than not go home with no more than sunburn or a few catfish, small sharks, rays and undersized pikey bream to show for their efforts!

While much of the estuary consists of mangrove-lined mud banks, there are plenty of sandy areas such as Wrights and Blackfellows creeks, and a hard clay bottom in the deep holes off the Old Bark Hut and the Sugar Terminal. Patches of reef and coral can also be found in the deeper sections of the inlet.

Most fishing in the Cairns Inlet is from small boats, as the shores are thickly lined with mangroves and local tides are large, exposing wide mud banks at low water. There are some wharves, but access is generally restricted as they are used for commerce or occupied by various trawlers and other professional boats.

The usual fishing methods around Cairns include live baiting, dead baiting, trolling and lure or fly casting. Gun local anglers tend to prefer live baits mostly gathered by cast netting.

Offshore from Cairns, the fishing improves somewhat, with some fine reef, cay and bombora fishing still in existence, particularly in shallow, reef-strewn areas surrounded by deeper water. Michaelmas Cay is one spot known for its lure-eating coral trout, red bass, cod, trevally and mackerel. Game and sport fishing wide of Cairns produces excellent action for Spanish mackerel at times, as well as tuna of several species, big trevally, queenfish, barracuda, juvenile marlin and sailfish. In deeper water outside the 'hard edge' of the Great Barrier Reef, these are joined by wahoo, dolphin fish, larger tuna and big marlin.

From the end of September until early December, giant black marlin are taken wide of Cairns, with several 'granders' (fish weighing more than the old-fashioned 1000-pound mark) being weighed or released each season. The main marlin fishing effort has moved from here northward to Cooktown and Lizard Island during the past few decades, however, and these days fewer boats make the three- or four-hour run out from Cairns Harbour to any of the more productive deep banks found offshore from this area.

Just a few kilometres north of Cairns, along the Cook Highway, there are several spots accessible to anglers who want to fish from river banks, spits, beaches or bridges. The Barron River mouth, Machans Beach, Holloways Beach, Yorkeys Knob and its adjacent creeks, Trinity Beach, Kewarra Beach and Clifton Beach all provide reasonable results from time to time around their various rocky outcrops and stands of mangrove trees for mangrove jack, fingermark, flathead, bream and whiting.

The beaches running north from Cairns also provide the odd threadfin salmon, queenfish and trevally, as well as small whiting and the like, while the rocky headlands between these beaches are always worth a throw for trevally, queenfish, school mackerel and other passing fish, especially on a high or rising tide.

Yabbies (nippers) can be pumped from the mud and sand banks at the mouths of Richters, Barrs and Reddens creeks, while there are very extensive yabby banks at the northern side of the Barron River.

At Yorkeys Knob, anglers can fish from the rock wall, the groyne and the rocks themselves, which extend right around the point. A boat of some sort is a great advantage when fishing these areas. The same is true of the other small to medium estuaries, tidal flats, beaches and rocky points extending north from Palm Cove to Port Douglas and beyond, all of which produce sporadic catches of the species already mentioned, as well as the odd barramundi.

Hot spots around Port Douglas include Crees and Packer creeks, Island Point, Four Mile Beach and, further offshore, Wentworth and Egmont reefs. Consistently reliable inshore and estuarine fishing results—especially for visiting anglers—are not really achieved, however, until one moves north beyond Port Douglas to the Daintree River region.

Daintree to Cape Tribulation

The Daintree River, north of Cairns, meanders through dense rainforest and mangrove lowlands, finally reaching the spectacularly beautiful coastline near Snapper Island, just south of Cape Kimberley. The lower Daintree offers anglers a wide variety of tropical fish species including barramundi, mangrove jack, fingermark, javelin fish (grunter), pikey bream, trevally, queenfish, barracuda, estuary cod, black jewfish, archer fish tarpon (ox-eye herring), permit (snub-nosed dart), tripletail and many others. Further upstream, these are joined by sooty grunter and jungle perch.

Live bait fishing and lure casting are the most productive ways of working the lower Daintree River, although trolling and dead baiting can also produce results. Hot spots include Stewart Creek, Virgil Island, the stretch just downstream of the ferry crossing, South Arm, the Broadwater and the Ballast Heap.

Boat launching facilities are available at the township of Daintree, next to the caravan park, or further downstream, beside the Daintree River ferry crossing. Small boats can be launched from beaches on the northern side of the Daintree River by those with 4WD vehicles. At the ferry launching ramp, anglers can hire small aluminium dinghies with outboard motors. Fuel and supplies are available at many of the service stations on the way to the Daintree River.

Offshore from the Daintree River are many coral reefs holding good numbers of tropical reef and open ocean species such as coral trout, wrasse, emperor, sea perch, sweetlip, giant trevally, jobfish, tuna, mackerel, marlin and sailfish. The best time of the year to fish the Daintree area and its adjacent coral reefs is during the warmer months, from late September until February or March each year, when the weather is generally very hot, humid and calm between tropical storms and the occasional cyclone.

North of the Daintree River (which can be crossed via the vehicular ferry), the often rough coastal road runs on through Thornton Beach and Noah Head to the prominent, rocky outcrop of Cape Tribulation, which has camping facilities and offers some interesting land-based fishing. Small estuaries and tidal flats in the area also provide reasonable to good results at times.

There is great reef fishing along this section of coast, too, with bottom bouncing for coral trout, sweetlip emperor and the like, as well as lure casting, poppering and jigging for the same species and more. Light to medium tackle trolling for mackerel, tuna, barracuda, trevally, sailfish and even small marlin is also possible here.

Some near-shore reefs have been rather hard hit over the years in this area, however, and anglers may need to look further afield than they once did to obtain really good results.

Barramundi are the fish every visitor most wants to catch

JESSIE RIVER, MELVILLE ISLAND

IN BRIEF

MAP REFERENCE: PAGE 174 D2

GETTING THERE Melville Island lies just off the coast of the Northern Territory near Darwin. Jessie River Camp lies on the northern side of the island, 1½ hours flight by light charter plane from Darwin
BEST TIME TO FISH April to December
BEST TIME TO TRAVEL June to October
MAJOR ANGLING SPECIES Barramundi, mangrove jack, fingermark (golden snapper), trevally, queenfish, mackerel, saratoga and various reef, sport and game species
SPECIAL RESTRICTIONS Permits and special entry restrictions apply in all Aboriginal lands. Catch-and-release is encouraged and barbless hooks are preferred in Andranangoe (Goose) Creek
WARNINGS Saltwater crocodiles inhabit all inshore areas, estuaries and river systems in the Top End, often extending above the upper tidal limits — observe all warning signs. Many roads are 4WD only, and may be totally impassable from November until late May or early June. Cyclones and severe tropical storms can occur at any time between November and May
CHARTER BOATS AND FISHING GUIDES Bookings for Jessie River Camp are handled by Angling Adventures in Geelong, telephone Freecall 1800 033 094

Melville Island is a sizeable body of land lying 75 to 100 km north of Darwin, across Beagle Gulf and the Clarence Strait. Along with neighbouring Bathurst Island to the west, this archipelago is known as the Tiwi Islands, and is home to a proud and culturally distinct group of Aboriginal peoples called the Tiwi.

Bathurst and Melville islands are also home to some of the finest and most exciting sport fishing available anywhere in the Top End. Several high-profile angling lodges, camps and guiding operations now exist expressly to cater for the needs of visiting anglers, who come from all over Australia and the rest of the world to cast a line in these remote, beautiful and fish-rich waters.

One of the finest of these guiding operations is the Jessie River Camp, on Melville Island's Jessie River — a business indicative of the latest generation of environmentally friendly sport fishing lodges catering exclusively to catch-and-release angling.

Changing Fortunes

Since first being established during the early 1990s as an outpost camp of Barra Base, on nearby Bathurst Island (see pp. 296–7), the Jessie River operation has undergone several significant transformations. In its earliest days, this was a rather basic and less-than-luxurious bush camp hewn from the scrub for the use of diehard anglers. Later, the operation was shifted to a mother ship which anchored itself in the mouth of the Jessie estuary for several months each year. Bookings for this live-aboard vessel were still handled, at that time, by Barra Base.

Most recently, however, this guided fishing business has become a separate entity and now operates from a much more comfortable cabin-style camp located near an airstrip upstream on the Jessie, towards that river's upper tidal limits.

Huge Range of Options

From this well-appointed riverside base, visiting anglers travel downstream in the camp's fast, stable boats to pursue the usual range of tropical targets in the lower river and estuary, as well as heading offshore in search of a host of pelagic and reef species. They may also choose (weather permitting) to range up and down the coast to other Melville creeks and river systems. The most notable of these are the famous waters of Goose (Andranangoe) Creek, which is is an hour's boat ride west of the Jessie River mouth.

The Jessie River itself and its tributary arms have a well-deserved reputation for producing consistently great action on barramundi, mangrove jacks, estuary cod, threadfin salmon, fingermark (golden snapper), pikey bream, trevally and queenfish. In particular, a major rock bar on the eastern side of the river's entrance is a famous hot spot for big saltwater barra. An hour or two of trolling here at the right stage of the tide can sometimes produce almost non-stop hook-ups on barra ranging anywhere from 2 to 20 kg in weight, with the 'average' fish being close to 8 kg on most occasions!

A three-way creek junction a little further upstream is another proven barra hot spot, especially as the first flush of a newly making tide reaches it, sending milling schools of mullet and other bait fish into an explosive frenzy of activity as they are ambushed by incoming predators. This junction may be trolled, like the more famous rock bar, or fished by casting and retrieving lures and flies from a drifting or anchored dinghy.

A fly-rod saratoga from Goose Creek

A solid mangrove jack from the Jessie River

BEYOND THE RIVER

Just offshore from Melville Island, beyond the broad mouth of the Jessie River, shallow coral reefs and isolated rocky outcrops produce excellent numbers of trevally, queenfish, coral trout, cod of several types, fingermark and various other common reef varieties such as Spanish flag or stripies, wrasse (parrot fish), emperor and sweetlip.

Trolling beyond this area or chasing surface-feeding schools of fish signposted by wheeling sea birds can add longtail tuna, mackerel tuna (kawa kawa) and Spanish or school mackerel to this growing list of options, especially in the months between June and November each year.

The odd cobia or black kingfish also turns up here from time to time, and some monster queenfish may be found feeding along the clearly marked current rips and colour changes close to points and reef corners.

GOOSE CREEK

In reasonably calm weather, a boat ride of an hour or so west along the coast from the mouth of the Jessie River brings adventurous anglers to the entrance of Goose Creek—a location that has become something of an icon in Australian sport fishing circles over the past couple of decades.

The lower and middle reaches of Goose Creek contain similar fishing to that on offer in the Jessie, although unbelievably large numbers of small to middling barra are often encountered here, occasionally resulting in 'cricket score' catches by individual anglers. (All these fish are caught and released, of course.)

However, it is the magnificent freshwater sections of upper Goose Creek—including many broad, lily-carpeted holes and bends—that reveal this delightful system's greatest appeal.

Here, bronze-flanked freshwater barra are joined by incredible numbers of prehistoric-looking northern saratoga, including more than a few specimens in the 4-kg plus class.

The freshwater reaches of Goose Creek are regarded as the finest saratoga fishing spot on earth and fly fishers, in particular, come from far and wide to chase these wonderful fish with surface flies among the lily pads and snags.

In the early days of this unique fishery, catches of a hundred saratoga and more a day by two or three anglers were far from unknown. Today, the saratoga have wised up a little and are somewhat more difficult to tempt. It is usually still possible, however, to enjoy a dozen or more encounters with these hard-mouthed, high-jumping and strong-fighting fish during a typical visit of three or four hours to the freshwater reaches of Goose Creek ... and it is certainly guaranteed that any such session will long burn in the memory of any visitor, especially a keen fly rodder, lucky enough to experience it!

Queenfish are plentiful offshore from the Jessie River.

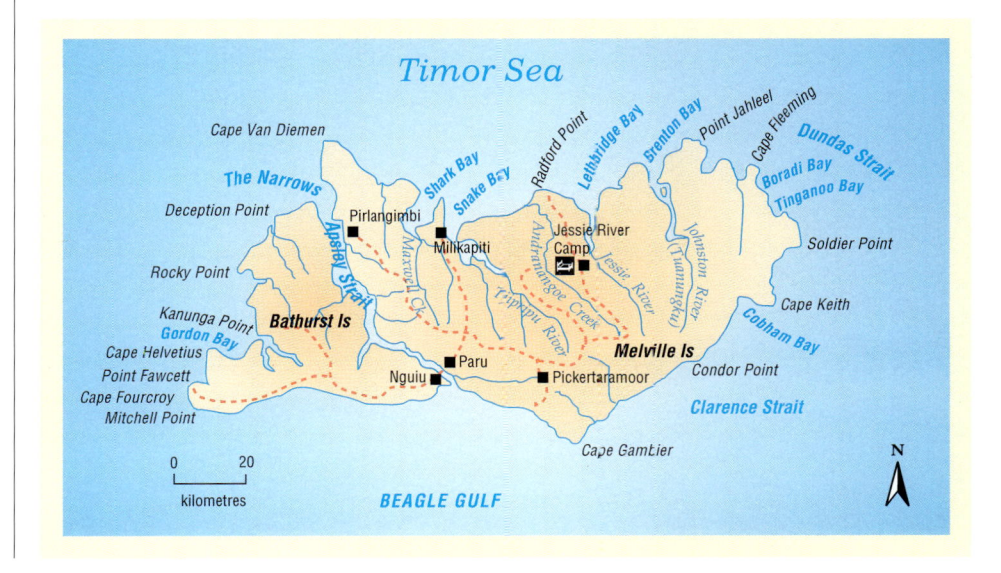

CAPE DON AND THE COBOURG PENINSULA

IN BRIEF

MAP REFERENCE: PAGE 174 E2

GETTING THERE The Cobourg Peninsula lies about 200 km by sea north-east of Darwin, across Van Diemen Gulf. If permits can be obtained, it may be reached by a long (9- to 12-hour) and often rough drive via western Arnhem Land (about 570 km). There are also air strips at Cape Don, Port Essington and Murgenella
BEST TIME TO FISH May to November
BEST TIME TO TRAVEL June to October
MAJOR ANGLING SPECIES Barramundi, mangrove jack, fingermark (golden snapper), trevally, queenfish, mackerel and various reef, sport and game species
SPECIAL RESTRICTIONS Permits and special entry restrictions apply in all Aboriginal lands
WARNINGS Saltwater crocodiles inhabit all inshore areas, estuaries and river systems in the Top End, often extending above the upper tidal limits — observe all warning signs. Many roads are 4WD only, and may be totally impassable from November until late May or early June. Cyclones and severe tropical storms can occur at any time between November and May
CHARTER BOATS AND FISHING GUIDES Bookings for Cape Don Lodge are handled exclusively by Angling Adventures in Victoria, telephone Freecall 1800 033 094

Cobourg Peninsula is an extended finger of land extending north-west from the corner of Arnhem Land, towards Melville and Bathurst islands. It partially encloses the waters of Van Diemen Gulf to the south, and is washed by the warm, blue Arafura Sea to the north.

Joined to the main body of Arnhem Land by a relatively narrow isthmus of land extending west from Murgenella and north of Endyalgout Island, Cobourg Peninsula is indented on its northern shores by a number of relatively deep, long inlets. The largest of these inlets is Port Essington, where an early attempt by European settlers to establish a coastal trading port ultimately met with disaster and failure. The ruins of this settlement still stand as mute testimony to the incredibly harsh nature of the country.

Cobourg Peninsula and nearby Croker Island are surrounded by fish-rich waters and traversed by a number of quite small, but fertile, mangrove-lined estuary systems. The area offers excellent angling opportunities for everything from barramundi and mangrove jacks to big trevally, queenfish, mackerel, coral trout and other reef species. The region is serviced by two excellent lodges—one at Cape Don and the other at Seven Spirit Bay—and some small, self-contained fishing huts or cabins on the shores near the eastern head of Port Essington.

CAPE DON LODGE

Cape Don, with its historic lighthouse, lies at the western extremity of the Cobourg Peninsula, where the rather milky, turbid waters of Van Diemen Gulf, with its very large tides, meet the cleaner, slightly less tidal-influenced seas of the open Arafura Sea to the north.

Currents and eddies rip and scour constantly around the reef-strewn point at Cape Don. Here, the mixing of different bodies of water in Dundas Strait acts as a giant meteorological engine, kickstarting many of the wet season storms and even cyclones that sweep south and west from here towards Darwin and the Tiwi Islands.

Some brilliant offshore and reef edge fishing is available around Cape Don, with schools of small tuna, lots of queenfish, packs of trevally and some big Spanish mackerel and barracuda regularly being encountered, along with numerous reef and bottom-dwelling species. South and east of Cape Don, several small estuaries and channels twist

Looking down on Cape Don Lodge, with a broad expanse of great fishing territory in the background

A massive barracuda taken on a sand cay near Cape Don

through the mangroves, and these hold jacks, fingermark, cod and a reasonable number of mostly small saltwater barra.

Cape Don Lodge is located in a restored 1930s homestead next to the historic lighthouse. Following a brief closure for renovations in 1997, the lodge now operates from April through November each year, catering to small parties of keen sport fishers from all over Australia and further afield. Bookings for this first-class guided fishing operation are handled exclusively by the Geelong-based Angling Adventures company.

East of Cape Don

Moving east along the north coast of Cobourg Peninsula from Cape Don, Vashon Head stands guard over the broad entrance to Port Essington. Trevally, queenfish, cod, coral trout and some big mangrove jacks all hunt the rocky edges of the port's entrance, while trevally and queenfish frequently attack bait fish schools near the various sand spits and cays further south, inside this natural harbour.

Smith Point, to the east of Port Essington's wide mouth, offers similar sport and has several comfortable fishing huts nestled behind its narrow, sandy beach. These are available for rent to visiting anglers.

East again from Smith Point and Danger Point lies Bowen Strait and Croker Island, with Cape Croker at its northern tip. This entire offshore area plays host to a superb run of large Spanish mackerel between September and November each year. The mackerel action typically peaks around the neap tides in October. Fish in excess of 25 kg are likely to be encountered at this time, along with the odd big cobia.

Each of these points and outcrops features current rips, isolated bomboras, reef patches and the occasional wreck, all of which provide ideal habitat for predators such as mangrove jacks, fingermark, coral trout, cod, barracuda, mackerel, trevally of several types and queenfish. Small estuaries and mangrove gutters at the backs of the bays are home to more representatives of the same species, as well as barramundi and delicious mud crabs.

Anglers intent on exploring this region usually opt for a stay at Seven Spirit Wilderness Lodge, Cape Don Lodge or one of the cabins at Smith Point. From any of these locations, it is possible to explore the coast, offshore grounds and estuaries of the Cobourg Peninsula by boat and sample some exceptional fishing, particularly from April until June and again in September, October and November.

The historic lighthouse at Cape Don

DRIVING TIPS FOR 4WD VEHICLES

Corrugations

Corrugations can make for very unpleasant driving conditons. They can be so bad they will seem to be vibrating the vehicle to pieces. Going too fast on these stretches can be dangerous as well as detrimental to you and your vehicle. Going too slow may not be as dangerous, but it will certainly be tiring on you and wearing on your vehicle.

In most cases, a speed of about 80 kph is the optimum, as at that speed the vehicle will tend to 'float' across the hollows, giving a smoother ride. Mind you, what sort of ride you get will depend on how good your suspension is — if you have poor shock absorbers, you are going to feel every bump!

Water Crossings

- Always check the crossing before you plunge in. A 4WD should be able to tackle a crossing of around 60 cm deep without any problems or preparation, but a soft, sandy bottom or a strong current flow can change all that.
- Spray electrical components with WD40 or similar, loosen the fan belt unless the fan has an auto clutch and, before crossing deep water, fit a canvas blind to the front of the vehicle.
- Enter the water at a slow pace — low second gear is generally the best — and keep the engine running even if you stop.
- Don't forget to dry the vehicle's brakes out once through the water crossing; if you did become stuck, check all your oils for contamination.

Mud

Speed and power are essential when driving in muddy conditions. In deep mud, low second or third are probably best. Keep a steady pace and, if possible, keep out of ruts.

BARRA BASE

IN BRIEF

MAP REFERENCE: PAGE 174 D2

GETTING THERE Bathurst Island lies just off the coast of the Northern Territory near Darwin. Barra Base lies on the western side of the island, $1^1/_2$ hours flight by light charter plane from Darwin
BEST TIME TO FISH March to December
BEST TIME TO TRAVEL March to December
MAJOR ANGLING SPECIES Barramundi, mangrove jack, golden snapper (fingermark bream), trevally species, queenfish, threadfin and blue salmon, Spanish mackerel and mud crabs
SPECIAL RESTRICTIONS Permits and special entry restrictions apply in all Aboriginal lands
ACCOMMODATION Comfortable, fully catered lodge accommodation at Barra Base
CHARTER BOATS AND FISHING GUIDES Angling Adventures, Victoria, can arrange extended guided fishing packages to Barra Base, telephone Freecall 008 089 175

Mangrove jacks are prolific in the estuaries around Barra Base

The oldest and most established fishing lodge in the Northern Territory is the operation known as the Barra Base. Built right on the beach at the entrance to expansive Port Hurd, on Bathurst Island, the Barra Base began as a remote fishing camp in the early 1980s.

Approximately 90 km from Darwin, Bathurst Island and the larger adjoining Melville Island form the Tiwi Islands, named after the Tiwi people who are their traditional owners.

Barra Base lodge was built in 1986 to provide remote, up-market accommodated guided fishing in a pristine location. Currently, it provides a range of fishing options spanning both islands.

EXPLORING PORT HURD

Port Hurd is a significant harbour with several arms and literally dozens of creeks. This is tidal saltwater barra country where an angler can spend many days exploring. Perhaps the single

Sunrise over Port Hurd, Bathurst Island

most famous spot is Second Creek, only five minutes boat ride from the lodge. Over the years, some of the biggest barramundi caught by the lodge's clients have come from Second Creek, particularly when trolling through the mouth on a making tide late in the afternoon.

Perhaps even more significant are the record-sized threadfin salmon which have latched on to lures in and around Second Creek. There is probably no more reliable place to catch a big salmon in Australia. There is also hardly a more frustrating experience than to see a school of huge threadfin finning in the current against a dead tree and completely ignoring all lures an angler has to offer! Such is the nature of the species, but the wait until feeding time can be well worthwhile.

The usual estuarine species are caught throughout Port Hurd, including mangrove jack and golden snapper (fingermark bream), but there are also a couple of reefs where anglers can try for black jewfish to 15 or 20 kg. This robust, tearaway species is usually best dealt with on a heavy handline. On the shallow jewie reefs at Port Hurd, however, anglers are encouraged to fish with 6- to 8-kg line on barra baitcasting tackle. Although anglers will lose some fish this way, the sporting thrill of the capture they will enjoy when it's made more than makes up for this.

At night, a favourite activity is to fish from the beach in front of the lodge for big sharks and jewfish. The occasional travelling barra will also take a bait, as will one of Port Hurd's resident Queensland gropers. Often beached after a mammoth tussle, these fish are quickly admired, photographed and carefully released unharmed.

Further Afield

Several creek systems along the coastline of Bathurst Island either side of Port Hurd are available to anglers staying at Barra Base, and these are often highly productive. As with all tropical tidal estuary fishing, tidal movements are critical to success. Some creeks are best fished by casting lures at the bottom of a big spring tide, while others are best trolled on a making neap tide when good water clarity is conducive to targeting travelling barramundi on lures. In this respect, anglers will find the lodge guides' expert local knowledge invaluable.

For anglers with an interest in large, edible crustaceans, it's not too difficult to pot a feed of mud crabs in the mangrove-lined creeks accessible to the Barra Base.

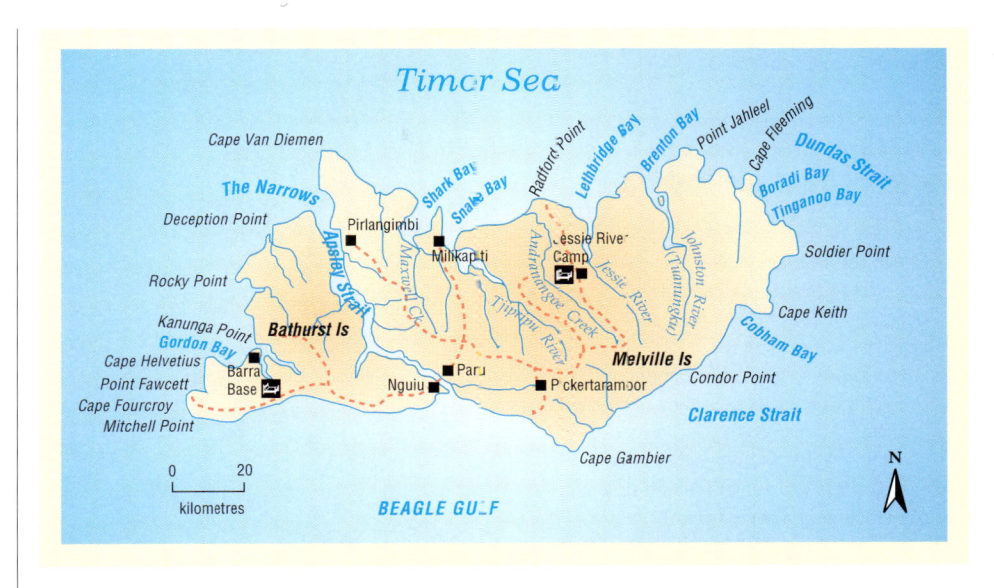

Excellent bluewater fishing is available along the coast from Port Hurd. There are queenfish grounds and recognised hot spots for giant trevally. Spanish mackerel run in season and reef anglers will be thrilled at the size of the golden snapper that inhabit the many inshore reefs. Wide of Port Hurd is the Bathurst Trench, a recognised sailfish and marlin ground, fished mainly by visiting game boats from Darwin. The biggest sailfish in Top End waters tend to turn up over the Bathurst Trench, and the near misses on big marlin, mostly hooked on tackle too light to handle them, have been well documented.

Black jewfish or northern mulloway are a prized catch in Bathurst Island waters

Barra Base is famous for its huge threadfin salmon

THE VICTORIA RIVER

IN BRIEF

MAP REFERENCE: PAGE 174 C9

GETTING THERE Timber Creek township on the Victoria River is about 500 km south of Darwin along the Stuart and Victoria highways

BEST TIME TO FISH March/April upriver; March to December downriver

BEST TIME TO TRAVEL March/April to December, depending on road access after the wet season

MAJOR ANGLING SPECIES Barramundi, threadfin salmon, blue salmon and black jewfish

WARNINGS Saltwater crocodiles inhabit these waters and anglers should stay out of the water and away from the water's edge. Rock bars and mud banks pose navigational hazards at different stages of flood and tide

ACCOMMODATION Timber Creek has budget hotel accommodation and camping and caravan parks

CHARTER BOATS AND FISHING GUIDES HotSpot Fishing Tours can arrange fishing safaris with accommodation to the Victoria River, telephone Freecall 1800 809 035

The Victoria River is the largest river system in the Northern Territory. It winds its way from practically the middle of the Territory, past the huge Gregory National Park and into the Joseph Bonaparte Gulf, on the western side of the Top End.

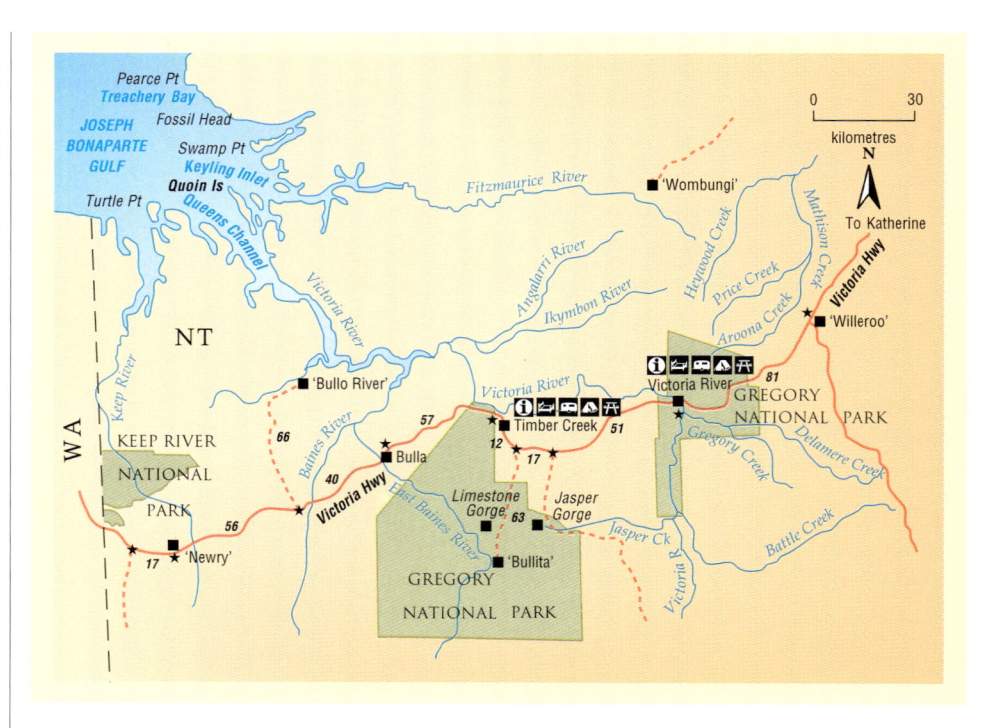

The unofficial fishing headquarters on the Victoria River (often referred to locally simply as the Vic) is the small township of Timber Creek. Timber Creek is approximately 300 km west of Katherine on the Victoria Highway, and about the same distance again from Kununurra, just over the border in Western Australia.

Each year, towards the end of the wet season, Timber Creek locals enjoy a brief period when barramundi in large numbers, and including some big ones, are caught from the shore at Policemans Point on the mouth of Timber Creek itself, and also at the mouth of Big Horse Creek, not far from the township. Mum, dad and the kids all line up at this time, chucking out lures and hooking great fish.

EXPLORING THE VICTORIA RIVER BY BOAT

For anglers with a boat, there is plenty of water to explore on the Victoria River. There is a concrete boat ramp at Big Horse Creek. Heading upstream from the ramp is more productive early in the dry season when water levels are still fairly high. There are many rock bars and shallow gravel beds which restrict progress once water levels drop. During this early season, barramundi can be caught both trolling and casting diving minnow lures around snags and rock bars. Fishing with live mullet baits suspended from a float around structures is also a popular technique.

Barramundi are caught right through the year downriver from the boat ramp. The run-off period straight after the wet does not last very long, as the region has an elevated topography which drains flood waters in the Victoria far more rapidly than other big Territory rivers.

Flowing feeder creeks in this scenic waterway are, however, capable of producing memorable barramundi fishing in their short life span. A fish a cast is not out of the question at even the smallest of creek mouth colour changes.

The Victoria River as it winds through Gregory National Park

By April, the Vic is usually settling into its dry season mode, but excellent fishing continues right through the year and into the following wet season. Tides are critical, however, in this part of the world. This is big tide country and on the high spring tides visibility is poor in the places where anglers need to concentrate their efforts.

Working the Tides

Live mullet baits account for nearly all the big barramundi taken during spring tides, and best action usually occurs at the bottom end of the tide and the first of the make.

There are many locations downriver where schools of popeye mullet swarm onto shallow mud flats as a big tide starts to rise. Able to see both above and below the water, the popeye mullet leap and dart across the surface. Often, their agitated antics attract barra in numbers, and the cacophony of feeding that takes place will stir the blood of any angler. There can be great frustration, however, for anglers trying to catch a popeye for bait.

Stealth is required to get close enough for a successful throw of the cast-net because these highly evolved mullet can see the angler and the net coming. On hard mud flats, the trick is to take a running charge at a school of flitting mullet, surprising them and hurling the cast-net once within range. Do not attempt this in water deeper than 30 cm, which is shallow enough for any large crocodiles in the vicinity to be clearly visible.

Depending on the size of the bait, a single 4/0 to 7/0 hook, pinned below the dorsal and above the backbone, and cast unweighted to the edge of the mud flat, will quickly be set upon when the barra are feeding. A dead mullet bait, scaled and pinned through both jaws, will often do the job when the live baits run out.

Lure Fishing on the Victoria River

For lure fishing, the prime time to fish the Victoria River is during the neap tidal phases, when tidal movement is minimal and there is reasonable water clarity right down the river.

The best fishing commences above the mouth of Angalarri Creek and ends below Green Island, not far above the huge, shallow mouth of the Baines River, which is a major tributary of the Victoria. Only the most experienced locals venture further down the river, or up into the Baines, as submerged rocks and deceptive, shallow mud flats are prevalent. In any event, even during phases of the most minimal tidal movement, below Green Island water clarity diminishes rapidly and is unsuitable for lure fishing.

Trolling medium to large lures past and over submerged snags accounts for most of the big barramundi caught in this prolific part of the river. Iridescent and dark colours seem to work best, and a bit of contrast doesn't hurt. A good depth sounder is essential because it enables anglers to troll banks and follow the contours of the bottom in search of snags and, hopefully, fish. Although most good trolling spots are within a short cast of the river bank, there are quite a few where big fish are caught practically in the middle of the river.

In contrast to other major barra rivers, most fish hooked in the Vic are in relatively shallow water—2 to 3.5 m. Anglers should fish the inside of the bends and along the straits, concentrating their efforts during the last half of the tide and ready for action just as it turns to come in.

Barra are not the only welcome predatory species to be caught using bait or lures. Threadfin and blue salmon are often encountered and lucky anglers sometimes stumble onto a school of black jewfish, which provide exciting sport on standard barramundi gear. Not so welcome are the big tidal river fork-tailed catfish and whaler sharks up to 2 m in length, which travel up the river with the tide.

The Victoria River is surrounded by some magnificent country

The Vic is famous for its big barramundi

VANDERLIN ISLAND

IN BRIEF

MAP REFERENCE: PAGE 175 N9

GETTING THERE Access to Vanderlin Island is by 4WD from Borroloola through a Gulf cattle station and then by boat. Borroloola is about 1000 km from Darwin along the Stuart and Carpentaria highways. There is also a daily air service

BEST TIME TO FISH May to November

BEST TIME TO TRAVEL May to December, depending on road access during early wet season rains

MAJOR ANGLING SPECIES Barramundi, mangrove jack, golden snapper (fingermark bream), trevally, queenfish, coral trout, Spanish mackerel and mud crabs

RESTRICTIONS Permits required to travel through mainland cattle stations and visit Vanderlin Island are arranged by the fishing tour operator

WARNINGS Vast areas of shallow water with obstructions, coupled with sometimes erratic tidal movements, pose navigational hazards. It is advisable to fish with an experienced operator

ACCOMMODATION Comfortable, fully catered, fishing cabin accommodation on the beach at Vanderlin Island

CHARTER BOATS AND FISHING GUIDES HotSpot Fishing Tours can arrange guided extended fishing packages to Vanderlin Island, telephone Freecall 1800 809 035

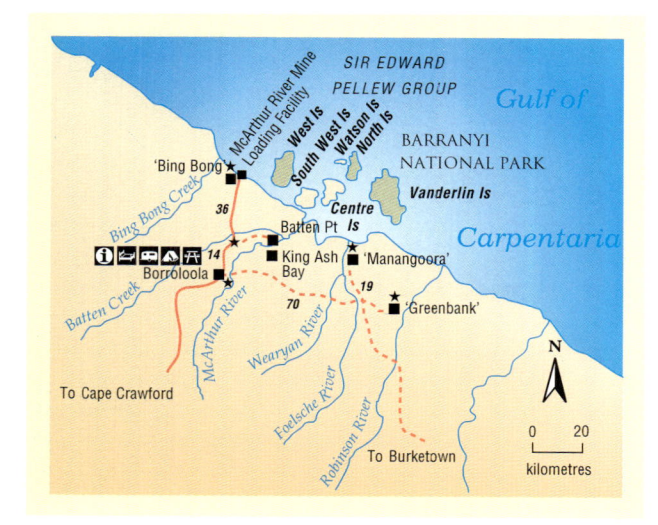

A large estuary cod from reef waters near Vanderlin Island

Vanderlin Island is the largest and most easterly island in the chain known as the Sir Edward Pellew Group. This vast archipelago is adjacent to the mainland deep in the Gulf of Carpentaria and about 200 km from the Queensland border. Locals from the Gulf town of Borroloola travel to these islands via the McArthur River.

Vanderlin Island itself is an extremely remote and exciting tropical fishing destination offering both estuary and bluewater fishing. The island is Aboriginal-owned, but visiting it is possible through an established fishing safari camp which has operated for several years in conjunction with the resident traditional owners.

BLUEWATER SPORT FISHING

Vanderlin Island is about 25 km long and 8 km wide. Around its circumference, anglers fish for a range of bluewater sport fish. High on the list is the queenfish or 'skinny fish', as Territorians tend to refer to it. These are found between the island and rocky outcrops where strong tidal currents surge over shallow reefs adjacent to quiet patches of water.

Schools of queenfish are often seen working these areas, feeding on the surface to the raucous accompaniment of flocks of terns above. Some very big specimens are caught in these waters—including fish in excess of 1 m in length and 9 kg in weight. Trolling surface poppers and diving minnows is a proven technique, but fly casters will also enjoy ample opportunities.

Various trevally species also inhabit the clear, blue waters around Vanderlin Island. Bigger specimens taken are invariably the giant trevally, but schools of golden trevally and gold-spot trevally are common. Tackle should be robust enough to prevent big trevally from reaching coral bommies, which provide typical habitat.

Vanderlin Island is famous for its population of coral trout. As with all coral trout in the Top End, these fish rarely exceed 4 kg, but they provide terrific sport on typical barramundi tackle. Most trout are caught while trolling small, deep-diving minnows with plenty of contrast and colour.

The best areas for trolling are around the rocky outcrops, and over adjacent coral in about 4 to 6 m of water. An adventurous but exciting tactic is to fish close in to the rocks, casting lures towards breaking water. This requires a reliable boat and competent driver.

In Northern Territory waters, Vanderlin Island is the most southerly domain of the vast Spanish mackerel schools which patrol the Top End coast on a seasonal basis. At times, anglers may encounter schools numbering in the thousands, and competition is fierce for deep-diving lures trolled at a fast pace.

For the reef angler, the options are numerous, with a variety of species on tap, including golden snapper (fingermark bream) and red emperor.

Anglers are often surprised at how shallow the water is where red emperor feed around Vanderlin Island. Anchored on a reef in only 5 m of water, with a berley stream running out the back, it is not uncommon to see red emperor swim halfway up to the boat and be clearly sighted. On these occasions, they may readily be caught with a jig or fly.

An indication of the extent of the island's remoteness are the number and size of huge Queensland groper which cruise around the reef edges and right into the shallows. It is a memorable experience to have a groper in excess of 150 kg appear suddenly from under the boat to devour whole a hooked trevally or reef fish!

MACKEREL MOUNTAIN

About an hour's run into the Gulf from the top of Vanderlin is an area known as Mackerel Mountain. This is a Spanish mackerel spawning ground where fish are often in such a frenzy that landing one is near impossible as other fish home in and bite at swivels, rings and even knots in the line.

Game boats that have visited the area in recent years have struck patches of both Indo-Pacific sailfish and marlin in significant numbers. As with the mackerel, however, these fish are attracted to the area by the presence of huge bait schools, and anglers targeting billfish are plagued by the mackerel.

INSHORE AND ESTUARY ACTION
Although there are no creeks on Vanderlin Island, barra are sometimes caught at high tide by casting off the rocks and sandy beach right in front of the fishing camp. For those targeting barramundi and other estuarine species, however, a number of mangrove systems are only a short boat drive away on the mainland.

Anglers will be pleasantly surprised by the number and variety of species in the mangrove systems. In addition to significant populations of barramundi and mangrove jack, at the top of the tide, there are also schools of queenfish and giant trevally that move well up the larger creeks.

The extent to which this takes place is surely an unusual phenomenon. On a big incoming tide, right up a wide creek, anglers may witness these aggressive sportfish erupting on the surface as they feed on vast mullet schools. These fish can be caught by casting and fast-retrieving minnows and poppers.

The nature of the estuarine terrain where these fish are encountered leads to the presence of barramundi, and one occasionally grabs a fast lure, much to the delight of the angler at the other end. Those anglers targeting barramundi and mangrove jack will enjoy most success casting small, medium-depth swimming minnows to dead, fallen trees, or snags, and around small creek junctions. The bottom half of a falling tide is the best period, but an early making tide can produce spirited fishing.

MUD CRABS AND ERRATIC TIDES
Mud crabbing is a popular fishing activity in these estuaries. Mud crabs are caught the traditional way in baited pots, but at low tide they are often seen free-swimming past the boat, or scurrying across shallow sand flats where a nimble angler can give chase with a landing net.

The tides in the Gulf of Carpentaria are difficult to predict. The Gulf is a vast area of relatively shallow water and wind direction and strength impacts on tide times and occurrences. In comparison to waters at the very top of the Northern Territory, tidal movement is minimal around Vanderlin Island and the adjoining mainland. Creeks can still be cut off at low tide, however, often in contravention of predicted tide times. This is one of several reasons why it pays to have local knowledge or the services of an experienced guide.

Trolling lures around reefy outcrops produces plenty of coral trout

An aerial view of Vanderlin Island

THE KIMBERLEY

IN BRIEF

MAP REFERENCE: PAGES 208 AND 209

GETTING THERE Broome is more than 2200 km north-east of Perth and around 1800 km south-west of Darwin. Wyndham is about 3280 km north-east of Perth
BEST TIME TO FISH March to November
BEST TIME TO TRAVEL May to October
MAJOR ANGLING SPECIES Mackerel, trevally, queenfish, sailfish, threadfin salmon, mangrove jacks, fingermark, barramundi, emperor, coral trout, cobia and various other reef, sport and game species
RESTRICTIONS Entry onto Aboriginal lands and reserves is via permit only
WARNINGS Saltwater crocodiles inhabit all inshore areas, estuaries and river systems in the Kimberley, often extending well above the upper tidal limits. Many roads are 4WD only, and may occasionally become impassable between December and late April or May. Cyclones and severe tropical storms can occur at any time between late November and May
CHARTER BOATS AND FISHING GUIDES Macka's Barra Camp, telephone (08) 9169 1759; Ultimate Adventures, telephone (08) 9168 2310; bookings for the Alligator Camp on the Drysdale River are handled by Angling Adventures, Victoria, telephone Freecall 1800 033 094

The Australian Aboriginal prehistory of the remote Kimberley region dates back many tens of thousands of years. This may even be the place where our continent's earliest human inhabitants first arrived on the Australian mainland from southern Asia, more than 40 000 years ago. A vivid reminder of this important link is provided by the presence in the Kimberley of dramatic indigenous rock art such as the extraordinary Wandjina figures, along with the more mysterious and possibly even older paintings widely known to Europeans as the Bradshaws.

Today, Aboriginal association with the land remains extremely strong in this area. Large tracts of the Kimberley have been set aside as Aboriginal land or Aboriginal reserves, with limited access and permit requirements in force for all non-indigenous people.

FIRST CONTACT

This remote region of Australia saw its first recorded European visitors during the 1600s, when numerous Dutch, Spanish, Portuguese and English sailing ships on their way to the Spice Islands, in what is now Indonesia, made often violent and catastrophic contact with Australia's rugged west coast. It is even possible that some European vessels sailed along this coastline as early as the late 1500s, and a few may have been wrecked here prior to the 17th century.

What we know for certain is that, in 1644, Abel Tasman mapped parts of what we now call the Kimberley coast. He was followed half a century later, in 1699, by William Dampier, who landed somewhere near the present site of Broome.

Today, this wild and extensive north-western coastline and its many rivers, gorges and waterholes remain largely unchanged since those very early days of European contact, and therefore offer a myriad of exciting angling opportunities.

Lake Argyle on the Ord River near Kununurra

Fishing near Kalumburu in the Northern Kimberley

With Broome as its southern base and Wyndham or Kununurra offering a stepping-off point for its even more remote north-western corner, near the border with the Northern Territory, the Kimberley offers a potential lifetime of excitement and exploration for the adventurous travelling angler.

THE NORTHERN KIMBERLEY

The Northern Kimberley is that vast area of land and indented coastline extending from the Northern Territory's border with Western Australia, just east of Kununurra, to about the Prince Regent River, which empties into St George Basin near the abandoned mission at Kwinana. This is a vast and largely uninhabited chunk of land larger than some European countries. It has an extensive and diverse coastline, ranging from the tidal mud flats of the broad Cambridge Gulf to the rocky points and islands of Admiralty Gulf, Cape Voltaire and the remote Bonaparte Archipelago.

The Northern Kimberley features many magnificent river systems including the Ord, Pentecost, Chamberlain, Berkeley, King George, Drysdale, King Edward, Mitchell and Prince Regent, to name just a few of the better known and more significant. Most of these rivers feature deep gorges and strings of isolated or partially isolated fresh waterholes along their upper reaches. Many waterholes only join up to form rivers during the heavy rainfall periods that sometimes occur through the northern wet season.

Further downstream, impressive waterfalls or narrow, rocky constrictions where the area's massive tides boil back and forth to create turbulent 'horizontal falls' can often be found. The mouths of many of these rivers consist of deep natural harbours and wide bays, often studded with uninhabited islands and shallow reefs.

Outstanding Fishing

This entire northern area of the Kimberley provides exceptional fishing opportunities. Good numbers of barramundi range up and down each river system as far as the first impassable waterfall or major barrier, often using floods to enter isolated lagoons and billabongs that may be cut off from the main river for years at a time.

Above these barriers to the migration of barramundi are to be found sooty, khaki and leathery grunter (called 'black bream' by many locals), as well as small chanda perch and big fork-tailed catfish.

Further downstream, the barramundi are joined by mangrove jacks, fingermark (golden snapper), estuary and gold spot cod, threadfin and blue salmon, pikey bream, tarpon (ox eye herring), trevally, queenfish, barracuda, long toms, giant herring, javelin fish, black jewfish

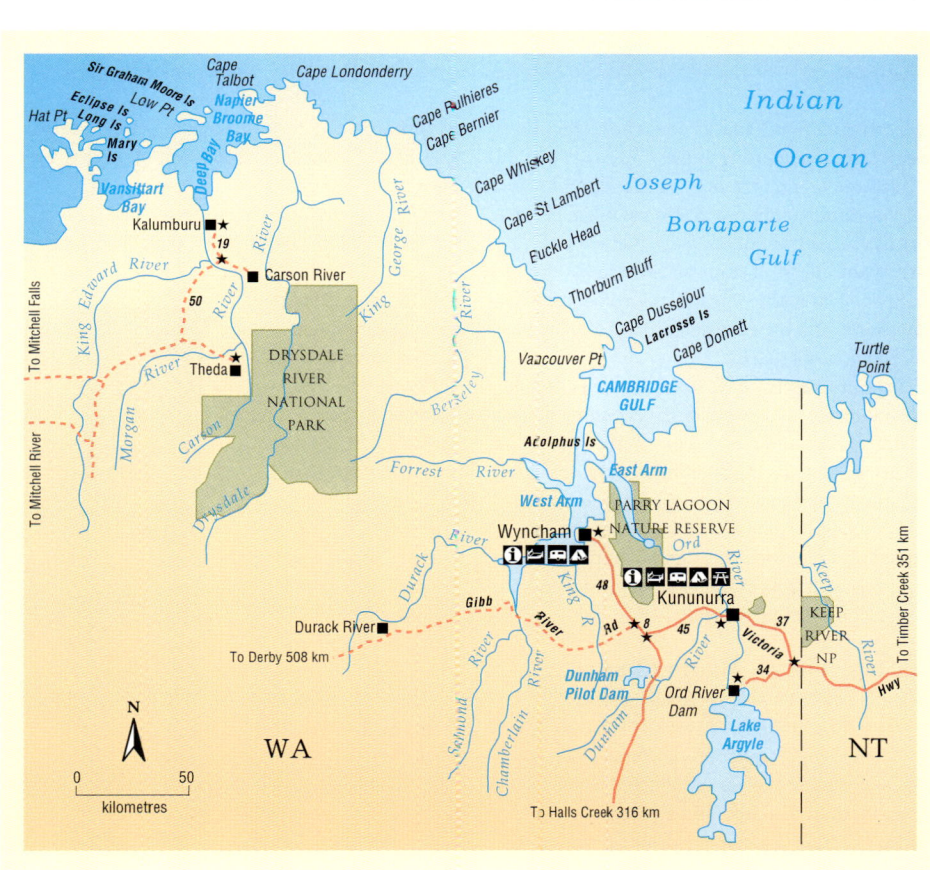

THE KIMBERLEY

El Questro Station overlooks Chamberlain Gorge, in the northern Kimberley region near Kununurra

(northern mulloway), sharks and a host of other species far too numerous to list.

Offshore, around the myriad islands and reefs, barramundi are much less common, but the other fish already mentioned are joined by coral trout, several types of emperor, wrasse, parrot fish, Spanish and school mackerel, cobia, tuna, large sharks and the occasional sailfish or small to middling black marlin.

There are several ways to explore this remote and sometimes rather challenging country. Some adventurous travellers use their 4WD vehicles and cartopper boats to gain limited coastal access, while others rely on the organised services of fishing guides, live-aboard charter vessels, mother ships and even fly-in and float plane operations with well-established outpost camps on rivers such as the Drysdale.

THE SOUTHERN KIMBERLEY

The many coastal rivers and major estuary systems strung along the stretch of remote coastline between the Fitzroy and the Prince Regent rivers — including the May, Meda, Robinson, Isdell, Charnley, Calder and Sale rivers — all offer bountiful barramundi fishing at times, along with abundant (and often big) mangrove jacks, fingermark, cod, tarpon, large fork-tailed catfish and, higher upstream, sooty grunter, archer fish and chanda perch.

Offshore, in King Sound, Strickland Bay, Yampi Sound, Doubtful Bay, Camden Sound and Brunswick Bay, there are literally hundreds of islands, isolated rocks, bomboras and reef patches where the racing, boiling tidal waters are home to chopping schools of queenfish, mackerel, trevally, longtail tuna and mackerel tuna, not to mention prolific reef species including cod, Queensland groper, wrasse, emperor, big fingermark and many, many others.

The coastal town of Derby, with a permanent population of around 3500 residents, makes an ideal staging point for any serious exploration of this fascinating and very challenging southern portion of the Kimberley region. Derby lies some 230 km by road northeast of Broome. It is also 260 km from Fitzroy Crossing, which offers access to some very good barra fishing in the Fitzroy River, and is 550 km from Halls Creek, on the long road to Darwin.

A beautiful, silvery barra from a Kimberley river

Dampier Land to Broome

Dampier Land is the name given to the sizeable wedge of country lying between King Bay, south of Derby, where the Fitzroy meets the sea, and the port of Broome, to the south.

This is another reasonably remote area, and some parts of it remain largely inaccessible, while most of the vehicular tracks should only be tackled in well-equipped 4WDs. Having said that, the rocky points around Beagle and Pender bays and at Cape Leveque and One Arm Point are certainly capable of producing some very good shore-based fishing for various types of trevally, queenfish, coral trout, cod, cobia and many other northern species. As a result, they offer some of the best angling opportunities in the entire Kimberley for those without boats.

Enormous tides (with movements of up to 9 and even 10 m on the springs) and occasional very strong winds can also make this rather hazardous country for the unwary visitor. However, there is certainly no shortage of fishing rewards on offer for the careful and well-prepared explorer!

At the southern extremity of this vast Kimberley region lies the lively and cosmopolitan town of Broome, with a permanent population somewhere in excess of 7000 people, and a great many more visitors each dry season.

Broome makes a great base for fishing and exploring the so-called Pearl Coast, at the southern end of the Kimberley, as well as for launching more ambitious expeditions further north. Its nearby waters offer bream, whiting, threadfin salmon, blue salmon, trevally, queenfish, tuna, mackerel, barracuda, mangrove jacks and an occasional barramundi, as well as all manner of reef and bottom-dwelling species.

Broome jetty, on the north-western side of Roebuck Bay, is a favourite spot with many visiting anglers, and the port is also home to a small fleet of modern charter vessels which regularly head offshore in search of piscatorial action.

Broome's offshore grounds are renowned for their abundant tuna, trevally, queenfish, mackerel, cobia, barracuda, sailfish and marlin, as well as for a host of tropical reef fish, including emperor, coral trout, fingermark and various wrasse and cod.

Above all, however, Broome is famous as one of the very best ports in the world for those interested in pursuing Indo-Pacific sailfish on light tackle or even fly gear. This aspect and the rest of Broome's outstanding fishing options are examined in far greater detail on pp. 306–7.

Harsh and Unforgiving

As mentioned, it is possible to spend weeks, months or even years exploring and fishing the Kimberley Coast, but visitors should never forget that this magnificent region can be a rather harsh and unforgiving place.

Landing a pair of giant trevally off the Kimberley coast

Extreme heat, massive tides (up to 10 m), strong currents, uncharted reefs, tropical storms, cyclones, crocodiles, sea wasps, stonefish, deadly cone shells and sharks all add a hard edge to the paradise known as the Kimberley. For many modern adventurers, however, these hurdles simply add to the challenge and excitement of visiting one of the globe's last true frontiers—a region some experienced travellers have fittingly called 'the best part of the best country on earth'!

BROOME AND THE PEARL COAST

IN BRIEF

MAP REFERENCE: PAGE 208 C8

GETTING THERE Broome is more than 2200 km north-east of Perth and around 1800 km south-west of Darwin
BEST TIME TO FISH March to November
BEST TIME TO TRAVEL May to October
MAJOR ANGLING SPECIES Mackerel, trevally, queenfish, sailfish, threadfin salmon, mangrove jack, fingermark, barramundi, emperor, coral trout, cobia and various other reef, sport and game species
SPECIAL RESTRICTIONS Entry onto Aboriginal lands and reserves is via permit only
WARNINGS Saltwater crocodiles inhabit all inshore areas, estuaries and river systems in the Kimberley, often extending well above the upper tidal limits. Many roads are 4WD only, and may occasionally become impassable between December and late April or May. Cyclones and severe tropical storms can occur at any time between late November and May
ACCOMMODATION Accommodation ranging from international-class hotels to motels, holiday units, caravan parks and camping grounds is available in this region

---

The north-western town of Broome is a diverse and cosmopolitan regional centre. Its fast-growing population is already in excess of 7000 people, and these numbers are swollen throughout the cooler, drier months of the years (from April to November) by thousands of visiting tourists from all over Australia and the rest of the world. Founded in 1883, Broome's European history is closely associated with the colourful pearling industry. This began with the pursuit of wild pearl shell and pearls, but shifted during the second half of the 20th century to the culturing of these natural gems in commercial pearl 'farms' up and down the coast.

Broome was also bombed several times by the Japanese during World War II and has survived a string of cyclones and major tropical storms to become the thriving town that it is today.

FISHING AROUND BROOME

Broome's port, situated on Roebuck Bay, has a major jetty, and this acts as a fine starting point for many visiting anglers. It provides shore-based access to some very good fishing at times for trevally, queenfish, mackerel, cod, small tuna of several types, various sharks and even the occasional barramundi, especially during the hotter, wetter months of the year.

This jetty is situated on the north-western side of Roebuck Bay. The eastern and north-eastern ends of this very large, shallow bay feature mangrove-lined shores and small creeks that regularly produce bream, whiting, threadfin salmon, blue salmon, various trevally, queenfish and mangrove jacks for boat anglers, as well as an occasional barramundi through the hotter months.

North and south of Roebuck Bay are long, sandy beaches where sand or yellowfin whiting, small queenfish, dart, trevally and even a few small bonefish are sometimes caught on baits, flies and small lures or jigs.

OFFSHORE FROM BROOME

Offshore from Broome, there is excellent fishing for tuna, trevally of several species, queenfish, mackerel, cobia, barracuda, sailfish and marlin. A big variety of tropical reef fish are also on offer, including several types of emperor, coral trout, fingermark (golden snapper) and various species of tropical cod.

Many sport and game anglers visit Broome specifically to sample its light-tackle, bluewater action, particularly the region's abundant stocks of Indo-Pacific sailfish.

Sailfish numbers off Broome tend to peak between June and September each year, although a few sails are on offer here any time from April to November. Their numbers and distance from shore fluctuate with the tidal cycle, and the very best fishing is usually experienced in the cleaner, bluer waters typically associated with the smaller rises and falls of the neap tides.

Broome's sailfish are mostly small, running from 10 to 30 kg on average, but are often present in very large numbers, attacking baits, lures and flies in packs or pods and providing world-class light-line fishing. Not surprisingly, several major tournaments, including a very successful fly fishing event, are run each year in conjunction with the sailfish season.

Rock fishing at Roebuck Bay near Broome

Above: *Broome Jetty is a popular fishing platform*
Right: *A free-swimming sailfish off Broome*

FURTHER AFIELD

North-east of Broome, the Fitzroy River and its various tributaries offer reasonable to very good numbers of barramundi in both the tidal and freshwater reaches. The best action here tends to be experienced by those visiting anglers willing to track down seasonal hot spots and talk to the locals.

Dampier Land, the name given to the large wedge of country between Broome and King Bay, where the Fitzroy meets the sea south of Derby, is quite remote and some parts of it remain largely inaccessible. The rocky points around Beagle and Pender bays and at Cape Leveque and One Arm Point, however, can produce some brilliant shore fishing at times for trevally, queenfish, coral trout, cod and many other northern species.

Huge tides and strong winds can also make this rather hazardous country for the unwary visitor, but there is certainly no shortage of fishing rewards for the adventurous and well-prepared traveller!

THE PILBARA COAST

IN BRIEF

MAP REFERENCE: PAGE 210 D5

GETTING THERE Karratha is more than 1500 km north of Perth and some 840 km south-west of Broome
BEST TIME TO FISH Year-round
BEST TIME TO TRAVEL April to October
MAJOR ANGLING SPECIES Mackerel, trevally, queenfish, threadfin salmon, mangrove jacks, barramundi, black jewfish (mulloway), emperor, coral trout, cobia and various other reef, sport and game species
SPECIAL RESTRICTIONS Permits are required to land and camp on some offshore islands
WARNINGS Small numbers of saltwater crocodiles inhabit certain inshore areas, estuaries and river systems on the Pilbara coast. Some roads are 4WD only, and may occasionally become impassable between December and late April. Cyclones and severe tropical storms are possible between late November and May
CHARTER BOATS AND FISHING GUIDES Tidal Zone Charters, telephone (08) 9185 2457

Sailing boats in a bay near Dampier

The mining town of Karratha, with a population of slightly fewer than 10 000 people, has grown from scratch since the late 1960s, largely as a regional service provider for the Hamersley Iron company and a dormitory centre for the nearby bulk ore port of Dampier. Karratha is also a very popular staging point for travelling anglers keen to sample the many piscatorial delights of the Pilbara Coast. It provides an ideal stepping-off point for exploring the extensive island group known as the Dampier Archipelago, as well as more distant offshore locations including Barrow Island and the fabulous but remote Montebello Islands.

The offshore fishing along this striking stretch of coast, although constrained at times by strong winds, can be nothing short of exceptional, offering everything from big queenfish, trevally, mackerel and sailfish to abundant tropical reef species such as emperor, cod and blue bone (a very popular and tasty type of wrasse). In addition, the Pilbara Coast boasts fine estuary, beach and rock angling for those anglers without offshore capabilities or desires.

KARRATHA AND THE DAMPIER ARCHIPELAGO

The Dampier Archipelago is a cluster of islands offshore to the north and north-east of Karratha. These include Enderby, Rosemary, Dolphin and Legendre islands, as well as many smaller islets, reefs and bomboras. The entire area is well endowed with fish life, especially queenfish, trevally of several species and mackerel, including some very large narrow-barred Spanish mackerel. There is also great reef and bottom-fishing to be enjoyed around these islands and reefs.

For shore-bound anglers or those with smaller trailer boats and car-toppers, the stretch of the Pilbara Coast between about Cape Preston and Balla Balla Harbour, halfway to Port Hedland, offers an attractive range of potential hot spots.

Situated just south of Cape Preston, the Fortescue River is 100 km south-west of Karratha along the Northwest Coastal Highway. The side road in to the river mouth is gravel and usually in good condition, remaining passable even to conventional vehicles. There is a good natural boat ramp on the side of the river about 15 km along this road, and even quite large trailer boats can be launched here at most stages of the tide.

The lower Fortescue River is navigable for about 6 or 7 km upstream and fishes well for mangrove jacks, bream and mulloway (black jewfish), especially in the hotter months of the year, from October to March. Larger trailer boats often travel out of the river mouth to work the reefs and islands offshore. Steamboat Island is located some 10 or 12 km out from the heads and produces good catches of trevally, Spanish mackerel and various tropical reef fish, as do half a dozen other islands within 20 km of the river mouth.

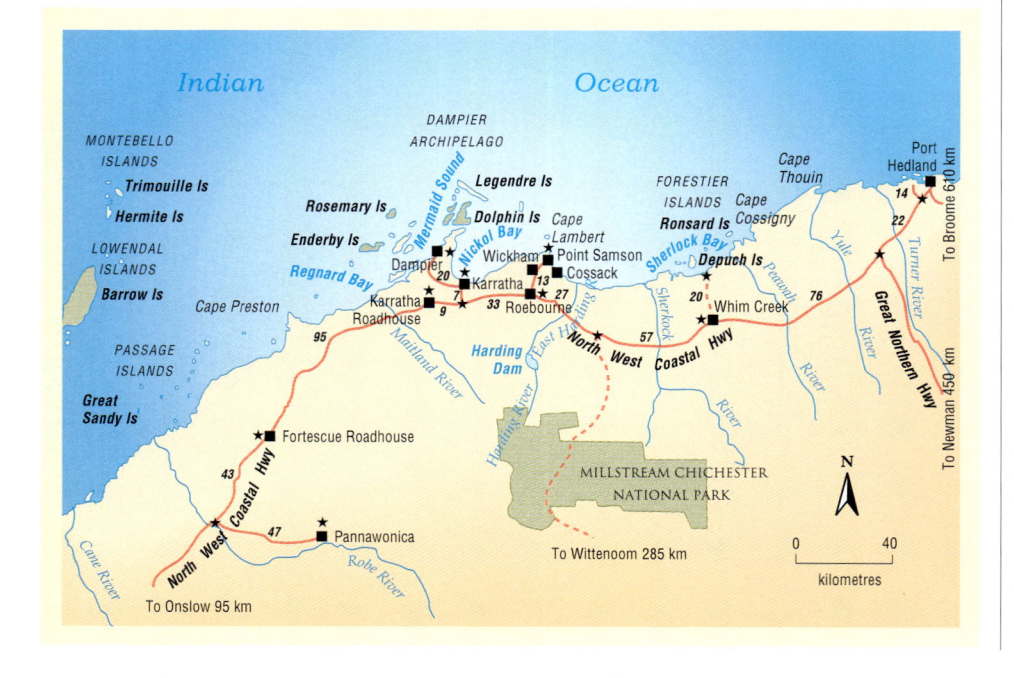

There are some excellent smaller creeks north and south of the Fortescue River, and the closest of these can be easily reached in a dinghy. There is a camp site of sorts at the river mouth, but it offers no shade and has plenty of sandflies.

Forty Mile Beach is so named not as a result of its length, but because it is located about 40 miles (60 km) south of Karratha. The turn-off from the highway is situated just south of Devils Creek, which is well signposted. The 10-km road to the beach has a gravel surface, but is usually in good to excellent condition. This beach itself is about 5 km long with a rocky headland at each end and is a very popular camping spot.

Whiting, golden trevally, sharks, bream, queenfish and several other tropical species are regularly taken from Forty Mile Beach, as well as from the rocks at either end of it. There is also a boat ramp at the southern end of the beach, which once consisted simply of hard sand, but has recently been replaced by a new concrete ramp.

Moving north-east, Withnell Bay is another great spot to launch a small boat or simply fish from the rocks and beaches. The turn-off to this location is on the Burrup Road, which runs off the Dampier to Karratha road. Simply take the Burrup Road all the way to the Northwest Shelf Project site and turn right just before the main gates onto a gravel road that eventually peters out to become a rather a rough track. This is not a major problem, however, as it is only about 3 km in all from the sealed road to the beach.

Fishing results at Withnell Bay tend to be especially good in winter, when most southern tourists choose to visit the area. Unfortunately, winter is also the time of the easterly winds, and these can present problems. Withnell Bay, however, is tucked into the south-western corner of the Burrup Peninsula and well protected.

Karratha Back Beach is only 2 km from town on a bitumen road and boasts a concrete ramp. It is only really usable, however when the tide is at 2.5 m or higher. This ramp offers access to all the creeks in Nickol Bay, as well as Airport Creek, the Nickol River, Fields Creek and Cleaverville Creek. These all fish well on the right tides (usually the neaps), producing jacks, trevally, cod, the odd barra and some very nice threadfin.

Cleaverville Beach is another popular camping and fishing spot some 20 km north of Karratha. The local council charges a small fee to camp here and supplies firewood. The beach itself is about 5 km long and there are plenty of leafy, shaded areas and sandy coves. From this beach, anglers can wade to the adjacent reef and catch many different types of fish.

Cleaverville Creek is at the southern end of the beach. It features a good natural ramp similar to the one at the Fortescue River. There are rock ledges at the mouth of the creek where land-based anglers can fish for mangrove jacks, bream,

Above: A golden trevally taken on a metal jig
Right: Mangrove jacks and fingermark abound in many estuaries along the Pilbara Coast

threadfin salmon and even the occasional barramundi. A deep hole at the mouth of Cleaverville Creek also yields some nice barra, threadfin salmon and mulloway (black jewfish). This hole is some 10 m deep, even on a low tide.

BALLA BALLA HARBOUR

Further east, past Point Samson and Cossack, is Balla Balla Harbour, about halfway between Port Hedland and Karratha. The turn-off for this spot is directly opposite the Whim Creek pub and there's a drive of about 20 km to the river mouth over a good gravel road. The estuary is referred to as a harbour because it was once used for shipping asbestos and copper from nearby mines. The old jetty is long gone, and only a few rotting pylons remain as mute testimony to the area's past.

The river at Balla Balla Harbour has a natural ramp on its bank, but boats may only be easily launched and recovered at high tide. There is a rock bar some 100 m from the ramp where mulloway (black jewfish), threadfin salmon and a few barramundi are caught. This river is large and offers plenty of tributaries and run-off drains capable of producing good fishing at times. There are also several more worthwhile creeks to the south of Balla Balla that can be reached by boat.

Not far off Balla Balla Harbour lies Depuch Island, along with several smaller islands. The offshore fishing for a whole host of pelagic species and reef fish is often very good to excellent in this area, just as it is further west in the Dampier Archipelago. Again, however, strong winds can be a problem, especially in winter.

Coastline at Cleaverville, east of Karratha

THE MACKEREL ISLANDS

IN BRIEF

MAP REFERENCE: PAGE 210 D7

GETTING THERE The Mackerel Islands group lies offshore from Onslow on the Pilbara Coast. Onslow is on the coast between Exmouth Gulf and Karratha, about 1390 km north of Perth

BEST TIME TO FISH March to October

BEST TIME TO TRAVEL March to May generally has the calmest weather, but this is cyclone country and storms are still possible at this time of year

MAJOR ANGLING SPECIES Mackerel (especially Spanish mackerel), queenfish, trevally of many types, spangled emperor, red emperor, cod, pink snapper, coral trout and striped sea perch

SPECIAL RESTRICTIONS Fish may be filleted offshore, but fillets must remain intact. Normal bag limits apply

WARNINGS Western Australia's north-west coast can be extremely windy at times. Poisonous creatures are common – watch for snakes, stonefish, sharks and sea snakes, and make sure you are familiar with toxic invertebrates such as cone shells if travelling to this area

ACCOMMODATION A Mackerel Islands holiday on Thevenard Island includes basic but comfortable living with meals provided. The holiday village, with large oil storage tanks as a backdrop, receives power and water from the oil facility with which it shares the island. There is a caravan park and units in the small town of Onslow

CHARTER BOATS AND FISHING GUIDES Sport fishing charters are run from Onslow by East Indian Charters, telephone 018 937 505; Montebello Islands Safaris, telephone (08) 9314 2034, operates a live-aboard pontoon boat for easy access to day activities

---

Few locations truly earn a place in the piscatorial 'hall of fame', but the Mackerel Islands certainly belong there. Fishing in this area, and around the other islands off the Pilbara Coast, is nothing short of sensational! Situated just offshore from the tiny town of Onslow, the Mackerel Island group's isolation has ensured that little people pressure has occurred. The archipelago's fishing possibilities reflect this, making it the perfect destination for a 'big trip'.

Large areas of this wild coast are inaccessible to vehicles and difficult to reach by boat because of prevailing sea conditions and hefty fuel requirements. Charter operations allow the best opportunities and a week's stay offers the chance to have one's arms stretched by monster fish.

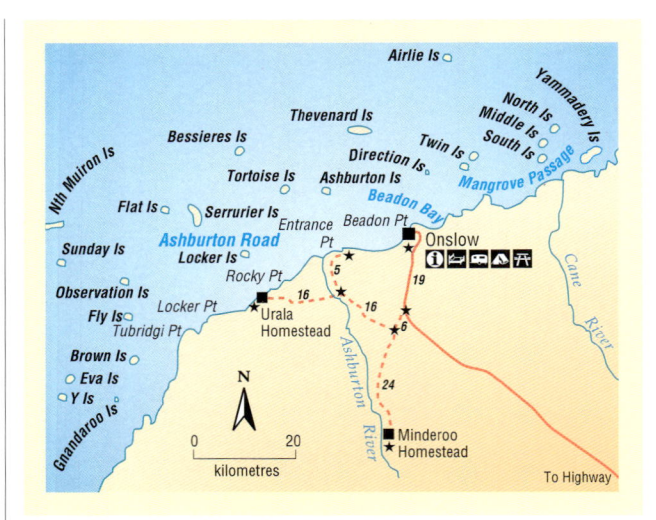

Shore fishing is certainly possible. Tidal creeks contain mangrove jack, cod of many types, bream, threadfin salmon, tarpon and even the mighty barramundi. Sharks are also plentiful and the mulloway (black jewfish) are sometimes unstoppable. Whiting make for a tasty meal in many locations, squid are prolific around weed areas and mud crabs are keenly chased.

The huge tidal range is the biggest constraint, with some creeks draining completely at low water.

BOATING BONANZA

If the shore fishing is good, then boat angling along this coast is brilliant. The Mackerel Islands offer fish capable of breaking the toughest gear. Even in shallow channels not far from shore, small boats will come across large trevally, queenfish, powerful northern mulloway (black jewfish) and many sharks.

LURES, FLIES AND BAITS

Near island and channel edges, a popper-style lure or a metal slice used in conjunction with say 8- to 10-kg spin gear allows for outstanding action, as queenfish, trevally of many species, threadfin salmon and long tom all attack with gusto. Hook-ups cast after cast are possible at times.

Nearer rock and reef areas, but still in shallow waters, one can add coral trout, masses of small cod and little school (doggie) mackerel to the list of likely lure takers.

Baits don't last long here. Most are snaffled by a cod almost instantly, but those that survive attract spangled emperor, coral trout, doggie mackerel, line-busting trevally, threadfin salmon, sharks and a heap of other inhabitants of these fish-rich waters.

These shallow places are a saltwater fly fisher's heaven, the fly being a perfect choice to entice a strike from small and large fish. Nine- and ten-weight outfits are enough for most situations, although the heaviest fly gear available is sometimes not enough to stop a giant trevally! Many Australian record captures have been made here.

Keen lure and fly casters are able to jump out of their boats onto the various sand banks exposed by the tides. Sandy Cay, off the north-western side of Thevenard Island, is a perfect illustration. A light spin rod and a couple of shallow-working lures are ideal here. Simply cast out and work the chosen lure back for non-stop action.

A tactic which works well is to find water about 6 to 10 m deep, where the bottom is visible. A spot is selected with a sandy bottom, but with

A spangled emperor landed at night

Above: *A large cod from Mackerel Island waters*
Left: *The hard-pulling Chinaman fish is usually released because it has been implicated in many cases of ciguatera poisoning*

reef or even weed banks close by. Anchoring carefully and casting a pilchard ('mulie') bait near the reef will draw all manner of fish from their hangouts. A small ball sinker running right down onto a gang (flight) of hooks (usually four 4/0s or 5/0s) or stopped by a swivel about 30 to 40 cm from the hooks is perfect. Wire is rarely used, as more hook-ups on highly prized table species occur without it. Even if mackerel come on the chew, not many will bite off a ganged set of hooks. Naturally, a gaff or large landing net is mandatory in this country.

It's also worth remembering that a few crushed-up mulies dropped into the water may stir some activity if things are a bit quiet at first.

In Deeper Water

Deeper water in this region yields massive fish, and bottom fishing is a popular activity for the likes of cod, members of the emperor family, the highly sought-after red emperor, various mackerel, cobia, barracuda of momentous proportions and even sailfish. Trevally of various types and sizes are common, too. Some fish hooked are simply too powerful to be landed, even on heavy lines.

A common problem in the region for either those trying to land fish for the table or for catch-and-release is the vast number of sharks, which quickly pick up the vibrations of a struggling fish. Little can be done at such times, aside from moving to another location.

Spanish mackerel fishing has a high priority in this region, as the archipelago's name implies. Trolling is the most common practice, with large bibbed minnow-style lures best, quickly taking hits from the toothy creatures, but also hooking cod, trevally or even coral trout.

Various colour schemes have their fans, but one of the first selected by most angling regulars features a red head and white body. This same colour scheme works well for bibless minnows, leadhead jigs and poppers, and has attracted a legion of proponents.

The Rosalie Shoals, near the Mackerel Islands resort on Thevenard Island, are an excellent place to try for mackerel. Trolling near the vast reef complex is often productive. Drifting, anchoring, lure fishing or any type of angling is sure to bring exciting action and big fish here. The tides play an important part in bottom angling, with strong currents meaning plenty of lead is required to hold your bait on the bottom.

Snorkling over the many shallow reef areas is popular, with painted crayfish sometimes taken as a bonus by those with thick gloves.

The Mackerel Islands group is one of the more accessible along this coast, courtesy of a fine lodge set up on Thevenard. The island is about 22 km off the coast of Onslow, and visitors are able to take their boat or use the island's dinghies. Seaworthy craft venture out from Onslow, heading for Direction Island or any of the other islands that dot this splendid ocean, and various charter boats are also available.

DIRK HARTOG ISLAND AND SHARK BAY

IN BRIEF

MAP REFERENCE: PAGE 210 D7

GETTING THERE Denham, on Shark Bay, is about 780 km north of Perth
BEST TIME TO FISH Year-round
BEST TIME TO TRAVEL April to October
MAJOR ANGLING SPECIES Snapper, tailor, mackerel, baldchin groper, cobia, whiting, flathead and various other reef, sport and game species
SPECIAL RESTRICTIONS Areas within Shark Bay are designated marine reserves and some activities are restricted — check before fishing
WARNINGS Great care should be exercised when fishing the exposed rock ledges and cliffs in this region. Large swells are common and crumbling rock strata can lead to potentially fatal falls. Travellers in this region should also carry additional water supplies in case of breakdowns
CHARTER BOATS AND FISHING GUIDES MV *Explorer* Charters and Cruises, telephone (08) 9968 1246; Dirk Hartog Island Tours, telephone (08) 9948 1211

Shark Bay is a massive area of relatively shallow water with abundant sea grass beds, areas of clean sand, rubble patches, reefs, beaches and islands. As well as being home to hordes of fish, it also supports the largest surviving population of dugong or sea cows in Australian waters.

The vast, fish-rich expanse of Shark Bay—one of our largest World Heritage areas—not only marks the most westerly point of the Australian mainland, but also serves as a fascinating intersection and overlap zone between the truly tropical waters further north and the subtropical and temperate seas stretching away to the south.

Here, in the clean, blue waters inside and adjacent to this magnificent and lightly fished bay, giant tailor regularly mix with Spanish mackerel, Samson fish overlap with cobia, and both mulloway and pink snapper are caught right alongside baldchin groper and nor'westers (spangled emperor). Few other areas in the world, let alone here in Australia, offer the same fascinating and diverse mix of fishing opportunities in such pristine and strikingly beautiful surroundings as those found at Western Australia's Shark Bay.

Dirk Hartog Island

Dirk Hartog Island holds a vitally important place in the European history of Australia. It was here, in 1616, that Dutch explorer, Dirk Hartog, came ashore and nailed a pewter plate to a wooden post. It was also here, in 1850, that Australia's first pearling base was established, well before the discovery of even richer pearl shell beds off Broome, further north.

Today, Dirk Hartog Island still looks much the same as it did in both 1616 and 1850. The only

Tailor are prolific around Dirk Hartog Island

A pelican and some of Monkey Mia's famed dolphins

STEEP POINT AND USELESS LOOP
In fishing circles, Shark Bay is justifiably famous for its monster tailor, some of which are caught in the shallow, inshore waters at the the south and south-eastern ends of the bay. Line class records, including many tailor weighing more than 7 kg, have been taken here. Dedicated anglers willing to invest the time and effort needed to locate the isolated schools of monster choppers that cruise these shallow, clear waters can have great success at times. Shark Bay offers a great deal more, however, than just big tailor.

Steep Point is situated on the outside tip of the southern arm of Shark Bay, facing the cliff-lined shores of Dirk Hartog Island. This is one of the most famous and productive rock or land-based fishing locations in all of Australia, if not the world.

The sky is literally the limit for rock-hoppers fishing from this rugged and isolated headland. Fish as large and exotic as marlin, sailfish and giant tiger sharks have been hooked from the shore here on a reasonably regular basis. There is also consistent action on big Spanish mackerel, shark mackerel, cobia, tuna, trevally and smaller sharks, as well as bottom and mid-water species such as mulloway, pink snapper, nor'westers, baldchin groper (wrasse), cod and so on.

Land-based specialists target game and sport fish from these high rocks using float-suspended live and dead baits or various lures and even saltwater flies. One of the most productive and exciting techniques is to drift whole or live garfish and long tom baits suspended beneath helium-filled balloons. The offshore (easterly) winds which prevail here for much of the year will carry these rigs hundreds of metres, causing the baits to skip and dance seductively across the surface. Strikes under these circumstances can be incredibly spectacular!

A cliff gaff is needed to land fish from most of the high ledges in this area, and extreme caution should always be exercised when fishing from these potentially dangerous rock platforms.

Nearby, South Passage and Useless Loop, which are located inside the bay, are most famous for their amazing runs of big pink snapper. These fish are taken in numbers by boat fishers and, to a lesser extent, shore and jetty anglers.

Monkey Mia is situated on the eastern side of the Peron Peninsula, a long finger of land that effectively splits Shark Bay into two sections. As well as being internationally renowned for the regular human interaction with its semi-tame dolphins, this area boasts abundant snapper, mulloway, trevally, barracuda and cobia. Similar action is available around Denham, on the western side of the Peron Peninsula.

Offshore, to the north-west of Shark Bay, Bernier and Dorre islands turn on some superb mackerel fishing at times, and have an almost untapped potential for marlin, sharks, cobia, wahoo and the like.

The town of Carnarvon, further afield again to the north of Shark Bay, offers jetty fishing for abundant mulloway (known as 'kingies' by the locals), mackerel, queenfish, big trevally, tailor and sharks. Offshore, those species are joined by schools of pink snapper that occasionally approach plague proportions!

significant concessions to the encroachment of modern civilisation are a few rough 4WD tracks, a fully operating sheep station and a comfortable eco-tourism resort that caters mostly to dedicated anglers keen to sample the incredibly fish-rich waters of this area.

Angling opportunities around Dirk Hartog Island range from sedately casting a line for abundant sand whiting and flathead on the shallow flats immediately in front of the lodge, right up to the adrenalin-charged pursuit of giant tailor, snapper and Spanish mackerel from the high, wave-battered cliffs along the ocean side of the island.

Offshore, on the many reef, gravel beds and sand patches, pink snapper are present in extraordinary numbers, along with more tailor, some big bluebone or baldchin groper (wrasse) and seasonal runs of Spanish mackerel, shark mackerel and the odd cobia. Further offshore again are tuna, wahoo, marlin and the occasional sailfish, as well as plenty of the toothsome critters for which nearby Shark Bay was first named.

At first glance, Dirk Hartog Island is a dry, sun-bleached and rather inhospitable looking spot, constantly pounded by the cobalt blue breakers of the Indian Ocean along the crumbling cliffs of its western and northern shores. For the adventurous angler, however, it is a genuine piscatorial paradise, where the fish are probably almost as abundant and willing today as they were when Hartog's sailing ship anchor was dropped not far from shore nearly four centuries ago.

Tropical species such as spangled emperor often range as far south as Dirk Hartog Island

KALBARRI AND THE MURCHISON

IN BRIEF

MAP REFERENCE: PAGE 204 B6

GETTING THERE Northampton is 476 km from Perth along the Brand Highway; Kalbarri is 115 km from Northampton
BEST TIME TO FISH March to May offers the best weather for boating and fishing; winter is big tailor time
BEST TIME TO TRAVEL Spring and autumn
MAJOR ANGLING SPECIES Tailor and mulloway from shore; West Australian jewfish, mackerel and pink snapper for boat anglers, or from the shore at Wagoe
SPECIAL RESTRICTIONS If the Murchison River is in flood, it is almost impossible to cross the river bar. The entrance is closed by authorities in this case
WARNINGS Always be aware of the danger posed by big waves — many inexperienced swimmers and snorkelers have lost their lives in this region. Coastal gorges have big undercuts where the force of the swell traps unwary divers
ACCOMMODATION A range of units, chalets, caravan parks and holiday homes to suit most budgets is available, but can be heavily booked during peak periods
CHARTER BOATS AND FISHING GUIDES A fast catamaran ventures out daily for deep sea fishing. Check the Yellow Pages for details or ask at local tackle stores

Combine beautiful scenery, stunning river and coastal gorges, carpets of wildflowers in season, a small but delightfully clean river and a pleasant climate for most of the year and you have Kalbarri, in Western Australia's mid-west. Swept by constant waves pushed from the Indian Ocean, the shoreline is both spectacular and awesome, and fishing from either land or a boat is productive. Inland from the town of Kalbarri, the Murchison River gorges are carved from variegated coloured rocks, forming breathtaking natural sculptures.

To the north, the rugged Zuytdorf Cliffs have kept humans at bay, with the coastal gorges south of the massive Red Bluff a few kilometres from the Kalbarri town site achieving the same effect. The high coastal gorges eventually give way to a long, surf-washed reef known as Wagoe, where numerous species are caught from shore.

Kalbarri has long existed as a commercial fishing location, but its wonderful river, bay and coast couldn't be kept secret from the recreational fraternity forever. Now the region is a magnet for thousands of visitors and supports various resorts, unit complexes and caravan parks. It offers something for everyone — kids, oldies, walkers, divers, surfers, snorkellers, swimmers, art lovers — and for those who just simply want to get away from it all, it's a marvellously peaceful place. For the angler, it nearly has it all!

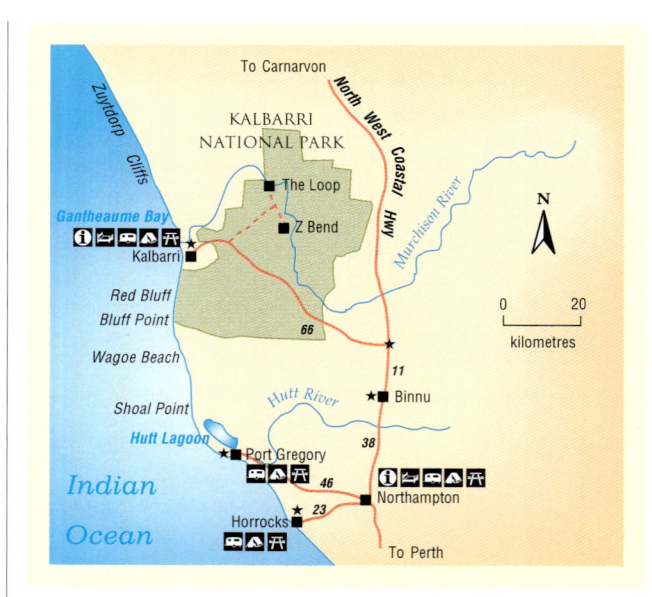

Quiet water beach fishing is popular below the massive Red Bluff headland at Witticara Creek, where tailor, whiting, mulloway, herring (tommy rough) and several species of shark are all caught.

Close to town, surf-washed holes such as Bluehole and Chinaman Rock turn on great tailor action in the morning and evening. Unweighted or lightly weighted 'mulies' (pilchards) are cast as far as possible, then slowly retrieved to entice the marauding tailor. Others throw out garfish laced with hooks, and many large tailor are also caught this way. Such baits also attract interest from mulloway, and some nights multiple captures are made, with gleaming fish weighing up to 25 kg and better brought onto the sand or reef.

Poppers are a favourite for lure fanciers, and this style is easily worked over rock and reef areas, where tailor love to hide.

Heavy metal lure styles are sometimes needed if the wind is really blowing or long distances are required — fast retrieves are best with these.

Without a boat, there is no easy way across the Murchison River, which flows to the ocean immediately in front of Kalbarri. A dinghy is fine for this purpose as it is just a short row or motor across, where it is left 'parked' as the anglers trudge north to fish Oyster Reef, which protects the estuary and allows reasonably safe passage to the ocean.

It is not at all unusual for Spanish mackerel to be caught from the shore at Oyster Reef, or from Frustration, a well-named spot just a bit further north. This latter location was named for the ease with which rigs become tangled with the reef, quickly leading to a break-off and re-rig, but it does turn on terrific fishing for tailor and mulloway.

Anglers need long rods to enable them to cast over the ever-present breakers, and 90- to 120-g spoon sinkers are also a big help here. A reef bag (shoulder bag) with pockets full of pilchards and a spare rig or two make for more fishing time at the edge of the reef.

Pelicans look on as anglers try their luck in the lower Murchison River

Adventurous souls who don't mind a hard walk may like to put some bait and gear in a backpack and head further north to waters largely untouched by anglers. Here they can fish holes and reefs for all manner of fish, including tailor, mulloway, spangled emperor, large and plentiful skippy (trevally), bream and many others. Chances are visitors will have the place to themselves. The rugged Kalbarri to Steep Point coastline is dotted with shipwrecks, indicative of its wild character, and it's visited by very few people each year.

HEADING SOUTH

South of Kalbarri, the pretty ocean gorges are fished for big tailor and reef species, and long gaffs or a cliff gaff are needed to secure the catch. It is dangerous to venture too close to the water's edge to gaff a fish along this stretch of coast.

The long, flat reef of Wagoe is among the very best land-based fishing platforms along the entire west coast. A variety of species, including mackerel and pink snapper, are within reach. Tailor, trevally, bream, reef fish, dart and mulloway are all caught from the long reef. At times, water laps gently at the reef edge, but mostly it has to be watched closely as robust seas easily flatten careless anglers. This stretch has only been accessible from Lucky Bay in recent times in a good 4WD vehicle.

McClintocks Station, immediately above Wagoe, has budget-priced cabins which are well equipped for angling parties, and accommodation here allows much easier and quicker access to both the reef and large rock fishing spots at the north end. Again, however, a 4WD vehicle (with tyres partially deflated) is essential.

Reef fishing, especially at Wagoe, requires solid footwear to ensure a good grip on the reef. Studded boots work well. Rigs should be kept simple, for snagging on the reef is common, especially when a big skippy is hooked.

Ballooning is also possible on the right day, and at night when fishing the reef is too risky, anglers move south to breaks in the reef for safe beach fishing. Many mulloway, tailor, dart, bream and sharks are caught at night. Camping on the wide beach or behind the sand dunes increases the adventure for Wagoe anglers.

OFFSHORE FROM KALBARRI

Boat anglers can enjoy a host of options offshore from Kalbarri, from trolling large lures along the cliffs near Wagoe for tuna and mackerel, to heading out deep for West Australian jewfish, baldchin groper, pink snapper, Samson fish, cod, mackerel and tuna.

The Murchison River near Kalbarri

Smaller craft are able to venture out of the river bar and sometimes head north, staying close to shore, yet still able to target highly desirable species such as West Australian jewfish and pink snapper. Use a sounder to look for reef and lumps, or even schools of fish. Don't, however, neglect places where you can see the bottom or spot sand holes and gutters among the reef. A lightly weighted pilchard is as deadly here as anywhere. Drift fishing is productive, with a sea anchor sometimes necessary to slow the drift.

THE MURCHISON RIVER

The Murchison River may be tiny, but it still provides entertainment for black bream anglers right near town or for those venturing by boat or along the bank further inland. The standard bream technique of using a single prawn or slab of fish is fine, although lures, too, are growing in popularity.

Mulloway and blue swimmer crabs are regularly caught here, and kids have a ball in perfect safety hooking whiting right near the river mouth with the most basic of gear.

Big mulloway are a major drawcard along this stretch of coastline

Crabbing is as simple as dropping a couple of nets off the jetty.

Kalbarri has all the options for the fishing trip of a lifetime. While it challenges the most experienced anglers, this region still allows the beginner to find out why angling is so popular, especially along this beautiful piece of coastline.

GREAT AUSTRALIAN BIGHT

IN BRIEF

MAP REFERENCE: PAGE 231 C9

GETTING THERE Via Port Lincoln for Western Eyre Peninsula or via Ceduna for far west coast beaches. Ceduna is about 800 km from Adelaide along the Main North Road and Eyre Highway
BEST TIME TO FISH November to March for mulloway; April to September for salmon
BEST TIME TO TRAVEL Year-round
MAJOR ANGLING SPECIES Mulloway, Australian salmon, snapper and sharks
SPECIAL RESTRICTIONS Camping permits must be obtained for Aboriginal land
ACCOMMODATION Caravan parks and motels in major towns, bush camping
CHARTER BOATS AND FISHING GUIDES Sam's Tours, telephone (08) 8332 3545

Ceduna is generally regarded as the gateway to South Australia's far west coast. This small, but well-serviced town is home to some of the state's keenest and most successful recreational anglers, many of whom specialise in fishing the surf beaches at the eastern end of the Great Australian Bight. This is wild and remote country, which generally enhances its appeal to adventurous anglers. Whale watching is another attraction in this area—groups of southern right whales are regularly spotted off this coastline during the winter months.

Hooked up to a big mulloway from a Bight beach

Ceduna is about 800 km by sealed bitumen road from Adelaide. Productive surf beaches begin just a few kilometres to the west of Ceduna, but the fishing definitely improves towards Head of Bight. As a rule of thumb, it's salmon in the cool months and mulloway in the summer, but there are some areas and some times of the year when these fish can be targeted together.

BIGHT MULLOWAY

There are few other parts of Australia where big mulloway (jewfish) are caught at such sizes and with such regularity as on South Australia's far west coast. As soon as the inshore Bight waters begin to warm with the onset of summer, the big jewies move in to feed along the surfline gutters. They vary in size from school fish up to 40-kg giants, with 20 kg a fair average.

Scotts Beach, near Fowlers Bay, is regarded as the first serious mulloway area beyond Ceduna. Scotts has produced hundreds of monster mulloway over the years and is undoubtedly the most convenient place for uninitiated anglers to start their quest. There is comfortable accommodation quite close by and it is possible to access Scotts Beach without 4WD by parking behind the sand dunes and walking in to the beach. This requires a bit of stamina, but it can be done. Other renowned mulloway beaches along this stretch include Tuckamore, the Dog Fence, Yalata and Twin Rocks, but these are more remote and require off-road transport of some sort to gain access.

Mulloway tackle for these beaches needs to be robust and well assembled, as sharks and the occasional big snapper are also likely when conditions are favourable. A 3- to 3.6-m fast taper surf rod is ideal and the reel, regardless of style, must hold at least 400 m of the chosen line class. Most serious mulloway chasers opt for 12- to 15-kg line, which provides the necessary 'grunt' if a truly big fish grabs the bait and bolts for the horizon.

Extra strong hooks in the 6/0 to 8/0 range are mandatory equipment, as is 30- to 40-kg monofilament trace material and a range of surf sinkers of up to 170 g. Surf conditions can often be turbulent, which calls for either star or grapnel sinkers to ensure the bait stays where it is intended to be.

Undoubtedly, live bait is the number one mulloway offering along the beaches

A monster mulloway of more than 30 kg

of the Great Australian Bight. It it isn't often easy to come by, however, although occasionally it is possible to berley a school of yellow-eye mullet or juvenile salmon within casting range. This shouldn't, however, be regarded as a sure thing. When the big jew are on the prowl, catching live bait is rarely easy.

Most experienced anglers set aside a day to catch bait before venturing on to the beach for their first try at mulloway. While big salmon aren't generally easy to locate during summer, they can be found in small, isolated pockets around rocky headlands and near inshore reefs. Fillets from freshly caught salmon are very effective on big mulloway, as they are very oily and carry a lot of blood. Unfortunately, whaler sharks love them, too, which can be annoying when there are better things to catch!

One of most critical aspects of mulloway fishing in the Bight is selecting the stretch of water to be fished. Although 'reading the beach' is something of a hackneyed term, it describes perfectly what is required before fishing is begun. Deep gutters, particularly those which run in quite close to the shoreline, are prime locations to prospect for mulloway. It is here that the predators actively seek out bait fish and crabs, sometimes venturing to within 15 or 20 m of the shore. Consequently, long casts are rarely necessary in order for baits to be in the strike zone.

Unlike most mulloway surf fishing situations, the great majority of fish are taken from far west coast beaches during daylight hours. Naturally, this is far more convenient than having to fish through the night.

THE SALMON SCENE

It is generally agreed that, kilo for kilo, the Australian salmon is one of the toughest and most spectacular opponents of all for the surf angler. South Australia's Bight beaches virtually teem with salmon during the winter and spring, attracting hordes of anglers from Adelaide and beyond. It is understandable that some folk can't see the sense in travelling 2000 km to catch fish that aren't particularly good to eat, but there's simply nothing like a 4-kg Australian salmon on the end of a light surf rod!

Just about all the well-formed beaches found between Ceduna and the Western Australia border hold salmon schools from May through to the end of September. An average fish would weigh 3.5 kg, but there are plenty of salmon taken each season of 5 kg or better, and these really pull hard in heavy surf.

Both lures and bait will take Bight salmon, with fresh West Australian pilchards undoubtedly at the top of the pile. Quality 6- to 8-kg surf tackle is all that is required and again long casts are the exception rather than the rule. Most of the better gutters run quite close to the beach—so close, in fact, that saltwater fly fishing for salmon is practical in many areas.

SOME IMPORTANT POINTS

Many of the more productive beaches lie on Aboriginal-owned land, which means that it is obligatory to obtain permission and a camping permit before venturing off the Eyre Highway.

Ceduna Jetty is a great fishing spot

Permits can be obtained in Ceduna or from the Yalata Roadhouse — being caught without one can mean ejection and a hefty fine.

These beaches are remote, so everything required for an extended visit has to be brought in with you. This includes ice, fuel, water and food supplies, all of which can be purchased in Ceduna at reasonable prices. A well-stocked first aid kit should also be packed, as medical assistance is often several hours away.

As the beaches of the Great Australian Bight are part of a delicate ecosystem, it is vital that they are treated with the utmost respect. Unfortunately, some thoughtless campers ignore this need, leaving behind rubbish and generally aggravating the relationship between anglers and the traditional land owners. Some beaches have actually been closed to non-Aboriginals as a result of this lack of respect from careless visitors.

Trail bikes and 4WD vehicles are very popular with Bight beach users, but these are under scrutiny in areas where they do regular damage to dunes and native vegetation. It is illegal to operate an unregistered vehicle on a far west coast beach and absolutely stupid to 'hoon' around in natural bushland on trail bikes or in 4WD vehicles. Consequently, these should only be operated on established tracks and at reasonable speeds. Failure to comply with these common sense rules may see off-road vehicles banned totally from the beaches, which would be a great pity indeed.

STEEL CITY SNAPPER

IN BRIEF

MAP REFERENCE: PAGE 233 H6

GETTING THERE Whyalla is about 370 km from Adelaide along the Main North Road and Lincoln Highway
BEST TIME TO FISH September to May offshore; April to August onshore
BEST TIME TO TRAVEL Year-round
MAJOR ANGLING SPECIES Snapper
ACCOMMODATION Abundant hotels, motels, caravan parks and units are found here
CHARTER BOATS AND FISHING GUIDES K&R Charters, telephone (08) 8645 4887

Whyalla is South Australia's second largest city. Situated on the north-western shore of Spencer Gulf, it attracts thousands of visiting anglers each year, most of whom are interested in one fish only—the magnificent snapper. And this situation is not without sound basis, as Whyalla is widely regarded as the home of 'big red'.

With a skyline dominated by the giant BHP steel mills, Whyalla isn't exactly the most picturesque city in Australia, but it does possess its own charm and extremely friendly residents. Keen anglers abound in the Steel City, which is undoubtedly why boating and general recreational fishing facilities in Whyalla are among the best in South Australia.

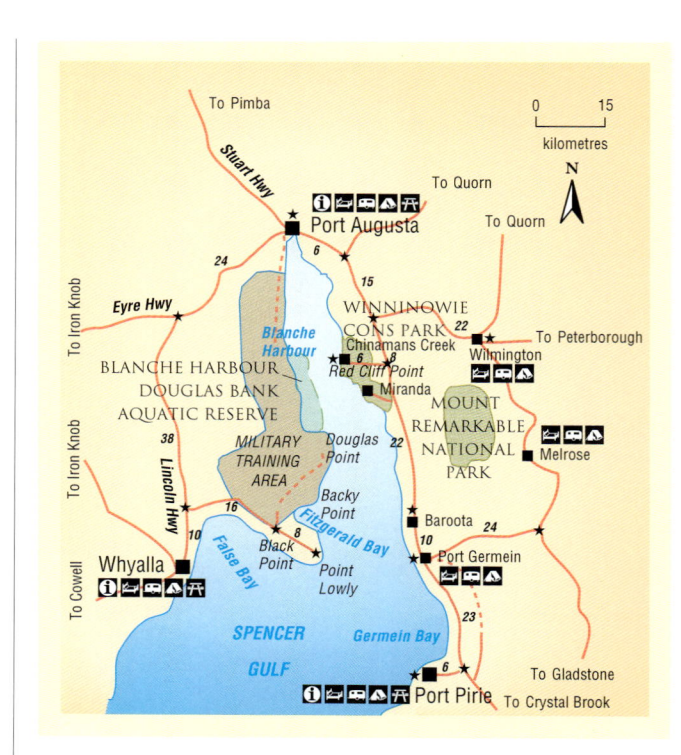

Unlike members of a lot of other country town populations, however, Whyalla folk always seem eager to share their great snapper fishing with anyone who goes to the trouble of travelling there. Members of the local sportfishing club, in particular, are always helpful towards visiting anglers and this club has hence developed a reputation for hospitality right across the country. The club's annual light tackle convention is always well attended, with competitors travelling from as far away as Melbourne to take part.

WHYALLA'S BOATING FACILITIES

Up until the early 1990s, launching a decent-sized trailer boat in Whyalla wasn't easy. The shipyard basin boat ramp was steep, slippery and difficult to negotiate at low tide, but this situation has now changed with the construction of a marina on the foreshore. Equipped with a four-lane launching ramp, washdown station, fish cleaning tables and expansive car park, this facility is probably the best in South Australia, outside of Adelaide.

There is another ramp located out near the Point Lowly lighthouse, 30 km or so from Whyalla, but this is suitable for smaller boats and 4WD tow

Snapper fishing is serious business in Whyalla, as can be seen from this overflowing boat ramp car park

Whyalla boasts excellent boat launching facilities

vehicles only. It can also be a tricky proposition in strong winds from the eastern sector.

WHERE, WHEN AND HOW?

One of the great things about snapper fishing in Whyalla is that it can be a year-round proposition. The rock fishing season begins in mid- to late April and concludes in early spring, while the best offshore action occurs between September and Easter. So, for the versatile angler who owns both surf rods and a suitable boat, big snapper are on tap most months, either from the shore or out in Spencer Gulf.

Although the land-based action around the shores of the rugged Point Lowly Peninsula isn't as reliable these days as it once was, giant snapper can still be taken from the rocks in several locations. Black Point, Fitzgerald Bay and Point Lowly itself all yield big reds, particularly when the inshore waters are stirred by strong southerly and south-easterly winds. The resultant heavy seas kill vast numbers of cuttlefish, which figure prominently on the snapper's list of favourite natural foods.

Early mornings produce the best rock fishing around Point Lowly, especially when the tide is still quite low at dawn. Waders are essential equipment, as are beefy 4-m surf rods, 10-kg line and plenty of spare sinkers. The bottom is incredibly snaggy, but losing a bit of tackle isn't a major hassle when 10- to 15-kg snapper are the likely reward.

By far the most productive rock fishing bait is the humble squid head, as it hangs on the hook securely during long casts and will rarely, if ever, be turned down by a hungry snapper. Fresh fish fillets such as salmon, mullet or tommy rough can also be effective, especially late in the season.

Out in the boat, both tackle and techniques for Whyalla snapper are considerably different. Line weight can drop back to 6 kg (or lighter for those who enjoy a real challenge) and short, fast taper rods with either threadline or overhead reels are the most popular choice. Any quality reel which holds 300 m of the desired line class is fine, so long as it has a good drag system. Some of today's up-market threadlines with free spool facility are close to the ultimate tools for big snapper.

The edges of Whyalla's two shipping channels still produce a few big reds for trailer boat anglers during the warmer months, but not as reliably as was once the case. Without doubt, the most consistent offshore snapper locations are now the artificial 'drops' — individual artificial reefs constructed from old car bodies, building refuse and similar waste material. Because the upper Spencer Gulf is devoid of natural bottom features, any structures of this kind tend to attract and hold snapper schools, providing plenty of action for those who know their whereabouts.

Some of these artificial grounds, such as the one called the 'Community Drop', are well known by most local and some visiting anglers, but others are held as top secret locations, to be fished only in private by their creators. This situation can cause friction between local snapper specialists at times, but the secrecy angle is understandable when a lot of work has gone into a new ground's construction.

As is the case with big snapper in most locations, dusk and dawn are the peak periods of feeding activity on Whyalla's offshore grounds. If a tide change coincides with either, then the chances of a good catch are much increased. On some artificial reefs, such as those well south of the city near the foot of Mount Young, the fish will bite through the night on occasion, and this is where boat-limit hauls become a formality.

Berley is the key to success on most of Whyalla's offshore snapper grounds, but its distribution is critical, particularly in areas of heavy tide run. Fish heads make great snapper berley and they are best loaded into a mesh bag, crushed under foot, then lowered to within a metre or so of the sea bed on a stout cord. A rock or half a house brick may be added to the bag to provide weight if tidal influence is strong.

Alternatively, fish heads, offal and frames may be simply dispersed by hand if the water isn't too deep. This works particularly well along the edges of the shipping channels, but all berley should be thrown well up into the tide so that it settles behind the boat in the general vicinity of the baits.

A huge snapper landed on light tackle as the sun sinks over Whyalla

KANGAROO ISLAND

IN BRIEF

MAP REFERENCE: PAGE 230 B1

GETTING THERE Kangaroo Island lies off the coast of South Australia opposite the Fleurieu Peninsula. There are regular air services from Adelaide to Kangaroo Island, as well as a fast ferry service from Glenelg and vehicular ferry from Cape Jervis
BEST TIME TO FISH Year-round, but autumn and early winter weather is most stable
BEST TIME TO TRAVEL Year-round
MAJOR ANGLING SPECIES King George whiting, snapper, Australian salmon, tommy rough, snook and trevally
ACCOMMODATION Resorts at Kingscote and American River, motels, on-site caravans and holiday units
CHARTER BOATS AND FISHING GUIDES Southern Freedom Charters, telephone (08) 8553 2349; Cooinda Charters, telephone (08) 8553 7063; Aquatic Charters, telephone (08) 8553 5338

The aptly named Remarkable Rocks in Flinders Chase National Park on Kangaroo Island

Kangaroo Island was named by the English explorer Matthew Flinders in 1802. Not counting Tasmania, Kangaroo Island (or simply 'KI' as it is best known in South Australia) is the second largest offshore island in the country. Only the Northern Territory's Melville Island is bigger.

Home to only a few thousand permanent residents, Kangaroo Island is basically a rural settlement, but several poor seasons on the land have seen tourism emerge as a significant service industry. Many farmers are now broadening their horizons in an effort to recoup lost income, with inland aquaculture (mainly marron farming) rapidly becoming a lucrative sideline.

Kangaroo Island's major attraction for visiting anglers lies in the diverse nature of available fishing. There are Australian salmon from the beaches, plenty of great table fish from the piers, huge King George whiting on the offshore reefs and both tuna and yellowtail kingfish for those with the right boat and the right tackle.

With tourism now so important to the island's economy, the standards of both accommodation and service facilities are constantly improving. Access is also far easier than it has ever been, with ferries and regular flights into Kingscote and a reliable vehicular ferry running between Cape Jervis and Penneshaw.

LAND-BASED FISHING

Unlike many other popular South Australian fishing holiday destinations, owning a boat is not mandatory in order to catch a good feed on Kangaroo Island. There are a couple of very productive jetties, kilometres of surf beach, several coastal rivers and some of the state's best rock platforms from which to choose.

Kingscote Jetty, used as a berthing facility by the new fast ferry service, is arguably the most consistent pier in South Australia for popular fish varieties such as tommy rough, snook, gar, squid and even King George whiting. Yellowtail kingfish turn up around the end of the jetty from time to time, too, as do large whaler sharks for those with the appropriate tackle and a sense of adventure.

Catching King George whiting from a jetty isn't at all common in South Australia, but nighttime anglers often pull a dozen or more in the space of a couple of hours at Kingscote. These are nice-sized fish as well, so they are definitely worth the effort.

Although the island's south coast surf beaches rarely produce big mulloway, they do become thick with salmon at times. Mouth Flat and Pennington Bay often hold vast schools of 3- to 4-kg salmon during the cooler months, providing both local and visiting surf casters with incredible action. Yellow-eye mullet and a few big King George whiting can also be expected from these beaches during calm weather.

Rock fishing on Kangaroo Island's north coast usually yields sweep, salmon of varying sizes, big tommy rough, silver trevally and whiting, while on the south coast it's big salmon, more sweep and a few blue groper. Land-based game fishers often do well on yellowtail kingfish from the rocks between Cape St Albans and Cape Willoughby, particularly when using live salmon as bait.

THE OFFSHORE SCENE

There are few locations in South Australia which offer trailer boat anglers more consistent fishing than Kangaroo Island. While reasonable launching facilities are limited to Kingscote, the Bay of Shoals, American River and Emu Bay, most of the better fishing grounds are within easy reach in favourable weather.

Kingscote's Nepean Bay literally teems with whiting at times, but these are mostly small- to medium-sized fish, many of which have to be measured for legal length. Even so, it is possible to pick up two or three dozen 'keepers' in a single session in the bay without travelling more than a couple of kilometres from the launch ramp.

Better whiting are available in nearby American River, an inlet on Backstairs Passage named by early American sealers. This is truly a wonderful place to include on any Kangaroo Island dream trip itinerary, as the waters are sheltered, there is abundant quality accommodation and the King George whiting are rarely difficult to find.

Although the big snapper for which Backstairs Passage was once famous are now less reliable, decent reds are still caught in this deep-water, big-tide area by those who know where and when to look. Backstairs Passage is easily accessible from Penneshaw, but it is prone to inclement weather and subject to tide rips of frightening proportions. This is no place for the inexperienced. Hiring the services of a local charter boat skipper is often a sensible alternative for any visiting angler wishing to try for a big snapper.

Kangaroo Island's north coast offers terrific offshore fishing and although it, too, receives its share of bad weather in summer and spring, this is perhaps the most popular area with those who own large trailer boats. Thumper King George whiting, many of which top the magic 1-kg mark, are available from Emu Bay all the way through to Cape Torrens. These fish inhabit low reef in water anywhere from 10 to 40 m deep and occasionally bite in big numbers.

Silver trevally weighing up to 5 kg or better regularly turn up on the recognised north coast whiting grounds and, although despised by whiting purists, they are terrific scrappers on any tackle. Trevally often make up the bulk of the charter boat catch in this area.

Right: *Harlequin fish are a reasonably common catch on the deeper reefs around the island*
Far right: *The tommy rough is one of South Australia's favourite fish*

An aerial view of the rugged coastline of Kangaroo Island

Blue morwong, small snapper, nannygai, harlequin fish, sharks and barracouta show up on most of the north coast reef systems according to season. The vast area of broken reef offshore from Western River Cove is perhaps the best location around the entire Kangaroo Island coast for a quality mixed bag, although trailer boat access is limited at the island's western end.

It is a pity that Kangaroo Island's south coast is so open to the brunt of South Australia's worst weather, as the offshore fishing between Cape Hart and Cape Du Couedic can be mind blowing. There are virtually no launching facilities except for Vivonne Bay, where the swell often wipes out access for days on end. Most big charter boats that venture to the south coast pull great fish such as massive blue groper, kings, Samson fish, sharks and southern bluefin tuna, and joining a charter group in these waters can provide truly memorable fishing.

ABOARD THE FALIE

IN BRIEF

GETTING THERE The *Falie* departs from Port Adelaide on Thursday evening and returns early the following Monday morning
BEST TIME TO FISH Autumn and early winter
BEST TIME TO TRAVEL Year-round
MAJOR ANGLING SPECIES Nannygai (red snapper), blue morwong, trevally, whiting, snapper and Samson fish
ACCOMMODATION On-board accommodation
CHARTER BOATS AND FISHING GUIDES *Falie* Charters, telephone (08) 8341 2004

The AK (Auxiliary Ketch) *Falie* is an 80-year-old former trading vessel, which was converted between 1982 and 1986 into an all-purpose charter ship. She is 40 m long, weighs 360 tonnes and accommodates 20 passengers and 10 crew—all of which makes her one of the largest charter fishing vessels operating in Australian waters.

Apart from duties as a fishing charter, the *Falie* also hosts groups of school children on sail training voyages, scuba divers, pleasure cruisers and those who enjoy viewing the magnificent great white shark from the security of a metal cage.

Because of the *Falie*'s bulk, range and ability to handle rough weather, she fishes consistently in some of South Australia's roughest and most notorious waters, namely Investigator Strait and the western end of Kangaroo Island. Not once in her serious charter fishing history (which began in 1993) has she been forced to cancel a trip due to bad weather, which must surely be unique within Australian charter fishing circles.

The *Falie* carries a broad cross-section of anglers on her safaris, ranging from those who have rarely, if ever, fished offshore to seasoned club anglers keen to expand their horizons. Although a degree of angling expertise is a decided advantage, it is not a prerequisite on one of these voyages.

A typical *Falie* fishing trip lasts three days and four nights and everything needed for an enjoyable stay on the water, including bait, restaurant quality food, wine and beer, and comfortable accommodation are provided. The crew members are highly experienced in catering for anglers and enjoy nothing better than dropping a line themselves from time to time between their rostered shifts.

The sailing vessel Falie *provides a unqiue fishing platform in South Australian waters*

A FALIE SAFARI ITINERARY

When charter clients board the ship at around 6.30 on a Thursday evening, everything is in readiness for a 7.30 p.m. departure from Port Adelaide. It takes approximately an hour for the ship to clear the Port River and Outer Harbor, and a course is then set for the north coast of Kangaroo Island via Investigator Strait. As the *Falie* was built for comfort rather than speed, she takes between 10 and 12 hours to reach the first fishing destination. As this lengthy run is completed during the hours of darkness, however, passengers have the opportunity to relax, prepare their gear and get a good night's sleep before the angling action begins.

Breakfast is served at 7.30 a.m., after which bait is distributed and the ship prepared for the first anchor drop. Fishing continues throughout the day, interrupted only by lunch and changes of location if required. Drinks and a three-course dinner are served at 7.30 p.m. and then anglers are free to fish as far into the night as their stamina allows.

A similar program continues for the next two full days, with final lines up at around 6 p.m. on Sunday. The *Falie* then weighs anchor and sets a return course for Port Adelaide, where she normally arrives at about 7.00 a.m. the next morning. The *Falie*'s on-board freezers are usually well loaded with all manner of great table fish, either whole or filleted, and most anglers have plenty to smile about on their departure.

THE FALIE CATCH

There is usually a fair mixture of fish varieties within the catch as the ship fishes an area with a diversity of bottom structure and water depth. Investigator Strait is one of the most lightly fished stretches of water in South Australia (both by amateurs and professionals), which means that *Falie* charter clients usually have the place to themselves for their entire stay and the action is traditionally thick and fast.

Red snapper (sometimes known as nannygai) are undoubtedly the most common fish on the reefs of Investigator Strait. These are most often caught at weights of between 1 and 3 kg, and can be expected in waters to 80 m in depth. Although red snapper are not the toughest fighters around, they often bite in vast numbers and are among the very best reef fish to eat.

Blue morwong (also known as queen snapper) inhabit both inshore and deep water reefs. They grow to more than 10 kg and whenever a lucky *Falie* angler hooks a good one, the ensuing struggle is invariably a spirited affair. To match their fighting ability, blue morwong are superb table fish and are always high on charter clients' wish lists.

Pink snapper often are found on the inshore reefs in huge schools. They are not the 10-kg plus giants caught in South Australia's gulf waters, but much smaller fish of between 1 and 3 kg. For some reason, big snapper are rarities in Investigator Strait, but most *Falie* anglers seem happy enough with a bag of succulent 'ruggers', as they are known in South Australia.

While Investigator Strait's snapper may be small, the King George whiting found here are enormous. Most whiting caught aboard the charter ship weigh between 800 g and 1.2 kg, with the latter size measuring around 55 cm in length. The largest King George whiting taken during a *Falie* safari came in at slightly more than 2 kg and there can be no argument that's the whiting of a lifetime! These fish will grab a whole pilchard on 4/0 hooks without hesitation, regularly surprising the lucky captor.

Silver trevally, although perhaps not highly regarded as table fish by some people, provide *Falie* anglers with hours of hectic action. It is not difficult to imagine the chaos when everyone on board simultaneously hooks up to silvers in the 3- to 4-kg class—silver trevally are among the toughest scrappers around the place, creating massive tangles and breaking lines all round the ship. Usually charter fishers release more silver trevally than they take for the table, which makes good sense when the gluttonous nature of these fish renders them so vulnerable to huge catches.

Undoubtedly, the Samson fish is the number one deep-water prize for most anglers who climb aboard the *Falie*. Samsons weren't commonly reported in South Australian waters until the *Falie* began prospecting the reefs of Investigator Strait, but this situation has now changed.

Although Samson fish are not taken on every charter voyage, they do turn up quite regularly, and mostly over reef in waters between 40 and 70 m deep. Like their close cousins the yellowtail kingfish, Samson fish are tough and uncompromising when hooked. And, as most encountered are 20 kg or better, boating one on the *Falie* is always touch and go. These fish run hard for the nearest reef edge when the hooks go in and often win their freedom if the angler or tackle involved aren't up to the task. In fact, the ratio of Samson fished hooked to those boated on the *Falie* charters is about 3:1.

So, whether it be the whiting of a lifetime, a bag of prime snapper fillets or a Samson fish to brag about forever, sailing aboard the *Falie* offers plenty for any keen angler—often a lot more than they have bargained for at that!

A pair of arm-stretching Samson fish landed by anglers aboard the Falie

Red snapper are members of the nannygai clan and are always welcome on the Falie

FLINDERS ISLAND

IN BRIEF

MAP REFERENCE: PAGE 255 (INSET)

GETTING THERE Flinders Island is part of the Furneaux Group and lies off the north-eastern coast of Tasmania. There are regular light plane and ferry services to the island

BEST TIME TO FISH Year-round depending on target species, but November to April is generally best

BEST TIME TO TRAVEL December to April as the winds are not so harsh during these months

MAJOR ANGLING SPECIES Albacore, striped trumpeter, blue-eye, flathead, snapper, gummy shark, Australian salmon, trevally, garfish, snook and yellowtail kingfish

SPECIAL RESTRICTIONS Tasmanian fishing rules and regulation apply on Flinders Island

WARNINGS The waters around Flinders Island have many reefy obstacles and should be navigated with care

ACCOMMODATION Accommodation can be organised through fishing tour operators

CHARTER BOATS AND FISHING GUIDES Corporate Fishing Charters, telephone (03) 9654 2022; Dreamtime Flights, telephone (03) 9205 0881; Mick and John Doran, telephone (03) 5688 1585; James Luddington, *Strait Lady* Charters, telephone (03) 6359 4507

Looking towards Mount Strzelecki from Trousers Point, on Flinders Island

After the last Ice Age, rising sea levels created a large group of islands off the north-east coast of Tasmania. These 52 islands are known as the Furneaux Group. At 137 000 ha, the largest island in the group, in both area and population, is Flinders Island.

Flinders Island is remote, and with a fluctuating population of 1000 or so people, its surrounding waters receive very little angling pressure. As a result, the fishing on Flinders Island is so consistent and so diverse that few people visit just once. It is the kind of place that draws the visiting angler back time after time.

The great thing about any Flinders Island dream trip holiday is that it need not be overly expensive, with the most costly exercise being actually getting there and back. Once the angler arrives, there are no inflated resort prices — just services supplied by down-to-earth country folk who go out of their way to make their guests feel at home during their stay.

Several charter boats work the area, operating out of Lady Barron, and everything from fishing to mutton bird watching trips is available at reasonable rates. If you can't afford to charter a vessel, however, there is still no need to feel disappointed as Flinders Island also has some fantastic land-based action.

Top Land-based Spots

The North East River is found at the island's northernmost point. The boulder that flanks the western entrance to the river is a local hot spot. This giant rock fishes up to six anglers in comfort as they target Australian salmon up to 3 kg, silver trevally, giant barracouta, gurnard and flathead, as well as gummy, seven-gill and thresher sharks. As the tide is making, fish slowly move into the North East River and are easy targets on a variety of small metal lures or pilchard tails fished on a paternoster rig.

Trousers Point is another popular land-based platform. It doesn't often produce the same sort of action as found at the North East River, but has scenic views that more than adequately compensate. From several large, flat rocks, good salmon and trevally will take a variety of lures and unweighted whole pilchards. Trousers Point is located on the south-west corner of the island, approximately 20 minutes drive from Lady Barron.

Roughly halfway up the eastern side of the island is Red Bluff, which looks directly across to Babel Island. Although visiting anglers will need a 4WD to get there, it is well worth the effort as the shark fishing off both the beach and the rocks is first class. As the sun begins to set, the gummies and seven-gills move in and the action hots up. It is not unusual to land a dozen good gummy sharks and a 30- or 40-kg seven-gill shark in an evening session.

Australian salmon weighing up to 3 kg, big barracouta and flathead will keep anglers interested between gummy strikes.

The Lady Barron Jetty is by far the most popular land-based haunt, due to its accessibility. Even though it is popular, it abounds with fish — more trevally than you could ever dream of catching, flathead to 3 kg, garfish, kingfish, large sharks and delicious calamari are all on tap. The ideal outfit for this action is a small overhead reel fished on a 3-kg 'flick stick' rod about 1.8 m long.

OFFSHORE FROM FLINDERS

As mentioned, several charter boats work out of Lady Barron, and these can almost guarantee a nominated species if it is the right time of year and the weather is favourable. Bread-and-butter bottom-bouncing species such as snapper, gummy sharks, flathead and leatherjackets are found in a variety of locations. A small granite ledge on the western side of the island produces snapper to 12 kg from December through to May.

If sharks are your quarry, head straight to the Pot Boil. Located offshore from Pot Boil Point, this spot on the south-east corner of the island produces gummies to 30 kg and school sharks, or tope as they are also known, of a similar weight.

Flathead to 4 or even 5 kg are a welcome bonus in most areas, and if anglers get bored with catching these, trolling for huge short-finned sea pike (snook) more than 1.2 m in length in and around the many islands is sure to entertain.

About 25 to 30 km due east of the island is the edge of the continental shelf. Here, warm water currents and pelagic species flow down from the north in late summer and autumn. Anglers trolling and live baiting in this area will encounter albacore, yellowfin tuna, bluefin tuna, a variety of sharks including blues, makos, and tigers and even striped marlin. A marlin has not yet been landed by a boat fishing out of Flinders Island, but several have been hooked and lost, and it will not be long before the drought is broken.

Tasmanian trumpeter are a prized deep-water species

This area is also home to the Tasmanian trumpeter, a reef fish that congregates around bottom structure on the edge of the continental shelf in around 60 to 150 m of water. Catching these fish is far from sporting as 500 g of lead is used to carry the baits to the ocean floor below. Light game tackle is needed to lift not only the lead, but also up to 25 kg of trumpeter from the sea bed. These succulent, white-fleshed fish range from 2 to 18 kg, with specimens weighing 10 kg considered a very good catch, and doubleheaders not being uncommon when using two or more hooks.

The long trip home from the shelf gives anglers a chance to clean the catch and prepare to eat the fish feast of a lifetime at the local tavern after a long, hot shower.

Regardless of the type of fishing preferred, Flinders Island and the Furneaux Group have something to offer everyone — from the hardcore, seasoned angler to the once-a-year fishing family.

A massive gummy shark taken off the Lady Barron Jetty

STRAHAN AND THE WILD WEST COAST

IN BRIEF

MAP REFERENCE: PAGE 254 B7

GETTING THERE Strahan is 304 km north-west of Hobart along the Lyell Highway. It is 4½ hours drive from both Hobart and Launceston

BEST TIME TO FISH October to March

BEST TIME TO TRAVEL Year-round

MAJOR ANGLING SPECIES Atlantic salmon, rainbow trout, Australian salmon, sharks, flounder, striped trumpeter and morwong

SPECIAL RESTRICTIONS Generally none apart from freshwater reaches of rivers where trout regulations apply

WARNINGS The west coast of Tasmania has some of the wildest seas in Australia. Every year, commercial fishers are lost to the huge seas which can appear from nowhere. Take extreme care, especially when fishing the ocean

ACCOMMODATION Strahan boasts a range of accommodation styles. The local YHA also has A-frame cabins offering excellent value for money, where anglers can stay in privacy and comfort

CHARTER BOATS AND FISHING GUIDES South West Adventure Tours, telephone (03) 6471 7157 or fax (03) 6471 7462, caters for all charter fishing needs, including accommodation

Australian salmon frequent the surf and estuary mouths of the wild west coast of Tasmania

Great fishing, amazing variety and spectacular scenery await anglers venturing onto Tasmania's wild west coast. Strahan, the perfect base for exploring the area, is located on Macquarie Harbour. Australia's second largest harbour after Port Phillip Bay, it covers an area of approximately 260 square km. The settlement of Strahan was established as a penal settlement in 1821 and the prison built on nearby Sarah Island quickly gained a reputation as the worst in Australia.

The prison here lasted only ten years and it was not until 1877 that the town re-established itself as a centre for local timber-fellers and then again in the late 19th century as a port for the copper mining industry. Today, although its industry has declined apart from the commercial fishing, the tiny settlement of Strahan draws visitors and anglers from far afield.

The west coast region is a major tourist destination, as well as becoming increasingly popular as a fishing locality. The entire area is an angler's haven, offering the waters of the harbour to fish, along with the coastline and a number of readily accessible rivers within 10 or 15 minutes drive of Strahan.

MACQUARIE HARBOUR

Macquarie Harbour is accessible to many types of angling—the most practical approach, though, is by boat. A boat allows easy movement throughout the harbour and access to some of its hot spots.

The most sought-after fish in Macquarie Harbour are the many large rainbow trout and Atlantic salmon that are a combination of escapees from the local fish farms, as well as a healthy local population (at least in the case of the rainbows). Casting from the many headlands jutting out into the harbour using metal and minnow-style lures often results in tremendous sport, and is an

Crayfish pots — commercial crayfishing is an important industry in Tasmania

excellent by-product of a thriving commercial fishery. Fish up to 9 kg in weight have been caught within sight of the Strahan township, and this knowledge certainly encourages the locals and visitors alike to pick up their rods.

Popular angling methods include bait fishing, spinning with lures and fly fishing. On still, warm evenings, fly fishing offers good sport, especially casting from a boat towards the shore. Trout sometimes rise throughout a number of bays and it is possible to choose a fish and cast to it. Sea-run trout are also common from the beach at Macquarie Heads, particularly between October and November.

During the warmer summer months, the harbour experiences an influx of cleaner, green water as the water level drops. This influx attracts schools of Australian salmon, which can be captured on the edges of the green water, where it meets the usual brown water of the harbour.

The favoured options here are trolling (which is also often the most productive), lure casting and bait fishing. A popular spot for Australian salmon is just inside the heads at Hells Gates. From this position, one can cast out to the channel that leads towards a long sand bar. There is also a camping ground near the beach.

In recent years, large numbers of flounder have been taken by spearing along the sandy shores and a good meal can usually be obtained. The most popular areas for this activity are around the heads, down towards Swan Basin and around Neck Island.

The harbour at Strahan offers visitors with their own boats a number of launching sites capable of catering to all trailerable boats. Within Strahan there are two concrete launching ramps: one at Mill Bay and the other at Letts Bay. Macquarie Heads also offers two gravel ramps with quick access to the best fishing spots. The variety of species caught within the harbour includes Atlantic salmon, trout, Australian salmon, flathead, flounder, small trumpeter, trevally, barracouta, morwong, cod and mullet.

THE RIVERS

For those who prefer river fishing, the Strahan area provides plenty of options that can produce great rewards.

The best and most popular of these include the Henty River, where anglers can launch at the bridge on the Zeehan road and troll lures either up or downstream. Those with 4WD vehicles can also gain access to an area known as Green Banks, downstream towards the mouth, and can either launch a small boat or fish from the shore.

During October and November, when sea-run trout chase whitebait upstream, these fish often make an incredible sight as they launch themselves halfway up the banks chasing the little fish. It pays to head out before daybreak so as to be on the river just as the sun peeks over the horizon. Once the sun gets too high, the fish are easily spooked and the only likely spots are the shadows at the bases of the hills.

Small, white baitfish flies are excellent early in the whitebait season, but a few changes will be required later in the season as the trout become a little fussy. Those who prefer to troll can do so literally from the mouth of the river to well upstream of the bridge.

Another productive river in the area, small though it is, is the Tully River. This river is more conducive to spin fishing or lure casting, due to its narrow and very snaggy nature. The fish here are often smaller than those taken from the Henty River, but nonetheless are in good numbers and excellent condition.

The Little Henty River is another of the west coast rivers that will produce fine fish, but it is difficult to gain access to unless equipped with a good 4WD vehicle.

The most picturesque of the rivers is definitely the Gordon. In recent times there have been good catches of large trout up to 7 kg from this famous river. The Gordon River is in a World Heritage Area, so anyone wanting to fish here must comply with all Parks and Wildlife regulations.

BEACH FISHING

Ocean Beach, 6 km due west of Strahan, offers some great beach fishing when the often rugged seas permit. This beach is claimed to be Tasmania's longest with 34 km of unbroken sand. The main fishing effort here is for Australian salmon, sharks and skate. One excellent spot is right at the mouth of the Henty River.

Anyone wishing to drive along Ocean Beach to gain access to its fishing spots should be very wary of the soft sand which is common throughout this area. It is best to seek local knowledge and direction before attempting this drive.

OUTSIDE THE HEADS

With the right boat and good weather, it is possible to venture beyond the heads to Cape Sorell or Pilot Bay, where sea fishing can be excellent at times. In this area, trolling or bait fishing with light gear can yield good results on a number of species. The main fish caught immediately outside the heads are trevally, barracouta and striped trumpeter.

One of the most prized catches in this region is certainly the local crayfish (southern rock lobster) and these crustaceans are trapped by both commercial and recreational fishers.

Not only does Strahan offer a variety of fishing, but it also makes an excellent family holiday destination. There are river cruises to the Gordon River, jet boat rides up the King River, trail rides, sea plane tours to a variety of areas, helicopter joy flights and 4WD and fishing tours.

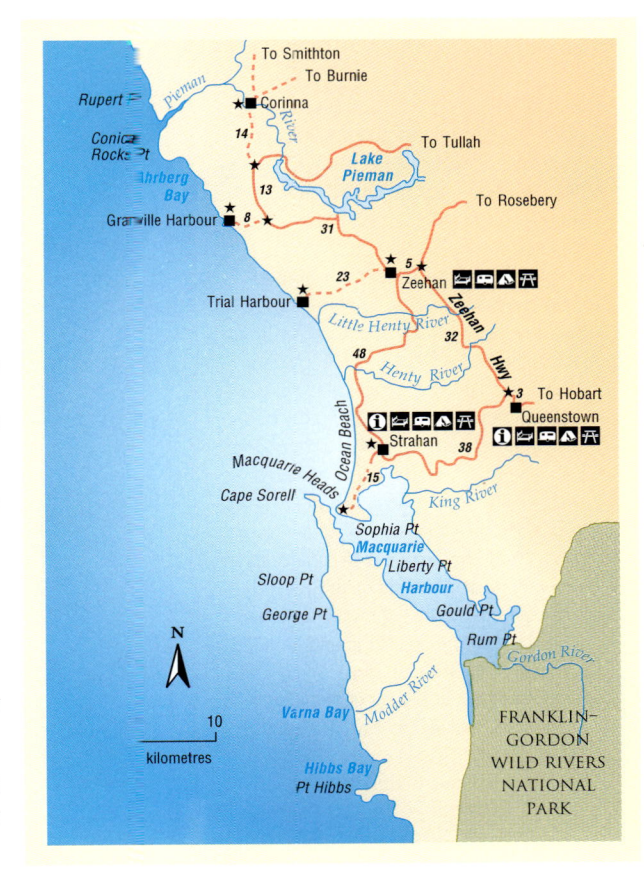

The Gordon River, part of the Franklin–Gordon Wild Rivers National Park, lies in a World Heritage area

TASMANIA'S CENTRAL HIGHLANDS

IN BRIEF

MAP REFERENCE: PAGE 254 F8

GETTING THERE Great Lake is about 140 km north-west of Hobart and 80 km south-west of Launceston; Queenstown is about 260 km north-west of Hobart and 220 km south-west of Launceston
BEST TIME TO FISH October to April
BEST TIME TO TRAVEL October to May
MAJOR ANGLING SPECIES Brown trout, rainbow trout and some pockets of brook trout (char)
SPECIAL RESTRICTIONS Strict rules and regulations apply to the taking of trout and salmon in all Tasmanian waters. There are also regulations on some activities within the Western Tiers, and many lakes in this area are only accessible on foot
WARNINGS Extreme weather conditions are possible at any time of the year in these high alpine regions. Check road conditions before travelling and always carry suitable clothing
CHARTER BOATS AND FISHING GUIDES Ken Orr's Tasmanian Trout Expeditions, telephone (03) 6289 1191; Peter Hayes Guided Fishing, telephone (03) 6259 8295

Tasmania's trout fishing is justifiably famous the world over. Also, in contrast to the saltwater scene, practically every Tasmanian wets a line in the state's many freshwater rivers and lakes at some time during his or her life. Many ultimately go on to become keen and skilful anglers.

The heart of this wonderful resource is the Central Highlands, an area roughly bounded by Poatina in the north, Lake Burbury in the west, the Midlands Highway to the east and the townships of Tarraleah and Ouse to the south. Within this extensive region of alpine and semi-alpine country lie hundreds of lakes, streams and canals, almost all of which hold trout in varying numbers and sizes. These delightful waterways offer an outstanding variety of fishing opportunities and options, from downrigging, trolling and bait soaking in the larger lakes, to careful wading and the stalking of individually sighted fish with light fly tackle in the shallow, gin-clear tarns and sloughs of the remote Western Tiers.

A Myriad of Lakes

This area includes a string of major lakes running south from Poatina, as well as countless smaller lakes, tarns, streams and canals extending to the south-west, deep into the Cradle Mountain–Lake St Clair National Park and Franklin–Gordon Wild Rivers National Park.

The best known and most easily accessible of these Central Tasmanian trout waters are Great Lake, Arthurs Lake, Lake Sorell, Lake Echo, Lake King William and Bronte Lagoon. Smaller, but nonetheless productive waters also include the Lagoon of Islands, Little Pine Lagoon, Dee Lagoon and Bradys Lake. Lake Crescent also lies within this region, but was closed to all recreational fishing activities at the time of publication, as part of an ongoing program to restrict and eradicate a relatively recent outbreak of noxious European carp in Tasmanian waters.

The shores of Great Lake, looking across the shallow margins which sometimes provide excellent fly fishing

All of the waters named hold good populations of trout. Some are dominated by browns, others by rainbows, while most hold a mix of the two species. The majority of these are 'wild' trout spawned in various feeder streams or canals, but some stocking also occurs in selected waters, particularly of rainbow trout. Included amongst these are specially bred 'triploid' rainbows which exhibit particularly fast growth rates and large maximum sizes.

FISHING STYLES

While most of these waterways are open to all legal styles of trout fishing—including bait fishing, lure casting, trolling and fly fishing—a few, such as Little Pine and two small areas of the Great Lake itself, have stricter regulations and are limited to fly fishing only. Still others are open only to fly and lure anglers, with bait fishing not being permitted. Obviously, the current status of these regulations should be carefully checked before going fishing.

Sadly, European carp have also appeared in two popular lakes in this region over recent years (Lakes Crescent and Sorell). This is most likely as the result of the illegal importation of live bait by anglers visiting Tasmania from the mainland. The state's Inland Fisheries Commission was working quite successfully at the time of publication to confine and eradicate these small populations of carp, but unfortunately had been forced to close Lake Crescent to angling and all other activities until further notice.

THE WESTERN LAKES

Further west lies a more remote and ruggedly beautiful area of mostly small glacial lakes and tarns, surrounded by low, thick bush, swampy bogs and high country heath or grasslands.

This rugged region is traversed by walking tracks and includes such truly delightful waters as Lakes Botsford, Augusta, Ada, Mackenzie, Meston, Myrtle and Louisa, to name just a few. All lie within the Central Plateau Conservation Area or Cradle Mountain–Lake St Clair National Park, and are part of a very important World Heritage listed area, with strict rules regarding all human activities that might prove detrimental to the often fragile environment.

Apart from Lake Mackenzie and Lake Augusta, waterways in this region are open only to fishing with artificial lures and flies during the designated season. This is also a fuel-stove-only area, and no open fires may be lit at any time.

While much of this wild and remote region is reasonably difficult to reach, the area known as the Nineteen Lagoons (around Lake Augusta) is readily accessible by family car and a short walk for much of the year, and is therefore very popular with less adventurous visitors. Waters within this vicinity include Lakes Ada, Botsford and Kay, as well as First, Howes Bay and Rocky lagoons. All hold good populations of wild trout.

QUALITY, NOT QUANTITY

Fishing within the western lakes region is mostly done on foot, with spinning (lure casting) or fly fishing tackle. It typically involves sighting one's quarry first, then carefully stalking it and presenting a fly or lure. Catching one or two fish per day under such demanding conditions may be regarded as something of an achievement, especially as they are likely to run anywhere from 1 to 4 kg apiece!

The emphasis here is very much on quality, rather than quantity. This is reflected in the western lakes' special regional bag limit of 5 fish per angler per day. Few fishers would be capable of filling this limit consistently, and even fewer would wish to kill that many of these wonderful, wild browns. Most visitors prefer to return the majority of their catch to the water, taking only photos and leaving no more than footprints.

Perhaps the greatest drawback to fishing in these high, Western Tiers lakes (as well as in most other parts of Tasmania, for that matter) is the unpredictable and often inclement weather. Strong winds are the norm, and rain, sleet or even snow can blow in with little notice at any time of year. Having said that, some wonderfully mild, blue-sky days are also likely, particularly in February and March... As they often say in Tasmania, if you don't like the weather now, just wait 10 minutes—it's sure to change!

Playing a big trout hooked on fly fishing tackle at St Clair Lagoon

Tasmania is world-famous for its big, wild brown trout

FURTHER AFIELD

At the south-western edge of this area lies the long, deep body of clean, sparkling water known as Lake St Clair. This is a truly delightful spot, with the cool waters of the big lake reflecting the surrounding mountain peaks and dense stands of vegetation along the rugged shorelines.

Lake St Clair also contains a good population of trout, although a boat is needed to reach the better spots. Fortunately, the overflow area at Lake St Clair's south-eastern end, between St Clair itself and Lake King William, often provides good sight fishing for wading anglers. Lake King William is another trout fishing hot spot, often producing large catches of generally smallish fish for lure and fly anglers.

Further afield again, Lake Burbury is one of Tasmania's newest hydroelectric water storages. Situated on the King River, since its construction in the 1980s and filling in the early 1990s, Burbury has emerged as one of the state's most exciting and productive new trout fisheries. This lake is covered in much greater detail on pp. 250–1.

LONDON LAKES

IN BRIEF

MAP REFERENCE: PAGE 252 G1

GETTING THERE London Lakes is about 140 km north-west of Hobart along the Lyell Highway, 26 km east of Derwent Bridge. It is two hours drive from Hobart
BEST TIME TO FISH October to April
BEST TIME TO TRAVEL September to May
MAJOR ANGLING SPECIES Brown and rainbow trout
SPECIAL RESTRICTIONS No boats, no landing nets, no public angling
WARNINGS Extreme weather conditions are possible at any time of the year in these high alpine regions. Check road conditions before travelling and always carry suitable clothing
ACCOMMODATION London Lakes is a private fishing lodge. Telephone (03) 6289 1159 or fax (03) 6289 1122 for further details

Frenchmans Cap mountain peak in the nearby Franklin–Gordon Wild Rivers National Park

Tasmanian lakes are renowned for their wild brown trout. Although an introduced species, these fish suit the clean, clear waters in Tasmania. Since their introduction in 1864, they have now come to inhabit nearly all Tasmanian waters. It is 'sight' fishing to these feeding brown trout that is the Tasmanian fly angler's forte.

Tasmanian waters have, in general, open and public access, and can be fished most of the year on payment of a trout fishing licence. Given the fact that most anglers can fish virtually anywhere in Tasmania for free, it was therefore unusual for a lodge operator to envisage a private fishery where a substantial fee would be charged.

In the early 1970s, Jason Garrett, a Tasmanian surveyor, decided that there was a future for a private fishery that would look after anglers in a way that was unknown in Australia at the time. Nestled away in what is almost the geographical centre of Tasmania, he created three private trout fishing waters and a lodge which collectively became known as London Lakes.

This plan to create trout fishing waters was developed just when Tasmania's Lake Pedder and its huge fish of 4.5 kg and more were capturing the minds of many anglers around the world. At the time, many thought a private fishery a foolhardy exercise. The critics, however, were quite wrong. Today, London Lakes is still going from strength to strength.

In 1978, after Lake Big Jim and Lake Samuel were created, 50 000 trout fry were added. The growth rate of these early fish was tremendous and fish of 2 to 3 kg were soon common. Little has changed and to this day 2-kg fish are regulars, with bigger fish not out of the ordinary. There has been no need to add more fish as both the rainbow and brown trout reproduce naturally in the many small spawning streams on the property.

The two lakes cover 340 and 200 hectares respectively and to see other anglers 'fishing your beat' is unusual. There is rarely a need to wade deep as trout tail and feed close to shore. During construction, wind rows of timber were felled and pushed up to give trout shelter, and

Releasing a plump brown trout captured in the margins of Lake Big Jim, part of the London Lakes complex

it is around these that anglers will often be found 'stalking' their prey. Eighty per cent of the fishing is with dry fly to 'sighted' fish as they cruise, tail and surface feed.

It is this type of fishing that visiting anglers can enjoy with tranquillity and the company of an experienced guide. Of course, native animals such as wallabies, wombats, quolls, platypus and any of the 86 varieties of birds may also join in. Anglers are generally directed by the highly professional lodge guides, who have vast experience in fishing and fly casting instruction. They do not fish—their only capture is anglers and fish on film.

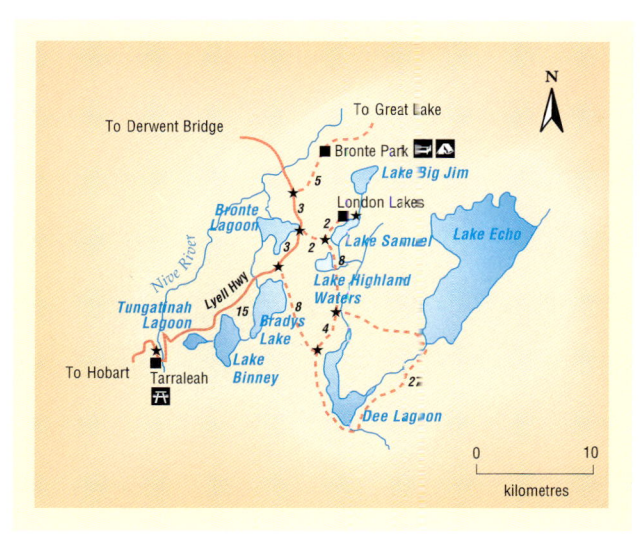

Accommodation is in a handsome lodge crafted from stone and timber, built amongst the gum trees on the banks of Lake Samuel. It caters for up to ten anglers and, like the fishing, everything is of the highest calibre. The food is gourmet standard, as are the wines and service. In fact, John Randolph, editor of *American Fly Fisherman* magazine, rated the lodge as one of the top five in the world. It exudes class and the fishing theme is never far away. There are also a library and fly-tying room, of course!

Twenty years on, the vision of Jason and Barbara Garrett has not changed. They were ahead of their time and Australia has benefited greatly from this development.

Interstate and overseas visitors make up the majority of anglers at London Lakes. A later expansion, Highland Waters, is reserved for a private development where anglers can build accommodation on their own private water. It is managed by Jason and the current ethos will be continued in this extension of his original dream.

Guided angling costs include all meals, accommodation, tackle, guiding from daylight to dark and pre-dinner drinks. Unguided costs are less and non-anglers accompanying an angler also enjoy a substantially reduced rate. On top of the excellent fishing available, visitors can enjoy bush walks, take photographs, or just relish the huge range of wildlife and birds, visit craft shops, go boating or visit the nearby Franklin–Gordon Wild Rivers National Park, a World Heritage listed area. There is always something to do at London Lakes!

The comfortable accommodation at London Lakes Lodge

Above: *First light breaks over a mirror-calm Lake Big Jim*
Left: *A typical brown trout from London Lakes*

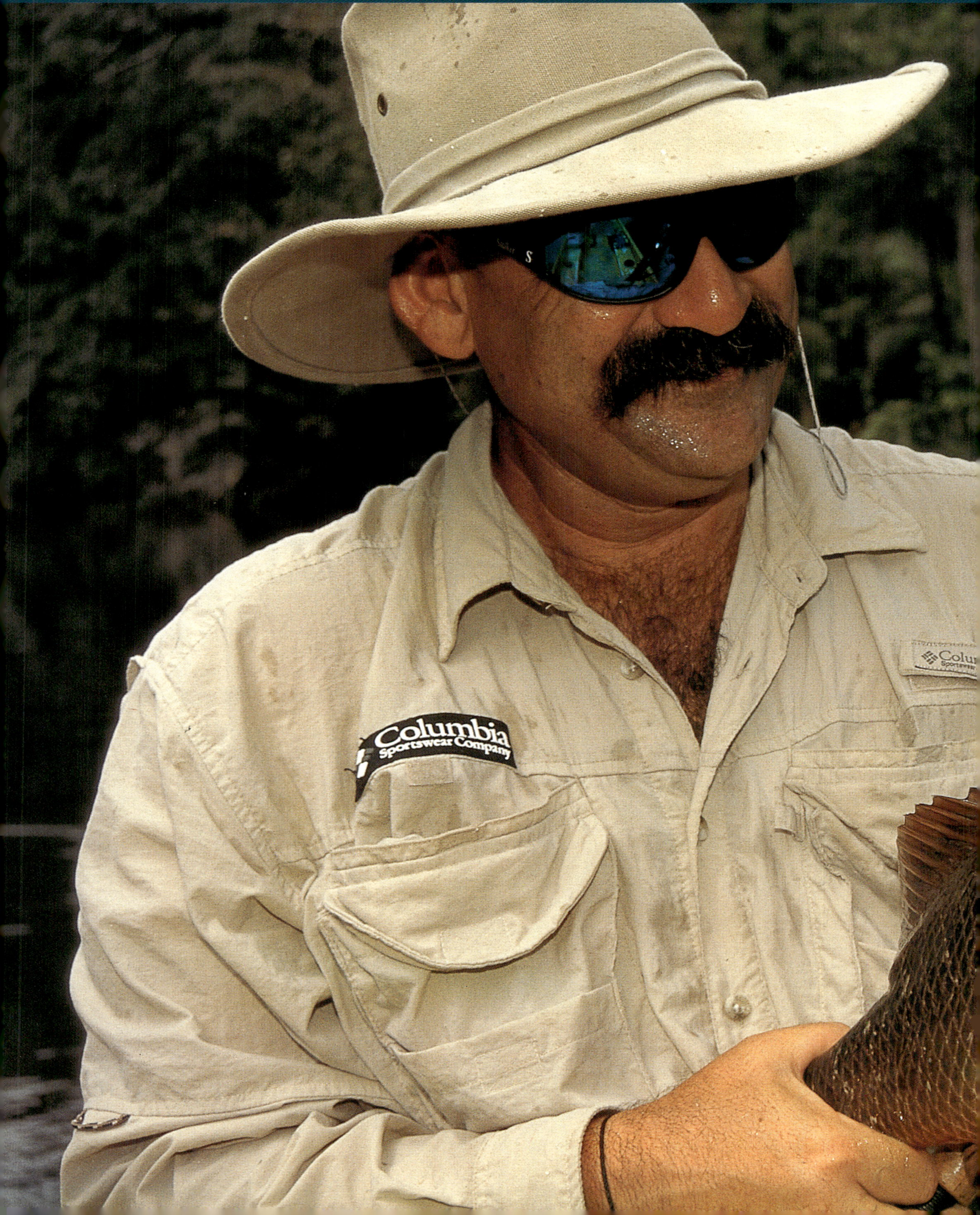
Columbia
Sportswear Company

Part 3

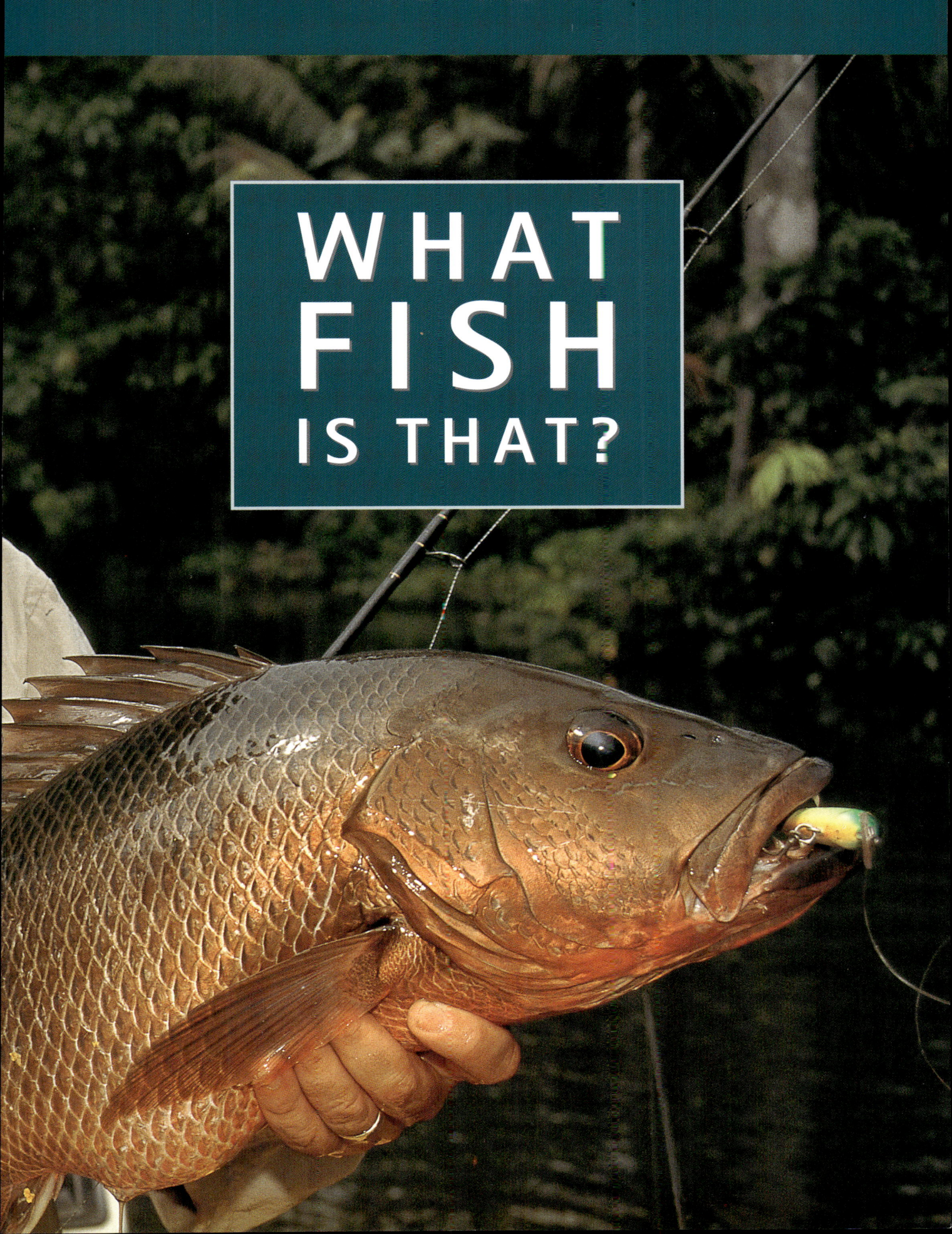

WHAT FISH IS THAT?

This A to Z guide looks at 80 or so of Australia's favourite salt and freshwater angling species that account for close to 90 per cent of the recreational fishing in our waters. With each species entry, we include the common and colloquial names, scientific names, description, size, distribution, fishing techniques and eating qualities.

One of the most diverse marine faunas in the world has evolved in Australian waters because of the country's isolation from other continents and the wide range of aquatic habitats. This fauna includes more than 3600 species of salt and freshwater fish representing at least 300 families — and those figures reflect only the species that have so far been identified and scientifically described. There may be others out there awaiting discovery and classification!

The vast majority of these 3600 fish species are of little more than academic interest to recreational anglers. Many live in very deep water far from shore, or don't grow large enough to be deliberately targeted by anglers. In fact, only about 150 to 200 species of salt and freshwater fish are taken by Australian anglers on a reasonably regular basis, and well under half of those could be regarded as common rod-and-reel captures.

We have listed each fish under its popular common name, followed by the most up-to-date scientific description. This is not always easy as there are great variations in common names and colloquial names depending on the locality. Similarly, the scientific names of species are by no means set in stone — they change when families are reclassified.

SCIENTIFIC NAMES

Many recreational anglers find the use of scientific names for fish rather daunting, and this is not surprising, considering the length and complexity of many of these titles. Nonetheless, it is well worth taking the time to study these scientific names.

Based loosely on the Latin language, most scientific names are divided into two parts. The first word denotes the fish's genus. Fish that share the same genus name are normally closely related. The second word (or words) identifies the individual species. Often, this part of the scientific name describes a particular physical feature of the fish, such as its body shape, colour or teeth. So don't be afraid of scientific names! It isn't necessary to be able to pronounce them correctly — simply to recognise them when comparing fish from different areas, or attempting to overcome the confusion so often surrounding the use of common and colloquial names.

ANATOMY OF A FISH

A fish is a cold-blooded, water-dwelling animal which breathes through gills, has a backbone and uses fins for propulsion. Strictly speaking, modern bony fishes are distinct from their more primitive relatives, the sharks and rays. The latter group are characterised by skeletons made from soft cartilage, rather than hard bone. For the purposes of this book, we will combine the true bony fishes and the sharks and rays, but maintain a distinct separation between fish generally and all of the other creatures to which people sometimes apply that generalised label. Dolphins, porpoises, whales and seals, for instance, are air-breathing mammals: they are not fish.

Beyond the basic definition of cold-blooded, water-dwelling animals with gills, fish vary enormously in size, shape, colour, behaviour and life cycle. There is a world of difference between a 5-cm whitebait and a 4-m tiger shark, yet both may be of interest to the angler at one time or another.

Having at least a basic idea of how a fish fits together, what its various parts do and the kind of existence it leads can be an enormous help to the angler. After all, the greater your store of knowledge about your quarry, the more you will enjoy the sport and, as a bonus, the better you will become at it!

Previous page: *A huge mangrove jack*

FISH DISTRIBUTION

A small distribution map is provided with each of the fish species or closely related group of fish described in this section of the book. The fish's common range is indicated as a shaded area on the map. The larger map shown above — complete with significant coastal features — may also prove useful in identifying the boundaries of each species' range. It should be remembered, however, that many fish are not especially common at the extreme boundaries of their known range, while others stray far beyond these boundaries on a regular basis. The distribution maps in this chapter are therefore intended only as a guide. Exceptions to the boundaries shown can and do occur from time to time. There are no borders or fences in the sea, and marine fish, in particular, may wander freely in search of their preferred habitat.

Similarly, the ranges and distribution zones of many freshwater fish are constantly being altered by human activity and development. Former habitats are sometimes degraded to the point where certain types of fish can no longer utilise them, while new habitats may also be created and the range of a particular fish expanded through the stocking or translocation of fingerlings, fry and adults.

So, when studying distribution maps, keep in mind that they can only ever be a guide to a fish's common range.

What fish is that?

Albacore
Thunnus alalunga

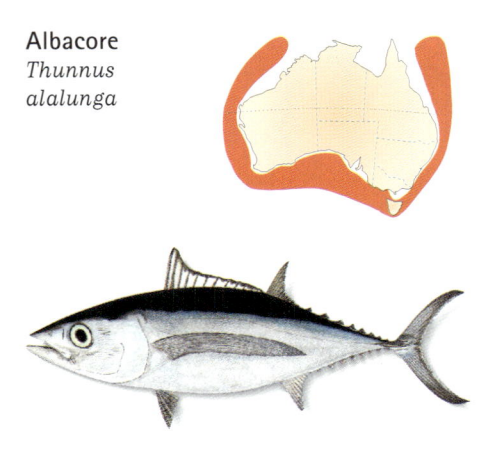

Common Names: This member of the tuna family is best known as albacore, but is also referred to as longfin tuna, white-meat tuna or 'chicken of the sea'. The albacore is occasionally confused with the yellowfin and bluefin tunas, although the albacore's elongated pectoral (side) fins easily distinguish it from these related species.

Description: The albacore has long, strap-like pectoral or side fins which, when pressed flat against its flanks, extend back beyond the base of the second dorsal and anal fins. It also has large, dark eyes. When fresh from the water, the albacore is dark, metallic blue on the back, changing quite suddenly along a somewhat irregular line to silvery blue on the flanks and fading more gradually to silvery white or white on the belly. A thin, iridescent band of electric blue is sometimes present along the fish's flanks when alive. After death, the albacore typically fades to a dull, gunmetal blue on the back, with silvery grey flanks.

Size: In some parts of the world, albacore have been recorded at weights in excess of 35 kg. In Australian and New Zealand waters, the species rarely tops 22 kg and is more common at weights between 3 and 12 kg. At times, large schools of juvenile albacore weighing from 500 g to 3 kg are encountered, especially in the cooler waters off Tasmania, western Victoria, South Australia and New Zealand.

Distribution: In common with the skipjack or striped tuna, the albacore is amongst the most prolific of all the tunas, and is found throughout the temperate and subtropical oceans of the world. Albacore prefer clean, blue ocean currents with water temperatures between 14°C and 20°C. This species is more at home in deep water along and beyond the edge of the continental shelf, and adult fish are rarely found in waters shallower than 150 m.

Fishing Techniques: The albacore responds to lure trolling, live baiting and dead baiting. This fish may also be taken by casting and retrieving lures, or allowing lures and jigs to sink beneath a school before retrieving them rapidly towards the surface. Small live baits are also readily accepted by the albacore, as are dead baits of whole or cut pilchards, herring and anchovies, or cut strips and slabs of fish flesh, especially those taken from oily, pink or red-fleshed species. A berley stream or chum trail of minced fish flesh, oil and chopped fish scraps will often attract and concentrate this species.

Eating Qualities: The albacore is regarded by many as the best tasting of all the tunas. It has finely textured pink flesh which turns white when cooked. This species is also suitable for raw fish or sashimi dishes, but is not as highly rated for this purpose as the bluefin, yellowfin and big-eye tunas. As with all the tunas, albacore should be killed, bled, cleaned and iced down promptly after capture to prevent deterioration of the rather delicate flesh.

This juvenile albacore was landed on fly fishing tackle and has been tagged prior to release

albacore • barracouta • barracuda

Barracouta
Leionura atun

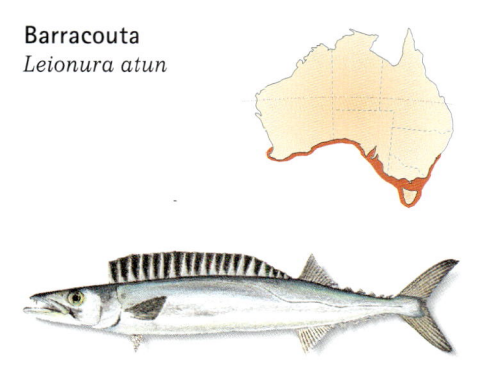

Common Names: The barracouta is frequently referred to as 'couta. Other colloquial names include pick-handle, axe-handle, hammer-handle, and its South African name, snoek (or snook).

Description: This slim, needle-toothed fish is usually dark, steely blue or green along the top of the back and bright, metallic silver on the flanks and belly. There is a distinct black patch near the leading edge of the long, relatively high first dorsal fin. The forked tail is dark, often black. The barracouta is sometimes confused with the tropical barracuda. Beyond vague similarities in body shape and teeth, however, the two have little in common and are unrelated. The gemfish or king barracouta (*Rexea solandri*) of deep, southern waters is much more closely related to the barracouta and an important commercial species.

Size: Although often caught at lengths between 50 and 140 cm, barracouta are very lightly built. Even exceptional specimens more than 150 cm long rarely weigh more than 4 or 5 kg. A more typical barracouta measures under a metre in length and weighs between 800 g and 1.5 kg. Much larger specimens, possibly up to 10 kg and more, have been reported from New Zealand waters.

Distribution: A cold-water fish, the barracouta is most numerous in the seas around Tasmania, Victoria, parts of South Australia and southern Western Australia. It is also reasonably common in New Zealand and South Africa.

Fishing Techniques: Barracouta are specifically fished for in the southern states, but are generally regarded as a pest in New South Wales. They respond to a range of techniques, but are best caught by casting or trolling with lures such as a flashy, chromed spoons and silver or white jigs. The addition of a diving paravane to the rig ahead of the lure can often improve trolling results. Strips of fish flesh or whole pilchards and garfish on ganged hook rigs make excellent baits. Live baits attract plenty of interest, but many strikes are missed. A wire trace or ganged hooks are practically essential when fishing for barracouta.

Eating Qualities: The barracouta has tasty, pinkish flesh which is firm and white when cooked,

A pair of barracouta from Tasmanian waters

and is also ideally suited to smoking. After cooking, the many long, flexible bones can be easily removed from the fish. The flesh of this fish can occasionally be infested with parasitic worms. Cooking destroys these worms and they appear to have no effect on the eating quality of the fish. Barracouta should never be eaten raw.

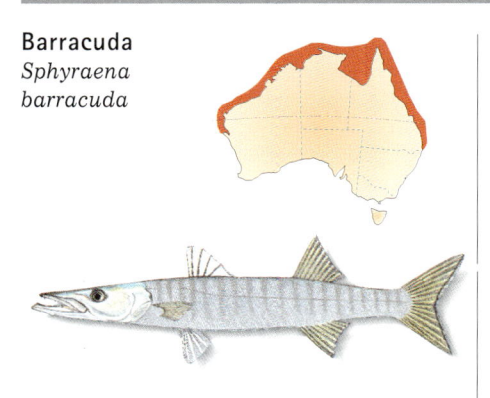

Barracuda
Sphyraena barracuda

Common Names: Best known as barracuda or 'cuda, this fish is occasionally referred to as the great barracuda, giant sea pike, dingo fish or pick-handle. There are several smaller but very similar species in the same family, and many of these are encountered in the same waters as the great barracuda.

Description: A long, almost cylindrical fish with a large mouth full of fearsome, canine teeth, the barracuda has a steely grey or dark green back and its silvery flanks carry between 18 and 24 faint, vertical stripes or bars when alive or freshly killed. There are often irregular dark blotches on the fish's sides, mainly towards the tail. The scalloped tail fin is sometimes tinged with yellow or edged in black. Although sometimes confused with the barracouta (*Leionura atun*) of southern waters, the two species are unrelated and have little in common beyond superficial similarities.

Size: In parts of the Atlantic and Caribbean, barracuda have a fearsome reputation and are reputed occasionally to exceed 2.2 m in length and weigh as much as 35 kg. In Australian waters, barracuda more than 1.7 m long and 25 or 30 kg in weight are exceptional, although rare specimens can exceed these dimensions. The majority of barracuda encountered by anglers will be a metre or less in length and weigh from 2 to 8 kg.

Distribution: This tropical and subtropical fish is found in all the warm oceans of the world. While stray barracuda have been caught as far south as Sydney and Perth, they are mainly found north of the Tropic of Capricorn. Their habitat ranges from the blue ocean currents of the open sea to the upper tidal reaches of mangrove-lined estuaries.

Fishing Techniques: Barracuda are rarely fished for deliberately. The smaller ones tend to be taken by estuary anglers targeting barramundi, mangrove jack, trevally, fingermark and the like, while offshore anglers chasing mackerel, trevally, cobia and even marlin and sailfish take most of the big barracuda caught on rod and reel. Barracuda respond well to trolled baits of garfish, mullet or scad, and will also take minnow lures, trolling heads with skirts and various metal spoons. Live and dead baits are also effective. A wire trace is helpful in landing barracuda, but some big ones have been taken on heavy nylon leaders.

Eating Qualities: Although quite popular as a table fish in some parts of the world, the barracuda has somewhat grey, coarse and rather strong-smelling flesh. This species is also a possible ciguatera poisoning risk, and larger fish should not be eaten if caught in known ciguatera locations. Always seek local advice before eating any potential ciguatera toxin carrier in northern, tropical regions. If in any doubt, always either release the fish or use it for bait or berley.

This large barracuda was landed in the Northern Territory

Barramundi
Lates calcarifer

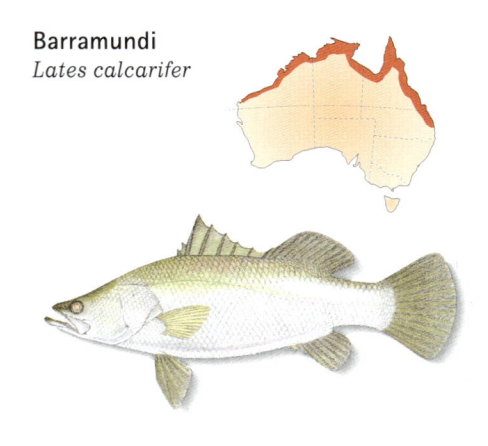

Common Names: Most Australians use the name barramundi or barra. In older magazines and books, it's sometimes referred to as the giant perch, palmer perch, palmer or 'cock-up', although these names are rapidly fading out. There is still some confusion about the names of the two species of saratoga (*Scleropages leichhardti* and *S. jardini*) found in our tropical fresh waters that were once known in certain circles as spotted barramundi or, in the case of *S. leichhardti*, as the Dawson River barramundi. These titles are rarely encountered today.

Description: The barramundi is a handsome fish with big scales, a large mouth, humped shoulders, a deeply scooped or concave forehead profile and characteristic, close-set eyes, which shine ruby red in artificial light or at certain angles in sunlight. The coloration of individual fish varies considerably, depending on environment. Freshwater barra—particularly those from seasonally landlocked billabongs and waterholes—are usually dark bronze or gold to chocolate brown on the back, with brassy or golden flanks and very dark fins and tails. At the other extreme, saltwater barra from reasonably clean tidal waters appear to wear suits of chrome-plated armour. Each scale is a metallic mirror and there is very little pigmentation apart from a mauve or purple sheen along the top of the back. The fins are very lightly coloured and the tail is often distinctly tinged with yellow.

Size: Barramundi in excess of 100 kg have reportedly been taken in nets in the Bay of Bengal, near the Indian coast. It is also likely that Australian waters once held a few monster barramundi of 60 kg or more, but today there would be little chance of a fish evading capture long enough to grow to such phenomenal dimensions. Commercial netters in the Northern Territory continue to take an occasional specimen of 30 kg or more, and it is possible that exceptional 35- to 40-kg barramundi still exist in very small numbers. Anglers mostly encounter specimens in the 1- to 12-kg range, although several fish in the 20- to 25-kg class are captured on rod and reel every year.

Distribution: Barramundi are found as far afield as the Bay of Bengal, Thailand and parts of Indonesia. They are reasonably prolific along the southern coast of Irian Jaya and Papua New Guinea. In Australia, barramundi range from the Mary River system in southern central Queensland to the Ashburton River, near Onslow, in Western Australia, although they are not commonly found at either extremity of this range. Barramundi numbers are greatest on the north-eastern and western sides of Cape York Peninsula, through the Gulf of Carpentaria, the Northern Territory and the Kimberley. They occupy a wide range of aquatic environments, from the inshore waters around rocky headlands

A 12-kg saltwater barramundi from the Kimberley

and shore-fringing reefs or islands, up through tidal estuaries and into freshwater creeks and rivers, billabongs and waterholes. Barramundi frequently inhabit bodies of water that are completely cut off from main river systems or estuaries for a year or more at a time.

Fishing Techniques: One of the most exciting and popular ways of fishing for barramundi is by casting and retrieving artificial lures or flies around snags, mangrove roots, rock bars, fallen trees and other cover, as well as creek and gutter inflows. This method accounts for a good percentage of the fish taken each year. However, at certain times, slow trolling with lures behind a moving boat produces more and larger fish than casting. The best lures for both casting and trolling are swimming minnows with timber or plastic bodies. Rubber-tailed jigs, surface lures and even metal spoons and jigs all attract barra, too. Bait fishing is also highly productive. Best baits for barramundi include small live mullet, live prawns or live macrobrachium (giant freshwater shrimp). These may be cast or drifted on unweighted or lightly weighted lines, rigged with a small running sinker, or suspended beneath a cork or float, depending on the terrain, water depth and strength of the current. Excellent barramundi are occasionally taken on dead baits.

Eating Qualities: Barramundi has a reputation as one of our finest eating fish—and a market price to match. Many would argue that this reputation is overrated, but there is certainly no denying the appeal of a properly cooked fillet of saltwater or tidal river barramundi. The meat is white, firm, fine grained and delicious. Barramundi which have spent weeks, months or even years in turbid, muddy billabongs are another story, and the flesh of these freshwater barra can range from tasty to almost inedible. Today, many sport anglers choose to release the majority of the barra they land.

Typical freshwater barramundi habitat

Bass, Australian
Macquaria novemaculeata

Common Names: The Australian bass is known throughout much of its range, especially by more senior anglers, simply as perch. However, this tends to cause some confusion between it and two other native species sometimes taken in the same waters: the Macquarie perch (*Macquaria australasica*), and the estuary perch (*M. colonorum*), which is a very close relative of the bass.

Description: This small native fish is usually found in fresh and brackish water. It has moderately large scales, large dark eyes, a scooped forehead profile and a relatively large mouth. Coloration varies with environment. Some are almost black on the back, with dark bronze or gold flanks and a creamy belly tinged with yellow, while others are bright coppery gold on the back with a silvery belly. Still others are silvery all over with a greenish silver upper back. The tail is usually relatively dark. The bass has a very fine, but well-defined, white leading edge or margin on each pelvic fin. This marking is sometimes the only feature that allows it to be readily distinguished from the nearly identical estuary perch, which has no such coloration.

Size: With an average of 200 to 800 g, any bass weighing more than 1.5 kg can be regarded as an exceptionally big fish, although specimens in excess of 2 kg are taken each year, especially in some of the dams and impoundments where they have been stocked. In fact, these waters are now producing small numbers of bass in the 3- to 4-kg range.

Distribution: The Australian bass is endemic to the south-eastern corner of Australia, from the Mary River system in southern central Queensland to the Gippsland Lakes of eastern Victoria. Its natural range is gradually being extended through stocking artificial dams and impoundments. The estuary perch ranges from about the Richmond River, in northern New South Wales, to the Murray Mouth in South Australia, but is rare at the extremities of this range. It was once found in rivers on the north coast of Tasmania.

Fishing Techniques: Traditionally, bass were taken on baits of live black crickets, grasshoppers, cicadas or shrimps often dangled or 'dapped' onto the surface of the water close to the bank. Practitioners of this style of fishing liked to use a long cane pole with the line fixed to the end,

Landing a bass in southern New South Wales

rather than a rod and reel—a set-up known as a Ned Kelly rig. Bass still respond enthusiastically to a live cricket or shrimp, but most sport anglers today prefer to cast and retrieve lures off a light, single-handed spin or baitcaster (plug) outfit, or throw flies on No. 5 to No. 9 weight outfits. Lure and fly casting is generally held to be more exciting and challenging than bait fishing and, as a bonus, most lure- and fly-caught fish are hooked in the mouth, which allows them to be released without undue injury.

Eating Qualities: Bass from clean, flowing water make very good to excellent table fish, rating amongst the best of our freshwater species. Fish from turbid or still waters may be slightly less palatable. Sport anglers now mainly choose to release bass, in recognition of their much reduced numbers and degraded habitat. Strict bag and size limits for bass are in force in most areas.

Bonito
Sarda australis and *Sarda orientalis*

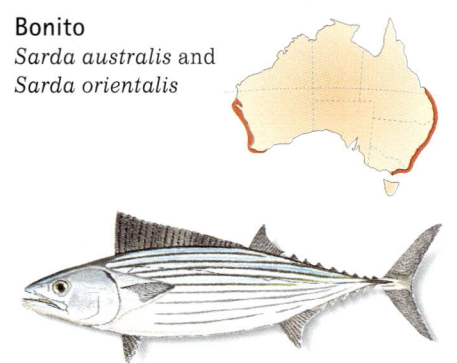

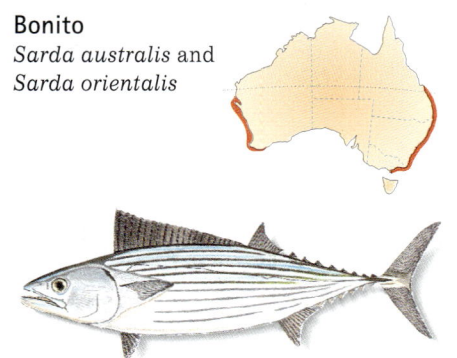

Common Names: These closely related fish are usually called bonito or Australian bonito, often shortened to bonny or bonnie. In some areas, they are known as horse mackerel or horsies. Both these species are sometimes confused with Watson's leaping bonito (*Cybiosarda elegans*), a smaller, subtropical species.

Description: The bonito has moderately large, strong jaws which carry a single row of relatively small, but distinct, conical teeth. It is generally dark green to blue on the back, silvery green on the sides and silvery white on the belly. A series of dark, longitudinal stripes are evident along the fish's upper and middle flanks. When fresh, these stripes may be broken into separate dashes by lighter, vertical bars. Bonito stripes are limited to the fish's upper and middle flanks, while those of the striped tuna or skipjack (*Katsuwonus pelamis*) are found on the lower flanks and belly.

Size: Bonito usually weigh from 800 g to 3.5 kg. Specimens of more than 4.5 kg are generally uncommon, although off parts of the New South Wales south coast, bonito weighing up to 7 kg and more are sometimes taken.

Distribution: These inshore predatory pelagic fish rarely venture outside the continental shelf and range from southern and central Queensland to about Wilsons Promontory in Victoria, with a similar subtropical to temperate distribution along the west coast.

Fishing Techniques: Bonito respond to the same techniques that take skipjack and mackerel tuna, and also fall for those employed to target salmon, tailor and kingfish. Boat anglers sometimes take good hauls by trolling diving minnows parallel with the shoreline, close to headlands and rock ledges, or by casting and retrieving lures or baits

A bonito taken while lure casting

around washes of broken white water adjacent to these areas. Land-based anglers can do well by casting and retrieving lures from the ocean rocks, jetties and breakwalls. Bonito will also attack pilchards and garfish rigged on ganged hooks, as well as live baits and strip baits or cubes of fish flesh, especially when these are free-lined in a berley trail.

Eating Qualities: The bonito's pink and flaky flesh is quite tasty, especially when eaten fresh rather than frozen. It tastes much better if the fish is bled immediately after capture.

What fish is that?

Bream, Eastern Black, Pikey and Southern
Acanthopagrus australis,
A. butcherii and
A. berda

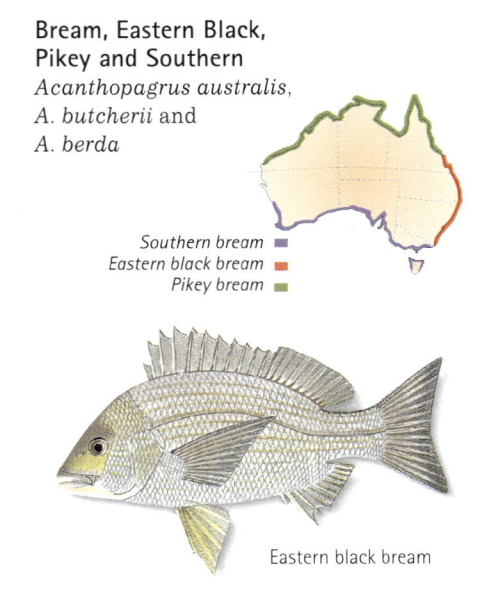

Southern bream
Eastern black bream
Pikey bream

Pikey bream

Eastern black bream

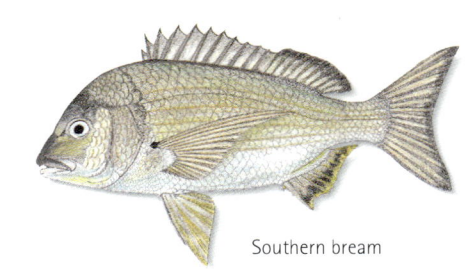

Southern bream

Common Names: There are several species of this vitally important family of angling fish in Australian waters, but the three discussed here are the best known. Referred to simply as bream by most anglers, they are also known as eastern black bream (*A. australis*), black bream (*A. australis* and *A. butcherii*), southern bream (*A. butcherii*), northern or pikey bream (*A. berda*) or silver bream. The eastern black bream is sometimes called yellowfin bream, although this name more correctly belongs to a closely related, but less prolific fish of Western Australian waters (*A. latus*). Very large bream of all species often exhibit a bluish tinge around the nose and upper jaw area, which earns them their nickname of blue-nose bream.

Description: The three species discussed here are deep-bodied, laterally compressed fish with moderately large scales, a forked tail and a smallish mouth lined with strong, peg-like teeth. Coloration varies considerably, depending upon habitat. Bream living in upper tidal estuaries or landlocked lagoons are often very dark — almost black — on the back, and bronze or gold on the flanks, while bream taken from the surf, ocean rocks or lower estuaries are usually bright silver. The eastern black bream's pelvic and anal fins are often yellowish to bright yellow. This bream's tail is typically dusky yellow with a black trailing edge. There is usually a small black blotch at the base of each pectoral fin, and this may also be evident on southern bream at times. In contrast, the pikey bream is generally much darker in hue than either the eastern black or southern variety, and its lips may also be thick and rubbery at times.

Size: Most bream landed by recreational anglers weigh between 200 g and 1.2 kg. Specimens weighing more than that are prize catches. An occasional specimen may top 2 kg, and records for the species stand at weights in excess of 4 kg. The eastern and southern species generally grow larger than the pikey bream of tropical waters.

Fishing for bream in an estuary near Bermagui in southern New South Wales

eastern black bream • pikey bream • southern bream • carp

A silvery-hued eastern black bream taken in New South Wales

Distribution: The eastern black bream's range extends from about Townsville or Cairns, in northern Queensland, southwards through New South Wales waters to about Lakes Entrance in eastern Victoria, where its range overlaps with that of the southern bream. The southern bream is primarily an estuary-, lake- and river-dwelling fish, ranging from the far south coast of New South Wales (rarely north of Merimbula) to about Geraldton in Western Australia. It is also found in the tidal rivers of Tasmania, the Bass Strait islands and on Kangaroo Island. The pikey bream is a northern species, ranging from central northern Queensland to about Exmouth, in Western Australia. All three species occupy a wide range of habitats from the freshwater reaches of rivers well above the upper tidal limits down through the estuaries and into harbours, inlets, bays and tidal lakes. Eastern black bream also range extensively along ocean surf beaches, rocky shorelines and into offshore waters; the other two species are mostly confined to the estuaries.

Fishing Techniques: The most productive techniques for taking bream in estuaries, bays and harbours are based on the use of light, sensitive tackle and live or fresh baits of marine worms, shellfish, yabbies (nippers), crabs, prawns or small bait fish species. Bream also succumb to an array of less conventional offerings such as bullock's heart, tripe, steak, chicken intestines and various 'pudding' mixtures of flour, water, cheese, tinned sardines and the like. Estuary and river-dwelling bream of all three species are also taken with reasonable consistency on small lures and flies, often by anglers targeting other species such as flathead or tailor. In New South Wales and southern Queensland, surf, rock and inshore boat anglers target eastern black bream using the same range of baits as estuary anglers, as well as whole and cut pilchards, fish fillets, strips and cubes. All three species respond well to the use of berley.

Eating Qualities: Bream are a much prized and highly rated table fish. Those taken from lower estuaries, harbours and the open ocean have moist, white flesh with a clean, sweet flavour. Upper estuary or freshwater dwelling fish often exhibit slightly softer flesh, and can have a slightly weedy or muddy taint at times.

Carp
Cyprinus carpio

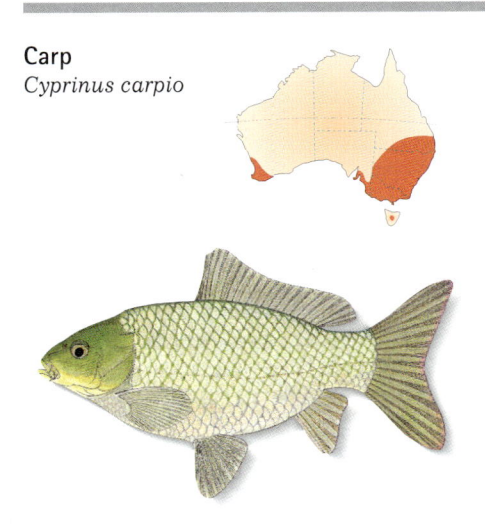

Common Names: The European or common carp actually comes from Asia. Popular Australian names include Euro', swamp trout or swampy.

Description: The carp is a heavily scaled, small-mouthed fish with rubbery lips, four barbels or whiskers and a single dorsal fin with one stout spine at its leading edge. The partially scaled mirror carp and the almost scaleless leather carp are variations of the same species, as is the multi-coloured and highly decorative koi carp. Their coloration varies from the standard coppery or bronze hues through dark olive green, gold, orange and mottled or piebald to completely white. Other members of the carp family introduced into Australia are the common goldfish (*Carassius auratus*), the tench (*Tinca tinca*) and the roach (*Rutilus rutilus*).

Size: Carp reach 1 to 6 kg; larger specimens are reasonably common in some areas. The heaviest recorded locally have weighed from 10 to 18 kg.

Distribution: These fresh and brackish water fish with their remarkable tolerance for varying temperatures and poor water quality are found on every continent except Antarctica. While carp generally prefer reasonably still, turbid and warm waters, they will tolerate cool, fast-running streams, polluted ponds and brackish estuaries. They are found throughout the Murray–Darling system, in many eastern and southern coastal streams, dams and lakes, and are common in ornamental ponds, lakes and permanent drains in areas south of the tropics. During the mid-1990s, they were discovered in Tasmanian lakes for the first time.

Fishing Techniques: Although carp are regarded as a noxious pest throughout Australia, anglers are increasingly fishing for them. They provide good sport and are often available in far greater quantities than more desirable freshwater species. Carp are usually fished for with lightly weighted, unweighted or float-suspended baits of bread, dough, maggots, par-boiled baby potatoes, sweetcorn kernels, earthworms, shrimps, yabby tails or freshwater mussels. They are also taken at times on flies and small lures. All European carp should be killed humanely and disposed of well away from the water.

Eating Qualities: Carp are gaining acceptance as table fish. The flesh is soft, watery and full of bones. It often tastes distinctly of mud or aquatic weed and needs to be heavily dressed in spices and sauces to disguise this.

A European or common carp taken on fly tackle

Catfish, Eel-tailed
Tandanus tandanus

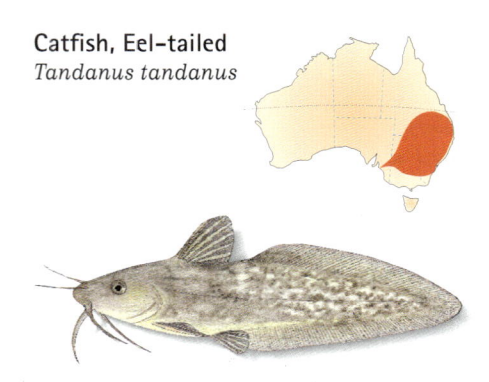

Common Names: This freshwater species has a range of common names, including eel-tailed catfish, eel-tail catfish, catfish, cattie, tandan, jewfish, dewfish, dhufish and kenaru. A closely related Western Australian fish (*Tandanus bostocki*) is commonly known as the cobbler, but this title is also applied to a less closely allied estuary catfish (*Cnidoglanis macrocephalus*), found in the coastal rivers of the south-west.

Description: Eel-tailed catfish are scaleless, whiskered, native freshwater fish with a distinctive, eel-like tail. They are usually black or blue-black to very dark brown on the back, slate grey or chocolate brown on the flanks and cream or creamy yellow on the belly. The flanks are often darkly mottled or spotted. Eel-tailed catfish have a stout, serrated spine in each pectoral fin, and another in the first dorsal fin. These spines can be locked in an erect position and are coated in a mildly venomous mucus which can cause severe pain and irritation if the spines penetrate the skin. Allergic reactions can be severe in some people, and may require hospitalisation.

Size: The eel-tailed catfish encountered by freshwater anglers usually weigh between 200 g and 2.2 kg, with occasional examples topping 3.5 kg. Rare specimens may weigh as much as 6 kg and measure 90 cm or so in length.

Distribution: This native Australian species was once found throughout most of the Murray–Darling system, as well as in the upper reaches of some eastern coastal streams, from South Australia to about Cairns, in Queensland. Identical or closely related tandans are also found in tropical rivers, the Coopers Creek inland drainage system and southern Western Australia. The range of the eel-tailed catfish has been reduced by dam and weir construction, and its numbers have declined dramatically in many regions, probably because of habitat alteration and direct competition with the introduced European carp. These fish prefer relatively slow flowing, warm and somewhat turbid waters. They are found in rivers, lakes and dams.

Fishing Techniques: Eel-tailed catfish are mainly caught using baits presented on or very near the bottom. Earthworms or scrub worms are favoured offerings, but many catfish are also taken on shrimps, whole small yabbies, yabby tails, mussels or even pieces of steak and other meat. Catfish will occasionally grab a lure, particularly a bobber or jig intended for redfin. At spawning time, they become particularly aggressive and are likely to strike at larger lures being used to target Murray cod and golden perch.

Eating Qualities: Although rather ugly, spiny, tough-skinned and slimy, the eel-tailed catfish is arguably one of the tastiest fish available from our outback rivers — rivalling even the highly regarded golden perch and Murray cod. A sharp knife and a pair of long-nosed pliers are required to skin this fish before it can be cooked.

Cobia
Rachycentron canadus

Common Names: The cobia or 'cobe' is still known in many areas as black kingfish or black king. Other, less common names for this species include sergeant fish, crab-eater, lemon fish and ling. When first hooked, cobia are often mistaken for sharks because of their prominent dorsal fin, large, dark pectoral fins and powerful forked tail. Once landed, they appear to have more in common with the catfish and remora clans, but can be easily identified by the very short, stout spines of their first dorsal fin.

Description: This dark, broad-headed and shark-like fish is the only member of its family and has no close relatives. It is occasionally confused with fork-tailed catfish and remoras or suckerfish, but is unrelated to these species. It is usually very dark in colour — chocolate brown to black on the back, fading to cream or creamy yellow on the belly. The flanks are typically marked with two lighter, longitudinal stripes. These stripes are often particularly well defined in live juveniles, but tend to fade after death or as the fish grows. The cobia's fins are dark brown to black, and its eyes are relatively large and very dark.

Size: Cobia may very occasionally reach 1.8 m or more in length and weigh as much as 75 kg, but they are more commonly encountered at weights between 2 and 20 kg, with 25- to 30-kg fish remaining reasonably common in some areas.

Distribution: The cobia is a widespread species, occurring sporadically throughout the tropical, subtropical and warm temperate waters of the Pacific, Indian and Atlantic oceans. Although not especially prolific in Australian waters, cobia may be encountered singly or in small groups anywhere around the northern coastline — from Geraldton in Western Australia to Port Stephens in New South Wales. However, in summer and autumn, stragglers occasionally extend this range much further south on both the east and west coasts, and rare examples have turned up as far afield as Batemans Bay, Eden or even Port Welshpool in the east and Cape Leeuwin or Albany in the west. Cobia have not yet been recorded in either New Zealand or Tasmania.

Fishing Techniques: An opportunistic feeder, the cobia will take such diverse prey as sand crabs, small stingrays, various reef and bait fish, squid, octopus and small tuna or mackerel. It is often found around floating objects such as marker buoys and logs, or in association with large marine creatures, including manta rays, whale sharks and even tiger sharks. Cobia respond to live and dead baits, lures and flies, but can be frustratingly difficult to tempt at times, particularly in very calm, clear water. Deep-bodied, flashy live baits such as bream, tarwhine, snapper and sweep, or strongly worked, surface-running popper-style lures, will sometimes produce results when all else fails. Once hooked, a large cobia will test an angler and his or her tackle to the limit, especially at the end of the fight. The cobia's shark-like gyrations have broken many gaffs and landing nets, and have even been known to cause injury to anglers. Tackle for cobia needs to be sturdy and well maintained.

Eating Qualities: A very good to excellent eating fish, the cobia has rather strong-flavoured and distinctive flesh that is firm, sweet and highly palatable. This versatile table fish can be prepared and cooked in a wide variety of ways.

The cobia has a broad, shark-like head

Cod, Estuary
Epinephelus spp.

Common Names: Several closely related members of this large family, including *Epinephelus malabaricus* and *E. coioides*, are commonly known as estuary cod or estuary rock cod. Other popular names include brown-spotted rock cod, north-west groper, spotted cod, Malabar cod, greasy cod, flowery cod and gold spot cod. Larger estuary cod are also occasionally confused with the Queensland groper (*E. lanceolatus*). However, the groper has a more rounded gill cover and a blunter head profile.

Description: The various fish known as estuary cod belong to the family Serranidae. They are large-mouthed, bottom- and snag-dwelling predators with cavernous mouths and rows of small, fine teeth. Their coloration is variable, but usually consists of a series of black, dark brown or gold spots and blotches over a vaguely barred or blotched creamy grey or light brown background. Larger specimens may be very dark.

Size: Some estuary cod grow to at least 1.8 m in length and reach weights well in excess of 250 kg, although it is doubtful that they can rival the maximum growth potential of the Queensland groper, which has been known to reach weights of 400 kg and more. Most of the cod taken in estuaries are juveniles and sub-adults, weighing between 800 g and 6 kg. Offshore, around reefs, islands and deep headlands, 10- to 40-kg cod are more common.

Distribution: Estuary cod are found in tropical and subtropical rivers, estuaries, harbours and inshore waters, and also around offshore reefs and islands. Isolated specimens sometimes stray as far south as Sydney on the east coast and Rottnest Island in Western Australia, but they are generally more common north of Brisbane in Queensland and Shark Bay in Western Australia.

Fishing Techniques: Within estuaries, smaller estuary cod up to about 6 to 8 kg often respond aggressively to lures of the type used to catch barramundi and mangrove jacks. They also bite strongly on a range of live and dead baits. The larger, reef-dwelling cod will take most types of cut, whole and live fish baits, as well as jigs and even deep-running trolling lures. Estuary cod are strong fighters and will dive powerfully for cover when hooked.

Eating Qualities: Small to medium estuary cod are very good to excellent table fish, although the flesh of larger, reef-dwelling specimens sometimes tends to be rather coarse and dry. Due to their relative scarcity and low meat yield in relation to total body weight, very large cod are usually released. Reef-dwelling cod weighing more than 8 kg are also potential ciguatera carriers in areas where this toxin occurs.

Top left: *This outback angler has taken an eel-tailed catfish (left) and a golden perch or yellowbelly (right)*
Top right: *A cobia taken off Dundee Beach in the Northern Territory*
Bottom left: *Unhooking a moderately large estuary cod in a Top End river*
Bottom right: *A small estuary cod taken on a lure in a Cape York estuary*

What fish is that?

Coral Trout
Plectropoma maculatum and other *Plectropoma* spp.

Common Names: There are several closely related members of the family Plectropoma in Australian waters, the most common being *Plectropoma maculatum*. Coral trout are often known simply as trout, although they are totally unrelated to the freshwater fish of the same name.

Description: These beautifully marked, robust, predatory reef fish of tropical waters belong to the same large group of groper-like fish as the tropical Australian saltwater cods (Serranidae). Coral trout have large mouths and sharp, widely spaced canine teeth. Coloration varies from greenish brown in shallow water, through brick red to bright red in deeper water, but always with an overlay of blue or red spots.

Size: Most coral trout caught in Australian waters weigh between 1 and 6 kg, although the larger, oceanic specimens found on outer reefs and around distant offshore islands can weigh 10 to 20 kg. Maximum growth potential of the largest members of this family may be upwards of 35 kg.

Distribution: The coral trout is a tropical, reef-dwelling species which occasionally strays into subtropical waters. It ranges from near-shore reefs and rock piles to deep, continental shelf drop-offs. The biggest coral trout are generally found well offshore.

Fishing Techniques: Most coral trout taken by anglers fall to traditional bottom-fishing techniques employing cut fish flesh, prawns or squid baits, but the species also responds well to more sophisticated sport fishing methods, including lure casting, jigging, trolling and even fly fishing, especially in shallower water. Coral trout strike savagely at all types of cast, jigged and trolled lures, live baits and rigged dead baits. Tackle for catching coral trout ranges from relatively heavy handlines to jig outfits and double or single-handed casting gear. These fish are strong fighters and will dive powerfully towards the sea bed when hooked. Strong lines are required to land larger specimens.

A coral trout taken in northern waters

Eating Qualities: The coral trout has moist, firm, white flesh and is a superb table fish. In some areas, larger coral trout are proven carriers of the potentially fatal ciguatera toxin; eating more than one meal from a coral trout weighing more than 8 kg is unwise at best.

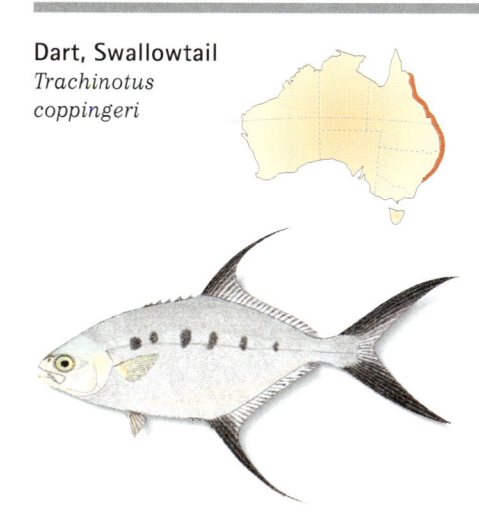

Dart, Swallowtail
Trachinotus coppingeri

Common Names: The dart, swallowtail dart or swallow-tailed dart has several close relatives in Australian waters, including the larger but less frequently caught common dart (*Trachinotus botla*) of Western Australian waters and the black spotted dart (*T. balloni*) of tropical seas. The more distantly related snub-nosed dart or oyster cracker (*T. blochii*) — a near-identical fish to the Atlantic permit — is also taken in Australian waters from time to time.

Description: Swallowtail dart are members of the family Carangidae, which also contains the various trevally and kingfish species. They are characterised by a deep, laterally compressed body, forked tail and a series of relatively large, dark blotches along the lateral line. Coloration is usually bluish to greenish silver on the back; bright, metallic silver on the flanks and silvery white on the belly. A row of dark grey 'thumb-prints' along the lateral line varies in intensity between individuals. The dart's fins are often darkly tipped or have dark margins.

Size: Swallowtail dart are relatively small fish, and most of those taken by anglers weigh less than 750 g. Any swallowtail dart of more than 1 kg is considered a truly exceptional catch.

Distribution: Swallowtail dart are a fish of tropical and subtropical waters, ranging about as far south as Jervis Bay and Rottnest Island. They are mainly found along ocean beaches, around sandy cays and inside lagoons. Dart generally favour clean, well-oxygenated and slightly turbulent water.

Fishing Techniques: Swallowtail dart are mostly taken incidentally by surf casters targeting whiting and bream using natural baits such as worms, pipis (cockles), crabs, prawns and yabbies or nippers. They will also take cut fish flesh baits, whole whitebait or small pilchards and strips of squid, and can sometimes be hooked on small lures, jigs and flies.

Eating Qualities: Dart are tasty, somewhat dry, white-fleshed fish, but are often overlooked by surf anglers targeting more desirable species such as bream, whiting, flathead and mulloway. Dart intended for the table should be bled and cleaned promptly after capture.

A pair of swallowtail dart landed from the beach on Fraser Island

Dolphin Fish
Coryphaena hippurus and *C. equiselis*

Adult male dolphin fish

Juvenile or female dolphin fish

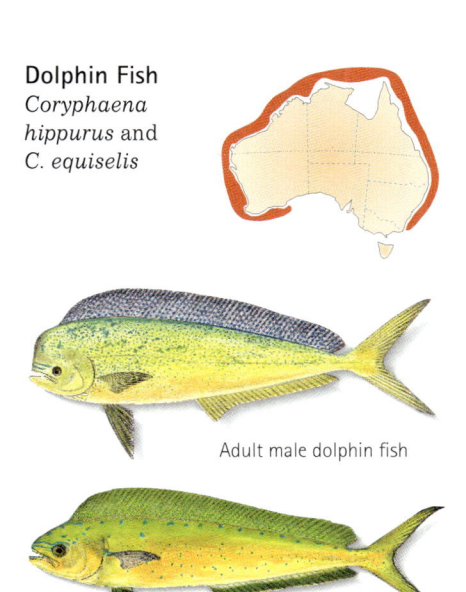

Common Names: The two similar and closely related types of dolphin fish — the more common *Coryphaena hippurus* and the much smaller and less abundant *C. equiselis* — are also known as mahi mahi, dorado, dolphin and dolphinfish. Despite their name, dolphin fish have nothing in common with the marine mammals also known as dolphins. Confusion arising from this shared name is best avoided by using the Polynesian title of 'mahi mahi' when referring to these fish.

Description: These two closely related species of dolphin fish are renowned the world over as especially colourful, spectacular and tasty pelagic fish. The larger and more common variety is characterised by distinct differences between the sexes. The female or 'cow' has a low, rounded head profile, while the adult male or 'bull' develops a high, steep and very blunt forehead. Dolphin fish coloration ranges from electric blue with numerous dark or gold spots, through intense green and gold to silver, depending on size, location and behaviour patterns. A hooked specimen may change colour several times while being fought and landed. The fish's tail is nearly always yellow, but may be tinged with blue or even silver.

Size: Dolphin fish grow to almost 2 m in length and may reach weights of close to 45 kg, although any specimen weighing more than 25 kg is an exceptional catch. Large schools of juvenile dolphin fish in the 400- to 3-kg range are seasonally abundant under floating debris and fish trap marker buoys in warm currents off our east and west coasts.

Distribution: The dolphin fish is a worldwide species, found in the tropical, subtropical and, more rarely, temperate waters of every ocean. In local waters, it ranges as far south as Eden, Albany and New Zealand's Bay of Islands, with occasional strays even turning up in South Australia. A true oceanic wanderer, the mahi mahi rarely ventures into waters shallower than 60 m, and is much more at home in continental shelf drop-off areas between 150 and 400 m deep.

Fishing Techniques: Dolphin fish caught in Australian waters are usually taken on small to medium trolling lures of the type used to catch tuna and other pelagic species. They will also attack live baits, rigged dead baits, fresh fish strips, bottle squid, jigs, plugs, poppers and flies.

A large male or 'bull' dolphin fish, or mahi mahi, weighing 15 kg

A keen-eyed and sometimes cautious fish, the mahi mahi will occasionally shy away from clumsy rigs or unnatural baits, unless competing strongly with fellow school members. Often, the school will cease biting altogether after one or two fish have been caught. However, a trace or leader of some sort — either light wire or heavy nylon — is advisable when pursuing large dolphin fish, which have hard, sharp jaws.

Eating Qualities: The dolphin fish is one of the tastiest of all the pelagic fishes. Pink-fleshed and delicious, it is regarded as a delicacy in many parts of the world and commands high prices. Dolphin fish intended for the table should be killed and bled immediately after capture. They must be handled carefully, as they frequently thrash wildly and throw themselves about when brought aboard. Smaller specimens are sometimes mushy and flavourless when cooked, but this can often be attributed to bad handling practices immediately after capture.

Drummer, Black
Girella elevata

Common Names: Few anglers use the official name eastern rock blackfish, as it tends to cause confusion with the closely related luderick or blackfish (*G. tricuspidata*). East coast anglers commonly call black drummer by the colloquial title of 'pig'.

Description: The black drummer is a robust, deep-bodied marine fish with a relatively small mouth and head. Its colour can vary from black, blue-black or purple-black to dark grey, slate grey or even a sooty off-white. Its belly is only slightly paler than the rest of its body.

Size: Most black drummer taken by anglers run from 400 g to 3 kg, but they can sometimes exceed 5 kg. There have been reports of exceptional specimens of 9 kg.

Distribution: Black drummer frequent temperate ocean shorelines from about Noosa Heads in southern Queensland to Wilsons Promontory in Victoria. They have also been taken along the north-eastern Tasmanian coast. A closely related fish is found in Western Australia. Drummer are generally found in the ocean or around bays and harbour mouths.

Fishing Techniques: Baits of cunjevoi flesh, cut crab, bread, abalone gut, peeled prawn-tail and squid or cuttlefish are most successful, particularly when used with a berley of soaked bread or bran and chopped green weed or cabbage. Drummer will often take weed baits used by luderick (blackfish) anglers. Most drummer are taken from the shore, but some small boat specialists enjoy success anchoring close to rock ledges, inshore bomboras, reefs or islands. Since the drummer is a very strong fighter and will dive for the seabed or make a run for a cave, double-strength hooks and lines from 6- to 15-kg breaking-strain are essential.

Eating Qualities: Black drummer are very tasty, particularly if cleaned, skinned and filleted soon after being caught. Smaller fish (800 g to 3 kg) are generally better eating than larger specimens, although even quite big drummer make excellent table fish if handled correctly.

What fish is that?

Drummer, Silver
Kyphosus sydneyanus

A silver drummer swimming amongst mullet schools at Lord Howe Island

Common Names: The silver drummer or drummer is also known as buffalo bream, particularly in Western Australia. It is closely related to the smaller low-finned drummer (*Kyphosus vaigiensis*) and the western buffalo bream (*K. cornelii*). None of these fish should be confused with the rock blackfish or black drummer (*Girella elevata*), which is often encountered in the same areas.

Description: A deep-bodied fish with moderately large scales, the silver drummer has a small mouth equipped with comb-like, weed-cropping teeth. Coloration varies from greenish or bluish silver to slate grey, sometimes with a vague longitudinal pattern of brownish yellow stripes. The fins are darker, and the tail may be almost black.

Size: Silver drummer grow to at least 90 cm in length and weigh up to 15 kg, although they are more common at half that size and less.

Distribution: Found around the southern half of Australia, from Moreton Bay to Shark Bay, as well as at Lord Howe Island, silver drummer prefer wave-washed inshore areas and shallow reefs.

Fishing Techniques: Silver drummer are mostly hooked incidentally by anglers targeting luderick (blackfish), black drummer (rock blackfish) and bream from the ocean rocks. They are omnivores and respond best to small, soft baits of bread, dough, cheese, weed, marine worms or peeled prawn tails. Once hooked, silver drummer are powerful opponents.

Eating Qualities: Silver drummer have tough, slightly grey flesh with a strong 'weed' or iodine flavour. They are not highly rated as table fish.

Emperor, Red
Lutjanus sebae

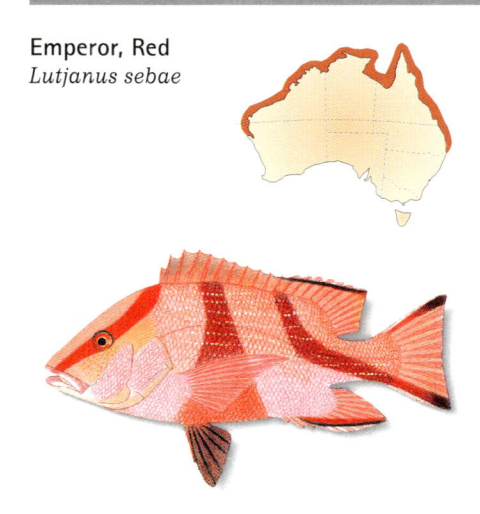

Common Names: The highly prized red emperor or emperor is also known as government bream, king snapper, red kelp or simply as a 'red'.

Description: The largest and most sought-after of all the emperor clan, the red emperor is a very deep-bodied fish with strong jaws and a large, powerful tail. Coloration varies with age. The arrowhead pattern of stripes is darker and much more clearly defined when the fish is young. Adults are salmon pink to pale or bright red with three vertical bands of darker red, one sloping back from the snout through the eye, a broader one running up through the pectoral fin area, and another slanting back down into the lower tail fin. The fins are reddish, particularly the first dorsal, which is often very bright along its upper edge.

Size: Red emperor grow to well over a metre in length and can weigh up to 20 to 25 kg, although such giants are rare. Weights between 1 and 8 kg are more common, although reasonable numbers of 10-kg plus 'reds' still continue to be taken in certain locations.

Distribution: Red emperor frequent tropical and subtropical waters, occasionally wandering as far south as northern New South Wales. These schooling fish prefer moderately deep coral reef areas, especially over gravel, sand, shell grit or 'marl' patches between hard coral outcrops.

Fishing Techniques: Most emperor are taken on bottom-fished baits of cut fish flesh, prawns or squid, particularly by nocturnal anglers operating from boats moored over coral reefs and gravel patches. Small live fish and rigged live squid will often take trophy-sized emperor if other methods fail. Red emperor will occasionally strike at jigged or deep-trolled lures, but such captures tend to be the exception rather than the rule.

Eating Qualities: Red emperor of all sizes are amongst the very best of the many fine table fish available in northern reef waters, with some people regarding it as second only to the delectable barramundi cod (*Cromileptes altivelis*). To date, there have been no published reports of ciguatera poisoning resulting from the consumption of red emperor in Australian waters. However, it is a potential carrier of this toxin, and should remain a suspect in areas where ciguatera is known to occur on a regular basis.

A red emperor from the Cape York Peninsula

Flathead, Dusky, Sand and Tiger
Platycephalus fuscus, P. arenarius,
P. caeruleopunctatus, P. speculator,
P. bassensis and
Neoplatycephalus
richardsoni

Dusky flathead

Common Names: The dusky (*Platycephalus fuscus*) is the largest member of the Platycephalidae family, which contains more than 30 species, at least 14 of which are taken by anglers. Most of the more common flathead may be separated and identified by carefully examining the coloration and markings on the tail or caudal fin. The dusky flathead or dusky is also known as the estuary flathead and mud flathead. It and other members of this extensive family are also commonly referred to as flatties, frogs, lizards, crocs and Yanks.

Description: Flathead are characterised by their flattened bodies (less flattened in the tiger flathead (*Neoplatycephalus richardsoni*)), broad, spade-like heads, large mouths and fine teeth. Sets of sharp spines covered in mildly venomous mucus are located on the gill covers. The camouflaged coloration is extremely variable, ranging from very light sandy white or fawn with darker bars and blue, red and black spots or 'stars' to brick red or almost jet black. The belly is almost always creamy, creamy yellow or white.

Size: Duskies are the giants of the flathead clan, very occasionally topping 1.2 m in length and 10 kg in weight. The other species rarely exceed 3 or 4 kg in weight and are much more common at sizes between 200 g and 1.5 kg.

Distribution: Flathead are found right around the Australian coastline, in rivers, estuaries, bays, harbours and offshore waters. The dusky is mostly an estuarine and inshore species of the east coast, ranging southwards from about Rockhampton or Mackay in Queensland to Wilsons Promontory and eastern Bass Strait in Victoria. The sand flathead are more wide ranging and usually occur in inshore areas, while the tiger flathead is a deeper water species with a range extending southwards from Sydney into Victorian and Tasmanian waters.

Fishing Techniques: Flathead may be fished for in a variety of ways. Many are taken on bottom-fished or drifted baits of small, live or dead poddy mullet or herring, pilchards, whitebait, sprats, anchovy and strips of mullet, tailor, yellowtail, tuna or garfish, as well as yabbies, nippers, marine worms, shellfish and prawns. When using dead baits, results are often improved by retrieving the bait slowly over the seabed, or by using the tide and current to keep the boat or rig moving. Flathead are also a recognised lure and fly fishing target. They respond particularly well to small- and

Two species of flathead

medium-sized metal spoons, rubber-tailed jigs, floating/diving or sinking minnows, plugs and streamer flies. These should be presented close to the bottom for best results.

Eating Qualities: Flathead are highly rated table fish with firm, white and flaky flesh which tends towards dryness in larger fish. They are best suited to recipes and cooking methods which retain moisture in the flesh.

Flounder
Pseudorhombus
arsius and
P. jenynsii

Small-toothed flounder

Common Names: There are many species of flounder in Australian waters, but only a few are large enough and common enough to be of interest to anglers. The large-toothed flounder (*Pseudorhombus arsius*) and small-toothed flounder (*P. jenynsii*) are the most common species taken by anglers in Australian waters. Less abundant types include the greenback flounder (*Rhombosolea tapirina*) and long-snouted flounder (*Ammotretis rostratus*). Flounder are occasionally confused with another group of flatfish known as sole. However, sole are tongue-shaped and do not have a separate tail.

Description: Flounder are relatively small, compressed, bottom-dwelling fish with both eyes on the same side of their head (in adults). Flounder alter their colour to suit the bottom strata on which they are lying. Most are brown, fawn, sandy or light khaki to green, usually overlaid with darker spots, blotches, 'stars' and halos. The underside of an adult flounder is almost always white, cream or creamy yellow, although rare specimens are coloured or partially coloured on both sides.

Size: The largest of the flounders may grow to 50 cm in length and 1.2 kg in weight, although fish weighing more than 800 g are regarded as exceptional specimens. An average flounder measures about 25 to 35 cm and weighs from 200 to 750 g.

Distribution: Flounder of one sort or another are found right around Australia, but these fish are more commonly caught in the southern half of the country. They prefer mud, sand or fine gravel bottom strata in tidal rivers, lakes and estuaries. They are also found in bays and on inshore grounds. Flounder occasionally penetrate upriver into fresh water but are more common in the lower stretches of estuaries.

Fishing Techniques: Voracious little hunters, flounder will take surprisingly large baits into

An attractively marked flounder

their tooth-lined mouths at times. Most flounder are caught on baits of prawns, worms, yabbies or nippers, fish flesh or squid strip. In most areas, they are usually an incidental catch by anglers fishing for flathead, bream and whiting. Flounder feed on or close to the bottom and prefer natural baits, although they will succumb to small lead-headed jigs, minnows, spoons or flies fished on or near the seabed.

Eating Qualities: Flounder are excellent and highly prized table fish, often given star billing on restaurant menus. However, fine bones can be something of a problem in smaller specimens. The flesh is white, moist and sweet, and has a delicate flavour. It should never be overcooked.

Garfish
Hemiramphidae spp.

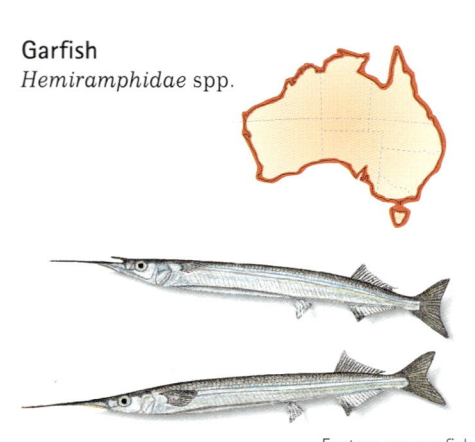

Common Names: This large family of worldwide fish species is well represented in Australia. The more common types found here include the near identical eastern and southern sea garfish (*Hyporhamphus australis* and *H. melanochir*), the river garfish (*H. regularis*), the robust garfish or 'three-by-two' (*Hemiramphus robustus*) and the snub-nosed garfish (*Arrhamphus sclerolepis*). They are commonly called gars, gardies and beakies in Australia. Very small garfish, which are popular as bait, are sometimes called pencil or splinter gar.

Description: Garfish are a widespread group of small, slender fish, most of which have a bottom jaw that extends into a bill or beak. Body colour varies between species, from bright, metallic silver to silvery green or silvery blue. Some have dark blotches, bands or bars. The belly is typically silvery white, white or pale and a red tip on the bill is common.

Size: The southern sea garfish and the robust or 'three-by-two' garfish occasionally reach more than 45 cm in length and 400 g in weight. Most garfish are more common at lengths of 25 to 35 cm and weights of 100 to 200 g.

Distribution: Garfish are present from the surface layers of oceanic waters far offshore, through inshore reef areas to bays and estuaries, and into freshwater reaches of some rivers. In fact, garfish of one type or another are found in practically every Australian estuary, harbour, bay and inshore area.

Fishing Techniques: Garfish are mainly taken on float-suspended baits of bread, dough, 'pudding' mix, fish strips, prawn pieces, marine worm, cut squid strips or maggots. Hooks should be small (No. 14 to No. 6) and long shanked. Garfish also respond well to a berley mix of pollard, crushed wheat or bread crumbs, especially if a little fish oil is added.

Eating Qualities: Garfish—particularly the larger varieties—are delectable table fish with sweet, moist flesh, but they have many fine bones. After capture, they should be squeezed from the head towards the tail to expel semi-digested vegetable matter and berley in the stomach, then kept cool until cleaned. Their scales dislodge easily, and those not rubbed off by handling at the time of capture are easily removed during cleaning.

Eastern sea garfish

A fillet of garfish on ganged (linked) hooks makes a great bait

Groper, Blue
Achoerodus viridis and *A. gouldii*

Common Names: These very closely related species, the eastern blue groper (*Achoerodus viridis*) and western blue groper (*A. gouldii*), are also known as groper, brown groper and red groper, the last two names referring to colour phases of the smaller female fish.

Description: These two near-identical, heavily scaled, barrel-bodied and peg-toothed members of the wrasse family (Labridae) exhibit well-defined colour differences between the smaller female and the larger male. Juvenile and female colouring ranges from green to brown to orange-red, often with a darker reddish spot on each scale. Very small specimens may also have whitish spots or blotches. Male groper are blue—from deep navy to brilliant cobalt—with darker blue and sometimes reddish lines or spots around their small, pig-like eyes.

Size: The western species of blue groper is the larger of the two, growing to 1.6 m in length and at least 40 kg in weight. The eastern blue groper, while rare these days at weights in excess of 15 kg, can approach 22 kg in isolated instances.

Distribution: The eastern blue groper ranges from about Hervey Bay in southern Queensland to Wilsons Promontory in Victoria, while the western blue groper extends from west of Melbourne to the Houtman Abrolhos off the coast of Geraldton in Western Australia.

Fishing Techniques: Strong line, heavy tackle and fresh crab baits are the tools of the groper specialist. Groper will also take shellfish, cunjevoi and sometimes even prawns, squid and cuttlefish. They will dive for cover among the rocks when hooked, so very strong tackle is required.

Eating Qualities: The groper is a delicious fish, particularly in the 3- to 9-kg range. Smaller fish can be rather soft and tasteless, and very large specimens may be a little coarse. Blue groper are best filleted and skinned, as their large scales are difficult to remove.

A large, male blue groper

garfish • blue groper • hairtail • giant herring   349

Hairtail
Trichiurus lepturus

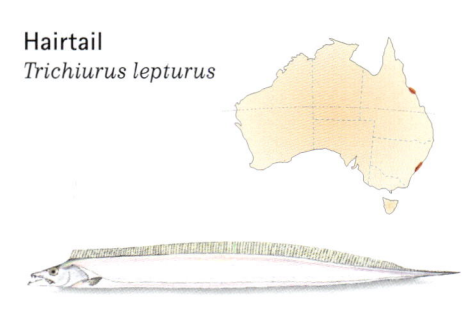

Common Names: These fish are usually known simply as hairtail or 'hairies' or, more rarely, as Australian hairtail or Cox's hairtail. Hairtail are occasionally confused with the closely related frostfish (*Lepidopus caudatus*). However, the latter has a tiny, forked tail, in contrast to the hairtail's whip-like rear end.

Description: The hairtail is a long, silvery, eel-like fish with no tail (caudal) fin and a large mouth full of sharp fangs. This fish is bright, reflective or metallic silver in colour, with a tinge of blue or green along the top of the back. The fins are almost transparent.

Size: Hairtail commonly reach lengths of between 1 and 1.8 m and weights of 1.5 to 3 kg, although outstanding examples may exceed 2 m in length and weigh as much as 5 or 6 kg.

Distribution: Hairtail or very closely related fish appear sporadically in many parts of the world, and are an important commercial catch in parts of South-East Asia and India. In Australia, they may at times turn up just about anywhere, but are common only in a few select estuarine and harbour environments between Newcastle and Wollongong on the New South Wales coast However, quantities of hairtail are occasionally reported in localities as widely separated as Townsville in Queensland and Bunbury in Western Australia. The hairtail remains something of a mystery fish. They are taken in deep, continental shelf waters by trawlers and, at times, in bays and large estuaries by anglers.

Fishing Techniques: Hairtail taken outside their few common haunts are almost always incidental captures. However, in the Hawkesbury River system and, to a lesser extent, Sydney Harbour, Botany Bay and Newcastle Harbour, the species has attracted a dedicated band of specialist anglers. The best hairtail fishing in these regions occurs at night or in deeper holes during the day. Most fish are caught in the cooler autumn and winter months. Small to medium live baits such as yellowtail, slimy mackerel and mullet, whole dead fish such as pilchards or garfish, and cut flesh strips account for most hairtail caught on hook and line. When biting well, hairtail will also strike savagely at lures, but their toothy mouth makes hooking these fish rather difficult. Wire traces or ganged hooks should be used to prevent hairtail biting through the line.

Eating Qualities: The hairtail has tasty, delicate flesh which should not be overcooked. Many people believe that rubbing the fish with a piece of rough cloth to remove the skin before cooking will improve the flavour.

Two anglers with a catch of smaller-than-average hairtail

Herring, Giant
Elops machnata

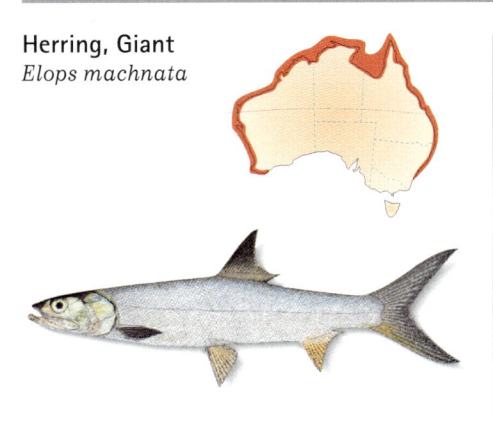

Common Names: The giant herring or 'GH' is also known simply as herring or, more rarely, by names such as pincushion fish, lady fish, banana fish, ten-pounder and elops. Although occasionally confused with two other herrings, the bonefish (*Albula neoguinaica*) and the milkfish (*Chanos chanos*), the giant herring's long, slender body and large mouth are identifying features. It also lacks the large, sharp teeth of the aptly named wolf herring (*Chirocentrus dorab*).

Description: The giant herring is a long, relatively slender fish with a nearly cylindrical body, a huge, forked tail, single dorsal fin and big, upturned mouth. Its moderately large, easily displaced scales are bright, metallic silver, although the fish is often gunmetal blue to dark grey or even yellow-green along the very top of the back. The giant herring's fins are dark, the tail sometimes showing a black border on the trailing edge.

Size: Giant herring encountered by Australian anglers most commonly weigh from 400 g to 2.5 kg, although the species is known to weigh as much as 10 kg and exceed 1.5 m in length occasionally.

Distribution: Giant herring are a highly rated and sought-after sport fish with a sporadic distribution through the tropical north, and are occasionally found in southern waterways such as Perth's Swan River or Sydney's Queenscliff Lagoon and Port Hacking, either singly or in small schools. Mainly a fish of the tidal estuaries, bays and saltwater lagoons, giant herring favour shallow, warm areas with plenty of prawns and small bait fish. They are rarely found very far offshore, unless the location is near an island or sand cay.

Fishing Techniques: Specifically fished for in just a few locations — such as the Gulf of Carpentaria — herring are more likely to be encountered incidentally during a hunt for mackerel, queenfish, trevally, longtail tuna or the like. Giant herring are taken on small live baits, fresh fish strips, prawns, small crabs, many different lures and various flies. Perhaps the most effective ploy is to use a small, cup-faced popper-style lure or surface running fly. With their lightning fast strikes, incredible bursts of speed and acrobatic leaps, herring always provide the angler with a real thrill, although they can be extremely difficult to keep on a line and often escape before being landed.

Eating Qualities: The giant herring is a poor to fair table fish. The flesh is full of fine bones — a trait common to the entire herring family.

A handsome giant herring taken on fly fishing tackle in the Gulf of Carpentaria

Javelin Fish
Pomadasys hasta

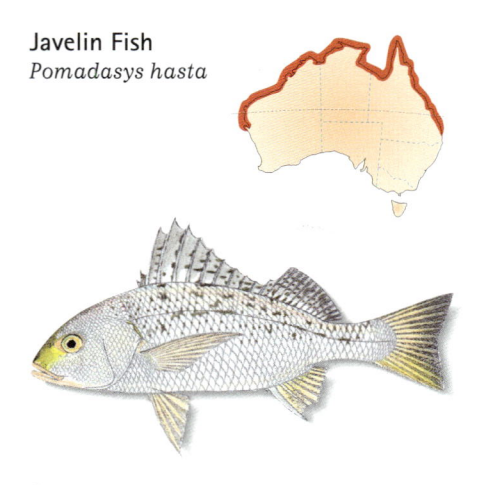

Common Names: There are three main species of javelin fish, although *Pomadasys hasta* is the best known. This fish is also known as the spotted javelin or grunter.

Description: The javelin fish is a handsome, speckled, deep-bodied fish, so named because of the stout spine or spear at the front edge of its anal fin and the grunting sound it sometimes makes after capture. Its typical coloration is purple-silver to dark silvery grey on the back, silver on the flanks and silver-white on the belly, overlaid by darker vertical bands and dark spots. The fins often have a yellowish tinge.

Size: The spotted javelin fish (*P. hasta*) is commonly caught at weights of between 400 g and 2 kg, although exceptional specimens may reach 6 or even 8 kg. The other two species are generally smaller than the spotted javelin fish.

Distribution: A fish of tropical estuaries and inshore waters, the javelin fish ranges from the central coast of Queensland around the northern half of the continent to at least Exmouth Gulf in Western Australia. Most javelin fish are found in estuaries or bays.

Fishing Techniques: Live prawns, fresh dead prawns, crabs, yabbies and fresh fish strips are the best baits for this sometimes shy biter. It will occasionally take lures, but is rarely targeted in this manner. Tackle should be kept light and sinker weights minimised when pursuing this fish. The javelin fish often runs with the bait held lightly in its mouth before swallowing it.

Eating Qualities: A fine table species held in high regard by most tropical anglers, the javelin fish has firm, white and slightly moist flesh. It handles well and can also be frozen.

A small javelin fish landed on diving lure

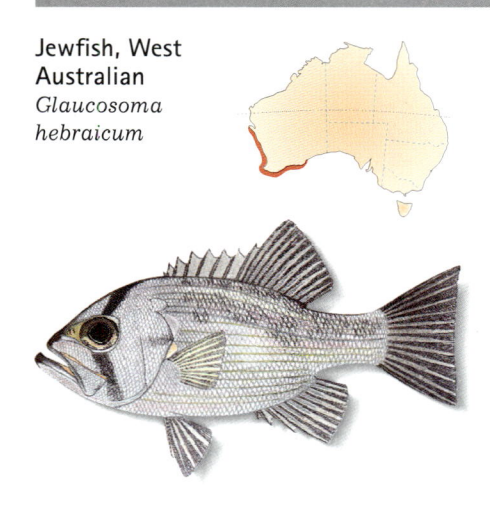

Jewfish, West Australian
Glaucosoma hebraicum

Common Names: The West Australian or Westralian jewfish is commonly known simply as jewfish or 'dhufish'. This species should not be confused with the mulloway, an unrelated fish frequenting the same waters and known in the eastern states as jewfish. The only known relative of the West Australian jewfish is the smaller pearl perch (*Glaucosoma scapulare*) of northern New South Wales and southern Queensland.

Description: A big, deep-bodied and strikingly attractive fish found only in the offshore waters of southern Western Australia, the jewfish has large eyes and a big, slightly undershot mouth. Typical coloration is purplish silver to metallic grey, overlaid with vague, lengthwise stripes of darker purple. Juveniles have a distinct, black, diagonal stripe through the eyes, but this fades as the fish approaches maturity. The eye stripe sometimes remains visible in freshly caught adults, but usually fades after death.

Size: The average size of West Australian jewfish taken by anglers has fallen in recent years, due to overharvesting. Most of those caught weigh from 2 to 8 kg, but many weighing more than 10 kg are still taken by anglers working deeper or less heavily fished reefs. Any jewfish of more than 20 kg is a real trophy, although specimens of up to 25 kg and more have been recorded.

Distribution: The West Australian jewfish is confined to southern Western Australia, ranging from about the Recherche Archipelago off the southern coastline to Shark Bay in the northwest. These fish are mostly found offshore over hard, but relatively flat bottom strata, especially limestone shelf country. They also frequent wrecks, reefs and rock piles.

Fishing Techniques: Bottom fishing with strong lines, heavy sinkers, big hooks and baits of octopus, squid, cut fish flesh or whole small fish is the favourite method for taking West Australian jewfish. The species also responds well to live baits fished close to the bottom and even to jigs or other deep-fished lures. Although not regarded as an outstanding sport fish on the tackle usually employed, jewfish hooked on lighter line, or encountered in the shallows, typically give a fine account of themselves.

Eating Qualities: The flesh of the West Australian jewfish is an acclaimed delicacy and certainly high on this country's short list of best table species. Specimens of all sizes are delicious and may be cooked in almost any way. However, the fish's superb flavour should not be masked by a strong sauce or overpowering flavourings.

The West Australian jewfish is one of the most sought-after of all West Australian reef fish

javelin fish • West Australian jewfish • John dory • yellowtail kingfish

John Dory
Zeus faber

Common Names: In Australia, John dory is the common name for this fish. It is occasionally called Peter's fish, Peter's dory or simply dory.
Description: This unusual looking, scaleless, plate-like fish has a deep, circular and laterally compressed body, a big head, huge extendible mouth, and long, filamentous dorsal fin. Coloration varies from greenish brown to olive or grey on the back and lighter on the flanks and belly. A large black spot or blotch bordered by a light edge is prominent on each flank.
Size: John dory commonly weigh between 500 g and 1.5 kg, and occasionally exceed 2.2 kg. Giants approaching 5 or 6 kg have been reported in New Zealand waters.
Distribution: John dory are found in cool and temperate waters all over the world. In Australia, they are confined to the southern half, from about south-eastern Queensland to South Australia, with sporadic appearances in the south of Western Australia and Tasmania. They frequent bays, harbours and estuaries, as well as deeper reefs.
Fishing Techniques: Many John dory taken by anglers are incidental captures landed while fishing with live baits for flathead, mulloway or kingfish. If slightly smaller baits are used, the chance of taking a John dory increases. Estuary and harbour anglers targeting John dory mostly use handlines or light rods and small live baits, sometimes trimming the tail of the bait with scissors to slow it down. Over deeper reefs, John dory take cut-flesh strips and whole small fish such as pilchards.
Eating Qualities: The John dory is a superb table fish. The flesh is pearly-white, firm and has an extremely fine grain. Once filleted, there are no bones in the flesh. John dory commands a very high price at market because of its quality.

A 2-kg John dory taken off Sydney

Kingfish, Yellowtail
Seriola lalandi

Common Names: This species is most commonly called kingfish, yellowtail kingfish, yellow-tailed kingfish, yellowtail, king, kingy or kingi. Colloquial names include hoodlum and bandit, while smaller specimens are often nicknamed rats or nor' headers. Some confusion exists between the kingfish and two of its near relatives—the amberjack (*Seriola dumerili*) and the Samson fish (*S. hippos*), while an unrelated species, the cobia (*Rachycentron canadus*), is also commonly called black kingfish.
Description: The yellowtail kingfish is a powerful, pelagic fish characterised by its bright yellow tail. Coloration varies slightly, but is usually dark green or blue on the back, shading through metallic blue-green to silver and white or off-white on the belly. A distinct gold or yellowish stripe runs along each flank of a freshly caught yellowtail kingfish.
Size: Large schools of yellowtail kingfish in the 1- to 4-kg range are often encountered, and school fish of 6 to 12 kg are relatively common in some areas, too. Bigger fish in the 15- to 30-kg range tend to form much smaller schools. The maximum growth potential of the yellowtail kingfish is in excess of 60 kg.
Distribution: Kingfish are found in the cool, temperate and subtropical waters of Australia, New Zealand and nearby islands, including Lord Howe and Norfolk. A similar or identical fish is found off the south-western coast of North America. Kingfish mainly frequent the waters around offshore reefs, pinnacles and islands, as well as inshore reef systems, large bays and even deep estuaries. They prefer fairly clean water with a temperature of 18°C or more, but will occasionally stray into cooler areas.
Fishing Techniques: The yellowtail kingfish is a strong, exciting game fish that strikes savagely at a wide range of lures, live baits and dead or cut flesh offerings. One of the most successful ways to take them is to present a live bait such as a slimy mackerel or yellowtail scad at the depth at which the kingfish are schooling. This may involve the use of a running or fixed sinker on the line. Slow-trolled, live baits, large, deep diving minnow lures and metal jigs worked vertically over the sea bed are also readily taken at times. Land-based anglers enjoy excellent sport with kingfish, especially when using high-speed metal lures, live baits and pilchards or garfish on ganged hooks. When all else fails, kingfish are particularly susceptible to a bait of whole, fresh or live squid.
Eating Qualities: The flavour and taste of kingfish flesh is good to very good in smaller fish, but tends towards dryness in large specimens. In some warmer areas, kingfish may be infested with parasites and occasionally suffer from a disease that causes the flesh to turn soft and milky when cooked, rendering the fish virtually inedible. For this reason, they are not a popular table fish in subtropical areas. It is important that all yellowtail kingfish intended for the table are bled and iced as soon as caught.

A yellowtail kingfish fresh from the water

Leatherjackets
Monacanthidae spp.

Rough leatherjacket

Yellow-finned leatherjacket

The six-spined leatherjacket is one of the most colourful members of this family

Common Names: There are at least 60 types of leatherjacket, 'leathery' or 'jacket' in Australian waters, 20 or more of which are sometimes taken by anglers. The more frequently captured species include the rough leatherjacket (*Scobinichthys granulatus*), six-spined leatherjacket (*Meuschenia freycineti*), yellow-finned leatherjacket (*M. trachylepis*), horseshoe leatherjacket (*M. hippocrepis*), Chinaman leatherjacket (*Nelusetta ayraudi*), mosaic leatherjacket (*Eubalichthys mosaicus*) and the estuary-dwelling fan-bellied leatherjacket (*Monacanthus chinensis*).

Description: This diverse and extensive group of relatively small, scaleless, rough-skinned fish has tiny mouths, beak-like teeth and a stout, serrated dorsal spine behind the head. Colour varies from the brightly hued six-spined leatherjacket to the drab and well-camouflaged rough and fan-bellied leatherjackets. Identifying each species can be difficult, but this is not usually important.

Size: Most leatherjackets are quite small. The estuarine fan-bellied leatherjackets rarely top 500 g, while at the other end of the scale, the six-spined and horseshoe varieties occasionally reach 2 kg. The giants of the family are the mosaic leatherjacket and the Chinaman, both of which occasionally exceed 3 kg.

Distribution: Leatherjackets are found right around Australia's coast, although they tend to be replaced by the closely allied trigger fishes (Balistidae) in tropical latitudes.

Fishing Techniques: Leatherjackets can be taken on almost any type of tackle. Most are caught on light handlines or the same rod and reel outfits used to catch bream, flathead and inshore snapper. When present in good numbers, leatherjackets are quite easy to catch, especially if a relatively small hook is used in conjunction with soft baits such as peeled prawns, worms, yabbies, cunjevoi, mussels, abalone gut or strips of fish flesh. Squid pieces make an excellent bait, too. Use long-shanked hooks or strong leaders so as to prevent leatherjackets biting through the line with their sharp, beak-like teeth.

Eating Qualities: The leatherjackets discussed here have white, sweet and slightly moist flesh and make very good to excellent table fish. There have been occasional reports of mild poisoning after eating some leatherjackets, particularly the Chinaman. This may be related to the fish's diet.

Long Tom
Belonidae family

Common Names: This group of very similar fish, all members of the family Belonidae, are usually called long tom, longtom, alligator gar or, more rarely, needlefish. Individual family members include the stout long tom (*Tylosurus gavialoides*), crocodilian long tom (*T. crocodilus*), slender long tom (*Strongylura leiura*), and barred long tom (*Ablennes hians*).

Description: These slender, silvery green fish, with their elongated jaws, are vaguely similar in appearance to garfish, but are distinguished by their two long jaws (garfish have only an extended lower jaw) and prominent, sharp teeth. Long tom also grow much larger than garfish. Coloration varies between long tom species, and ranges from green through blue to steely black on the back. Most are bright, metallic silver on the flanks and belly. Some species are barred or marked with dark 'thumbprints' or blotches along the flanks. Interestingly, the bones of most long tom are blue-green, like those of some wrasse and parrot fish.

Size: Depending on the species, long tom may be long and slender, or shorter and more stout. Some individuals grow to 1.8 m in length and may weigh more than 5 kg, although most measure 1 m or less, and weigh 200 g to 2 kg.

Distribution: Long tom are widespread throughout the tropical, subtropical and warmer temperate seas of the world. A species of long tom is also found in tropical freshwater rivers. Long tom will enter estuaries, particularly on a rising tide, although they usually prefer clear, warm and saline water. Travelling in ocean currents, long tom sometimes migrate well down the east coast and are taken from time to time around Newcastle, Sydney and even Jervis Bay.

Fishing Techniques: Long tom are rarely fished for specifically, and are usually taken on baits or lures intended for other tropical and subtropical species. Because of their long, tooth-filled jaws, they are very difficult to hook, especially on lures, which they often chase and strike at enthusiastically. Baits of fish strip, squid, pink nippers (yabbies) or prawns presented on sharp, long-shanked hooks or a ganged flight of hooks provide the best chance of landing a long tom.

Eating Qualities: Long tom are reasonable table fare, although there is little flesh on the more lightly built species. They also make useful baits. Smaller ones may be used live, and are popular among land-based anglers targeting tuna, big Spanish mackerel and sailfish from the ocean rocks, particularly in Western Australia.

Luderick
Girella tricuspidata

Common Names: This fish is rarely called by its official name anywhere outside of Victoria. In New South Wales and southern Queensland where most luderick are caught, they are widely known as blackfish or blackies. Big, sea-going luderick are sometimes nicknamed bronzies or square-mouths, while on Queensland's Gold Coast and Sunshine Coast, the species is erroneously referred to as black bream.

Description: The luderick is a small- to medium-sized omnivorous fish of the ocean and estuaries characterised by a small, relatively square mouth and comb-like teeth. Its coloration varies with its habitat. Estuary-dwelling fish are usually dark grey to purplish brown, overlaid by nine or more darker vertical stripes. Their bellies are creamy. Ocean fish often take on a brassy or bronze hue over their purple-brown base colour. However, they may also be a light blue-grey or grey with distinct dark stripes. Luderick fins, especially the tail, are darker.

Size: Most luderick taken by anglers weigh between 400 g and 1.2 kg. However, an occasional exceptional specimen may approach 3 kg, and the species has the potential to exceed 4 kg.

Distribution: Luderick are found around the south-eastern seaboard of Australia, from about Fraser Island or Maryborough in Queensland to western Victoria and north-eastern Tasmania. They are also reasonably prolific in New Zealand waters, particularly around the North Island.

Fishing Techniques: Blackfishing or 'riggering' is the traditional and time-proven method for taking these fish. A centrepin reel, long, fine rod and stemmed float are used to suspend a bait of green weed or 'cabbage' between 1 and 5 m beneath the surface of the water. The line to the hook should be fine, the hook small and sharp, and the float weighted so that the softest bite will sink it. Luderick are also taken on baits of peeled prawn, sand, squirt or bloodworm, cunjevoi, yabbies (nippers) and hermit crabs. In most areas, they take these baits best in late winter and spring. Whatever the method, the gear should be light, and hooks small.

Eating Qualities: Luderick are regarded as a fair to good eating fish, but should be bled and cleaned promptly. Those caught around the ocean rocks generally taste better than fish taken inside estuaries and rivers. Fillet and skin luderick intended for the table to help remove the slight taste of weed sometimes present in the flesh.

A luderick or blackfish taken from the ocean rocks

Mackerel, School, Spanish and Spotted
Scomberomorus commerson,
S. munroi,
S. niphonia and
S. queenslandicus

Spanish mackerel

Queensland school mackerel

Common Names: The larger narrow-barred Spanish mackerel (*Scomberomus commerson*) is commonly known as Spanish mackerel, Spanish or Spaniard. Other names include narrow-bar, mack and macko. In some parts of the world this species is called tanguigue, while in Fiji it is known as walu. A very closely related fish, the broad-barred Spanish or grey mackerel (*S. semifasciatum*), is sometimes confused with the narrow-barred Spanish mackerel. The smaller school and spotted mackerel are known by these names, as well as being called Queensland school mackerel, spotty, schoolie and doggie mackerel.

Description: The narrow-barred Spanish mackerel and various school mackerel are elongate fish with pointed noses and a row of very sharp teeth in each jaw. Their tails are deeply forked and there are a number of small finlets between the second dorsal and anal fins and the tail. The Spanish mackerel is usually green to dark green or blue on the back and silver on the flanks, with shimmers of purple and violet when fresh. Its flanks are overlaid with dark, wavy vertical bars of grey, dark green or purple-blue. The number of bars increases with the size of the fish. The smaller spotted and school mackerel are similar, but are characterised by the presence of spots or small blotches instead of the vertical bars of their larger cousin.

Size: Narrow-barred Spanish mackerel commonly weigh from 2 to 20 kg, although specimens from 40 to 55 kg are occasionally reported. Spotted and school mackerel are mostly taken at weights ranging from 1.5 to 6 kg, although they may, on rare occasions, top the 10-kg mark.

Distribution: The Spanish, school and spotted mackerels are tropical and subtropical, Indo-Pacific species. Although mainly found in northern latitudes, these fish do range as far south as Port Macquarie and Port Stephens on the east coast, and Rottnest Island in Western Australia. They are mainly open ocean and inshore fish, but will sometimes venture into bays, harbours and lower estuary reaches.

Fishing Techniques: These fast-swimming fish regularly fall to trolled or drifted live baits, whole dead fish and fish strips. They will also take whole or cut squid. Baits of dead garfish, mullet, tailor or wolf herring, rigged to swim in a natural manner when trolled behind a boat at 3 to 6 knots, are particularly effective. Lures such as skirted trolling heads, feather jigs, spoons and minnows — both bibbed and bibless — also account for excellent catches. From the shore, cast-and-retrieved metal lures, minnows or pilchards and garfish on ganged hooks work well.

Eating Qualities: The popular Spanish mackerel and its smaller cousins are delicious, white-fleshed table fish. They should be bled and iced immediately after capture for best results. Specimens weighing more than 10 kg or so are regarded as a definite ciguatera toxin poisoning risk in certain areas.

What fish is that?

Mackerel, Slimy
Scomber australicus

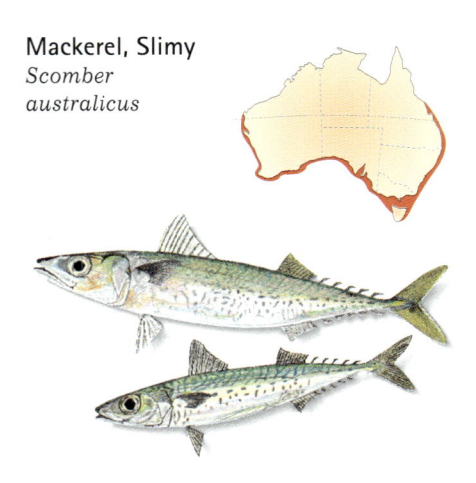

Common Names: Called blue mackerel in southern states and slimy mackerel or 'slimies' in the east, this fish is also known as the common or Pacific mackerel. It belongs to a worldwide family of small, but commercially important pelagic fishes.

Description: The slimy mackerel is a small, tuna-like fish of the family Scombridae, characterised by a nearly cylindrical body, narrow tail wrist, small finlets and a deeply forked tail. Coloration is dark blue to blue-green on the back when alive, turning silver-green after death. This base colour is overlaid with very dark blue or green wavy lines, dots and dashes. The belly is bright silver to silvery white, with mother-of-pearl reflections. The fins are lighter, except for the tail, which is dusky, sometimes with a tinge of yellow. Fish taken from offshore waters are generally more blue than green.

Size: Most slimy mackerel caught by anglers measure 20 to 35 cm and weigh from 100 to 700 g, although schools of 500-g to 1-kg fish sometimes move in to inshore areas, and rare specimens may top 1.5 kg.

Distribution: Slimy mackerel are found right around the southern part of the continent, in bays, harbours and large estuaries, and also far offshore in deep water near or even beyond the continental shelf. Juveniles and young adults generally frequent inshore grounds, while large adults form dense schools over reefs in 40 to 200 m of water.

Fishing Techniques: These hard-fighting little fish are usually taken on lightly weighted or unweighted baits of fish flesh strip, squid or peeled prawns presented on a small hook. Long-shanked hooks make unhooking easier. Slimy mackerel respond well to a berley trail of soaked bread and fish scraps mixed with a little tuna oil. Once excited, mackerel will bite ferociously and can be taken on small lures, white-painted barrel sinkers, flies, bait catching rigs and even bare hooks!

Eating Qualities: Although dark-fleshed and oily, the slimy mackerel has a fine flavour and makes an excellent smoked or pickled fish. However, most of those caught by anglers are used as bait, and they are superb for this purpose, especially when used live to tempt large predators such as kingfish and tuna. Mackerel also make fine dead baits, either whole, 'cubed' or cut into strips.

A slimy or blue mackerel taken on a minnow-style lure

Mangrove Jack
Lutjanus argentimaculatus

Common Names: The mangrove jack or jack is also called red bream or red chopper in some areas and, less commonly, dog bream or red perch. Mangrove jacks are occasionally confused with two similar or closely related fish: the sometimes poisonous red bass (*Lutjanus bohar*) and the fingermark bream (*L. johnii*).

Description: This deep-bodied, medium-sized member of the family Lutjanidae is characterised by large, dark eyes, powerful jaws and strong, canine teeth. The base colour varies from olive green through grey to a rusty ochre or brick red, usually overlaid with lighter or darker vertical stripes, but these are not always evident. A common colour variation features a darker centre on each scale, giving a spotted or chequered effect. Juveniles are particularly striking. Their vertical bands are pronounced and they have fine, electric blue lines around their eyes and a flush of crimson and yellow in their white-tipped ventral fins.

Size: Most jacks caught on hook and line weigh from 400 g to 2 kg, although 2.5- to 4-kg fish are reasonably abundant in more remote areas. Exceptional fish weighing up to 12 kg and more mainly come from offshore reefs.

Distribution: Although more common in tropical waters, mangrove jacks are found from about Sydney Harbour in the south-east, right around the northern half of the country to Shark Bay in Western Australia. They range from freshwater rainforest streams, down through the tidal reaches of coastal rivers, bays and harbours and out to adjacent headlands and reefs. Large adults may move several kilometres offshore to take up residence on deeper reefs or wrecks.

Fishing Techniques: The mangrove jack is one of the most sought-after tropical estuarine species. Many are taken on live or dead baits fished close to cover, or on lures—especially minnow-style plugs or wobblers—cast and retrieved or trolled from a boat, or cast from the river bank. Jacks are powerful, no-holds-barred battlers that will dive back into the snags and cut a line if given the slightest chance. Their strike is sudden and hard, often taking the angler by surprise.

Eating Qualities: The mangrove jack is a delicious, sweet-fleshed fish, although very large specimens tend to have somewhat dry and coarse flesh. If there is any doubt about its identity (such as with large, reef-caught fish) do not eat it, as the related red bass is a regular carrier of the ciguatera toxin.

A handsomely marked mangrove jack

Marlin, Black, Blue and Striped

Makaira indica, M. mazara and *Tetrapturus audax*

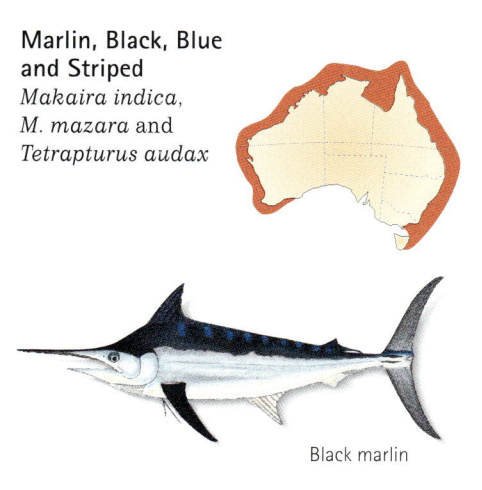

Black marlin

Common Names: All three marlin species are sometimes known as beakie, beak or stick-face, and may be collectively referred to as billfish. They are at times incorrectly called swordfish. Each species is commonly referred to by a shortening of its correct title: black, blue and striped or stripey.

Description: A heavy-shouldered, solidly built fish, the black marlin has a relatively short, stout bill and a low dorsal fin. It is characterised by rigid, non-folding, airfoil-shaped pectoral fins, although these fins are not necessarily fixed in fish less than about 45 kg in weight. The blue marlin is slightly less heavily built, and is usually longer for a given weight. The blue marlin's bill or spear is also longer than that of the black marlin, and its dorsal fin is higher, but not as high as that of the striped marlin. The striped marlin is the most lightly built and streamlined of the marlin found in our waters. It has a long, fine bill; flat, flexible pectoral fins and a very high dorsal fin which is higher than the fish's maximum body depth through the shoulders. Colour varies considerably between species and individuals, although live striped marlin usually display 12 to 14 clearly defined vertical bars on their flanks.

Size: Australian black marlin run from tiny juveniles weighing less than 10 kg up to world record-class fish in excess of 500 kg. Blue marlin in our waters are usually between 80 and 400 kg, while striped marlin rarely exceed 160 kg in weight.

Distribution: Black, blue and striped marlin are wide-ranging pelagic fish of the Pacific and Indian oceans, turning up in tropical, sub-tropical, temperate and even cool waters around our coastline. They prefer the open ocean, but often travel quite close to the coast of Australia, which has a relatively narrow continental shelf. Over the years, many small to medium black marlin have been landed by rock anglers in southern New South Wales.

Fishing Techniques: Because of their large size and strength, catching marlin demands the use of quality tackle kept in good repair. Trolling with lures and trolling with baits—either live or dead—and fishing at anchor or from a drifting boat with baits, live or dead, accounts for more than 90 per cent of the marlin taken in our waters. The best lures are Konahead-style skirted heads that run freely on the leader or trace. A lure of this pattern with a flat or slightly angled head, called a 'pusher', trolled at between 7 and 12 knots behind a moving boat, is a proven method of attracting marlin. Suitable live and dead baits range from 15-cm yellowtail scad or mullet, through 3-kg striped tuna and 5-kg mackerel tuna to whole 15-kg Spanish mackerel.

A large striped marlin taken in New Zealand waters clearly exhibits the vertical bars which give this species its name

A black marlin of more than 100 kg from southern New South Wales

Bait choice depends on location, strength of tackle and the ambitions of the angler. Rigging baits for trolling, especially dead baits which are pulled fairly quickly, is an acquired skill. Fine marlin have also been taken on live baits of tuna, bonito, salmon or kingfish hooked through the top jaw or bridle-rigged and trolled at walking pace near a current line or patch of bait. In lure fishing, the strike is instantaneous, as the drag is usually set at about a quarter to a third of the line's breaking strain. The hook either punches home or misses in the instant of the strike. However, if taken on a bait, marlin should be allowed to turn and run with the bait against minimal resistance for anything between 1 and 30 seconds before being struck.

Eating Qualities: Marlin of all sizes are fair to good table fish, although their relatively high mercury content precludes them from some commercial markets. The striped marlin, with its pinkish orange flesh, is generally considered the tastiest of the three.

What fish is that?

Morwong, Silver or Common
Nemadactylus douglasii

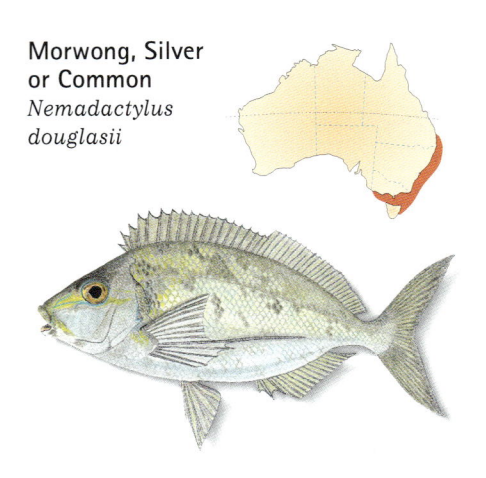

Common Names: The silver morwong is commonly known as the blue morwong in eastern waters, although this name can cause considerable confusion with the larger, more brilliantly coloured blue morwong or queen snapper of southern and western waters (*Nemadactylus valenciennesi*). Other names for the common silver morwong are rubberlip or blubberlip morwong, mowie and sea bream. The last is mainly used by fish shops and restaurants as a marketing ploy. A closely related, but smaller fish, the jackass morwong (*N. macropterus*), is a common trawl catch in southern waters and is taken by anglers fishing deep waters.

Description: The silver or rubberlip morwong is a deep-bodied fish with a small mouth and large, fleshy lips. As with all morwongs, several soft rays in each pectoral or side fin are extended into long 'fingers'. The morwong's colour ranges from smoky blue through grey to silver or silvery blue, although this species is never as brightly hued as the striking queen snapper (*N. valenciennesi*).

Size: The silver or rubberlip morwong grows in excess of 80 cm in length and may weigh more than 6 kg, although any specimen of more than 4 kg is exceptional. The typical size range of line-caught morwong is 600 g to 3 kg.

Distribution: The silver or rubberlip morwong is a fish of temperate and cool southern seas ranging from about southern Queensland to eastern Victoria and north-east Tasmania. These fish prefer deep reefs and gravel beds, but are often found in shallower waters than the closely related jackass morwong.

Fishing Techniques: Jackass and silver morwong are stand-bys of many deep sea anglers, and the mainstay of the 'head boat' or 'cattle boat' bottom-fishing charter industry in many areas. In deep water, morwong are taken on heavily weighted handlines or deck winch lines rigged with several hooks and baited with fish flesh, prawns or squid pieces.

Eating Qualities: The silver or rubberlip morwong is a highly palatable and popular table fish, although its flavour is perhaps inferior to snapper and flathead. It is also a little less tasty than the smaller jackass morwong and the larger queen snapper. For best results, morwong should be filleted and skinned before cooking, to help remove the slight iodine taint sometimes evident in their flesh. Remove the black lining inside the stomach cavity of these fish if baking them or cooking whole.

A common, silver or rubberlip morwong

Mullet, Sand, Sea and Yellow-eye
Myxus elongatus, Mugil cephalus and *Aldrichetta forsteri*

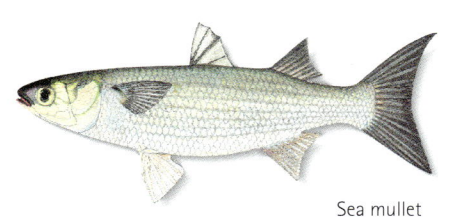

Sea mullet

Yellow-eye mullet

Common Names: The sand mullet is commonly known as the lano or tellegalene mullet in some areas, while the sea mullet is called bully mullet or simply bully, as well as hard-gut mullet and river mullet. The yellow-eye mullet is sometimes known as 'pilch' in some places, while juveniles of all three species are often called poddy mullet or 'poddies'.

Description: The sea mullet is a fat, cylindrical fish characterised by a thick, transparent, gelatinous covering over the eyes. Its colour varies, but is generally dark grey or green on the back with bright silver flanks and a silvery white belly. The sand mullet is much more streamlined, with a more pointed head and smaller eyes. A small, dark blotch is evident at the base of the sand mullet's pectoral fins. The yellow-eye mullet is characterised by its yellowish eyes and smaller, more easily dislodged scales.

Size: The sea or bully mullet is the giant of the mullet clan, although it is possibly rivalled by the tropical diamond-scaled mullet. Sea mullet commonly weigh from 600 g to 1.5 kg or more. Those taken commercially in beach netting operations often weigh between 1.5 and 3 kg, with exceptional giants approaching 5 kg. Sand and yellow-eye mullet are much smaller, rarely exceeding 700 g.

Distribution: Sea mullet are found right around Australia, but are more common along the stretch of east coast between central Queensland and southern New South Wales. They are a schooling fish at all sizes, especially when migrating along the coast, which they tend to do in autumn and early winter. The sand mullet is an estuarine and inshore fish of the southern half of the continent, ranging from southern Queensland to southern Western Australia, while the closely related yellow-eye mullet's range is confined to more southerly waters.

Fishing Techniques: Many mullet species are difficult to catch, but both the sand and yellow-eye can be taken on light tackle and small hooks baited with bread, dough, peeled prawn, cockle or pipi, worm pieces or maggots. Yellow-eye mullet are the more willing biters, and will even take flesh baits, squid strips and pieces of pilchard or whitebait. Most of the successful rigs for these species incorporate a light float, such as a quill or small bobby cork, although the fish can be taken on unweighted or very lightly weighted lines. They respond well to a berley trail of soaked bread. Sea mullet are generally harder to catch, but will bite at times.

Eating Qualities: Sea mullet rate as fair to good table fish, their oily, somewhat fatty flesh being well suited to smoking. Sand mullet are arguably the tastiest of the mullet clan. All mullet should be cleaned promptly if intended for the table.

Mulloway
Argyrosomus hololepidotus

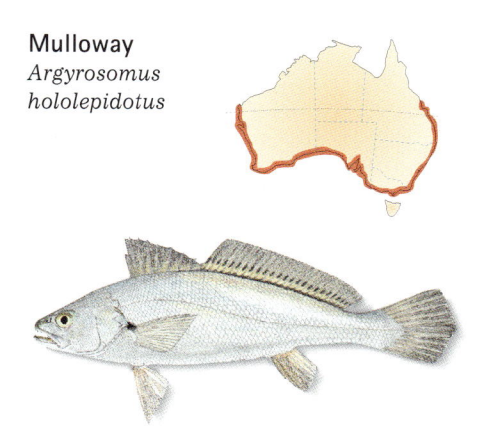

Many mulloway are taken from surf beaches, especially when tailor or other species are prolific

Common Names: In Queensland and New South Wales, the mulloway is almost exclusively known as jewfish, 'jew' or 'jewie'. In Victoria, South Australia and Western Australia, the official name of mulloway is more widely accepted. In South Australia, it is sometimes called a butterfish or buttery, while in the west it may be referred to as a river kingfish, silver kingfish or simply king. On the eastern seaboard, juvenile mulloway up to about 3 kg are frequently nicknamed soapies, while fish from 3 to 8 kg or so are commonly called schoolies. These fish should not be confused with the totally unrelated Western Australian jewfish or 'dhufish' (*Glaucosoma hebraicum*) of south-western waters, or with the eel-tailed catfish of freshwater rivers and lakes (Tandan family), which are also called jewfish in certain areas.

Description: A large, long-bodied, predatory fish of the ocean, estuaries and tidal rivers, the mulloway has a generous mouth, heavy scales and a convex spade-like tail. Colour varies with size and location from dark bronze or brassy green on the back to blue-green or even purple-blue. The flanks are lighter, often overlaid with a purplish sheen. The belly is silvery white. Sometimes the fish exhibits a distinct reddish tinge. Juveniles may be silvery all over. The fins are mainly dark and there is a well-defined black patch just above the base of the pectoral fins. When alive or freshly killed, mulloway have a string of bright spots along the lateral line. These and their rose-red eyes glow under artificial light.

Size: Soapies are small fish in the 400-g to 2.5-kg bracket; schoolies run up to about 8 kg; and adult fish range from 8 to 35 kg with rare giants to 45 kg and very occasionally beyond. The mulloway's maximum growth potential is probably in the order of 55 or 60 kg.

Distribution: Mulloway belong to a worldwide family of croakers, grunter and drum. In Australia, they are found from about Rockhampton in Queensland, around the southern half of the continent to at least Carnarvon and possibly Exmouth in the north of Western Australia. The mulloway is practically unknown in Tasmania. A closely related and very similar fish called the black jewfish occurs in northern, tropical waters. While mulloway can tolerate water that is almost completely fresh, they are rarely found so far upstream. Their usual haunts lie between the upper tidal limits of coastal rivers and inshore reefs a few kilometres off the coast.

Fishing Techniques: Smaller mulloway mainly succumb to baits of prawns, worms, yabbies or fish pieces intended for bream or flathead. They will also take small live baits. Larger fish are best sought with live baits such as mullet, yellowtail, slimy mackerel, pike, tailor and sweep, or dead baits of whole or cut fish. Tailor, luderick, pilchards and pike fillets are favourites in some areas. Squid, octopus and cuttlefish are also very good baits, especially if used live or very fresh. Despite their generous mouths, mulloway often fumble a bait or run with it for some distance before spitting it out. Using big sharp hooks and being willing to strike while the fish is running usually give the best results. Heavy rain and discoloured run-off are excellent for mulloway fishing. When flood waters cause a distinct colour change in the water at a river mouth, mulloway can readily be caught on lures. White, or red and white lead-head feathers, soft plastic-tailed jigs, large, strong-actioned minnows and so-called 'chair-leg' poppers or darters are the favoured choices of mulloway spinning specialists. These fish may also be taken on lures at other times, particularly at night in and around the pools of light created under illuminated bridges, breakwalls and wharves or piers. Mulloway are a strong, reasonably hard-fighting fish, and the capture of large specimens demands the use of sturdy tackle maintained in good working order.

Eating Qualities: The flesh quality of small fish is generally inferior to that of adults. Mulloway weighing more than 5 or 6 kg are very good table fare, despite their fairly strong smell. At weights of less than 3 kg, the flesh is often soft and rather flavourless, hence the nickname 'soapy'. Very large mulloway may have rather dry and slightly coarse flesh. Nonetheless, they are a popular table fish and command a high price at market.

A 16-kg mulloway from offshore waters in southern New South Wales

What fish is that?

Murray Cod
Maccullochella peeli

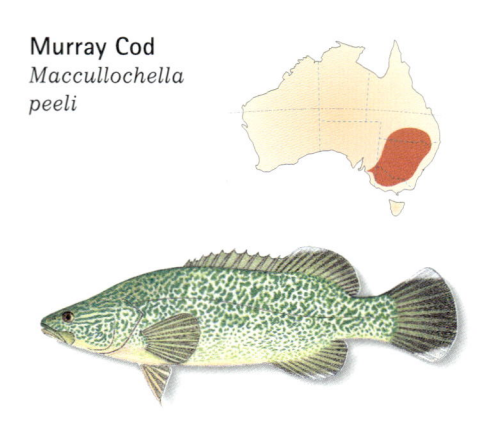

Common Names: Australia's most famous freshwater fish is nearly always known as Murray cod, or simply cod or Murray. It is unrelated to the true cod family and is actually a distant member of the perch group, which also contains the golden perch and Australian bass. Some anglers use the Aboriginal term 'goodoo' when referring to Murray cod. At least three or four closely related species of freshwater cod once also occurred in the eastern-flowing Clarence, Richmond, Brisbane and Mary River systems of northern New South Wales and southern Queensland. However, only the Clarence and Mary River species are known to have survived, and both populations remain threatened in the wild. The Clarence River or eastern cod (*M. ikei*) is protected in New South Wales waters, while catches of Mary River cod (*Maccullochella* spp.) are strictly controlled through bag limits and various other restrictions.

Description: The Murray cod is big, robust and barrel shaped, with a cavernous mouth and small eyes set well forward on the head. Colour varies depending on the environment, particularly on water clarity. Most Murray cod are olive green to yellow-green on the back, becoming yellowish on the flanks and creamy yellow or white on the belly. The back is overlaid with darker green or brownish green mottling and reticulations, which often extend well down the flanks. The eyes are usually brown. The second dorsal and tail or caudal fins typically have white margins, and sometimes such a margin is also found on the ventral fins. These white margins are particularly distinct and striking on fish from clear, fast-flowing streams.

Size: The giant of Australian outback rivers, and among the three or four largest freshwater species in the world, the Murray cod has the potential to reach more than 100 kg—early records tell of Murray cod up to 112 kg. Today, a 40-kg fish is very large indeed, and most of those seen by anglers weigh from 600 g to 10 kg, with a few 10- to 45-kg specimens still taken each year.

Distribution: The Murray cod was once found throughout almost the entire Murray–Darling river system, with the exception of its cold alpine and subalpine headwaters. Although its range has been reduced by dam and weir construction, de-snagging, pollution and overfishing, cod are still present in reduced numbers through most of their traditional distribution area. They have also been introduced into many dams and some eastern-flowing or coastal drainage systems. As already mentioned, a group of subspecies or separate species once existed in the eastern-flowing Clarence, Richmond, Brisbane and Mary rivers of northern New South Wales and southern Queensland.

Fishing Techniques: Traditionally, Murray cod were taken on heavy set-lines baited with yabbies, whole fish, rabbit pieces or even galah (parrot) breasts, or pieces of rabbit and kangaroo meat. Today, anglers have come to appreciate the sporting qualities of these fine fish and they are more often sought on medium or even lightweight tackle baited with live yabbies, bardi grubs, shrimps or small, live fish. Murray cod respond actively to lures, especially if visibility through the water exceeds 30 cm. Deep-diving plugs, metal spoons, spinnerbaits and bladed spinners all work well. A slow, steady retrieve or walking-pace troll is best.

Eating Qualities: The Murray cod is regarded as one of Australia's best outback table fish. The flavour of smaller fish is excellent, especially those taken from clearer streams. However, they tend to be rather oily over about 15 or 20 kg, and fish from very dirty water may have a muddy taint to their flesh. In deference to the Murray cod's increasing scarcity, many anglers release most of their catch. There is a closed season to protect spawning cod in many areas, usually from September until the end of November. There are also strict bag and size limits governing the taking of this very important, increasingly threatened freshwater native fish.

The Murray cod's marbled patterning is quite variable

A smaller fish from more discoloured water. Deep diving lures or plugs work well on the cod

A beautifully marked Murray cod from the New England plateau

Murray cod • nannygai • golden perch

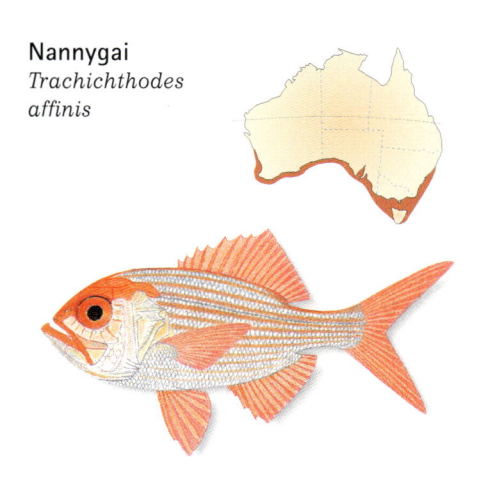

Nannygai
Trachichthodes affinis

Common Names: The nannygai, gai or nanny is also nicknamed 'goat' or 'nanny goat' by some anglers, and is almost always marketed commercially under the title of 'redfish'. Several related species occur around the Australian coastline, with the swallow-tail nannygai (*Centroberyx lineatus*) and red snapper (*C. garradi*) of Victoria, South Australia and southern Western Australian waters being the most significant.

Description: The nannygai is a small, deep-bodied and laterally compressed species, characterised by oversized eyes, large, rough scales and a cavernous mouth. Overall coloration varies from bright red to reddish orange, and grading to silvery white on the belly. The eyes are red around a large, black pupil.

Size: Most nannygai taken by anglers measure between 15 and 30 cm and weigh less than 750 g. However, in deeper water, 1-kg specimens are occasionally reported, and rare examples may approach or even exceed 1.4 kg. The red snapper of south-western waters grows considerably larger.

Distribution: The nannygai is a cool and temperate water fish, mainly found on offshore reefs, gravel beds and trawling grounds of 40 to 200 m in depth. It ranges from northern New South Wales to eastern Victoria, Bass Strait and eastern Tasmania.

Fishing Techniques: Nannygai are mostly an incidental catch taken while fishing over deep reefs for snapper and morwong, or drifting on broken ground for these same species and flathead. Nannygai will take most cut fish flesh baits, as well as prawns, squid and the like. They are also easily caught on multi-hook bait-catching jig rigs and small lures.

A large catch of nannygai aboard a commercial trawler

Eating Qualities: The nannygai is a fine table fish, with sweet, slightly moist, pinkish white flesh. There is a good deal of wastage with this species because of the large size of the fish's head in proportion to the rest of its body. As large bags of nannygai are common, however, this does not present a major problem. Nannygai should be filleted and skinned for best results. It should be noted that this species also makes an effective live bait for big yellowfin tuna, yellowtail kingfish and even marlin.

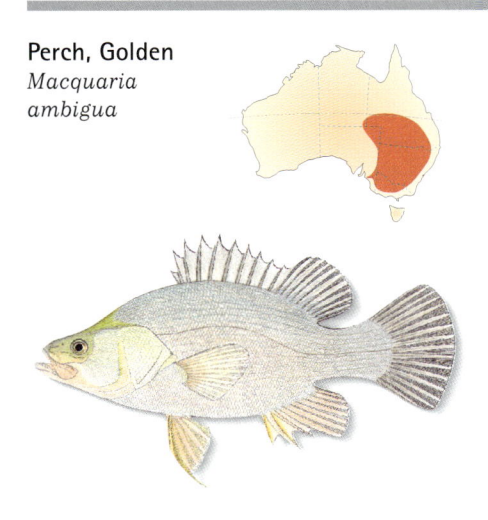

Perch, Golden
Macquaria ambigua

Common Names: This inland species is widely known throughout outback New South Wales and Queensland as the yellowbelly or yellow-belly. In South Australia and parts of Victoria, it is called callop, and at the fish markets, it is sometimes presented as Murray perch.

Description: A relatively large perch, this species has a convex tail margin and strongly concave or 'scooped' forehead profile. Body colour ranges from a handsome, dark coppery bronze with green reflections in clear water, though to pale, yellowish white in muddy locations. This fish is sometimes fairly barred or irregularly speckled, especially in clear water. The belly is usually creamy yellow, but sometimes appears bright lemon yellow.

Size: Most golden perch taken by anglers weigh from 200 g to 3 kg, although in some areas (particularly in lakes and dams) 4- to 6-kg specimens are not uncommon. Fish weighing more than 7 kg are highly prized, and 10-kg plus golden perch are exceptional. In the past, weights as great as 23 kg have been reported.

Distribution: The golden perch is the most widespread and prolific of all our large inland native fish, and is found in four states and both territories. Its natural range is thought to encompass most of the Murray–Darling river system, excluding the highest alpine headwaters; the Dawson–Fitzroy drainage system of central Queensland; Lake Eyre and the Coopers Creek system, and some coastal rivers in northern New South Wales and Queensland. These hardy fish have been introduced successfully into many dams and pondages from Townsville to Perth.

Fishing Techniques: The golden perch or yellowbelly taken by outback anglers are mainly caught on natural baits such as yabbies, shrimps, earthworms, wood or bardi grubs, and small live fish presented on or near the riverbed and close to snags. A willing lure striker, golden perch will

A very large golden perch of more than 6 kg

also take a variety of diving plugs, spoons, spinners, spinnerbaits, soft-tailed jigs and even flies. Bigger golden perch will hit very large lures intended for Murray cod.

Eating Qualities: The golden perch is rated by many experts as one of the tastiest of our inland natives. Specimens weighing less than 2 kg are generally superior in table quality to their larger kin. Fish from clean, slightly cooler water taste much better than those from hot, muddy waterholes or dams.

Perch, Macquarie
Macquaria australasica

Common Names: The Macquarie perch or Macquarie is also known as the 'Macca', mountain perch, white-eyed perch, bream or black bream. It is sometimes confused with silver perch (*Bidyanus bidyanus*), but the silver perch has a slightly concave or forked tail, as opposed to the Macquarie perch's convex or outwardly curving tail.

Description: The Macquarie perch is a medium-sized perch with a moderately large eye, small, slightly overshot mouth, prominently developed 'shoulder' or dorsal hump, scooped forehead profile and slightly convex or outwardly curving tail. A light-coloured area around the pupil of the eyes in adults is distinctive, explaining the common name of white-eyed perch. Coloration ranges from almost coal black through smoky grey to greenish brown on the back, paler on the flanks and cream or creamy yellow on the belly. Juveniles may be mottled. The Macquarie perch's fins are dark, sometimes with a purplish tinge, although the pelvic fins are lighter, often with a white leading margin.

Size: These days, the average Macquarie perch caught on rod and reel weighs between 200 and 800 g, although in Victoria's Dartmouth Dam, 900-g to 1.4-kg fish are reasonably common, and 2-kg specimens are not completely unknown. This relatively short-lived perch may very occasionally reach weights of more than 3 kg, if optimum conditions prevail.

Distribution: The Macquarie perch frequents the higher, cooler reaches of the Murray–Darling system, ranging well into subalpine waters at times. An identical or very closely related fish is also found in the headwaters of coastal drainages, including the Shoalhaven, Nepean and Woronora Rivers of coastal New South Wales, and in the Mitta Mitta and Snowy River systems of Victoria. It also occurs in a few dams or impoundments in both states, and in the Australian Capital Territory. Macquarie perch have been successfully introduced into Melbourne's Yarra River. They prefer slightly faster, clearer and cooler water than golden perch.

Fishing Techniques: Techniques for catching Macquarie perch are basically the same as those described for golden and silver perch, but with increased emphasis on small baits, lures and flies. This species will also take insect and insect larvae baits, such as grasshoppers and mudeyes, as well as artificial flies intended for trout.

Eating Qualities: The Macquarie perch is a very good to excellent table fish, with a taste and texture not unlike, but possibly superior to, that of the Australian bass. Populations of this fish have seriously declined in many areas, and it is now totally protected in New South Wales. In Victoria, many anglers opt to release the majority of Macquarie perch taken, especially during the spawning run in spring and late summer.

This large Macquarie perch from Victoria's Dartmouth Dam clearly shows the light-coloured eyes and body coloration typical of the species

---

Perch, Silver
Bidyanus bidyanus

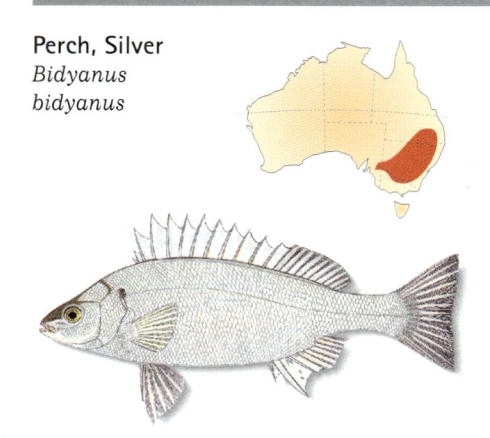

Common Names: The silver perch or 'silver' is also known as the bidyan, grunter, perch, black bream, bream and terapon. With its relatively tiny scales and slightly concave or forked tail, the silver perch is quite distinctive. It is unlikely to be confused with any other southern and central freshwater fish, native or exotic, with the possible exception of the smaller spangled perch or 'bobby cod' (*Leiopotherapon unicolour*), which has a stouter body and larger mouth than the silver perch, and is usually mottled.

Description: The silver perch actually belongs to the Teraponidae or grunter family. This perch species is characterised by its slightly concave or inwardly curving tail margin, relatively small mouth, small scales, small eyes and fairly straight forehead profile, which contrasts with the scooped foreheads of both golden and Macquarie perch. Silver perch vary in colour from nearly jet black through smoky grey to olive green, gold or silver. Most are lighter on the belly, and juveniles may be mottled or faintly barred. A distinct scale pattern is usually visible.

Size: The majority of silver perch taken by anglers weigh between 200 g and 1.8 kg, with very rare specimens reaching 3 kg or more, especially in dams. The species' maximum growth potential is probably close to 7 or 8 kg, but they are almost never seen at such sizes.

Distribution: The silver perch is a native Australian freshwater fish found through most of the Murray–Darling system, including subalpine regions, and also in the Coopers Creek drainage system. Silver perch have been introduced into many dams and lakes, and some eastern-flowing streams. A very similar or identical species occurs in the Fitzroy–Dawson and some other Queensland coastal systems. Silver perch prefer running water with a sand, mud or gravel bottom, but also thrive in dams—both large and small. Sadly, their numbers have declined dramatically in many outback rivers, due to habitat modification, pollution and overfishing.

Fishing Techniques: When silver perch are specifically targeted, anglers tend to use lighter tackle, smaller hooks and a little more finesse than is commonly employed in catching the larger outback natives. Silver perch spend much of their time feeding on algae and freshwater plankton, but will readily take baits of worm, shrimp, insects or peeled yabby tail. Small spoons, spinners and diving plugs also attract them, and occasionally these territorial and aggressive little fish will chase and hit big lures intended for cod or golden perch.

Eating Qualities: The silver perch, with its fine bones, is often rated as the least appealing of the outback natives when it comes to the culinary department. Nonetheless, it is rapidly becoming a popular and profitable subject for aquaculture or fish farming. Silver perch from turbid waters often have a weedy or muddy flavour, although those from clean water are quite tasty.

Macquarie perch • silver perch • queenfish   361

Queenfish
Scomberoides commersonnianus and *S. lysan*

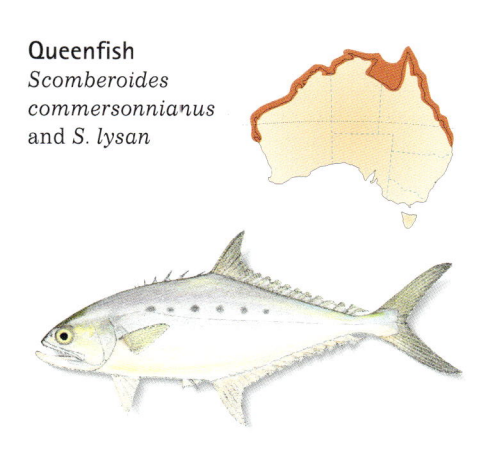

Common Names: The queenfish or queenie is popularly known in the Northern Territory and in other parts of tropical Australia as the skinny fish or skinny. In other parts of the world, this species or closely related fish are also called leatherskin or whitefish. Although several species of queenfish are found in Australian waters, the common queenfish (*Scomberoides commersonnianus*) and *S. lysan* are by far the largest and most important species to anglers.

Description: The common queenfish (*Scomberoides commersonnianus*) is a long, fairly deep and extremely laterally compressed saltwater and estuarine fish of tropical waters. It is typically dark green along the top of the back and metallic silver to silvery white on the flanks and belly, sometimes with a yellowish tinge. A series of oval-shaped blotches forms a broken line along each flank of this fish.

Size: Most queenfish caught by anglers weigh from 800 g to 8 kg, with occasional specimens weighing up to 10 or even 12 kg, and very rare giants of about 15 kg being taken.

Distribution: A tropical fish, the queenfish is rarely found in large numbers far south of the Tropic of Capricorn, although stragglers are sometimes taken in Queensland's Hervey Bay and even Moreton Bay and the Southport Seaway in southern Queensland. They also turn up in reasonable numbers in and around Shark Bay in Western Australia.

Fishing Techniques: This exciting sport fish falls for live baits, dead baits, fish strips and pilchards or garfish on ganged hooks, as well as various lures and flies. With lures, the emphasis should be on movement and speed, which will excite the fish. Fast trolled or rapidly retrieved sliced chrome lures, poppers, spoons, minnows and saltwater flies are all excellent choices. A wire or heavy monofilament nylon leader is advisable when pursuing queenfish, as their hard, sharp-edged jaws and small teeth can easily damage light nylon fishing line.

Eating Qualities: The queenfish has firm, white meat with an excellent flavour, although it does tend towards dryness. Smaller specimens are not generally popular for eating because of the very thin fillets and excessive wastage. This fish should be bled and iced after capture. As well as lending itself to a range of cooked dishes, queenfish flesh is also well suited to serving raw, marinating, pickling and smoking. Small, whole queenfish also make excellent baits for marlin, sailfish and other large tropical predators.

Top left: A 500-g silver perch from an inland lake. These fish are also known as grunter or bream
Bottom left: Silver perch have been stocked in many dams and lakes around the country
Top right: This 3- or 4-kg queenfish was taken on light fly fishing tackle in northern Queensland

What fish is that?

Redfin
Perca fluviatilis

A better-than-average redfin weighing more than 1 kg

Common Names: This introduced freshwater fish is commonly known in Australia as the redfin, redfin perch or 'reddie'. However, its more correct name is European perch or English perch. In western and central Europe, this species is simply called perch.

Description: A relatively deep-bodied fish with a smallish head and scooped or concave forehead profile, the redfin is characterised by its very high, spiky first dorsal fin. The tail is small in relation to the rest of its body. Coloration is olive green on the back, creamy on the belly with six or more dark green to khaki bands running down each flank. The fins, particularly the pectoral, ventral and anal fins, are usually bright red or crimson.

Size: In the years immediately following the introduction of redfin to a waterway, catches of 500-g to 2-kg specimens are reasonably common. Overpopulation quickly stunts the average length to 15 or 20 cm, however, and reduces weights to less than 300 g. Rare examples have been known to exceed 3 kg and the species has been recorded in Australia to at least 5 kg, which is heavier than the largest perch found in European waters.

Distribution: Native to Europe, the introduced redfin is now widespread throughout much of the Murray–Darling river system, as well as in many other inland rivers, lakes, dams, ponds and swamps throughout New South Wales, the Australian Capital Territory, Victoria, South Australia, Tasmania and southern Western Australia. The redfin prefers warm, slow-moving water with plenty of cover, weed growth and a good population of small fish. It does well in dams, lakes and pondages below alpine levels.

Fishing Techniques: Redfin are mainly taken on worms, shrimps, yabbies, as well as live minnows, gudgeons and other small fish species (where the use of such baits is permitted by law). They are very susceptible to a wide range of lures — particularly spinners, spoons, jigs, bobbers and minnows — and also to various wet flies. One of the most productive techniques is to drop a weighted lure, jig or specially designed bobber to the bottom near cover such as drowned timber, and to jig this offering up and down using short, erratic jerks of the rod tip.

Eating Qualities: A tasty, if slightly dry table fish, the redfin should be skinned, as its scales are almost impossible to remove in the conventional manner. All redfin caught should be killed, as they are regarded as something of a pest in our waters. On no account should live redfin be transported from one area to another.

Sailfish, Indo-Pacific
Istiophorous platypetrus

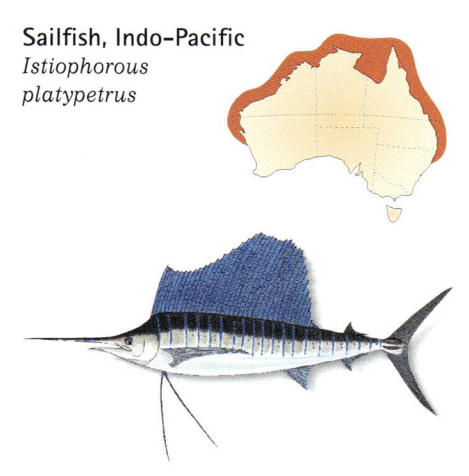

Preparing to release an Indo-Pacific sailfish

Common Names: The Indo-Pacific sailfish is also known as the sail, spear-chucker or spearfish, although the two latter names may cause confusion with the related, but rare, short-billed spearfish (*Tetapturus angustirostris*).

Description: The Indo-Pacific sailfish is a long but lightly built pelagic game fish, with a top jaw that extends into a long, slender bill or spear, and an extremely high and ornate dorsal fin. Colouring is usually electric blue to blue-green, darker on the back and overlaid with broken vertical bars and dashes of lavender or powder blue. Some sailfish have a golden or coppery flush to the gill covers and flanks when alive, especially if stressed or tired. The sail-like dorsal fin is dark, steely blue with many blue-black or purple spots and broken dashes.

Size: Sailfish grow to almost 4 m in length and up to 100 kg in weight, but are more common at half that length and weights of 15 to 45 kg. The biggest sailfish found in Australian waters have come from the Whitsunday Islands in Queensland, and the waters around Lord Howe Island.

Distribution: Indo-Pacific sailfish are found throughout the tropical and subtropical areas of the Indian and Pacific oceans. A very closely related fish is found in the Atlantic, where it is usually smaller in size. Sailfish are surface and mid-water wanderers, preferring to hunt in warm currents and upwellings over inshore grounds and out towards the edge of the continental shelf.

Fishing Techniques: Sailfish caught by anglers in Australia are mainly taken on trolled, rigged baits of garfish or mullet, pulled behind a boat travelling at 4 to 8 knots, or small to medium live baits drifted or cast close to feeding 'pods' of sails or bait fish schools. They will readily strike fast-trolled lures such as jet-heads and straight-running skirted heads pulled at 8 to 15 knots. However, many of these strikes fail to result in hook-ups, because of the sailfish's long bill and hard mouth. In northern Western Australia, a growing number of sailfish are being taken on live baits from the ocean rocks. In the same area as well as in Queensland and Northern Territory waters, adventurous fly rodders also target these fish on saltwater fly tackle after teasing them to the surface with hookless baits or lures trolled behind a boat. In Australia, Indo-Pacific sailfish are pursued primarily for the superb sport they provide on light tackle, and the majority of those caught are tagged and released.

Eating Qualities: Although not regarded as good table fare by some people, the Indo-Pacific sailfish is quite palatable. Its dark, somewhat sinewy flesh is ideally suited for smoking.

Salmon, Australian
Arripis trutta

Common Names: Unrelated to the true salmon of the northern hemisphere, the Australian salmon is nicknamed 'sambo' by some anglers, and known in its juvenile stages in Victoria, Tasmania and South Australia as a salmon trout or bay trout. Very large examples are sometimes called black backs. In New Zealand, this species is called kahawai.

Description: The Australian salmon or kahawai is a medium-sized, elongate marine fish with a nearly cylindrical body and a large, forked tail. It is almost always bluish green to black on the upper back, silver to greenish silver or purplish silver on the flanks and silvery white on the belly. The back is patterned with darker green spots which extend down onto the flanks. The eye is yellowish around the dark pupil. The fins are light coloured, except that the dusky tail often has a dark trailing edge and a light leading margin to the lower lobe.

Size: Most Australian salmon taken by anglers weigh between 200 g and 3.5 kg. The eastern sub-species may very occasionally reach 6 kg, while the western fish has been reported at weights of up to 10 kg or slightly more. New Zealand kahawai grow even larger on rare occasions.

Distribution: A migratory, pelagic or semi-pelagic species of our cool and temperate waters, salmon are found right around the southern seaboard, up the east coast at least as far as Port Macquarie in New South Wales and sometimes northwards along the west coast to about Geraldton. The fish is also prolific around much of New Zealand's coastline. The Australian salmon is a near-shore species, found largely in estuaries, bays, harbours, along beaches and rocky shorelines and also out on deeper reefs, particularly in the south. Salmon frequently hunt in areas of strong wave or current action.

Fishing Techniques: Australian salmon are commonly taken on baits of cut fish flesh, whole pilchards and garfish on ganged hooks, bottle squid or squid pieces, prawns, beach worms and pipis. They will also occasionally take crabs, cunjevoi or even bread, particularly in a berley trail. Large specimens will take live yellowtail or mullet baits.

An Australian salmon or kahawai taken on fly fishing tackle

They prefer lightly weighted or moving baits rather than those anchored to the bottom. Salmon are also avid lure and fly takers. They succumb to cast and retrieved or trolled metal slices, lead slugs, spoons, spinners, jigs, minnows, plugs, poppers, and streamer flies. Because of their habit of jumping and shaking their heads, many salmon hooked on lures are lost.

Eating Qualities: The Australian salmon provides reasonable table fare. A dark-fleshed, strongly flavoured fish, it is suitable for smoking, baking or being made into fish cakes. Australian salmon is popular in Tasmania, Victoria and parts of South Australia and Western Australia, but not highly regarded as a table fish in New South Wales. In areas where it is unpopular table fare, this fine sporting fish should always be carefully released to fight again.

What fish is that?

Salmon, Threadfin
Polynemidae spp.

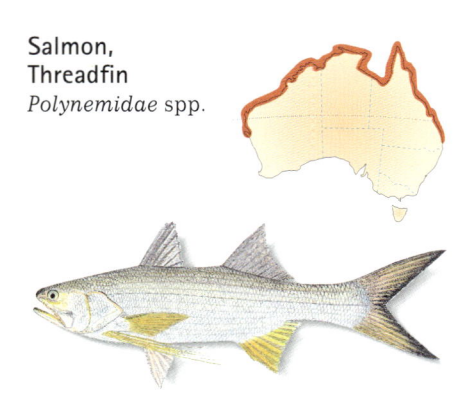

Common Names: There are several species of this tropical inshore and estuarine fish found in Australian waters. The best known and most popular are the blue threadfin (*Polydactylus sheridani*) and the larger golden or giant threadfin, also known as the king salmon (*Eleutheronema tetradactylum*). Other names for these fish include Sheridan's threadfin, Burnett salmon, Cooktown salmon and giant salmon.

Description: Members of this group of related fish are characterised by their overshot upper jaws; hard, bony head; and long, filamentous rays ahead of the pectoral fin area. They also have a thick, transparent, gelatinous covering over the eyes, known as an adipose eyelid. The coloration of threadfin salmon varies from blue to bluish grey or green on the back, through to brassy gold in some species. The flanks are usually silvery white or grey, and the belly creamy. The fins are mainly dusky, although the ventral and anal fins may sometimes be strongly tinged with yellow.

Size: The average size of threadfin salmon varies with species and location. The more commonly caught blue threadfin (*P. sheridani*) usually weighs from 500 g to 3 kg. The larger golden threadfin or king salmon (*E. tetradactylum*), however, often weighs from 5 to 10 kg, or even up to 15 kg. Rare specimens can top 18 kg in weight.

Distribution: An inshore family of the tropical north, the threadfin extends as far south as Hervey Bay in the east and Shark Bay in the west. These fish are mainly found in northern estuaries, where they range upstream at least as far as the tidal limit. Threadfin are also encountered in bays, inlets, harbours and over coastal mud and sand flats. They are rarely found far from shore or in deep water.

Fishing Techniques: Threadfin salmon are taken both deliberately and incidentally, often by anglers pursuing barramundi and other tropical sport fish. They show a preference for live or very fresh baits of herring, mullet, prawns or crabs, but will also take cut fish flesh, particularly a strip or slab of wolf herring or some other oily fish with a bright, silvery skin. Threadfin salmon will strike at lures and flies, particularly smaller models. The blue threadfin is a more common lure-fishing catch in most areas than the larger golden or giant threadfin.

Eating Qualities: Threadfin are superb table fish. In the north, they are rated more highly by some than the barramundi, although their flesh does not respond well to freezing or rough handling. All specimens intended for the table should be cleaned promptly and chilled.

Blue salmon are generally smaller than golden or giant threadfin and lack prominent sensory 'whiskers' ahead of their pectoral fins

Samson Fish
Seriola hippos

Common Names: The Samson fish or Samsonfish is also known as the sea kingfish, particularly in Western Australia, where it is reasonably prolific. This species is often confused with the amberjack (*Seriola dumerili*) and, more rarely, with the yellowtail kingfish (*S. lalandi*), both of which are closely related to the Samson fish.

Description: The Samson fish is a medium to large, deep-bodied predatory fish, distinguished from the amberjack primarily by the number of its fin rays and gill rakers. The Samson fish has from 23 to 25 soft rays in its second dorsal fin, while the amberjack has between 29 and 35 soft fin rays. The coloration of the Samson fish is variable. Adults are normally blue-green to green-gold or bronze on the back, paler on the flanks and yellowish white on the belly. Younger fish are often reddish bronze with fairly distinct vertical blotches and bars of very dark brown or black on the back and upper flanks. These bars tend to fade with age. The Samson fish's teeth and mouth lining are often red-tinged, but this is not a diagnostic feature. The fins are typically reddish yellow or dusky.

Size: Samson fish grow to at least 50 kg in weight, although specimens weighing more than 30 kg are exceptional. Juveniles in the 500-g to 5-kg range are seasonally abundant in some areas.

Distribution: The Samson fish is an Australian species, confined mainly to temperate and sub-tropical waters, but occasionally found in cooler southern seas. Healthy populations occur off some southern Queensland ports and offshore from Coffs Harbour, South West Rocks and Nambucca Heads in northern New South Wales. The fish are relatively uncommon, however, elsewhere on the east coast, although schools of juveniles sometimes frequent the Jervis Bay area of southern New South Wales during summer. Samson fish are far more frequently found in the west, where they range from the Recherche Archipelago to about Shark Bay. This species prefers similar habitats to the yellowtail kingfish.

Fishing Techniques: Methods and tackle used for taking Samson fish are much the same as those described for yellowtail kingfish, with particular emphasis on deep-fished live and dead baits, squid and heavy jigs. The Samson fish is a strong, determined fighter and big specimens demand the use of quality tackle.

Eating Qualities: Small- to medium-sized Samson fish make quite good table fare. They have white, slightly dry meat. Larger fish, however, tend to be too dry and coarse for most tastes. All Samson fish intended for the table should be killed promptly, bled and kept on ice.

threadfin salmon • Samson fish • saratoga

Saratoga
Scleropages leichhardti and *S. jardini*

Common Names: The two closely related and almost identical saratoga species found in Australian waters are sometimes distinguished by the names northern saratoga (*Scleropages jardini*) and Dawson River saratoga (*S. leichhardti*). Both are also called 'toga by some anglers. These fish were once known as spotted barramundi or Dawson River barramundi. These latter two names should be discouraged, however, as they lead to considerable confusion with the true barramundi (*Lates calcarifer*).

Description: These striking, rather prehistoric-looking members of the small, ancient and international family of fresh and brackish water fish called Osteoglossids are characterised by an elongated, very laterally compressed body; a huge, upturned mouth; very large scales and the presence of small barbels or whiskers under the lower lip. Both species of saratoga are greenish grey to brown on the back and silvery green or coppery gold on the flanks. The belly is lighter. An orange spot on each scale is common. The saratoga's fins are similar to, or darker than, its body colour. These species are mouth-brooders. Their relatively few, large eggs are hatched in the mouth of the female where the juveniles stay until ready to fend for themselves.

Size: Saratoga encountered by anglers usually weigh from 500 g to 3 kg, with prize specimens reaching more than 4 kg in weight. The northern species is generally considered to grow larger than its southern cousin, but both may very rarely weigh as much as 8 kg. In Papua New Guinea, a saratoga similar or identical to *S. jardini* very occasionally exceeds 12 or 13 kg.

Distribution: As mentioned, there are two species of saratoga in Australia: one found in the Dawson–Fitzroy system of central Queensland (*S. leichhardti*) and the other ranging widely, but discontinuously, through western Cape York, the Gulf Country and the eastern Northern Territory (*S. jardini*), west to about Darwin or slightly beyond. This species of saratoga may also occur in small numbers in a few eastern-flowing drainages near the tip of Cape York Peninsula, and a similar or identical fish also occurs in southern Papua New Guinea and Irian Jaya. The Dawson River species (*S. leichhardti*) has been introduced into several other rivers in central and southern Queensland, as well as dams as far south as Brisbane and Noosa.

Fishing Techniques: Many saratoga are caught by anglers pursing barramundi in tropical waterholes, lagoons and rivers. However, these days more and more sport anglers are specifically targeting these exciting and challenging fish. Baits of live or fresh dead herring, frogs and large insects will all take saratoga, but this fine sporting fish responds more readily to lure-casting with spoons, spinners, plugs, smaller minnows and poppers. Saratoga are also superb fly-rod targets.

Eating Qualities: The saratoga is an inferior table fish with soft, rather tasteless flesh and many fine bones. All saratoga should be released unharmed because of their slow growth rate, poor eating qualities and limited habitats.

Top left: The long sensory 'whiskers' of the threadfin salmon are one of this species' key characteristics
Bottom left: A juvenile Samson fish from northern New South Wales showing clearly defined patterning and a dark, diagonal stripe through the eyes
Top right: A large northern saratoga taken on fly fishing tackle on the western side of Cape York Peninsula

Shark, Gummy and School
Mustelus antarcticus and *Galeohinus galeus*

Gummy shark

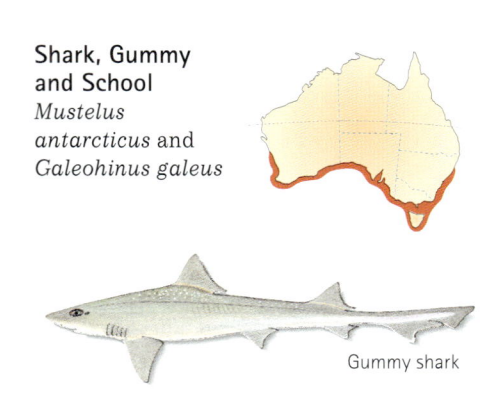

Common Names: The gummy shark or gummy (*M. antarcticus*) is often confused with the similar-looking school shark (*G. galeus*). Both belong to the family Triakidae. Other names for the school shark include tope and snapper shark, and the flesh of both species is usually marketed as 'flake'.

Description: The gummy shark is a long, relatively lightly built shark. The second dorsal fin is almost as large as the first, and both are slightly rounded at the top. There is a small tentacle or whisker adjacent to each nostril. Its back is dusky grey to greenish grey or greenish brown, fading to white or cream on the belly. The back and upper flanks are sprinkled with small, light-coloured spots. The school shark or tope is more streamlined. The first dorsal fin is considerably larger than the second and the snout is more pointed, giving it a whaler-like appearance. There are no obvious tentacles or whiskers around the nostrils. The school shark's back is grey to bronze, fading gradually to white or cream on the belly, and it has no obvious light spots. The most conclusive way of distinguishing these two edible sharks is by examining their teeth. The gummy shark has flat, grinding molars arranged like the cobbles in a footpath, while the school shark has small, sharp, cutting teeth.

Size: The gummy shark grows to a maximum of about 1.7 m in length and 30 kg in weight, although it is more common at half that size. The school shark or tope is larger, occasionally reaching 1.8 m in length and 30 to 35 kg.

Distribution: Gummy sharks are found in the waters of central and southern New South Wales, Victoria, Tasmania, South Australia and around the Western Australian coast to about Geraldton or Shark Bay. They prefer deeper, offshore waters, but will range along beaches and rocky foreshores and occasionally enter large, deep estuaries, harbours and bays. School sharks range through our temperate and cool to cold waters, from southern Queensland to about Geraldton in Western Australia. They are also found in Tasmania and New Zealand. Their habitat preferences are similar to those of the gummy shark.

Fishing Techniques: Both these shark species, particularly the gummy, are eagerly targeted by southern anglers. Most are taken by surf-casting anglers along ocean beaches and around the mouth of larger estuaries and bays, but many are also landed by boat anglers working offshore grounds, bays and harbour waters. Many are also taken, or at least hooked, by anglers targeting snapper, flathead and salmon. Best baits for both species are reasonably large slabs of fresh fish, whole pilchards or garfish, squid or octopus. In their larger sizes, both these sharks are strong and active fighters.

A small whaler shark from tropical waters. Whalers are often mistaken for school sharks

Eating Qualities: These are highly rated table fish, especially in southern states, where flake is the standard accompaniment to potato chips. Both species have firm, white meat and no true bones. To improve the flavour, kill and bleed by severing the head and tail immediately after capture.

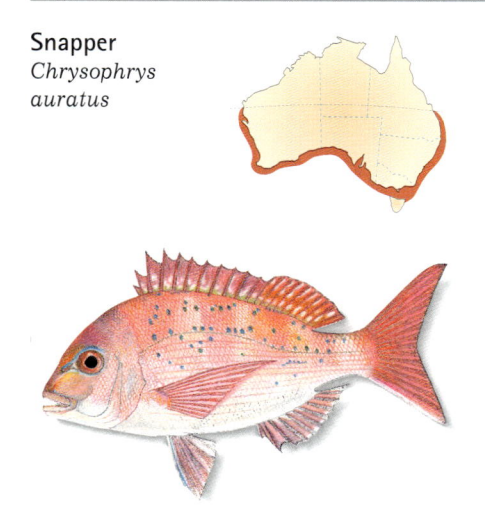

Snapper
Chrysophrys auratus

Common Names: As one of Australia's most popular and important species, the snapper has an array of alternative names. Red, big red and reddie are amongst the most common. Throughout much of Western Australia, it is called pink snapper, in order to distinguish it from several unrelated species, while for international record-keeping purposes, the same fish is also referred to as squire fish. Snapper also have different names at various sizes in some regions. There was once a strongly established system of size-gradation amongst east coast snapper anglers. The smallest fish were known as cockney bream, cockneys or cockies, the next size up were red bream, then squire, then snapper and, finally, the largest were old man snapper. Thankfully, this archaic system is now largely a thing of the past. However, in Victoria and parts of New South Wales smaller snapper—from legal length up to 1 kg or so in weight—are often called pinkies, while the same fish in South Australia are known as ruggers.

Description: The snapper is a deep-bodied fish with powerful jaws and strong, peg-like teeth. Larger adults often exhibit a distinct hump or bump on the head, and sometimes an enlarged nose area, but this is by no means universal. In New Zealand waters, snapper almost never develop these humps and lumps, and in Victoria and South Australia, some very large specimens have practically no hump. Coloration varies from

A catch of small snapper

one locality to another. Fish caught in deep water over hard reef tend to be a much brighter red than those taken on sand or mud. Typical coloration is red to pinkish silver or coppery on the head and back, rosy silver with blue reflections on the flanks, and silver or silvery white on the belly. The flanks are heavily peppered with small, iridescent blue spots. Fins are usually dusky red and the anal fin is often edged with blue. The bottom lobe of the tail may be white along its leading edge.

Size: Outside South Australia and New Zealand, an 8- or 9-kg snapper is the catch of a lifetime. The majority of snapper taken off the east and south-east coasts today weigh from 400 g to 5 kg. Even in Victoria's Port Phillip Bay — once renowned for big reds — fish weighing more than 9 kg cause large crowds to gather at the cleaning tables. Many 8-kg plus snapper are still taken around New Zealand's North Island, although, even here, 10-kg plus specimens are rare. In parts of South Australia, snapper sometimes average 8 or 9 kg and regularly exceed 12 kg. The one location where snapper grow even larger is Norfolk Island, where occasional specimens as heavy as 18 kg have been recorded.

Distribution: A member of a worldwide family with close relatives in Japan, North America, the Mediterranean and South Africa, the snapper is found right around the southern half of the continent, from at least Rockhampton in Queensland to Carnarvon in Western Australia. However, it is practically unknown in Tasmanian waters, at least outside of Flinders Island, the Tamar estuary and certain other north coast locations. In New Zealand, this fish is found right around the North Island, and as far down the east coast of the South Island as Christchurch. Snapper also occur around Norfolk Island and, sporadically, near Lord Howe Island. Ideal habitat for snapper includes open ocean reef or gravel-bottomed grounds 20 to 150 m deep, particularly those close to structures such as pinnacles, headlands, islands and bomboras. In southern waters, large spawning-related migrations of snapper occur in relatively shallow sand- and mud-bottomed bays

Fishing Techniques: Because of the diversity of environments in which they live and the size range of the fish themselves, techniques and tackle for snapper fishing vary immensely. For example, a surf-caster on New Zealand's Ninety Mile Beach will use very different gear to that employed by a party boat customer fishing the sea bed in 100 m of water off Coffs Harbour, or a small boat angler chasing finicky winter reds in the shallows of Geelong's Corio Bay. However, there are some basic guidelines. In water of less than 40 m, the best results will usually be enjoyed by anglers using unweighted or lightly weighted baits of cut fish flesh, particularly tuna, bonito, whole or cut pilchards, garfish pieces, squid, octopus, prawn and crabs. In deeper water, sinkers weighing between 100 g and 1 kg may be needed to take the bait or baits to the fish. Here prawns, squid and cut fish are often the favoured options. Rock-hoppers and surf-casters mainly use 60- to 120-g sinkers and baits of octopus, squid, pilchard or cut fish flesh. However, at dawn and dusk, and after heavy seas, good fish can be taken close to the rocks on unweighted or lightly weighted 'floaters' Big snapper will also succumb to live baits, and will occasionally strike lures, particularly jigs.

A pan-sized snapper from offshore waters

Eating Qualities: Snapper are very highly rated as table fish and have a high commercial value. They have white moist and slightly flaky flesh, which occasionally tends towards dryness in very large specimens. Fish in the 600-g to 5-kg range are usually regarded as being the best, although they are delicious at all sizes. They freeze well and lose little of their flavour or texture if frozen soon after being caught.

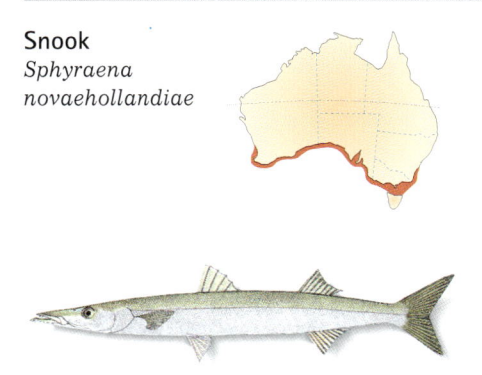

Snook
Sphyraena novaehollandiae

Common Names: The snook, a southern saltwater species distantly related to the northern barracuda, is also known as the short-finned pike or short-fin sea pike, although snook is the most common name. There is occasional confusion between this fish and the unrelated long-finned pike (*Dinolestes lewini*), which is found in many of the same southern waters, as well as further north along the coast of New South Wales.

Description: The snook is characterised by its elongated, almost cylindrical body, sharp teeth and widely separated, short-based dorsal fins. Its coloration is greenish to bluish purple or brown on the back, silvery on the flanks, often with two or three darker green or brown longitudinal stripes along each side. Vertical stripes, bars or dashes may also be evident. The fins are lightly coloured, the tail sometimes yellowish, but never as bright yellow as that of the long-finned pike.

Size: Most snook taken by anglers weigh between 200 g and 1.5 kg, although fish in excess of 3 kg are not unknown, and the species may have a maximum growth potential in excess of 4 kg.

Distribution: Snook range throughout our cooler coastal waters from the far south coast of New South Wales through Victoria, northern Tasmania, South Australia and into southern Western Australia. They are inshore predators of the bays, harbours, sea grass beds and shallow reefs, but occasionally can be found close to the bottom over deeper reefs and around offshore islands.

Fishing Techniques: Most snook are taken on lightly weighted or unweighted baits of whitebait, anchovies or pilchards presented on ganged hooks or single, long-shanked hooks. They also fall to fish flesh strips, small live baits and pieces or strips of squid. These baits should be lightly weighted and kept moving. A gentle jigging motion will often attract snook. Snook are also keen lure and fly takers, and fall to slow-trolled spoons, jigs, feathers and minnows, particularly when these are trolled on weighted lines or rigged behind paravanes.

A pair of snook from South Australian waters

Eating Qualities: The snook is a very good to excellent table fish, much prized in southern waters. The flesh is white, moist and sweet, although a little soft. Care should be taken not to bruise the meat and all snook should be cleaned and iced promptly after capture. This species does not respond particularly well to freezing, and should always be eaten fresh for best results.

Sooty Grunter
Hephaestus spp.

Common Names: The name 'sooty grunter' covers several closely allied members of the family Theraponidae, which are also related to the silver perch and spangled perch of Australia's outback rivers. The most common and widespread of the clan is *Hephaestus fuliginosus*. Other common titles for this species and its close relatives are black bream, khaki bream, 'blubber-lips', grunter and sooty.

Description: The term 'sooty grunter' covers a variable group of tropical freshwater fish, not all of which have yet come under close scientific scrutiny. Most are small to medium-sized, deep-bodied fish with squared-off or slightly concave tails and rubbery lips. They are usually coal black to smoky grey, green, olive or khaki in colour, often with off-white or yellowish patches or blotches. The fins are dark, as is the tail. However, coloration may vary significantly between species, areas and even individuals of the same species, and a rare golden form is known to occur occasionally.

Size: Most sooty grunter encountered by anglers weigh from 200 g to 1.5 kg, but outstanding specimens sometimes top 2.5 kg and, on rare occasions, reach or even exceed 3 kg.

Distribution: This wide-ranging family is found in the freshwater reaches of the tropical north, from central and northern Queensland to the Kimberley and Pilbara regions in Western Australia. Sooty grunter inhabit tropical freshwater streams, lakes and billabongs. They prefer relatively clean, flowing water with gravel or sand beds, rocks and snags. However, they have also been successfully introduced into dams.

Fishing Techniques: Sooty grunter respond well to unweighted or lightly weighted baits of shrimps, earthworms, yabbies, prawns or insects. They are also enthusiastic lure-takers and will strike at a wide range of lures and flies

Eating Qualities: Sooty grunter make fair to good table fare, although their slightly 'weedy' flavour deters some people.

A small sooty grunter from the Kimberley region

Sweep
Scorpis spp.

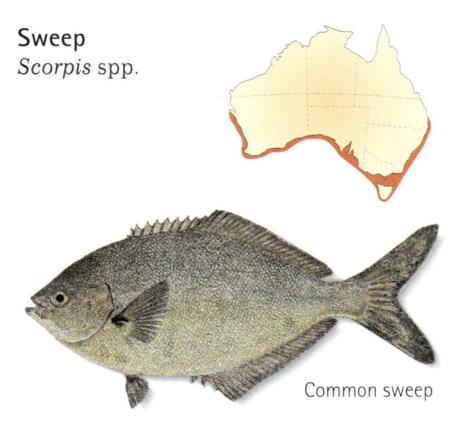

Common Names: There are three reasonably common southern sea fishes in the Scorpididae family. The sea or southern sea sweep (*Scorpis aequipinnis*) is the largest and most sought-after member of the family. Other species include the less abundant banded sweep (*S. georgianus*) of southern waters and the smaller, but very prolific, common or silver sweep (*S. lineolatus*) of the east and south-east coasts. In western Victoria, sea sweep are sometimes called snap-jacks, while in New South Wales, silver or common sweep are occasionally referred to as Newcastle bream.

Description: Sweep are deep-bodied fish with relatively small mouths and small scales. Their coloration ranges from slate grey to steely blue on the back and bluish grey to silvery grey on the flanks and belly. The sea sweep usually has an indistinct dark vertical band on each flank. This band or saddle is wider at the top, tapering to a point behind the pectoral fin. A less clearly defined band may also be evident under the base of the second dorsal fin. However, these bands are never as clearly defined in the sea sweep as they are on the banded sweep. The sea sweep also has a small, yellow patch under the lower jaw. The smaller and less sought-after common or silver sweep has a more laterally compressed body and a smaller mouth, and is uniformly blue-grey to slate on the back and flanks.

Size: Sea sweep are the largest fish in the clan, occasionally reaching weights of 3.5 kg. However, fish of 600 g to 1.2 kg are more common. Banded sweep may reach weights of 2.2 kg, while silver sweep mostly weigh from 100 to 800 g, with exceptional specimens topping 1 kg.

Distribution: The sea sweep is a fish of cool southern seas, and ranges from the far south coast of New South Wales around the coastlines of Victoria, South Australia and southern Western Australia. It is also found around Tasmania. The banded sweep is found from far western Victoria through South Australia to Western Australia, north to about Geraldton or Shark Bay. The common or silver sweep ranges along the east coast, from about Moreton Bay to Wilsons Promontory.

Fishing Techniques: Sweep are mainly taken on small, soft baits such as prawns, mussels, worms, cockles or pipis, cut fish flesh and squid pieces.

Eating Qualities: The sea sweep is the best table fish in this family. Its firm, white, moist flesh is superior in taste and texture to that of both the banded and the common sweep.

A common or silver sweep from New South Wales (right) and an eastern black bream (left)

A handsome sea sweep from South Australia

sooty grunter • sweep • sweetlip • tailor

Sweetlip
Lethrinus chrystostomus

Common Names: The sweetlip, sweetlips or sweetlip emperor is also known as the red-throated sweetlip, red-throated emperor, red-throat or 'lipper'. Around Norfolk Island, where it is common, the same species is also erroneously referred to as 'trumpeter'. This fish is closely related to the other emperors, and is often confused with the grass sweetlip (*Lethrinus laticaudis*) and, less commonly, with the spangled emperor (*L. nebulosus*) and long-nosed emperor (*L. olivaceus*).

Description: The sweetlip is an attractive member of the Lethrinid clan, with a steep forehead and a pointed nose and mouth. Coloration varies, but is most often golden to yellowish brown overlaid with darker vertical blotches and bars. The head is often red, especially around the throat-latch area and under the gills. The inside of the mouth is bright red. The sweetlip's fins are also red, especially the dorsal fin, which is often very bright. There is also a bright red blotch or patch around the base of each pectoral fin.

Size: Most line-caught sweetlip weigh between 800 g and 2.2 kg. Bigger specimens sometimes reach 3 to 3.5 kg, but only rarely top 4 kg.

Distribution: The sweetlip is a fish of tropical reef waters, rarely straying far south of Moreton Island in Queensland or Carnarvon in Western Australia. This species favours coral reef areas ranging from the inshore shallows to deep, continental shelf drop-offs.

Fishing Techniques: The sweetlip is a popular species with tropical reef anglers and is often landed in large numbers. It is mostly taken on baits of cut fish flesh presented near the sea bed, but will eagerly devour crabs, shellfish, prawns, squid and octopus. Sweetlip are more rarely taken on lures, usually in shallower areas around bomboras and reef edges.

Eating Qualities: This tasty member of the emperor clan is generally rated ahead of the spangled emperor in the culinary department, but behind the red emperor and coral trout. Sweetlip are potential carriers of ciguatera toxin, but cases of poisoning involving this species are virtually unknown.

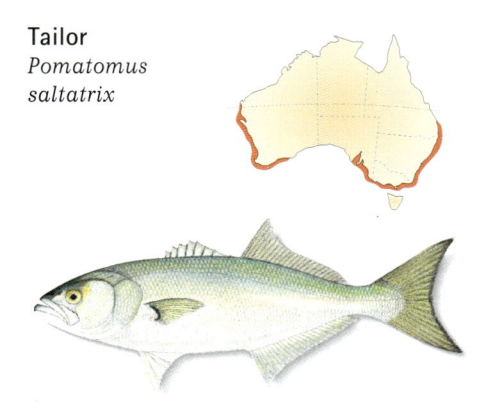

Tailor
Pomatomus saltatrix

Common Names: This worldwide saltwater fish is called bluefish in the United States, and elf in South Africa. In Australia, anglers usually call it tailor (sometimes incorrectly spelt tailer or taylor), or use its popular nicknames of chopper or green back. Tailor are sometimes known as skipjack or skippy in Victoria.

Description: The tailor is a mid-sized predatory fish with a relatively elongated body, forked tail and a large mouth lined with fairly small, but very sharp, teeth. Typical colouring is green to greenish blue, grey or gunmetal on the back, silver on the flanks and silvery white on the belly. Fish caught well offshore tend to have distinctive steely blue backs. Fin colour is variable, but the tail is almost always darker, usually with a black trailing edge.

Size: The majority of tailor caught in Australia weigh from 200 g to 2.5 kg. Smaller schools of big fish in the 2- to 5-kg range are regularly encountered in some areas, while outsize tailor, which are often caught further offshore than their smaller brethren, may weigh as much as 6 or 8 kg. The very largest specimens taken in Australia have topped the 10-kg mark.

Distribution: In Australia, tailor are found in temperate and subtropical waters, being most prolific on the east coast between Wilsons Promontory and Fraser Island, and in the west from Albany to Carnarvon. They also occur sporadically along the southern seaboard, including South Australia, but are very rare in Tasmania. They make use of a wide range of habitats from the upper, almost freshwater reaches of estuaries, through bays, harbours and inlets to inshore grounds, shallow reefs, islands and out to the edge of the continental shelf — and perhaps even beyond it.

Fishing Techniques: Tailor are fished for in a variety of ways. One of the most productive techniques is to cast and slowly retrieve unweighted or very lightly weighted pilchards and garfish rigged on ganged or linked hooks. These gang-hooked rigs can also be used under bobby cork floats, or with heavier sinkers when casting distance is required, particularly on the beach. Fish flesh strips and small live baits will also attract tailor, and they are one of the commonest lure-caught fish in our waters. They strike at a wide range of cast-and-retrieved or trolled chrome slices, spoons, lead slugs, minnows, jigs and flies. A light wire trace is helpful to resist the tailor's razor sharp teeth, although this fish rarely bites off ganged hooks or large, hard-bodied lures.

Eating Qualities: Fresh tailor are quite tasty, although their soft, slightly grey meat bruises very easily and does not respond well to freezing. The flesh is mildly flavoured, flaky and somewhat oily. It is ideally suited to smoking. All tailor destined for the table should be killed and bled as soon as possible, and cleaned within an hour or two of capture. Avoid dropping the fish, stacking them on top of each other or allowing rigor mortis to set in while they are bent or curled up.

A 'chopper' tailor taken from the rocks at sunset

What fish is that?

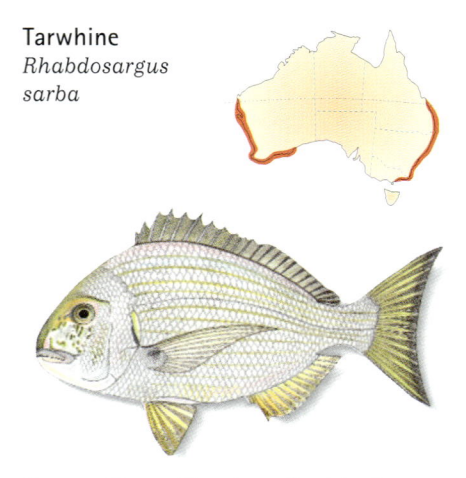

Tarwhine
Rhabdosargus sarba

Common Names: This close ally of the three common bream species is known in some areas as the silver bream. The tarwhine is often confused with the other members of the family, particularly with the eastern black bream (*Acanthopagrus australis*).

Description: The tarwhine is distinguishable from its bream relatives by virtue of its more rounded head profile, slightly larger eye and, most noticeably, the small gold spot or blotch on each scale. These spots give the tarwhine's body the appearance of being lined with horizontal gold stripes. Apart from this gold patterning, the tarwhine is almost identical to the eastern black bream, and often has the same bright yellow pelvic fins, yellow anal fins and yellow-tinged tail. However, tarwhine always have six or seven rows of scales above the lateral line, as opposed to the bream's four or five rows. A final distinguishing feature is the fact that all tarwhine have a distinctive black lining to the gut or stomach cavity. This lining is not evident in bream.

Size: A typical tarwhine is similar in size to an average bream—about 20 to 40 cm long and 300 g to 1.2 kg in weight. The tarwhine's maximum growth potential is probably close to 3 kg, although it is rarely seen at such large sizes.

Distribution: The tarwhine is an inshore fish of the east and west coasts of Australia, ranging from about southern Queensland to the Gippsland Lakes, Victoria, in the east and Albany to Carnarvon in the west. Juvenile tarwhine are often found in large numbers in estuaries, while adults are generally confined to ocean surf beaches and rocky shorelines, and may also range offshore to deeper reefs.

Fishing Techniques: Tarwhine are rarely prolific enough to be specifically targeted, although they are reasonably common in the bags of surf anglers fishing the south-west corner of Western Australia. The tarwhine generally responds to the same techniques as those described for the eastern black bream, and exactly the same tackle may be used to catch this species.

Eating Qualities: The tarwhine's rating as a table fish is much the same as that of the eastern black bream, although some people maintain that the tarwhine's flesh is of slightly inferior quality. The fish's black stomach lining should be removed by scrubbing with a nylon brush or a square of hessian bag after the fish has been cleaned.

Tarwhine are very similar in appearance to bream, but have a more rounded head profile, yellow or gold horizontal stripes and a different scale count

Teraglin
Astractoscion eaquidens

Common Names: The teraglin, trag or trag-jew is very closely related to the mulloway or jewfish (*Argyrosomus hololepidotus*), and is often confused with this larger species.

Description: While teraglin and mulloway look very much alike, the shape of each fish's tail is distinctive. The mulloway's tail is spade-like, with an outward curving (convex) trailing margin, while that of the teraglin or trag is slightly concave or inwardly curving along the rear edge. The teraglin's scales are also smaller than those of the mulloway. Teraglin are usually bluish, purple or brown on the back and silvery grey or slightly brassy on the flanks. The tail is darker. The inside of the teraglin's mouth is typically orange or yellow, and this colour sometimes shows on the fish's lips, even when the mouth is closed. The inside of the gill covers is also yellow.

Size: Exceptional teraglin may measure 1 m in length and weigh close to 10 kg, although any specimen weighing more than 6 kg is considered a prize catch. Most teraglin caught by anglers weigh from 700 g to 3.5 kg.

Distribution: The teraglin is confined to offshore waters along the east coast, between about Moreton or Fraser Islands in Queensland and Merimbula on the far south coast of New South Wales. However, it is more common in the northern part of its range—from Sydney to Moreton Island.

Fishing Techniques: Once prolific on many offshore grounds along the east coast, teraglin populations declined dramatically through the 1970s and 1980s, before staging a partial recovery in the early 1990s. This fish is mostly taken on small live baits, fillets or strip baits presented on relatively large hooks. It also responds well at times to offerings of bottle squid and large prawns. Very few keen teraglin specialists use rods and reels, preferring the direct contact afforded by a handline. Once a school is located and induced to bite, large catches are possible. However, losing a hooked fish often scatters the school and brings an abrupt end to the bite.

Eating Qualities: The teraglin is a highly rated table fish, considered by many to be superior in this department to its close cousin, the mulloway.

Fresh from the sea, teraglin or 'trag' typically exhibit a purplish sheen and are yellow or orange around the lips and mouth

tarwhine • teraglin • tommy rough • giant trevally • golden trevally

Tommy Rough
Arripis georgianus

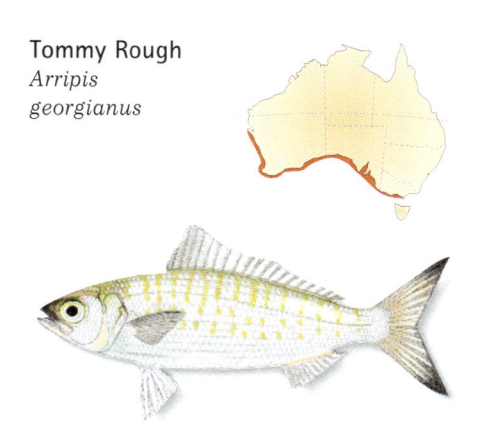

Common Names: In Western Australia and parts of South Australia, this small cousin of the more widely distributed Australian salmon (*Arripis trutta*) is known almost exclusively as herring or Australian herring, while in Victoria and eastern South Australia, tommy rough, tommy ruff, tommy, roughie or ruffy are the preferred names. The tommy rough is also commonly confused with juvenile Australian salmon, and occasionally lumped with this species under the rather inappropriate title of 'salmon trout' or 'bay trout'.

Description: The tommy rough is very similar in body shape to the Australian salmon, but has noticeably larger eyes and a scale pattern which is slightly rough or textured to the touch. Coloration is green on the back, greenish silver to silver on the flanks, and silvery white on the belly. There are rows of gold spots along the flanks, sometimes giving an overall yellow-gold hue when viewed from the side. The tail of the tommy rough is dusky grey or yellowish with distinctly black tips. These black tips are one of the main features readily distinguishing tommy rough from juvenile Australian salmon.

Size: Tommy rough or herring are mainly captured at weights from 100 to 400 g, and lengths ranging from 15 to 30 cm. These little fish rarely top 700 g, although isolated exceptional specimens weighing close to 1 kg may occasionally be encountered in more remote areas.

Distribution: The tommy rough or ruff is a cool water fish, largely confined to the inshore waters of western Victoria, South Australia and southern Western Australia. It is most common from Port Phillip Bay, Victoria, to a little north of Perth, but occasionally ranges north to Shark Bay in the west. Reports of tommy rough from southern New South Wales and eastern Victoria almost always turn out to be juvenile Australian salmon or so-called 'salmon trout'.

Fishing Techniques: In Western Australia, traditional herring anglers often use a large, wooden float called a 'blob', fitted with a fish oil or berley disperser, and baits of maggots (gents) presented on several small hooks set a short distance below the float. Tommy rough also take various marine worms, prawns, squid flesh and cut fish baits. They will strike readily at small lures, jigs and flies, too. These little fish respond well to a berley trail of soaked bread, bran or pollard with a little fish oil added.

Eating Qualities: The tommy rough is a rather oily and strong-flavoured species that enjoys considerable regional popularity as a table fish in South Australia and Western Australia. It is best grilled, but is also well suited to smoking or pickling. Tommy rough intended for the table should be bled and cleaned soon after capture.

Tommy rough are an abundant inshore species in southern and south-western Australia

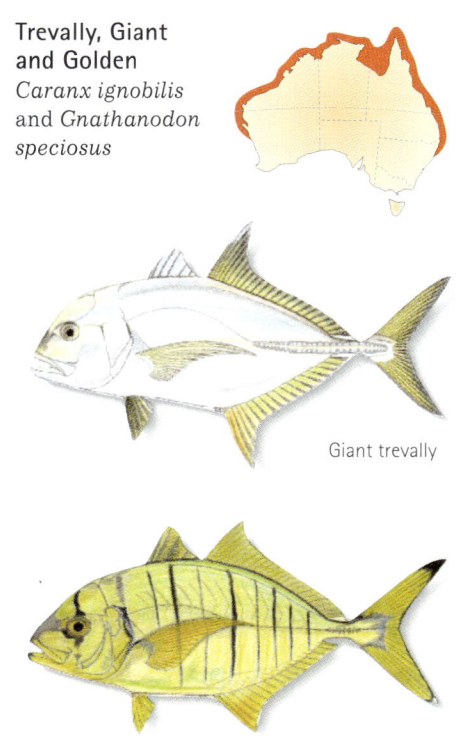

Trevally, Giant and Golden
Caranx ignobilis and *Gnathanodon speciosus*

Giant trevally

Golden trevally

Common Names: The giant trevally or 'GT' was once commonly (and erroneously) referred to as 'turrum'. It was also known as the lowly trevally, before having its name changed to great trevally and, finally, to giant trevally. The golden trevally is often referred to simply as golden. Both species are sometimes nicknamed 'blurter' or 'trevor'.

Description: The giant trevally is the largest and most robust member of the trevally clan. It has a steep forehead, powerful jaws, canine teeth and heavy scutes or sharp, modified scales on the tail wrist. Giant trevally coloration ranges from almost black to blue-green or purple-grey on the back, silvery on the flanks, and silvery white on the belly. The flanks sometimes exhibit irregular spots and blotches, while the belly may carry a yellowish flush, and the tail is often yellow. In contrast, the golden trevally is characterised by its more rounded head profile, extendible (protractile), toothless mouth and tough, rubbery lips. Golden trevally are usually greenish grey to blue-grey on the back, silvery gold on the flanks and lemon yellow on the belly, overlaid with vague, dark, vertical bands that are much more distinct on juveniles. Most adult golden trevally have at least one or two fairly large black spots or patches on the lower rear half of their body.

A fly-rod golden trevally

Size: Giant trevally very occasionally reach lengths of 1.8 m and weights in excess of 50 kg, with a maximum potential of more than 70 kg. Although golden trevally can grow to 16 or 18 kg, they are uncommon at more than 12 kg.

Distribution: Both the giant and golden trevally range widely through the Indian and Pacific oceans and their adjacent seas to our tropical north, and are common around the northern half of the Australian continent. They occasionally roam as far south as Sydney and Perth. They inhabit areas ranging from upper estuaries to deep, offshore reefs, although the golden trevally prefers sand or mud-bottomed flats, shallow bars, beaches and estuary mouths.

Fishing Techniques: Both giant and golden trevally are relatively common catches in tropical waters. They are often fished for deliberately by sport anglers seeking a powerful and exciting adversary, but they are also taken as incidental catches. Bottom and mid-water fishing with cut fish flesh, live baits, whole dead bait fish, squid and the like are very effective, and these fish also respond well to trolled, cast-and-retrieved or jigged lures, especially metal spoons, minnows, plugs and poppers. For best results, cast or troll these lures close to cover or along submerged drop-offs and channels. Tackle for both species should be sturdy and in good order, as both giant and golden trevally put up an exceptionally spirited struggle when hooked.

Eating Qualities: Although denigrated by many in the north when it comes to eating, the giant and golden trevally are both good to very good table fish, particularly in their smaller sizes. These species are well suited to curries and sauced dishes, but should be killed and bled immediately after capture for best results.

The giant trevally or 'GT' is the largest member of its extensive family

Trevally, Silver
Pseudocaranx dentex

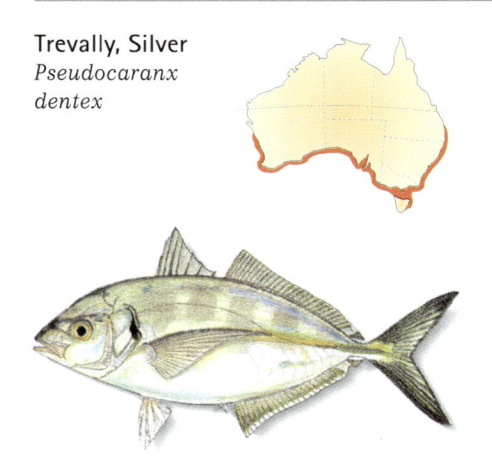

Common Names: The silver trevally is also known as trevally, white trevally, skipjack or skippy, the last two names being most prevalent in Western Australia. One of the silver trevally's popular nicknames is 'blurter', a term referring to the grunting noise freshly landed specimens make. They are also incorrectly referred to as silver bream in some areas.

Description: A deep-bodied, laterally compressed fish, this species has a relatively small, toothless mouth and rubbery lips. Typical colouring is dark grey to blue-green on the back, silvery with a blue and purple sheen on the flanks and silvery white on the belly. A yellow, longitudinal stripe along the flanks is often evident in freshly caught fish.

Size: The silver trevally typically runs between 200 g and 2.5 kg, although schools of 2- to 4-kg fish are occasionally encountered. Silver trevally of more than 6 kg are exceptional, although specimens in excess of 12 kg have been reported from Lord Howe Island.

Distribution: The silver trevally is a fish of our subtropical, temperate and cool southern waters ranging from southern Queensland to about Geraldton in Western Australia. It is also found in Tasmania and is prolific around the North Island of New Zealand and at Lord Howe Island. The trevally's chosen habitat ranges from estuaries and bays to beaches, rocky shorelines, inshore reefs and offshore sand, mud and gravel patches.

Fishing Techniques: Silver trevally are mainly taken on baits of cut fish flesh strips, small whole fish such as anchovies, whitebait and pilchards, or on baits of whole or cut squid, prawns, crab and cunjevoi. These baits are best used unweighted or very lightly weighted. Trevally are also reasonably regular lure takers in some areas. They seem to prefer metal spoons, chrome slices, lead slugs, small minnows, plugs and flies. In most cases, these artificial lures should be presented in mid-water or close to the sea bed. Trevally respond well to a berley trail of soaked bread, minced fish and tuna oil.

Eating Qualities: The flavour of silver trevally is fair to good, even very good in small, fresh specimens, although the flesh can be somewhat strong flavoured and dry in larger ones. Large silver trevally are sometimes infested with worms and often have unusual air or gas spaces or gaps in their flesh, especially along the rear and upper backbone.

A 1-kg silver trevally

Trout, Brown and Rainbow
Salmo trutta and *Oncorhyncus mykiss*

Brown trout

Rainbow trout (female)

Rainbow trout (male)

Common Names: These introduced sport fish from the northern hemisphere have a number of common names in Australia. The brown trout is often called brown or brownie, while sea-run or estuary-dwelling stocks may be called sea trout. The rainbow trout is known as rainbow or bow, while its sea-run populations are sometimes called steelhead.

Description: All Salmonidae fishes are characterised by their relatively elongated bodies, soft dorsal fins, fleshy adipose fins and the placement of the ventral fins well back on the belly. Brown trout have a relatively large mouth and a squared-off or slightly forked tail which either lacks spots completely, or has a small number of relatively large spots only along its upper edge. Brown trout coloration varies considerably, but is usually olive green to dark brown on the back and flanks and cream or creamy white on the belly. This base colour is overlaid with black and red spots, often with a lighter halo around each spot. There are large, widely spaced spots on the gill covers. In contrast, the rainbow trout usually has a slightly smaller mouth than the brown trout, and its tail is typically a little more forked and peppered with small, dark spots. Most Australian rainbow trout are olive green to deep steely blue on the back, silvery on the flanks and silvery white underneath. The back and flanks are overlaid with a peppering of dark spots, and many rainbow trout have a bright crimson or pink slash along both flanks and gill covers, although this may be rather vague at times. As with all trout and salmon, these colours change and intensify during the spawning season (late autumn, winter and early spring).

Size: In their native waters, both brown and rainbow trout have been known to reach weights of 20 kg in exceptional circumstances. In Australia, most trout caught by anglers weigh from 200 g to 3 kg, with record-breaking fish (particularly browns) very occasionally approaching the 10-kg mark.

Distribution: Brown trout were originally native to Britain and Europe, while the rainbow is a native of the Pacific watersheds in North America (from southern California to Alaska), as well as parts of eastern Siberia. Both species have been successfully introduced to many parts of the world, including Australia and New Zealand. In Australia, these trout prefer cool, clean rivers, creeks, lakes and dams, mainly in alpine and subalpine areas. Their distribution in mainland Australia is limited to the higher, cooler areas of New South Wales, Victoria, the Australian Capital Territory, South Australia and southern Western Australia. Both species are more widespread and prolific in Tasmania and on both islands of New Zealand.

Fishing Techniques: Trout are usually taken on light tackle and fairly fine lines baited with earthworms, grubs, shrimps, insects and insect larvae such as mudeyes (dragonfly larvae). Baits should be float suspended or very lightly weighted, rather than anchored to the bottom, and smallish hooks tend to work best. Trout respond well to lures such as metal spoons and spinners, small minnows and tiny jigs. These may be cast and retrieved from the shoreline of a lake or river, or slowly trolled from a moving boat. Trout are also ideally suited to fly fishing, a technique that originated with this group of fish as its primary target.

Eating Qualities: Trout provide good to very good or even excellent table fare, although some specimens tend to be a little dry. Trout flesh varies from white or pale pink to bright orange or even red, depending on the individual fish's diet. The more strongly coloured orange or red flesh is generally the tastiest and most sought-after. Trout flesh is also ideally suited to smoking, pickling and sugar-and-salt curing to produce gravlax.

A rainbow trout (top) and brown trout (below)

A silvery rainbow trout landed on light spinning gear

Fly fishing for trout in the shallow margins of Rocklands Reservoir in Victoria

What fish is that?

Trumpeter, Tasmanian
Latris linaeta

Common Names: The Tasmanian trumpeter or Tassie trumpeter is more commonly known simply as trumpeter or striped trumpeter in its home state. Elsewhere, it is usually referred to by its full title. The related silver or bastard trumpeter (*Latridopsis forsteri*) is a smaller inshore species, sometimes confused with the larger and more sought-after Tasmanian trumpeter. The plankton-feeding real bastard trumpeter (*Mendosoma allporti*) of south-eastern Tasmania is rarely, if ever, caught on a baited line.

Description: The Tasmanian trumpeter is a medium to large, relatively deep-bodied fish with a long, sloping forehead and large, semi-extendible (protractile) mouth with powerful, fleshy lips. Typical coloration is chocolate brown on the back, lighter brown on the flanks and creamy below, with several longitudinal stripes of creamy yellow running through the dark background colour on the upper flanks. The trumpeter's fins are dusky, and sometimes tinged with red or yellow.

Size: Tasmanian trumpeter commonly run from 1 to 8 kg, although 10- to 15-kg fish are far from rare on some deeper grounds. Exceptional specimens may very occasionally exceed 25 or 30 kg.

Distribution: This fish of Australia's cool southern seas ranges from Tasmania north to the south coast of New South Wales. They are rarely found far north of Montague Island, but do occur sporadically on very deep reefs as far north as Sydney, especially in winter. The Tasmanian trumpeter also ranges westward through the deeper waters off South Australia and southern Western Australia to about Albany.

Fishing Techniques: Most Tasmanian trumpeter are taken on bottom-fished baits of squid, prawn or cut fish flesh. They will also take small, whole fish and live baits, and may very occasionally succumb to jigs and lures. In Tasmania, smaller trumpeter are often taken close inshore or even in estuarine waters. However, larger fish—both in Tasmania and further north—are usually fished for in waters deeper than 50 m.

A large Tasmanian or striped trumpeter

Eating Qualities: Tasmanian trumpeter of all sizes are exceptionally fine table fish. This species is often rated as one of the very best of our cool water reef species.

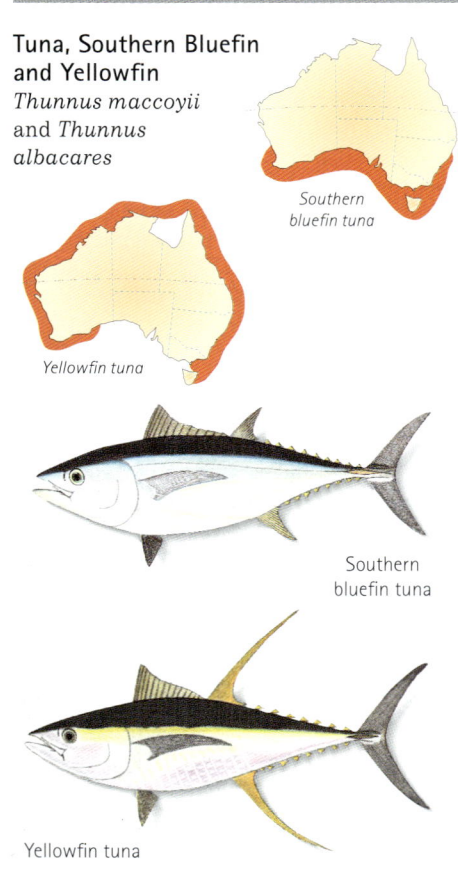

Tuna, Southern Bluefin and Yellowfin
Thunnus maccoyii and *Thunnus albacares*

Southern bluefin tuna

Yellowfin tuna

Southern bluefin tuna

Yellowfin tuna

Common Names: Southern bluefin tuna are also called southern blues, bluefin, blueys and sometimes tunny. The yellowfin tuna, yellow-finned tuna or yellowfin was once known as the Allison tuna, long-finned Allison tuna or Allison tunny, although these names are rarely used today. Sport and game anglers sometimes nickname this species fin, while in Hawaii it is known as 'ahi'.

Description: The southern bluefin is a very heavily built tuna with a cylindrical body and short fins. It is blue-black on the back and bluish silver on the belly, often with broken vertical white bars and dashes on the flanks and belly, especially when young. The fins and finlets are yellowish, but never as bright as those of the yellowfin tuna. However, the caudal keels on the tail wrist, ahead of the tail, are conspicuously yellow, especially in smaller fish. Yellowfin coloration is the most striking of all the tunas. Freshly caught or live specimens are blue to steel black on the back, silver to silvery gold on the flanks, and silvery white on the belly. A band of bright gold or iridescent blue (sometimes both colours, one above the other) runs along the upper flanks, separating the dark back from the lighter belly. The stomach area sometimes carries oval, colourless patches and vague, broken vertical bars of white or off-white. As its name implies, the yellowfin's fins are bright yellow, particularly the small finlets. However, the caudal keels, ahead of the tail, are dark or dusky. Larger yellowfin (weighing more than 30 or 40 kg) are characterised by extended, strap-like second dorsal and anal fins, sometimes called sickles.

Size: Both southern bluefin and yellowfin tuna grow to at least 2 m in length and reach weights of more than 150 kg, although in both species fish weighing more than 100 kg are relatively uncommon, especially in inshore waters. The much rarer central Pacific bluefin—a near identical fish to the giant Atlantic bluefin (*Thunnus thynnus*)—grows to more than 350 kg, and any tuna weighing more than 200 kg taken in our waters are most likely to be representatives of this central Pacific species.

Distribution: The southern bluefin is a cool and temperate water fish of the southern Pacific, Indian and Southern Oceans. It is rarely encountered north of Sydney or Geraldton, although it is known to spawn in tropical waters. In contrast, the yellowfin tuna is a worldwide fish of tropical, subtropical and temperate waters.

Fishing Techniques: Both these tuna are taken using a range of angling techniques. These include trolling with lures as well as live baiting, dead baiting, lure casting and even fly fishing. A favoured technique for taking larger yellowfin tuna is to use unweighted flesh-strip baits or whole and cut pilchards in conjunction with a berley trail of fish pieces. This is called cubing or strip baiting. Big tuna are extremely powerful and demand the best in tackle, rigs and gaffs.

Eating Qualities: The southern bluefin tuna has dark, red meat with a high oil content, and is well regarded by the Japanese for use in sashimi or sushi. The yellowfin's flesh is slightly lighter in colour and less oily, but this fish also demands a high price on the sashimi market and is rated just behind the albacore in terms of its cooked flavour. All tuna should be killed by a solid blow to the head immediately after capture, and bled by severing one or more arteries. The carcass should then be cooled as quickly as possible using ice or an iced brine slurry, before being eaten fresh or snap frozen for future consumption.

Tasmanian trumpeter • tuna • skipjack tuna

Tuna, Longtail
Thunnus tonggol

Common Names: Other common names for the longtail or long-tailed tuna include northern bluefin tuna, northern blue, bluefin and, more rarely, Oriental bonito, although it should not be confused with one of the true bonitos (*Sarda orientalis*), which is also referred to in some literature as an Oriental bonito. Until recent times, the longtail tuna was known almost exclusively in Australia as the northern bluefin tuna. However, the continued use of this name causes considerable confusion between this relatively small species and the giant northern bluefin tuna (*Thunnus thynnus*) of the Atlantic.

Description: The longtail is a medium-sized tuna with a narrow, tapering tail section. It is more lightly built than many other tunas, and weighs less for a given length than either the yellowfin or southern bluefin tunas. Coloration is blue-black on the back and silver to silvery white on the belly. Live specimens usually exhibit an iridescent blue band along each flank and may also have a golden flush adjacent to this band. The lower portion of the body is often marked with vague spots and blotches of white or off-white. The longtail tuna's fins are dusky to dirty yellow. Its finlets are dark-edged.

Size: In the northern, tropical part of its range, the longtail tuna is mainly encountered at weights from 2 to 12 kg. Further south, larger fish are more likely to be encountered, and along the New South Wales coast there are seasonal influxes of adult longtails in the 12- to 30-kg range, with rare 40-kg giants turning up sporadically.

Distribution: The longtail is an Indo-Pacific species confined to the seas off Australia, Papua New Guinea and parts of Southeast Asia. Although mostly a tropical and subtropical species, this tuna makes summer and autumn forays southward, reaching the area around Green Cape in the east and Cape Leeuwin in the west. Longtail tuna are rarely found more than a few kilometres off the coast, especially in southern waters. The only exceptions occur around a few offshore islands within the continental shelf.

Fishing Techniques: In the tropics, the majority of small to medium longtail tuna are taken by anglers spinning or trolling with small lures. Many larger longtails are also caught on various minnows and poppers. However, larger fish often prefer live baits of yellowtail, mullet, slimy mackerel or garfish. They will also take dead baits, including pilchards and garfish.

Eating Qualities: The meat of the longtail tuna is dark and blood-rich, but has a good flavour if longtails are killed and bled promptly after capture. The meat is well suited to curries, casseroles and stews, and may also be baked, barbecued or smoke-cured with very good results. Longtail tuna may also be eaten raw.

Longtail or northern bluefin tuna are commonly encountered by land-based game anglers

Tuna, Skipjack
Katsuwonus pelamis

Common Names: The skipjack or striped tuna is also known by many Australian anglers as the stripey. In Hawaii, the Polynesian name for this prolific species is 'aku'. As with all the tunas, the name tunny is still sometimes used, and skipjacks are often confused with bonito (*Sarda australis* and *S. orientalis*), to which they bear a superficial resemblance, but are only distantly related.

Description: The skipjack is a small to medium fish with a very thickset, barrel-like body that tapers abruptly to a relatively small, upright tail. This fish is characterised by its belly stripes, which contrast with the upper back and flank stripes of the true bonitos. Skipjack coloration is typically steel blue to purple on the back, silvery blue on the flanks and silvery white on the belly. The belly area carries four to six longitudinal dark stripes. There are no stripes on the skipjack's back.

Size: Most striped tuna or skipjack caught by Australian anglers weigh from 1 to 6 kg, with a few giants of close to 10 kg turning up occasionally. Record catches in other parts of the world, such as Hawaii and Mauritius, have topped 18 kg, but such fish are uncommon.

Distribution: A worldwide species of tropical, subtropical, temperate and even cool waters, the skipjack ranges from the lower reaches of larger estuaries, harbours and bays, through inshore areas to the continental shelf and well beyond, into open ocean areas. Striped tuna prefer relatively clean water with a temperature range of about 16°C to 26°C, but will sometimes swim in both cooler or warmer seas, and are known to spawn in tropical waters.

Fishing Techniques: Skipjack are mainly pursued as bait, although they are brilliant sport fish in their own right, and provide one of the toughest battles, for their size, of any species. The vast majority of skipjack tuna fall to small lures trolled quickly behind boats or cast-and-retrieved from boats, deep shorelines or jetties and wharves. They will also take unweighted pilchards or small flesh-strip baits and even small live baits at times.

Eating Qualities: In the past, skipjack were not often eaten in Australia because of their dark, blood-rich meat and strong flavour. However, if bled promptly and kept on ice, skipjack tuna are quite palatable in casseroles, pies or when baked. They are also well suited to canning, smoking, salting and drying, and may be eaten raw in sushi or sashimi. They make superb baits, and can be used whole or alive for marlin, sharks and big tuna, or cut into strips, cubes or slabs for practically any carnivorous saltwater fish.

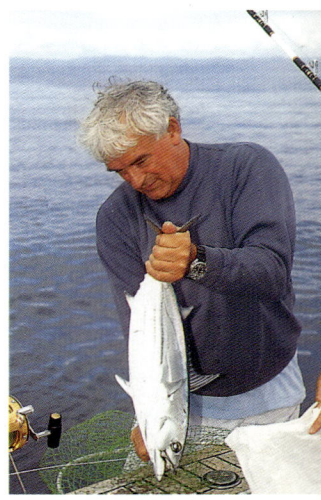

A skipjack or striped tuna

What fish is that?

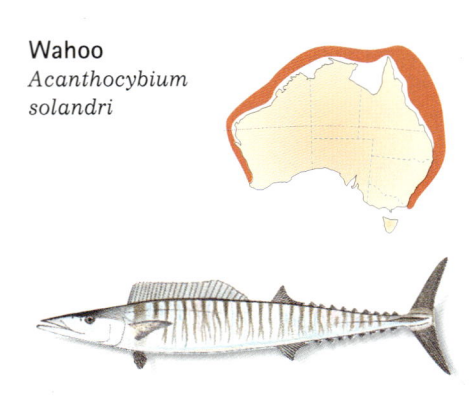

Wahoo
Acanthocybium solandri

Common Names: This worldwide oceanic speedster is known in Hawaii as ono, in parts of North America as peto and, incorrectly, in many areas as mackerel. Wahoo is the most widely accepted name in Australia, although the nickname 'hoo is also used at times. This fish should not be confused with the much smaller and totally unrelated warehou or snotty trevalla (*Seriolella brama*) of cool, southern seas.

Description: The wahoo is a very elongate, rather cylindrical, mackerel-shaped fish with scissor-like jaws and very sharp teeth. It is similar in shape to the Spanish mackerel, but with a more cylindrical body; a relatively small, almost upright tail and a long first dorsal fin of roughly even height (unlike the mackerel's dorsal fin, which is higher at the front and lower behind). Although wahoo vary in colour, they are typically steely blue-black to brilliant blue on the back, silver to silvery blue on the flanks and silver underneath. Fresh specimens have slightly wavy vertical bars, which may be either inconspicuous or very distinct. In some cases, these bars give the fish a striking tiger or zebra pattern while alive. However, most wahoo fade to a uniform gunmetal grey or blue-grey shortly after death.

Size: The majority of wahoo caught by Australian anglers weigh between 8 and 30 kg. Specimens weighing less than 6 kg are almost unknown in Australian inshore waters, and very large wahoo in excess of 40 kg are taken each year. Elsewhere, particularly around Fiji and in the Caribbean, wahoo in excess of 50 kg are regularly encountered. The maximum growth potential of this species may be in the order of 75 to 80 kg.

Distribution: The wahoo is found throughout the tropical, subtropical and warm temperate oceans of the world. In Australia, wahoo are caught most commonly off Queensland, New South Wales and Western Australia. They are also common around offshore islands such as Lord Howe, and may be present well offshore in Northern Territory waters at times. This fish very occasionally visits the Northland region of New Zealand, but is rarely captured there. The wahoo is an open ocean, pelagic species favouring clean, blue currents with water temperatures of 21°C to 30°C.

Fishing Techniques: Wahoo are mainly taken on fast-trolled lures such as Konahead-style skirted heads, pushers, rubber squid, feather jigs, bibless minnows and various diving minnows. They are also fond of rigged skip and swimming baits such as mullet, garfish, scad and small tuna. A wire trace or leader is regarded as essential when fishing for wahoo, although many anglers are lucky enough to land large fish on monofilament nylon leaders, mainly because of the fish's tail-biting mode of attack. Wahoo are rarely targeted specifically in our waters. They are usually taken

While alive, wahoo often exhibit 'zebra' stripes

while fishing for tuna, marlin, sailfish, mackerel, kingfish and other species. However, they are nearly always a welcome catch because of their striking looks, incredible bursts of speed and erratic direction changes when hooked, and also because of their superb table qualities.

Eating Qualities: The wahoo is a very good to excellent table fish, with firm, white and sweet flesh that tastes not unlike that of the Spanish mackerel. Large, slug-like parasites commonly found in the wahoo's gut do not affect the fish's flesh in any way.

Whiting, King George and Sand
Sillaginodes punctatus and *Sillago ciliata*

Sand whiting
King George whiting

King George whiting

Sand whiting

Common Names: The King George whiting is also known as the spotted whiting and occasionally abbreviated to the letters 'KG'. The smaller sand whiting, silver whiting, yellow-finned whiting or summer whiting should not be confused with the even smaller winter or diver whiting (*Silago maculata*) of southern Queensland. Very large sand whiting are often called blue nose whiting, because of the bluish tinge around their semi-transparent snouts.

Description: The King George or spotted whiting of southern waters is a long, almost cylindrical fish with a tapering tail portion and a small, slightly underslung mouth. Typical colouration of the King George whiting is light brown to dark brown or even reddish on the back, silver or

This sand whiting took a beach worm bait on a long shanked hook

silvery brown on the flanks and silvery white on the belly, overlaid with many dark brown or red-brown spots on the back and flanks. These dark spots are often arranged in irregular, longitudinal lines, especially along the middle and lower flanks. The sand whiting is a relatively small, elongate, silvery fish, lacking the spots of the King George whiting. Its typical colouring is

wahoo • King George whiting • sand whiting • yellowtail

A sand whiting taken from a surf beach

golden yellow through light brown to green on the back, silvery gold on the flanks and silvery white on the belly. The sand whiting's fins are yellowish, particularly the anal, ventral and pectoral fins, and the pectorals are usually distinctly edged with white.

Size: The King George is the largest and most sought-after of all Australian whiting, with most specimens taken by anglers running between 300 and 800 g. Exceptional King George whiting of 2 and even 3 kg have been recorded from time to time, mainly from offshore areas such as Kangaroo Island in South Australia and Rottnest Island in Western Australia. The average weight of sand whiting taken by anglers is generally smaller, running from 200 to 600 g, and only very rarely exceeding 800 g. Record fish occasionally top 1 kg, but such giants are exceptionally uncommon.

Distribution: King George whiting range through the inshore waters of our cooler southern coastline, from the far south coast of New South Wales to about Geraldton in Western Australia. They are also found in parts of northern Tasmania and around the islands of Bass Strait, preferring coastal sandy areas, gravel or mud patches and sea grass beds in waters less than 10 or 15 m deep, although larger individuals may sometimes be found in deeper water near reef systems. Sand whiting tend to take over where the King George leave off, ranging northwards along the eastern seaboard from about Lakes Entrance, in Victoria to Cape York in north Queensland. A very similar fish (*S. schomburgkii*) occurs along a similar stretch of coastline in Western Australia, and a smaller but nearly identical member of the whiting clan is also found in Northern Territory waters. The sand whiting is an inshore species of our estuaries, bays, harbours, tidal lakes and ocean beaches, and is rarely found far from shore or in water deeper than about 10 m.

Fishing Techniques: Both King George and sand whiting respond best to fresh, natural baits such as marine worms, pink nippers or bass yabbies, cockles, clams, pipis, mussels and prawns. Larger fish are often taken on squid pieces, and occasionally succumb to fish flesh strips or even pilchards and pilchard pieces. Much more rarely, a whiting will grab a small lure, jig or fly worked near the sea bed. Tackle should be light and sensitive for best results. In general, sinkers should be kept as light as possible, and these fish often respond well to a slowly moving bait.

Eating Qualities: The King George whiting is a superb and highly rated food fish, and is regularly listed among the very best table fish available in Australian waters. The sand whiting is also a delicate, sweet-fleshed fish held in extremely high esteem by many seafood fanciers. However, fine bones can be a problem when eating smaller sand whiting and, where possible, these should be carefully cut away when the fish is filleted and prepared for cooking. The flesh of both whiting species freezes well.

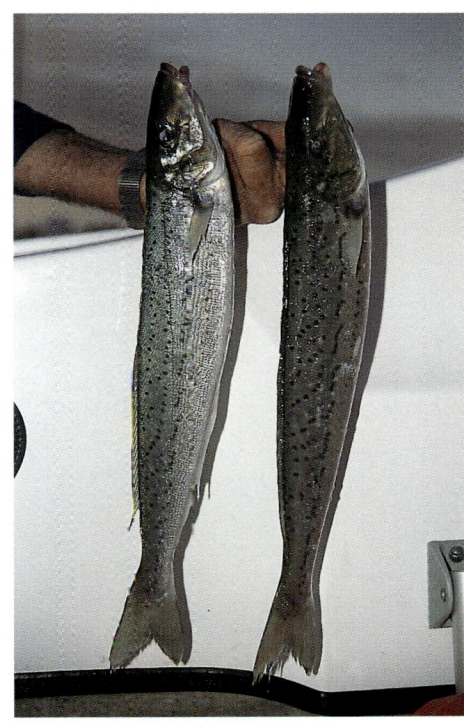

A pair of large King George whiting

Yellowtail
Trachurus novaezelandiae

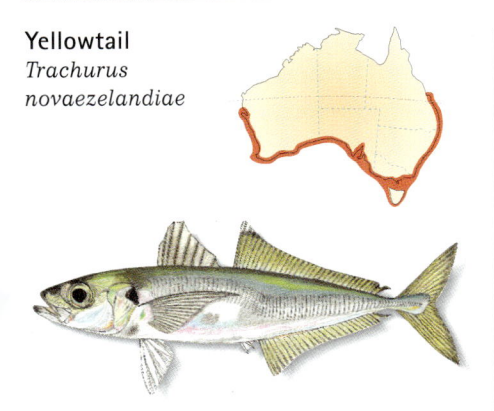

Common Names: The yellowtail or yellowtail scad has many regional names, including 'bung' and 'yakka' in New South Wales and 'chow' in South Australia. Several almost identical fish are prolific in New Zealand, and one of these is known as the koheru. Larger yellowtail are easily confused with cowanyoung or jack mackerel (*Trachurus declivis*), Russells mackerel scad (*Decapturus russelli*) and southern mackerel scad (*D. muroadsi*). All these fish belong to the same widespread and prolific family of scads, which are abundant in Australia's cool, temperate and tropical waters.

Description: A small, reasonably elongate member of the scad group of fishes distinguished by its prominent scutes (sharp, plate-like scales on the lateral line ahead of the tail). The coloration of the yellowtail varies slightly between open ocean and estuarine or harbour-dwelling individuals, but is usually green to yellowish brown on the back, silvery green on the flanks and silvery white on the belly. The fins are yellowish, particularly the tail. A large sea louse called a tongue biter or 'doctor' is commonly found in the mouth of freshly caught yellowtail and often crawls out when the fish dies.

Size: Most yellowtail caught by anglers weigh from 50 to 400 g, although occasional schools of larger fish are encountered. Fish from such schools may occasionally top 750 g. However, many of these larger specimens turn out, on closer examination, to in fact be cowanyoung or mackerel scad.

Distribution: The yellowtail is a fish of Australia's temperate and cool seas, although very similar and closely related members of the same family also occur in tropical waters. This species is usually found in mid-water over broken reef, kelp and sand patches in estuaries, harbours, bays and inshore reef areas between 2 and 20 m deep. It is particularly common around wharves, jetties and breakwalls.

Fishing Techniques: The yellowtail is mainly targeted for use as bait (either live or dead), or is caught by younger anglers fishing from piers and jetties. Yellowtail will take lightly weighted or unweighted baits of cut fish flesh, prawn, squid, bread or mincemeat presented on small, long-shanked hooks. They also strike at tiny lures, flies or multi-jig, sabiki-style bait catching rigs. A berley of soaked bread, bran or pollard with fish scraps and a little tuna oil helps to attract and excite these fish.

Eating Qualities: Yellowtail are not often eaten except by the family cat. Most are used as bait, either live or dead. However, their flesh is quite palatable, if a little oily and rather strongly flavoured. They are quite well suited to smoke curing and pickling, and can also be eaten raw.

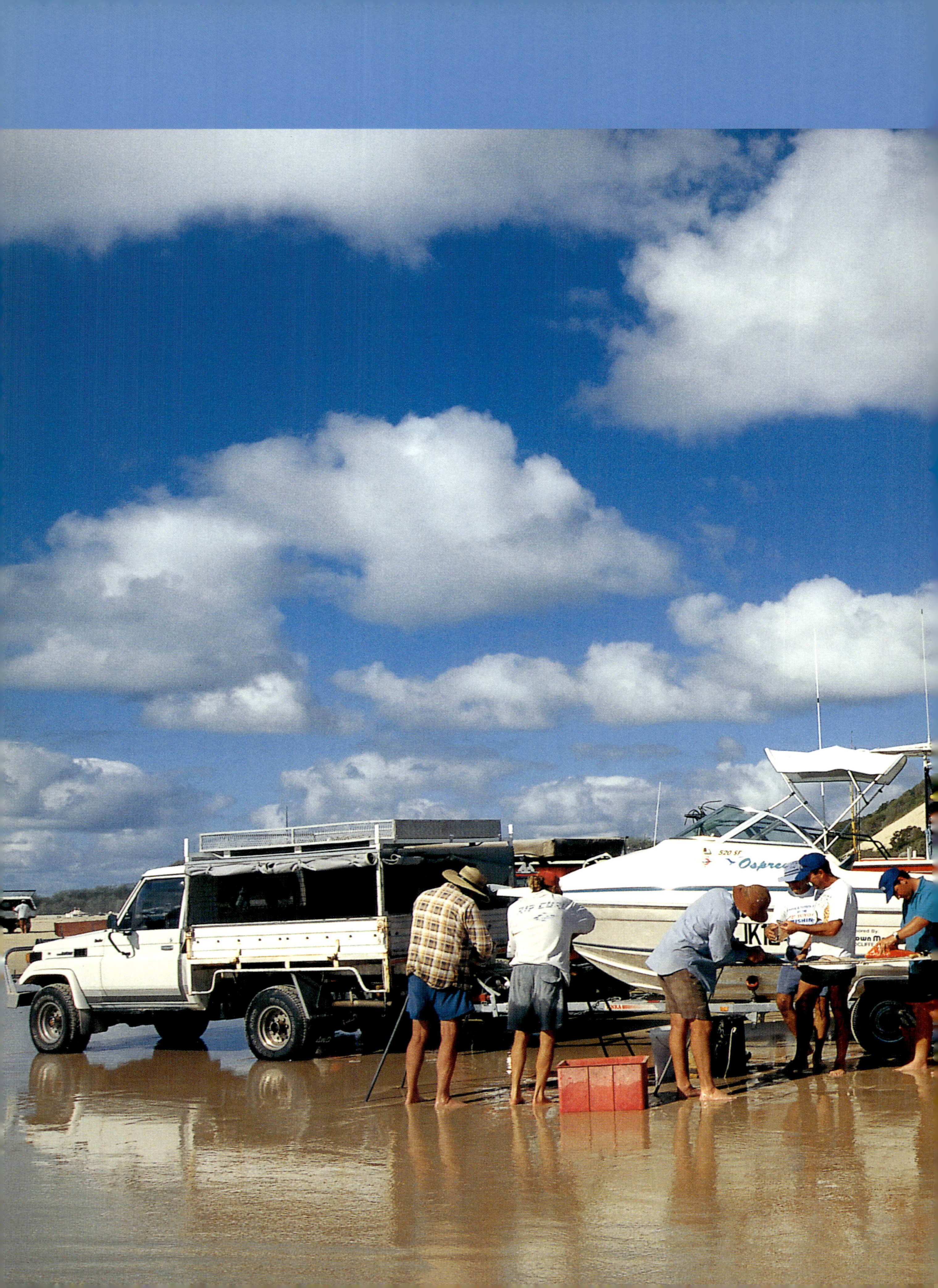
520 SF

Part 4

FISHING RULES & REGULATIONS

Fishing rules and regulations

This section is a state-by-state summary of Australian fisheries rules and regulations. The summary emphasises:

- the recreational pursuit of finfish (as opposed to crustaceans, molluscs and other invertebrates);
- hook-and-line angling methods;
- accepted recreational fishing practices; and
- permissible equipment and techniques for recreational angling.

The rules summarised here are only a few of a large range in force nationwide and were up to date at the time of going to press. This summary is simply a guide and rules change, so always check on the latest state of play **before** you go fishing.

We haven't included all the regulations governing invertebrates, the classification of various controlled waterways (sanctuaries, reserves, etc.), some specific seasonal closures affecting anglers and various laws controlling the activities of commercial fishers, spearfishermen, divers, boat owners and bait gatherers.

- **Remember—rules and regulations change!** To be sure of the rules in your chosen fishing area check with the authorities and get a copy of their latest regulations **before** going fishing.
- **Size limit** means the minimum legal limit, unless otherwise stated.
- **Bag limit** is the daily possession limit per person, unless otherwise stated.

If in doubt, check with the relevant authorities first.

At the end of the section on each state or territory for recreational anglers you will find a list of useful contact numbers.

GREAT WHITE AND GREY NURSE SHARKS NOW PROTECTED

The Federal Government has listed great white and grey nurse sharks on the Commonwealth's endangered species list. This means that these sharks will be protected throughout Australia's fishing zone (AFZ) and in waters over the continental shelf beyond the 3-nautical mile limit.

It is currently estimated that there may be only some 10 000 great whites in Australian waters, of which as many as 500 are caught and killed annually. The vast majority of these sharks are killed inadvertently during commercial fishing operations. The Commonwealth plans to develop a recovery plan for the species and to help the fishing industry find ways to exclude great whites from its bycatch. Although grey nurse sharks pose little or no threat to humans, their numbers were severely depleted by anglers and spearfishermen in the 1960s and 1970s.

Great white shark in South Australian waters

Fishing Information

VICTORIA
Victorian Fisheries Information Line	(03) 9643 3533

NEW SOUTH WALES
NSW Fisheries Information Service	(02) 9566 7802
Fisherman's Watch Hot Line	1800 043 536

QUEENSLAND
Fisheries Enforcement Hot Line	1800 017 116

NORTHERN TERRITORY
Recreational Fishing Office	(08) 8999 4395
Police Fisheries Enforcement Hotline	1800 89 1136

WESTERN AUSTRALIA
Fish Watch Hot Line	1800 815 507

SOUTH AUSTRALIA
Fishwatch Hot Line (24 hours)	1800 065 522
Recfish Australia	1800 686 818

TASMANIA
Inland Fisheries Commission	(03) 6233 4140
Parks and Wildlife	(03) 6233 6556
Marine Resources	(03) 6233 7042
Fisherman's Watch (24 hours)	1800 005 555

Previous page: *Cleaning the catch*

VICTORIA

Recreational fishing in Victoria is controlled by the Fisheries Division of the Department of Conservation and Natural Resources (DCNR). Detailed rules and regulations exist for both fresh and saltwater angling. The guide book to Victorian rules and regulations is available free from many tackle outlets and DCNR offices throughout the state.

Amateur Fishing Licences

Amateur fishing licences are required for all adult anglers (except certain pensioners) intending to fish in 'inland waters'. The Victorian definition of 'inland waters' includes many brackish tidal waters where the species sought may be marine fish such as bream.

New Trout and Salmon Regulations

Trout and freshwater salmon fishing regulations in Victoria underwent a major upgrade in 1997. The new regulations include the reintroduction of a closed season on the taking of trout and salmon from all Victorian streams and at least one lake, as well as size limits, bag limits and additional tackle and fishing method regulations.

The following summary of these new regulations is intended as a guide only. Anglers should seek clarification of the waterways covered under each schedule and the specifics of the various rules. It should also be noted that additional changes to the trout and salmon regulations in Victoria are likely before the year 2000.

Summary of the New Regulations

- The new closed season on the taking of trout and salmon applies in all Victorian rivers and streams as well as Lake Wendouree. It also applies to boat fishing on Lake Purrumbete. All other lakes and dams remain open to trout fishing all year.
- The closed season runs from midnight on the Monday of the Queen's Birthday long weekend in early June until midnight of the Friday prior to the first Saturday in September.
- On all Schedule 3 waterways (most stocked waters), the new bag limit is as follows: A total of 10 salmonid fishes, of which not more than 5 trout may be under 30 cm in length, and not more than 5 of which may be chinook (quinnat) salmon.
- On all Schedule 4 waterways (specially stocked waters), the new bag limit is as follows: A total of 5 trout. (Salmon are not included in this bag limit.)
- On all Schedule 5 waterways ('quality' waters), the new bag limit is as follows: A total of 5 trout, of which not more than 2 may be greater than 30 cm in length, and of those 2 no more than 1 may be greater than 40 cm in length.
- On all other waters, there is a blanket bag limit of 10 trout per angler per day. All of these daily limits are also possession limits in, on or adjacent to the waters to which each limit applies.
- The use of trout or salmon ova (eggs or roe) as bait or berley is now also banned in all Victorian waters

Protected Species

The *Flora and Fauna Guarantee Act 1988* affords protection to threatened species. Once listed, fish may not be taken or kept in possession without a licence issued under that Act. By Special Orders of the Governor-in-Council, Australian grayling, Murray cod and Macquarie perch may be taken by rod and line. Bag and size limits and closed seasons apply to the taking of Murray cod and Macquarie perch. Listed fish are as follows:

- Aggassiz's chanda perch
- Australian grayling
- Barred galaxias
- Cox's gudgeon
- Dwarf galaxias
- Freshwater herring
- Macquarie perch
- Mallacoota burrowing crayfish
- Murray cod
- Murray hardyhead
- Narracan burrowing crayfish
- Non-speckled hardyhead
- Orbost spiny freshwater crayfish
- Southern purple-spotted gudgeon
- Tasmanian mudfish
- Trout cod
- Variegated pygmy perch
- Yarra pigmy perch
- Warragul burrowing crayfish

Protection of the great white shark is under consideration in Victoria. Check with your local fisheries officer.

Size and Bag Limits

Fish Species	Bag Limit* (person/day)	Size Limit (cm)
Australian bass	—	25
Australian salmon	—	21
Blackfish, river (Limit applies only to waters south of the Great Dividing Range.)	—	22
Bream (all)	10, only 2 over 36 cm	26
Butterfish (dusky morwong)	—	23
Chinook salmon	10	—
Eel (freshwater)	—	30
Estuary (Gippsland) perch	—	25
Flathead (all)	—	25
Flounder (all)	—	23
Grass whiting (stranger)	—	20
King George whiting	20	27
Ling	—	33
Luderick	—	22
Macquarie perch	10	25
Murray cod	2	50
Pike, short-finned (snook)	—	36
Rock cod	—	22
Shark, gummy	—	45 (from last gill slit)
Shark, snapper or school	—	40 (from last gill slit)
Silver trevally	—	20
Snapper (under 40 cm)	10	27
Snapper (over 40 cm)	5	27
Sweep (all)	—	23
Sole (all)	—	20
Tailor (skipjack)	—	23
Trout and salmon	See accompanying text (this page)	

*Bag limit is the daily possession limit in, on or adjacent to Victorian waters

Fishing rules and regulations

Closed Seasons

Closed seasons existed for several Victorian species at the time of going to press. Some of these were general, whilst others applied only to specific waterways. Closures included the following:

Species	Closure Period (dates are inclusive)	Closed Area
Blackfish, river	1 September to 31 December	South of the Great Dividing Range
Macquarie perch	1 October to 18 December	Lake Dartmouth and tributaries
Macquarie perch	Until 18 December 1999	Lake Eildon and tributaries
Murray cod	1 September to 30 November	All Victorian and NSW waters
Trout and salmon	See New Trout and Salmon Regulations (pp. 381-2)	

Contact Numbers

For the latest information on Victorian regulations call one of the numbers shown below:

FISHERIES INFORMATION LINE
(03) 9643 3533

DEPARTMENT OF CONSERVATION AND NATURAL RESOURCES OFFICES

Alexandra	(03) 5772 0200	Horsham	(03) 5381 1255	Portland	(03) 5523 3232
Bairnsdale	(03) 5152 0400	Kerang	(03) 5452 1237	Sale	(03) 5144 3048
Ballarat	(03) 5337 0782	Lakes Entrance	(03) 5155 1539	Shepparton	(03) 5831 1777
Benalla	(03) 5761 1611	Mallacoota	(03) 5158 0219	Swan Hill	(03) 5033 1290
Bendigo	(03) 5444 6666	Melbourne	(03) 9651 3728	Traralgon	(03) 5172 2111
Box Hill	(03) 9296 4400	Mildura	(03) 5022 3000	Wangaratta	(03) 5721 5022
Colac	(03) 5233 5533	Mornington	(03) 5975 4779	Warrnambool	(03) 5561 9950
Cowes	(03) 5952 2509	Noojee	(03) 5628 9507	Wodonga	(03) 6055 6111
Geelong	(03) 5226 4667	Orbost	(03) 5161 1222	Yarram	(03) 5182 5155

Trout and freshwater salmon fishing regulations in Victoria underwent a major upgrade in 1997. The new regulations include the reintroduction of a closed season on the taking of trout and salmon from all Victorian streams and at least one lake, as well as size limits, bag limits and additional tackle and fishing method regulations

NEW SOUTH WALES

Recreational angling in New South Wales is controlled by the New South Wales Fisheries Department. Current rules and regulations are to be found in the Fisheries Department's separate freshwater and saltwater guide books. These are available free of charge from many tackle shops, bait outlets and boat hire sheds, or by calling one of the Fisheries Department numbers shown at the end of this section.

Saltwater Regulations

The size and bag limits shown in the following tables apply to saltwater and brackish-water fish in New South Wales. It should be noted that size and bag limits also exist for the taking of many species of invertebrates (crustaceans, molluscs, etc.). These limits are not shown here, but should always be checked carefully with the authorities before you gather invertebrate organisms for bait or food.

Freshwater Regulations

The freshwater size and bag limits shown in the table on the next page apply to the taking of fresh and brackish water species from all waterways within New South Wales. The table sets out the current regulations, plus changes proposed but not formally approved at the time of going to press. Note that in most cases possession limits also apply to freshwater fishing, and these possession limits are generally double the daily bag limit. However, this situation should be carefully checked with the relevant authorities before fishing. A recreational freshwater fishing fee will be introduced during 1998 for all non-tidal waters. Licences may be purchased at tackle shops and other outlets. The cost of this fishing fee will range from $10.00 (28 days), to $25.00 (yearly) and $72.00 (three-yearly).

The taking of silver perch from rivers and streams in New South Wales is now prohibited. Silver perch may only be taken from the backed-up waters of lakes or dams, in accordance with existing size and bag limits, etc.

Closed Seasons

Closed seasons apply for the taking of certain freshwater fish species in New South Wales' waters. For example, there is a general fishing closure on all designated flowing trout waters (gazetted trout streams) from midnight on the Monday of the Queen's Birthday long weekend in June until midnight on the Friday of the Labour Day long weekend in October.

There is also a ban on the keeping or killing of Murray cod between 1 September and 30 November (inclusive) each year. For more details on specific closures and designated waterways, consult the latest guide books, or call one of the numbers shown at the end of this section.

Gear and Technique Restrictions

There are restrictions on the amount and style of fishing tackle that may be used in New South Wales. In saltwater, for example, each angler may use up to 4 rods and/or handlines with up to 3 hooks or sets of ganged hooks attached to each line. In freshwater, the general limit is 2 attended lines (these must be no more than 10 metres away from the angler).

In some trout waters only artificial flies or lures may be used (no baits), and the use of certain baits (including trout or salmon eggs, frogs and live fish) is prohibited in all fresh waters.

Protected Species

The following saltwater and freshwater species are totally protected throughout the state of New South Wales:

- All marine mammals
- Australian grayling
- Ballina angel fish
- Black rock cod
- Eastern blue devil
- Eastern freshwater cod (all)
- Elegant wrasse
- Estuary cod
- Giant Queensland groper
- Great white shark
- Grey nurse and Herbsts nurse sharks
- Macquarie perch
- Trout cod
- Turban snails (north of Seal Rocks)
- Weedy (common) sea dragon

If caught, these fish and other creatures must be returned carefully to the water.

Saltwater Size and Bag Limits

Fish Species	Bag Limit (number per person)	Legal Length (cm)
Australian salmon	5	—
Blackfish, rock (black drummer)	10	30
Bream (all)	20	25
Eels, short and long-finned	—	30
Flathead, dusky	10	33
Flathead, sand and tiger	20 in total (all species)	33
Flathead, other	20 in total (all species)	—
Deep-sea fishes: hapuka, blue-eye trevalla, bar cod and bass groper	5 in total (all species)	—
Groper; blue, red and brown	2 (by line only)	—
Hairtail	10	—
Kingfish, yellowtail	5	60
Luderick (blackfish)	20	25
Mackerel: Spanish and spotted	5 in total (all species)	—
Morwong: jackass and rubberlip	—	28
Morwong, red	5	25
Mullet, sea or bully	—	30
Mullet, poddy (for bait)	20	under 15
Mulloway (jewfish)	5 (only 2 over 70 cm)	45
Shark, school	—	91
Snapper	10	28
Tailor	20	30
Tarwhine	—	20
Teraglin	5	38
Trevally (all)	20	—
Tuna: bluefin, bigeye, yellowfin and albacore	— / 2	under 90 / over 90
Whiting (sand)	20 in total (all species)	27
Whiting (all other)	20 in total (all species)	—

Fishing rules and regulations

Freshwater Size and Bag Limits

Fish Species	Waters	Old Size (cm)	New Size (cm)	Old Bag Limit	New Bag Limit	Possession Limit
Golden perch	All waters	25	30	10	5	10
Murray cray/freshwater spiny cray	All waters	8	9	10	No change	No change
Murray cod	All waters	50	No change	2	No change	4 (only 1 of which can be longer than 100 cm)
Silver perch	Backed-up waters of impoundments	25	No change	5	No change	10
	All other waters	25	N/A	2	0	0
Australian bass/ estuary perch	Backed-up waters of impoundments	N/A	N/A	2	No change	4
	All other waters	N/A	N/A	2	No change	4 (only 1 of which can be longer than 35 cm)

NOTE: Some of these changes had not been formally approved and signed by the New South Wales Fisheries Minister at the time of publication. The zero bag limit for silver perch in all waters except impoundments (dams) is a closure under Section 8 of the Fisheries Management Act 1994, and was signed by the Minister in February 1998

Contact Numbers

Anglers and others wishing to obtain additional information on fisheries rules and regulations in New South Wales should contact one of the fisheries offices on the numbers shown below:

FISHERIES INFORMATION SERVICE
(02) 9566 7802

FISHERMAN'S WATCH (24 hours)
1800 043 536

REGIONAL OFFICES (business hours)

Albury	(02) 6021 2954	Narrandera	(02) 6959 1393
Ballina	(02) 6686 2018	Nelson Bay	(02) 4982 1311
Batemans Bay	(02) 4472 4032	Newcastle	(02) 4929 4530
Bathurst	(02) 6333 4480	Nowra	(02) 4423 2200
Bourke	(02) 6872 2481	Port Macquarie	(02) 6583 1102
Brooklyn (Hawkesbury)	(02) 9985 7256	South West Rocks	(02) 6566 6386
Coffs Harbour	(02) 6652 3977	Swansea	(02) 4971 1201
Condobolin	(02) 6895 2099	Sydney Metropolitan	(02) 9438 5046
Cooma	(02) 6452 3996	Sydney South Metropolitan	(02) 9529 6021
Dareton	(02) 5027 4409	Tamworth	(02) 6765 4591
Deniliquin	(02) 5881 9908	Taree	(02) 6552 6799
Eden	(02) 6496 1377	Tea Gardens	(02) 4997 0214
Gosford	(02) 4329 1819	The Entrance	(02) 4332 2147
Inverell	(02) 6722 1129	Toronto	(02) 4959 2433
Jindabyne	(02) 6456 2115	Toukley	(02) 4396 4990
Karuah	(02) 4997 5248	Tumut	(02) 6947 2916
Lake Illawarra South	(02) 4295 1809	Tuncurry	(02) 6554 6078
Maclean	(02) 6645 2147	Tweed Heads	(07) 5523 1822
Menindee	(02) 8091 4301	Ulladulla	(02) 4455 1725
Merimbula	(02) 6495 2347	Wellington	(02) 6845 1866
Nambucca Heads	(02) 6568 6131	Yass	(02) 6226 2199
Narooma	(02) 4476 2072		

The taking of silver perch from rivers and streams in New South Wales is now prohibited. Silver perch may only be taken from the backed-up waters of lakes, dams or impoundments in accordance with existing size and bag limits. See table above

QUEENSLAND

Recreational angling in the state of Queensland is governed by the Queensland Fisheries Management Authority (QFMA). The Authority should be consulted on the current state of play before going fishing in Queensland. A listing of the phone numbers for regional QFMA offices and the fisheries enforcement 'hot line' number are given at the end of this section.

Many activities within the waters of the Great Barrier Reef and those seas immediately adjacent to it are controlled by the Great Barrier Reef Marine Parks Authority (GBRMPA). Consult this Authority for up-to-date information on zoning restrictions and other regulations for all waters under its control.

Size and Bag Limits

The following tables give size and bag limits for both saltwater and freshwater species that may be taken by recreational anglers in Queensland waters. It should be noted that specific bag limits for the taking of certain species, notably lobsters, apply in the waters of Torres Strait, and these are detailed in full in the Fisheries Regulations 1995. It is also unlawful to take or possess more than the bag limit listed for reef fish species, or more than a total of thirty (30) of the listed reef fish combined. Furthermore, the skin must not be removed from the fillets of any of these fish while at sea.

Size Limits

The following minimum size limits (and, where indicated, maximum size limits) apply throughout Queensland:

Species	Legal Lengths (cm)
Reef Fish	
Black kingfish (cobia)	75
Black-spot tuskfish	30
Broad-barred or grey mackerel	50
Coral trout (all)	38
Dolphin fish (mahi-mahi)	45
Estuary cod	35 (min) 120 (max)
Grass sweetlip	30
Hussar	25
Jew teraglin	45
Large-mouthed nannygai	40
Large-scale sea perch	35
Mangrove jack	35
Maori wrasse	75
Moses perch	25
Mulloway (jewfish)	45
Narrow-barred (Spanish) mackerel	75
Pearl perch	30
Potato cod	35 (min) 120 (max)
Purple tuskfish	30
Queensland groper	35 (min) 120 (max)
Queensland school mackerel	50
Red emperor	45
Red-throat emperor	35
Rosy jobfish	30
Shark (scaley) mackerel	50
Silver jewfish	45
Silver teraglin	30
Small-mouthed nannygai	40
Snapper	30
Spangled emperor	40
Spotted or black jewfish	45
Stripey (Spanish flag)	25
Venus tuskfish	30
Wahoo	75
Yellowtail kingfish	50
Other Fish	
Australian bass	30
Barramundi	58 (min) 120 (max)
Bar-tailed flathead	30
Black-lipped pearl oyster	9
Blue swimmer crab (carapace)	15
Burnett salmon	40
Cooktown salmon	40
Freshwater eel	30
Golden-lined whiting	23
Golden perch (yellowbelly)	30
Gold-lipped oyster	13 (min) 23 (max)
Luderick (blackfish)	23
Mud crab (carapace)	15
Mud (dusky) flathead	30
Moreton Bay bug (carapace)	6.2
Pikey bream	23
Sand or blue crab (carapace)	15
Sand flathead	30
Sand whiting	23
Saratoga	35
Sea mullet	30
Silver perch	30
Small-spotted javelin fish	30
Spanner crab (carapace)	10
Spotted javelin fish	30
Tailor	30
Tarwhine	23
Trochus	8 (min) 12.5 (max)
Yellow-finned bream	23

Bag Limits

In all Queensland waters, a person may not take or possess more than the following:

Species	Bag/ Possession Limit (per person)
Australian bass	2
Barramundi	5
Golden perch (yellowbelly)	10
Mary River cod*	1
Molluscs (excluding oysters)	50
Mud crabs	10
Murray cod	5
Saratoga	1
Silver perch	10
Reef Fish	
Potato cod	1
Queensland groper	1
Maori wrasse	1
Estuary cod	10
Red emperor	10
Red throat emperor	10
Spangled emperor	10
Fingermark	10
Large scale sea perch	10
Spotted black jew	10
Rosy jobfish	10
Black kingfish (cobia)	10
Broad-barred (grey) mackerel	10
Narrow-barred (Spanish) mackerel	10
Mulloway (jewfish)	10
Large-mouth nannygai	10
Small-mouth nannygai	10
Pearl perch	10
Black-spot tuskfish	10
Purple tuskfish	10
Venus tuskfish	10
Teraglin jew	10
Coral trout	10
Wahoo	10
School mackerel	30
Spotted mackerel	30
Snapper	30

* A person may take or possess one Mary River cod from waters upstream of the following dams: Bill Gunn, Cressbrook, Hinze, Maroon, Moogerah, North Pine, Somerset and Wivenhoe. Elsewhere, the limit is zero

Fishing rules and regulations

Closed Seasons

Closed seasons exist for the taking of the following species during the inclusive periods specified:

Species	Closed Season
BARRAMUNDI	
Gulf of Carpentaria and adjoining waterways south of the intersection of longitude 142°9' east with shore at high-water mark	Variable from year to year depending upon the spawning season
Elsewhere	Midday 1 November to midday 1 February
SPANNER OR FROG CRABS	Midday 20 November to midday 20 December

Protected Species

The following species must not be taken or harmed in Queensland waters:

- Ceratodus or lungfish
- Helmet, trumpet and clam shells
- Female mud and sand (blue swimmer) crabs
- Whales, porpoises, dugongs and dolphins
- Turtles (all)
- Egg-bearing female spanner crabs
- Egg-bearing female Moreton Bay bugs (and other egg-bearing sea bugs)
- Egg-bearing female slipper lobsters
- Mary River cod (except where specified)

Contact Numbers

Additional information on fisheries rules and regulations in Queensland can be obtained during business hours on the numbers below:

Bowen	(07) 4786 3444
Brisbane	(07) 3860 3506
Bundaberg	(07) 4153 7800
Cairns	(07) 4052 7404
Gladstone	(07) 4976 0729
Gold Coast	(07) 5583 5500
Hervey Bay	(07) 4125 3989
Ingham	(07) 4776 1611
Karumba	(07) 4745 9142
Mackay	(07) 4951 8724
Maryborough	(07) 4123 7722
Mooloolooba	(07) 5444 4599
Noosa	(07) 5449 7555
Port Douglas	(07) 4099 5160
Rockhampton	(07) 4936 0218
Roma	(07) 4622 9999
Thursday Island	(07) 4069 1772
Townsville	(07) 4772 7311

FISHERIES ENFORCEMENT HOT LINE
(24 Hours)
1800 017 116

Many activities within the waters of the Great Barrier Reef and the seas surrounding it are controlled by the Great Barrier Reef Marine Parks Authority. Consult the authority for up-to-date information on zoning restrictions and other regulations

NORTHERN TERRITORY

The Fisheries Division of the Department of Primary Industry and Fisheries is responsible for the management of recreational fishing in the Northern Territory. The department's rules and regulations are explained in the *Northern Territory Fishing and Boating Guide*, available from the Recreational Fishing Office in Darwin.

You don't need a fishing licence in the Northern Territory, but you may not sell or barter your catch. Some special controls do apply in Kakadu National Park. Contact Parks Australia North for advice, telephone (08) 8938 1100.

It is essential that anglers make themselves familiar with the details of the latest regulations before going fishing.

Legislation in the Northern Territory includes personal possession limits for managed species: barramundi (*Lates calcarifer*), narrow-barred Spanish mackerel (*Scomberomorus commerson*), black jewfish (*Protonibea diacanthus*) and mud crab (*Scylla serrata*). There is also a general personal fish possession limit for recreational fishing to enhance the long-term sustainability of fish stocks in the Northern Territory.

To assist with identification, the entire skin must be left on fillets or trunks of all non-managed fish species caught.

General Personal Fish Possession Limits

In the Northern Territory, you may not possess a combination of fish and fillets exceeding the equivalent of 30 whole fish, other than in your place of permanent residence.

Species exempt from the general possession limit are:

- managed species (see following)
- crustaceans (including prawns)
- molluscs (including squid)
- bait fish (mullet, whiting, garfish, pilchards, sardines and herring)
- marine bream (*Acanthopagrus berda*)
- echinoderms (sea urchins and starfish)
- aquarium fish

Size and Possession Limits for Managed Species

Species	Minimum Size Limit (cm)	Possession Limit
Barramundi	55	5 per person 2 per person in Mary River
Jewfish, black	–	5 per person
Spanish mackerel, narrow-barred	–	5 per person
Mud crabs*	carapace width: 13 (male) 14 (female)	10 per person (both) 30 per boat (both)
Cod and groper	A maximum size limit applies to all cod and groper, which must not be taken if larger than 1.2 metres	

* Female mud crabs bearing eggs may not be taken

The general possession limit enables you to possess up to:

- 30 fish in total of the non-managed species;
- 5 of each of the managed species (note that a 2 barramundi possession limit applies in the Mary River Management Zone);
- 10 mud crabs;
- any exempt non-managed species.

Note that the general possession limit is the maximum allowable number of fish each person may have in possession at any time. It is not a boat limit or a daily limit.

Managed Species Possession Limits

The personal possession limits on the managed species list have been designed to conserve stocks of these popular species and ensure long-term sustainability. The size and possession limits are set out in the table above.

To allow practical enforcement, any fish or fillets from managed species must be kept in separate packing or containers from fillets of other species. For further information, there are brochures on each of the managed species available from the Northen Territory Fisheries Division, PO Box 990, Darwin NT 0801.

Seasonally Closed Areas

From 1 October through 31 January (inclusive), recreational fishing is not permitted in the area downstream of the Shady Camp barrage on the Mary River system or on the Daly River downstream of the Moon Billabong outlet.

Contact Numbers

Anglers and others wishing to purchase maps or the video 'Sportfishing Australia's Northern Territory' or to obtain additional information on rules and regulations from the Fisheries Division of the Northern Territory Department of Primary Industry and Fisheries should contact the Fisheries Division Licensing Office, GPO Box 990, Darwin NT 0801.

Contact Numbers

RECREATIONAL FISHING OFFICE
(08) 8999 4395

Reports of illegal fishing activity should be directed immediately to:

POLICE FISHERIES
ENFORCEMENT HOTLINE
1800 89 1136

Fishing rules and regulations

WESTERN AUSTRALIA

Recreational fishing in Australia's largest state is controlled by the Fisheries Department of Western Australia. The following information is only a summary of Western Australia's extensive recreational fishing regulations. For more details, consult the latest guide books and pamphlets available from the Fisheries Department at one of the offices listed.

Size and Bag Limits
In Western Australia, the most popular and important angling species are divided into categories (e.g. Prize Fish, Reef Fish, Bread and Butter Fish, etc.). Most categories have a total mixed bag limit (covering a combination of species from each list), and individual species or groups of species from within each category may also have separate limits.

Bag and size limits and other restrictions governing the taking of shellfish, lobsters and marron have not been included here. These should be checked carefully before harvesting. Strict penalties exist for the illegal harvesting of these invertebrates. Finally, it should be noted that (at the time of publication) a special recreational licence was required for catching or harvesting abalone, rock lobsters and marron, as well as recreational net fishing and south-western freshwater angling (for trout and redfin).

Closed Seasons
At the time of publication, there was a closed season on the taking of trout in most Western Australian waters from 1 May until 31 August each year (inclusive). Other closures for specific species, particularly lobsters and marron, should be checked with the authorities before harvesting.

Protected Species
The following species are totally protected at all times in Western Australian waters:
- Great white shark
- Leafy seadragon
- Potato cod
- Whale shark

Contact Numbers

Information on rules and regulations in Western Australia can be obtained from the following offices during business hours:

Perth	(08) 9482 7333
Bunbury	(08) 7212 598
Mandurah	(08) 9535 1240

FISHWATCH HOT LINE (24 hours)
1800 815 507

Size and Bag Limits

Fish Species or Category	Size Limit (mm)	Bag Limit
Prize Fish		4 of each, 8 combined
Billfish (marlin, sailfish, etc.)	—	Mixed bag of 4
Cobia (black kingfish)	—	4
Cod (all saltwater)	1200 maximum	Mixed bag of 4
Coral trout	450	4
Jewfish, Westralian	500	4
Mackerel, Spanish and broad barred	750	4
Mackerel, shark, spotted and school	500	4
Mahi-mahi (dolphin fish)	—	4
Mulloway (all, combined)	450	Mixed bag of 4
Queenfish	—	4
Salmon, Australian	300	4
Samson fish	600	4
Sharks (all, except whale sharks)	—	Mixed bag of 4
Trout (all, combined)	300	4
Tuna, southern bluefin	—	4
Yellowtail kingfish	—	4
Wahoo	750	4
Reef Fish		Mixed bag of 8 combined with other reef fish
Emperor, red	410	8
Emperor, spangled	410	8
Groper (baldchin) and tuskfish	400	8
Snapper, pink	410	8
Snapper, queen (blue morwong)	410	8
Snapper (nor' west or tricky)	280	8
Key Angling Fish		8 per angler
Cobbler	430	8
Fingermark bream	—	8
Giant threadfin salmon	—	8
Mangrove jack	—	8
Tailor	250	8
Table Fish		20 per angler
Bream (all)	250	20
Flathead (all) and flounder (all)	300 (flathead) 250 (flounder)	20 (combined)
Leatherjackets (all)	250	20
Pike and snook	280 (pike) 330 (snook)	20 (combined)
Skipjack trevally	200	20
Snapper, red (nannygai)	230	20
Tarwhine	230	20
Threadfin (blue, etc.)	—	20
Whiting, King George	250 280 (south coast)	20
Bread and Butter Fish*	No size limit	40 per angler
Garfish (all)	—	40
Herring, Australian (Tommy ruff)	—	40
Mackerel, blue or slimy	—	40
Mullet, sea and yellow-eye	—	40
Whiting, western sand, school and yellowfin	—	40
Special Bag Limits		
Barramundi	550	5 (possession limit)
Groper, western blue	400	1 (daily bag limit)
Cephalopods		
Squid, octopus and cuttlefish		15 (combined) 30 (per boat)

All fish species not listed in other specific categories are automatically classified as Bread and Butter Fish

SOUTH AUSTRALIA

Recreational angling in South Australia is governed by the Fisheries Division of the South Australian Department of Primary Industry. The Department's guide books provide all necessary information regarding rules and regulations and are freely available from both tackle shops and the offices listed at the end of this section.

Size Limits

Anglers are bound by size limits, bag limits, and boat limits. It should be noted that the table shown here does not include the many invertebrate species (abalone, crabs, lobsters, cockles, razorfish, etc.) also covered by bag, size and boat limits in South Australia.

Note also that in South Australia specific size, bag and boat limits apply for certain species in specific locations (such as those for mulloway in the Coorong estuary system, or snapper in the Gulf St Vincent, Investigator Strait and Backstairs Passage).

Finally, close attention should be given to the regulations applying to snapper and King George whiting. These two species are South Australia's most important recreational fish, and rules affecting them have been fine-tuned in recent years.

Contact Numbers

Anglers and any other people wishing to obtain further information on fisheries rules and regulations in South Australia should contact one of the following offices by telephoning one of the numbers listed below during business hours:

Adelaide	(08) 8226 2311
Kadina	(08) 8821 3242
Kingston	(08) 8767 2358
Mount Gambier	(08) 8724 2942
Port Adelaide	(08) 8449 1432
Port Lincoln	(08) 8688 3488
Streaky Bay	(08) 8626 1247
Whyalla	(08) 8648 8187

FISHWATCH HOT LINE
(24 Hours)
1800 065 522

RECFISH AUSTRALIA
1800 686 818

Closed Seasons

There is a closed season on the taking of black bream from the Onkaparinga River, upstream of the Main South Road Bridge at Noarlunga, from 1 November to 31 January each year (inclusive). There is also a state-wide closed season on the taking of Murray cod from 1 September to 31 December each year (inclusive). There are also various other restricted areas and periodic closures which should be checked carefully in current guide books available from South Australia's Department of Primary Industry.

Protected Species

The following species are protected by law in South Australia:

- All marine mammals
- Blue crabs with eggs attached
- Eel-tailed catfish
- Giant crabs with eggs attached
- Great white shark
- Groper in Gulf waters, Investigator Strait and Backstairs Passage
- Leafy sea dragons
- Murray river crayfish
- River blackfish
- Rock lobsters with eggs attached
- Silver perch
- Trout cod
- Yabbies with eggs attached
- Also all fish of the genera *Ambassis* (glass perchlets), *Mogurnda* (purple spotted gudgeons), and *Nannoperca* (pygmy perch)

Note that alterations to the regulations for 1998 include a bag limit of 200 yabbies per person per day.

Size and Bag Limits

Fish Species	Size Limit (cm)	Bag Limit (number per person)	Boat Limit (number per boat)
Bream, black	28	—	—
Callop (golden perch)	33	6	—
Flounder (all)	—	20	60
Garfish*	21	80	240
Groper, blue**	60	2	6
Kingfish, yellowtail	40	—	—
Mullet (all)	21	—	—
Mulloway (within Coorong)	46	10	—
Mulloway (all other waters)	75	3	—
Murray cod	50 minimum 110 maximum	2	—
Salmon, Australian	21–35	—	—
Salmon, Australian	over 35	15	45
Shark, gummy***	45	—	—
Shark, school***	40	—	—
Silver perch	33	—	—
Snapper (Gulf St Vincent, Investigator Strait, Backstairs Passage)	38–60	5	15
Snapper (other waters)	38–60	10	30
Snapper (all waters)	over 60	2	6
Snook	36	25	75
Squid (calamari)	—	15	45
Sweep (all)	24	—	—
Trout (all)	28	—	—
Whiting, King George	30	20	60
Whiting, yellowfin or sand	24	25	75

* Garfish are measured from the tip of the upper jaw to the tip of the tail
** The taking of groper is prohibited in Gulf St Vincent waters, as well as in Investigator Strait and Backstairs Passage
*** These sharks are measured from the fifth gill slit to the base of the tail

Fishing rules and regulations

TASMANIA

In Tasmania, saltwater fishing is controlled by the Marine Resources Division of the Department of Primary Industries and Fisheries. Inland or freshwater angling comes under the umbrella of the Inland Fisheries Commission. Comprehensive guides are available detailing the rules and regulations for both salt and freshwater fishing, and anglers are advised to seek copies of these from tackle shops or the state authorities.

Angling Licences
A licence is required to fish in fresh water in Tasmania. Different forms of licence are available, from one day to full season duration, and with varying rates for adults, pensioners and juveniles.

Saltwater Regulations
The following tables show the size and bag limit regulations and the open seasons that apply to saltwater recreational fishing in Tasmania. Some size and bag limits and seasons are set each year. Check with the Marine Resources Division for the latest details.

Freshwater Regulations
When your licence for inland fishing is purchased, the authorities supply a very comprehensive booklet containing all necessary information regarding the various controls and restrictions on when, where, and how anglers may fish, particularly for trout. These regulations may vary from season to season, so it is important to refer to the current booklet.

Protected Species
- Elephant snail
- Female freshwater crayfish
- Grayling (cucumber herring)
- Great white shark
- Handfish
- Limpets
- Pipehorse, pipefish, seahorse and sea dragon
- Threefin blenny

Saltwater Bag Limits

Species	Bag Limit (per person)
Abalone*	10 per day
Crayfish (rock lobster)**	5 per day
Octopus (Eaglehawk Bay)	5 per day
Scallop	Set each year
Shark (school and gummy)	2 per day

* Possession limit 20 for licence holders, 5 for non-licence holders
** Possession limit 10 for licence holders, 5 for non-licence holders

Contact Numbers

For additional information on rules and regulations, contact one of the following:

INLAND FISHERIES COMMISSION
(03) 6223 6622

PARKS AND WILDLIFE
(03) 6233 6556

MARINE RESOURCES (Recreational)
(03) 6233 6234

FISHERMAN'S WATCH
(24 Hours)
1800 005 555

FISHWATCH HOT LINE (24 hours)
1800 815 507

Freshwater Size and Bag Limits

Fish Species or Category	Minimum Length (mm)	Bag Limit (person/day)
Trout and salmon (all)	220	12 (in any combination, including Tasmanian blackfish)
Tasmanian blackfish	220	12 (in any combination, including trout and salmon)
Bream	230	—
Flounder	250	—
Giant crayfish (carapace)	130	3 (male only)

Saltwater Seasons

Open seasons exist for the taking of the following species during the inclusive periods specified:

Species	Open Season
Male crayfish*	2nd Saturday in November to 31 August
Female crayfish*	2nd Saturday in November to 30 April
Banded morwong	By notice
Queen scallop	By notice
Commercial scallop	By notice
Doughboy scallop	By notice

*Note: Any crayfish retained by a recreational fisher must be clipped or punched indicating that it must not be sold

Minimum and Maximum Legal Sizes

Fish Species	Minimum Length (mm)	Maximum Length (mm)
Australian salmon	250	—
Banded morwong	330	430
Bastard (silver) trumpeter	330	—
Bream	230	—
Commercial scallop	80	—
Crayfish (rock lobster), female	105	—
Crayfish (rock lobster), male	110	—
Doughboy scallop	80	—
Flathead (all)	300	—
Flounder	250	—
Garfish	230	—
Gummy shark	750	—
Mullet (all)	200	—
Perch (morwong)	230	—
Queen scallop	100	—
Real trumpeter	350	—
School shark	710	—
Wrasse (*Notolobrus*)	280	430

INDEX OF FISH SPECIES

Acanthocybium solandri 376
Acanthopagrus australis 340–1
Acanthopagrus berda 340–1
Acanthopagrus butcherii 340–1
Achoerodus gouldii 348
Achoerodus viridis 348
albacore 336
Aldrichetta forsteri 356
Argyrosomus hololepidotus 357
Arripis georgianus 371
Arripis trutta 363
Astractoscion eaquidens 370

barracouta 337
barracuda 337
barramundi 338
bass, Australian 339
Belonidae family 352
Bidyanus bidyanus 360
blackfish *see* luderick
bonito 339
bream, eastern black 340–1
bream, pikey 340–1
bream, southern 340–1

Caranx ignobilis 371–2
carp 341
catfish, eel-tailed 342
Chrysophrys auratus 366–7
cobia 342
cod, estuary 343
coral trout 344
Coryphaena equiselis 345
Coryphaena hippurus 345
Cyprinus carpio 341

dart, swallowtail 344
dhufish *see* jewfish, West Australian
dolphin fish 345
drummer, black 345
drummer, silver 346

eastern rock blackfish *see* drummer, black
Elops machnata 349
emperor, red 346
Epinephelus spp. 343

flathead, dusky 347
flathead, sand 347
flathead, tiger 347
flounder 347

Galeohinus galeus 366
garfish 348

Girella elevata 345
Girella tricuspidata 353
Glaucosoma hebraicum 350
Gnathanodon speciosus 371–2
groper, blue 348

hairtail 349
Hemiramphidae spp. 348
Hephaestus spp. 368
herring, Australian *see* tommy rough
herring, giant 349
Istiophorous platypetrus 362–3

javelin fish 350
jewfish *see* mulloway
jewfish, West Australian 350
John dory 351

kahawai *see* salmon, Australian
Katsuwonus pelamis 375
kingfish, yellowtail 351
Kyphosus sydneyanus 346

Lates calcarifer 338
Latris lineata 374
leatherjackets 352
Leionura atun 337
Lethrinus chrystostomus 369
long tom 352
luderick 353
Lutjanus argentimaculatus 354
Lutjanus sebae 346

Maccullochella peeli 358
mackerel, blue *see* mackerel, slimy
mackerel, school 353
mackerel, slimy 354
mackerel, Spanish 353
mackerel, spotted 353
Macquaria ambigua 359
Macquaria australasica 360
Macquaria novemaculeata 339
mahi mahi *see* dolphin fish
Makaira indica 355
Makaira mazara 355
mangrove jack 354
marlin, black 355
marlin, blue 355
marlin, striped 355
Monacanthidae spp. 352
morwong, common 356
morwong, silver 356
Mugil cephalus 356
mullet, sand 356

mullet, sea 356
mullet, yellow-eye 356
mulloway 357
Murray cod 358
Mustelus antarcticus 366
Myxus elongatus 356

nannygai 359
Nemadactylus douglasii 356
Neoplatycephalus richardsoni 347

Oncorhyncus mykiss 373

Perca fluviatilis 362
perch, English *see* redfin
perch, European *see* redfin
perch, golden 359
perch, Macquarie 360
perch, silver 360
Platycephalus arenarius 347
Platycephalus bassensis 347
Platycephalus caeruleopunctatus 347
Platycephalus fuscus 347
Platycephalus speculator 347
Plectropoma maculatum 344
Plectropoma spp. 344
Polynemidae spp. 364
Pomadasys hasta 350
Pomatomus saltatrix 369
Pseudocaranx dentex 372
Pseudorhombus arsius 347
Pseudorhombus jenyrsii 347

queenfish 361

Rachycentron canadus 342
redfin 362
Rhabdosargus sarba 370

sailfish, Indo-Pacific 362–3
Salmo trutta 373
salmon, Australian 363
salmon, threadfin 364
Samson fish 364
saratoga 365
Sarda australis 339
Sarda orientalis 339
Scleropages jardini 365
Scleropages leichhardti 365
Scomber australicus 354
Scomberoides commersonnianus 361
Scomberoides lysan 361
Scomberomorus commerson 353
Scomberomorus munroi 353

Scomberomorus niphonia 353
Scomberomorus queenslandicus 353
Scorpis spp. 368
Seriola hippos 364
Seriola lalandi 351
shark, gummy 366
shark, school 366
Sillaginodes punctatus 376–7
Sillago ciliata 376–7
skinny fish *see* queenfish
snapper 366–7
snook 367
sooty grunter 368
Sphyraena barracuda 337
Sphyraena novaehollandiae 367
sweep 368
sweetlip 369

tailor 369
Tandanus tandanus 342
tarwhine 370
teraglin 370
Tetrapturus audax 355
Thunnus alalunga 336
Thunnus albacares 374
Thunnus maccoyii 374
Thunnus tonggol 375
tommy rough 371
Trachichthodes affinis 359
Trachinotus coppingeri 344
Trachurus novaezelandiae 377
trevally, giant 371–2
trevally, golden 371–2
trevally, silver 372
Trichiurus lepturus 349
trout, brown 373
trout, rainbow 373
trumpeter, striped *see* trumpeter, Tasmanian
trumpeter, Tasmanian 374
tuna, longtail 375
tuna, northern bluefin *see* tuna, longtail
tuna, skipjack 375
tuna, southern bluefin 374
tuna, yellowfin 374

wahoo 376
whiting, King George 376–7
whiting, sand 376–7

yellowbelly *see* perch, golden
yellowtail 377

Zeus faber 351

INDEX OF PLACE NAMES

Numbers in **bold** indicate main entry, those in *italics* indicate photographs

Abbreviations used in the index
CA Conservation Area
CP Conservation Park
CR Conservation Reserve
FP Forest Park
FR Forest Reserve
GR Game Reserve
NP National Park
NR Nature Reserve
PA Protected Area
RP Recreation Park
RR Regional Reserve
SF State Forest
SP State Park
SR State Reserve
SRA State Recreation Area
WP Wildlife Park
WPA Wilderness Protection Area

A1 Mine Settlement Vic 65 N1, 72 E9
Abbeyard Vic 70 B2, 72 G7
Abbieglassie Qld 144 C6
Abbotsford NSW 114 G10, 116 G1
Abbotsham Tas 254 F5
Aberbaldie NSW 111 J1, 113 J9
Abercorn Qld 145 J2
Abercrombie NSW 109 D1, 110 C9
Abercrombie River NSW 110 D9
Aberdeen NSW 110 G4
Aberfeldy Vic 65 N2, 72 F10
Aberfoyle NSW 113 K7
Aberfoyle Qld 151 N5
Abergowrie Qld 149 L8
Abermain NSW 111 H5
Abingdon Downs Qld 149 H6
Abington NSW 113 H7
Abminga SA 234 C1
Abydos WA 211 J6
Acacia Store NT 174 D5
Acheron Vic 72 D8
Acland Qld 145 K6
Acraman Creek CP SA 232 A5
Acton Downs Qld 151 K3
Adaminaby NSW 109 B6
Adavale Qld 153 M4
Adcock Gorge WA 209 J6
Addington Vic 64 B1, 67 K4
Adelaide SA **214–15**, **216–17**, 221, 233 J10
Adelaide Lead Vic 67 K3
Adelaide River NT 174 D5
Adelong NSW 109 A5, 117 P6
Adels Grove Qld 148 B8
Adjungbilly NSW 109 B4
Admiralty Gulf WA 209 J2, 302
Advance Qld 153 K3
Advancetown Lake Qld 121, **136–7**, *136–7*
Adventure Bay Tas 253 K8
Afton Downs Qld 151 L4
Agery SA 233 H8
Agnes Water Qld 134, 147 M10
Agnew Qld 154 C5
Agnew WA 205 K7
Aileron NT 178 G4
Ailsa Vic 68 F10
Aireys Inlet Vic 64 D6, 67 L8
Airlie Beach Qld 146 F2, 289
Airly Vic 70 C7
Ajana WA 204 C7
Alawoona SA 233 N9
Alba Qld 151 L4
Albacutya Vic 68 D8
Albany WA 202 F10
Albany Downs Qld 144 D6
Albatross Bay Qld 154 B6, 281
Albemarle NSW 114 E9
Alberrie Creek SA 234 G8
Albert NSW 115 N9
Alberton Vic 70 B9
Alberton West Vic 65 P7, 70 A9
Albion Downs WA 205 K6
Albion Park NSW 109 G3
Albro Qld 146 C7
Albury NSW 117 M8, 264
Alcala Qld 148 D10, 150 E1

Alcomie Tas 254 C4
Alcoota NT 179 J4
Alderley Qld 150 D6
Aldersyde WA 202 E5
Aldinga SA 230 A5, 233 J10
Aldinga Beach SA 230 A5
Aldingham Qld 151 K6
Alectown NSW 110 A6, 115 P10, 117 P1
Alehvale Qld 148 G8
Alexander Morrison NP WA 202 B1, 204 D10
Alexandra Vic 72 D8
Alexandra River Qld 148 C7, 285
Alexandria NT 177 M7
Alford SA 233 H7
Alfred NP Vic 71 M5
Alfred Town NSW 117 N6
Ali-Curung NT 177 J10, 179 J1
Alice NSW 113 L3
Alice Downs Qld 146 A10, 151 N10, 153 N1
Alice Downs WA 209 M8
Alice Springs NT 179 H6
Alkira Qld 145 H6
Allambee Vic 65 M6
Allambee South Vic 65 M6
Allambi NT 179 J7
Allambie NSW 114 E8
Allan Qld 145 L8
Allandale SA 234 D4
Allandy NSW 114 D4
Allans Flat Vic 73 H4
Allansford Vic 66 F8
Allawah Qld 145 J8
Alleena NSW 117 M4
Allendale Vic 64 C1, 67 K4
Allendale East SA 230 G9
Allies Creek Qld 145 J4
Alligator Creek Qld 149 N9
Allora Qld 145 L8
Allworth NSW 111 K5
Allynbrook NSW 111 J4
Alma NSW 117 H3
Alma SA 233 J8
Alma Vic 67 K3
Alma Park NSW 117 M7
Almaden Qld 149 K6, 155 B9
Almonds Vic 72 E4
Almoola Qld 146 E3
Almora Qld 148 C8
Alonnah Tas 253 K7
Alpha Qld 144 A6, 153 P6
Alpha Qld 146 C10
Alpha Qld 146 C9
Alpine NP Vic 70 B4, 72 G9, 73 M7
Alroy Qld 151 K8
Alroy Qld 153 M7
Alroy Downs NT 177 L7
Alsace Qld 146 G8
Alsace Qld 148 C10, 150 D1
Alstonville NSW 113 P3
Althorpe Islands CP SA 230 A2
Altona Vic 64 G3, 67 N6
Alum Cliffs SR Tas 254 G7
Alva Qld 146 D1, 149 P9
Alva Qld 153 N2
Alvie Vic 64 A5, 67 J7
Alyangula NT 175 M6
Amamoor Qld 145 M5
Amanbidji NT 176 B2
Amaroo Qld 153 N2
Amata SA 231 D1
Ambalindum NT 179 J5
Ambathala Qld 153 N4
Amboola Qld 144 D5
Ambrose Qld 147 K9
Ambulbinya Peak NT 179 K5
Amburla NT 178 G5
Amby Qld 144 D5
Amby Downs Qld 144 E5
Amelup WA 202 F8
Amen Corner SA 230 B3
American River SA 230 B4, 321
Amery WA 202 E3
Amherst Vic 67 K3
Amity Point Qld 124, 145 N7
Ammaroo NT 179 K3
Amoonguna NT 179 H6

Amor Downs Qld 151 L9
Amosfield NSW 113 K2
Amphitheatre Vic 67 J3
Amungee Mungee NT 177 H2
Anakie Qld 146 E8
Anakie Vic 64 D4, 67 L6
Anavale Qld 146 B1, 149 M10
Andado NT 179 K9
Andamooka SA 232 G1
Andamooka SA 234 F10
Anderson Vic 65 J7
Ando NSW 109 C8
Andoom Qld 154 B5
Andover Tas 253 K2
Andranangoe Creek NT see Goose Creek NT
Andrews SA 233 J7
Angahook-Lorne SP Vic 64 C6, 67 L8
Angalarri Creek NT 299
Angas Downs NT 178 F8
Angas Valley SA 233 L9
Angaston SA 233 K9
Angellala Qld 144 B5
Angellala Qld 144 C4
Angepena SA 233 K1, 235 K10
Angip Vic 68 E9
Angle Point WA 210 E6
Angledool NSW 115 P2
Anglers Reach NSW 109 B6
Anglers Rest Vic 70 E2, 73 K7
Anglesea Vic 64 D6, 67 L8
Angourie NSW 113 N5, 266
Angurugu NT 175 M7
Anketell WA 205 H7
Anna Bay NSW 111 K5
Anna Creek SA 234 E7
Anna Plains WA 211 M3
Annaburroo NT 174 E5
Annean WA 204 G5
Anningie NT 178 G3
Annitowa NT 177 M10, 179 M2
Annuello Vic 68 G4
Ansons Bay Tas 255 P4
Answer Downs Qld 150 F5
Anthony Lagoon NT 177 K5
Antill Plains Qld 149 N9
Antill Ponds Tas 253 K1, 255 L10
Antwerp Vic 68 E9
Apamurra SA 233 K10
Aparatjara Homeland SA 231 B1
Aparawatatja SA 231 A1
Apoinga SA 233 K8
Apollo Bay Vic 64 B8, 67 K9
Appealinna Station SA 233 J2
Appila SA 233 J6
Appin NSW 109 G2, 110 G10
Appin South Vic 69 K8
Apple Tree Flat NSW 111 L2
Apsley NSW 110 C5
Apsley Vic 66 B3
Apsley River NSW 113 K9
Aqua Downs Qld 144 B6
Arabella Qld 144 B5
Arakoon NSW 113 N9
Araluen NSW 109 E6
Araluen North NSW 109 E6
Aramac Qld 151 N7
Arapunya NT 179 L4
Ararat Vic 66 G4
Arawata Vic 65 L6
Arawee Qld 153 L4
Arcadia Vic 72 B5
Archdale Vic 67 J2
Archdale Junction Vic 67 J2
Archer Bend NP Qld 154 C7
Archer River Roadhouse Qld 154 D7
Archervale Qld 150 G6
Archies Creek Vic 65 K7
Archipelago of the Recherche WA 203 N8
Arckaringa SA 234 C5
Arcoona SA 232 G2
Arcturus Downs Qld 146 F9
Ardath WA 202 F4
Ardglen NSW 110 G2
Ardlethan NSW 117 M4
Ardmona Vic 72 B4
Ardmore Qld 150 C5
Ardno Qld 144 E5

Ardno Vic 66 A6
Ardoch Qld 153 L7
Ardrossan Qld 144 A7, 153 P7
Ardrossan SA 233 H9
Area Vic 68 B7
Areegra Vic 68 F9
Areyonga NT 178 F6
Argadargada NT 179 M2
Argyle Qld 144 D8
Argyle Vic 67 N3
Ariah Park NSW 117 M4
Arizona Qld 148 E10, 150 F1
Arkaba SA 233 J3
Arkaroola SA 235 L10
Arkaroola – Mount Painter Sanctuary SA 235 K9
Arkaroola Village SA 235 L10
Arklay Creek Tas 255 L6
Arkona Vic 66 E1, 68 E10
Arlparra NT 179 J3
Arltunga Historical Reserve NT 179 J5
Armadale WA 202 C5
Armatree NSW 110 A2, 112 A10
Armdobilla Qld 153 N6
Armidale NSW 113 J8
Armraynald Qld 148 C7
Armstrong Vic 66 G4
Armstrong Beach Qld 146 G4
Armuna Qld 146 E2
Arnhem Land NT 28, 172, 175 J5, 284, 294
Arno Qld 153 K1
Arno Bay SA 232 F7
Arnold Vic 67 K2
Aroona SA 233 J2
Arrabury Qld 152 F5
Arranfield Qld 153 N5
Arrawarra NSW 113 N6
Arrilalah Qld 151 L9
Arrino WA 204 D9
Arthur Pieman PA Tas 254 A7
Arthur Range Tas 252 F6
Arthur River Tas 254 A4
Arthur River WA 202 D7
Arthurs Creek Vic 65 H2, 67 P5, 72 B10
Arthurs Lake Tas **248–9**, 255 J9, 328
Arthurs Seat SP Vic 64 G6
Arthurton SA 233 H8
Arthurville NSW 110 B5
Artimore SA 233 K2
Arubiddy WA 207 C7
Arumpo NSW 116 D3
Ascot Vale NSW 114 B8
Ashbourne SA 230 A6
Ashburton Downs WA 210 F9
Ashburton River WA 210 D8
Ashens Vic 66 F2
Ashford NSW 113 H4
Ashley NSW 112 E4
Ashmont NSW 114 D9
Ashover Qld 150 D4
Ashton Qld 151 M4
Ashville SA 230 B7
Astrebla Downs NP Qld 150 E10
Atartinga NT 179 J4
Atherfield Qld 151 N4
Atherton Qld 149 L6, 155 D8
Athlone Vic 65 L5
Atley WA 205 J7
Atnarpa NT 179 J6
Attunga NSW 112 G9
Atula NT 179 M5
Aubrey Vic 68 E9
Auburn Qld 145 J6
Auburn SA 233 J8
Auburn River NP Qld 145 J3
Augathella Qld 144 B4
Augusta WA 195, 197, 202 B8
Augustus Downs Qld 148 C8
Aurukun Aboriginal Community Qld 154 B7
Auski Roadhouse WA 211 H8
Austin Downs WA 204 G6
Austral Downs NT 177 P9
Australia Plains SA 233 K8
Australind WA 202 B7
Auteuil Qld 151 N8

Authoringa Qld 144 B5
Auvergne NT 174 B10, 176 B1
Avalon Vic 64 E4, 67 M7
Avenel NSW 114 A5
Avenel Vic 72 B7
Avenue SA 230 E9
Avoca Qld 146 D9
Avoca Tas 255 M8
Avoca Vic 67 J3
Avoca Downs WA 203 M3
Avoca River Vic 69 H10
Avon NSW 114 D9
Avon SA 233 J8
Avon Downs NT 177 N8
Avon Downs Qld 146 D5
Avon Downs Police Station NT 177 N8
Avon River Vic 50
Avon Valley NP WA 202 C4
Avon Wilderness Park Vic 70 B5, 73 H10
Avondale NSW 115 H4
Avondale SA 235 J10
Avonmore Qld 146 C9
Avonmore Vic 67 M1, 69 M10
Avonsleigh Vic 65 J4
Axe Creek Vic 67 M2
Axedale Vic 67 M2
Aylmerton NSW 109 F3, 110 F10
Ayr Qld 146 D1, 149 P10
Ayrford Vic 66 G8
Ayton Qld 149 L4, 155 C4

Baan Baa NSW 112 E8
Baandee WA 202 F4
Babakin WA 202 F5
Babbiloora Qld 144 C2
Babel Island Tas 255 K2, 325
Babinda NSW 115 L8
Babinda Qld 149 M6, 155 E9
Bacchus Marsh Vic 64 E2, 67 M5
Back Creek Vic 73 H4
Back Springs NSW 115 H2
Back Yamma NSW 117 P2
Backstairs Passage SA 220, 221, 230 B4, 321
Backwater NSW 113 K6
Backwell NSW 114 B9
Badalia Qld 150 C7
Baddaginnie Vic 72 D5
Baden Tas 253 K2
Baden Park NSW 114 G8
Badgebup WA 202 F7
Badgingarra WA 202 B2, 204 D10
Badgingarra NP WA 202 B2
Badja WA 204 F8
Badjaling WA 202 E4
Badu Island Qld 154 C1, 279
Bael Bael Vic 69 K7
Baerami NSW 110 F4
Baerami Creek NSW 110 F5
Bagdad Tas 253 J3
Bagnoo NSW 111 L2
Bagot Well SA 233 K8
Bagshot Vic 67 M2
Bagshot North Vic 67 M1
Bahgallah Vic 66 C5
Baikal NT 179 L4
Baines River NT 174 B9, 299
Baird Bay SA 232 B6
Bairnsdale Vic 70 E6, 261
Bajool Qld 147 J9
Bakara SA 233 L9
Bakara CP SA 233 M9
Bakers Beach Tas 255 H5
Bakers Creek Qld 146 G4
Bakers Swamp NSW 110 B5
Baladjie WA 202 G3
Baladjie Lake NR WA 202 G2
Balah SA 233 L7
Balaklava SA 233 J8
Balbirini NT 177 L3
Balcanoona SA 233 L1, 235 L10
Bald Hills Vic 64 B1, 67 K4
Bald Nob NSW 113 K5
Bald Rock Vic 69 L8
Bald Rock NP NSW 113 K3
Baldersleigh NSW 113 H7
Baldivis WA 202 C5
Baldry NSW 110 A6

INDEX OF PLACE NAMES 393

Balfes Creek Qld 146 A2, 151 P2
Balfour Tas 254 B5
Balfour Downs WA 211 L8
Balgo WA 206 F2
Balgowan SA 232 G9
Balgownie NSW 109 G2, 110 G10
Balhannah SA 233 K10
Balingup WA 202 C7
Balkuling WA 202 E4
Balla Balla Harbour WA 308, 309
Balladonia WA 207 A8
Balladonia Hotel WA 203 P5, 207 A8
Balladoran NSW 110 B3
Ballalaba NSW 109 D5
Ballandean Qld 145 L9
Ballangeich Vic 66 F7
Ballara SA 233 N4
Ballarat Vic 64 B2, 67 K5
Ballatherie NSW 117 J2
Ballatta NSW 115 M9
Ballbank NSW 116 F7
Balldale NSW 117 L8
Ballendella Vic 69 N9
Balliang Vic 64 E3, 67 M6
Balliang East Vic 64 E3, 67 M6
Ballidu WA 202 D2
Ballimore NSW 110 B4
Ballina NSW 113 P3
Balls Pyramid NSW 270, *270*
Ballyrogan Vic 67 H4
Balmoral Qld 147 J7
Balmoral Vic 66 D4
Balmoral Village NSW 109 F2, 110 F10
Balnarring Vic 65 H6, 67 P8
Balonne River Qld 144 E 9
Balook Qld 146 G5
Balook Vic 65 P6, 70 A8
Balranald NSW 116 F5
Bamaga Qld 154 C2, 278, 279, 280
Bamawm Vic 69 M9
Bamawm Extension Vic 69 N9
Bambaroo Qld 149 M8
Bambill Vic 68 C3
Bamboo Creek WA 211 K6
Bamboo Springs NT 176 A3
Bamboo Springs WA 211 J7
Bambra Vic 64 C6, 67 L8
Bamganie Vic 64 C4, 67 L6
Ban Ban Qld 151 K10
Ban Ban Spring NT 174 E6
Ban Ban Springs Qld 145 L3
Banana Qld 145 H1, 147 J10
Bandiana Vic 73 H3
Bandon Grove NSW 111 J4
Bandon Grove Qld 151 K9
Bandya WA 205 M6
Banealla SA 230 C9
Bang Bang Qld 148 D8
Bangalow NSW 113 P2
Bangham SA 230 D10
Bangham CP SA 230 D10
Banjawarn WA 205 M6
Banka Banka NT 177 H6
Banks Strait Tas 255 N3
Banksia Qld 147 H7
Bankstown NSW 109 G1, 111 H9
Bannerton Vic 68 G4
Bannister WA 202 D6
Banoon NSW 116 D4
Banora Point NSW 113 P1
Banyena Vic 66 G1, 68 G10
Banyena South Vic 66 G1
Banyenong Vic 69 H9
Baradine NSW 112 C9
Barakula Qld 145 H5
Baralaba Qld 147 H10
Barataria Qld 151 K7
Baratta SA 233 K4
Barbalin WA 202 F2
Bare Sand Island NT 161
Barbigal NSW 110 B4
Barcaldine Qld 146 A8, 151 N9
Barellan NSW 117 L4
Barenya Qld 151 L5
Barfield Qld 145 H1
Barfold Vic 67 M3
Bargara Qld 145 M2
Bargo NSW 109 F2, 110 F10
Barham NSW 116 G7

Baring Vic 68 E6
Baringhup Vic 67 L3
Barjarg Vic 72 E7
Barkers Creek Vic 67 L3
Barkly Vic 67 H3
Barkly Downs Qld 150 B3
Barkly Homestead Roadhouse NT 177 L8
Barkly Tableland NT 177 M8
Barlee Range NR WA 210 E9
Barmah Vic 69 P8, 72 A3
Barmah SP Vic 69 P8, 72 A2
Barmedman NSW 117 N4
Barmera SA 233 N8
Barmundu Qld 147 K10
Barna Qld 232 F6
Barnadown Vic 67 M2
Barnato NSW 115 H7
Barnawartha Vic 72 G3
Barnawartha South Vic 72 G4
Barnes Bay Tas 253 K6
Barngo Qld 144 C2
Barnie Bolac Vic 67 H6
Barnong WA 204 E8
Barongarook Vic 64 A6, 67 J8
Barooga NSW 117 K8
Baroona NSW 112 B5
Baroona Qld 153 P8
Baroona Downs Qld 150 G3
Baroondah Qld 144 F3
Barpinba Vic 64 B5, 67 K7
Barraba NSW 112 G7
Barradale NSW 114 E7
Barradeen Qld 144 B4
Barrakee NSW 115 H4
Barrakee Vic 69 J9
Barram Qld 145 J2
Barrambie WA 205 J6
Barramornie Qld 145 H6
Barramunga Vic 64 B7, 67 K9
Barranyi NP NT 175 M9, 177 N1
Barraport Vic 69 K8
Barraroo NSW 114 D8
Barrenjoey Peninsula NSW *78*
Barretts Creek NSW 113 M4
Barrington Tas 254 G6
Barrington Tops NP NSW 111 H4
Barringun NSW 115 K1
Barron River Qld 291
Barrow Creek NT 179 H2
Barrow Island NR WA 210 D5, 308
Barry NSW 109 C1, 110 C8
Barry NSW 111 H2
Barrys Beach Vic 55, 65 P8, 70 A10
Barrys Reef Vic 64 D1, 67 M4
Bartle Frere Qld 149 M6, 155 E9
Bartlett Bluff WA 207 B4
Barton SA 231 F8
Barton Vic 66 G4
Barton Plains WA 209 K2
Barton Springs Qld 144 F4
Barunduda Vic 73 H4
Barunga NT 174 G8
Barunga Gap SA 233 H7
Barwell CP SA 232 D7
Barwell CR SA 232 D7
Barwidgee WA 205 L5
Barwidgee Creek Vic 73 H5
Barwidgi Qld 149 K7, 155 A10
Barwo Vic 69 P8, 72 B3
Barwon Downs Vic 64 B6, 67 K8
Barwon Heads Vic 64 E6, 67 M8
Barwon Park Qld 146 F8
Barwon River NSW 112 A5, 115 L3
Baryulgil NSW 113 M4
Basalt Creek Qld 144 F1
Bascombe Well CP SA 232 D7
Bass Vic 65 K7
Bass Reef NT 161, 163
Bat Cave Point WA 203 J8
Batavia Downs Qld 154 D6
Batavia Outstation Qld 154 B5
Batchelor NT 174 D5
Batchica Vic 68 F9
Batehaven NSW 109 E6
Batemans Bay NSW 97, 109 E5, 272
Batemans Bay NSW **96–7**, 109 F6
Bates SA 231 E8
Batesford Vic 64 D5, 67 L7
Batheaston Qld 146 F6
Bathurst NSW 110 D7

Bathurst Head Qld 149 J1, 154 F9
Bathurst Island NT 174 C3, 292, 294, **296–7**, *296*
Batlow NSW 109 A5, 117 P7
Battery Qld 146 A1, 149 L9, 151 P1
Battle Camp Qld 149 K3, 154 G10, 155 B3
Bauhinia Downs NT 175 K10, 177 K2
Bauhinia Downs Qld 144 F1, 146 G10
Bauple Qld 145 M4
Baw Baw Alpine Village Vic 65 N3
Baw Baw NP Vic 65 N4
Bawley Point NSW 109 F5
Baxter Vic 65 H5, 67 P7
Baxter Cliffs WA 207 C8
Bay of Fires Coastal Reserve Tas 255 P5
Bay of Shoals SA 230 B3, 321
Bayindeen Vic 67 H4
Baykool Qld 153 N3
Bayles Vic 65 K5
Bayrick Qld 144 A3, 153 P3
Beachmere Qld 145 N6
Beachport SA 230 F8
Beachport CP SA 230 F8
Beacon WA 202 F2
Beaconsfield Qld 151 M8
Beaconsfield Tas 255 J5
Beaconsfield Vic 65 J4
Beagle Bay WA 208 D7, 305, 307
Beagle Gulf NT 174 C4, 292
Bealba NSW 115 P6
Bealiba Vic 67 J2
Beames Brook Qld 148 C7
Bearbung NSW 110 B2
Beardmore Vic 65 P3, 70 A6
Bearii Vic 72 B2
Bears Lagoon Vic 69 L10
Beatrice Downs Qld 151 J10
Beauchamp Vic 69 J7
Beaudesert Qld 145 M8
Beaudesert Qld 150 F5
Beaufort Qld 146 C9
Beaufort Qld 146 C9
Beaufort SA 233 J8
Beaufort Vic 67 J4
Beaumaris Tas 255 P6
Beaumaris Vic 40
Beaumont NR WA 203 N7
Beauty Point Tas 255 J5
Beazleys Bridge Vic 67 H2
Bedford Downs WA 209 L7
Bedgerebong NSW 117 N2
Bedooba NSW 115 K9
Bedourie Qld 144 F2
Bedourie Qld 150 C10, 152 C1
Bee Creek SA 231 F2
Beeac Vic 64 B5, 67 K7
Beebo Qld 145 J9
Beech Forest Vic 64 A7, 67 J9
Beechford Tas 255 J4
Beechwood NSW 111 M2, 113 M10
Beechworth Vic 72 G4
Beechworth Park Vic 72 G4
Beecroft Peninsula NSW 94
Beedelup NP WA 202 C9
Beekeepers NR WA 204 D9
Beelbangera NSW 117 K4
Beenleigh Qld 145 N7
Beerbarrel Beach Tas *244*
Beerburrum Qld 145 M6
Beerwah Qld 145 M6
Beetaloo NT 177 H3
Beetoomba Vic 73 L4
Bega NSW 109 E8
Bega River NSW 274
Beggan Beggan NSW 109 A3, 117 P5
Beilpajah NSW 114 F10, 116 F1
Bejoording WA 202 D3
Belah NSW 115 J5
Belair SA 230 A5, 233 J10
Belalie East NSW 233 J6
Belalie North SA 233 J6
Belarabon NSW 115 H8
Belaringar NSW 115 N7
Belconnen ACT 109 C5
Beldene Qld 144 E6
Belele WA 204 G4
Belfast Qld 151 H5
Belford NSW 111 H5
Belgamba NSW 110 G1, 112 G10
Belgrave Vic 65 J4

Belinar NSW 116 D3
Belka WA 202 F4
Bell Cd 145 K6
Bell Bay Tas 255 J5
Bellalie Qld 153 J6
Bellancry NSW 111 M1, 113 M10
Bellarine Vic 64 F5, 67 N7
Bellarine Peninsula Vic 41, 44
Bellata NSW 117 M4
Bellata Qld 112 E6
Bellbird NSW 111 H6
Bellbird Creek Vic 71 K5
Bellbrae Vic 64 D6, 67 L8
Bellbridge Vic 73 J3
Bellbrook NSW 113 L9
Belle Creek Qld 144 D7
Bellellen Vic 66 G3
Bellencen Ker Qld 149 M6, 155 E8
Bellevue NSW 116 G2
Bellevue Qld 149 J5
Bellfield Qld 149 H9
Bellingen NSW 113 M8
Bellinger River NSW 269
Bellingham Tas 255 K4
Bellman Qld 148 D10, 150 E1
Bellmount Forest NSW 109 C4
Bellrose Qld 144 B4
Belltrees NSW 111 H3
Belmont NSW 111 J6
Belmont Vic 64 E5, 67 M7
Belmore NSW 116 A3
Belmunjing WA 202 E4
Beloka NSW 109 B8
Beltana SA 233 J1
Beltana Roadhouse SA 233 J1
Belton SA 233 K4
Belvedere SA 230 A6
Belvidere NSW 115 K3
Beyuen NT 174 C4
Bemboka NSW 109 D8
Bemboka NP NSW 109 D8
Benm River NSW 109 C8
Benm River Vic 49, 71 K4
Ben Boyd NP NSW 109 E9, 272
Ben Bullen NSW 110 E7
Ben Lomond NSW 113 J6
Ben Lomond NSW 115 K5
Ben Lomond CA Tas 255 M7
Ben Lomond NP Tas 247, 255 M7
Bena NSW 117 M2
Bena Vic 65 L6
Beralla Vic 72 E5
Berambre Vic 70 E2, 73 L7
Beranee NSW 116 D5
Beraraby Qld 147 L9
Berayeo Vic 66 B2
Bercubbin WA 202 F2
Benda SA 233 M5
Bendalorg NSW 109 F5
Bendemeer NSW 113 H9
Bendemeer Qld 151 H5
Bendemere Qld 144 F5
Bendering WA 202 F5
Bendick Murrell NSW 109 B2, 110 A9
Bendigo SA 233 L6
Bendigo Vic 67 M2
Bendigo Park Qld 148 E10, 150 F2
Bendoc Vic 71 K3
Bendoc North Vic 71 K3
Bendolba NSW 111 J4
Bendora Dam ACT 104, 107, 109 B5
Benetook Vic 68 E2
Bengerang NSW 112 D4
Bengworden Vic 70 E6
Beni NSW 110 B4
Benjaberring WA 202 E3
Benjeroop Vic 69 K7
Benli di Qld 151 M10, 153 M1
Bennara NT 177 M5
Bennison Vic 65 N8
Bentinck Island Qld 148 C6, 285
Bentley NSW 113 N3
Benwerrin Vic 64 C7, 67 K8
Berangabah NSW 115 H9
Berembok NSW 64 D3, 67 L6
Beresfield NSW 111 J6
Beresford Qld 146 C6
Beresford SA 234 F8
Beringarra WA 204 F5
Berkeley River WA 209 L3, 302
Berkshire Valley WA 202 C2
Bermagui NSW 109 E8, 273, **274**

Bermagui South NSW 109 E8
Bernacchi Tas 255 H8
Bernfels Qld 151 J5
Bernier and Dorre Islands NR WA 204 A2, 313
Berowra Waters NSW 111 H8
Berri SA 233 N8
Berridale NSW 109 C7
Berrigan NSW 117 K7
Berrima NSW 109 F3, 110 F10
Berrimal Vic 67 J1, 69 J10
Beringama Tas 73 L4
Berriwillock Vic 69 H7
Berrook Vic 68 A5
Berry NSW 109 G3
Berry Springs NT 174 D4
Berrybank Vic 64 A4, 67 J6
Bertiehaugh Qld 154 C5
Berwick Vic 65 J4
Bessiebelle Vic 66 D7
Beswick NT 174 G8
Bet Bet Vic 67 K3
Beta Qld 146 B9
Bete Bolong Vic 71 H5, 73 N10
Bethanga Vic 73 J3
Bethungra NSW 117 P5
Betka River VIC 71 M4, 259
Betley Vic 67 K3
Betoota Qld 152 E3
Beulah NSW 115 L2
Beulah Tas 254 G6
Beulah Vic 68 F8
Beulah East Vic 68 F8
Beulah West Vic 68 E8
Bevendale NSW 109 C3
Beverford Vic 69 J6
Beveridge Vic 64 G1, 67 P5, 72 A9
Beverley WA 202 D5
Beverley Group NP Qld 147 J4
Beverley Springs WA 209 H6
Bews SA 230 A9
Bexhill NSW 113 N3
Beyondie WA 205 K2
Biala NSW 109 C3
Biamanga NP NSW 109 E8
Bibbenluke NSW 109 D9
Bibochra Qld 149 L5, 155 D7
Bicheno Tas **242–3**, 255 P8
Bicton Qld 144 B6
Biddon NSW 110 B2
Bidgeemia NSW 117 L7
Bidgemia WA 204 D3
Bidura NSW 116 E4
Bierbank Qld 153 N5
Big Creek Qld 153 M7
Big Desert Wilderness Park Vic 68 B7
Big Heath CP SA 230 E9
Big Hill Vic 67 L2
Big Horse Creek NT 298
Big River Vic 65 M1
Big River Country NSW **266–7**
Bigga NSW 109 C2, 110 C9
Biggara Vic 73 M4
Biggenden Qld 145 L3
Biambil NSW 113 N1
Bilbah Downs Qld 151 L10, 153 L1
Bilbarin WA 202 F5
Bilbul NSW 117 K4
Billa Kalina SA 234 E9
Billabalong WA 204 E6
Billenbah Qld 144 F7
Billengarrah NT 177 L2
Billeroy NSW 112 A8
Billiatt CP SA 233 M10
Billilla NSW 114 E8
Billiluna WA 206 E1
Billimari NSW 109 B1, 110 B8
Billinncoka WA 211 L9
Billybingbone NSW 115 M4
Billyrimba NSW 113 L4
Billys Creek NSW 113 L7
Biloela Qld 145 H1, 147 J10
Bilpa Morea Claypan Qld 152 D2
Bilpin NSW 110 F8
Bimbi NSW 109 A2, 117 P4
Bimbijy WA 204 G9
Bimbowrie SA 233 M4
Bimerah Qld 151 K10, 153 K1
Binalong NSW 109 B3
Binalong Bay Tas 245, 255 P5
Binbee Qld 146 E2
Binda NSW 109 D2, 110 C10

394 INDEX OF PLACE NAMES

Binda NSW 116 F3
Bindara NSW 114 C10, 116 C1
Bindawalla Qld 147 K10
Bindebango Qld 144 C7
Bindi NSW 115 J8
Bindi Vic 70 F3, 73 L8
Bindi Bindi WA 202 C2
Bindle Qld 144 E7
Bindogundra NSW 110 A6
Bindoon WA 202 C3
Binerah Downs NSW 114 B1
Bing Bong NT 175 M10, 177 M1
Bingara NSW 112 F6
Bingil Bay Qld 149 M7, 155 E10
Binginwarri Vic 65 P7, 70 A9
Bingo Munjie North Vic 70 E2, 73 L7
Biniguy NSW 112 F5
Binjour Qld 145 K3
Binnaway NSW 110 D2
Binningup WA 195, 202 B6
Binnu WA 204 C7
Binnum SA 230 D10
Binthalya WA 204 C2
Binya NSW 117 L4
Binyeah Qld 150 B5
Birchip Vic 68 G8
Birchs Bay Tas 253 K7
Birdsville Qld 152 C4
Birdwood SA 233 K10
Birdwoodton Vic 68 E2
Birkhead Qld 144 A1, 146 B10
Birralee Qld 146 E3
Birralee Tas 255 J6
Birrego NSW 117 L6
Birregurra Vic 64 B6, 67 K8
Birricannia Qld 151 M5
Birrimba NT 176 E2
Birrindudu NT 176 B6
Birriwa NSW 110 D4
Bishopsbourne Tas 255 J7
Bittern Vic 65 H6, 67 P8
Black Flag WA 203 L2
Black Gate NSW 114 D8
Black Hill SA 233 L9
Black Hill WA 205 J7
Black Hills Tas 253 J4
Black Mountain NSW 113 J7
Black Mountain Qld 146 G5
Black Mountain NP Qld 149 L3, 155 C4
Black Range WA 205 J7
Black Range SP Vic 66 E3
Black Rock SA 233 K5
Black Rock Vic 40
Black Springs NSW 109 E1, 110 D9
Black Springs SA 233 K8
Blackall Qld 146 A10, 151 N10, 153 N1
Blackboy Lake NSW 114 B10, 116 B1
Blackbraes Qld 149 J9, 151 L1
Blackbull Qld 148 F7
Blackbutt Qld 145 L6
Blackdown Qld 149 J6
Blackdown Tableland NP Qld 146 G9
Blackfellows Caves SA 230 G9
Blackheath NSW 109 F1, 110 F8
Blackheath Vic 66 E1, 68 E10
Blackmans Bay Tas 253 K5
Blackmans Point NSW 111 M1, 113 M10
Blacktown NSW 109 G1, 110 G8
Blackville NSW 110 F2
Blackwall Tas 255 J6
Blackwarry Vic 70 A8
Blackwater Qld 146 F9
Blackwood Vic 64 D1, 67 M5
Blackwood Creek Tas 255 J8
Blackwood NP Qld 146 C4
Blackwood River WA 197, 200, 202 B8
Bladensburg NP Qld 151 J7
Blair Athol Qld 146 D7
Blair Athol Qld 150 D7
Blairgowrie Qld 151 M10, 153 M1
Blairgowrie Vic 64 F6, 67 N8
Blairmore Qld 144 B8
Blakeville Vic 64 D1, 67 L5
Blakney Creek NSW 109 C3
Blamey WA 203 M3
Blampied Vic 64 C1, 67 L4
Blanchetown SA 233 L9
Blanchewater SA 235 K2

Bland NSW 117 N3
Blandford NSW 110 G3
Blanket Flat NSW 109 C2, 110 C9
Blantyre Qld 151 M3
Blaxland NSW 109 F1, 110 G8
Blayney NSW 110 C8
Blenheim Qld 144 G7
Blessington Tas 255 L7
Blighty NSW 117 J7
Blina WA 208 G8
Blinman SA 233 J2
Bloods Creek SA 234 C1
Bloomfield NSW 110 C7
Bloomfield NSW 115 J8
Bloomfield Qld 153 N1, 287
Bloomsbury Qld 146 F3
Blow Clear NSW 115 P10, 117 P1
Blow Clear NSW 117 M3
Blowering Reservoir NSW 109 A5
Blue Creek Qld 152 G2
Blue Hills Qld 144 G1, 147 H10
Blue Knob NSW 113 N2
Blue Lake NP Qld 124
Blue Mountain Qld 146 G5
Blue Mountains NSW 1, 74, 80, 102
Blue Mountains NP NSW 109 F2, 110 F9
Blue Range Qld 149 L9
Blue Rock Lake Vic 63
Blue Rocks Tas 255 J2
Blue Water Springs Roadhouse Qld 149 L9
Bluewater Qld 149 M9
Blueys Beach NSW 111 L4
Bluff Qld 146 G9
Bluff Downs Qld 146 A1, 149 L10, 151 P1
Bluff Rock NSW 113 K4
Blumont Tas 255 L5
Blyth SA 233 J8
Blythdale Qld 144 F5
Boambee NSW 113 N7, 268, 269
Boat Harbour NSW 111 K5
Boat Harbour Tas 254 D4
Boat Harbour Beach Tas 254 D4
Boatman Qld 144 B6
Bobadah NSW 115 L9
Bobawaba Qld 146 D1, 149 P10
Bobby Towns Hut Qld 148 G6
Bobin NSW 111 L2
Bobinawarrah Vic 72 G5
Bobundara NSW 109 C8
Bodalla NSW 109 E7
Bodallin WA 202 G3
Boddington WA 202 D6
Bogan Gate NSW 115 N10, 117 N2
Bogangar NSW 113 P1
Bogantungan Qld 146 D9
Bogarella Qld 144 C3
Bogee NSW 110 E6
Bogewong Qld 151 K9
Boggabilla NSW 112 F2
Boggabri NSW 112 E8
Bogolo NSW 115 L10, 117 L1
Bogong Qld 144 D8
Bogong Vic 70 D1, 73 J6
Bogong High Plains Vic 60, 73 J7
Bohemia Downs WA 206 D1, 209 J10
Bohnock NSW 111 L3
Boho South Vic 72 D6
Boigbeat Vic 68 G7
Boinka Vic 68 C5
Boisdale Vic 70 C6
Bokhara Plains NSW 115 M3
Bolgart WA 202 D3
Bolinda Vic 64 F1, 67 N4
Bolingbroke Qld 146 G5
Bolivia NSW 113 K4
Bollards Lagoon SA 235 N7
Bollon Qld 144 C8
Bolton Vic 68 G5
Boltons Beach Coastal Reserve Tas 253 N2
Bolwarra Qld 149 J6
Bolwarra Vic 66 C7
Bomaderry NSW 109 F4
Bomali NSW 115 N2
Bombah NSW 115 M9
Bombah Point NSW 111 L5
Bombala NSW 109 C9
Bombo Beach NSW 92
Bomera NSW 110 E2

Bon Bon SA 234 D10
Bonalbo NSW 113 M3
Bonang Vic 71 J3
Bonaparte Archipelago WA 208 G2, 302
Bonathorne Qld 144 E9
Bond Springs NT 179 H6
Bondi Junction NSW 111 H9
Bondo NSW 109 B5
Bonegilla Vic 73 H3
Boneo Vic 64 G6, 67 N8
Boney Point NT 175 M3
Bongaree Qld 122, 145 N6
Bonna Vonna Qld 144 B8
Bonney Downs WA 211 K8
Bonnie Brae SA 233 L4
Bonnie Doon Qld 146 F9
Bonnie Doon Qld 153 N2
Bonnie Doon Vic 72 D7
Bonnie Rock WA 202 F2
Bonnie Vale WA 203 L2
Bonny Hills NSW 111 M2
Bonrook NT 174 E6
Bonshaw NSW 113 H3
Bonton NSW 114 F9, 116 F1
Bonus Downs Qld 144 D5
Bonville NSW 113 N7
Bonville Creek NSW 269
Boobera Qld 153 N7
Booberoi Qld 144 G9
Booborowie SA 233 K7
Boobyalla Tas 255 M4
Boodarockin WA 202 G3
Boogardie WA 204 G7
Book Book Qld 144 D9
Bookabie SA 231 F10
Bookaloo SA 232 G3
Bookar Vic 67 H7
Bookham NSW 109 B4
Bool Lagoon SA 230 E9
Bool Lagoon GR SA 230 E9
Boola Boolka NSW 114 E9
Boolambayte NSW 111 L4
Boolardy WA 204 E5
Boolaroo NSW 111 J6
Boolarra Vic 65 N6
Boolarra South Vic 65 N6
Boolba Qld 144 D8
Boolbanna Qld 153 L5
Boolburra Qld 147 H9
Boolcoomata SA 233 N4
Booleroo Centre SA 233 J6
Booligal NSW 117 H3
Boolite Vic 68 F10
Boologooro WA 204 B2
Boomahnoomoonah Vic 72 E3
Boomi NSW 112 D2
Boomley NSW 110 C3
Boonah Qld 145 M8
Boonarga Qld 145 J6
Boonarring NR WA 202 C3
Boondandilla Qld 145 H8
Boondarra NSW 117 H2
Boonderoo Qld 151 L2
Boongoondoo Qld 146 B7, 151 P7
Boonoo Boonoo NSW 113 K3
Boonoo Boonoo NP NSW 113 K3
Boorabbin WA 203 J3
Boorabbin NP WA 203 J3
Booral NSW 111 K5
Boorara Qld 146 A9, 151 P9
Boorara Qld 153 L9
Boorcan Vic 67 H7
Boorhaman Vic 72 F4
Boorolite Vic 72 E8
Boorongie Vic 68 F5
Boorooma NSW 115 N4
Booroondarra Downs NSW 115 J6
Booroopki Vic 66 B2
Boororban NSW 117 H6
Boorowa NSW 109 B3, 110 B10
Boort NSW 69 K9
Boort East Vic 69 K9
Boothulla Qld 153 N5
Bootra NSW 114 D4
Booyal Qld 145 L2
Booylgoo Spring WA 205 K7
Boppy Mount NSW 115 L7
Borambil NSW 110 E3
Borambola NSW 117 N6
Borden WA 202 F8
Border Cliffs SA 233 P8

Border Downs NSW 114 A4
Border Ranges NP NSW 113 N2
Border Village SA 231 A9
Bordertown SA 230 C10
Boree NSW 110 B7
Boree Qld 151 L3
Boree Creek NSW 117 L6
Boree Plains NSW 116 E3
Boreen Qld 145 M5
Borenore NSW 110 B7
Boro NSW 109 D4
Bororen Qld 145 K1, 147 L10
Borrika SA 233 M10
Borroloola NT 175 M10, 177 M1, 300
Borung Vic 69 K9
Boscabel WA 202 E7
Bostobrick NSW 113 M7
Bostock Creek Vic 67 H7
Bosworth SA 232 G1
Botany NSW 111 H9
Botany Bay NSW 82–3, 82, 85, 111 H9
Bothwell Tas 253 J2
Bottom Lake Vic 48, 48–9, 258, 259
Bouddi NP NSW 87, 111 J8
Bouillia NSW 114 B4
Boulder WA 203 L2
Bouldercombe Qld 147 J9
Boulia Qld 150 D7
Boundary Bend Vic 69 H4
Bountiful Island Qld 148 C5, 285
Bourke NSW 115 K4
Bournda NP NSW 109 E9
Bow NSW 110 F4
Bow Bridge WA 202 D10
Bow River WA 209 M6
Bowalli Qld 153 L6
Bowan Park NSW 110 B7
Bowelling WA 202 D7
Bowen Qld 146 E2, 288
Bowenville Qld 145 K6
Bower SA 233 L8
Bowes River WA 199
Bowgada WA 204 E9
Bowhill SA 233 L10
Bowie Qld 146 B5, 151 P5
Bowillia SA 233 J8
Bowling Alley Point NSW 111 H1, 113 H10
Bowling Green Bay NP Qld 149 N9
Bowmans SA 233 J8
Bowmans Creek NSW 111 H4
Bowna NSW 117 M8
Bowning NSW 109 B3
Bowral NSW 109 F3, 110 F10
Bowraville NSW 113 M8
Bowser Vic 72 F4
Box Creek SA 234 D7
Box Hill NSW 109 G1, 110 G8
Box Hill Vic 65 H3, 67 P6
Boxvale Qld 144 E3
Boxwood Hill WA 202 G9
Boyanup WA 202 B7
Boyben NSW 110 C3
Boyeo Vic 68 C9
Boyer Tas 253 J4
Boyne Island Qld 147 L9
Boyup Brook WA 202 C8
Brachina SA 233 J2
Brackendale NSW 111 J1, 113 J10
Brackenley Qld 146 G10
Bracknell Tas 255 J7
Braddon ACT 109 C5
Bradvale Vic 67 J6
Bradys Lake Tas 252 G1, 254 G10, 328
Braefield NSW 110 G2
Braemar NSW 112 E3
Braemar Qld 151 L4
Braemar SA 233 L6
Braeside Qld 146 F5
Braeside Qld 150 G5
Braidwood NSW 109 E5
Braidwood Qld 153 J2
Bramfield SA 232 C7
Bramston Beach Qld 149 M6, 155 E9
Bramwell Qld 154 C5
Brandon Qld 146 D1, 149 N10
Brandy Creek Vic 65 M5
Bransby Qld 153 H8
Branxholm Tas 255 M5
Branxholme Vic 66 D6
Branxton NSW 111 H5

Braunstone NSW 113 M6
Brawlin NSW 109 A3, 117 P5
Brayfield SA 232 E8
Breadalbane NSW 109 D4
Breadalbane Qld 150 C9
Breadalbane Tas 255 K7
Break O'Day Vic 65 J1, 72 B9
Breakaway Ridge NR WA 202 G6
Breakfast Creek NSW 109 B2, 110 B9
Breakfast Creek NSW 110 E5
Breaksea Spit QLD 132, 133
Bream Creek Tas 253 M4
Breamlea Vic 64 E6, 67 M8
Bredbo NSW 109 C6
Breelong NSW 110 B3
Breeza NSW 110 F1, 112 F10
Breeza Plains Outstation Qld 149 J2, 154 F10
Bremer Bay WA 203 H9
Brenda NSW 115 N1
Brenda Gate Qld 144 C10
Brentwood SA 232 G10
Brentwood Vic 68 E8
Breona Tas 255 H8
Bretti NSW 111 K3
Brewarrina NSW 115 M3
Brewongle NSW 110 D8
Brewster Vic 64 A1, 67 J5
Briaba Qld 146 E2
Briagolong Vic 70 C6
Bribbaree NSW 117 P4
Bribie Island QLD 122, 123, 125, 145 N6
Bribie Island NP Qld 145 N6
Bridge Creek Vic 72 E7
Bridgenorth Tas 255 J6
Bridgetown WA 202 C8
Bridgewater Tas 253 K4
Bridgewater Vic 67 K1
Bridport Tas 255 L4
Brierfield NSW 113 M8
Brigalow NSW 110 B1, 112 B10
Brigalow Qld 145 J6
Bright Vic 39, 70 C1, 73 H6
Brightlands Qld 150 E4
Brighton SA 214, 215, 216, 233 J10
Brighton Tas 253 J4
Brighton Vic 64 G4, 67 P6
Brighton Downs Qld 150 G8
Brim Vic 68 F9
Brim East Vic 68 F9
Brimbago SA 230 C9
Brimboal Vic 66 C4
Brimpaen Vic 66 E3
Brinawa Qld 148 B7
Brindabella NSW 109 B5
Brindingabba NSW 115 H2
Brindiwilpa NSW 114 D3
Bringagee NSW 117 K5
Bringalbert Vic 66 B2
Bringelly NSW 109 G1, 110 G9
Bringle NSW 110 B1, 112 B10
Brinkley SA 230 A7, 233 K10
Brinkworth SA 233 J7
Brisbane Qld 145 N7
Brisbane Ranges NP Vic 64 D3, 67 M6
Brisbane River Qld 122, 123, 140, 141, 145 L5
Brisbane Water NSW 78, 86–7
Brisbane Water NP NSW 86, 87, 111 J8
Brit Brit Vic 66 D5
Brittons Swamp Tas 254 B4
Brixton Qld 151 N8
Broad Arrow WA 203 L2, 205 L10
Broadford Qld 151 L5
Broadford Vic 67 P4, 72 A8
Broadleigh Downs Qld 146 B3
Broadmarsh Tas 253 J4
Broadmeadow NSW 111 J6
Broadmeadows Vic 64 G2, 67 N5, 72 A10
Broadmere NT 177 K2
Broadmere Qld 144 G3
Broadmount Qld 147 K8
Broadwater NSW 113 P3
Broadwater Vic 66 E7
Broadwater NP NSW 113 P4
Brocklehurst NSW 110 B4
Brocklesby NSW 117 L7
Brodribb River Vic 71 J5, 73 P10
Brogo NSW 109 E8

Broke NSW 111 H5
Broke Inlet WA 202 C10
Broken Bay NSW 78-9, 78, 80, 86, 111 H8
Broken Hill NSW 114 B8
Brolgan NSW 115 P10, 117 P2
Bromelton Qld 145 M8
Bronte Qld 153 N3
Bronte Lagoon Tas 252 F1, 328
Bronte Park Tas 252 F1, 254 G10
Bronzewing Vic 68 F5
Brookdale Qld 148 C7
Brooker SA 232 E8
Brookfield NSW 111 J5
Brookfield CP SA 233 L9
Brooking Gorge CP WA 209 H8
Brooking Springs WA 209 H9
Brooklana NSW 113 M7
Brooklands Qld 149 J7
Brooklyn NSW 111 H8
Brooklyn Qld 151 J5
Brookstead Qld 145 K7
Brookton WA 202 D5
Brookville Vic 70 E4, 73 L9
Brooloo Qld 145 M5
Broome WA 19, 29, 30, 208 C8, 211 N1, 257, 302, 304, 305, 306-7, 307, 312
Broomehill WA 202 E8
Brooms Head NSW 113 N5, 267
Broughton Qld 146 B2, 149 M10
Broughton Vic 68 B9
Broughton River SA 226-7, 233 H6
Broulee NSW 109 E6
Brownleigh NSW 112 E3
Brownlow SA 233 L8
Browns Plains Qld 145 N7
Browns Plains Vic 72 G3
Bruce SA 233 J5
Bruce Rock WA 202 F4
Brucedale Qld 144 F6
Bruinbun NSW 110 D6
Brumbys Creek Tas 246-7
Brunchilly NT 177 J6
Brunette Downs NT 177 L6
Brungle NSW 109 A4, 117 P6
Brunkerville NSW 111 J6
Brunswick Vic 64 G3, 67 P6
Brunswick Bay WA 208 G4, 304
Brunswick Heads NSW 113 P2
Brunswick Junction WA 202 C7
Bruny Island Tas 239, 253 K6
Bruthen Vic 70 F5, 73 L10
Bryah WA 205 H3
Bryans Gap NSW 113 K3
Buangor Vic 67 H4
Bubialo Qld 146 F2
Bucasia Qld 146 G4
Buccaneer Archipelago WA 208 E5
Buccarumbi NSW 113 L6, 267
Buccleuch SA 230 A8
Buchan Vic 70 G4, 73 N9
Buchan South Vic 70 G5, 73 N10
Bucheen Creek Vic 73 K5
Buckalow NSW 114 A9, 116 A1
Buckenderra NSW 109 B7
Bucket Claypan Qld 150 B9
Bucketty NSW 111 H6
Buckeys Creek Qld 144 A3
Buckhorst Vic 68 A8
Buckingham SA 230 C9
Buckland Tas 253 L3
Buckland Vic 70 B1, 73 H6
Buckleboo SA 232 E5
Buckleboo SA 232 E6
Buckley Swamp Vic 66 E6
Buckrabanyule Vic 69 J9
Buckwaroon NSW 115 J6
Budawang NP NSW 109 E5
Buddabaddah NSW 115 M8
Buddigower NSW 117 M4
Buderim Qld 128, 145 N5
Budgee Budgee NSW 110 D5
Budgeree Vic 65 N6
Budgerum Vic 69 J7
Budgerygar Qld 153 K3
Budgewoi NSW 111 J7
Buffalo Vic 65 M7
Buffalo Creek Vic 72 G5
Buffalo River Vic 70 B1, 72 G6
Bugaldie NSW 110 C1, 112 C10
Bugilbone NSW 112 B6

Bugtown NSW 109 B6
Bukalong NSW 109 C9
Bukkula NSW 113 H5
Bukulla NSW 112 A4
Bulahdelah NSW 111 L4
Bulart Vic 66 D5
Buldah Vic 71 L3
Bulga NSW 111 H5
Bulga NSW 111 L2
Bulga Downs WA 205 J8
Bulgamurra NSW 114 E10, 116 E2
Bulgandramine NSW 115 P9
Bulgandry NSW 117 L7
Bulgary NSW 117 M6
Bulgroo Outstation Qld 153 K4
Bulgunnia SA 234 C10
Bulimba Qld 149 H5
Bulingary NSW 113 M8
Bulla NSW 115 H7
Bulla Vic 64 G2, 67 N5
Bullabulling WA 203 K3
Bullamon Plains Qld 144 F9
Bullara WA 210 B8
Bullardoo WA 204 D7
Bullargreen NSW 115 P7
Bullaring WA 202 F5
Bullarto Vic 64 D1, 67 L4
Bullawarrie Qld 144 E9
Bullecourt Qld 150 A3
Bullen Bullen Qld 144 D2
Bullenbong NSW 117 M6
Bullengarook Vic 64 E1, 67 M5
Buller River WA 199
Bulleringa NP Qld 149 J6
Bullfinch WA 203 H3
Bullhead Creek Vic 73 K4
Bullioh Vic 73 K4
Bullita NT 174 C10, 176 C2
Bulliwallah Qld 146 C5
Bullo River NT 174 B9
Bullock Creek Qld 149 K7, 155 A10
Bulloo Creek SA 233 N4
Bulloo Downs Qld 153 J9
Bulloo Downs WA 205 J1, 211 J10
Bulloo River Qld 153 L7
Bulls Gully Qld 153 M4
Bullsbrook WA 202 C4
Bullumwaal Vic 70 E5, 73 K10
Bulman NT 175 J6
Buln Buln Vic 65 M5
Bulwer Qld 124, 125
Bulyee WA 202 E5
Bulyeroi NSW 112 C6
Bumberry NSW 110 A7
Bumbunga SA 233 J8
Bunbartha Vic 72 B4
Bunbury Vic 181, 194-5, 196, 202 B7
Bunda NT 176 A5
Bunda Bunda Qld 148 F10, 151 H2
Bundaberg Qld 130, 145 L2
Bundaburrah NSW 117 N2
Bundalaguah Vic 70 B7
Bundaleer Qld 144 B9
Bundalong Vic 72 E3
Bundalong South Vic 72 E3
Bundanoon NSW 109 F3
Bundarra NSW 113 H7
Bundarra NSW 114 E3
Bundeena NSW 111 H9
Bundeena Qld 153 J7
Bundella NSW 110 E2
Bundemar NSW 110 A3, 115 P8
Bundjalung NP NSW 113 N4, 266
Bundoo Qld 144 B4
Bundooma NT 179 J8
Bundoora Vic 153 M8
Bundure NSW 117 K6
Bung Bong Vic 67 J3
Bunga NSW 109 E8
Bungador Vic 67 J8
Bungal Vic 64 D2, 67 L5
Bungalien Qld 150 D4
Bungalla WA 202 E4
Bungaree Vic 64 C2, 67 L5
Bungaringa Qld 144 D4
Bungeet Vic 72 E4
Bungendore NSW 109 D5
Bungil Vic 73 K3, 264
Bungobine Qld 146 D4
Bungonia NSW 109 E4

Bungowannah NSW 117 M8
Bunguluke Vic 69 J9
Bungunya Qld 144 G9
Bungwahl NSW 111 L4
Buninyong Vic 64 C2, 67 K5
Bunjil WA 204 E9
Bunketch WA 202 E2
Bunna Bunna NSW 112 C6
Bunnaloo NSW 117 H7
Bunnan NSW 110 G3
Bunnawarra WA 204 F8
Bunnerungee NSW 116 B3
Buntine WA 202 D1, 204 F10
Bunya Mountains NP Qld 145 K5
Bunyah NSW 111 L4
Bunyan NSW 109 C7
Bunyip Vic 65 L5
Bunyip River Vic 62, 63
Bunyip SP Vic 65 K4
Bunyung SA 233 L7
Burakin WA 202 E2
Burcher NSW 117 M2
Burdekin Downs Qld 146 B1, 149 M10
Burdett South NR WA 203 M7
Burekup WA 202 C7
Burgooney NSW 117 L2
Burgoyne Qld 146 B9, 151 P9
Burkan Qld 146 G8
Burke and Wills Roadhouse Qld 148 D9
Burkes Flat Vic 67 J2
Burketown Qld 148 C7, 284-5
Burleigh Qld 151 J2
Burleigh Heads Qld 145 N8
Burlington Qld 149 J7, 155 A10
Burma Road NR WA 204 D8
Burnabinmah WA 204 G8
Burnbank Vic 67 J4
Burngrove Qld 146 F9
Burnie Tas 254 E4
Burns Bay Tas 245
Burns Creek Tas 255 L6
Burnside Qld 151 L5
Burnt Yards NSW 110 B8
Buronga NSW 116 C4
Burra Qld 151 N3
Burra SA 233 K7
Burra Bee Dee NSW 110 D1, 112 D10
Burra NR WA 203 L3
Burraboi NSW 116 G7
Burracoppin WA 202 G3
Burraga NSW 109 D1, 110 D9
Burragate NSW 109 D9
Burramine Vic 72 D3
Burrandana NSW 117 N7
Burrangong NSW 109 A2, 110 A10, 117 P4
Burrapine NSW 113 M8
Burraway NSW 110 A3, 115 P8
Burrell Creek NSW 111 L3
Burren Junction NSW 112 B7
Burrenbilla Qld 153 P8
Burrereo Vic 66 G1, 68 G10
Burrill Lake NSW 109 F5
Burringbar NSW 113 P2
Burrinjuck NSW 109 B4
Burrinjuck Dam NSW see Lake Burrinjuck NSW
Burrowa - Pine Mountain NP Vic 73 L3
Burrowye Vic 73 K3
Burrum Heads Qld 130, 145 M2
Burrumbeet Vic 64 B1, 67 K5
Burrumbuttock NSW 117 M8
Burslem Qld 151 L6
Burta NSW 114 A9
Burthong NSW 115 L9
Burtle Qld 146 C8
Burton Downs Qld 146 E5
Burtundy NSW 116 C3
Burua Qld 147 K9
Burunga Qld 144 G4
Busbys Flat NSW 113 M3
Bushy Park NT 179 H4
Bushy Park Qld 150 D4
Bushy Park Tas 253 H4
Bushy Park Vic 70 C6
Busselton WA 194-5, 194, 196, 197, 202 B7
Bustard Bay Qld 135, 147 L10
Bustard Head Qld 134, 135
Butcher Lake WA 206 E4
Butchers Creek Qld 149 L6, 155 D9

Butchers Ridge Vic 70 G3, 73 N8
Bute SA 233 H8
Butler Tanks SA 232 E8
Butru Qld 150 D4
Buxton NSW 109 F2, 110 F10
Buxton Vic 65 L1, 72 D9
Byabarra NSW 111 L2
Byaduk Vic 66 D6
Byaduk North Vic 66 D6
Byalong Qld 144 E8
Byawong Qld 146 E4
Byerawering NSW 115 M2
Byerwen Qld 146 E4
Byfield Qld 147 J7
Byfield NP Qld 147 K7
Byford WA 202 C5
Bylands Vic 64 G1, 67 P4, 72 A9
Bylong NSW 110 E4
Bylong Qld 151 J2
Bynoe Harbour NT 162-3, 163, 167
Byrneside Vic 67 P1, 69 P10, 72 B5
Byrneville Vic 66 E1, 68 E10
Byro WA 204 E4
Byrock NSW 115 L5
Byron Bay NSW 113 P2
Bywong NSW 109 D4

C Lake NSW 114 E10, 116 E2
Cabana Qld 149 J7
Cabanandra Vic 71 J3
Cabanda Qld 150 G2
Cabbage Lake NSW 116 G3
Cabbage Tree Creek Vic 71 J5
Cable Beach WA 29
Caboolture Qld 145 M6
Cabramurra NSW 109 B6
Caddens Flat Vic 66 C8
Cadelga Outstation SA 235 N1
Cadell SA 233 L8
Cadney Homestead (Roadhouse) SA 234 A5
Cadney Park SA 234 A5
Cadoux WA 202 E2
Cahills Crossing NT 172, 173, 174 G4
Caiguna WA 207 C8
Cairn Curren Reservoir Vic 67 L3
Cairns Qld 30, 118, 149 L5, 155 D7, 278, 288, 290-1
Cairns Bay Tas 253 H7
Cairo Qld 146 D6
Caiwarra Qld 150 F3
Caiwarro Qld 153 M8
Cal Lal NSW 116 A4
Calala NSW 110 G1, 112 G10
Calca SA 232 B6
Calcifer Qld 149 K6, 155 A8
Calcium Qld 146 C1, 149 N10
Calder Tas 254 D5
Calder River WA 209 H5, 304
Caldermeade Vic 65 K5
Caldervale Qld 144 B2
Caldwell NSW 116 G7
Calen Qld 146 F3
Calga NSW 111 H7
Calindary NSW 114 D4
Calingiri WA 202 D3
Calivil Vic 69 L9
Callagiddy WA 204 B8
Callala Bay NSW 109 G4
Callanna SA 235 H9
Callawa WA 211 K5
Callawadda Vic 66 G2
Calleen NSW 117 M3
Callide Qld 145 H1, 147 J10
Callington SA 230 A6, 233 K10
Calliope Qld 147 K9
Callytharra Springs WA 204 D4
Calomba SA 233 J9
Caloola NSW 110 D8
Caloona NSW 112 C3
Caloundra Qld 122, 126, 128, 145 N6
Calpatanna Waterhole CP SA 232 B6
Calperum SA 233 N8
Calton Hills Qld 148 C10, 150 C2
Caltowie SA 233 J6
Calvert Vic 66 G5
Calvert Hills NT 177 N3
Calwynyardah WA 208 G8
Camballin WA 208 F8
Cambarville Vic 65 L2, 72 D10
Camberwell NSW 111 H5
Camberwell Vic 65 H3, 67 P6
Camboon Qld 145 H2

Cambooya Qld 145 L7
Cambrai SA 233 L9
Cambridge Tas 253 K5
Cambridge Gulf WA 209 M3, 302
Camburinga Village NT 175 M5
Camden NSW 81, 109 G2, 110 G9
Camden Sound WA 208 F4, 304
Camel Creek Qld 149 L8
Camel Lake NR WA 202 F8
Camena Tas 254 F5
Camfield NT 176 D3
Camira Creek NSW 113 M4
Camooweal Qld 148 A10, 150 A1
Camooweal Caves NP Qld 148 A10, 150 A2
Campania Tas 253 K4
Campbell Range WA 209 M3
Campbell Town Tas 255 L9
Campbellfield Vic 64 G2, 67 F5, 72 A9
Campbells Bridge Vic 66 G2
Campbells Creek Vic 67 L3
Campbells Forest Vic 67 L1
Campbelltown NSW 84, 109 G2, 110 G9
Campbelltown Vic 67 L4
Camperdown Vic 67 H7
Camurra NSW 112 E4
Canaga Qld 145 J5
Canary Qld 150 E8
Canary Island Vic 69 K8
Canaway Downs Qld 153 L4
Canbelego NSW 115 L7
Canberra ACT 104-5, 104, 109 C5
Candelo NSW 109 D8
Cane Grass SA 233 M7
Cane River WA 210 D7
Cangai NSW 113 L5, 267
Cania Gorge NP Qld 145 J1
Cann River Vic 49, 71 L5
Canna WA 204 E8
Cannawigara SA 230 C9
Canning River WA 190-1
Cannington Qld 150 F5
Cannonvale Qld 146 F2
Canobie Qld 148 E9, 150 F1
Canonba NSW 115 N6
Canoona Qld 147 J8
Canopus SA 233 N7
Canowie SA 233 K6
Canowindra NSW 110 B8
Canteen Creek NT 177 L9, 179 L1
Canterbury Qld 152 G3
Canunda NP SA 230 F8
Canyonleigh NSW 109 E3
Cap Island CP SA 232 C8
Capalaba Qld 145 N7
Capamauro NR WA 202 C1, 204 E10
Cape Arid NP WA 203 P7, 207 A9
Cape Barren Island Tas 255 P1
Cape Bougainville WA 209 J1
Cape Bouguer WPA SA 230 C2
Cape Bridgewater Vic 66 C8
Cape Clear Vic 64 A3, 67 J6
Cape Crawford NT 177 L3
Cape Croker NT 174 F2, 295
Cape du Couedic SA 230 C2, 321
Cape Don NT 174 E2, 294-5, 295
Cape Gantheaume CP SA 230 B3
Cape Hart SA 230 B4, 321
Cape Hart CP SA 230 B2
Cape Hotham CR NT 174 D4
Cape Hotham Forestry Reserve NT 174 D3
Cape Jaffa SA 230 E7
Cape Jervis SA 220, 221, 230 B4, 320
Cape Kimberley Qld 149 L4, 155 D6, 291
Cape Le Grand NP WA 203 N8
Cape Leeuwin WA 196, 196, 202 B9
Cape Leveque WA 208 D6, 305, 307
Cape Londonderry WA 209 K1
Cape Melville Qld 149 K1, 154 F8, 278
Cape Melville NP Qld 149 K2, 154 G9, 155 B1, 278
Cape Moreton Qld 124, 125, 145 N6
Cape Naturaliste WA 194, 195, 196, 202 A7
Cape Nelson SP Vic 66 C8
Cape Onslow WA 209 M2
Cape Palmerston NP Qld 147 H5
Cape Paterson Vic 65 K8, 262

396 INDEX OF PLACE NAMES

Cape Pillar Tas 241, *241*, 253 N7
Cape Pillar SR Tas 253 M7
Cape Preston WA 210 E6, 308
Cape Range NP WA 210 B7
Cape Raoul SR Tas 253 M7
Cape Riche WA 202 G9
Cape River Qld 146 A3, 151 N3
Cape St Albans SA 230 B4, 320
Cape Schanck Vic 64 G6, 67 N8, 262, *262*
Cape Sorell Tas 252 A1, 254 C10, 327
Cape Torrens SA 230 B2, 321
Cape Torrens WPA SA 230 B2
Cape Tribulation Qld 149 L4, 155 D5, **290–1**
Cape Tribulation NP Qld 149 L4, 155 D5
Cape Upstart NP Qld 146 E1, 149 P10
Cape Voltaire WA 209 H2, 302
Cape Willoughby SA 230 B4, 320
Cape Woolamai Vic 65 J7, 263
Cape York Peninsula Qld 28, 154 C5, **278–81**, *278*, *281*, 284
Capel WA 202 B7
Capella Qld 146 E8
Capels Crossing Vic 69 L7
Capertee NSW 110 E7
Capietha SA 232 C5
Capricorn Coast Qld 147 K8, 288–9
Capricorn Group Qld 147 M8, 289
Capricorn Roadhouse WA 211 K9
Captain Billy Landing Qld 154 D4
Captains Flat NSW 109 D5
Carabost NSW 117 N7
Caradoc NSW 114 E5
Carag Carag Vic 67 N1, 69 N10, 72 A5
Caragabel NSW 117 N3
Caralue SA 232 E7
Caramut Vic 66 F6
Carandotta Qld 150 B5
Carapooee Vic 67 J2
Carapook Vic 66 C5
Carawa SA 232 B5
Carbeen NSW 112 C7
Carbeen Park NT 174 E8
Carbine WA 203 K2
Carbla WA 204 C4
Carboor Vic 72 G5
Carboor Upper Vic 70 A1, 72 G6
Carcoar NSW 109 C1, 110 C8
Carcoory Qld 152 D3
Carcuma CP SA 230 B8
Cardabia WA 210 B9
Cardigan Qld 146 C2
Cardigan Village Vic 64 B1, 67 K5
Cardington Qld 146 C1, 149 N10
Cardinia Vic 65 J5
Cardinia Reservoir Vic 65 J4
Cardowan Qld 146 G6
Cardross Vic 68 E2
Cardstone Qld 149 L7, 155 D10
Cardwell Qld 149 M7
Carey Downs WA 204 D3
Carfax Qld 146 F6
Cargo NSW 110 B7
Cargoon Qld 149 K10, 151 M2
Cariewerloo SA 232 G5
Carina Vic 68 B6
Carinda NSW 115 N5
Caringbah NSW 111 H9
Carinya NSW 116 F2
Carinya Qld 144 E4
Carisbrook Vic 67 K3
Carlindi WA 211 J5
Carlisle River Vic 67 J9
Carlisle SP Vic 64 A7, 67 J9
Carlsruhe Vic 67 M4
Carlton Tas 253 L5
Carlton Hill WA 209 N4
Carlyarn NR WA 202 E1, 204 G10
Carmichael Qld 146 B5, 151 P5
Carmila Qld 146 G5
Carmor Plain NT 174 E4
Carnac Island WA 186, *187*, 193
Carnamah WA 204 E9
Carnarvon Qld 144 D2
Carnarvon WA 204 B2, 313
Carnarvon NP Qld 144 D1
Carnarvon Range WA 205 L3
Carne Outstation SA 234 B10

Carnegie WA 205 N4
Carney NSW 115 H5
Carngham Vic 64 A2, 67 J5
Caroda NSW 112 F6
Caroona NSW 110 F1, 112 F10
Caroona SA 233 K7
Carpa SA 232 F7
Carpendeit Vic 67 H8
Carpentaria Downs Qld 149 J8
Carpenter Rocks SA 230 G9
Carpet Springs Qld 153 M8
Carpolac Vic 66 B2
Carrabin WA 202 G3
Carrajung Vic 70 B8
Carrajung South Vic 70 B8
Carranballac Vic 67 H5
Carranya Qld 153 H3
Carranya WA 206 E1
Carrarang WA 204 B5
Carrathool NSW 117 J4
Carrick Tas 255 J7
Carrickalinga SA 230 A5
Carrieton SA 233 J5
Carroll NSW 112 F9
Carroll Gap NSW 112 F9
Carron Vic 68 G9
Carron River Qld 148 E7, 284
Carrum Qld 150 G3
Carrum Downs Vic 65 H5, 67 P7
Carson River WA 209 K2
Carwarp Vic 68 E3
Carwell Qld 144 B2
Cascade NSW 113 M7
Cascade WA 203 K7
Cashew Nut Farm NT 174 E4
Cashmere Qld 144 E8
Cashmere Downs WA 205 J8
Cashmore Vic 66 C8
Casino NSW 113 N3
Cassidy Gap Vic 66 F5
Cassilis NSW 110 E3
Cassilis Vic 70 E3, 73 L8
Casterton Vic 66 C5
Castle Doyle NSW 113 J8
Castle Forbes Bay Tas 253 H6
Castle Rock NSW 110 G4
Castle Tower NP Qld 147 L10
Castleburn Vic 70 D5, 73 J10
Castlemaine Vic 67 L3
Castlevale Qld 144 B1, 146 C10
Cataby WA 202 B2
Catamaran Tas 253 H9
Cathcart NSW 109 D9
Cathcart Vic 66 G4
Cathedral Hill Qld 151 H6
Cathedral Range SP Vic 65 L1, 72 D9
Cathedral Rock NP NSW 113 L7
Catherine Hill Bay NSW 111 J7
Cathkin Vic 72 C8
Cathundral NSW 115 P8
Cattai NSW 110 G8
Cattle Creek NT 176 E4
Catumnal Vic 69 K9
Caurnamont SA 233 L10
Cavan NSW 109 C4
Cave Creek NSW 112 G7
Cave Hill NR WA 203 L4
Caveat Vic 72 C8
Cavendish Vic 66 E5
Caveside Tas 254 G7
Cavillon Qld 144 D9
Cawarral Qld 147 J8
Cawnalmurtee NSW 114 E5
Cawongla NSW 113 N2
Cecil Plains Qld 145 J7
Cedar Bay NP Qld 149 L4, 155 C4
Cedar Brush Creek NSW 111 H6
Cedar Party NSW 111 L2
Cedar Point NSW 113 N2
Ceduna SA 212, 232 A4, 231 G10, 317, *317*
Central Castra Tas 254 F6
Central Highlands Tas 250, 251, **328–9**
Central Lansdowne NSW 111 L2
Central Mangrove NSW 111 H7
Central Mt Stuart Historical Reserve NT 179 H3
Central Plateau CA and PA Tas 255 H8, 329
Central Plateau PA Tas 255 J9
Central Tilba NSW 109 E7

Ceres Vic 64 D5, 67 L7
Cerito Qld 146 E4
Cervantes WA 202 B2
Cessnock NSW 111 H6
Chadinga CR SA 231 F10
Chadshunt Qld 148 G7
Chaffey Reservoir NSW 98, 111 H1
Chain of Lagoons Tas 255 P7
Chakola NSW 109 C7
Chalk Cliffs SA 233 K7
Chalky Well NSW 114 C10, 116 C2
Challa WA 205 H7
Challambra Vic 68 F9
Chamberlain River WA 209 L6, 302
Chambers Pillar Historical Reserve NT 179 H8
Chandada SA 232 B5
Chandler SA 231 G2
Chandlers Creek Vic 71 L4
Channing Qld 144 G5
Chapple Vale Vic 67 J9
Charam Vic 66 C3
Charbon NSW 110 E6
Charles Point NT 161, 174 C4
Charles Point Patches NT 161
Charlestown NSW 111 J6
Charleville Qld 144 A5
Charleyong NSW 109 E5
Charleys Creek Vic 64 A7, 67 J9
Charlotte Plains Qld 144 A8, 153 P8
Charlotte Plains Qld 151 L2
Charlotte Vale Qld 144 A7, 153 P7
Charlotte Waters NT 179 K10
Charlottes Pass NSW 109 A8, 117 P9
Charlton NSW 115 M4
Charlton Vic 69 J9
Charnley River WA 209 H5, 304
Charters Towers Qld 146 B2, 149 M10
Chartwell Vic 64 F3, 67 N6
Chatsbury NSW 109 E5
Chatswood NSW 111 H8
Chatsworth NSW 113 N4
Chatsworth Qld 150 E6
Chatsworth Vic 66 G6
Cheadanup NR WA 203 K7
Cheepie Qld 153 M5
Chelmer Qld 144 F8
Chelsea Vic 65 H4, 67 P7
Cheriton Qld 144 F8
Cherrabun WA 206 C1, 209 H10
Cherry Tree Hill NSW 113 H5
Cherrypool Vic 66 E3
Chesalon Qld 146 C9
Cheshire Qld 144 B1, 146 B10
Cheshunt Vic 70 A1, 72 F6
Cheshunt South Vic 72 F7
Chesney Vic 72 E5
Chesterfield Qld 146 D5
Chesterton Range NP Qld 144 C4
Chetwynd Vic 66 C4
Chewton Vic 67 M3
Cheyne Bay WA 202 G9
Cheyne Beach WA 202 F9
Chichester NSW 111 J4
Chichester Range WA 210 G7
Chiddarcooping NR WA 202 G2
Chidlow WA 202 C4
Chidna Qld 148 C9, 150 C1
Chifley WA 203 N3
Childers Qld 145 L2
Childers Vic 65 M6
Chilla Well NT 178 D2
Chillagoe Qld 149 K6, 155 A8
Chillagoe – Mungana Caves NP Qld 149 K6, 155 A8
Chillingham NSW 113 N1
Chillingollah Vic 69 H6
Chilpanunda SA 232 B5
Chiltern Vic 72 G3
Chiltern Hills Qld 150 G7
Chiltern SP Vic 72 G3
Chinaman Creek SA 233 H5
Chinaman Wells SA 232 G9
Chinbi Qld 151 K4
Chinbingina SA 232 A4
Chinchilla Qld 142, 145 J5
Chinderah NSW 113 P1
Chinkapook Vic 68 G5
Chinocup NR WA 202 F7
Chirrup Vic 69 H9
Chorregon Qld 151 K7
Chowilla SA 233 N8

Chowilla GR SA 233 N8
Chowilla RR SA 233 N7
Christmas Creek Qld 149 L9
Christmas Creek Vic 70 E1, 73 K6
Christmas Creek WA 206 C1, 209 J10
Christmas Hills Tas 254 B4
Christmas Point Qld 148 F1, 154 B9
Chudleigh Tas 254 G7
Chudleigh Park Qld 149 J10, 151 L1
Church Plain Camp NSW 112 F4
Churchill Vic 65 P6, 70 A8
Churinga NSW 114 D7
Chute Vic 67 J4
Circle Valley WA 203 L6
Clackline WA 202 D4
Clairview Qld 147 H6
Clandulla NSW 110 E6
Clarafield Qld 151 H4
Claravale NT 174 E7
Claravale Qld 144 D4
Claraville NT 179 J5
Claraville Qld 148 F8
Clare NSW 116 D2
Clare Qld 146 A7, 151 P7
Clare Qld 146 D1, 149 N10
Clare SA 233 J7
Clare Calpa NSW 116 G3
Claremont Tas 253 K4
Clarence Point Tas 255 J5
Clarence River NSW 29, 113 L2, **266–7**, *266*
Clarence Strait NT 174 C3, 292
Clarence Town NSW 111 K5
Clarendon SA 230 A5, 233 J10
Clarendon Tas 255 K7
Clarendon Vic 64 C3, 67 L5
Clarke Hills Qld 149 K10, 151 M1
Clarke River Qld 149 L9
Clarkefield Vic 64 F1, 67 N5
Clarkes Hill Vic 64 C1, 67 L5
Clarrie Hall Dam NSW **75**
Claude Road Tas 254 G6
Claverton Qld 144 A7, 153 P7
Clay Wells SA 230 E8
Clayton SA 230 A6
Clayton SA 235 J8
Clear Lake Vic 66 D3
Clear Ridge NSW 117 N3
Cleary WA 202 E2, 204 G10
Clermont Qld 146 D7
Cleve SA 232 F7
Cleveland Qld 145 N7
Cleveland Tas 255 L8
Cliffdale Qld 153 P6
Clifford Qld 144 F4
Cliffordville WA 202 E6
Clifton Qld 145 L8
Clifton Qld 153 J3
Clifton Beach Qld 149 L5, 155 D7, 291
Clifton Beach Tas 253 L5
Clifton Creek Vic 70 E5, 73 L10
Clifton Downs NSW 114 D3
Clifton Hills SA 235 J3
Clifton Springs Vic 44, 64 E5, 67 M7
Clinton Centre SA 233 H8
Clinton CP SA 233 H8
Clio Qld 151 J5
Clive Qld 146 G7
Clonagh Qld 148 D10, 150 E2
Cloncose Qld 145 J3
Cloncurry Qld 150 E3
Clontarf Qld 145 K8
Clouds Creek NSW 113 M6
Clough Creek NT 179 N3
Clovelly Qld 151 M9
Cloverlea Vic 65 M5
Cloyna Qld 145 L4
Cluan Tas 255 J7
Club Terrace Vic 71 K5
Clunes Vic 67 K4
Cluny Qld 150 C10, 152 C1
Clybucca NSW 113 M9
Clyde Vic 65 J5
Clyde River NSW **96–7**, *96*, *97*, 272
Clydebank Vic 70 D7
Coal Mines Historic Site Tas 253 L5
Coalcliff NSW 109 G2, 110 G10
Coaldale NSW 113 M4
Coalstoun Lakes Qld 145 L3
Coalville Vic 65 N5
Coan Downs NSW 115 K9, 117 K1
Cobains Vic 70 C7

Cobar NSW 115 K7
Cobargo NSW 109 E7
Cobbadah NSW 112 F7
Cobbannah Vic 70 D5, 73 J10
Cobbora NSW 110 C3
Cobbrum Qld 144 A7
Cobden Vic 67 H8
Cobdogla SA 233 N8
Cobera SA 233 N9
Cobham NSW 114 C4
Cobourg Marine Park NT 174 F1
Cobourg Peninsula NT 174 F2, **294–5**
Cobra WA 204 E1
Cobram Vic 72 C2, 265
Cobrico Vic 67 H8
Coburn WA 204 C5
Cocamba Vic 68 G5
Cocata CP SA 232 C6
Cocata CR SA 232 D6
Cochranes Creek Vic 67 J2
Cockaleechie SA 232 D8
Cockatoo Qld 145 H3
Cockatoo Vic 65 K4
Cockburn SA 233 N4
Cockburn Sound WA **186–7**, *187*, 193, 202 B5
Cockenzie Qld 146 F5
Cocklarina Qld 153 N7
Cockle Creek Tas 253 H9
Cocklebiddy WA 207 D7
Cocoparra NP NSW 117 L4
Codrington Vic 66 D7
Coen Qld 149 H1, 154 D8, 278
Coffin Bay SA 232 D9
Coffin Bay NP SA 232 C9
Coffs Harbour NSW 113 N7, **268–9**, 270
Coghills Creek Vic 64 B1, 67 K4
Cogla Downs WA 205 H6
Cohuna Vic 69 L8
Coimadai Vic 64 E2, 67 M5
Cokum Vic 69 H7
Colac Vic 56, 64 A6, 67 J8
Colac Colac Vic 73 L4
Colane NSW 114 E3
Colbinabbin Vic 67 N1, 69 N10
Colbinabbin West Vic 67 N1
Coldstream Vic 65 J3, 72 B10
Coldstream River NSW 267
Coleambally Irrigation Area NSW 117 K5
Colebrook Tas 253 K3
Coleman Bend Vic 73 M4
Coleraine Qld 151 J4
Coleraine Vic 66 D5
Coles Bay Tas *237*, 242, 253 P1, 255 P10
Colignan Vic 68 F3
Colinroobie NSW 117 L5
Colinton NSW 109 C6
Collapy Qld 146 C1, 149 N10
Collarenebri NSW 112 B5
Collaroy Qld 144 A5
Collaroy Qld 146 G6
Collector NSW 109 D4
Collerina NSW 115 L3
Colley SA 232 B6
Collie NSW 110 A2, 115 P7
Collie WA 201, 202 C7
Collie River WA 194
Collier Bay WA 208 F5
Collier Range NP WA 205 J2
Collingullie NSW 117 M6
Collingwood Qld 145 H4
Collingwood Qld 151 H6
Collinsvale Tas 253 J5
Collinsville Qld 146 E3
Collinsville SA 233 K6
Collymongle NSW 112 B5
Colo Heights NSW 110 G7
Colo River NSW 79, 80, 81, 110 F7
Colossal NSW 115 M5
Colosseum Qld 145 K1, 147 L10
Colreavy WA 202 G2
Colston Qld 151 J7
Colston Park Qld 146 G5
Columboola Qld 145 H5
Colwell Qld 150 F4
Comara NSW 113 L8
Combaning NSW 117 N5

INDEX OF PLACE NAMES 397

Combara NSW 110 A1, 112 A10
Combienbar Vic 71 K4
Comboyne NSW 111 L2
Comboyuro Point QLD 124
Come by Chance NSW 112 A7
Comeroo NSW 115 H2
Comet Qld 146 F9
Commodore SA 233 J2
Commonwealth Hill SA 234 A9
Como NSW 85, 111 H9
Como Qld 153 L5
Comobella NSW 110 C4
Comongin Qld 153 L5
Compton Downs NSW 115 L4
Conara Tas 255 L8
Conargo NSW 117 J6
Concongella Vic 66 G3
Condada SA 232 C5
Condah Vic 66 D6
Condamine Qld 145 H6
Condamine River Qld 142, 143, 145 J6
Condingup WA 203 N7
Condobolin NSW 115 M10, 117 M1
Condong NSW 113 P1
Condoulpe NSW 116 F5
Condowie SA 233 J7
Congie Qld 153 K6
Congo NSW 109 E6
Congupna Vic 72 C4
Conimbla NP NSW 109 A1, 110 A8
Coningham Tas 253 K6
Coniston NT 178 F3
Coniston Qld 144 B7
Coniston SA 153 J3
Conjola NSW 109 F5
Conjuboy Qld 149 K8
Conmurra SA 230 E9
Connells Lagoon CR NT 177 M6
Connemara Qld 144 B3
Connemara Qld 151 H10, 153 H1
Connemarra NSW 110 D2
Connemara Qld 146 E9
Connewarre Vic 64 E5, 67 M7
Connewirrecoo Vic 66 C4
Connolly Qld 146 C2
Conoble NSW 115 H10, 117 H1
Conondale Qld 145 M5
Conondale NP Qld 145 M5
Conway Qld 146 F2
Conway Beach Qld 146 F3, 289
Conway NP Qld 146 G3
Cooba NSW 117 P6
Coober Pedy SA 234 C7
Cooberrie Qld 147 K8
Coobowie SA 230 A4, 233 H10
Cooby Dam Qld **141**
Coodardy WA 204 G6
Coogee Beach WA 183
Cooinda NT 174 F5
Coojar Vic 66 C4
Cook SA 231 C8
Cookamidgera NSW 110 A7, 117 P2
Cookardinia NSW 117 M7
Cooke Plains SA 230 A7
Cooks Well Outstation Qld 152 G5
Cooktown Qld 149 L3, 155 C3, 278, 286, 287, 288, 291
Cool Creek Vic 65 M3, 72 E10
Coolabah NSW 115 L6
Coolabah Qld 153 N6
Coolabara Qld 153 M2
Coolabri Qld 144 B3
Coolabunia Qld 145 L5
Coolac NSW 109 A4, 117 P6
Cooladdi Qld 153 N5
Coolah NSW 110 D3
Coolamon NSW 117 M5
Coolangatta Qld 145 N8
Coolangubra NP NSW 109 D9
Coolanie SA 232 F7
Coolatai NSW 112 G4
Coolbaggie NSW 110 A3
Coolcalalaya WA 204 D6
Coolcha SA 233 L10
Coolgardie WA 203 L3
Coolibah NT 174 D9
Coolimba WA 202 A1, 204 D10
Coolongolook NSW 111 L4
Cooloola Beach Qld 126, 129
Cooloola NP Qld see Great Sandy NP Qld
Cooltong SA 233 N8

Coolullah Qld 148 D10, 150 D1
Coolum Beach Qld 126, 129, 145 N5
Coolup WA 202 C6
Cooma NSW 109 C7
Cooma Qld 144 F7
Cooma Qld 153 J5
Cooma Vic 67 P1, 69 P10, 72 A5
Coomaba SA 232 D8
Coomallo NR WA 202 B1, 204 D10
Coomandook SA 230 A7
Coomba NSW 111 L4
Coombabah Lake Qld 120
Coombah Roadhouse NSW 114 B10, 116 B1
Coombell NSW 113 M3
Coomberdale WA 202 C2
Coombie NSW 115 J10, 117 J1
Coombogolong NSW 115 P5
Coomera River Qld 120
Coomeratta NSW 114 G7
Coominglah Qld 145 J1
Coominya Qld 145 M7
Coomooboolaroo Qld 147 H9
Coomoora Vic 64 D1, 67 L4
Coomrith Qld 144 G7
Coomunga SA 232 D9
Coonabarabran NSW 110 C1, 112 C10
Coonalpyn SA 230 B8
Coonamble NSW 112 A9
Coonana WA 203 N3
Coonawarra SA 230 E10
Coondambo SA 232 D2
Coondarra Qld 145 H4
Cooneel Qld 147 J9
Coonerang NSW 109 C8
Coongan WA 211 J5
Coongie Qld 152 D6
Coongie SA 235 M3
Coongie Lake SA 235 M3
Coongoola Qld 144 A7, 153 P7
Coongulla Vic 70 B6
Coonooer Bridge Vic 67 J1, 69 J10
Cooper Creek Qld 152 G5
Cooper Creek SA 235 J6
Coopernook NSW 111 M3
Coopracambra NP Vic 71 L3
Coorabah Qld 146 A7
Coorabah Qld 151 N7
Coorabelle Qld 151 K5
Coorabie SA 231 E10
Coorabulka Qld 150 E9
Coorada Qld 144 G2
Cooralya WA 204 C2
Cooran Qld 145 M5
Cooranbong NSW 111 J6
Cooranga North Qld 145 K5
Coordewandy WA 204 E3
Cooriemungle Vic 67 H8
Coorong NP SA **222–3**, 230 B6
Cooroorah Qld 146 F8
Coorow WA 202 C1, 204 E10
Cooroy Qld 138, 145 M5
Cootamundra NSW 109 A3, 117 P5
Cootawundi WA 204 D6
Cooyal NSW 110 D4
Cooyar Qld 145 L6
Coparella Qld 153 M6
Cope Cope Vic 67 H1, 69 H10
Copeland NSW 111 K3
Copeton Dam NSW 113 H6
Copeville SA 233 M10
Copley SA 233 J1, 235 J10
Copmanhurst NSW 113 M5, 267
Coppabella Qld 146 F5
Copper Hill SA 234 B5
Copperfield WA 205 K8
Copping Tas 253 M5
Cora Lynn Vic 65 K5
Corack East Vic 69 H9
Corackerup NR WA 202 G8
Coragulac Vic 64 A5, 67 J7
Coraki NSW 113 N3
Coral Bank Vic 73 J5
Coral Bay WA 210 B9
Coral Sea Qld 149 N5
Coralie Qld 148 F7
Coralville NSW 111 M3
Coramba NSW 113 N7
Cordelia Qld 149 M8
Cordering WA 202 D7
Cordillo Downs SA 235 N2
Corea Plains Qld 146 B3, 151 P3

Coreen NSW 117 L7
Corella NSW 115 L3
Corella SA 233 N4
Corella Lakes NSW 115 M3
Corfield Qld 151 K8
Corin Dam ACT 104, 107, 109 C5
Corndhap Vic 64 B3, 67 K6
Corndi Beach NSW 113 N6
Cornella NSW 117 N2
Cornella Vic **42**, 43, 65 J6, 263
Cornna Tas 254 B7
Corinthia WA 203 H3
Corio Vic 64 E4, 67 M7
Corio Bay Vic **44–5**, **44**, 64 E5
Cork Qld 151 N7
Corella Vic 67 N2
Corella East Vic 67 N2
Corner Camp NSW 112 G7
Corner Inlet Vic **54–5**, 65 N8
Cornwall Qld 144 E4
Cornwall Tas 255 N7
Corny Point SA 232 G10
Corobimilla NSW 117 L5
Coromby Vic 66 F1, 68 F10
Corona NSW 114 B6
Corona Qld 153 M4
Coronation Bay WA 199
Coronet Bay Vic 65 J6
Coronga Peak NSW 115 L5
Corop Vic 67 N1, 69 N10
Corrobe Vic 64 A6, 67 J8
Corowa NSW 117 L8, 264
Corricegery NSW 117 N2
Corrie Downs Qld 150 D6
Corrigin WA 202 F5
Corrimal NSW 109 G2, 110 G10
Corroboree Park Tavern NT 174 E5
Corrong NSW 116 G4
Corrowong NSW 109 B9
Corryong Vic 73 M4, 264
Corunna SA 232 G5
Corunna Downs WA 211 K6
Cosgrove Vic 72 C4
Cosmo Newbery WA 205 N7
Cosmos Qld 145 F7
Cossack WA 210 F5, 309
Costerfield Vic 67 H3
Cotabena SA 233 J3
Cotswold Qld 150 E2
Cotter Dam ACT 104, 107
Cotter River ACT 106, **107–8**, 107
Cottesloe Beach WA **182**, 183
Couangalt Vic 64 F2, 67 N5
Cougal NSW 113 M1
Coulson Qld 145 M8
Coulta SA 232 D9
Countegany NSW 109 D7
County Downs WA 208 D7
Coura SA 232 B5
Couta Rocks Tas 254 A5
Coutts Crossing NSW 113 M6
Cowabbie West NSW 117 M5
Cowan Cowan Qld 123, 124
Cowan Downs Qld 148 D9
Cowangie Vic 68 C6
Cowaramup WA 202 B8
Coward Springs SA 234 F8
Cowarie SA 235 J4
Cowarna Downs WA 203 M3
Cowary NSW 114 F8
Cowcowing Lakes WA 202 E3
Cowell SA 232 F7
Cowes Vic 43, 65 J6
Cowl Cowl NSW 117 J3
Cowley Qld 149 M7, 155 E10
Cowley Qld 153 M6
Cowra NSW 109 B1, 110 B9
Cowwarr Vic 70 B7
Cowwarr Weir Vic 70 B6
Coxs River NSW 102
Coyrecup WA 202 F7
Crabbon Qld 151 H0 D3
Crabtree Tas 253 J5
Cracow Qld 145 H3
Cradle Mountain Tas 254 F8
Cradle Mountain Lake St Clair NP Tas 254 E8, 328, 329
Cradle Valley Tas 254 E7
Cradoc Tas 253 J6
Cradock SA 233 J4
Craigie NSW 109 C9
Craigieburn Vic 64 G2, 67 P5, 72 A10

Craiglie Qld 149 L5, 155 D6
Craigmore Qld 146 E9
Cramenton Vic 68 F4
Cramps Tas 255 J9
Cramsie Qld 151 L8
Cranbourne Vic 65 J5
Cranbrook Tas 255 N9
Cranbrook WA 202 E8
Cranebrook NSW 109 G1, 110 G8
Craven NSW 111 K4
Craven Qld 146 D8
Crayfish Creek Tas 254 D4
Crediton Qld 146 F4
Credo WA 203 K3
Creighton Creek Vic 72 C7
Cremorne Qld 145 G5
Cremorne Tas 253 L5
Crendon Qld 151 H4
Crescent Head NSW 111 M1, 113 M10
Cressbrook Dam Qld **141**
Cresswell Downs NT 177 L5
Cressy Tas 246, 255 K8
Cressy Vic 64 B4, 67 K7
Creswick Vic 64 C1, 67 K4
Creswick North Vic 64 C1, 67 K4
Crew Qld 152 F8
Crib Point Vic 65 H6, 67 P8
Cringadale NSW 116 E5
Croajingolong NP Vic **48–9**, **49**, 71 N5, 258
Crocodile Qld 149 K3, 155 B4
Croker Island NT 174 F2, 294, 295
Cronulla NSW 111 H9
Crooble NSW 112 F4
Crooked Corner NSW 109 D2, 110 C10
Crooked River Vic 70 C4, 73 J9
Crookhaven Heads NSW 93
Crookhaven River NSW 92, 93
Crookwell NSW 109 D3, 110 D10
Croppa Creek NSW 112 F4
Crossley Vic 66 E8
Crossman WA 202 D6
Crossmoor Qld 151 M7
Crowdy Bay NP NSW 111 M2
Crowdy Head NSW 111 M3
Crowlands Vic 67 H3
Crows Nest Qld 141, 145 L6
Crowther NSW 109 B2, 110 A9
Croydon Qld 146 G5
Croydon Qld 148 G7
Croydon Vic 65 J3
Crusher NSW 112 E9
Cryon NSW 112 B6
Crystal Brook SA 233 J7
Crystalbrook Qld 144 D3
Cuba Plains Qld 149 K10, 151 N1
Cuballing WA 202 E6
Cubbaroo NSW 112 C7
Cubbaroo Qld 148 D10, 150 E2
Cuckadoo Qld 150 E3
Cuckoo Tas 255 L5
Cudal NSW 110 B7
Cuddapan Qld 152 G3
Cudgee Vic 66 G8
Cudgegong River NSW 98, 99
Cudgewa Vic 73 L4
Cudgewa North Vic 73 L3
Cudmirrah NSW 109 F4
Cue WA 204 G6
Culbin WA 202 D6
Culburra NSW 109 G4
Culburra SA 230 B8
Culcairn NSW 117 M7
Culfearne Vic 69 L7
Culgoa Vic 69 H7
Culgoa Floodplain NP Qld 144 C9
Culgoora NSW 112 D7
Culgowie Qld 144 G4
Culla Vic 66 C4
Culladar Qld 151 K6
Cullculli WA 205 H6
Cullen Bullen NSW 110 E7
Culloden Vic 70 C6
Cullulleraine Vic 68 C2
Culpataro NSW 116 G3
Culpaulin NSW 114 E7
Cultowa NSW 114 G7
Cumberland Downs Qld 146 E6
Cumbijowa NSW 117 F2
Cumboogle NSW 110 B4
Cumborah NSW 115 N3

Cummins SA 232 D8
Cumnock NSW 110 B6
Cundeelee Community WA 203 P2, 207 A6
Cunderdin WA 202 E4
Cundumbul NSW 110 B6
Cungelella Qld 144 C1
Cungena SA 232 B5
Cunliffe SA 233 H8
Cunnamulla Qld 153 P8
Cunningar NSW 109 B3
Cunningham SA 233 H9
Cunno Creek Qld 144 B2
Cunyu WA 205 K4
Cuprona Tas 254 F5
Curban NSW 110 B2
Curbur WA 204 E5
Curdie Vale Vic 66 G8
Curdimurka SA 234 G8
Curlewis NSW 110 F1, 112 F10
Curlwaa NSW 116 C4
Curnamona SA 233 L3
Curra Creek NSW 110 B5
Currabubula NSW 110 G1, 112 G10
Curragh NSW 116 F3
Curragh Qld 146 F8
Currajong Qld 144 G7
Currajong Qld 145 H8
Currambene Creek NSW 95
Currumulka SA 233 H9
Curravera Qld 153 J3
Currarong NSW 93, 94, 109 G4
Currawarna NSW 117 M6
Currawilla Qld 152 F3
Currawinya NSW 153 M9
Currawinya NP Qld 153 L9
Currawong Qld 144 E10
Currency Creek SA 230 A6
Currie Tas 254 F2
Curtin WA 203 M2
Curtin Springs NT 178 E9
Curtis Channel Qld 147 L8
Curtis Island Qld 147 K9
Curtis Island NP Qld 147 K8
Curyo Vic 68 G8
Cuthero NSW 114 C10, 116 C1
Cuttabri NSW 112 C7
Cygnet Tas 253 J6
Cygnet River SA 230 B3
Cytherea Qld 144 D6

Daandine Qld 145 J6
Dadswells Bridge Vic 66 F3
Daguragu NT 176 C4
Dagworth Qld 149 H7
Dagworth Qld 151 H5
Darwilly NSW 117 H7
Daintree Qld 149 L4, 155 C5, 287, 291
Daintree Qld 151 K6
Daintree NP Qld 149 K4, 155 C5
Daintree River Qld 288, **290–1**, 290
Dairy Creek WA 204 E3
Daisy Hill Vic 67 K3
Daisy Plains NSW 113 L9
Dajarra Qld 150 C5
Dalbeg Qld 146 D2
Dalby Qld 142, 145 K6
Dalgaranga WA 204 F7
Dalgety NSW 109 B8
Dalgety Downs WA 204 E3
Dalgonally Qld 148 E10, 150 F2
Dalgouring WA 202 F2
Dalhousie SA 234 D2
Dallarnil Qld 145 L3
Dalma Qld 147 J8
Dalman NSW 113 L1
Dalmeny NSW 109 E7
Dalmore Qld 151 L8
Dalmorino NSW 114 E10, 116 E1
Dalmorton NSW 113 L6
Dalmuir NSW 114 C4
Dalton NSW 109 C3
Dalveen Qld 145 L9
Dalwallinu WA 202 D1, 204 F10
Dalwood NSW 115 L2
Daly River NT **168–9**, 174 C6
Daly Waters NT 176 G2
Dalyston Vic 65 K7
Dalyup WA 203 L7
Damboring WA 202 D2
Dampier WA 210 F5, 308

INDEX OF PLACE NAMES

Dampier Archipelago WA 210 E5, 308, 309
Dampier Downs WA 208 E9, 211 P2
Dancers Valley Qld 150 G5
Dandaloo NSW 115 N8
Dandaraga Qld 151 M9
Dandaraga WA 205 J7
Dandaragan WA 202 B2
Dandenong Vic 65 H4, 67 P6
Dandenong Park Qld 146 C3
Dandenong Ranges NP Vic 65 H3
Dandongadale Vic 70 B1, 72 G6
Dangarfield NSW 110 G4
Danggali CP SA 233 N6
Dangin WA 202 E4
Danyo Vic 68 B6
Dapto NSW 109 G3, 110 G10
Daradgee Qld 149 M6, 155 E9
Darby River Vic 54
Darbys Falls NSW 109 C1, 110 B9
Darbyshire Vic 73 K3
Dardanup WA 202 C7
Dareton NSW 116 C4
Dargo Vic 70 D4, 73 J9
Dargo High Plains Vic 70 C2, 261
Dargo River Vic 73 K8, 261
Darkan WA 202 D7
Darke Peak SA 232 E7
Darkwood NSW 113 M8
Darling River NSW 114 D8, 115 H5, 116 C3
Darlington Tas 253 N3
Darlington Vic 67 H7
Darlington Point NSW 117 K5
Darnick NSW 114 F10, 116 F1
Darnum Vic 65 M5
Daroobalgie NSW 117 P2
Darr Qld 151 L8
Darraweit Vic 64 G1
Darraweit Guim Vic 67 N4, 72 A9
Darriman Vic 70 C9
Dartmoor Vic 66 B6
Dartmouth Vic 60, 73 K5
Dartmouth Reservoir Vic 60–1, 73 K5
Darwin NT 156, 157, 158–9, 158, 159, 160–1, 174 D4, 292, 294
Daubeny NSW 114 D6
Daunia Qld 146 F6
Davenport Downs Qld 150 F10
Davenport Range NT 177 J9
Davenport Range NP NT 177 J10, 179 J1
Davis Creek NSW 111 H4
Davyhurst WA 203 K1, 205 L10
Dawes Qld 145 J1
Dawesville WA 202 B5
Dawson SA 233 K5
Dawson City Vic 70 E4, 73 L9
Dawson Vale Qld 145 H3
Dawson Vale Qld 146 B4
Dayboro Qld 145 M6
Daylesford Vic 64 D1, 67 L4
Daymar Qld 144 F9
Daysdale NSW 117 L7
Daytrap Vic 68 G5
De Grey WA 211 J5
De La Poer Range NR WA 205 N6
De Rose Hill SA 231 G1
Deakin WA 207 G6
Dean Vic 64 C1, 67 L5
Deans Marsh Vic 64 C6, 67 K8
Debella Qld 148 G10, 150 G1
Debesa WA 208 F8
Deception Bay Qld 145 N6
Deddick Vic 71 H2, 73 P7
Deddington Tas 255 L7
Dederang Vic 73 H5
Dee Tas 252 G2
Dee Lagoon Tas 252 G1, 255 H10, 328
Deep Creek WA 210 D9
Deep Creek CP SA 230 B4
Deep Lead Vic 66 G3
Deep Well NT 179 H7
Deepwater NSW 113 K5
Deepwater NP Qld 145 L1, 147 M10
Deer Park Vic 64 F3, 67 N6
Deeral Qld 149 M6, 155 E8
Degarra Qld 149 L4, 155 C5
Delalah House NSW 114 E2
Delamere NT 174 E9, 176 E1
Delamere SA 230 B4

Delatite River Vic 58
Delegate NSW 109 C9
Delegate River Vic 71 K2
Dellicknora Vic 71 J3
Dellyannie WA 202 E7
Delmore Downs NT 179 J4
Delny NT 179 J4
Deloraine Tas 247, 255 H7
Delray Beach Vic 70 D8
Delta Qld 146 E2
Delta Downs Qld 148 E3
Delta South Qld 146 A9, 151 N9
Delungra NSW 112 G5
Delvine Vic 70 D6
Denham WA 204 B4
Denham Island Qld 148 B5, 285
Denham Sound WA 204 A4
Denial Bay SA 231 G10
Denian NSW 114 E9
Denicull Creek Vic 66 G4
Deniliquin NSW 117 H7
Denison Vic 70 B7
Denman NSW 110 G4
Denman SA 231 B8
Denmark WA 202 E10
Dennes Point Tas 253 K6
Dennington Vic 66 F8
D'Entrecasteaux NP WA 202 C9
Depot Creek SA 233 H4
Depot Springs WA 205 K7
Deptford Vic 70 E5, 73 L10
Depuch Island WA 210 G5, 309
Derby Tas 255 M5
Derby Vic 67 L2
Derby WA 208 E7, 304, 305
Dereel Vic 64 B3, 67 K6
Dergholm Vic 66 B4
Dergholm SP Vic 66 E4
Dering Vic 68 E6
Deringulla NSW 110 C1, 112 C10
Derrinallum Vic 67 H6
Derriwong NSW 115 N10, 117 N2
Derry Downs NT 179 K3
Derwent NT 178 F5
Derwent Bridge Tas 252 E1, 254 F10
Detpa Vic 68 D9
Deua NP NSW 109 E6
Devenish Vic 72 D4
Deverill Qld 146 F6
Devils Marbles CR NT 177 J9
Deviot Tas 255 J5
Devlins Bridge Vic 65 K1, 72 C9
Devon Tas 114 D7
Devon Vic 70 A9
Devonborough Downs SA 233 M5
Devoncourt Qld 150 E4
Devonport Tas 254 G5
Devonshire Qld 151 M9
Dharug NP NSW 111 H7
Dhuragoon Vic 116 G6
Dhurringile Vic 72 E5
Diamantina Lakes Qld 150 F9
Diamantina NP Qld 150 F9
Diamantina River Qld 151 H7, 152 E2
Diamond Beach NSW 111 L3
Diamond Creek Vic 65 H2, 67 P5, 72 B10
Diamond Downs Qld 146 D5
Diamond Well WA 205 J4
Diapur Vic 68 C10
Diemals Qld 205 J9
Digby Vic 66 C6
Diggers Rest Vic 64 F2, 67 N5
Diggora Vic 69 M10
Diggora West Vic 67 M1, 69 M10
Dillalah Qld 144 A3, 153 P6
Dillcar Qld 151 K6
Dilpurra NSW 116 F6
Dilston Tas 255 K6
Dilulla Qld 151 M8
Dimboola Vic 66 E1, 68 E10
Dimbulah Qld 149 K6, 155 C8
Dimora Vic 151 H4
Dingee Vic 67 L1, 69 L10
Dingo Qld 146 G5
Dingo Beach Qld 146 F2
Dingwall Vic 69 K3
Dinner Plain Vic 70 D2, 73 J7
Dinninup Vic 202 D8
Dinoga NSW 112 G6
Dinyarrak Vic 68 B10
Dipperu NP Qld 146 F5

Dirk Hartog Island WA 204 A3, 312–13
Dirnasser NSW 117 N5
Dirranbandi Qld 144 E9
Dirrung NSW 117 J3
Disaster Bay NSW 109 E10, 275
Discovery Bay Vic 66 B7
Discovery Bay Coastal Park Vic 66 B7
Disney Qld 146 C5
Dittmer Qld 146 F3
Dixie Vic 66 G8
Dixie Outstation Qld 149 H2, 154 E10
Dixons Creek Vic 65 J2, 72 B10
Dlorah Downs SA 233 M5
Dneiper NT 179 K4
Dobbyn Qld 148 C10, 150 D1
Dobie Vic 67 H4
Docker Vic 72 F5
Doctors Flat Vic 70 F3, 73 L8
Dodges Ferry Tas 253 L5
Dogs Grave Vic 70 D3, 73 K8
Dogtown Vic 70 E4, 73 L9
Dollar Vic 65 N7
Dolphin Island NR WA 210 F5
Don Qld 148 A10, 150 A2
Don Tas 254 G5
Don Valley Vic 65 K3, 72 C10
Donald Vic 66 G1, 69 H10
Doncaster Qld 151 K2
Doncaster Vic 65 H3, 67 P6
Donga Qld 144 F7
Dongara WA 198–9, 204 C9
Donnelly WA 202 C8
Donnelly River WA 200
Donnybrook Vic 64 G2, 67 P5, 72 A9
Donnybrook Qld 202 C7
Donnyville Qld 149 H8
Donors Hill Qld 148 D8
Donovans SA 230 G10
Doobibla Qld 153 N6
Dooboobetic Vic 67 H1, 69 H10
Doodlakine WA 202 F4
Dooen Vic 66 E2
Dookie Vic 72 C4
Dookie College Vic 72 D4
Dooley Downs WA 204 F1, 210 F10
Doolgunna WA 205 J4
Doomadgee Qld 148 B7
Doongmabulla Qld 146 B6
Dooralong NSW 111 H7
Doorawarrah WA 204 C2
Doorstop Bay Tas 252 E8
Dooruna Qld 146 D5
Dora Creek NSW 111 J6
Dora Vale Qld 148 E9, 150 F1
Doreen NSW 112 C6
Dorisvale NT 174 F6
Dornock WA 202 G6
Dorodong Vic 66 B4
Dorrigo NSW 113 M7
Dorrigo NP NSW 113 M7
Dorunda Qld 148 F5
Dotswood Qld 146 B1, 149 M10
Double Bridges Vic 70 F5, 73 M10
Double Gates NSW 115 J7
Double Island Point QLD 126, 128, 129, 154 E3
Double Lagoon Qld 148 E6
Double Sandy Point Coastal Reserve Tas 255 K4
Doubtful Bay WA 208 G5, 304
Doubtful Creek NSW 113 M3
Doughboy River Qld 154 C3, 280–1
Douglas Vic 66 D3
Douglas Apsley NP Tas 237, 255 N8
Douglas Downs Qld 150 B5
Douglas Hot Springs NP NT 174 D6
Dover Qld 150 F7
Dover Tas 253 J7
Dowerin WA 202 D3
Downside NSW 117 N6
Doyalson NSW 111 J7
Doyles Creek NSW 110 G5
Dragon Rocks NR WA 202 G5
Dragon Tree Soak NR WA 206 A2, 211 P4
Drain C SA 230 E8
Drake NSW 113 L3
Drakesbrook Reservoir WA 201
Dreeite Vic 64 A5, 67 J7
Driftway NSW 109 A1, 117 P3
Drik Drik Vic 66 B6

Dripstone NSW 110 C5
Dromana Vic 64 G6, 67 P8
Dromedary Tas 253 J4
Dronfield Qld 150 D4
Dropmore Vic 72 B7
Drouin Vic 65 L5
Drovers Cave NP WA 202 B1, 204 D10
Drumanure Vic 72 C3
Drumborg Vic 66 C7
Drumduff Qld 149 H4
Drummond Qld 146 D9
Drummond Vic 67 M4
Drummond Cove WA 199, 204 C8
Drung Drung Vic 66 F2
Drung Drung South Vic 66 E2
Dry Creek Vic 72 D7
Dry Creek WA 207 D6
Dry River NT 174 F9
Dryander NP Qld 146 F2
Drysdale Vic 64 F5, 67 M7
Drysdale River WA 209 K4, 302, 304
Drysdale River NP WA 209 L3
Duaringa Qld 147 H9
Dubbo NSW 110 B4
Dublin SA 233 J9
Duchess Qld 150 D4
Duck Creek WA 210 F8
Dudinin WA 202 F6
Dudley CP SA 230 B4
Dudley Qld 146 E4
Dudley South Vic 65 K7
Duff Creek SA 234 D6
Duffield NT 179 J10
Dulacca Qld 144 G5
Dulkaninna SA 235 J7
Dululu Qld 147 J9
Dumaresq River Qld 143, 145 H9
Dumbalk Vic 65 M7
Dumbalk North Vic 65 N7
Dumbleyung WA 202 E7
Dumbleyung Lake WA 202 E7
Dumosa Vic 69 H8
Dunach Vic 67 K4
Dunalley Tas 240, 253 M5
Dunbar Qld 148 G4
Dundas NR WA 203 N5
Dundas Strait NT 174 E2, 294
Dundee NSW 113 K5
Dundee Qld 151 J4
Dundee Beach WA 166–7, 166, 167
Dundee Rail NSW 113 K5
Dundoo Qld 153 M7
Dundula Qld 146 G4
Dundurrabin NSW 113 L7
Dunedoo NSW 110 D3
Dungarubba NSW 113 N3
Dungarvon NSW 115 H2
Dungog NSW 111 J4
Dungowan NSW 111 H1, 113 H10
Dungowan NT 176 F3
Dunham River WA 209 M5
Dunk Island Qld 149 M7, 155 E10, 288, 288
Dunkeld Qld 144 D6
Dunkeld Vic 66 F5
Dunkerry Qld 145 H6
Dunmarra NT 176 F3
Dunmora NSW 115 P9, 117 P1
Dunmore Vic 66 E7
Dunn Rock NR WA 203 H7
Dunneworthy Vic 67 H4
Dunnstown Vic 64 C2, 67 L5
Dunoak NSW 114 G6
Dunolly Vic 67 K2
Dunoon NSW 113 N2
Dunorlan Tas 255 H7
Dunrobin Qld 146 B7, 151 P7
Dunrobin Vic 66 C5
Dunrobin Bridge Tas 252 G3
Dunsborough WA 195, 196, 197, 202 B7
Duntroon NSW 114 E6
Duntulla Qld 150 C5
Dunwich QLD 124
Durack River WA 209 L5
Durah Qld 145 J4
Duramana NSW 110 D7
Duranillin WA 202 D7
Durdidwarrah Vic 64 D3, 67 L6
Durella Qld 144 C5
Durham Qld 149 H7
Durham Downs Qld 144 F4

Durham Downs Qld 152 G6
Durham Ox Vic 69 K9
Duri NSW 110 G1, 112 G10
Durong South Qld 145 J5
Durras NSW 109 F6
Durras North NSW 109 F6
Durrie Qld 152 E3
Dutson Vic 70 D7
Dutton SA 233 K9
Dutton Bay SA 232 D9
Dwarda WA 202 D6
Dwellingup WA 201, 202 C6
Dwyers NSW 115 L5
Dyers Crossing NSW 111 L3
Dynevor Downs Qld 153 L8
Dyraaba Central NSW 113 M2
Dysart Qld 146 F7
Dysart Tas 253 J3

Eagle Bay WA 208 G5
Eagle Point Vic 70 E6
Eagle Vale NSW 109 G2, 110 G9
Eaglebar Qld 144 G8
Eaglefield Qld 146 E4
Eaglehawk NSW 114 B9
Eaglehawk Vic 67 L2
Eaglehawk Neck Tas 240, 253 M6
Earaheedy WA 205 M3
Earlando Qld 146 F2
East Alligator River NT 172–3, 173, 174 F4
East Boyd NSW 109 E9
East Creek Qld 146 E7
East End Qld 147 K9
East Jindabyne NSW 109 B7
East Loddon Vic 67 L1, 69 L10
East Lynne NSW 109 F5
East Lynne Qld 144 A1, 146 A10, 151 P10, 153 P1
East Sassafras Tas 255 H6
East Vernon Island NT 160, 174 D3
East Yuna NR WA 204 D7
Eastbourne NSW 109 B7
Eastbrook Qld 146 G9
Eastbrook WA 202 C9
Eastern View Vic 64 C6, 67 L8
Eastmere Qld 146 B6, 151 P6
Eastville Vic 67 L2
Eastwood Qld 153 N2
Ebden Vic 73 H3
Ebor NSW 113 L7
Echo Hills Qld 146 D10
Echuca Vic 69 N9, 264, 265, 265
Echuca Village Vic 69 N9
Echunga SA 230 A6, 233 K10
Ecklin South Vic 66 G8
Edaggee WA 204 C3
Eddington Qld 150 G3
Eddington Vic 67 K2
Eden NSW 109 E9, 274–5
Eden Creek NSW 113 M2
Eden Vale Qld 149 H7
Eden Valley SA 233 K9
Edenhope Vic 66 B3
Edeowie SA 233 J3
Edgecombe Vic 67 M4
Edgeroi NSW 112 E7
Edi Vic 70 A1, 72 F6
Edillilie SA 232 D9
Edith NSW 109 E1, 110 E8
Edith Creek Tas 254 C4
Edith Downs Qld 151 H3
Edithburgh SA 230 A4, 233 H10
Edjudina WA 205 N10
Edmonton Qld 149 L5, 155 D8
Edmund WA 204 E1, 210 E10
Edmund Kennedy NP Qld 149 M7
Edwards Creek SA 234 D6
Edwinstowe Qld 146 B8, 151 P8
Eenaweenah NSW 115 N7
Eganstown Vic 64 C1, 67 L4
Egelabra NSW 115 N5
Egera Qld 146 B4, 151 P4
Egg Lagoon Tas 254 F1
Eginbah WA 211 K6
Eglinton NSW 110 D7
Ehlma Qld 145 J6
Eidsvold Qld 145 K3
Eighty Mile Beach WA 211 L4
Eildon Vic 72 D8
Eildon Park Qld 151 H8

INDEX OF PLACE NAMES 399

Eildon Pondage Vic 59
Eildon SP Vic 72 E8
Eimeo Qld 146 G4
Einasleigh Qld 149 J8
Ejanding WA 202 E3
El Alamein SA 233 H5
El Arish Qld 149 M7, 155 E10
El Dorado NSW 114 F10, 116 F1
El Questro WA 28, 209 M5, *304*
El Trune NSW 115 L6
Elabbin WA 202 F3
Elaine Vic 64 C3, 67 L6
Elanda Point Qld 139
Elands NSW 111 L2
Elbow Hill SA 232 F7
Elderslie Qld 149 K3, 154 G10, 155 C2
Elderslie Tas 253 J3
Eldon Tas 253 K3
Eldorado Qld 151 L4
Eldorado Vic 72 G4
Electrona Tas 253 K6
Elgin Down Qld 146 C5
Elgin Vale Qld 145 L5
Elizabeth SA 233 J9
Elizabeth Beach NSW 111 L4
Elizabeth Downs NT 174 C6
Elizabeth Town Tas 255 H7
Elkedra NT 177 K10, 179 K2
Ella Vale NSW 115 J2
Ellalong NSW 111 H6
Ellam Vic 68 E9
Ellangowan NSW 113 N3
Ellavalla WA 204 C3
Ellenborough NSW 111 L2, 113 L10
Ellenbrae WA 209 L5
Ellendale Tas 252 G3
Ellendale WA 208 G8
Ellerside Vic 65 L7
Ellerslie Vic 66 G7
Ellerston NSW 111 H3
Elliminyt Vic 64 A6, 67 J8
Ellinbank Vic 65 L5
Elliot Price CP SA 234 G7
Elliott NT 177 H4
Elliott Tas 254 E5
Elliott Heads Qld 130, 145 M2
Ellis Crossing Vic 66 D1, 68 D10
Elliston SA 232 C7
Elmhurst Vic 67 H4
Elmina Qld 144 B7
Elmore Vic 148 G10, 151 J2
Elmore Vic 67 N1, 69 N10
Elong Elong NSW 110 C3
Elphin WA 202 D2
Elphinstone Qld 146 E5
Elphinstone Vic 67 M3
Elrose Qld 150 D7
Elrose Qld 150 F4
Elsey NT 174 G8
Elsey NP NT 174 G8
Elsie Hills Qld 146 B10, 151 P10
Elsmore NSW 113 H6
Eltham Vic 65 H3, 67 P5, 72 B10
Elton Downs Qld 151 K4
Elverston Qld 144 B6
Elvira Qld 151 K4
Elvo Qld 151 H8
Emaroo NSW 114 G4
Emerald Qld 146 E8
Emerald Vic 65 J4
Emerald Beach NSW 113 N7
Emerald Hill NSW 112 E9
Emerald Springs Roadhouse NT 174 E6
Emily and Jessie Gap NP NT 179 H6
Emita Tas 255 J2
Emmaville NSW 113 J5
Emmdale Roadhouse NSW 114 G2
Emmet Qld 153 M1
Emmet Downs Qld 153 M2
Empire Vale NSW 113 P3
Emu Vic 67 J2
Emu Bay SA 230 B3, *321*
Emu Creek Vic 67 M2
Emu Flat Vic 67 N3
Emu Downs SA 233 K8
Emu Junction SA 231 E5
Emu Lake WA 211 N10
Emu Mountain Qld 150 E4
Emu Park Qld 147 K8
Emu Plains Qld 146 E3
Emu Springs SA 230 B8
Emudilla Qld 153 L4

Encounter Bay SA 230 B5
Endeavour Qld 149 K3, 155 C3
Endeavour River NP Qld 149 L3, 155 C3
Endyalgout Island NT 174 F3, *294*
Eneabba WA 202 B1, 204 D10
Enfield Vic 64 B3, 67 K5
Englefield Vic 66 D4
Engoordina NT 179 J8
Enmore NSW 113 J8
Enngonia NSW 115 K2
Ennisvale NSW 116 A2
Enryb Downs Qld 151 K5
Ensay Qld 151 L4
Ensay Vic 70 F4, 73 M9
Ensay North Vic 70 F4, 73 M9
Epala Qld 147 K9
Eppalock Vic 67 M2
Epping Vic 65 H2, 67 P5, 72 A10
Epping Forest Qld 146 C6
Epping Forest Tas 255 L8
Epping Forest NP Qld 146 C6
Epsilon Qld 152 F8
Epsom Qld 146 F5
Epsom Vic 67 M2
Erambie Qld 144 G6
Eremaran NSW 115 L9
Eribung NSW 115 N9, 117 N1
Erica Vic 65 P4, 70 A6
Erigolia NSW 117 L3
Erikin WA 202 F4
Eringa SA 233 M4, 234 B1
Erldunda NT 178 G9
Erlistoun WA 205 M7
Erne Qld 144 A1, 146 B10, 151 P10, 153 P1
Eromanga Qld 153 K5
Erong Springs WA 204 F3
Errabiddy WA 204 F3
Erriba Tas 254 F6
Errinundra Vic 71 K4
Errinundra NP Vic 71 K4
Erskine Park NSW 109 G1, 110 G8
Erudgere NSW 110 D5
Erudina SA 233 L3
Erudina Woolshed SA 233 L3
Escombe Qld 151 K5
Escott Qld 148 C7
Esk Qld 140, 145 L6
Esk River NSW 267
Eskdale Qld 151 L6
Eskdale Vic 60, 61, 73 J5
Esmeralda Qld 148 G8
Esperance WA 203 M8
Essex Downs Qld 151 J4
Etadunna SA 235 J7
Ethel Creek WA 211 K9
Etheldale Qld 148 G10, 151 J1
Etona Qld 144 B4
Etta Plains Qld 148 E10, 150 F1
Ettrick NSW 113 M2
Etty Bay Qld 149 M6, 155 E9
Euabalong NSW 115 L10, 117 L2
Euabalong West NSW 115 L10, 117 L1
Euchareena NSW 110 C6
Eucla WA 207 G7
Eucla NP WA 207 G7
Eucumbene NSW 109 B7
Eucumbene River NSW 276, 276
Eudamullah WA 204 D2
Eudunda SA 233 K8
Eugenana Tas 254 G5
Eugowra NSW 110 A7
Eulo NSW 116 D2
Eulo Qld 153 N8
Eulolo Qld 150 G4
Eulomogo NSW 110 B4
Euminbah NSW 115 P3
Eumundi Qld 145 M5
Eumungerie NSW 110 B3
Eungai NSW 113 M9
Eungella Qld 146 F4
Eungella NP Qld 146 F3
Eurack Vic 64 B5, 67 K7
Euramo Qld 149 M7
Eurardy WA 204 C6
Eureka Plains NSW 115 K1
Eurelia SA 233 J5
Eurimbula NSW 110 B6
Eurimbula Creek Qld 134
Eurimbula NP Qld 134, 147 L10

Euroa Vic 72 C6
Eurobin Vic 70 B1, 73 H6
Eurobodalla NSW 109 E7
Euroka Qld 145 J3
Euroka Springs Qld 148 F10, 150 G1
Eurong Qld 145 N3
Eurongilly NSW 117 N6
Euston NSW 116 D5
Euston Qld 151 K8
Eva Downs NT 177 J5
Eva Valley NT 174 G7
Evandale Tas 247, 255 K7
Evangy Qld 151 J10, 153 J1
Evans Head NSW 113 P4
Evansford Vic 67 K4
Eveleigh Qld 149 J7
Evelyn Downs SA 234 B5
Evercreech FR Tas 255 N6
Everton Vic 72 G4
Evesham Qld 151 K8
Evora Qld 146 A10, 151 N10
Ewan Qld 149 L9
Ewaninga NT 179 H6
Ewaninga Rock Carvings CR NT 179 H6
Exeter NSW 109 F3
Exeter Tas 255 J6
Exevale Qld 146 F4
Exford Vic 64 F3, 67 M6
Exmoor Qld 146 E3
Exmoor Qld 151 J4
Exmouth WA 210 C7
Exmouth Gulf WA 210 C7
Exmouth Gulf WA 210 B8
Expedition NP Qld 144 F2

Failford NSW 111 L3
Fairfield Qld 144 F1
Fairfield Qld 151 M8
Farfield WA 209 H8
Fairhaven Vic 64 C6, 67 L8
Fairhaven Vic 71 N4
Fairhill Qld 146 F8
Fairholme NSW 117 N2
Fairlight NSW 115 M5
Fairlight Qld 149 J3
Fairview Qld 149 J3, 155 A3
Fairview CP SA 230 D9
Fairy Hill NSW 113 M3
Fairyland Qld 145 H3
Fairyland Qld 145 J5
Falls Creek NSW 109 F4
Falls Creek Vic 70 D2, 73 J7
Falmouth Tas 255 P7
Fanning River Qld 146 B1, 149 M10
Far South Coast NSW **272–5**
Faraway Hill SA 233 L6
Farina SA 235 J9
Farleigh Qld 146 G4
Farrel Flat SA 233 K8
Farrerdale NSW 115 P9
Faulkland NSW 111 K3
Fawcett Vic 72 D8
Feilton Tas 253 H4
Felton East Qld 145 K8
Fenton Patches NT 160–1
Fertonbury Tas 253 H4
Fertons Creek Vic 67 J1, 69 J10
Fermoy Qld 151 J8
Fern Bay NSW 111 K6
Fern Hill Vic 64 E1, 67 M4
Fern Tree Tas 253 K5
Fernbank Vic 70 D6
Fernbrook NSW 113 L7
Ferndale Qld 144 B7
Ferrihurst NSW 116 K9
Ferrlee Qld 144 C8
Ferrlees Qld 146 E9
Fernshaw Vic 65 K2, 72 C10
Fernvale Qld 145 M7
Fernvale Vic 73 J4
Fiddlers Green Vic 65 P2, 70 A5, 72 F10
Fifield NSW 115 N10, 117 N1
Finch Hatton Qld 146 F4
Fingal Tas 255 N7
Fingal Head NSW 113 P1
Finke NT 179 J9
Finke Gorge NP NT 178 F7
Finke River NT 178 G7

Finley NSW 117 J7
Finniss SA 230 A6
Finniss River NT 167, 174 C5
Finniss Springs SA 234 G9
Fischerton Qld 149 J6, 155 A9
Fish Creek Vic 65 M8
Fish Point Vic 68 K6
Fish River Reserve NT 174 D8
Fisher SA 231 D3
Fisherman Bay SA 233 H7
Fiskville Vic 64 C2, 67 L5
Fitzgerald Tas 247, 255 G4
Fitzgerald WA 203 H7
Fitzgerald Bay SA 233 H6, *319*
Fitzgerald River NP WA 203 H8
Fitzroy NT 174 D9, 176 D1
Fitzroy Crossing WA 209 H9, *304*
Fitzroy Island NP Qld 149 M5, 155 E7, *288*
Fitzroy River Vic 66 C7
Fitzroy River WA 208 F8, 304, 305, 307
Five Day Creek NSW 113 L8
Five Ways NSW 115 M8
Flaggy Rock Qld 146 G5
Flamingo NSW 115 M10, 117 M1
Flamingo Beach Vic 70 D8
Fletcher Vale Qld 146 A1, 149 L10, 151 P1
Fleurieu Peninsula SA 212, **220–1**, *221*, 230 A5
Flinders Vic 65 H7, 67 P8
Flinders Bay WA 97, 202 B9
Flinders Chase NP SA 230 B2, *320*
Flinders Group NP Qld 149 J1, 154 F8
Flinders Island Tas 30, 255 J2, 257, **324–5**, *324*
Flinders Ranges NP SA 233 K2
Flinders River Qld 148 E8, 151 K3, 284
Flintstone Tas 255 J9
Floods Creek NSW 114 B6
Flora Valley WA 209 N9
Floraville Qld 148 C7
Florence Vale Qld 146 D8
Florida NSW 115 L7
Florieton SA 233 L3
Florina NT 174 E7
Florina SA 233 M4
Flowerdale Tas 254 E4
Flowerdale Vic 65 J1, 72 B9
Fluorspar Qld 149 K6, 155 A8
Flyers Creek NSW 110 C8
Flying Fish Point Qld 149 M6, 155 E8
Flynn Vic 70 B7
Flynns Creek Vic 70 A8
Fog Bay NT 166, 174 C5
Fog Creek Qld 149 H9
Fogg Dam CR NT 174 D4
Foleyvale Qld 147 H3
Footscray Vic 64 G3, 67 N6
Forbes NSW 117 P2
Forbes River NSW 111 L1, 113 L10
Forbesdale NSW 111 K3
Forcett Tas 253 L4
Fords Bridge NSW 115 J3
Fords Lagoon SA 233 L7
Fordsdale Tas 253 H4
Forest Tas 254 C3
Forest Den NP Qld 151 N6
Forest Hill NSW 117 N6
Forest Hills Qld 144 J2
Forest Home Qld 146 B2, 149 M10
Forest Home Qld 149 H7
Forest Reefs NSW 110 C7
Forest Vale Qld 144 D4
Forestier Peninsula Tas 240
Forge Creek Vic 70 E5
Forktown Vic 70 E4, 73 L9
Forrest Vic 64 B7, 67 K8
Forrest WA 207 F6
Forrest Beach Qld 143 M8, 288
Forrester Qld 146 C7
Forsayth Qld 149 H8
Forsyth Island Qld 143 B5, 285
Forsyth Islands Qld 148 B5, 285
Forster NSW 111 L4
Forster Keys NSW 111 L4
Fort Constantine Qld 150 E3
Fort Grey NSW 114 A4
Fort William Outstation Qld 150 D6
Fortescue Bay Tas 241, 253 M6
Fortescue River WA 210 E6, 308–9

Fortescue Roadhouse WA 210 E6
Forth Tas 254 G5
Fortland Qld 144 B6
Fortuna Qld 146 A7, 151 N7
Fortville House WA 114 A1
Forty Mile Scrub NP Qld 149 K7
Fossil Downs WA 209 J9
Foster Vic 65 N7
Fosterton NSW 111 J4
Fosterville Vic 67 M2
Foul Bay SA 230 A3, 232 G10
Four Brothers SA 233 L4
Four Corners NSW 117 J5
Four Mile Clump NSW 112 D3
Four Mile Creek NSW 110 B7
Four Mile Creek Tas 255 P7
Four Pegs Qld 145 H7
Four Ways NSW 110 A7
Fowlers Bay SA 231 F10, 316
Fowlers Gap NSW 114 B6
Fox Creek Qld 148 G2, 154 D9
Foxdale Qld 146 F2
Foxhow Vic 64 A4, 67 J7
Framlingham Vic 66 G7
Frances SA 230 D10
Francois Peron NP WA 204 B4
Frank Hann NP WA 203 J6
Frankfield Qld 146 C6
Frankford Tas 255 H6
Frankland WA 202 E9
Franklin Qld 150 G7
Franklin Tas 253 J6
Franklin Harbor CP SA 232 F7
Franklin River Tas 252 D3, 254 E10
Franklin-Gordon Wild Rivers NP Tas 252 D2, 328, **330**, 331
Franklyn SA 233 K6
Frankston Vic 65 H5, 67 P7
Frankton SA 233 K8
Fraser Island Qld *119*, 129, **130–1**, *130*, *131*, **132–3**, 145 N2
Fraser NP Vic 72 D8
Fraser Range WA 203 N4
Frazier Downs WA 208 C10, 211 M3
Frederick Henry Bay Tas 241, 253 L5
Frederickton NSW 113 M9
Freeburgh Vic 70 C1, 73 H6
Freeling SA 233 K9
Fregon SA 231 E2
Fremantle WA 182, 183, 184, 186, 190, 192, 193, 202 C4
French Island SP Vic 65 J6
French Park NSW 117 M6
Frenchman Bay WA 202 F10
Frenchmans Cap Tas 252 D1, 254 E10, 330
Freshwater Bay WA 184, 185
Freshwater Creek Vic 64 D5, 67 M7
Frewhurst Qld 149 J7
Freycinet NP Tas 242, 253 P1, 255 P10
Freycinet Peninsula Tas *237*, **242–3**, *242*, *243*, 253 P1
Friendly Beaches Tas 243, 255 P9
Frogmore NSW 109 C2, 110 B10
Frome Downs SA 233 L2
Fry Qld 147 K10
Fryerstown Vic 67 L3
Fulham Vic 70 C7
Fumina South Vic 65 M4
Furneaux Group Tas 255 K2, 324, 325
Furnell Landing Vic 49, 71 L5
Furner SA 230 F9
Fyansford Vic 64 D5, 67 M7
Fyshwick ACT 109 C5

Gabaninta WA 205 H5
Gabbin WA 202 E2
Gabo Island Vic 71 P5, 259
Gabyon WA 204 F7
Gaffneys Creek Vic 65 N1, 72 E9
Gairdner WA 202 G8
Galah Vic 68 E5
Galah Creek NT 175 K6
Galaquil Vic 68 F8
Galaquil East Vic 68 F8
Galbraith Qld 148 F5
Galena WA 204 C7
Galga SA 233 M9
Galiwinku NT 175 L3
Gallipoli NT 177 P7
Galong NSW 109 B3
Galore NSW 117 M6

INDEX OF PLACE NAMES

Galway Downs Qld 153 J2
Gama Vic 68 F7
Gambier Islands CP SA 230 A1
Gamboola Qld 149 H5
Gammon Ranges NP SA 235 K10
Ganmain NSW 117 M5
Gannawarra Vic 69 L7
Gapuwiyak NT 175 L4
Garah NSW 112 D4
Garbutt Qld 149 N9
Garden Island SA 215, 218, 219
Garden Island WA 186, 193, 202 B5
Garden Island Creek Tas 253 J7
Garden Vale NSW 114 F4
Gardners Bay Tas 253 J7
Garema NSW 117 P3
Garfield Qld 146 B8, 151 P8
Garfield Vic 65 K5
Gargett Vic 146 F4
Garlands NSW 115 K3
Garlandtown NSW 109 E6
Garnpung Lake NSW 116 E2
Garrawilla NSW 110 D1, 112 D10
Garthowen NSW 112 G9
Gartmore Qld 144 A2
Garvoc Vic 66 G8
Gascoyne Junction WA 204 D3
Gascoyne River WA 204 B2
Gatton Qld 145 L7
Gatum Vic 66 D4
Gavial Qld 147 J8
Gawler SA 233 K9
Gawler Tas 254 F5
Gawler Ranges SA 232 D4
Gawler Ranges CR SA 232 C5
Gayndah Qld 145 K3
Gaza Qld 151 L10
Geehi NSW 109 A7, 117 P9
Geelong Vic 44–5, 64 E5, 67 M7
Geera Qld 146 A9, 151 N9
Geeveston Tas 253 H6
Geikie Gorge NP WA 209 J9
Gelantipy Vic 71 H3, 73 N8
Gellibrand Vic 64 A7, 67 J8
Gelorup WA 202 B7
Gem Creek Qld 146 A4, 151 P4
Gembrook Vic 65 K4
Gemoka Qld 151 J3
Gemtree Roadhouse NT 179 J5
Genoa Vic 71 M4
Genoa NP NSW 109 D9
Genoa River Vic 49, 71 M3, 258, 259
Geographe Bay WA 194–5, 195, 196–7, 202 B7
George Town Tas 255 J5
Georges Bay Tas 244, 245, 255 P6
Georges Creek NSW 113 K8
Georges Plains NSW 110 D8
Georges River NSW 82, 82, 84–5
Georges River Tas 245, 255 N6
Georges River NP NSW 85
Georgetown Qld 149 H7
Georgetown SA 233 J7
Georgina NT 177 P10, 179 P1
Georgina River Qld 148 A10, 285
Geraldton WA 198–9, 204 C8
Gerang Gerung Vic 66 D1, 68 D10
Geranium SA 230 A8
Gerara NSW 115 L2
Gerard SA 233 N9
Gerata NSW 148 C10, 150 D2
Germantown Vic 70 C1, 73 H6
Gerogery NSW 117 M8
Gerringong NSW 75, 92, 93, 109 G3
Gerroa NSW 92, 93, 109 G3
Geurie NSW 110 B4
Ghin Ghin Vic 72 B8
Gibb River WA 209 K5
Gibihi Qld 145 H1
Gibraltar Range NP NSW 113 L5
Gibson WA 203 M7
Gibson Desert WA 206 C7
Gibson Desert NR WA 206 C8
Gidgealpa SA 235 M4
Gidgee NSW 115 J6
Gidgee WA 205 J6
Gidgegannup WA 202 C4
Gidginbung NSW 117 N4
Giffard Vic 70 C8
Giffard West Vic 70 C8
Gifford Creek WA 204 E1, 210 E10
Gilbert River Qld 148 G7

Giles Meteorological Station WA 206 F8
Gilgai NSW 113 H6
Gilgandra NSW 110 B2
Gilgooma NSW 112 A8
Gilgunnia NSW 115 K9
Giligulgul Qld 145 H5
Gilliat Qld 150 G3
Gillieston Vic 72 B4
Gillingall Vic 70 G4, 73 N9
Gillingarra WA 202 C2
Gilmore NSW 109 A5, 117 P6
Gilroyd WA 204 D4
Gin Gin NSW 115 P8
Gin Gin Qld 145 L2
Gina SA 234 B9
Ginburra Qld 150 E3
Gindie Qld 146 E9
Gingerella Qld 149 K7, 155 B10
Gingin WA 202 C3
Ginninderra ACT 109 C4
Gippsland Lakes Vic 50–1, 52–3, 63, 260
Gippsland Lakes Coastal Park Vic 50, 70 E7
Gipsy Point Vic 49, 71 N4
Giralia WA 210 C8
Girgarre Vic 67 P1, 69 P10, 72 A5
Girgarre East Vic 67 P1, 69 P10, 72 A5
Girilambone NSW 115 M6
Girragulang NSW 110 D3
Girral NSW 117 M3
Girrawheen NP Qld 145 L9
Girrawheen NSW 114 F10, 116 F1
Giru Qld 146 D1, 149 N9
Girvan NSW 111 K5
Gisborne Vic 64 F1, 67 N5
Gladfield Vic 69 L8
Gladstone NSW 113 M9
Gladstone Qld 147 K9, 289
Gladstone SA 233 J6
Gladstone Tas 255 N4
Gladstone WA 204 C4
Glandore Qld 145 H2
Glanworth Qld 153 P3
Glastonbury Qld 145 M4
Glaziers Bay Tas 253 J6
Gleeson Qld 148 D10, 150 D1
Glen WA 204 G6
Glen Afton Qld 151 L10, 153 L1
Glen Albyn NSW 114 F9
Glen Alice NSW 110 F6
Glen Alvie Vic 65 K7
Glen Aplin Qld 145 L9
Glen Avon Qld 146 C10
Glen Creek Vic 73 H5
Glen Davis NSW 110 F6
Glen Elgin NSW 113 K5
Glen Eva Qld 146 D4
Glen Florrie WA 210 E9
Glen Forbes Vic 65 K6
Glen Gallic NSW 110 G5
Glen Garland Qld 149 H2, 154 E10
Glen Gowrie NSW 114 E6
Glen Harding Qld 149 L7
Glen Helen NT 178 F5
Glen Helen Tourist Camp NT 178 F6
Glen Hill WA 209 N6
Glen Hope NSW 114 E5
Glen Hope NSW 115 L6
Glen Huon Tas 253 H6
Glen Innes NSW 113 J6, 267
Glen Isla Qld 150 E2
Glen Morrison NSW 111 J1, 113 J10
Glen Ora NSW 114 F9
Glen Ruth Qld 149 L7
Glen Valley Vic 70 E2, 73 K7
Glen Waverley Vic 65 H3, 67 P6
Glen Wills Vic 70 E1, 73 K6
Glenaire Vic 64 A8, 67 J9
Glenaladale Vic 70 D5, 73 K10
Glenalbyn Vic 67 K1, 69 K10
Glenarbon Qld 145 J9
Glenariff NSW 115 L5
Glenarlie Qld 153 J1
Glenaroua Vic 67 P3, 72 A8
Glenavon Qld 146 D5
Glenayle WA 205 M3
Glenbervie Qld 150 G4
Glenbrae Vic 64 A1, 67 J4
Glenburgh WA 204 E3
Glenburn Vic 65 J1, 72 C9

Glenburnie SA 230 F10
Glencairn Vic 65 P2, 70 A4, 72 G9
Glencoe NSW 113 J6
Glencoe Qld 145 J2
Glencoe SA 230 F9
Glendambo SA 232 D2
Glenden Qld 146 E4
Glendevie Tas 253 H7
Glendilla Qld 153 N7
Glendinning Vic 66 D4
Glendon Brook NSW 111 H5
Glenelg SA 214, 215, 216, 217, 233 J10
Glenelg River Vic 66 B7
Glenfern Tas 253 H5
Glengalla Qld 148 G10, 151 H2
Glengarry Qld 144 E4
Glengarry Qld 144 G7
Glengarry Tas 255 J6
Glengarry Vic 65 P5, 70 A7
Glengeera NSW 110 B4
Glengower Vic 67 K4
Glengyle Qld 152 D2
Glenhaughton Qld 144 F3
Glenhope NSW 114 G2
Glenhope NSW 116 G5
Glenhope Vic 67 N3
Glenidal Qld 144 F2
Glenisla Vic 66 E4
Glenlee Vic 68 D9
Glenlofty Vic 67 H3
Glenloth Vic 69 J9
Glenlusk Tas 253 J5
Glenlyon Qld 145 K9
Glenlyon Qld 151 J4
Glenlyon Vic 67 L4
Glenmaggie Vic 70 A6
Glenmaggie Reservoir Vic 70 B6
Glenmore Qld 144 F7
Glenmore Downs Qld 146 D7
Glenmorgan Qld 144 G6
Glennies Creek Dam NSW 100
Glenora NSW 114 C7
Glenora NSW 115 H4
Glenora SA 233 L7
Glenora Tas 253 H4
Glenoran WA 202 C8
Glenorchy WA 233 L3
Glenorchy Tas 253 K5
Glenorchy Vic 66 G3
Glenore Qld 148 E7
Glenore Tas 255 J7
Glenormiston Qld 150 B7
Glenormiston Vic 66 G7
Glenorn WA 205 M9
Glenpatrick Vic 67 J3
Glenprairie Qld 147 H7
Glenreagh NSW 113 M6
Glenrock Qld 149 K2, 154 G10, 155 C2
Glenrowan Qld 145 H5
Glenrowan Vic 72 F5
Glenroy Qld 151 K10, 153 K1
Glenroy WA 209 J7
Glenthompson Vic 66 F5
Glenusk Qld 146 A10, 151 N10, 153 N1
Glenvalley Qld 153 J2
Glenwood NSW 115 K8
Glenwood Qld 145 M4
Glomar Beach Vic 70 D8
Glossop SA 233 N8
Gloucester NSW 111 K3
Gloucester Island NP Qld 146 F2, 288
Gnalta Qld 150 F6
Gnaraloo WA 204 B1, 210 B10
Gnarwarre Vic 64 D5, 67 L7
Gnotuk Vic 67 H7
Gnowangerup WA 202 F8
Gobarralong NSW 109 A4, 117 P6
Gobur Vic 72 C7
Gocup NSW 109 A4, 117 P6
Godfreys Creek NSW 109 B2, 110 B9
Gogango Qld 147 H9
Gogeldrie NSW 117 L5
Gogo WA 209 H9
Gol Gol NSW 116 C4
Gol Gol NSW 116 E2
Golconda Tas 255 K5
Gold Coast Qld 120–1, 121, 122, 136, 136–7, 145 N8
Golden Beach Vic 70 D8

Golden Grove WA 204 F8
Golden Valley Tas 255 H7
Golden West Qld 142–3
Goldsborough Vic 67 K2
Goldsworthy WA 211 J5
Gollan NSW 110 C4
Golspie NSW 109 D2, 110 D10
Goneaway NP Qld 151 H9
Gongolgon NSW 115 M4
Goobang NSW 110 A6, 115 P10, 117 P1
Goobarragandra NSW 109 B5
Goode River Qld 145 K4
Goodooga NSW 115 N2
Goodparla NT 174 F5
Goodradigbee River NSW 106–7, 106
Goodwill Point Tas 254 A2
Goodwood NSW 114 E5
Goodwood Qld 150 D7
Googong Reservoir NSW 108, 109 C5
Goold Island NP Qld 149 M7
Goolgowi NSW 117 K3
Goolma NSW 110 C4
Goolmangar NSW 113 N3
Gooloogong NSW 109 B1, 110 A8
Goolwa SA 222, 223, 224, 230 A6
Goomalibee Vic 72 D5
Goomalling WA 202 D3
Goomally Qld 144 F1, 146 G10
Goomarin WA 202 G3
Goombie Qld 153 L4
Goomboorian Qld 145 M4
Goombungee Qld 145 L6
Goomburra Qld 145 L8
Goomeri Qld 145 L4
Goon Goon Qld 151 K10, 153 K1
Goon Nure Vic 70 E6
Goonalah Qld 145 H5
Goonalga NSW 114 F7
Goondah NSW 109 B3
Goondi Qld 149 M6, 155 E9
Goondiwindi Qld 142, 145 H9
Goondoola Qld 144 F8
Goondooloo NT 174 G8
Gooneengerry NSW 113 P2
Goonery NSW 115 H4
Goongarrie WA 203 K1, 205 L10
Goongarrie NP WA 203 L1, 205 M10
Goongee Vic 68 B5
Goongerah Vic 71 J4
Goonoo Goonoo NSW 110 G1, 112 G10
Goora Qld 153 N7
Gooram Vic 72 C7
Gooramadda Vic 72 G3
Goorambat Vic 72 D5
Gooray Qld 145 H9
Goorianawa NSW 112 B9
Goorimpa NSW 114 G4
Goornong Vic 67 M1
Gooroc Vic 67 H1, 69 H10
Goose Creek NT 292, 293
Goovigen Qld 147 J10
Gooyer Qld 153 L3
Gorae Vic 66 C7
Gorae West Vic 66 C7
Goranba Qld 145 H6
Gordon SA 233 J4
Gordon Tas 253 K7
Gordon Vic 64 C2, 67 L5
Gordon Brook NSW 113 M5
Gordon Downs WA 209 N10
Gordon River Tas 252 C3, 327, 327
Gordon River NSW 110 E4
Gordonvale Qld 149 L6, 155 E8
Gorge Rock WA 202 F5
Gormandale Vic 70 B8
Gormanston Tas 254 D10
Goroke Vic 66 C2
Gorrie NT 174 F9, 176 F1
Goschen Vic 69 J7
Gosford NSW 86–7, 111 H7
Gosnells WA 202 C4
Gostwyck NSW 113 J8
Gough Bay Vic 72 E8
Goulburn NSW 109 D3
Goulburn River Vic 58, 72 B8
Goulburn River NP NSW 110 E4
Goulburn Weir Vic 67 P2, 72 A6
Goulds Country Tas 255 N5
Govana Qld 145 H6

Gove Peninsula NT 175 M4
Gowan NSW 110 C7
Gowan Hills Qld 151 M10, 153 M1
Gowanford Vic 69 H6
Gowangardie Vic 72 D5
Gowar East Vic 67 J1, 69 J10
Gowrie Park Tas 254 G7
Goyura Vic 68 F8
Grabben Gullen NSW 109 D3
Gracemere Qld 147 J8
Gracetown WA 202 A8
Gradgery NSW 115 P6
Gradule Qld 144 F9
Grafton NSW 113 M5, 266
Graman NSW 112 G5
Grampians NP Vic 66 F4
Granada Qld 148 D10, 150 E2
Granite Downs SA 231 G2
Granite Peak WA 205 L3
Granite Point Coastal Reserve Tas 255 L4
Grant Qld 146 A8, 151 P8
Grantham Qld 145 L7
Grantham Downs Qld 144 F6
Grantleigh Qld 147 H9
Granton Tas 253 J4
Grantville Vic 65 K6
Granville Harbour Tas 254 B8
Granya Vic 73 K3
Grasmere NSW 114 D7
Grass Patch WA 203 L7
Grass Valley WA 202 D4
Grassdale Vic 66 C6
Grassmere Qld 144 C7
Grasstree Qld 146 G4
Grasstree Hill Tas 253 K4
Grassville SA 233 L7
Grassy Tas 254 F3
Grassy Head NSW 113 N9
Grassy Point Vic 44
Gravelly Beach Tas 255 J6
Gravesend NSW 112 F5
Graytown Vic 67 P2, 72 A6
Gre Gre Vic 67 H2
Gre Gre North Vic 67 H1
Great Australian Bight SA 231 B10, 316–17
Great Barrier Reef Qld 118, 147 K3, 256, 286–9, 287, 290
Great Barrier Reef Marine Park (Cairns Section) Qld 149 M3, 155 E4
Great Barrier Reef Marine Park (Central Section) Qld 146 F1, 149 N7
Great Barrier Reef Marine Park (Far North Section) Qld 154 G5
Great Barrier Reef Marine Park (Mackay–Capricorn Section) Qld 145 M1, 147 M6
Great Basalt Wall NP Qld 146 A2, 149 L10, 151 N2
Great Dividing Range NSW 109 D6, 110 E5, 113 L3
Great Dividing Range Qld 146 A2
Great Keppel Island Qld 147 K8, 289
Great Lake Tas 246, 248, 255 H9, 328, 328, 329
Great Oyster Bay Tas 242, 253 N1
Great Sandy Desert WA 206 B2
Great Sandy Island NR WA 210 D6
Great Sandy NP Qld 119, 128, 133, 138, 139, 145 N2, 145 N4
Great Victoria Desert SA 231 B4
Great Victoria Desert WA 207 C4
Great Victoria Desert NR WA 207 F4
Great Western Vic 66 G3
Great Western Tiers Tas 255 H8
Gredgwin Vic 69 K8
Green Cape NSW 109 E10, 274, 275
Green Head WA 202 A1, 204 D10
Green Hill Creek Vic 67 J3
Green Island NP Qld 149 M5, 155 E7
Green Lake SA 233 M1
Green Patch SA 232 D9
Green Point SA 232 C9
Greenbank NT 175 N10, 177 N2
Greenbushes WA 202 C8
Greendale Vic 64 D2, 67 M5
Greenethorpe NSW 109 B1, 110 A9
Greenhills WA 202 D4
Greenland NSW 111 H4
Greenly Island CP SA 232 C9
Greenmount Qld 145 L7

INDEX OF PLACE NAMES 401

Greenmount Vic 70 B9
Greenock SA 233 K9
Greenough WA 198, *199*, 204 C8
Greenough River WA 198, 204 C8
Greenough-on-Sea WA 204 C8
Greenridge NSW 113 N3
Greens Beach Tas 255 H5
Greens Creek Vic 66 G3
Greenvale NSW 116 C2
Greenvale NSW 117 L6
Greenvale Qld 149 K9
Greenvale Qld 149 K9
Greenvale Vic 64 G2, 67 N5
Greenwald Vic 66 C6
Greenways SA 230 E8
Greenwell Point NSW 92, 93
Greenwood Qld 150 F3
Greenwoods Qld 151 L10
Gregadoo NSW 117 N6
Gregory WA 204 C7
Gregory Downs Qld 148 C8
Gregory NP NT 174 C10, 174 D10, 176 C2, 176 D1, *298*, **298**
Gregory Range Qld 148 G8
Gregory Range WA 211 L6
Gregory River Qld 148 A9, 285
Grenfell NSW 109 A1, 117 P3
Grenfield Qld 153 M4
Grenville Vic 64 C3, 67 K6
Gresford NSW 111 J4
Greta NSW 111 H5
Greta Vic 72 F5
Greta South Vic 72 F6
Greta West Vic 72 F5
Gretna Tas 253 H4
Grevillia NSW 113 M2
Grey WA 202 B2
Grey Peaks NP Qld 149 L6, 155 E8
Grey Range Qld 152 G10
Greycroft Qld 151 N10
Griffith NSW 117 K4
Griffiths NR WA 203 L7
Grimwade WA 202 C7
Gringegalgona Vic 66 D4
Gritjurk Vic 66 D5
Grogan NSW 117 P4
Groganville Qld 149 J5, 155 A6
Grong Grong NSW 117 M5
Groote Eylandt NT 175 M7
Grose Islands NT 161, 174 C4
Grosvenor Downs Qld 146 E6
Grove Tas 253 J5
Grove Creek Qld 154 D5
Grovedale Vic 64 E5, 67 M7
Gruyere Vic 65 J3, 72 C10
Gubbata NSW 117 L3
Gudgenby River ACT **106**
Guilderton WA 202 B3
Guildford Tas 254 E6
Guildford Vic 67 L3
Guildford WA 190, 202 C4
Guim Vic 64 G1
Gular NSW 110 A1, 112 A10
Gulargambone NSW 110 A1, 112 A10
Gulera Qld 145 J6
Gulf Creek NSW 112 G7
Gulf of Carpentaria NT 28, 175 M8, 300, 301
Gulf of Carpentaria Qld 28, 148 C3, 278, 282, **284–5**, *284*
Gulf St Vincent SA 212, 214, 215, **216–17**, *216*, *217*, 218, 220, 226, 233 H10
Gulgong NSW 110 D4
Gulley Point Tas 252 A3
Gulnare SA 233 J7
Guluguba Qld 145 H4
Gum Creek NSW 117 J5
Gum Creek Qld 148 F7
Gum Flat NSW 113 H6
Gum Lagoon CP SA 230 C8
Gum Lake NSW 114 E9, 116 E1
Gum Vale NSW 114 B2
Gumahah Qld 153 N9
Gumbalie NSW 115 J3
Gumbardo Qld 153 M4
Gumble NSW 110 B6
Gumeracha SA 233 K10
Gumlu Qld 146 E1, 149 P10
Gunalda Qld 145 M4
Gunbar NSW 117 J3
Gunbar NSW 117 J4

Gunbarwood Qld 145 H6
Gunbower Vic 69 M8
Gundagai NSW 109 A4, 117 P6
Gundaring WA 202 E7
Gundaroo NSW 109 C4
Gundary Qld 153 M4
Gundowring Vic 73 J5
Gundy NSW 111 H3
Gunebang NSW 115 L10, 117 L1
Gungal NSW 110 F4
Gungarlin River NSW 276
Gunn Point NT 160, 174 D4
Gunnawarra Qld 148 B6
Gunnawarra Qld 149 L7, 155 C10
Gunnedah NSW 112 F9
Gunnewin Qld 144 E4
Gunning NSW 109 C3
Gunningbland NSW 115 P10, 117 P2
Gunns Plains Tas 254 F6
Gunpowder Qld 148 C10, 150 C1
Guntawang NSW 110 D4
Gununa Qld 148 B5, 282
Gunyidi WA 202 C1, 204 E10
Gurig NP NT 174 E2
Gurley NSW 112 E5
Gurner NT 178 D4
Gurrai SA 230 A9, 233 N10
Gutha WA 204 E8
Guthalungra Qld 146 E1, 149 P10
Guthega NSW 109 A7
Guy Fawkes River NP NSW 113 L6
Guyra NSW 113 J7, 267
Guys Forest Vic 73 L3
Gwabegar NSW 112 B8
Gwambagwine Qld 144 G3
Gwambygine WA 202 D4
Gwandalan NSW 111 J6
Gwydir River NSW 112 C5
Gymbowen Vic 66 C2
Gympie Qld 145 M4
Gypsum Vic 68 F6

Habana Qld 146 G4
Haddon Vic 64 B2, 67 K5
Haddon Rig NSW 115 P7
Haden Qld 145 L6
Hadleigh NSW 112 F5
Hadspen Tas 247, 255 K7
Hagley Tas 255 J7
Hahndorf SA 233 K10
Haig WA 207 D6
Haines Junction Vic 64 B7, 67 K9
Halbury SA 233 J8
Halfway Creek NSW 113 N6
Halidon SA 233 M10
Halifax Qld 149 M8
Hall ACT 109 C4
Hallam Vic 65 H4
Hallett SA 233 K7
Hallidays Point NSW 111 L3
Halls Creek WA 209 L9, 304
Halls Gap Vic 66 F3
Hallsville NSW 112 G9
Halton NSW 111 J4
Hambidge CP SA 232 D7
Hamel WA 202 C6
Hamelin WA 204 C5
Hamelin Bay WA 202 A8
Hamelin Pool Marine NR WA 204 B4
Hamersley WA 210 G8
Hamersley Range WA 210 F7
Hamilton NSW 114 F7
Hamilton SA 233 K8
Hamilton SA 234 C2
Hamilton Tas 253 H3
Hamilton Vic 66 D6
Hamilton Downs NT 178 G6
Hamilton Downs Youth Camp NT 178 G6
Hamilton Hotel Qld 150 E7
Hamilton Island Qld 146 G2, 289
Hamilton Park NSW 115 J4
Hamley Bridge SA 233 J9
Hammond SA 233 J5
Hammond Downs Qld 153 J3
Hammond Island SA 154 C2, 279
Hampden Downs Qld 150 G5
Hampshire Tas 254 E5
Hampton NSW 109 E1, 110 E8
Hampton Park Vic 65 J4
Hampton Tableland WA 207 F7
Hanging Rock NSW 111 H2

Hann River Qld 149 J2, 278–9
Hann River Roadhouse Qld 149 J3, 154 E10
Hannaford Qld 145 H7
Hannahs Bridge NSW 110 D3
Hannan NSW 117 L3
Hannaville Qld 146 F4
Hansborough SA 233 K8
Hanson SA 233 K7
Hanwood NSW 117 K4
Happy Valley Qld 145 N3
Happy Valley Vic 68 G4
Happy Valley Vic 73 H5
Haran Qld 145 H7
Harcourt Vic 67 L3
Harden NSW 109 A3
Harding Falls FR Tas 255 N8
Hardings Ranges Qld 150 G10
Hardington Qld 151 M6
Hardwicke Bay SA 232 G10
Hardy Inlet WA 197, 202 B8
Harefield NSW 117 N6
Herford Tas 255 H5
Hargraves NSW 110 D5
Harrami Qld 145 J2
Harriedale NSW 114 B10, 116 B1
Harrietville Vic 70 C2, 73 J7
Harrington NSW 111 M3
Harris NR WA 202 G6
Harrismith WA 202 F6
Harrisville Qld 145 M7
Harrogate SA 233 K10
Harrow Vic 66 C3
Harrys Creek Vic 72 D6
Harrys Hut Qld 138–9
Harston Vic 67 P1, 69 P10, 72 B5
Hart SA 233 J7
Hartley NSW 110 E8
Hartley SA 230 A6, 233 K10
Harts Range Police Station NT 179 K5
Hartz Mountains NP Tas 253 H7
Harvest Home Qld 146 C3
Harvey WA 202 C6
Harvey Dam WA 201
Harvey Weir WA 200, 201
Harwood NSW 113 N5, 266
Haslam SA 232 B5
Hassell NP WA 202 F9
Hastings NSW 115 L4
Hastings Vic 42, 43, 65 H6, 67 P8
Hat Head NSW 113 N9
Hat Head NP NSW 111 N1, 113 N9
Hatches Creek NT 177 K10, 179 K1
Hatfield NSW 116 F3
Hatherleigh SA 230 F9
Hattah Vic 68 E4
Hattah-Kulkyne NP Vic 68 E3
Hatton Vale Qld 145 M7
Havelock Vic 67 K3
Haven Vic 66 E2
Havilah Qld 146 E3
Hawker SA 233 J3
Hawkesbury River NSW **78–9**, **80–1**, *80*, *81*
Hawkesdale Vic 66 E7
Hawkesdale West Vic 66 E7
Hawks Nest NSW 111 K5
Hawkwood Qld 145 J4
Hawley Beach Tas 255 H5
Hay NSW 117 H5
Hay Point Qld 146 G4
Haydens Bog Vic 71 K3
Haydon Qld 148 F7
Hayes Tas 253 J4
Hayes Creek NT 174 D6
Hayman Island Qld 146 F2, 289
Haysdale Vic 69 H4
Hazel Park Vic 65 P7
Hazelbush Qld 146 B8
Hazelmere Qld 146 A6, 151 P6
Hazelmere Qld 149 K3, 155 C3
Hazelwood Qld 151 J3
Hazelwood Qld 151 J3
Head of Bight SA 231 D9, 316
Headingly Qld 150 A4
Healesville Vic 65 K2, 72 C10
Healesville West Vic 65 K2, 72 C10
Heathcote NSW 109 G2, 111 H9
Heathcote Vic 67 N3

Heathcote Junction Vic 65 H1, 67 F4, 72 A9
Heather Qld 144 C8
Heather Downs Qld 144 D5
Heathfield NSW 115 P3
Heathfield West Qld 146 C2, 149 M10
Heathlands Qld 154 C4
Heathmere Vic 66 C7
Heatvale Vic 66 E3
Hebel Qld 144 D10
Hedley Vic 65 P7, 70 A9
Heggaton CR SA 232 F7
Heidelberg Qld 146 D3
Heidelberg Vic 65 H3, 67 P6, 72 A10
Heka Tas 254 F6
Helen Springs NT 177 H5
Helen Vale Qld 146 B9, 151 F9
Helensburgh NSW 109 G2, 110 G10
Helenvale Qld 149 L3, 155 C4
Helidon Qld 145 L7
Hell Hole Gorge NP Qld 153 L3
Hells Gate Roadhouse Qld 148 A6
Hellyer Tas 254 D4
Hellyer Gorge SR Tas 254 D5
Henbury NT 178 G7
Henbury Meteorite CR NT 178 G7
Henlow Vic 73 K4
Henrietta Tas 254 E5
Henty NSW 117 M7
Henty Vic 66 C5
Henty River Tas 254 C9, 327
Hepburn Springs Vic 67 L4
Herbert Downs Qld 150 C8
Herbert Vale Qld 148 A9
Herberton Qld 149 L6, 155 C9
Hereward Qld 151 L7
Hermansburg NT 178 F6
Hermidale NSW 115 L7
Hernani NSW 113 L7
Herons Creek NSW 111 M2
Herrick Tas 255 M5
Hervey Bay Qld 130, 132, *133*, 145 M2
Hervey Bay Qld 130, 131, 132, *133*, 145 M3
Hervey Bay Marine Park Qld 145 M1
Hesket Vic 64 F1, 67 N4
Hesso SA 232 G4
Hester WA 202 C8
Hewart Downs NSW 114 A2
Hexham Qld 151 J6
Hexham Vic 66 G6
Heybridge Tas 254 F5
Heyfield Vic 70 B6
Heywood Vic 66 C7
Heywood Islands WA 208 G4
Hi-Way Inn NT 176 G2
Hiamdale Vic 70 B6
Hiawatha Vic 65 P7, 70 A9
Hibiscus Coast Qld 147 G4
Hidden Valley NT 176 G2
Hidden Valley Qld 146 D3
Hidden Valley Qld 149 M9
Hidden Valley NP WA 209 N4
Hideaway Bay Tas 253 J7
Higginsville WA 203 L4
High Camp Vic 67 N4, 72 A8
High Range NSW 109 F2, 110 F10
Highbury Qld 149 H5
Highbury WA 202 E6
Highclere Tas 254 E5
Highcroft Tas 255 H5
Highland Waters Tas 331
Highlands Qld 144 A1
Highlands Qld 153 M2
Highlands Vic 72 B8
Highton Vic 64 D5, 67 M7
Hill End NSW 110 D6
Hill End Vic 65 N4
Hill Grange SA 233 L6
Hill Springs WA 204 C2
Hill Top NSW 109 F2, 110 F10
Hill View NSW 115 K7
Hillarys Boat Harbour WA 183, **188–9**
Hillcroft NSW 110 C4
Hillgrange SA 233 K6
Hillgrove NSW 113 K8
Hillgrove Qld 146 A1, 149 L10, 151 P1
Hillside NSW 114 F2
Hillside West Vic 65 K2, 72 C10
Hillside Qld 144 C3
Hillside WA 211 J7
Hillston NSW 117 J2

Hilltown SA 233 J7
Hillview NSW 144 D1, 146 E10
Hillview Qld 151 L4
Hillview WA 205 H5
Hillwood Tas 255 J5
Hiltaba SA 232 E8
Hilton Qld 150 C3
Hinchinbrook Island NP Qld 149 M8
Hincks CP SA 232 E8
Hindmarsh Island SA 222, 230 A6
Hindmarsh River SA 226
Hinemoa Qld 144 G1, 147 H10
Hines Hill WA 202 F4
Hinnomunjie Vic 70 E2, 73 L7
Hinze Dam Qld *see* Advancetown Lake Qld
Hivesville Qld 145 K4
Hobart Tas 238–9, *238*, *239*, 253 K5
Hobartville Qld 146 B8
Hobbys Yards NSW 109 D1, 110 C8
Hoddle Vic 65 M8
Hoddles Creek Vic 65 K3
Hodgson Qld 144 E5
Hodgson Downs NT 175 H9
Hodgson River NT 175 H9, 177 H1
Hog Back SA 233 K7
Hoganthulla Qld 144 C3
Holbrook NSW 110 F5
Holbrook NSW 117 N7
Holey Creek NT 174 C7
Holey Plains SP Vic 70 B7
Holland Landing Vic 51, 70 D7
Hollow Tree Tas 253 H3
Holly Downs Qld 144 B4
Hollybank FR Tas 255 K6
Holmwood NSW 109 B1, 110 B8
Holowilena SA 233 J3
Holowilena South SA 233 K4
Holstons Vic 70 F4, 73 M9
Holt Rock WA 203 H6
Holwell Tas 255 J6
Home Hill Qld 146 D1, 149 P10
Home Rule NSW 110 D4
Home Valley WA 209 M4
Homeboin Qld 144 C7
Homebush Qld 146 G4
Homebush Vic 67 J3
Homecroft Vic 68 F9
Homestead Qld 146 A2, 151 P2
Homevale Qld 146 F4
Homevale NP Qld 146 F4
Homewood Vic 72 B8
Honan Downs Qld 151 M9
Honiton SA 230 A3, 233 H10
Hook Island Qld 146 F2, 289
Hooley WA 211 H7
Hoomooloo Park Qld 153 M4
Hope Vale Aboriginal Community Qld 149 L3, 155 C3
Hopefield NSW 117 L8
Hopetoun Vic 68 F7
Hopetoun WA 203 J8
Hopetoun West Vic 68 E7
Hopevale Vic 68 E8
Hopkins River Vic 66 G7
Hoppers Crossing Vic 64 F3, 67 N6
Horn Island Qld 154 C2, 278, 279
Hornet Bank Qld 144 G4
Hornsby NSW 109 G1, 111 H8
Hornsdale SA 233 J6
Horrocks WA 199, 204 C7
Horseshoe Bend NT 179 J9
Horseshoe Creek NSW 113 N2
Horsham Vic 66 E2
Horton Vale Qld 153 P8
Hoskinstown NSW 109 D5
Hotham Heights Vic 70 C2, 73 J7
Hotspur Vic 66 C6
Houtman Abrolhos WA 198, 199, 204 B7
Hovells Creek NSW 109 C2, 110 B9
Howard Qld 145 M3
Howard Springs NT 174 D4
Howden Tas 253 K6
Howes Bay Lagoon Tas 329
Howes Valley NSW 110 G6
Howick Group NP Qld 149 K2, 154 G9
Howittville Vic 70 C4, 73 H9
Howqua Vic 72 E7
Howqua River Vic 58
Howth Tas 254 F5
Hoyleton SA 233 J8

INDEX OF PLACE NAMES

Huckitta NT 179 K4
Huddleston SA 233 J6
Hugh River NT 179 H7
Hugh River NT 179 H7
Hughenden Qld 151 L3
Hughes SA 231 B8
Hull Heads Qld 149 M7, 288
Humbert River Ranger Station NT 176 C2
Humboldt Qld 146 F10
Humbug Point SRA Tas 255 P5
Hume Weir NSW 117 M8, 264
Humeburn Qld 153 N7
Humevale Vic 65 H1, 67 P5, 72 B9
Humpty Doo NT 174 D4
Humula NSW 117 N7
Hungerford Qld 153 M10
Hunter Vic 67 M1, 69 M10
Hunter River NSW 100, 110 G5
Hunterson Vic 70 B9
Huntingfield NSW 116 A3
Huntly Vic 67 M2
Huon Vic 73 J4
Huon River Tas 253 J7
Huonville Tas 253 J6
Hurricane Qld 149 K5, 155 B6
Hurstbridge Vic 65 H2, 67 P5, 72 B10
Hurstville NSW 111 H9
Huskisson NSW 95, 109 G4
Hy Brazil WA 204 G7
Hyden WA 202 G5
Hynam SA 230 D10
Hyperna SA 233 N7

Ibis Creek Qld 146 D4
Icy Creek Vic 63, 65 M3
Ida Bay Tas 253 H8
Ida Valley WA 205 K8
Idalia Qld 148 G8
Idalia NP Qld 153 M2
Idracowra NT 179 H8
Iffley Qld 146 F6
Iffley Qld 148 E8
Iguana Creek Vic 70 D5, 73 K10
Ibilbie Qld 146 G5
Ilford NSW 99, 110 E6
Ilfracombe Qld 151 M8
Illabarook Vic 64 B3, 67 K6
Illabo NSW 117 N5
Illawarra Vic 66 G3
Illawong WA 204 D9
Ililliwa NSW 117 H4
Illintjitja Homeland SA 231 C1
Illistrin Qld 148 D10, 150 E1
Illowa Vic 66 F8
Iltur Homeland SA 231 C3
Iluka NSW 113 N4, **266–7**
Imanpa NT 178 F8
Imbil Qld 145 M5
Impadna NT 179 H8
Indee WA 211 H6
Indented Head Vic 41, 44, 64 F5, 67 N7
Indian Head Qld *119*, 132, 133
Indian Island NT 162, 163, 174 C4
Indiana NT 179 K5
Ingeberry Qld 153 L6
Ingebyra NSW 109 B8
Ingham Qld 149 M8
Ingleby Vic 64 C6, 67 K8
Inglewood Qld 145 J9
Inglewood Vic 67 K1, 69 K10
Ingomar SA 234 B8
Injinoo Aboriginal Community Qld 154 C3
Injune Qld 142, 144 E4
Inkerman Qld 146 D1, 149 P10
Inkerman Qld 148 E4
Inkerman SA 233 J9
Inman River SA 226
Inman Valley SA 230 A5
Innamincka SA 235 N4
Innamincka RR SA 235 M3
Innes NP SA 213, 230 A2
Innesowen NSW 115 H6
Inneston SA 230 A2
Innesvale NT 174 D9
Innis Downs Qld 144 A2, 153 P2
Innisfail Qld 149 M6, 155 E9
Innot Hot Springs Qld 149 L7, 155 C10
Innouendy WA 204 E3
Inorunie Qld 148 G7

Inskip Point Qld 129
Interlaken Tas 253 J1, 255 K10
Inveralochy NSW 109 D4
Invergordon Vic 72 C3
Inverleigh Qld 148 D7
Inverleigh Vic 64 C5, 67 L7
Inverloch Vic 65 L7
Inverway NT 176 B5
Investigator Group CP SA 232 B8
Investigator Strait SA 230 A2, 322, 323
Inyarinyi SA 231 F1
Iona NSW 116 E3
Iona WA 204 G7
Ipolera NT 178 F6
Ipswich Qld 145 M7
Irishtown Tas 254 C4
Iron Baron SA 232 G6
Iron Knob SA 232 G5
Iron Range Qld 154 E6
Iron Range NP Qld 154 E6, 278
Ironbark Dam Camp NSW 112 G4
Ironhurst Qld 149 H7
Ironpot Qld 145 K5
Irrapatana SA 234 F7
Irrewarra Vic 64 A6, 67 K8
Irrewillipe Vic 67 J8
Irvinebank Qld 149 L6, 155 C9
Irymple Vic 68 E2
Isdell River WA 208 G6, 304
Isis Downs Qld 151 M10
Isisford Qld 151 H3, 153 M1
Isla Gorge NP Qld 144 G2
Isla Plains Qld 145 H2
Island Bend NSW 109 B7
Island Lagoon SA 232 F3
Israelite Bay WA 207 A9
Italian Gully Vic 64 B3, 67 K5
Ivanhoe NSW 114 G10, 116 G1
Ivanhoe Qld 144 A2
Ivanhoe WA 209 N4
Iwantja (Indulkana) SA 231 G2
Iwupataka NT 179 H6

Jabiru NT *171*, 172, 174 G4
Jabuk SA 230 A8
Jackadgery NSW 113 L5, 267
Jackson Qld 144 G5
Jackson Vic 66 F2
Jackson River Qld 154 B4, 280–1
Jacky Jacky System Qld 279
Jacobs Well Qld 123, 145 N7
Jalbarragup WA 202 B8
Jallukar Vic 66 G4
Jallumba Vic 66 D3
Jamberoo NSW 109 G3
Jamberoo Qld 144 G2
Jambin Qld 147 J10
Jamestown SA 233 J6
Jamieson Vic 72 E8
Jamieson River Vic 58
Jan Juc Vic 64 D6, 67 M8
Jancourt East Vic 67 H8
Jandowae Qld 145 J5
Jane River Tas 254 D7
Janina NSW 115 H4
Japoon Qld 149 M7, 155 E10
Jardine River Qld 154 C3, 280, 281
Jardine River NP Qld 154 C3, 278
Jarklin Vic 69 L9
Jarrahdale WA 202 C5
Jarrahmond Vic 71 H5, 73 P10
Jarrahwood WA 202 B8
Jarvis Field Qld 151 H7
Jarvisfield Qld 146 D1, 149 P10
Jaspers Brush NSW 109 G3
JC Hotel Qld 152 G3
Jecundars Park WA 202 D2
Jeedamya WA 205 L9
Jeffcott Vic 69 H9
Jefferson Lakes WA 205 K9
Jellat Jellat NSW 109 E8
Jellinbah Qld 146 F8
Jennacubbine WA 202 D3
Jennapullin WA 202 D3
Jenolan Caves NSW 109 E1, 110 E8
Jeogla NSW 113 K8
Jeparit Vic 68 D9
Jerangle NSW 109 D6
Jericho Qld 146 B9, 151 P9
Jericho Tas 253 K2

Jerilderie NSW 117 K6
Jerona Qld 146 D1, 149 N9
Jerramungup WA 202 G8
Jerrys Plains NSW 110 G5
Jerseyville NSW 113 N9
Jervis Bay NSW 93, **94–5**, *94*, *95*, 109 G4
Jervis Bay NP NSW 94, 109 G4
Jervois NSW 179 L5
Jervois SA 230 A7
Jessie River NT **292–3**
Jetsonville Tas 255 L5
Jibberding WA 202 D1, 204 F10
Jigalong WA 211 L9
Jil Jil Vic 69 H8
Jilbadji NR WA 203 J4
Jilliby NSW 111 H7
Jimba Jimba WA 204 D3
Jimboola Qld 150 B6
Jimbour Qld 145 K6
Jimna Qld 145 L5
Jindabyne NSW 109 B8
Jindalee NSW 109 A3, 117 P5
Jindare NT 174 E7
Jindera NSW 117 M8
Jindivick Vic 65 L4
Jingellic NSW 117 N8
Jingemarra WA 204 F7
Jingera NSW 109 D6
Jinka NT 179 L5
Jitarning WA 202 F6
Jobs Gate NSW 115 M1
Joel Vic 67 H3
Joel South Vic 67 H3
Johanna Vic 67 J9
Johnburgh SA 233 K5
Johns River NSW 111 M2
Johnsonville Vic 70 F6
Jomara NSW 112 A3
Jondaryan Qld 145 K7
Jones Bay Vic 71 E6, 261
Jooro Qld 147 J10
Jordan Avon Qld 146 B7
Joseph Bonaparte Gulf NT 174 A8, 298
Joseph Bonaparte Gulf WA 209 N2
Joulnie NSW 114 A5
Joycedale Qld 146 B9, 151 P9
Joyces Creek Vic 67 L3
Joylands Qld 144 B5
Jubilee Downs WA 209 H9
Jubilee Lake WA 207 D4
Judbury Tas 253 H5
Jugiong NSW 109 A4, 117 P5
Jugiong Qld 151 K8
Julatten Qld 149 L5, 155 C7
Julia SA 233 K8
Julia Creek Qld 150 G3
Julius River FR Tas 254 B5
Jumpinpin Qld 120, 122, 123
Juna Downs WA 211 H9
Junction Village Vic 65 J5
Jundah Qld 153 J2
Jundee WA 205 L4
Junee NSW 117 N5
Jungien Qld 146 G7
Junee Reefs NSW 117 N5
Jung Vic 66 F1
Junortoun Vic 67 M2
Jurema Qld 146 E8
Jurien WA 202 A1, 204 D10

Kaarimba Vic 72 B3
Kaban Qld 149 L6, 155 D9
Kabelbara Qld 146 E8
Kabra Qld 147 J8
Kadina SA 233 H8
Kadji Kadji WA 204 E9
Kadnook Vic 66 C3
Kadungle NSW 115 N10, 117 N1
Kaimkillenbun Qld 145 K6
Kainton SA 233 H8
Kaiuroo Qld 146 G8
Kajabbi Qld 148 D10, 150 D2
Kajuligah NSW 115 H9
Kajuligah NR NSW 115 H9, 117 H1
Kakadu NP NT 28, **170–1**, *170*, *171*, 172, 174 F5
Kalabity SA 233 M4
Kalala NT 174 G10, 176 G2
Kalamurina SA 235 J4
Kalanbi SA 232 A3, 231 G10

Kalang Qld 146 D6
Kalangadoo SA 227, 230 F9
Kalannie WA 202 E2, 204 F10
Kalarka Qld 147 H6
Kalaru NSW 109 E8
Kalbar Qld 145 M8
Kalbarri WA 204 C7, **314–15**
Kalbarri NP WA 204 C6
Kaleno NSW 115 H8
Kalgoorlie WA 203 L2
Kalimna Vic 53, 70 F6
Kalimna West Vic 70 F6
Kalinga Qld 149 J3, 154 E10
Kalkadoon Qld 151 H6
Kalkallo Vic 64 G2, 67 P5, 72 A9
Kalkarindji NT 176 D4
Kalkaroo NSW 114 F6
Kalkaroo SA 233 N3
Kalkee Vic 66 E1, 68 E10
Kallara NSW 114 G5
Kalli WA 204 F5
Kalmeta Qld 148 E10, 150 F1
Kalpienung Vic 69 H8
Kalpowar Qld 149 J2, 154 F10
Kalpower Qld 145 K1
Kaltukatjara Community (Docker River) NT 178 A8
Kalumburu WA 209 K2, *302*
Kaluwiri WA 205 K6
Kalyan SA 233 M10
Kalyeeda WA 208 G10
Kamarah NSW 117 M4
Kamaran Downs Qld 150 C10, 152 C1
Kamarooka Vic 67 M1, 69 M10
Kamarooka East Vic 67 M1, 69 M10
Kamarooka SP Vic 67 M1, 69 M10
Kambalda WA 203 L3
Kambalda NR WA 203 L3
Kambalda West WA 203 L3
Kambalup WA 202 F9
Kameruka NSW 109 D8
Kamileroi Qld 148 D9
Kanagulk Vic 66 D3
Kanandah WA 207 B6
Kanangra-Boyd NP NSW 109 E1, 110 E9
Kanawalla Vic 66 E5
Kancoona Vic 73 H5
Kandanga Qld 145 M5
Kandos NSW 110 E6
Kangaloon NSW 109 F3
Kangan WA 211 H6
Kangarilla SA 230 A5, 233 J10
Kangaroo Bay SA 230 C3
Kangaroo Camp NSW 113 H6
Kangaroo Flat NSW 111 K1, 113 K10
Kangaroo Flat Vic 67 L2
Kangaroo Hills Qld 149 L9
Kangaroo Island SA 220, 221, 230 B2, **320–1**, *320*, *321*, 322
Kangaroo River NSW 92, 93
Kangaroo Valley NSW 109 F3
Kangaroo Well SA 232 D3
Kangawall Vic 66 C2
Kangiara NSW 109 B3
Kaniva Vic 66 B1, 68 B10
Kanoloo Qld 146 D9
Kanowna Qld 144 C9, 146 E8
Kanowna WA 203 L2
Kantappa NSW 114 A7
Kanumbra Vic 72 C7
Kanunnah Bridge Tas 254 B5
Kanya Vic 67 H2
Kanyaka SA 233 J4
Kanyapella NSW 69 N9, 72 A3
Kanyapella South Vic 69 N9
Kanypi SA 231 B1
Kaoota Tas 253 J6
Kapinnie SA 232 D8
Kapunda SA 227, 233 K9
Kara NSW 114 C5
Kara Kara SP Vic 67 J2
Karabeal Vic 66 E5
Karadoc Vic 68 E2
Karalee WA 203 J3
Karalundi NSW 205 H4
Karanja Tas 253 H4
Karara Qld 145 K8
Karara WA 204 F9
Karatta SA 230 B2
Karawinna Vic 68 D3
Karbar WA 204 G6

Karcultaby SA 232 C5
Kardella Vic 65 L6
Kariah Vic 67 H7
Karidi Creek NT 178 E2
Karijini NP WA 211 H9
Kariong NSW 111 H7
Karkoo SA 232 D8
Karlgarin WA 202 G5
Karlo Creek Vic 71 M4
Karmona Qld 152 G7
Karn Vic 72 E6
Karnak Vic 66 C2
Karnup WA 202 C5
Karonie WA 203 N3
Karoola NSW 114 C10, 116 C1
Karoola Tas 255 K6
Karoonda SA 230 A8, 233 M10
Karpa Kora NSW 114 E10, 116 E1
Karragullen WA 202 C5
Karratha WA 210 F5, 308, 309
Karratha WA 210 F6
Karratha Roadhouse WA 210 F5
Karridale WA 202 B8
Karroun Hill NR WA 202 F1, 205 H10
Kars NSW 114 C8
Kars Springs NSW 110 F3
Karte SA 230 A9, 233 N10
Karte CP SA 230 A9, 233 N10
Karuah NSW 111 K5
Karumba Qld 148 E6, 284
Karwarn NSW 115 J9
Karween Vic 68 B2
Karyrie Vic 68 G8
Katamatite Vic 72 D3
Katamatite East Vic 72 D3
Katandra Qld 151 L5
Katandra Vic 72 C4
Katandra West Vic 72 C4
Katanning WA 202 E7
Katarvon Qld 144 D6
Katherine NT 168, 174 F7, 298
Kathida NSW 113 J4
Katoomba NSW 109 F1, 110 F8
Katunga Vic 72 C3
Katyil Vic 68 E10
Kau Rock NR WA 203 M7
Kawarren Vic 64 A7, 67 J8
Kayena Tas 255 J5
Kayrunnera NSW 114 D5
Kearsley NSW 111 J6
Keelambra NSW 114 G5
Keep River WA 209 P4
Keep River NP NT 174 A10, 176 A1
Keeroongooloo Qld 153 J4
Keewong NSW 115 J4
Keilor Vic 64 G3, 67 N5
Keith SA 230 C9
Kellalac Vic 66 F1, 68 F10
Kellerberrin WA 202 E4
Kellevie Tas 253 M4
Kellidie Bay CP SA 232 D9
Kelmscott WA 202 C5
Kelsey Creek Qld 146 F2
Kelso NSW 110 D7
Kelso Tas 255 H5
Kelvin NSW 112 F9
Kemps Creek NSW 109 G1, 110 G9
Kempsey NSW 113 M9
Kempton NSW 109 D2, 110 D10
Kempton Tas 253 J3
Kendall NSW 111 M2
Kendenup WA 202 E9
Kenebri NSW 112 C8
Kenilworth Qld 145 M5
Kenley Vic 69 J4
Kenmare Vic 68 E8
Kenmore NSW 109 E3
Kenmore Qld 144 A6
Kennedy Qld 149 M7
Kennedy Range WA 204 D2
Kennedy Range NP WA 204 D2
Kennedy River Qld 148 J2, 278–9
Kennedys Creek Vic 67 H9
Kennett River Vic 64 B8, 67 K9
Kentbruck Vic 66 B7
Kentucky NSW 113 J8
Kentucky Qld 145 H5
Keppel Sands Qld 147 K8
Keppoch SA 230 D9
Kerang Vic 69 K7
Kerang East Vic 69 L8
Kerein Hills NSW 115 M9

INDEX OF PLACE NAMES

Kergunyah Vic 73 H4
Kergunyah South Vic 73 J4
Keri NT 174 C5
Kerrabee NSW 110 F4
Kerrisdale Vic 72 B8
Kerriwah NSW 115 N9
Kersbrook SA 233 K9
Keswick Point NT 162
Ketchowla SA 233 K6
Kettering Tas 253 K6
Kevington Vic 65 N1, 72 E9
Kew NSW 111 M2
Kew Vic 65 H3, 67 P6
Kewell Vic 66 F1, 68 F10
Keyneton SA 233 K9
Keysbrook WA 202 C5
Khancoban NSW 109 A7, 117 P8, 264
Ki Ki SA 230 B8
Kia Ora NSW 115 N3
Kia Ora Qld 144 C1, 146 D10
Kia Ora SA 233 L7
Kiacatoo NSW 115 M10, 117 M1
Kiah NSW 109 E9
Kialla Vic 72 C5
Kialla West Vic 72 B5
Kiama NSW 92, 93, 109 G3
Kiama NSW 115 H8
Kiamal Vic 68 E5
Kiana NT 177 L4
Kiandool NSW 112 D7
Kiandra NSW 109 B6
Kiandra Qld 153 L7
Kianga NSW 109 E7
Kianga Qld 145 H2
Kianinny Bay NSW 274
Kiata Vic 66 D1, 68 D10
Kiata East Vic 68 D9
Kickabil NSW 110 A3
Kiddell Plains Qld 144 G1
Kidston Qld 149 J8
Kielpa SA 232 E7
Kiewa Vic 73 H4
Kiewa River Vic 73 J5, 264
Kihee Qld 153 J7
Kikoira NSW 117 L3
Kilcowera Qld 153 L9
Kilcoy Qld 140, 145 M6
Kilcummin Qld 146 D6
Kilcunda Vic 65 K7
Kilfeera Vic 72 E5
Kilfera NSW 114 G10, 116 G1
Kilkerran SA 233 H9
Kilkivan Qld 145 L4
Killara WA 205 J4
Killarney NT 176 E2
Killarney Qld 145 L8
Killarney Qld 149 H3
Killarney Qld 149 L10, 151 N2
Killarney Vic 66 E8
Killarney Park Qld 144 B1
Killawarra NSW 111 L3
Killawarra Qld 145 H5
Killawarra SA 233 L3
Killawarra Vic 72 F4
Killcare NSW 86, 111 H8
Killeen Qld 151 K3
Killiecrankie Tas 255 H2
Killora Tas 253 K6
Kilmany Vic 70 B7
Kilmany South Vic 70 C7
Kilmore Vic 67 P4, 72 A8
Kilmorey Qld 144 D4
Kiln Corner SA 233 H9
Kilterry Qld 151 H2
Kilto WA 208 D8, 211 N1
Kimba Qld 149 H3
Kimba SA 232 F6
Kimberley NSW 114 A10, 116 A1
Kimberley Tas 254 G6
Kimberley Downs WA 208 G7
Kimberley, The WA 28, 28, 31, 302–5
Kimbriki NSW 111 L3
Kimovale NSW 109 A4, 117 P6
Kin Kin Qld 138, 145 M4
Kinaba Qld 139
Kinalung NSW 114 C8
Kinchega NP NSW 114 C9
Kinchela NSW 113 M9
Kincora Qld 144 D5
Kindee NSW 111 L1, 113 L10

Kindon Qld 145 J8
Kindred Tas 254 G5
King Ash Bay NT 175 M10, 177 M1
King Edward River WA 209 J4, 302
King George River WA 209 L2, 302
King George Sound WA 202 F10
King Island Tas 254 F2
King Junction Qld 149 H4
King Leopold Ranges WA 209 H7
King River Tas 252 B1, 254 D10, 327, 329
King River WA 202 F9
King Sound WA 208 E7, 304
King Valley Vic 70 A1, 72 F6
Kingaroy Qld 145 L5
Kinglake Vic 65 J2, 72 B9
Kinglake NP Vic 65 J1, 72 B10
Kinglake West Vic 65 J1, 72 B9
Kingoonya SA 232 D1
Kingower Vic 67 K1
Kings Canyon Resort NT 178 E7
Kings Creek NT 178 E7
Kings Plains NSW 113 J5
Kings Plains NP NSW 113 H5
Kingsborough Qld 149 K5, 155 C7
Kingsborough Qld 151 N7
Kingscliff NSW 113 P1
Kingscote SA 230 B3, 320, 321
Kingsdale NSW 109 D3
Kingston Qld 146 C8
Kingston Tas 253 K5
Kingston Vic 64 C1, 67 L4
Kingston-on-Murray SA 233 M8
Kingston SE SA 230 D8
Kingstown NSW 113 H8
Kingsvale NSW 109 A3, 110 A10, 117 P4
Kinimakatka Vic 66 C1, 68 C10
Kinkuna NP Qld 145 M2
Kinnabulla Vic 68 G8
Kinnoul Qld 144 G3
Kio Ora Vic 66 G5
Kioloa NSW 109 F5
Kiora Qld 146 A2, 151 N2
Kirk Point Vic 40
Kirkalocka WA 204 G8
Kirkdune WA 202 D1, 204 F10
Kirkimbie NT 176 A4
Kirkstall Vic 66 F8
Kirrama Qld 149 L7
Kirup WA 202 C7
Kitchener NSW 111 H6
Kitchener WA 207 B6
Kiwirrkurra WA 206 E6
Klori NSW 112 G9
Knebsworth Vic 66 D7
Knockwood Vic 65 N1, 72 F9
Knowsley Vic 67 N2
Koah Qld 149 L5, 155 D7
Koberinga Qld 146 D1, 149 P10
Kobyboyn Vic 72 B7
Koetong Vic 73 K3
Kogan Qld 145 J6
Koimbo Vic 68 G4
Kojonup WA 202 E8
Kokardine WA 202 E2
Kokatha SA 232 C2
Kokotungo Qld 147 H10
Kolendo SA 232 E5
Koloona NSW 112 G5
Komungla NSW 109 D4
Kondinin WA 202 F5
Kondoolka SA 232 C4
Kondut WA 202 D2
Kongorong SA 230 G9
Kongwak Vic 65 K7
Konnongorring WA 202 D3
Konong Wootong Vic 66 C5
Koo-Wee-Rup Vic 62, 65 K5
Kooba Qld 147 H10
Koojan WA 202 C2
Kookaburra NSW 113 L9
Kookynie WA 205 M9
Koolamarra Qld 150 E2
Koolan WA 208 F5
Koolanooka WA 204 E9
Koolatah Qld 148 G4
Koolburra Outstation Qld 149 J3
Koolgera CR SA 232 B4
Kooline WA 210 E9
Koolkhan NSW 113 M5
Kooloonong Vic 69 H4

Koolpinyah NT 174 D4
Kooltandra Qld 147 H7
Koolunga SA 233 J7
Koolyanobbing WA 203 H2
Koolywurtie WA 233 H9
Koombooloomba Qld 149 L7, 155 D10
Koomooloo SA 233 L7
Koonadgin WA 202 G4
Koonalda SA 231 B9
Koonamore SA 233 L4
Koonawarra NSW 114 C6
Koonda Vic 72 D5
Koondoo Qld 153 N2
Koondrook Vic 69 L7
Koongawa SA 232 E6
Koongie Park WA 208 G4
Koonibba Community SA 231 G10
Koonkool Qld 145 H1, 147 J10
Koonmarra WA 204 G4
Koonoomoo Vic 72 C2
Koonunga SA 233 K9
Koonwarra Vic 65 M7
Koonya Tas 253 M6
Koorawatha NSW 109 B2, 110 A9
Koorboora Qld 149 K6, 155 B9
Koorda WA 202 E2
Koordarrie WA 210 D8
Kooreh Vic 67 J1
Koorkab Vic 69 H4
Koornalla Vic 65 P6, 70 A8
Koorongara Qld 145 K8
Kooroora Qld 150 G4
Kootaberra SA 232 G4
Kootchee Qld 153 P2
Koothney NSW 112 A6
Kootingal NSW 113 H9
Kooyoora SP Vic 67 K1, 69 J10
Kopi SA 232 D7
Koppio SA 232 D9
Kopyje NSW 115 L7
Korbel WA 202 F4
Korcha Qld 144 E3
Korenan Qld 145 K1, 147 L10
Koriella Vic 72 C8
Korobeit Vic 64 E2, 67 M5
Koroit Vic 66 F8
Korong Vale Vic 69 K10
Koroop Vic 69 L7
Korora NSW 113 N7
Korrelocking WA 202 E3
Korumburra Vic 65 L6
Kosciuszko NP NSW 109 B7, 117 P9
Kotta Vic 69 M9
Koumala Qld 146 G5
Koumala South Qld 146 G5
Kowanyama Aboriginal Community Qld 148 F3
Kowguran Qld 145 H5
Koyuga Vic 69 N9, 72 A4
Krambach NSW 111 L3
Krowera Vic 65 K6
Ku-ring-gai Chase NP NSW 111 H8
Kubill Qld 144 A7, 153 P7
Kudardup WA 202 B8
Kudriemitchie Outstation SA 235 M4
Kuender WA 202 G6
Kukerin WA 202 F6
Kulde SA 230 A7, 233 L10
Kulgera NT 178 G10
Kulgera Rail Head NT 178 G10
Kulin WA 202 F6
Kulja WA 202 E2
Ku kami SA 230 A9, 233 M10
Kulkyne Vic 68 F3
Kulkyne Park Vic 68 F4
Kuliparu CP SA 232 C6
Kuliparu CR SA 232 C6
Kulnine Vic 68 C2
Kulnura NSW 111 H7
Kulpara SA 233 H8
Kulpi Qld 145 K6
Kultanaby SA 232 D2
Kulwin Vic 68 F5
Kulwyne Vic 68 G5
Kumari WA 203 L6
Kumarina Roadhouse WA 205 J2
Kumbarilla Qld 145 J7
Kumbia Qld 145 K5

Kunamata SA 231 C2
Kunat Vic 69 J7
Kundabung NSW 111 M1, 113 M10
Kundip NR WA 203 J7
Kungala NSW 113 N6
Kunghur NSW 113 N2
Kunjir WA 202 F5
Kunmunya Mission WA 208 G4
Kununoppin WA 202 F3
Kununurra WA 209 N5, 298
Kunwarara Qld 147 J7
Kunytjanu Homeland SA 231 A4
Kupingarri Community WA 209 J6
Kuranda Qld 149 L5, 155 D7
Kurbayia Qld 150 D4
Kuri Bay WA 208 G4
Kuridala Qld 150 E4
Kurnwill Vic 68 C3
Kurraca West Vic 67 J1, 69 J10
Kurrajong NSW 110 G8
Kurrajong Qld 145 H1
Kurray Qld 144 E8
Kuri Kuri NSW 111 J6
Kurrimine Beach Qld 149 M7, 155 E10
Kurting Vic 67 K1, 69 K10
Kurundi NT 177 J9
Kuttabul Qld 146 G4
Kwinana WA 202 C5, 302
Kwobrup WA 202 F7
Kyabra Qld 153 J4
Kyabram Vic 69 P9, 72 A4
Kyalite NSW 116 E6
Kyancutta SA 232 D6
Kybeyan NSW 109 D7
Kybunga SA 233 J8
Kybybolite SA 230 D10
Kyeamba NSW 113 N7
Kyndalyn Vic 68 G4
Kyneton Vic 67 M4
Kynnersley Qld 144 A6, 153 P6
Kynuna Qld 150 G5
Kyogle NSW 113 N2
Kyvalley Vic 69 P9, 72 A4
Kywong NSW 117 M6
Kywong Qld 151 K6

Laanecoorie Vic 67 K2
Laanecoorie Reservoir Vic 67 K2
Laang Vic 66 G8
Labelle Downs Outstation NT 174 C5
Labillardiere SR Tas 253 J8
Laceby Vic 72 F5
Lacepede Bay SA 230 D7
Lachlan Tas 253 J5
Lachlan River NSW 109 C2, 110 C10, 116 G4
Lacmalac NSW 109 A5
Lady Barron Tas 255 K3, 324, 325
Lady Musgrave Island Qld 147 M9, 289
Ladys Pass Vic 67 N2
Laen Vic 66 G1, 68 G10
Laen East Vic 66 G1, 68 G10
Laen North Vic 66 G1, 68 G10
Lagaven Qld 150 G4
Laggan NSW 109 D2, 110 D10
Laglan Qld 146 D5
Lagoon of Islands Tas 328
Lagrange WA 208 C10, 211 M2
Laguna NSW 111 H6
Laguna Qld 144 A3
Laguna Quays Qld 146 F3
Lah Vic 68 F9
Lah-Arum Vic 66 E3
Laheys Creek NSW 110 C4
Laidley Qld 145 L7
Lajamanu NT 176 C5
Lake Ace NR WA 203 J6
Lake Ada Tas 254 G9, 329
Lake Albacutya Vic 68 D7
Lake Albert SA 222, 230 B7
Lake Alexandrina SA 222, 224, 226, 230 A6
Lake Amadeus NT 178 C7
Lake Argyle WA 209 N5, 302–3
Lake Argyle Tourist Village WA 209 N5
Lake Augusta Tas 254 G8, 329
Lake Auld WA 206 A5
Lake Austin WA 204 G6
Lake Ballard WA 205 L9
Lake Barambah Qld 142, 145 L5

Lake Barlee WA 205 J9
Lake Barlee WA 205 J9
Lake Bathurst NSW 109 D4
Lake Benetook Vic 68 E2
Lake Biddy WA 202 G6
Lake Big Jim Tas 252 G1, 255 H10, 330, 330, 331
Lake Birdegolly NP Qld 153 L8
Lake Blanche SA 235 L8
Lake Boga Vic 69 K6
Lake Bolac Vic 66 G5
Lake Bolac Vic 66 G5
Lake Boondooma Qld 142, 143, 145 K4
Lake Botsford Tas 329
Lake Brewster NSW 117 K2
Lake Brown WA 202 F3
Lake Buloke Vic 68 G9
Lake Burbury WA 250–1, 254 E9, 328, 329
Lake Burley Griffin ACT 104–5, 108, 109 C5
Lake Burragorang NSW 80, 109 F1, 110 F9
Lake Burrendong NSW 110 C5
Lake Burrinjuck NSW 98, 106, 109 B4
Lake Burrumbeet Vic 64 E2, 67 K5
Lake Cadibarrawirracanna SA 234 D7
Lake Callabonna SA 235 M9
Lake Campion NR WA 202 G3
Lake Carey WA 205 N9
Lake Cargelligo NSW 117 L2
Lake Carnegie WA 205 N4
Lake Cathie NSW 111 M2
Lake Charm Vic 69 K7
Lake Chisholm FR Tas 254 B5
Lake Colac Vic 64 A6
Lake Condah Vic 66 D7
Lake Conjola NSW 109 F5
Lake Connewarte Vic 64 E5
Lake Cooloola NSW 128
Lake Cooroibah Qld 128, 145 N5
Lake Cootharaba Qld 128, 139, 145 N4
Lake Corangamite Vic 64 A5, 67 J7
Lake Cowal NSW 117 N3
Lake Cowan WA 203 M4
Lake Crescent Tas 253 J1, 255 K10, 328, 329
Lake Dalrymple Qld 146 C3
Lake Dartmouth Vic 73 L5
Lake De Burgh NT 177 L7
Lake Deborah East WA 203 H2
Lake Deborah West WA 202 G2
Lake Delusion SA 235 J9
Lake Disappointment WA 211 N10
Lake Doonella Qld 128
Lake Dora WA 211 P8
Lake Dundas WA 203 M5
Lake Echo Tas 252 G1, 255 H10, 328
Lake Eildon Vic 58–9, 59, 72 D8
Lake Eppalock Vic 67 M2
Lake Eppalock Vic 67 M2
Lake Eucumbene NSW 109 B7, 276–7
Lake Eulo NSW 114 E8
Lake Everard SA 232 C2
Lake Everard SA 232 C3
Lake Eyre North SA 234 G6
Lake Eyre NP SA 234 G6
Lake Eyre South SA 234 G8
Lake Frome SA 233 L1, 235 M10
Lake Frome RR SA 233 L1
Lake Gardner SA 232 E3
Lake Gardner NP SA 232 D2
Lake Galilee Qld 151 P6
Lake George NSW 109 D4
Lake Gilles SA 232 F5
Lake Gilles CP SA 232 F6
Lake Ginninderra ACT 104–5, 105
Lake Glenbawn NSW 98, 100–1, 101, 110 G3
Lake Glenlyon Qld 142, 143, 145 K8
Lake Goldsmith Vic 67 J5
Lake Goran NSW 112 E10
Lake Gordon Tas 252 E4
Lake Grace WA 202 G6
Lake Gregory SA 235 K7
Lake Harry SA 235 J8
Lake Hattah Vic 68 F4
Lake Hindmarsh Vic 68 D8
Lake Honey SA 231 D5
Lake Hope WA 203 J5

INDEX OF PLACE NAMES

Lake Hopkins WA 206 F7
Lake Hume NSW 117 M8, 264
Lake Hume Vic 73 J4, 264
Lake Hurlstone NR WA 203 H5
Lake Illawarra NSW **90–1**, *91*, 109 G3
Lake Innes NR NSW 111 M2
Lake Jindabyne NSW 109 B7, **276–7**
Lake John SA 235 K4
Lake Johnston WA 203 K5
Lake Jones WA 206 B7
Lake Kay Tas 329
Lake Keepit NSW 112 F9
Lake King Vic 50, 51, 70 F6, *260–1*, 261
Lake King WA 203 H6
Lake King NR WA 203 H6
Lake King William Tas 254 G10, 328, 329
Lake Leake Tas 255 M9
Lake Learmonth Vic 64 B1
Lake Lefroy WA 203 L3
Lake Leslie Qld *142*, 145 K8
Lake Lewis NT 178 F5
Lake Logue NR WA 202 B1, 204 D10
Lake Lonsdale Vic 66 F3
Lake Louisa Tas 254 G8, 329
Lake Lucy Qld 149 L8
Lake Lyell NSW **102–3**, *103*
Lake Macfarlane SA 232 F4
Lake Mackay NT 178 A4
Lake Mackay WA 206 F5
Lake Mackenzie Tas 254 G8, 329
Lake MacLeod WA 204 B1, 210 B10
Lake Macquarie NSW 86, 111 J6
Lake Magenta NR WA 202 E2
Lake Marmal Vic 69 J9
Lake Martin Vic 64 A5
Lake Mason WA 205 J6
Lake Meran Vic 69 K8
Lake Mere NSW 115 H4
Lake Meston Tas 254 F9, 329
Lake Mindona NSW 116 C2
Lake Minigwal WA 205 P9
Lake Mokoan Vic 72 E5
Lake Moore WA 202 E1, 204 G9
Lake Muir WA 202 D9
Lake Muir NR WA 202 D9
Lake Mulwala NSW 117 K8, 264–5
Lake Mulwala Vic 72 E3, 264–5
Lake Mundi Vic 66 B5
Lake Munmorah NSW 111 J7
Lake Murdeduke Vic 64 C5
Lake Myrtle Tas 254 F9, 329
Lake Nash NT 177 P10, 179 P1
Lake Neale NT 178 B7
Lake Newland CP SA 232 C7
Lake Noondie WA 205 J8
Lake Parrarra NT 178 D8
Lake Pedder Tas 252 F5
Lake Pieman Tas 254 C8
Lake Raeside WA 205 M9
Lake Rason WA 207 B3
Lake Rebecca WA 203 M1, 205 N10
Lake Reeve Vic 50, 51, 70 D8
Lake Robin WA 203 J4
Lake Rowan Vic 72 E4
Lake St Clair NSW 100, 111 H4
Lake St Clair Tas 254 F9, 329
Lake Samuel Tas 252 G1, 255 H10, 330, 331
Lake Sharpe WA 203 K6
Lake Somerset Qld **140**, 141, *141*, 143, 145 M6
Lake Sorell Tas 255 K10, 328, 329
Lake Stewart NSW 114 A2
Lake Sylvester NT 177 L6
Lake Tay WA 203 K6
Lake Theo WA 204 F7
Lake Thistle WA 207 E2
Lake Thompson Vic 65 N3
Lake Timboram Vic 69 H6
Lake Tinaroo Qld 118, 155 D8
Lake Torrens SA 233 H1, 234 G10
Lake Torrens SA 233 H3
Lake Torrens NP SA 233 H2
Lake Trevallyn Tas 247, 255 J6
Lake Tuggeranong ACT **104–5**
Lake Tyers Vic 52, 70 G6
Lake Tyers SP Vic 70 G5
Lake Tyrrell Vic 68 G6
Lake Valerie NT 179 M7
Lake Varley NR WA 203 H6

Lake Victoria NSW 116 A3
Lake Victoria Vic 50, 51, 70 E7
Lake View NSW 114 C7
Lake View SA 233 J7
Lake Violet WA 205 L5
Lake Wahpool Vic 68 G6
Lake Wallace NSW 114 B4
Lake Wallambin WA 202 E3
Lake Wasby NSW 114 D2
Lake Waukarlycarly WA 211 M6
Lake Way WA 205 K5
Lake Way WA 205 K5
Lake Wellington Vic 50, 51, 63, 70 D7
Lake Wells WA 205 P5
Lake Weyba Qld 128, 145 N5
Lake Windamere NSW *see* Windamere Dam NSW
Lake Wivenhoe Qld *119*, **140–1**, 145 M6
Lake Woods NT 176 G5
Lake Wooloweyah NSW 266
Lake Wyangala NSW 98, 109 C1, 110 C9
Lake Yamma Yamma Qld 152 G5
Lake Yarrunga NSW 93, 109 F3
Lake Yindarlgooda WA 203 M2
Lakefield Qld 149 J2, 154 F10, 155 A2
Lakefield NP Qld 149 J2, 154 F10, 155 A2
Lakeland Qld 149 K4, 155 B4
Lakes Entrance Vic 50, **52–3**, *52*, *52–3*, 70 G6
Lakeside WA 204 G6
Lal Lal Vic 64 C2, 67 L5
Lal Lal Reservoir Vic 64 C2
Lalbert Vic 69 J7
Lalbert Road Vic 69 J7
Lalla Tas 255 K6
Lalla Rookh WA 211 J6
Lambina SA 234 A3
Lamboo WA 209 L9
Lameroo SA 230 A9
Lamington NP Qld 145 N8
Lamorbey Qld 146 C8
Lamplough Vic 67 J3
Lana Downs Qld 151 J5
Lancaster Vic 69 P10, 72 B4
Lancefield Qld 147 J9
Lancefield Vic 67 N4
Lancelin WA 182, 202 B3
Lancevale Qld 146 B9, 151 P9
Lancewood Qld 146 E4
Landor WA 204 F3
Landreath Qld 144 E5
Landsborough Qld 145 M6
Landsborough Vic 67 H3
Landsborough West Vic 67 H3
Landsdowne Qld 144 A2
Lane Poole Reserve WA 202 C6
Lanena Tas 255 J6
Lang Creek Vic 69 L9
Lang Lang Vic 43, 65 K5
Lang Lang River Vic 63
Langdale Qld 151 J3
Langhorne Creek SA 230 A6
Langi Ghiran FP Vic 67 H4
Langi Logan Vic 66 G4
Langidoon NSW 114 C7
Langkoop Vic 66 A3
Langley Qld 146 G7
Langley Vic 67 M3
Langleydale NSW 116 F3
Langlo Crossing Qld 153 P4
Langlo Downs Qld 153 P3
Langtree NSW 117 J3
Langville Vic 69 K8
Langwarrin Vic 65 H5, 67 P7
Langwell NSW 114 B9
Lankeys Creek NSW 117 N7
Lansdale NSW 115 M8
Lansdowne NSW 111 L2
Lansdowne WA 209 K8
Lapoinya Tas 254 D4
Lara Vic 64 E4, 67 M7
Laravale Qld 145 M8
Lardner Vic 65 L5
Largs Bay SA 215, 233 K5
Laroona Qld 149 M9
Larpent Vic 64 A6, 67 J8
Larras Lee NSW 110 B6
Larrawa WA 206 D1, 209 K10
Larrimah NT 174 G9, 176 G1

Lascelles Qld 146 B3, 151 P3
Lascelles Vic 68 F7
Latham WA 204 E9
Lathami CP SA 230 B3
Latrobe Tas 254 G5
LaTrobe River Vic 50, 63, 65 M4
Lauderdale Tas 253 L5
Launceston Tas **246–7**, 255 K6
Laura Qld 149 K3, 155 A3, 278
Laura SA 233 J6
Laura Bay SA 232 A4, 231 G10
Lauradale NSW 115 J3
Laurieton NSW 111 M2
Lauriston Vic 67 M4
Lavers Hill Vic 67 J9
Laverton Vic 64 F3, 67 N6
Laverton WA 205 N8
Laverton Downs WA 205 N8
Lavington NSW 117 M8
Lavinia NR Tas 254 F1
Lawloit Vic 66 C1, 68 C10
Lawn Hill Qld 148 B8
Lawn Hill NP Qld 148 A8
Lawrence NSW 113 N5, 266
Lawrenny Tas 253 H3
Lawson NSW 97, 109 F1, 110 F8
Lea Creek Qld 148 D8
Leadville NSW 110 D3
Leaghur Vic 69 K8
Leaghur SP Vic 69 K8
Leander NSW 115 M2
Learmonth Vic 64 B1, 67 K4
Learmonth WA 210 B8
Lebrina Tas 255 K5
Ledcourt Vic 66 F3
Ledge Point WA 202 B3
Ledgerwood Tas 255 M5
Lee Point NT 160, *161*, 174 D4
Leechs Gully NSW 113 K3
Leeka Tas 255 H2
Leeman WA 202 A1, 204 D10
Leeor Vic 66 B1, 68 B10
Leeson Qld 151 J6
Leeton NSW 117 L5
Leeuwin-Naturaliste NP WA 202 A8
Leeville NSW 113 M3
Lefroy Tas 255 J5
Lefroy WA 203 L3
Lefroy Brook WA 200
Legana Tas 255 J6
Legume NSW 113 L2
Legune NT 174 B9
Leichardt Vic 67 L2
Leichhardt Range Qld 146 D2
Leigh Creek SA 233 J1, 235 J10
Leigh Creek Vic 64 C2, 67 K5
Leinster WA 205 L7
Leinster Downs WA 205 L7
Leitchville Vic 69 M8
Leith Tas 254 G5
Leitpar Vic 68 G5
Lemana Tas 255 H7
Lemnos Vic 72 C4
Lemont Tas 253 L2
Leneva Vic 73 H4
Lennox Qld 146 B7, 151 P7
Lennox Head NSW 113 P3
Leonards Hill Vic 64 D1, 67 L4
Leongatha Vic 65 M7
Leongatha South Vic 65 L7
Leonora WA 205 L8
Leonora Downs NSW 114 C9
Leopold Vic 64 E5, 67 M7
Leopold Downs WA 209 H8
Lerderderg Gorge FP Vic 64 E2, 67 M5
Lerida NSW 115 K7
Leschenault Estuary WA 194
Leslie Manor Vic 67 J7
Leslie Vale Tas 253 K5
Lesueur NP WA 202 B1, 204 D10
Lethbridge Vic 64 D4, 67 L6
Lethebrook Qld 146 F3
Leura NSW 109 F1, 110 F8
Leura Qld 147 H8
Leven Beach CP SA 232 G10
Levendale Tas 253 L3
Lewis Ponds NSW 110 C7
Lewisham Tas 253 L5
Lexton Vic 64 A6, 67 J8
Leyburn Qld 145 K8
Liawenee Tas 255 H9
Licola Vic 70 A5, 72 G10

Liena Tas 254 G7
Liffey Tas 255 H8
Liffey FR Tas 255 J8
Lightning Creek Vic 70 D1, 73 K6
Lightning Ridge NSW 115 P2
Lila NT 178 E7
Lilarea Qld 151 M6
Lileah Tas 254 C4
Lilla Creek NT 179 H9
Lillimur Vic 66 B1, 68 B10
Lillimur South Vic 66 B1, 68 B10
Lilliput Vic 72 F3
Lily Vale Qld 149 H1, 154 E9
Lilydale SA 233 M6
Lilydale Tas 255 K5
Lilydale Vic 65 J3, 72 B10
Lilyvale NSW 115 H7
Lilyvale Downs Qld 144 G3
Lima Vic 72 E5
Lima South Vic 72 E6
Limbla NT 179 K6
Limbri NSW 113 H9
Limbunya NT 176 B3
Lime Bay NR Tas 253 L5
Limebumers Bay Vic 45
Limebumers Creek NSW 111 K5
Limebumers Creek NR NSW 111 M1, 113 M10
Limestone Vic 72 C8
Limevale Qld 145 J9
Limmen Bight NT 175 K8
Lincoln NSW 110 C4
Lincoln Gap SA 232 G5
Lincoln NP SA 232 D10
Lind NP Vic 71 K5
Linda Downs Qld 150 B6
Lindeman Group Qld 146 G2, 289
Linden NSW 109 F1, 110 F8
Lindenow Vic 70 E6
Lindenow South Vic 70 D6
Lindesay View NSW 113 M2
Lindfield Qld 150 G2
Lindsay Vic 66 A5
Lindsay Point Vic 68 A1
Linga Vic 68 C5
Linton Vic 64 A2, 67 J5
Linville Qld 145 L6
Lipson SA 232 E8
Lirambenda NSW 109 A2, 117 P4
Lisle Tas 255 K5
Lismore Qld 145 J4
Lismore NSW 113 N3
Lismore Vic 67 J6
Lissadell WA 209 N6
Liston NSW 113 K2
Listowel Downs Qld 153 N2
Listowel Valley Qld 153 N3
Litchfield NT 174 C6
Litchfield Vic 68 G9
Litchfield NP NT 174 D5
Lithgow NSW 102, 110 F7
Littabella NP Qld 145 L1
Little Billabong NSW 117 N7
Little Desert NP Vic 66 C1, 68 C10
Little Dip CP SA 230 E8
Little Finniss River NT 167
Little Hampton Vic 64 D1, 67 M4
Little Hartley NSW 110 F8
Little Henty River Tas 254 C9, 327
Little Pine Lagoon Tas 255 H9, 328, 329
Little Plain NSW 112 G5
Little River Vic 64 E4, 67 M6
Little Sandy Desert WA 205 M1
Little Snowy Creek Vic 73 J5
Little Swanport Tas 243, 253 M2
Little Topar Roadhouse NSW 114 C7
Littlemore Qld 145 K1, 147 L10
Liveringa WA 208 F9
Liverpool NSW 84, 85, 109 G1, 110 G9
Liverpool Range NSW 110 F3
Lizard Island NP Qld 149 L2, 155 D1, 278, 291
Llanelly Vic 67 K2
Llangothlin NSW 113 J7
Llidem Vale NSW 144 G8
Llorac Qld 151 M6
Lobethal SA 233 K10
Loch Vic 65 L6
Loch Lilly NSW 114 A10, 116 A1
Loch River Vic 63

Loch Sport Vic 51, 70 E7
Loch Valley Vic 65 M3
Loch Winnoch SA 233 L6
Lochanger Qld 144 F7
Lochern Qld 151 K10
Lochern NP Qld 151 K10
Lochiel NSW 109 E9
Lochiel SA 233 J8
Lochnagar Qld 146 A9, 151 P9
Lochnagar Qld 148 F3
Lock SA 232 D7
Lockhart NSW 117 L6
Lockhart River Aboriginal Community Qld 154 E6
Lockington Vic 69 M9
Locksley Vic 72 B6
Lockwood NSW 110 B7
Lockwood Vic 67 L2
Loddon Qld 153 P5
Loddon River Vic 69 K8
Loddon Vale Vic 69 L8
Logan Vic 67 J1
Logan Downs Qld 146 E6
Loganholme Qld 145 N7
Logie Brae NSW 117 J7
Logue Brook Dam WA 200, 201, *201*
Lolworth Qld 151 N2
Lombadina WA 208 D6
London Lakes Tas 252 G1, 255 H10, **330–1**, *331*
Londonderry NSW 109 G1, 110 G8
Lonesome Creek Qld 145 H2
Long Beach NSW 109 F6
Long Plains SA 233 J9
Long Plains Vic 68 G6
Long Pocket Qld 149 M8
Longerenong Vic 66 F2
Longford NSW 113 H8
Longford Qld 150 F3
Longford Qld 153 J2
Longford Tas 255 K7
Longford Vic 70 C7
Longlea Vic 67 M2
Longley Tas 253 J5
Longreach Qld 151 L8
Longs Corner NSW 110 B7
Longton Qld 146 B3, 151 P3
Longwarry Vic 62, 65 L5
Longwood Vic 72 B6
Lonnavale Tas 253 H5
Loomberah NSW 111 H1, 113 H10
Loongana Tas 254 F6
Loongana WA 207 E6
Loorana Tas 254 F2
Lord Howe Island NSW **6–7**, **270–1**, *270*
Lords Well SA 233 M7
Lorinna Tas 254 F7
Lorna Downs Qld 150 D8
Lorna Glen WA 205 M4
Lorna Shoal NT 161, 163
Lorne Qld 144 C3
Lorne Qld 153 N2
Lorne SA 233 J9
Lorne Vic 64 C7, 67 L8
Lorne FP Vic 64 C7, 67 K8
Lornesleigh Qld 146 C3
Lornvale Qld 149 H8
Lorquon Vic 68 D9
Lorraine Qld 148 C9
Lorraine Station Qld 151 K7
Lorrett Downs Qld 150 E6
Lotus Vale Qld 148 E6
Lou Lou Park Qld 146 B6
Louis Point NSW 113 L6
Louisa Downs WA 209 K10
Louisiana Qld 149 K3, 155 C3
Louisville Tas 253 M3
Louth NSW 115 J5
Louth Bay SA 232 E9
Lovely Banks Vic 64 D4, 67 M7
Low Head Tas 255 J5
Lowan Vale SA 230 C9
Lowanna NSW 113 M7
Lowden WA 202 C7
Lowdina Tas 253 K3
Lower Barrington Tas 254 G6
Lower Beulah Tas 254 G7
Lower Boro NSW 109 E4
Lower Glenelg NP Vic 66 C7
Lower Light SA 233 J9
Lower Longley Tas 253 J5

INDEX OF PLACE NAMES 405

Lower Mookerawa NSW 110 C5
Lower Mount Hicks Tas 254 E4
Lower Norton Vic 66 E2
Lower Quipolly NSW 110 G1, 112 G10
Lower Turners Marsh Tas 255 K5
Lower Wilmot Tas 254 F6
Lowesdale NSW 117 L7
Lowlands NSW 115 J10, 117 J2
Lowmead Qld 134, 145 K1, 147 L10
Lowood Qld 144 B5
Lowther NSW 109 E1, 110 E8
Loxton SA 233 N9
Loxton North SA 233 N9
Lubeck Vic 66 F2
Lucaston Tas 253 J5
Lucinda Qld 149 M8
Lucindale Qld 151 J3
Lucindale SA 230 E9
Lucknow NSW 110 C7
Lucknow Qld 150 F7
Lucknow Vic 70 E6
Lucky Bay SA 232 G7
Lucy Creek NT 179 M4
Lucyvale Vic 73 L4
Lue NSW 110 E5
Luina Tas 254 D7
Luluigui WA 208 F9
Lulworth Tas 255 J4
Lumholtz NP Qld 149 M8
Lunawanna Tas 253 J8
Lundavra Qld 144 G8
Lune River Tas 253 H8
Lurnea Qld 144 B5
Lyal Vic 67 M3
Lymington Tas 253 J7
Lymwood Tas 254 F2
Lynchford Tas 252 C1, 254 D10
Lyndavale NT 178 G9
Lyndbrook Qld 149 K7, 155 A10
Lyndhurst NSW 109 C1, 110 C8
Lyndhurst Qld 149 J9
Lyndhurst SA 235 J10
Lyndoch SA 233 K9
Lyndon WA 204 D1, 210 D10
Lynwood Qld 153 K3
Lyons SA 232 A1
Lyons Vic 66 C7
Lyons River WA 204 D2
Lyonville Vic 64 D1, 67 L4
Lyrian Qld 148 E9, 150 F1
Lyrup SA 233 N8
Lysterfield Vic 65 J4

Mabel Creek SA 234 A7
Mabel Downs WA 209 M7
Mac Clark (Acacia Peuce) CR NT 179 L8
McAlinden WA 202 C7
Macalister Qld 145 J6
Macalister Qld 148 D7
Macalister River Vic 70 A4
Macaroni Qld 148 F5
Macarthur Vic 66 E7
McArthur River NT 177 L2, 300
McCallum Park NSW 114 D5
Macclesfield SA 230 A6, 233 K10
McClintock Range WA 209 L10
McColl Vic 69 M10
McCoys Well SA 233 K5
McCrae Vic 64 G6, 67 N8
MacDonald Downs NT 179 K4
Macdonald River NSW 80, 110 G6
McDonald River Qld 154 C4, 280–1
MacDonnell Ranges NT 179 K6
McDouall Peak SA 234 B9
McDougalls Well WA 114 A6
Macedon Vic 64 F1, 67 M4
McGullys Gap NSW 110 G4
Machans Beach Qld 149 L5, 155 D7, 291
Macintyre River NSW 112 C3, 143
Mackay Qld 146 G4
McKenzie Creek Vic 66 E2
Mackenzie River Vic 66 E2
Mackerel Islands WA **310–11**
McKinlay Qld 150 F4
Macknade Qld 149 M8
Macks Creek Vic 70 A9
Macksville NSW 113 M8
Mackunda Downs Qld 150 F6
McLachlan SA 232 D7
McLaren Creek NT 177 H9

McLaren Vale SA 230 A5, 233 J10
Maclean NSW 113 N5, 266
Macleay River NSW 113 L9, 269
McLoughlins Beach Vic 70 B9
McMahons Creek Vic 65 L3, 72 D10
McMahons Reef NSW 109 B3
Macorna Vic 69 L8
Macquarie Harbour Tas 252 B2, **326–7**
Macquarie Marshes NR NSW 115 N5
Macquarie Plains Tas 239, 253 H4
Macquarie River NSW 110 B4, 115 N7
Macquarie River Tas **246**
Macrossan Qld 146 B2, 149 M10
Macs Cove Vic 72 E8
Macumba SA 234 D3
Macumba River SA 234 C3, 234 F4
Madoonga WA 204 G5
Madura WA 207 E7
Madura Hotel WA 207 E7
Mafeking Qld 146 A9, 151 P9
Mafeking Vic 66 F4
Maffra Vic 70 B6
Maffra West Upper Vic 70 B6
Magela Creek NT 172–3
Magenta NSW 116 F3
Maggea SA 233 M9
Maggieville Qld 148 E6
Maggot Point Tas 253 J7
Maggy Creek Qld 150 E5
Magnetic Island NP Qld 149 N9, 288
Magowra Qld 148 E7
Magra Tas 253 J4
Magrath Flat SA 230 B7
Mahanewo SA 232 E3
Mahrigong Qld 151 K6
Maiala NP Qld 145 M7
Maiden Gully Vic 67 L2
Maiden Springs Qld 149 J10, 151 L1
Maidenhead Qld 145 K10
Mailors Flat Vic 66 F8
Main Creek NSW 111 K4
Main Range NP Qld 145 L8
Main Ridge Vic 64 G6, 67 P8
Maindample Vic 72 E7
Mainoru NT 175 H7
Maison Dieu NSW 111 H5
Maitland NSW 111 J5
Maitland SA 233 H9
Maitland Downs Qld 149 K4, 155 B5
Majorca Vic 67 K3
Majors Creek NSW 109 E5
Malacura Qld 149 H8
Malanda Qld 149 L6, 155 D9
Malbina Tas 253 J4
Malbon Qld 150 E4
Malbooma SA 232 B1
Malcolm WA 205 M8
Maldon Vic 67 L3
Malebelling WA 202 D4
Malebo NSW 117 N6
Maldon Qld 145 M5
Malinong SA 230 B7
Mallacoota Vic 48, 71 N5, 258
Mallacoota Inlet Vic **48**, 48–9, 71 N5, **258–9**, 258
Mallala SA 233 J9
Mallanganee NSW 113 M3
Mallapunyah NT 177 L3
Mallee WA 204 D7
Mallee Cliffs NP NSW 116 D4
Mallett SA 233 K6
Mallina WA 210 G6
Mallowa NSW 112 C5
Malmsbury Vic 67 M3
Maloneys Qld 144 G1
Maltee SA 232 A4
Malua Bay NSW 109 F6
Malverton Qld 151 N10, 153 N1
Mambray Creek SA 233 H5
Manangatang Vic 68 G5
Manangoora NT 175 M10, 177 M1
Manara NSW 114 E10, 116 E1
Manara NSW 114 G7
Manberry WA 204 C1, 210 C10
Manbulloo NT 174 F8
Manchester NSW 112 A5
Mandagery NSW 110 A7
Mandalay NSW 114 E5
Mandemar NSW 109 F3, 110 F10
Mandora WA 211 L4
Mandorah NT 159, 174 C4

Mandurah WA 182, *182*, 202 B5
Mandurama NSW 109 C1, 110 C8
Maneroo Qld 151 L8
Manfred NSW 116 F2
Manfred WA 204 E5
Manfred Downs Qld 150 G2
Mangalo SA 232 F7
Mangalore NSW 115 L7
Mangalore Tas 253 K4
Mangalore Vic 67 P3, 72 B7
Mangana Tas 255 M7
Mangaroon WA 204 D1, 210 D10
Mangkili Claypan NR NSW 206 B9
Mangooya Vic 68 G4
Mangoplah NSW 117 M7
Manguel Creek WA 208 E8, 211 P1
Manguri SA 234 B7
Manildra NSW 110 B7
Manilla NSW 112 G8
Manilla NSW 116 C2
Maningrida NT 175 J3
Manjimup WA 200, 202 C8
Manly NSW 111 H8
Manmanning WA 202 E2
Mann River NSW 113 K5, 267
Mann River NR NSW 113 K5
Mannahill SA 233 M5
Mannanarie SA 233 J6
Mannerim Vic 64 F5, 67 M7
Manners Creek NT 179 P3
Mannibadar Vic 64 A3, 67 J6
Manning Point NSW 111 M3
Mannum SA 233 L10
Mannus NSW 109 A6, 117 P7
Manobalai NSW 110 G4
Manoora SA 233 K8
Mansfield Vic 72 E7
Manton Dam Park NT 174 D5
Mantung SA 233 M9
Mantuan Downs Qld 144 C1, 146 D10
Manumbar Qld 145 L5
Manunda SA 233 M5
Many Peaks Qld 145 K1, 147 L10
Manya Vic 68 B5
Manypeaks WA 202 F9
Mapala Qld 144 F2
Mapleton Qld 145 M5
Mapoon Aboriginal Community Qld 154 B4
Mapperley Park Qld 150 F3
Maralinga SA 231 D7
Marambir NSW 112 E5
Maranalgo WA 204 G9
Maranboy NT 174 F8
Marandoo WA 210 G8
Marathon Qld 151 K3
Marble Bar WA 211 J6
Marburg Qld 145 M7
March NSW 110 C7
Marchagee WA 202 C1, 204 E10
Marcoola Beach Qld 126, 129
Marcus Beach Qld 126, 129
Mardan Vic 65 M6
Mardathuna WA 204 C2
Mardie WA 210 E6
Mareeba Qld 149 L5, 155 D8
Marengo Vic 64 B8, 67 K9
Marengo Plain NSW 113 L7
Marfield NSW 114 G9
Margaret River WA 194, 196–7, *196*, 202 A8
Margaret River WA 202 B8
Margaret River WA 209 K10
Margate Tas 253 K6
Maria Downs Qld 144 E6
Maria Island Tas 253 N3
Maria Island NP Tas 253 N4
Mariala NP Qld 153 N4
Marian Qld 146 G4
Maribyrnong River Vic 47
Marillana WA 211 J8
Marimo Qld 150 E3
Marina Plains Qld 149 J2, 154 E9
Marion Bay SA 230 A2, 232 F10
Marion Downs Qld 150 D8
Marita Downs Qld 151 K6
Markwell NSW 111 K4
Markwood Vic 72 G5
Marla SA 234 A4, 231 G3
Marlborough Qld 147 H7

Marlo Vic 71 J6
Marmion Marine Park WA 202 B4
Marnoo Vic 66 G2
Marnoo East Vic 66 G2
Maronan Qld 150 F4
Marong Vic 67 L2
Maronga Qld 144 E7
Maroochy River Qld 126, 127, 128–7
Maroochydore Qld 126, 128, 129
Maroon Qld 145 M8
Maroona Vic 66 G4
Maroonah WA 210 D9
Maroota NSW 111 H7
Marqua NT 179 N4
Marrabel SA 233 K8
Marradong WA 202 D6
Marrakai CR NT 174 D4
Marramarra NP NSW 111 H8
Marrapina WA 114 C6
Marrar NSW 117 N5
Marrawah Tas 254 A4
Marree SA 235 H8
Marrilla WA 210 C9
Marron WA 204 C3
Marryat SA 231 G1
Marsden NSW 117 N3
Marshall Vic 64 E5, 67 M7
Martin Washpool CP SA 230 C8
Martins Creek NSW 111 J5
Martins Well SA 233 K3
Marton Qld 149 L3, 155 C3
Marulan NSW 109 E3
Marungi Vic 72 C4
Marvel Loch WA 203 H3
Mary Kathleen Qld 150 D3
Mary River NT 164, 174 E6
Mary River 130, 145 M3
Mary River CR NT 174 E4
Mary River Roadhouse NT 174 F5
Mary Springs WA 204 C6
Maryborough Qld 130, 145 M3
Maryborough Vic 67 K3
Maryfarms Qld 149 L5, 155 C6
Maryfield NT 174 G10, 176 G1
Maryknoll Vic 65 K4
Marysville Vic 65 L2, 72 D9
Maryvale NSW 110 B5
Maryvale NT 179 K7
Maryvale Qld 145 L8
Maryvale Qld 144 B5
Maryvale Qld 149 L10, 151 N1
Massey Vic 68 G9
Massey Downs Qld 144 E5
Matakana NSW 115 K10, 117 K1
Mataranka NT 174 G8
Matheson NSW 113 J5
Mathiesons Vic 67 P1, 72 A5
Mathinna Tas 247, 255 M7
Mathoura NSW 117 H7
Matlock Vic 65 N2, 72 F10
Matong NSW 117 M5
Maude NSW 116 G5
Maude Vic 64 D4, 67 L6
Maudville NSW 111 J3
Maules Creek NSW 112 E8
Mawbanna Tas 254 D4
Mawson WA 202 E4
Maxwelton Qld 151 J3
Maxwelton Qld 151 J3
May Downs Qld 146 G7
May River WA 208 F7, 304
May Vale Qld 148 F7
Maya WA 202 D1, 204 E10
Mayanup WA 202 D8
Mayberry Tas 254 G7
Maybole NSW 113 J6
Maydena Tas 252 G4
Mayfield Qld 144 A5, 153 P5
Mayfield Bay Coastal Reserve Tas 253 N1, 255 N10
Maynards Well SA 233 K1, 235 K10
Mayneside Qld 151 H8
Mayrung NSW 117 J7
Maytown (ruins) Qld 149 J4, 155 A5
Mayvale Qld 144 A8, 153 P8
Mazeppa NP Qld 146 D6
Mead Vic 69 L8
Meadow Downs SA 233 K5
Meadow Flat NSW 110 E7
Meadow Glen NSW 115 J7
Meadowbank Qld 149 K7

Meadows SA 230 A6, 233 K10
Meadowvale Qld 146 C1, 149 M10
Meandarra Qld 144 G6
Meander Tas 255 H7
Meander River Tas 246, **247**
Meatian Vic 69 J7
Meckering WA 202 D4
Meda WA 208 F7
Meda River WA 208 F7, 304
Medlow Bath NSW 109 F1, 110 F8
Medowie NSW 111 K5
Meeberrie WA 204 E5
Meedo WA 204 C4
Meekatharra WA 205 H5
Meeline WA 205 H8
Meelup WA 196
Meeniyan Vic 65 M7
Meeragoolia WA 204 C2
Meerlieu Vic 70 D6
Meetus Falls FR Tas 255 M9
Megan NSW 113 M7
Megine Qld 144 E6
Meka WA 204 F6
Mekaree Qld 153 M1
Melangata WA 204 F7
Melbourne Vic **38**, **46–7**, *46*, 64 G3, 67 P6
Melinda Downs Qld 148 D10, 150 E1
Melita WA 205 M8
Mella Tas 254 B3
Mellenbye WA 204 E8
Melmoth Qld 146 G8
Melrose NSW 115 M9, 117 M1
Melrose Qld 233 J5
Melrose Tas 254 G5
Melrose WA 205 L7
Melton SA 233 H8
Melton SA 233 L4
Melton Vic 64 F2, 67 M5
Melton Grove NSW 116 F2
Melton Mowbray Tas 253 J3
Melton South Vic 64 F3, 67 M5
Melville Forest Vic 66 D5
Melville Island NT 174 D2, **292–3**, 294, 296
Memana Tas 255 J2
Memerambi Qld 145 L5
Mena Murtee NSW 114 E7
Mena Park Qld 146 A10, 151 N10
Mena Park Vic 64 A2, 67 J5
Menangina WA 203 M1, 205 M10
Mendooran NSW 110 C3
Mengha Tas 254 C4
Menin Downs Qld 150 G6
Menindee NSW 114 D9
Menindee Lake NSW 114 C9
Meningie SA 222, 230 B7
Mentone Vic 65 H4, 67 P6
Mentor Outstation SA 234 C10
Menzies WA 205 L9
Merah North NSW 112 C7
Meran West Vic 69 K8
Merapah Qld 154 C8
Merbein Vic 68 E2
Merbein South Vic 68 D2
Mercadool NSW 112 A6
Mercunda SA 233 M9
Meredith Vic 64 C3, 67 L6
Mergenia SA 233 K5
Meribah SA 233 N9
Merildin SA 233 K8
Merimbula NSW 109 E9, **274**
Merimbula Lake NSW 274
Meringandan Qld 141, 145 L7
Meringur Vic 68 B2
Meringur North Vic 68 B2
Merino Vic 66 C5
Merivale Qld 144 E3
Merluna Qld 154 C6
Mernda Vic 65 H2, 67 P5, 72 A10
Mernmerna SA 233 J3
Merolia WA 205 N8
Merredin WA 202 F3
Merriang Vic 65 H1, 67 P5, 72 A9
Merriang Vic 72 G5
Merricks Vic 65 H6, 67 P8
Merrigang Qld 144 B5
Merrigum Qld 69 P1, 69 P10, 72 B4
Merrijig Vic 72 F8
Merrinee Vic 68 D2

INDEX OF PLACE NAMES

Merrinee North Vic 68 D2
Merriot Qld 144 F9
Merriton SA 233 J7
Merriula Qld 151 J3
Merriwa NSW 110 F4
Merriwagga NSW 117 J3
Merrygoen NSW 110 C3
Merrywinebone NSW 112 B5
Merseylea Tas 254 G6
Merton Vic 72 D7
Merton Vale NSW 117 L8
Mertondale WA 205 M8
Merty Merty SA 235 M6
Merungle NSW 117 H3
Messent CP SA 230 C8
Metcalfe Vic 67 M3
Metford NSW 111 J5
Methul NSW 117 M5
Metung Vic 51, 53, 70 F6
Meunna Tas 254 D5
Mexico Qld 146 B9
Mia Mia Vic 67 M3
Mia Mia WA 210 C9
Miakite Vic 66 D6
Miallo Qld 149 L5, 155 C6
Miandetta NSW 115 M7
Miawood Qld 144 F5
Michaelmas Reef Qld 149 M5, 155 E6
Michelago NSW 109 C6
Mickibri NSW 110 A6, 115 P10, 117 P1
Mickleham Vic 64 G2, 67 N5
Middalya WA 204 C1, 210 C10
Middle Beach SA 233 J9
Middle Camp NSW 114 B9, 116 B1
Middle Creek Qld 134, 135
Middle Harbour NSW 76–7
Middle Park Qld 149 H10, 151 K1
Middle Point NT 174 D4
Middle Tarwin Vic 65 L8
Middleback SA 232 G6
Middlemount Qld 146 F7
Middleton Qld 150 G6
Middleton SA 230 A5
Middleton Tas 253 K6
Middleton Park Qld 150 G6
Midge Point Qld 146 F3
Midgee Qld 147 J8
Midgee SA 232 G7
Midland WA 202 C4
Midway Point Tas 253 L4
Miena Tas 255 H9
Miepoll Vic 72 C5
Miga Lake Vic 66 C3
Mil Lel SA 230 F10
Mila NSW 109 C9
Milabena Tas 254 D4
Milang SA 230 A6
Milang Well SA 233 K4
Milawa Vic 72 F5
Milbong Qld 145 M8
Milbrulong NSW 117 M6
Mildura Vic 68 E2, 267
Miles Qld 145 H5
Mileura WA 204 G5
Milgarra Qld 148 E7
Milgery Qld 150 G4
Milgun WA 205 H3
Milguy NSW 112 F4
Milikapiti NT 174 C2
Miling WA 202 C2
Milingimbi NT 175 K3
Milkengay NSW 116 C2
Milkshakes Hills FR Tas 254 C5
Millaa Millaa Qld 149 L6, 155 D9
Millajiddee WA 208 G10
Millaroo Qld 146 D2, 149 N10
Millbillillie WA 205 K5
Millbrook Vic 64 C2, 67 L5
Millers Creek SA 234 E4
Millgrove Vic 65 K3, 72 C10
Millicent SA 230 F9
Millie NSW 112 D6
Millie Windie WA 209 J7
Millmerran Qld 142, 145 K8
Milloo Vic 69 M10
Millrose WA 205 L5
Millstream WA 210 F7
Millstream-Chichester NP WA 210 G6
Millthorpe NSW 110 C7
Milltown Vic 66 D7
Millungera Qld 148 F10, 150 G1

Millwood NSW 117 M6
Milly Milly WA 204 F4
Milman Qld 147 J8
Milo Qld 153 M3
Milparinka NSW 114 C3
Milray Qld 146 A3, 151 P3
Milton NSW 109 F5
Milton Park NT 178 G5
Milton Park Qld 153 N1
Milvale NSW 117 P4
Milyakburra NT 175 L6
Mimili SA 231 F2
Mimong Qld 150 G4
Mimosa NSW 117 N5
Mimosa Park Qld 147 H10
Mimosa Rocks NP NSW 109 E8, *274*
Minamere Qld 151 H3
Minara WA 205 M8
Minburra SA 233 K5
Mincha Vic 69 L8
Minda NSW 116 D2
Mindarie SA 233 M10
Minderoo WA 210 D7
Mindie Qld 150 E3
Miners Rest Vic 64 B1, 67 K5
Minetta NSW 115 H3
Mingah Springs WA 205 H2
Mingary SA 233 N4
Mingay Vic 67 J6
Mingela Qld 146 C1, 149 N10
Mingenew WA 204 D9
Mingoola NSW 113 J3
Minhamite Vic 66 E6
Minilya WA 204 B1, 210 B10
Minilya Roadhouse WA 204 B1, 210 B10
Minimay Vic 66 B2
Mininera Vic 66 G5
Minjah Vic 66 F7
Minjilang NT 174 F2
Minlaton SA 233 H9
Minmindie Vic 69 K8
Minnamoolka Qld 149 K7
Minnamurra NSW 109 G3
Minnamurra River NSW 92, 93
Minnel Qld 144 G8
Minnie Creek WA 204 D1, 210 D10
Minnie Water NSW 113 N6, 267
Minnies Outstation Qld 148 G6
Minnipa SA 232 C5
Minnivale WA 202 E3
Minore NSW 110 A4
Mintabie SA 231 G3
Mintaro SA 233 K8
Minyip Vic 66 F1, 68 F10
Miram Vic 68 B10
Miram South Vic 66 C1, 68 C10
Miranda Downs Qld 148 F6
Mirani Qld 146 F4
Mirboo Vic 65 N7
Mirboo East Vic 65 N7
Mirboo North Vic 65 N6
Miriam Vale Qld 134, 135, 145 K1, 147 L10
Mirikata SA 234 C9
Mirimbah Vic 70 A3, 72 F8
Miriwinni Qld 149 M6, 155 E9
Mirool NSW 117 M4
Mirtna Qld 146 B4
Missabotti NSW 113 M8
Mission Beach Qld 149 M7, 155 E10, 288
Mistake Creek NT 176 A3
Mitakoodi Qld 150 E3
Mitchell Qld 144 D5
Mitchell and Alice Rivers NP Qld 148 F3
Mitchell River Qld 148 F3
Mitchell River Vic 50, 53, 70 D5, **260–1**
Mitchell River WA 209 J3, 302
Mitchell River NP Vic 70 D5, 73 K10
Mitchells Flat NSW 113 J8
Mitchellstown Vic 67 P2, 72 A6
Mitchellville SA 232 G7
Mitiamo Vic 69 L9
Mitre Vic 66 D2
Mitta Junction Vic 73 H3
Mitta Mitta Vic 60, 73 K5
Mitta Mitta River Vic **60–1**, *61*, 73 J4, 264

Mittagong NSW 109 F3, 110 F10
Mittagong Qld 148 G8
Mittebah NT 177 N6
Mittyack Vic 68 G5
Moa Island Qld 154 C1, 279
Moalie Park WA 114 D3
Moama NSW 117 H8
Moble Qld 153 L6
Moble Springs Qld 153 M5
Mockinya Vic 66 E3
Moculta NSW 115 K4
Modanville NSW 113 N2
Modella Vic 65 L5
Moe Vic 65 N5
Mogal Plain NSW 115 M9
Moglonemby Vic 72 C6
Mogo NSW 109 E6
Mogong NSW 110 B7
Mogriguy NSW 110 B3
Mogumber WA 202 C3
Moina Tas 254 F7
Mokepilly Vic 66 F3
Mole Creek Tas 254 G7
Mole River NSW 113 J3, 143
Molesworth Qld 151 J3
Molesworth Tas 253 J4
Molesworth Vic 72 C8
Moliagul Vic 67 K2
Molka Vic 72 C6
Mollerin WA 202 E2
Mollerin NR WA 202 E2
Mollongghip Vic 64 C1, 67 L5
Mollymook NSW 109 F5
Mologa Vic 69 L9
Molong NSW 110 B6
Molonglo River ACT 104, 108
Moltema Tas 255 H6
Momba NSW 114 F6
Momba Qld 148 F9
Mona Qld 144 D8
Mona Vale NSW 111 H8
Mona Vale Qld 153 M4
Monadnocks CP WA 202 C5
Monak NSW 116 C4
Monarto South SA 230 A6, 233 K10
Monash SA 233 N8
Monbulk Vic 65 J3
Mondure NSW 115 K4
Monegeeta Vic 64 F1, 67 N4
Mongarlowe NSW 109 E5
Monia Gap NSW 117 K3
Monivea NSW 114 G10, 116 G1
Monkey Mia WA 204 B4, 313
Monkira Qld 152 E2
Monogorilby Qld 145 J4
Monolon NSW 114 E4
Mons Qld 151 M10, 153 M1
Monstraven NSW 148 E10, 150 F1
Montagu Tas 254 B3
Montague Island NSW 109 F7, **272–4**
Montana Tas 255 H7
Monteagle NSW 109 A2, 110 A10
Montebello Islands CP WA 210 D5, 308
Montefiores NSW 110 B5
Montejinni NT 176 E2
Monto Qld 145 J2
Montumana Tas 254 D4
Montville Qld 145 M5
Montys Hut Vic 65 M2, 72 E10
Moockra SA 233 J5
Moodiarrup WA 202 D7
Moogara Tas 253 H4
Moojebing WA 202 E7
Mooka WA 204 C2
Moolah NSW 115 H9
Moolawatana SA 235 L9
Moolbong NSW 117 H2
Mooleulooloo SA 233 N3
Mooleyarrah NSW 114 G2
Mooloo Downs WA 204 E3
Mooloogool WA 205 J3
Mooloolaba Qld 126, 145 N5
Mooloolah River Qld 126
Mooloolerie NSW 114 D10, 116 D1
Moolooloo SA 233 J2
Moolooloo Outstation NT 176 E2
Moolort Vic 67 K3
Moolpa NSW 116 F6
Moomba SA 235 M5
Moombidary Qld 153 L10

Moomboldool NSW 117 L4
Moona Plains NSW 113 K9
Moonagee NSW 115 M6
Moonan Flat NSW 111 H3
Moonaran NSW 112 G9
Moonaree SA 232 D4
Moonbah NSW 109 B8
Moonbi NSW 113 H9
Moondarra Vic 65 N4
Moondarra SP Vic 65 N4
Moondene NSW 114 G10, 116 G1
Moonford Qld 145 J2
Moongobulla Qld 149 M9
Moonee Beach NSW 113 N7
Moonie Qld 145 H7
Moonlight Flat SA 232 C6
Moonta SA 233 H8
Moonta Bay SA 232 G8
Moonyoonooka WA 204 C8
Moopina WA 207 Q7
Moora WA 202 C2
Moorabbin Vic 65 H4, 67 P6
Mooraberree Qld 152 F2
Moorabie NSW 114 A4
Moorak Qld 144 C4
Mooral Creek NSW 111 L2
Mooralla Vic 66 E4
Mooramanna Qld 144 E8
Moorarie WA 204 G4
Moore NSW 112 G9
Moore Qld 145 L6
Moore Park Qld 145 L1
Moore River NP WA 202 B3
Mooreland Downs NSW 114 G2
Mooren Creek NSW 110 D2
Mooreville Tas 254 E5
Moorine Rock WA 203 H3
Moorinya NP Qld 151 M4
Moorland NSW 111 M3
Moorland Qld 145 L2
Moorlands SA 230 A7
Moorleah Tas 254 D4
Moorooduc Vic 65 H5, 67 P7
Moorook SA 233 M8
Mooroopna Vic 72 B5
Mooroopna North Vic 72 B4
Moorumbine WA 202 E5
Moothandella Qld 153 J3
Mootwingee NSW 114 C6
Mootwingee NP NSW 114 D6
Moppin NSW 112 D4
Moquilambo NSW 115 K6
Moraby Qld 144 G6
Morago NSW 117 H6
Moranbah Qld 146 E6
Morang South Vic 65 H2, 67 P5, 72 A10
Morangarell NSW 117 N4
Morapoi WA 205 M9
Morawa WA 204 E9
Moray Downs Qld 146 C5
Morbining WA 202 E5
Morchard SA 233 J5
Morden NSW 114 C5
Mordialloc Vic 40, 65 H4, 67 P6
Morecambe Qld 149 K7, 155 C10
Moree NSW 112 E5
Moree Vic 66 C4
Moreenia SA 232 E8
Morehead River Qld 278–9
Morella Qld 151 L7
Morestone Qld 150 B1
Moreton Bay Qld **122–3**, 145 N6
Moreton Island Qld *119*, 122, 123, **124–5**, *124–5*, 145 N6
Moreton Island NP Qld 145 N6
Morgan SA 233 L8
Morgan Vic 70 C5
Morgan Vale SA 233 N6
Moriac Vic 64 D5, 67 L7
Moriarty Tas 254 G5
Morisset NSW 111 J6
Morkalla Vic 68 B2
Morney Qld 152 G3
Morning Side NSW 114 G10, 116 G1
Mornington Vic *41*, 65 H5, 67 P7
Mornington WA 209 J8
Mornington Island Qld 148 C5, **282–3**, *282*, *283*, 285
Mornington Peninsula NP Vic 64 F6, 67 N8
Moroak NT 175 H8

Morongla Creek NSW 109 B1, 110 B9
Mororo NSW 113 N4
Morpeth NSW 111 J5
Morpeth Qld 146 F6
Morri Morri Vic 66 G2
Morstone Qld 148 A9
Mortchup Vic 64 A2, 67 J5
Mortlake Vic 66 G7
Morton NP NSW 109 E4
Morton Plains NSW 115 L1
Morton Plains Vic 68 G9
Morundah NSW 117 L6
Moruya NSW 109 E6
Moruya Heads NSW 109 E6
Morven Qld 144 C5
Morwell Vic 65 P5, 70 A8
Morwell NP Vic 65 P6
Moselle Qld 151 K3
Mosman Bay WA 185, 190
Moss Vale NSW 109 F3
Mossgiel NSW 116 G2
Mossiface Vic 70 F5, 73 L10
Mossman Qld 149 L5, 155 C6
Mossy Point NSW 109 E6
Motpena SA 233 J2
Moulamein NSW 116 G6
Moulyinning WA 202 F7
Mount Aberdeen Qld 146 E2
Mount Aberdeen NP Qld 146 E2
Mount Adrah NSW 117 P6
Mount Alfred Qld 153 N6
Mount Alfred Vic 73 L3
Mount Amhurst WA 209 L9
Mount Anderson WA 208 F9
Mount Arapiles – Tooan SP Vic 66 C2
Mount Arrowsmith NSW 114 B4
Mount Augustus WA 204 F2
Mount Augustus NP WA 204 F2
Mount Barker SA 230 A6, 233 K10
Mount Barker WA 202 E9
Mount Barkly NT 178 F2
Mount Barnett WA 209 J6
Mount Barney NP Qld 145 M8
Mount Barry SA 234 C6
Mount Beauty Vic 60, 70 D1, 73 J6
Mount Beckworth Vic 64 B1, 67 K4
Mount Benson SA 230 E8
Mount Best Vic 65 N7
Mount Bogong Vic 60, 73 K6
Mount Boothby CP SA 230 B7
Mount Brockman WA 210 F8
Mount Brown CP SA 233 H5
Mount Bryan SA 233 K7
Mount Buangor SP Vic 67 H4
Mount Buckley Qld 146 E2
Mount Buffalo Vic 60
Mount Buffalo NP Vic 70 B1, 73 H6
Mount Buller Alpine Village Vic 70 A3, 72 F8
Mount Burges WA 203 K2
Mount Burr SA 230 F9
Mount Bute Vic 64 A3, 67 J6
Mount Campbell Qld 151 H5
Mount Carbine Qld 149 K5, 155 C6
Mount Cavenagh NT 178 G10
Mount Celia WA 205 N9
Mount Charlton Qld 146 F4
Mount Christie SA 231 G8
Mount Clarence SA 234 B7
Mount Clear Vic 64 C2, 67 K5
Mount Clere WA 204 G3
Mount Compass SA 230 A5
Mount Cook NP Qld 149 L3, 155 C3
Mount Coolon Qld 146 D4
Mount Cornish Qld 151 M7
Mount Damper SA 232 C6
Mount Dandenong Vic 65 J3
Mount Dangar Qld 146 E2
Mount Dare SA 234 C1
Mount Darrah NSW 109 D9
Mount David NSW 109 D1, 110 D8
Mount Denison NT 178 E3
Mount Direction Tas 255 J5
Mount Doran Vic 64 C3, 67 L5
Mount Douglas Qld 146 C5
Mount Driven Qld 144 F8
Mount Dutton SA 234 D5
Mount Eba SA 235 D10
Mount Ebenezer NT 178 F8
Mount Eccles Vic 65 M6
Mount Eccles NP Vic 66 D7
Mount Edgar WA 211 K6

INDEX OF PLACE NAMES 407

Mount Egerton Vic 64 D2, 67 L5
Mount Eliza Vic 65 H5, 67 P7
Mount Elizabeth WA 209 J5
Mount Elsie Qld 146 C4
Mount Emu Vic 64 A2, 67 J5
Mount Emu Plains Qld 149 K10, 151 M2
Mount Etna Qld 151 H5
Mount Evelyn Vic 65 J3
Mount Farmer WA 204 G7
Mount Featherchop Vic 61, 73 J7
Mount Field NP Tas 252 G3
Mount Fitton SA 235 L9
Mount Florance WA 210 G7
Mount Frankland NP WA 202 D9
Mount Freeling SA 235 K9
Mount Gambier SA 226, 227, 230 F10
Mount Gap NSW 115 H6
Mount Garnet Qld 149 K7, 155 C10
Mount George NSW 111 K3
Mount Gibson WA 204 G9
Mount Gipps NSW 114 B7
Mount Gipps NSW 114 B8
Mount Gould WA 204 G4
Mount Granya SP Vic 73 K3
Mount Grenfell NSW 115 J6
Mount Hale WA 204 G4
Mount Harden Qld 153 M2
Mount Hart WA 208 G6
Mount Helen Vic 64 C2, 67 K5
Mount Hill SA 232 E8
Mount Hope NSW 115 K10, 117 K1
Mount Hope Qld 146 C4
Mount Hope SA 232 D8
Mount Hopeless SA 235 L8
Mount Horeb NSW 109 A4, 117 P6
Mount House WA 209 J7
Mount Howe Qld 144 D2
Mount Howitt Qld 153 H5
Mount Hyland NR NSW 113 L7
Mount Imlay NP NSW 109 D9
Mount Irvine NSW 110 F7
Mount Isa Qld 150 C3
Mount Ive SA 232 E5
Mount Jack NSW 114 F5
Mount Jackson WA 203 H1, 205 J10
Mount James WA 204 F2
Mount Jowlaenga WA 208 E8, 211 P1
Mount Julian Qld 146 F2
Mount Kaputar NP NSW 112 E7
Mount Keith WA 205 K6
Mount Kokeby WA 202 D5
Mount Kosciuszko NSW 109 A8
Mount Larcom Qld 147 K9
Mount Lawson SP Vic 73 K3
Mount Leonard Qld 152 E3
Mount Lewis NSW 115 L7
Mount Liebig NT 178 D5
Mount Lion NSW 113 M2
Mount Lloyd Tas 253 H5
Mount Lofty Ranges SA 226, 233 K10
Mount Lonarch Vic 67 J4
Mount Lonsdale Qld 144 D5
Mount Lyndhurst SA 235 J10
Mount Macedon Vic 64 F1, 67 N4
Mount Madden WA 203 J7
Mount Magnet WA 204 G7
Mount Manara NSW 114 F9
Mount Manning NR WA 203 J1, 205 J10
Mount Manning Range WA 205 J10
Mount Margaret Qld 153 K6
Mount Margaret WA 205 N8
Mount Maria Qld 144 C5
Mount Marlow Qld 153 K2
Mount Martha Vic 39, 65 H5, 67 P7
Mount Mary SA 233 L8
Mount McConnel Qld 146 C3
Mount McLaren Qld 146 E6
Mount Mee Qld 145 M6
Mount Mercer Vic 64 C3, 67 K6
Mount Minnie WA 210 D7
Mount Mistake NP Qld 145 L8
Mount Mitchell NSW 113 K6
Mount Molloy Qld 149 L5, 155 C7
Mount Monger WA 203 M3
Mount Morgan Qld 147 J9
Mount Moriac Vic 64 D5, 67 L7
Mount Morris Qld 153 N4
Mount Mulgrave Qld 149 J4
Mount Mulligan Qld 149 K5, 155 B7
Mount Mulyah NSW 114 G4

Mount Murchison NSW 114 F7
Mount Napier SP Vic 66 E6
Mount Narryer WA 204 E5
Mount Nebo Qld 145 M7
Mount Norman Qld 149 H10, 151 K1
Mount Ossa Qld 146 F3
Mount Padbury WA 204 G4
Mount Pelion Qld 146 F3
Mount Perry Qld 145 K2
Mount Phillips WA 204 E2
Mount Pierre WA 209 J10
Mount Playfair Qld 144 B2
Mount Pleasant NSW 114 F6
Mount Pleasant Qld 144 E1
Mount Pleasant Qld 146 D9
Mount Pleasant SA 233 K9
Mount Poole NSW 114 B3
Mount Prospect Vic 64 C1, 67 L4
Mount Remarkable WA 205 M9
Mount Remarkable NP SA 233 H5
Mount Rescue CP SA 230 B9
Mount Richmond Vic 66 C7
Mount Richmond NP Vic 66 C7
Mount Riddock NT 179 J5
Mount Ringwood NT 174 D5
Mount Russell NSW 112 G5
Mount Samaria SP Vic 72 E7
Mount Sandiman WA 204 D2
Mount Sanford NT 176 C3
Mount Sarah SA 234 C3
Mount Scott CP SA 230 D8
Mount Seaview NSW 111 K1, 113 K10
Mount Serle SA 233 K1, 235 K10
Mount Seymour Tas 253 K2
Mount Shannon NSW 114 B3
Mount Shaugh CP SA 230 B10
Mount Skinner NT 179 H3
Mount Strzelecki Tas 255 J3, 324
Mount Stuart NSW 114 C2
Mount Stuart Qld 146 F7
Mount Stuart WA 210 E8
Mount Sturgeon Qld 149 J10, 151 L2
Mount Sturt NSW 114 B3
Mount Surprise Qld 149 J7
Mount Taylor Vic 70 E5, 73 L10
Mount Tenandra NSW 110 B1, 112 B10
Mount Timothy SA 230 B9
Mount Torrens SA 233 K10
Mount Tyson Qld 145 K7
Mount Vernon WA 205 H1
Mount Vetters WA 203 L1, 205 L10
Mount Victor SA 233 L4
Mount Victoria NSW 110 F8
Mount Victoria FR Tas 255 M6
Mount Vivian SA 232 D1, 234 D10
Mount Walker WA 202 G5
Mount Wallace Vic 64 D3, 67 L6
Mount Walsh NP Qld 145 L3
Mount Wedge NT 178 E4
Mount Wedge SA 232 C7
Mount Wedge FR Tas 252 F5
Mount Weld WA 205 N8
Mount Wellington Tas 253 J5
Mount Westwood NSW 114 B6
Mount Willoughby SA 234 A5
Mount Wilson NSW 110 F8
Mount Windsor Qld 150 G9
Mount Wittenoom WA 204 F6
Mount Wood NSW 114 C2
Mount Woowoolahra NSW 114 A6
Mount Worth SP Vic 65 M6
Mountain River Tas 253 J5
Mountain Valley NT 175 H7
Mountain View Qld 146 D1, 149 N10
Mountain View Qld 146 D7
Moura Qld 144 G1
Mourilyan Qld 144 D8
Mourilyan Qld 149 M6, 155 E9
Mourilyan Harbour Qld 149 M6, 155 E9
Mouroubra WA 202 E1, 204 G10
Moutajup Vic 66 E5
Mowanjum Community WA 208 F7, 211 P1
Mowbray Tas 255 K6
Mowla Bluff WA 208 E10, 211 P2
Moyhu Vic 72 F5
Moyston Vic 66 G4
Muccan WA 211 K5
Muchea WA 202 C4
Muckadilla Qld 144 E5

Muckatah Vic 72 C3
Muckaty NT 177 H6
Mudamuckla SA 232 A4
Mudgeacca Qld 150 D8
Mudgee NSW 99, 110 D5
Mudgeegonga Vic 73 H5
Mudgeeraba Qld 145 N8
Mudginberri NT 174 F4
Mudjimba Beach Qld 126, 129
Mudjimba Island Qld 127
Muggleton Qld 144 F5
Muggon WA 204 D5
Mukinbudin WA 202 F2
Mulga Downs WA 211 H7
Mulga Park NT 178 E10
Mulga Valley NSW 114 E4
Mulga View SA 233 K1
Mulgaria SA 234 G9
Mulgathing SA 234 A10
Mulgowie Qld 145 L7
Mulgul WA 205 H2
Mulka SA 235 J6
Mullaley NSW 110 E1, 112 E9
Mullaloo WA 202 B4
Mullamuddy NSW 110 D5
Mullengandra NSW 117 M8
Mullengudgery NSW 115 N7
Mullewa WA 204 D8
Mullion Creek NSW 110 C6
Mulloway Point NSW 113 N4
Mullumbimby NSW 113 P2
Muloorina SA 235 H8
Mulpata SA 230 A9, 233 N10
Multi Qld 145 H2
Muludja Community WA 209 J9
Mulwala NSW 117 K8
Mulya NSW 115 J5
Mulyandry NSW 117 P2
Mulyungarie SA 233 N3
Mumballup WA 202 C7
Mumbannar Vic 66 B6
Mumbil NSW 110 C5
Mummulgum NSW 113 M3
Mumu Qld 151 L3
Munarra WA 205 H4
Munburra Qld 149 K2, 154 G10, 155 C1
Mundabullangana WA 210 G5
Mundadoo NSW 115 M5
Mundaring WA 202 C4
Mundarlo NSW 117 P6
Munderoo NSW 117 P8
Mundijong WA 202 C5
Mundiwindi WA 205 K1, 211 K10
Mundoo Bluff Qld 146 A5, 151 N5
Mundoona Vic 72 B3
Mundoora SA 233 H7
Mundowdna SA 235 J9
Mundrabilla WA 207 E6
Mundrabilla WA 207 E7
Mundrabilla Motel WA 207 F7
Mundubbera Qld 145 K3
Mundulla SA 230 C9
Munduran Qld 150 G7
Mungabroom NT 177 J5
Mungala SA 231 F8
Mungallala Qld 144 C5
Mungana Qld 149 J6, 155 A8
Mungeranie SA 235 K5
Mungeranie Roadhouse SA 235 J5
Mungeribar NSW 115 P8
Mungerup WA 202 F8
Mungery NSW 115 P9
Mungindi NSW 112 C3, 142
Mungle NSW 112 F3
Munglinup WA 203 N9
Mungo NSW 116 E3
Mungo Brush NSW 89, 111 L5
Mungo NP NSW 116 E3
Mungunburra Qld 146 A2, 151 P2
Munni NSW 111 J4
Munro Vic 70 C6
Muntadgin WA 202 G4
Muntz NR WA 203 N7
Munyaroo CP SA 232 G7
Munyaroo CR SA 232 G7
Muradup WA 202 D8
Muralgarra WA 204 F8
Murbko SA 233 L8
Murchison Vic 67 P1, 72 B5
Murchison Downs WA 205 J5
Murchison East Vic 72 B5

Murchison House WA 204 C6
Murchison River WA 204 E5, 314–15, 315
Murchison Roadhouse WA 204 E5
Murdinga SA 232 D7
Murdong WA 202 E7
Murdunna Tas 240, 253 M5
Murgenella NT 174 G2, 294
Murgheboluc Vic 64 D5, 67 L6
Murgon Qld 142, 145 L4
Murgoo WA 204 E6
Murkaby SA 233 L7
Murmungee Vic 72 G5
Murninnie Beach SA 232 G7
Murnpeowie SA 235 K8
Muronbong NSW 110 B4
Murphys Creek Qld 145 L7
Murra Murra Qld 144 B8
Murra Warra Vic 66 E1, 68 E1
Murrabit Vic 69 L7
Murramarang NP NSW 96, 97 109 F5
Murrami NSW 117 L4
Murranji NT 176 G3
Murrawal NSW 110 C2
Murray Bridge SA 230 A7, 233 L10
Murray Downs NSW 116 F6
Murray Downs NT 177 J10, 179 J1
Murray Mouth SA 222, 223, 224–5, 225, 230 B6, 265
Murray River NSW 109 A7, 117 J8, 264–5, 264, 265
Murray River SA 212, 222, 228–9, 228, 229, 233 L9
Murray River Vic 68 F3, 69 K6, 72 A2
Murray River WA 201, 224, 225
Murray River NP SA 233 N9
Murray Town SA 233 J6
Murray-Kulkyne NP Vic 68 F4
Murray-Sunset NP Vic 68 B4
Murrayville Vic 68 B6
Murrin Bridge NSW 117 L2
Murrincal Vic 73 N9
Murrincindi Vic 65 K1, 72 C9
Murringo NSW 109 B2, 110 A10
Murroon Vic 64 B6, 67 K8
Murrum WA 204 G7
Murrumbateman NSW 109 C4
Murrumbidgee River NSW 109 J07, 116 F5, 276
Murrumburrah NSW 109 A3
Murrungowar Vic 71 J5
Murrurundi NSW 110 G2
Murtoa Vic 66 F1
Murwillumbah NSW 113 P1
Musgrave Qld 149 H2, 154 E1, 278
Musk Vic 64 D1, 67 L4
Muskerry East Vic 67 N2
Musselroro Tas 255 L7
Muswellbrook NSW 100, 110 H4
Mutchilba Qld 149 L6, 155 C8
Mutooroo SA 233 N5
Muttaburra Qld 151 M7
Muttama NSW 109 A4, 117 P5
Mutton Hole Qld 148 E6
Muttonbird Island NSW 268, 269
Myall NSW 114 F1
Myall Vic 69 L7
Napier Broome Bay WA 209 K2
Myall Creek NSW 112 G6
Myall Creek SA 153 P2
Myall Creek SA 232 G5
Myall Lakes NP NSW 89, 111 L5
Myalla Tas 254 D4
Myalup WA 195, 202 B6
Myamyn Vic 66 D6
Myaring Vic 66 B6
Myers Flat Vic 67 L2
Mylestom NSW 113 N8
Mylor SA 233 K10
Myola Qld 148 E9
Myola Vic 67 N1
Mypolonga SA 230 A7, 233 L10
Myponga SA 230 A5
Myponga Beach SA 230 A5
Myra Vae Qld 148 E6
Myrniong Vic 64 E2, 67 M5
Myrnong NSW 114 F3
Myro NSW 114 E4
Myroodah WA 208 F9
Myrrhee Vic 65 N3
Myrrlumbing Qld 146 A2, 149 N10, 151 P2
Myrtle Bank Tas 255 L6

Myrtle Scrub NSW 111 K1, 113 K10
Myrtle Springs SA 235 J10
Myrtle Vale NSW 115 J4
Myrtlebank Vic 70 C7
Myrtleford Vic 72 G5
Myrtleville NSW 109 E3, 110 E10
Myrtleville Qld 144 E3
Mysia Vic 69 K9
Mystic Park Vic 69 K7
Myubee Qld 150 D4
Myuna Qld 151 J4
Mywee Vic 72 C2
Mywyn Qld 149 J8

Nabageena Tas 254 C4
Nabarlek NT 174 G4
Nabawa WA 204 C8
Nabiac NSW 111 L3
Nabowla Tas 255 L5
Nackara SA 233 K5
Nadgee NR NSW 109 E10
Nagambie Vic 67 P2, 72 A6
Nagoorin Qld 145 K1, 147 K10
Nairana Qld 146 C5
Nairne SA 233 K10
Nalangil Vic 64 A6, 67 J8
Nalbarra WA 204 G8
Nalcoombie Qld 144 D1, 146 E10
Naldera Qld 144 E6
Nalinga Vic 72 D5
Nalkain WA 202 E3
Nallan WA 204 G6
Namadgi NP ACT 109 C6
Nambi WA 205 M7
Nambour Qld 128, 145 M5
Nambrok Vic 70 B7
Nambrok West Vic 70 B7
Nambucca Heads NSW 113 N8, 269
Nambucca River NSW 269
Nambung NP WA 202 B2
Namming NR WA 202 B3
Namoi River NSW 112 E8
Nana Glen NSW 113 N7
Nanami NSW 110 A8
Nanango Qld 145 L5
Nanardine NSW 115 P10, 117 P1
Nandaly Vic 68 G6
Nanga WA 204 B4
Nangar NP NSW 110 A7
Nangara NSW 114 G6
Nangeela Vic 66 B5
Nangeenan WA 202 F4
Nangerybone NSW 115 L9
Nangiloc Vic 68 F3
Nangus NSW 117 P6
Nangwarry SA 230 F10
Nanneella Vic 69 N9
Nannup WA 200, 202 C8
Nanson WA 204 C8
Nantawarra SA 233 J8
Nantawarrina SA 233 K1
Nantilla NSW 114 F4
Nanutarra WA 210 D8
Nanutarra Roadhouse WA 210 D8
Nanya NSW 116 A2
Nanya Qld 146 E7
Napier Broome Bay WA 209 K2
Napier Downs WA 208 G7
Napoleons Vic 64 B2, 67 K5
Nappa Merrie Qld 152 F7
Napperby NT 178 F4
Napperby SA 233 H6
Napranum Qld 154 B6
Napunyah NSW 114 G5
Naracoopa Tas 254 G2
Naracoorte SA 230 E9
Naradhan NSW 117 L3
Naraling WA 204 C8
Narbethong Vic 65 K2, 72 C10
Narcowla NSW 114 C2
Nardoo NSW 114 G2
Nardoo Qld 144 A7, 153 P7
Nardoo Qld 148 C8
Nareen Vic 66 C4
Narellan NSW 109 G2, 110 G9
Narembeen WA 202 F5
Naretha SA 153 L5
Naretha WA 207 B6
Nariel Vic 73 L5
Nariel Creek Vic 73 L4
Narine Qld 144 E10
Naringal Vic 66 G8

INDEX OF PLACE NAMES

Narkal WA 202 E2
Narline Qld 144 D9
Narloo WA 204 E7
Narndee WA 205 H8
Narooma NSW 109 E7, **272–3**
Narounyah Qld 146 C9
Narrabarba NSW 109 E10
Narrabeen NSW 111 H8
Narrabri NSW 112 E7
Narrabri West NSW 112 D7
Narraburra NSW 117 N4
Narracan Vic 65 N5
Narran Lake NSW 115 N3
Narran Park NSW 115 N3
Narrandera NSW 117 L5
Narraport Vic 69 H8
Narrawa NSW 109 C3, 110 C10
Narrawa Qld 149 J8
Narrawong Vic 66 D7
Narraway NSW 115 P6
Narre Warren Vic 65 J4
Narrewillock Vic 69 J9
Narridy SA 233 J7
Narrien Qld 146 C7
Narrien Range NP Qld 146 C7
Narrierra NSW 114 D2
Narrikup WA 202 E9
Narrina SA 233 K1
Narrogin WA 202 E6
Narromine NSW 110 A4, 115 P8
Narrung SA 230 B6
Narrung Vic 69 H4
Narwietooma NT 178 F5
Naryilco Qld 152 G9
Nashua NSW 113 P3
Natal Downs Qld 151 P4
Nathalia Vic 69 P9
Nathan River NT 175 K9, 177 K1
Natimuk Vic 66 D2
National Park Tas 252 G4
Native Point NT 166
Natone Tas 254 E5
Nattai NP NSW 109 F2, 110 F10
Natte Yallock Vic 67 J3
Naturi SA 230 A7, 233 L10
Natya Vic 69 H5
Nauiyu Nambiyu NT 174 C6
Navarre Vic 67 H2
Nayook Vic 65 M4
N'Dhala Gorge NP NT 179 J6
Nea NSW 110 F1, 112 F10
Neale Junction NR WA 207 C3
Nebo Qld 146 F5
Nectar Brook SA 233 H5
Neds Corner Vic 68 C2
Neds Creek WA 205 J3
Needle Creek Qld 153 K1
Needles Tas 255 H7
Neerabup NP WA 202 B4
Neerim Vic 65 M4
Neerim South Vic 62, 65 M4
Neeworra NSW 112 C3
Neika Tas 253 J5
Neilrex NSW 110 C2
Nelia Qld 151 H3
Nelia Ponds Qld 151 H3
Nelligen NSW 109 E6
Nellys Hut Qld 148 G6
Nelshaby SA 233 H6
Nelson Vic 66 A7
Nelson Bay NSW 111 K5
Nelson Springs NT 176 A4
Nelwood SA 233 N8
Nemeena NSW 115 M5
Nemingha NSW 113 H10
Nene Valley SA 230 G9
Nene Valley CP SA 230 G9
Nepabunna SA 233 K1, 235 K10
Nepean Bay SA 230 B3, 321
Nepean River NSW **80–1**, 110 F9
Nerang Qld 145 N8
Nerang River Qld 120, 121, 136, 137
Nereena Qld 151 L9
Nerong NSW 111 L5
Nerren Nerren WA 204 C6
Nerriga NSW 109 E4
Nerrigundah NSW 109 E7
Nerrigundah Qld 153 L6
Nerrima WA 208 G9
Nerrin Nerrin Vic 67 H6
Nerring Vic 64 A1, 67 J5
Netherby Vic 68 C9

Netherton SA 230 A8
Netley NSW 114 B9
Netley Gap SA 233 M5
Neuarpur Vic 66 B2
Neumayer Valley Qld 148 D8
Neutral Junction NT 179 H2
Nevertire NSW 115 N8
Neville NSW 109 C1, 110 C8
New Alton Downs SA 235 L2
New Armraynald Qld 148 C7
New Bamboo Qld 149 H2, 154 E9
New Chum NSW 115 H5
New Crown NT 179 J9
New Deer Qld 153 L1
New Dixie Qld 149 H2, 154 E10
New Dunmore Qld 145 J7
New England NP NSW 113 L8
New Forest WA 204 D6
New Gisborne Vic 64 F1, 67 N4
New Mollyan NSW 110 C2
New Moon Qld 149 L9
New Norcia WA 202 C3
New Norfolk Tas 239, 253 J4
New Springs WA 205 K4
New Strathgordon Qld 148 G2, 154 C10
New Victoria Downs Qld 146 B3
Newborough Vic 65 N5
Newbridge NSW 110 C8
Newbridge Vic 67 K2
Newbury Vic 64 D1, 67 M4
Newcastle NSW 111 J6
Newcastle Waters NT 176 G4
Newdegate WA 202 G6
Newell Qld 149 L5, 155 D6
Newham Vic 67 N4
Newhaven NT 178 D4
Newhaven Vic 43, 65 J7, 262
Newland Head CP SA 230 B5
Newlyn Vic 64 C1, 67 L4
Newman Qld 211 J9
Newmerella Vic 71 H5, 73 P10
Newminster WA 202 E5
Newnes NSW 110 F7
Newport Qld 147 H6
Newry NT 174 A10, 176 A1
Newry Vic 70 B6
Newstead Qld 144 F6
Newstead Vic 67 L3
Newton Boyd NSW 113 L6
Newtown Vic 64 B2, 67 K5
Ngangganawili WA 205 K5
Ngarkat CP SA 230 B9
Nguiu NT 174 C3
Ngukurr NT 175 J8
Nhill Vic 68 C10
Nhulunbuy NT 175 M4
Niagara Qld 146 D6
Niall Qld 149 L9
Niangala NSW 111 J1, 113 J10
Nicholls Rivulet Tas 253 J6
Nicholson Vic 70 F6
Nicholson WA 209 N9
Nicholson River Qld 148 A7, 285
Nicholson River Vic 50, 53, 70 E4, 73 K9, **260–1**
Nickol Bay WA 210 F5, 309
Nidgery Downs NSW 115 M5
Nietta Tas 254 F6
Nightcap NP NSW 113 N2
Nildottie SA 233 L9
Nile Tas 255 K7
Nilgen NR WA 202 B3
Nilma Vic 65 M5
Nilpena SA 233 J2
Nilpinna SA 234 E6
Nimaru Qld 144 A5, 153 P5
Nimbin NSW 113 N2
Nimboy Qld 153 N5
Nimby Creek NSW 109 B2
Nimmitabel NSW 109 D8
Ninda Vic 68 G6
Nindigully Qld 145 N7
Nineteen Lagoons Tas 329
Ninety Mile Beach SA 222–3
Ninety Mile Beach Vic 51, 52, **52**, 70 C9
Ningaloo WA 210 B8
Ningaloo Marine Park WA 210 B8
Ninghan WA 204 F9
Ninnes SA 233 H8
Ninyeunook Vic 69 J8

Nipan Qld 145 H2
Nippering WA 202 E7
Nirranda Vic 66 G8
Nita Downs WA 208 C10, 211 M3
Nithsdale Qld 150 F5
Nitmiluk NP NT 174 F7
Nive Downs Qld 144 B3
Noarlunga SA 230 A5, 233 J10
Noble Park Vic 65 H4
Noccundra Qld 153 J7
Nockatunga Qld 153 J7
Nocoleche NSW 114 G3
Nocoleche NR NSW 114 G3
Noella Qld 144 A3, 153 P3
Nome Qld 149 N9
Nonda Qld 151 H3
Nonnamah NSW 114 F4
Nonning SA 232 F5
Noojee Vic 65 M4
Nook Tas 254 G6
Nookawarra WA 204 F4
Noonamah NT 174 D4
Noonbah Qld 151 J10
Noonbinna NSW 109 B1, 110 B9
Noondie WA 204 F6
Noondoo Qld 144 E9
Noondoonia WA 203 P5, 207 A8
Noonga Qld 144 G5
Noongal WA 204 F7
Noonkanbah WA 208 G9
Noorama Qld 144 A9, 153 P9
Noorat Vic 66 G7
Noorinbee Vic 71 L4
Noorinbee North Vic 71 L4
Noosa Heads Qld 126, 127, **128–9**, **128**, 145 H8
Noosa NP Qld 127, 128, **129**, 145 N5
Noosa River Qld 127, 128, **138–9**, **139**
Nooyeah Downs Qld 153 K8
Nora Creina SA 230 E8
Noradjuha Vic 66 D2
Noraville NSW 111 J7
Noreena Downs WA 211 K8
Norfolk Qld 148 A9
Norfolk Bay Tas 241, 253 M6
Norie WA 205 H5
Norlane Vic 64 E5, 67 M7
Norley Qld 153 L7
Norman River Qld 148 E6, 284, **284**
Normanby River Qld 149 J1, 154 F9, 278–9
Normanton Qld 148 E7, 284
Normanville Vic 69 K8
Normanville SA 220, **221**, 230 A5
Nornalup WA 202 D10
Norong Vic 72 F3
Norong Central Vic 72 F3
Norseman WA 203 M5
North Bannister WA 202 D5
North Bourke NSW 115 K4
North Dandalup WA 202 C5
North Dorrigo NSW 113 M7
North East Island NP Qld 147 J5
North East River Tas 324
North Esk River Tas 246, **247**, 255 K7
North Haven NSW 111 M2
North Head Qld 149 H8
North Huntly Vic 67 M1
North Karlgarin NR WA 202 G5
North Keppel Island NP Qld 147 K8
North Molle Island Qld 146 F2
North Moolooloo SA 233 J1
North Motton Tas 254 F5
North Mulga SA 235 L10
North Peake SA 234 D5
North Peron Island NT 167, 174 B5
North Scottsdale Tas 255 L5
North Shields SA 232 D9
North Star NSW 112 F3
North Stradbroke Island Qld 122, 123, **124–5**, 145 N7
North Sydney NSW 111 H8
North Well SA 232 D1
North West Vernon Island NT 160, 174 D3
Northam WA 202 D4
Northampton WA 204 C7
Northcliffe WA 202 C9
Northdown Tas 254 G5
North-Eastern Estuaries Vic **48–9**

Northern Gully WA 204 C8
Norval Vic 66 G4
Norway NSW 109 E1, 110 E8
Norwich Park Qld 146 F7
Norwood Tas 255 K6
Nottingham Downs Qld 151 K4
Notts Well SA 233 L9
Nowa Nowa Vic 70 G5, 73 M10
Nowendoc NSW 111 J2
Nowhere Else SA 232 D8
Nowie North Vic 69 J6
Nowingi Vic 68 E3
Nowley NSW 112 C6
Nowra NSW 92, 109 F4
Nubeena Tas 240, 253 M6
Nuga Nuga NP Qld 144 E2
Nugadong WA 202 D1, 204 F10
Nugent Tas 253 M4
Nuggetty Vic 67 L3
Nukarni WA 202 F3
Nulla Qld 153 P8
Nulla Nulla Qld 149 L10, 151 N1
Nullagine WA 211 K7
Nullah Outstation Qld 152 F5
Nullamanna NSW 113 H5
Nullarbor NP SA 231 B9
Nullarbor Plain SA 231 B7
Nullarbor Plain WA 207 F6
Nullarbor Roadhouse SA 231 C9
Nullarbor RR SA 231 B8
Nullawa NSW 115 P2
Nullawarre Vic 66 G8
Nullawil Vic 69 H8
Nulty NSW 115 J4
Number One NSW 111 K2
Numbla Vale NSW 109 B8
Numbugga NSW 109 D8
Numbulwar NT 175 L7
Numeralla NSW 109 D7
Numery NT 179 K6
Numil Downs Qld 148 E10, 150 G1
Numinbah NSW 113 N1
Numinbah Valley Qld 145 N8
Numurkah Vic 72 C3
Nunamara Tas 255 K6
Nundle NSW 111 H2
Nundora NSW 114 C5
Nundroo SA 231 E10
Nunga Vic 68 F5
Nungarin WA 202 F3
Nungatta NSW 109 D10
Nungunyah NSW 114 G2
Nunjikompita SA 232 B4
Nunnyah CR SA 232 B4
Nunthewrungie NSW 114 D5
Nurcoung Vic 66 D2
Nurina WA 207 D6
Nuriootpa SA 233 K9
Nurrabiel Vic 66 E3
Nutwood Downs NT 175 H10, 177 H1
Nuyts Reef SA 231 E10
Nuytsland NR WA 207 B8
Nyabing WA 202 F7
Nyah Vic 69 J5
Nyah West Vic 69 J5
Nyamup WA 202 C8
Nyang WA 210 D9
Nyapari SA 231 C1
Nyarrin Vic 68 G5
Nychum Qld 149 K5, 155 A7
Nymagee NSW 115 L8
Nymboida NSW 113 M6
Nymboida NP NSW 113 L5
Nymboida River NSW 113 L5, 267
Nyngan NSW 115 M7
Nyngynderry NSW 114 E8
Nyora Vic 65 K6
Nypo Vic 68 E7

O B Flat SA 230 G10
Oak Park Qld 149 J9
Oak Park SA 233 L6
Oak Vale NSW 114 D5
Oak Vale Qld 151 N2
Oak Valley Qld 149 J10, 151 L1
Oakagee River WA 199
Oakbank SA 233 N6
Oakdale NSW 109 F2, 110 F9
Oakden Hills SA 232 G3
Oakenden Qld 146 G4
Oakey Qld 145 K7
Oakey Creek NSW 110 D2

Oakey Park Qld 144 D9
Oakham Qld 153 K3
Oaklands NSW 117 K7
Oaklands Junction Vic 64 G2, 67 N5
Oakleigh Qld 144 A4, 153 P4
Oakleigh Qld 146 C9
Oakleigh Vic 65 H4, 67 P6
Oakley Qld 151 N4
Oakpark NSW 144 A4, 153 P4
Oaks Tas 255 J7
Oakvale SA 233 N6
Oakvale Vic 69 J8
Oakwood NSW 113 H5
Oakwood Qld 144 A3, 153 P3
Oasis Roadhouse Qld 149 K8
Oatlands Tas 253 K2
Oban Qld 150 C4
Oberon NSW 109 E1, 110 E8
Obley NSW 110 A5
OBX Creek NSW 113 M6
Ocean Beach Tas 252 A1, 254 C10, 327
Ocean Grove Vic 64 E5, 67 M7
Ocean Shores NSW 113 P2
O'Connell NSW 110 D8
Oenpelli NT 174 G4
Offham Qld 144 A7, 153 P7
Officer Vic 65 J4
Ogmore Qld 147 H7
Ogunbil NSW 111 H1, 113 H10
Olary SA 233 M4
Old Adaminaby NSW 109 B7
Old Andado NT 179 K9
Old Banchory Qld 146 D7
Old Bar NSW 111 L3
Old Beach Tas 253 K4
Old Bonalbo NSW 113 L2
Old Bowenfels NSW 110 E8
Old Burren NSW 112 B6
Old Cherrabun WA 209 H9
Old Cork Qld 150 G7
Old Creek Vic 67 L2
Old Delamere NT 174 E10, 176 E1
Old Grevillia NSW 113 M2
Old Junee NSW 117 N5
Old Koomooloo SA 233 L7
Old Koreelah NSW 113 L2
Old Laura Qld 149 K3, 155 A3
Old May Downs Qld 150 C2
Old Pender WA 208 D6
Old Roseberth Qld 152 C3
Old Rowena NSW 114 C6
Old Silver Plains Qld 149 H1, 154 E8
Old Strathgordon Qld 148 F2, 154 C9
Old Warrah NSW 110 G2
Oldina Tas 254 E5
Olinda NSW 110 E6
Olio Qld 151 K5
Olive Downs NSW 114 B1
Olive Island CP SA 232 A5
Olive Vale Qld 149 K3, 155 A3
Olympic Dam SA 232 F1, 234 F10
Oma Qld 151 L10, 153 L1
O'Malley SA 231 D8
Omeo Vic 70 E3, 73 L8
Omicron Qld 152 F9
One Arm Point WA 208 E6, 305, 307
One Tree NSW 114 C4
One Tree NSW 117 H4
Onepah NSW 114 C1
Ongerup WA 202 G8
Onkaparinga River SA 226, 227
Onoto Qld 151 H10
Onslow WA 210 D7, 310, 311
Oobagooma WA 208 F6
Oodla Wirra SA 233 K6
Oodnadatta SA 234 D4
Oodoorou SA 151 J6
Oolloo NT 174 D7
Oolloo Crossing NT 174 D7
Oombabeer Qld 144 G1, 147 H10
Oombulgurri WA 209 M4
Oondooroo Qld 151 J6
Oonoomurra Qld 150 E3
Ooratippra NT 179 L3
Oorindi Qld 150 F3
Ootann Qld 149 K6, 155 B9
Ootha NSW 115 N10, 117 N2
Opalton Qld 151 J8
Ophir NSW 110 C7
Opium Creek NT 174 E4
Opossum Bay Tas 253 K5

INDEX OF PLACE NAMES 409

Ora Banda WA 203 K2, 205 L10
Orana NSW 114 G10, 116 G1
Orange NSW 110 C7
Orange Creek NT 178 G7
Orange Grove NSW 116 F3
Oraparinna SA 233 K2
Orara River NSW 267, 269
Orbost Vic 71 H5, 73 P10
Orchid Beach Qld *131*, 132, 133, 145 N2
Ord River WA 209 N4, 302
Ord River NT 209 N7
Ord River NR WA 209 N3
Orford Tas 253 M3
Orford Vic 66 E7
Orielton Tas 253 L4
Orientos Qld 152 G8
Orion Downs Qld 146 F10
Oroners Outstation Qld 148 G3
Orpheus Island NP Qld 149 M8
Orroroo SA 233 J5
Osborne NSW 117 M6
Osborne Well NSW 117 K7
Osbornes Flat Vic 73 H4
O'Shannassey River Qld 148 A9, 285
Osmaston Tas 255 H7
Osmond Valley WA 209 M7
Osterley Tas 253 H2
OT Downs NT 177 K2
Otway NP Vic 64 A8, 67 J9
Otway Range Vic 64 A8, 67 K9
Ouchy Qld 148 E10, 150 F1
Oulnina Park SA 233 M5
Ourimbah NSW 111 H7
Ourimbah NSW 114 F2
Ournie NSW 117 P8
Ouse Tas 252 G3, 328
Outalpa SA 233 M4
Outer Harbor SA 217, *217*, **218–19**, 233 J9, 322
Outtrim Vic 65 L7
Ouyen Vic 68 E5
Ovens Vic 73 H5
Overlander Roadhouse WA 204 C5
Overnewton NSW 114 F10, 116 F1
Owen SA 233 J8
Owen Downs NSW 114 E2
Owens Gap NSW 110 G3
Owieandana SA 235 K10
Oxenford Qld 145 N8
Oxenhope Outstation Qld 146 A4, 151 P4
Oxford Downs Qld 144 A3
Oxley NSW 116 G4
Oxley Vic 72 F5
Oxley Vale NSW 112 G9
Oxley Wild Rivers NP NSW 113 K9
Oyster Cove Tas 253 J6
Ozenkadnook Vic 66 B2

Paaratte Vic 66 G8
Pacific Palms NSW 111 L4
Packsaddle NSW 114 C5
Paddington NSW 115 H8
Paddys Flat NSW 113 L3
Paddys Plain NSW 113 L7
Paddys Ranges SP Vic 67 K3
Padthaway SA 230 D9
Padthaway CP SA 230 D9
Pago WA 209 K2
Paignie Vic 68 E5
Painters Bore Camp NSW 112 F4
Pajingo Qld 146 B3, 151 P3
Pakenham Vic 65 K5
Pakenham South Vic 65 K5
Pakenham Upper Vic 65 K4
Palana Tas 255 J1
Palgarup WA 202 C8
Paling Yards NSW 110 D7
Pallamallawa NSW 112 E5
Pallamana SA 230 A6, 233 K10
Pallarang Vic 68 B5
Pallarenda Qld 149 N9
Pallarup NR WA 203 H6
Palm Beach NSW 111 J8
Palmer SA 233 K10
Palmer River Roadhouse Qld 149 K4, 155 B5
Palmer Valley NT 178 G8
Palmerston NT 174 D4
Palmerville Qld 149 J4
Palmgrove NP Qld 144 G2

Palmwoods Qld 145 M5
Paloona Tas 254 G6
Palparara Qld 152 G2
Paluma Qld 149 M9
Paluma Range NP Qld 149 M9
Palumpa NT 174 B7
Pambula NSW 109 E9, **274**
Pambula Beach NSW 109 E9
Panaramitee SA 233 L5
Pancake Creek Qld 134, 135
Pandanus Creek Qld 149 K9
Pandappa CP SA 233 N10
Pandie Pandie SA 235 L1
Pandora Park Qld 151 K10, 153 K1
Paney SA 232 D5
Panitya Vic 68 A6
Panmure Vic 66 G8
Pannawonica WA 210 E7
Pantapin WA 202 E4
Pantijan WA 209 H5
Panton Hill Vic 65 H2, 67 P5, 72 B10
Paper Beach Tas 255 J5
Pappinbarra NSW 111 L1, 113 L10
Papulankutja WA 206 F10
Papunya Aboriginal Community NT 178 E5
Paraburdoo WA 210 G9
Parachilna SA 233 J2
Paradise Tas 254 G6
Paradise Vic 66 H4, 67 J9
Paradise Vic 67 H2
Paradise WA 208 G9
Paradise Beach Vic 70 D7
Paradise Point Qld 145 N8
Parakylia SA 234 E10
Parara SA 233 H9
Paratoo SA 233 L5
Parattah Tas 253 K2
Parawa SA 230 B5
Parawee Tas 254 D6
Parcoola SA 233 M7
Pardoo WA 211 J5
Pardoo Roadhouse WA 211 K4
Parenna Tas 254 F2
Parham SA 233 J9
Parilla SA 230 A9
Paringa NSW 114 B7
Paringa SA 233 N8
Park Ridge Qld 145 N7
Parkes NSW 110 A6, 115 P10, 117 P2
Parkham Tas 255 H6
Parkhurst Qld 147 J8
Parklea NSW 109 G1, 110 G8
Parkside Tas 255 P6
Parkville NSW 110 G3
Parnabal Qld 146 G9
Parndana SA 230 B3
Parnella Tas 255 P6
Paroo WA 205 J4
Parrakie SA 230 A9
Parramatta NSW 109 G1, 111 H8
Parramatta River NSW 77
Parry Lagoons NR WA 209 N4
Partacoona SA 233 H4
Partridge Lakes SA 234 B10
Paru NT 174 C3
Paruna SA 233 N9
Parwan Vic 64 E3, 67 M5
Paschendale Vic 66 C5
Pasha Qld 146 D5
Paskeville SA 233 H8
Pata SA 233 N9
Patchewollock Vic 68 E6
Pateena Tas 255 K7
Paterson NSW 111 J5
Paterson Bay Vic 64 C7, 67 L8
Patersonia Tas 255 K6
Patho Vic 69 M8
Patyah Vic 66 B2
Paupong NSW 109 B8
Pawleena Tas 253 L4
Pawtella Tas 253 L2
Paxton NSW 111 H6
Paynes Find WA 204 G9
Paynesville Vic 51, 70 E6
Peachna CR SA 232 D7
Peak Charles NP WA 203 L6
Peak Creek NSW 110 B8
Peak Downs Qld 146 E7
Peak Hill NSW 110 A5, 115 P9, 117 P1
Peak Hill WA 205 H3

Peak Vale Qld 146 D8
Peak View NSW 109 D7
Peaka NSW 116 D2
Peake SA 230 A8
Pearcedale Vic 65 H5
Pearl Coast WA 305, **306–7**
Pearlah SA 232 D9
Peats Ridge NSW 111 H7
Peawaddy Qld 144 E1
Pedirka SA 234 C2
Pedirka Desert SA 234 B3
Peebinga SA 233 N10
Peebinga CP SA 233 N10
Peechelba Vic 72 E4
Peechelba East Vic 72 F3
Peedamulla WA 210 D7
Peekadoo Qld 144 G4
Peel NSW 110 D7
Peel Island Qld 122, 123
Peelwood NSW 109 D2, 110 D9
Pegarah Tas 254 F2
Pekina SA 233 J5
Pelaw Main NSW 111 J6
Pelham Qld 148 G9, 151 J1
Pelham Tas 253 J3
Pella Vic 68 D8
Pelverata Tas 253 J6
Pemberton WA 200, 202 C9
Pembrooke NSW 111 M1, 113 M10
Penarie NSW 116 F4
Pencil Pine Tas 254 F7
Pender Bay WA 208 D6, 305, 307
Penguin Tas 254 F5
Penneshaw SA 230 B4, 320
Penola SA 230 E10
Penola CP SA 230 E9
Penong SA 231 F10
Penrice Qld 151 M3
Penrith NSW 80, 81, 109 G1, 110 G8
Penshurst Vic 66 E6
Pentecost Downs WA 209 L5
Pentecost River WA 209 M4, 302
Pentland Qld 146 A3, 151 N3
Penwortham SA 233 J8
Peppers Plains Vic 68 E9
Peppimenarti NT 174 C7
Peranga Qld 145 K6
Perch Creek Qld 147 H10
Percival Lakes WA 206 B4
Peregian Beach Qld 126, 129
Perekerten NSW 116 F6
Perenjori WA 204 E9
Perenna Vic 68 D9
Pericoe NSW 109 D9
Perisher Valley NSW 109 B8
Pernatty SA 232 G3
Peron WA 204 B4
Peron Islands NT 166, 167
Peronne Vic 66 C2
Perponda SA 233 M10
Perrinvale Outcamp WA 205 K8
Perry Bridge Vic 70 D7
Perth Tas 247, 255 K7
Perth WA 181, **182–3**, **184–5**, *185*, **188–9**, **190–1**, 202 C4
Perthville NSW 110 D8
Petcheys Bay Tas 253 J7
Peterborough SA 233 J6
Peterborough Vic 66 G9
Petersville SA 233 H9
Petford Qld 149 K6, 155 B9
Petina SA 232 B5
Petita NSW 114 E4
Petrie Qld 145 M6
Petro NSW 116 D3
Pettit NSW 109 A4, 117 P6
Pheasant Creek Vic 65 J1, 72 B9
Phillip Creek NT 177 H7
Phillip Island Vic 43, 65 H6, **262–3**
Piallamore NSW 111 H1, 113 H10
Piallaway NSW 110 F1, 112 F10
Piambie Vic 69 H4
Piambra NSW 110 D2
Piangil Vic 69 J5
Piangil North Vic 69 H5
Piavella Vic 69 M9
Piawaning WA 202 C2
Picaninny Outstation NT 176 B8
Picardy Qld 151 F7
Piccaninnie Ponds CP SA 230 G10
Pickabox Qld 144 B5
Pickering Brook WA 202 C4

Pickertaramoor NT 174 D3
Picnic Bay Qld 149 N9
Picola Vic 69 P8, 72 A3
Picton NSW 109 G2, 110 G1
Picton WA 202 B7
Piedmont Vic 65 M4
Piednippie SA 232 B5
Pieman River SR Tas 254 B8
Pier Millan Vic 68 G6
Piesseville WA 202 E6
Pigeon Hole NT 176 D3
Pigeon Ponds Vic 66 C4
Pikedale Qld 145 K9
Pilbara WA 210 E8
Pilbara Coast WA 210 F5, **308–9**, 310
Pilga WA 211 J7
Pillana SA 232 D9
Pillar Valley NSW 113 N6
Pilliga NSW 112 B7
Pilliga NR NSW 112 D9
Pilot Bay Tas 327
Pimba SA 232 F2
Pimbee WA 204 C3
Pimpama Qld 145 N7
Pimpara Lake NSW 114 B4
Pimpinio Vic 66 E1
Pincally NSW 114 B4
Pindabunna WA 204 G9
Pindar WA 204 E8
Pindera Downs NSW 114 D2
Pindi Pindi Qld 146 F3
Pine Clump NSW 115 P7
Pine Corner SA 232 E7
Pine Creek NT 174 E6
Pine Creek SA 233 L6
Pine Creek SA 233 L6
Pine Gap NT 179 H6
Pine Grove NSW 112 B9
Pine Lodge Vic 72 C4
Pine Lodge South Vic 72 C5
Pine Plains Vic 68 D6
Pine Point SA 233 H9
Pine Ridge NSW 110 F2
Pine Valley NSW 113 M6
Pine View NSW 114 A5
Pine View NSW 115 J3
Pinedale Qld 145 H4
Pinegrove WA 204 D7
Pinery SA 233 J9
Piney Range NSW 109 A1, 117 P3
Pingandy WA 204 G1, 210 G10
Pingaring WA 202 G6
Pingelly WA 202 E5
Pingine Qld 153 M5
Pingrup WA 202 G7
Pinjarra WA 202 C5
Pinjarrega NR WA 202 C1, 204 E10
Pinjin WA 203 N1, 205 N10
Pinkawillinie CP SA 232 D5
Pinkawillinie CR SA 232 D6
Pinkett NSW 113 K6
Pinkilla Qld 153 K5
Pinnacle Qld 146 F4
Pinnacle Reefs NSW 117 P3
Pinnacles Qld 149 H3
Pinnacles WA 205 K7
Pinnaroo SA 230 A10, 233 N10
Pintharuka WA 204 E9
Pioneer Qld 146 D1, 149 N9
Pioneer Qld 146 D7
Pioneer Tas 255 N5
Pipalyatjara SA 231 A1
Pipers Brook Tas 255 K5
Pipers River Tas 255 K5
Pira Vic 69 J6
Pirlta Vic 68 D2
Pirron Yallock Vic 64 A6, 67 J8
Pitfield Vic 64 A3, 67 J6
Pithara WA 202 D2, 204 F10
Pittong Vic 64 A2, 67 J5
Pittsworth Qld 142, 145 K7
Pittwater NSW 78–9, 78
Plain Creek Qld 146 C5
Planet Downs Qld 148 C8
Planet Downs Outstation Qld 152 F5
Pleasant Hills NSW 117 M7
Plenty Tas 253 H4
Plevna Downs Qld 153 J5
Plumbago SA 233 M4
Plumridge Lakes NR WA 207 B4

Pmara Jutunta NT 178 G3
Poatina Tas 255 J8, 328
Poinsetta Qld 146 E8
Point Blaze NT 166, 167, 174 C5
Point Cook Vic 40, 64 F4, 67 N6
Point Coulomb NR WA 208 C7, 211 N1
Point Davenport CP SA 230 A3, 232 G10
Point Gordo WA 202 G9
Point Hicks Vic 49
Point Jenny NT 166
Point Lillias Vic 44, 45
Point Lonsdale Vic 64 F6, 67 N8
Point Lookout Qld 124, 125, 145 N7
Point Lowly WA 233 H6, 318, 319
Point Moore WA 199, 204 C8
Point Pass SA 233 K8
Point Pearce SA 232 G9
Point Percy Vic 66 E8
Point Richard Vic 44
Point Samson WA 210 F5, 309
Point Stuart Coastal Reserve NT 174 E4
Point Turton SA 232 G10
Point Wilson Vic 44
Poison Gate NSW 112 C5
Poitrel Qld 146 E6
Poldinna SA 232 C6
Polelle WA 205 H5
Police Point Tas 253 J7
Policemans Point SA 230 C7
Polkemmet Vic 66 D2
Pollappa Qld 149 H1, 154 D9
Polocara NSW 114 G5
Poltalloch SA 230 A7
Pomborneit Vic 67 J8
Pomona Qld 145 M5
Pomonal Vic 66 F4
Pompoota SA 233 L10
Ponto NSW 110 B4
Pontville Tas 253 K4
Pony Hills Qld 144 F4
Poochera SA 232 C5
Pooginook CP SA 233 M8
Poolaijelo Vic 66 B4
Poolamacca NSW 114 B7
Poole Tas 255 N3
Poona NP Qld 145 M3
Pooncarie NSW 116 D2
Poonindie SA 232 E9
Poonunda SA 233 K7
Pootilla Vic 64 C2, 67 L5
Pootnoura SA 234 A6
Poowong Vic 65 L6
Poowong East Vic 65 L6
Popanyinning WA 202 E6
Popiltah NSW 116 B2
Popiltah Lake NSW 116 B2
Popio NSW 114 B10, 116 B1
Porcupine Flat Vic 67 L3
Porcupine Gorge NP Qld 151 L2
Porepunkah Vic 70 C1, 73 H6
Pormpuraaw Aboriginal Community Qld 148 F2, 154 B10
Porongurup WA 202 F9
Porongurup NP WA 202 F9
Port Adelaide SA 214, 215, 219, *219*, 233 J10, 322
Port Adelaide River SA 214, **218–19**, *218*, *219*, 322
Port Albert Vic 55, 70 B9
Port Alma Qld 147 K9
Port Arthur Tas 240, 241, 253 M6
Port Augusta SA 212, 233 H5
Port Botany NSW 82
Port Broughton SA 233 H7
Port Campbell Vic 67 H9
Port Campbell NP Vic 67 H9
Port Clinton SA 233 H8
Port Davis SA 233 H6
Port Denison WA 204 C9
Port Douglas Qld 149 L5, 155 D6, 288, 291
Port Elliot SA 222, 230 B5
Port Essington NT 174 E2, 294, 295
Port Fairy Vic 66 E8
Port Franklin Vic 55, 65 N8
Port Gawler SA 217, 233 J9
Port Germein SA 233 H6
Port Gibbon SA 232 F7
Port Giles SA 233 H10

INDEX OF PLACE NAMES

Port Hacking NSW 111 H9
Port Hedland WA 211 H5, 308, 309
Port Hughes SA 232 G8
Port Huon Tas 253 H6
Port Jackson NSW 76–7, 111 H9
Port Julia SA 233 H9
Port Kembla NSW 109 G3, 110 G10
Port Kenny SA 232 B6
Port Latta Tas 254 C3
Port Lincoln SA 232 B10
Port MacDonnell SA 230 G9
Port Macquarie NSW 111 M2, 113 M10, 270
Port Minlacowie SA 232 G10
Port Moorowie SA 230 A3, 232 G10
Port Musgrave Qld 154 B4, 280, 281
Port Neill SA 232 E8
Port Noarlunga SA 213, 214–15, 215, 216, 217, 226
Port Phillip Bay Vic 39, 40–1, 42, 44–5, 47, 64 G4
Port Pirie SA 233 H6
Port Prime SA 233 J9
Port Rickaby SA 232 G9
Port River SA *see* Port Adelaide River SA
Port Roper NT 175 K8
Port Sorell Tas 255 H5
Port Stephens NSW 88–9, 111 K5
Port Victoria SA 232 G9
Port Vincent SA 233 H10
Port Wakefield SA 233 J8
Port Warrender WA 209 J2
Port Welshpool Vic 55, 65 P8, 70 A10
Portarlington Vic 40, 44, 64 F5, 67 N7
Porters Retreat NSW 109 E1, 110 D9
Portland NSW 110 E7
Portland Vic 66 C8
Portland Bay Vic 66 D8
Portland Downs Qld 151 M10
Portland North Vic 66 C8
Portland Roads Qld 154 E6
Portsea Vic 41, 64 F6, 67 N8
Poseidon Qld 144 B3
Possession Island NP Qld 154 C2, 279
Pot Boil Point Tas 255 K3, 325
Potato Point NSW 109 E7
Pottsville Beach NSW 113 P2
Powell Creek NT 177 H5
Powelltown Vic 65 L3
Powers Creek Vic 66 B3
Powlathanga Qld 146 B2, 151 P2
Powlett Plains Vic 67 K1, 69 K10
Powlett River Vic 65 K7
Prairie Qld 151 M3
Prairie Qld 153 L7
Prairie Vic 69 L9
Prairie Downs WA 211 J10
Pranjip Vic 72 B6
Pratten Qld 145 K8
Precipice NP Qld 145 H3
Premaydena Tas 240, 253 M6
Premer NSW 110 E2, 112 E10
Premier Downs WA 207 C6
Prenti Downs WA 205 N5
Preolenna Tas 254 D5
Preston Qld 144 C6
Preston Tas 254 F6
Preston Vic 64 G3, 67 P6, 72 A10
Preston Beach WA 202 B6
Pretty Bend Qld 146 E2
Pretty Plains Qld 149 K10, 151 L2
Prevelly WA 202 A8
Price SA 233 H8
Primrose Sands Tas 253 L5
Prince Frederick Harbour WA 209 H3
Prince of Wales Island Qld 154 C2, 279
Prince Regent NR WA 209 H4
Prince Regent River WA 209 H4, 302, 304
Princess Charlotte Bay Qld 149 J1, 154 E9, 278–9
Princetown Vic 67 H9
Princhester Qld 147 H7
Prooinga Vic 69 H5
Proserpine Qld 146 F2, 289
Prospect Qld 144 A2, 153 P2
Prospect Qld 148 G9
Prospect Tas 255 K6
Proston Qld 145 K4
Prubi Qld 151 J6

Prungle NSW 116 E4
Pucawan NSW 117 N4
Puckapunyal Vic 67 P3, 72 A7
Pudman Creek NSW 109 C3
Pukatja (Ernabella) SA 231 E1
Pularumpi NT 174 C2
Pulgamurtie NSW 114 C4
Pullabooka NSW 117 N3
Pullagaroo WA 204 G9
Pulletop NSW 117 N7
Pullut Vic 68 E8
Pumicestone Passage Qld 122, 123
Pumphreys Bridge WA 202 D6
Pungalina NT 177 N3
Punjaub Qld 148 B7
Puntabie SA 232 B4
Punthari SA 233 L10
Pura Pura Vic 67 H6
Puralka Vic 66 B6
Purbrook WA 144 E2
Pureba CP SA 232 B4
Purga Qld 145 M7
Purlewaugh NSW 110 D1, 112 D10
Purnanga NSW 114 E4
Purnim Vic 66 F8
Purnong SA 233 L10
Purnululu CR WA 209 M8
Purnululu NP WA 209 N7
Purple Downs SA 232 F1
Putty NSW 110 G6
Pyalong Vic 67 N3
Pyengana Tas 255 N6
Pygery SA 232 D6
Pymble NSW 111 H8
Pyramid Qld 146 D3
Pyramid WA 210 G6
Pyramid Hill Vic 69 L9
Pyramul NSW 110 D6

Quaama NSW 109 E8
Quail Island NT 161
Quairading WA 202 E4
Qualco SA 233 M8
Quambatook Vic 69 J8
Quambetook Qld 151 H4
Quambone NSW 115 P6
Quamby Qld 150 E2
Quamby Brook Tas 255 H7
Quanbun WA 209 H9
Quandialla NSW 117 P4
Quandong NSW 114 C8
Quangallin WA 202 E7
Quantong Vic 66 E2
Quarrum NR WA 202 D9
Quarry View NSW 114 D4
Queanbeyan NSW 109 C5
Queanbeyan River NSW 106, 107, 108
Queen Victoria Spring NR WA 203 P1, 205 P10, 207 A5
Queens Beach Qld 146 E2
Queenscliff Vic 41, 64 F5, 67 N7
Queenstown Tas 254 D10
Quellington WA 202 D4
Questa Park NSW 114 E4
Quibet Qld 144 E7
Quida Downs Qld 144 C4
Quilpie Qld 153 L5
Quinalow Qld 145 K6
Quindanning WA 202 D6
Quindinup NR WA 202 D9
Quinninup WA 202 C9
Quinns Rocks WA 202 B4
Quinyambie SA 233 N1
Quirindi NSW 110 G2
Quobba WA 204 B2
Quondong Vale SA 233 M6
Quorn SA 233 H4

RAAF East Sale Vic 70 C7
Rabbit Flat Roadhouse NT 176 B9
Raft Point NT 162
Raglan NSW 110 D7
Raglan Qld 147 K9
Raglan Vic 67 J4
Railton Tas 254 G6
Rainbar NSW 115 H3
Rainbow Vic 68 E8
Rainbow Beach Qld 126, 129, 145 N4
Rainbow Flat NSW 111 L3
Rainbow Valley CR NT 179 H7
Rainsby Qld 151 N5

Raleigh NSW 113 N8
Ralphs Bay Tas 239, 253 K5
Raluana NSW 117 M7
Ramco SA 233 M8
Raminea Tas 253 H7
Ramingining NT 175 K4
Ranceby Vic 65 L6
Rand NSW 117 L7
Ranelagh Tas 253 J6
Ranga Tas 255 J3
Ranges Valley Qld 150 G5
Rangeview Qld 146 D2
Ranken NT 177 M8
Rankins Springs NSW 117 L3
Rannes Qld 147 J10
Rapid Bay SA 220, 221, 230 B4
Rapid Head SA 221
Rappville NSW 113 M4
Rathdowney Qld 145 M8
Rathscar Vic 67 J3
Raukkan SA 230 B6
Ravendale NSW 114 C6
Ravenshoe Qld 149 L6, 155 D9
Ravensthorpe WA 203 J7
Ravenswood Qld 146 A7, 151 N7
Ravenswood Qld 146 C2, 149 N10
Ravenswood Vic 67 L2
Ravenswood WA 202 C5
Ravenswood South Vic 67 L3
Ravensworth NSW 111 H4
Ravine des Casoars WPA SA 230 B1
Rawbelle Qld 145 J2
Rawdon Vale NSW 111 J3
Rawlinna WA 207 C6
Rawson Vic 65 P4, 70 A6
Ray Qld 153 K4
Raymond Terrace NSW 111 J5
Raymore Qld 153 J4
Raywood Vic 67 L1, 69 L10
Recherche Archipelago NR WA 203 N8
Red Bank Qld 146 G9
Red Bluff WA 204 C7, 314
Red Cap Creek Vic 66 B5
Red Cliffs SA 232 G9
Red Cliffs Vic 68 E2
Red Creek WA 205 D2
Red Hill NSW 65 H6, 67 P8
Red Hill WA 210 E7
Red Hills Tas 255 H7
Red Lake WA 203 L6
Red Range NSW 113 K6
Red Rock NSW 113 N6
Redbank Qld 145 H3
Redbank Vic 67 J3
Redbournberry NSW 111 H5
Redcastle Vic 67 N2
Redcliffe Qld 122, 123, 125, 145 N6
Redcliffe Qld 144 G1, 147 H10
Redcliffe SA 233 L7
Reddford WA 144 C4
Redesdale Vic 67 M3
Redford WA 144 C4
Redgate WA 197
Redhead NSW 111 J6
Redhill SA 233 J7
Redmond WA 202 E9
Redpa Tas 254 A4
Redrock Qld 146 D7
Reedy Corner NSW 115 N7
Reedy Creek SA 230 D8
Reedy Creek Vic 67 P4, 72 A8
Reedy Dam Vic 68 G8
Reedy Marsh Tas 255 H6
Reedy Spring Qld 149 K10, 151 M2
Reedys WA 205 H6
Reefton NSW 117 N4
Reekara Tas 254 F1
Regatta Point Tas 252 B1, 254 C10
Reid WA 207 F6
Reid River Qld 146 C1, 149 N10
Reids Creek Vic 72 G4
Reids Flat NSW 109 C2, 110 C9
Reindeer Lake NT 176 C8
Relbia Tas 255 K7
Remington NSW 115 N3
Remlap WA 202 E1, 204 G10
Rendelsham SA 230 F9
Renison Bell Tas 254 D8
Renmark SA 233 N8
Renner Springs NT 177 H5
Rennick Vic 66 A6
Rennie NSW 117 K7

Reola NSW 114 E3
Repton NSW 113 N8
Retreat Qld 153 K2
Retreat Tas 255 K5
Retro Qld 146 E7
Revilo Qld 144 D5
Reynella SA 230 A5, 233 J10
Reynolds Neck Tas 255 H8
Rheban Tas 253 M3
Rheola Vic 67 K2
Rhyll Vic 43, 65 J6
Rhyndaston Tas 253 K3
Rhynie SA 233 J8
Riachella Vic 66 G2
Riamukka NSW 111 J1, 113 J10
Riana Tas 254 F5
Rich Avon Vic 66 G1, 68 G10
Richlands NSW 109 E2, 110 E10
Richmond NSW 79, 80, 81, 110 G8
Richmond Qld 151 J3
Richmond Tas 253 K4
Richmond Downs Qld 144 F5
Richmond Hills Qld 146 A8, 151 P8
Richmond Plains Vic 67 J1, 69 J10
Riddells Creek Vic 64 F1, 67 N5
Ridgeland Qld 141 E3
Ridgelands Qld 147 J8
Ridgeway Tas 253 K5
Ridgley Tas 254 E5
Rifle Creek Qld 150 C3
Rimbanda Qld 151 K7
Ringarooma Tas 255 M5
Ringarooma Coastal Reserve Tas 255 N3
Ringwood NT 179 K6
Ringwood Vic 65 J3
Ripplebrook Vic 65 L5
Ripponhurst Vic 66 E7
Risdon Vale Tas 253 K4
Rita Island Qld 146 D1, 149 P10
River Derwent Tas 238–9, 238, 239, 252 G3, 253 H3
River Finniss SA 226–7
River Heads Qld 130, 145 M3
River Light SA 226, 233 J9
River Tamar Tas 255 J5
River View Qld 146 A3, 151 N3
River View Vic 70 B1
Riverdale Qld 151 K3
Riveren NT 176 C5
Riverina WA 205 K9
Riverside NSW 114 E7
Riverside Qld 144 C1, 146 D10
Riverslea Vic 70 C7
Riversleigh Qld 144 B5
Riversleigh Qld 148 B9
Riverton SA 233 K8
Riverview Qld 149 H8
Rivington Qld 146 C9
Robbins Island Tas 254 B3
Robe SA 230 E8
Robertson NSW 109 F3
Robertson Range WA 211 L9
Robertstown SA 233 K8
Robin Hood Vic 65 L4
Robinhood Qld 149 J8
Robins Qld 151 H6
Robinson River NT 177 N3
Robinson River WA 208 F6, 304
Robinvale Vic 68 G3, 265
Roche Reefs NT 163, 166
Rocherlea Tas 255 K6
Rochester SA 233 J7
Rochester Vic 67 N1, 69 N10
Rochford Vic 67 N4, 67 N4
Rock Flat NSW 109 C7
Rock Valley NSW 113 N2
Rockbank Vic 64 F3, 67 N6
Rockbrae Qld 145 L8
Rockdale Qld 144 F6
Rockhampton Qld 147 J8
Rockhampton Downs NT 177 K6
Rockingham WA 186, 187, 202 B5
Rocklands Qld 148 A10, 150 A1
Rocklands Reservoir Vic 66 D4
Rocklea WA 210 G9
Rockleigh SA 233 K10
Rockley NSW 109 D1, 110 D8
Rocksville NSW 114 A4, 153 P4
Rockvale Qld 151 H3
Rocky Qld 144 B5

Rocky Cape Tas 254 D4
Rocky Cape NP Tas 254 D4
Rocky Creek NSW 112 F6
Rocky Creek NT 176 A3
Rocky Dam NSW 112 G4
Rocky Glen NSW 112 D9
Rocky Gully WA 202 D9
Rocky Islets NP Qld 149 L2, 155 D2
Rocky Lagoon Tas 329
Rocky Plains NSW 109 B7
Rocky Ponds Qld 146 D1, 149 P10
Rocky River NSW 113 J8
Rocky River SA 230 B2
Rodds Bay Qld 134, 135
Rodds Peninsula Qld 134, 135
Rodinga NT 179 H7
Rodney Downs Qld 151 M8
Roebourne WA 210 F6
Roebuck Bay WA 208 C9, 305, 306, 306
Roebuck Plains WA 208 D8, 211 N1
Roebuck Roadhouse WA 208 D8, 211 N1
Roeburne Qld 144 G2
Roger Corner SA 232 G10
Roger River Tas 254 B4
Rokeby Qld 151 L3
Rokeby Qld 154 C8
Rokeby Tas 253 K5
Rokeby Vic 65 M4
Rokeby National Park Qld 154 D7
Rokewood Vic 64 B4, 67 K6
Rokewood Junction Vic 64 B3, 67 K6
Roland Tas 254 G6
Rollands Plains NSW 111 M1, 113 M10
Rolleston Qld 144 E1, 146 F10
Rollingstone Qld 149 M9
Roma Qld 142, 144 F5
Romani NSW 115 J3
Romsey Vic 64 F1, 67 N4
Rooken Glen Qld 146 D9
Rookhurst NSW 111 K3
Rookwood Qld 149 J6, 155 A8
Rooney Point Qld 133
Rooster Point Tas 253 P2
Roper Bar NT 175 J8
Rosa Brook WA 202 B8
Rosebank NSW 113 N2
Rosebank Qld 153 P4
Roseberry NSW 113 M2
Roseberth Qld 152 C4
Rosebery Tas 254 D8
Rosebery Vic 68 F8
Rosebery Downs Qld 151 M7
Rosebery East Vic 68 F8
Rosebrook Vic 66 E8
Rosebud Vic 40, 41, 64 G6, 67 N8
Rosedale NSW 109 C6
Rosedale Qld 145 L1
Rosedale Qld 146 B8, 151 P8
Rosedale Qld 146 G5
Rosedale Vic 70 B7
Rosegarland Tas 253 H4
Rosella Plains Qld 149 K8
Roseneath Vic 66 B4
Rosevale Qld 145 M8
Rosevale Qld 144 A6, 153 P6
Rosevale Qld 145 K1, 147 L10
Rosevale Tas 255 J6
Rosevears Tas 255 J6
Rosewood NSW 114 F5
Rosewood NSW 117 P7
Rosewood NT 176 A2
Rosewood Qld 145 M7
Roseworthy SA 233 K9
Roslyn NSW 109 D3, 110 D10
Roslynmead Vic 69 M9
Ross Tas 255 L9
Ross Creek Vic 64 B2, 67 K5
Ross River NT 179 J6
Rossarden Tas 255 M8
Rossbridge Vic 66 G5
Rossi NSW 109 D5
Rossmoya Qld 147 J7
Rossville Qld 149 L3, 155 C4
Rostella NSW 113 J1
Rostock Qld 144 G6
Rostron Vic 67 H2
Rothbury NSW 111 H5
Rothwell Vic 64 E4, 67 M6

INDEX OF PLACE NAMES 411

Roto NSW 115 J10, 117 J1
Rottnest Island WA 186, **192–3**, *192–3*, 202 B4
Round Hill Qld **134–5**, *135*, 147 L10
Round Hill Head Qld 134, 135
Round Hill NR WA 115 K10, 117 K1
Round Lake Vic 66 C2
Rowella Tas 255 J5
Rowena NSW 112 B6
Rowles Lagoon NR WA 203 K2, 205 L10
Rowley Shoals Marine Park WA 211 J1
Rowsley Vic 64 E3, 67 M5
Roxburgh Downs Qld 150 B6
Roxby Downs SA 232 F1
Roxby Downs SA 232 F1, 234 F10
Roy Hill WA 211 K8
Royal George Tas 255 M8
Royal NP NSW 111 H9
Royal Oak NSW 114 D5
Royalla NSW 109 C5
Royston Qld 144 E6
Rubicon Vic 65 L1, 72 D9
Ruby Vic 65 L6
Ruby Gap Nature Park NT 179 K5
Ruby Plains WA 209 L9
Rubyvale Qld 146 E8
Rudall SA 232 E7
Rudall River NP WA 211 N8
Ruffy Vic 72 C7
Rufus River NSW 116 A4
Rugby NSW 109 C2, 110 C10
Rules Beach Qld 145 L1, 147 M10
Rules Point NSW 109 B6
Rum Jungle NT 174 D5
Rumbalara NT 179 J9
Rumula Qld 149 L5, 155 C6
Rundle Range NP Qld 147 K9
Running Creek Vic 73 J5
Running Stream NSW 110 E6
Runnymede Qld 144 C8
Runnymede Qld 151 J2
Runnymede Tas 253 L4
Runnymede Vic 67 N1, 69 N10
Rupanyup Vic 66 F1
Rupanyup North Vic 66 F1, 68 F10
Rushworth Vic 67 P1, 69 P10, 72 A5
Russell Park Qld 146 E6
Rutchillo Qld 150 G3
Rutherford NSW 111 J5
Rutherglen Vic 72 F3
Rutland Qld 146 D9
Rutland Park Qld 151 M10, 153 M1
Rutland Plains Qld 148 F3
Rydal NSW 110 E7
Rye Vic 41, 64 G6, 67 N8
Rye Park NSW 109 C3, 110 B10
Ryeford Qld 145 K8
Rylstone NSW 110 E5
Ryton Vic 65 P7
Rywung Qld 145 H5

Saddleworth SA 233 K8
Safety Beach Vic 64 G6, 67 P8
St Albans NSW 110 G7
St Albans Qld 146 F5
St Andrews Vic 65 J2, 72 B10
St Andrews Beach Vic 64 G6, 67 N8
St Anns Qld 146 C4
St Arnaud Vic 67 H1
St Clair NSW 111 H4
St Clair Vic 65 N2, 72 E10
St Columba Falls SR Tas 255 N6
St Fillans Vic 65 K2, 72 C10
St George Qld 142, 144 E8
St George Basin NSW 209 H4, 302
St Georges Head NSW 95, 109 G4
St Germains Vic 69 P9, 72 B4
St Helens Tas **244–5**, 255 P6
St Helens Vic 66 E7
St Helens Beach Qld 146 F3
St Helens Plains Vic 66 F2
St Helens Point SRA Tas 255 P6
Saint Hilliers Qld 145 H7
St James Vic 72 D4
St Kilda SA 214, 233 J9
St Kilda Vic 64 G3, 67 P6
St Lawrence Qld 147 H6
St Leonards Vic 44, 64 F5, 67 N7
St Marys NSW 109 G1, 110 G8
St Marys Tas 255 P7
St Patricks River Tas 236, **247**

St Vidgeon NT 175 K8
Sale Vic 70 C7
Sale River WA 208 G5, 304
Salisbury NSW 111 J4
Salisbury SA 233 J9
Salisbury Vic 68 D10
Salisbury Downs NSW 114 D3
Sallys Flat NSW 110 D6
Salmon Gums WA 203 L6
Salt Creek Qld 154 B9
Salt Creek SA 222, 223, 230 C7
Salt Lake NSW 114 G4
Salt Water Point NT 174 F3
Saltbush Park Qld 146 F6
Saltwater Bay NSW *272*
Saltwater River Tas 253 L6
Samford Qld 145 M7
Samson Dam WA 201
Samson Well SA 233 L7
San Remo Vic 65 J7
Sandalwood SA 233 M10
Sandergrove SA 230 A6
Sandfire Roadhouse WA 211 L4
Sandfly Tas 253 J5
Sandford Tas 253 L5
Sandford Vic 66 C5
Sandgate NSW 111 J6
Sandgate Qld 145 N6
Sandhill Lake Vic 69 K7
Sandigo NSW 117 L6
Sandilands SA 233 H9
Sandmount Vic 72 C3
Sandon NSW 113 N5
Sandon River NSW 266, 267, 269
Sandringham Qld 150 C9
Sandringham Vic 40, 65 H4, 67 P6
Sandsmere Vic 68 B9
Sandspit River FR Tas 253 M4
Sandstone WA 205 J7
Sandy Beach NSW 113 N7
Sandy Camp NSW 115 N5
Sandy Creek Vic 73 J4
Sandy Flat NSW 113 K4
Sandy Hill NSW 113 L3
Sandy Hollow NSW 110 F4
Sandy Lake WA 208 E9, 211 P2
Sandy Point NSW 109 E4
Sandy Point Vic 65 M8
Sangar NSW 117 K7
Sanpah NSW 114 A5
Santa Teresa NT 179 J7
Santos Qld 152 G8
Sapphire NSW 113 H5
Sapphire Qld 146 E8
Sardine Creek Vic 71 J4, 73 P9
Sarina Qld 146 G4
Sarina Beach Qld 146 G4
Sarsfield Vic 70 E5, 73 L10
Sassafras NSW 109 F4
Sassafras Tas 254 G6
Saunders Beach Qld 149 N9
Savage River Tas 254 C7
Savernake NSW 117 K7
Sawmill Settlement Vic 72 F8
Sawpit Creek NSW 109 B7
Sawtell NSW 113 N7
Saxa NSW 110 C4
Saxby River Qld 284
Sayers Lake NSW 114 E9, 116 E1
Scaddan WA 203 L7
Scamander Tas 255 P6
Scamander FR Tas 255 P6
Scamander River Qld 245
Scarborough WA 183, 189, 202 C4
Scarsdale Vic 64 B2, 67 K5
Scartwater Qld 146 C4
Sceale Bay SA 232 B6
Schouten Island Tas 242–3, 253 P2
Schouten Passage Tas 243, 253 P2
Scone NSW 110 G3
Scoria Qld 145 H1, 147 J10
Scorpion Springs CP SA 230 A10
Scotsburn Vic 64 C2, 67 K5
Scott Creek NT 174 E8
Scott NP WA 202 B8
Scotts Creek Vic 67 H8
Scotts Head NSW 113 N8
Scottsdale Tas 255 L5
Sea Lake Vic 68 G7
Seabird NSW 202 B3
Seabrook Tas 254 E4
Seacombe Vic 70 D7

Seaford Vic 65 H5, 67 P7
Seaforth NSW 111 J5
Seaham NSW 111 J5
Seal Bay CP SA 230 B3
Seal Rocks NSW 111 L4
Seaspray Vic 70 D8
Seaton Vic 70 A6
Sebastapol NSW 117 N5
Sebastian Vic 67 L1
Sebastopol Vic 64 B2, 67 K5
Second Valley SA *212*, 220, 230 B5
Sedan SA 233 L9
Sedan Dip Qld 148 E10, 150 F2
Sedgwick Vic 67 M2
Seemore Downs WA 207 C6
Seisia Qld 278, 280, *280*
Selbourne Tas 255 J6
Seldom Seen Vic 70 E4, 73 K9
Sellicks Beach SA 230 A5
Selwyn Qld 150 E5
Separation Creek Vic 64 C7, 67 K9
Serpentine Vic 67 L1, 69 L10
Serpentine WA 202 C5
Serpentine NP WA 202 C5
Serpentine River WA 181, 201
Serviceton Vic 66 A1, 68 A10
Sesbania Qld 151 J4
Settlement Point Vic 42
Seven Emu NT 177 N2
Seven Mile Beach NSW 75, 92, 92, 93
Seven Mile Beach Tas 253 L5
Seven Mile Beach PA Tas 253 L5
Sevenhill SA 233 J8
Seventeen Seventy Qld **134–5**, *135*, 147 L10
Severn River NSW 143, *143*
Seville Vic 65 K3
Seymour Tas 255 P8
Seymour Vic 67 P3, 72 B7
Shackleton WA 202 F4
Shadeville Qld 146 E10
Shadforth NSW 110 C7
Shady Camp NT **164–5**, *164–5*, 174 F4
Shady Lagoon Qld 148 E7
Shallow Crossing NSW 96, 97
Shandon Vale Qld 146 A8, 151 N8
Shannon NP WA 202 D9
Shannon River WA 200
Shannons Flat NSW 109 C6
Shark Bay WA 204 B3, **312–13**
Shark Bay Marine Park WA 204 B3
Sharon Point Tas 255 P5
Shaw Vic 65 M2, 72 E10
Shay Gap WA 211 K5
She Oak Flat SA 233 H9
Sheans Creek Vic 72 C6
Sheep Hills Vic 68 F10
Sheffield Tas 254 G6
Sheila Outstation Qld 150 B4
Shelbourne Vic 67 L2
Shelford Vic 64 C4, 67 L7
Shelley Vic 73 K4
Shellharbour NSW 109 G3
Shenandoah NT 176 G3
Sheoak Hill CR SA 232 F7
Sheoaks Vic 64 D4, 67 L6
Shepparton Vic 72 C4
Sheringa SA 232 C8
Sherlock SA 230 A8
Sherlock WA 210 G6
Sherwood NSW 113 M9
Sherwood WA 205 H5
Shinfield Qld 146 G4
Shirley Qld 144 E9
Shirley Vic 67 H4
Shoal Bay NSW 111 K5
Shoal Bay NT 160, 174 D4
Shoalhaven Heads NSW 92, 93, 109 G4
Shoalhaven River NSW 92–3, 109 E4
Shoalwater Islands Marine Park WA 202 B5
Shooters Hill NSW 109 E1, 110 E9
Shoreham Vic 65 H6, 67 P8
Shortys Point Tas 255 K4
Shovel Lake WA 211 M3
Shute Harbour Qld 146 F2, 289
Shuttleworth Qld 146 B6, 151 P6
Shy Creek NSW 115 L7
Siam SA 232 E5
Sidmouth Tas 255 J5

Silent Grove WA 209 H7
Silkwood Qld 149 M7, 155 E10
Silky Oak Creek Qld 149 M7
Silvan Vic 65 J3
Silver Hills Qld 151 J3
Silver Plains Qld 149 H1, 154 E3
Silver Spur Qld 145 K10
Silverton NSW 114 A8
Simmie Vic 69 N9
Simpson Vic 67 H8
Simpson Desert NT 179 M9
Simpson Desert SA 234 F2
Simpson Desert CP SA 235 H1
Simpson Desert NP Qld 152 A3
Simpson Desert RR SA 234 G3
Simpsons Bay Tas 253 K7
Sims Reef NT 162
Simson Vic 67 K3
Sinclair Vic 66 C7
Singleton NSW 111 H5
Singleton NT 177 J9, 179 J1
Sir Edward Pellew Group NT 175 M9, 300
Sir Joseph Banks Group CP SA 232 F9
Sisters Beach Tas 254 D4
Sisters Creek Tas 254 D4
Six-Pack Creek NT 167
Skardon River Qld 154 B4, 280–1
Skenes Creek Vic 64 B8, 67 K9
Skipton Vic 67 J5
Skye Vic 65 H5, 67 P7
Slade Point Qld 146 G4
Slamannon NSW 114 F8
Slashers Creek Qld 150 E7
Slaty Creek Vic 67 J1, 69 J10
Smeaton Vic 64 C1, 67 K4
Smiggin Holes NSW 109 B7
Smith Island NP Qld 146 G3
Smithfield Qld 145 J9
Smithfield SA 233 K9
Smithton Tas 254 C3
Smithtown NSW 113 M9
Smithville House NSW 114 A4
Smokers Bank Tas 254 C4
Smoky Bay SA 232 A4
Smoky Creek NSW 117 N5
Smythesdale Vic 64 B2, 67 K5
Snake Creek NT 177 J2
Snake Creek WA 202 D2
Snake Range NP Qld 146 D10
Snake Valley Vic 64 A2, 67 J5
Snapper Island Qld 149 L4, 155 D6, 291
Snowball NSW 109 D6
Snowtown SA 233 J7
Snowy Mountains NSW 74, 257, **276–7**, *277*
Snowy River NSW 109 B8, 276
Snowy River Vic 71 H3, 73 N9
Snowy River NP Vic 71 H3, 73 P8
Snug Tas 253 K6
Sofala NSW 110 D6
Soil Creek Qld 149 H6
Soldiers Point NSW 111 K5
Solitary Islands NSW 269
Somers Vic 65 H6, 67 P8
Somers Park Vic 65 L2, 72 D10
Somerset Qld 146 B1, 149 M10, 151 P1
Somerset Qld 151 L9
Somerset Vic 154 C2
Somerset Tas 254 E4
Somerset Dam Qld 145 M6
Somerton NSW 112 G9
Somerton Vic 64 G2, 67 P5, 72 A10
Somerville Qld 148 G10, 151 J2
Somerville Vic 65 H5, 67 P7
Sophie Downs WA 209 M9
Sorell Tas 253 L4
Sorrel Hills Qld 147 H9
Sorrento Vic 41, 64 F6, 67 N8
Sorrento WA 183, 188
Soudan NT 177 N8
South Alligator NT 174 F4
South Alligator River NT **170–1**, 174 F4
South Arm Tas 253 K6
South Blackwater Qld 146 F9
South Bruny Island Tas 253 K8
South Burracoppin WA 202 F4
South Canberra ACT 109 C5
South Coast NSW **92–3**

South Comongin Qld 153 L6
South Cumberland Islands NP Qld 147 H3
South End Qld 147 L9
South Eneabba NR WA 202 B1, 204 D10
South Esk River Tas 236, **247**, *247*, 255 K8
South Flinders Ranges SA 233 J4
South Forest Tas 254 C4
South Franklin Tas 253 H6
South Galway Qld 153 H3
South Gap SA 233 H3
South Glen Qld 145 H7
South Grafton NSW 113 M5
South Head Qld 149 H9
South Island NP Qld 147 J5
South Ita NSW 114 B10, 116 B1
South Johnstone Qld 149 M6, 155 E9
South Kempsey NSW 111 M1, 113 M9
South Kilkerran SA 233 H9
South Kumminin WA 202 F5
South Mission Beach Qld 149 M7, 155 E10
South Mount Cameron Tas 255 N4
South Nietta Tas 254 F6
South Peron Island NT 167, 174 D3
South Riana Tas 254 F5
South Solitary Island NSW *268*
South Springfield Tas 255 L5
South Stradbroke Island Qld 120, 122, 145 N7
South Trayning WA 202 F3
South Wellesley Islands Qld 148 C5, 285
South West Rocks NSW 113 N9, 269
South West Vernon Island NT 160, 174
Southend SA 230 F8
Southern Beekeepers NR WA 202 B2, 204 D10
Southern Brook WA 202 D4
Southern Cross Qld 146 B2, 149 M10, 151 F2
Southern Cross WA 203 H3
Southern Hills WA 203 N5
Southport Qld 120, 122, 123, 136, 145 N8
Southport Tas 253 H8
Southwest CA Tas 252 B4
South-West Corner WA **196–7**
Southwest NP Tas 252 F7
Southwood NP Qld 145 H7
Spalding SA 233 J7
Spalford Tas 254 F5
Spargo Creek Vic 64 D1, 67 L5
Specdingup WA 203 M7
Speed Vic 68 F6
Speewa Vic 69 J5
Spencer Gulf SA 232 F8, 319
Spencers Brook WA 202 D4
Spicer Flat SA 233 H9
Spicers Creek NSW 110 C4
Split Rock Qld 148 B10, 150 B1
Sportsmans Creek NSW 267
Sprent Tas 254 F6
Spreyton Qld 150 G4
Spreyton Tas 254 G5
Spring Beach Tas 253 M3
Spring Creek NT 177 M2
Spring Creek Qld 145 L8
Spring Creek Qld 149 K8
Spring Creek WA 209 N6
Spring Grove Qld 144 F6
Spring Hill NSW 110 C7
Spring Hill Qld 144 E1, 146 E10
Spring Hill Vic 67 M4
Spring Mount Qld 144 G8
Spring Plain NSW 112 C6
Spring Plains Qld 151 K9
Spring Ridge NSW 110 C4
Spring Ridge NSW 110 F1, 112 F10
Spring Vale Qld 146 B9, 151 P9
Spring Valley Qld 151 L3
Springbank Vic 64 C2, 67 L5
Springbrook NP Qld 145 N8
Springdale NSW 117 N5
Springfield Qld 144 D6
Springfield Qld 149 K7
Springfield Qld 153 J4
Springfield Tas 255 L5
Springhurst Vic 72 F4

INDEX OF PLACE NAMES

Springside Qld 145 K7
Springsure Qld 146 E10
Springton SA 233 K9
Springvale Qld 146 C7
Springvale Qld 149 K4, 155 B4
Springvale Qld 150 E9
Springvale Vic 65 H4, 67 P6
Springvale WA 209 L8
Springwood NSW 109 F1, 110 F8
Springwood NSW 116 B2
Staaten River NP Qld 148 G5
Staceys Bridge Vic 65 P7, 70 A9
Staghorn Flat Vic 73 H4
Stagmount Qld 151 N7
Stamford Qld 151 L4
Stanage Qld 147 H6
Stanborough NSW 113 H6
Standley Chasm NT 178 G6
Stanhope Vic 67 P1, 69 P10, 72 A5
Stanley Tas 254 C3
Stanley Vic 72 G5
Stanley Park NSW 110 G7
Stanley River Qld 140
Stannifer NSW 113 H6
Stannum NSW 113 J4
Stansbury SA 233 H10
Stanthorpe Qld 142, 143, 145 L9
Stanwell Qld 147 J8
Stanwell Park NSW 109 G2, 110 G10
Star Qld 149 M9
Starcke Qld 149 K2, 154 G10, 155 C2
Starcke NP Qld 149 K2, 154 G10, 155 C2
Stavely Vic 66 F5
Staverton Tas 254 F6
Stawell Vic 66 G3
Steep Point WA 204 A4, 313, 315
Steiglitz Vic 64 D3, 67 L6
Stenhouse Bay SA 230 A2
Stephens Creek NSW 114 B8
Steppes Tas 253 H1, 255 J10
Stieglitz Tas 255 P6
Stirling NT 179 H2
Stirling Qld 144 E4
Stirling Qld 148 F6
Stirling SA 233 K10
Stirling Vic 70 F4, 73 L9
Stirling Dam WA 201
Stirling North SA 233 H5
Stirling Range NP WA 202 F9
Stirrat Qld 147 K9
Stockdale Vic 70 C6
Stockinbingal NSW 117 P5
Stockmans Reward Vic 65 M2, 72 E9
Stockport Qld 150 D7
Stockport SA 233 J9
Stockton NSW 111 J6
Stockyard Hill Vic 67 J5
Stockyard Point Vic 43
Stokes Bay SA 230 B3
Stokes NP WA 203 K8
Stone Hut SA 233 J6
Stonecraft Qld 144 G2
Stonefield SA 233 L9
Stonehaven Vic 64 D5, 67 L7
Stonehenge NSW 113 J6
Stonehenge Qld 151 K10, 153 K1
Stoneville WA 203 L2
Stoneyford Vic 67 J8
Stonor Tas 253 K2
Stony Creek NSW 110 D5
Stony Creek SA 234 A3
Stony Creek Vic 65 M7
Stony Point Vic 65 H6, 67 P8, 263
Stony Rivulet Tas 253 L3
Store Creek NSW 110 C6
Storm Bay Tas 239, 253 L7
Storys Creek Tas 255 M7
Stowport Tas 254 F5
Stradbroke Vic 70 C8
Stradbroke West Vic 70 C8
Strahan Tas 252 B1, 254 C10, **326–7**
Stratford NSW 111 K4
Stratford Qld 149 L5, 155 D7
Stratford Vic 70 C6
Strath Creek Vic 67 P4, 72 B8
Strathalbyn Qld 146 D2
Strathalbyn SA 230 A6, 233 K10
Strathallan Vic 69 N9
Stratham WA 202 B7
Strathaven Qld 149 H2, 154 D10
Strathblane Tas 253 H7

Strathbogie NSW 113 J5
Strathbogie Qld 146 D2
Strathbogie Vic 72 D6
Strathbogie Ranges Vic 72 C7
Strathbowen Qld 146 D3
Strathburn Qld 148 G1, 154 D9
Strathdownie Vic 66 B5
Strathearn SA 233 M3
Strathelbiss Qld 150 D7
Strathern NSW 115 J2
Strathewen Vic 65 J2, 72 B10
Strathfield Qld 146 F5
Strathfield Qld 150 F4
Strathfieldsaye Vic 67 M2
Strathfillan Qld 151 J6
Strathgordon Tas 252 E4
Strathkellar Vic 66 E5
Strathlea Vic 67 L3
Strathleven Qld 149 H4
Strathmay Qld 148 G2, 154 D10
Strathmerton Vic 72 C2
Strathmore Qld 146 D3
Strathmore Qld 148 G7
Strathmore Qld 151 L8
Strathpark Qld 149 H10, 151 J1
Strathpine Qld 145 M6
Stratton Vic 68 F6
Streaky Bay SA 232 B5
Streatham Vic 67 H5
Strelley WA 211 J5
Strickland Tas 252 G2
Strickland Bay WA 208 E6, 304
Striped Lake WA 205 N2
Stroud NSW 111 K4
Stroud Road NSW 111 K4
Strzelecki Vic 65 L6
Strzelecki Desert SA 235 L6
Strzelecki NP Tas 255 J3, 255 N1
Strzelecki RR SA 235 L7
Stuart Qld 149 N9
Stuart Creek SA 234 G9
Stuart Mill Vic 67 H2
Stuart Town NSW 110 C6
Stuarts Point NSW 113 M9
Stuarts Well NT 178 G7
Sturt Meadows WA 205 L8
Sturt NP NSW 114 B2
Sturt Stony Desert SA 235 K4
Sturt Vale SA 233 M6
Sturts Meadows NSW 114 B6
Styx Qld 147 H7
Sudley Qld 154 C6
Sue City Camp NSW 109 A6
Suffolk Park NSW 113 P2
Sugar River NSW 111 J2
Suggan Buggan Vic 71 H2, 73 N7
Sullivan WA 204 E8
Sullivans Vic 65 P3, 70 A6
Sulphur Creek Tas 254 F5
Summerfield Vic 67 L1, 69 L10
Summervale Qld 153 N2
Sunbury Vic 64 F2, 67 N5
Sunday Creek NT 174 G10, 176 G2
Sundown Qld 149 K7, 155 B10
Sundown NP Qld 145 K9
Sunny Corner NSW 110 E7
Sunnyside NSW 113 K3
Sunnyside Tas 254 G6
Sunrise Qld 144 D3
Sunset Vic 68 A5
Sunset Country Vic 68 B3
Sunset Strip NSW 114 C8
Sunshine Vic 64 G3, 67 N6
Sunshine Beach Qld 126, 127, 128, 129
Sunshine Coast Qld **126–7**, 128–9, 145 N5
Supplejack NT 176 B7
Surat Qld 144 F6
Surbiton Qld 146 C8
Surface Hill NSW 113 L4
Surfers Paradise Qld *121*, 136, *136*, 145 N8
Surges Bay Tas 253 J7
Surveyors Bay Tas 253 J7
Surveyors Lake NSW 114 F9
Sussex NSW 115 L7
Sussex Inlet NSW 109 F4
Sutherland NSW 109 G2, 111 H9
Sutherland Vic 67 H1, 69 H10
Sutherlands SA 233 K8
Sutton NSW 109 C4

Sutton Vic 69 H7
Sutton Grange Vic 67 M3
Swan Bay NSW 111 K5
Swan Bay Vic 44, 64 F5
Swan Hill Vic 69 J6, 265
Swan Marsh Vic 67 J8
Swan Reach SA 233 L9
Swan Reach Vic 70 F6
Swan Reach CP SA 74, 233 L9
Swan River Tas 243, 255 N9
Swan River WA *181*, 183, **184–5**, *185*, **190–1**, *190*, 202 C4
Swan Vale NSW 113 J6
Swan Vale Qld 153 K1
Swanlean Qld 151 P6
Swanpool Vic 72 E6
Swansea NSW 111 J6
Swansea Tas 242, 253 N1, 255 N10
Swanwater Vic 67 H1, 69 H10
Swanwater West Vic 67 H1, 69 H10
Sweers Island Qld 148 C6, 285 285
Swifts Creek Vic 70 F3, 73 L8
Swim Creek Plains NT 174 E4
Sydenham Vic 64 F2, 67 N5
Sydenham Inlet Vic 49, 71 K6
Sydenham West Vic 64 F2, 67 N5
Sydney NSW *35*, *75*, 111 H9
Sydney Harbour NSW *35*, **76–7**, *76–7*, *77*
Sydney Island Qld 148 C5, 285
Sylvania WA 211 K10
Synnot Range WA 209 H6

Tabba Tabba WA 211 H6
Tabberabbera Vic 70 D5, 73 K10
Tabbimoble NSW 113 N4
Tabbita NSW 117 K4
Table Top NSW 117 M8
Tableland WA 209 K7
Tabletop Qld 148 G7
Tabletop Qld 149 M9
Tabor Vic 66 E6
Tabourie Lake NSW 109 F5
Tabratong NSW 115 N8
Tabulam NSW 113 L3
Taggerty Vic 65 L1, 72 D9
Tahara Vic 66 D6
Tahara West Vic 66 C5
Tahmoor NSW 109 F2, 110 F10
Tahune FR Tas 253 H6
Tailem Bend SA 230 A7, 233 L10
Taincrow WA 204 G6
Takone Tas 254 D5
Talarm NSW 113 M8
Talaroo Qld 149 J7
Talavera Qld 146 A1, 149 L10, 151 N1
Talawa Tas 255 M6
Talawanta NSW 115 M2
Talawanta Qld 148 D8
Talbingo NSW 109 A5, 117 P7
Talbot Vic 67 K3
Talbot Well NT 176 B7
Talbragar River NSW 110 B4
Taldora Qld 148 E9
Taldra SA 233 N9
Taleeban NSW 117 L3
Talgarno Vic 73 J3, 264
Talia SA 232 C6
Talisker WA 204 D4
Tallageira Vic 66 A2
Tallalara NSW 114 F5
Tallandoon Vic 73 J5
Tallangatta Vic 73 J4
Tallangatta East Vic 73 J4
Tallangatta Valley Vic 73 K4
Tallaringa CP SA 234 A7, 231 G5
Tallarook Vic 67 P3, 72 A8
Tallebung NSW 115 L9, 117 L1
Tallering WA 204 E7
Tallimba NSW 117 M3
Tallong NSW 109 E3
Tallowa Dam NSW 92, 93, 109 F3
Tallygaroopna Vic 72 C4
Talmalmo NSW 117 N8
Talwood Qld 144 G9
Talyawalka NSW 114 E9
Tamala WA 204 B5
Tamarang NSW 110 E2
Tambar Springs NSW 109 G2, 111 H9
Tambellup WA 202 E8
Tambo Qld 144 A2
Tambo Crossing Vic 70 F4, 73 L9

Tambo River Vic 50, 51, 53, **260–1**, *261*
Tambo Upper Vic 70 F6
Tamboon Vic 71 L5
Tamboon Inlet Vic 49, 71 L5
Tamborine Qld 145 N8
Tambua NSW 115 J7
Taminick Vic 72 E5
Tamleugh Vic 72 C5
Tamleugh North Vic 72 C5
Tamleugh West Vic 72 C5
Tammin WA 202 E4
Tamworth NSW 110 G1, 112 G9
Tanami Desert NT 176 D9
Tanami Downs NT 176 B9
Tanby Qld 147 K8
Tandarook Vic 67 H8
Tandarra Vic 67 L1, 69 L10
Tanderra Qld 144 D1
Tandou NSW 114 C10, 116 C1
Tangadee WA 205 H2
Tangalooma Qld 123, **124–5**, *125*
Tangambalanga Vic 73 H4
Tangorin Qld 151 L5
Tanja NSW 109 E8
Tanjil Bren Vic 65 N3
Tanjil River Vic 63
Tanjil South Vic 65 N5
Tankerton Vic 65 J6
Tanners Spring NSW 110 A5
Tannum Sands Qld 147 L9
Tansey Qld 145 L4
Tantangara Reservoir NSW 106, 109 B6
Tantanoola SA 230 F9
Tantawangalo NP NSW 109 D8
Tanumbirini NT 177 J2
Tanunda SA 233 K9
Tanwood Vic 67 J3
Tapa Bay NT 163
Taplan SA 233 N9
Tara NSW 115 H5
Tara Qld 145 H6
Taradale Vic 67 M3
Tarago NSW 109 D4
Tarago Vic 65 L4
Tarago Reservoir Vic 62, 63, 65 L4
Tarago River Vic 62, 63
Taragoro SA 232 E7
Taralba NSW 115 M2
Taralga NSW 109 E2, 110 E10
Tarana NSW 110 E8
Taranna Tas 240, 253 M6
Taravale Qld 149 M9
Tarban NSW 113 K3
Tarcombe Vic 72 B7
Tarcoola SA 232 B1
Tarcoon NSW 115 L4
Tarcowie SA 233 J6
Tarcutta NSW 117 N6
Tardie WA 204 E7
Tardun WA 204 E8
Taree NSW 111 L3
Taree Qld 146 A8, 151 N8
Tareleton Tas 254 G5
Tarella NSW 114 E6
Targa Tas 255 L6
Tarin Rock WA 202 F6
Tarin Rock NR WA 202 F6
Taringo Downs NSW 115 J8
Tarlee SA 233 K8
Tarlo NSW 109 E3
Tarlo River NP NSW 109 E3, 110 E10
Tarlton Downs NT 179 M4
Tarmoola Qld 144 E7
Tarmoola WA 205 L8
Tarnagulla Vic 67 K2
Tarnma SA 233 K8
Tarnook Vic 72 D5
Taroborah Qld 146 E8
Tarome Qld 145 M8
Taroom Qld 142, 144 G3
Taroona Tas 253 K5
Tarpeena SA 230 F10
Tarra Valley Vic 65 P7, 70 A9
Tarra-Bulga NP Vic 70 A8
Tarragal Vic 66 C8
Tarragona Qld 151 L6
Tarraleen Tas 252 F2, 328
Tarranginnie Vic 68 C10
Tarrango Vic 68 D3
Tarranyurk Vic 68 E9

Tarraville Vic 70 B9
Tarrawingee Vic 72 F5
Tarrayoukyan Vic 66 C4
Tarrenlea Vic 66 D5
Tarrina Qld 144 A2, 153 P2
Tarrington Vic 66 E6
Tarrion NSW 115 M4
Tartrus Qld 146 G7
Tarvano Qld 151 K5
Tarwin Lower Vic 65 L8
Tarwong NSW 116 G3
Tarzali Qld 149 L6, 155 D9
Tasman NSW 115 H9
Tasman Island Tas 241, *241*
Tasman Peninsula Tas **240–1**, *241*
Tatham NSW 113 N3
Tathra NSW 109 E8, **274**
Tathra NP WA 202 B1, 204 D10
Tatong Vic 72 E6
Tatura Vic 67 P1, 69 P10, 72 B5
Tatyoon Vic 66 G5
Tatyoon North Vic 67 H5
Taunton Qld 145 L1, 147 L10
Tawallah NT 177 L2
Tawonga Vic 70 C1, 73 J6
Tayene Tas 255 L6
Taylors Flat NSW 109 C2, 110 C10
Tchelery NSW 116 G5
Tea Gardens NSW **88**, 89, 111 K5
Tea Tree Tas 253 K4
Teal Point Vic 69 L7
Teatree Outstation SA 233 L1
Tebin Qld 153 L5
Teddywaddy Vic 69 J9
Teddywaddy West Vic 69 H9
Teds Beach Tas 252 E4
Teesdale Vic 64 C4, 67 L7
Teewah Beach Qld 126, *126*, 129
Teewah Creek Qld 138, 139
Tego Qld 144 B9
Teilta NSW 114 A6
Telangatuk East Vic 66 D3
Telegraph Point NSW 111 M1, 113 M10
Telfer Mine WA 211 N7
Telford SA 235 J10
Telford Vic 72 D3
Telleraga NSW 112 D5
Telopea Downs Vic 68 B9
Telowie Gorge CP SA 233 J6
Temma Tas 254 A5
Temora NSW 117 N4
Tempe Downs NT 178 F7
Templestowe Vic 65 H3, 67 P6, 72 A10
Templeton Qld 148 G8
Tempy Vic 68 F6
Ten Mile Vic 65 N1, 72 E9
Tenham Qld 153 J3
Tenindewa WA 204 D8
Tennant Creek NT 177 H8
Tennappera Qld 152 G8
Tennyson Vic 69 M9
Tent Creek NSW 113 K4
Tent Hill NSW 113 J5
Tent Hill SA 233 H4
Tent Island NR WA 210 C7
Tenterden NSW 113 J7
Tenterden WA 202 E9
Tenterfield NSW 142, 143, 113 K3
Tepko SA 233 K10
Terang Vic 66 G7
Teridgerie NSW 112 B9
Termeil NSW 109 F5
Tero Creek NSW 114 D4
Terowie NSW 115 P9
Terowie SA 233 K6
Terragong NSW 110 F3
Terrey Hills NSW 111 H8
Terrick Terrick Qld 153 N2
Terrick Terrick Vic 69 L9
Terrigal NSW 86, 111 J7
Terry Hie Hie NSW 112 E6
Teryawynia NSW 114 E8
Tetoora Road Vic 65 L6
Teurika NSW 114 D2
Teutonic WA 205 L7
Teviot Qld 151 J6
Tewantin Qld 138, 145 M5
Tewkesbury Tas 254 E5
Texas Qld 145 J9
Texas Qld 146 A8, 151 P8

INDEX OF PLACE NAMES 413

Texas Downs WA 209 N7
Thalia Vic 69 H9
Thallon Qld 144 F9
Thane Qld 145 K8
Thangoo WA 208 D9, 211 N2
Thangool Qld 145 H1, 147 J10
Thargomindah Qld 153 K8
Tharwa ACT 109 C5
The Banca Tas 255 M4
The Bark Hut Inn NT 174 E5
The Bluff NSW 115 K7
The Broadwater Qld 120–1, *121*, 122, 123, 136
The Brothers Vic 70 F2, 73 L7
The Cap Vic 64 C5, 67 K7
The Cascade Vic 73 K4
The Caves Qld 147 J8
The Channon NSW 113 N2
The Chase Qld 146 G4
The Coorong SA *222–3, 222, 223,* 224, *225*, 230 B6
The Cove Vic 66 G8
The Cups Vic 64 G6, 67 N8
The Dutchmans Stern CP SA 233 H4
The Entrance NSW 86, 111 J7
The Fingerboards Vic 70 D6
The Gap SA 213
The Garden NT 179 J5
The Gardens Tas 255 P5
The Granites NT 176 C9, 178 C1
The Gums Qld 145 H7
The Gums SA 233 L8
The Gurdies Vic 65 K6
The Heart Vic 70 C7
The Honeysuckles Vic 70 D8
The Lagoon NSW 110 D8
The Lagoon NSW 115 L3
The Lake Qld 146 A7, 151 P7
The Lakes WA 202 C4
The Lakes NP Vic 39, 54, *51*, 70 E6
The Lynd Qld 149 K9
The Monument Qld 150 D5
The Nobbies Vic 43, 65 H7, 252
The Oaks Qld 147 J7
The Oaks Qld 149 J8
The Oaks Vic 65 N2, 72 E10
The Peaks Qld 144 D5
The Quiet Corner NSW 115 P6
The Ranch Qld 151 K8
The Range NSW 114 F4
The Range WA 210 D8
The Rock NSW 117 M6
The Rookery NSW 115 K7
The Sisters Vic 66 G7
The Summit Qld 145 L9
The Twins SA 234 D9
The Vale NSW 116 F3
The Veldt NSW 114 B5
The Whitsundays Qld 146 G2, 288, **289**
Theda WA 209 K3
Theodore Qld 145 H2
Theresa Creek NSW 113 M3
Thevenard SA 232 A4, 231 G10
Thevenard Island WA 210 D7, 310, 311
Thirlstone Qld 146 A5, 151 N5
Thirlstane Tas 255 H5
Thirroul NSW 109 G2, 110 G10
Thistlebank Qld 151 N6
Thistlebeds SA 233 K7
Thomastown Vic 65 H2, 67 P5, 72 A10
Thomby Qld 144 F8
Thomby Qld 144 G2
Thompson River Vic 50, 70 A6
Thomson Bay WA *192–3*
Thomson River Qld 151 L8
Thoona Vic 72 E4
Thoopara Qld 146 F3
Thora NSW 113 M7
Thordon Park Qld 144 G4
Thornborough Qld 149 K5, 155 C8
Thornhill Qld 144 E5
Thornleigh Qld 151 M10, 153 M1
Thornton Qld 151 M6
Thornton Vic 72 D8
Thornton Beach Qld 149 L4, 155 D5, 291
Thorntonia Qld 148 B9, 150 B1
Thorpdale Vic 65 N6
Thoura NSW 115 H2
Thowgla Vic 73 M4

Thowgla Upper Vic 73 M4
Thredbo River NSW 276
Thredbo Village NSW 109 A8
Three Bridges Vic 65 K3
Three Rivers WA 205 J3
Three Springs WA 204 E9
Three Ways Roadhouse NT 177 J7
Thrushton NP Qld 144 D7
Thuddungra NSW 109 A2, 117 P4
Thule NSW 116 G7
Thulloo NSW 117 M3
Thunda Qld 153 J3
Thundelarra WA 204 F8
Thurgoona NSW 117 M8
Thuringowa Qld 149 N9
Thurla Vic 68 E2
Thurlga SA 232 D5
Thurloo Downs NSW 114 E2
Thurra River Vic *49*
Thurrulgoonia Qld 153 P9
Thursday Island Qld 154 C2, 279
Thylungra Qld 153 K4
Ti-Tree NT 178 G3
Ti-Tree NT 178 G3
Ti-Tree Farm NT 178 G3
Tiaro Qld 145 M3
Tiarri NSW 115 H10, 117 H1
Tibarri Qld 150 F3
Tibbuc NSW 111 K3
Tibooburra NSW 114 C2
Tichborne NSW 117 P2
Tickalara Qld 153 H9
Tickera SA 233 H7
Tidal River Vic *39*, 54–5, 65 N9
Tieri Qld 146 F8
Tieyon SA 234 A1, 231 G1
Tilba Tilba NSW 109 E7
Tilboroo Qld 153 N7
Tilmouth Well NT 178 F4
Tilpa NSW 114 G6
Tilpilly NSW 114 G6
Tiltagoona NSW 115 H6
Timbarra Vic 70 G4, 73 M9
Timber Creek NT 174 C9, 176 C1, 298
Timber Lake Vic **56–7,** *57*
Timberfield WA 203 J2
Timberoo South Vic 68 E6
Timbillica NSW 109 D10
Timboon Vic 67 H8
Timmering Vic 69 N10
Timor NSW 111 H2
Timor Qld 144 E3
Timor Vic 67 K3
Timora Qld 148 F7
Tims Channel Vic 69 H6
Tin Can Bay Qld 126, **128–9,** 145 M4
Tinamba Vic 70 B6
Tinderbox Tas 239, 253 K6
Tinderry NSW 153 L7
Tindo Qld 151 L3
Tingha NSW 113 H6
Tingoora Qld 145 K5
Tinnenburra Qld 153 N9
Tinonee NSW 111 L3
Tinowon Qld 144 F6
Tintaldra Vic 73 M3
Tintinara SA 230 B8
Tipperary NT 174 D6
Tiranna Qld 153 N5
Tiree Qld 151 N5
Tireen Qld 145 J3
Tirlta NSW 114 C6
Tirranna Roadhouse Qld 148 C7
Tittybong Vic 69 J7
Tiverton SA 233 L5
Tjukayirla Roadhouse WA 207 B1
Tnorala CR NT 178 F6
Tobermory NT 179 P3
Tobermory Qld 153 K6
Tocumwal NSW 117 J7, 265
Todd River NT 179 J6
Todmorden SA 234 B3
Tods Tas 255 J9
Togari Tas 254 B4
Togganoggera NSW 109 D6
Toiberry Tas 255 J7
Tolga Qld 149 L6, 155 D8
Tolmie Vic 72 F7
Tom Groggin NSW 109 A8, 117 P9
Tom Price WA 210 G8
Tomahawk Qld 146 B6, 151 P6
Tomahawk Tas 255 M4

Tomakin NSW 109 E6
Tomerong NSW 109 F4
Tomingley NSW 110 A5, 115 P9
Tomoo Qld 144 C6
Toms Cap Creek Vic 70 B8
Toms Lake NSW 117 H3
Tonderburine NSW 110 B1, 112 B10
Tongala Vic 69 P9, 72 A4
Tonganah Tas 255 L5
Tonghi Creek Vic 71 K4
Tongio Vic 70 E3, 73 L8
Tongio West Vic 70 E3, 73 L8
Tongo NSW 114 F5
Tonkoro Qld 151 H9
Tooan Vic 66 D2
Toobanna Qld 149 M8
Toobeah Qld 144 G9
Tooborac Vic 67 N3
Toodyay WA 202 F4
Toogong NSW 110 B7
Toogoolawah Qld 145 L6
Toolakea Qld 149 M9
Toolamba Vic 72 B5
Toolamba West Vic 72 B5
Toolangi Vic 65 K2, 72 C9
Toolebuc Qld 150 F6
Toolern Vale Vic 64 F2, 67 M5
Tooleybuc NSW 116 E6
Toolibin WA 202 E6
Tooligie SA 232 D8
Tooligie Hill SA 232 D7
Toolleen Vic 67 N2
Toolondo Vic 66 D3
Toolondo Reservoir Vic 66 D3
Toolong Vic 66 E8
Toolonga NR WA 204 D5
Tooloom NSW 112 A9, 115 P6
Tooloom Qld 153 H2
Tooloombah Qld 147 H7
Tooloombilla Qld 144 D4
Tooloon NSW 112 A9, 115 P6
Tooma NSW 109 A6, 117 P8
Toomba Qld 146 A2, 149 L10, 151 N2
Toombullup Vic 72 F7
Toompine Qld 153 L6
Tooms Lake CA Tas 246, 253 L1, 255 M10
Toongabbie Vic 70 A7
Toongi NSW 110 B4
Toora Vic 65 N7
Tooradin Vic 43, 65 J5
Toorale NSW 115 J4
Toorale East NSW 115 J4
Tooraweenah NSW 110 B2
Toorongo Vic 65 M3
Toorongo River Vic 63
Toorooka NSW 113 M9
Tootool NSW 117 M6
Tootoolah Qld 146 F5
Toowoomba Qld 141, 142, 143, 145 L7
Top Hut NSW 116 D3
Top Lake Vic 48, 49, 358, 359
Top Springs NT 176 E2
Topiram Vic 65 L6
Torbanlea Qld 145 M3
Torbreck Station Vic 65 M1, 72 E9
Torndirrup NP WA 202 F10
Toronto NSW 111 J6
Torquay Vic 64 D6, 67 M8
Torrens Creek Qld 151 N3
Torrens Island SA 218, 219
Torrens Vale SA 230 B5
Torres Strait Qld 154 B1, 279, 280
Torrington NSW 113 J4
Torrita NSW 68 D5
Torrumbarry Vic 69 M9
Torryburn NSW 113 H8
Tortilla Flats NT 174 D5
Torver Valley Qld 151 L3
Torwood Qld 149 J6
Tostaree Vic 70 G5, 73 N10
Tothill Creek SA 233 K8
Tottenham NSW 115 N8
Tottington Vic 67 H2
Toulby Gate NSW 115 M1
Towallum NSW 113 M6
Towamba NSW 109 D9
Towan Vic 69 H5
Towaninny NSW 69 J8
Towaninny South Vic 69 J8
Tower Hill Vic 66 F8
Townson Qld 145 L8

Townsville Qld 30, 149 N9, 288
Towong Vic 73 M3
Towong Upper Vic 73 M4
Towrana WA 204 D3
Towrang NSW 110 E3
Trafalgar Qld 153 K2
Trafalgar Vic 65 N5
Tragowell Vic 69 L8
Trangie NSW 115 P8
Traralgon Vic 65 P5, 70 A7
Traralgon South Vic 65 P6, 70 A8
Travellers Lake NSW 116 C2
Trawalla Vic 64 A1, 67 J4
Trawool Vic 67 P3, 72 B8
Trayning WA 202 F3
Traynors Lagoon Vic 67 H1, 69 H10
Treasure Vic 70 D3, 73 J8
Treasures Vic 70 D3, 73 J8
Trebonne Qld 149 M8
Tregoning Qld 144 C5
Treleca NSW 116 C2
Trent Qld 146 A9, 151 N9
Trentham Vic 64 E1, 67 M4
Trentham East Vic 64 E1, 67 M4
Trephina Gorge Nature Park NT 179 J6
Tresco Vic 69 K7
Trewalla Qld 153 J1
Trewalla Vic 66 C8
Trewilga NSW 110 A5, 115 P9, 117 P1
Triabunna Tas 253 M3
Trial Harbour Tas 254 C9
Triamble NSW 110 C6
Triangle Flat NSW 109 D1, 110 D8
Trida NSW 115 H10, 117 H1
Trigg Point WA 183, **188–9**
Trigwell Qld 202 B7
Trinidad Qld 153 L3
Trinita Vic 68 E4
Trinity Beach Qld 149 L5, 155 D7, 291
Troubridge Island CP SA 230 A4, 233 H10
Troubridge Point SA 217, 230 A4
Trousers Point Tas 255 J3, 324
Trowutta Tas 254 B4
Truganina Vic 64 F3, 67 N6
Trundle NSW 115 N10, 117 N1
Trungley Hall NSW 117 N4
Trunkey NSW 109 D1, 110 C8
Truro SA 233 K9
Truslove WA 203 L7
Truslove Townsite NR WA 203 L7
Tuan Qld 145 M3
Tuart Forest NP WA 202 B7
Tubbul NSW 109 A2, 117 P4
Tubbut Vic 71 J2, 73 P7
Tucabia NSW 113 N5
Tuckanarra WA 204 G6
Tucklan NSW 110 D4
Tuckurimba NSW 113 N3
Tudor Vic 69 H5
Tuen Qld 153 P9
Tuena NSW 109 D2, 110 C9
Tuggerah NSW 111 J7
Tuggeranong ACT 109 C5
Tulendeena Tas 255 M5
Tulka SA 232 D10
Tulkara Vic 67 H3
Tullah Tas 254 D8
Tullakool NSW 116 G7
Tullamarine Vic 64 G2, 67 N5
Tullamore NSW 115 N9
Tullaroop Reservoir Vic 67 K3
Tullibigeal NSW 117 M2
Tulloh Vic 64 A6, 67 J8
Tully Qld 149 M7, 155 E10
Tully Heads Qld 149 M7
Tully River Tas 254 C9, 327
Tulmur Qld 151 H7
Tumbar Qld 146 B9
Tumbarumba NSW 109 A6, 117 P7
Tumblong NSW 109 A4, 117 P5
Tumbulgum NSW 113 P1
Tumby Bay SA 232 E9
Tummaville Qld 145 K8
Tumorrama NSW 109 B4
Tumut NSW 109 A5, 117 P6
Tumut River NSW 109 A5
Tunbridge Tas 253 K1, 255 L10
Tuncurry NSW 111 L4
Tungamah Vic 72 D3

Tungkillo SA 233 K10
Tunnack Tas 253 K2
Tunnel Tas 255 K5
Tunnel Creek NP WA 208 G8
Tunney WA 202 E8
Tuppal NSW 117 J7
Turee NSW 110 E3
Turee Creek WA 211 H10
Turill NSW 110 E3
Turkey Beach Qld 134, 135, 147 L10
Turkey Creek Qld 146 F9
Turkey Creek WA 209 M7
Turlee NSW 116 E3
Turlinjah NSW 109 E7
Turner WA 209 M8
Turners Beach Tas 254 G5
Turners Flat NSW 113 M9
Turners Marsh Tas 255 K6
Tuross Head NSW 109 E7
Turrawalla Qld 146 E4
Turrawan NSW 112 E8
Turriff Vic 68 F6
Turriff West Vic 68 F6
Turtons Creek Vic 65 N7
Tutanning NR WA 202 E5
Tutye Vic 68 C5
Tweed Heads NSW 113 P1
Twelve Mile NSW 110 C5
Twin Hills Qld 146 C5
Twin Peaks WA 204 E6
Twin Wells NSW 114 B10, 116 B2
Two Mile Flat NSW 110 D4
Two Peoples Bay NR WA 202 F10
Two Rocks WA 202 B4
Two Wells SA 233 J9
Twofold Bay NSW 109 E9, 274–5
Twyford Qld 149 L4, 155 C6
Tyaak Vic 67 P4, 72 B8
Tyabb Vic 65 H5
Tyagong NSW 109 A2, 110 A9, 117 P4
Tyalgum NSW 113 N1
Tycannah NSW 112 E5
Tyenna Tas 252 G4
Tyers Vic 65 P5, 70 A7
Tyers Junction Vic 65 N4
Tyers Park Vic 65 P5, 70 A7
Tylden Vic 64 E1, 67 M4
Tyndale NSW 113 N5
Tynong Vic 65 K4
Tyntynder Central Vic 69 J6
Typo Vic 70 A2, 72 G7
Tyraman NSW 111 J4
Tyrendarra Vic 66 D7
Tyrendarra East Vic 66 D7
Tyringham NSW 113 L7
Tyrrell Downs Vic 68 G6

Uanda Qld 151 M5
Uarbry NSW 110 D3
Uardry NSW 117 J4
Uaroo WA 210 D8
Ubobo Qld 145 K1, 147 L10
Ucharonidge NT 177 J4
Udialla WA 208 F8, 211 P1
Uki NSW 113 N2
Ulalie NSW 114 F6
Ulamambri NSW 110 D1, 112 D10
Ulan NSW 110 D4
Uley NSW 117 M4
Ulimaroa Qld 144 G5
Ulinda NSW 110 D2
Ulladulla NSW 109 F5
Ullawarra WA 210 E9
Ullina Vic 67 L4
Ullswater Vic 66 C3
Ulmarra NSW 113 N5
Ulong NSW 113 M7
Ultima Vic 69 H6
Uluru-Katatjuta NP NT 178 D9
Ulva Qld 151 N4
Ulverstone Tas 254 F5
Umbakumba NT 175 M6
Umbango NSW 117 N7
Umbeara NT 179 H9
Umberatana SA 235 K10
Umbrawarra Gorge NP NT 174 E7
Umina NSW 111 H8
Unanderra NSW 109 G3, 110 G10
Undara Volcanic NP Qld 149 K8
Undera Vic 69 P9, 72 B4
Underbank NSW 111 J4

414 INDEX OF PLACE NAMES

Underbool Vic 68 D5
Undercliff Qld 146 G5
Underwood Tas 255 K6
Undilla Qld 148 B10, 150 B1
Undina Qld 150 F3
Undoolya NT 179 H6
Undulla Qld 144 G6
Ungarie NSW 117 M3
Ungarra SA 232 E8
Ungo Qld 153 L2
Unicup NR WA 202 D8
Unnamed CP SA 231 A4
Uno SA 232 F5
Upalinna SA 233 K3
Uplands Vic 70 E2, 73 L7
Upper Beaconsfield Vic 65 J4
Upper Bingara NSW 112 G6
Upper Blessington Tas 255 L7
Upper Bowman NSW 111 J3
Upper Castra Tas 254 F6
Upper Horton NSW 112 F7
Upper Manilla NSW 112 G8
Upper Mount Hicks Tas 254 E5
Upper Natone Tas 254 E5
Upper Rollands Plains NSW 111 L1, 113 L10
Upper Scamander Tas 255 N6
Upper Stone Qld 149 M8
Upper Stowport Tas 254 E5
Upper Swan WA 202 C4
Upper Yarra Reservoir Vic 72 D10
Upson Downs NSW 116 E4
Urala WA 210 C7
Uralla NSW 113 J8
Urambie Qld 151 N9
Urana NSW 117 L6
Urana West Qld 144 B6
Urandangi Qld 150 A5
Urangan Qld 130, 132, 133
Urangeline NSW 117 L7
Urangeline East NSW 117 L7
Urania SA 233 H9
Urannah Qld 146 F3
Uranquinty NSW 117 N6
Urapunga NT 175 J8
Urawa NR WA 204 D7
Urbenville NSW 113 L2
Urella Downs NSW 114 E3
Urisino NSW 114 F3
Urquhart Qld 150 E2
Urunga NSW 113 N8, 269
Useless Loop WA 204 B4, 313
Uteara NSW 115 J4
Utopia NT 179 J3
Uxbridge Tas 253 H4

Vacy NSW 111 J5
Valencia Creek Vic 70 C6
Valery NSW 113 M7
Valla Beach NSW 113 N8
Valley of Lagoons Qld 149 K8
Valley of Lakes Qld **140–1**
Valroona NSW 117 K2
Van Diemen Gulf NT 174 E3, 294
Van Lee Qld 149 J7
Vanderlin Island NT 175 N9, **300–1**, *301*
Vandyke Qld 146 E10
Vanrook Qld 148 F5
Varley WA 203 H6
Vasey Vic 66 D4
Vashon Head NT 174 E2, 295
Vasse WA 202 B7
Vaughan Vic 67 L3
Vaughan Springs NT 178 D3
Veitch SA 233 N9
Velox Hut Qld 148 G6
Vena Park Qld 148 E8
Ventnor Vic 65 H7, 67 P8
Venus Bay SA 232 B6
Venus Bay Vic 65 L8
Venus Bay CP SA 232 B6
Venus Bay CR SA 232 B6
Verdun Valley Qld 150 G8
Verdure Qld 149 K6, 155 C8
Vergemont Qld 151 J9
Vermont Qld 146 F6
Vermont Hill NSW 115 M9
Vernon Islands NT 160, 174 D3
Verona Sands Tas 253 J7
Verran SA 232 E8
Vervale Vic 65 K5

Victor Harbor SA 220, 221, *221, 222*, 226, 230 B5
Victoria Downs Qld 146 B3
Victoria Point Qld 145 N7
Victoria River NT 174 B9, 176 D4, **298–9**
Victoria River Downs NT 176 D2
Victoria River Wayside Inn NT 174 D9, 176 D1
Victoria Rock NR WA 203 K3
Victoria Vale Qld 148 G9
Victoria Valley Vic 66 E5
Victory Downs NT 178 G10
View Point Outstation NSW 114 G4
Viewmont NSW 114 D8
Villa Dale Qld 151 K3
Villafranca Qld 146 E6
Vimy Qld 147 J9
Vinabel Qld 146 C8
Vincentia NSW 95, 109 G4
Vindex Qld 151 K7
Vinifera Vic 69 J5
Violet Town Vic 72 D6
Violet Vale Qld 148 E10, 150 F1
Virginia SA 233 J9
Vite Vite Vic 67 H6
Vite Vite North Vic 67 H6
Vivian Wells SA 234 D10
Vivonne Bay SA 230 B2, 321
Vivonne Bay CP SA 230 C2
Volo NSW 114 F7
Vrilya Point Qld 154 C3, 280

Waaia Vic 72 B3
Waar Waar Qld 145 J7
Wabba Wilderness Park Vic 73 L4
Waddamana Tas 253 H1, 255 H10
Waddi NSW 117 K5
Waddikee SA 232 E6
Waddington WA 202 C2
Wade Hill Qld 153 M4
Waddy Point Qld 131, 132, *132*, 133, 145 N2
Wadeye NT 174 B7
Wadnaminga SA 233 M5
Wagant Vic 68 F5
Wagga Wagga NSW 117 N6
Wagga Wagga WA 204 F7
Waggarandall Vic 72 D4
Wagin WA 202 E7
Wagoe Beach WA 204 B7, 314, 315
Wagonga Inlet NSW 109 E7, 272–3
Wagoora Qld 146 F3
Wahgunyah Vic 72 F3
Wahgunyah CR SA 231 E10
Wahring Vic 67 P2, 72 B6
Wahroonga WA 204 C3
Waikerie SA 233 M8
Wail Vic 66 E1, 68 E10
Wairewa Vic 70 G5, 73 N10
Wairuna Qld 149 L8
Waitara Qld 146 F5
Waitchie Vic 69 H6
Waite River NT 179 J4
Waitpinga SA 220, 221, 230 B5
Waiwera SA 233 N4
Waka NSW 114 A2
Wakefield River SA 226–7, 233 J8
Wakes Lagoon Qld 153 M3
Wakooka Outstation Qld 149 K2, 154 F9
Wakool NSW 116 G7
Wal Wal Vic 66 F2
Walba Qld 144 G1, 147 H10
Walbundrie NSW 117 L7
Walcha NSW 113 J9
Walcha Road NSW 113 J9
Waldburg WA 204 G2
Waldegrave Islands CP SA 232 C7
Walebing WA 202 C2
Walenda NSW 114 G9, 116 G1
Walgett NSW 115 P4
Walgoolan WA 202 G3
Walgun NSW 211 L9
Walhalla Vic 65 P4, 70 A6
Walhallow NT 177 L4
Walkamin Qld 149 L6, 155 D8
Walkaway WA 204 C8
Walker Flat SA 233 L9
Walkers Hill NSW 115 M9
Walkerston Qld 146 G4

Walkerville Vic 65 M9
Walla Walla NSW 117 M7
Wallabadah NSW 110 G2
Wallabadah NSW 148 G7
Wallabella Qld 144 F6
Wallabi Point NSW 111 L3
Wallace Vic 64 C2, 67 L5
Wallace Rockhole NT 178 G7
Wallacedale Vic 66 D6
Wallagaraugh River Vic 49, 258, 259
Wallagoot Lake NSW 109 E8, 274
Wallal Qld 144 A5, 153 P5
Wallalong NSW 111 J5
Wallaloo Vic 67 H6
Wallaloo East Vic 66 G2
Wallamunga NT 176 A5
Wallan Vic 64 G1, 67 P4, 72 A9
Wallan East Vic 65 H1, 67 P4, 72 A9
Wallangarra Qld 145 L10
Wallangra NSW 112 G4
Wallareenya WA 211 H5
Wallarobba NSW 111 J5
Wallaroo Qld 147 H9
Wallaroo SA 233 H8
Wallen Qld 153 P7
Wallendbeen NSW 109 A3, 117 P5
Wallerawang NSW 102, 110 E7
Wallerberdina SA 233 H3
Walleroobie NSW 117 M5
Walli NSW 109 C1, 110 B8
Wallinduc NSW 64 A3, 67 J6
Walling Rock WA 205 K9
Wallington Vic 64 E5, 67 M7
Walls of Jerusalem NP Tas 254 G8
Wallsend NSW 111 J6
Wallumbilla Qld 144 F5
Wallumburrawang NSW 110 B2
Wallundry NSW 117 N4
Wallup Vic 68 E10
Walmer NSW 110 B5
Walpa Vic 70 D6
Walpeup Vic 68 E5
Walpole WA 202 D10
Walpole-Nornalup NP WA 202 D10
Walungurru NT 178 A5
Walwa Vic 73 L3
Walyahmoning NR WA 202 G2
Wamberra NSW 116 C3
Wamboin NSW 115 M5
Wamboyne NSW 117 N3
Wammadoo Qld 151 K8
Wammutta Qld 150 D4
Wamoon NSW 117 L5
Wampo NSW 116 E3
Wampra NSW 115 H3
Wamuran Qld 145 M6
Wanaaring NSW 114 G3
Wanbi SA 233 M9
Wanda NSW 114 D9
Wandagee WA 204 C1, 210 C10
Wandana SA 232 A4, 231 G10
Wandana NR WA 204 D7
Wandandian NSW 109 F4
Wandearah East SA 233 H7
Wandearah West SA 233 H7
Wandering WA 202 D6
Wandiligong Vic 70 C1, 73 H6
Wandilo SA 230 F10
Wandin Vic 65 J3
Wandina WA 204 D7
Wando Bridge Vic 66 C5
Wando Vale Vic 66 C5
Wandoan Qld 144 G4
Wandong Vic 65 H1, 67 P4, 72 A9
Wandoona NSW 112 C4
Wandsworth NSW 113 J6
Wandsworth Qld 153 K2
Wanganella NSW 117 H6
Wangarabell Vic 71 M4
Wangaratta Vic 72 F4
Wangareena NSW 114 G3
Wangary SA 232 D9
Wangianna NSW 235 H9
Wangoom Vic 66 F8
Wanilla SA 232 D9
Wanjarri NR WA 205 L6
Wanna WA 204 F1, 210 F10
Wannamal WA 202 C3
Wannarra WA 204 F9

Wanneroo WA 202 C4
Wannerup WA 195
Wannon Vic 66 D5
Wannon Vic 66 F4
Wannon River Vic 66 D5
Wannoo Billabong Roadhouse WA 204 C5
Wanora Downs Qld 151 H5
Wantabadgery NSW 117 N6
Wantagong Qld 151 J9
Wanwin Vic 66 B6
Wapengo NSW 109 E8
Wapengo Lake NSW 109 E8, 274
Wapet Camp WA 210 D6
Wappinguy NSW 110 F4
Warambie WA 210 F6
Waranga Basin Vic 72 A5
Waratah NSW 115 L2
Waratah NSW 115 M4
Waratah Tas 254 D6
Waratah Bay Vic 65 M8
Waratah Bay Vic 65 M9
Waratah North Vic 65 M8
Warbreccan Qld 151 J10, 153 J1
Warburn NSW 117 K4
Warburton Vic 65 L3, 72 D10
Warburton WA 206 D10
Warburton Creek SA 234 G5
Warburton East Vic 65 L3, 72 D10
Warby Range SP Vic 72 F4
Warcowie SA 233 J3
Wardell NSW 113 P3
Wards Mistake NSW 113 K7
Wards River NSW 111 K4
Wareek Vic 67 K3
Warenda Qld 150 E7
Wareo Qld 153 M6
Wargambegal NSW 117 L2
Warge Rock WA 115 N9
Warialda NSW 112 F5
Warialda Rail NSW 112 F5
Warianna Qld 151 L4
Warida NSW 144 C5
Warkton NSW 110 C1, 112 C10
Warkworth NSW 111 H5
Warnamboo Downs Qld 151 J7
Warncoort Vic 64 B6, 67 K8
Warne Vic 69 H8
Warnecliffe NSW 110 C6
Warneet Vic 43, 65 J5
Warner Glen WA 202 B9
Warners Bay NSW 111 J6
Warnertown SA 233 J6
Warooka SA 232 G10
Waroon Qld 144 F7
Waroona WA 202 C6
Waroona Dam WA 200, 201
Waroula Qld 147 J8
Warra Qld 145 J6
Warra Qld 150 E8
Warrabah NP NSW 112 G8
Warrabin Qld 153 K5
Warrabkook Vic 66 E6
Warrachie SA 232 D7
Warrachuppin WA 202 G3
Warracknabeal Vic 68 F9
Warraderry NSW 109 A1, 110 A8, 117 P3
Warragamba NSW 109 F1, 110 G9
Warragamba Dam NSW 80, 81
Warragoon NSW 117 K8
Warragul Vic 65 M5
Warrak Vic 67 H4
Warrakimbo SA 233 H4
Warral NSW 110 G1, 112 G10
Warralakin WA 202 G3
Warralong WA 211 J5
Warrambine Vic 64 B4, 67 K6
Warramboo SA 232 D6
Warrananga NSW 116 B3
Warrawagine WA 211 L6
Warraweena SA 233 J1
Warrayure SA 66 E5
Warreah Qld 151 M3
Warregal Qld 151 H7

Warregal Qld 146 D5
Warrego Park Qld 144 A6, 153 P6
Warrego River NSW 115 J3
Warrego River Qld 144 A5
Warrell Creek NSW 113 M8
Warren NSW 115 P7
Warren NP WA 202 C9

Warren River WA 200
Warren Vale Qld 148 E8
Warrenbayne Vic 72 D6
Warrenben CP SA 230 A2, 232 G10
Warrenmang Vic 67 J3
Warrentinna Tas 255 M5
Warriedar WA 204 F9
Warrigal NSW 115 N7
Warrigal Qld 146 A3, 151 N3
Warrill View Qld 145 M8
Warrimbah WA 209 H9
Warrina SA 234 D5
Warringa Tas 254 F6
Warrinilla NSW 112 A5, 115 P2
Warrion Vic 64 A5, 67 J7
Warrnambool Vic 66 F8
Warrong Qld 144 D2
Warrong Vic 66 E7
Warroo NSW 117 N2
Warrow SA 232 D9
Warrumbungle NSW 110 B1, 112 B10
Warrumbungle NP NSW 110 C1, 112 C10
Warrumbungle Range NSW 110 C1
Warruwi NT 174 G3
Wartaka SA 232 G5
Wartook Vic 66 F3
Wartook Reservoir Vic 66 F3
Warwick Qld 145 L8
Warwick Vic 146 F7
Washpool SA 233 J7
Washpool NP NSW 113 L4, 266
Wasleys SA 233 J9
Watarrka NP NT 178 D7
Watchem Vic 68 G9
Watchupga Vic 68 G7
Waterbag NSW 114 C7
Waterfall NSW 109 G2, 111 H9
Waterford Vic 70 D4, 73 J9
Waterhouse PA Tas 255 L4
Waterloo NT 176 A4
Waterloo Qld 144 E7
Waterloo SA 233 K8
Waterloo Tas 253 H7
Waterloo Vic 64 A1, 67 J4
Watermark NSW 110 F1, 112 F10
Watervale SA 233 J8
Watheroo WA 202 C1, 204 E10
Watheroo NP WA 202 C1, 204 E10
Wathumba Creek Qld 132–3
Watson SA 231 D8
Watsons Bay NSW 75
Watsons Creek NSW 113 H8
Watsons Creek Vic 65 J2, 72 B10
Wattamondara NSW 109 B1, 110 B9
Wattle Vic 67 H9
Wattle Creek Vic 67 H3
Wattle Flat NSW 110 D6
Wattle Grove Tas 253 J6
Wattle Hill Tas 253 L4
Wattle Vale NSW 114 E4
Waubra Vic 64 A1, 67 K4
Wauchope NSW 111 M2
Wauchope NT 177 J9, 179 J1
Waukaringa SA 233 L4
Wauraltee SA 232 G9
Waurn Ponds Vic 67 M7
Wave Hill NSW 114 F8
Wave Hill NSW 115 L4
Wave Hill NT 176 D4
Waverley Downs NSW 114 F2
Wayatinah Tas 252 G2
Waychinicup NP WA 202 F9
Waygara Vic 71 H5, 73 N10
Weabonga NSW 111 H1, 113 H10
Wealwandangie Qld 144 D1, 146 E10
Weaner Creek Qld 153 P5
Weavers SA 233 H10
Wedderburn Vic 67 J1, 69 J10
Wedderburn Junction Vic 67 K1, 69 K10
Weddin Mountains NP NSW 109 A1, 117 P3
Wedge Island WA 202 B2
Wee Jasper NSW 109 B4
Wee Waa NSW 112 D7
Wee Wee Rup Vic 69 M8
Weeaproinah Vic 64 A7, 67 J9
Weebo WA 205 L7
Weegena Tas 254 G7
Weekeroo SA 233 M4
Weelamurra Qld 144 A8

INDEX OF PLACE NAMES 415

Weelarrana WA 205 K1, 211 K10
Weemelah NSW 112 C3
Weeragua Vic 71 L4
Weeraman NSW 110 D3
Weerangourt Vic 66 D6
Weerite Vic 67 H7
Weetah Tas 255 H6
Weetalaba Qld 146 E4
Weetaliba NSW 110 D2
Weethalle NSW 117 L3
Weetulta SA 233 H8
Wehla Vic 67 J1
Weilmoringle NSW 115 M2
Weimby NSW 116 E5
Weipa Qld 154 B6, 278, 281
Weira WA 202 G3
Weja NSW 117 M3
Welaregang NSW 109 A7, 117 P8
Welbourn Hill SA 234 A4
Welbungin WA 202 F2
Weldborough Tas 255 M5
Welford NP Qld 153 J2
Wellesley Islands Qld 148 C5, 285
Wellingrove NSW 113 J5
Wellington NSW 110 B5
Wellington SA 230 A9
Wellington Dam WA 201, 202 C7
Wellington Mills WA *201*
Wellshot Qld 151 M9
Wellstead WA 202 G9
Welltree NT 174 C5
Welshmans Reef Vic 67 L3
Welshpool Vic 65 P8, 70 A9
Wemen Vic 68 G4
Wendouree Vic 64 B2, 67 K5
Wengenville Qld 145 K6
Wenlock (ruins) Qld 154 D7
Wentworth NSW 116 C4, 265
Wentworth Falls NSW 109 F1, 110 F8
Weranga Qld 145 J6
Weribone Qld 144 F7
Werna Qld 151 J5
Wernadinga Qld 148 C7
Werneth Vic 64 A4, 67 K6
Werombi NSW 109 F1, 110 G9
Werrap Vic 68 D8
Werri Beach NSW *75*, 92, 93, 109 G3
Werribee Vic 64 F3, 67 N6
Werribee Gorge SP Vic 64 D2, 67 M5
Werribee South Vic 64 F4, 67 N6
Werrikimbe NP NSW 111 L1, 113 L10
Werrimull Vic 68 C3
Werrina Qld 150 G2
Werrington Qld 149 J9
Werris Creek NSW 110 G1, 112 G10
Wertaloona SA 233 L1, 235 L10
Wesburn Vic 65 K3
Wesley Vale Tas 254 G5
West Cape Howe NP WA 202 E10
West Frankford Tas 255 H6
West Hill Qld 146 G5
West Hill NP Qld 147 H5
West Kalgoorlie WA 203 L2
West Kentish Tas 254 G6
West Lynne NSW 109 B8
West MacDonnell NP NT 178 G5
West Pine Tas 254 F5
West Point Qld 147 H6
West Ridgley Tas 254 E5
West Scottsdale Tas 255 L5
West Tamworth NSW 112 G9
West Wyalong NSW 117 M3
Westbourne Qld 151 N9
Westbrook NSW 117 P7
Westbury Tas 255 J7
Westby NSW 117 N7
Westby Vic 69 L7
Westcourt Qld 144 C6
Western Creek NT 174 F10, 176 F1
Western Creek Tas 255 H7
Western Flat SA 230 D10
Western Junction Tas 255 K7
Western Port Vic **42–3**, 62, 65 J5, 262
Western River Cove SA 230 B2, 321
Western Tiers Tas 247, 251, 328, 329
Western River WPA SA 230 B2
Westerton Qld 151 J9
Westerway Tas 253 H4
Westgrove Vic 144 E3
Westland Qld 151 L9
Westlea Tas 153 P9
Westmar Qld 144 G8

Westmere Vic 66 G5
Westmoreland Qld 148 A6
Weston Creek ACT 109 C5
Westonia WA 202 G3
Westward Ho Qld 150 E8
Westwood Qld 147 J9
Westwood Tas 255 J7
Westwood Downs NSW 114 B5
Wet Creek NT 174 E9
Wetlands Qld 144 C3
Weymouth Tas 255 K4
Wharminda SA 232 E8
Wharparilla Vic 69 N9
Wharparilla North Vic 69 N9
Whealbah NSW 117 J3
Whetstone Qld 145 J9
Whidbey Islands CP SA 232 C10
Whim Creek WA 210 G6
Whiporie NSW 113 M4
Whipstick SP Vic 67 M1
Whirily Vic 69 H8
White Beach Tas 253 M6
White Cliffs NSW 114 E5
White Cliffs WA 205 N8
White Creek SA 233 N5
White Flat SA 232 D9
White Gate Vic 72 E6
White Hills Tas 255 K7
White Hut SA 230 A2, 232 G10
White Leeds NSW 114 B8
White Mountains Qld 151 M2
White Mountains NP Qld 151 M2
White Rock Qld 149 L5, 155 D8
Whitefoord Tas 253 L2
Whiteheads Creek Vic 72 B7
Whitemark Tas 255 J3
Whitemore Tas 255 J7
Whitewells WA 204 F9
Whitewood Qld 151 K5
Whitfield Vic A1, 72 F6
Whitlands Vic 72 F6
Whitsunday Group Qld 146 G2, 288, **289**, *289*
Whitsunday Islands NP Qld 146 G3
Whittata SA 232 G3
Whittlesea Vic 65 H2, 67 P5, 72 A9
Whitton NSW 117 K5
Whitwarta SA 233 J8
Whorouly Vic 72 G5
Whorouly East Vic 72 G5
Whroo Vic 67 P2, 72 A6
Whyalla NSW 112 A4
Whyalla SA 232 G6, **318–19**, *318*, *319*
Whyalla CP SA 232 G6
Whyjonta NSW 114 D3
Whyralla Qld 151 H7
Whyte Yarcowie SA 233 K6
Wialki WA 202 F2
Wiangaree NSW 113 M2
Wickepin WA 202 E6
Wickham WA 210 F5
Wickliffe Vic 66 G5
Widbury Qld 145 J3
Widden NSW 110 F5
Widgelli NSW 117 K4
Widgeman Qld 146 B7, 151 P7
Widgiemooltha WA 203 L3
Widgiewa NSW 117 L6
Wietalaba Qld 145 K1, 147 K10
Wilangee NSW 114 A7
Wilban WA 207 C6
Wilburville Tas 255 J9
Wilby Vic 72 E3
Wilcannia NSW 114 E7
Wilcherry SA 232 E5
Wild Duck Island NP Qld 147 H6
Wild Horse Plains SA 233 J9
Wilfred Downs Qld 151 L4
Wilga NSW 114 F7
Wilga Downs NSW 115 K5
Wilga South SA 145 H6
Wilgalong NSW 115 L7
Wilgaroon NSW 115 K5
Wilgena SA 232 C1
Wilkatana SA 233 H4
Wilkawatt SA 230 A9
Wilkur Vic 68 G8
Wilkur South Vic 68 F9
Wilkurra NSW 114 E10, 116 E2
Willa Vic 68 E6
Willaba NSW 114 C10, 116 C1

Willalooka SA 230 C9
Willandra NP NSW 117 H2
Willandspey Qld 146 C5
Willara Qld 144 B3
Willare Bridge Roadhouse WA 208 F8, 211 P1
Willarie Qld 144 F9
Willaroy NSW 114 E4
Willatook Vic 66 E7
Willaura Vic 66 G5
Willawa Qld 144 H2
Willawarrin NSW 113 M9
Willbriggie NSW 117 K5
Willenabrina Vic 68 E9
Willeroo NT 174 E9
Willesley Qld 146 D6
William Creek SA 234 E7
Williambury WA 204 D1, 210 D10
Williams WA 201, 202 D6
Williamsdale ACT 109 C5
Williamsford Tas 254 D8
Williamstown SA 233 K9
Williamstown Vic 47, 64 G3, 67 N6
Williamtown NSW 111 K6
Willippa SA 233 K3
Willis Vic 71 H2, 73 P7
Willochra SA 233 J4
Willow Grove Vic 65 N4
Willow Tree NSW 110 G2
Willow Waters SA 233 J4
Willowie SA 233 J5
Willowmavin Vic 67 N4, 72 A8
Willowra NT 176 F10, 178 F2
Willows Qld 146 D9
Willowvale Vic 64 A3, 67 J6
Willung Vic 70 B8
Willung South Vic 70 B8
Willunga SA 230 A5
Wilmington Qld 146 E2, 149 P10
Wilmington SA 233 H5
Wilmot Tas 254 F6
Wilora NT 179 H2
Wilpena SA 233 J3
Wilpoorinna SA 235 J9
Wilroy WA 204 D8
Wilson SA 233 J4
Wilsons Hut Qld 148 F6
Wilsons Promontory Vic *39*, **54–5**, *54*, *55*, 65 N9
Wilsons Promontory NP Vic *39*, 54, *54*, *55*, 65 N9
Wilton NSW 109 G2, 110 G10
Wilton Qld 151 M7
Wiltshire Tas 254 C3
Wiluna WA 205 K5
Winbar NSW 115 H5
Winchelsea Vic 64 C5, 67 L7
Winchester WA 202 C1, 204 E10
Windah Qld 147 J9
Windamere Dam NSW 20, **98–9**, *98*, *99*, 110 E5
Windara NSW 115 H7
Windarra WA 205 N8
Windellama NSW 109 E4
Windera NSW 115 K6
Windera Qld 145 L4
Winderie WA 204 D3
Windermere Tas 255 J6
Windermere Vic 64 B1, 67 K5
Windeyer NSW 110 D5
Windidda SA 205 N5
Windimurra WA 205 H7
Windjana Gorge NP WA 208 G8
Windorah Qld 153 J3
Windsor NSW 79, 80, 81, 109 G1, 110 G8
Windsor SA 233 J9
Windsor WA 205 H7
Windsor Park Qld 150 D6
Windurong NSW 110 B2
Windy Harbour WA 202 C9
Wineglass Bay Tas 242, 253 P1, 255 P10
Wingadee NSW 112 A8
Wingan Bay Vic 71 N5
Wingan Inlet Vic 49
Wingan Swamp Vic 71 M4
Wingeel Vic 64 B4, 67 K7
Wingelinna WA 206 G10
Wingello NSW 109 E3
Wingen NSW 110 G3
Wingfield Qld 145 J2

Wingham NSW 111 L3
Winiam Vic 66 C1, 68 C10
Winiam East Vic 66 D1, 68 D10
Winjallok Vic 67 H2
Winkie SA 233 N9
Winkle Creek NT 177 M7
Winkleigh Tas 255 J6
Winlaton Vic 69 K7
Winnaleah Tas 255 M5
Winnambool Vic 68 G5
Winnap Vic 66 B6
Winnathee NSW 114 A3
Winneba Qld 144 C4
Winnindoo Vic 70 B7
Winning WA 210 C9
Winninowie SA 233 H5
Winninowie CP SA 233 H5
Winnungra NSW 117 M3
Winslow Vic 66 F7
Wintinna SA 234 A4
Winton Qld 151 J6
Winton Vic 72 E5
Winulta SA 233 H8
Wirega NSW 109 A1, 110 A9, 117 P3
Wirha SA 230 A9, 233 N10
Wirra Wirra Qld 149 K3
Wirrabara SA 233 J6
Wirraminna SA 232 E2
Wirrappa SA 232 F3
Wirrawa NSW 115 N2
Wirrawarra NSW 115 J2
Wirrealpa SA 233 K2
Wirrega SA 230 C9
Wirrida SA 234 B8
Wirrimah NSW 109 A2, 110 A9
Wirrinya NSW 117 P3
Wirrulla SA 232 B5
Wiseleigh Vic 70 F5, 73 L10
Wisemans Creek NSW 109 D1, 110 D8
Wisemans Ferry NSW 80, 81, *81*, 111 H7
Witchcliffe WA 202 B8
Witchelina SA 235 H9
Witchitie SA 233 K4
Witera SA 232 B6
Withersfield Qld 146 D9
Withnell Bay WA 210 E5, 309
Withywine Qld 151 K9
Witjira NP SA 234 D1
Wittenbra NSW 112 C9
Wittenoom WA 211 H8
Woden Valley ACT 109 C5
Wodonga Vic 73 H3, 264
Wogarl WA 202 G4
Wogarno WA 204 G7
Woggoon NR NSW 115 M10, 117 M1
Woko NP NSW 111 J2
Wokurna SA 233 H7
Wolfe Creek Crater NP WA 206 E1, 209 M10
Wolffdene Qld 145 N7
Wolfram Qld 149 K6, 155 B8
Wollar NSW 110 E4
Wollemi NP NSW 110 F5
Wollert Vic 65 H2, 67 P5, 72 A10
Wollogorang NT 177 P3
Wollogorang Qld 148 A6
Wollombi NSW 111 H6
Wollombi Qld 146 E4
Wollomombi NSW 113 K8
Wollongbar NSW 113 P3
Wollongong NSW 90, 92, 109 G3, 110 G10
Wollun NSW 113 J9
Wololla Qld 146 B9, 151 P9
Wolonga Camp NSW 112 F3
Wolseley SA 230 C10
Wolseley Park NSW 117 P7
Wolumla NSW 109 E9
Wolverton Qld 154 D7
Wolvi Qld 145 M4
Womal Park Qld 144 D5
Womalilla Qld 144 D5
Wombat NSW 109 A3, 110 A10, 117 P4
Wombelano Vic 66 C3
Womblebank Qld 144 D3
Womboota NSW 117 H8
Wombramurra NSW 111 H2
Wombungi NT 174 D8
Wompah House NSW 114 C1
Wonaminta NSW 114 C5

Wonboyn Lake NSW 109 E10, **274–5**
Wondai Qld 145 L5
Wondinong WA 205 H7
Wondoola Qld 148 E8
Wonga NSW 114 A9
Wonga NSW 114 E3
Wonga Qld 149 L4, 155 D6
Wonga Creek Vic 73 J5
Wonga Lilli NSW 114 F4
Wonga Park Vic 65 J3, 72 B10
Wongabinda NSW 112 E4
Wongalara NSW 114 G7
Wongalea NSW 117 J4
Wongalee Qld 151 M3
Wongamere Qld 144 B7
Wongan Hills WA 202 D2
Wonganoo WA 205 M6
Wongarbon NSW 110 B4
Wongarra Vic 64 B8, 67 K9
Wongawol WA 205 M4
Wongoni NSW 113 C3
Wongoondy WA 204 D8
Wongungarra Vic 70 C4, 73 J9
Wongwibinda NSW 113 K7
Wonnangatta River Vic 70 B3, 261
Wonoka SA 233 J3
Wonolga Qld 144 E8
Wonthaggi Vic 65 K7
Wonthaggi North Vic 65 K7
Wonwondah North Vic 66 E2
Wonwron Vic 70 E9
Wonyip Vic 65 P7, 70 A9
Woobera Qld 150 D4
Wood Wood Vic 69 J5
Woodanilling WA 202 E7
Woodbourne Vic 64 C3, 67 L6
Woodbridge Tas 253 K6
Woodbrook WA 210 F6
Woodburn NSW 113 N4, 266
Woodbury Tas 253 K1, 255 L10
Woodchester SA 230 A6, 233 K10
Woodenbong NSW 113 M2
Woodend Vic 64 E1, 67 M4
Woodend North Vic 64 F1, 67 M4
Woodford NSW 109 F1, 110 F8
Woodford Qld 145 M6
Woodford Vic 66 F8
Woodford Dale NSW 113 N5
Woodgate Qld 130, 145 M2
Woodgate NP Qld 145 M2
Woodglen Vic 70 D6
Woodhouse Qld 146 D1, 149 N10
Woodhouselee NSW 109 D3
Woodie Woodie WA 211 L7
Woodlands Qld 144 A7
Woodlands Qld 144 D6
Woodlands WA 204 G2
Woodlawn Qld 144 F8
Woodleigh Vic 65 K6
Woodleigh WA 204 C4
Woodman Point WA 183, 187, 202 B5
Woods Point Vic 65 N2, 72 F10
Woods Well SA 230 C7
Woodsdale Tas 253 L3
Woodside Qld 144 B5
Woodside SA 233 K10
Woodside Vic 70 B9
Woodside Beach Vic 70 C9
Woodstock NSW 109 C1, 110 B8
Woodstock NSW 115 K4
Woodstock Qld 146 C1, 149 N10
Woodstock Qld 150 G6
Woodstock Tas 253 J6
Woodstock Vic 67 L2
Woodstock WA 211 H7
Woodvale Qld 144 37
Woodvale Vic 67 L2
Woodview NSW 113 M3
Woodville NSW 111 J5
Woohlpocer Vic 66 E4
Wool Bay SA 233 H10
Wool Wool Vic 64 A5, 67 J7
Woolabra Qld 144 B4
Woolamai Vic 65 K7
Woolamai Waters Vic 65 J7
Woolbrook NSW 113 H9
Woolcunda NSW 114 B10, 116 B1
Wooleen WA 204 E5
Woolerbilla Qld 144 D9
Woolerina Qld 144 C9
Woolfield Qld 145 H6
Woolfield Qld 151 K5

INDEX OF PLACE NAMES

Woolgangi SA 233 L7
Woolgangie WA 203 K3
Woolgoolga NSW 113 N7, 269
Woolgorong WA 204 E7
Wooli NSW 113 N6, 269
Woolibar WA 203 L3
Woolla Downs NT 179 H3
Woolner NT 174 D4
Woolnorth Tas 254 A3
Woolomin NSW 111 H1, 113 H10
Woolooga Qld 145 L4
Woolooma NSW 111 H3
Wooloweyah Estuary NSW 113 N5
Woolshed Corner Vic 67 L1, 69 L10
Woolshed Flat SA 233 H5
Woolsthorpe Vic 66 F7
Wooltana SA 235 L10
Woomargama NSW 117 N8
Woomelang Vic 68 G7
Woomera SA 232 F2
Woomera Prohibited Area SA 232 C1, 234 D8, 231 F7
Woongoolba Qld 145 N7
Woonigan Qld 150 D4
Woorabinda Qld 146 G10
Woorak Vic 68 D9
Woorak West Vic 68 D9
Wooramel WA 204 C4
Wooramel Roadhouse WA 204 C4
Woorarra Vic 65 P7, 70 A9
Wooreen Vic 65 M6
Woori Yallock Vic 65 K3
Woorinen Vic 69 J6
Woorndoo Vic 66 G6
Woorndoo Upper Vic 66 G6
Wooroloo WA 202 C4
Wooroonook Vic 69 H9
Woorragee Vic 72 G4
Woosang Vic 69 J10
Wootton NSW 111 L4
Wooyung NSW 113 P2
Wotonga Qld 146 E5
Wotto NR WA 204 D9
Wowan Qld 147 J9
Woy Woy NSW 87, 111 H8
Wrangrawally NSW 115 P4
Wrightley Vic 72 E6
Wrotham Park Qld 149 J5
Wroxham Vic 71 M4
Wubbera NSW 112 E5
Wubin WA 202 D1, 204 F10
Wudinna SA 232 D6
Wujal Wujal Qld 149 L4, 155 C5
Wulgulmerang Vic 70 G2, 73 N7
Wumalgi Qld 147 H6
Wumbulgal NSW 117 L4
Wundowie WA 202 C4
Wunghnu Vic 72 C3
Wunkar SA 233 M9
Wunurra NT 177 M8
Wurarga WA 204 E8
Wurruk Vic 70 C7
Wurung Qld 148 D9
Wutul Qld 145 K6
Wy Yung Vic 70 E6
Wyalkatchem WA 202 E3
Wyalong NSW 117 M3
Wyan NSW 113 M4
Wyandotte Qld 149 K8
Wyandra Qld 144 A6, 153 P6
Wyangala NSW 109 C1, 110 B9
Wycarbah Qld 147 J9
Wycheproof Vic 69 H9

Wychitella Vic 69 J9
Wycliffe Well Roadhouse NT 177 J10, 179 J1
Wye River Vic 64 C7, 67 K9
Wyee NSW 111 J7
Wyeebo Vic 73 K4
Wyelangta Vic 64 A7, 67 J9
Wyena Qld 146 D5
Wyena Tas 255 K5
Wylie Creek NSW 113 K2
Wylie Scarp WA 207 A9
Wyloo WA 210 E8
Wymah NSW 117 N8
Wynarka SA 230 A8, 233 L10
Wynbring SA 231 G8
Wyndham NSW 109 D9
Wyndham WA 209 M4, 302
Wyndonga NSW 114 B5
Wynyangoo WA 205 H7
Wynyard Tas 254 E4
Wyong NSW 111 J7
Wyperfeld NP Vic 68 C7
Wyreema Downs Qld 151 H5
Wyseby Qld 144 E2
Wyuna Vic 69 P9, 72 A4
Wyuna Downs NSW 115 L5

Yaamba Qld 147 J8
Yaapeet Vic 68 E7
Yabba North Vic 72 D4
Yabulu Qld 149 M9
Yacka SA 233 J7
Yackabindie WA 205 K6
Yackandandah Vic 73 H4
Yadboro Flat NSW 97, 109 F5
Yadlamalka SA 233 H4
Yahl SA 230 G10
Yakara Qld 153 L9
Yalamurra Qld 153 N5
Yalardy WA 204 D4
Yalata SA 231 E9
Yalata Roadhouse SA 231 E9
Yalbalgo WA 204 C3
Yalbarrin WA 202 F4
Yalboroo Qld 146 F3
Yalbra WA 204 E3
Yalca North Vic 72 B2
Yalca South Vic 72 B3
Yalgogrin NSW 117 M3
Yalgoo WA 204 F7
Yalgorup NP WA 202 B6
Yalla Y Poora Vic 67 H5
Yallalong WA 204 D6
Yallaroi NSW 112 F4
Yalleen WA 210 E7
Yalleroi Qld 146 A10, 151 P10
Yallingup WA 195, 202 A7
Yallock NSW 115 H9
Yallourn North Vic 65 P5
Yallunda Flat SA 232 E9
Yalwal NSW 109 F4
Yalymboo SA 232 F3
Yamala Qld 146 F9
Yamarna WA 205 P7, 207 A3
Yamba NSW 113 N5, **266-7**
Yamba NSW 114 E3
Yambacoona NSW 115 L3
Yambacoona Tas 254 F1
Yambah NT 179 H5
Yambuk Vic 66 E8
Yambungan Qld 148 D10, 150 E1
Yampi Sound WA 208 E5, 304
Yan Yan Qld 146 F8

Yan Yean Vic 65 H2, 67 P5, 72 A10
Yanac Vic 68 C9
Yanakie Vic 65 N8
Yancannia NSW 114 D4
Yanchep WA 202 B4
Yanchep NP WA 202 B4
Yanco NSW 117 L5
Yanco Glen NSW 114 B7
Yandal WA 205 L6
Yandama NSW 114 B3
Yandaminta NSW 114 B3
Yandaminta South NSW 114 B3
Yandanooka WA 204 D9
Yandaran Qld 145 L1
Yandarlo Qld 144 B2
Yandaroo NSW 115 J4
Yandeearra WA 211 H6
Yanderra NSW 109 F2, 110 F10
Yandi WA 204 C7
Yandil WA 205 K5
Yandilla Qld 151 K8
Yandina Qld 145 M5
Yando Vic 69 K9
Yandoit Vic 67 L4
Yanerbie Beach SA 232 A6
Yaninee SA 232 C6
Yanipy Vic 66 B1, 68 B10
Yankalilla SA 230 A5
Yankaninna SA 235 K10
Yannathan Vic 65 K5
Yannergee NSW 110 E2
Yanrey WA 210 C8
Yantabangee NSW 114 F5
Yantabulla NSW 115 H2
Yantara NSW 114 C3
Yaouk NSW 109 B6
Yaraka Qld 153 L2
Yarck Vic 72 C8
Yard Creek NSW 209 L7
Yardanogo NR WA 204 D9
Yardea SA 232 D4
Yaringa WA 204 C4
Yarlarweelor WA 204 G3
Yarloop WA 202 C6
Yarmouth Qld 144 A7
Yarooomba Beach Qld 126, 129
Yarra NSW 109 D3
Yarra Glen Vic 65 J2, 72 B10
Yarra Junction Vic 65 K3
Yarra Ranges NP Vic 65 K2, 72 C10
Yarra River Vic *38, 46-7, 46*
Yarra Yarra Lakes WA 204 E9
Yarrabah Qld 149 L5, 155 E7
Yarrabandai NSW 115 N10, 117 N2
Yarraberb Vic 67 L1
Yarrabin NSW 110 C5
Yarrabubba WA 205 H6
Yarraden Qld 149 H1, 154 E9
Yarragadee WA 204 D8
Yarragon Vic 65 M5
Yarragrin NSW 110 C2
Yarrah Creek Tas 254 F2
Yarralin NT 176 D2
Yarraloola WA 210 E7
Yarram Vic 70 B9
Yarrama NSW 115 L8
Yarramalong NSW 111 H7
Yarraman NSW 110 F2
Yarraman Qld 145 L6
Yarramba SA 233 N3
Yarrangobilly NSW 109 B6

Yarranlea Qld 145 K7
Yarranvale NSW 115 K8
Yarrara Vic 68 C3
Yarras NSW 111 L1, 113 L10
Yarrawalla Vic 69 L9
Yarrawalla South Vic 69 L9
Yarrawin NSW 115 M4
Yarrawonga Vic 72 E3, 265
Yarriambiack Creek Vic 68 F10
Yarrie WA 211 K5
Yarrock Vic 68 B9
Yarronvale Qld 153 N6
Yarroweyah Vic 72 C2
Yarrowford NSW 113 K5
Yarrowitch NSW 111 K1, 113 K10
Yarrowmere Qld 146 A4, 151 P4
Yarrowyck NSW 113 H8
Yarrum Qld 148 C7
Yarto Vic 68 E7
Yarwun Qld 147 K9
Yass NSW 109 C4
Yatchaw Vic 66 E6
Yathong NSW 115 J9
Yathong NR NSW 115 J9
Yatina SA 233 J6
Yatpool Vic 68 E2
Yatteyattah NSW 109 F5
Yea Vic 72 B8
Yeal NR WA 202 C3
Yealering WA 202 E5
Yearinan NSW 110 C1, 112 C10
Yearinga Vic 68 B9
Yednalue SA 233 J4
Yednia Qld 145 M5
Yeeda WA 208 E8, 211 P1
Yeelanna SA 232 D8
Yeelirrie WA 205 K6
Yeerip Vic 72 E4
Yelarbon Qld 145 J9
Yelbeni WA 202 E3
Yeldulknie CP SA 232 F7
Yelka NSW 114 B5
Yellabinna RR SA 231 F8
Yellangip Vic 68 E9
Yellingbo Vic 65 K3
Yellow Lake SA 232 E3
Yellow Waters NT 171, 174 F5
Yellowdine WA 203 H3
Yellowdine NR WA 203 H3
Yeltacowie SA 232 G2
Yelty NSW 114 G10, 116 G1
Yelvertoft Qld 150 B2
Yenda NSW 117 L4
Yendon NSW 64 C2, 67 L5
Yengo NP NSW 110 G6
Yenlora Qld 153 L9
Yenyening Lakes NR WA 202 E5
Yeo Lake WA 207 B2
Yeo Lake NR WA 207 B2
Yeo Yeo NSW 109 A3, 117 P5
Yeodene Vic 64 B6, 67 K8
Yeoval NSW 110 B5
Yeppoon Qld 147 K8, 289
Yerda SA 232 C2
Yerecoin WA 202 C2
Yerilla Qld 145 J3
Yering Vic 65 J2, 72 B10
Yerong Creek NSW 117 M7
Yerrinbool NSW 109 F2, 110 F10
Yethera NSW 115 N9
Yetholme NSW 110 E7
Yetman NSW 112 G3
Yeungroon Vic 67 J1, 69 J10

Yeungroon East Vic 69 J10
Yiddah NSW 117 N4
Yilliminning WA 202 E6
Yindi WA 203 N2, 205 N10
Yinkanie SA 233 M9
Yinnar Vic 65 N6
Yinnetharra WA 204 E2
Yirrkala NT 175 M4
Yo Yo Creek Qld 144 B3
Yo Yo Park Qld 144 B4
Yolla Tas 254 E5
Yongala SA 233 K6
Yoogali NSW 117 K4
Yoorooga Qld 144 F7
Yoothapina WA 205 H5
York WA 202 D4
York Plains Tas 253 K2, 255 L10
Yorketown SA 233 H10
Yorkeys Knob Qld 149 L5, 155 D7, 291
Yorklea NSW 113 N3
Yorkrakine WA 202 E3
Yorkshire Downs Qld 150 G3
Yornaning WA 202 E6
Yornup WA 202 C8
You Yangs FP Vic 64 E4, 67 M6
Youangarra WA 205 H8
Youanmi Downs WA 205 H8
Youanmite Vic 72 D3
Youndegin WA 202 E4
Young NSW 109 A2, 110 A10, 117 P4
Younghusband Peninsula SA 222, *223*, 230 B6
Youngs WA 202 E10
Youngtown Tas 255 K7
Youno Downs WA 205 J6
Yowah Qld 153 M8
Yowaka NP NSW 109 E9
Yoweragabbie WA 204 G7
Yowrie NSW 109 E7
Yudnapinna SA 232 G4
Yuelamu NT 178 F3
Yuendumu NT 178 E3
Yugilbar NSW 112 B8
Yuin WA 204 E7
Yuinmery WA 205 J8
Yulabilla Qld 144 G6
Yulama NSW 117 L6
Yulara NT 178 D8
Yuleba Qld 144 F5
Yulecart Vic 66 E6
Yullundry NSW 110 B6
Yumali SA 230 B8
Yumbarra CP SA 231 F9
Yuna WA 204 D7
Yundamindra WA 205 M9
Yunderup WA 202 C5
Yundool Vic 72 D4
Yungaburra Qld 149 L6, 155 D8
Yunta SA 233 L5
Yurammie NSW 109 D9
Yuraraba Qld 145 K9
Yuraygir NP NSW 113 N5, 266
Yurgo SA 230 A8, 233 M10
Yuroke Vic 64 G2, 67 N5
Yuulong Vic 67 J9

Zanthus WA 203 P3, 207 A6
Zeehan Tas 254 C9
Zenonie Qld 153 K9
Zumsteins Vic 66 F3
Zuytdorp Cliffs WA 204 B6, 314
Zuytdorp NR WA 204 C6